Big Data Meets Survey Science

Big Data Meets Survey Science

A Collection of Innovative Methods

Edited by
Craig A. Hill
Paul P. Biemer
Trent D. Buskirk
Lilli Japec
Antje Kirchner
Stas Kolenikov
Lars E. Lyberg

This edition first published 2021
© 2021 John Wiley & Sons

All rights reserved. No part of this publication may be reproduced, stored in a retrieval system, or transmitted, in any form or by any means, electronic, mechanical, photocopying, recording or otherwise, except as permitted by law. Advice on how to obtain permission to reuse material from this title is available at http://www.wiley.com/go/permissions.

The right of Craig A. Hill, Paul P. Biemer, Trent D. Buskirk, Lilli Japec, Antje Kirchner, Stas Kolenikov, and Lars E. Lyberg to be identified as the editorial material in this work has been asserted in accordance with law.

Registered Office
John Wiley & Sons, Inc., 111 River Street, Hoboken, NJ 07030, USA

Editorial Office
111 River Street, Hoboken, NJ 07030, USA

For details of our global editorial offices, customer services, and more information about Wiley products visit us at www.wiley.com.

Wiley also publishes its books in a variety of electronic formats and by print-on-demand. Some content that appears in standard print versions of this book may not be available in other formats.

Limit of Liability/Disclaimer of Warranty
While the publisher and authors have used their best efforts in preparing this work, they make no representations or warranties with respect to the accuracy or completeness of the contents of this work and specifically disclaim all warranties, including without limitation any implied warranties of merchantability or fitness for a particular purpose. No warranty may be created or extended by sales representatives, written sales materials or promotional statements for this work. The fact that an organization, website, or product is referred to in this work as a citation and/or potential source of further information does not mean that the publisher and authors endorse the information or services the organization, website, or product may provide or recommendations it may make. This work is sold with the understanding that the publisher is not engaged in rendering professional services. The advice and strategies contained herein may not be suitable for your situation. You should consult with a specialist where appropriate. Further, readers should be aware that websites listed in this work may have changed or disappeared between when this work was written and when it is read. Neither the publisher nor authors shall be liable for any loss of profit or any other commercial damages, including but not limited to special, incidental, consequential, or other damages.

Library of Congress Cataloging-in-Publication Data
Names: Hill, Craig A., 1956- editor. | Biemer, Paul P., editor. | Buskirk,
   Trent D., 1971- editor. | Japec, Lilli, 1966- editor. | Kirchner, Antje,
   1982- editor. | Kolenikov, Stanislav, editor. | Lyberg, Lars, editor. |
   John Wiley & Sons, publisher.
Title: Big data meets survey science : a collection of innovative methods /
   edited by Craig A. Hill, Paul P. Biemer, Trent D. Buskirk, Lilli Japec,
   Antje Kirchner, Stas Kolenikov, Lars Erik Lyberg.
Description: Hoboken, NJ : John Wiley & Sons, Inc., 2021. | Includes index.
Identifiers: LCCN 2020022652 (print) | LCCN 2020022653 (ebook) | ISBN
   9781118976326 (cloth) | ISBN 9781118976333 (adobe pdf) | ISBN
   9781118976340 (epub)
Subjects: LCSH: Big data. | Social surveys–Methodology.
Classification: LCC QA76.9.B45 B5563 2021 (print) | LCC QA76.9.B45
   (ebook) | DDC 001.4/33028557–dc23
LC record available at https://lccn.loc.gov/2021022652
LC ebook record available at https://lccn.loc.gov/2021022653

Cover Design: Wiley
Cover Image: Courtesy of RTI International

Set in 9.5/12.5pt STIXTwoText by SPi Global, Chennai, India

10 9 8 7 6 5 4 3 2 1

Contents

List of Contributors *xxiii*

Introduction *1*
Craig A. Hill, Paul P. Biemer, Trent D. Buskirk, Lilli Japec, Antje Kirchner, Stas Kolenikov, and Lars E. Lyberg
Acknowledgments *7*
References *7*

Section 1 The New Survey Landscape *9*

1 Why Machines Matter for Survey and Social Science Researchers: Exploring Applications of Machine Learning Methods for Design, Data Collection, and Analysis *11*
Trent D. Buskirk and Antje Kirchner
1.1 Introduction *11*
1.2 Overview of Machine Learning Methods and Their Evaluation *13*
1.3 Creating Sample Designs and Constructing Sampling Frames Using Machine Learning Methods *16*
1.3.1 Sample Design Creation *16*
1.3.2 Sample Frame Construction *18*
1.3.3 Considerations and Implications for Applying Machine Learning Methods for Creating Sampling Frames and Designs *20*
1.3.3.1 Considerations About Algorithmic Optimization *20*
1.3.3.2 Implications About Machine Learning Model Error *21*
1.3.3.3 Data Type Considerations and Implications About Data Errors *22*
1.4 Questionnaire Design and Evaluation Using Machine Learning Methods *23*
1.4.1 Question Wording *24*
1.4.2 Evaluation and Testing *26*
1.4.3 Instrumentation and Interviewer Training *27*

	1.4.4	Alternative Data Sources 28
	1.5	Survey Recruitment and Data Collection Using Machine Learning Methods 28
	1.5.1	Monitoring and Interviewer Falsification 29
	1.5.2	Responsive and Adaptive Designs 29
	1.6	Survey Data Coding and Processing Using Machine Learning Methods 33
	1.6.1	Coding Unstructured Text 33
	1.6.2	Data Validation and Editing 35
	1.6.3	Imputation 35
	1.6.4	Record Linkage and Duplicate Detection 36
	1.7	Sample Weighting and Survey Adjustments Using Machine Learning Methods 37
	1.7.1	Propensity Score Estimation 37
	1.7.2	Sample Matching 41
	1.8	Survey Data Analysis and Estimation Using Machine Learning Methods 43
	1.8.1	Gaining Insights Among Survey Variables 44
	1.8.2	Adapting Machine Learning Methods to the Survey Setting 45
	1.8.3	Leveraging Machine Learning Algorithms for Finite Population Inference 46
	1.9	Discussion and Conclusions 47
		References 48
		Further Reading 60
	2	**The Future Is Now: How Surveys Can Harness Social Media to Address Twenty-first Century Challenges** **63**
		Amelia Burke-Garcia, Brad Edwards, and Ting Yan
	2.1	Introduction 63
	2.2	New Ways of Thinking About Survey Research 67
	2.3	The Challenge with … Sampling People 67
	2.3.1	The Social Media Opportunities 68
	2.3.1.1	Venue-Based, Time-Space Sampling 68
	2.3.1.2	Respondent-Driven Sampling 70
	2.3.2	Outstanding Challenges 71
	2.4	The Challenge with … Identifying People 72
	2.4.1	The Social Media Opportunity 73
	2.4.2	Outstanding Challenges 73
	2.5	The Challenge with … Reaching People 74
	2.5.1	The Social Media Opportunities 75
	2.5.1.1	Tracing 75

2.5.1.2	Paid Social Media Advertising	76
2.5.2	Outstanding Challenges	77
2.6	The Challenge with ... Persuading People to Participate	77
2.6.1	The Social Media Opportunities	78
2.6.1.1	Paid Social Media Advertising	78
2.6.1.2	Online Influencers	79
2.6.2	Outstanding Challenges	80
2.7	The Challenge with ... Interviewing People	81
2.7.1	Social Media Opportunities	82
2.7.1.1	Passive Social Media Data Mining	82
2.7.1.2	Active Data Collection	83
2.7.2	Outstanding Challenges	84
2.8	Conclusion	87
	References	89

3 Linking Survey Data with Commercial or Administrative Data for Data Quality Assessment 99
A. Rupa Datta, Gabriel Ugarte, and Dean Resnick

3.1	Introduction	99
3.2	Thinking About Quality Features of Analytic Data Sources	101
3.2.1	What Is the Purpose of the Data Linkage?	101
3.2.2	What Kind of Data Linkage for What Analytic Purpose?	102
3.3	Data Used in This Chapter	104
3.3.1	NSECE Household Survey	104
3.3.2	Proprietary Research Files from Zillow	105
3.3.3	Linking the NSECE Household Survey with Zillow Proprietary Datafiles	107
3.3.3.1	Nonuniqueness of Matches	107
3.3.3.2	Misalignment of Units of Observation	110
3.3.3.3	Ability to Identify Matches	110
3.3.3.4	Identifying Matches	112
3.3.3.5	Implications of the Linking Process for Intended Analyses	114
3.4	Assessment of Data Quality Using the Linked File	116
3.4.1	What Variables in the Zillow Datafile Are Most Appropriate for Use in Substantive Analyses Linked to Survey Data?	116
3.4.2	How Did Different Steps in the Survey Administration Process Contribute to Representativeness of the NSECE Survey Data?	119
3.4.3	How Well Does the Linked Datafile Represent the Overall NSECE Dataset (Including Unlinked Records)?	123

3.5	Conclusion *125*
	References *127*
	Further Reading *129*

Section 2 Total Error and Data Quality *131*

4 Total Error Frameworks for Found Data *133*
Paul P. Biemer and Ashley Amaya
- 4.1 Introduction *133*
- 4.2 Data Integration and Estimation *134*
- 4.2.1 Source Datasets *135*
- 4.2.2 The Integration Process *137*
- 4.2.3 Unified Dataset *137*
- 4.3 Errors in Datasets *138*
- 4.4 Errors in Hybrid Estimates *141*
- 4.4.1 Error-Generating Processes *141*
- 4.4.2 Components of Bias, Variance, and Mean Squared Error *145*
- 4.4.3 Illustrations *148*
- 4.4.4 Error Mitigation *153*
- 4.4.4.1 Sample Recruitment Error *153*
- 4.4.4.2 Data Encoding Error *156*
- 4.5 Other Error Frameworks *156*
- 4.6 Summary and Conclusions *158*
- References *160*

5 Measuring the Strength of Attitudes in Social Media Data *163*
Ashley Amaya, Ruben Bach, Frauke Kreuter, and Florian Keusch
- 5.1 Introduction *163*
- 5.2 Methods *165*
- 5.2.1 Data *165*
- 5.2.1.1 European Social Survey Data *166*
- 5.2.1.2 Reddit 2016 Data *167*
- 5.2.1.3 Reddit Survey *169*
- 5.2.1.4 Reddit 2018 Data *169*
- 5.2.2 Analysis *170*
- 5.2.2.1 Missingness *171*
- 5.2.2.2 Measurement *173*

5.2.2.3	Coding *173*	
5.3	Results *174*	
5.3.1	Overall Comparisons *174*	
5.3.2	Missingness *175*	
5.3.3	Measurement *177*	
5.3.4	Coding *178*	
5.4	Summary *180*	
5.A	2016 German ESS Questions Used in Analysis *184*	
5.B	Search Terms Used to Identify Topics in Reddit Posts (2016 and 2018) *186*	
5.B.1	Political Ideology *186*	
5.B.2	Interest in Politics *186*	
5.B.3	Gay Rights *186*	
5.B.4	EU *187*	
5.B.5	Immigration *187*	
5.B.6	Climate *187*	
5.C	Example of Coding Steps Used to Identify Topics and Assign Sentiment in Reddit Submissions (2016 and 2018) *188*	
	References *189*	
6	**Attention to Campaign Events: Do Twitter and Self-Report Metrics Tell the Same Story?** *193*	
	Josh Pasek, Lisa O. Singh, Yifang Wei, Stuart N. Soroka, Jonathan M. Ladd, Michael W. Traugott, Ceren Budak, Leticia Bode, and Frank Newport	
6.1	What Can Social Media Tell Us About Social Phenomena? *193*	
6.2	The Empirical Evidence to Date *195*	
6.3	Tweets as Public Attention *196*	
6.4	Data Sources *197*	
6.5	Event Detection *198*	
6.6	Did Events Peak at the Same Time Across Data Streams? *204*	
6.7	Were Event Words Equally Prominent Across Data Streams? *205*	
6.8	Were Event Terms Similarly Associated with Particular Candidates? *206*	
6.9	Were Event Trends Similar Across Data Streams? *207*	
6.10	Unpacking Differences Between Samples *211*	
6.11	Conclusion *212*	
	References *213*	

7	**Improving Quality of Administrative Data: A Case Study with FBI's National Incident-Based Reporting System Data** *217*
	Dan Liao, Marcus E. Berzofsky, G. Lance Couzens, Ian Thomas, and Alexia Cooper
7.1	Introduction *217*
7.2	The NIBRS Database *220*
7.2.1	Administrative Crime Statistics and the History of NIBRS Data *220*
7.2.2	Construction of the NIBRS Dataset *221*
7.3	Data Quality Improvement Based on the Total Error Framework *222*
7.3.1	Data Quality Assessment for Using Row–Column–Cell Framework *224*
7.3.1.1	Phase I: Evaluating Each Data Table *224*
7.3.1.2	Row Errors *225*
7.3.1.3	Column Errors *226*
7.3.1.4	Cell Errors *226*
7.3.1.5	Row–Column–Cell Errors Impacting NIBRS *227*
7.3.1.6	Phase II: Evaluating the Integrated Data *227*
7.3.1.7	Errors in Data Integration Process *227*
7.3.1.8	Coverage Errors Due to Nonreporting Agencies *228*
7.3.1.9	Nonresponse Errors in the Incident Data Table Due to Unreported Incident Reports *229*
7.3.1.10	Invalid, Unknown, and Missing Values Within the Incident Reports *230*
7.3.2	Improving Data Quality via Sampling, Weighting, and Imputation *231*
7.3.2.1	Sample-Based Method to Improve Data Representativeness at the Agency Level *231*
7.3.2.2	Statistical Weighting to Adjust for Coverage Errors at the Agency Level *232*
7.3.2.3	Imputation to Compensate for Unreported Incidents and Missing Values in the Incident Reports *233*
7.4	Utilizing External Data Sources in Improving Data Quality of the Administrative Data *234*
7.4.1	Understanding the External Data Sources *234*
7.4.1.1	Data Quality Assessment of External Data Sources *234*
7.4.1.2	Producing Population Counts at the Agency Level Through Auxiliary Data *235*
7.4.2	Administrative vs. Survey Data for Crime Statistics *236*
7.4.3	A Pilot Study on Crime in the Bakken Region *238*
7.5	Summary and Future Work *239*
	References *241*

8	**Performance and Sensitivities of Home Detection on Mobile Phone Data** *245*	

Maarten Vanhoof, Clement Lee, and Zbigniew Smoreda

8.1	Introduction *245*	
8.1.1	Mobile Phone Data and Official Statistics *245*	
8.1.2	The Home Detection Problem *247*	
8.2	Deploying Home Detection Algorithms to a French CDR Dataset *249*	
8.2.1	Mobile Phone Data *249*	
8.2.2	The French Mobile Phone Dataset *251*	
8.2.3	Defining Nine Home Detection Algorithms *252*	
8.2.4	Different Observation Periods *253*	
8.2.5	Summary of Data and Setup *255*	
8.3	Assessing Home Detection Performance at Nationwide Scale *255*	
8.3.1	Ground Truth Data *256*	
8.3.2	Assessing Performance and Sensitivities *256*	
8.3.2.1	Correlation with Ground Truth Data *256*	
8.3.2.2	Ratio and Spatial Patterns *258*	
8.3.2.3	Temporality and Sensitivity *258*	
8.4	Results *258*	
8.4.1	Relations between HDAs' User Counts and Ground Truth *258*	
8.4.2	Spatial Patterns of Ratios Between User Counts and Population Counts *260*	
8.4.3	Temporality of Correlations *260*	
8.4.4	Sensitivity to the Duration of Observation *266*	
8.4.5	Sensitivity to Criteria Choice *266*	
8.5	Discussion and Conclusion *267*	
	References *270*	

Section 3 Big Data in Official Statistics *273*

9	**Big Data Initiatives in Official Statistics** *275*	

Lilli Japec and Lars Lyberg

9.1	Introduction *275*	
9.2	Some Characteristics of the Changing Survey Landscape *276*	
9.3	Current Strategies to Handle the Changing Survey Landscape *280*	
9.3.1	Training Staff *281*	
9.3.2	Forming Partnerships *281*	
9.3.3	Cooperation Between European NSIs *282*	
9.3.4	Creating Big Data Centers *282*	
9.3.5	Experimental Statistics *283*	

9.3.6	Organizing Hackathons	*283*
9.3.7	IT Infrastructure, Tools, and Methods	*284*
9.4	The Potential of Big Data and the Use of New Methods in Official Statistics	*285*
9.4.1	Wider and Deeper	*285*
9.4.1.1	Green Areas in the Swedish City of Lidingö	*285*
9.4.1.2	Innovative Companies	*285*
9.4.1.3	Coding Commodity Flow Survey	*286*
9.4.2	Better Statistics	*287*
9.4.2.1	AIS	*287*
9.4.2.2	Expenditure Surveys	*288*
9.4.2.3	Examples of Improving Statistics by Adjusting for Bias	*288*
9.4.3	Quicker Statistics	*289*
9.4.3.1	Early Estimates	*289*
9.4.4	Cheaper Statistics	*289*
9.4.4.1	Consumer Price Index (CPI)	*289*
9.4.4.2	Smart Meter Data	*289*
9.4.4.3	ISCO and NACE Coding at Statistics Finland	*290*
9.5	Big Data Quality	*290*
9.6	Legal Issues	*293*
9.6.1	Allowing Access to Data	*293*
9.6.2	Providing Access to Data	*294*
9.7	Future Developments	*295*
	References	*296*
10	**Big Data in Official Statistics: A Perspective from Statistics Netherlands**	***303***
	Barteld Braaksma, Kees Zeelenberg, and Sofie De Broe	
10.1	Introduction	*303*
10.2	Big Data and Official Statistics	*304*
10.3	Examples of Big Data in Official Statistics	*305*
10.3.1	Scanner Data	*305*
10.3.2	Traffic-Loop Data	*306*
10.3.3	Social Media Messages	*307*
10.3.4	Mobile Phone Data	*308*
10.4	Principles for Assessing the Quality of Big Data Statistics	*309*
10.4.1	Accuracy	*310*
10.4.2	Models in Official Statistics	*311*
10.4.3	Objectivity and Reliability	*312*

10.4.4	Relevance	*314*
10.4.5	Some Examples of Quality Assessments of Big Data Statistics	*315*
10.5	Integration of Big Data with Other Statistical Sources	*316*
10.5.1	Big Data as Auxiliary Data	*316*
10.5.2	Size of the Internet Economy	*317*
10.5.3	Improving the Consumer Confidence Index	*319*
10.5.4	Big Data and the Quality of Gross National Product Estimates	*321*
10.5.5	Google Trends for Nowcasting	*322*
10.5.6	Multisource Statistics: Combination of Survey and Sensor Data	*323*
10.5.7	Combining Administrative and Open Data Sources to Complete Energy Statistics	*324*
10.6	Disclosure Control with Big Data	*325*
10.6.1	Volume	*326*
10.6.2	Velocity	*326*
10.6.3	Variety	*326*
10.7	The Way Ahead: A Chance for Paradigm Fusion	*327*
10.7.1	Measurement and Selection Bias	*328*
10.7.2	Timeliness	*329*
10.7.3	Quality	*329*
10.7.4	Phenomenon-Oriented Statistics	*330*
10.8	Conclusion	*330*
	References	*331*
	Further Reading	*337*
11	**Mining the New Oil for Official Statistics**	*339*
	Siu-Ming Tam, Jae-Kwang Kim, Lyndon Ang, and Han Pham	
11.1	Introduction	*339*
11.2	Statistical Inference for Binary Variables from Nonprobability Samples	*341*
11.3	Integrating Data Source *B* Subject to Undercoverage Bias	*343*
11.4	Integrating Data Sources Subject to Measurement Errors	*344*
11.5	Integrating Probability Sample *A* Subject to Unit Nonresponse	*345*
11.6	Empirical Studies	*347*
11.7	Examples of Official Statistics Applications	*350*
11.8	Limitations	*353*
11.9	Conclusion	*354*
	References	*354*
	Further Reading	*357*

12	**Investigating Alternative Data Sources to Reduce Respondent Burden in United States Census Bureau Retail Economic Data Products** *359*
	Rebecca J. Hutchinson
12.1	Introduction *359*
12.1.1	Overview of the Economic Directorate *360*
12.1.2	Big Data Vision *361*
12.1.3	Overview of the Census Bureau Retail Programs *361*
12.2	Respondent Burden *362*
12.3	Point-of-Sale Data *366*
12.3.1	Background on Point-of-Sale Data *366*
12.3.2	Background on NPD *368*
12.4	Project Description *369*
12.4.1	Selection of Retailers *370*
12.4.2	National-Level Data *371*
12.4.3	Store-Level Data *375*
12.4.4	Product Data *377*
12.5	Summary *381*
	Disclaimer *384*
	Disclosure *384*
	References *384*

Section 4 Combining Big Data with Survey Statistics: Methods and Applications *387*

13	**Effects of Incentives in Smartphone Data Collection** *389*
	Georg-Christoph Haas, Frauke Kreuter, Florian Keusch, Mark Trappmann, and Sebastian Bähr
13.1	Introduction *389*
13.2	The Influence of Incentives on Participation *390*
13.3	Institut für Arbeitsmarkt- und Berufsforschung (IAB)-SMART Study Design *392*
13.3.1	Sampling Frame and Sample Restrictions *393*
13.3.2	Invitation and Data Request *394*
13.3.3	Experimental Design for Incentive Study *397*
13.3.4	Analysis Plan *397*
13.4	Results *398*
13.4.1	App Installation *398*
13.4.2	Number of Initially Activated Data-Sharing Functions *400*
13.4.3	Deactivating Functions *401*

13.4.4	Retention	*402*
13.4.5	Analysis of Costs	*403*
13.5	Summary	*405*
13.5.1	Limitations and Future Research	*407*
	References	*412*

14 Using Machine Learning Models to Predict Attrition in a Survey Panel *415*
Mingnan Liu

14.1	Introduction	*415*
14.1.1	Data	*417*
14.2	Methods	*418*
14.2.1	Random Forests	*418*
14.2.2	Support Vector Machines	*419*
14.2.3	LASSO	*420*
14.2.4	Evaluation Criteria	*420*
14.2.4.1	Tuning Parameters	*422*
14.3	Results	*423*
14.3.1	Which Are the Important Predictors?	*425*
14.4	Discussion	*425*
14.A	Questions Used in the Analysis	*428*
	References	*431*

15 Assessing Community Wellbeing Using Google Street-View and Satellite Imagery *435*
Pablo Diego-Rosell, Stafford Nichols, Rajesh Srinivasan, and Ben Dilday

15.1	Introduction	*435*
15.2	Methods	*437*
15.2.1	Sampling Units and Frames	*437*
15.2.2	Data Sources	*438*
15.2.2.1	Study Outcomes from Survey Data	*438*
15.2.2.2	Study Predictors from Built Environment Data	*440*
15.2.2.3	Study Predictors from – Geospatial Imagery	*447*
15.2.2.4	Model Development, Testing, and Evaluation	*450*
15.3	Application Results	*451*
15.3.1	Baltimore	*451*
15.3.2	San Francisco	*455*
15.3.3	Generalizability	*456*
15.4	Conclusions	*457*
15.A	Amazon Mechanical Turk Questionnaire	*459*
15.B	Pictures and Maps	*461*

15.C	Descriptive Statistics 463
15.D	Stepwise AIC OLS Regression Models 469
15.E	Generalized Linear Models via Penalized Maximum Likelihood with k-Fold Cross-Validation 472
15.F	Heat Maps – Actual vs. Model-Based Outcomes 477
	References 485

16   Nonparametric Bootstrap and Small Area Estimation to Mitigate Bias in Crowdsourced Data: Simulation Study and Application to Perceived Safety *487*
David Buil-Gil, Reka Solymosi, and Angelo Moretti

16.1	Introduction 487
16.2	The Rise of Crowdsourcing and Implications 489
16.3	Crowdsourcing Data to Analyze Social Phenomena: Limitations 490
16.3.1	Self-Selection Bias 490
16.3.2	Unequal Participation 491
16.3.3	Underrepresentation of Certain Areas and Times 492
16.3.4	Unreliable Area-Level Direct Estimates and Difficulty to Interpret Results 492
16.4	Previous Approaches for Reweighting Crowdsourced Data 492
16.5	A New Approach: Small Area Estimation Under a Nonparametric Bootstrap Estimator 493
16.5.1	Step 1: Nonparametric Bootstrap 494
16.5.2	Step 2: Area-Level Model-Based Small Area Estimation 496
16.6	Simulation Study 496
16.6.1	Population Generation 497
16.6.2	Sample Selection and Simulation Steps 497
16.6.3	Results 499
16.7	Case Study: Safety Perceptions in London 503
16.7.1	The Spatial Study of Safety Perceptions 503
16.7.2	Data and Methods 504
16.7.2.1	Place Pulse 2.0 Dataset 504
16.7.2.2	Area-Level Covariates 506
16.7.3	Results 506
16.7.3.1	Model Diagnostics and External Validation 506
16.7.3.2	Mapping Safety Perceptions at Neighborhood Level 510
16.8	Discussion and Conclusions 511
	References 513

17	**Using Big Data to Improve Sample Efficiency** *519*
	Jamie Ridenhour, Joe McMichael, Karol Krotki, and Howard Speizer
17.1	Introduction and Background *519*
17.2	Methods to More Efficiently Sample Unregistered Boat-Owning Households *523*
17.2.1	Model 1: Spatial Boat Density Model *525*
17.2.2	Model 2: Address-Level Boat-Ownership Propensity *526*
17.3	Results *530*
17.4	Conclusions *533*
	Acknowledgments *534*
	References *534*

Section 5 Combining Big Data with Survey Statistics: Tools *535*

18	**Feedback Loop: Using Surveys to Build and Assess Registration-Based Sample Religious Flags for Survey Research** *537*
	David Dutwin
18.1	Introduction *537*
18.2	The Turn to Trees *538*
18.3	Research Agenda *539*
18.4	Data *540*
18.5	Combining the Data *541*
18.6	Building Models *543*
18.7	Variables *545*
18.8	Results *545*
18.9	Considering Systematic Matching Rates *552*
18.10	Discussion and Conclusions *554*
	References *557*

19	**Artificial Intelligence and Machine Learning Derived Efficiencies for Large-Scale Survey Estimation Efforts** *561*
	Steven B. Cohen and Jamie Shorey
19.1	Introduction *561*
19.2	Background *562*
19.2.1	Project Goal *563*
19.3	Accelerating the MEPS Imputation Processes: Development of Fast-Track MEPS Analytic Files *563*

19.3.1	MEPS Data Files and Variables *566*	
19.3.2	Identification of Predictors of Medical Care Sources of Payment *567*	
19.3.2.1	Class Variables Used in the Imputation *571*	
19.3.3	Weighted Sequential Hot Deck Imputation *572*	
19.4	Building the Prototype *572*	
19.4.1	Learning from the Data: Results for the 2012 MEPS *573*	
19.5	An Artificial Intelligence Approach to Fast-Track MEPS Imputation *575*	
19.5.1	Why Artificial Intelligence for Health-Care Cost Prediction *577*	
19.5.1.1	Imputation Strategies *578*	
19.5.1.2	Testing of Imputation Strategies *580*	
19.5.1.3	Approach *580*	
19.5.1.4	Raw Data Extraction *581*	
19.5.1.5	Attribute Selection *582*	
19.5.1.6	Inter-Variable Correlation *584*	
19.5.1.7	Multi-Output Random Forest *584*	
19.5.2	Evaluation *585*	
19.6	Summary *588*	
	Acknowledgments *592*	
	References *593*	

20 Worldwide Population Estimates for Small Geographic Areas: Can We Do a Better Job? *597*

Safaa Amer, Dana Thomson, Rob Chew, and Amy Rose

20.1	Introduction *597*	
20.2	Background *598*	
20.3	Gridded Population Estimates *600*	
20.3.1	Data Sources *600*	
20.3.2	Basic Gridded Population Models *601*	
20.3.3	LandScan Global *601*	
20.3.4	WorldPop *602*	
20.3.5	LandScan HD *603*	
20.3.6	GRID3 *604*	
20.3.7	Challenges, Pros, and Cons of Gridded Population Estimates *605*	
20.4	Population Estimates in Surveys *608*	
20.4.1	Standard Sampling Strategies *608*	
20.4.2	Gridded Population Sampling from 1 km × 1 km Grid Cells *609*	
20.4.2.1	Geosampling *609*	
20.4.3	Gridded Population Sampling from 100 m × 100 m Grid Cells *611*	

20.4.3.1	GridSample R Package *611*	
20.4.3.2	GridSample2.0 and www.GridSample.org *611*	
20.4.4	Implementation of Gridded Population Surveys *613*	
20.5	Case Study *613*	
20.6	Conclusions and Next Steps *616*	
	Acknowledgments *617*	
	References *617*	

Section 6 The Fourth Paradigm, Regulations, Ethics, Privacy *625*

21 Reproducibility in the Era of Big Data: Lessons for Developing Robust Data Management and Data Analysis Procedures *627*
D. Betsy McCoach, Jennifer N. Dineen, Sandra M. Chafouleas, and Amy Briesch

21.1	Introduction *627*	
21.2	Big Data *627*	
21.3	Challenges Researchers Face in the Era of Big Data and Reproducibility *629*	
21.4	Reproducibility *630*	
21.5	Reliability and Validity of Administrative Data *632*	
21.6	Data and Methods *632*	
21.6.1	The Case *632*	
21.6.2	The Survey Data *633*	
21.6.3	The Administrative Data *634*	
21.6.4	The Six Research Fallacies *635*	
21.6.4.1	More Data Are Better! *635*	
21.6.4.2	Merging Is About Matching by IDs/Getting the Columns to Align *637*	
21.6.4.3	Saving Your Syntax Is Enough to Ensure Reproducibility *639*	
21.6.4.4	Transparency in Your Process Ensures Transparency in Your Final Product *641*	
21.6.4.5	Administrative Data Are Higher Quality Than Self-Reported Data *643*	
21.6.4.6	If Relevant Administrative Data Exist, They Will Help Answer Your Research Question *644*	
21.7	Discussion *646*	
	References *649*	
	Further Reading *654*	

22	**Combining Active and Passive Mobile Data Collection: A Survey of Concerns** *657*
	Florian Keusch, Bella Struminskaya, Frauke Kreuter, and Martin Weichbold
22.1	Introduction *657*
22.2	Previous Research *659*
22.2.1	Concern with Smartphone Data Collection *659*
22.2.2	Differential Concern across Subgroups of Users *661*
22.3	Methods and Data *661*
22.3.1	Sample 1 *662*
22.3.2	Sample 2 *662*
22.3.3	Sample 3 *662*
22.3.4	Sample 4 *663*
22.3.5	Measures *663*
22.3.6	Analysis Plan *664*
22.4	Results *666*
22.5	Conclusion *670*
22.A	Appendix *673*
22.A.1	Frequency of Smartphone Use *673*
22.A.2	Smartphone Skills *673*
22.A.3	Smartphone Activities *674*
22.A.4	General Privacy Concern *674*
22.B	Appendix *675*
	Funding *679*
	References *679*

23	**Attitudes Toward Data Linkage: Privacy, Ethics, and the Potential for Harm** *683*
	Aleia C. Fobia, Jennifer H. Childs, and Casey Eggleston
23.1	Introduction: Big Data and the Federal Statistical System in the United States *683*
23.2	Data and Methods *684*
23.2.1	Focus Groups 2015 and 2016 *685*
23.2.2	Cognitive Interviews *689*
23.3	Results *690*
23.3.1	What Do Respondents Say They Expect and Believe About the Federal Government's Stewardship of Data? *690*
23.3.1.1	Confidentiality *690*
23.3.1.2	Privacy *695*
23.3.1.3	Trust in Statistics *697*

23.3.2	How Do Expectations and Beliefs About the Federal Government's Stewardship of Data Change or Remain When Asked About Data Linkage or Sharing?	*698*
23.3.3	Under What Circumstances Do Respondents Support Sharing or Linking Data?	*701*
23.3.4	What Fears and Preoccupations Worry Respondents When Asked About Data Sharing in the Federal Government?	*706*
23.3.4.1	Individual Harm	*706*
23.3.4.2	Community Harm	*707*
23.4	Discussion: Toward an Ethical Framework	*708*
23.4.1	Data Security	*709*
23.4.2	Transparency in Need for Data and Potential Uses of Data	*709*
23.4.3	Connecting Data Collections to Benefits	*709*
	References	*710*
24	**Moving Social Science into the Fourth Paradigm: The Data Life Cycle**	*713*
	Craig A. Hill	
24.1	Consequences and Reality of the Availability of Big Data and Massive Compute Power for Survey Research and Social Science	*717*
24.1.1	Variety	*717*
24.1.2	Volume	*718*
24.1.3	Velocity	*718*
24.1.4	Validity	*718*
24.2	Technical Challenges for Data-Intensive Social Science Research	*718*
24.2.1	The Long Tail	*719*
24.2.2	Uncertainty Characterization and Quantification Or True, Useful, and New Information: Where Is It?	*720*
24.2.3	Reproducibility	*722*
24.3	The Solution: Social Science Researchers Become "Data-Aware"	*723*
24.4	Data Awareness	*725*
24.4.1	Acquire/Create/Collect	*725*
24.4.2	Munge	*725*
24.4.3	Use/Reuse	*726*
24.4.4	Disseminate	*726*
24.4.5	Stewardship	*727*
24.5	Bridge the Gap Between Silos	*727*
24.6	Conclusion	*729*
	References	*729*

Index *733*

List of Contributors

Ashley Amaya
RTI International
Research Triangle Park
NC, USA

Safaa Amer
RTI International
Research Triangle Park
NC, USA

Lyndon Ang
Australian Bureau of Statistics
ABS House
Belconnen, ACT 2617, Australia
School of Mathematics
National Institute for Applied
Statistical Research
Australian University of Wollongong
Keiraville, NSW 2500, Australia

Ruben Bach
Department of Sociology
School of Social Sciences
University of Mannheim
Germany

Sebastian Bähr
Institute for Employment Research
Nuremberg, Germany

Marcus E. Berzofsky
RTI International
Research Triangle Park
NC, USA

Paul P. Biemer
RTI International
Research Triangle Park
NC, USA

Leticia Bode
Communication, Culture, and
Technology
Georgetown University
Washington, DC, USA

Barteld Braaksma
Statistics Netherlands
The Hague/Heerlen, The Netherlands

Amy Briesch
Bouve College of Health Sciences
Northeastern University
Storrs, CT, USA

Ceren Budak
School of Information
University of Michigan
Ann Arbor, MI, USA

David Buil-Gil
University of Manchester
Department of Criminology
Manchester, UK

Amelia Burke-Garcia
NORC
University of Chicago
Bethesda, MD, USA

Trent D. Buskirk
Applied Statistics and Operations
Research Department
College of Business, Bowling Green
State University
Bowling Green, OH, USA

Sandra M. Chafouleas
The Neag School of Education
University of Connecticut
Storrs, CT, USA

Rob Chew
RTI International
Research Triangle Park
NC, USA

Jennifer H. Childs
US Census Bureau
Center for Behavioral Science Methods
Washington, DC, USA

Steven B. Cohen
RTI International
Research Triangle Park
NC, USA

Alexia Cooper
Bureau of Justice Statistics
Washington, DC, USA

G. Lance Couzens
RTI International
Research Triangle Park
NC, USA

A. Rupa Datta
Center for Excellence in Survey
Research
NORC at the University of Chicago
Chicago, IL, USA

Sofie De Broe
Statistics Netherlands
The Hague/Heerlen, The Netherlands

Pablo Diego-Rosell
The Gallup Organization
Washington, DC, USA

Ben Dilday
The Gallup Organization
Washington, DC, USA

Jennifer N. Dineen
The Department of Public Policy
University of Connecticut
Storrs, CT, USA

David Dutwin
NORC at the University of Chicago
Chicago, IL 60603, USA

Brad Edwards
Westat
Rockville, MD, USA

List of Contributors

Casey Eggleston
US Census Bureau
Center for Survey Measurement
Washington, DC, USA

Aleia C. Fobia
US Census Bureau
Center for Behavioral Science Methods
Washington, DC, USA

Georg-Christoph Haas
Institute for Employment Research
Nuremberg, Germany
Joint Program in Survey Methodology
University of Maryland
College Park, MD, USA

Craig A. Hill
RTI International
Research Triangle Park
NC, USA

Rebecca J. Hutchinson
US Census Bureau
Economic Indicators Division
Washington, DC, USA

Lilli Japec
Statistics Sweden
Stockholm, Sweden

Florian Keusch
Department of Sociology
School of Social Sciences
University of Mannheim
Germany
Joint Program in Survey Methodology
University of Maryland
College Park, MD, USA

Jae-Kwang Kim
Department of Statistics
Iowa State University
Ames, IA 50011, USA

Antje Kirchner
RTI International
Research Triangle Park
NC, USA

Stas Kolenikov
Abt Associates
Cambridge, MA, USA

Frauke Kreuter
Institute for Employment Research
Nuremberg, Germany
Joint Program in Survey Methodology
University of Maryland
College Park, MD, USA
Department of Sociology
School of Social Sciences
University of Mannheim
Germany

Karol Krotki
RTI International
Research Triangle Park
NC, USA

Jonathan M. Ladd
Massive Data Institute
Georgetown University
Washington, DC, USA
McCourt School of Public Policy
Georgetown University
Washington, DC, USA
Department of Government
Georgetown University
Washington, DC, USA

Clement Lee
Department of Mathematics and Statistics
Lancaster University
Lancaster, UK

Dan Liao
RTI International
Research Triangle Park
NC, USA

Mingnan Liu
Independent Researcher
San Mateo, CA, USA

Lars E. Lyberg
Inizio
Stockholm, Sweden

D. Betsy McCoach
The Neag School of Education
University of Connecticut
Storrs, CT, USA

Joe McMichael
RTI International
Research Triangle Park
NC, USA

Angelo Moretti
Manchester Metropolitan University
Department of Computing and Mathematics
Manchester, UK

Frank Newport
Gallup Inc.
Washington, DC, USA

Stafford Nichols
The Gallup Organization
Washington, DC, USA

Josh Pasek
Department of Communication & Media
University of Michigan
Ann Arbor, MI, USA
Center for Political Studies
Institute for Social Research
University of Michigan
Ann Arbor, MI, USA

Han Pham
Australian Bureau of Statistics
ABS House
Belconnen, ACT 2617, Australia
School of Mathematics
National Institute for Applied Statistical Research
Australian University of Wollongong
Keiraville, NSW 2500, Australia

Dean Resnick
Center for Excellence in Survey Research
NORC at the University of Chicago
Chicago, IL, USA

Jamie Ridenhour
RTI International
Research Triangle Park
NC, USA

Amy Rose
Oak Ridge National Laboratory
Oak Ridge, TN, USA

Jamie Shorey
RTI International
Research Triangle Park, NC, USA

Lisa O. Singh
Computer Science Department
Georgetown University
Washington, DC, USA
Massive Data Institute
Georgetown University
Washington, DC, USA

Zbigniew Smoreda
SENSE
Orange Labs
Paris, France

Reka Solymosi
University of Manchester
Department of Criminology
Manchester, UK

Stuart N. Soroka
Department of Communication &
Media
University of Michigan
Ann Arbor, MI, USA
Center for Political Studies
Institute for Social Research
University of Michigan
Ann Arbor, MI, USA

Howard Speizer
RTI International
Research Triangle Park
NC, USA

Rajesh Srinivasan
The Gallup Organization
Washington, DC, USA

Bella Struminskaya
Department of Methodology and
Statistics
Utrecht University
The Netherlands

Siu-Ming Tam
Australian Bureau of Statistics
ABS House
Belconnen, ACT 2617, Australia
School of Mathematics
National Institute for Applied
Statistical Research
Australian University of Wollongong
Keiraville, NSW 2500, Australia

Ian Thomas
RTI International
Research Triangle Park
NC, USA

Dana Thomson
WorldPop
University of Southampton
UK
Flowminder Foundation
Stockholm, Sweden

Mark Trappmann
Institute for Employment Research
Nuremberg, Germany
University of Bamberg
Bamberg, Germany

Michael W. Traugott
Center for Political Studies
Institute for Social Research
University of Michigan
Ann Arbor, MI, USA

Gabriel Ugarte
Center for Excellence in Survey Research
NORC at the University of Chicago
Chicago, IL, USA

Maarten Vanhoof
The Bartlett Centre for Advanced Spatial Analysis
University College London
London, UK

Yifang Wei
Computer Science Department
Georgetown University
Washington, DC, USA

Martin Weichbold
University of Salzburg
Austria

Ting Yan
Westat
Rockville, MD, USA

Kees Zeelenberg
Statistics Netherlands
The Hague/Heerlen, The Netherlands

Introduction

Craig A. Hill[1], Paul P. Biemer[1], Trent D. Buskirk[2], Lilli Japec[3], Antje Kirchner[1], Stas Kolenikov[4], and Lars E. Lyberg[5]

[1] *RTI International, Research Triangle Park, NC, USA*
[2] *Applied Statistics and Operations Research Department, College of Business, Bowling Green State University, Bowling Green, OH, USA*
[3] *Statistics Sweden, Stockholm, Sweden*
[4] *Abt Associates, Cambridge, MA, USA*
[5] *Inizio, Stockholm, Sweden*

When we started this endeavor several years ago, our main intent was to produce a volume that would sew together the most promising new technologies and methodologies for exploiting massive datasets to improve, supplement, or replace processes, data, and estimates from complex surveys and censuses. As we began, we, like many others from various fields of research and practice, thought that the so-called Big Data revolution would be a one-way street affording lots of potential for improving both survey and social science research. Over the course of several years, what we have seen and learned has confirmed much of this potential. But the more we learned and the further we traveled along this path, the more we realized that it is a two-way street whereby the Big Data revolution can benefit from the research and experience of survey and social scientists. In particular, survey and social science researchers have a longstanding history of, and experience in, designing data collection processes that both provide context and answer "how" and "why" questions. Survey and social science researchers also understand how to identify, measure, and improve the quality of data. This knowledge and experience can afford much insight into the Big Data ecosystem including, for example, the introduction of survey-related variables that relay context about how and why outcomes may be occurring that have great potential for improving the signals used to create predictive models. Data poverty issues that lead to so-called "algorithmic biases" can be recast as coverage error issues; furthermore, understanding how to evaluate and mitigate impacts of these biases creates additional

Big Data Meets Survey Science: A Collection of Innovative Methods, First Edition. Edited by Craig A. Hill, Paul P. Biemer, Trent D. Buskirk, Lilli Japec, Antje Kirchner, Stas Kolenikov, and Lars E. Lyberg.
© 2021 John Wiley & Sons, Inc. Published 2021 by John Wiley & Sons, Inc.

opportunities for survey researchers and social scientists to improve the quality of data streams within the Big Data ecosystem.

Collectively, the fields of survey research and social science have extensive experience with both data generation of varying scale and data quality, realizing that estimates and insights require data of adequate quality. Under the "fit-for-purpose" paradigm, we are also exploring the use of other types of data and a larger, different array of quality indicators. These alternative new data sources, including those afforded by the Big Data revolution along with new and emerging methods, can add value and improve the quality of official statistics and estimates of human populations.

This edited volume presents a collection of snapshots from both sides of the Big Data perspective. We have assembled an array of tangible tools, methods, and approaches that illustrate (i) how Big Data sources and methods are being used in the survey and social sciences to improve official statistics and estimates for human populations along with (ii) examples of how survey data are being used to evaluate and improve the quality of insights derived from Big Data. Taken together, we believe this collection of innovative methods, tools, and examples will serve both the survey and social science communities as they learn to capitalize on this new revolution. We hope this collection serves as well the broader data and computer science communities looking for new areas of application for emerging methods and data sources.

In contrast to censuses or surveys that generate designed and sampled data, we view Big Data as nonsampled data that are organic or "found" in sources for which the primary purpose is not statistical inference *per se*. In particular, in this book we use the term *Big Data* to refer to a collection of datasets so large, complex, and rapidly changing that they become difficult to process using extant database management tools or traditional data processing applications. With rapid changes in data generation, computing, and digitization, the reality is that Big Data represent an ever-expanding collection of datasets, where the sheer size, variety, and speed of generation make them potentially powerful, but also quite difficult to manage and challenging to extract information contained therein. Certainly, "Big" may be the operative word, but we realize that "big" is relative and can have different meanings to different organizations. Petabytes of data might not pose a problem for some organizations, whereas terabytes might be a challenge for smaller organizations.

Perhaps more variable than size of data are the types or sources of Big Data: data now emanate from video surveillance and traffic cameras, sensors, retail scanners, mobile phones, web scraping, internet queries, GPS, social media, clickstreams, satellites, and credit card transactions, among many others. Big Data now proliferate across virtually every scientific domain and business sector, including agriculture, genomics, banking, health care, sports, and sales, just to name a few. Although not yet fully adopted, Big Data sources are also being embraced by many national statistical agencies now actively investigating their utility for official statistics: already, examples exist for road and marine traffic surveillance, tourism assessments, consumer confidence statistics, consumer and retail price indices, crop yield forecasting, and energy use. Increasingly, Big Data and other sources of nontraditional data are becoming available for use for an array of statistical products that have been primarily, if not exclusively, based on survey data. These new data sources are also becoming available at a time when survey data are increasingly more expensive and difficult to collect spawning greater interest to explore their viability as a lower-cost alternative.

Survey researchers and government officials are focusing on Big Data because of their potential to replace traditional data collection, supplement it, or provide new information that can improve statistical estimates. In fact, numerous Big Data developments and initiatives are under way, many of which will generate new theories, methods, and applications including, for example, the UNECE Big Data project; the European Statistical System's ESSnet on Big Data, and the Committee on Using Multiple Data Sources in U.S. Federal Statistics.

Although the rewards seem apparent, the risks of using Big Data are not as well understood or quantified. Several challenges with using Big Data sources for statistical estimation still exist, including data quality and technology-related issues. More specifically, data quality issues include: identification and treatment of errors, particularly due to incompleteness and (questionable) data content; the lack of a framework quantifying and characterizing data quality; issues related to privacy and confidentiality; the often univariate, cross-sectional nature of the available data; new legal structures associated with data ownership; and lack of universal tools. Technology-related issues include gaining access to proprietary datasets; reproducibility of technical algorithms used in generating data; potential algorithmic engineering bias; storage and processing of massive datasets and the possibility of using, as of yet, unfamiliar tools. One could argue, though, that these challenges may be more than offset by the potential advantages of using Big Data for statistics production; in fact, the potential to use various data sources and methods to reduce sampling errors, lower respondent burden, make data collection more affordable, minimize processing and production times, reduce missing or erroneous data rates and decrease the cost of information yield per unit may yet outweigh the risks.

We have no doubt that, as these data quality and technology-related challenges are studied and, subsequently, better understood, many survey researchers and government statistical agencies will move from merely exploring to implementing these alternative data sources to produce official statistics and other population estimates. That said, literature is rather limited on the use of Big Data and data science methods (within survey research) to collect, process, and analyze data to describe or estimate characteristics of finite populations. In this specific subfield,

Lane et al. (2014) deals primarily with confidentiality and privacy issues; Biemer et al. (2017) contains a few chapters on Big Data and its implications for survey science; and, Salganik (2018) discusses social science research in the digital age, including approaches, opportunities, and ethics.

By compiling the best of the papers presented at the first conference on Big Data Meets Survey Science (BigSurv18), we hope this book contributes to the current literature. Conducted under the auspices of the European Survey Research Association at the Universitat Pompeu Fabra's Research and Expertise Centre for Survey Methodology in Barcelona, Spain, BigSurv18 brought together over 400 survey researchers, social, computer, and data scientists from 45 countries. During the conference, attendees and speakers explored the potential and pitfalls of using Big Data sources and methods to examine and solve social science problems to which we have long applied survey research approaches. This book captures a representative sample (see what we did there?) of the best papers, and is organized into six sections:

Section 1: The New Survey Landscape. The BigSurv18 conference provided a unique opportunity to discuss, brainstorm, and learn how to leverage both the power of Big Data and data science to better estimate public opinion and improve official statistics. As noted, the field of public opinion research is in flux. Within this so-called "new landscape," social and survey researchers – along with government officials – are expanding their choices of methods and data sources. Specifically, these new developments and approaches are in four broad domains: (i) reimagining traditional survey research by leveraging new machine learning methods that improve efficiencies of traditional survey data collection, processing, and analysis; (ii) augmenting traditional survey data with nonsurvey data (administrative, social media, or other Big Data sources) to improve estimates of public opinion and official statistics; (iii) comparing estimates of public opinion and official statistics derived from survey data sources to those generated from Big Data or other nonsurvey data exclusively; and (iv) exploring new methods for enhancing survey data collection as well as automating the collection of nonsurvey web data. This section has three chapters that provide examples of work conducted in these domains and provide a broad overview of how machine learning methods and Big Data sources can be evaluated and used in the survey research process.

Section 2: Total Error and Data Quality. This section focuses on errors in administrative data and other Big Data sources, particularly social media data. Although a total error framework exists for complex survey data (c.f., Biemer et al. 2017), no such framework has been developed for data acquired from Big Data provenance. These chapters in this section describe efforts to understand – and quantify – these errors and their effects on data quality and substantive conclusions.

Section 3: Big Data in Official Statistics. Producers of official statistics currently face challenges from increasing expectations associated with the near-ubiquity of data: users want and expect data that are both more timely and are made richer by tapping into new data sources. At the same time, official statistics based on traditional survey data are falling out of favor because nonresponse is increasing at alarming rates, threatening validity – and costs for survey data collection are increasing at equally alarming rates. Coupled with now-common demands for reduced respondent burden, statistical agencies have been forced to investigate new ways to produce official statistics. More and more frequently, statistical agencies are now considering using Big Data in its various forms more systematically and more routinely, sometimes in combination with other data sources (including surveys), to replace current data collection procedures. Chapters in this section provide examples of this strategy in practice.

Section 4: Combining Big Data with Survey Statistics: Methods and Applications. The exponential growth of computing power and the availability of cheap data storage have given rise to Big Data applications, including artificial intelligence and machine learning. This section presents papers investigating the potential of these applications and methods for survey research, demonstrating, for example, how Big Data can be used to improve sampling efficiencies in traditional survey data collection, how Big Data can be used to complement or replace traditional survey data, or how machine learning can be used to improve the accuracy of estimates.

Section 5: Combining Big Data with Survey Statistics: Tools. This section showcases a broad cross-section of the new computational tools that are becoming available to, and more often used by, survey methodologists and social scientists. Chapters in this section demonstrate the use of machine learning methods to enhance address-based sampling frames; the use of machine learning methods to augment complicated, labor- and time-intensive imputation tasks; and new high-resolution geographic information system (GIS) grid frames for areal population sampling.

Section 6: The Fourth Paradigm: Regulations, Ethics, and Privacy. Arriving at what some would call an idealized future state in which data are shareable, discoverable, and accessible by virtually-connected communities of researchers (the Fourth Paradigm: see Hey, Tansley, and Tolle 2009) will almost necessarily entail reworking regulations and the culture surrounding data privacy and ethics. Increasingly, science – even social science – is a team sport, requiring close collaboration across multiple institutions and researchers (and their data). How do we make that utopia a reality? In this section, our authors are already considering these issues.

As the editors of this book, we believe we have started to thread together various disciplines and perspectives under the same cover to provide both novel applications of technology and data to enhance survey research *and* frontier-extending research advancing multiple scientific disciplines. In our view, this book illuminates two primary intersection points between survey research and computer science, including the use of survey data and Big Data together and the application of data science methods and approaches for refining and improving the survey research process.

Several chapters show how survey data and Big Data are used together for the benefit of one or more sources of data. More specifically, several chapters provide consistent illustrations and examples of survey data enriching the evaluation of Big Data sources. This collection of work offers a clear, fresh, and bold view of the utility and place for survey data within the broader Big Data ecosystem. Although some have argued that administrative data are considered Big Data (Connelly et al. 2016), there is less of a consensus that survey data are considered Big Data. Integrating administrative data, paradata, and, for example, sensor-derived (and other similar peripherals) data to survey respondents' records *does* make survey data bigger – not in the number of cases, but in the number of variables available per case; put another way, some survey datasets are getting bigger because they are "wider" rather than "longer." Moreover, the value proposition of survey data in the broader Big Data ecosystem could also hinge on the fact that surveys are often designed to maximize information about context and provide signals related to the "why" question. Leveraging information related to context or answers to "why" questions might improve models that are relying on other Big Data sources that do not already include such content. To this end, we see a future where researchers advocate for the utility of survey data not just as the source of national estimates or statistics, but for the role information collected using the survey process can play in enhancing prediction problems. Several chapters offer practical evidence for how organic datasets, created through technology (e.g. customer and electronic transaction data, physical sensor measurements, smartphone app ownership, web-browsing histories), are crosschecked or combined with survey data. For many of these examples, the result is greater context, richness, and insight than either source of data could have achieved alone. This extra robustness was foreshadowed by, among others, Groves (2011), Hill et al. (2013), and the AAPOR Task Force on Big Data (Japec et al. 2015). Furthermore, this ongoing line of research provides new insights into evaluating Big Data sources and incorporating them into data collection and analysis, which has wide-ranging implications and benefits to the Big Data ecosystem, itself.

Several chapters include examples of how machine learning, data mining, and other data science techniques are inserted into virtually every stage of the survey lifecycle. Taken together, these examples illustrate how data science methods are being applied to (i) assist or automate sample frame construction and the sampling process itself; (ii) provide real-time insights to monitor data collection efforts; and (iii) aid in the analysis of collected data, including identifying error sources and imputing missing data. The data science and artificial intelligence methods deployed are varied, ranging from decision trees and clustering methods for numeric data to natural language processing for enhancing the use of textual data in qualitative and quantitative analyses to cutting-edge deep learning approaches, such as convolutional and recurrent neural networks, for understanding spatial and sequential data. Although much of this work explores the application of these current methods to the survey research process, we anticipate a future where many of these methods will be adapted to the finite population framework that can incorporate aspects of survey designs and weighting, much like the work of Toth (2017) who adapted regression trees to survey data. We also see a future that includes development of new methods for improving data triangulation as well as new methods for better analyzing data from multiple sources. Such techniques will allow better fusion between survey data and other Big Data sources, for example, but will also extend to the Big Data ecosystem to improve insights by having more complete or rich data upon which to build predictive models.

To us, this collection of innovative methods evinces a willingness to improve, adapt, and enhance survey research at the corner where Big Data meets survey science. The book also illustrates how this conversation offers insights into how Big Data can be leveraged to improve official statistics and other estimates of human populations as well as expressing new perspectives for the utility and value of survey data for refining, evaluating, and improving the quality of Big Data. We hope these chapters will provide insights into how you might begin to explore the many possibilities at this rich intersection between survey science and Big Data. See you at BigSurv20 and beyond!

Acknowledgments

The editors wish to acknowledge the invaluable and tireless contributions of Susan Occoquan for her efforts in coordinating the entire process and of Laura Small for her very careful reading and editing suggestions.

References

Biemer, P.P., de Leeuw, E., Eckman, S. et al. (eds.) (2017). *Total Survey Error in Practice*, Wiley Series in Survey Methodology. Hoboken, NJ: Wiley.

Connelly, R., Playford, C.J., Gayle, V. et al. (2016). The role of administrative data in the big data revolution in social science research. *Social Science Research* 59: 1–12. https://doi.org/10.1016/j.ssresearch.2016.04.015.

Groves, R.M. (2011). Three eras of survey research. *Public Opinion Quarterly* 75 (5): 861–871. https://doi.org/10.1093/poq/nfr057.

Hey, T., Tansley, S., and Tolle, K. (2009). *The Fourth Paradigm: Data-Intensive Scientific Discovery*. Redmond, WA: Microsoft Research.

Hill, C.A., Dean, E., and Murphy, J. (2013). *Social Media, Sociality, and Survey Research*. Hoboken, NJ: Wiley.

Japec, L., Kreuter, F., Berg, M. et al. (2015). *AAPOR Report: Big Data*. Oakbrook Terrace, IL: AAPOR https://www.aapor.org/Education-Resources/Reports/Big-Data.aspx.

Lane, J., Stodden, V., Bender, S. et al. (2014). *Privacy, Big Data, and the Public Good: Frameworks for Engagement*. Cambridge, MA: Cambridge University Press.

Salganik, M.J. (2018). *Bit by Bit. Social Research in the Digital Age*. Princeton, NJ: Princeton University Press.

Toth, D. (2017). rpms: Recursive Partitioning for Modeling Survey Data. R package version 0.2.0. https://cran.r-project.org/web/packages/rpms/vignettes/rpms_2018_01_22.pdf (accessed 22 June 2019).

Section 1

The New Survey Landscape

1

Why Machines Matter for Survey and Social Science Researchers: Exploring Applications of Machine Learning Methods for Design, Data Collection, and Analysis

Trent D. Buskirk[1] and Antje Kirchner[2]

[1] *Applied Statistics and Operations Research Department, College of Business, Bowling Green State University, Bowling Green, OH, USA*
[2] *RTI International, Research Triangle Park, NC, USA*

1.1 Introduction

The earliest hard drives on personal computers had the capacity to store roughly 5 MB – now typical personal computers can store thousands of times more (around 500 GB). Data and computing are not limited to supercomputing centers, mainframe or personal computers, but have become more mobile and virtual. In fact, the very definition of "computer" is evolving to encompass more and more aspects of our lives from transportation (with computers in our cars and cars that drive themselves) to everyday living with televisions, refrigerators, doorbells, thermostats, and many other devices that are Internet-enabled and "smart." The rise of the Internet of things, smart devices, and personal computing power relegated to mobile environments and devices, like our smartphone, has certainly created an unprecedented opportunity for survey and social researchers and government officials to track, measure, and better understand public opinion, social phenomena, and the world around us.

A review of the current social science and survey research literature reveals that these fields are indeed at a crossroads transitioning from methods of active observation and data collection to a new landscape where researchers are exploring, considering, and using some of these new data sources for measuring public opinion and social phenomena. Connelly et al. (2016) comment that "whilst there may be a 'Big Data revolution' underway, it is not the size or quantity of these data that is revolutionary. The revolution centers on the increased availability of new types of data which have not previously been available for social research." In our

Big Data Meets Survey Science: A Collection of Innovative Methods, First Edition. Edited by Craig A. Hill, Paul P. Biemer, Trent D. Buskirk, Lilli Japec, Antje Kirchner, Stas Kolenikov, and Lars E. Lyberg.
© 2021 John Wiley & Sons, Inc. Published 2021 by John Wiley & Sons, Inc.

view, advances in this new landscape are taking place in seven major dimensions including

(1) reimagining traditional survey research by leveraging new machine learning methods (MLMs) that improve efficiencies of traditional survey data collection, processing, and analysis;
(2) augmenting traditional survey data with nonsurvey data (administrative, social media, or other Big Data sources) to improve estimates of public opinion and official statistics;
(3) enhancing official statistics or estimates of public opinion derived from Big Data or other nonsurvey data;
(4) comparing estimates of public opinion and official statistics derived from survey data sources to those generated from Big Data or other nonsurvey data exclusively;
(5) exploring new methods for enhancing survey and nonsurvey data collection and gathering, processing, and analysis;
(6) adapting and modifying current methods for use with new data sources and developing new techniques suitable for design and model-based inference with these data sources;
(7) contributing survey data, methods, and techniques to the Big Data ecosystem.

Weaved within this new landscape is the perspective of assimilating these new data sources into the process as substitutes, augments, or auxiliary to existing survey data. Computational social science continues to evolve as a social sciences subfield that uses computational methods, models, and advanced information technology to understand social phenomena. This subfield is particularly suited to take advantage of alternative data sources including social media and other sources of Big Data like digital footprint data generated as part of social online activities. Survey researchers are exploring the potential of these alternate data sources, especially social media data. Most recently, Burke et al. (2018) explored how social media data create opportunities for not only sampling and recruiting specific populations but also for understanding a growing proportion of the population who are active on social media sites by mining the data on such sites.

No matter the Big Data source, we need data science methods and approaches that are well suited to deal with these types of data. Although some have made the case that administrative data be considered as Big Data (Connelly et al. 2016), the general consensus in both the data science and survey research communities is that they are not. However, with the increased collection of paradata and the increased use of sensors and other similar peripherals used in data collection, one could argue that survey data are getting bigger – not in the number of cases, but in the number of variables that are available per case. Put another way, some survey datasets are getting bigger because they are "wider" rather than "longer." So we could also make the case that surveys themselves are creating bigger data and could benefit from such applying these types of methods.

This chapter explores how techniques from data science, known collectively as MLMs, can be leveraged in each phase of the survey research process. Success in the new landscape will require adapting some of the analytic and data collection approaches traditionally used by survey and social scientists to handle this more data rich reality. In his recent MIT Press' Essential Knowledge book entitled *Machine Learning*, computer engineering professor Ethem Alpaydin notes, "Machine learning will help us make sense of an increasingly complex world. Already we are exposed to more data than what our sensors can cope with or our brains can process." Although the use of MLMs seems fairly new in survey research, machines and technology have long been part of the survey and social sciences' DNA. At the 1957 AAPOR conference Frederick Stephan pointed out that "Computers will tax the ingenuity, judgment and skill of technically proficient people to (a) put the job on the machine and (b) put the results in form for comprehension of human beings; and determine the courses of action we might take based on what the machines have told us" in the context of data collection. This adage still holds today, but we are moving from machines to MLMs.

This chapter provides a brief overview of MLMs and a deeper exploration of how these data science techniques are applied to the social sciences from the perspective of the survey research process including sample design and constructing sampling frames; questionnaire design and evaluation; survey recruitment and data collection; survey data coding and processing; sample weighting and survey adjustment; and data analysis and estimation. We present a wide array of applications and examples from current studies that illustrate how these methods can be used to augment, support, reimagine, improve, and in some places replace the current methodologies. Machine learning is likely not to replace all human aspects of the survey research process, but these methods can offer new ways to approach traditional problems and can provide more efficiency, reduced errors, improved measurement, and more cost-effective processing. We also discuss how errors in the machine learning process can impact errors we traditionally manage within the survey research process.

1.2 Overview of Machine Learning Methods and Their Evaluation

MLMs are generally flexible, nonparametric methods for making predictions or classifications from data. These methods are typically described by the algorithm that details how the predictions are made using the raw data and can allow for a larger number of predictors, referred to as high-dimensional data. These methods can often automatically detect nonlinearities in the relationships between independent and dependent variables and can identify interactions automatically. Generally, MLMs can be divided into two broad categories: supervised and unsupervised machine learning techniques. The goal of supervised learning is to optimally predict a dependent variable (also referred to as output, target, class, or label), based on a range of independent variables (also referred to as inputs, features, or attributes). When a supervised method is applied to predict continuous outcomes, it is generally referred to as a regression problem and a classification problem when used to predict levels of a categorical variable. Ordinary least squares regression is a classic example of supervised machine learning. Such a technique relies on a single (continuous) dependent variable and seeks to determine the best linear fit between this outcome and multiple independent variables. MLMs can also be used to group cases based on a collection of variables known for all the cases. In these situations, there is no single outcome of interest and MLMs that are used in this context are referred to as unsupervised learners. One of the most common unsupervised methods with which social scientists and market researchers might have some familiarity is hierarchical cluster analysis (HCA) – also known as segmentation. In this case, the main interest is not on modeling an outcome based on multiple independent variables, as in regression, but rather on understanding if there are combinations of variables (e.g. demographics) that can segment or group sets of customers, respondents, or members of a group, class, or city. The final output of this approach is the actual grouping of the cases within a dataset – where the grouping is determined by the collection of variables available for the analysis.

Unlike many traditional modeling techniques such as ordinary least squares regression, MLMs require a specification of hyperparameters or tuning parameters before a final model and predictions can be obtained. These parameters are often estimated from the data prior to estimating the final model. It could be useful to think of these as settings or "knobs" on the "machine" prior to hitting the start button to generate the predictions. One of the simplest examples of a tuning parameter comes from k-means clustering. Prior to running a k-means clustering algorithm, the method needs to know how many clusters it should produce in the end (i.e. K). The main point is that these tuning parameters are needed before computing final models and predictions. Many machine learning algorithms have only one such hyperparameter (e.g. K-means clustering, least absolute shrinkage and selection operator (LASSO), tree-based models), while others require more than one (e.g. random forests, neural networks).

In contrast to many statistical modeling techniques that have a form specified in advance, MLMs are algorithmic and focus on using data at hand to describe the data-generating mechanism. In applying these more empirical methods in survey research, one must understand the distinction between models created and used for explanation vs. prediction. Breiman (2001) refers to these two end goals as the two statistical modeling cultures, and Shmueli (2010) refers to them as two modeling paths. The first consists of traditional methods or explanatory models that focus on explanation, while the second consists of predictive models that focus on prediction of continuous outcomes or classification for categorical outcomes. Although machine learning or algorithmic methods can be used to refine explanatory models, their most common application lies in the development of prediction or classification models. The goals and methods for constructing and evaluating models from these two paths overlap to some degree, but in many applications, specific differences can occur that should be understood to maximize their utility in both research and practice.

Explanatory models are commonly used in research and practice to facilitate statistical inferences rather than to make predictions, per se. The underlying shape (e.g. linear, polynomial terms, and nonlinear terms) and content of these models is often informed by the underlying theory, experience of the researcher, or prior literature. Well-constructed explanatory models are then used to investigate hypotheses related to the underlying theory as well as to explore relationships among the predictor variables and the outcome of interest. These models are constructed to maximize explanatory power (e.g. percentage of observed variance explained) and are evaluated by goodness of fit measures and effect sizes. On the other hand, MLMs are often constructed solely to predict or classify continuous or categorical outcomes, respectively, for new cases not yet observed. In contrast to many explanatory models, the actual functional form of the predictive model is often not specified in advance and is often not of primary interest since the main objective in evaluating these models revolves around the overall prediction accuracy (Shmueli 2010) and not on the individual evaluation of the predictors themselves.

Compared to traditional statistical methods, MLMs are more prone to overfitting the data, that is, to detecting patterns that might not generalize to other data. Model development in machine learning hence usually relies on so-called *cross-validation* as one method to curb the risk of overfitting. Cross-validation can be implemented in different ways but the general idea is to use a subsample of the data, referred to as a *training* or *estimation sample*, to develop a predictive model. The remaining sample, not included in the training subsample, is referred to as a *test* or *holdout sample* and is used to evaluate the accuracy of the predictive model developed using the training sample. Some machine learning techniques use a third subsample for tuning, that is, the *validation sample*, to find those tuning parameters that yield the most optimal prediction. In these cases, once a model has been constructed using the training sample and refined using the validation sample, its overall performance is then evaluated using the test sample.

For supervised learners, these three samples contain both the predictor variables (or features) and the outcome (or target) of interest.

The predictive accuracy for machine learning algorithms applied to continuous outcomes is usually quantified using a root mean squared error statistic that compares the observed value of the outcome to predicted value. In classification problems, the predictive accuracy can be estimated using a host of statistics including sensitivity, specificity, and overall accuracy. Generally, the computation of these and related measures of accuracy are based on a *confusion matrix*, which is simply a cross-tabulated table with the rows denoting the actual value of the target variable for every sample or case in your test set and the columns representing the values of the predicted level of the target variable for every sample or case in your test set. Buskirk et al. (2018b) describe confusion matrices in more detail along with a host of accuracy metrics that can be derived from the confusion matrix and used to evaluate classification models, in particular. Kuhn and Johnson (2013) and James et al. (2013) also provide a deeper discussion of using such metrics for evaluating models within a cross-validation framework.

1.3 Creating Sample Designs and Constructing Sampling Frames Using Machine Learning Methods

1.3.1 Sample Design Creation

Many early applications of MLMs for sample design development focused on using these algorithms to create partitions of known population units into optimal groupings to facilitate stratified sampling or some other type of sampling designs. In particular, these approaches apply various types of unsupervised machine learning algorithms such as k-means clustering or Gaussian mixture models (GMMs) to an array of frame data and other auxiliary information to segment population units into groups for use as primary sampling units or strata for sampling designs. The population might also refer to a survey panel and auxiliary information might refer to typical frame-related variables as well as survey variables collected during prior phases. In either case, the goal of these approaches is to optimize segmentation of population units into groups that are efficient for sampling rather than on optimizing model fit. Evaluation of the final groupings obtained from the MLMs considers implications for both sampling errors and operational issues.

Although the literature illustrating applications of these types of unsupervised machine learning algorithms for developing sampling designs is small, it is growing. Burgette et al. (2019) compared three different unsupervised learning methods to create sampling strata to understand the range of care delivery structures and processes being deployed to influence the total costs of caring for patients over time. More specifically, their team compared k-means clustering to a mixture of normals (also referred to as GMMs) and mixture of regression models for clustering annual total cost of care statistics over a three-year period for some 40 physician organizations participating in the Integrated Healthcare Association's value-based pay-for-performance program. Of primary interest was the total cost of care and its pattern over this period, so developing a design that groups physician organizations by total cost trajectories and magnitude was crucial. The cluster groupings from each of the three methods considered formed the basis of sampling strata. Burgette et al. (2019) evaluated the results from each method and decided on the results produced using the mixture of normals for their final sampling strata.

The work of Burgette and colleagues highlighted some key, important differences in the assumptions and mechanics of the three clustering methods. Most notably, the k-means clustering algorithm is concerned with differences about the cluster means and assumes that the within-cluster variances are equal, and the algorithm seeks to group units so as to minimize this within-cluster variance across the k-clusters. A common assumption in many models such as ANOVA is that the assumption of equal stratum variances may be too restrictive and not reasonable. The optimal number of clusters generated from the k-means algorithm taken as strata will be too heterogeneous relative to other stratifications that focus on grouping sampling units to reduce variation within each stratum without the restriction or assumption that this reduced variance is the same for every stratum. Burgette et al. (2019) note that the mixture of normal models does not have the assumption of equal variance within each of the clusters and allows this variance to vary within the resulting clusters. The mixture of normal models also allows researchers to incorporate a unit of size as an additional input into the modeling process separate from the variables upon which clustering is based.

Despite the limitations of k-means clustering, it is widely used because of its speed and ease of implementation and interpretation. Buskirk et al. (2018a) also explored the utility of the k-means clustering algorithm applied to telephone exchange data. The goal was to create a stratified sampling design to be used to select households from 13 council districts in an urban county in the northeastern United States. Using the 13 district geographical boundaries and information about assigned landline telephones, the team created auxiliary information consisting of the percentage of each of the 13 local districts covered by each landline telephone exchange in this county. The k-means algorithm grouped telephone exchanges based on these coverage statistics, resulting in eight clusters. Because the final goal was to create nonoverlapping sampling strata for an random digit-dial (RDD) sample that could be used to create estimates of sufficient size from all 13 council districts, the eight clusters were combined into a smaller number of strata. The first stratum consisted of the union of two of these eight clusters and covered four council districts, whereas the second stratum combined the remaining six clusters to cover the remaining nine council districts. Based on cross-validation information collected during the survey, this design achieved an estimated 97% overall coverage rate with 95% from the first stratum and 98% from the second.

1.3.2 Sample Frame Construction

The applications discussed in Section 1.3.1 have assumed that a population or frame already exists and have focused on leveraging known information about these units to create sample partitions or subsets using unsupervised MLMs. In some situations, however, the frames may overcover the target population and may require modification prior to segmentation to create sampling units that have a higher incidence for the target population. In yet other situations, no known frames or systematic collection of population units are available. To this end, a growing body of literature is focused on applying MLMs to *create* sampling frames or revise existing frames to improve coverage for the intended target population. Some of these applications use existing frame data, auxiliary data, and survey data to create models predicting whether or not population units in an existing frame belong to the target population while other applications use Big Data sources, such as satellite images, to create models that will identify locations of sampling units.

Garber (2009) used classification trees to predict eligibility of units included in a master mailing list for a survey targeting farms. Reductions in data collection inefficiencies due to overcoverage resulted from removing those units with low likelihood of eligibility. Bosch et al. (2018) discuss how they added web address information to a business register composed of a list of enterprises using a focused web scraping approach. Because the crawler might have misidentified the uniform record locator (URL), the team used MLMs to predict whether the URL was appropriate for each enterprise in the database. In this application, MLMs were not applied directly to identify population units or to segment them, but rather as part of the process for editing information on the frame obtained via web scraping methods. Chew et al. (2018) combine the approaches of frame refinement with frame creation by applying a two-category classification task to predict whether a satellite image scene is residential or nonresidential within a gridded population sampling framework.

Gridded samples use a geographic information system to partition areas of interest into logistically manageable grid cells for sampling (Thomson et al. 2017; Amer 2015). These designs typically involve several stages with one of the key stages selecting a series of primary grid units (PGUs) followed by a subselection of many secondary grid units (SGUs) within the PGUs. In many applications of this approach in developing countries, these SGUs are sparsely populated and

1.3 Creating Sample Designs and Constructing Sampling Frames Using Machine Learning Methods

consequently may have no eligible household units within them. To improve sampling efficiency, a layer of coding is often deployed within the selected PGUs to eliminate SGUs that contain no eligible population units prior to the phase of sampling that selects a subset of the SGUs. Human coders have traditionally been used to perform these important frame revision tasks but costs for this labor continue to rise and press against budget constraints. Chew et al. (2018) explored how a collection of machine learning algorithms compare to human coders for accurately determining whether SGUs, within selected PGUs from two different developing counties, contain residential units making them eligible for inclusion in further sampling stages of the gridded population design. The team compared MLMs (such as random forests, decision trees, and support vector machines, among others) that used predictors from an administrative database along with other algorithms such as convolutional neural networks (CNNs) (as described in Eck 2018, for example) that used satellite images to predict whether SGUs should be classified as residential (and thus eligible) or nonresidential. They found that although administrative data helped predict whether SGUs were residential, neural network models using aerial images performed much better, nearly as well as human coders for one country, and outperformed human coders in another. This performance is encouraging, but the authors note that the processing and availability of aerial images may not be ubiquitous for all regions or countries.

Whereas the work of Chew et al. (2018) focused on object recognition tasks, with the primary objective of classifying the object in the image (e.g. residential or nonresidential), other research has focused on applying similar machine learning algorithms for object detection, with the primary task of counting the number and/or locations of specific images (e.g. houses). Eck et al. (2018) applied CNN models to aerial images of land plots from across a Midwestern state in the United States to generate a sampling frame of windmills. They were interested not only in classifying a sample of land plots into those with and without windmills but also in determining the location of the windmills within those land plots. Based on processing images from 10 counties within this state, the algorithm exhibited about 95% sensitivity missing only 95 of the 1913 windmills within these 10 counties. The specificity was also high at nearly 98% – however, because many land plots have no windmills, even this 2% misclassification results in nearly 8000 land plots incorrectly identified as having a windmill. However, human coders might be able to examine all images predicted to be windmills and provide final classifications for these images reducing the problem, in this case, from looking at about 9800 images instead of 300 000. So the machine learning algorithm can provide a focused set of land plots that need final adjudication by human coders, thus reducing the total costs in constructing a final sampling frame.

Identifying whether a unit belongs in the sampling frame is an important aspect of frame refinement or digitization of eligibility. Such an application though assumes that sampling units are already identified, either from the beginning, or via some earlier stage of sampling. Another application of machine learning involves the actual identification of sampling units from a collection of aerial images. In these applications, it is not sufficient to know only that an image contains sampling units because some images may contain more than one such population unit and ultimately, the population will be sampled at the unit level. Eck et al. (2018) applied CNNs to a series of aerial images to determine the location of windmills in counties across Iowa in the United States. They found that the neural networks model was adequate for correctly identifying land plots that contained a windmill, but at the cost of a large number of false positives. Eck et al. (2018) also sought to use these models to generate estimates of the total number of windmills from each county in Iowa. Such an estimate could be used by designs as a measure of size to facilitate selection of counties proportional to the number of windmills or stratification of counties based on the number of windmills. Because of the high number of false positives from the CNN model applied to the land plots, the estimated total number of windmills varied widely across the counties with all estimates being too high by between 95 and just over 1300 windmills. Eck and colleagues refined their approach in 2019 to include a stratification step prior to training the CNN models that ensured more variability in images without windmills that found that this step greatly reduced the number of false positives. They also examined the relationship between the source of the images and various tuning parameters and the coverage properties of the resulting sampling frame. They found that coverage rates were consistent across a range of tuning parameters and that the number of images used for training had relatively little impact on the accuracy measures. Including stratification in the selection of training data was important for reducing the number of false negatives (i.e. increased sensitivity) but had relatively little impact on the false negative rate. They posit that refinements in the stratification approach may be needed to improve the false negative rates moving forward.

1.3.3 Considerations and Implications for Applying Machine Learning Methods for Creating Sampling Frames and Designs

The synthesis of this small collection of studies suggests that the application of MLMs for sampling frame and design development is not automatic and algorithmic, and data error implications should be considered and balanced carefully. We discuss each of these broad considerations in turn here.

1.3.3.1 Considerations About Algorithmic Optimization

The results deemed optimal for grouping population units into groups based on an MLM may not be optimal for sampling or data collection. For example, some results from unsupervised learning models may produce groups with a single or too few population units to support the sampling design or estimation of sampling variance. Generally, for stratification, one wants a sample of at least two population units selected per group and in some cases, larger samples may be needed for other analytic objectives including comparisons across groups. In these cases, we need to ensure that the final segmentation has sufficient numbers of population units per unit. As Burgette et al. (2019, p. 6) point out "we are less concerned with model fit and more concerned with the sample characteristics that result from using the clusters [segments] as sample strata."

The MLMs are using an objective for optimization that is related to what researchers desire – a natural grouping of population units into segments. However, to be useful for sampling, these segments may need to have a minimum size or the number of such segments may need to be constrained to meet sampling field operations requirements or data collection cost constraints, none of which are considered in the algorithms. That is, the requirements of sample designs and survey operations are not seen by current clustering algorithms during their processing of available data to create potential sampling strata or primary sampling unit groupings. As a result, the results from the MLM serve as the basis or first step that is then refined to meet additional sampling requirements or data collection constraints.

1.3.3.2 Implications About Machine Learning Model Error

Although using MLMs has notable advantages for creating sampling designs, these methods are not without error. Misclassification errors result when MLMs fail to correctly classify units. In sample frame development, machine learning algorithms are applied to classify an image, land plot, or some other related unit as eligible for inclusion in the frame or ineligible. A false positive misclassification error results in a frame that might result in overcoverage of the actual population and lead to inefficiencies in survey data collection. A false negative misclassification error results in undercoverage and may lead to biased estimates if there is a systematic difference between population units correctly included on the frame and those excluded. To our knowledge, there is little work on the impact of this type of machine learning error on final survey estimates although Eck et al. (2019) discuss this as a future area of research. Moreover, there is even less understanding of how tuning parameter selection in these machine learning algorithms might be related to these potential survey errors and how one might incorporate this aspect of survey estimation into the classification algorithm.

By default, most machine learning algorithms optimize classifications to balance false positives with false negatives; however, one can use additional cost functions within these algorithms to penalize false positives at a higher rate than false negatives or vice versa. In frame development, one might argue that false negatives (leading to undercoverage) may be the more critical error. However, if there are no systematic differences on the survey outcome between correctly included and incorrectly excluded cases, then there might be more tolerance for this type of error. On the other hand, one could argue that if data collection costs are expensive (as in in-person or on-the-ground data collection or collection via expensive sensor equipment), then false positives might be the more critical error. If the false positive rate is high, for example then an eligibility screener may be necessary as an additional survey process step to ensure that only eligible population units be included in final analyses. In any case, it seems important to be able to quantify the impact of these errors before using MLMs for sampling frame development so that either the final results or choices of which of many MLMs lead to the best possible sample frame for use in the final sampling design can be assessed accordingly.

1.3.3.3 Data Type Considerations and Implications About Data Errors

Most of the unsupervised MLMs create population groupings using a collection of continuous covariates. Cluster solutions are often sensitive to variable scaling so if the continuous variables have different scales, transforming the variables so they are all on the same scale is often recommended (Hastie, Tibshirani, and Friedman 2001). However, not all frame or auxiliary variables that are available for use in such segmentation are continuous. Scaling binary or nominal variables and treating them as continuous variables does not make much sense and could impact interpretability of results. Sampling designs seeking to leverage auxiliary information that is a mix of continuous, ordinal, and nominal variables may need to be modified by selecting a different proximity measure or using a method that allows for a mix of variable types such as hierarchical clustering with an appropriate distance measure. Boriah et al. (2008) compared 14 different similarity measures for categorical data for use with a k-nearest neighbors algorithm for outlier detection. Their experimental results suggest that there is no one best performing similarity measure, and the authors urge researchers to carefully consider how a particular similarity measure handles the different characteristics of the categorical variables in a given dataset *prior to* selecting the measure. Rather than focusing on different proximity measures for clustering data based on categorical variables, researchers have also explored using different statistics for creating the clusters including k-modes (Huang 1998) or fuzzy k-modes (Huang and Ng 1999; Kim, Lee, and Lee 2004). These methods use a single distance function appropriate for categorical variables. For datasets with categorical and continuous variables, Huang (1998) proposes a k-prototypes clustering algorithm based on a combination of two distance functions applied to categorical and continuous variables, respectively. When cases are to be clustered using only categorical variables or a mix of categorical and continuous variables, as often occurs in survey research applications, the results of the clustering will likely be more reproducible and interpretable and more likely to represent the underlying constructs, if any, within the collection of variables. Sampling designs seeking to give variables unequal influence on the creation of population segments may also benefit from using an additional weighting variable in the unsupervised MLM where the weights specify each variable's relative influence on the overall segmentation.

Regardless of the type of data used in the machine learning algorithms, the impact of error within the variables themselves on the overall segmentation results is not well understood. Errors in the measurement of auxiliary, frame, or survey variables that are used in unsupervised machine learning algorithms to create population segments are of particular interest since we readily experience and quantify this type of error within the total survey error framework. Pankowska et al. (2018) explored the impact of survey measurement error on the correct classification of respondents into known groups using both GMMs as well as density-based spatial clustering of applications with noise (DBSCAN). Their simulation experiment varied the type of measurement error, the number of variables considered in the clustering that had error, the error rate, and the magnitude of the error. Pankowska and colleagues found that GMM is less sensitive to measurement errors compared to DBSCAN. Measurement error, regardless of method, has a very strong biasing effect for correctly recovering the true underlying grouping structure if the measurement error is systematic, rather than random, and all variables have high levels of measurement error. This work provides insights into the interplay between measurement error in surveys and the results of the clustering algorithms and suggests that cluster algorithms are not equally sensitive or robust to these types of survey errors. The measurement error found in survey variables that might be used to create sampling designs may have a compounding effect under certain conditions as suggested by the work of Pankowska et al. (2018). More work is needed to understand the degree of this compounding and whether other popular clustering methods may be robust against it. This example is just one of many where survey methodologists and statisticians might be able to improve these types of algorithms. The implications of revised algorithms that can incorporate error properties of data within them have a great potential for not only survey data but also for other Big Data sources, especially for Big Data sources with error properties similar to measurement error.

1.4 Questionnaire Design and Evaluation Using Machine Learning Methods

Questionnaire design, pretesting, and evaluating survey questions, improving instrument design, and incorporating alternative measures alongside survey data are other components in the survey lifecycle that can benefit from recent developments in MLMs.

1.4.1 Question Wording

Although applications demonstrating the potential of machine learning for questionnaire design (or developing question wording in the more traditional sense) have been developed successfully, users may not know that many of these tools rely on MLMs.

The free online application Survey Quality Predictor (SQP) *2.0* (http://sqp.upf.edu/) is one such example. SQP allows researchers to assess the quality of their questions, including suggestions for improvements, either prior to data collection or if this assessment is done after data collection, to allow researchers to quantify (and correct for) potentially biasing impact of measurement error (Oberski and DeCastellarnau 2019). For this assessment to work, researchers first have to code their question along several different dimensions including topic, wording, response scale, and administration mode (using the coding system developed by Saris and Gallhofer 2007, 2014). The second step is that the system then predicts the quality of said question, or more specifically, two indicators of measurement error: the reliability and the validity of the survey question.[1] This prediction task is where machine learning comes in: while SQP 1.0 relied on linear regression modeling, SQP 2.0 uses random forests consisting of 1500 individual regression trees to account for possible multicollinearity of question characteristics, nonlinear relationships, and interaction effects (Saris and Gallhofer 2007, 2014; Oberski, Gruner, and Saris 2011; Oberski and DeCastellarnau 2019).[2] These random forests explain a much higher portion of the variance, namely 65% of the variance in reliability and 84% of validity across the questions in the test sample, compared to the linear regression used in the first version of SQP (reliability: 47%; validity: 61%) (Saris and Gallhofer 2014; Oberski 2016). SQP also provides researchers with an importance measure, that is prioritization, as to which question characteristic is the most influential and how changing a particular question feature, say a 5-point response scale to an 11-point response scale would alter the predicted reliability and validity. Another tool with a slightly different approach is QUAID (question-understanding-aid) (Graesser et al. 2000; Graesser et al. 2006).

---

1 Reliability in the context of SQP refers to the "theoretical correlation between the true value and the observed answer," whereas validity refers to the "hypothetical spurious correlation between two otherwise unrelated questions" asked using the same method (Oberski and DeCastellarnau 2019, p. 8)).

2 The predictions of a question's quality in SQP 2.0 and higher are based on data from an extensive meta-analysis consisting of 98 survey experiments conducted in 22 countries between 1979 and 2006, with about 3500 questions and about 60 question characteristics (Oberski and DeCastellarnau 2019).

QUAID uses computational linguistics (i.e. lexicons and syntactic parsers) to assist researchers and practitioners in improving the wording, syntax, and semantics of questions.

Other applications in this domain investigate the use of machine learning in respondent and interviewer instructions, or scripted probes. Belli et al. (2016) used classification trees to uncover respondent and interviewer behavioral sequences that predicted respondents engaging in different retrieval strategies in calendar interviews which, as the authors showed, ultimately affect data quality. The challenges with these data are the dependencies within each sequence of behaviors and the (non)occurrence of behaviors at each stage that prohibits the use of more traditional approaches. These results are relevant for questionnaire design because they can directly impact placement and scripting of interviewer probes and interviewer training in how to use these probes. Machine learning can also provide insights as to how to redesign questionnaires based on (real-time) respondent behaviors, for example, to minimize item-level nonresponse, or to prevent break-offs or straight lining. If a participant is estimated to have a high likelihood of breaking off from a web survey while they are in the process of taking it, adaptations can be made to perhaps mitigate the risk of a partial complete due to break-off. One of the main issues is the speed by which models can estimate these propensities as well as being able to make adaptations in real time for online surveys based on these predictions. The other issue to tackle is at what points within the survey is break-off propensity estimated and how frequently an adaptation is made. For now these are open questions, but research into some of these areas is under way. For example, Mittereder and West (2018) used a dynamic Cox survival model based on page invariant respondent characteristics as well as page variant response behavior during the first portion of an annual survey to predict break-off from that point. A separate warning screen was displayed for those respondents with high predicted likelihood of break-off with a message encouraging respondents to continue because their answers were crucial to the goals of the study. The team determined the place where most break-offs occurred and generated a propensity model using survey data from prior years. Using Markov chains (MCs) and recurrent neural networks (RNN) to account for the sequential data, Eck et al. (2015) predict whether a respondent will break off from an online survey, based on paradata collected about respondents interactions with the survey. The authors showed that, compared to MCs, the RNNs achieve a better performance and have a higher precision in that they almost always predict break-offs correctly. More recently, Eck and Soh (2017a) extended these models to predict straight lining in survey grids before it occurs again using paradata. The authors showed that grids placed later in the survey tend to be predicted more accurately, i.e. when there were more opportunities for the algorithm to learn the behavior under investigation, and that the models perform better with more instances of "bad" behaviors. Using the knowledge from these studies in real time would allow questionnaire designers to incorporate motivation probes or other adaptive survey interventions to retain respondent motivation and prevent straight lining or break-offs (e.g. Eck and Soh 2017b; Mittereder and West 2018; Mittereder 2019).

1.4.2 Evaluation and Testing

In addition to the tools and applications targeted to improve question wording, researchers have used machine learning in question evaluation and testing. The insights from these studies, e.g. which questions contribute to interviewer misreading and which operations in reporting cause respondent reporting errors, can be used to redesign and improve existing questionnaires, serve as a tool to assess interviewer performance and to target interviewers for retraining, and potentially help identify the type of respondent to include for testing.

For example, Timbrook and Eck (2018, 2019) investigated the respondent-interviewer interaction or more specifically interviewer reading behaviors – that is, whether a question was read with or without changes and whether those changes were minor or major. The traditional approach to measure interviewer reading behaviors is behavior coding, which can be very time-consuming and expensive. Timbrook and Eck (2018, 2019) demonstrated that it is possible to partially automate the measurement of these interviewer question reading behaviors using machine learning. The authors compared string comparisons, RNNs, and human coding. Unlike string comparisons that only differentiate between reading with and without changes, RNNs like human coders should be able to reliably differentiate between reading questions with minor or with major changes. Comparing RNNs to string matching (read with change vs. without), the authors showed that exact string comparisons based on preprocessed text were comparable to the other methods. Preprocessing text, however, is resource intensive. If the text was left unprocessed, they showed that the exact string comparisons were less reliable than any other method. In contrast, RNNs can differentiate between different degrees of deviations in question reading. The authors showed that RNNs trained on unprocessed text are comparable to manual, human coding if there is a high prevalence of deviations from exact reading and that the RNNs perform much worse when there is a low prevalence of deviations. Regardless of this prevalence, RNNs performed slightly worse identifying minor changes in question wording. McCarthy and Earp (2009) retrospectively analyzed data from the 2002 Census of Agriculture using classification trees to identify respondents with higher rates of reporting errors in surveys (more specifically, when reporting land size such as total acreage and broken down by individual components depending on land use).

Data from focus groups are also useful for evaluating and pretesting questionnaires, but often the data generated from these sessions is digitized and stored as text. The potential for MLMs to aid in processing this type of textual data along with others gathered throughout the survey process are discussed in more detail in Section 1.6.1.

1.4.3 Instrumentation and Interviewer Training

Finally, other studies exemplified the use of machine learning with a focus on instrumentation, interface development, and interviewer training. Arunachalam et al. (2015) showed how MCs and artificial neural networks (ANNs) can be used to improve computer-assisted telephone interviewing for the American Time Use Survey. Using algorithms that are particularly useful for temporal pattern recognition in combination with paradata, the authors' goal was to predict a respondent's next likely activity. This next likely activity would then be displayed live for interviewers on their computer assisted telephone interviewing (CATI)-screens based on time of day and previous activity to facilitate probing and data entry reducing item nonresponse. This process should ultimately improve data quality and increase data collection efficiencies. Although both algorithms predicted the respondents' activity sequence accurately, the authors found a higher predictive accuracy for the ANNs. Machine learning has also been used to improve the survey instrument for open-ended questions, such as questions regarding occupation (see Section 1.6.1). To facilitate respondent retrieval, decrease respondent burden, and reduce coding errors, Schierholz et al. (2018) investigated computer-assisted coding. More specifically, they assessed the performance of matching algorithms in combination with gradient-boosting decision trees, suggesting a potential occupation based on a verbatim response initially provided by the respondent. Respondents then selected their occupation from this list of suggestions (including an option "different occupation"). The authors showed that the algorithm detected possible categories for 90% of all respondents, of which 80% selected a job title and 15% selected "different occupation" thereby significantly reducing the resources needed for postinterview coding. Other applications of machine learning algorithms, such as regularization networks, test-time feature acquisition, or natural language processing can be used to reduce respondent burden and data collection cost by informing adaptive questionnaire designs (e.g. for nonresponse conversion) in which individuals receive a tailored number or order of questions or question modules, tailored instructions, or particular interventions in real time, depending on responses to earlier questions and paradata (e.g. for surveys more generally, Early 2017; Morrison et al. 2017; Kelly and Doriot 2017; for vignette surveys or conjoint analysis in marketing, Abernethy et al. 2007; for intelligent, dialogue-based or conversational, tutoring systems, or knowledge assessments, Niraula and Rus 2014).

1.4.4 Alternative Data Sources

Other areas of application of MLMs for questionnaire design include the collection or extraction and processing of data from alternative (Big) Data sources. For example, collecting data from images (e.g. expenditure data from grocery or medical receipts, Jäckle et al. 2019), or websites and apps such as Flickr, Facebook, Instagram or Snapchat (Agarwal et al. 2011), or sensors (e.g. smartphone sensors capturing geo-location and app use, fitness trackers, or eye trackers) may allow researchers to simplify the survey questionnaire and reduce the data collection burden for respondents by dropping some questions entirely. Processing these Big Data, is however, often impossible with standard techniques and requires the use of MLMs to extract features. Among these are deep learning for image processing (e.g. student transcripts,[3] photos of meals or receipts to keep food logs in surveys about food or health,[4] or aerial images to assess neighborhood safety) (Krizhevsky, Sutskever, and Hinton 2012); natural language processing (e.g. to understand spoken meal descriptions (Korpusik et al. 2016); code student transcripts (Shorey et al. 2018)), or the use of Naïve Bayesian classifiers or density-based spatial clustering algorithms (e.g. applied to high-dimensional sensor data from smartphones to optimize the content, frequency, and timing of intervention notifications (e.g. Morrison et al. 2017), to detect home location (e.g. Vanhoof et al. 2018), or to investigate the relationship between location data and an individual's behavior such as exercise frequency (e.g. Eckman et al. 2019)).

1.5 Survey Recruitment and Data Collection Using Machine Learning Methods

Machine learning can also be useful for survey recruitment to monitor and manage data collection and to tailor data collection protocols in terms of expected response rates, nonresponse or measurement bias, or cost considerations.

---

3 While Shorey et al. (2018) focus primarily on the application of deep learning techniques enhanced with structured prior knowledge in the Minerva™ Knowledge Graph to improve coding, imputation, and quality control of survey data in postsecondary education, they also briefly discuss data extraction when processing transcripts, e.g. using optical character recognition software to extract information from pdfs.
4 Calorie Mama AI (https://www.caloriemama.ai/) is one example of an app-based food AI API to identify and track food items based on deep learning and image classification.

1.5.1 Monitoring and Interviewer Falsification

Opportunities for interviewer monitoring and the detection of fabricated interviews during survey recruitment and data collection using machine learning instead of principal component analysis, multiple correspondence analysis, or logistic regression (e.g. Blasius and Thiessen 2015; De Haas and Winker 2016) are now being explored. Using survey and paradata, for example, Birnbaum (2012) investigated different scenarios[5] using supervised (logistic regression and random forest) and unsupervised techniques (e.g. outlier detection via local correlation integral algorithms) to detect fabricated interviews and describes the anomalies found in datasets. Although the logistic regression performed comparably to the random forest at the individual level, the random forest outperformed logistic regression (92% accuracy) at the interviewer level (97% accuracy). The unsupervised algorithms also performed significantly above chance. Sun et al. (2019) took a different approach to detect interviewer falsification and performance issues. The authors relied on audio-recordings of survey interviews and speech recognition to identify fabrication (via the number of speakers) and performance issues (via interviewer reading behaviors; see also Timbrook and Eck (2018, 2019)). They could accurately detect the number of speakers and question misreading in their lab study, but the authors also showed that detecting the number of speakers was highly dependent on the quality of the audio recording.

1.5.2 Responsive and Adaptive Designs

In 2012, the US Census Bureau set out to develop a new model-based hard-to-count score by organizing the Census Return Rate Challenge that researchers and practitioners could use to tailor data collection protocols by "stratify[ing] and target[ing] geographic areas according to propensity to self-respond in sample surveys and censuses" (Erdman and Bates 2017, p. 144). The challenge asked teams to predict the 2010 Census mail-return rates using data from the census planning database (PDB). Interestingly, the three winning models used some form of ensemble methods (more specifically, gradient boosting or random forests), and the winning model included over 300 predictor variables. Using MLMs to prioritize variables, the Census Bureau then proceeded to derive their new low response score (using ordinary least squares including 25 predictors identified as most important in the winning models). These data are now available for researchers and practitioners to use at the block group and the tract level of the PDB to adjust and tailor their data collection protocols. MLMs

---

5 Assuming a training dataset in which it is known which interviews are fabricated and a scenario in which this is unknown, and whether or not researchers want to investigate fabrication at the question(s), the individual or the interviewer-level.

have also been applied in federal settings to prioritize resources. In particular, Earp and McCarthy (2009) used classification trees to determine characteristics of units most likely to respond both with and without incentives for the Agricultural Resource Management Survey (ARMS). From these models, the team was able to create an efficient allocation plan that provided incentives to those units for which they would likely be most effective.

Chew and Biemer (2018) presented another approach to improve the efficiency of adaptive and responsive survey designs by dynamically adjusting designs during data collection using multi-armed bandits (MABs). Stochastic MABs rely on reinforcement learning at different steps of the data collection process (e.g. using sample batches) to balance the tradeoff between "exploiting" the currently most successful intervention (e.g. with respect to response rates) while also "exploring" alternative interventions. Instead of randomly allocating the entire sample into a fixed control and treatment group prior to data collection and then assessing the effectiveness of interventions after data collection ends, the MAB algorithm iteratively assesses treatment effectiveness of each condition during data collection starting with a smaller sample replicate and iteratively assigns remaining replicates. This iterative approach allows more sampled cases to be allocated to the superior treatment earlier compared to a traditional experimental approach (however, potentially at the cost of unequal variances). Chew and Biemer (2018) compared the performance of a traditional experiment with that of a batched MAB simulating unit response and showed a modest improvement in response rates with MAB that tended to increase with larger effect sizes. The authors also showed that MABs never perform worse than the experiment: even if there is no superior treatment, MABs will always default to continue with random assignment and in that situation can be considered a special case of a traditional experiment.

Another approach to tailor interventions, or rather to optimize the frequency, timing, and content of notifications to deliver cognitive-behavioral interventions (e.g. to use a stress management app) was presented by Morrison et al. (2017).[6] Comparing the performance of intelligent, sensor-driven notifications (accounting for contextual information based on a Naïve Bayesian classifier), to daily and occasional notifications with predefined time frames, the authors showed there is little difference in the percentage of notifications viewed (intelligent 30%, daily 28%, and occasional 30%). However, they also showed that the optimized timing of the intelligent intervention increased the percentage of individuals participating in the intervention suggested by the notification (intelligent 25%, daily 19%, and occa-

---

[6] Just-in-Time Adaptive Interventions (JITAIs) are a class of mobile health interventions for tailored, real-time behavior change support that is system-triggered, e.g. via the use of sensor information (e.g. Hardeman et al. 2019; Spruijt-Metz and Nilsen 2014; Nahum-Shani et al. 2018; Schembre et al. 2018).

sional 19%). These findings are particularly relevant for survey researchers aiming to optimize and tailor the timing and frequency of contact attempts to increase unit response and for researchers using ecological momentary assessments (e.g. in combination with global positioning system (GPS) and accelerometer data) to trigger measurements based on activities (e.g. Stone and Shiffman 1994; Stone et al. 2007).

MLMs can be useful for recruitment in longitudinal settings (panels and repeated cross-sections with a similar data-generating process), for example, to predict panel attrition to ultimately tailor data collection protocols in subsequent waves (e.g. Liu and Wang 2018; Kolb, Kern, and Weiß 2018; Mulder and Kieruj 2018) or mode preferences (Megra et al. 2018). Kern et al. (2019) compared five different tree-based algorithms to a standard logistic regression model predicting panel attrition. The authors showed that each of the different tree-based algorithms had certain advantages that "can be utilized in different contexts" (Kern et al. 2019, p. 87). While the ensemble methods, that is random forests and extreme gradient boosting, performed particularly well for predicting nonresponse, other tree-based methods, such as model-based recursive partitioning or conditional inference trees, provided insights into distinct attrition patterns for certain subgroups. Liu and Wang (2018) took a similar approach but compared three different MLMs – random forests, support vector machines, and LASSO – to a traditional logistic regression model to predict the likelihood to attrite in a follow-up survey using prior wave information. Since these MLMs require (almost) no model specification regardless of whether the true relationships are relevant, linear or not, monotonic or not, or a product of self-selection, they have the potential to increase prediction accuracy and decrease bias by more accurately detecting the true complexity of the underlying model. The MLMs that Liu and Wang (2018) explored did not outperform logistic regression in terms of accuracy, sensitivity, or specificity, but these models provided valuable insights into the relative importance and prioritization of individual variables for the prediction of attrition.

The use of MLMs to derive propensity models and to adapt or tailor data collection designs is not limited to panel studies. Buskirk et al. (2013) compared the use of logistic regression and random forest models to derive response propensity models for a large periodic, national, cross-sectional survey. The models were estimated using responses from one cross-sectional sample along with available household characteristics as well as aggregated census block-group information. These models were then applied to an entirely new sample selected in a subsequent quarter of the year using the same sampling design to estimate temporal and external validity of the response propensity models. Buskirk et al. (2013) found that the random forest propensity model had slightly lower temporal validity, as measured by model accuracy and area under the curve statistics, when compared to a logistic regression model constructed using principal components. Earp et al. (2014) applied an ensemble of trees to predict nonresponse using census data and response status from multiple years of an establishment survey. They used this model to predict response of establishments for the next survey and found a weak, but significant, relationship between actual and estimated survey response. These studies highlight the importance of considering temporal and external validity measures of performance for models developed and applied in a responsive/adaptive survey design context, especially if we suspect that respondents from future waves of data collection might have different response patterns or if the relationship between predictors and response changes over time.

As these examples illustrate, many types of variables are included in the propensity models deployed within a responsive or tailored survey design and range from only frame or auxiliary variables to a combination of these variables and survey data. A growing body of work is exploring the application of MLMs to paradata to create variables for inclusion in these propensity models, such as information regarding respondent's prior survey experience or unstructured text from interviewer comments. Lugtig and Blom (2018) showed that paradata such as break-offs in the prior survey wave, the time between the survey invitation and completion, whether or not respondents needed reminders, and interview duration were among the best predictors of panel attrition and that these predictors were largely consistent across waves. More importantly, using classification and regression trees (CARTs), the authors demonstrated that complex interactions between these paradata indicators contributed to the prediction of panel attrition. MLMs can also be used to extract indicators from paradata including unstructured interviewer comments. Guzman (2018) used two natural language processing methods – sentiment analysis and topic modeling – to extract information from interviewer comments to then investigate the relationship between these open-ended interviewer comments and panel attrition (see also Ward and Reimer 2019 for a sentiment analysis of interviewer comments and panel attrition). The author showed that both negative sentiments and the topics covered in the interviewer notes were significant predictors of survey completion. Ward and Reimer (2019) noted, however, that while the sentiments found in interviewer comments were predictive, they also tended to correlate with other paradata such as number of contact attempts. Other challenges when working with interviewer comments in particular pertained to the fact that interviewer comments tended to be in shorthand, include abbreviations, and incomplete sentences (Guzman 2018; Ward and Reimer 2019).

These examples illustrate how propensity scores have been developed with MLMs to improve unit-level responses in an adaptive or responsive survey design context. Applications of MLMs for estimating propensity scores used for calibrating and adjusting samples are further explored in Section 1.7.

1.6 Survey Data Coding and Processing Using Machine Learning Methods

One of the most labor-intensive aspects of the survey research process apart from interviewing is the coding and processing of survey data. We consider processing and coding to encompass data validation, editing, imputation, and data linkage. Research applying MLMs to each of these aspects of coding and processing is beginning to emerge, and we explore a great number of these in turn in this section.

1.6.1 Coding Unstructured Text

For the processing of unstructured text and open-ended responses, survey researchers often spend a lot of time and resources to manually code this type of response or discard them altogether (e.g. Conrad et al. 2016; see Couper and Zhang 2016 for an exploration how to incorporate technology in web surveys to assist respondents). Text mining or natural language processing can help to at least partially automate some of this process, and unsupervised algorithms can help researchers to infer topics from the data rather than applying a predefined set of categories (for earlier approaches to automation see, e.g. Creecy et al. 1992 or the literature review for coding and classifying medical records by Stanfill et al. 2010). Schonlau and Couper (2016), for example demonstrated that gradient boosting can categorize 47–58% of the open-ended responses to single categories in surveys with an accuracy of 80% or higher, thereby significantly increasing efficiencies particularly in large surveys. Given these results, the authors suggested using hybrid approaches, that is, automated categorizations, where possible, complemented with manual categorizations where necessary. An extension of this approach using support vector machines (e.g. Schonlau, Gweon, and Wenemark 2018), L1-regularized logistic regression, or RNN (e.g. Card and Smith) is more flexible in that it allows for the coding of multi-categorical data. The study by Schierholz et al. (2018; see Section 1.4.3) also supported the arguments for a hybrid approach, however, in the context of predictive occupation coders suggesting candidate job categories to respondents during the survey interview. In a follow-up study Schierholz (2018) compared the performance of 10 algorithms – among those multinomial logistic regression, gradient boosting with decision trees, adapted nearest-neighbor matching, memory-based reasoning, and an algorithm based on string similarities and Bayesian ideas. The author showed that depending on the goal of the prediction task (e.g. fully automated coding vs. computer-assisted coding), different algorithms tended to perform better, although their approach, based on string similarities and Bayes, tended to outperform the other algorithms.

Shorey et al. (2018) used a knowledge graph developed for natural language processing tasks to incorporate prior domain knowledge (e.g. about the US education system) to prepare student transcripts for statistical analyses. The advantage of combining knowledge graphs with neural networks to (partially) automate coding courses from transcripts is improved information extraction and classification, that is, improved modeling power and decreased computational cost. More specifically, the authors showed that their system can make successful recommendations to human coders 94% of the time (i.e. the correct course code is suggested in the top five most likely predictions), thereby increasing intercoder reliability between 3% and 5% points (e.g. from 84% to 87% for the general course category) and coding efficiency.

Korpusik et al. (2016) investigated coding of text and spoken meal descriptions (for the latter using a deep neural network acoustic model for the speech recognition) comparing different algorithms to assign semantic labels to these spoken descriptions (e.g. k-means clustering) and then in a second step comparing different algorithms (e.g. Naïve Bayes, logistic regression, and random forests) to associate food-properties with the given label. They showed that adding word vector features significantly improved model performance in both stages.

Instead of using supervised learners that require a labeled dataset and prespecified categories, a series of more recent studies investigated the use of topic modeling to create clusters of categorizations that are not predetermined by researchers (e.g. Can, Engel, and Keck 2018; McCreanor, Wronski, and Chen 2018; Ye, Medway, and Kelley 2018). Areas of application for topic modeling are manifold:

- Topic modeling can be used to analyze open-ended responses. For example, Can et al. (2018) discussed how open-ended questions on data privacy in surveys compare to publicly available comments in newspaper articles on the same topic. The authors also compared topic modeling with the more traditional content analysis for each data source and showed that different data sources and different modeling approaches may lead to different substantive conclusions. Roberts et al. (2014) used semiautomated structural topic modeling to analyze open-ended responses. Structural topic models have the advantage of incorporating contextual information about the document (e.g. covariates such as, gender, or treatment assignment), allowing topic prevalence and topic content to vary, and thereby allowing the estimation of treatment effects.
- Topic modeling can also be used to analyze larger bodies of unstructured text. One example for the analyses of unstructured text involved the use of two different topic modeling approaches to identify research on emerging and published topics and trends in survey statistics and methodology by mining 10 years of abstracts from relevant conferences and journals (Thaung and Kolenikov 2018).

- Topic modeling can also assist researchers to categorize question characteristics. Sweitzer and Shulman (2018), for example, used topic modeling to code question topics in their analysis of the relationship between language difficulty and data quality in public opinion questions.

1.6.2 Data Validation and Editing

Data validation and data editing, that is, the examination and correction of data for errors, has also benefited from recent developments in machine learning. For surveys that are repeated periodically, instead of having subject-matter experts specify the conditions that data edits need to satisfy, tree-based methods can be used to automatically identify logical statements about the edits to be performed using the historic, clean data as a training dataset (e.g. Petrakos et al. 2004; Ruiz 2018). TREEVAL is one example of an automated data editing tool and validation strategy that derives the optimal functional form of the edits and of statistical criteria based on the training data to edit the raw incoming data (Petrakos et al. 2004). An extension of this approach would be to use unsupervised machine learning algorithms to "identify expected patterns, systematic mistakes (unexpected patterns) or to observe cases that do not fall into any patterns" both during and after data collection (Ruiz 2018, p. 10).

1.6.3 Imputation

Another area of application for MLMs is imputation at the unit or item level (e.g. Lu, Li, and Pan 2007; Borgoni and Berrington 2013; Beretta and Santaniello 2016; Loh et al. 2019). More traditional imputation methods addressing item nonresponse often face challenges. These approaches (i) often assume a (too) simplistic missing data pattern and implement either univariate or simple multivariate imputation (such as a monotone missing data patterns instead of more complex missing data patterns), (ii) can be computationally inefficient, (iii) can be impossible to estimate if there are too many auxiliary variables, or a high rate of missing data in these auxiliary variables. To address these challenges, researchers recently started investigating alternative approaches including tree-based techniques. Borgoni and Berrington (2013), for example, demonstrated the flexibility of an iterative sequential tree-based imputation assuming a complex missing data pattern and showed that the results compare to existing techniques. Because these tree-based models are nonparametric (an advantage), they are less sensitive to model misspecification and outliers while being computationally efficient even with many variables to be imputed (see also Fischer and Mittereder 2018). Loh et al. (2019) exposed CART and forest to a series of robustness analyses and showed that tree- and forest-based methods are always applicable, fast, and efficient even under what they call "real data" situations where other methods, such as likelihood-based approaches fail. At the unit level, Drechsler and Reiter (2011) provided an example of using tree- and forest-based methods as well as support vector machines to create synthetic data in instances in which intense redaction was needed (see also Caiola and Reiter 2010 to create partially synthetic categorical data). The authors showed that tree-based methods provide reliable estimates and minimize disclosure risks.

1.6.4 Record Linkage and Duplicate Detection

Record linkage – e.g., linking records of individuals from administrative records and survey data, traditionally either using rule-based or probabilistic approaches – can also benefit from recent developments in machine learning (Winkler 2006). Supervised machine learning algorithms, such as random forests, develop a matching strategy based on a set of training data that can then be applied out of sample (e.g. Christen 2012; Ventura, Nugent, and Fuchs 2015). The advantage of using machine learning algorithms over more traditional approaches is that (i) they allow the researcher to start with a range of predictor variables and then assess variable importance to tailor the linkage strategy and determine whether a field is relevant for linkage; and (ii) they allow predictor variables to be continuous contrary to some of the more traditional approaches. Morris (2017) investigates the use of logistic regression, classification trees, and random forests to investigate the quality of administrative records composite matching a person to their (US) census day address using administrative records, characteristics of the person, and the housing unit. Their approach ultimately allowed researchers to address the question as to whether or not administrative data can be used as a proxy for nonrespondents in the 2010, and potentially the 2020, US Census and thus contribute to cost savings if a case that was successfully matched could be excluded from fieldwork (this is also an example of responsive designs, see Section 1.5.2). The author showed how the choice of a particular classification technique can imply a tradeoff between simplicity and predictive accuracy.

Unsupervised techniques have the advantage in that they do not require a labeled training dataset and can be used to assess proximity between cases from different datasets. Supervised and unsupervised MLMs have also been used in sample matching (see Section 1.7.2). Related to record linkage is the detection of duplicate records. Elmagarmid et al. (2007) presented a comprehensive review of existing traditional and machine learning algorithms used to detect nonidentical duplicate entries in datasets (for record linkage and deduplication, see Christen 2012).

1.7 Sample Weighting and Survey Adjustments Using Machine Learning Methods

Probability sample survey data is often adjusted to account for the probabilities of inclusion as well as to mitigate potential biases due to various sources of nonsampling error including coverage and response. Similar adjustments are also made to nonprobability samples to account for nonsampling errors, most notably for coverage and self-selection (Valliant, Dever, and Kreuter 2013). Although raking and poststratification (Kalton and Flores-Cervantes 2003; Valliant et al. 2013) are two of the most widely applied techniques to correct for coverage related issues for both probability and nonprobability samples, to our knowledge there has been little to no work applying MLMs to these calibration techniques. On the other hand, a steady stream of research has explored various MLMs for propensity score modeling and sample matching – two of the more common methods for adjusting for nonresponse and self-selection (Valliant and Dever 2011; Elliott and Valliant 2017; Mercer et al. 2017). We discuss recent developments in applying MLMs to sample matching and propensity score estimation as it relates to sample weighting and adjustment. Propensity score models constructed to identify respondents or used for sample management or recruitment were discussed in Section 1.5.

1.7.1 Propensity Score Estimation

Propensity score adjustments trace their origins to observational studies that are used to compare treatment affects when treatments are not assigned at random (Rosenbaum and Rubin 1983). This method was since adapted to adjust for nonresponse in probability sample settings (Brick 2013; Valliant et al. 2013; Baker et al. 2013) and for self-selection in nonprobability sample settings (Valliant et al. 2013; Valliant and Dever 2011; Lee 2006). For probability samples, the propensity scores represent the inverse probability of response modeled as a function of available covariates. In the nonprobability survey setting, propensity score estimation is also used to derive so-called quasi-randomization weights that are estimated from the model using nonprobability data as well as data from a probability-based reference sample (Valliant and Dever 2011; Elliott and Valliant 2017). In either setting, logistic regression was by far the most common approach for estimating propensity models (Lee 2006; Valliant et al. 2013). However, as discussed in Mendez et al. (2008), limitations about specifying the parametric model form, convergence, and possible under specification associated with logistic regression models create opportunities for considering other modeling approaches.

Valliant et al. (2013) discussed how tree-based MLMs may be used for modeling response adjustments and how CARTs have more flexibility over chi-square automatic interaction detector (CHAID) models (Kass 1980) in that they can create predictions using a combination of continuous and categorical variables. As a case in point, Lee et al. (2010) explored the use of supervised machine learning algorithms for estimating propensity scores in an epidemiological observational study. More specifically, they compared propensity scores derived from main effects logistic regression models and a host of MLMs including CART, pruned CART and several ensemble methods including bagged CART, boosted CART, and random forests using various metrics of model performance. Generally, they reported adequate performance across the various models, but note that under moderate nonadditivity and moderate nonlinearity, the logistic regression models fared worse than models developed from ensemble methods such as boosted CART models.

Survey researchers are making similar comparisons about various MLMs used to derive propensity score models used for nonresponse adjustment. Much of the current work on propensity score estimation within the survey context has started to include many supervised machine learning algorithms, especially tree-based methods. In probability settings, the applications of MLMs to propensity scores explored both direct adjustments and adjustments made through propensity score stratification (Bethlehem, Cobben, and Schouten 2011; Brick 2013; Valliant et al. 2013). Schouten and de Nooij (2005) presented a classification tree method to construct weighting strata that simultaneously account for the relation between response behavior, survey questions, and covariates. Phipps and Toth (2012) applied regression trees to data from the Occupational Employment Statistics Survey to estimate response propensities for sampled establishments.

Lohr et al. (2015) also explored propensity estimation with an expanded collection of methods including CART (Breiman et al. 1984), conditional trees (Strobl et al. 2007), random forests (Breiman 2001), and trees with random effects (Sela and Simonoff 2012). Lohr et al. (2015) also evaluated mean squared errors for survey-related estimates based on propensity weights derived using several different approaches including direct adjustment, propensity stratification adjustment, and terminal nodes for the CART and conditional tree models as suggested by Toth and Phipps (2014). Propensity models for each of the MLMs included both a regression approach (e.g. treating binary response as a continuous 0/1 variable) as well as classification (e.g. treating the outcome as binary/categorical). The team tested the performance of these MLMs and adjustment approaches under 32 different sample scenarios formed by varying the response rates, nonresponse mechanisms, number of primary sampling units, and the degree of latent nonresponse within primary sampling units (PSUs). Within each particular MLM, Lohr and colleagues also varied particular tuning parameters such as minimum node size and other process settings such as the use of pruning or not and incorporating weights or not, among others. This study represents one of the most comprehensive comparisons of propensity methods, theoretical response mechanisms, and MLMs to date. In the end, Lohr et al. (2015) found that unadjusted settings, which included no pruning, no use of weights and other adjustment factors resulted in better performance. They also reported that regression versions of trees and forests performed better than classification versions and found that conditional tree models outperformed CART models in almost every scenario they considered. The team noted that of all the methods, random forests fared the best under direct propensity adjustment but did not fare as well under propensity stratification.

The results reported by Lohr et al. (2015) regarding random forests were fairly consistent with those reported by Buskirk and Kolenikov (2015) who also compared random forest models to logistic regression models for deriving propensity adjustments to sample surveys using both the direct and stratification approaches. However, the results of Buskirk and Kolenikov for random forest models using propensity stratification were far less favorable because the resulting survey estimates had much larger variances compared to direct propensity estimation or to logistic regression models with either direct or stratification adjustments. The team noted that large ranges in estimated propensities resulted in respondents being assigned to different propensity strata across bootstrap resamples that were used in evaluating the variances. Lohr et al. (2015) did not evaluate mean squared errors using replicate variance but instead relied on repeated subsamples taken from a larger population. Differences in these two studies also illuminated an important point when comparing various applications of MLMs to derive and apply propensity adjustments. Namely, to examine differences in results, it is important to consider both the type of adjustment method (e.g. direct vs. stratification) and the type of MLM as well as the tuning parameters and other related settings along with the method of evaluation. Although most MLMs are robust to a wide range of tuning parameters, differences in them can impact the results even when all other settings, data sources, covariates, methods, and adjustment techniques are equal.

Within the nonprobablity framework, estimation of propensity models to create so-called pseudo-weights under the quasi-randomization framework (Valliant and Dever 2011; Elliott and Valliant 2017) have been generated in large part using logistic regression models but a growing body of research is also exploring a wide array of MLMs. The choice of how weights are computed from derived propensities can be an important factor in comparing various MLMs and approaches. Nearly all of the studies we reviewed used the Hajek weights, which equal the quotient of the estimated probability for being in the probability sample divided by the estimated probability the case was from the nonprobability sample as explained by Schonlau and Couper (2017) and Elliott and Valliant (2017). Mercer (2018) used

Bayesian Adaptive Regression Trees to create propensity-based pseudo-weights and doubly robust estimates for several nonprobability surveys. Mercer et al. (2018) expanded the use of tree-based approaches to an ensemble approach by applying random forest models based on two different sets of covariates to derive propensity models for creating pseudo-weights for an array of nonprobability samples. They also apply a calibration step to created pseudo-weights to balance the final weighted nonprobability sample to known population benchmarks as a way to smooth out or minimize the impact of extreme weights. They found that the combination of propensity models along with a final raking step performed better than raking alone, but also that propensity models alone fared worse than just raking. They also note that beyond the method of adjustment what mattered most was the choice of covariates citing that the expanded covariate set consisting of both demographic and politically related variables reduced biases more than just using demographics alone. This result reiterates the strong ignorability assumption that Schonlau and Couper (2017) reference when emphasizing that the success of the propensity scoring adjustments depends strongly on whether the available auxiliary variables adequately capture the difference between the nonprobability sample and the reference sample for all outcomes of interest.

Garcia and Rueba (2018) expanded further still the MLMs applied to deriving pseudo-weights based on propensity models estimated using several decision tree methods, k-nearest neighbors, Naïve Bayes, random forests, and gradient-boosting machines under various scenarios that varied the number of covariates and sample sizes for the nonprobability sample. They reported that nearest-neighbor methods provided good performance as long as the number of covariates was small and Naïve Bayes created unstable estimates for most scenarios. They reported that beyond these results, the performance of MLMs varied according to the sample size of the nonprobability sample as well as the type of underlying mechanism governing self-selection.

Although many of these studies used tree-based methods for estimating response propensities, either as adjustment factors in probability samples or as the basis of pseudo-weights in the nonprobability setting, the approach used to estimate these propensities as well as methods to bin them into strata is important. Lohr et al. (2015) as well as Buskirk and Kolenikov (2015) noted that regression approaches to these decision tree-based models proved better for estimating propensities – that is decision trees were applied to binary 0/1 outcome treated as a continuous variable. Settings in the MLMs such as minimum node size might impact the overall range of estimated propensities, making some of these estimated to be 0 and others 1, which will create irregularities in the weighting adjustments. Buskirk and Kolenikov (2015) explicitly transformed the propensities derived from forest models slightly to prevent these irregularities.

Provost and Domingos (2003) encouraged the use of probability estimating tree approaches to creating propensities from these types of MLMs by applying a Laplace correction to the estimated propensities that is a function of the sample size and number of classes underling the prediction problem (e.g. two classes, in the case of response). Their early work on applying this adjustment approach indicated increased accuracy and stability in the resulting estimated propensity scores. Of course, when propensity stratification is used, there is less concern about the irregularities imposed by estimated propensities that are 0. In most of the survey research literature a general rule of 5–10 propensity strata is used (Cochran 1964). However, as Buskirk and Kolenikov (2015) point out, the range of propensities estimated from MLMs is often wider than that observed for logistic regression models, largely because these MLMs often include more complex model structures incorporating important interactions and higher-order effects that might not be included in parametric models based on logistic regression. For propensity stratification to be effective, the values of the propensity scores should be similar within strata (see Lee 2006) and so for the case of MLMs, the common practice of using five groups may be insufficient for the range of estimated propensities often seen with MLMs.

1.7.2 Sample Matching

Sample matching is another technique currently being explored for mitigating the effects of nonresponse in probability surveys and self-selection in nonprobability surveys (Baker et al. 2013; Bethlehem 2015; Elliott and Valliant 2017). Simply put, sample matching in the nonprobability sample setting matches a subset of members from the nonprobability sample to members of a smaller, reference probability sample using a set of common covariates (Elliott and Valliant 2017; Bethlehem 2015). Mercer et al. (2017) drew parallels between sample matching for observational studies and how this approach can be adapted to the nonprobability framework. Essentially, sample matching can be done at the population level, as in quota sampling, or at the individual or case level. MLMs have been almost exclusively applied to facilitating matches at the individual level. Cases are identified as matches by using some type of proximity measure computed based on a set of covariates measured from both the nonprobablity sample and the reference sample. Proximity measures can be computed using MLMs based on any number and combination of categorical and continuous variables offering an advantage over more traditional metrics such as the simple matching coefficient or Euclidean distance which suffer from the so-called "curse of dimensionality" and generally require all variables to be of the same type. These proximity measures can also be used to facilitate record linkage and more applications of MLMs in this context are described in the Section 1.6.4.

Regardless of the number of variables used in sample matching, Mercer et al. (2017) noted that the utility of the method hinges on identifying variables related to the survey outcomes of interest as well as those that ensure at least conditional exchangeability within the nonprobability sample. For a given nonprobability survey, these variables may not be available on the reference survey but could be added rather easily if a small probability-based reference survey was available as was the case in the applications of sample matching employed by Buskirk and Dutwin (2016). Valliant et al. (2013), Bethlehem (2016), and Mercer et al. (2017) noted that the reference survey must be a good representation of the target population for sample matching to be effective in reducing biases. Generally, there is a tradeoff in the flexibility afforded by smaller target samples and the representation offered by larger government surveys, for example (Elliott and Valliant 2017). Mercer et al. (2018) applied a clever method of creating a synthetic reference sample by first imputing variables from the Current Population Survey and the General Social Survey to cases in the American Community Survey using a hot deck procedure powered by a random forest model. An expanded so-called synthetic sample resulted that expanded the possible variables in the American Community Sample available for use in the matching process. They created matches between this reference sample and various nonprobability samples using proximity measures derived from a random forest that classified cases in a combined dataset as being from the reference or nonprobability datasets. Mercer et al. (2018) noted that estimates produced with sample matching using both demographic and political variables resulted in the lowest average bias across the full set of benchmarks that were considered. They also noted that using raking alone resulted in just slightly more biased estimates, overall. Matching also tended to improve as the ratio of the sample size of the nonprobability sample to the reference dataset increased.

Buskirk and Dutwin (2016) also applied random forest models to match nonprobability sample cases to a small probability-based reference survey. However, in their approach, they used an unsupervised version of random forest methods to create a forest model describing the structure present in the probability reference set using two different sets of covariates measured from both samples. Proximity measures between cases in the probability reference sample and nonprobability sample were then estimated using this random forest model. Similar to the work of Mercer et al. (2018), Buskirk and Dutwin explored a simple set of covariates as well as an expanded set of covariates and varied the ratio of the nonprobability sample to the probability sample. They found that the matched samples generated using proximities computed using random forest models were generally consistent with those computed using the simple matching coefficient but in some scenarios were more stable across multiple replicate samples.

To date, we know of no study directly comparing the use of supervised vs. unsupervised applications of random forest models or other MLMs to estimate proximity measures that can be used in the matching process. One advantage of using the unsupervised approach is inherent in the desired outcome to generate proximity measures within a full range so the matching process can better discern the best matching case. With supervised methods, the algorithms are optimized to create final nodes that are pure in terms of sample parity – putting cases from the probability samples in the same nodes and the same for nonprobability cases. Of course, there are exceptions, and not every node is completely pure allowing for some variability in the proximity measures derived from these supervised tree-based models – which base proximity calculations on a function of the proportion of times two different cases in the combined file fall in the same final node. With the unsupervised approach, there is no label of sample parity that allows the algorithm to naturally find patterns in the datasets based on the variables used in the matching process. One might argue that using the reference sample only in this step is important, especially if it is a better representation of the target population so that these patterns are not spurious or driven by self-selection or other issues possibly present in the nonprobability samples. Then using this model as the basis of measuring proximity between probability and nonprobability is more of a function of the relationships present among the matching variables and as such should lead to a wider range of proximity measures. Buskirk and Dutwin's work illustrated differences in the range of proximity measures created from using unsupervised random forests and those computed using the simple matching coefficient from the same covariate sets and found that the measures from the simple matching coefficient were very negatively skewed and concentrated very close to 1, while those from the random forest model were more evenly spread between 0 and 1.

1.8 Survey Data Analysis and Estimation Using Machine Learning Methods

Analysis of probability-based survey data requires understanding of the sampling design structure and generally, estimates are derived that incorporate this structure and a set of final sampling weights. Two broad frameworks are used to analyze and produce estimates from survey data – the so-called design-based framework that focuses on repeated sampling to generate inference and a model-based framework that leverages a postulated statistical model for the relationships among variables to create estimates. Models can be incorporated into the design-based approach to improve the efficiency of estimates using the model-assisted approach as described by Breidt and Opsomer (2017). Although the model-based framework is not as common for generating estimates from probability samples, it is becoming popular for generating population estimates using nonprobability samples (Elliott and Valliant 2017). Applications of MLMs for estimation in the survey context are concentrated around three main areas, the first of which leverages capabilities of MLMs to identify key correlates of a survey outcome of interest from among many possible variables measured within the survey context and to gain insights into possible complexities in relationships among these variables. The second area encapsulates adaptations of these MLMs to incorporate survey design and weighting features for use in design-based population inference. And finally, the third area leverages the predictive nature of these MLMs within a model-assisted framework to improve finite population inference for both probability and nonprobability surveys. We review some of the current advances in each of these areas, in turn.

1.8.1 Gaining Insights Among Survey Variables

Arpino et al. (2018) used survival random forests to model changes in marital status over time in Germany based on data from the German Socio-Economic Panel survey to understand determinants of marriage dissolutions in Germany over the past two decades. They used variable importance measures to identify influential variables with the largest impact on predicting dissolution of marriages and partial dependence plots to gain insights into the direction of the association between the most influential variables and marriage dissolution status. Their investigation revealed that relationship between key continuous predictors and the marriage dissolution status may not be linear and that other effects may be affecting the outcome not as a main effect but through the moderation of another variable. These insights highlight future work in confirming these more complex relationships among a key set of predictors and marriage dissolution status.

As the previous example illustrates, variable importance measures, for example, derived from random forest models can be helpful in providing focus on a much smaller set of influential covariates. However, importance measures derived using regular random forests are often biased in the presence of many variables that might be correlated or might be of different variable types (Strobl et al. 2007). In the survey setting, some level of correlation or association almost always exists between the variables for any given prediction problem, and we certainly have a mix of variable types. So to identify a smaller set of important variables within the survey context, an alternate version of variable importance is needed. The fuzzy forests method applies a recursive feature elimination process and has been noted to offer estimates of variable importance that are nearly as unbiased as those computed for the more computationally expensive conditional forests (Conn et al. 2015). Dutwin and Buskirk (2017) applied a series of fuzzy random forest models to first identify a smaller set of important predictors for predicting household Internet status, from a collection of over 500 variables identified from 15 probability-based surveys. The goal was to identify a small, manageable set of variables that could be used to create a model for predicting Internet status and then be used to create weighting adjustments for coverage in subsequent online samples that fielded this small collection of questions. A probability-based RDD survey was fielded that identified about the same number of Internet and non-Internet households that asked the three dozen questions identified as important by the fuzzy forest models. Another fuzzy random forest model applied to the RDD survey data identified a final set of about a total of about 12 demographic and nondemographic variables that were most important for predicting Internet status. A final regular random forest model predicting non-Internet status was fit using data from the RDD survey and model performance measures for this model revealed that the demographic variables were important for identifying households without Internet (e.g. high sensitivity), while the core set of nondemographic variables were most powerful for identifying those households with Internet (e.g. high specificity).

1.8.2 Adapting Machine Learning Methods to the Survey Setting

Although the number of studies making adaptations of existing MLMs to incorporate sample design and weighting information is rather limited to date, we anticipate that such studies will continue to increase in the near future and will collectively represent an important contribution of survey research, statistics, and methodology to data science. McConville et al. (2017) adapted the LASSO and adaptive LASSO approaches to the survey setting. Their work established the theory for applying these methods to probability survey data and proposed two versions of lasso survey regression weights so that this method can be used to develop model-assisted, design-based estimates of multiple survey outcomes of interested. In a similar vein, Toth and Eltinge (2011) developed a method for adapting regression trees via recursive partitioning to the probability survey context by incorporating information about the complex sample design, including design weights. Toth (2017) later developed the R-package, rpms, that makes estimation of regression trees numerically possible and accessible for probability-based survey data. Toth and Eltinge's work also unlocked the potential for using regression trees within the model-assisted approach to design-based inference. McConville and Toth (2019) explored regression tree estimators to automatically determine poststratification adjustment cells using auxiliary data available for all population units. They noted that one strength of this method over other model-assisted approaches is how naturally regression trees can incorporate both continuous and categorical auxiliary data. These poststrata have the ability to capture complex interactions between the variables, and as shown in the simulations, they can increase the efficiency of the model-assisted estimator. Additionally, the estimator is calibrated to the population totals of each poststratum.

Although not explicitly applicable only to survey data, Zhao et al. (2016) adapted random forest models to handle missing values on covariates and for facilitating improved estimation of proximity measures that rely on all observations rather than just those that are out of bag. Although individual decision trees have the ability to handle missing data via surrogates, this advantage is lost within the general random forest approach by virtue of the mechanics of only selecting a subset of variables for node splitting at each node. Zhao et al. applied this adapted random forest method to examine impacts of smoking on body mass index (BMI) using data from the National Health and Nutrition Examination Survey. Missing values were implicitly handled within their revised approach via surrogates and thus eliminated the need to explicitly imputing missing values for any of the covariates used in the model.

1.8.3 Leveraging Machine Learning Algorithms for Finite Population Inference

Breidt and Opsomer (2017) explored how MLMs can be used as the basis of the working models in the model-assisted approach to design-based estimation for probability samples. They provided a general framework within which predictions from various MLMs can be incorporated and used to derive finite population estimates and inference. They specifically illustrated how methods like k-nearest neighbors, CARTs and neural networks could be used within this framework. More recently, Buelens et al. (2018) explored similar approaches for using MLMs for inference from nonprobability samples. Their work compares quasi-randomization methods to model-based methods (or super-population models, as more formally explained by Elliott and Valliant (2017)), where various MLMs are used in creating the models. More specifically, Buelens et al. (2018) compared sample mean estimation, quasi-randomization pseudo-weighting based on poststratification via a known auxiliary variable for the entire population, generalized linear models, and a host of MLMs including k-nearest neighbors, ANNs, regression trees and support vector machines as the basis of generating model-based estimates. They tuned each of the MLMs using a repeated split-sample scenario based on 10 bootstrap replications, and the optimal values of the respective tuning parameters were then used to form models upon which final estimates were generated. In predicting a continuous outcome, Buelens and colleagues reported generally adequate, although varied, results from the MLMs compared to using either the sample mean or the pseudo-weighted quasi-randomization based estimator. Generally, the MLMs removed more or nearly the same amount of bias due to self-selection compared to either the sample mean or pseudo-weighted estimator, especially under moderate to severe levels of self-selection. They also identified support vector machines as a top performer compared to all other methods in almost all scenarios they examined.

Model-based estimates generally work well if the predictions made using the model are well suited for population members not included in the sample. The models are estimated using data from the sample (be it probability or nonprobability) based on a set of covariates that are available from members of the sample and population. If these covariates fail to fully represent the self-selection bias mechanism, the range of values on the outcome of interest may differ between the sample and population members not included in the sample. If so, some models will not be able to generate predicted values that extrapolate beyond the range of values observed from the population and this limitation will result in biased model-based estimates. Buelens and colleagues noted this limitation for the sample mean, pseudo-weighted estimator, k-nearest neighbors, and regression trees. They noted that generalized linear models, neural networks, and support vector machines (from among the MLMs they explored) are stronger choices in this situation. Reiterating points of exchangeability made by Mercer et al. (2017), the ability to have auxiliary information that can explain this self-selection and a predictive algorithm that can utilize it are very important. As this current work demonstrates, MLMs are not all equal in their ability to use such information adequately and some have limitations for such applications making method selection an important component in addition to variable selection for creating finite population inference using nonprobability samples.

1.9 Discussion and Conclusions

This collection of examples, while not exhaustive, provides a glimpse into how survey researchers and social scientists are applying an assortment of data science methods within the new landscape. These examples show that data science methods are and can add value to the survey research process. But what is not as clear, yet, is just how the social sciences can add value to the broader data science community and Big Data ecosystem. Grimmer (2015) was quick to identify strengths that social scientists and survey researchers can bring to this conversation by stating, "Data scientists have significantly more experience with large datasets but they tend to have little training in how to infer causal effects in the face of substantial selection. Social scientists must have an integral role in this collaboration; merely being able to apply statistical techniques to massive datasets is insufficient. Rather, the expertise from a field that has handled observational data for many years is required." In fact, the much-reported algorithmic bias among data scientists is a problem almost certainly related to coverage bias – an issue survey researchers have been investigating and mitigating for decades. More generally, advances on understanding and quantifying data error sources are yet another example where survey researchers can add value to the Big Data ecosystem. But apart from methodology, we believe that survey data in and of itself can add much needed insights into this ecosystem with the value proposition being directly related to the fact that surveys are often designed to maximize information about context and provide signals related to the "why" question. In this vein, survey data offer valuable additional sources of information that can enhance prediction accuracy.

This chapter is in no way comprehensive. Our goal was to provide survey researchers and social scientists, as well as data and computer scientists with some examples and ideas that illustrate how MLMs are and can be used throughout the main phases of the survey research process. If we were to cluster these examples in terms of how MLMs have been used, we would find four major uses simply labeled as processing, preparation, prioritization, and prediction. Within each of these four main application areas we saw many cases where MLMs offered considerable benefit to the survey process. We saw examples that leveraged both human effort and MLMs to create better outcomes with respect to the survey research process. We also saw many examples where the MLMs enhanced the process by providing insights into how best to use human effort and machine effort. However, we saw very few examples where MLMs were working completely autonomously within the survey research process. Collectively, these studies seem to suggest that while MLMs offer efficiencies not realized without their use, human decision-making and engineering the application and deployment of these methods is tantamount to their success throughout the survey research process. Nonetheless, in the new landscape, the rise of MLMs has provided survey and social scientists with additional resources that – while certainly no cure-all for the challenges our fields face – are meaningful and warrant further exploration.

References

Abernethy, J., Evgeniou, T., Toubia, O., and Vert, J.-P. (2007). Eliciting consumer preferences using robust adaptive choice questionnaires. *IEEE Transactions on Knowledge and Data Engineering* 20 (2): 145–155.

Agarwal, S., Furukawa, Y., Snavely, N. et al. (2011). Building Rome in a day. *Communications of the ACM* 54 (10): 105–112. https://doi.org/10.1145/2001269.2001293.

Amer, S.R. (2015). Geo-sampling: from design to implementation. 70th Annual Conference of the American Association for Public Opinion Research, Hollywood, FL (14–17 May 2015).

Arpino, B., Le Moglie, M., and Mencarin, L. (2018). Machine-learning techniques for family demography: an application of random forests to the analysis of divorce determinants in Germany. http://hdl.handle.net/10230/34425 (accessed 5 July 2019).

Arunachalam, H., Atkin, G., Wettlaufer, D., et al. (2015). I know what you did next: predicting respondent's next activity using machine learning. Paper presented at the 70th Annual Conference of the American Association for Public Opinion Research, Hollywood, FL (17 May 2015).

Baker, R., Brick, J.M., Bates, N.A. et al. (2013). Summary report of the AAPOR task force on non-probability sampling. *Journal of Survey Statistics and Methodology* 1 (2): 90–143. https://doi.org/10.1093/jssam/smt008.

Belli, R., Miller, L.D., Al Baghal, T. et al. (2016). Using data mining to predict the occurrence of respondent retrieval strategies in calendar interviewing: the quality of retrospective reports. *Journal of Official Statistics* 32 (3): 579–600. https://doi.org/10.1515/jos-2016-0030.

Beretta, L. and Santaniello, A. (2016). Nearest neighbor imputation algorithms: a critical evaluation. *BMC Medical Informatics and Decision Making* 16 (S3, Suppl 3): 74. https://doi.org/10.1186/s12911-016-0318-z.

Bethlehem, J. (2015). Essay: Sunday shopping-the case of three surveys. *Survey Research Methods* 9 (3): 221–230.

Bethlehem, J. (2016). Solving the nonresponse problem with sample matching? *Social Science Computer Review* 34 (1): 59–77.

Bethlehem, J., Cobben, F., and Schouten, B. (2011). *Handbook of Nonresponse in Household Surveys*, Chapter 11. Hoboken, NJ: Wiley https://doi.org/10.1002/9780470891056.

Birnbaum, B. (2012). Algorithmic approaches to detecting interviewer fabrication in surveys. Doctoral thesis. Department of Computer Science & Engineering, University of Washington, Seattle, WA.

Blasius, J. and Thiessen, V. (2015). Should we trust survey data? Assessing response simplification and data fabrication. *Social Science Research* 52: 479–493. https://doi.org/10.1016/j.ssresearch.2015.03.006.

Borgoni, R. and Berrington, A. (2013). Evaluating a sequential tree-based procedure for multivariate imputation of complex missing data structures. *Quality & Quantity* 47 (4): 991–2008. https://doi.org/10.1007/s11135-011-9638-3.

Boriah, S., Chandola, V., and Kumar, V. (2008). Similarity measures for categorical data: a comparative evaluation. *Proceedings of the SDM, SIAM*, Atlanta, GA (April 24–26, 2008). https://doi.org/10.1137/1.9781611972788.22.

Breidt, F.J. and Opsomer, J.D. (2017). Model-assisted survey estimation with modern prediction techniques. *Statistical Science* 32 (2): 190–205. https://doi.org/10.1214/16-STS589.

Breiman, L. (2001). Statistical modeling: the two cultures (with comments and a rejoinder by the author). *Statistical Science* 16 (3): 199–231. https://doi.org/10.1214/ss/1009213726.

Breiman, L., Friedman, J.H., Olshen, R.A. et al. (1984). *Classification and Regression Trees*. Belmont, CA: Wadsworth.

Brick, J.M. (2013). Unit nonresponse and weighting adjustments: a critical review. *Journal of Official Statistics* 29 (3): 329–353. https://doi.org/10.2478/jos-2013-0026.

Buelens, B., Burger, J., and van den Brakel, J.A. (2018). Comparing inference methods for non-probability samples. *International Statistical Review* 86 (2): 322–343. https://doi.org/10.1111/insr.12253.

Burgette, L.F., Escarce, J.J., Paddock, S.M. et al. (2019). Sample selection in the face of design constraints: use of clustering to define sample strata for qualitative research. *Health Services Research* 54 (2): 509–517. https://doi.org/10.1111/1475-6773.13100.

Burke, A., Edwards, B., and Yan, T. (2018). The future is now: how surveys can harness social media to address 21st-century challenges. Paper presented at the BigSurv18 Conference, Barcelona, Spain (25–27 October 2018). https://www.europeansurveyresearch.org/bigsurv18/uploads/167/178/BigSurv_PPT_Burke_Garcia_Edwards_Yan_FINAL_FOR_DISSEMINATION_181025.pptx (accessed 5 July 2019).

Buskirk, T.D., Bear, T., and Bareham, J. (2018a). Machine made sampling designs: applying machine learning methods for generating stratified sampling designs. Paper presented at the BigSurv18 Conference, Barcelona, Spain (25–27 October 2018). https://www.bigsurv18.org/conf18/uploads/177/203/BuskirkBearBarehamBigSurv18ProgramPostedVersionFinal.pdf (accessed 20 June 2019).

Buskirk, T.D. and Dutwin, D. (2016). Matchmaker, data scientist or both? Using unsupervised learning methods for matching nonprobability samples to probability samples. Paper presented at the 2016 Joint Statistical Meetings, Chicago, IL (30 July–4 August 2016).

Buskirk, T.D., Kirchner, A., Eck, A. et al. (2018b). An introduction to machine learning methods for survey researchers. *Survey Practice* 11 (1): 1–10. https://doi.org/10.29115/SP-2018-0004.

Buskirk, T.D. and Kolenikov, S. (2015). Finding respondents in the forest: a comparison of logistic regression and random forest models for response propensity weighting and stratification. *Survey Insights: Methods from the Field, Weighting: Practical Issues and 'How to' Approach*. http://surveyinsights.org/?p=5108. https://doi.org/10.13094/SMIF-2015-00003 (accessed 2 January 2019).

Buskirk, T.D., West, B.T., and Burks, A.T. (2013). Respondents: who art thou? Comparing internal, temporal, and external validity of survey response propensity models based on random forests and logistic regression models. Paper presented at the 2013 Joint Statistical Meetings, Montreal, Canada (3–8 August 2013).

Caiola, G. and Reiter, J. (2010). Random forests for generating partially synthetic, categorical data. *Transactions on Data Privacy* 3: 27–42.

Can, S., Engel, U., and Keck, J. (2018). Topic modeling and status classification using data from surveys and social networks. Paper presented at the BigSurv18 Conference, Barcelona, Spain (25–27 October 2018).

Chew, R. and Biemer, P. (2018). Machine learning in adaptive survey designs. Paper presented at the BigSurv18 Conference, Barcelona, Spain (25–27 October 2018). https://www.europeansurveyresearch.org/bigsurv18/uploads/165/21/BigSurv18_Bandits.pptx (accessed 5 July 2019).

Chew, R.F., Amer, S., Jones, K. et al. (2018). Residential scene classification for gridded population sampling in developing countries using deep convolutional neural networks on satellite imagery. *International Journal of Health Geographics* 17 (1): 12. https://doi.org/10.1186/s12942-018-0132-1.

Christen, P. (2012). *Data Matching: Concepts and Techniques for Record Linkage, Entity Resolution, and Duplicate Detection*. Heidelberg, Germany: Springer Science & Business Media https://doi.org/10.1007/978-3-642-31164-2.

Cochran, W.G. (1964). *Sampling Techniques*, 2e. New York, NY: Wiley.

Conn, D., Ngun, T., Li, G. et al. (2015). *Fuzzy Forests: Extending Random Forests for Correlated, High-Dimensional Data*. Technical Research Report; eScholarship. Los Angeles, CA: University of California http://escholarship.org/uc/item/55h4h0w7.

Connelly, R., Playford, C.J., Gayle, V. et al. (2016). The role of administrative data in the big data revolution in social science research. *Social Science Research* 59: 1–12. https://doi.org/10.1016/j.ssresearch.2016.04.015.

Conrad, F.G., Couper, M.P., and Sakshaug, J.W. (2016). Classifying open-ended reports: factors affecting the reliability of occupation codes. *Journal of Official Statistics* 32 (1): 75–92. https://doi.org/10.1515/jos-2016-0003.

Couper, M.P. and Zhang, C. (2016). Helping respondents provide good answers in web surveys. *Survey Research Methods* 10 (1): 49–64. https://doi.org/10.18148/srm/2016.v10i1.6273.

Creecy, R.H., Masand, B.M., Smith, S.J. et al. (1992). Trading MIPS and memory for knowledge engineering. *Communications of the ACM* 35 (8): 48–64. https://doi.org/10.1145/135226.135228.

De Haas, S. and Winker, P. (2016). Detecting fraudulent interviewers by improved clustering methods – the case of falsifications of answers to parts of a questionnaire. *Journal of Official Statistics* 32 (3): 643–660. https://doi.org/10.1515/jos-2016-0033.

Drechsler, J. and Reiter, J. (2011). An empirical evaluation of easily implemented, nonparametric methods for generating synthetic datasets. *Computational Statistics & Data Analysis* 55 (12): 3232–3243. https://doi.org/10.1016/j.csda.2011.06.006.

Dutwin, D. and Buskirk, T.D. (2017). Apples to oranges or gala versus golden delicious?: Comparing data quality of nonprobability internet samples to low response rate probability samples. *Public Opinion Quarterly* 81 (S1): 213–239. https://doi.org/10.1093/poq/nfw061.

Early, K. (2017). Dynamic question ordering: obtaining useful information while reducing user burden. Doctoral thesis. Machine Learning Department, Carnegie Mellon University, Pittsburgh, PA.

Earp, M., Mitchell, M., McCarthy, J., and Kreuter, F. (2014). Modeling nonresponse in establishment surveys: using and ensemble tree model to create nonresponse propensity scores and detect potential bias in an agricultural survey. *Journal of Official Statistics* 30 (4): 701–719.

Earp, M. S. and McCarthy, J. S. (2009). Using respondent prediction models to improve efficiency of incentive allocation. United States Department of Agriculture, National Agricultural Statistics Service. http://purl.umn.edu/235087 (accessed 3 July 2019).

Eck, A. (2018). Neural networks for survey researchers. *Survey Practice* 11 (1): 1–11. https://doi.org/10.29115/SP-2018-0002.

Eck, A., Buskirk, T. D., Fletcher, K., et al. (2018). Machine made sampling frames: creating sampling frames of windmills and other non-traditional sampling units using machine learning with neural networks. Paper presented at the BigSurv18 Conference, Barcelona, Spain (25–27 October 2018).

Eck, A., Buskirk, T. D., Shao, H., et al. (2019). Taking the machines to class: exploring how to train machine learning methods to understand images for survey sampling. Paper presented at the 74th Annual American Association of Public Opinion Research Conference, Toronto, Canada (18–21 May 2017).

Eck, A. and Soh, L.-K. (2017a). Sequential prediction of respondent behaviors leading to error in web-based surveys. Paper presented at the 72nd Annual Conference of the American Association for Public Opinion Research, New Orleans, LA (18–21 May 2017).

Eck, A. and Soh, L.-K. (2017b). Can an automated agent anticipate straightlining answers? Paper presented at the 72nd Annual Conference of the American Association for Public Opinion Research, New Orleans, LA (18–21 May 2017).

Eck, A., Soh, L.-K., and McCutcheon, A. L. (2015). Predicting breakoff using sequential machine learning methods. Paper presented at the 70th Annual Conference of the American Association for Public Opinion Research, Hollywood, FL (18–21 May 2017).

Eckman, S., Chew, R., Sanders, H., et al. (2019). Using passive data to improve survey data. Paper presented at the MASS Workshop, Mannheim, Germany (4–5 March 2019).

Elliott, M. and Valliant, R. (2017). Inference for nonprobability samples. *Statistical Science* 32 (2): 249–264.

Elmagarmid, A.K., Ipeirotis, P.G., and Verykios, V.S. (2007). Duplicate record detection: a survey. *IEEE Transactions on Knowledge and Data Engineering* 19 (1): 1–16. https://doi.org/10.1109/TKDE.2007.250581.

Erdman, C. and Bates, N. (2017). The Low Response Score (LRS). A metric to locate, predict, and manage hard-to-survey populations. *Public Opinion Quarterly* 81 (1): 144–156. https://doi.org/10.1093/poq/nfw040.

Fischer, M. and Mittereder, F. (2018). Can missing patterns in covariates improve imputation for missing data? Paper Presented at the BigSurv18 Conference, Barcelona, Spain (25–27 October 2018). https://www.bigsurv18.org/conf18/uploads/42/64/MF_FM_MissInd_BigSurv18.pdf (accessed 1 June 2019).

Garber, S.C. (2009). *Census Mail List Trimming Using SAS Data Mining* (RDD Report 09-02). Fairfax, VA: Department of Agriculture, National Agricultural Statistics Service.

Garcia and Rueba. (2018). Efficiency of classification algorithms as an alternative to logistic regression in propensity score adjustment for survey weighting. Paper Presented at the BigSurv18 Conference; Barcelona, Spain (25–27 October 2018). https://www.bigsurv18.org/conf18/uploads/132/117/ExpBigSurv18.pdf (accessed 1 June 2019).

Graesser, A.C., Cai, Z., Louwerse, M.M. et al. (2006). Question Understanding Aid (QUAID) a web facility that tests question comprehensibility. *Public Opinion Quarterly* 70 (1): 3–22. https://doi.org/10.1093/poq/nfj012.

Graesser, A.C., Wiemer-Hastings, K., Kreuz, R. et al. (2000). QUAID: a questionnaire evaluation aid for survey methodologists. *Behavior Research Methods, Instruments, & Computers* 32 (2): 254–262. https://doi.org/10.3758/BF03207792.

Grimmer, J. (2015). We are all social scientists now: how big data, machine learning, and causal inference work together. *PS: Political Science & Politics* 48 (1): 80–83. https://doi.org/10.1017/S1049096514001784.

Guzman, D. (2018). Mining interviewer observations. Paper presented at the BigSurv18 Conference, Barcelona, Spain (25–27 October 2018). https://www.europeansurveyresearch.org/bigsurv18/uploads/139/174/bigSurv18_daniel_guzman.pptx (accessed 5 July 2019).

Hardeman, W., Houghton, J., Lane, K. et al. (2019). A systematic review of just-in-time adaptive interventions (JITAIs) to promote physical activity. *International Journal of Behavioral Nutrition and Physical Activity* 16 (1): 31. https://doi.org/10.1186/s12966-019-0792-7.

Hastie, T., Tibshirani, R., and Friedman, J. (2001). *The Elements of Statistical Learning: Data Mining, Inference and Prediction*. New York, NY: Springer https://doi.org/10.1007/978-0-387-21606-5.

Huang, Z. (1998). Extensions to the K-modes algorithm for clustering large data sets with categorical values. *Data Mining and Knowledge Discovery* 2 (3): 283–304. https://doi.org/10.1023/A:1009769707641.

Huang, Z. and Ng, M.K. (1999). A fuzzy K-modes algorithm for clustering categorical data. *IEEE Transactions on Fuzzy Systems* 7 (4): 446–452. https://doi.org/10.1109/91.784206.

Jäckle, A., Burton, J., Couper, M.P. et al. (2019). Participation in a mobile app survey to collect expenditure data as part of a large-scale probability household panel: coverage and participation rates and biases. *Survey Research Methods* 13 (1): 23–44. https://doi.org/10.18148/srm/2019.v13i1.7297.

James, G., Witten, D., Hastie, T. et al. (2013). *An Introduction to Statistical Learning*, vol. 112. New York, NY: Springer https://doi.org/10.1007/978-1-4614-7138-7.

Kalton, G. and Flores-Cervantes, I. (2003). Weighting methods. *Journal of Official Statistics* 19 (2): 81–97.

Kass, G.V. (1980). An exploratory technique for investigating large quantities of categorical data. *Journal of the Royal Statistical Society: Series C* 29 (2): 119–127.

Kelly, F. and Doriot, P. (2017). Using data mining and machine learning to shorten and improve surveys. [Article ID: 20170526-1]. *Quirk's Media*.

Kern, C., Klausch, T., and Kreuter, F. (2019). Tree-based machine learning methods for survey research. *Survey Research Methods* 13 (1): 73–93. https://doi.org/10.18148/srm/2019.v13i1.7395.

Kim, D.W., Lee, K.H., and Lee, D. (2004). Fuzzy clustering of categorical data using fuzzy centroids. *Pattern Recognition Letters* 25 (11): 1263–1271. https://doi.org/10.1016/j.patrec.2004.04.004.

Kolb, J.-P., Kern, C., and Weiß, B. (2018). Using predictive modeling to identify panel dropouts. Paper presented at the BigSurv18 Conference, Barcelona, Spain (25–27 October 2018).

Korpusik, M., Huang, C., Price, M., et al. (2016). Distributional semantics for understanding spoken meal descriptions. *IEEE SigPort*. http://sigport.org/676 (accessed 14 April 2019).

Krizhevsky, A., Sutskever, I., and Hinton, G.E. (2012). ImageNet classification with deep convolutional neural networks. *Advances in Neural Information Processing Systems* 1: 1097–1105.

Kuhn, M. and Johnson, K. (2013). *Applied Predictive Modeling*, vol. 26. New York, NY: Springer https://doi.org/10.1007/978-1-4614-6849-3.

Lee, B.K., Lessler, J., and Stuart, E.A. (2010). Improving propensity score weighting using machine learning. *Statistics in Medicine* 29 (3): 337–346. https://doi.org/10.1002/sim.3782.

Lee, S. (2006). Propensity score adjustment as a weighting scheme for volunteer web panel surveys. *Journal of Official Statistics* 22 (2): 329–349.

Liu, M. and Wang, Y. (2018). Using machine learning models to predict follow-up survey participation in a panel study. Paper presented at the BigSurv18 Conference, Barcelona, Spain (25–27 October 2018). https://www.europeansurveyresearch.org/bigsurv18/uploads/93/87/BigSurv_presentation_Liu_upload.pdf (accessed 18 June 2019).

Loh, W.-Y., Eltinge, J., Cho, M.J. et al. (2019). Classification and regression trees and forests for incomplete data from sample surveys. *Statistica Sinica* 29 (1): 431–453. https://doi.org/10.5705/ss.202017.0225.

Lohr, S., Hsu, V., and Montaquila, J. (2015). Using classification and regression trees to model survey nonresponse. In: *Proceedings of the Joint Statistical Meetings, 2015 Survey Research Methods Section: American Statistical Association*, 2071–2085. Alexandria, VA: American Statistical Association (8–13 August).

Lu, C., Li, X.-W., and Pan, H.-B. (2007). Application of SVM and fuzzy set theory for classifying with incomplete survey data. In: *2007 International Conference on Service Systems and Service Management*, Chengdu, China, 1–4. https://doi.org/10.1109/ICSSSM.2007.4280164.

Lugtig, P. and Blom, A. (2018). Advances in modelling attrition: the added value of paradata and machine learning algorithms. Paper presented at the BigSurv18 Conference, Barcelona, Spain (25–27 October 2018). https://www.europeansurveyresearch.org/bigsurv18/uploads/192/47/Lugtig_and_Blom_big_surv_paradata_and_attrition_machine_learning.pdf (accessed 18 June 2019).

McCarthy, J.S. and Earp, M.S. (2009). *Who makes mistakes? Using data mining techniques to analyze reporting errors in total acres operated* (RDD Research Report Number RDD-09-02). Washington, DC: U.S. Departmente of Agriculture https://pdfs.semanticscholar.org/dee9/cf6187b6a77a1e8e1f64a76a4942dc2e0f6d.pdf?_ga=2.139828851.1790488900.1562077670-74454473.1562077670.

McConville, K.S., Breidt, F.J., Lee, T.C. et al. (2017). Model-assisted survey regression estimation with the lasso. *Journal of Survey Statistics and Methodology* 5 (2): 131–158. https://doi.org/10.1093/jssam/smw041.

McConville, K.S. and Toth, D. (2019). Automated selection of post-strata using a model-assisted regression tree estimator. *Scandinavian Journal of Statistics* 46 (2): 389–413. https://doi.org/10.1111/sjos.12356.

McCreanor, R., Wronski, L., and Chen, J. (2018). Automated topic modeling for trend analysis of open-ended response data. Paper presented at the BigSurv18 Conference, Barcelona, Spain (25–27 October 2018). https://www.bigsurv18.org/program2018?sess=38#286 (accessed 18 June 2019).

Megra, M., Medway, R., Jackson, M., et al. (2018). Predicting response mode preferences of survey respondents: a comparison between traditional regression and data mining methods. Paper presented at the BigSurv18 Conference, Barcelona, Spain (25–27 October 2018).

Mendez, G., Buskirk, T.D., Lohr, S. et al. (2008). Factors associated with persistence in science and engineering majors: an exploratory study using random forests. *Journal of Engineering Education* 97 (1): 57–70. https://doi.org/10.1002/j.2168-9830.2008.tb00954.x.

Mercer, A.W., Kreuter, F., Keeter, S., and Stuart, E.A. (2017). Theory and practice in nonprobability surveys: parallels between causal inference and survey inference. *Public Opinion Quarterly* 81 (S1): 250–271.

Mercer, A., Lau, A. and Kennedy, C. (2018) For weighting online opt-in samples, what matters most? Pew Research Center Report released on January 26, 2018. https://www.pewresearch.org/methods/2018/01/26/for-weighting-online-opt-in-samples-what-matters-most/ (accessed 2 June 2019).

Mercer, A., Lau, A., and Kennedy, C. (2018). For weighting online opt-in samples, what matters most? Pew Research Center. https://www.ewresearch.org/methods/2018/01/26/for‐weighting‐online‐opt‐in‐samples‐what‐matters‐most/ (accessed 30 June 2019).

Mittereder, F. and West, B. (2018). Can response behavior predict breakoff in web surveys? Paper presented at the General Online Research Conference, Cologne, Germany. https://www.gor.de/gor18/index.php?page=downloadPaper&filename=Mittereder-Can_Response_Behavior_Predict_Breakoff_in_Web_Surveys-135.pdf&form_id=135&form_version=final (accessed 3 July 2019).

Mittereder, F. K. (2019). Predicting and preventing breakoffs in web surveys. Doctoral dissertation. Survey Methodology, University of Michigan, Ann Arbor, MI.

Morris, D.S. (2017). A modeling approach for administrative record enumeration in the decennial census. *Public Opinion Quarterly* 81 (S1): 357–384. https://doi.org/10.1093/poq/nfw059.

Morrison, L.G., Hargood, C., Pejovic, V. et al. (2017). The effect of timing and frequency of push notifications on usage of a smartphone-based stress management intervention: an exploratory trial. *PLoS One* 12 (1): e0169162. https://doi.org/10.1371/journal.pone.0169162.

Mulder, J. and Kieruj, N. (2018). Preserving our precious respondents: predicting and preventing non-response and panel attrition by analyzing and modeling longitudinal survey and paradata using data science techniques. Paper presented at the BigSurv18 Conference, Barcelona, Spain (25–27 October 2018).

Nahum-Shani, I., Smith, S.N., Spring, B.J. et al. (2018). Just-in-Time Adaptive Interventions (JITAIs) in mobile health: key components and design principles for ongoing health behavior support. *Annals of Behavioral Medicine* 52 (6): 446–462. https://doi.org/10.1007/s12160-016-9830-8.

Niraula, N. B. and Rus, V. (2014). A machine learning approach to pronominal anaphora resolutionin dialogue based intelligent tutoring systems. *Proceedings of the Computational Linguistics and Intelligent Text Processing. Proceedings (Part 1) of the 15th International Conference CICLing*, Kathmandu, Nepal (pp. 307–318). Berlin, Heidelberg: Springer.

Oberski, D.L. (2016). Questionnaire science. In: *The Oxford Handbook of Polling and Survey Methods* (eds. L.R. Atkeson and R.M. Alvarez), 113–140. New York, NY: Oxford University Press https://doi.org/10.1093/oxfordhb/9780190213299.013.21.

Oberski, D. L. and DeCastellarnau, A. (2019). Predicting measurement error variance in social surveys. (Unpublished Manuscript).

Oberski, D.L., Gruner, T., and Saris, W.E. (2011). The prediction of the quality of the questionsbased on the present data base of questions. In: *The Development of the Program SQP 2.0 for the Prediction of the Quality of Survey Questions* (eds. W.E. Saris, D. Oberski, M. Revilla, et al.), 71–81. Spain: Barcelona.

Pankowska, P., Oberski, D., and Pavlopoulos, D. (2018). The effect of survey measurement error on clustering algorithms. Paper presented at the BigSurv18 Conference, Barcelona, Spain (25–27 October 2018). https://www.europeansurveyresearch.org/bigsurv18/uploads/219/239/clustering_measurement_error.ppt (accessed 29 June 2019).

Petrakos, G., Conversano, C., Farmakis, G. et al. (2004). New ways of specifying data edits. *Journal of the Royal Statistical Society. Series A (General)* 167 (2): 249–274. https://doi.org/10.1046/j.1467-985X.2003.00745.x.

Phipps, P. and Toth, D. (2012). Analyzing establishment nonresponse using an interpretable regression tree model with linked administrative data. *The Annals of Applied Statistics* 6 (2): 772–794. https://doi.org/10.1214/11-AOAS521.

Provost, F. and Domingos, P. (2003). Tree induction for probability-based ranking. *Machine Learning* 52 (3): 199–215. https://doi.org/10.1023/A:1024099825458.

Roberts, M.E., Stewart, B.M., Tingley, D. et al. (2014). Structural topic models for open-ended survey responses. *American Journal of Political Science* 58 (4): 1064–1082. https://doi.org/10.1111/ajps.12103.

Rosenbaum, P.R. and Rubin, D.B. (1983). The central role of the propensity score in observational studies for causal effects. *Biometrika* 70 (1): 41–55. https://doi.org/10.1093/biomet/70.1.41.

Ruiz, C. (2018). Improving data validation using machine learning. Paper presented at the Conference of European Statisticians, Workshop on Statistical Data Editing, Neuchatel, Switzerland (18–20 September 2018).

Saris, W.E. and Gallhofer, I.N. (2007). Estimation of the effects of measurement characteristics on the quality of survey questions. *Survey Research Methods* 1 (1): 29–43. https://doi.org/10.1002/9780470165195.ch12.

Saris, W.E. and Gallhofer, I.N. (2014). *Design, Evaluation, and Analysis of Questionnaires for Survey Research*. Hoboken, NJ: Wiley https://doi.org/10.1002/9781118634646.

Schembre, S.M., Liao, Y., Robertson, M.C. et al. (2018). Just-in-time feedback in diet and physical activity interventions: systematic review and practical design framework. *Journal of Medical Internet Research* 20 (3): e106. https://doi.org/10.2196/jmir.8701.

Schierholz, M. (2018). A comparison of automatic algorithms for occupation coding. Paper presented at the BigSurv18 Conference, Barcelona, Spain (25–27 October 2018). https://www.europeansurveyresearch.org/bigsurv18/uploads/56/82/Schierholz_Barcelona_26_10_2018.pdf (accessed 5 July 2019).

Schierholz, M., Gensicke, M., Tschersich, N. et al. (2018). Occupation coding during the interview. *Journal of the Royal Statistical Society. Series A (General)* 181 (2): 379–407. https://doi.org/10.1111/rssa.12297.

Schonlau, M. and Couper, M. (2017). Options for conducting web surveys. *Statistical Science* 32 (2): 279–292. https://doi.org/10.1214/16-STS597.

Schonlau, M. and Couper, M.P. (2016). Semi-automated categorization of open-ended questions. *Survey Research Methods* 10 (2): 143–152. https://doi.org/10.18148/srm/2016.v1012.6213.

Schonlau, M., Gweon, H., and Wenemark, M. (2018). Classification of open ended questions with multiple labels. Paper presented at the BigSurv18 Conference, Barcelona, Spain (25–27 October 2018). https://www.europeansurveyresearch.org/bigsurv18/uploads/173/39/all_that_apply_barcelona.pdf (accessed 5 July 2019).

Schouten, B. and de Nooij, G. (2005). *Nonresponse Adjustment Using Classification Trees*. The Netherlands: CBS, Statistics Netherlands.

Sela, R.J. and Simonoff, J.S. (2012). RE-EM trees: a data mining approach for longitudinal and clustered data. *Machine Learning* 86 (2): 169–207. https://doi.org/10.1007/s10994-011-5258-3.

Shmueli, G. (2010). To explain or to predict? *Statistical Science* 25 (3): 289–310. https://doi.org/10.1214/10-STS330.

Shorey, J., Jang, H., Spagnardi, C., et al. (2018). Enriching surveys with knowledge graphs. Paper presented at the BigSurv18 Conference, Barcelona, Spain (25–27 October 2018).

Spruijt-Metz, D. and Nilsen, W. (2014). Dynamic models of behavior for just-in-time adaptive interventions. *IEEE Pervasive Computing* 13 (3): 13–17. https://doi.org/10.1109/MPRV.2014.46.

Stanfill, M.H., Williams, M., Fenton, S.H. et al. (2010). A systematic literature review of automated clinical coding and classification systems. *Journal of the American Medical Informatics Association* 17 (6): 646–651. https://doi.org/10.1136/jamia.2009.001024.

Stone, A.A. and Shiffman, S. (1994). Ecological momentary assessment (EMA) in behavioral medicine. *Annals of Behavioral Medicine* 16 (3): 199–202. https://doi.org/10.1093/abm/16.3.199.

Stone, A.A., Shiffman, S., Atienza, A.A. et al. (2007). *The Science of Real-Time Data Capture: Self-Reports in Health Research*. New York, NY: Oxford University Press.

Strobl, C., Boulesteix, A.-L., Zeileis, A. et al. (2007). Bias in random forest variable importance measures: illustrations, sources and a solution. *BMC Bioinformatics* 8 (25): 25. https://doi.org/10.1186/1471-2105-8-25.

Sun, H., Rivero, G., and Yan, T. (2019). Identifying interviewer falsification using speech recognition: a proof of concept study. Paper presented at the 74th Annual Conference of the American Association for Public Opinion Research, Toronto, Canada (16–19 May 2019).

Sweitzer, M.D. and Shulman, H.C. (2018). The effects of metacognition in survey research experimental, cross-sectional, and content-analytic evidence. *Public Opinion Quarterly* 82 (4): 745–768. https://doi.org/10.1093/poq/nfy034.

ten Bosch, O., Windmeijer, D., van Delden, A., et al. (2018). Web scraping meets survey design: combining forces. Paper presented at the BigSurv18 Conference, Barcelona, Spain (25–27 October 2018). https://www.bigsurv18.org/conf18/uploads/73/61/20180820_BigSurv_WebscrapingMeetsSurveyDesign.pdf (accessed 30 June 2019).

Thaung, A. and Kolenikov, S. (2018). Detecting and comparing survey research topics in conference and journal abstracts. Paper presented at the BigSurv18 Conference, Barcelona, Spain (25–27 October 2018).

Thomson, D.R., Stevens, F.R., Ruktanonchai, N.W. et al. (2017). GridSample: an R package to generate household survey primary sampling units (PSUs) from gridded population data. *International Journal of Health Geographics* 16 (1): 25. https://doi.org/10.1186/s12942-017-0098-4.

Timbrook, J. and Eck, A. (2018). Comparing coding of interviewer question-asking behaviors using recurrent neural networks to human coders. Paper presented at the BigSurv18 Conference, Barcelona, Spain (25–27 October 2018). https://www.europeansurveyresearch.org/bigsurv18/uploads/158/193/Timbrook_Eck_BigSurv_2018.pdf (accessed 5 July 2019).

Timbrook, J. and Eck, A. (2019). Humans vs. machines: comparing coding of interviewer question-asking behaviors using recurrent neural networks to human coders. Paper presented at the Interviewers and Their Effects from a Total Survey Error Perspective Workshop, University of Nebraska-Lincoln (26–28 February 2019). https://digitalcommons.unl.edu/cgi/viewcontent.cgi?article=1025&context=sociw (accessed 5 July 2019).

Toth, D. (2017). rpms: Recursive partitioning for modeling survey data. R Package Version 0.2.0. https://CRAN.R-project.org/package=rpms (accessed 20 October 2017).

Toth, D. and Eltinge, J.L. (2011). Building consistent regression trees from complex sample data. *Journal of the American Statistical Association* 106 (496): 1626–1636. https://doi.org/10.1198/jasa.2011.tm10383.

Toth, D. and Phipps, P. (2014). Regression tree models for analyzing survey response. In: *Proceedings of the Government Statistics Section*, 339–351. American Statistical Association.

Valliant, R., Dever, J., and Kreuter, F. (2013). *Practical Tools for Designing and Weighting Survey Samples*. New York, NY: Springer https://doi.org/10.1007/978-1-4614-6449-5.

Valliant, R. and Dever, J.A. (2011). Estimating propensity adjustments for volunteer web surveys. *Sociological Methods & Research* 40 (1): 105–137. https://doi.org/10.1177/0049124110392533.

Vanhoof, M., Lee, C., and Smoreda, Z. (2018). Performance and sensitivities of home detection from mobile phone data. Paper presented at the BigSurv18 Conference, Barcelona, Spain (25–27 October 2018). https://www.europeansurveyresearch.org/bigsurv18/uploads/135/169/BigSurv_MainText_Performance_and_sensitivities_of_home_detection_from_mobile_phone_data.pdf (accessed 30 June 2019).

Ventura, S.L., Nugent, R., and Fuchs, E.R.H. (2015). Seeing the non-stars: (some) sources of bias in past disambiguation approaches and a new public tool leveraging labeled records. *Research Policy* 44 (9): 1672–1701. https://doi.org/10.1016/j.respol.2014.12.010.

Ward, C. and Reimer, B. (2019). Using natural language processing to enhance prediction of panel attrition in a longitudinal survey. Paper presented at the 74th Annual Conference of the American Association for Public Opinion Research, Toronto, Canada (16–19 May 2019).

Winkler, W.E. (2006). *Overview of Record Linkage and Current Research Directions* (Technical Report Statistical Research Report Series RRS2006/02). Washington, DC: U.S. Bureau of the Census.

Ye, C., Medway, R., and Kelley, C. (2018). Natural language processing for open-ended survey questions. Paper presented at the BigSurv18 Conference, Barcelona, Spain (25–27 October 2018).

Zhao, P., Su, X., Ge, T. et al. (2016). Propensity score and proximity matching using random forest. *Contemporary Clinical Trials* 47: 85–92. https://doi.org/10.1016/j.cct.2015.12.012.

Further Reading

Buskirk, T.D. (2018). Surveying the forests and sampling the trees: an overview of classification and regression trees and random forests with applications in survey research. *Survey Practice* 11 (1): 1–13. https://doi.org/10.29115/SP-2018-0003.

Cochran, W.G. (1968). The effectiveness of adjustment by subclassification in removing bias in observational studies. *Biometrics* 25 (2): 295–313.

Dutwin, D. and Buskirk, T. D. (2017). A deep dive into the digital divide. Paper presented at the 72nd annual American Association of Public Opinion Research Conference, New Orleans, LA (18–21 May 2017).

Ferri-García, R. and del Mar Rueda, M. (2018). Efficiency of classification algorithms as an alternative to logistic regression in propensity score adjustment for survey weighting. Paper presented at the BigSurv18 Conference, Barcelona, Spain (25–27 October 2018). https://www.europeansurveyresearch.org/bigsurv18/uploads/132/117/ExpBigSurv18.pdf (accessed 28 June 2019).

Gower, J.C. (1971). A general coefficient of similarity and some of its properties. *Biometrics* 27 (4): 857–874. https://doi.org/10.2307/2528823.

Gray, J. (2009). On eScience: a transformed scientific method. In: *The Fourth Paradigm* (eds. T. Hey, S. Tansley and K. Tolle), xvii–xxxi. Redmond, WA: Microsoft Research.

Han, B. and Baldwin, T. (2011). Lexical normalization of short text messages: makn sens a #twitter. In: *Proceedings of the 49th Annual Meeting of the Association for Computational Linguistics*, Portland OR (19–24 June), 368–378.

Japec, L., Kreuter, F., Berg, M. et al. (2015). Big data in survey research: Aapor task force report. *Public Opinion Quarterly* 79 (4): 839–880. https://doi.org/10.1093/poq/nfv039.

Khoshrou, A., Aguiar, A.P., and Pereira, F.L. (2016). Adaptive sampling using an unsupervised learning of GMMs applied to a fleet of AUVs with CTD measurements. In: *Robot 2015: Second Iberian Robotics Conference. Advances in Intelligent Systems and Computing* (eds. L. Reis, A. Moreira, P. Lima, et al.), 321–332. Cham: Springer https://doi.org/10.1007/978-3-319-27149-1.

Kim, J.K. and Wang, Z. (2019). Sampling techniques for big data analysis in finite population inference. *International Statistical Review* S1: S177–S191. https://doi.org/10.1111/insr.12290.

Kirchner, A. and Signorino, C.S. (2018). Using support vector machines for survey research. *Survey Practice* 11 (1): 1–14. https://doi.org/10.29115/SP-2018-0001.

Krantz, A., Korn, R., and Menninger, M. (2009). Rethinking museum visitors: using K-means cluster analysis to explore a museum's audience. *Curator* 52 (4): 363–374. https://doi.org/10.1111/j.2151-6952.2009.tb00358.x.

Lee, S. and Valliant, R. (2009). Estimation for volunteer panel web surveys using propensity score adjustment and calibration adjustment. *Sociological Methods & Research* 37 (3): 319–343. https://doi.org/10.1177/0049124108329643.

Linden, A. and Yarnold, P.R. (2017). Using classification tree analysis to generate propensity score weights. *Journal of Evaluation in Clinical Practice* 23 (4): 703–712. https://doi.org/10.1111/jep.12744.

McCaffrey, D.F., Griffin, B.A., Almirall, D. et al. (2013). A tutorial on propensity score estimation for multiple treatments using generalized boosted models. *Statistics in Medicine* 32 (19): 3388–3414. https://doi.org/10.1002/sim.5753.

Mercer, A.W., Kreuter, F., Keeter, S. et al. (2017). Theory and practice in nonprobability surveys: parallels between causal inference and survey inference. *Public Opinion Quarterly* 81 (S1): 250–271. https://doi.org/10.1093/poq/nfw060.

Pirracchio, R., Petersen, M.L., and van der Laan, M. (2015). Improving propensity score estimators' robustness to model misspecification using super learner. *American Journal of Epidemiology* 181 (2): 108–119. https://doi.org/10.1093/aje/kwu253.

Signorino, C.S. and Kirchner, A. (2018). Using LASSO to model interactions and nonlinearities in survey data. *Survey Practice* 11 (1): 1–10. https://doi.org/10.29115/SP-2018-0005.

Timpone, R., Kroening, J., and Yang, Y. (2018). From big data to big analytics: automated analytic platforms for data exploration. Paper presented at the BigSurv18 Conference, Barcelona, Spain (25–27 October 2018). https://www.europeansurveyresearch.org/bigsurv18/uploads/307/367/From_Big_Data_to_Big_Analytics_102618_paper.pdf (accessed 30 June 2019).

2

The Future Is Now: How Surveys Can Harness Social Media to Address Twenty-first Century Challenges

Amelia Burke-Garcia[1], Brad Edwards[2], and Ting Yan[2]

[1] NORC, University of Chicago, Bethesda, MD, USA
[2] Westat, Rockville, MD, USA

2.1 Introduction

This century has brought tremendous social and economic shifts with major global implications. Mass migration and population displacement have made populations more mobile and harder to reach than ever. The general decline in trust in most institutions hinders populations from participating in civic activities. These trends have made *all* populations increasingly difficult to survey in this new world (Brick and Williams 2013; Curtin, Presser, and Singer 2005; De Heer and De Leeuw 2002; Egley 2002; Tourangeau et al. 2014; Uslaner and Brown 2005).

One of the more powerful shifts that has occurred – with the potential to greatly affect survey research operations – is the acceleration of technological advances. The ubiquitous use of mobile phones and the advent of online social networks, specifically social media, are drastically increasing the speed and scale of communication globally.

Since its inception, social media has generally been considered purely as a channel of *communication*, similar to the written word or the telephone. We argue that it has become much more than that: the Internet age has brought an increasing share of our entire lives online. For example, in the 60 seconds it might take to read this paragraph, Americans will have used more than 2.5 million GB of Internet data, conducted more than 3 million Google searches, sent more than 15 million text messages, sent nearly 500 000 tweets, and posted nearly 50 000 photos on Instagram (WERSM 2017). Moreover, mobile and social are no longer considered separate platforms; in 2018, more than 60% of social media usage was on mobile devices (Statista 2018).

Big Data Meets Survey Science: A Collection of Innovative Methods, First Edition. Edited by Craig A. Hill, Paul P. Biemer, Trent D. Buskirk, Lilli Japec, Antje Kirchner, Stas Kolenikov, and Lars E. Lyberg.
© 2021 John Wiley & Sons, Inc. Published 2021 by John Wiley & Sons, Inc.

Compounding these events is the emergence of the Internet of things, or the network of physical devices, vehicles, home appliances, and other items embedded with electronics, software, sensors, actuators, and Internet connectivity. This phenomenon has extended the traditional communication role that social media has played by enabling these "things" to connect and exchange data (Hassan 2018). As Stephen Hawking said, "We are all now connected by the Internet, like neurons in a giant brain" (Swartz 2014). To provide a sense of the size and scope of some of these platforms, Table 2.1 lists some of the most popular social networking-related sites globally by number of monthly active users.

Thus, the line between communication and technology has become blurred, leading us to propose a broader conceptualization of social media that includes the context of who, what, and where we are, not just the explicit message (text or images) we communicate. This broader conceptualization suggests that vast amounts of new data have become available via these channels, data that

Table 2.1 Social networking sites by total number of active users.[a]

Platform	Location of headquarters	Number of monthly active global users (in millions)
Facebook	United States	2230
Google	United States	2000
YouTube	United States	1800
Reddit	United States	1600
Instagram	United States	1000
WeChat	China	1000
Apple	United States	1000
Qzone	China	600
Weibo	China	340
Amazon	United States	310
RenRen	China	257
Pinterest	United States	200
Twitter	United States	68
Alexa	United States	8.2
Online influencers	Global	1.1
MTurk	United States	0.5

[a] As a point of reference, the global population ages 15–64 years was 4.92 billion in 2017 (The World Bank 2017).

may enhance survey research as the field moves farther into the twenty-first century.

Among these data, we can differentiate two broad classes of data (i) the social media data itself, and (ii) the paradata, or the data about the process by which the data are collected. For the first type, a wealth of data on individuals and their behaviors is available across various platforms including Facebook, Twitter, and Instagram (all from the United States) as well as the microblogging site, Weibo; the messaging, social media, and mobile payment application, WeChat; and the online social network, Qzone (all from China). These data have never been so easily accessible. Twitter is one example of a social media platform where user demographics (geographic location, gender, age, etc.) as well as user perspectives (knowledge, attitudes, beliefs, actions, etc.) have been easy to obtain through Twitter's own application program interface (API) or via the plethora of mining or scraping tools (e.g. Radian6 and Crimson Hexagon; Burke-Garcia and Stanton 2017). Such easy access has led scholars to use Twitter to examine a multitude of patterns across many topics (Boyd and Crawford 2012; Golder and Macy 2011; Lotan et al. 2011; Shamma, Kennedy, and Churchill 2010; Wu et al. 2011). However, many other available social media platforms (e.g. Facebook, Instagram, Reddit) can also be mined using these tools, and they have also been the focus of academic research (Burke-Garcia and Stanton 2017).

For the second type of data, paradata, or data about the process by which the data were collected in social media can be documented by the researchers themselves as part of administrative procedures. In addition, they may be collected through objective observation because the implementation of these methods is often publicly visible to users. For example, conversations by social media users often happen publicly. Social media ads, while targeted to users, are publicly available to those to whom they are shown. Social media users can join online, often private, groups, which provide access to membership lists. Many social media users often attend public virtual events and document their participation by using a hashtag. We discuss details of these examples later in the chapter.

Use of both classes of data comes with multiple challenges. First, they are fundamentally different from traditional survey data. The systems that contain these opinions were not designed to produce data for social science researchers. How participants understand the activity in which they are engaged differs – e.g. taking a survey vs. how a social media post may be collected and analyzed (Schober et al. 2016). The data produced by survey responses compared to social media posts differ in context and quality (Schober et al. 2016). They are also unstructured and messy. Moreover, the extent to which researchers can make sense of these data also differs – e.g. social media users often use slang or code terms that may be unfamiliar to researchers (Schober et al. 2016).

Second, the practical and ethical considerations about using the data also differ as user knowledge of consent is almost universally lacking (Schober et al. 2016). Thus, the simple availability of data does not necessarily mean that it should always be used. As Zimmer (2010, p. 323) writes, "[There are] considerable conceptual gaps in the understanding of the privacy implications of research in social networking spaces." Understanding consent, properly identifying and respecting expectations of privacy on social network sites, developing strategies for data anonymization prior to public release, and addressing the relative expertise of institutional review boards when confronted with research projects using social media data must be considered before using social media data in survey research (Zimmer 2010).

Despite these challenges, survey researchers should be tracking these types of data – or at least having earnest discussions about their utility for survey research. In fact, the American Association for Public Opinion Research's Task Force on Big Data stated in its 2015 report, "The change in the nature of the new types of data, their availability, the way in which they are collected, and disseminated are fundamental. The change constitutes a paradigm shift for survey research" (Japec et al. 2015).

Moreover, while the Internet has been around for decades, what is important about the current moment is the increasing proportion of our lives that is now implemented, shared, and displayed online. Social media technology is not just an aspect of our lives – we now live through technology. Consequently, vast amounts of opinions are shared online – about food, people, travel and tourism, transportation and commuting, political affiliations and policy issues, among many others. These kinds of opinions, which survey researchers have been attempting to obtain for many decades, are now available with the click of a button or a quick keyword search.

In this context, and using this broad definition of social media, we envision a new survey world "that uses multiple data sources, multiple modes, and multiple frames" to help make the whole world more accessible to survey researchers (Lyberg and Stukel 2017). Specifically, this new world leverages social media in different ways to advance the survey research paradigm for the twenty-first century – from one that has traditionally been a researcher-centered "structured conversation" with a willing and randomly selected respondent to one that is more people-centered, efficient, and relevant. Already we have seen social media used extensively in the more qualitative survey activities such as cognitive interviewing. This chapter explores the potential for applying social media methods to key stages in quantitative survey operations (Tourangeau et al. 2014). It discusses a wide array of opportunities for survey research to be supported, enhanced, and even transformed by social media.

2.2 New Ways of Thinking About Survey Research

We believe that, today, surveying most individuals using traditional methods has become very difficult. Tourangeau's typology of hard-to-survey populations traditionally assessed the ways some populations can be difficult to survey throughout the stages of survey operations. Defining these populations in relation to general household populations and suggesting that comparative analyses may be used to describe them, he maintains that some segments of the population are hard to sample, whereas others are hard to find, still others are hard to persuade to participate in surveys, and many are hard to interview (Tourangeau et al. 2014). Taken together, these difficulties present challenges throughout the whole survey research process.

Through this lens, he (and his team of international contributors) examined a wide range of populations (e.g. immigrants, people with intellectual difficulties, and political extremists) as well as settings (e.g. war zones and homeless shelters) that present special problems or unusual challenges for surveys. They then proposed methods for addressing these challenges (e.g. respondent-driven sampling (RDS) and advertising).

However, in defining these groups, Tourangeau also notes that, "In an era of falling response rates ... it may seem that *all* household populations are hard to survey" (Tourangeau et al. 2014, p. 1). We agree with this assertion and believe the application of this typology has great utility for surveying general populations today. In this chapter, we apply this typology to general populations with a particular focus on applying social media platforms and their data to this framework. Specifically, in this chapter, we discuss pertinent challenges and possible opportunities that social media platforms and data provide for survey researchers at each stage of the hard-to-reach framework (Tourangeau et al. 2014).

2.3 The Challenge with ... Sampling People

Although many developed countries have complete lists of current populations (European and Social Research Council 2017), others such as the United States, do not. When complete lists of current populations are not available, survey researchers must find other methods to sample their population of interest. One way is to use a two-stage approach where households are first sampled and then individuals living in the sampled households are listed and randomly selected to achieve a nationally representative sample of general population. Households can be sampled with both telephone numbers (both landline and cell phone) and with addresses. In sampling by telephone numbers, random-digit-dial (RDD) is usually used. The major weakness with RDD is very low response rates: the vast majority of households screen their calls and do not answer calls from unknown numbers. And coverage has decreased markedly because many American households now do not have a landline telephone number.

To sample households by addresses, researchers first need an address list. When such an address list does not exist, one can be created using human "listers" (Eckman 2010) or virtual tools such as Google Earth (Wampler, Rediske, and Molla 2013). The former approach, however, is quite expensive and while the latter holds promise, it can be labor-intensive and time-consuming (Eckman 2010; Wampler et al. 2013). In a recent survey of US commercial buildings, researchers reduced the cost of human listers by having staff complete the listing task using satellite images from Google Earth (Amsbary and Dulaney 2018). Eck et al. (2018) developed an application that systematically selects a random sample of satellite or aerial images from a desired geographic region and then processes those images using neural networks to identify the presence of sampling units of interest such as windmills, playgrounds, or park benches. Regardless of approach, the quality of addresses is threatened by coverage problems in rural areas and access issues in multiunit structures (especially locked buildings) and gated communities.

Finally, there are large movements of populations across borders; internal displacement in war-torn areas; large numbers of undocumented, homeless, and marginally housed people; and many people suspicious of government and concerned about privacy. As a result, many people in a general population may be missing from such samples, or they may seek to avoid having their names, telephone numbers, or addresses included in such a sampling frame.

2.3.1 The Social Media Opportunities

Traditional methods to sample people through telephone number or household address are neither efficient nor effective with hard-to-sample populations (Tourangeau et al. 2014), and they can also be problematic with general populations. Social media provides the means to supplement traditional sampling methods as well as apply these methods to a digital environment. We discuss two main methods below – venue/time sampling and RDS. The former represents an opportunity for social media to supplement traditional approaches, whereas the latter could allow social media to replace traditional nonprobability methods.

2.3.1.1 Venue-Based, Time-Space Sampling

Venue-based, time-space sampling (VBTS) is used in traditional sampling for rare and iterant populations when no sampling frame exists for such a population. Going to locations these populations frequent for a period of time is the best way to obtain a frame. For instance, to obtain a sample of gay men, one could frequent an establishment where gay men congregate at a time many of them will be there (e.g. a bar on a weekend night) in an attempt to obtain a sample of them for a study.

This approach can be conducted in social media by going where researchers' populations of interest spend their time on social media – e.g. online groups, networks, mobile apps – obtaining a list of members (if available) and selecting a sample of those users. This approach is recommended as a supplement to traditional methods because of how people coalesce in these virtual spaces, which is different from how they might convene in real-life venues. Because many social media platforms allow asynchronous communication and interaction, just hanging out in an online group for a time will probably not result in many participants being sampled. Instead, researchers can create a sample from the list they obtained or they can seek out and coordinate virtual events – e.g. Facebook live, Reddit Ask Me Anything – within these online communities to proactively gather a group of respondents in one virtual place at one time. This strategy helps ensure a larger number of participants. Although this method is not a solution for obtaining a probability sample of the general population, sampling members of various subgroups with VBTS through social media may be the best approach for obtaining a sample.

Key to this discussion of VBTS online is the issue of gaining access to these groups. Whether open or closed, online groups remain a challenge in sampling. Some have conditions that must be met to join – e.g. acknowledging certain permissions that limit use of the group members' names or signing terms-of-service agreements. Still others require those who want to join to answer screening questions first. All private groups require approval to gain access, yet even with public groups, enumerating the members, despite them being public, is hard because often the platforms do not make it easy to access or download these lists.

To overcome some of these barriers – and as with everything in social media – transparency is of the utmost importance. Trying to obtain access or information under false pretenses will not result in positive outcomes (e.g. researchers may be removed from a group or prohibited from participating with the group in the future). Researchers need to look at the engagement with these groups as relationship building. They must work through the community or group manager to be able to successfully engage the larger group. By approaching these group managers as gatekeepers and being explicit about their research aims, researchers can be successful in sampling populations via these online groups.

Studies that have piloted this approach are limited. One study compared VBTS in traditional and face-to-face settings with recruitment via Facebook (Hernandez-Romieu et al. 2014). For the traditional VBTS, bars, dance clubs, fitness clubs or gymnasiums, Gay Pride events, parks, restaurants, retail businesses, sex establishments, social organizations, street locations, and other special events were included in the sampling frame. Venue-date-time units were randomly sampled. At sampled venue-day-time units, study staff members systematically sampled male attendees, then approached them and administered a recruitment script and screening questions using a hand-held device. For Facebook sampling, paid banner advertisements were placed in the Facebook advertising interface. Advertisements were delivered only to men 18 years of age or older who selected residing in Atlanta and interest in relationships with other men as demographic options on their Facebook profiles. Participants clicking on the banner advertisements were redirected to a web-based survey where, after giving consent to screening, they were administered the same screening questions used for VBTS recruitment. Both methods yielded similar samples of men who have sex with men (MSM) in terms of HIV-testing patterns, and prevalence of HIV/STI, with no differences in study retention (Hernandez-Romieu et al. 2014). The study found that most Facebook-recruited men also attended venues where VBTS recruitment was conducted and that studies may recruit via Facebook with little evidence of bias, relative to VBTS (Hernandez-Romieu et al. 2014).

Another similar study of MSM compared two web-based approaches (advertising to recruit men on 24 sites and using online VBTS) with traditional venue-based sampling (Raymond et al. 2010). VBTS resulted in only a small number of completed interviews. Given the findings from these two studies, and the relative lack of exploration of VBTS online as a supplemental sampling method, methodological testing of VBTS online is a worthy area of future investigation.

2.3.1.2 Respondent-Driven Sampling

RDS has become a popular approach for obtaining a probability sample of a hard-to-survey group, but it depends on some stringent assumptions that may not often hold. For example, it assumes a closed group, where each member is known (and can be identified) by at least one other member in the group. Sample weights can be developed by starting with a small number of seeds within the group and following branches in their social networks until individuals are reached who can name no other members (Heckathorn 1997; Lee et al. 2014). RDS has not been applied in the large-scale context of social media networks for general population studies, and one quickly encounters a number of issues in considering it.

Setting aside the general population issues, many online networks have already enumerated all network members. For instance, groups in Facebook often manage their membership closely – especially if they are private groups. The membership list may not be available as a frame for sampling directly, but because it is a closed group and all members are known, it meets an RDS requirement. Groups are run by moderators who often require new members to request to join the group – and even answer questions to confirm who they are. Groups such as "Show me Your Stethoscope," a private group of nurses with more than 650 000 members and a daily active discussion, can be leveraged by using their already-enumerated list of members for possible sampling. Additionally, there are private online communities, such as The "New" Prostate Cancer InfoLink Social Network, an online community of prostate cancer patients and their families. Membership in this network requires vetting and approval by the community manager who maintains the roster of members.

Other similar types of networks with membership lists include online influencer networks. Newer to the social media space, online influencers are celebrity and layperson opinion leaders who market messages or products via peer-to-peer recommendation. More than 1 million influencers (estimated) operate globally (Upfluence 2018), and many belong to numerous influencer networks, which help to bring paid campaign opportunities to their membership. These networks maintain databases of their memberships, which not only enumerate them, but also include data on various aspects of them, their lifestyles and families, and hobbies and interests. A model of RDS that uses these online influencers as the "nodes" or the "seeds" would be an interesting design, one worth testing in this new paradigm.

Studies that have used RDS in social media to sample rare populations are limited. One study used a modified RDS approach to recruit participants to a sexually transmitted infection (STI)-focused intervention study (Bull et al. 2012). Along with other traditional methods, the social media channels used to select RDS seed participants included online personal social media channels and postings on popular blogs and websites (Bull et al. 2012). Then, the seeds were asked to invite an additional three friends (Bull et al. 2012). Results revealed success in recruitment of youth of color and youth living in geographic regions with high STI and HIV prevalence and success in reaching large numbers of people with STI- and HIV-related content through Facebook (Bull et al. 2012). No prior work using online influencers as possible RDS lists was found. They are an important area of future study.

2.3.2 Outstanding Challenges

Social media may not be able to support sampling for probability surveys, but it could possibly be used to support nonprobability surveys – albeit not without challenges. Researchers must still weed out the large groups of ineligibles – e.g. "users" of Facebook who are not active, who are bots or spam accounts, or those who are considered "undesirable" (Kleinman 2013). As of 2012, Facebook estimates that 1.5% of its 2.23 billion monthly active users are "undesirable" or spam accounts (Facebook 2018). They may choose to use the platform for a while and then stop, or they may use it for a specific purpose and when that task is complete, they never return.

These issues are not just Facebook-related, however. As Crawford (2009) writes,

> Twitter does not represent 'all people', although many journalists and researchers refer to 'people' and 'Twitter users' as synonymous. Neither is the population using Twitter representative of the global population. Nor can we assume that accounts and users are equivalent. Some users have multiple accounts. Some accounts are used by multiple people. Some people never establish an account, and simply access Twitter via the web. Some accounts are 'bots' that produce automated content without involving a person. Furthermore, the notion of an 'active' account is problematic. While some users post content frequently through Twitter, others participate as 'listeners' (Crawford 2009, p. 532).

Finally, The Pew Research Center's 2018 study about the role of so-called social media bots further supports this theory, purporting that bots are responsible for most of the content we engage with on social media (Wojcik et al. 2018). Thus, appropriate enumeration of lists in social media, being able to confirm that someone is who she/he says she/he is, and appropriate use of the data are key to ensuring the successful application of these sampling methodologies to social media contexts.

2.4 The Challenge with ... Identifying People

As Tourangeau notes, successful survey research requires a respondent who is "willing and able to answer the screener questions accurately" (Tourangeau et al. 2014). Yet, globally, "the willing" are becoming a smaller part of the general population. In face-to-face surveys in the United States (which traditionally achieve higher response rates than other modes), screener response rates are falling below 50% (Czajka and Beyler 2016). Even when people choose to complete the screener, people are reluctant to identify themselves or others in the household, leading to nonresponse or noncoverage error (Tourangeau, Kreuter, and Eckman 2012).

Certain people are more likely to decline identifying themselves if they do not know why the information is sought. Specifically, populations of color are often underrepresented in research due to mistrust based on historical precedent (e.g. the Tuskegee syphilis experiment) or because of the risk of disclosure of private information (e.g. immigration status).

The general population's concerns about privacy have intensified in the past decade with breaches such as Equifax (Timberg, Dwoskin, and Fung 2017) in 2017 and Facebook (Lapowsky 2018) in 2018. Yet identification in research must extend beyond just personally identifiable information to characteristics of interest to the survey researcher that distinguish one person or group from another.

Thus, identifying participants and respect of privacy may be at odds. Finally, in designing screening operations, researchers must recognize a classic total survey error tradeoff between response and accuracy. A complete enumeration of household members has been shown to be more accurate than other screening methods, but imposes more burden and can be perceived as more invasive than other methods, and thus yields a lower response rate (Tourangeau et al. 2012).

2.4.1 The Social Media Opportunity

Social media provides the means to supplement traditional identification methods by allowing certain characteristics of users to be confirmed without having to ask these questions of the participants themselves via a screener. Social networks such as Facebook, Twitter, RenRen, and Qzone allow social media users to disclose publicly key demographic variables such as gender, age, and geographic locations. For those who choose to make this data public and who are part of a sample pulled via social media, accessing these data passively can help reduce survey burden on these participants. Other, more intricate variables that a survey may be seeking to use to identify its participants may also be available via passively collected social media data. For instance, membership to certain types of groups that signify political leanings, personal interests or passions, and professional and financial situations can be collected via social media if users have selected these types of interests and made these associations known.

Studies that have used social media data to help identify respondents and reduce burden during the screening process are limited. Sloan et al.'s (2015) work suggests that "It is possible to detect 'signatures' of both occupation and age from Twitter meta-data with varying degrees of accuracy (particularly dependent on occupational groups)." Cesare, Grant, and Nsoesie (2017) conducted a meta-analysis of studies that propose methods for inferring the age, race, ethnicity, and gender of social media and blog users. Their findings suggest that gender is the easiest trait to accurately infer – with measures of accuracy higher than 90% in some studies – while race, ethnicity, and age tend to be more challenging to predict.

Moreover, whereas 2016 American National Election Studies research suggests that these data are not accurate enough for most government statistical programs, they may be enough to be used for more general market research (DeBell et al. 2018). Schober et al. (2016), suggest further that "Traditional population coverage may not be required for social media content to effectively predict social phenomena to the extent that social media content distills or summarizes broader conversations that are also measured by surveys" (Schober et al. 2016, p. 180).

2.4.2 Outstanding Challenges

The availability of these data types – while they do indeed help reduce the need to screen and identify people – raises questions about household composition and the accuracy of these data in capturing all members who comprise a household, including the personal characteristics of each. Issues with privacy remain as researchers and participants alike try to balance their understanding and respect of third-party data use. Participants might not realize the extent to which their data might be shared and/or the breadth of their use. Researchers may struggle to understand how to effectively use these data while still respecting the privacy of their participants.

For example, in his article, "'But the data is already public': On the ethics of research in Facebook," Michael Zimmer relates the story of a group of researchers who publicly released profile data collected from the Facebook accounts of an entire cohort of college students from a US university in 2008 (Zimmer 2010). Although good-faith attempts were made to hide the identity of the institution and protect the privacy of the subjects, the source of the data was quickly identified, placing the privacy of the students at risk (Zimmer 2010). Thus, even when the conventional expectations of privacy are not in question, accountability concerns may arise. Zimmer writes, "In order to act ethically, it is important that researchers reflect on the importance of accountability: both to the field of research and to the research subjects" (Zimmer 2010, p. 20). Zimmer (2010) posits further,

> How a Facebook user might decide to share her profile information only with other students, but wants to remain private to the rest of the world. The Harvard [research assistants] (RAs) employed for the project, being from the same network as the subject, would be able to view and download a subject's profile data that was otherwise restricted from outside view. Thus, her profile data – originally meant for only those within the Harvard network – is now included in a dataset released to the public. As a result, it is likely that profile information that a subject explicitly restricted to only 'in network' participants in Facebook has been accessed from within that network, but then extracted and shared outside those explicit boundaries.
> (Zimmer 2010, p. 318)

This scenario reveals a lack of understanding about privacy settings and what connotes "consent" for use of these data.

2.5 The Challenge with ... Reaching People

Among the myriad issues survey researchers face today is the increasing difficulty in reaching people, which has two aspects – locating and contacting members of the general population. Locating people has become challenging because, in the developed world, people spend less time at home. The Bureau of Labor

Statistics found in their 2018 American Time Use Survey that employed people spent more time working at the workplace than at home: 83% of employed people performed some or all of their work at their workplace (Economic News Release 2018). Further, data suggests that when they are home, confirming their location and contacting them are still difficult because they are less likely to open the door to a stranger, answer a phone call from a strange number, or open a piece of unexpected mail. Finally, certain populations live at the margins of society and reaching them is very difficult – e.g. the homeless, some drug users, sex workers, and other highly stigmatized groups. These occurrences suggest that today's general population differs from those of prior generations.

2.5.1 The Social Media Opportunities

Social media provides the means to supplement traditional methods for locating and contacting respondents, while applying these methods for a digital-first survey environment. In this section, we discuss two main methods – tracing respondents and use of paid advertising to contact respondents. Both can be supplemental approaches to traditional methods, but they also can replace traditional methods, depending on the population.

2.5.1.1 Tracing

Although researchers often have names, addresses, telephone numbers, and e-mail addresses for their respondents, they may still have difficulty locating them for follow-up data collection – especially in longitudinal research (Alderman et al. 2001) – because respondents change their addresses, telephone numbers, and e-mail addresses without informing the researchers (Calderwood 2012). By contrast, users of social networking sites such as Facebook, RenRen, and Qzone have profiles that rarely change, even when they move or switch to a new e-mail provider. These sites contain contact information that does not change and, therefore, can act as a channel for contacting respondents and tracing, or allow locating participants lost to follow up. Particularly with certain groups, these sites would seem to be especially promising to reach key demographics of respondents. For instance, Census Bureau data suggest that the top two most mobile groups are 55 to 59-year-olds and 20 to 24-year-olds (US Census Bureau 2017). These groups are both more likely to use social networking websites (older adults use Facebook more often (Pew Research Center 2018b) and youth use YouTube, Instagram, and Snapchat (Anderson and Jiang 2018)) and disproportionately likely to become unreachable in longitudinal studies (Littman et al. 2010; Seed, Juarez, and Alnatour 2009; Young, Powers, and Bell 2006).

The literature on respondent tracing using this method is rich. Prior research suggests that sending private messages to Facebook users who had been identified as respondents has worked well and that private messages do not disclose publicly a participant's potential involvement in a study (Schneider, Burke-Garcia, and Thomas 2015). Privacy is a central concern for some in survey research where the mere association of an individual respondent (or potential respondent) with the survey is considered a breach. Some commercial survey houses and statistical agencies in the United States go to great lengths to avoid the possibility of anyone being able to infer that a specific individual or household might have been sampled for or might be participating in a particular survey (Mneimneh, Lyberg, and Sharma 2015; National Center for Health Statistics 2018). This method also lessens the burden of responding (compared to a public message) if users are uncomfortable with publicly disclosing that they are participating. Recommendations from one study include wording messages carefully so recipients can quickly see that the messages are legitimate, not spam; keeping messages brief, since many recipients will read them on the small screen of a smartphone or other mobile device; and creating messages that motivate including a call-to-action for the recipient to respond with confirmation they are indeed the respondent (Schneider et al. 2015).

2.5.1.2 Paid Social Media Advertising

Another approach for contacting people to participate in a survey is to use paid advertising messages that either promote the survey brand or serve them a direct link to a web survey. Social media advertisements can be designed to fit specific platforms such as Google, Facebook, Instagram, YouTube, Weibo, RenRen, WeChat, Pinterest, Twitter, and Qzone. Ads can also be run via Amazon and Apple products and services. Finally, smart speakers like Alexa are also beginning to feature ads in the form of paid audio content included in listeners' daily "Flash Briefings" (Social Report Blog 2018). These paid social ads can help achieve contact at-scale because a single advertisement can potentially reach millions of users.

To contact social media users – and potential survey respondents – ads can be developed and tailored to respondent demographic and psychographic subgroups using very sophisticated criteria. These platforms allow users to be targeted based on demographics (e.g. age, location, job title), interests, and behaviors (Chevalier 2015). Custom audiences can be built based on a set of users for whom researchers have specific data (e-mail, phone, mobile phone ID, Facebook Fans, etc.; Chevalier 2015). These users may have already been exposed to prior surveys, brands, or websites (Chevalier 2015). These sites allow users to be targeted based on their similarities to other users (Chevalier 2015). Finally, these basic criteria may be enhanced by using third-party data that feature consumer purchase behavior – e.g. what products and services users are buying, historical behavior, and other types of psychographic data (e.g. entertainment media consumption; Chevalier 2015). Such targeting allows more tailored and specific groups to be reached – e.g. hiring managers (which could include Chief Executive Officers (CEOs) of small businesses as well as human resource professionals at large companies) who know of the availability of certain hiring tools but do not use them. Depending on the population, paid advertising in social media can replace traditional paid advertising a study might use, or it might act as a supplement to a larger advertising strategy that includes multiple channels.

The literature on this topic – e.g. using social media advertising to locate participants – is well developed. One study examined Facebook as a mechanism to reach and survey young adults about tobacco and other substance use (Ramo and Prochaska 2012). It found that despite the varying success of individual ads and concerns about sample representativeness, Facebook was a useful and cost-effective channel by which to locate and contact young-adult smokers to complete a survey (Ramo and Prochaska 2012). Another study described the use of both social media ads and in-person intercepts for the US Food and Drug Administration's *This Free Life* campaign evaluation targeting lesbian, gay, bisexual, and transgender (LGBT) young adults who smoke cigarettes occasionally (Guillory et al. 2018). Findings included that social media ads combined with the intercepts successfully provided access to important LGBT subpopulations and created a more diverse sample (Guillory et al. 2018). Although the study acknowledged that the social media method had more data quality issues, locating and contacting respondents were achieved faster and less expensively than intercepts (Guillory et al. 2018).

2.5.2 Outstanding Challenges

Social media users are increasingly employing ad blockers, which means that ads may not be reaching their intended audience. Moreover, the increasingly frequent reports of data breaches on social media sites continue to erode users' trust. Additionally, these data breaches have resulted in more scrutiny by the platforms themselves about how people are using this information (Facebook 2018; Marketing 2018); therefore, as users are more protected, which data are available for targeting will change. Finally, as noted earlier, issues with privacy remain outstanding as researchers and participants alike try to balance their understanding and respect of third-party data use (Zimmer 2010).

2.6 The Challenge with ... Persuading People to Participate

Contributing factors to the issue of declining response rates include researchers' inability to locate and contact respondents, respondents' perception that participating in surveys is increasingly burdensome, and the widespread trend of declining trust in institutions. Yet researchers' methods of persuasion have also not changed for decades, relying heavily on mailed letters and brochures, a warm greeting on the phone, a friendly face at the door, prepaid and promised incentives, and a refusal conversion program. Recent web experiments featuring the researcher's face and use of avatars have not fared much better (Couper, Tourangeau, and Steiger 2001). The public seems increasingly resistant to attempts to gain cooperation in surveys, making researchers' inability to successfully persuade respondents to participate in survey research another contributing factor to the issue of declining response rates.

2.6.1 The Social Media Opportunities

If the respondent and the message about the survey are optimally matched, social media tools appear to be influential in persuading participants to participate. We discuss two main methods in this section – paid advertising and online influencer outreach – both of which may be used as supplements as well as replacements to traditional methods, given the population.

2.6.1.1 Paid Social Media Advertising

As previously discussed, social media ads can easily be developed and disseminated via social networking sites such as Facebook, Twitter, RenRen, and Qzone. The messaging in those ads, however, is critical to the discussion of persuasion. Communication theory provides frameworks that researchers aiming to better persuade respondents to participate may use. For instance, social norms theory suggests that normative information about what others think and how they behave can be a primary tool for changing socially significant behaviors (Schultz et al. 2007). This can help respondents situate their participation in survey research as part of a larger normative culture and make them more comfortable with participating.

Weick's Model of Organizing (1979) is another theory that could be applied to survey research persuasion as it describes how uncertainty can be reduced and understanding increased through the process of iterative communication. This theory may help researchers understand how respondents view survey research, questions they might have that may lead them to be resistant to participating, and ultimately strategies that can help bridge the gap between respondents' perceptions of why participating in survey research is important and their willingness to do so.

Operationally, social media ad messaging can be text-based or use imagery and video. Text-only ads can be developed for platforms such as Reddit and Google Search, and video-only ads can be developed for platforms like YouTube. These days, however, text-only content approaches rarely obtain the level of visibility that content featuring a visual does. For instance, the use of color in visuals is proven to increase people's willingness to read a piece of content by 80% (CrowdRiff Blog 2019). As well, when paired with a visual, retention of heard information increases from 10% to 65% (CrowdRiff Blog 2019). Video, however, is the dominant content type in social media. It is projected that in 2019, 45 minutes of an average person's daily Internet time will be spent watching mobile video (Social Report Blog 2018). Video is eye-catching and engaging, and it can convey a message in an effective but streamlined way.

The use of advertising in support of survey research – and persuading populations to participate – has a lengthy and successful history. For instance, more recent work in this area includes the US Census Bureau's comprehensive media campaign for the 2010 Decennial Census (Evans, Datta, and Yan 2014; Yan and Datta 2015). The media campaign improved the survey-taking climate and positively affected the decision to participate in the Census (Evans et al. 2014; Yan and Datta 2015). The Census Bureau also conducted a pilot of digital advertising use as part of the 2015 Census Test in Savannah, Georgia (Virgile et al. 2016). This test marked the first time the Census Bureau used digital communications and paid advertising (Virgile et al. 2016). Additionally, it was the first opportunity for some households to participate without receiving any mailed materials (Virgile et al. 2016). For this pilot, the Census Bureau selected 120 000 households to receive mailed materials, yet all remaining households (approximately 320 000) who were also eligible to respond learned of it through a variety of communication channels including digital advertising (Virgile et al. 2016). The experiment produced many encouraging results: 80% of respondents completed the test questionnaire via the Internet (Virgile et al. 2016). Of those submissions, nearly half (49.2%) were directly attributable to the advertising campaign (Virgile et al. 2016). These respondents entered the online response instrument and completed the test by either typing in the advertising campaign URL (35.5%) or by clicking an advertisement online (13.7%; Virgile et al. 2016).

2.6.1.2 Online Influencers

A newer method of persuading audiences to participate is via online influencers, which have been discussed previously. The act of influencing requires a specific result: a change in thinking or behavior (Dada 2017) and an influencer (someone who has the power to influence the perception of others or gets them to do something different; Dada 2017). These layperson opinion leaders can share information with their readers about the importance of these surveys and, because their readers and followers trust them (Burke-Garcia 2017), they can be incredibly influential in motivating them to consider participating.

Abundant public opinion and market research literature describes and explains the roles that these layperson opinion leaders play in changing the knowledge, attitudes, and behaviors of their readers and followers. First, research suggests that consumers are 92% more likely to trust their peers compared to advertising when making purchasing decisions (Little 2015). Second, research suggests that consumers, especially younger people, increasingly tune out paid promotions (Klara 2017). Third, research indicates that – especially among younger generations – blocking social ads is growing: 67% of 18 to 24-year-olds using ad-blocking technology on at least one of their devices (Silvia 2018). Thus, the influence that these lay person opinion leaders wield with their audiences appears to be powerful for garnering increased survey participation.

Studies examining the role of online influencers are increasing. Burke-Garcia et al.'s work (2018) illustrates that there are rich opportunities for working with online influencers, especially "mommy bloggers," to communicate with key health decision-makers (mothers) on important health issues. Burke-Garcia et al.'s earlier work (Burke-Garcia et al. 2017a) explored the feasibility of leveraging online mommy bloggers as thought leaders and sources of influence in the promotion of human papilloma virus (HPV) vaccine messages. They found that mommy bloggers have substantial vaccine hesitancy but that certain messaging approaches can help engage online influencers to discuss HPV vaccination with their readers in the blogosphere. Finally, in support of the Bayley Short Form Formative Study, conducted as part of the National Children's Study (NCS), traditional recruitment methods were proving to be ineffective; therefore, online influencers were engaged as part of a multichannel outreach approach (Burke-Garcia and Mathew 2017). Results included successful recruitment of over 1800 infant and toddler participants to the study (Burke-Garcia and Mathew 2017). Studies that have examined this role specifically in relation to survey research are more limited.

2.6.2 Outstanding Challenges

The challenges with social media ads noted above apply here as well. In addition, the paid social media campaign may not be feasible for many surveys with a limited budget. Although social media advertising has helped open up advertising options available to researchers since costs in digital tend to be lower and required spend amounts are more nimble than traditional media, it still requires an advertising budget that many surveys may not have and it still puts research budgets in competition with other advertisers who are vying to reach those same audiences. Moreover, as online influencers come under more scrutiny related to disclosure and transparency (about whom they are working with and whether they will make money by promoting something via their blog or social media), we can expect that the space of influencers will face increased scrutiny and regulation in the future.

2.7 The Challenge with ... Interviewing People

Tourangeau lists three population subgroups that can be difficult to interview (vulnerable populations, those who have cognitive or physical disabilities, and those who do not speak or understand the language of the interview), but suggests these difficulties affect only small proportion of the general population. Of course, if large proportions of a population speak different languages, the language mismatch can be addressed by translating the survey interview into those languages (Tourangeau et al. 2014). We contend the general population in many countries has become hard to interview because of a combination of physical and cognitive factors: the small screens on mobile devices and shortened attention spans.

As of early 2018, the vast majority of Americans (95%) own a cellphone of some kind, and 77% of these own smartphones (Pew Research Center 2018a). A large percentage of our lives is now spent with a smartphone in hand, and we choose to conduct much of our lives on its small screen – e.g. shopping, consumption of news and entertainment, and staying in touch with family and friends. Early challenges to using mobile devices to share and capture data included limited smartphone display space, navigation issues, distractions on one's mobile devices (such as e-mail, texts, and other notifications), and how to appropriately and successfully translate complex data into a simple visual or narrative; yet it is estimated that these kinds of tasks are increasingly happening (Innovation Enterprise 2017).

Similar challenges still exist in survey design. Designing questions that work on smartphones is a challenge even with responsive software, because the small screen can limit readability and comprehension (Buskirk and Andres 2012). Some designs that might help the respondent understand more complex content on a larger screen (such as grids) must be adapted or abandoned (Buskirk and Andres 2012). Finally, long questions that require the respondent to scroll to see the whole question with the response categories are suboptimal (Buskirk and Andres 2012).

Convenience often trumps usability. For instance, when confronted with a task, many respondents prefer to answer the questions on the small screen, even if they realize the task might be easier on a larger screen, and even when a larger screen is available. This could perhaps be viewed as survey satisficing behavior in a more generalized form.

A second factor that makes interviewing more difficult is humans' shrinking attention span. Since the year 2000 (or about when the mobile revolution began), the average attention span has dropped from 12 to 8 seconds (Microsoft 2018). The average person now reads *at most* 28% of the words during an average website visit (Doolittle 2017). The challenge for survey research in the era of waning attention spans is rethinking how we write research questions and what other ways questions may be conveyed to retain respondents and quickly gather their feedback.

2.7.1 Social Media Opportunities

Ultimately, as survey researchers, we aim to create a better match between our respondents and the questions we are asking them to obtain the best data possible to answer our research questions. Social media is aiding in this effort. Here we discuss two main methods – passive social media data mining and active data collection vis-à-vis crowdsourcing. Both are envisioned as supplemental approaches to traditional methods of interviewing and data collection.

2.7.1.1 Passive Social Media Data Mining

As noted earlier, social media users create millions of pieces of content a minute – and the use cases for this participation are numerous. Respondents' mobile devices have the potential to provide real-time data continuously over a period of time – e.g. day, week, month, and year (Moy and Murphy 2016). This can include location-based or event-based survey data captured via global positioning software (Moy and Murphy 2016); health data (e.g. steps, heart rate); diet data (e.g. food consumption patterns and exercise habits); and photos or videos that can supplement survey data (Moy and Murphy 2016).

People also use social media to make new friends, connect with old friends, ask and answer questions, share experiences (both good and bad), and participate in movements or current events. To understand these trends, social data (organic and often unstructured) can be collected and analyzed using any number of data mining tools (Burke-Garcia and Stanton 2017). Understanding what questions may be more easily answered via passively collected social media data and working with respondents to obtain consent to collect and use this data can help supplement traditional methods of survey data collection.

The literature regarding passive data mining is rich. Table 2.2 summarizes some of the emerging work in this field. These topics are organized first by platform and then by year starting with the most recent.

Thus, as Hampton et al. write,

> Examples of successes in sharing and collaboratively integrating ecological data are abundant among the scientific contributions that have emerged from networks of individual ecologists who have teamed up to analyze and synthesize disparate, highly heterogeneous datasets. The integration of scientific results from multiple research projects through meta-analysis is becoming more common in ecology (Chaudhary et al., 2010) and has had an increasing impact on the ecological literature over the past 10 years (Cadotte et al., 2012).
>
> (Hampton et al. 2013, p. 160)

Table 2.2 Examples of emerging work in the area of data mining.

Platform	Topic	Contributing authors
Twitter	Twitter as a means to answer research questions that might have previously been informed by surveys	Hsieh and Murphy (2017)
Twitter	The structure and content of the political conversations that took place through the microblogging platform Twitter in the context of the 2011 Spanish legislative elections and the 2012 US presidential elections	Barbera and Rivero (2015)
Twitter	A review of the state of the predictive power of Twitter data and considerations to advance the field	Gayo-Avello (2013)
Facebook	Increasing Facebook usage and engagement and steady adoption of other platforms	Greenwood, Perrin, and Duggan (2016)
Facebook	How personality influences usage or nonusage of Facebook	Ryan and Xenos (2011)
Multiple (Facebook, Twitter)	Internet users and demographic variables in Great Britain	Blank and Lutz (2017)
Multiple (Twitter, Instagram, Pinterest)	Issues that are endemic to the study of human behavior through large-scale social media datasets and strategies that can be used to address them	Ruths and Pfeffer (2014)
Multiple (Facebook, Twitter)	Friends' networks and politics	Rainie and Smith (2012)

2.7.1.2 Active Data Collection

One method of active data collection is crowdsourcing, which is the practice of obtaining needed services, ideas, or content by soliciting contributions from a large group of people and especially from the online community rather than from traditional employees or suppliers (Merriam-Webster 2018). Crowdsourcing has had a dramatic impact on the speed and scale at which scientific research can be conducted. Traditional benefits of crowdsourcing include a readily available sample of research study participants and streamlined recruiting and payment systems. Moreover, the use of crowdsourcing in research is becoming quite commonplace. The most well-known and used platforms for this kind of data collection is MTurk; a quick Google Scholar search returned approximately 22 000 results containing the keyword "MTurk." MTurk is certainly one of the better-understood crowd-sourcing platforms today.

Crowdsourcing (coupled with web probing/web debriefing) is a faster and cheaper way to pretest survey items than cognitive interviews done in a lab setting. Traditionally, researchers have assessed data comparability either quantitatively or qualitatively, yet Meitinger's study (2017) demonstrates how the combination of multigroup confirmatory factor analysis and online probing can uncover and explain issues related to cross-national comparability.

Any conversation about crowdsourcing has to include discussions of reliability, representativeness, and data linkage. A review of the literature suggests several key findings. Results of one study suggested that treatments deployed in crowd-sourced experiments caused similar responses for many subject types (Coppock 2018). Another study compared a large MTurk sample to two benchmark national samples – one conducted online and one conducted face to face – and found that all three samples produced substantively identical results with only minor variations in effect sizes (Turker Nation 2016). A final study found that MTurk respondents did not appear to differ fundamentally from population-based respondents (Levay, Freese, and Druckman 2016). However, limitations, such as human error and the prevalence of "professional respondents," suggest that such active data collection should be considered a supplement to traditional methods.

2.7.2 Outstanding Challenges

Passive and active data collection in social media still presents challenges. Passively collected data have both fundamental theoretical and operational issues. Data passively collected may not directly map to the construct being measured so use of passively collected data may require some transformation of that data to match what analysts need. Exploratory research could be conducted ahead of time to assess what, if any, passive data would map to the theoretical constructs being measured. Researchers could then identify which data could be used to answer which questions prior to beginning a survey.

Identifying the right tool for mining social data also has operational issues, including quality and validity of the data, and cost and usability of the tool (Burke-Garcia and Stanton 2017). For example, each tool delivers results based on individual algorithms that employ a mix of keywords, users, and geotags, but the algorithms lack documentation and change over time, which makes data validation challenging (Burke-Garcia and Stanton 2017). These tools also vary in price and ease of use but evaluating these differences can be hard to decipher for the inexperienced researcher (Burke-Garcia and Stanton 2017).

Finally, Twitter's enterprise API provides varying levels of access to tweets (Burke-Garcia and Stanton 2017). Twitter offers three levels of data – 1% of the data; the "Gardenhose" (otherwise known as the "Decahose"), or 10% of the data; and the "Firehose," or full access, all of which have different price points and provide differing coverage levels of conversations (Burke-Garcia and Stanton 2017). Although accessing and mining social media data have become easier and more ubiquitous, using any data mining tool has drawbacks. Even Twitter's API has its limitations. Both of the larger datasets (i.e. the "Gardenhose" and "Firehose") come with a cost – and these costs are related to both accessing the data and storing and analyzing the data (Morstatter et al. 2013; Valkanas et al. 2014).

Compounding these issues with variability in Twitter data collection methods is the existence of online activities intentionally conducted, especially on Twitter, to sway or skew what trends online. One example is "Twitter bombings," which according to Joyce (2010, p. 221), are the act of "flooding the microblogging site Twitter with similar hashtags, keywords, and links using multiple accounts, with the objective of attracting more viewers to the website, product, service, or idea." This proactive and intentional attempt to alter the content on Twitter means that the data available to be sampled can be skewed.

Individual sources of social media data – specifically Twitter – will have both costs and benefits that researchers must weigh when selecting a data source. Twitter's "Gardenhose" or "Firehose" samples provide more comprehensive coverage of a topic, but come at a cost (Morstatter et al. 2013; Valkanas et al. 2014); whereas others (e.g. Radian6) may be easier to use and cost less but may only provide a fraction of the conversations to be analyzed. Thus, while Twitter has historically been frequently referenced in the literature for data mining, this abates investigation into the nuances of the platform's data itself as well as other data mining options (Burke-Garcia and Stanton 2017).

Active data collection, or crowdsourcing, also has potential pitfalls. These include human error, which exists in traditional survey research but also here, and response bias, as many of the respondents are taking many surveys at a time, and therefore can act as "professional respondents," which increases the risk of lower quality data. The platforms for this kind of data collection often are nuanced in how they are built, so using them requires a certain level of expertise, and when things go wrong, there is little feedback on how to improve (Chandler, Paolacci, and Mueller 2013). Finally, many of the same issues already discussed also hold true with crowdsourcing (e.g. transparency, disclosure, and ethics). Similar protocols should be followed in addressing these issues.

Collecting data via social media can also lead to contamination as a result of the social networking aspect of social media – e.g. social media users participate inherently because of the ability to share with and learn from others. However, for research, this may impact both the confidentiality of the study as well as the parameters of the study itself if participants start to change their behaviors because of their participation in the research (the Hawthorne effect). A related concern is conditioning in panel surveys, where panel survey participation has been found not only to affect the reporting of a behavior but also alter respondents' actual behavior (Bach and Eckman 2019).

Exemplifying how to deal with this risk of contamination for research studies seeking to use social media is Burke-Garcia et al.'s social media substudy, which was conducted under the NCS, led out of the *Eunice Kennedy Shriver* National Institute of Child Health and Human Development at the National Institutes of Health (NIH; Burke-Garcia et al. 2017b). This study arose because the NCS sought to evaluate the feasibility, acceptability, and cost of using social media to support participant retention in longitudinal research, given the reach and influence of social media with the study's target population – parents (Burke-Garcia et al. 2017b). Because of this unique pilot – the use of social media (which is traditionally an open medium for discussion) among a group of study participants (for whom privacy and security are of the utmost importance) – steps had to be taken to ensure that any private online community developed for the NCS would meet the security protocols required of a federally funded research study (Burke-Garcia et al. 2017b). Participants' information needed to remain private and anonymous (Burke-Garcia et al. 2017b). Therefore, the substudy developed a private online community, designed similarly to other popular online social networks, to be able to institute adjustments to maintain users' privacy (Burke-Garcia et al. 2017b). For instance, it allowed personalization, but rather than having members use their own photo and name, they were prompted to choose a profile image, or avatar from a selection of colorfully illustrated images and create a playful username from predetermined sets of nouns and adjectives to protect their identities (Burke-Garcia et al. 2017b).

The private online community also had a terms-of-service agreement that users had to accept before joining (Burke-Garcia et al. 2017b). Similar to traditional terms-of-service agreements to which social media users consent, this agreement outlined what content would be allowed and what content would be removed if posted (Burke-Garcia et al. 2017b). We have addressed the concept of consent previously in this chapter, and that social media users' understanding of what they have consented to regarding availability of their data may not always be accurate. For these reasons, survey consent traditionally defined does not necessarily translate into the social media data capture environment.

Moreover, the terms of service or online consent must also respect any applicable third-party use clauses/restrictions, or at least waive them for said study. In the case of the NCS, to ensure that the participants understood the purpose of the private online community and any protocols that required adherence, the research team and designers developed an escalation and communications policy to identify and respond to private online community posts (Burke-Garcia et al. 2017b). This policy stipulated that participants refrain from sharing their names, locations, or other identifying information in the private online community. The policy was written in plain language to ensure comprehension, outlined policies to protect privacy, and provided parameters for what kind of information could be shared. This policy guided the daily monitoring of the private online community and responses to participant inquiries. The community manager monitored comments and questions daily, responding as necessary. Violators were privately messaged to alert them that their content would be removed and to answer any questions from them about this process and avoid any issues.

Although this study focused solely on retention in longitudinal research, it offers numerous lessons for researchers who aim to use social media to support, amplify, or replace traditional research methods while still maintaining appropriate privacy and confidentiality protocols and controlling for possible reactive effects.

A final note worth mentioning here is about how longitudinal research is just beginning to employ innovative methods to create a more optimal fit between a study's aims and its participants. Most notably, NIH's *All of Us* study, which aims to accelerate research and improve health, is providing feedback to participants based on the data they share (Rutter 2018). Participants will know approximately where they rank in comparison to the rest of the participant cohort (Rutter 2018). Although it may influence participant behavior, the researchers working on *All of Us* appear to be shifting the design of this study from a researcher-centered one to a people-centered design to do a better job of engaging and retaining participants over time.

2.8 Conclusion

This chapter discussed challenges that survey research is facing today, such as declining response rates, loss to follow up, and increasing costs. Such challenges, in turn, result in lower participation, which can lead to lower response rates and ultimately, questionable response quality. Many of today's surveys may not be "fit for purpose" because of their expense or because they take so long to design and implement that the results are not timely.

Rather than fearing social media, however, and reacting defensively, survey researchers have much to gain by using social media to adapt and strengthen the survey paradigm. Social media – broadly defined in this chapter – may be a solution to other challenges the field is facing, and can play numerous roles within the traditional survey research paradigm. In this chapter, we have examined how traditional survey methods (e.g. time/venue sampling) can be applied in an online context using social media methods. We also explored how social media provides a wealth of data that can supplement and possibly even replace aspects of traditional survey research. Table 2.3 overlays Tourangeau's hard-to-survey

Table 2.3 Social media platform by survey research typology.

Platform	Typology				
	Sampling	Identifying	Reaching	Persuading	Interviewing
Facebook	X	X	X	X	X
Google			X	X	X
YouTube	X	X	X	X	X
Reddit	X		X	X	X
Instagram	X	X	X	X	
WeChat		X	X	X	X
Apple			X	X	
Qzone	X	X	X	X	X
Weibo		X	X	X	X
Amazon			X	X	
RenRen	X	X	X	X	X
Pinterest		X	X	X	
Twitter	X	X	X	X	X
Alexa			X	X	
Online influencers	X	X	X	X	X
MTurk					X

typology on various social media platforms to highlight the roles they may play through key stages in survey operations. This table summarizes the applications of various social media platforms to each phase of the framework.

At the outset of this chapter, we laid our vision for a new survey world "that uses multiple data sources, multiple modes, and multiple frames" to help make the whole world more accessible to survey researchers (Lyberg and Stukel 2017). To make this vision a reality, survey researchers and data scientists need to engage in new discussions that question their starting assumptions and analytic traditions to understand the potential points of alignment and nonalignment. One of the most paramount questions of the day is whether it is still imperative to have representative samples drawn from frames that fully cover the population. Schober et al. (2016) suggest that estimates are likely to align to differing degrees depending on the topic, the population of study, unique aspects of the survey, the social media sites involved, and the techniques used to extract opinions and experiences from these sites. Traditional population coverage may not be required for social media content to effectively predict social phenomena to the extent that social media content distills or summarizes broader conversations that are also measured by surveys (Schober et al. 2016).

Investment in pilot and feasibility studies to advance the field in this way are required. Reporting on findings from these pilot studies is critical to know what works and what does not. Yield in terms of reach, engagement, participation, and completion rates is needed to know how many responses came through social media and how many of those successfully completed the task at hand. Comparisons with traditional methods are required to be able to evaluate approaches, including reporting and comparing costs associated with each method tested. New frameworks for how to successfully integrate such data into survey research are required, which is particularly important as we try to merge data points obtained via different modes. Finally, protocols for appropriately and successfully using social media in this way are required to provide researchers with guidance and ensure that the risk of unintended consequences is minimized. The wide array of opportunities in social media discussed in this chapter present opportunities to support, enhance, and adapt survey research as the twenty-first century unfolds.

References

Alderman, H., Behrman, J., Kohler, H.-P. et al. (2001). Attrition in longitudinal household survey data. *Demographic Research* 5 (4): 79–124.

Amsbary, M. and Dulaney, R. (2018). The view from above – virtual listing using GIS. *Proceedings of the BigSurv18*, Barcelona, Spain (25–27 October 2018). Barcelona, Spain: BigSurv18.

Anderson, M. and Jiang, J. (2018). Teens, social media & technology 2018. http://www.pewinternet.org/2018/05/31/teens-social-media-technology-2018/ (accessed 25 March 2020).

Bach, R.L. and Eckman, S. (2019). Participating in a panel survey changes respondents' labour market behaviour. *Journal of the Royal Statistical Society: Series A (Statistics in Society)* 182 (1): 263–281.

Barbera, P. and Rivero, G. (2015). Understanding the political representativeness of Twitter users. *Social Science Computer Review* 33 (6): 712–729. https://doi.org/10.1177/0894439314558836.

Blank, G. and Lutz, C. (2017). Representativeness of social media in Great Britain: investigating Facebook, LinkedIn, Twitter, Pinterest, Google+, and Instagram. *American Behavioral Scientist* 61 (7): 741–756. https://doi.org/10.1177/0002764217717559.

Boyd, D. and Crawford, K. (2012). Critical questions for big data: provocations for a cultural, technological, and scholarly phenomenon. *Information, Communication & Society* 15 (5): 662–679. https://doi.org/10.1080/1369118X.2012.678878.

Brick, J.M. and Williams, D. (2013). Explaining rising nonresponse rates in cross-sectional surveys. *The Annals of the American Academy of Political and Social Science* 645 (1): 36–59. https://doi.org/10.1177/0002716212456834.

Bull, S.S., Levine, D.K., Black, S.R. et al. (2012). Social media-delivered sexual health intervention: a cluster randomized controlled trial. *American Journal of Preventive Medicine* 43 (5): 467–474. https://doi.org/10.1016/j.amepre.2012.07.022.

Burke-Garcia, A. (2017). Opinion leaders for health: formative research with bloggers about health information dissemination. Dissertation. George Mason University, Fairfax, VA.

Burke-Garcia, A. and Mathew, S. (2017). Leveraging social and digital media for participant recruitment: a review of methods from the Bayley Short Form Formative Study. *Journal of Clinical and Translational Science* 1 (3): 205–207. https://doi.org/10.1017/cts.2017.9.

Burke-Garcia, A. and Stanton, C.A. (2017). A tale of two tools: reliability and feasibility of social media measurement tools examining e-cigarette Twitter mentions. *Informatics in Medicine Unlocked* 8: 8–12. https://doi.org/10.1016/j.imu.2017.04.001.

Burke-Garcia, A., Berry, C. N., Kreps, G. L., et al. (2017a). The power & perspective of mommy bloggers: formative research with social media opinion leaders about HPV vaccination. *Proceedings of the 50th Hawaii International Conference on System Sciences* (3–7 January 2017). Hawaii, United States: HICSS.

Burke-Garcia, A., Winseck, K., Jouvenal, L.C. et al. (2017b). A review of social media methods and lessons learned from the National Children's Study. *Journal of Clinical and Translational Science* 1 (4): 260–264. https://doi.org/10.1017/cts.2017.19.

Burke-Garcia, A., Kreps, G.L., and Wright, K.B. (2018). Perceptions about disseminating health information among mommy bloggers: quantitative study. *JMIR Research Protocols* 7 (4).

Buskirk, T.D. and Andres, C. (2012). Smart surveys for smart phones: exploring various approaches for conducting online mobile surveys via smartphones. *Survey Practice* 5 (1): 1–12. https://doi.org/10.29115/SP-2012-0001.

Cadotte, M.W., Mehrkens, L.R., and Menge, D.N.L. (2012). Gauging the impact of meta-analysis on ecology. *Evolutionary Ecology* 26: 1153–1167.

Calderwood, L. (2012). Tracking sample members in longitudinal studies. *Survey Practice* 5 (4): 1–6. https://doi.org/10.29115/SP-2012-0024.

Cesare, N., Grant, C., and Nsoesie, E. O. (2017). Detection of user demographics on social media: a review of methods and recommendations for best practices. Preprint *arXiv:1702.01807*.

Chandler, J., Paolacci, G., and Mueller, P. (2013). Risks and rewards of crowdsourcing marketplaces. In: *Handbook of Human Computation* (ed. P. Michelucci), 377–392. New York: Springer.

Chevalier, V. (2015). Facebook advertising 101 – ads creation.

Chaudhary, V.B., Walters, L.L., Bever, J.D. et al. (2010). Advancing synthetic ecology: a database system to facilitate complex ecological meta-analyses. *Bulletin of the Ecological Society of America* 91: 235–243.

Coppock, A. (2018). Generalizing from survey experiments conducted on Mechanical Turk: a replication approach. *Political Science Research and Methods* 7 (3): 613–628.

Couper, M. P., Tourangeau, R., and Steiger, D. M. (2001). Social presence in web surveys. *SIGCHI Conference on Human Factors in Computing Systems*, Seattle, WA, pp. 412–417. https://doi.org/10.1145/365024.365306.

Crawford, K. (2009). Following you: disciplines of listening in social media. *Continuum: Journal of Media & Cultural Studies* 23 (4): 532–533.

CrowdRiff Blog. (2019). 20 visual marketing statistics you need to know [infographic]. https://crowdriff.com/blog/visual-marketing-statistics/.

Curtin, R., Presser, S., and Singer, E. (2005). Changes in telephone survey nonresponse over the past quarter century. *Public Opinion Quarterly* 69 (1): 87–98. https://doi.org/10.1093/poq/nfi002.

Czajka, J.L. and Beyler, A. (2016). *Declining Response Rates in Federal Surveys: Trends and Implications. Background Paper*. Princeton, NJ: Mathematica Policy Research https://aspe.hhs.gov/system/files/pdf/255531/Decliningresponserates.pdf.

Dada, G. A. (2017). What is influencer marketing and how can marketers use it effectively? https://www.forbes.com/sites/forbescommunicationscouncil/2017/11/14/what-is-influencer-marketing-and-how-can-marketers-use-it-effectively/#15de59f123d1 (accessed 25 March 2020).

De Heer, W. and De Leeuw, E. (2002). Trends in household survey nonresponse: a longitudinal and international comparison. *Survey Nonresponse* 41: 41–54.

DeBell, M., Amsbary, M., Meldener, V. et al. (2018). *Methodology Report for the ANES 2016 Time Series Study*. Palo Alto, CA, and Ann Arbor, MI: Stanford University and the University of Michigan https://www.electionstudies.org/wp-content/uploads/2016/02/anes_timeseries_2016_methodology_report.pdf.

Doolittle, E. (2017). Humans are changing – how to adapt your brand.

Eck, A., Buskirk, T., Fletcher, K., et al. (2018). Machine made sampling frames: creating sampling frames of windmills and other non-traditional sampling units using machine learning with neural networks. *Proceedings of the BigSurv18*, Barcelona, Spain (25–27 October 2018). Barcelona, Spain: BigSurv18.

Eckman, S. (2010). Errors in housing unit listing and their effects on survey estimates. Dissertation. University of Maryland, College Park, MD.

Economic News Release (2018). American time use survey summary. https://www.bls.gov/news.release/atus.nr0.htm (accessed 25 March 2020).

Egley, A. (2002). *National Youth Gang Survey Trends from 1996 to 2000*. FS-200203 . Washington, DC: US Department of Justice, Office of Justice Programs, Office of

Juvenile Justice and Delinquency Prevention. https://www.ncjrs.gov/pdffiles1/ojjdp/fs200203.pdf (accessed 25 March 2020).

European and Social Research Council (2017). European Social Survey (ESS). https://esrc.ukri.org/research/our-research/european-social-survey-ess/ (accessed 25 March 2020).

Evans, W.D., Datta, R., and Yan, T. (2014). Chapter 25: Use of paid media to encourage 2010 Census participation among the hard-to-count. In: *Hard-to-Survey Populations* (eds. R. Tourangeau, B. Edwards, T.P. Johnson, et al.), 519–540. Cambridge University Press.

Facebook (2018). Company info. https://newsroom.fb.com/company-info/ (accessed 6 September 2018).

Gayo-Avello, D. (2013). A meta-analysis of state-of-the-art electoral prediction from Twitter data. *Social Science Computer Review* 31 (6): 649–679. https://doi.org/10.1177/0894439313493979.

Golder, S.A. and Macy, M.W. (2011). Diurnal and seasonal mood vary with work, sleep, and daylength across diverse cultures. *Science* 333 (6051): 1878–1881. https://doi.org/10.1126/science.1202775.

Greenwood, S., Perrin, A., and Duggan, M. (2016). Social media update 2016. http://www.pewinternet.org/2016/11/11/social-media-update-2016/ (accessed March 25 2020).

Guillory, J., Wiant, K.F., Farrelly, M. et al. (2018). Recruiting hard-to-reach populations for survey research: using Facebook and Instagram advertisements and in-person intercept in LGBT bars and nightclubs to recruit LGBT young adults. *Journal of Medical Internet Research* 20 (6): e197. https://doi.org/10.2196/jmir.9461.

Hampton, S.E., Strasser, C.A., Tewksbury, J.J. et al. (2013). Big data and the future of ecology. *Frontiers in Ecology and the Environment* 11 (3): 156–162. https://doi.org/10.1890/120103.

Hassan, Q.F. (2018). *Internet of Things A to Z: Technologies and Applications*. Hoboken, NJ: Wiley-IEEE Press.

Heckathorn, D.D. (1997). Respondent-driven sampling: a new approach to the study of hidden populations. *Social Problems* 44 (2): 174–199. https://doi.org/10.1525/sp.1997.44.2.03x0221m.

Hernandez-Romieu, A.C., Sullivan, P.S., Sanchez, T.H. et al. (2014). The comparability of men who have sex with men recruited from venue-time-space sampling and facebook: a cohort study. *JMIR Research Protocols* 3 (3): e37. https://doi.org/10.2196/resprot.3342.

Hsieh, Y.P. and Murphy, J. (2017). Chapter 2: Total Twitter error. In: *Total Survey Error in Practice* (eds. P.P. Biemer, E. Leeuw, S. Eckman, et al.), 23–46. Hoboken,

NJ: Wiley. https://doi.org/10.1002/9781119041702.ch2 https://onlinelibrary.wiley.com/doi/abs/10.1002/9781119041702.ch2.

Innovation Enterprise (2017). Data visualization top trends for 2017. https://channels.theinnovationenterprise.com/articles/data-visualization-top-trends-for-2017 (accessed 25 March 2020).

Japec, L., Kreuter, F., Berg, M. et al. (2015). *AAPOR Report: Big Data*. Oakbrook Terrace, IL: AAPOR https://www.aapor.org/Education-Resources/Reports/Big-Data.aspx.

Joyce, M.C. (2010). *Digital Activism Decoded: The New Mechanics of Change*. New York, NY: International Debate Education Association.

Klara, R. (2017). Are the most valuable celebrity brand endorsements the ones brands don't actually pay for? https://www.adweek.com/brand-marketing/why-the-most-valuable-celebrity-brand-endorsements-are-the-ones-brands-dont-pay-for/ (accessed 25 March 2020).

Kleinman, A. (2013). Facebook user numbers are off: 10 percent of reported users are not humans. https://www.huffingtonpost.com/2013/05/17/facebook-user-numbers_n_3292316.html (accessed 25 March 2020).

Lapowsky, I. (2018). Facebook exposed 87 million users to Cambridge Analytica. https://www.wired.com/story/facebook-exposed-87-million-users-to-cambridge-analytica/ (accessed 25 March 2020).

Lee, S., Wagner, J., Valliant, R. et al. (2014). Chapter 25: Recent developments of sampling hard-to-survey populations: an assessment. In: *Hard-to-Survey Populations* (eds. R. Tourangeau, B. Edwards, T.P. Johnson, et al.), 424–444. New York: Cambridge University Press. https://doi.org/10.1017/CBO9781139381635.025 https://search.proquest.com/docview/1674697805?accountid=28100.

Levay, K.E., Freese, J., and Druckman, J.N. (2016). The demographic and political composition of Mechanical Turk samples. *Sage Open* 6 (1): 2158244016636433. https://doi.org/10.1177/2158244016636433.

Little, J. (2015). Who do you trust? 92% of consumers trust peer recommendations over advertising. https://www.linkedin.com/pulse/who-do-you-trust-92-consumers-peer-recommendations-over-joey-little/.

Littman, A.J., Boyko, E.J., Jacobson, I.G. et al. (2010). Assessing nonresponse bias at follow-up in a large prospective cohort of relatively young and mobile military service members. *BMC Medical Research Methodology* 10: 99. https://doi.org/10.1186/1471-2288-10-99.

Lotan, G., Graeff, E., Ananny, M. et al. (2011). The revolutions were tweeted: information flows during the 2011 Tunisian and Egyptian revolutions. *International Journal of Communication* 5: 1375–1405.

Lyberg, L.E. and Stukel, D.M. (2017). Chapter 1: The roots and evolution of the total survey error concept. In: *Total Survey Error in Practice* (eds. P.P. Biemer, E. Leeuw, S. Eckman, et al.), 1–22. Hoboken, NJ: Wiley. https://doi.org/10.1002/9781119041702.ch1 https://onlinelibrary.wiley.com/doi/abs/10.1002/9781119041702.ch1.

Marketing (2018). Facebook's cut off with third-party data partners: who stands to lose? https://www.marketing-interactive.com/facebooks-cut-off-with-third-party-data-partners-who-stands-to-lose/ (accessed 25 March 2020).

Meitinger, K. (2017). Necessary but insufficient: why measurement invariance tests need online probing as a complementary tool. *Public Opinion Quarterly* 81 (2): 447–472. https://doi.org/10.1093/poq/nfx009.

Merriam-Webster (2018). Crowdsourcing [Definition]. https://www.merriam-webster.com/dictionary/crowdsourcing (accessed 25 March 2020).

Microsoft (2018). Microsoft advertising. https://advertising.microsoft.com/home (accessed 25 March 2020).

Mneimneh, Z., Lyberg, L., and Sharma, S. (2015). Case studies on monitoring interviewer behavior in cross-national and international surveys. *International Conference on Total Survey Error*, Baltimore, MD.

Morstatter, F., Pfeffer, J., Liu, H., et al. (2013). Is the sample good enough? Comparing data from Twitter's streaming API with Twitter's firehose *arXiv preprint arXiv:1702.01807*: arXiv:1306.5204.

Moy, P. and Murphy, J. (2016). Problems and prospects in survey research. *Journalism and Mass Communication Quarterly* 93 (1): 16–37. https://doi.org/10.1177/1077699016631108.

National Center for Health Statistics (2018). Confidentiality and security of information collected by The National Center for Health Statistics. https://www.cdc.gov/nchs/about/policy/confidentiality.htm (accessed 25 March 2020).

Pew Research Center (2018a). Mobile fact sheet. http://www.pewinternet.org/fact-sheet/mobile/ (accessed 25 March 2020).

Pew Research Center (2018b). Social media fact sheet. http://www.pewinternet.org/fact-sheet/social-media/ (accessed 25 March 2020).

Rainie, L. and Smith, A. (2012). Social Networking Sites and Politics. Pew Internet & American Life Project. https://core.ac.uk/download/pdf/30679670.pdf (accessed 25 March 2020).

Ramo, D.E. and Prochaska, J.J. (2012). Broad reach and targeted recruitment using Facebook for an online survey of young adult substance use. *Journal of Medical Internet Research* 14 (1): e28. https://doi.org/10.2196/jmir.1878.

Raymond, H.F., Rebchook, G., Curotto, A. et al. (2010). Comparing internet-based and venue-based methods to sample MSM in the San Francisco Bay Area. *AIDS and Behavior* 14 (1): 218–224. https://doi.org/10.1007/s10461-009-9521-6.

Ruths, D. and Pfeffer, J. (2014). Social media for large studies of behavior. *Science* 346 (6213): 1063–1064. https://doi.org/10.1126/science.346.6213.1063.

Rutter, J. (2018). All of us. *Proceedings of the 2018 NIEHS BCERP Annual Meeting*, Washington, DC (7–8 November 2018). Research Triangle, NC: NIH/NIEHS.

Ryan, T. and Xenos, S. (2011). Who uses Facebook? An investigation into the relationship between the Big Five, shyness, narcissism, loneliness, and Facebook usage. *Computers in Human Behavior* 27 (5): 1658–1664. https://doi.org/10.1016/j.chb.2011.02.004.

Schneider, S., Burke-Garcia, A., and Thomas, G. (2015). Facebook as a tool for respondent tracing. *Survey Practice* 8 (1): 1–6.

Schober, M.F., Pasek, J., Guggenheim, L. et al. (2016). Social media analyses for social measurement. *Public Opinion Quarterly* 80 (1): 180–211. https://doi.org/10.1093/poq/nfv048.

Schultz, P.W., Nolan, J.M., Cialdini, R.B. et al. (2007). The constructive, destructive, and reconstructive power of social norms. *Psychological Science* 18 (5): 429–434. https://doi.org/10.1111/j.1467-9280.2007.01917.x.

Seed, M., Juarez, M., and Alnatour, R. (2009). Improving recruitment and retention rates in preventive longitudinal research with adolescent mothers. *Journal of Child and Adolescent Psychiatric Nursing* 22 (3): 150–153. https://doi.org/10.1111/j.1744-6171.2009.00193.x.

Shamma, D., Kennedy, L., and Churchill, E. (2010). Tweetgeist: can the Twitter timeline reveal the structure of broadcast events. *CSCW Horizons*: 589–593.

Silvia, A. (2018). Spotlight on ad blocking: awareness of new Chrome feature is low. https://www.mediapost.com/publications/article/315291/spotlight-on-ad-blocking-awareness-of-new-chrome.html.

Sloan, L., Morgan, J., Burnap, P. et al. (2015). Who tweets? Deriving the demographic characteristics of age, occupation and social class from Twitter user meta-data. *PLoS One* 10 (3): e0115545. https://doi.org/10.1371/journal.pone.0115545.

Social Report Blog (2018). 7 digital marketing trends that will own 2019 [blog]. https://www.socialreport.com/insights/article/360000663006-7-Digital-Marketing-Trends-That-Will-Own-2019 (accessed 25 March 2020).

Statista (2018). Mobile social media – statistics & facts. https://www.statista.com/topics/2478/mobile-social-networks/ (accessed 25 March 2020).

Swartz, J. (2014). Q&A with Stephen Hawking. https://www.usatoday.com/story/tech/2014/12/02/stephen-hawking-intel-technology/18027597/ (accessed 25 March 2020).

The World Bank (2017). Population ages 15–64, total. https://data.worldbank.org/indicator/SP.POP.1564.TO (accessed 25 March 2020).

Timberg, C., Dwoskin, E., and Fung, B. (2017). Data of 143 million Americans exposed in hack of credit reporting agency Equifax. https://www.washingtonpost

.com/business/technology/equifax-hack-hits-credit-histories-of-up-to-143-million-americans/2017/09/07/a4ae6f82-941a-11e7-b9bc-b2f7903bab0d_story.html?noredirect=on (accessed 25 March 2020).

Tourangeau, R., Kreuter, F., and Eckman, S. (2012). Motivated underreporting in screening interviews. *Public Opinion Quarterly* 76 (3): 453–469. https://doi.org/10.1093/poq/nfs033.

Tourangeau, R., Edwards, B., Johnson, T.P. et al. (eds.) (2014). *Hard-to-Survey Populations*. New York: Cambridge University Press.

Turker Nation (2016). Are samples drawn from Mechanical Turk valid for research on political ideology?.

U.S. Census Bureau (2017). Migration/geographic mobility. https://www.census.gov/topics/population/migration/data/tables.html (accessed 25 March 2020).

Upfluence (2018). The future of influence marketing. https://search.upfluence.com/ (accessed 25 March 2020).

Uslaner, E.M. and Brown, M. (2005). Inequality, trust, and civic engagement. *American Politics Research* 33 (6): 868–894. https://doi.org/10.1177/1532673x04271903.

Valkanas, G., Katakis, I., Gunopulos, D., et al. (2014). Mining twitter data with resource constraints. *Proceedings of the 2014 IEEE/WIC/ACM International Joint Conferences on Web Intelligence (WI) and Intelligent Agent Technologies (IAT)*, pp. 157–164. Washington, DC, USA: IEEE Computer Society.

Virgile, M., Vines, M., Bates, N., et al. (2016). Digital advertising: encouraging participation in the decennial census. https://www.census.gov/newsroom/blogs/research-matters/2016/05/digital-advertising-encouraging-participation-in-the-decennial-census.html (accessed 25 March 2020).

Wampler, P.J., Rediske, R.R., and Molla, A.R. (2013). Using ArcMap, Google Earth, and global positioning systems to select and locate random households in rural Haiti. *International Journal of Health Geographics* 12: 3. https://doi.org/10.1186/1476-072x-12-3.

Weick, K.E. (1979). *The Social Psychology of Organizing*, Topics in Social Psychology Series. Columbus, OH: McGraw-Hill Humanities.

WERSM (2017). Ever wondered how much data is generated every minute? https://wersm.com/much-data-generated-every-minute/ (accessed 25 March 2020).

Wojcik, S., Messing, S., Smith, A., et al. (2018). Bots in the Twittersphere. http://www.pewinternet.org/2018/04/09/bots-in-the-twittersphere/ (accessed 25 March 2020).

Wu, S., Hofman, J. M., Mason, W. A., et al. (2011). Who says what to whom on Twitter. *Proceedings of the 20th International Conference on World Wide Web*, pp. 705–714 (28 March–1 April 2011). Hyderabad, India: Association for Computing Machinery.

Yan, T. and Datta, A. R. (2015). Altering the survey-taking climate: the case of the 2010 U.S. Census. *Survey Methods: Insights from the Field*. https://doi.org/10.13094/SMIF-2015-00014.

Young, A.F., Powers, J.R., and Bell, S.L. (2006). Attrition in longitudinal studies: who do you lose? *Australian and New Zealand Journal of Public Health* 30 (4): 353–361.

Zimmer, M. (2010). "But the data is already public": on the ethics of research in Facebook. *Ethics and Information Technology* 12 (4): 313–325. https://doi.org/10.1007/s10676-010-9227-5.

3

Linking Survey Data with Commercial or Administrative Data for Data Quality Assessment

A. Rupa Datta, Gabriel Ugarte, and Dean Resnick

Center for Excellence in Survey Research, NORC at the University of Chicago, Chicago, IL, USA

3.1 Introduction

As response rate challenges and data collection costs continue to climb, survey sponsors and data collection organizations face constant pressures to find less costly means of answering high-priority research questions. As surveys have grown more challenging to conduct, administrative and commercial data sources have become increasingly ubiquitous and accessible. A hybrid strategy is to link these data sources with survey data at the record level to create expanded datafiles. Administrative or commercial data can potentially enhance survey data through linkage in a variety of ways, including

(1) expanding the set of feasible analyses by supplementing survey responses with additional variables, possibly on new topics, at new time points, or at a level of precision or accuracy that cannot be obtained in the survey data;
(2) introducing efficiencies or quality improvements into survey processes such as constructing more efficient sampling frames, assessing quality of survey responses, or informing data collection processes; and
(3) achieving cost or schedule efficiencies by using already available administrative or commercial data to reduce the scope of survey data collection, for example, shortening questionnaires, reducing sample sizes, or collecting data at fewer time points.

The defining feature of the linkage is that data are available for the same unit or level of observation from multiple data sources, for example, survey interviews with specific individuals for whom data are also available in administrative datafiles.[1]

Analyses of linked survey and administrative data have a decades-long history, e.g. in the Framingham Health Study (Kannel 1976) and other health studies that combined health records with survey data and education studies, beginning with the Coleman Report on Equality of Educational Opportunity (Coleman et al. 1966) that combined surveys of teachers, students, and parents with test scores and other administrative information. In these earlier instances, however, collecting and processing the administrative data was often borne as a study expense, so the advantages of administrative data were in improved measurement, not reduced cost. Today's emphasis on linkages primarily exploits data that already exist in a mostly processable form and can therefore be accessible to survey researchers at low cost and outside of the original study design (Künn 2015; O'Hara, Shattuck, and Goerge 2016).

Since at least some of the interest in linking datafiles comes from the cost or time advantages of doing so (relative to creating only survey-based datafiles), we need to be able to assess the tradeoffs in cost and quality of different types of datafiles. Although survey data quality is defined primarily by representativeness and sample size, comparing the value of a survey-administrative linked file with a survey-only file or another linked file is more complex. The particular quality issues of interest vary somewhat across survey data, administrative data, or other types of data and are often related to the processes that generated the data. Linking the two types of data not only introduces additional sources of quality concerns but also opens the possibilities of better understanding the data quality features of each source and linkage. This chapter reviews some general issues in data quality considerations of analytic datafiles, then examines the specific case of a linkage of survey data to a commercially available compilation of administrative data sources in which we assessed quality features of each component datafile as well as the linked file. The case offers a generalizable approach for investigating the quality of other data sources and illustrates how such investigation can inform and improve analyses using linked data.

The chapter proceeds as follows: Section 3.2 offers a general discussion of assessing and improving data quality through linking survey data to other data sources; Section 3.3 describes the two data sources we linked in our study, including the linkage process; Section 3.4 presents two analyses of the linked data, one focusing on understanding the administrative data, and one focusing on understanding bias introduced in different phases of the data collection process for the survey; and Section 3.5 concludes with our inferences about the value of our link-

---

[1] In the remainder of this chapter, we generally use the term *administrative data* to refer to both administrative and commercial datafiles. For our purposes, the features of the two types of data are quite similar.

age for assessing data quality and for developing a data source that supports our analytical objectives.

3.2 Thinking About Quality Features of Analytic Data Sources

3.2.1 What Is the Purpose of the Data Linkage?

The objectives for a data linkage dictate the necessary quality features of possible data sources to be linked and how they would be linked. Common data quality features might include the population represented by the data, the extent of coverage of that population, the accuracy of key measures, and other systematic errors that might bias analyses. Consider these examples of data linkages:

(1) *Expanding the set of feasible analyses*: In some cases, the purpose of the linkage is to be able to combine measures that do not exist in the same data source (either survey or administrative). Administrative data, though potentially rich on the details of government program participation, can be limited in the range of demographic characteristics or other contextual information that might be available in survey data. By linking survey responses to administrative data, Henly et al. (2017) calculated precise spell lengths for childcare subsidy receipt that would not have been possible through survey reports, then explored the determinants of spell length using survey data collected from program participants regarding their work schedules, demographic characteristics, and experiences participating in the program.

(2) *Informing or improving survey processes*: Some analyses of linked survey and administrative data seek to assess the quality of a specific survey variable, again with the premise that the administrative data source is more accurate. This can be the case where surveys are more easily able to ask respondents about arrest histories, for example, but rap sheets are thought to be more accurate. The purpose of these analyses is to inform other surveys as to whether self-reports can be of acceptable quality, given the significant obstacles to linking to arrest records for most surveys. The suspected survey error need not be measurement error, but could similarly be processing error in the coding of verbatim responses, for example classification of medical treatment received, degree earned, or retirement benefits awarded (Kane, Rouse, and Staiger 1999; Meyer and Goerge 2011).

The US Census Bureau has been interested in the use of administrative data sources to enhance the American Community Survey or the decennial Census. Researchers are investigating the potential of administrative data to inform the survey process or improve survey data through imputation or other techniques (Seeskin 2018).

(3) *Reducing the scope of survey data collection for cost or schedule savings*: Spillman and Waidman (2014) linked a survey of residents of senior long-term care with later administrative data from Medicare and Medicaid to understand provisions of those public health-care finance programs. The research thus constructed a longitudinal datafile with one survey time point and later administrative data time points, supplanting a second survey round with administrative data to lessen both cost and schedule requirements.

3.2.2 What Kind of Data Linkage for What Analytic Purpose?

Each analytic purpose for linkage is associated with distinctive features of what data would be appropriate for linkage. The most common questions pertain to the availability and quality of the linkage variables (for example, name, address, geography), the match in populations covered by the respective datasets, the availability of relevant and comparable constructs in both datasets, the existence of a "gold standard" measure if desired, and the extent of variation in each dataset as necessary for accomplishing the desired analysis. Additional constraints also sometimes exist that limit what linkages would be appropriate for a given purpose.

If the linkage is intended to add essential variables to a dataset for analysis, the data quality requirements for each data source and their linkage are quite high. Similarly, strict requirements pertain if the purpose of the analysis is to assess the accuracy of a survey item. In this case, a survey item as well as a gold standard administrative data item that can be compared must be used, and the dataset must contain enough cases to be able to assess their agreement or lack thereof.

Some analyses use administrative data to add or improve a specific variable, for example supplementing survey data with earnings from unemployment insurance (UI) records. However, the combined data can only be used to make inferences about the population covered by the two datasets. Although UI data on earnings are excellent for the population of workers covered by UI, many low-income workers, self-employed workers, or gig economy workers are not covered. Thus, although the survey dataset may have been broadly representative of the population, the linked datafile will exclude categories of workers who may be important to the analysis or whose absence can introduce bias.

Recent program evaluations have linked survey data from one time period with administrative data from another time period to construct longitudinal datafiles (Shattuck 2017; Lorden et al. 2016). To support this analysis, not only do the linkages and the covered populations need to be adequate but also the ability to make comparative inferences about treatment and control groups also depends on the linkage rates and the quality of the linked files for the treatment and controls separately, not just as pooled data. If, as is common, the treatment group has more accurate linking variables, then there may be more error in the control group portion of the linked data, introducing bias into the comparisons.

The literature on survey errors closely follows the survey process in classifying errors – coverage, sampling, nonsampling, measurement, processing, and editing (from a common framework) (Biemer 2010). Similarly, the literature on administrative data quality also identifies potential errors based on the processes that generate those data – completeness, accuracy, relevance, timeliness, coherence/consistency, and clarity/interpretability (Seeskin, Datta, and Ugarte 2018). It makes sense for linked data to identify possible errors based on the processes that generated each component data source and then the linkage process in turn. In particular, it is useful to be aware that even two "perfect" data sources could be linked together to yield a datafile with significant errors with respect to an analytic question, depending on the linkage mechanism. For example imagine nationally representative survey data that are linked to complete state-level program records of a human service agency. Even if the linkage mechanism is flawless, a problem may exist if the survey data are nationally representative but not state-representative. As long as there are some differences from state to state in the consistency of the state administrative data, these "perfectly" linked data may yield biased analyses because of systematic errors introduced from each of the states' datasets (differences in definitions, thresholds, or covered populations across states) (Lucas 2014).

In survey process improvements or assessments, the data quality requirements may be much less stringent. Even imperfect measures, data sources with significant coverage gaps, or other data quality concerns may still provide valuable insights into the survey process or how it might be improved, at least to generate hypotheses or for certain segments of the population.

Two additional constraints are worth noting in the context of linking survey data with administrative data. First, record-level linkage to survey data often requires consent from the survey respondent. Even when such consent is collected at the time of the survey (rather than later), consent may not be secured from all respondents, and those who provide consent may be a biased subset of the full survey sample (Sakshaug and Kreuter 2012; Sala, Burton, and Knies 2010). The properties of the consenting sample are a critical determinant of the quality of any data linkage, although weighting techniques can sometimes correct for consent-related bias.

A second constraint is potential reporting limitations as a tool for protection of respondent identities. Data using confidential identifiers and possibly also commercial or proprietary data sources will often be subject to a wide range of reporting restrictions to protect against disclosure of respondent identities or features of the private datasets. These reporting constraints likely need to be considered in designing analyses of the linked data and may impose challenging restrictions on what analyses are feasible to conduct.

In addition to all of these considerations, we note that linkages of survey data with administrative datasets are still often opportunistic – the linkage is conducted because it can be, not necessarily because it is the best possible linkage that can be imagined. Because many linkages are opportunistic, assessing the quality of the linked file is critical to conduct and interpret analyses that are appropriate to the linked file.

3.3 Data Used in This Chapter

This chapter links household survey data from the National Survey of Early Care and Education (NSECE) by street address to proprietary real estate and property tax information from Zillow.com. This section includes more information about the two contributing data sources and our process of linking them by street address. The linked data offer the potential of having financial and property-related data from Zillow data for the same households who completed the survey interview on childcare topics, allowing investigations of how household wealth and housing choice relate to childcare usage. Key details of the linkage process, as well as the subsequent explorations of data quality that we report, contribute to the inferences about the analytic promise of the NSECE-Zillow linkage with which we conclude this chapter.

3.3.1 NSECE Household Survey

The 2012 NSECE consists of four integrated, nationally representative surveys of (i) households with children under 13, (ii) home-based providers of early care and education (ECE), (iii) center-based providers of ECE, and (iv) the center-based provider workforce. The study was sponsored by the US Department of Health and Human Services, and conducted by NORC at the University of Chicago. The four surveys were conducted in all 50 states and the District of Columbia; the sample was found in 219 counties or county clusters across the country, and in 755 clusters of census tracts within the sampled counties/clusters. Areas with high-densities of low-income families were oversampled for the study.

This chapter uses data from the NSECE household survey (NSECE Project Team 2013). Using a two-stage probability design, the household survey sample was constructed using an address-based sample of housing units and included nearly 100 000 US households. A mail screening effort was followed by a telephone screening and interviewing effort, followed by field outreach combining telephone and in-person efforts. After the location was determined as residential and occupied, interviewers attempted to conduct a household screening. Although 65 712 households were successfully screened, 5940 households were occupied but not screened. Eligibility for the household interview was determined by presence of a child under age 13 in the household. Only these screened households with children under age 13 were invited for a household interview, to be conducted with a parent or guardian. At the close of data collection, 11 630 eligible households had been interviewed (either by phone or in-person), and 5180 had not. The NSECE household survey had an overall weighted response rate including screening and interview completion of 62.2%. The number of completed household interviews per state varied widely: 13 states had fewer than 80 interviews at the low-end and 5 states had 600 or more interviews at the high-end.

The NSECE Household Survey data documented the nation's demand for ECE services and included key topics such as the usage and cost of nonparental care, the balance of parental employment with childcare needs and availability, and differences across household characteristics in these areas. The NSECE team and other researchers linked the NSECE surveys with relevant administrative data with different objectives. For example, researchers linked NSECE household survey data to administrative data on childcare subsidy records for the state of Illinois to better understand families who may be eligible for childcare subsidies based on income and employment status but not participating in the subsidy program (NSECE Project Team 2016). The linkage to state data used parental consents to link to administrative records that were requested as part of the interview. Because of the wide range of policy and practice data available about ECE practice, the NSECE was designed to make available a tremendous variety of linkage opportunities (subject to protection of respondent privacy), quite rare for large-scale US surveys. For example, researchers could seek to link households to government program participation records, households or childcare providers to proximity to educational institutions, or providers to applicable policies or regulations on ECE, which are primarily geographically defined. To facilitate these analyses, many identifiers were retained and archived for future analytic purposes, public use data were deidentified so that many linkages can be conducted without re-dentification of individual respondent identities, and a routine process was established to allow researchers to use restricted identifiers to conduct linkages to NSECE data. To date, more than 100 researchers have conducted research using this process.

3.3.2 Proprietary Research Files from Zillow

Zillow is an online real estate company that has developed one of the most comprehensive databases of US residential real estate information. Zillow has data on more than 110 million US homes, including homes not currently on the market. It provides consumers with home value and rent estimates, as well as with detailed information about the residence. Using a proprietary formula, Zillow also provides an estimate of the market value of all homes, known as a Zestimate, using publicly available data as well as information from comparable properties in the neighborhood.[2] These data, Zillow's signature products, are freely available online at www.zillow.com.

Zillow aggregates public records that it obtains from a major third-party provider and information it gathers from county records. The transactions data are obtained from the municipal offices responsible for recording real estate transactions, while the assessment tables are sourced ultimately from the county assessors' offices. Because of the emphasis on market transactions and residential property tax assessments, data for multiunit dwellings, especially within a residential income improvement, are seldom available. In many cases, units within a residential income improvement like an apartment are not identified; thus, only information at the building level is available. In contrast, residential buildings such as condominiums typically have information at the unit level.

Zillow has public databases on its website with different levels of aggregation from neighborhood to national level, but only for a very restricted set of variables. These databases are available by market segments (single family, condos, one bedroom, etc.), and by certain characteristics of the dwelling such as the number of bedrooms. Additionally, the public databases have different levels of completeness due to the absence of data or quality concerns,[3] which is especially an issue when working with finer levels of geography such as county or zip code.

The confidential address-level Zillow datafiles are available in two sets of tables called ZTRAX. The first set records real estate transactions, of which there can be many for one property. There are more than 300 million records from the past two decades; the tables include information related to sales, loans, and foreclosures, among other variables. The second set of tables, known as assessors' tables, store property characteristics, detailed geographic information, and prior assessor valuations on the parcel/lot. Each parcel/lot may have zero, one, or more improvements, such as single-family residences (SFRs), apartment buildings, etc. The information in these tables includes market value, assessed value, tax amount, land use, characteristics of the building such as the number of rooms and units, among many others. Current tables store the most updated record for each parcel/lot, while historical tables store previous records. The restricted-use ZTRAX data include a much broader set of variables than the public datafiles. For example, the public data do not include aggregate metrics of the tax value,

---

2 From www.zillow.com extracted in August 2018.
3 https://www.zillow.com/research/zhvi-methodology-6032/.

market value, number of rooms, etc. Since the ZTRAX data are directly from administrative and commercial data sources, they do not include created or derived fields such as the Zestimate.

Zillow makes ZTRAX files available to researchers at academic institutions at no cost, but subject to submission and approval of a data use agreement approved for a specific research project. The data use agreement restricts the reporting of information that could be used to recover individual records or values, and grants Zillow a three-week review period before any release of information to individuals not covered under the data use agreement. All references to Zillow data in this chapter pertain to variables extracted from the ZTRAX files.

3.3.3 Linking the NSECE Household Survey with Zillow Proprietary Datafiles

In creating a linked NSECE/Zillow datafile, our objective was to create a new datafile containing both NSECE survey data and Zillow property-related data for the same households. Focusing on the almost 12 000 households that completed the NSECE household interview, we sought to attach such property-specific Zillow variables as market value and property tax assessment to each household for an expanded datafile. Given the two datasets, residential street address was our linking variable; we sought one and only one record in the Zillow data to link to each NSECE record. The linked file, if of good quality, would support a wider range of analyses than either dataset independently; in this case, in-depth explorations of how property values and property tax assessments influence households' choice of and expenditure on ECE. This chapter reports on assessing that quality.

Although residential street address appeared in both files, we identified three conceptual challenges to linking Zillow data to NSECE survey data: (i) nonuniqueness of matches, (ii) misalignment of units of observation, and (iii) ability to identify matches. All three challenges contributed to the final match rate, an essential quality of the linked file: What is the percentage of survey records that find a match in the Zillow files? With these various insights into the linkage process, we can better understand possible weaknesses in the linked file as well as the potential analytic value of the linked file.

3.3.3.1 Nonuniqueness of Matches

Whereas Zillow data are organized by housing unit, in most cases, there are multiple records for each unit, annotated in the Zillow files according to dates of extract from source datafiles. This happens because Zillow data are a compilation of many different types of data sources and transactions, for example one for each time a property is assessed or sold. A fictitious address might be associated with dates of extract as given in Table 3.1.

Table 3.1 Fictitious address associated with dates of extract.

Housing unit address: 123 main st, Apt 45	
Extract #	Date of extract
1	7/1/1999
2	7/1/2003
3	7/1/2005
4	7/1/2006
5	7/1/2007
6	7/1/2009
7	7/1/2010
8	7/1/2011
11	7/1/2014
12	3/31/2016
13	7/1/2016
14	3/1/2017

Figure 3.1 shows the distribution of extracts per housing unit for a set of approximately 1200 NSECE addresses within a few states. (States cannot be identified due to NSECE disclosure guidelines, but constitute approximately 15% of the nation, and differ in region, population size, and extent of urbanicity.) Almost one-half (42%) of NSECE street addresses had between 11 and 15 records available in Zillow files received in 2017.

Because the NSECE data were collected in the first half of 2012 and our primary interest was time-variant property finance variables such as market value and property tax burden, our preference would have been to match to a record as close as possible to 2012. In attempting such a match, we found that data completeness varied significantly across records so that a record from 2013 might include data that were then missing from the 2014 record, even on seemingly time-invariant characteristics such as the number of stories or year of construction. Our solution was to link to the record closest in date to 2012, and if there was more than one, to the most complete record among those closest to 2012. Figure 3.2 shows the distribution by extract year for the linked data for the same addresses as in Figure 3.1, prior to selection of a single record. Many addresses had multiple records for a single year. For comparability of financial constructs such as market value and tax payments, the dataset might ideally include one record for each housing unit for each year.

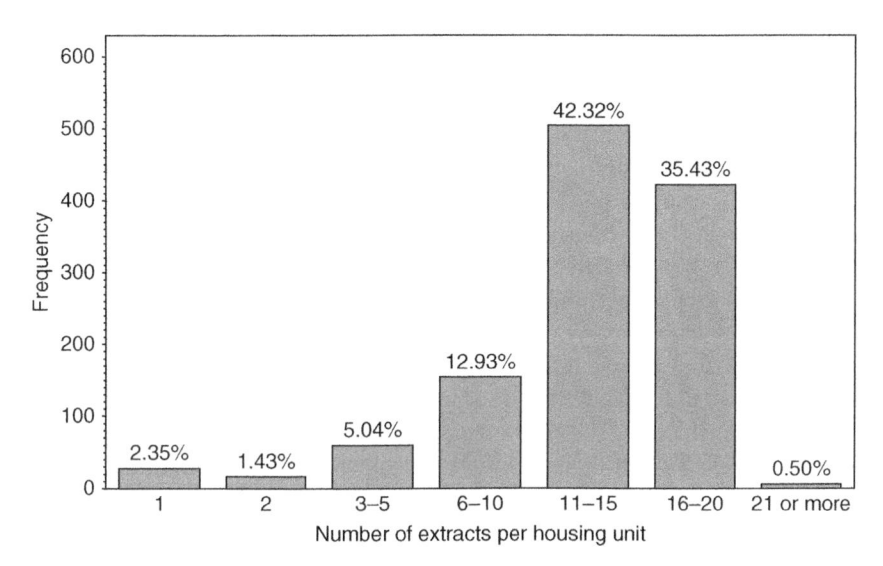

Figure 3.1 Distribution of number of Zillow extracts per housing unit.

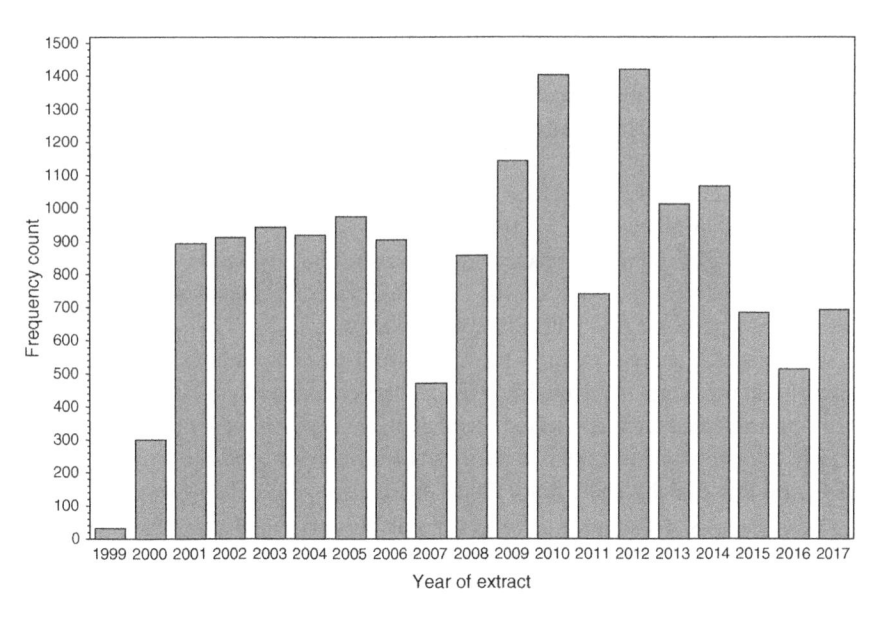

Figure 3.2 Distribution of extract years for individual housing units.

3.3.3.2 Misalignment of Units of Observation

In principle, we preferred a unit-level match, in which we could feel confident that the surveyed household would be accurately described by the linked Zillow variables on property value, tax assessment, or characteristics of the structure (e.g. room count or number of floors). For multiple-unit dwellings, a single residential address from the survey perspective represents a housing unit such as an apartment or a single-family home. In the Zillow data, however, the smallest unit of observation may be an apartment building, in which case the exact dwelling inhabited by the surveyed household is not measured in the Zillow data.

For multiunit dwellings, we were wary of allowing matches across nonmatching unit numbers (for example, 1A to 2B) because we did not have adequate data to know if the two units might differ in value-related characteristics like number of rooms or square footage. The Zillow datafiles included such variables as "number of units," which we had thought to use to estimate financial variables for units within lot-level matches, but we were not able to develop methods to use these variables to construct unit-level values within multiunit properties. One decision we had to make in linking by address was whether to link at the "lot level," that is, 123 Elm St, or further at the "unit level," so 123 Elm St, Apt 2B. As we show below, we preserved both lot-level and unit-level matches because of significantly lower match rates at the unit level.

3.3.3.3 Ability to Identify Matches

In data linkages, we were always concerned about the quality of the linkage itself. Could we find the same unit in both datafiles and accurately link them to one another? For example, 11651-53 E North Avenue in the Zillow data may appear in the survey datafile as 11651/11653 E North Avenue, but we may be unable to determine that these are the same address. Alternatively, we may believe 1322 Englewood Parkway is a match with 1322 Englewood Parkway East, but the two address may pertain to distinct residential locations.

The approach we used to link the Zillow and NSECE data was deterministic rather than probabilistic, using the street address in each file to identify matches. In a deterministic match, a selected set of identifiers in both files either do or do not match. In a probabilistic match, a wider set of variables is used, and any given pair of records is assigned a score that reflects the relative odds of being a match. Analyses can then use different probabilities to include more definite or more uncertain matches. For example, in a deterministic match on street–city–state–ZIP, 703 Rand Avenue, Oakland CA 94610 would not match to 703 Rand Avenue, Piedmont CA 94610 because the city names are different. In a probabilistic match, the fact that the street number, street name, state, and ZIP match would generate a high probability (but less than 1) that the two records are a match. More sophisticated matching might be able to identify that there are no other Rand Avenues within the 94610 ZIP code and further increase the probability of the two records being a match. Generally, the issue with deterministic linkage is that it does not identify links where one or several of the linkage identifiers being compared are different (i.e. due to transcription error or some other cause). However, the advantage of the deterministic approach is that it tends to reduce the incidence of nonmatching links (type I errors).

In a complete street address (house number, unit number, street name, city, state, ZIP code), the street name is the most likely to vary due to alternative formatting: i.e. with differences in capitalization, street name spelling, punctuation abbreviations, and directional indicators. However, this potential issue is mitigated by rendering the street address using a common address standardizer software. Nevertheless, we conducted a quality control review to see to what degree common lots/structures were not identified as links by this join. If we had found cases where matches were not linked by this deterministic linkage, we would have attempted a probabilistic linkage process to improve match rates (but ultimately, that step was unnecessary).

We evaluated the completeness of the deterministic linkage by conducting merges using selected components of the street address. For example, these test joins were done after removing all directional indicators (e.g. "N," "SW," etc.) and street suffix types (e.g. "RD," "ST," "AVE"), and we reviewed the additional linked cases that were identified (i.e. that had not been identified in the basic join) to see if indeed these were valid matches. We reviewed all unmatched cases in the same selected states individually (by "eye") using Internet geography tools such as Google Maps. For linkage at the unit level, we were only comparing the unit identifiers, not the unit types (e.g. "Floor," "Apt," "Unit"). Our review manually examined every unmatched address in approximately 15% of the NSECE sample locations: just over 500 unmatched addresses in different states, regions of the country, and levels of urbanicity. Our review identified very few cases (less than 20) where the broader join caught a match not returned by the deterministic linkage routine, and more cases (up to 100) where a broader join might identify questionable matches that would be hard to exclude outside of the narrower match rules. Thus, we concluded there was no need to replace the deterministic linkage with a probabilistic linkage. More specifically, we concluded that when the survey address did not match to an address in the Zillow data, the lack of match was because the address simply was not present in the Zillow data. Having developed matching techniques on the approximately 1700 addresses in our selected states and determining that further matching improvements could not be achieved, we then implemented those matching techniques on all 11 630 addresses within the NSECE sample.

We had expected to require probabilistic or "fuzzy" matching techniques, but ultimately concluded that deterministic approaches would suffice because the primary reason for lack of match was absence of a record to match in the Zillow data. Fuzzy matching techniques would be useful where deterministic methods were missing matches or there were many candidate matches that are difficult to choose between. None of these occurred in our linkage. We believe some of the success in deterministic matching occurred because both the Zillow addresses and the NSECE addresses were standardized in similar ways and were well-curated. We hypothesize that as with the Zillow data, other linkages using unique identifiers (such as social security numbers) could likely also be achieved deterministically, while linkages using names, dates of birth, or other text strings or common identifiers might be more likely to require probabilistic matching methods. With the use of such methods, one would also want to employ a variety of sensitivity analyses to better understand the implications on analytic findings of different matching choices.

The quality of the linking variables and the resultant linkage may result in bias as well as undercoverage. A common example might be if linkages must be done only with names and dates of birth; in many datasets, some East Asian and some Hispanic names may exhibit less variation than names for other racial/ethnic subgroups. If duplicate names cannot be effectively disentangled using dates of birth or other available linking information, then the linked dataset may under-represent some racial/ethnic subgroups or there may be more error in the linked data for those groups than for others.

3.3.3.4 Identifying Matches

We defined two types of matches between the NSECE household data and the Zillow datafiles: lot level and unit level. A lot-level match may be for an apartment building or townhomes on a shared lot, while unit-level matches apply to single-family homes or when the exact unit identifier matches in a multiunit dwelling. Any unit-level match is also a lot-level match. For either type of match, we selected exactly one Zillow record for that address, as close as possible to 2012 and as complete as possible among those closest to 2012, but we did not exclude any matches on the basis of dates too far from 2012 or records that were incomplete.

The match rate (whether at the lot level or the unit level) is the percentage of all NSECE household addresses with a match according to these criteria. The overall lot-level matching rate (unweighted) was 81%, and the overall unit-level match rate was 63%; both varied significantly across geographic areas. Because the ZTRAX data are drawn heavily from local jurisdictions such as municipalities, counties, or other taxing bodies, we hypothesized that geographic variation in match rates might occur. Figure 3.3 shows the distribution of states' lot-level (a) and unit-level (b) match rates for the 50 states and District of Columbia, our study population. Two states had rates below 50%, while four states were above 90%. For unit-level

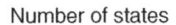

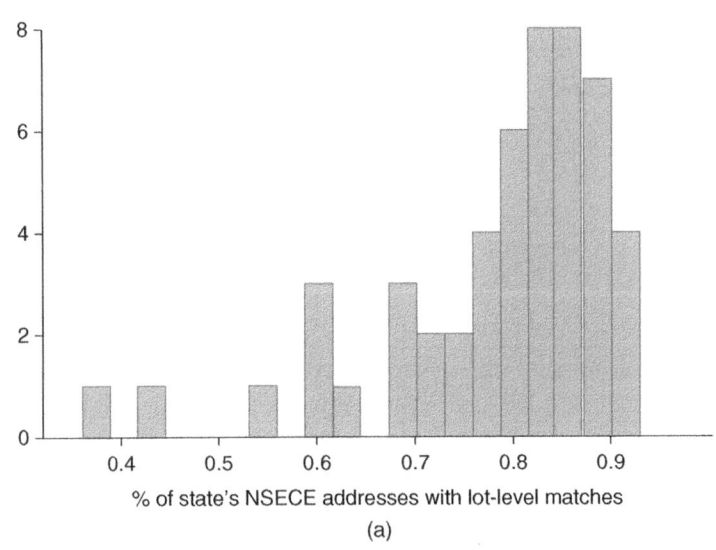

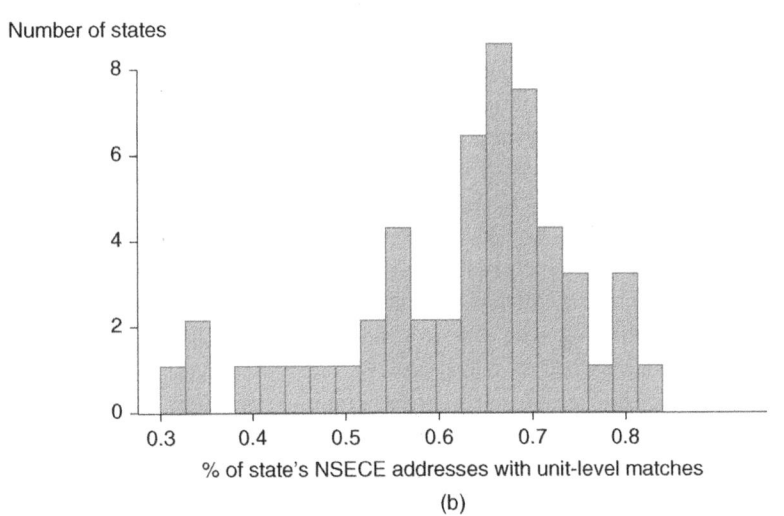

Figure 3.3 Distribution of the state match rates at the lot level (a) and the unit level (b).

match rates, the distribution shifted to the left, with seven states under 50% and no states above 90%. The state-level match rate could have been affected by characteristics of the NSECE sample in a given state as well as state-specific features of the data sources represented in the Zillow data.

Table 3.2 Match rate of NSECE household records to Zillow data by home own/rent status.

Survey-reported home ownership status	Unweighted count	Unweighted match rate	
		% Lot-level match	% Unit-level match
Own	5280	95	87
Rent	5740	68	40
Other	540	85	72
Missing	60	89	73
Total	11 620	81	63

Note: A few households did not report if the home was rented or owned (Missing category). All unweighted counts were rounded to the nearest 20.

The match rates adjusted for survey sampling weights were higher: 85% at the lot level and 70% at the unit level. Given the design of the NSECE, the differences between weighted and unweighted match rates were likely due to higher nonmatch rates for the households oversampled in low-income areas (and therefore having lower sampling weights), where sampled units were more likely to be multiple-unit dwellings than in higher-income areas.

The match rates varied considerably by the characteristics of the dwelling. Table 3.2 shows the match rates by the own/rent status of the home as reported in the NSECE interview. Households with owner-occupied residences had a 95% lot-level match rate and 87% unit-level match rate. In contrast, rental households had lower match rates, especially at the unit level, where the match rate was 40%.

NSECE respondents were not asked about the type of residence (i.e. SFR, multifamily, etc.), so information on type of residence was only available for those NSECE records that matched to Zillow data. We did, however, assess lot-level vs. unit-level matches using structure type information in the Zillow data. Table 3.3 shows the proportion of cases matched at the lot level that were also matched at the unit level for each type of residence. Almost all (96%) SFRs that matched across the two files matched at the unit level, while about 42% of non-SFRs that matched across the two files matched at the unit level.

3.3.3.5 Implications of the Linking Process for Intended Analyses

Recalling our analytic objective of linking property-specific values such as market value and property tax assessment to nationally representative survey data on ECE usage, we reflect on the findings presented in Figure 3.3, Tables 3.2, and 3.3. Figure 3.3 showed substantial variation in state-level match rates. States with very low match rates may have other differences in their contributing data sources

Table 3.3 Percentage of NSECE-Zillow lot-level matches also matching at unit-level by Zillow indicator of type of dwelling.

Zillow category	Unweighted count	% Unit-level match
Single family	6360	96
Not single family	2640	42
Other	340	25
Missing	80	62
Total	9420	78

Note: All unweighted counts were rounded to the nearest 20. NSECE addresses with no lot-level match were excluded from table ($n = 2180$).

so that their Zillow variables are either not comparable to other states' or their samples of linked households may not be comparable to those in others states. For example, states may vary in the jurisdiction types that maintains property-related data, or they may differ in how they classify or tax different property types, resulting in differences in administrative data sources that Zillow can acquire. Comparing Tables 3.2 and 3.3, we see that structure type is more strongly associated with unit-level match rates than ownership status. (Households may own their dwellings as single-family structures or as condominiums or other unit types in multiunit structures. Similarly, many households rent single-family homes.) This pattern suggests that the linked data cover the population of households living in SFRs (whether or not they rent) better than the population of households who live in owner-occupied housing (including condominiums and townhouses as well as single-family homes). The relevance of property tax values and property values for renters is less clear than for home owners, since renters may not directly pay property taxes, nor experience wealth increases when property values rise. Similarly, households living in single-family structures are not typically an inferential population of interest (i.e. for the analysis of public or poverty support benefits), and especially not for childcare research. Although the overall NSECE-Zillow match rates may be good, the systematic patterns in match rates documented in Figure 3.3, Tables 3.2, and 3.3 begin to raise concerns about the quality of the linked datafile for analytic purposes.

Model-based weights can correct for unequal match rates, for example, using a weight that is inversely proportional to the likelihood of match. This can be an excellent strategy, for example when lack of consent to match is a reason for nonmatch. In the consent scenario, the reason for nonmatch (refusal to consent) may be unrelated to the quality of the data that would have been matched. In our case, the reason for nonmatch was specifically the coverage properties of the

Zillow data. For this reason, we were not sure that the assumptions underlying a weights-based correction of the linked file would be met. We chose not to implement a model-based weighting approach because we did not find it plausible that the unlinked records would be well-represented even by differentially weighted linked cases.

3.4 Assessment of Data Quality Using the Linked File

In this section, we describe three assessments we undertook to understand the quality features of our two data sources and our linked datafile: (i) inspection of Zillow variables to determine possibilities for analytic use; (ii) use of Zillow data to understand errors introduced in the NSECE survey process; and (iii) tabulation of key sample characteristics to understand the representativeness of the linked file relative to the NSECE survey data alone. For each of these analyses, we constructed a slightly different file, varying the variables included from each of the two source datafiles, as well as which records were included in the analytic dataset.

One challenge of exploring data quality through linked files was adopting assumptions about which file provided better quality. For this study, we treated each file as the more reliable source in its respective domain. That is, we saw the NSECE as a nationally representative sample of households and exploited that statistical dimension of the file. We treated the Zillow data as more authoritative regarding property value-related issues, which are absent from the NSECE data. A great value of the techniques we demonstrate here is that neither data source need be unimpeachable for the linked file to provide valuable information on the qualities of each. Rather, there can be information content in any systematic and statistically significant patterns we see in the quality tabulations, as long as suspected sources of error in each file are not likely to be correlated with the quality dimension being assessed.

The remainder of this section presents the results of the three data quality assessments we conducted.

3.4.1 What Variables in the Zillow Datafile Are Most Appropriate for Use in Substantive Analyses Linked to Survey Data?

Understanding the quality of administrative or commercial datafiles can be especially difficult because the datasets themselves do not often describe well-defined populations. For example, datasets may frequently not only have duplicate records for many entities but also have gaps in coverage that are difficult to detect. Such data often also describe transactions, properties, or other nonhuman entities where less statistical data are available as benchmarks. One advantage of linking administrative data to a nationally representative sample is to put some structure on the data to allow for better interpretation of exploratory statistics.

To understand the relative analytic value of different variables in the Zillow proprietary files, we began with almost all of the ZTRAX variables. Our inspection of the full ZTRAX datafiles indicated that the variable list for the datafiles was essentially the union of all variables available from any source file or jurisdiction. Thus, many variables were missing almost everywhere or took on a single value almost everywhere. We created a linked Zillow-NSECE datafile that included only one variable from the NSECE dataset: the address itself. We used the NSECE sample only to put structure on the Zillow datafiles (for example, to remove duplicate records across multiple years), and we analyzed only the linked file – that is, a file that contained exactly once any NSECE address that had a completed interview and matched to a Zillow record at the unit or lot level. From the ZTRAX files, we retained only variables that were available in a large number of jurisdictions, exhibited some variation, and were potentially of interest to us analytically. All data from Zillow reported in these analyses were variables appearing in the ZTRAX data; we did not construct any variables based on ZTRAX information or manipulate the ZTRAX fields in any way.

We began by reviewing categorical variables, for which we tabulated frequencies and verified that the levels of the identifiers were consistent with those shown in documentation we received. As part of this process, we counted separately the number (and rate) at which these fields were left unfilled. Because we understood that the data compiled from each state differed substantially, for our categorical variables of interest, we computed the completeness rate on a state-by-state basis. Table 3.4 shows that variation across states was substantial. For example, the third row of the table describes the variable, "Effective Year Built." Across the 50 states and DC, the average completeness rate of this variable was 11.8%. Although at least the first quartile of states had no values for this variable, in the top 5% of states (3 of them), 64.2% of records in the linked data had valid information for this variable.

As a next step, for continuous variables such as "assessed value" and other dollar amounts, we explored the variation in values across states. Table 3.5 shows quantiles for the state means of each variable. In the first row of the table, eight states had missing values for the variable land assessed value, making the mean not computable. Across states with computable mean values, we saw a significant range from $3000 at the 5th percentile of state means to $19 600 at the 95th percentile of state means.

Additionally, we wanted to understand how each variable added to the total information that was available on the file. In particular, knowing the total market value for each unit and also how this relates to tax amount would be quite helpful. Figure 3.4 plots these data for addresses in the same selected states as above, where tax amount was less than $50 000 and total market value was less than $1 million.

Table 3.4 Rates of completeness for 50 states and DC for selected Zillow categorical variables.

		Percentile in completeness rate distribution across 50 states + DC				
Categorical variable	Mean	5%	25%	50%	75%	95%
Assessment year (%)	99.8	99.4	100	100	100	100
Building or improvement number (%)	100	100	100	100	100	100
Effective year built (%)	11.8	0.0	0.0	4.7	12.2	64.2
Market value year (%)	70.5	0.0	36.3	96.3	100	100
Number of units (%)	99.9	100	100	100	100	100
Tax year (%)	93.4	63.7	91.5	100	100	100
Total rooms (%)	99.9	100	100	100	100	100
Year built (%)	80.1	21.9	72.9	88.2	96.9	100
Year remodeled (%)	7.7	0.0	0.0	3.4	10.1	29.7
Building condition standard code (%)	47.6	0.0	21.1	51.0	75.0	97.0
Building quality standard code (%)	37.2	0.0	0.0	32.8	63.6	97.1
Occupancy status standard code (%)	58.3	32.5	49.0	59.9	67.1	78.0
Property land use standard code (%)	99.0	98.2	100	100	100	100
Number of stories (%)	99.9	100	100	100	100	100

Table 3.5 Distribution of state mean values of selected continuous Zillow variables.

Variable	# with computable statistics	Percentile of state mean value distribution (in 1000's)				
		5%	25%	50%	75%	95%
Land assessed value	43	$3	$9	$31	$70	$196
Improvement assessed value	43	$9	$30	$96	$203	$326
Total assessed value	51	$13	$31	$109	$233	$514
Land market value	43	$8	$32	$56	$119	$224
Improvement market value	43	$56	$117	$158	$207	$633
Total market value	44	$65	$139	$204	$283	$545
Tax amount	50	$1	$2	$3	$4	$11

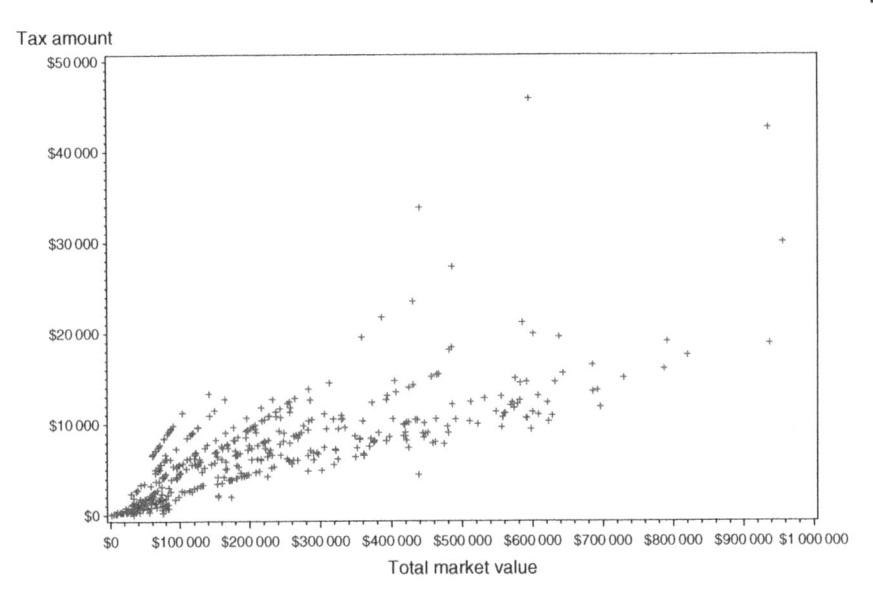

Figure 3.4 Total market value vs. tax amount in linked NSECE-Zillow data for selected states.

As we might expect, plotting total market values against tax amounts suggested linear patterns that might reflect the different taxing rates across different jurisdictions. On the one hand, the data appeared to exhibit sufficient variation – at least across diverse geographic settings – in relationships of total market value to tax amount to allow investigation of questions such as whether tax burdens and market value make independent contributions to household behavior. On the other hand, the strict linearity of the plots within jurisdiction raised the question of how much added information can be extracted from the total market value over and above information about assessed value and tax amount. In addition, since the survey sample was geographically clustered, the variation in jurisdictions and tax rates was limited.

3.4.2 How Did Different Steps in the Survey Administration Process Contribute to Representativeness of the NSECE Survey Data?

To assess NSECE data quality, we were particularly interested in understanding the extent to which key steps in the survey process contributed error relative to variables found in the Zillow data. Survey researchers typically have limited data for understanding bias or other error introduced in screening or interviewing, primarily because data are not available on units that could not be screened or interviewed. For this analysis, we constructed a datafile of all 99 820 sampled housing units for the NSECE fielding effort, not just those with completed household interviews. These were to be a nationally representative set of housing units, before almost any sources of survey error are likely to have intruded, except frame coverage weaknesses and sampling error in the selection process. We used the same linkage processes as described in Section 3.3.3.4. Variables from the NSECE file were two survey process outcomes (screened, interviewed if eligible), while from the Zillow data we selected those variables that our initial inspection indicated to be most complete and most consistent in coding across jurisdictions. Although we used the same linkage procedures described in Section 3.3, this linked file of 99 820 sampled units was larger than the linked file of 11 630 units with completed interviews described in Section 3.3.1. There may be some differences in the attributes of the two linked files, for example, in lot-level and unit-level match rates.

To study how the survey administration process contributed to the representativeness of the survey data, we evaluated whether households systematically differed in key observable characteristics across different steps of the data collection process. To analyze this pattern, we employed a logistic regression and tested for the individual statistical significance of selected Zillow housing unit characteristics in predicting data collection outcomes. We studied two different data collection outcomes: (i) screener nonresponse among occupied households, and (ii) interview nonresponse among households screened as eligible. In both cases, we measured unit nonresponse – no participation in the survey stage – rather than item nonresponse in which a participating household may have declined to answer a subset of questions. As described in Section 3.2, screening activities included mail, phone and in-person outreach to all sampled housing units as needed, while interviews were attempted only with screened households including at least one child under age 13. Approximately hour-long interviews were conducted in English or Spanish by phone or in-person with an adult parent or guardian in the household.

The linked file allowed us to examine lot-level matches on two questions: to what extent are occupied households more or less likely to get screened based on structure type, and to what extent are eligible households (screened units with children) more or less likely to complete the interview based on structure type? The four structure types are: SFRs, non-SFRs that are not residential income properties (for example row houses or town houses, duplex homes, or larger condominium complexes), the reference category of residential income properties (such as larger rental buildings), and other residential or mixed-use structures.

Using multivariate logistic regression, we modeled the data collection outcome as a dependent variable, explained by a set of variables available in the Zillow database. For each outcome, we estimated two models. The first used all lot-level linked observations and included only one variable that characterized the type of dwelling: residential income, SFR, residential but not SFR, and other. Because this model used all lot-level linked observations, we can think of the Model 1 comparisons as describing differences among lot-linked addresses of different types of housing structures. We were limited in the variables for this lot-level model, since for many variables, the interpretation or relevance of a lot-level variable to a household living on that lot was limited. For example, the meaning of market value for a lot is unclear for a household's finances if the household is renting and the presence of additional dwellings on the lot is undocumented.

The second model included only SFRs that were matched at the unit level, thus significantly reducing the number of observations in the model and focusing on a narrower segment of the population. We chose this subpopulation because the unit level matching rates for SFRs were particularly high compared to the other categories. This model was explained by continuous variables measuring the total assessed and market value of the property, the tax amount paid, the age of the building, and the size of the lot in acres. Because the second model ran only on SFRs that linked at the unit level, the interpretation of these estimates is more challenging, although because these were unit-level matches, we had a larger set of relevant variables from which to choose. In all models, we included state-fixed effects to account for the heterogeneity of the Zillow data by state (Tables 3.6 and 3.7).

Relative to residential income properties, SFRs were more likely to complete a screener (less likely to result in screener nonresponse). However, among eligible households, those living in SFRs were less likely to complete the interview. Both

Table 3.6 Odds ratios using structure type (relative to residential income structures) to predict screener and interview nonresponse among lot-level linked addresses.

Structure type (from Zillow)	Screener nonresponse	Survey nonresponse
Residential, not single-family residence (SFR)	0.88	1.15
Residential SFR	0.72***	1.40***
Other	0.84	1.17
N event	4560	4860
N no event	54 220	9380
Likelihood ratio test (joint sign)	6.55***	3.53***

Note: The dependent variable was an indicator variable for an occupied household not screening (second column), or an eligible household not completing the interview (third column). Asterisks denote: *$p < 0.05$, **$p < 0.01$, ***$p < 0.001$. Cluster (PSU) corrected standard errors. Data were unweighted; counts were rounded to the nearest 20. Design-adjusted Rao–Scott likelihood ratio χ^2-test to test the global null hypothesis.

Table 3.7 Odds ratios using structure characteristics to predict screener and interview nonresponse among unit-level linked single-family residences.

Zillow variables	Screener nonresponse	Survey nonresponse
Total assessed value (×100 000)	0.96	1.17
Tax amount (×1000)	1.05	0.97
Age of building (decades)	0.92***	0.97*
Lot size (acres)	1.00	0.99
Total market value (×100 000)	1.00	1.11*
N event	1140	1380
N no event	13 420	2260
Likelihood ratio test (joint sign)	1.63	6.20***

Note: The dependent variable was an indicator variable for an occupied household not screening (second column), or an eligible household not completing the interview (third column). Asterisks denote: $^{*}p < 0.05$, $^{**}p < 0.01$, $^{***}p < 0.001$. Cluster (PSU) corrected standard errors. Data were unweighted; counts were rounded to the nearest 20. Design-adjusted Rao–Scott likelihood ratio χ^2-test to test the global null hypothesis.

of these results are consistent with on-the-ground fielding experience. SFRs may have fewer barriers to an initial approach, such as doormen, locked gates, inaccessible mailboxes, or ability to mask whether individuals are home. Thus, we might expect better screening success with such households. However, residents of single-family homes may also be more protective of their privacy and able to evade interviewers.

Table 3.7 shows the odds ratios from the logistic regressions among households in SFRs matched at the unit level. The model predicting screener nonresponse shows that the only statistically significant variable is the age of the building, where occupied households living in older buildings were slightly more likely to be screened (i.e. had lower odds of screener nonresponse). Interestingly, the age of the building was statistically significant for both screener nonresponse and interview nonresponse. It is possible that age of structures was a proxy for certain types of older neighborhoods in more dense urban cores, but we were not able to test this assumption. Finally, among eligible households, we found that higher market values were associated with greater interview nonresponse. Every additional $100 000 in market value was associated with an increase of 10% in likelihood of interview nonresponse, when comparing unit-linked SFRs.

The lot-level analyses suggest that structure-related characteristics may be systematically related to screening and interviewing, but that these may offset one another, especially for single-family homes. The unit-level analysis indicates potentially large differences by building age, but the sample is quite diminished, and comparing older and more expensive single-family homes to other single-family homes yields limited inferences about the overall quality of the NSECE household survey data.

3.4.3 How Well Does the Linked Datafile Represent the Overall NSECE Dataset (Including Unlinked Records)?

Our final assessment asked how similar the linked file was compared to the original (unlinked) household survey datafile. The question is particularly salient given our observations about differential match rates by structure type and variability across states. For this analysis, we retained a variety of NSECE variables, but only the indicator of lot-level or unit-level match from the linked file. Results shown in Table 3.8 compare weighted proportions of household characteristics between households that were and were not matched to the Zillow database at the lot and at the unit levels. In the table, we compare matched households across brackets of household income-to-poverty ratio, whether the home was owned or rented, the household composition in terms of the number of children and adults, the community poverty density, the degree of urbanicity of the community where the households were located, and the household's use of regular and center-based care for young children. Analysis of differences in means of the selected categories of variables between the matched and nonmatched sample were conducted using t-tests where the null hypothesis was no difference between the means (or proportions) of the two groups. Standard errors were adjusted to account for the NSECE survey complex design.

In Table 3.8, we observed that for both unit-level and lot-level matching, matched addresses differed in statistically significant ways from the corresponding sets of unmatched addresses. The differences between matched and unmatched addresses were very similar whether we analyzed lot-level matches or unit-level matches. In two primary instances, the two match definitions yielded dissimilar patterns. Although both lot-level and unit-level matched addresses were less likely to have a unit number than unmatched addresses, the difference was much larger for unit-level matches, where just 2% of matched addresses had a unit number compared with 61% of unmatched addresses. The other difference was a measure of urbanicity. Unit-level matches were more likely than nonmatches to be high or moderate density urban, but equally likely to be rural. In contrast, lot-level matches were less likely to be rural than were nonmatches, but both were equally likely to be high- or moderate-density urban.

As suggested in earlier tabulations, the matched addresses (whether lot level or unit level) were more likely to be owned (vs. rented). Household income differed at all levels: poor households were twice as likely to be nonmatched than

Table 3.8 Characteristics of NSECE households by match status at the lot and unit level.

Household characteristic	Full NSECE sample	Lot-level Match	Lot-level No match	Unit-level Match	Unit-level No match
Own	53%	60%***	14%	69%***	18%
Rent	41%	34%***	83%	25%***	79%
Has unit number (proxy for multi-unit)	20%	16%***	44%	2%***	61%
Income below Federal Poverty Level (FPL)	26%	23%***	43%	19%***	42%
Income 100–199% FPL	22%	21%***	31%	19%***	29%
Income 200–299% FPL	15%	16%***	11%	16%***	12%
Income 300% or more FPL	37%	41%***	15%	45%***	17%
Avg. no. of children < 13 in HH	1.8	1.8	1.8	1.8	1.8
Avg. no. of children ≤ 5 in HH	0.8	0.8***	1.0	0.8***	0.9
Avg. no. of adults (>17) in HH	2.1	2.1***	1.9	2.2***	1.9
Avg. no. of earners in HH	1.5	1.6***	1.4	1.6***	1.4
Low-poverty density	59%	61%***	45%	66%***	43%
Moderate-poverty density	22%	21%*	27%	19%***	30%
High-poverty density	19%	18%***	28%	16%***	28%
High-density urban	69%	69%	67%	67%*	72%
Moderate-density urban	21%	21%	19%	23%**	17%
Rural	10%	10%**	14%	10%	11%
HHs with child(ren) under 5:					
At least one child < 5 attends center-based care	27%	28%***	21%	30%***	22%
No children < 5 attend any regular care	46%	45%**	52%	43%***	52%
Number of households (weighted)	29 500 000	25 100 000	4 410 000	20 700 000	8 780 000

HH = household.
Note: The asterisks in the third (fifth) column indicate statistical significance in mean differences between lot-level (unit-level) matched and nonmatched cases. Asterisks denote: *$p < 0.05$, **$p < 0.01$, ***$p < 0.001$. Standard errors account for the complex survey design. Due to NSECE disclosure guidelines, weighted estimates were rounded to no more than three significant digits.

matched (42% vs. 19% for unit level), whereas households with incomes at least triple the poverty level were almost three times as likely to be matched as nonmatched (41% vs. 15% for lot level). Matched households had the same number of children under age 13 as unmatched households, but matched households had fewer children under age 5, more adults, and more earners than did unmatched households. Mirroring the income patterns, matched households were more likely to be located in communities with low-poverty density (66% unit-matched to 43% unmatched) and less likely to be in high-poverty density areas (28% unit-matched to 16% unmatched) than were unmatched households.

Finally, the analytical motivation for this file linkage had been to explore the role of property taxes and housing values in childcare usage, which has been documented to be closely tied to household income. Matched and unmatched addresses differ on use of center-based care for young children and on use of any regular child care for young children, but the magnitudes of differences are somewhat smaller than for some other measures in Table 3.8.

Overall, the differences between matched and unmatched households cause concern about the ability of the linked datafile to provide meaningful insights into the nationally representative population of households represented by the NSECE survey data alone.

3.5 Conclusion

For most data quality assessments, we wish to determine the suitability of the data for a particular substantive analysis. In this study, we had three objectives for data quality assessment:

1) What can we learn about bias or other error in the survey process for gathering NSECE data? This information is relevant for any analyses using the NSECE household survey data, and perhaps for other studies using similar data collection methodologies.
2) What can we learn about the data quality properties of newly available research datafiles from Zillow.com? This information helps inform a variety of potential research efforts that seek to exploit administrative and commercial data to enhance survey data sources.
3) What are the properties of a linked NSECE-Zillow datafile, and what do those properties indicate about potential uses of the linked data to answer substantive questions about ECE usage by different types of families in different types of communities?

Our data quality assessments allowed us to learn about each component dataset. Imposing the structure of a nationally representative sample allowed inspection of the Zillow data with more of a population focus than is natural for a property-based dataset. We found that national analysis would likely need to be limited to two or three of the hundreds of available variables based on availability and consistency across jurisdictions. However, we were able to use the linked data to explore patterns of nonresponse in the NSECE survey data collection process. These explorations would not have been feasible without the Zillow variables. In addition to gaining insights about each dataset individually, we also drew some conclusions about the linked datafile. Specifically, we had very good match rates for SFRs, including when those residences were rented rather than owned. Conversely, linkage quality was poor for multifamily residences, especially when the units were rented. As a result of differential match rates, the linked file exhibited a marked bias toward higher-income households (who are more likely to be found in owned SFRs).

Our inferences about the appropriate use of Zillow data for national analyses are very similar to inferences in Seeskin (2018) about the use of CoreLogic data, a similar proprietary dataset that gathers property information from jurisdictions into a single national dataset. Seeskin's assessment too is that these data are best used for SFRs only and even then there is considerable variability across the jurisdictions that are the original data sources.

We embarked on this research anticipating we could use a variety of techniques to create a linked dataset that would expand research questions that could be addressed with the NSECE survey data alone. For example, we anticipated using probabilistic matching to improve the size and quality of our linked file over and above what deterministic matching methods could achieve, employing multiple imputation or other modeling techniques to be able to include units in multi-family dwellings as well as single-family dwellings in analyses, and developing model-based weights to correct for bias in representativeness of the linked file. As discussed, in each case, we examined the available data and concluded that these methods would not improve the linked data or their analyses, given the coverage and characteristics of the Zillow data.

With specific reference to the linkage we implemented, we conclude that the potential analytic use of Zillow proprietary research datafiles in combination with household survey data is best limited to single-family homes given the high rates of missing data for multifamily dwellings. In addition, the significant variability and apparent inconsistency of data across the jurisdictions that originally generated these data is a substantial deterrent to using the data for analyses across jurisdictions. These research datafiles would be most successfully used for analyses involving only single-family homes and ideally within jurisdictions (for example, a study of single-family home residents in a single large jurisdiction).[4]

This chapter provides a model for using linkages between survey data and other administrative datasets to understand the data quality features of each dataset individually and of the linked datafile. Our analyses demonstrate both that such data quality assessments can reveal information about each dataset and provide important guidance on how best to use the linked file for analytic purposes.

References

Biemer, P.P. (2010). Total survey error: design, implementation, and evaluation. *Public Opinion Quarterly* 74 (5): 817–848. https://doi.org/10.1093/poq/nfq058.

Coleman, J.S., Campbell, E.Q., Hobson, C.J. et al. (1966). *Equality of Educational Opportunity*. Washington, DC: U.S. Government Printing Office.

Henly, J.R., Kim, J., Sandstrom, H. et al. (2017). What explains short spells on child-care subsidies? *Social Service Review* 91 (3): 488–533. https://doi.org/10.1086/693751.

Kane, T.J., Rouse, C.E., and Staiger, D. (1999). *Estimating Returns to Schooling When Schooling Is Misreported*. Working Paper No. 7235. Cambridge, MA: National Bureau of Economic Research https://EconPapers.repec.org/RePEc:nbr:nberwo:7235.

Kannel, W.B. (1976). Some lessons in cardiovascular epidemiology from Framingham. *The American Journal of Cardiology* 37 (2): 269–282. https://doi.org/10.1016/0002-9149(76)90323-4.

Künn, S. (2015). The challenges of linking survey and administrative data. *IZA World of Labor* https://doi.org/10.15185/izawol.214.

Lorden, A.L., Radcliff, T.A., Jiang, L. et al. (2016). Leveraging administrative data for program evaluations: a method for linking data sets without unique identifiers. *Evaluation & the Health Professions* 39 (2): 245–259. https://doi.org/10.1177/0163278714547568.

Lucas, S.R. (2014). An inconvenient dataset: bias and inappropriate inference with the multilevel model. *Quality & Quantity* 48: 1619–1649. https://doi.org/10.1007/s11135-013-9865-x.

---

4 We did not have adequate sample size to determine what we would need to define the jurisdiction; for example, Cook County in Illinois generates property tax bills and assessments for millions of housing units in the Chicago area, but those bills reflect tremendous variety in taxing rates across the hundreds of suburbs and taxing bodies within the county.

Meyer, B.D. and Goerge, R. (2011). *Errors in Survey Reporting and Imputation and Their Effects on Estimates of Food Stamp Program Participation*. Washington, DC: U.S. Census Bureau, Center for Economic Studies https://www2.census.gov/ces/wp/2011/CES-WP-11-14.pdf.

National Survey of Early Care and Education (NSECE) Project Team (2013). *National Survey of Early Care and Education: Summary Data Collection and Sampling Methodology*. (OPRE Report #2013-46). Washington, DC: Office of Planning, Research and Evaluation, Administration for Children and Families, U.S. Department of Health and Human Services.

National Survey of Early Care and Education (NSECE) Project Team (2016). *Examining Child Care Subsidy Receipt: An Analysis of Matched NSECE and Illinois Administrative Data*. (OPRE Report #2016-12). Washington, DC: Office of Planning, Research and Evaluation, Administration for Children and Families, U.S. Department of Health and Human Services https://www.acf.hhs.gov/sites/default/files/opre/nsece_summarymethodology_toopre_102913.pdf.

O, Hara, A., Shattuck, R.M., and Goerge, R.M. (2016). Linking federal surveys with administrative data to improve research on families. *The Annals of the American Academy of Political and Social Science* 669 (1): 63–74. https://doi.org/10.1177/0002716216678391.

Sakshaug, J. and Kreuter, F. (2012). Assessing the magnitude of non-consent biases in linked survey and administrative data. *Survey Research Methods* 6 (2): 113–122. https://doi.org/10.18148/srm/2012.v6i2.5094.

Sala, E., Burton, J., and Knies, G. (2010). *Correlates of Obtaining Informed Consent to Data Linkage: Respondent, Interview and Interviewer Characteristics*. (ISER Working Paper Series, No. 2010-28). Colchester, UK: University of Essex, Institute for Social and Economic Research.

Seeskin, Z.H. (2018). Evaluating the utility of a commercial data source for estimating property tax amounts. *Statistical Journal of the IAOS* 34 (4): 543–551. https://doi.org/10.3233/SJI-180452.

Seeskin, Z.H., Datta, A.R., and Ugarte, G. (2018). Constructing a toolkit to evaluate quality of state and local administrative data. *International Journal of Population Data Science* 3 (5) https://doi.org/10.23889/ijpds.v3i5.1053.

Shattuck, R. (2017). *Is Subsidized Childcare Associated with Lower Risk of Grade Retention for Low-Income Children? Evidence from Child Care and Development Fund Administrative Records Linked to the American Community Survey*. (CARRA Working Paper 2017-06). Washington, DC: U.S. Census Bureau.

Spillman, B. and Waidman, T. (2014). *Rates and Timing of Medicaid Enrollment among Older Americans*. Washington, DC: Office of Assistant Secretary for Planning and Evaluation. U.S. Department of Health and Human Services.

Further Reading

Daas, P., Ossen, S., Tennekes, M., et al. (2011). List of Quality Groups and Indicators Identified for Administrative Data Sources. First deliverable of work package 4 of the BLUE Enterprise and Trade Statistics project (Blue-Ets Project – SSH-CT-2010-244767). Available on: http://www.pietdaas.nl/beta/pubs/pubs/BLUE-ETS_WP4_Del1.pdf (accessed 26 March 2020).

Eurostat (2000). Assessment of the quality in statistics. *Proceedings of the Eurostat/A4/Quality/00/General/Standard Report*, Room Ampere, Bech Building, Luxembourg (4–5 April 2000).

National Survey of Early Care and Education (NSECE) Project Team (2016). *Early Care and Education Usage and Households' Out-of-pocket Costs: Tabulations from the National Survey of Early Care and Education (NSECE)*. (OPRE Report #2016-09). Washington, DC: Office of Planning, Research and Evaluation, Administration for Children and Families, U.S. Department of Health and Human Services.

Sinai, T. and Souleles, N.S. (2005). Owner-occupied housing as a hedge against rent risk. *Quarterly Journal of Economics* 120 (2): 763–789. https://doi.org/10.1093/qje/120.2.763.

United Nations Economic Commission for Europe (2007). *Register-Based Statistics in the Nordic Countries*. Geneva, Switzerland: United Nations Publications.

Vale, S. (2008). *Using Administrative Source for Official Statistics – A Handbook of Principles and Practices*. Geneva, Switzerland: United Nations Economic Commission for Europe.

Section 2

Total Error and Data Quality

4

Total Error Frameworks for Found Data

Paul P. Biemer and Ashley Amaya

RTI International, Research Triangle Park, NC, USA

4.1 Introduction

The survey world is relying more heavily on "found" data for inference and decision-making rather than survey or "designed" data. Found data are those not primarily collected for statistical purposes, but rather contain information that might be useful for inference or to gain insights about a population or phenomenon. For example, administrative data are a type of found data from systems that register persons or other entities, record transactions, and other information for later retrieval, track participants, and so on. Big Data refers to data of extreme volume, variety, and velocity, often unstructured and created from system "exhaust" with no particular purpose other than data preservation. These data become found data when they are used to achieve some analytic purpose through data mining or analysis. National statistical offices such as Statistics New Zealand (https://www.stats.govt.nz/integrated-data/integrated-data-infrastructure), Central Bureau of Statistics in The Netherlands (https://www.cbs.nl/en-gb/our-services/unique-collaboration-for-big-data-research), the Office of National Statistics in the United Kingdom (Duhaney 2017), and Statistics Canada (StatCan; Rancourt 2017) have established program areas devoted to the discovery of statistical uses of found for official statistics. For example, at StatCan, integrating administrative data into the official statistics program has become a central focus. These national statistical offices understand that administrative data can enhance relevance, reduce respondent burden, increase efficiency,

---

Big Data Meets Survey Science: A Collection of Innovative Methods, First Edition. Edited by Craig A. Hill, Paul P. Biemer, Trent D. Buskirk, Lilli Japec, Antje Kirchner, Stas Kolenikov, and Lars E. Lyberg.
© 2021 John Wiley & Sons, Inc. Published 2021 by John Wiley & Sons, Inc.

and produce more timely and detailed statistics. In Europe, particularly the Nordic countries, population registers serve both administrative and statistical purposes, so these countries are also quite familiar with the concept of employing found data in official statistics. The integrated-data movement throughout the government sector mirrors similar activities taking place in private and academic survey organizations across the world.

Social scientists once considered sample survey data to be the gold standard for research data, but no longer regard them so highly as a result of errors that have increasingly plagued the methodology. These errors include frame deficiencies, increasing nonresponse, and item missing data rates, and measurement errors (Citro 2014). As these problems have increased for surveys, data producers are beginning to view alternative data sources, like administrative records and Big Data, as reasonable alternatives to surveys. Besides saving costs, data quality for these alternative sources may compare well with survey data and, in some cases, may exceed current survey quality. The main deficiency with such sources is that the data-generating mechanism is unknown and likely depends on the very data it is generating (Spiegelhalter 2014). Thus, the usual assumptions for statistical inference do not apply. However, when combined with survey data, nonsurvey data sources can overcome this deficiency so they can be used to address some of the data quality issues in survey data.

Today, the search is on for ways to integrate nontraditional data sources such as administrative records, transactional data, social media data, and other found data with survey data to produce so-called hybrid estimates that have improved costs, quality, and timeliness compared with estimates derived from a single source.

This chapter focuses on the accuracy of data produced by integrating two or more datasets, particularly when one dataset is from a survey and the other may be created purely for administrative purposes or is otherwise obtained from non-survey methods. The next section considers the data integration process as well as the process by which (hybrid) estimates are derived from integrated datasets. Section 4.3 provides an error framework for evaluating the quality of the integrated dataset itself, and Section 4.4 focuses on a related error framework that can be applied to the hybrid estimate produced from such a dataset. Finally, Section 4.6 provides a summary and a conclusion.

4.2 Data Integration and Estimation

The literature and this volume in particular provide examples of combining a survey and a found dataset so that both datasets contribute directly to the statistical outputs (see, for example Künn (2015) for a comprehensive review as well as Chapters 5–8). Thus, the flow diagram in Figure 4.1 depicts the essential

Figure 4.1 Flow diagram of a simple hybrid estimation process.

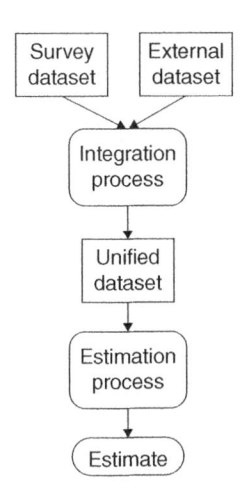

```
Survey dataset    External dataset
        ↓             ↓
      Integration process
            ↓
       Unified dataset
            ↓
      Estimation process
            ↓
         Estimate
```

steps in integrating a survey dataset with an external dataset to produce a so-called hybrid estimate (because it is a blend of disparate datasets). Although only two source datasets are shown, the process can be generalized for any number of datasets. Step 1 is to identify the source datasets that will be unified or integrated in some way. In addition, generalizing the process for generic (probability or nonprobability) datasets is straightforward. Once the datasets are assembled and prepared, the integration process proceeds. As we describe later, this process may involve linking and merging records based upon common variables or simply aligning the data fields and concatenating data files. Integration could also involve statistical modeling where cells of one or both datasets are imputed or entire records are synthesized. Limitations on integration methods that are within the scope of the methodology to follow will become evident when the methodology is described.

4.2.1 Source Datasets

Survey datasets have been traditionally generated from probability samples from a well-defined target population. They have relatively small sample sizes (megabytes of data as compared to gigabytes or more for Big Data), low response rates (e.g. 60% is considered a high response rate for general populations surveys), and high relevance for researchers because of their flexibility and customizable content. A 60-minute survey interview can generate data on hundreds of variables covering many topics. Surveys based upon random samples can easily be generalized to the target population, although selection biases introduced by nonresponse and frame noncoverage can invalidate inferences if not properly addressed in the design and estimation process. Nevertheless, survey datasets have strong population representativity that can be used to full potential when integrated with nonprobability samples.

Administrative datasets are common in many private, academic, and government organizations for recording data on their program participants, employees, students, affiliates, members registrants, transactions, and so on, primarily for administrative uses. Data contained in administrate datasets include driver's licenses issued, federal taxes paid, medical transactions, and expenditures, births and deaths, and membership lists of professional organizations. Survey practitioners are well aware of the value of administrative records for adjusting survey weights for coverage error, evaluating survey data quality, constructing sampling frames, and adding variables to survey records that can be more conveniently and, often, more accurately obtained from administrative data sources. However, administrative records are often subject to specification error – i.e. the constructs represented by the administrative data may not align well with the construct required for research. For example, the tax record income may be household income, while personal income is required for the application.

Several new data sources have high potential for adding value to traditional, probability survey data. These include Internet panel survey data (e.g. nonprobability panels, opt-in or volunteer panels, proprietary panels), social media data (e.g. Twitter Tweets, LinkedIn postings, and Facebook data), transaction records (e.g. Google searches, loyalty card grocery purchases, and credit card data), and sensor and image data (e.g. traffic sensors, satellite imagery, and drone sensors). Nonprobability Internet panel surveys, social media data, and transaction records all suffer from a common limitation – poor and ill-defined representativity. The populations represented by these datasets are necessarily limited to persons having Internet access, which, for the United States, eliminates about 5% of the general population (see, for example Statistica (2019)). In addition, the process for recruiting sample members is determined by self-selection, which may be highly related to the outcomes being measured. As we discuss later, a selection process that differentially recruits sample members using a mechanism related to their personal characteristics may result in estimation bias.

In addition to errors from sample recruitment, the data contents themselves may have high levels of error. While so-called content errors are a universal problem for all types of data, unstructured data from such social media, sensors, and images are particularly at risk. Unstructured data must be transformed into data records with well-defined features (or characteristics) to be analyzed and/or integrated with other structured data. This data encoding process creates analyzable data elements from bits and pieces of information embedded in a mass of data fragments (e.g. Tweets and pixels). Hsieh and Murphy (2017) describe the data encoding process in fine detail for Twitter data and study its error characteristics.

For the purposes of this chapter, we assume each dataset to be integrated can be represented by a rectangular data file with rows corresponding to population (or sample) units, columns corresponding to features (or variables), and cells containing alphanumeric data.

4.2.2 The Integration Process

Data integration is the process of combining or unifying two or more datasets to form a third dataset that is suitable for estimation and analysis. A common practice is to use one of the datasets to calculate weights for the other dataset. For example, control totals from administrative datasets have often been merged with survey datasets to calibrate the survey dataset. Likewise, survey datasets have been used to calculate propensity scores for opt-in online survey datasets (see, for example Valliant and Dever (2011)).

In cases where two data sources represent two distinct populations with the same data fields, the two data files might be simply concatenated to provide greater coverage for the resulting unified dataset. A problem arises when the populations represented by the datasets substantially overlap. In that case, concatenation is still possible; however, now it may be important to identify the population to which each member in the unified file belongs so that multiplicity counts can be assigned and the units in the unified dataset can be properly weighted.

Sometimes the survey dataset is augmented through linking individual records from the external dataset. This requires methods for uniquely identifying the same individuals in each file. Even when exact matching is not possible, models built on one data source can be used to impute variables for the other data source. A related approach is statistical matching (see, for example D'Orazio et al. (2006)), which appends data fields from one source to records in the other source that match on a set of common characteristics.

4.2.3 Unified Dataset

In its most general form, the format of a found dataset will not conform to the traditional, rectangular file with rows, columns, and cells. Multiple files of varying structures and formats are possible and commonplace. Indeed, for analyzing massive datasets of a terabyte or more, a single computer may not hold all the data. But, as noted in Japec et al. (2015), most researchers and all statistical software packages assume the data are structured as rows and columns. Therefore, we shall assume that both the input and output datasets to the integration process are rectangular, with rows representing the units in the sample or population and columns representing features or characteristics of those units. Section 4.3 summarizes the errors associated with generic datasets, including unified datasets.

4.3 Errors in Datasets

As noted in last section, errors in an integrated dataset can have many and varied root causes. First, each input dataset has its own inherent errors, which may include missing data, content error, and specification error. The magnitudes of these errors may vary across inputs, and their root causes depend on the methodologies used to generate and process the data. The process of integrating the inputs into a single dataset can create additional errors. For example, the record linkage process may fail to link records for the same unit or erroneously link records from two different units. Likewise, during the harmonization process, variables that measure the same construct are created and merged. However, variables that are labeled as measuring the same construct may actually measure different constructs and, thus, specification error can occur. The integration process may also involve imputing missing data elements that are imperfect representation of the unit true characteristics.

Figure 4.2 depicts a typical dataset as an array of N rows and p columns. Both single-source and integrated, multiple-source datasets can be represented by this structure, at least conceptually if not physically. As described in Japec et al. (2015), even datasets that may reside in hierarchical or federated data structures are often reformatted as rectangular files to conform to the input requirements of almost all major statistical software packages. Typically, the rows in the dataset correspond to a subset of units in a well-defined target population, columns correspond to characteristics or variables of the population units and cells contains the values of the column variables for row units.

As described in Biemer (2016), a key concept describing the errors in an integrated dataset is the so-called row/column/cell model. This model states that, regardless of the root causes of the errors, be they inherent in the inputs files or created during the integration process, all errors in a dataset can be categorized into only three types: row error, column error, or cell error. Thus, a simple

Record #	V_1	V_2	....	V_p
1				
2				
...				
N				

Figure 4.2 Generic dataset with n records and p variables.

expression for the total error (TE) for a dataset is given by the following heuristic formula:

Total error = Row error + Column error + Cell error

That is, all error in the dataset must relate to the rows, columns, or cells. Next, we consider the subcomponents of each of these three major error components.

Row error: The first step for traditional inference is usually defining the target population to which inferences will be made, which can be exceedingly difficult for found datasets. For example, what target population is implied by a Twitter data set, respondents to a volunteer web survey, or the grocery store shoppers who scanned their loyalty cards upon checkout in a given month? Yet, defining the target population in an analysis is essential for defining possibly the most egregious errors that can afflict a dataset – namely, row errors.

Three types of errors may be attributed to row error: omissions, duplications, and erroneous inclusions. Omissions mean that some rows are missing and, thus, some units in the target population are not represented in the dataset. For survey datasets, omissions include population units that are either inadvertently or deliberately absent from the sampling frame as well nonsampled frame units and sample unit nonrespondents. For nonprobability datasets, omissions include all members of the target population who do not occupy at least one row in the dataset and may depend upon the selectivity of the sample recruitment or data encoding process. For example, some online surveys invite participation from whomever sees the survey invitation online. Thus, persons not seeing the invitation as well as persons who do see it, but then decline the invitation, should be considered as omission errors when making inferences from this dataset to more broadly defined populations such as all Internet users. The integration process may combine the rows across the multiple inputs in the hope that the resulting integrated dataset covers a greater proportion of the target population. However, target population units that are not in any input file will remaining missing. In addition, the integration process may create duplicate rows.

Duplications occur when two or more rows of the dataset correspond to the same population unit. Undetected, duplications present in the input datasets will carry forward to the integrated dataset. For example, a dataset containing Google searches during some prior week may have the same person represented multiple times. People who conducted many searches during the sample recruitment period would be disproportionately represented relative to those who conducted fewer searchers. Whether such duplications should be regarded as errors depends upon the goals of the analysis. For example, if the goal is to characterize Google searches during the recruitment week, having multiple searches per Google searcher may be valid. But if the goal is to characterize the Google searchers for that week, then allowing duplicate searches per person (without appropriately weighting the data to compensate for duplications) may be biasing.

Erroneous inclusions (also called overcoverage errors) occur when some rows correspond to units or entities that are not part of the target population. For example, Google searches or Tweets may not be generated by a person, but rather by a computer either maliciously or as part of an information-gathering or publicity-generating routine. Likewise, some rows may not satisfy the criteria for inclusion in an analysis – for example, an analysis by age or gender may include some row elements that do not satisfy the criteria. If the criteria can be applied accurately, the rows violating the criteria can be excluded prior to analysis. Otherwise, if some out-of-scope elements are included in the estimates, biased inferences will result. An integrated dataset will contain erroneous inclusions if these errors exist in the input files and are not corrected in the integration process.

Column error: The most common type of column error in survey data analysis is caused by inaccurate or erroneous labeling of the column data – an example of metadata error. In the total survey error (TSE) framework, this is referred to as a *specification* error. For example, a business register may include a column labeled "number of employees" defined as the number of persons in the company who received a paycheck in the preceding month. Instead, the column may contain the number of persons on the payroll whether or not they received a check in the prior month, thus including, for example, persons on leave without pay. For many types of external datasets, such errors would seem to be common because of the complexities involved in producing a dataset.

As noted above, data harmonization is often an important step in data integration. Specification errors in the input files often remain after integration. In addition, new specification errors can arise when variables purported to measure the constructs of interest are derived during data integration using other variables in the input files. For example, the variable "number of rooms" for a set of housing units obtained from an online database may use a definition for a "room" that is quite different from the official (say, Census Bureau) definition, where the latter definition is used to interpret the variable.

Cell errors: Content error and missing data are two types of cell errors. A content error occurs when the value in a cell satisfies the column definition but still deviates from the true value, whether or not the true value is known. Content errors may result from the measurement process, data processing (e.g. keying, coding, and editing), record linkage error (e.g. linking record units that are not the same and should not be linked), logic or statistical modeling (e.g. imputation, extrapolation/interpolation, and derived values), or some other cause. For example, a cell value may satisfy the definition of "number of employees," but the value may be outdated and not agree with the current number of employees.

Finally, missing data, as the term implies, is just an empty cell that should have a value. One cause of missing data specific to integrated data arises when two datasets with different variables are concatenated. For example, consider an integrated dataset, formed by concatenating a survey dataset, whose sampling frame consists of survey nonrespondents and nonsampled population members. The nonsampled population in the frame will have missing values for the items collected in the survey. As described in Kreuter and Peng (2014), datasets derived from Big Data are notoriously affected by both types of cell errors, particularly missing or incomplete data. Missing data is the most obvious deficiency since content errors are often undetectable in a dataset.

The dataset error framework can be applied to essentially any dataset that conforms to the format in Figure 4.1. However, the price of its generality is the limitation that it makes no attempt to describe how the processes that generated the data may have contributed to what could be construed as data errors. In many practical situations, these processes constitute a "black box" and the only option is to simply evaluate the quality of the end product with no ability to link the data errors to their root causes.

For survey data, the TSE framework provides a fairly complete description of the error-generating processes for survey data and survey frames (see, for example Biemer (2016)). In addition, these processes for population registers and register-based surveys and censuses have been described in the literature (Wallgren and Wallgren 2007). Zhang (2012), whose research is discussed in detail later in this chapter, also contributed some important ideas to the concept of TE of register data and data generated from integrating registers and other administrative datasets. At this writing, however, little effort has been devoted to enumerating the error sources and the error-generating processes that affect Big Data.

4.4 Errors in Hybrid Estimates

4.4.1 Error-Generating Processes

As with most existing error frameworks for estimation, the simplest way to illustrate the basic ideas is to consider the estimation of the target population mean using the sample or dataset mean. This section considers the TE of estimates of the population mean, denoted by $\overline{X} = \sum_1^N X_j$, of a population consisting of N units. Since the rows correspond to units in the population, the sample constitutes the recruited and observed sample from the population. This sample may be randomly selected or nonrandomly recruited by essentially any process, passive, or active, externally selected or self-selected. The focus of this examination of TE is to consider how errors that may occur in the estimation process affect inferences about $\overline{X}$.

For a given variable (column) in the dataset, two sample averages can be defined: the average of the n observations in the dataset, given by $\bar{y} = \sum_1^n y_i/n$, and the average of the constructs those observations are intended to represent, given by $\bar{x} = \sum_1^n x_i/n$. In the first average, y_i denotes the observation on the ith unit that may be subject to specification error, measurement error, and data processing error. For the second average, x_i denotes the true value of the unit for the intended construct.

For example, a well-known problem in the measurement of imports and exports is the assessment of the "statistical value" of an import, which includes shipping costs from a shipment's origin to its destination, excluding the costs of shipping within the destination country's borders. Unfortunately, the only known shipping cost for a shipment is the "invoice value," which does not separate out these within-border shipping costs. Consequently, invoice value is taken as the statistical value even though they are clearly different constructs. To obtain valid measures of gross domestic product (GDP), national accountants must then somehow adjust the invoice values for these shipping costs that should be excluded. In this example, $\bar{y}$ is the average value of imports using invoice values and $\bar{x}$ is an analogous average but based instead on statistical values.

Consistent with the TSE framework (see, for example, Biemer and Lyberg (2003)), the TE of $\bar{y}$ as an estimator of $\bar{X}$ is just the difference $\bar{y} - \bar{X}$. The TSE framework decomposes this difference into small and then smaller components, where each component can be associated with either some aspect of the data collection or estimation process or an error that may arise from these processes. However, the TSE framework is too specialized for general hybrid estimation in that it focuses solely on activities, processes, and errors that are primarily survey related. Here, we generalize the TSE framework so that it is more applicable to generic estimators, which may be hybrid or traditional single-source estimates.

The simplest decomposition of TE involves only two subcomponents: the data encoding error (DEE) and the sample recruitment error (SRE). DEE is a generalization of the concept of "errors of observation" (Groves 2004). It is a catch-all term for the combined error due to specification error, measurement error, and data processing error. Likewise, SRE is a generalization of the concept of errors of nonobservation (Groves 2004). It is a catch-all term for several error components: coverage error, sampling error, and nonresponse/missing data. Thus, the TE in the sample mean can be written as

$$\text{TE} = \text{DEE} + \text{SRE} \tag{4.1}$$

which essentially means the TE in an estimate is a function of what is in the dataset (DEE) plus what is not in the dataset (SRE). Letting DEE = $(\bar{y} - \bar{x})$ and SRE = $\bar{x} - \bar{X}$ leads to the equation

$$\bar{y} - \bar{X} = (\bar{y} - \bar{x}) + (\bar{x} - \bar{X}) \tag{4.2}$$

Decomposing both DEE and SRE further into mutually exclusive and exhaustive subcomponents is often desirable for several reasons. First, knowing the causes of DEE, SRE, or both are valuable and such decompositions allow us to better identify the root causes of the errors. Decompositions can also aid in the estimation of TE if they are aligned with the subprocesses embedded in the data encoding and sample recruitment processes. In addition, decompositions to smaller error components can facilitate error mitigation, often the ultimate goal of the error evaluation. Next, we discuss some of the subcomponents contained in the DEE and SRE terms.

Figure 4.3 is a flow diagram of a generic sample recruitment process. The recruitment process may be either active – that is, population members are sampled, contacted, and requested to complete a questionnaire or otherwise encode their data – or passive – that is, the data may be collected incidentally with the active involvement of the population member. An example of an active process is a sample survey, while a passive process could be a traffic sensor that collects data on vehicles as they pass a collection point. Note that Figure 4.3 suggests the process begins with a well-defined target population. While this is true for most designed data collections, it may not be true for found datasets for which the definition of the target population may be decided much later, for example, after the data have been collected and some use for it has been determined. However, modifications of chronological ordering of the recruitment events will not alter the error structure of the process.

There are essentially four "gates" or decision points toward the actual encoding of a value for a population unit: (i) having a nonzero probability of encountering the recruitment activity, (ii) actually encountering the recruitment activity, (iii) receiving a stimulus for data input, and (iv) responding to that stimulus by

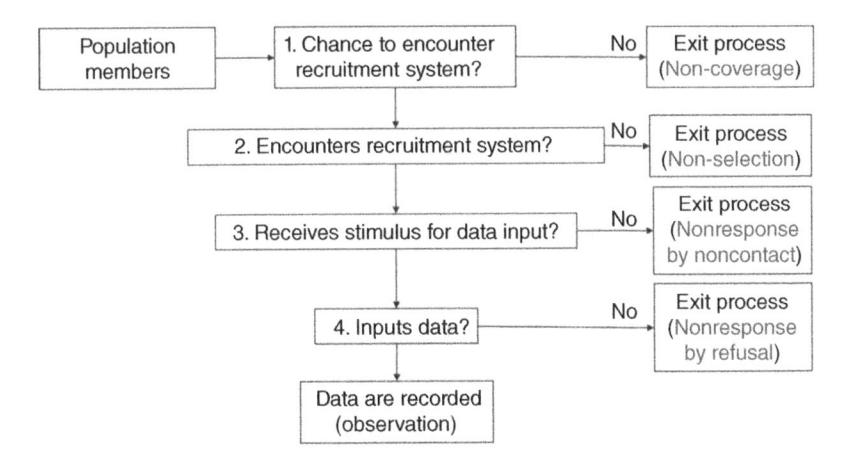

Figure 4.3 Sample recruitment process.

encoding a value for X. A noncoverage error occurs when a population unit fails to pass through gate 1. For example, the unit is not listed on the sampling frame for a survey, does not have access to a computer in the case of an online survey, or does not own a credit card in the case of a credit card transaction file. A nonselection occurs when population units with a positive probability of encountering the recruitment system do not encounter it. For surveys, these may be units on the frame that are not sampled. For nonprobability datasets, these may be units with miss encounters with the system by chance or circumstances; for example a person with access to a computer does not visit the website associated with the online survey and, thus, never receives an invitation to participate. For a database of credit card transactions, the individual owns a credit card but did not use it. Gate 3 refers to a situation where, although one or more stimuli for data encoding is triggered by the sample recruitment system, the population member fails to receive the stimuli. Survey noncontacts are a form of nonresponse that results from the failure to pass gate 3. However, this could also happen in passive data collections such as satellite imagery where data may be missing due to cloud cover or other obstructions. Finally, the population unit receiving the stimuli to encode data may choose not to comply, which is a failure at gate 4. This source of missing data primarily affects active data collection systems.

Of course, for some populations and sample recruitment systems, not all four gates will apply. For our TE model development, for those gates that are applicable, data are only encoded when all applicable gates are passed.

Given that a population unit has been recruited into the sample, a value, y, for the variable, X, must be recorded or encoded by the data collection system, which generates a value for the record in the dataset corresponding to that unit. Figure 4.4 describes the key error components for the data encoding process: specification error, measurement error, and data processing error. Specification

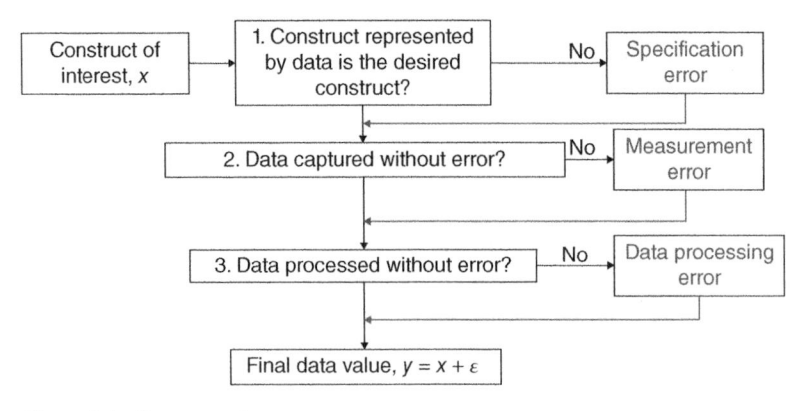

Figure 4.4 Data encoding process.

error was defined previously as column error in the dataset error framework. However, this error may also carry forward to the estimation process unless it is mitigated somehow. As previously noted, specification error arises when the construct represented by the encoded data value, y, differs from the desired construct, x – the construct that data analysts and other users require to meet their analytical objectives. Measurement error, which is often confused with specification error, is a form of cell error (described previously for the dataset framework) where the encoded value differs from the true value of the construct. For example, suppose X is defined as the annual personal income for the recruited person. A measurement error occurs when an individual only roughly estimates his or her personal income and this reported value differs from the person's actual income.

Finally, data processing error results from editing, coding, record linkage, and other data processing activities. For example to correct for specification error, some adjustments might be made to the value of y so that it better represents the construct x. In the situation described earlier of statistical value vs. invoice value for imports, the invoice value can be corrected to reflect statistical value if an estimate of the shipping costs within the destination countries borders is available. In many statistical agencies, evaluation studies are conducted to estimate these within-country shipping costs to transform invoice values into statistical values. However, such corrections will create statistical adjustment errors (that may be assigned to the data processing error component) even while they are removing some of the specification error. The hope is that the residual errors in the corrected invoice values are closer to their true statistical values.

4.4.2 Components of Bias, Variance, and Mean Squared Error

In this section, we derive an expression for the total mean squared error (MSE) of the dataset mean, $\bar{y}$ as an estimate of $\overline{X}$. The MSE is defined as MSE = $E(\bar{y} - \overline{X})^2$, where the expectation is over both the data encoding and SRE-generating mechanisms. Using Eq. (4.1), MSE is rewritten as

$$E(\bar{y} - \overline{X})^2 = E(\bar{y} - \bar{x})^2 + E(\bar{x} - \overline{X})^2 + 2E(\bar{y} - \bar{x})(\bar{x} - \overline{X}) \tag{4.3}$$

In that expression, the MSE_{SRE} component is defined as

$$\text{MSE}_{\text{SRE}} = [E(\bar{x}_n - \overline{X}_N)^2 + E(\bar{y}_n - \bar{x}_n)(\bar{x}_n - \overline{X}_N)] \tag{4.4}$$

and the DEE component as

$$\text{MSE}_{\text{DEE}} = [E(\bar{y}_n - \bar{x}_n)^2 + E(\bar{y}_n - \bar{x}_n)(\bar{x}_n - \overline{X}_N)] \tag{4.5}$$

Note that in this formulation, the cross-product term in Eq. (4.3) is divided between the two components since it reflects both types of error. Next, we propose expressions for each of these two MSE components that will provide greater insights regarding what specifically drives the magnitude of each component. First, we consider MSE_{SRE}.

Define R_j as the sample recruitment (or "response") indicator, which takes the value 1 if the jth population member passes through all applicable gates in the sample recruitment flow diagram (Figure 4.3) and 0 otherwise. Bethlehem (1988) showed that the bias due to sample recruitment can be written as

$$E(\bar{x} - \bar{X}) = \frac{\text{Cov}(X_j, R_j)}{E(R_j)} \tag{4.6}$$

Meng (2018) further extended this result to derive the following similar formula for the bias,

$$E(\bar{x} - \bar{X}) = E_R(\rho_{RX})\sigma_X \sqrt{\frac{1-f}{f}} \tag{4.7}$$

where $\rho_{RX} = \text{Corr}(R_j, X_j)$, f is the sampling fraction n/N, and $E_R(\cdot)$ denotes expectation for the sample recruitment mechanism, which may be random or deterministic. For simple random sampling or any sample design that provides constant inclusions probabilities, the term $E_R(\rho_{RX})$ is 0 and thus the bias is also 0. Note also that the bias is a decreasing function of f as expected. Likewise, for small samples, even a small $E_R(\rho_{RX})$ can result in a large bias.

It follows from Eq. (4.7) that

$$E(\bar{x} - \bar{X})^2 = E_R(\rho_{RX}^2)\sigma_X^2 \frac{(1-f)}{f} \tag{4.8}$$

which, under the assumption of no DEE, is MSE_{SRE}. This equation essentially states that the MSE_{SRE} component is the product of the expected squared correlation between the in-data indicator, R, and the outcome variable, X, the population variance of the outcome variable, and a term that behaves like a finite population correction. For simple random sampling, $E_R(\rho_{RX}^2) = (N-1)^{-1}$ Eq. (4.8) simplifies to the textbook formula $(1 - n/N)S_X^2/n$.

Not much is known about the distribution of ρ_{RX} for nonprobability samples. It is likely to vary considerably from one dataset to the next, depending on the source, the type of data, and the recruitment mechanism operating for the data-generating process. For probability samples, more is known about ρ_{RX} because it has been studied extensively for decades. In addition, researchers generally will have more control over the magnitude of ρ_{RX} because more control can be exercised on who or what passes through gates 1–3. For example, gate 1 is controlled by the creation of a sampling frame, gate 2 by the sample design, and gate 3, to a large extent, by the data collection process. Note, however, respondents also have some control over gate 3, for example, by avoiding contact, and complete control over gate 4 by ultimately refusing to provide data once contact has been established. A number of studies have shown that the bias due to nonresponse may be small in sample surveys even though f in (4.7) is very small, say less than 1% (see, for example Groves et al. (2001)), which suggests that ρ_{RX} is also quite small for sample surveys.

For found data, researchers often have no control over all four gates and thus, the magnitude of ρ_{RX} is less predictable and may be considerably larger. Still, the methods for estimating ρ_{RX} for surveys can still be applied for other nonsurvey datasets. This will certainly require information on units in the population not in the dataset (i.e. units for which $R_j = 0$) and, consequently, the estimation of ρ_{RX} often is quite challenging, perhaps even more so than for survey data. Section 4.4 discusses methods for reducing the magnitude of ρ_{RX} that do not require knowledge of the magnitude.

This formulation of the MSE of a dataset mean is based upon weak assumptions about the sample recruitment mechanism – assumptions that are satisfied for virtually any dataset and variable within a dataset. Its generality makes it well-suited for describing the selection bias in found data, so we adopt it for our use in this chapter. However, Meng (2018) did not consider the errors associated with the data encoding process; thus, the component of the TE will be added to the MSE so that it is useful for describing and exploring the TE of an estimator.

To consider the DEE component, we adopt the traditional measurement error model $y_i = x_i + \varepsilon_i$ which assumes that the error, ε_i, is independently and identically distributed with mean B_ε and variance σ_ε^2. The data encoding bias is $E_\varepsilon(\bar{y} - \bar{x}) = B_\varepsilon$ and the variance is $\text{Var}_\varepsilon(\bar{y} - \bar{x}) = \sigma_\varepsilon^2/n$, where $E_\varepsilon(\cdot)$ and $\text{Var}_\varepsilon(\cdot)$ denote conditional expectation and variance, respectively, with respect to the error distribution given the sample (i.e. given $R_i = 1$). Thus,

$$E_\varepsilon(\bar{y} - \bar{x})^2 = B_\varepsilon^2 + \frac{\sigma_\varepsilon^2}{n} \tag{4.9}$$

Finally, the cross-product term in (4.3) is given by

$$E(\bar{y} - \bar{x})(\bar{x} - \bar{X}) = \sqrt{\frac{N-n}{n}} \sigma_X B_\varepsilon E_S(\rho_{RX}) \tag{4.10}$$

It, therefore, follows from (4.3) that

$$\text{MSE}(\bar{y}) = B_\varepsilon^2 + \frac{\sigma_\varepsilon^2}{n} + \frac{N-n}{n}\sigma_X^2 E_S(\rho_{RX}^2) + 2\sqrt{\frac{N-n}{n}}\sigma_X B_\varepsilon E_S(\rho_{RX}) \tag{4.11}$$

where

$$\text{MSE}_{SRE} = \frac{N-n}{n}\sigma_X^2 E_S(\rho_{RX}^2) + \sqrt{\frac{N-n}{n}}\sigma_X B_\varepsilon E_S(\rho_{RX}) \tag{4.12}$$

and

$$\text{MSE}_{DEE} = B_\varepsilon^2 + \frac{\sigma_\varepsilon^2}{n} + \sqrt{\frac{N-n}{n}}\sigma_X B_\varepsilon E_S(\rho_{RX}) \tag{4.13}$$

We can rewrite (5.11) in terms of the relative MSE, i.e. RelMSE = $\text{MSE}/\overline{X}^2$, as

$$\text{RelMSE}(\bar{y}) = \text{RB}_\varepsilon^2 + \frac{\text{CV}_X^2}{n}\left[\frac{1-\tau_y}{\tau_y} + (N-n)E_R(\rho_{RX}^2)\right]$$

$$+ 2\text{CV}_X \text{RB}_\varepsilon \sqrt{\frac{N-n}{n}} E_R(\rho_{RX}) \quad (4.14)$$

where $\text{RB}_\varepsilon = B_\varepsilon/\overline{X}$ is the relative bias, $\text{CV}_X = \sigma_X/\overline{X}$ is the coefficient of variation of $\bar{x}$, and $\tau = \sigma_X^2/(\sigma_X^2 + \sigma_\varepsilon^2)$ is the reliability ratio.

4.4.3 Illustrations

This section illustrates how these results for the total MSE can be used to answer the following question. Which is more accurate:

1) An estimate of the population average based upon an administrative dataset with almost 100 million records and over 80% coverage? or
2) A national survey estimate based upon a probability sample of 6000 respondents with a 45% response rate?

Many data users might choose option 1 because the size of the administrative dataset is almost 16 000 times the size of the survey dataset. However, as this illustration shows, option 1 may not be the better choice when the TE is considered. One option not considered in this illustration is some combination of options 1 and 2, that is, a hybrid estimate formed from integrating the survey and administrative datasets. Although that analysis has not been conducted, later we speculate on how the hybrid option might perform relative to options 1 and 2.

The data used for the illustration come from the 2015 Residential Energy Consumption Survey (RECS). RECS is an in-person computer-assisted personal interview (CAPI) survey of US households that collects energy characteristics, energy usage patterns, and household demographics. The Energy Information Agency (EIA) has conducted this survey since 1978 and most recently in 2015. The target variable in this illustration is housing unit square footage – a critical variable for household energy consumption modeling. We compare the MSEs of average housing unit square footage from the survey with the average based on square footage from a commercial real estate database.

In 2015, the RECS had a very low CAPI response rate as well as other issues in the field. So, about halfway through data collection, all incomplete CAPI cases were moved to the mail/web mode (EIA 2018). For this illustration, we use only data from the CAPI survey because this analysis requires both interviewer and respondent assessments of square footage, and interviewer assessments are not available for the 2015 mail/web component. The sample size for the 2015 RECS was around 12 750 housing units, yielding about 5700 completed interviews for a 45% response rate. Thus, our illustration assumes a sample size of $n = 6000$ and uses the estimates of relevant sample and nonsampling error estimated for the 2015 RECS.

For reasons discussed below, the quality of the square footage data collected from respondents is a concern. A better approach might be to rely on external sources for housing square footage. Several commercial databases are available that collect housing square footage data from US households, including Zillow, Acxiom, and CoreLogic. Of particular interest in this illustration is the Zillow data. Zillow obtains its data from county, municipal, and jurisdictional records. In addition, Zillow allows realtors and owners to edit these entries.

For the 2015 RECS, interviewers were trained in the proper methods for collecting and, if necessary, estimating the square footage of housing units. For the CAPI component, housing unit square footage was obtained from both the respondent and, with respondent consent, the interviewer who estimated the square footage from actual measurements of the housing unit. For this illustration, we considered the interviewer measurements (labeled "Official" in Figure 4.5) as the gold standard and estimated the error in the respondent and Zillow reports through direct comparisons with interview data for the same households. One finding from this analysis is that both respondent and Zillow reports are both negatively biased. Using the data in Figure 4.5, we calculated that the relative DEE bias for the respondent reports is −8.2% compared with −14% for the Zillow reports. We suspect that the Zillow reports may be more biased as a result of specification error due to differences in the definitions of what is to be included in the square footage calculations.

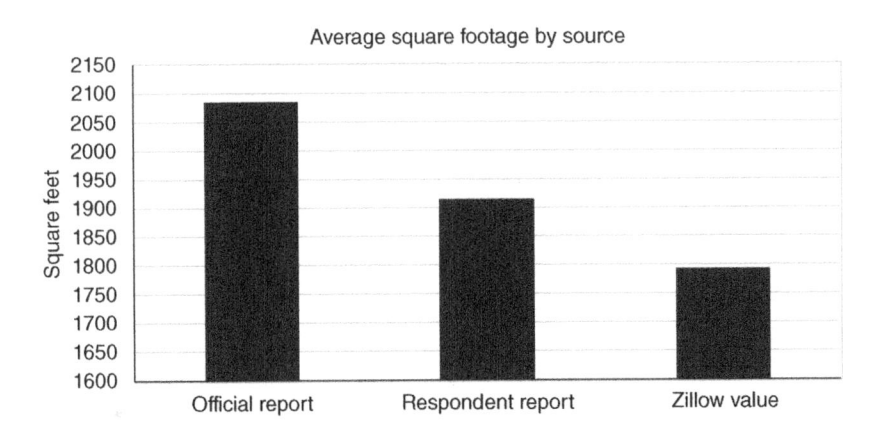

Figure 4.5 Residential energy consumption survey (RECS) average square footage by data source.

Linking and merging the RECS square footage data with the three external databases (namely, Zillow, Acxiom, and CoreLogic), EIA (2017) estimated the reliability and bias associated with respondent and each commercial source. These results for respondent and Zillow results are used in the following discussion.

Suppose a researcher wants to estimate the average square footage (using EIA's definition) of housing units in the United States. The researcher can choose to use the entire Zillow database, which contains about 120 million records but only covers about 82% of all housing units in the United States or a sample survey of $n = 6000$ completed interviews (45% response rate) but nearly full coverage of all US housing units. To ascertain which of these two approaches provides the most accurate estimate, we use some of the results from EIA (2017), which appear in Table 4.1.

Using the EIA (2017) estimated bias in the RECS due to nonresponse, the estimate of ρ_{RX} was obtained by the formula (Meng 2018):

$$\hat{\rho}_{RX} = \frac{\widehat{RB}_{SRE}}{CV_X \sqrt{(1-f)/f}} \tag{4.15}$$

where $\widehat{RB}_{SRE}$ is an estimate of the relative bias due to nonresponse. For the Zillow data, no information was available to estimate ρ_{RX}. However, using the results in Meng (2018), we can obtain a range of plausible estimates of ρ_{RX}. Thus, the plausible range of possible values that appears in Table 4.1 is used in our analysis.

Finally, note that $E_R(\rho_{RX}^2) = \text{Var}_R(\rho_{RX}^2) + E^2(\rho_{RX})$. Our illustration assumes that $\text{Var}_R(\rho_{RX}^2) = 0$ for simplicity. To gain some insights as to the impact of this assumption on the results to follow, we can use the well-known result that, for a bivariate normal distribution, $\text{Var}(\hat{\rho}) \approx \frac{(1-\rho^2)^2}{N}$ (see, for example Kendall and Stuart 1958,

Table 4.1 Parameters used for computing mean squared errors (MSEs) for survey and Zillow estimates of average housing unit square footage.

MSE component	Survey	Zillow
Relative bias (RB_ε)	−0.082	−0.14
Population coefficient of variation (CV_X)	0.64	0.64
Reliability (τ)	0.59	0.66
Selection correlation (ρ_{RX})	−0.000 295	[−0.27,0.22]
Population size (N)	118 208 250	118 208 250
Sample size (n)	6000	96 930 765
Response rate (%)	55.4	
Coverage rate (%)	≈99	
Selection rate (%)	0.009	82

p. 236), and thus $E(\hat{\rho}^2) \approx \rho^2 + \frac{(1-\rho^2)^2}{N}$. When this formula was used for $E_R(\rho_{RX}^2)$ rather than ρ_{RX}^2, the results of comparisons of the survey and Zillow relative mean squared errors (RelMSEs) defined as $\text{MSE}/\overline{X}^2$, did not change appreciably.

It is interesting to first consider the two MSEs assuming there is no error due to data encoding – that is, setting $RB_\varepsilon = \tau = 0$. Figure 4.6a shows these results. Clearly, the survey estimate has uniformly greater RelMSE over the entire feasible

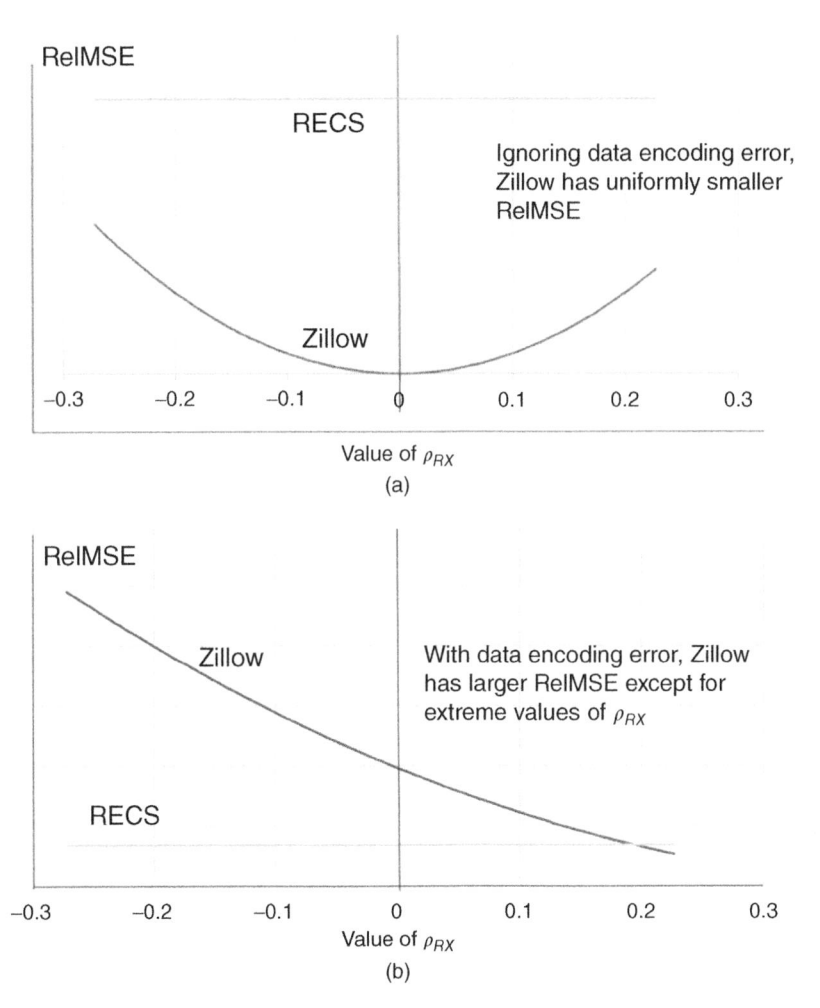

Figure 4.6 (a) RelMSE of survey and Zillow data for range of values for ρ_{RX} ignoring data encoding error. (b) RelMSE of survey and Zillow data for range of values for ρ_{RX} with data encoding error. (c) RelMSE of survey and Zillow data for range of values for ρ_{RX} showing DEE and SRE components separately.

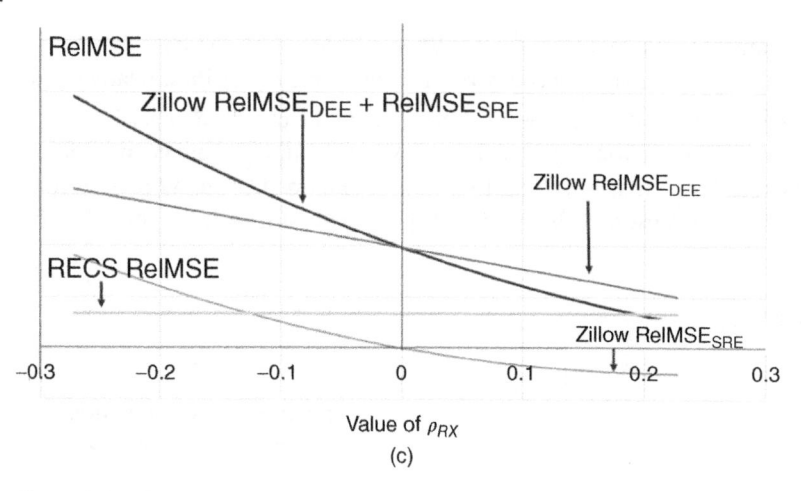

Figure 4.6 (Continued)

range of ρ_{RX} for Zillow data. This result is probably expected given that the Zillow sample size is almost 20 000 times larger than the survey. Figure 4.6b repeats the comparison, this time setting RB_ε and τ to the values in Table 4.1. Here the comparison changes dramatically. The RelMSE for Zillow is larger than its counterpart for the survey except for extreme, positive values of ρ_{RX}. In this comparison the Zillow MSE_{SRE} and MSE_{DEE} components have the same sign for lower values of ρ_{RX}, which causes the relative MSE to be large when ρ_{RX} is in this range. Note that when $\rho_{RX} = 0$, the RelMSE only reflects the DEE component. As ρ_{RX} increases, the MSE_{DEE} component is offset by the SRE component until, at approximately $\rho_{RX} = 0.2$, the two components offset one another to the point where the survey and Zillow MSEs are about equal. As ρ_{RX} increases further, the RelMSE for Zillow becomes smaller than its survey counterpart. This effect is clearly illustrated in Figure 4.6c, which plots the DEE and SRE components separately.

This illustration emphasizes the need for evaluating the TE in a comparison of estimates from alternate sources rather than just focusing on a subset of MSE components.

As noted above, a third, unevaluated option is a hybrid estimate based upon an integrated RECS and Zillow dataset. The methodology described by Tam et al. (see Chapter 11) seems ideally suited for these data because it addresses situations where the outcome variable is subject to both SRE and DEE. In their approach, data from Zillow is used to reduce the sample recruitment bias (primarily due to nonresponse) for the RECS, and the RECS interviewer data is used to reduce the data encoding bias in the Zillow data. Thus, both sources of error in the integrated data can possibly be mitigated by a hybrid approach to produce an estimate with better error properties than either single-source estimate. Error mitigation strategies for single-source estimates are described in Section 4.4.4.

Meng (2018) provides a second illustration of how the size of a Big Data dataset can be misleading, using data from the 2016 US presidential election. His illustration only considers the SRE – that is, no DEE. Combining all state and national election polls results yields a combined sample size of $n \approx 2\,315\,570$, for a sampling fraction of $f \approx 0.01$. From these data, the selection correlation in the pre-election vote share for candidate Donald Trump vs. Hillary Clinton can be estimated as $\hat{\rho}_{RX} = -0.005\,02$. A comparison of the resulting MSE of an estimate of the Trump vote share with that of a simple random sample (SRS) of size n_{SRS} suggests that the pre-election sample of over 2 million respondents yields the same accuracy as an SRS of $n_{SRS} = 400$ respondents. This assumes, of course, a perfect SRS. A question not addressed in this illustration is how the comparison might change should SRE (i.e. nonresponse) be introduced for the SRS sample and/or DEEs be introduced in both data collection processes. Meng's formulation does not consider the latter type of errors.

4.4.4 Error Mitigation

The Zillow example in the previous section illustrates the importance of TE analysis in comparing estimates from alternate data sources. However, it also illustrates an untenable situation when the accuracy of an estimation process is determined by two large components of error that may offset one another. The situation is untenable in that when error from one of the sources is reduced, the total MSE will increase, which defeats the purpose of error mitigation.

As an example, house sellers may tend to overestimate the square footage of their housing units for various reasons, not the least of which is to increase their unit's market value. Specification error may also be responsible for some positive bias in that Zillow's definition of square footage may differ from the official (EIA) definition, which may also tend in a positive direction (i.e. including areas in the calculus that EIA does not include). However, these positive encoding errors may be offset to some extent by selection errors in that larger housing units tend to be missed and, thus, the net bias is likely smaller. If square footage measurement was improved by, say, correcting the specification error, the magnitude of the net bias would effectively increase. Thus, a strategy of simultaneous mitigation of major sources is usually more desirable than one that focuses on a single source of error. This section briefly discusses some approaches for reducing the RelMSE of an estimator by reducing both the SRE and DEE components.

4.4.4.1 Sample Recruitment Error

As noted in the previous section, the size of the SRE component in the absence of encoding error depends upon three quantities: the sampling fraction (f), the variance of the population (σ_X^2), and the sample recruitment process correlation (ρ_{XR}). While the former two quantities are often known or can be readily estimated from the data, the latter parameter is seldom known and can be exceedingly difficult to estimate. Estimating ρ_{XR} is possible if data on both sampled and non-sampled population units can be used to model the recruitment mechanism (see, for example Chapter 11). One strategy for reducing the magnitude of ρ_{XR} for a given dataset is to weight the sample units by the inverse of their recruitment probabilities. However, Buelens et al. (2018) suggest that weighting may be less effective than machine learning methods at removing selection bias from found data. An important disadvantage of these methods is that they require data of sufficient quality to "train" the algorithms how to adjust for sample selectivity – data that are seldom unavailable in practical applications. Thus, in this section, we only consider the effects of weighting on the SRE component. The mitigation of DEE is discussed subsequently.

Let $\pi_j = \Pr(R_j = 1)$ denote the (unknown) recruitment probability (or response propensity) for the jth unit in the population. Meng (2018) notes that the weighted mean, $\bar{x}_w = \sum_{i \in s} \omega_i y_i / \sum_{i \in s} \omega_i$, where $\omega_i = \pi_i^{-1}$, will have zero bias. Meng provides an expression for the SRE component of the bias for some arbitrary w_i. Using his expression, the relative bias in the weighted mean is

$$\text{RB}_{\text{SRE}} = E_S(\rho_{Rw,X})\text{CV}_X\sqrt{\frac{1+\text{CV}_w^2-f}{f}} \qquad (4.16)$$

where $\rho_{Rw,X} = \text{Corr}(w_j R_j, x_j)$ and CV_w is the coefficient of variation of the weights. Note that when $w_i = \omega_i$, then $E(\rho_{Rw,X}) = 0$ and, thus, $B_{\text{SRE}} = 0$. However, given the difficulty of estimating ω_i in practice, B_{SRE} is seldom 0 but may be small provided that w_i is close to ω_i. An expression for the relative MSE of the weighted mean is given by

$$\text{RelMSE}_{\text{SRE}} = E_S(\rho_{Rw,X}^2)\text{CV}_X^2\left(\frac{1+\text{CV}_w^2-f}{f}\right) \qquad (4.17)$$

When $w_i = \omega_i$, this can be rewritten as $\text{Var}(\rho_{R\omega,X})\text{CV}_X^2\left(\frac{1+\text{CV}_\omega^2-f}{f}\right)$, which could still be large if the variation in the weights is large.

Much has been written regarding the consequences of error in the weights when the error is correlated with the outcome variable – an issue known as missingness not at random (MNAR; see, for example Little and Rubin 2002). However, not much has been written about uncorrelated errors in the weights. Such errors are common when the π_i's are estimated and subject to sampling errors and other random nonsampling errors.

Let $\delta_i = w_i - \omega_i$ and note that

$$\text{Cov}(R_j w_j, X_j) = \text{Cov}(R_j \omega_j, X_j) + \text{Cov}(R_j \delta_j, X_j) \qquad (4.18)$$

Thus, if the error, δ_j is uncorrelated with ω_j, we can write

$$\rho_{Rw,X} = \mathrm{Corr}(R_j\omega_j, X_j)\sqrt{\gamma_w} + \mathrm{Corr}(R_j\delta_j, X_j)\sqrt{1-\gamma_w} \tag{4.19}$$

which simplifies to

$$\rho_{Rw,X} = \rho_{R\delta,X}\sqrt{1-\gamma_w} \tag{4.20}$$

because $\mathrm{Corr}(R_j\omega_j, X_j) = 0$, where $\gamma_w = \frac{\mathrm{Var}(R_j\omega_j)}{\mathrm{Var}(R_jw_j)}$ is the reliability ratio of the weights. Note further that $\mathrm{CV}_w^2 = \mathrm{CV}_\omega^2(1-\gamma)^{-1}$ and therefore the relative bias in the sample recruitment process can be rewritten as

$$\mathrm{RB}_{\mathrm{SRE}} = E_S(\rho_{R\delta,X})\sqrt{1-\gamma}\sqrt{\frac{1+\mathrm{CV}_\omega^2/(1-\gamma)-f}{f}}\mathrm{CV}_X \tag{4.21}$$

where $\rho_{R\delta,X} = \mathrm{Corr}(R_j\delta_j, X_j)$. Again, the bias could be substantial if the weight variation is large, which will be the case if γ is small. Finally, the RelMSE in (4.17) can be rewritten by replacing $\rho_{Rw,X}$ in (4.17) with the expression in (4.19). However, rather than considering the analytical form of the RelMSE, greater insights can be obtained by simulating errors in the weights and then assessing the impact of the errors on the RelMSE.

Figure 4.7 shows some results from such a simulation. The simulations depicted in this figure all regard repeated sampling from a population of 10 000 units with X following a continuous distribution. The average RelMSEs of the sample mean from 1000 repetitions of the recruitment process is plotted on the y-axis. On the x-axis is the reliability of the weights, γ, which varies from about 0.18 to 0.95. The two curves in the figure represent the RelMSEs of nonprobability samples having sampling fractions of $f = 0.58$ for the upper curve and $f = 0.76$ for the lower curve.

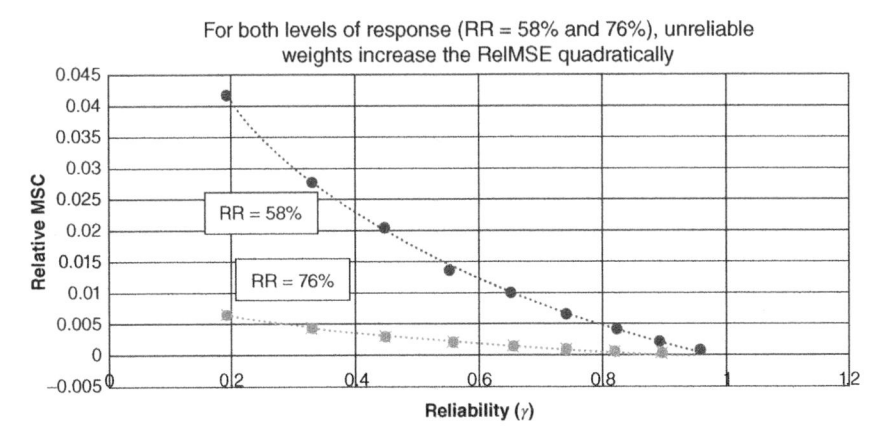

Figure 4.7 Effect of random errors in the weights on the relative mean squared error of the mean.

In all cases, recruitment selection was proportional to $\pi_j = [1+\exp(X)]^{-1}$, X was generated according to a gamma distribution with mean 36 000 and $CV_X = 1.8$, and the weight attached to the ith sample unit was computed as $w_i = \omega_i + \delta_i$ where $\omega_i = \pi_i^{-1}$, δ_i is sampled from a uniform distribution having 0 mean and variance, $\mathrm{Var}(\omega_j)/\gamma$.

Figure 4.7 suggests that the impact of random errors in the weighting process becomes more important for smaller sampling fractions. However, as the figure shows, the increase in the RelMSE from $\gamma = 0.3$ to 0.7 is approximately the same in both cases, that is, about 500%. These results suggest that random errors in the computation of adjustment weights can have a profound impact on the RelMSE. Even a small reduction in reliability can have a large multiplicative effect on the RelMSE.

4.4.4.2 Data Encoding Error

The survey science literature is rife with examples of how to reduce DEE through the reduction of its major components, namely specification error, measurement error, and data processing error (see, for example Biemer and Lyberg (2003), especially Chapter 8). Unfortunately, many of these approaches require modifications of the data collection approach, which, while they are applicable in design datasets, do not apply to found datasets. To the extent that the researcher introduces DEE in the data processing step, survey data processing error mitigation methods may be applicable. For example, several chapters in Biemer et al. (2017) discuss methods for mitigating data processing errors including editing, coding, and data linkage errors.

For Big Data analysis, the RECS example described an almost universally applicable, useful approach. It required determinations of X that could be considered highly accurate (for example the interviewer measurements of square footage). Then the DEE term, $\mathrm{DEE} = \bar{y} - \bar{x}$, and its contributions to the total MSE can be estimated directly. Likewise, this estimator of DEE also can be taken as an estimate of the bias, B_ε. Note, however, that the adjusting the estimator of $\overline{X}$ by $\widehat{B}_\varepsilon$ will increase its variance. Thus, in the final analysis, the MSE of the adjusted estimator of $\overline{X}$ may not be much reduced from the unadjusted estimator.

4.5 Other Error Frameworks

Three other error frameworks are noteworthy for their applicability to integrated microdata datasets produced by national statistical offices, especially the integration of population registers and other administrative data. These are the framework proposed by Zhang (2012), the extensions of that framework by Statistics New Zealand (2016) and Reid et al. (2017), and the framework proposed by Biemer

(2016), which covers generic datasets such as registers, frames, and administrative data, and estimators from surveys, as well as other probability samples and compilations such the GDP.

Zhang proposed a "two-phase life-cycle model of integrated statistical microdata," where Phase 1 describes the potential error sources for a single microdata source and Phase 2 depicts the sources of error, characterizing the integrated microdata, including transformations of the initial inputs so that the two sets of data can be harmonized to reduce specification errors. Zhang's Phase 1 framework is essentially the TSE framework produced by Groves et al. (2009) but with the error sources renamed to achieve greater generality and applicability. Similar to the framework in Section 4.4, both Groves and Zhang divide the data generation process into components for observation and nonobservation error and then define components such as specification, measurement, and data processing errors on the observation side and define frame, sampling, and nonresponse error on the nonobservation side. However, while the output of the Groves et al. (2009) framework is an estimate, the output of Zhang's Phase 1 is a dataset. In this way, it is comparable to the framework in Section 4.3.

As noted in Section 4.2, administrative data (such as a population register) often have to be combined with data from other sources before they can be used for a statistical purpose. Thus, Zhang takes the Groves and colleagues framework a step further in Phase 2 to produce an integrated microdata dataset as its end product. Zhang depicts the various steps in the data integration process and their associated error risks. On the "observation error" side of the dichotomy, he defines errors of relevance, mapping, and comparability and on the "nonobservation error" side, he defines errors of coverage, identification, and unit. Zhang's framework may be a useful vehicle for dissecting the data integration process to reveal the errors it generates. In this way, the integration errors can be both evaluated and mitigated.

Zhang's framework was recently adopted by Statistics New Zealand to maximize use of administrative data supplemented by survey data collection when needed (Holmberg and Bycroft 2017). In 2016, Statistics New Zealand (2016) issued a *Guide to Reporting on Administrative Data Quality*, which uses Zhang's framework to provide an elaborate system of quality indicators for both Phases 1 and 2 that should be reported for integrated datasets.

Reid et al. (2017) extended Zhang's framework by adding a third phase, which can be used for assessing the quality of estimates. Thus, Reid and colleagues' Phase 3 is directly comparable to the framework in Section 4.3 of this chapter. However, Reid et al. incorporate specific error components for the possible application of complex models, including postintegration statistical adjustments. In this sense, Reid and colleagues aim for greater generality in the types of errors considered, much like the framework developed in Biemer (2016), except focused on integrated data.

Reid and colleagues present several case studies that were used to test and further develop the three-phase framework. These studies illustrate different approaches for evaluating the quality of estimates derived from integrated data. One study examined the redesign of New Zealand's Building Activity Survey where a sample survey component was replaced with a model based upon building permits. Another example compared household survey personal income measures with comparable data from tax records. A third example examined the accuracy of an administrative population census using linked administrative sources with linkage error.

Finally, Biemer (2016) combines the row/column/cell framework with the framework proposed by Groves et al. (2009) for survey estimators. The framework is illustrated on nine of Statistics Sweden's most critical statistical products using a system for scoring overall data quality called ASPIRE, which stands for *A System for Product Improvement, Review, and Evaluation*. In addition, the authors illustrate how their general approach can be extended to statistical products that are integrations or compilations of many diverse data sources using Statistics Sweden's GDP program as an illustration.

4.6 Summary and Conclusions

For many data scientists and analysts, TE is not a familiar concept. Sampling error has been the traditional foe of statistical inference, and the massive datasets available today seem to provide a ready solution to that problem. However, while they may be less apparent, nonsampling errors may limit statistical inference to the same extent as a small sample size would. For example, Meng's example from Section 4.3 illustrates how SRE can reduce the information of a sample of more than 2 million respondents to the equivalent of a random sample of only 400 respondents, even before other types of nonsampling errors are considered. Some analysts are aware of the debilitating effects of missing data but may not be aware of other, less obvious sources of uncertainty such as measurement errors, data linkage errors, editing errors, and specification errors. An important benefit of a TE framework is that it focuses attention on these less apparent errors and may prompt data providers and users to consider the implications of nonsampling errors for the range of applications envisioned for the dataset.

Fortunately, a number of frameworks are available for evaluating data quality, and new frameworks can be readily customized for any particular use. The simple row/column/cell framework described in Section 4.3 is a convenient starting point for describing the error in a dataset, be it from found or designed data. It simply enumerates the various kinds of errors that might affect the rows, columns, or cells of a typical rectangular dataset. The more elaborate framework proposed by Zhang

(2012) and extended by Reid et al. (2017) digs deeper into the construction of the datasets and defined error components in the integration, linkage, and harmonization processes. These frameworks are useful for tracing the origins or causes of the errors in the current data, which is important for improving the data generation, preparation, integration, and estimation processes. While their frameworks were developed explicitly for registers, their approaches for describing the error in the integration and estimation processes are more general and can usually be adapted to the situation at hand.

For estimation, the frameworks proposed by Groves et al. (2009) and Biemer et al. (2014) seek to decompose the MSE of the sample mean into components that align somewhat with the row/column/cell errors but may also include errors in weighting, imputation, calibration, statistical adjustments, and other types of modeling errors. Meng's (2018) formulation of the MSE does not require that the units in the dataset be randomly selected; rather, the selection mechanism may be solely due to the process of sample recruitment. However, Meng's framework is limited because it ignores measurement errors and other DEEs. This chapter incorporates those errors to formulate an expression for the TE of a dataset mean. We illustrated this approach using housing unit square footage data from the Zillow website and the RECS survey. This example emphasizes the importance of considering all error sources when comparing the quality of alternative estimates, particularly estimates based upon different datasets, or when comparing estimates from integrated vs. single-source datasets.

The survey field has entered a new era, one where nonprobability samples are equated to probability samples in their quality and utility, while their cost disparities (in favor of the former) are emphasized. This does not mean the end of designed data in favor of found data because, despite its flaws, designed data can provide information unavailable in found data. In addition, the errors in both types of data can be better addressed by data integration rather than the exclusion of one in favor of the other. We can only conclude from this explosion of interest in found data that hybrid estimation is the future of survey research. As such, it is essential that researchers enter this new era with heightened awareness that data are inherently flawed and it is important to carefully consider these flaws in any application that may employ them.

Another key message from this work is that TE must be considered when evaluating alternative datasets, methods of data integration, and the construction of estimates. Focusing only on the size of the sample or whether the sample recruitment mechanism is known or unknown risks choosing greater inferential uncertainty rather than a nontraditional estimation approach having smaller MSE. While much has been done over the years to better understand the TE in datasets and estimators, more work still needs to be done, particularly in estimating error components or computing indicators of their magnitudes.

References

Bethlehem, J.G. (1988). Reduction of nonresponse bias through regression estimation. *Journal of Official Statistics* 4: 251–260.

Biemer, P.P. (2016). Errors and inference. In: *Big Data and Social Science: A Practical Guide to Methods and Tools* (eds. I. Foster, R. Ghani, R. Jarmin, et al.), Chp. 10, 265–298. Boca Raton, FL: CRC Press.

Biemer, P.P. and Lyberg, L. (2003). *Introduction to Survey Quality*. Hoboken, NJ: Wiley.

Biemer, P., Trewin, D., Bergdahl, H. et al. (2014). A system for managing the quality of official statistics. *Journal of Official Statistics* 30 (3): 381–415. https://doi.org/10.2478/JOS-2014-0022.

Biemer, P.P., de Leeuw, E., Eckman, S. et al. (eds.) (2017). *Total Survey Error in Practice*. (Wiley Series in Survey Methodology). Hoboken, NJ: Wiley.

Buelens, B., Burger, J., and van den Brakel, J.A. (2018). Comparing inference methods for non-probability samples. *International Statistical Review* 86 (2): 322–343. https://doi.org/10.1111/insr.12253.

Citro, C.F. (2014). From multiple modes for surveys to multiple data sources for estimates. *Survey Methodology* 40 (2): 137–161.

D'Orazio, M., Di Zio, M., and Scanu, M. (2006). *Statistical Matching: Theory and Practice*. Chichester, UK: Wiley.

Duhaney, D. (2017). Building capability and community through the Government Data Science Partnership. https://gds.blog.gov.uk/2017/07/20/building-capability-and-community-through-the-government-data-science-partnership.

Energy Information Administration (EIA). (2017). 2015 RECS square footage methodology. https://www.eia.gov/consumption/residential/reports/2015/squarefootage/pdf/2015_recs_squarefootage.pdf (Accessed 20 December 2018).

Energy Information Administration (EIA). (2018). Residential Energy Consumption Survey (RECS) 2015 consumption and expenditures technical documentation summary. https://www.eia.gov/consumption/residential/reports/2015/methodology/pdf/2015C&EMethodology.pdf (Accessed 20 December 2018).

Groves, R.M. (2004). *Survey Errors and Survey Costs*. Hoboken, NJ: Wiley https://doi.org/10.1002/0471725277.

Groves, R.M., Dillman, D.A., Eltinge, J.L. et al. (2001). *Survey Nonresponse*. Hoboken, NJ: Wiley.

Groves, R.M., Fowler, F.J. Jr.,, Couper, M. et al. (2009). *Survey Methodology*, Revisede. Hoboken, NJ: Wiley.

Holmberg, A. and Bycroft, C. (2017). Statistics New Zealand's approach to making use of alternative data sources in a new era of integrated data. In: *Total Survey Error in Practice* (eds. B.T. West, N.C. Tucker, L.E. Lyberg, et al.), Vol. 74. (Wiley Series in Survey Methodology). Hoboken, NJ: Wiley.

Hsieh, Y. and Murphy, J. (2017). Total twitter error: decomposing public opinion measurement on twitter from a total survey error perspective. In: *Total Survey Error in Practice* (eds. B.T. West, N.C. Tucker, L.E. Lyberg, et al.), Vol. 74, 23–46. (Wiley Series in Survey Methodology). Hoboken, NJ: Wiley.

Japec, L., Kreuter, F., Berg, M. et al. (2015). Big data in survey research. *Public Opinion Research* 79 (4): 839–880. https://doi.org/10.1093/poq/nfv039.

Kendall, M. and Stuart, A. (1958). *The Advanced Theory of Statistics, Volume 1. Distribution Theory*. London: Charles Griffin.

Kreuter, F. and Peng, R.D. (2014). Extracting information from big data: issues of measurement, inference and linkage. In: *Privacy, Big Data, and the Public Good: Frameworks for Engagement*, Chp, vol. 12 (ed. J. Lane), 257–275. New York: Cambridge University Press https://doi.org/10.1017/CBO9781107590205.016.

Künn, S. (2015). *The Challenges of Linking Survey and Administrative Data*. IZA World of Labor https://doi.org/10.15185/izawol.214.

Little, R. and Rubin, D. (2002). *Statistical Analysis with Missing Data*, 2e. Hoboken, NJ: Wiley.

Meng, X. (2018). Statistical paradises and paradoxes in big data (I): law of large populations, big data paradox, and the 2016 U.S. presidential election. *Annals of Applied Statistics* 12 (2): 685–726. https://doi.org/10.1214/18-AOAS1161SF.

Rancourt, E. (2017). Admin-first as a statistical paradigm for Canadian official statistics: meaning, challenges and opportunities. In: *Paper Presented at the Statistics Canada 2018 International Methodology Symposium, Ottawa, Canada*.

Reid, G., Zabala, F., and Holmberg, A. (2017). Extending TSE to administrative data: a quality framework and case studies from Stats NZ. *Journal of Official Statistics* 33 (2): 477–511. https://doi.org/10.1515/Jos-2017-0023.

Spiegelhalter, D.J. (2014). Statistics. The future lies in uncertainty. *Science* 345 (6194): 264–265. https://doi.org/10.1126/science.1251122.

Statistica (2019). *Leading Online Markets Based on Penetration Rate: 2019*. The Statistica Portal https://www.statista.com/statistics/227082/countries-with-the-highest-internet-penetration-rate.

Statistics New Zealand. (2016). Guide to reporting on administrative data quality. http://www.stats.govt.nz.

Valliant, R. and Dever, J.A. (2011). Estimating propensity adjustments for volunteer web surveys. *Sociological Methods & Research* 40 (1): 105–137. https://doi.org/10.1177/0049124110392533.

Wallgren, A. and Wallgren, B. (2007). *Register-Based Statistics: Administrative Data for Statistical Purposes*. Hoboken, NJ: Wiley.

Zhang, L.C. (2012). Topics of statistical theory for register-based statistics and data integration. *Statistica Neerlandica* 66 (1): 41–63. https://doi.org/10.1111/j.1467-9574.2011.00508.x.

5

Measuring the Strength of Attitudes in Social Media Data

Ashley Amaya[1], Ruben Bach[2], Frauke Kreuter[2,3,4], and Florian Keusch[2,3]

[1] RTI International, Research Triangle Park, NC, USA
[2] Department of Sociology, School of Social Science, University of Mannheim, Mannheim, Germany
[3] Joint Program in Survey Methodology, University of Maryland, College Park, MD, USA
[4] Institute for Employment Research, Nuremburg, Germany

5.1 Introduction

The amount of stored data is expected to double every two years for the next decade (Quartz 2015). The advances in social science research will be enormous even if only a fraction of these data can be used. Official statistics could be produced more quickly and less expensively than currently possible using surveys (Kitchin 2015). Big Data may also provide statistics for small areas to make informed policy and program decisions (Marchetti et al. 2015). Researchers have already begun to harness Big Data from social media for a variety of purposes, including research into disease prevalence, consumer confidence, and household characteristics (Butler 2013; O'Connor et al. 2010; Citro 2014).

In researchers' excitement to capitalize on Big Data, many have published papers in which they attempt to create point estimates from Big Data. Unfortunately, there are as many examples of biased estimates created from Big Data as there are success stories. For example, Twitter data has successfully been used to predict the 2010 UK, 2011 Italian, and 2012 French elections (Kalampokis et al. 2017; Ceron et al. 2014). However, Chung and Mustafaraj (2011) found Twitter to be an unreliable source to predict the 2010 US Senate special elections in Massachusetts while Gayo-Avello (2013) was unable to reproduce Ceron and colleagues' findings using similar data and methods. Similarly, in 2008, Google Flu Trends was touted as being able to successfully predict the number of individuals suffering from the flu (Ginsberg et al. 2009). However, in 2009 and again in 2013, this same data source severely misestimated flu prevalence (Butler 2013; Cook et al. 2011). In a final example, researchers have used Twitter

Big Data Meets Survey Science: A Collection of Innovative Methods, First Edition. Edited by Craig A. Hill, Paul P. Biemer, Trent D. Buskirk, Lilli Japec, Antje Kirchner, Stas Kolenikov, and Lars E. Lyberg.
© 2021 John Wiley & Sons, Inc. Published 2021 by John Wiley & Sons, Inc.

data to successfully measure and track change in consumer sentiment over time (O'Connor et al. 2010; Bollen, Mao, and Pepe 2011). However, these trends broke down after 2011 (Pasek et al. 2018; Conrad et al. 2020).

Each example of creating point estimates using Big Data, regardless of success, is useful in helping researchers think outside the box and find more creative ways to collect and analyze data. However, these types of papers are not generalizable. They use one type of Big Data to produce one estimate using one type of model. When Big Data can be manipulated to produce unbiased estimates, consideration is rarely given to why it worked. When the application fails to produce unbiased estimates, most researchers have limited their explanation of the failure to untestable hypotheses or specific reasons that are, once again, not generalizable to other applications.

It is critical to understand the underlying reasons for the successes and failures of different applications of Big Data to allow researchers more foresight into the ways in which Big Data may be used and the ways it may not (Japec et al. 2015). To this end, several researchers have developed theoretical frameworks that decompose error from Big Data sources into components. Frequently cited error components include (i) missingness when individuals do not subscribe to the given data source; (ii) inappropriate use of the data (i.e. the data were not intended for the researcher's purpose so may measure the researcher's preferred construct); and (iii) researcher's inaccurate modeling or coding (Baker 2017; Schober et al. 2016; Biemer 2016; Hsieh and Murphy 2017). However, these frameworks are mostly theoretical and have not been applied to actual applications to identify how much each of these errors is contributing to the overall error.

Another limitation of the existing literature is its focus on proportions, prevalence estimates, and other dichotomous outcomes (e.g. election outcomes and flu prevalence).[1] These data points are important in official statistics. However, researchers often depend on other types of data, such as scales used, to measure attitude strength. For example, dichotomous indicators are useful to predict the outcome of an election, but scales are useful to identify swing votes during the campaign. Similarly, sociologists depend on scales to identify the types of individuals who may be affected by a social intervention. Individuals who fall on the extreme ends of the spectrum are unlikely to be swayed by politicians or affected by a social intervention, whereas individuals who feel less strongly may be more likely to change their opinion (Dalege et al. 2017; Bos, Sheets, and Boomgaarden 2018; Doherty and Adler 2014). Therefore, it is important to accurately measure attitude strength and understand the potential for measurement error on such scales.

In this chapter, we extend the current literature by attempting to use social media data to produce similar attitude distributions as survey data. We then dive

---

1 An exception to this statement is the consumer sentiment analysis described above.

deeper into each distribution to determine the source of any observed dissimilarities. We use a combination of several datasets stemming from the European Social Survey (ESS) and Reddit to measure six scalar attitudes (political ideology, interest in politics, support for gay rights, support for the European Union [EU], views on immigration, and belief in climate change). Error was evaluated both overall, and by three commonly cited error components of Big Data: (i) missingness, (ii) measurement, and (iii) coding.

5.2 Methods

5.2.1 Data

To address our first objective, producing attitude distributions using social media data, we compared sentiment scores derived from Reddit comments and posts made between October 2016 and March 2017 to survey estimates from the 2016 German ESS. Reddit.com is the self-proclaimed "front page of the Internet." Registered users may post text, a link, images, or video onto any of thousands of subreddits (individual pages that cover a given topic, originally designed to be similar to a section of a newspaper). Other individuals may read, vote them up or down, or comment on the post. Although anyone may read Reddit content (to be sure, Reddit receives 14 billion screen views per month, worldwide [https://www.redditinc.com]), one must login with an anonymous username to participate (e.g. submit a post or comment).

The ESS is a repeating cross-sectional survey that measures attitudes on a host of topics in several countries throughout Europe. Six sentiments or attitudes were compared: political ideology, interest in politics, gay rights, the EU, immigration, and climate change. Unfortunately, the attitude distributions produced using the Reddit posts and comments were not comparable to those observed in the ESS data (details to follow), and we turned our attention to the second objective – understanding the cause of the difference.

To address the latter objective, we isolated error due to missingness, measurement error, and coding error. In this chapter, we define these terms broadly. Missingness refers to any individual or attitude missing from the dataset. This conflates two types of errors from the Total Survey Error (TSE) framework, undercoverage, and nonresponse, and we attempt to separate these two types of missingness in the analysis (Biemer and Amaya 2020; Groves and Lyberg 2010; Groves 2004). Measurement error includes any data that do not accurately represent the desired construct. Again, this conflates specification error and traditional measurement error from TSE. Unfortunately, we cannot parse these error components in this analysis. Finally, coding error includes bias introduced by researcher mishandling of the data such as including off-topic posts or assigning the incorrect sentiment score to the Reddit text data. This definition is similar to the TSE definition, although it is less common in survey research since much of the "coding" is done by the respondent (e.g. respondents provides their own sentiment score on a predefined scale).

To isolate the different error components, we conducted a series of comparisons using data from two additional data sources: (i) a 2018 nonprobability survey conducting using the Reddit platform, and (ii) one year of Reddit submissions made by 2018 Reddit Survey respondents. Throughout this chapter, we refer to the various datasets as the ESS, Reddit 2016, Reddit Survey, and Reddit 2018, respectively. In the rest of this section, we describe each data source and how each was used in the analysis.

5.2.1.1 European Social Survey Data

In Germany, the ESS was conducted using a stratified, two-stage probability sample of 9456 residents 15 years or older drawn from the local residents' registration offices' official registers. A total of 2852 German in-person interviews were conducted between 23 August 2016 and 26 March 2017 using the standard ESS questionnaire (AAPOR RR1 = 30.61%; European Social Survey 2016). In this chapter, we limited our analysis to interviews conducted with individuals 16 years and older ($n = 2829$) to be comparable to Reddit users (who are restricted to 16 and older in Germany [https://www.redditinc.com/policies/user-agreement]) and maximize comparability.

Although the ESS covers a host of topics, we limited our analysis to data from questions covering six areas: political ideology, interest in politics, gay rights, the EU, immigration, and climate change. These topics were chosen to span a broad array of issues and were hypothesized to vary in our ability to identify Reddit submissions on the same topics. For example, people use a set of finite words to discuss climate change (e.g. climate change or global warming), whereas submissions to express the lack of political interest may not use a fixed set of words. Appendix 5.A includes a list of all questions used in analysis and the topic to which they belong. All questions were combined to create a singular index for each topic. Although all questions used in the analysis were asked on a scale, the scales varied (i.e. 2-point, 4-point, 5-point, or 11-point). Where necessary, factors were assigned to convert scales to an 11-point scale. Then, questions on a given topic were summed and divided by the count of items, creating an average score across items that ranged from 0 to 10. Mathematically, this took the form:

$$x_{q,\text{Revised}} = x_{q,\text{Original}} \times \frac{10}{s_q - 1}$$

$$X = \frac{\sum_1^Q x_{q,\text{Revised}}}{Q}$$

where $x_{q,\text{Original}}$ is the original sentiment value and s_q is the number of points on the scale for the question. Q is the total number of questions, and X is the overall sentiment score.

The ESS data were poststratified to population targets from the EU Labour Force Survey 2016 (Eurostat). Unless otherwise noted, the final weights that account for sample selection and poststratification were used in the analysis.

5.2.1.2 Reddit 2016 Data

We downloaded[2] all submissions made between October 2016 and March 2017 that originated from a selection of 367 subreddits, overlapping with approximately 85% of the ESS field period in Germany. The chosen subreddits were identified from a list that is meant to include all subreddits originating from German-speaking countries (i.e. Germany, Austria, Lichtenstein, Luxembourg, and Switzerland; DACH Reddit wiki page [https://www.reddit.com/r/dach/wiki/k]). This list is maintained by users, and there was no method to confirm its completeness. Moreover, our goal was to use Reddit data to make inferences about attitudes in Germany. However, given the anonymity of redditors, location was unknown. It is possible that individuals who participated on the selected subreddits do not live in Germany or that German residents posted on other subreddits. To the extent that the mismatch between the target universe of all German residents' submissions and our frame of all posts on the identified subreddits is systematic and not random, this method introduced bias into our analysis, which we discuss later.

The 367 included subreddits originated in German-speaking countries, but submissions were in multiple languages. We used R package CLD3 to identify the language of the submission: 68.7% were categorized as German, 10.6% as English, and 20.7% as undeterminable or language other than English or German. Only submissions categorized as German or English ($n = 463\,234$ submissions by $25\,742$ authors) were available for analysis. Including all posts would have improved coverage, but we excluded these because we assumed that these posts were unlikely to concern the six topics of interest.

We removed all punctuation and converted all text to lowercase to reduce error caused by case-sensitive searches. Each original post and its accompanying comments were collapsed into a single entry (as opposed to one entry for a post and one entry for each comment) for topic identification. A dictionary-based search was applied to the collapsed data to identify submissions on the six topics of interest (i.e. political ideology, interest in politics, gay rights, the EU, immigration, and climate change; Appendix 5.B). Comments and posts were initially collapsed to

---

2 Data were downloaded from http://files.pushshift.io/reddit. Reddit content has been scraped and posted monthly to this site since 2005.

ensure relevant material was not missed, given the brevity of some posts and comments and the widespread use of pronouns.[3] We then brainstormed search terms; we used a thesaurus to add more words and also reviewed additional words that Google recommended once a topic was entered into the search box. Some Boolean operators (e.g. "and" or "or") were used to minimize false positive and false negative errors.

All relevant submissions on a given topic were re-separated (one entry per post and one entry per comment), then collapsed by language and author, creating one entry per author per language per topic. The entries were tokenized, and a sentiment analysis was conducted using the AFINN Sentiment Lexicon for English entries (Nielsen 2011) and the SentimentWortschatz (SentiWS) Lexicon for German entries (Goldhahn, Eckart, and Quasthoff 2012). These lexicons were chosen because they provide weights for each word (as opposed to just labeling a word as positive or negative), which was critical to reproduce scaled attitude scores. They are also widely used lexicons in their respective languages. The team calculated sentiment for each individual and each topic as the average score of all words used by the author that were found in the lexicons. Scores could range from −5 to 5 and were recentered to range from 0 to 10 to be directly comparable to the ESS scale. Table 5.1 displays the counts of records at each stage of the coding process. All analyses were conducted using the cases in the final column – one record per author for which a sentiment score was calculated on a given topic. Sentiment

Table 5.1 Number of entries by type and summarization metric.

	Authors with data on relevant topics			Authors with measurable sentiment		
	German	English	Total	German	English	Total
Total	14 549	4 733	16 643	11 850	3 779	14 051
Political ideology	11 172	3 497	12 712	9 190	2 842	10 830
Interest in politics	13 416	4 181	15 217	10 929	3 312	12 826
Immigration	9 404	2 605	10 505	7 770	2 093	8 857
EU	5 500	1 204	6 036	4 489	958	5 005
Gay rights	7 777	1 701	8 452	6 453	1 307	7 107
Climate change	4 428	1 132	4 964	3 700	939	4 250

Source: Reddit (2016).

---

3 For example, an original post could be "I support Merkel," and a response could be "I support her, too." If we had run the dictionary-based search on each submission individually, we would have picked up the original post but not the comment. We collapsed them to determine if any mention was relevant, flagged all submissions within relevant posts than reformatted the data back to the one row per submission for later analysis (see Appendix 5.C).

scores for a given topic were possible if an author had at least one word that was found in either sentiment lexicon.

5.2.1.3 Reddit Survey

Between 29 June and 13 July 2018, we conducted a survey by posting a link on 244 of the 367 previously identified subreddits. One hundred twenty-three (123) subreddits were excluded because they were private, meant to teach German (i.e. the readers likely did not reside in a German-speaking country), did not allow posts that contained links, or the subreddit moderator explicitly asked us to exclude their subreddit from the survey. The survey included all questions used in the analysis of the ESS data with modification made as necessary to adapt for the difference in mode. To make the survey of interest to a wider population, we also included questions about Reddit at the beginning of the survey. Finally, we asked respondents to provide their Reddit username so it could be linked to their Reddit submissions. Although anyone who saw the link could take the survey, we screened individuals who were under 18 years old. The survey was only available in German, but English translations of the questions are available in the appendix.

A total of 746 individuals clicked on our link.[4] Among them, 75 completed the survey, resulting in a completion rate of 10.1%. Of the 75 completes, 24 did not provide a valid username. Depending on the analysis, we used the full 75 completed interviews or the subset of 51 completed interviews for which a username was available. This sample size limits the power of all analyses below. We advise readers to consider any analyses conducted using the Reddit Survey as preliminary and would encourage any researcher to repeat these analyses with a larger, more robust sample.

5.2.1.4 Reddit 2018 Data

For the 51 Reddit Survey respondent who provided a valid username, we used the Reddit application programming interface (API) to scrape all of their submissions made between 14 July 2017 and 13 July 2018 (the day on which the Reddit Survey closed). A total of 18 279 submissions were identified (3625 in German, 10 056 in English, and 4598 in an undetectable language). The resulting data were cleaned and coded in the same manner as the Reddit 2016 data. They were subset to English and German posts, flagged as being on or off topic, summarized by language and author, and run through the sentiment analysis models.

---

4 There is no way to measure post views on Reddit, so the number of individuals who saw the link but opted not to click on it is unknown. However, Reddit's CEO, Steve Huffman, estimates that two-thirds of new Reddit users are lurkers, meaning they consume information but opt not to participate (Protalinski 2017). Many more individuals are likely active Reddit contributors but opted not to participate in our survey. For additional perspective, the median click rate for Twitter ads is 1.51% (Rodriguez 2018). We expect that this is likely comparable to the click rate for our Reddit survey.

Table 5.2 Number of entries by type and summarization metric.

	Authors with data on relevant topics			Authors with measurable sentiment – modeled			Authors with measurable sentiment – manually coded[a]
	German	English	Total	German	English	Total	Total
Total	10	18	19	8	17	17	15
Political ideology	8	14	16	7	14	15	11
Interest in politics	9	16	17	7	16	16	14
Immigration	7	9	26	7	7	11	8
EU	3	10	12	3	10	12	3
Gay rights	3	8	9	3	8	9	3
Climate change	4	8	8	4	8	8	2

a) Hand-coded sentiment was not calculated by language, so only a total count is available.
Source: Reddit (2018).

We manually coded all 13 681 English and German submissions. Each submission was coded as a given topic, with a small subsample double-coded to evaluate coder variance.[5] We then read all items flagged as relevant for a given author and topic altogether to determine a sentiment score. Phrases such as "I voted for the AFD" resulted in sentiment codes at the ends of the spectrum, while phrases that included more than one viewpoint (e.g. "I understand why people are afraid of the effect immigrants may have on the economy, but I also want to be sympathetic to refugees in need") were assigned codes toward the middle. This coding scheme and the limited data available were prone to researcher subjectivity and cannot be considered a gold standard. This scheme can only be used to demonstrate consistency or inconsistency with the sentiment models. Table 5.2 includes the same information as Table 5.1 for the Reddit 2018 data and has additional columns for the counts of authors who could be assigned a sentiment via manual coding.

5.2.2 Analysis

For all analyses, we assumed that the Reddit data would be used in isolation (i.e. it would not be combined with survey data to create hybrid estimators). We made this assumption for three reasons. First, it is real world. As evidenced by the examples in the introduction, several researchers are attempting to use

---

5 We did this check at the beginning of the coding process to ensure both coders were coding the data consistently. When differences were identified, they were discussed and rules were edited/clarified before coding the rest of the entries.

social media data without supplementing with other sources. For even more examples of how Big Data (including social media) are being used independently of survey data, please see Stephens-Davidowitz (2017). Second, we believe it is important to understand all sources of error even if using social media data in combination with other data sources. Understanding the flaws in each data source independently help researchers to identify ways in which to combine data (if desired). Third, social media data could be combined with survey data in numerous ways and create more ways errors could be introduced or mitigated. We have considered several of these methods in the summary.

To address our first research objective, i.e. whether social media data can be used to produce similar attitude distributions as survey data, we compared the means, medians, and standard deviations of the sentiment scores from the Reddit 2016 data to the comparable indices from the ESS. We made comparisons using two-sample, two-sided t-tests on the final weighted ESS data and unweighted Reddit 2016 data.[6] Reddit is anonymous; therefore, weights cannot be constructed for any Reddit data.[7]

To answer the second question concerning the source of the observed differences, we analyzed three potential sources of error: missingness, measurement, and coding. The definitions and analysis plan for each are described in this section and summarized for easy reference in Table 5.3. Each comparison is meant to isolate, to the best of our abilities, one error source while holding all other error sources constant. Unfortunately, some of the comparisons do not entirely isolate one error source, and we note this as a limitation of the analysis and discuss the implications on our ability to draw inference in the discussion. As mentioned previously, one weakness in most of these analyses is the sample size of the Reddit Survey and the Reddit 2018 datasets. We are cognizant of this limitation and have accounted for this in our discussion of the results.

5.2.2.1 Missingness

Missingness occurs when there is no submission to be analyzed and may introduce error if the individuals who choose not to post on Reddit have different opinions than those who do post. Missingness can be further broken down into two

---

6 t-Tests are designed for random samples and may not be appropriate on nonprobability samples such as the Reddit 2016 data. We also compared the data using the Mann–Whitney U test, which does not rely on the same assumptions as the t-test but also did not allow us to apply the ESS weights (Mann and Whitney 1947; Fay and Proschan 2010). The results between the t-tests and Mann–Whitney tests were similar, so we opted to report the t-tests. We conducted a similar comparison for all other analyses mentioned in this section.
7 Although redditors are not required (or even asked) to provide personal information, algorithms have been developed to assign attributes to individuals based on their posts (see https://snoopsnoo.com). Researchers should consider the ethical implications in addition to the accuracy of these algorithms before using them.

Table 5.3 Summary of analyses

Error component	Datasets used	Test conducted
Overall	ESS vs. Reddit 2016	t-test
Missingness	ESS vs. Reddit Survey	t-test and χ^2
	Reddit Survey respondents with username vs. Reddit Survey respondents with username and topical posts	t-test
Measurement	Reddit Survey vs. Reddit 2018 (auto-coded sentiment scores)	Paired t-test and correlation
	Reddit Survey vs. Reddit 2018 (manually coded sentiment scores)	Paired t-test and correlation
Coding	Reddit 2018 auto-coded sentiment score vs. Reddit 2018 manually coded sentiment score	t-test
	Reddit 2018 auto-coded topic model "Relevance" flag vs. Reddit 2018 manually coded "Relevance" flag	κ

subcomponents. First, if individuals do not use Reddit in the first place, no text is available to analyze. For survey researchers, this type of missingness is similar to undercoverage in surveys. To assess this type of missingness, we compared the average sentiments as calculated by the Reddit Survey responses to the average sentiment scores using the ESS using two-sample, two-sided t-tests. We also compared demographic distributions across the two sources. Significant differences may suggest that the Reddit population is different from the ESS population, introducing bias. This comparison assumed that the Reddit Survey respondents were similar to the Reddit population as a whole, and there was no self-selection or nonresponse bias. It also assumed that any measurement error typically found in surveys (e.g. social desirability bias) was consistent in both the ESS and Reddit Survey and that the individuals who posted on Reddit would submit similarly honest responses as those who opt not to post. We discuss the likelihood of these assumptions and the effect on the overall conclusions in the results section.

Second, active redditors may not post on a given topic because they are not interested in the topic or do not want to share their opinion through this medium. In other words, they are a member of Reddit, so they have the opportunity to post but opt not to. This is similar to the concept of nonresponse in survey research. To identify whether this may be a source of error in these data, we used two-sample, two-sided t-tests to compare the average Reddit Survey sentiment scores among all respondents who provided a username to the average Reddit Survey sentiment scores among respondents who also submitted at least one post or comment on the topic of interest. Given that one group is a subset of the other, we used the repeated measures analysis method to account for the violation of the independence assumption (Center for Behavioral Health Statistics and Quality 2015). Significant differences would suggest that some error is attributable to this source of missingness.

5.2.2.2 Measurement

Measurement error may also be present in the Reddit 2016 data. Individuals often use social media to present the most favorable version of themselves (Van Dijck 2013). Using Reddit text data to create estimates of the strength of social attitudes will be biased if the content posted to Reddit is not representative of the individuals' views. To identify measurement error in these data, we compared the sentiment scores using the Reddit 2018 data to the survey responses using the Reddit Survey. This comparison has the potential to confound coding error with the measurement since we cannot be certain whether any observed differences in the scores are the result of misrepresentation on the part of the respondent or faulty modeling on the part of the researcher. To address this issue, we conducted the comparison using both the model-based sentiment scores and the manually coded scores. Both the model-based and manually coded sentiment scores likely contain some coding error, but if we find differences between the survey values and the values derived from text, then we can be relatively confident that at least some of the difference is caused by the redditor's misrepresentation. Comparisons were limited to individuals for which a survey value and a sentiment score were available. We conducted two types of analyses. First, we compared the average sentiment scores for all individuals across the two sources using a paired sample t-test. Second, we created a correlation coefficient to determine whether the two scores for a given individual were correlated. A significant t-statistic or low correlation coefficient would suggest measurement error.

5.2.2.3 Coding

Unlike the ESS and Reddit Survey data, the Reddit 2016 and Reddit 2018 submissions (i.e. text) had to be coded by topic and onto a scale before it could be analyzed. In theory, individuals could represent their attitudes accurately and completely online, but our attitude distributions derived from these submissions could still be biased due to poor models. The models could fail in two ways: (i) they may not appropriately identify relevant submissions or (ii) they may not correctly assign attitude strength. To assess the extent of bias introduced by coding error, we conducted two comparisons. Using the Reddit 2018 data, we first conducted a two-sided, two-sample t-test to compare the average manually coded sentiment scores to the average dictionary-coded sentiment. Although both coding methods likely have error, we assumed the error was primarily due to poor models and attributed the differences to bias in the models. Second, we further assessed the source of the bias by comparing the dictionary-based topic model flags (i.e. on or off topic) to the manually coded topic flags using a κ statistic. A high κ would indicate that the models worked well, whereas a low κ would demonstrate that the dictionary search was not identifying the correct submissions for analysis.[8]

5.3 Results

5.3.1 Overall Comparisons

The first two columns of each cluster in Figure 5.1 display the average attitude for the ESS and Reddit 2016, respectively. For most variables, the higher the value, the more support (e.g. a 10 would be complete support of the EU, while a 0 would be no support). In the case of political ideology, higher scores represent right-leaning

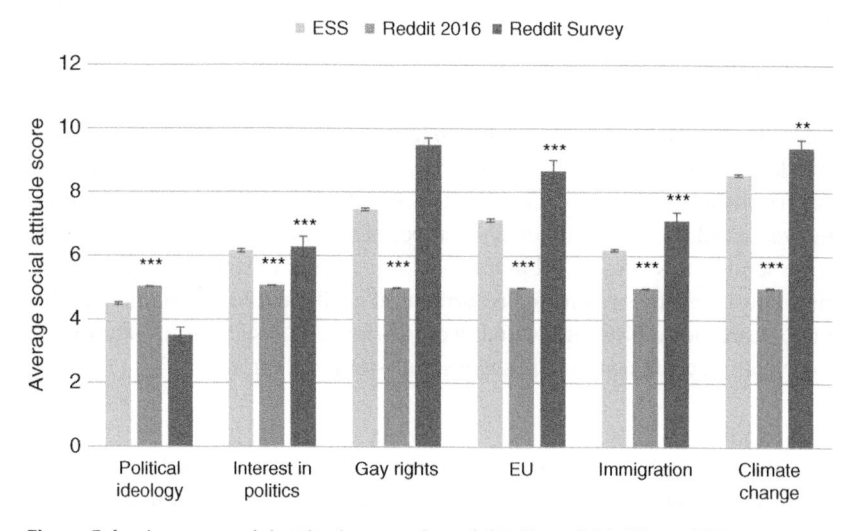

Figure 5.1 Average social attitude score. * $p < 0.05$, ** $p < 0.01$, *** $p < 0.001$ (compared to the ESS). Source: ESS, Reddit 2016, Reddit Survey.

---

[8] We intended to conduct a third comparison in which we subset the data to submissions that were flagged by both topic assignment methods as being on topic and calculate the correlation between the sentiment score as coded by the researchers and the sentiment score as coded using the lexicons. A high correlation would have indicated that the lexicons well represented the sentiment in the text, whereas low correlations indicated poor representation. Unfortunately, small sample sizes precluded this analysis.

views, and for climate change, a higher score means a stronger belief in its existence. There are two interesting findings from the ESS and Reddit 2016 comparison. First, the Reddit 2016 data produced significantly different averages compared to the ESS for all attitude measures. The Reddit 2016 averages were consistently more conservative than their ESS counterparts – further to the political right, less support for gay rights, less support for the EU, less favorable perceptions of immigrants and immigration, and less likely to believe in climate change. Redditors were also less interested in politics. This finding was similar when we reviewed the medians and used base-weighted ESS data (not shown). One could argue that the significance level is an artifact of the sample sizes (n ranged from 2829 to 12 826 for each group), but the magnitude of the differences is quite large in some instances (e.g. 3.56 for climate change) and would remain significant with smaller samples.

Second, there is little variability across the Reddit 2016 averages. All hover around 5.0 (the midpoint on the 11-point scale). We hypothesized that this finding may be the result of Reddit culture. As "the front page of the Internet," submissions should be about fact, not about opinion. However, we did not find support for this hypothesis. The methods used to construct the sentiment scores discarded all posts about the topic that did not contain any words in the sentiment lexicon. The only submissions included were those with some positive or negative value, so the unopinionated submissions could not have added noise to the models. Additionally, while the means did not fluctuate across variables, all variables had individuals who were coded into all possible values in the range (0–10). This suggests that people are posting opinions to Reddit, but differing opinions appear to balance out.

Based on this analysis, we were unsuccessful at achieving our first objective – to use social media data to construct a similar attitude distribution as that created from ESS data. Whereas the ESS skewed toward more liberal attitudes, the Reddit 2016 data were more centrist and normally distributed.

5.3.2 Missingness

To assess the source of the observed differences between the ESS and the Reddit 2016 data, we isolated the various error components, beginning with error caused by missingness. As mentioned in the methods section, we evaluated two types of missingness. First, we assessed error caused by individuals who do not use Reddit (i.e. the uncovered). The third column in each cluster in Figure 5.1 displays the average sentiment scores from the Reddit Survey. Overall, the Reddit Survey respondents were significantly more liberal than their ESS counterparts – they identified further to the left of the political spectrum, were more likely to believe that climate change is real, and demonstrated more support for gay rights, the EU, and acceptance of immigrants and immigration. This ideological bias is consistent

Table 5.4 Weighted percentages, means, and distributions of sociodemographic variables.

	Reddit Survey	ESS	p-value
Female (%)	5.0	51.0	<0.0001
Age (mean)	27.4	48.7	<0.0001
Married (%)	17.0	53.5	<0.0001
Years of education (mean)	16.6	13.6	<0.0001
Urbanicity (% distribution)			
Big city	40.0	14.4	<0.0001
Suburbs	16.7	13.8	
Town or small city	35.0	35.3	
Country village, farm, or countryside	8.3	36.5	

Source: Reddit Survey, ESS.

with the demographic distribution of the Reddit Survey respondents (Table 5.4). These respondents were significantly more likely to be male, be younger, have more education, and are more likely to live in urban areas than the ESS respondents, all attributes correlated with more liberal attitudes (Gallego 2007).

As previously noted, this analysis assumes that the Reddit Survey respondents are representative of the Reddit population. Although exact statistics are not available on the Reddit population, the distributions in Table 5.3 are consistent with Reddit's estimates of its users' sociodemographics (https://www.digitaltrends.com/social-media/reddit-ads-promoted-posts) and others' research on the topic (Shatz 2017; Singer et al. 2014; Duggan and Smith 2013). This information lends support to our assumption that the differences observed between the Reddit Survey and ESS are the result of coverage, not self-selection bias. However, our sample sizes are small and these data should not be considered conclusive.

Second, we analyzed whether there were missing attitudes among redditors. That is, are redditors who submit relevant content to Reddit different from redditors who do not submit content and are thus missing from our sentiment models? Figure 5.2 displays the average survey responses among individuals who posted on each topic and those who did not. Although none of the comparisons reached significance, this is not surprising given the small sample size. However, the magnitude of the difference among four of the seven comparisons (political ideology, gay rights, EU, and immigration) was smaller than 0.2 and varied in the direction of difference.

Given these analyses, we suspect that missingness error is large and is driven by the difference between the Reddit population and the general population

■ Respondents with username ■ Respondents with username and topical post

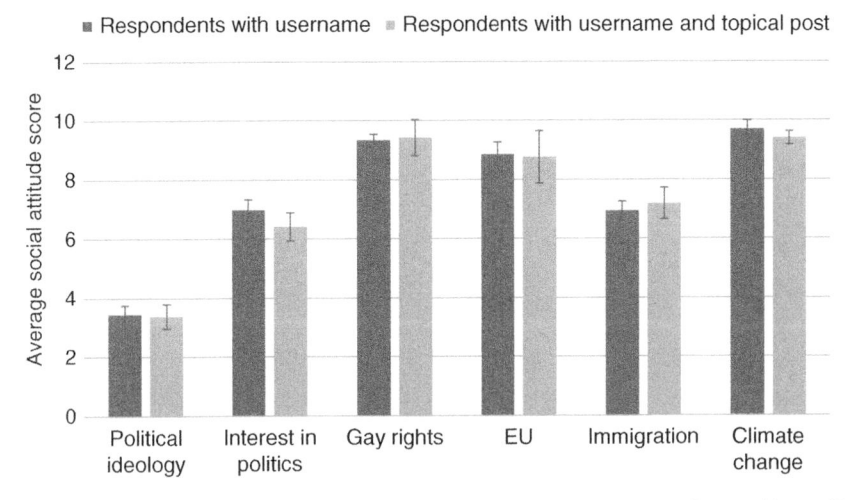

Figure 5.2 Average social attitude score among Reddit Survey respondents with a valid username by presence of submissions. * $p < 0.05$, ** $p < 0.01$, *** $p < 0.001$. Source: Reddit Survey.

(i.e. coverage bias, in TSE). These data and others' suggest that Reddit underrepresents older, married, and lesser educated individuals, females, and those living in rural areas. As a result, Reddit posts express more liberal attitudes than the general population. The data also suggest that while the Reddit population is not representative of the general population, redditors who post about a given topic appeared to be similar to redditors who do not post. If demographics are strongly correlated with the measures of interest, then this finding suggests there will be minimal nonresponse bias. However, we are cautious about placing too much credence in this conclusion given the small sample size.

5.3.3 Measurement

Next, we attempted to isolate the contribution of measurement error to the differences between the ESS and social media attitude distributions. Figure 5.3 displays the results of our analysis – the average difference between an individual's survey response on the Reddit Survey to the same individual's sentiment value (both auto-coded and manually coded). All of the comparisons between the auto-coded sentiment scores and the survey responses were significantly different, whereas two of the five manually coded versus survey comparisons reached significance. Despite a difference in significance, the direction of the difference was consistent in five of the six variables (exception: interest in politics). These findings suggest that while we are likely conflating some coding error with measurement error, individuals are not posting material that adequately depicts their full set of

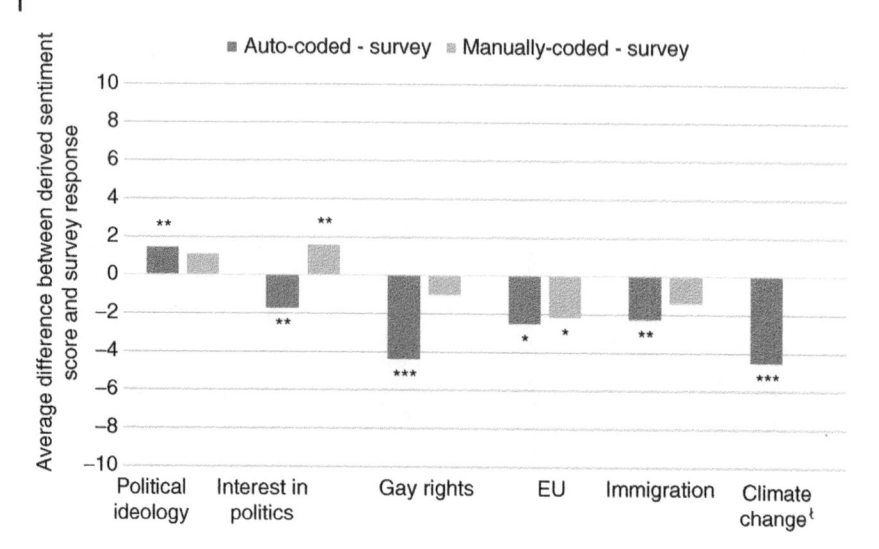

Figure 5.3 Average difference between derived sentiment score and Reddit Survey response. * $p < 0.05$, ** $p < 0.01$, *** $p < 0.001$. (ⱡ A paired t-test was not available given the lack of variance for the manually coded values.) Source: Reddit 2018 vs. Reddit Survey.

attitudes. Redditors appear to be more liberal than their posted content would indicate. When compared to their survey responses, individuals' Reddit content skewed toward the political right, was less supportive of gay rights, the EU, and immigrants or immigration, and was less likely to agree that climate change is real. Their exclusion of their full set of views resulted in significant measurement error that contributed to the overall differences. These findings were affirmed using a correlation matrix (not shown).

5.3.4 Coding

Figure 5.4 displays the average sentiment scores produced using the sentiment models versus those produced through manual coding. Similar to the results in Figure 5.1, the auto-coded scores were centered near the midpoint of the scale (e.g. near 5) and were normally distributed. This was inconsistent with the manually coded sentiment scores that tended to show more liberal attitudes. Despite the large differences observed in Figure 5.4, only two of the six comparisons reached statistical significance – interest in politics and support for immigrants and immigration. This is a result of the exceptionally small sample sizes (n ranged from 2 to 17) and all results in this section should be interpreted with extreme caution.

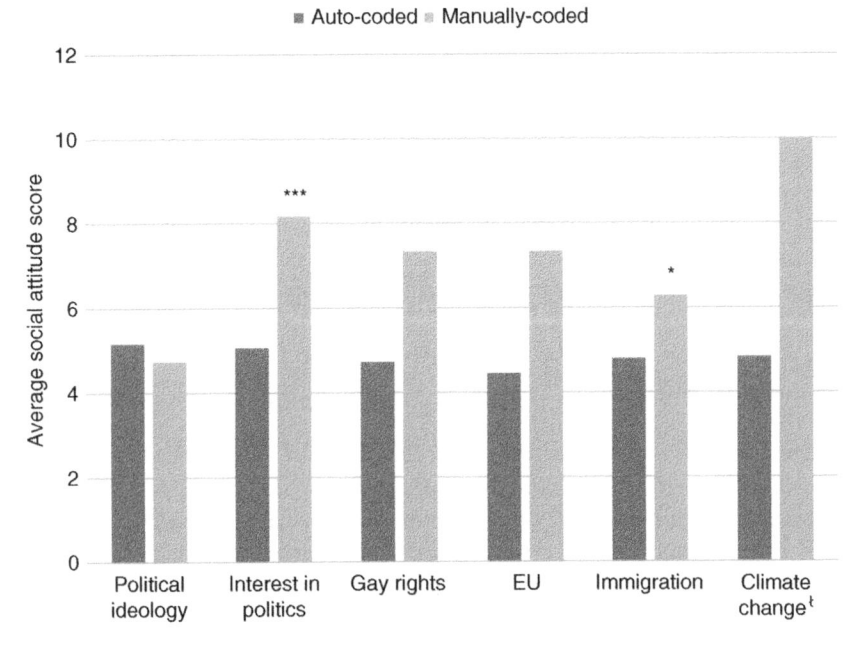

Figure 5.4 Average social attitude score by coding scheme. * $p < 0.05$, ** $p < 0.01$, *** $p < 0.001$. († A paired t-test was not available given the lack of variance for the manually coded values.) Source: Reddit (2018).

The data in Figure 5.4 only compare the averages by coding method and the net effect of coding. However, there were two steps in the coding process – (i) topic modeling in which Reddit posts were flagged as relevant or not and (ii) sentiment models applied to the relevant posts. κ statistics (not shown) were calculated to identify whether the difference in coding outcomes were a function of flagging different entries. κ values ranged from 0.096 for support of the EU to 0.515 for support of gay rights, suggesting significant disagreement between coding methods in the identification of relevant posts.

Based on these analyses, we hesitantly (due to small sample sizes) concluded that coding error further contributed to our inability to use social media data to create similar attitude distributions as those produced by the ESS. Not only were the sentiment scores different between coding methods, but these differences were the result of flagging different cases for consideration in determining sentiment. Although our ability to draw strong conclusions is limited by the data, additional qualitative evidence suggests that coding error could be sizeable. In Appendix 5.C, we walk through an example of how the topic and sentiment models were applied. We provide a sample post (for illustrative purposes only):

>
> Post 1 : I think climate change is real.(Author 1)
>
> Comment 1.1 : I disagree.(Author 2)
>
> Comment 1.2 : I can prove it.(Author 1)

In this example, Author 1 has clearly stated that she believes in climate change. However, the AFINN lexicon used in sentiment coding would have coded her as having expressed no sentiment because none of the words used (I think climate change is real. I can prove it.) are in the lexicon. If this example is indicative of real content, the current modeling approach will suffer from significant coding error.

5.4 Summary

Unfortunately, we were unable to meet our first objective – to use social media data to create similar attitude distributions as those observed on the ESS. The Reddit data, as analyzed in this chapter, produced more centrist and normally distributed scores than the ESS, skewing estimates toward the conservative end of the spectrum on all attitude measures. This conservative skew was driven by two types of error: measurement and coding. Individuals posted more conservative sentiment on Reddit than they reported in surveys. Our models also contributed to error in that they did not identify the correct Reddit submissions for inclusion in the sentiment analysis. These findings were moderated by missingness due to undercoverage. The Reddit population was younger, more urban, and had a higher level of education than the general population (16 and over). These individuals pushed the overall sentiment scores back toward the liberal side of the distribution. However, the error introduced by missingness did not completely offset the other two errors, and the overall estimates still showed more conservative attitudes than those produced by the ESS.

Despite our best efforts to conduct thorough analyses and isolate various error components, these analyses suffer several limitations. First, and most importantly, several of these analyses have extremely small sample sizes, reducing power, and our ability to draw conclusions. Our overall analyses of the attitude distributions were conducted using sufficient sample sizes, but several of the other comparisons were conducted on as few as eight cases. Some of the analyses conducted using small case counts were further supported with anecdotal evidence or findings from other surveys, but we still caution readers from placing too much credibility in the statistics presented here. Instead, we encourage researchers to reproduce this research on a larger scale with Reddit and, in general, to be more cognizant of the potential for and sources of error in Big Data.

Second, we have insinuated that the ESS is the more accurate data source, but that assumption may be incorrect. Surveys are prone to social desirability bias, resulting in individuals reporting more liberal beliefs than they actually hold (DeMaio 1984; Goffman 1959). As a result, it is possible that the Reddit data may be less prone to some types of error than the ESS. For example, Reddit is anonymous, and individuals may feel freer in expressing less socially desirable attitudes than when sitting across from an interviewer. Although this scenario is possible, there are also limits to the freedom that anonymity provides. Germany recently passed a law that requires social media platforms, including Reddit, to remove all hate speech within 24 hours or face a fine (the Netzwerkdurchsetzungsgesetz [NetzDG]). This law could influence the types of posts or comments submitted or those available for analysis. Even if redditors felt freer to express their true perspectives, redditors are not representative of the general populations, and missingness error (i.e. coverage bias) in the Reddit data is likely to swamp any improvement in measurement error. Overall, we believe that our initial assumption is appropriate – the ESS data are more accurate than the social mediate data. However, we note this limitation because researchers should consider whether this assumption holds for their own data sources.

Third, in an ideal setting, we would have been able to further isolate the error sources. We could have done this if ESS collected information on whether respondents had a Reddit account and collected their username. We could have linked their posts to their ESS survey responses. Unfortunately, we could not, and we had to isolate the various error sources by using a combination of different data sources. Not only did this approach introduce a level of complexity into the analysis, but it also required assumptions that the various data sources suffer from similar errors. Throughout this chapter, we note where these assumptions likely hold and where they are more questionable. Researchers will continue to need to make decisions using imperfect data, and we believe that these data are a good starting point. But we continue to encourage researchers to continue to research this topic area to validate or refute these findings.

Finally, one error source we were not capable of isolating and investigating was related to geography. Data are available on the ESS to identify and limit analyses to individuals living in Germany. Given the anonymity of Reddit, we had to focus on using data from subreddits based in German-speaking countries. To the extent that we included Austrians or individuals from other countries, we have introduced error that could add noise, increase or reduce the observed differences.

Given our findings, these limitations, and the growing need for a large amount of high-quality but cheap data, we recognize researchers' desire to find ways to use social media data to replace or supplement survey attitude data. Our results suggest that Reddit may not currently be a strong candidate to create similar attitude scales as those researchers typically use on surveys such as ESS, but we encourage them to keep working on finding ways in which social media data can be used for attitudinal research. First, researchers should focus on improving the models and modeling methods. We used a simple lexicon to conduct our analyses since this is a common approach by social scientists. However, there are multiple types of topic and sentiment models, each with strengths and weaknesses (Choi and Lee 2017). More research is necessary to evaluate and improve these models so they are appropriate for short entries (e.g. tweets), accommodate the social media lexicon, and account for sarcasm, emojis, and punctuation. Many of these models are also limited to processing one language at a time. To the extent to which language is nontransferrable – that equivalent words are not used to express equivalent attitudes – sentiment models that accommodate multiple language will be subject to error. These models were also limited to posts. Researchers may investigate methods and the utility of incorporating additional data such as up/down votes, likes, and retweets to improve the accuracy of these models. As these sentiment and topic models improve, we expect that the ability to use social media in attitudinal research will also improve.

Second, researchers should continue to consider and test for various error components when assessing the feasibility of using Big Data as a supplement or replacement for survey data. Even when overall estimates produced from Big Data appear consistent with survey estimates, competing, and canceling error sources may exist. We must understand these errors to identify how they may affect the estimate's variance or alter the correlations between variables. These types of analyses also increase the usefulness to other researchers who may have data with slightly different attributes. By breaking down error sources, they may be able to identify the reason their results may differ and, ideally, improve their methods.

Third, and counter-intuitively, we encourage researchers to wait patiently. As evidenced by this chapter, a significant amount of the differences between Reddit and the ESS attitude scales were the result of missingness from undercoverage. The effect of undercoverage will change over time as some social media platforms become more or less popular and as more individuals gain access to the Internet. Reddit is the fifth most popular website in Germany as of October 2018, but we estimate that only 12.9% of the population uses it (Alexa 2018),[9] Just as telephone penetration had to reach a critical mass before telephone surveys were able to create similar estimates as their face-to-face counterparts, social media needs time to gain further popularity and uptake.

---

9 Exact usage statistics are not available. We calculated 12.9% using the following formula: number of active Reddit users per month (330 million) * proportion of Reddit page views that originate from Germany (3.24%)/German population (82.79 million; https://www.redditinc.com, https://www.similarweb.com/website/reddit.com). This estimate should be used only to illustrate the vast growth potential for social media.

Fourth, researchers may accept the error and account for it by developing or applying different analytic methods. For example, survey researchers typically use frequentist models when imputing missing values. These models assume limited error in the observed data on which they are based. However, we know that this assumption does not hold on the Reddit data. Researchers are experimenting with the application of Bayesian models to avoid the limited error assumption, more accurately impute missing values, and create more accurate overall estimates (Arima, Datta, and Liseo 2015). This work has been limited to other applications to date (small area estimation is discussed in the above cite), but it could be applicable to Big Data as well. This research is a work in progress and only one example of a method that accepts the error and adjusts other steps in the estimation process to accommodate and correct for it. These methods are encouraging, but they reinforce the need to understand the type of error that exists in the social media (or any Big Data source). Without understanding the type of error, researchers will not know which model assumptions may be violated and which types of models may be adapted to correct for the error.

Finally, we encourage researchers to look into alternative uses of social media data for which they may be better suited. For example, hybrid estimates that are created from a combination of social media and surveys may allow researchers to reduce costs over current designs that exclusively use survey data but minimize the risk of bias found in social media data. Even though it is not an example of using social media data, Oberski and his colleagues create hybrid estimates from administrative and survey data using generalized multitrait-multimethod models. This approach accounted for both random and systematic errors and could accommodate the types of distributions that occur in nonsurvey records (e.g. nonlinearity; Oberski et al. 2017). Alternatively, social media may be used to enhance survey efficiencies. Topic models could be used to identify rare populations (e.g. smokers, individuals with a rare disease). Once identified, individuals may opt to reach out to the identified individuals and invite them to participate in a survey. Or they could separate all individuals in the topic models into two strata – those likely and unlikely to be in the target population – and use this to draw a stratified sample. If used to supplement frame construction or to stratify a sample, the error we observed in the models may be acceptable or could be accounted for in the survey weights. These and other methods to use Big Data and survey data in tandem are discussed in more detail by Lohr and Raghunathan (2017). Given the anonymity of Reddit (no information is required to open a Reddit account), weighting was not possible while using Reddit in isolation. We hope that researchers do not finish this chapter deflated but with a greater respect for the potential errors in Big Data and the goal of understanding those errors when choosing a data source or analysis plan.

5.A 2016 German ESS Questions Used in Analysis

	German wording	English wording	Number of scale points
Political interest	Wie sehr sind Sie an Politik interessiert?	How interested are you in politics?	4
Political ideology	In der Politik spricht man manchmal von "links" und "rechts." Wo auf der Skala würden Sie sich selbst einstufen, wenn 0 für links steht und 10 für rechts?	In politics people sometimes talk of "left" and "right." Where would you place yourself on this scale, where 0 means the left and 10 means the right?	11
Gay rights	Bitte sagen Sie mir, wie sehr Sie jeder der folgenden Aussagen zustimmen oder wie sehr Sie diese ablehnen: Schwule und Lesben sollten ihr Leben so führen dürfen, wie sie es wollen.	Please say to what extent you agree or disagree with each of the following statements: Gay men and lesbians should be free to live their own life as they wish.	5
Gay rights	Bitte sagen Sie mir, wie sehr Sie jeder der folgenden Aussagen zustimmen oder wie sehr Sie diese ablehnen: Wenn ein nahes Familienmitglied schwul oder lesbisch wäre, würde ich mich schämen.	Please say to what extent you agree or disagree with each of the following statements: If a close family member was a gay man or a lesbian, I would feel ashamed.	5
Gay rights	Bitte sagen Sie mir, wie sehr Sie jeder der folgenden Aussagen zustimmen oder wie sehr Sie diese ablehnen: Schwule und lesbische Paare sollten die gleichen Rechte haben, Kinder zu adoptieren, wie Paare, die aus Mann und Frau bestehen.	Please say to what extent you agree or disagree with each of the following statements: Gay male and lesbian couples should have the same rights to adopt children as straight couples.	5
EU	Jetzt kommen wir zum Thema Europäische Union. Manche Leute sagen, dass die europäische Einigung weiter gehen sollte. Andere sagen, dass sie schon jetzt zu weit gegangen ist.	Now thinking about the European Union, some say European unification should go further. Others say it has already gone too far.	11
EU	Stellen Sie sich vor, morgen würde eine Volksabstimmung in Deutschland über die Mitgliedschaft in der Europäischen Union stattfinden. Würden Sie für die Fortsetzung der Mitgliedschaft Deutschlands in der Europäischen Union oder für einen Austritt Deutschlands aus der Europäischen Union stimmen?	Imagine there were a referendum in Germany tomorrow about membership of the European Union. Would you vote for Germany to remain a member of the European Union or to leave the European Union?	2

5.A 2016 German ESS Questions Used in Analysis

	German wording	English wording	Number of scale points
Immigration	Nun geht es zunächst um die Zuwanderer, die derselben Volksgruppe oder ethnischen Gruppe angehören wie die Mehrheit der Deutschen. Wie vielen von ihnen sollte Deutschland erlauben, hier zu leben?	Now it is first about the immigrants which have are of the same race or ethnic group as most Germans. To what extent do you think Germany should allow them to come and live here?	4
	Wie ist das mit Zuwanderern, die einer anderen Volksgruppe oder ethnischen Gruppe angehören als die Mehrheit der Deutschen?	How about people of a different race or ethnic group from most German people?	4
	Und wie ist das mit Zuwanderern, die aus den ärmeren Ländern außerhalb Europas kommen?	How about people from the poorer countries outside Europe?	4
	Was würden Sie sagen, ist es im Allgemeinen gut oder schlecht für die deutsche Wirtschaft, dass Zuwanderer hierher kommen?	Would you say it is generally bad or good for Germany's economy that people come to live here from other countries?	11
	Würden Sie sagen, dass das kulturelle Leben in Deutschland im Allgemeinen durch Zuwanderer untergraben oder bereichert wird?	Would you say that Germany's cultural life is generally undermined or enriched by people coming to live here from other countries?	11
	Wird Deutschland durch Zuwanderer zu einem schlechteren oder besseren Ort zum Leben?	Is Germany made a worse or a better place to live by people coming to live here from other countries?	11
Climate change	Sie haben vielleicht von der Auffassung gehört, dass sich das Klima auf der Erde verändert, weil die Temperaturen über die letzten 100 Jahre gestiegen sind. Wie ist Ihre persönliche Meinung dazu? Denken Sie, dass sich das globale Klima gegenwärtig verändert?	You may have heard the idea that the world's climate is changing due to increases in temperature over the past 100 years. What is your personal opinion on this? Do you think the world's climate is changing?	4
	Wie viel haben Sie vor dieser Umfrage über den Klimawandel nachgedacht?	How much have you thought about climate change before this survey?	5

5.B Search Terms Used to Identify Topics in Reddit Posts (2016 and 2018)

5.B.1 Political Ideology

polid = "(links & politik) | (left & politic) | (rechts & politik) | (right & politic) | extremismus | nazis | (links & extrem) | (left & extrem) | (rechts & extrem) | (right & extrem) | antifa | faschist | rechter flügel | right.wing | rightwing | afd | nationalismus | nationalism | heimatliebe | homeland love | linker flügel | left.wing | leftwing | nsu | rechtsruck | right jerk | linksruck | left jerk | konservativ | conservatism | spd | die grüne | green party | sozialdemokratie | social democracy | csu | cdu | linkspartei | mitte.links | middle.left | demokrat | democrat | fdp | liberal | sozialist | socialist"

5.B.2 Interest in Politics

polint = "(links & politik) | (left & politic) | (rechts & politik) | (right & politic) | extremismus | nazis | (links & extrem) | (left & extrem) | (rechts & extrem) | (right & extrem) | antifa | faschist | rechter flügel | right wing | rightwing | afd | nationalismus | nationalism | heimatliebe | homeland love | linker flügel | left.wing | leftwing | nsu | rechtsruck | right jerk | linksruck | left jerk | konservativ | conservatism | spd | die grüne | green party | sozialdemokratie | social democracy | csu | cdu | linkspartei | mitte.links | middle.left | demokrat | democrat | fdp | liberal | sozialist | socialist | erstwähler | geht wählen | go vot | wahlbeteiligung | vote | politic | demokratie | democracy | verfolgen aktueller nachrichten | (follow & news) | teilnahme an wahl | participating in election | parteimitgliedschaft | party member | beteiligung an demonstrationen | participation in demonstration | merkel | schulz | nahles | seehofer | steinmeier | maas | von der leyen | scholz | altmeier | gabriel | schäuble | de maiziere | kretschmann | gauland | weidel | lucke | helmut kohl | brandt | schröder | adenauer"

5.B.3 Gay Rights

gay = "ehe für alle | marriage for everyone | schwul | gay | lesbisch | lesbian | homosexualität | homo | lieb doch wen du willst | love whoever you want |

csd | christopher street day | bunt | colorful | regenbogen fahne | rainbow flag | gleichgeschlechtlich | same.sex | tunte | pansy | schwuchtel | faggot | kampflesbe | combat lesbian | dyke | frühsexualisierung | early sexual | sexuelle orientierung | sexual orientation | sexuelle vorlieben | sexual preference | bisexu | queer | analverkehr | sodomy"

5.B.4 EU

EU = "european uni | europäische einigung | pulse of europe | pulse of europe | zukunft europas | future of europe | pro.europ | junge europäische förderalisten | young european federalits | jef | europäische uni | internationale solidarität | international solidarity | brexit | eu.austritt | eu.withdrawal | nato | schengen | außengrenzen | external borders | blaue karte | blue card | abendland | occident"

5.B.5 Immigration

immig = "balkan route | refugee | immigra | foreigner | national community | we are the people | pegida | dominant culture | asylum | deportation | migration | immigrat | nigger | subhuman | moslems | men with kni(v|f)es | guests of merkel | people exchange | girl with headscarf | islamization | immigrant | we make it | balkanroute | obergrenze | flüchtling | zuwanderung | ausländer raus | volksgemeinschaft | wir sind das volk | leitkultur | asyl | abschiebung | asylkrisen | eger | untermenschen | muselmanen | musels | kanacken | messermänner | merkels gäste | volksaustausch | kopftuchmädchen | islamisierung | immigrant | einwander | wir schaffen das"

5.B.6 Climate

clmt = "erderwärmung | global warming | temperaturanstieg | temperature increase | klima | climate | energiewende | energy transition | eisbären | icebear | (pole & schmelzen) | (polar & melting) | co2 | kohlenstoffdioxid | carbon dioxide | treibhausgase | greenhouse gases | ozonschicht | ozone layer | umweltzerstörung | environmental destruction | dieselskandal | diesel scandal | ökoterroristen | ecological terrorists | umweltschütz | environment | naturschutz | nature protection"

5.C Example of Coding Steps Used to Identify Topics and Assign Sentiment in Reddit Submissions (2016 and 2018)

Original Post and Associated Comments

>Post 1 : I think climate change is real.(Author 1)
>>Comment 1.1 : I disagree.(Author 2)
>>Comment 1.2 : I can prove it.(Author 1)
>Post 2 : I like cats.(Author 3)
>>Comment 2.1 : Me too!(Author 4)

Collapsed Post and Associated Comments to Identify Topic, Remove Punctuation, and Convert to Lowercase

Entry 1: i think **climate change** is real i disagree
Entry 2: i like cats me too

> * "climate change" is a keyword, so the algorithm would label Post 1 and all associated comments as being about climate change. There are no key words in Entry 2, so Post 2 and all associated comments would be discarded from additional analysis.

Subset Relevant Posts and Associated Comments and Transpose by Author

Author 1: i think climate change is real i can prove it
Author 2: i disagree

Tokenize Entries for Sentiment Analysis

Author 1: i, think, climate, change, is, real, i, can, prove, it
Author 2: i, disagree

> * commas delineate tokens (they should not be considered punctuation).

Apply AFINN Lexicon to Obtain Initial Sentiment Score

Author 1: i, think, climate, change, is, real, i, can, prove, it = N/A (no words with sentiment score in lexicon)
Author 2: i, disagree = -2 ("disagree" has a value of -2)

Shift Scale from −5 to 5 to 0–10 for Final Sentiment Score

Author 1: N/A
Author 2: $-2 + 5 = 3$

References

Alexa. (2018). The top 500 sites on the web. https://www.alexa.com/topsites (accessed 01 October 2018).

Arima, S., Datta, G.S., and Liseo, B. (2015). Bayesian estimators for small area models when auxiliary information is measured with error. *Scandinavian Journal of Statistics* 42 (2): 518–529. https://doi.org/10.1111/sjos.12120.

Baker, R. (2017). Big data: a survey research perspective. In: *Total Survey Error in Practice* (eds. P.P. Biemer, E. de Leeuw, S. Eckman, et al.), 47–67. (Wiley Series in Survey Methodology). Hoboken, NJ: Wiley.

Biemer, P.P. (2016). Errors and inference. In: *Big Data and Social Science: A Practical Guide to Methods and Tools* (eds. I. Foster, R. Ghani, R. Jarmin, et al.), Chp. 10, 265–298. Boca Raton, FL: CRC Press.

Biemer, P. and Amaya, A. (2020). Total error frameworks for found data. In: *Big Data Meets Survey Science: A Collection of Innovative Methods* (eds. C.A. Hill, P.P. Biemer, T.D. Buskirk, et al.), Chp. 4, 133–162. Hoboken, NJ: Wiley.

Bollen, J., Mao, H., and Pepe, A. (2011). Modeling public mood and emotion: twitter sentiment and socio-economic phenomena. In: *Paper Presented at the International AAAI Conference on Weblogs and Social Media*, Barcelona, Spain (17–21 July), 450–453.

Bos, L., Sheets, P., and Boomgaarden, H.G. (2018). The role of implicit attitudes in populist radical-right support. *Political Psychology* 39 (1): 69–87.

Butler, D. (2013). When Google got flu wrong. *Nature* 494 (7436): 155–156. https://doi.org/10.1038/494155a.

Center for Behavioral Health Statistics and Quality. (2015). 2013 National Survey on Drug Use and Health: Methodological Resource Book (Section 13, Statistical Inference Report). Rockville, MD: Substance Abuse and Mental Health Services Administration. https://www.samhsa.gov/data/sites/default/files/NSDUHmrbStatInference2013.pdf.

Ceron, A., Curini, L., Iacus, S.M. et al. (2014). Every tweet counts? How sentiment analysis of social media can improve our knowledge of citizens' political preferences with an application to Italy and France. *New Media & Society* 16 (2): 340–358. https://doi.org/10.1177/1461444813480466.

Choi, Y. and Lee, H. (2017). Data properties and the performance of sentiment classification for electronic commerce applications. *Information Systems Frontiers* 19 (5): 993–1012. https://doi.org/10.1007/s10796-017-9741-7.

Chung, J. E. and Mustafaraj, E. (2011). Can collective sentiment expressed on Twitter predict political elections? *Twenty-Fifth AAAI Conference on Artificial Intelligence*, San Francisco, CA (7–11 August).

Citro, C.F. (2014). From multiple modes for surveys to multiple data sources for estimates. *Survey Methodology* 40 (2): 137–161.

Conrad, F.G., Gagnon-Bartsch, J.A., Ferg, R.A. et al. (2020). Social media as an alternative to surveys of opinions about the economy. In: *Big Data Meets Survey Science: A Collection of Innovative Methods* (eds. C.A. Hill, P.P. Biemer, T.D. Buskirk, et al.), Chp. 10. Hoboken, NJ: Wiley.

Cook, S., Conrad, C., Fowlkes, A.L. et al. (2011). Assessing Google flu trends performance in the United States during the 2009 influenza virus A (H1N1) pandemic. *PLoS One* 6 (8): e23610. https://doi.org/10.1371/journal.pone.0023610.

Dalege, J., Borsboom, D., van Harreveld, F. et al. (2017). Network structure explains the impact of attitudes on voting decisions. *Scientific Reports* 7 (1): 4909. https://doi.org/10.1038/s41598-017-05048-y.

DeMaio, T.J. (1984). Social desirability and survey measurement: a review. In: *Surveying Subjective Phenomena*, vol. 2 (eds. C.F. Turner and E. Martin), 257–282. New York, NY: Russell Sage Foundation.

Doherty, D. and Adler, E. S. (2014). Campaign mailers can affect voter attitudes, but the effects are strongest early in the campaign and fade rapidly. LSE USCentre [Blog]. Internet http://blogs.lse.ac.uk/usappblog/2014/09/10/campaign-mailers-can-affect-voter-attitudes-but-the-effects-are-strongest-early-in-the-campaign-and-fade-rapidly (accessed 16 March 2020).

Duggan, M. and Smith, A. (2013). *Cell Internet Use 2013*. Washington, DC: Pew Research Center.

European Social Survey. (2016). ESS8—2018 Documentation Report. Edition 2.0. Bergen, European Social Survey Data Archive, NSD—Norwegian Centre for Research Data for ESS ERIC.

Fay, M.P. and Proschan, M.A. (2010). Wilcoxon–Mann–Whitney or *t*-test? On assumptions for hypothesis tests and multiple interpretations of decision rules. *Statistics Surveys* 4: 1–39. https://doi.org/10.1214/09-SS051.

Gallego, A. (2007). Unequal political participation in Europe. *International Journal of Sociology* 37 (4): 10–25.

Gayo-Avello, D. (2013). A meta-analysis of state-of-the-art electoral prediction from Twitter data. *Social Science Computer Review* 31 (6): 649–679. https://doi.org/10.1177/0894439313493979.

Ginsberg, J., Mohebbi, M.H., Patel, R.S. et al. (2009). Detecting influenza epidemics using search engine query data. *Nature* 457 (7232): 1012–1014. https://doi.org/10.1038/nature07634.

Goffman, E. (1959). *The Presentation of Self in Everyday Life*. Garden City, NY: Doubleday/Anchor.

Goldhahn, D., Eckart, T., and Quasthoff, U. (2012). Building large monolingual dictionaries at the Leipzig Corpora Collection: from 100 to 200 languages. *Proceedings of the 8th International Conference on Language Resources and Evaluation (LREC'12)*, Istanbul, Turkey (21–27).

Groves, R.M. (2004). *Survey Errors and Survey Costs*. Hoboken, NJ: Wiley https://doi.org/10.1002/0471725277.

Groves, R.M. and Lyberg, L. (2010). Total survey error: past, present, and future. *Public Opinion Quarterly* 74 (5): 849–879. https://doi.org/10.1093/poq/nfq065.

Hsieh, Y. and Murphy, J. (2017). Total Twitter error: decomposing public opinion measurement on twitter from a total survey error perspective. In: *Total Survey Error in Practice*, vol. 74 (eds. B.T. West, N.C. Tucker, L.E. Lyberg, et al.), 23–46. (Wiley Series in Survey Methodology). Hoboken, NJ: Wiley.

Japec, L., Kreuter, F., Berg, M. et al. (2015). *AAPOR Report on Big Data*. Oakbrook Terrace, IL: American Association for Public Opinion Research https://www.aapor.org/Education-Resources/Reports/Big-Data.aspx (accessed 16 March 2020).

Kalampokis, E., Karamanou, A., Tambouris, E. et al. (2017). On predicting election results using twitter and linked open data: the case of the UK 2010 election. *Journal of Universal Computer Science* 23 (3): 280–303.

Kitchin, R. (2015). Big data and official statistics: opportunities, challenges and risks. *Statistical Journal of the International Association of Official Statistics* 31 (3): 471–481. https://doi.org/10.2139/ssrn.2595075.

Lohr, S. and Raghunathan, T. (2017). Combining survey data with other data sources. *Statistical Science* 32 (2): 293–312. https://doi.org/10.1214/16-STS584.

Mann, H.B. and Whitney, D.R. (1947). On a test of whether one of two random variables is stochastically larger than the other. *Annals of Mathematical Statistics* 18 (1): 50–60. https://doi.org/10.1214/aoms/1177730491.

Marchetti, S., Giusti, C., Pratesi, M. et al. (2015). Small area model-based estimators using big data sources. *Journal of Official Statistics* 31 (2): 263–281. https://doi.org/10.1515/Jos-2015-0017.

Nielsen, F.A. (2011). A new ANEW: evaluation of a word list for sentiment analysis in microblogs. In: *Proceedings of the ESWC2011 Workshop on 'Making Sense of Microposts': Big Things Come in Small Packages 718 in CEUR Workshop Proceedings*, Heraklion, Crete (30 May), 93–98. http://arxiv.org/abs/1103.2903.

Oberski, D.L., Kirchner, A., Eckman, S. et al. (2017). Evaluating the quality of survey and administrative data with generalized multitrait-multimethod models. *Journal of the American Statistical Association* 112 (520): 1477–1489. https://doi.org/10.1080/01621459.2017.1302338.

O'Connor, B., Balasubramanyan, R., Routledge, B.R. et al. (2010). From tweets to polls: linking text sentiment to public opinion time series. In: *Proceedings of the International AAAI Conference on Weblogs and Social Media*, 122–129. AAAI.

Pasek, J., Yan, H.Y., Conrad, F.G. et al. (2018). The stability of economic correlations over time. *Public Opinion Quarterly* 82 (3): 470–492. https://doi.org/10.1093/poq/nfy030.

Protalinski, E. (2017). Reddit CEO Steve Huffman on the site's redesign, coming in Q1 2018, Venture Beat. https://venturebeat.com/2017/11/09/reddit-ceo-huffman-on-the-sites-redesign-coming-in-q1-2018 (accessed 3 October 2018).

Quartz Marketing Team. (2015). Data is expected to double every two years for the next decade. https://qz.com/472292/data-is-expected-to-double-every-two-years-for-the-next-decade.

Rodriguez, J. (2018). Twitter ads CPM, CPC, & CTR benchmarks for Q1 2018. https://blog.adstage.io/2018/05/31/twitter-ads-benchmarks-q1-2018.

Schober, M.F., Pasek, J., Guggenheim, L. et al. (2016). Social media analyses for social measurement. *Public Opinion Quarterly* 80 (1): 180–211. https://doi.org/10.1093/poq/nfv048.

Shatz, I. (2017). Fast, free, and targeted: reddit as a source for recruiting participants online. *Social Science Computer Review* 35 (4): 537–549. https://doi.org/10.1177/0894439316650163.

Singer, F. F., Meinhart, C., Zeitfogel, E., et al. (2014). Reddit research and data. https://f-squared.org/reddit/#survey.

Stephens Davidowitz, S. (2017). *Everybody Lies: Big Data, New Data, and What the Internet Can Tell Us about Who We Really Are*. New York, NY: HarperCollins.

Van Dijck, J. (2013). 'You have one identity': performing the self on Facebook and LinkedIn. *Media, Culture & Society* 35 (2): 199–215.

6

Attention to Campaign Events: Do Twitter and Self-Report Metrics Tell the Same Story?

Josh Pasek[1,2], Lisa O. Singh[3,4], Yifang Wei[3], Stuart N. Soroka[1,2], Jonathan M. Ladd[4,5,6], Michael W. Traugott[2], Ceren Budak[7], Leticia Bode[8], and Frank Newport[9]

[1] *Department of Communication & Media, University of Michigan, Ann Arbor, MI, USA*
[2] *Center for Political Studies, Institute for Social Research, University of Michigan, Ann Arbor, MI, USA*
[3] *Computer Science Department, Georgetown University, Washington, DC, USA*
[4] *Massive Data Institute, Georgetown University, Washington, DC, USA*
[5] *McCourt School of Public Policy, Georgetown University, Washington, DC, USA*
[6] *Department of Government, Georgetown University, Washington, DC, USA*
[7] *School of Information, University of Michigan, Ann Arbor, MI, USA*
[8] *Communication, Culture, and Technology, Georgetown University, Washington, DC, USA*
[9] *Gallup Inc., Washington, DC, USA*

6.1 What Can Social Media Tell Us About Social Phenomena?

In recent years, scholars have been increasingly interested in whether various types of digital trace data can be used to make inferences about society. Researchers from computer science and across the social sciences have used data from social media sites, smartphones, and official sources to learn about broad national populations (Barberá 2016; Blevins and Mullen 2015; Chen et al. 2015; Conover et al. 2012; Culotta, Kumar, and Cutler 2015; Golbeck and Hansen 2011; Lampos, Preoțiuc-Pietro, and Cohn 2013; Mahmud, Nichols, and Drews 2012; Mislove et al. 2011; Mitchell and Hitlin 2013). This rush to understand the potential uses of social media data stems from a series of both challenges and opportunities. The dominant model for understanding public opinion has long been probability sample survey research. Yet traditional surveys have suffered recently from declining response rates (see Keeter et al. 2006), increasing costs (Roberts, Vandenplas, and Stähli 2014), and new challenges in translating between survey results and target populations (see e.g. Kolenikov and Kennedy 2014). At the same time, the emergence of digital trace data allows researchers

Big Data Meets Survey Science: A Collection of Innovative Methods, First Edition. Edited by Craig A. Hill, Paul P. Biemer, Trent D. Buskirk, Lilli Japec, Antje Kirchner, Stas Kolenikov, and Lars E. Lyberg.
© 2021 John Wiley & Sons, Inc. Published 2021 by John Wiley & Sons, Inc.

to observe behaviors as well as expressions of attitudes and beliefs among broad populations of ordinary citizens in real time (see, e.g. Achrekar et al. 2011; Golder and Macy 2011). Although these expressions are substantively interesting in and of themselves – indeed, they constitute a novel form of public opinion (Murphy et al. 2014) – the possibility that they could supplement or even replace survey-based approaches is particularly tantalizing given the challenges that surveys face.

Digital trace data in general, and social media data in particular, may yield vast new insights into public attitudes and behaviors. The scope of data available to researchers is far larger than what can be ascertained in traditional surveys. Data generation occurs in real time: public responses can be observed as they occur, not merely recalled after the fact. Trace data are organically generated, rather than solicited by researchers, meaning that social expressions are ecologically valid and responsive to whatever forces render those expressions salient in the real world. In each of these respects, social media data have the potential to enable analyses that were either impossible or infeasible with survey methods.

Two central questions, however, raise concerns about the validity of inferences from social media. First, the community of social media users and particularly of those who post on social media differs in notable ways from the public at large (Greenwood, Perrin, and Duggan 2016). Second, the data-generating process underlying social media data differs substantially from that of survey methods (Schober et al. 2016). Hence, to assess the quality of inferences from social media data, we need to know both what populations digital trace data are describing and what the digital trace data are revealing about those populations. Absent this sort of understanding, social media data will be telling us about unknown parameters about an unknown population – a situation that makes meaningful social inference all but impossible.

Despite these challenges, many studies using social media data have begun with strong assumptions about the data under examination. Social media expressions are often treated as if they should be identical to the opinions solicited from nationally representative samples of the public on similar topics. Although the individuals posting on social media about any given topic are clearly a self-selected group with distinct motivations, this set of assumptions is not unreasonable. Because social media posts are public expressions designed for an audience (Marwick and Boyd 2011), individual posters may be motivated to tailor what they post to reflect broader societal considerations (Conrad et al. 2015; Schober et al. 2016). Such processes may explain why social media expressions sometimes predict real-world phenomena with little or no adjustment (and also why the results of social media data collections could differ from those of survey methods). But the lack of consistent evidence for these sorts of predictions shows that assumptions about the data need to be tested, and their validity must be established empirically.

This chapter examines one possible explanation for what social media data might be revealing; social media may well provide a window into public attention rather than attitudes and opinions. We provide an empirical test of this possibility by comparing tweets about candidates in the 2016 elections with open-ended survey responses that directly measure public attention.

6.2 The Empirical Evidence to Date

A number of early studies connecting social media data with real-world phenomena seemed to indicate that social media data could yield inferences similar to those of traditional surveys. O'Connor and colleagues (2010) found that sentiments surrounding tweets about "Jobs" closely tracked survey questions about economic confidence. And a number of papers reported that analyses of social media posts enabled them to forecast election outcomes (Anstead and O'Loughlin 2015; Smailović, Kranjc, and Grčar 2015; Tumasjan et al. 2011). Many of the scholars involved in these studies have argued that tweets constitute a form of public opinion, albeit a different one from that measured with survey questions. Simple textual analyses of the data gathered from tweets – such as the number of mentions of various candidates/parties and the sentiment of those mentions – have been treated as proxies for political attitudes.

Failed replications of these results as well as some more recent studies have instead revealed that the assumption of one-to-one compatibility between survey and social media results was likely naïve. Key research decisions – such as the set of parties to include in political forecasts (Jungherr, Jürgens, and Schoen 2012), the group of users whose posts are analyzed (Barberá 2016), the specific social media metrics employed (Gayo-Avello 2012), and the time period of analysis (Pasek et al. 2018) – can lead to wildly different conclusions. These variations suggest an inherent instability in linking social media metrics with ostensibly similar survey data. And some results indicating instability suggest that the problem is simply an analytical issue, but directly related to the data-generating process that might have produced the Twitter data in the first place.

In response to these issues, some researchers have attempted to account for differences between the community of social media users or individuals posting on a topic and the population at large. Most have involved attempts to estimate demographic information about the individuals whose data comprise the social media corpus and to adjust results to address differences between the data generators and the public (see, e.g. Barberá 2016; Diaz et al. 2016). But this approach has some key challenges, as demographic information is not available for many social media sites and efforts to infer this information can result in bias (Freelon 2019; Hsieh and Murphy 2017). An alternative to testing this assumption is adjusting survey data to look more like the population of social media users or posters, but this too has yielded mixed results (Pasek et al. 2018; 2019). Therefore, not only are the dynamics of users different, but what is being measured can also introduce important distinctions between social media and survey data.

Newer work has begun to contemplate more seriously the ways in which digital traces may be qualitatively different from their traditional counterparts. Although posting is a very different behavior from responding to a survey, the implications of this for analyses have been unclear. Contemporary news events influence the topics that people are tweeting about as well as the articles they retweet (Hermida 2010; Jang and Pasek 2015). As a public expression, tweets are also tailored to an audience: perceptions of that audience can also shape the content of posts (Marwick and Boyd 2011). Thus, tweets do not necessarily tell us about the individuals who are posting, but they may instead say something about society (or at least Twitter society) more broadly.

6.3 Tweets as Public Attention

A recent paper by Jungherr et al. (2016) contends that Twitter metrics may tell more about public attention rather than about attitudes and opinions per se – both the models of tweets as a reflection of news (Kwak et al. 2010) and as expressions for an audience (Marwick and Boyd 2011). It also could suggest that it may not be necessary to account for differences between the set of individuals who tweet and the public at large to achieve successful topic coverage (Schober et al. 2016).

The tweets-as-attention model also resonates with a long line of research in political communication suggesting that media – traditional and social – track and even set the public agenda (see Ceron et al. 2014; McCombs and Shaw 1972). That is, that media tell people what kinds of topics to think about and, in so doing, manage the allocation of public attention. Twitter, in particular, might serve this role effectively, as it represents both a reflection of what a broad swath of individuals are thinking about and a medium where those topics of relevance can themselves "trend" and thereby set the agenda for others.

There are a number of reasons to prefer treating social media metrics as a measure of attention rather than a portrait of public opinion. One central difference between social media and survey data stems from the data-generating process. Unlike survey data, which are produced in explicit response to a researcher query (and therefore are subject to potential measurement errors associated with social desirability, memory issues, and the like), social media data emerge based on what people who use the sites are already thinking and talking about (Schober et al. 2016). Social media data are likely to respond to events in the news and matters of public concern in more dynamic ways than surveys. And to the extent that message dissemination on social media sites reflects what is in the news, the same processes that drive public attention may drive online posting behaviors (see Karpf 2016).

The value of regarding Twitter as a measure of attention is extenuated in that traditional surveys do not accurately measure what people are actually thinking about, because most survey questions are closed-ended (cf. Schuman and Presser 1981). That is, researchers provide the question to be asked and the available response options prior to beginning the study. To the extent that changes in attention are driven by news events, researchers may not have provided appropriate responses to capture these shifts. Indeed, traditional studies of public attention have largely focused on broad issue areas – such as the economy or healthcare – rather than the specific happenings that may captivate the public on any particular occasion (McCombs and Shaw 1993). Thus, in many cases, survey researchers simply are not in the field with questions that could elicit an understanding of what people are attending to (though the open-ended survey data used for the current study constitutes an exception).

Although tweets may have some comparative advantages in tracking public attention, what they track may not be what the public is actually thinking about. Instead, the public attention assumption is speculative until we can concretely show that users of these sites are attending to whatever garners the interest of the larger population. And given concerns about the unrepresentativity of social media users (e.g. Couper 2013), this possible difference needs to be formally examined.

This chapter describes an empirical test of the assumption that Twitter might provide a window into what Americans were thinking about in the run-up to the 2016 US Presidential election. To do so, we compared answers to a series of open-ended survey questions about what Americans had heard about the candidates with the content of posts about those same candidates at the same time on Twitter. Specifically, we examined whether the frequency of mentions of event-related terms from these two types of data displayed similar patterns over time.

6.4 Data Sources

To assess whether public attention on Twitter mirrors public attention in the population at large, we juxtaposed two daily data streams in the run-up to the 2016 US Presidential election. These data included tweets mentioning the presidential candidates and open-ended survey questions about the candidates from the Gallup Daily Survey. Across both data streams, we looked for spikes in the use of particular keywords that tap political events. We then compare the relative salience of these keywords across data streams. The objectives were to ascertain whether events that received attention on Twitter reflected those that yielded open-ended responses in the survey data and whether the attention levels afforded to particular events were similar across streams.

Twitter data for the current analyses were collected using the Sysomos firehose access tool, which allows subscribing researchers to download a random sample of tweets related to any given keyword on a particular date. On each day between 10 July and 8 November 2016, we collected a simple random sample of up to 5000 tweets per day from the full set of daily tweets mentioning the keyword "Trump" and an identical sample was collected from all tweets mentioning "Clinton" that were classified by Sysomos as US-based tweets in English.[1] In total, the current study examines data from 609 831 tweets containing "Clinton" and 610 000 tweets containing "Trump." Thirty-two percent of Clinton tweets also contained the word "Trump" and 12.2% of Trump tweets also contained the word "Clinton." Because of these overlaps, 8.7% of tweets were present for both candidates, indicating that the samples gathered captured a large proportion of the tweets that fit all search parameters.

Survey data came from two open-ended survey questions fielded as part of the Gallup Daily Survey. Respondents were asked, "Did you read, hear, or see anything about [CANDIDATE] in the last day or two?" for both Donald Trump and Hillary Clinton (asked in random order). Respondents who said "yes," were asked "What have you read, seen or heard about [CANDIDATE]?" To the best of their ability, telephone interviewers recorded individuals' responses verbatim (approximately, 60% cellphone and 40% landline). Gallup asked these questions of a random sample of 500 respondents daily between 9 July and 7 November 2016. In total, 58 909 individuals provided a substantive response to the follow-up Trump question and 58 905 to the Clinton question (see Bode et al. 2020 for additional details about the survey). All interviews were conducted during evening hours.

6.5 Event Detection

To detect events, we did not want to rely on any existing lists of occurrences from the campaign. Journalists typically compile these lists, which reflect a mix of items that were heavily covered by the news and that seemed politically salient. These sorts of lists could therefore bias the set of events considered in ways that might

---

1 Sysomos also purports that these tweets were cleaned of spam, though they were not forthcoming on how spam was detected or how language and location were identified. For a variety of reasons, both practical and theoretical, we made no attempt to identify bot accounts beyond those cleaned by Sysomos. Sampling was done at the Tweet level, and Sysomos reports that their algorithm takes a simple random sample of all tweets that fit the search parameters.

induce similarity across data streams. Hence, to identify events that attracted some public attention, we looked for words that had three features: they were mentioned with sufficient frequency that they could be analyzed, needed to be at least somewhat congregated on particular dates, and needed to only appear in some time periods. To do this, we searched the survey data for words that were mentioned at least 10 times in a single day and 50 times total, but that were not present for at least 40% of days. These parameters were chosen based on a sensitivity analysis that varied all three parameters and considered the set of words that emerged. Making them less restrictive did not introduce any additional words that could be easily linked to events, whereas more restrictive parameters removed words that could be easily linked to events. Text preprocessing involved removing select punctuation,[2] converting all terms to lowercase, and removing stop words (i.e. words like "the," "and," and "her" that appear frequently in English but do not convey much meaningful information). We then searched Google News for these words and the dates at which their use peaked in the survey mentions to determine whether we could associate the terms with some substantive news happening(s). Finally, we bundled terms that appeared to relate to the same event (or set of term-related events). We dropped any events that were only linked to a single word in our data because alternate uses of those words could be confused with attention to the event.

Using this procedure, we found 304 terms that followed the event-related pattern we described and linked 242 of those terms with 39 distinct events mentioned in the news. These distinct events are presented in chronological order of peak survey mentions, with all associated terms in Table 6.1, accompanied by the peak number of mentions of event-related terms in each data stream for each candidate. Because the initial event detection employed terms from both the Clinton and Trump open-ended questions, some terms that were regarded as events did not register as an event connected to one of the two candidates in particular. For instance, words related to the shooting of six police officers in Baton Rouge, LA, met the minimum event criteria, but fewer than 50 of these mentions were present for Hillary Clinton. We considered these terms when comparing mentions across candidates, but not when comparing the mentions in survey and Twitter data within a single candidate. Because of the number of events identified, we were only able to include a very short description of each event in Table 6.1. Readers hoping to learn more about these events are encouraged to Google the dates and the identified keywords.

Even when an event was closely linked to only one of the two candidates, words associated with that event often peaked in both survey responses and tweets linked to the other candidate at the same time. For instance, when Trump traveled to

---

2 These were commas, apostrophes, dashes, periods, and carats.

Table 6.1 List of events and attention metrics.

Event	Words	Candidate	Survey			Twitter			Correlation	
			Maximum	Total	Date of maximum	Maximum	Total	Date of maximum	Daily	3-day
Dallas shooting	Police; Dallas; shootings; officers; shooting; lives; Texas	Clinton	138	612	10-Jul	242	6253	18-Jul	0.66	0.67
		Trump	161	787	10-Jul	191	6321	10-Jul & 17-Jul	0.65	0.73
Sanders endorsed Clinton	Bernie; Sanders; endorsed; endorsing; endorsement	Clinton	243	1005	12-Jul	5469	28 254	12-Jul	0.88	0.90
		Trump	50	284	6-Aug	748	10 613	12-Jul	0.45	0.41
Ginsberg disparages Trump	Court; supreme; justice	Trump	46	214	14-Jul	238	3828	14-Jul	0.77	0.84
Vice-presidential announcements	Mike; Pence; picking; mate; vice; VP; pick; picked; announcement; announced; selected; decision; Kaine; Tim; announcing; choice; governor; selection	Clinton	425	1764	23-Jul	3756	26 642	22-Jul	0.55	0.78
		Trump	513	2873	16-Jul	2839	28 696	15-Jul	0.85	0.89
Terrorist attack in Nice, FR	France; terrorist; Nice	Clinton	81	222	15-Jul	177	2071	15-Jul	0.81	0.91
		Trump	92	288	15-Jul	214	2489	15-Jul	0.74	0.90
Shooting in Baton Rouge, LA	Baton; Rouge	Trump	15	63	17-Jul	146	446	19-Aug	0.59	0.77
Party conventions	GOP; convention; Wifes; Michelle; nomination; acceptance; RNC; DNC; nominee; nominated; accepted	Clinton	210	1780	27-Jul	1147	22 654	26-Jul	0.66	0.82
		Trump	287	2039	22-Jul	1397	26 766	19-Jul	0.88	0.91
Ted Cruz endorses Trump	Cruz; Ted	Trump	60	211	23-Jul	1102	5938	23-Sep	0.41	0.60

Event	Keywords	Candidate								
Trump asks Russia to hack Clinton Emails	Russians; Russian; hacking; hack; hacked; missing	Clinton	20	276	30-Jul	296	7493	30-Jul	0.47	0.78
		Trump	117	523	28-Jul	496	5227	27-Jul	0.75	0.81
Khzir Kahn	Son; Father; Mother; tour; Muslim; parents; star; Soldier; Muslims; MR; Soldiers; died; Khan; veteran; heart; purple; gold; Kahn	Clinton	34	421	1-Aug	694	13 749	9-Aug	0.86	0.88
		Trump	316	2075	1-Aug	1548	25 709	31-Jul	0.63	0.72
Trump: Second amendment people could stop Clinton	Amendment; second; rights; 2nd	Clinton	31	272	10-Aug	1101	5630	9-Aug	0.35	0.65
		Trump	267	822	10-Aug	953	5291	9-Aug	0.69	0.85
Iran executes former nuclear scientist	Nuclear; Iran	Clinton	11	100	3-Aug	314	3092	3-Aug	0.63	0.83
		Trump	44	136	5-Aug	276	2364	3-Aug	0.72	0.88
Biden campaigns for Clinton	Pennsylvania; Joe; Biden	Clinton	39	171	15-Aug	331	3352	15-Aug	0.82	0.84
Trump staff shakeup	Staff; changed; hired; manager; fired	Clinton	11	192	17-Oct	201	5204	30-Oct	0.09	0.27
		Trump	79	516	19-Aug	159	4783	21-Aug	0.42	0.57
Louisiana flooding	Louisiana; victims; flood	Clinton	15	77	19-Aug & 21-Aug	210	3062	19-Aug	0.66	0.83
		Trump	103	533	20-Aug	988	3763	19-Aug	0.87	0.92
Trump meets Mexican President	Mexico; visiting; meet; trip; visit; Mexican; met	Clinton	34	224	31-Aug	521	5006	31-Aug	0.75	0.79
		Trump	409	2295	31-Aug	1712	8950	31-Aug	0.79	0.87
Trump visits Detroit Church	Church; African; Detroit; visited	Trump	131	671	4-Sep	1002	5388	3-Sep	0.72	0.88
Trump: I know more than generals	Forum; Iraq; hall; chief; commander; generals	Clinton	81	226	8-Sep	538	5462	8-Sep	0.88	0.89
		Trump	102	374	8-Sep	604	4655	8-Sep	0.90	0.92

(Continued)

Table 6.1 (Continued)

Event	Words	Candidate	Survey				Twitter			Correlation	
			Maximum	Total	Date of maximum	Maximum	Total	Date of maximum		Daily	3-day
Matt Lauer forum	Matt; Lauer	Clinton	22	73	9-Sep	440	1364	1-Sep		0.41	0.54
		Trump	24	75	10-Sep	440	843	8-Sep		0.55	0.76
Clinton overheats at 9/11 memorial	911; memorial; leave; ceremony; ill; passed; pneumonia; sick; illness; fainting; fainted; 9; 11	Clinton	352	2120	12-Sep	3833	17621	11-Sep		0.81	0.89
		Trump	68	442	12-Sep	1517	13798	11-Sep		0.37	0.75
Clinton: Basket of deplorables	Basket; deplorable	Clinton	21	118	11-Sep	776	2281	10-Sep		0.54	0.81
		Trump	32	84	13-Sep	565	2619	10-Sep		0.41	0.67
Candidate medical records on Dr. Oz	Medical; records; Oz; doctor; dr	Clinton	36	256	14-Sep	653	5474	11-Sep		0.72	0.81
		Trump	111	389	14-Sep	693	4377	14-Sep		0.82	0.84
Flint water crisis	Flint; Michigan	Trump	43	153	15-Sep	280	1781	15-Sep		0.95	0.97
Jimmy Fallon touches Trump hair	Jimmy; hair; Fallon	Trump	52	177	16-Sep	350	1201	16-Sep		0.82	0.94
Trump ends Birther claims	Birth; admitted; born; Barack; Birther; citizen	Clinton	28	159	16-Sep	839	4536	16-Sep		0.75	0.84
		Trump	192	727	17-Sep	759	4352	16-Sep		0.71	0.81
NJ/NY bombing	Bomb; bombing; bombings; Jersey; terrorism; NY	Clinton	73	261	20-Sep	424	3727	18-Sep		0.78	0.90
		Trump	115	360	19-Sep	742	4357	18-Sep		0.61	0.84
Charlotte riots	Riots; Carolina; Charlotte	Clinton	39	209	23-Sep	164	2179	21-Sep		0.79	0.88
		Trump	39	196	23-Sep	107	1671	18-Aug		0.83	0.91
Debate preparation	Preparing; ready; tomorrow; tonight; upcoming; preparation	Clinton	90	646	26-Sep	249	4707	26-Sep		0.38	0.52
		Trump	83	479	26-Sep	271	6459	7-Nov		0.32	0.51

Event	Keywords	Candidate							
Debates	Performance; won	Clinton	40	222	28-Sep	209	2553	27-Sep	0.33	0.46
		Trump	27	210	28-Sep	277	2804	27-Sep	0.61	0.79
Trump attacks Former Ms Universe	Miss; universe; ms; tweets; girl; beauty; tweeting; fat; pageant; former; weight	Clinton	43	240	1-Oct	445	26 923	30-Sep	0.53	0.62
		Trump	223	1139	30-Sep	768	29 640	30-Sep	0.75	0.85
NY Times releases Trump tax return	Returns; income; dollars; federal; return; 18	Clinton	40	313	13-Aug	379	6635	12-Aug	0.67	0.80
		Trump	125	593	3-Oct	450	8065	2-Oct	0.63	0.80
Access hollywood tapes	Leaked; street; 2005; recording; bus; bush; Billy; hot; audio; hollywood; recorded; tape; room; locker; tapes; 10; ten	Clinton	60	578	8-Oct	913	21 032	7-Oct	0.60	0.77
		Trump	197	1399	8-Oct	1394	16 973	7-Oct	0.69	0.87
Sexual assault allegations against Trump	Accusing; sexually; sexual; allegations; assault; accusations; groping; inappropriate; harassment; assaulted; sex; Gettysburg; sue; abuse; accused	Clinton	16	264	14-Oct	464	10 040	8-Oct	0.42	0.58
		Trump	259	2404	15-Oct	1085	13 845	14-Oct	0.82	0.85
Trump: elections might be rigged	Rigged; elections; claiming; results; accept	Trump	93	874	17-Oct	533	6917	20-Oct	0.67	0.88
WikiLeaks	WikiLeaks; wiki	Clinton	70	1069	17-Oct & 27-Oct	625	13 386	11-Oct	0.64	0.81
Al Smith Dinner	Dinner; charity; event; al; Smith; catholic	Clinton	153	456	21-Oct	567	8077	21-Oct	0.82	0.91
		Trump	156	415	21-Oct	602	5298	21-Oct	0.76	0.88
Trump opens DC hotel	Washington; hotel; opened; DC	Trump	84	359	26-Oct	270	5237	26-Oct	0.62	0.72
Comey Reopens Clinton E-mail investigation	Reopening; reopened; case; opening; investigating; computer; Comey; director; Anthony; Weiner; letter; cleared; closing	Clinton	176	1143	29-Oct	1834	19 712	28-Oct	0.91	0.96
		Trump	39	378	29-Oct	692	9080	28-Oct	0.69	0.86
Trump whisked offstage at NV Rally	Service; secret; stage; Nevada	Trump	98	256	6-Nov	648	6055	5-Nov	0.27	0.66

Mexico City on 31 August to meet with Mexican President Enrique Peña Nieto, associated words peaked for Clinton as well (Mexico; visiting; meet; trip; visit; Mexican; met). The same was true when Clinton felt overheated at a September 11th memorial after which he was eventually diagnosed with pneumonia. Although associated candidates received more attention in relation to these events than their opponents, the typical pattern was that the prevalence of associated terms increased for both candidates.

There were some exceptions to these general patterns. For some events, terms associated with one candidate were not strongly associated with the other candidate. For instance, terms related to Trump's August staff shakeup, which elevated Steve Bannon and Kellyanne Conway to leadership roles and demoted then-campaign chairman Paul Manafort, did not register as a corresponding event in the Clinton data stream. Other events, such as the vice-presidential announcements preceding the two conventions employed similar terms but were associated with different dates for each of the candidates. Of the 39 events considered in the dataset, 28 produced discernable events ($\geq$50 total survey mentions and $\geq$10 survey mentions on the peak day) for both candidates, two were identifiable only in the Clinton data (Biden campaigning, and WikiLeaks), and nine were identifiable only in the Trump data. This yielded 67 distinct candidate–event combinations for analysis.

6.6 Did Events Peak at the Same Time Across Data Streams?

Across the 67 distinct candidate–event combinations identified in the survey data, 22 events (32.8%, see Figure 6.1) peaked the same day in the Twitter and survey data streams. In 25 additional cases (37.3%), the Twitter data preceded the survey data by a single day. This indicated that Twitter may have been quicker to respond to some events. Twitter may have responded more rapidly because it was somehow setting the agenda (cf. Neuman et al. 2014), because events occurred at times where they would only make the following day's survey responses, or because Twitter simply picks up on things more quickly. Notably, there were no events for which survey responses preceded tweets by a single day. For 11 events (16.4%), however, Twitter and survey peaks differed by more than five days. Collectively, the results suggest that the two data streams often identify the same events, but not always.

Lags between dates of Twitter and survey maximums

[Bar chart showing proportion of cases for each lag category:
- Twitter >10 days before
- Twitter 6–10 days before
- Twitter 2–5 days before
- Twitter one day before
- Same day
- Survey one day before
- Survey 2–5 days before
- Survey 6–10 days before
- Survey 6>10 days before

X-axis: Proportion of cases, 0.00 to 0.35]

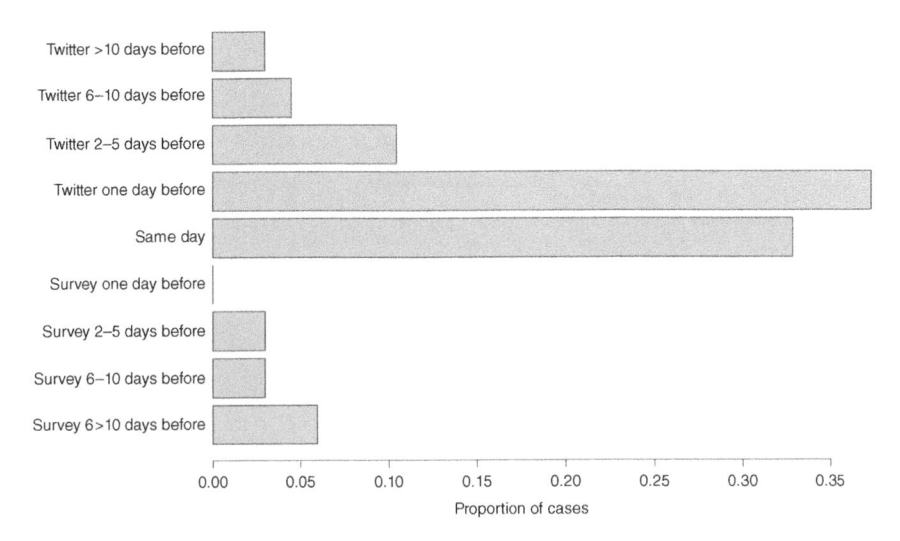

Figure 6.1 Correspondence of Twitter and survey maximums across data streams for 67 event–candidate combinations.

6.7 Were Event Words Equally Prominent Across Data Streams?

On average, the words associated with events spiked more prominently and over narrower windows of time in the survey data stream compared to the social media data stream. On the most prominent individual date for each wording, 20.5% of the overall survey mentions of each event-related term could be expected to emerge compared to 11.9% of the term mentions in the Twitter data stream. This pattern was not due to a subset of the words, but instead reflected a nearly universal trend. For only 9 of the 67 candidate–event combinations, 13.4% was the Twitter peak more prominent than the survey peak (Figure 6.2).

One important question about this pattern was whether the Twitter data simply had more uniform mentions of event-style terms over time or whether tweets and surveys differentially responded to the campaign events we examined. To assess this, we looked at the 11 cases where a set of terms was associated with only one of the two candidates and examined the patterns for those terms in the candidate

Relative prominance of Twitter and survey data maximums as a proportion of total mentions in each stream

- Survey > 10 × as peaked
- Survey 2–10 × as peaked
- Survey 1.5–2 × as peaked
- About equal
- Twitter 1.5–2 × as peaked
- Twitter 2–10 × as peaked
- Twitter > 10 × as peaked

Proportion of cases

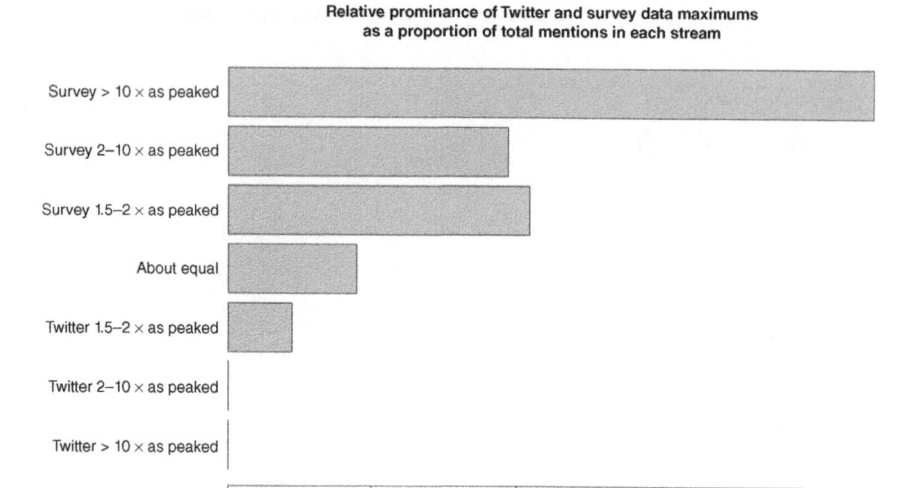

Figure 6.2 Relative prominence of survey and Twitter data peaks for 67 event-candidate combinations.

with whom they were not associated. Here, we found that the pattern we had observed when an event was not associated with a particular candidate was the same as when they were not. Tweets, it seems, were simply more dispersed than survey responses.

6.8 Were Event Terms Similarly Associated with Particular Candidates?

Twenty events were much more strongly related to Donald Trump than they were to Hillary Clinton, peaking at more than three times as many mentions. Not a single event was associated with Hillary Clinton more than three times as much as it was associated with Donald Trump. Indeed, the closest such event was when the FBI announced that it was reopening the Clinton e-mail server investigation, with 2.7 times as much attention for Clinton as for Trump in the survey data. Seven sets of event-related words peaked in their survey attention at very different dates across candidates. One of these – the vice-presidential announcements – was unsurprising given that it referred to two different events that occurred. Another three events with different peak dates associated with Trump never received much attention linked to Hillary Clinton (Trump's staff shakeup, his visit to an African–American church in Detroit, and a security breach where he was whisked offstage in Nevada). The remaining three were associated with release of the two candidates' tax returns (12 August 2016 for Clinton vs. an old return from Donald Trump that was leaked on 2 October 2016), concerns about rigged elections by Donald Trump on 17 October 2016 (the terms for which also captured Clinton's acceptance of the Democratic nomination on 29 July 2016), and discussions about the Supreme Court (Trump mentions peaked when Justice Ginsberg walked back her criticism of the candidate on 14 June 2016 and Clinton mentions peaked when the Court was a principal topic in the third debate on 20 October 2016).

In general, event-related terms that were more associated with Clinton or Trump in the survey data had similar associations among the tweets. Whether we compared the total number of mentions or the peak volume of mentions across the two data streams, events tended to retain their associations with one of the other candidates in similar ways across both data streams. The Pearson's correlation between the proportion of mentions associated with Trump vs. Clinton in the two streams was 0.75 and for maximum mentions was 0.79 (Figure 6.3).

6.9 Were Event Trends Similar Across Data Streams?

To assess whether survey and Twitter data captured the same public attention over time, we compared the over-time trends in the data mentioning each set of terms for each candidate across the two types of data. That is, we looked at whether patterns of attention to campaign-related events for Clinton correlated strongly with survey mentions for those same terms and did the same for Trump. We used Pearson's correlation coefficients between the Twitter and survey data streams for each candidate to see how closely the volume across dates for each type of attention corresponded. Because of the evidence that tweets sometimes responded more rapidly than survey responses, we also conducted a smoothed version of this analysis where the data streams were smoothed over a three-day rolling window (where our measure of tweeting about each word on a particular day was instead treated as the sum of that day, the prior day, and the subsequent day) before they were correlated. That is, our measure of tweeting about each word on a particular day was instead treated as the sum of that day, the prior day, and the subsequent day.

We found that levels of attention to most terms were moderately correlated across the survey and Twitter data streams for each candidate (Figure 6.4). The average over-time correlation across the 67 candidate–event combinations was 0.65. The variation in these correlations, however, was large. The strongest correlations in attention were when Trump was discussed in connection with the Flint water crisis (Pearson's $r = 0.98$), when Clinton was mentioned related to the reopening of the Comey investigation ($r = 0.91$), and for Trump's claim that

Comparing total mentions
Correlation = 0.75

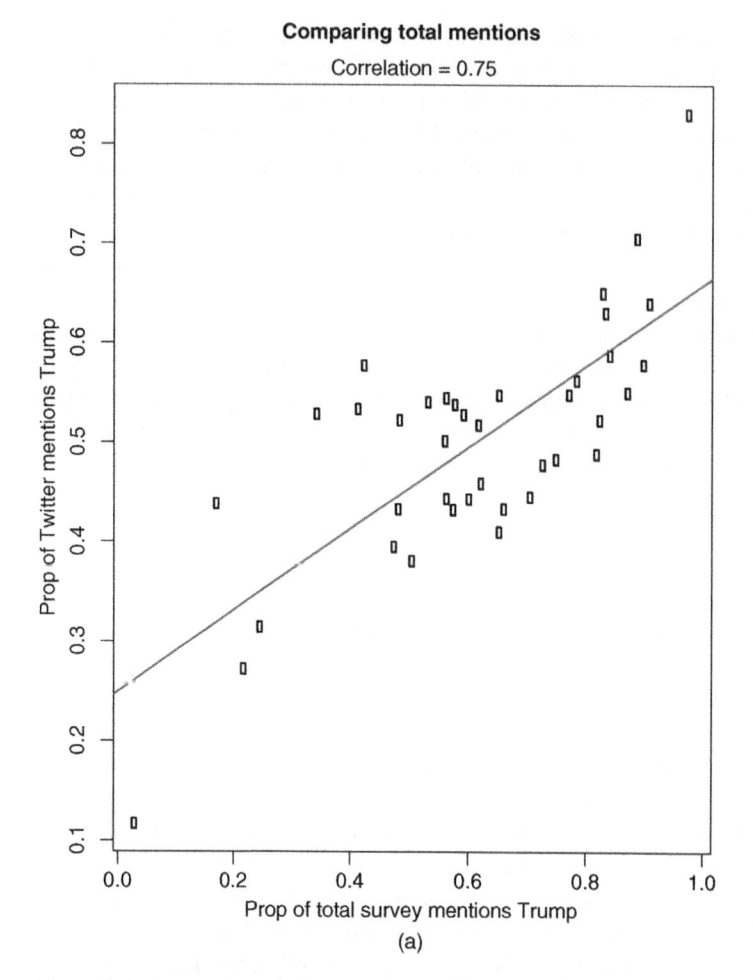

Figure 6.3 Comparing relative attention to Trump vs. Clinton event-related words across data streams for total mentions (a) and maximum attention (b).

he knew more than the generals about ISIS ($r = 0.90$). The weakest for Clinton surrounded Trump's staff shakeup ($r = 0.09$), when Trump was whisked offstage after an incident at a Nevada rally ($r = 0.27$) and for Trump's debate preparation ($r = 0.32$). In total, correlations for 31 of the events (46%) were above the 0.70 threshold that is typically used for inter-item reliability.

Correlations were typically somewhat higher for the three-day smoothed data. Smoothed correlations for the 67 candidate–event combinations ranged from 0.27 to 0.97 with an average value of 0.79. Further, 79.1% of these correlations were above the 0.70 threshold, which indicated a relatively strong degree of similarity

Comparing Maximums
Correlation = 0.79

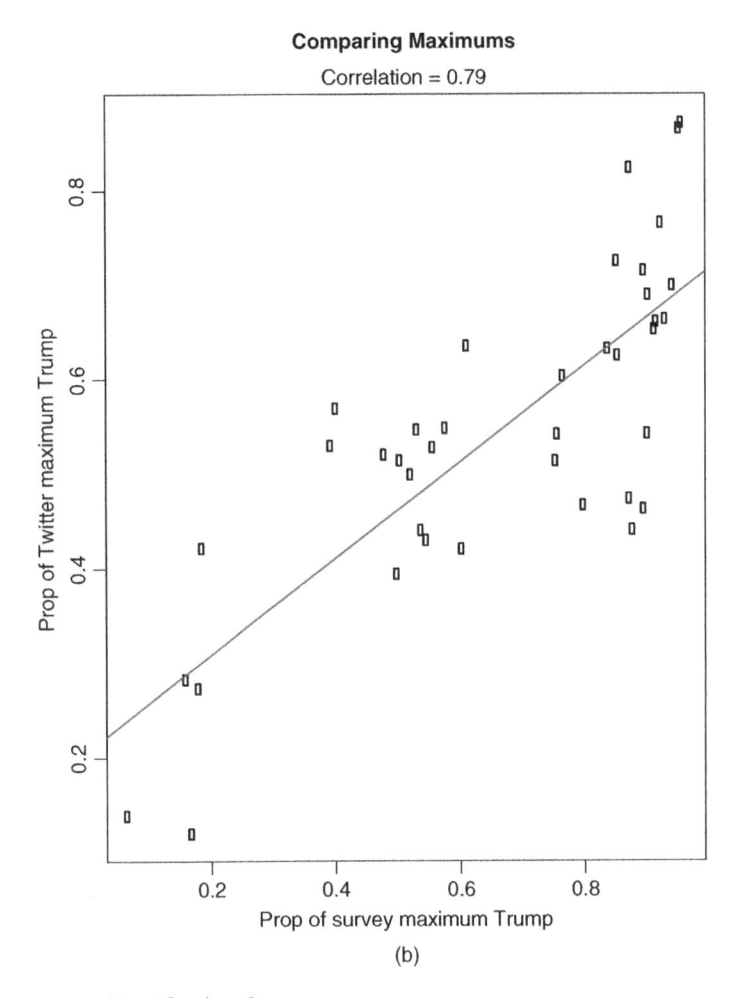

Figure 6.3 (Continued)

across data streams. The implication is that differences in the time it took for Twitter and survey responses to react to events may have artificially reduced the raw correlations.

At the same time, some systematic differences were evident in how Twitter and survey streams reacted to the same events. In particular, terms related to events were for a few extra days in the open-ended survey responses than they were in the Twitter data. That is, survey respondents would often continue to mention an event as something they had recently seen, read, or heard about the candidates for a few days following each event where Twitter users appeared to quickly move on (though events would reemerge in Twitter with more frequency). In contrast,

Correlations between Tweets and survey mentions

Average correlation = 0.65

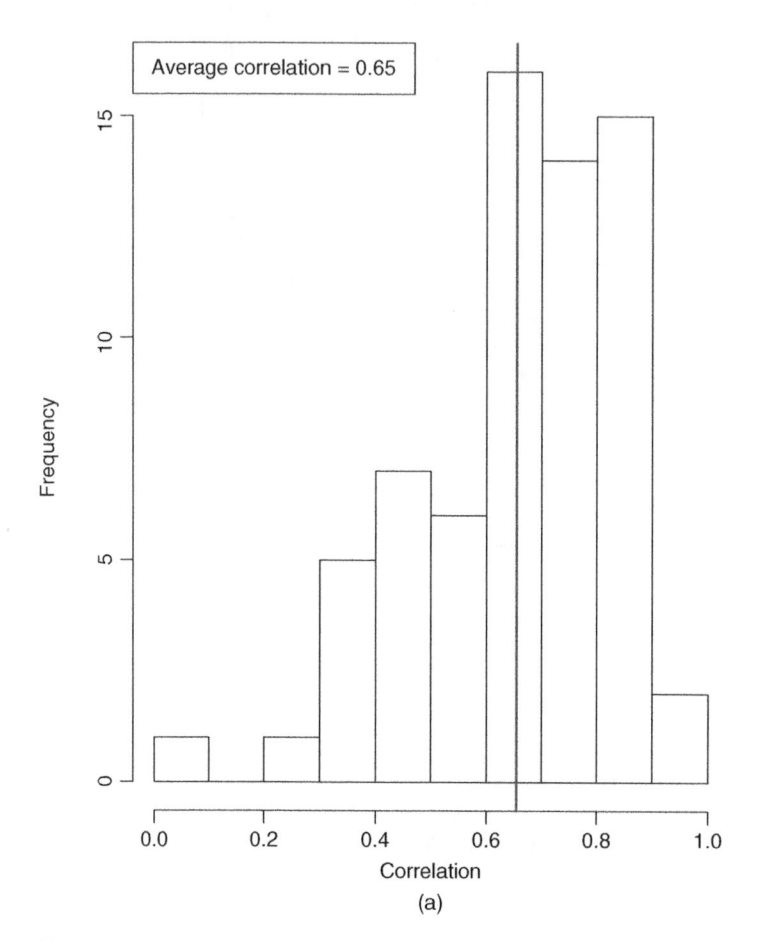

(a)

Figure 6.4 Correlations between mentions of event-related words in Twitter (a) and survey time trends (b).

the Twitter data stream often experienced smaller spikes in attention that could be associated with relevant terms. These smaller spikes were sometimes related occurrences and sometimes alternative events that also attracted social media attention. Notably, however, the smaller spikes were far less frequent (and often less pronounced) in the survey data, suggesting that the distribution of survey attention is more closely tied to large events than the distribution of Twitter attention, at least in the context of political campaigns. These differences may be less surprising if Twitter is viewed as a hybrid of public opinion and a news medium, but additional research is needed to understand why this is the case.

3–day smoothed correlations between tweets and survey mentions

Average correlation = 0.79

Correlation
(b)

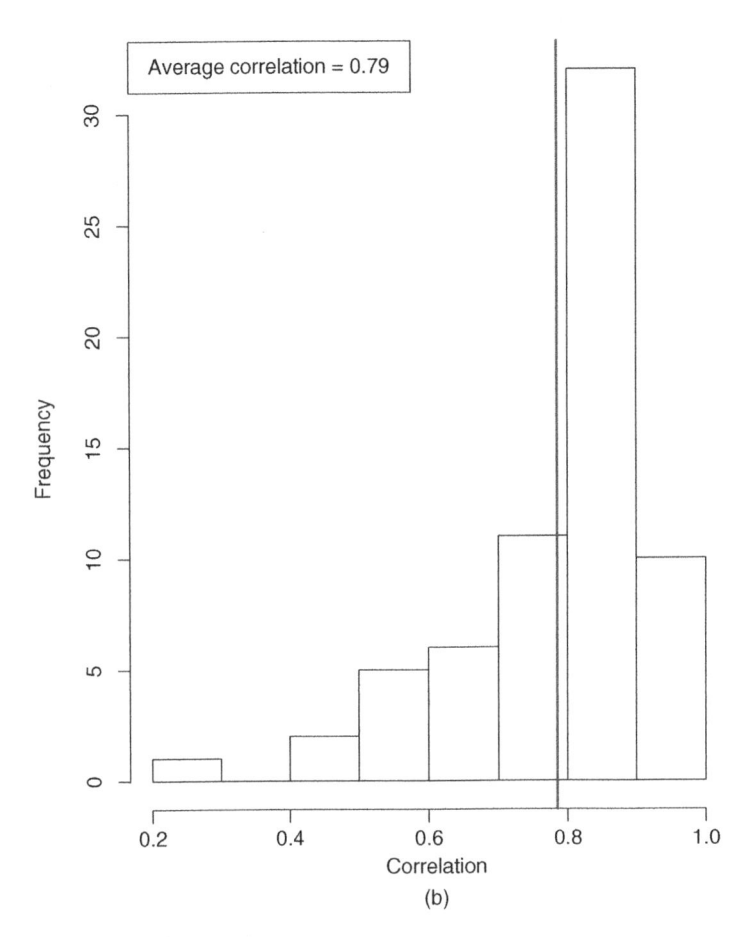

Figure 6.4 *(Continued)*

6.10 Unpacking Differences Between Samples

Differences in attention allocation between survey respondents and Twitter users are important both for understanding the communicative processes involved in creating both types of data and in considering how social media data can be used. The results of this analysis provide some support for the notion that tweets can track public attention over time, but highlight both that the patterns of attention in the two data streams behaved somewhat differently and that the attention allocated in Twitter did not always mirror the attention garnered in surveys.

Some differences we observed between Twitter and survey data are easily understood. For example, tweets logically often preceded surveys by a single day in attending to event-related words. Even the daily surveys conducted by Gallup were far less sensitive to current events than a medium that often seems to track what is in the news (Rogstad 2016). In contrast, however, the occasions when tweets and survey responses hit their relative maximums a number of days apart were more surprising and indicate that sometimes these data collection methods really were picking up on different phenomena.

A cursory look at the cases where these data streams were more vs. less similar suggested that the larger the event, the more the pattern of responses was similar across the two media. In other words, large-scale events might have been inducing similarities across diverse types of data and communities of respondents in ways that smaller-scale events did not share (cf. Pasek et al. 2018). But it is unclear how we should attribute these differences; when Twitter and survey data diverge, are the differences due to their data-generating processes, the communities of people who produced the data, some combination of these, or something else entirely?

In addition, the relatively discrete words used to identify events or the specific metrics used to establish their properties might have served to either inflate correspondence in some cases or to produce divergence in others. We examined a few other methods, such as weighting all keywords equally as indicators of each event, to discern whether the patterns observed would be consistent, and found that the results generally held. Notably, however, the number of arbitrary decisions involved was considerable, and we have not yet tested the impact of each systematically. It would be valuable to examine whether some additional transformations of the patterns we observed or tweaks in the analytic process could increase correspondence across multiple of the metrics we present. We could also examine whether different types of events differ systematically in their correspondence. Indeed, political occurrences may be unusual beasts either in the similarities in the attention they attract across surveys and tweets or in the differences.

Nonetheless, we believe the results presented here provide a valuable window into the extent to which one can reasonably assume that survey and Twitter metrics tell similar stories. By all indications, the answer is that they often do. Relying on tweets as opposed to surveys, however, likely produces a slightly different understanding of which events mattered and when they were most salient. So, as a measure of attention, we can conclude that these two types of data are not simply interchangeable.

6.11 Conclusion

Scholars hoping to use social media data to track attitudes and behaviors have a difficult task. They need to find a way to wrangle data produced as a social response to real-world events into a metric that can be the subject of scholarly analyses and that can yield meaningful inferences about society. As a growing body of research shows, this task is not simple. Models that were invented to understand survey responses and the implications of those responses for political and social behaviors have, time and again, proven limited in their ability to accomplish this feat. Social media data are a different beast from survey responses.

The current study continues to build on this basic conclusion. In it, we examine one relatively simple model for what a single type of social media data might tell us about attention to the candidates in the 2016 US Presidential election. When comparing tweets with open-ended survey responses about candidates, we find some support for the notion that social media attention – in this arena – might echo what we could get from surveys. But this support is coupled with evidence that some systematic differences need to be better understood. In this narrow arena, Twitter data do not appear to be a stand-in for survey data, but may be a useful tool for thinking about political events. Pragmatic survey methodologists might be able to use social media data to select topics that could garner valuable insights into the key events and issues of the day. Events detected using survey responses from Twitter users could possibly display patterns more similar to the events observed on Twitter, but there was no Twitter use variable in the study that could be used to identify these cases. Also important is that the type of survey question used here is a rarity: tweets may often be the best window we have into the state of public attention. Hence, more research is needed, but we believe that the attention-based model provides a fruitful avenue for thinking about how these two kinds of public opinion data might relate.

References

Achrekar, H., Gandhe, A., Lazarus, R. et al. (2011). Predicting flu trends using Twitter data. In: *Proceedings of the 2011 IEEE Conference on Computer Communications Workshops (INFOCOM WKSHPS)*, 702–707. Shanghai, P.R. China: IEEE https://doi.org/10.1109/INFCOMW.2011.5928903.

Anstead, N. and O'Loughlin, B. (2015). Social media analysis and public opinion: the 2010 UK general election. *Journal of Computer-Mediated Communication* 20 (2): 204–220. https://doi.org/10.1111/jcc4.12102.

Barberá, P. (2016). *Less is more? How demographic sample weights can improve public opinion estimates based on Twitter data*. Working paper. https://doi.org/10.1101/095778.

Blevins, C. and Mullen, L. (2015). Jane, John… Leslie? A historical method for algorithmic gender prediction. *DHQ: Digital Humanities Quarterly* 9 (3) http://www.digitalhumanities.org/dhq/vol/9/3/000223/000223.html.

Bode, L., Budak, C., Ladd, J.M. et al. (2020). *Words That Matter: How the News and Social Media Shaped the 2016 Presidential Campaign*. Washington, DC: Brookings Institution Press.

Ceron, A., Curini, L., Iacus, S.M. et al. (2014). Every tweet counts? How sentiment analysis of social media can improve our knowledge of citizens' political preferences with an application to Italy and France. *New Media & Society* 16 (2): 340–358. https://doi.org/10.1177/1461444813480466.

Chen, X., Wang, Y., Agichtein, E., et al. (2015). A comparative study of demographic attribute inference in Twitter. Presented at the Ninth International AAAI Conference on Web and Social Media.

Conover, M. D., Gonçalves, B., Ratkiewicz, J., et al. (2012). Predicting the political alignment of Twitter users. *Presented at the 2011 IEEE Third International Conference on Privacy, Security, Risk and Trust (PASSAT)*, pp. 192–199. IEEE. https://doi.org/10.1109/PASSAT/SocialCom.2011.34.

Conrad, F. G., Schober, M. F., Pasek, J., et al. (2015). A collective-vs-self hypothesis for when Twitter and survey data tell the same story. *6th Conference of the European Survey Research Association*, Reykjavic, Iceland (13–17 July 2015).

Couper, M.P. (2013). Is the sky falling? New technology, changing media, and the future of surveys. *Survey Research Methods* 7 (3): 145–156.

Culotta, A., Kumar, N. R., and Cutler, J. (2015). Predicting the demographics of Twitter users from Website traffic data. *Presented at the Twenty-Ninth AAAI Conference on Artificial Intelligence*, pp. 72–78 (25–29 Jan 2015). Austin, TX: AAAI.

Diaz, F., Gamon, M., Hofman, J.M. et al. (2016). Online and social media data as an imperfect continuous panel survey. *PLoS One* 11 (1): e0145406. https://doi.org/10.1371/journal.pone.0145406.

Freelon, D. (2019). Inferring individual-level characteristics from digital trace data: issues and recommendations. In: *Digital Discussions: How Big Data Informs Political Communication* (eds. N.J. Stroud and S. McGregor). New York: Routledge.

Gayo-Avello, D. (2012). No, you cannot predict elections with Twitter. *IEEE Internet Computing* 16 (6): 91–94. https://doi.org/10.1109/MIC.2012.137.

Golbeck, J. and Hansen, D. (2011). Computing political preference among twitter followers. *Proceedings of the SIGCHI Conference on Human Factors in Computing Systems*, Vancouver, BC, Canada, pp. 1105–1108. Association for Computing Machinery (ACM). https://doi.org/10.1145/1978942.1979106.

Golder, S.A. and Macy, M.W. (2011). Diurnal and seasonal mood vary with work, sleep, and daylength across diverse cultures. *Science* 333 (6051): 1878–1881. https://doi.org/10.1126/science.1202775.

Greenwood, S., Perrin, A., and Duggan, M. (2016). *Social Media Update 2016*. Washington, DC: Pew Research Center.

Hermida, A. (2010). Twittering the news. *Journalism Practice* 4 (3): 297–308.

Hsieh, Y. and Murphy, J. (2017). Total Twitter error: decomposing public opinion measurement on Twitter from a total survey error perspective. In: *Total Survey Error in Practice*, vol. 74 (eds. B.T. West, N.C. Tucker, L.E. Lyberg, et al.), 23–46. (Wiley Series in Survey Methodology). Hoboken, NJ: John Wiley & Sons.

Jang, S.M. and Pasek, J. (2015). Assessing the carrying capacity of Twitter and online news. *Mass Communication and Society* 18 (5): 577–598. https://doi.org/10.1080/15205436.2015.1035397.

Jungherr, A., Jürgens, P., and Schoen, H. (2012). Why the pirate party won the German election of 2009 or the trouble with predictions: a response to Tumasjan, A., Sprenger, T. O., Sander, P. G., & Welpe, I. M. "predicting elections with Twitter: what 140 characters reveal about political sentiment". *Social Science Computer Review* 30 (2): 229–234. https://doi.org/10.1177/0894439311404119.

Jungherr, A., Schoen, H., Posegga, O. et al. (2016). Digital trace data in the study of public opinion. *Social Science Computer Review* 35 (3): 336–356. https://doi.org/10.1177/0894439316631043.

Karpf, D. (2016). *Analytic Activism*. New York: Oxford University Press.

Keeter, S., Kennedy, C., Dimock, M. et al. (2006). Gauging the impact of growing nonresponse on estimates from a national RDD telephone survey. *Public Opinion Quarterly* 70 (5): 759–779. https://doi.org/10.1093/poq/nfl035.

Kolenikov, S. and Kennedy, C. (2014). Evaluating three approaches to statistically adjust for mode effects. *Journal of Survey Statistics and Methodology* 2 (2): 126–158.

Kwak, H., Lee, C., Park, H., et al. (2010). What is Twitter, a social network or a news media? *Proceedings of the 19th International Conference on World Wide Web*, Raleigh, NC, pp. 591–600. Association for Computing Machinery (ACM).

Lampos, V., Preoţiuc-Pietro, D., and Cohn, T. (2013). A user-centric model of voting intention from social media. Presented at the 51st Annual Meeting of the Association for Computational Linguistics, Sofia, Bulgaria, pp. 993–1003.

Mahmud, J., Nichols, J., and Drews, C. (2012). Where is this Tweet from? Inferring home locations of Twitter users. *Proceedings of the Sixth International AAAI Conference on Weblogs and Social Media*, Dublin, Ireland, pp. 511–415. AAAI

Marwick, A.E. and Boyd, D. (2011). I tweet honestly, I tweet passionately: Twitter users, context collapse, and the imagined audience. *New Media & Society* 13 (1): 114–133. https://doi.org/10.1177/1461444810365313.

McCombs, M.E. and Shaw, D.L. (1972). The agenda-setting function of mass media. *Public Opinion Quarterly* 36 (2): 176–187. https://doi.org/10.1086/267990.

McCombs, M.E. and Shaw, D.L. (1993). The evolution of agenda-setting research: twenty-five years in the marketplace of ideas. *Journal of Communication* 43 (2): 58–67. https://doi.org/10.1111/j.1460-2466.1993.tb01262.x.

Mislove, A., Lehmann, S., Ahn, Y.-Y., et al. (2011). Understanding the demographics of Twitter users. *Proceedings of the Fifth International AAAI Conference on Weblogs and Social Media*, Barcelona, Spain, pp. 554–557. AAAI.

Mitchell, A. and Hitlin, P. (2013). *Twitter Reaction to Events Often at Odds with Overall Public Opinion*. Washington, DC: Pew Research Center.

Murphy, J., Link, M.W., Childs, J.H. et al. (2014). *Report of the Emerging Technologies Task Force of the American Association for Public Opinion Research*. Washington, DC: American Association for Public Opinion Research. http://www.aapor.org/Social_Media_Task_Force_Report.htm.

Neuman, W.R., Guggenheim, L., Mo Jang, S. et al. (2014). The dynamics of public attention: agenda-setting theory meets big data. *Journal of Communication* 64 (2): 193–214. https://doi.org/10.1111/jcom.12088.

O'Connor, B., Balasubramanyan, R., Routledge, B. R., et al. (2010). From tweets to polls: linking text sentiment to public opinion time series. *Proceedings of the International AAAI Conference on Weblogs and Social Media*, pp. 122–129. AAAI

Pasek, J., McClain, C.A., Newport, F. et al. (2019). Who's Tweeting about the President? What big survey data can tell us about digital traces. *Social Science Computer Review* https://doi.org/10.1177/0894439318822007.

Pasek, J., Yan, H.Y., Conrad, F.G. et al. (2018). The stability of economic correlations over time. *Public Opinion Quarterly* 82 (3): 470–492. https://doi.org/10.1093/poq/nfy030.

Roberts, C., Vandenplas, C., and Stähli, M.E. (2014). Evaluating the impact of response enhancement methods on the risk of nonresponse bias and survey costs. *Survey Research Methods* 8 (2): 67–80. https://doi.org/10.18148/srm/2014.v8i2.5459.

Rogstad, I. (2016). Is Twitter just rehashing? Intermedia agenda setting between Twitter and mainstream media. *Journal of Information Technology & Politics* 13 (2): 142–158. https://doi.org/10.1080/19331681.2016.1160263.

Schober, M.F., Pasek, J., Guggenheim, L. et al. (2016). Social media analyses for social measurement. *Public Opinion Quarterly* 80 (1): 180–211. https://doi.org/10.1093/poq/nfv048.

Schuman, H. and Presser, S. (1981). *Questions and Answers in Attitude Surveys*. New York: Academic Press.

Smailović, J., Kranjc, J., and Grčar, M. (2015). Monitoring the Twitter sentiment during the Bulgarian elections. 2015 IEEE International Conference on Data Science and Advanced Analytics (DSAA), Paris, pp. 1–10.

Tumasjan, A., Sprenger, T.O., Sandner, P.G. et al. (2011). Election forecasts with Twitter. *Social Science Computer Review* 29 (4): 402–418. https://doi.org/10.1177/0894439310386557.

7

Improving Quality of Administrative Data: A Case Study with FBI's National Incident-Based Reporting System Data

Dan Liao[1], Marcus E. Berzofsky[1], G. Lance Couzens[1], Ian Thomas[1], and Alexia Cooper[2]

[1] *RTI International, Research Triangle Park, NC, USA*
[2] *Bureau of Justice Statistics, Washington, DC, USA*

7.1 Introduction

With the dramatic growth in computational power and data storage sources in the past two decades, government agencies, organizations, and corporations have made great efforts to modernize administrative procedures that collect detailed, complex qualitative and quantitative information via electronic systems. Because this information is collected typically for administrative purposes, such as registration, record keeping, or transaction monitoring, this type of information is referred to as *administrative data*. Aside from administrative purposes, the increased collection of these types of data also presents exciting opportunities for statisticians, researchers, and policymakers to address important topics in a timely manner without requiring additional resources to collect the data by traditional experiments or surveys.

Many statistical institutes and researchers worldwide have explored producing official statistics with administrative data (e.g. Connelly et al. 2016; Holt 2007; Statistics Finland 2004; Wallgren and Wallgren 2007). However, like other data sources, the need to understand and control for data quality issues in administrative data before putting them in statistical use becomes crucial. Literature in the past decade has been committed to establishing structured and systematic frameworks to assess data quality issues in administrative data and to facilitating decision-making when designing the data processing and estimation procedures. Eurostat (2009) developed a quality framework for official statistics consisting of

Big Data Meets Survey Science: A Collection of Innovative Methods, First Edition. Edited by Craig A. Hill, Paul P. Biemer, Trent D. Buskirk, Lilli Japec, Antje Kirchner, Stas Kolenikov, and Lars E. Lyberg.
© 2021 John Wiley & Sons, Inc. Published 2021 by John Wiley & Sons, Inc.

six dimensions: relevance, accuracy, timeliness and punctuality, accessibility and clarity, comparability, and coherence. The United Nations Economic Commission for Europe (UNECE) (2011) discussed possibilities and limitations when applying these criteria to administrative data. These criteria may be used to assess the quality of resulting statistics based on administrative data. However, some dimensions, such as accuracy, might be difficult to measure for the administrative data themselves. Zhang (2012) developed a two-phase quality assessment framework by applying the total survey error (TSE) paradigm (Groves and Lyberg 2010; Biemer 2010), a theoretical data quality assessment framework for survey data, to administrative data and integrated data with combined data sources that encompass both survey data and administrative data. Reid, Zabala, and Holmberg (2017) extended Zhang's two-phase framework to three phases. Phase I assesses the quality of each data source. Phase II determines the impact of the identified data errors in each data source on the integrated data. Phase III evaluates the final statistical outputs based on the integrated data. Because maintaining and improving data quality can be a long-term process, Biemer et al. (2014) suggested a general framework, named ASPIRE (A System for Product Improvement, Review, and Evaluation), to achieve continual improvements in data quality for statistical programs that supply a continuous flow of statistical data to users and stakeholders. In their paper, they emphasized the accuracy component of product quality, whereas the other quality dimensions can be considered constraints during the production process. Furthermore, to improve the accuracy of integrated data, Biemer and Amaya (Chapter 4 in this book (2019)) describe a practical row–column–cell error framework for evaluating the quality of the unified dataset itself and a related error framework to evaluate the hybrid estimate produced from the unified dataset.

Although these frameworks are general and can be widely applicable to improve data quality for administrative data and data of other types, implementing them in practical statistical projects can still be challenging for practitioners. First, these frameworks are conceptual and can be very abstract. Each data source may have its own unique features and problems. Defining and measuring different error components require careful deliberation and may entail a learning curve to get to the root of the problems. Second, unlike sample survey data that are often considered *primary* in that the data are purposefully collected for well-defined statistical goals, administrative data are often *secondary* in that they are put to statistical uses distinct from their original purpose. Analysts sometimes have little information on the data collection procedures and are limited in their ability to examine some error components, such as specification errors (i.e. how the concept implied by the data variables differs from the concept meant to be measured in the target research problem) or measurement errors (i.e. how the method of obtaining the data affects the recorded values). Therefore, practitioners need to carefully design their data quality assessment plan based on the theoretical frameworks while accounting for the potential barriers. In addition, practitioners must also consider concrete technical limitations within budgetary and time constraints, especially when dealing with data of large volume.

This chapter describes a statistical estimation project that aims to use administrative data collected from a national incident-based crime-reporting system to estimate the prevalence and characteristics of crimes and arrests in the United States. Like other administrative data, this data source contains various data quality problems. To produce national estimates on crime, a comprehensive data quality assessment and strategy development to improve the quality of these administrative data had to be undertaken. As described in Section 7.2, the data studied here have some special features that are common in administrative data or other types of Big Data. For instance, the data are incident based and reported by law enforcement agencies (LEAs) and collected using a hierarchical data structure, with higher level information on the reporting LEA and incident, and lower level information on the characteristics of victim, offender, offense, property, and other related information under the incident. Moreover, because the data are reported by LEAs, the size and the characteristics of the reporting LEAs affect the representativeness of the data considerably. Finally, auxiliary data from other sources can be used in the process of evaluating and improving data quality. However, their quality and accessibility must also factor into the entire data quality improvement process.

The work described in this chapter concentrates on improving the quality of the dataset itself to put it into statistical use, while final statistical estimation is treated as out of scope. Section 7.2 provides some background information on the National Incident-Based Reporting System (NIBRS) database, the focus of this study. Section 7.2.1 provides an overview of crime statistics with both administrative data and survey data in the United States to help readers better understand the history of these data and their target statistical usage. Section 7.2.2 describes the strategies used in constructing the database and forming the analytic platform to facilitate and expedite the analytic activities under this work. Section 7.3 adopts the row–column–cell framework suggested in Chapter 4 to assess the quality of the NIBRS dataset and presents strategies to mitigate the errors and improve the quality of this dataset. Section 7.4 shares our unique experiences and insights gained from this project that can be applied to other statistical projects involving data quality improvement. This work can be considered a concrete case study in dealing with data quality issues and, we hope, can provide additional insights for practitioners on designing and implementing their own data quality assessments, for either administrative data or more generic Big Data.

7.2 The NIBRS Database

7.2.1 Administrative Crime Statistics and the History of NIBRS Data

Administrative data sources of crime statistics, the focus of this chapter, are collected from local LEAs. In the United States, LEAs *voluntarily* submit counts of reported crimes by type of crime to the Federal Bureau of Investigation (FBI) through the Uniform Crime Report (UCR) Program. The UCR program, which was conceived in 1929, is the only data collection that includes information at a national, state, and local level on the amount of crime (by type) occurring in the United States. From its inception, the goal of the UCR program, similar to other administrative data sources, was to establish a system to collect information on crime in a uniform, standardized way across numerous LEAs. As of 2015, the UCR program collected data from LEAs covering 99% of the US population (Criminal Justice Information Services Division 2016).[1]

Between the UCR program's inception and the 1980s, LEAs reported crime data to the FBI through the Summary Reporting System (SRS). The SRS provides summary-level counts of seven main crime types by law enforcement with limited or no information about reported incidents beyond the type of crime that occurred. In other words, characteristics of the victim, the perpetrator, or the incident itself are not included in the SRS data. As a consequence, some types of crimes, specifically those defined by the characteristics of the crime, are not explicitly reported and/or cannot be uniquely identified. For example, the SRS cannot be used to quantify crimes such as firearm violence, crimes committed by gangs, domestic violence, and crimes against children. To provide additional detail of each incident and allow for a broader array of crimes to be reported, the FBI developed the NIBRS in the 1980s. Strom and Smith (2017) detail several benefits of NIBRS over the SRS. For example, NIBRS provides a level of detail and context about the crime, victim, and offender not available in the SRS. Additionally, NIBRS has greater flexibility in the aggregation of crime data than the SRS allows. Moreover, NIBRS offers better quality data by incorporating checks on each incident rather than a check on a total number of reported crimes.

Despite its benefits, as of 2016, only about 6900[2] of the roughly 18 000 LEAs in the United States reported crime through NIBRS. Moreover, the 6900 LEAs that do report to NIBRS do not include any of the LEAs in major metropolitan service areas. In terms of total crimes in the United States, the NIBRS-reporting agencies

---

[1] Although participation in the UCR program is voluntary, law enforcement agencies are not eligible for federal funding opportunities, such as Byrne JAG funding, if they do not participate in the UCR program. Therefore, almost all agencies participate in the Summary Reporting System program.
[2] Numbers are from https://ucr.fbi.gov/nibrs/2016/resource-pages/nibrs-2016_summary.pdf.

have very low coverage: about 29% of the US residential population (Strom and Smith 2017). Even though many LEAs collect the NIBRS data elements for each incident, most LEAs do not report data to NIBRS – but rather continue to report through the SRS – because their record management systems (RMSs) do not comport with the way in which NIBRS requires data to be submitted. The cost to update or modify an LEA's RMS is the most common reason to maintain the status quo rather than transition to NIBRS.

In an effort to motivate agencies to report using NIBRS, the FBI has decided to retire the SRS in 2021 and collect crime data only through NIBRS. In other words, after 2021, agencies will no longer be able to report UCR data through the SRS – leaving NIBRS as the only option. To help encourage and facilitate the transition to NIBRS, the FBI and Bureau of Justice Statistics (BJS) are providing grants to LEAs to update their RMS.

7.2.2 Construction of the NIBRS Dataset

NIBRS, like many administrative datasets, is a hierarchical system and has a very large volume of data. Figure 7.1 illustrates the six main file-type levels in this hierarchical system: administrative, offense, property, victim, offender, and arrestee.[3] An agency has a record for each incident that was reported. Each incident contains information about each offense, the offenders, and the victims. If there are multiple offenses, offenders, or victims for an incident, a specific record is associated with each. The hierarchical structure is maintained through a series of unique identifiers (IDs) that allow users to link victims and offenders within an incident and agency.

The NIBRS data used for this analysis come from the FBI's Crime Data Explorer[4] (CDE). The CDE allows users to download the NIBRS data in an easy-to-use format for one state for one year at a time. This state–year pair is delivered as a collection of comma-separated text files, along with scripts for importing the data into a relational database. Each file can be connected through a series of unique identifier keys. The data files at the CDE site were downloaded and merged into a large relational database holding all publicly available years and states of data and storing data from different file-type levels across 43 unique data tables.

Based on the 2016 data files, and with only one-third of LEAs participating in NIBRS, there are more than five million incident reports for that single year alone. Once all agencies report through NIBRS, we anticipate that the size of the data files could increase to 15–20 million records per year. Because NIBRS data is hierarchical, a relational database is an ideal way to store and access these data. By using the

---

3 A more detailed diagram that demonstrates the NIBRS data structure is available at the Crime Data Explorer' website: https://crime-data-explorer.fr.cloud.gov/downloads-and-docs.
4 See https://crime-data-explorer.fr.cloud.gov/.

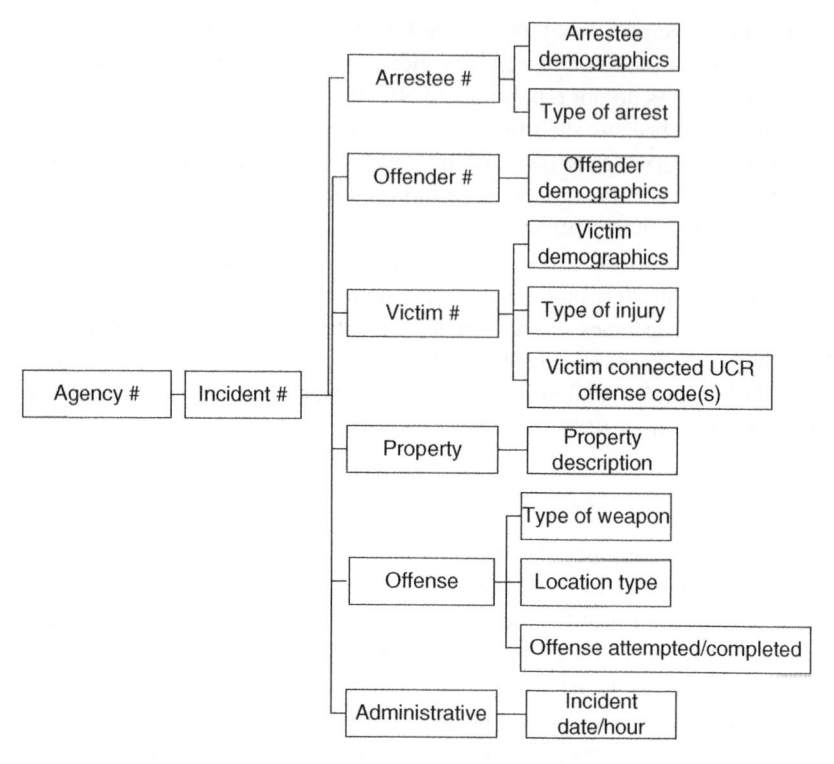

Figure 7.1 Hierarchical structure of the NIBRS data. UCR = uniform crime report.

database's natural ability to interlink tables, the CDE NIBRS data can be accessed much more efficiently than data stored in the rectangular or flat data files such as the NIBRS data files available through the National Archive of Criminal Justice Data at Inter-University Consortium for Political and Social Research (ICPSR).[5] In addition, the CDE data are now formatted with more human-readable column names and a simpler, and well-documented, table structure.

7.3 Data Quality Improvement Based on the Total Error Framework

Quality of administrative data for statistical use can be assessed in two phases: (i) a source-specific assessment and (ii) a product-specific assessment (Eurostat 2003).

---

[5] See https://www.icpsr.umich.edu/icpsrweb/. The ICPSR provides the NIBRS data in different formats (e.g. SAS, Stata, SPSS, and R) and is a popular source for researchers to obtain the NIBRS data.

A source-specific quality assessment focuses on the data collection and reporting procedures conducted by submitting agencies. To maintain the data quality from the source, the FBI UCR program has implemented rigorous quality checks in its data submission software. It rejects and asks for resubmission if an NIBRS incident report from an LEA fails its quality checks (see more details in the NIBRS Technical Specifications[6]). A product-specific assessment, which is the focus of this work, aims at identifying the analytic need or statistical use of the administrative data and assessing whether they can meet the need or use. In this project, the statistical use of the NIBRS data is to generate national estimates of crime and arrests. The design of our data quality assessment and improvement centers on this purpose.

In this section, a row–column–cell total error framework developed by Biemer et al. (2014) and described in Biemer and Amaya (Chapter 4, (2019)) is adopted to identify potential errors in the entire NIBRS database. As mentioned in Japec et al. (2015) and Biemer and Amaya (Chapter 4 (2019)), data are often reformatted as rectangular files with rows and columns to be analyzed in all major statistical software packages, even though the datasets may be stored in hierarchical or federated data structures. Based on this fact, Biemer and Amaya suggested the row–column–cell framework to assess total error for a rectangular dataset given a heuristic formula that can be expressed as follows: total error = row error + column error + cell error (defined in detail in Section 7.3.1). The three major error components can then be assessed separately. Their framework is chosen over the TSE framework adopted in Zhang (2012) and Reid, Zabala, and Holmberg (2017), because, as most of the secondary data users, we have very limited information and resources to understand the generating process of the NIBRS data; the most efficient method is to evaluate the quality of the dataset itself.

As described in Section 7.2.2, the constructed NIBRS database contains 43 data tables with hundreds of variables and an intricate hierarchical structure. Evaluating the entire database as one big rectangular dataset is impractical. To simplify this situation and improve efficiency, the three-phase concept used by Reid, Zabala, and Holmberg (2017) is applied in this work. Phase I evaluates the key data tables at different levels (e.g. agency level or victim level) separately. Phase II evaluates the integrated data as well as the data integration process when multiple data tables are integrated. Although this chapter focuses on the dataset itself, a Phase III evaluation should be conducted when generating final statistical estimates based on the integrated data. This phase should evaluate the quality of the final estimates by accounting for all error sources, including the error sources discovered in the first two phases and the bias or variance introduced by estimation

---

6 Available at: https://www.fbi.gov/services/cjis/ucr/data-documentation.

methods (e.g. weighting, imputation, assumptions made when performing statistical modeling). Finally, strategies to mitigate identified error components such as probability sampling, statistical weighting, and imputation are discussed.

7.3.1 Data Quality Assessment for Using Row–Column–Cell Framework

As shown in Figure 7.1, the NIBRS database contains multiple file-type levels, each of which is stored in a separate set of data tables. For illustration purposes, we have selected five data tables for discussion in this section, including an agency data table, an incident data table, a victim data table, an offender data table, and an offense data table. As illustrated in Figure 7.2, these five data tables represent three typical file levels that can be seen in administrative records. The agency data table contains information on the source of the data, which can be schools in administrative records for education, or hospitals in administrative records for medical expenditures. The incident data table contains information on each individual report, which can be a student's test reports in education, or an expense report in medical context. The victim, offender, and offense data tables include detailed information in the individual report and can be linked to explore the associations across variables from different data tables. Although the following discussion concentrates on these data tables in NIBRS, readers can associate our discussion with their data and data tables when performing their own data quality assessment.

7.3.1.1 Phase I: Evaluating Each Data Table

In Phase I, the five data tables are evaluated separately based on Biemer and Amaya's total error framework. Each data table could carry different types of errors. This process should also distinguish the error components that can be addressed or adjusted based on the information available from the error components where examination is limited due to lack of adequate information. For

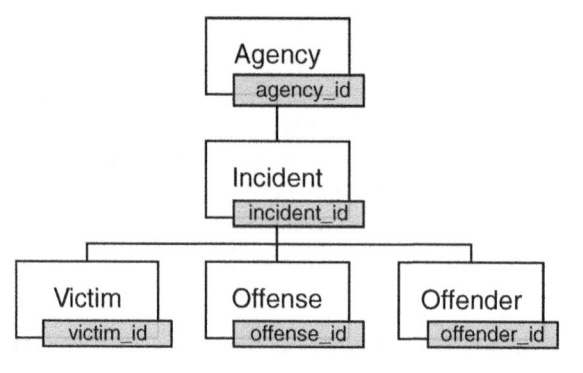

Figure 7.2 Five data tables selected for discussion in Section 7.3.

example, coverage error due to nonresponding agencies may be reduced through statistical weighting with auxiliary information available on the target population, whereas measurement error in a variable (e.g. ethnicity of the offender) will be difficult to evaluate without a greater depth of understanding as to how the police made the judgment when inputting this information.

7.3.1.2 Row Errors

Three types of potential errors are considered to examine the rows: omissions, duplications, and erroneous inclusions. In the agency data table, omission error is of concern because of the large proportion of the NIBRS nonreporting agencies in the target population. If an LEA does not have an RMS that is compliant with NIBRS, then that LEA can report UCR data only through the SRS. Agencies with a non-NIBRS-capable RMS, although a part of the target population, are not covered by the NIBRS-capable portion of the population. Therefore, in this case, this type of error is also known as a *coverage error* because NIBRS is not available to all agencies. In 2016, about 6900 of about 18 000 LEAs in the United States reported their crime and arrest data in the NIBRS format. The ID variable in the agency data table is the originating agency identifier (ORI) number officially assigned to each LEA. We did not find any duplication error in the agency table (by confirming no ORI occurs more than once). The erroneous inclusion error can be translated into an eligibility issue when examining the agency data table. The statistical purpose of this project is to produce national estimates of crime for 50 states (and the District of Columbia) but excluding other territories. Any agencies from other territories should be considered as ineligible and excluded if they are listed in the agency table. In the incident data table, omission error is also a concern because an agency could fail to submit an incident report, or a submitted incident report could fail to pass quality checks and get rejected by the UCR edit checks. This type of error is also known as a *nonresponse error*. Duplications are mainly controlled by the design of the NIBRS data collection system that assigns unique incident ID numbers to each incident report to avoid duplications caused by resubmissions (see the NIBRS Technical Specifications for more detail). Duplication error is found by checking whether multiple rows in this data table have the same incident number. Erroneous inclusions are minor in the incident data table, given that each incident in the database has already passed all the quality checks developed by the data collection program that have excluded the ineligible reports.

Row errors in the offender, victim, and offense tables could occur if officers make flawed inputs into the system. These could be omissions, or duplications, or erroneous inclusions. The quality of the incident reporting can vary across agencies and be influenced by individual reporting officers. However, the row errors within the data tables under the incident level could be very difficult to assess without an in-depth investigation of the reporting agencies.

7.3.1.3 Column Errors

Specification error is the most common type of column error. It occurs when the concept captured by the measure (usually in the form of one or more columns) in the data differs from the target concept meant to be measured for particular research questions. The NIBRS data, as a data source from administrative collections, usually aligns the measure with the target concept well because the information measured is mainly factual, such as the agency type (e.g. state police or municipal police), whether a weapon was present in the incident, the victim's gender, and the relationship between victim and offender. The specification errors are usually smaller in this type of measurement compared with conceptually complex survey questions on an individual's behaviors and attitudes. Yet when generating final statistical outputs using the NIBRS data, one still needs to confirm that the measures align with the target concepts or constructs. For example, the definition of an offense type (e.g. rape) in NIBRS can be different in the target research questions.

7.3.1.4 Cell Errors

Two types of potential errors are considered to examine the cells: content errors and missing data. The variables in the agency data file are generated from the UCR administrative system and thus do not have either type of errors. The other four data tables, however, could have these errors in varying degrees and must be assessed further.

Content errors can be caused by measurement errors, or by keying or coding errors made by the reporting units (reporting officers in our case). For the data tables, content errors are evaluated mainly by identifying invalid values based on intercorrelation across two or more variables in the database. The quality checks developed by the UCR programs have already incorporated a variety of outlier detection algorithms and logic checks that focus on marginally examining single variables. Checking invalid values based on intercorrelation across multiple variables can be the next step to further detect invalid values. For instance, if the victim–offender relationship in an incident indicates that the victim is the offender's grandfather and the victim's gender in the data is female, then it indicates that either the victim–offender relationship or victim's gender is invalid in this incident.

NIBRS has two types of missing data: unknowns and missing values (i.e. blanks). There is an "Unknown" category under some variables in the incident reports (e.g. offender's age, the value of the damaged property). The mechanisms that yield unknowns and truly missing data can be very different and, thus, need to be assessed separately. For example, for an incident in which an arrest has not been successfully made, the offender's age can be truly unknown. If the offender's age in the data is shown as "Unknown," the response is legitimate, indicating that the police don't know the offender's age, whereas if the offender's age is shown as "blank" (i.e. missing), the offender's age might be known to the police but was not successfully reported to NIBRS.

7.3.1.5 Row-Column-Cell Errors Impacting NIBRS
Through the Phase I evaluation, we identified several major error sources that need to be addressed:

Row: coverage errors in the agency data table due to nonreporting agencies
Row: nonresponse errors in the incident data table due to unreported incident reports
Cell: invalid values within the incident reports (i.e. in the incident, victim, offender, offense data tables)
Cell: "unknown" values within the incident reports
Cell: missing (blank) values within the incident reports

7.3.1.6 Phase II: Evaluating the Integrated Data
Multiple data tables can be linked together so that the errors identified in Phase I can be further assessed by taking advantage of intercorrelations among variables in different data tables. The linked data tables can also be combined with external data sources to facilitate data quality assessment at this stage. In our project, several different external data sources are publicly available and can be used, including (i) the UCR SRS data with monthly crime counts of major offense types reported by almost all the LEAs in the nation, (ii) the Law Enforcement Officers Killed and Assaulted (LEOKA) Program data with characteristics (e.g. agency's number of sworn officers, agency type) of all LEAs in the nation, and (iii) Census Bureau population data. This yields the Phase II evaluation, which focuses on assessing errors within the integrated data as well as the data integration process itself.

7.3.1.7 Errors in Data Integration Process
Given that improper data integration may be a source of errors (especially row error), the data integration procedure should be validated before assessing the integrated data. Managing the data integration process is critical in data quality assessment when working with a database-like NIBRS with many different data tables and data linkage variables.

For example, consider a case of merging incident, victim, and offense data tables. The linkage relationship among these three data tables is shown in Figure 7.3. Each white rectangle in this figure represents a data table with its corresponding ID variable name. Each pair within the set of these three tables can be merged by their ID variables. One incident could involve multiple offenses and multiple victims. Within this incident, one victim could be related to one or more offenses but not all the offenses.

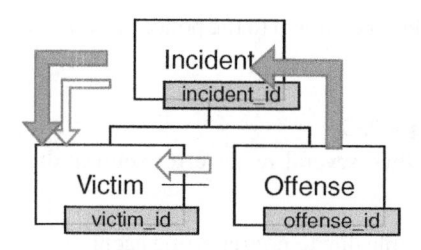

Figure 7.3 Correct (white) and wrong (gray) data linkage among incident, victim, and offense data tables.

When integrating the three data tables, if an analyst overlooked the direct linkage between the offense data table and the victim data table, he or she may link the offense data table to the incident data table first and then link the merged data table with the victim data table based on the linkage between incident ID and victim ID. This incorrect linkage is shown in gray arrows in Figure 7.3. This linkage leads to a scenario in which each victim has rows for all the offense ID values under this incident, a type of erroneous inclusion. The correct way to link the three data tables is shown in white arrows in Figure 7.3. Both the incident data table and the offense data table should be linked to the victim data table directly.

7.3.1.8 Coverage Errors Due to Nonreporting Agencies

After validating the data integration process, the data errors identified in Phase I can be further assessed using the integrated data. First, the coverage errors due to nonreporting agencies in the agency data table can be assessed after merging the agency data table with the SRS data file that contains aggregate monthly tallies of crimes reported by almost all LEAs in the nation. Some studies (Addington 2008; McCormack, Pattavina, and Tracy 2017) found that the mix of all reporting LEAs does not support generating national estimates of crime based on their reported NIBRS data, especially considering the lack of crime data from the largest agencies, including the New York and Los Angeles police departments.

The coverage of an administrative source is often correlated with the size of the reporting units. In the 2016 SRS data, the total number of crimes reported by the 110 LEAs with more than 750 sworn officers (fewer than 1% of all the LEAs in the nation) accounts for more than 20% of the total number of crimes reported. By 2016, of these 110 LEAs, 24 were NIBRS reporters. Therefore, evaluating the impact of coverage error at the level of the reporting sources should consider the characteristics of the reporting units.

In this analysis, after combining the 2016 SRS data with the 2016 NIBRS data, we calculated the total number of crimes reported to SRS by the NIBRS-reporting LEAs, as well as the total number of crimes reported to SRS by all LEAs in the nation, for each major SRS crime. The NIBRS coverage ratio for a given crime type was then calculated by dividing the former number by the latter number. The results are shown in Table 7.1. Nationally, 37.1% of LEAs reported about

Table 7.1 NIBRS coverage ratio by crime types: 2016.

Crime type	Total number of crimes reported to SRS by the NIBRS-reporting LEAs	Total number of crimes reported to SRS by all LEAs in the nation	Coverage ratio (%)
All crimes	3 893 567	11 719 297	33.2
Murder	4861	17 134	28.4
Manslaughter	329	710	46.3
Rape	48 160	126 597	38.0
Robbery	75 753	328 987	23.0
Assault	1 273 513	3 480 533	36.6
Aggravated assault	239 697	761 049	31.5
Simple assault	1 033 816	2 689 874	38.4
Burglary	480 600	1 478 181	32.5
Larceny	1 783 264	5 529 455	32.3
Vehicle theft	227 087	757 700	30.0

Source: The FBI's National Incident-Based Reporting System, 2016 and the FBI's Summary Reporting System, 2016.

33.2% of crimes to SRS. This coverage ratio ranges from 23.0% (robbery) to 46.3% (manslaughter). These results indicate that the coverage errors due to nonreporting agencies could have varying levels of impact on crime estimates, depending on the crime type. Figure 7.4 shows the coverage ratio by state in 2016. As can been seen in this figure, 37 out of the 50 states have at least 1 NIBRS-reporting agency; 9 out of these 37 states (including Washington, DC) have fewer than 20% of all their LEAs as NIBRS reporters in 2016. In Section 7.3.2.2, we discuss remedies for this type of errors, noting that the remedies should account for discrepancies in coverage ratios across crime types.

7.3.1.9 Nonresponse Errors in the Incident Data Table Due to Unreported Incident Reports

The magnitude and causes of nonresponse errors due to unreported incidents are difficult to gauge. No information is available to understand the mechanism of the failures of the incident report submissions, and only very limited information is available on the incident reports that are rejected by the individual state UCR programs or the FBI (the UCR programs have documented some information on the rejected incident reports and reasons for the rejections). Therefore, when we examine the monthly crime counts in an agency, a zero-crime count might be a "true zero" (i.e. no crime occurred in that month) or the zero might be "missing"

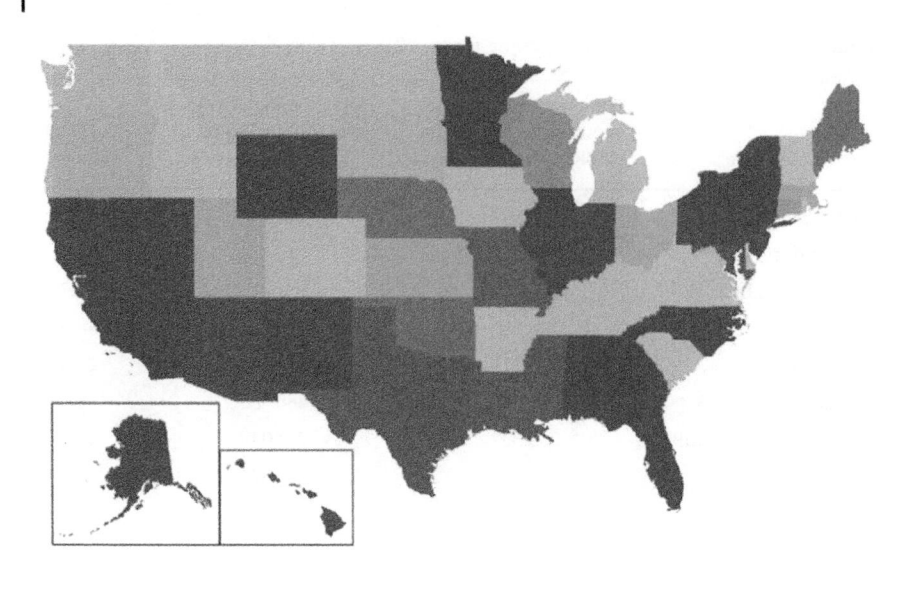

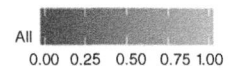

Figure 7.4 NIBRS coverage ratio by state: 2016. Source: FBI's National Incident-Based Reporting System, 2016 and the FBI's Summary Reporting System, 2016.

(i.e. unreported crime incident). With the integrated information from the agency data table and incident data table, LaValle et al. (2013) and LaValle, Haas, and Nolan (2014) developed a guideline for classifying agencies' monthly crime counts of zero as true zeros or missing data based on each agency's monthly reporting patterns in total violent, property, nonindex, and annual property crime in NIBRS. They also developed outlier detection methods to identify irregular crime counts at the monthly-agency level. The SRS data file can also be utilized to identify missing incident reports by comparing the crime counts in the SRS data file with crime counts for NIBRS reporters in the NIBRS data file (Liao et al. 2015). Both LaValle et al. (2013); LaValle, Haas, and Nolan (2014) and Liao et al. (2015) proposed imputation strategies to compensate for missing incident reports after classifying the crime counts of zero as missing data.

7.3.1.10 Invalid, Unknown, and Missing Values Within the Incident Reports

Invalid, unknown, and missing values can be studied with integrated data tables by observing the intercorrelation among different variables. Because the source of the NIBRS data is decentralized, the patterns of invalid, unknown, and missing data can be examined by agency as well. The examination of these patterns can inform the improvement of the NIBRS data-generation process (e.g. the reporting officers' training, the design of the electronic forms) and can also provide insight into the data editing and imputation procedures that can be used to correct for these errors. The NIBRS database has hundreds of variables. Examining, editing, and imputing all of them can be very time consuming and expensive. In collaboration with subject-matter experts, we identified about 20 variables to form the primary indicators of crime and arrests in the nation and to become the focus in this work. Furthermore, these variables are grouped into different content clusters, or segments, including those relating to the victim or offender. Variables in each segment are evaluated simultaneously given the similar correlations they have with other variables. Subject-matter experts are also heavily involved to determine the intercorrelations among different variables and to make final decisions on whether an invalid value, or unknown, or missing value should be treated as missing and requiring imputation.

7.3.2 Improving Data Quality via Sampling, Weighting, and Imputation

As discussed in Section 7.3.1, several different error components affect the NIBRS data. Each error component has the potential to introduce bias in any statistical outputs derived from these data. As is common with administrative data, multiple error types can occur, including nonresponse, noncoverage, specification, data processing, and measurement. Because it is not always possible to mitigate all error types, when determining how to best minimize the impact of the errors, it is important to determine which types contribute most to the data errors. For NIBRS, we believe that noncoverage and nonresponse were the largest components of error and, therefore, made them the focus of our mitigation strategy. To mitigate noncoverage and nonresponse errors, we considered a variety of statistical methods in sampling, weighting, and data imputation as illustrated in this section. Note that although these procedures are intended to reduce data errors and improve data quality, they can also introduce other types of errors that should be carefully evaluated and controlled for. Especially, the two postsurvey adjustment procedures, weighting and data imputation, may cause data processing errors under the TSE paradigm. Hence, assessments must be incorporated in these procedures to evaluate their effectiveness in improving the data quality.

7.3.2.1 Sample-Based Method to Improve Data Representativeness at the Agency Level

Recognizing that the NIBRS data are not nationally representative (as shown in Figure 7.4), BJS and FBI/CJIS in 2012 launched the National Crime Statistics Exchange (NCS-X) initiative. This program utilized survey sampling techniques targeting conversion of 400 additional agencies to NIBRS to supplement data provided by the existing NIBRS reporters and to produce national estimates of crime. These agencies were selected from among NIBRS nonreporting agencies in 2011 via a stratified probability (random) sampling scheme that contains 12 strata based on the government type of the LEA (i.e. state, county or township, municipal, or tribal) and number of sworn officers. All 72 of the largest nonreporting agencies (those with more than 750 sworn officers) were selected with certainty under this sampling scheme. Prior to the sample selection, a simulation study was performed with the 2009 UCR SRS data. The study validated that the sample size and the sample design of 400 sample agencies can meet the target precision level for the final national crime estimates when using the data provided by these 400 agencies in conjunction with the NIBRS data provided by all the NIBRS reporters in 2009. Although the ideal scenario is to have the complete census of all the LEAs to report NIBRS data, concentrating resources to convert 400 LEAs can be much more efficient than converting all of the 10 000+ LEAs at once. Hence, the NCS-X sample-based method can be considered as the initial step to generate national crime estimates, and experience gained from converting the 400 agencies can be applied in planning for the broader transition among other nonreporting LEAs.

7.3.2.2 Statistical Weighting to Adjust for Coverage Errors at the Agency Level

Since 2012, some nonreporting LEAs other than those 400 sampled for NCS-X also completed their conversions to NIBRS without the support of NCS-X. However, the set of current NIBRS reporters is still far from a complete census. Approximately 6900 LEAs in the United States participated in NIBRS in 2016; this rate increased to 43% in 2018. To generate estimates based on data from a sample of the target population, statistical weights should be developed and used to mitigate against errors resulting from noncoverage or unit nonresponse. Weight calibration is a commonly used method that can be used to compensate for unit nonresponse and to force the sample distributions to align with known population distributions across key characteristics.

The NIBRS dataset can be considered a dataset collected from a two-phase setting in which the first phase is a nonprobability sample consisting of all reporting agencies that voluntarily enrolled in NIBRS and the second phase is a probability sample consisting of the 400 NCS-X sample agencies. Several different weighting strategies can be considered within this setting. The first option is to weight the sample agencies in both phases together. The downside of this option is that the utility of the 400 sample agencies selected from among the nonreporters can be limited in the nonresponse bias reduction because they are treated equally with the reporters in the weighting. The second option is to set the weights for all agencies in the first phase to one to just represent themselves in the final estimation, while assigning the base weights for the agencies in the second phase as the inverse of their initial selection probabilities. These base weights would then be adjusted using either a propensity score or calibration weighting method to align the sample distribution of the second phase agencies with the distribution of the nonreporters. The drawback of this option is that some or even all the nonresponse bias reduction benefits gained from the second phase can be lost through the increase in variance due to variation in the final weights overall given the differences between weights in the first and second phases. The mean squared error (MSE), which is a common measure to evaluate the accuracy of the final estimate, is a composition of bias and variance. Therefore, the weighting process should control for both bias and variance simultaneously to minimize the MSE and maximize the accuracy of estimation. Literature on weighting strategies for nonresponse follow-up (e.g. Laaksonen and Chambers 2006; Singh, Iannacchione, and Dever 2003) and nonprobability samples (e.g. Baker et al. 2013; Mercer et al. 2017; Valliant and Dever 2017) can be used as a reference here when developing the weighting strategies. The UCR SRS data with monthly crime counts of almost all the LEAs in the population can be used to evaluate the effectiveness of different weighting strategies.

7.3.2.3 Imputation to Compensate for Unreported Incidents and Missing Values in the Incident Reports

The unique hierarchical structure of the NIBRS data should also be considered when developing strategies to address the missing data problem. Today, statistical imputation for hierarchical data is still an active research area. Zhang et al. (2017) used the weighted sequential hot deck method proposed by Cox (1980) and Iannacchione (1982) to impute missing data in the birth certificate data that were linked to the Centers for Disease Control and Prevention's National Assisted Reproductive Technology Surveillance System database. These data had a hierarchical data structure with infants (as observations) nested within fertility clinics, and the authors performed the imputation by fertility clinics to adapt this data structure. This approach may not be suitable for the NIBRS data, however, because, unlike infants, the observations in the NIBRS data are incidents that can have very different attributes (e.g. violent crime vs. property crime). Van Buuren (2011) summarized the literature on imputation for multilevel data up to the year of 2008. Van Buuren (2012) discussed two methods for imputing multilevel data: one is a method developed under a Bayesian framework for multilevel modeling and the other is a bootstrap method developed under a linear normal model with variances across units at higher level. Grund, Lüdtke, and Robitzsch (2016) introduced the R package "pan" to perform multiple imputation for multilevel missing data. Another R package "micemd" was also created to perform multiple imputations using chained equation based on imputation methods provided in Resche-Rigon et al. (2013), Resche-Rigon and White (2018), and Audigier et al. (2018). As this project progresses, statistical assessments will be conducted to compare different imputation methods for addressing the missing data problem in the NIBRS data.

7.4 Utilizing External Data Sources in Improving Data Quality of the Administrative Data

As mentioned in Section 7.3, additional external data sources can be used to assess or improve the quality of the administrative data or assist in the final estimation process. For either use, one needs to be mindful of the quality of any external data sources being used. In this section, we discuss several external data sources, including other administrative sources and survey data sources. We then present an example of how external data sources can be used to assess and improve the quality of the NIBRS data in the area of north central United States called the Bakken region.

7.4.1 Understanding the External Data Sources

7.4.1.1 Data Quality Assessment of External Data Sources

Although external data sources can provide valuable auxiliary information for improving the quality of administrative data or more generic Big Data, auxiliary data are reasonably accurate. In other words, users need to be certain the data being integrated with the administrative data do not suffer from error sources that could create additional issues when estimates are produced through the administrative data. For example, one must confirm that the auxiliary dataset is comparable to the administrative dataset – that the auxiliary dataset will cover the same time period and define common fields similarly. If the auxiliary dataset is not comparable, then it may introduce bias into the administrative dataset if it is used to make adjustments (e.g. imputation or weights) in the administrative dataset. Biemer and Amaya's row–column–cell framework is also an effective tool to assess data quality of the auxiliary dataset, and the integrated data procedure needs to be inspected when incorporating them into the main dataset. Consider the UCR SRS data file, for example. These data, as an auxiliary administrative data source, could suffer from coverage and nonresponse errors in different degrees. The impact of these errors on the effectiveness of using this auxiliary data source to improve the administrative data needs to be evaluated. The result of the evaluation may determine that certain adjustments are required before using the auxiliary data to assess and improve the data quality of NIBRS.

7.4.1.2 Producing Population Counts at the Agency Level Through Auxiliary Data

The auxiliary data sometimes cannot be linked with the main dataset directly and may require transformation and adjustment. The data integration process then becomes even more complicated and should be executed systematically. One example is to produce population counts at the agency level using the US Census Bureau population estimates. NIBRS contains the number of crimes in each LEA, but without a sense of the size of the population being served by an LEA, it is difficult to compare crime counts across LEAs or collections of LEAs. Consequently, researchers standardize estimates using crime rates per 1000 persons (or households for property crime). To compute these rates, auxiliary data are needed to provide the population counts.

The population count under each LEA, however, can be difficult to estimate as agencies may have complex jurisdictional relationships with one another and do not necessarily conform to the geographies used for general population estimation. Currently, the FBI, using the SRS, publishes crime totals for LEAs in the United States. Although crime rates are not explicitly provided by the FBI at the agency level, estimated police employment rates (the number of officers per 1000 people), and the estimated sizes of the populations residing within the jurisdictional boundaries of LEAs (the denominators of these rates), are published at the LEA level. Police officer employment rates are substantively important for understanding of law enforcement presence in a given agency's jurisdiction, but the population estimates released alongside them can also be used with published crime totals to calculate crime rates at the agency level. Under the UCR SRS, these population figures are based on Census Bureau estimates for standard geographic entities such as cities and counties that are in some cases adjusted by the FBI to account for year-to-year population change. Although the existing estimation process suits the FBI's needs, the detailed algorithms, inputs, and adjustments used to arrive at final population figures for each LEA are not available to the public.

Because the FBI population served estimation process is not available to all persons in the public, an independent population estimation methodology is developed; it is based on three primary phases: (i) identifying agencies with zero population, (ii) matching nonzero-population agencies to standard geographic entities with associated US Census Bureau population estimates, and (iii) reconciling populations across agencies with overlapping jurisdictions.

In the first phase, agencies that are not the primary law enforcement entity in their jurisdictions are coded with populations of zero. This class of agencies is primarily composed of all law enforcement entities that are not local police departments, county sheriff's offices, or state police agencies, although these agencies can have zero populations as well. This situation can occur for several reasons, such as when a county's population is completely covered by the jurisdictions of one or more local police agencies. In such a case, the county sheriff's department would have a population of zero because it is not the primary law enforcement entity for any area or population within its jurisdiction.

In the second phase, nonzero population agencies are matched to geographies recognized by the US Census Bureau, which may be cities, villages, towns, Census-designated places, counties, or county subdivisions. The population estimate associated with each geography is then taken as the starting point for estimating the population directly served by a given agency. For this component to work, it is critical to ensure that the time period of the Census data corresponds to the time period of the NIBRS data. This can sometimes be difficult in that agencies (e.g. the FBI and Census Bureau) do not always release data for a given year at the same time.

In the third phase, local police agency populations are deducted from the populations of the county or state police agencies with overlapping jurisdictions. This process of population residualization ensures that each person is counted only once for the purpose of crime rate estimation: in the jurisdiction of the agency having direct authority, be it a local police department, county sheriff's office, or state police agency.

7.4.2 Administrative vs. Survey Data for Crime Statistics

For many constructs, researchers can use administrative data or survey data for their analysis. When both data sources are an option, researchers need to understand the differences in these two data sources. Administrative data are data reported to a government agency. As such, they contain only the data as they were collected. Administrative data do not usually make adjustments to address potential coverage issues to compensate for unit nonresponse (i.e. row error). Furthermore, administrative data may come from multiple sources each of which may define attributes differently (i.e. column error). On the other hand, survey data are data that come from a random sample of persons in the population. Because it costs more to collect survey data, these data sources often contain many fewer records. By design, these sources contain survey weights to allow for generalizations to the population of interest, but, as such, have sampling error that needs to be indicated when presenting estimates. In addition, although all respondents are being asked about constructs in the same way, some may not understand them the same way, or an interviewer may have an impact on how a respondent answers (i.e. column error). Moreover, surveys are subject to nonresponse from some of the selected sample members (i.e. row error). However, surveys, unlike administrative data, can ask questions about the construct directly from the person affected, which allows survey data to include information to which the administrative source is not privy.

In the case of crime statistics, the UCR – either SRS or NIBRS – serves as the administrative data source, and the National Crime Victimization Survey (NCVS) serves as the survey data source. When assessing the two sources, the first, obvious, difference is the size of the files. In NIBRS data, a single year of data has millions of records, whereas the NCVS has about 200 000. This difference creates a lot more variability due to sampling error in the NCVS. Another difference is how crime is measured. Both the UCR and the NCVS measure a crime incident. However, the UCR covers only those incidents *reported* to the police. The NCVS, because incidents are identified directly by the victim, includes victimizations reported to the police as well as those not reported to the police. These crime victimizations not reported to police are known as "the dark figure of crime" (Biderman and Reiss 1967). For some types of crime, the number of unreported crimes is nonnegligible (Langton et al. 2012). Another difference in measurement is how crimes are collected for the UCR. For the UCR, crimes are reported to the FBI through individual LEAs that categorize the crime prior to submission. Therefore, the UCR is subject to specification error (a type of column error) if different jurisdictions categorize crimes differently. However, for the NCVS, all crimes are coded by a standard set of rules ensuring that crimes are comparably measured across geographic areas. Both the UCR and NCVS suffer from row error, but the type of error is different. For the UCR (especially for NIBRS), there is nonresponse error due to not all LEAs' reporting their crimes. For the NCVS, nonresponse error occurs because some sampled households' do not participate. In terms of cell error, both NIBRS and the NCVS suffer from item nonresponse.

As Strom and Smith (2017) argue, the differences in the NIBRS and NCVS data make them complementary rather than competing data sources. For example, the two sources come from two different perspectives: law enforcement (NIBRS) and the victim (NCVS). NIBRS can provide information on the adjudication of the incident, whereas the NCVS can provide information about what happened to the victim after the crime was reported (if it was reported). In addition, NIBRS allows for additional disaggregation that the NCVS does not provide. Although work has been done to produce subnational estimates in the NCVS, it is currently able to produce only national estimates. NIBRS allows for detailed disaggregation of crime characteristics at the state and local levels. Furthermore, NIBRS and the NCVS assign the location of a crime differently. NIBRS identifies a crime based on where the crime was reported, whereas the NCVS identifies a crime based on where the victim lives. For national estimates, this distinction does not matter, but, for subnational estimates, this distinction can make a difference, especially in areas with a large number of transient populations such as cities with commuters or tourists. Moreover, NIBRS fills in a coverage gap by including crimes against a business or commercial entity. As a household survey, the NCVS covers only person or household crimes. NIBRS includes any crime reported to the police regardless of whether the victim is a person, household, or business.

7.4.3 A Pilot Study on Crime in the Bakken Region

When developing methods to improve the quality of a dataset as massive as NIBRS, researchers often find it beneficial to start with a subset of the data that represents a "best case" scenario. This type of analysis offers a baseline of the types of problems that will need to be resolved in the more complicated portions of the dataset. Furthermore, it allows users to isolate the basic types of issues and resolve them in their most simplified form rather than having to deal immediately with the more nuanced situation.

For our pilot assessment of NIBRS, the Bakken formation underlying North Dakota (ND), South Dakota (SD), and Montana (MT) provided an ideal test case. The Bakken region has been a major oil boom site in the most recent two decades (see Figure 7.5). Observers (Brown 2012; Horwitz 2014) speculated an increase in crime in the areas that surround the drilling because of the arrival of temporary

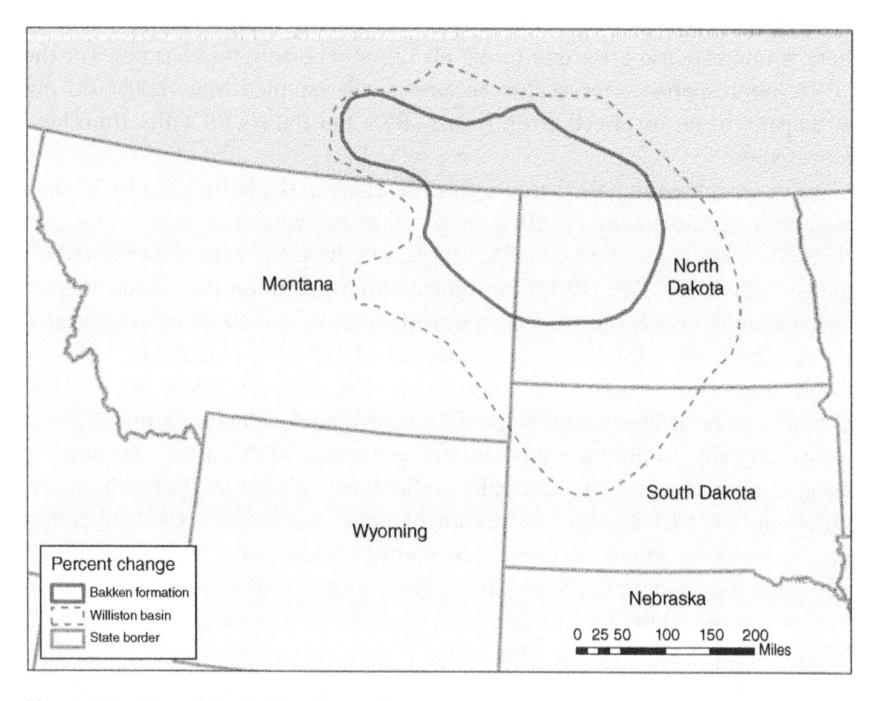

Figure 7.5 Map of the Bakken formation.

oil workers. Therefore, it was of interest to see if NIBRS and other available data sources could identify an increased trend in crime from 2006 to 2012 compared with their counterparts in the non-Bakken regions in ND, MT, and SD.

The assessment of the Bakken region is ideal for developing methods to improve quality for several reasons. First, ND, SD, and MT are 100% NIBRS-reporting states. In other words, all LEAs in the three states submit data through NIBRS, which mitigates any potential coverage error due to nonreporting agencies. Second, the comparison of crime in the Bakken region focused on only a small subset of crime indicators (e.g. overall violent or property crimes; injury occurred), which reduced the amount of cell errors that needed to be assessed. In this setup, the focus becomes dealing with the missing data problem in a hierarchical dataset that could have the entire incident missing or a certain variable within a reported incident missing.

In general, missing data can be remedied through either weighting or imputation. Often, when dealing with a flat rectangular file – as in a survey sample – weighting is used to address unit nonresponse (e.g. missing incidents) and imputation is used to address item nonresponse (e.g. missing victim or offender characteristics). However, when dealing with hierarchical data like NIBRS, weighting missing incidents within each LEA may be too cumbersome or even impossible. Therefore, to be as flexible as possible, we determined that imputing at both the incident and within-incident level was best. As detailed in Liao et al. (2015), we developed a hierarchical imputation approach with multiple imputation to compensate for both unreported incidents and missing values within the reported incidents. Multiple imputation was used to ensure that the additional variability due to imputation could be taken into account in the estimation process. Based on suggestions from subject-matter experts, several external data sources, such as the UCR SRS data and LEOKA data, were assessed and integrated in the imputation process. In the current project, we will continue to refine this imputation approach by adopting the newly developed imputation methods and software packages as described in Section 7.3.2.3.

7.5 Summary and Future Work

The emergence of administrative data has great potential to change the landscape of social research and official statistics worldwide. Administrative data sources provide abundant information that creates new research opportunities and fills some gaps in primary data collected from surveys or experiments. However, like other types of data, administrative data can contain various data errors that limit its use for statistical and research purposes. Therefore, establishing effective and systematic methods to assess the quality of administrative data and developing the strategies to address detected data errors becomes a pressing need to make administrative data fit for use. Although literature in the past decade (e.g. Reid, Zabala, and Holmberg 2017; Zhang 2012) has developed theoretical frameworks for quality assessment with administrative data, the perfection of these frameworks requires empirical tests and continuous improvement.

This chapter illustrates our experience in applying the theoretical data quality assessment frameworks in improving the quality of an administrative dataset that is collected from a national incident-based crime-reporting system in the United States. The overarching goal of this work is to use this dataset to produce nationally representative estimates of crime. The data quality assessment conducted in this work concentrates on this goal while also considering various practical issues, such as whether the data errors can be examined and addressed, how to improve the efficiency when conducting data quality assessment and addressing the uncovered data errors, and how to put external data sources in proper use in improving the data quality. Furthermore, some special features of the dataset, which are similar to other administrative data sources and more generic Big Data sources, are also part of this work – for example, complex and hierarchical data structures, data being stored in a relational database due to their large volume, a decentralized data collection, and voluntary participation by reporting entities.

The next steps in the quality process surround the evolving NIBRS data, e.g. evaluating the representativeness of the NIBRS dataset to produce national estimates as new LEAs transition from the traditional Summary Reporting System (i.e. SRS) to NIBRS. Collaborating with subject-matter experts, the mechanisms of invalid, unknown, and missing values will be investigated based on intercorrelations among different variables from the database itself as well as from auxiliary data sources (e.g. auxiliary data on LEA characteristics). When it comes to LEA reporting and coding of crimes, the quality of reported administrative data can vary markedly across officers and agencies. The effects of differences across the officers who report NIBRS information and the reporting rules of each individual agency will be evaluated on different dimensions of the data quality, including nonresponse errors, specifications, and measurement errors. Alternative weighting and imputation strategies will be developed and compared to determine final statistical adjustment procedures for the NIBRS dataset. The final selected statistical adjustment procedures will be implemented in a prototype system that can produce analytic products based on the NIBRS, including national estimates of key crime indicators. To this end, improving the quality of administrative data can be a long-term process and requires collaborative efforts across experts and organizations from different fields. The experience gained from decades of methodological work in survey research is highly relevant for administrative data, although new methods are still needed to account for the special features of administrative data.

References

Addington, L.A. (2008). Assessing the extent of nonresponse bias on NIBRS estimates of violent crime. *Journal of Contemporary Criminal Justice* 24 (1): 32–49. https://doi.org/10.1177/1043986207312936.

Audigier, V., White, I.R., Jolani, S. et al. (2018). Multiple imputation for multilevel data with continuous and binary variables. *Statistical Science* 33 (2): 160–183. https://doi.org/10.1214/18-sts646.

Baker, R., Brick, J.M., Bates, N.A. et al. (2013). Summary report of the AAPOR task force on non-probability sampling. *Journal of Survey Statistics and Methodology* 1 (2): 90–143. https://doi.org/10.1093/jssam/smt008.

Biderman, A.D. and Reiss, A.J. (1967). On exploring the "dark figure" of crime. *The Annals of the American Academy of Political and Social Science* 374 (1): 1–15. https://doi.org/10.1177/000271626737400102.

Biemer, P.P. (2010). Total survey error: design, implementation, and evaluation. *Public Opinion Quarterly* 74 (5): 817–848. https://doi.org/10.1093/poq/nfq058.

Biemer, P., Trewin, D., Bergdahl, H. et al. (2014). A system for managing the quality of official statistics. *Journal of Official Statistics* 30 (3): 381–415. https://doi.org/10.2478/JOS-2014-0022.

Brown, M. (2012). As Bakken oil booms, so does crime. https://www.mprnews.org/story/2012/04/23/bakken-crime (accessed 09 March 2020).

Connelly, R., Playford, C.J., Gayle, V. et al. (2016). The role of administrative data in the big data revolution in social science research. *Social Science Research* 59: 1–12. https://doi.org/10.1016/j.ssresearch.2016.04.015.

Cox, B.G. (1980). The weighted sequential hot deck imputation procedure. In: *Joint Statistical Meetings Proceedings, Survey Research Methods Section*, 721–726. Alexandria, VA: American Statistical Association.

Criminal Justice Information Services Division (2016). About UCR. https://ucr.fbi.gov/crime-in-the-u.s/2015/crime-in-the-u.s.-2015/resource-pages/aboutucrmain_final (accessed 09 March 2020).

Eurostat (2003). Quality Assessment of Administrative Data for Statistical Purposes. Working group "Assessment of Quality in Statistics", Luxembourg (2–3 October 2003). Web publication, Eurostat. https://ec.europa.eu/eurostat/documents/64157/4374310/36-QUALITY-ASSESSMENT-ADMINISTRATIVE-DATA-STATISTICAL-PURPOSES_2003.pdf/37373e67-d69c-4215-b727-5b036393b80f.

Eurostat (2009). Regulation (EC) No 223/2009 of the European Parliament and of the Council of 11 March 2009 on European statistics and repealing Regulation (EC, Euratom) No 1101/2008 of the European Parliament and of the Council on the transmission of data subject to statistical confidentiality to the Statistical Office of the European Communities, Council Regulation (EC) No 322/97 on Community Statistics, Council Decision 89/382/EEC Stat. Official Journal of the European

Union, L 87, Volume 52 (31 March 2009). https://eur-lex.europa.eu/LexUriServ/LexUriServ.do?uri=OJ:L:2009:087:0164:0173:En:PDF.

Groves, R.M. and Lyberg, L. (2010). Total survey error: past, present, and future. *Public Opinion Quarterly* 74 (5): 849–879. https://doi.org/10.1093/poq/nfq065.

Grund, S., Lüdtke, O., and Robitzsch, A. (2016). Multiple imputation of multilevel missing data: an introduction to the R package pan. *SAGE Open* 6: 1–17. https://doi.org/10.1177%2F2158244016668220.

Holt, D.T. (2007). The official statistics Olympic challenge. *The American Statistician* 61 (1): 1–8. https://doi.org/10.1198/000313007x168173.

Horwitz, S. (2014). Dark side of the boom: North Dakota's oil rush brings cash and promise to reservation, along with drug-fueled crime, *The Washington Post*. https://www.washingtonpost.com/sf/national/2014/09/28/dark-side-of-the-boom/?utm_term=.d3533f55cf78 (accessed 09 March 2020).

Iannacchione, V. (1982). Weighted sequential hot deck imputation macros. *Proceedings of the Seventh Annual SAS User's Group International Conference* (February 1982), pp. 759–763, Cary, NC: SAS Institute. https://support.sas.com/resources/papers/proceedings-archive/SUGI82/Sugi-82-139%20Iannacchione.pdf.

Japec, L., Kreuter, F., Berg, M. et al. (2015). *AAPOR Report on Big Data*. Oakbrook Terrace, IL: American Association for Public Opinion Research https://www.aapor.org/Education-Resources/Reports/Big-Data.aspx.

Laaksonen, S. and Chambers, R. (2006). Survey estimation under informative nonresponse with follow-up. *Journal of Official Statistics* 22 (1): 81–95.

Langton, L., Berzofsky, M., Krebs, C.P. et al. (2012). *Victimizations Not Reported to the Police, 2006–2010 (NCJ 238536; Contract No. 2011-NV-CX-K068)*. Washington, DC: Bureau of Justice Statistics, Office of Justice Programs, U.S. Department of Justice https://bjs.gov/content/pub/pdf/vnrp0610.pdf.

LaValle, C.R., Haas, S.M., Turley, E. et al. (2013). *Improving State Capacity for Crime Reporting: An Exploratory Analysis of Data Quality and Imputation Methods Using NIBRS Data*. Charleston, WV: Criminal Justice Statistical Analysis Center, Office of Research and Strategic Planning, Division of Justice and Community Services http://citeseerx.ist.psu.edu/viewdoc/download?doi=10.1.1.400.5066&rep=rep1&type=pdf.

LaValle, C.R., Haas, S.M., and Nolan, J.J. (2014). *Testing the Validity of Demonstrated Imputation Methods on Longitudinal NIBRS Data*. Charleston, WV: Criminal Justice Statistical Analysis Center, Office of Research and Strategic Planning, Division of Justice and Community Services https://djcs.wv.gov/ORSP/SAC/Documents/WV_Impute2ReportJan2014_Final.pdf.

Liao, D., Berzofsky, M.E., Heller, D.C. et al. (2015). Treatment of missing data in the FBI's National Incident Based Reporting System: a case study in the Bakken Region. In: *Joint Statistical Meetings Proceedings, Survey Research Methods Section*,

1970–1981. Alexandria, VA: American Statistical Association http://www.asasrms.org/Proceedings/y2015/files/234045.pdf.

McCormack, P.D., Pattavina, A., and Tracy, P.E. (2017). Assessing the coverage and representativeness of the National Incident-Based Reporting System. *Crime & Delinquency* 63 (4): 493–516. https://doi.org/10.1177%2F0011128717694595.

Mercer, A.W., Kreuter, F., Keeter, S. et al. (2017). Theory and practice in nonprobability surveys. *Public Opinion Quarterly* 81 (S1): 250–271. https://doi.org/10.1093/poq/nfw060.

Reid, G., Zabala, F., and Holmberg, A. (2017). Extending TSE to administrative data: a quality framework and case studies from Stats NZ. *Journal of Official Statistics* 33 (2): 477–511. https://doi.org/10.1515/Jos-2017-0023.

Resche-Rigon, M. and White, I.R. (2018). Multiple imputation by chained equations for systematically and sporadically missing multilevel data. *Statistical Methods in Medical Research* 27 (6): 1634–1649. https://doi.org/10.1177/0962280216666564.

Resche-Rigon, M., White, I.R., Bartlett, J.W. et al. (2013). Multiple imputation for handling systematically missing confounders in meta-analysis of individual participant data. *Statistics in Medicine* 32 (28): 4890–4905. https://doi.org/10.1002/sim.5894.

Singh, A.C., Iannacchione, V.G., and Dever, J.A. (2003). Efficient estimation for surveys with nonresponse follow-up using dual-frame calibration. In: *Joint Statistical Meetings Proceedings, Survey Research Methods Section*, 3919–3930. Alexandria, VA: American Statistical Association http://www.asasrms.org/Proceedings/y2003/Files/JSM2003-000872.pdf.

Statistics Finland (2004). *Use of Registers and Administrative Data Sources for Statistical Purposes – Best Practices in Statistics Finland*. Helsinki, Finland: Statistics Finland.

Strom, K.J. and Smith, E.L. (2017). The future of crime data. *Criminology & Public Policy* 16 (4): 1027–1048. https://doi.org/10.1111/1745-9133.12336.

United Nations Economic Commission for Europe (2011). Using Administrative and Secondary Sources for Official Statistics: A Handbook of Principles and Practices. https://statswiki.unece.org/display/adso/Using+Administrative+and+Secondary+Sources+for+Official+Statistics (accessed 09 March 2020).

Valliant, R. and Dever, J.A. (2017). *Survey Weights: A Step-by-Step Guide to Calculation*. College Station, TX: Stata Press.

Van Buuren, S. (2011). Multiple imputation of multilevel data. In: *Handbook of Advanced Multilevel Analysis* (eds. J.J. Hox and J.K. Roberts), 173–196. New York, NY: Routledge.

Van Buuren, S. (2012). *Flexible Imputation of Missing Data*. Boca Raton, FL: CRC Press.

Wallgren, A. and Wallgren, B. (2007). *Register-Based Statistics: Administrative Data for Statistical Purposes*. Hoboken, NJ: Wiley.

Zhang, L.C. (2012). Topics of statistical theory for register-based statistics and data integration. *Statistica Neerlandica* 66 (1): 41–63. https://doi.org/10.1111/j.1467-9574.2011.00508.x.

Zhang, Y., Crawford, S., Boulet, S.L. et al. (2017). Using multiple imputation to address the inconsistent distribution of a controlling variable when modeling an infrequent outcome. *Journal of Modern Applied Statistical Methods* 16 (1): 744–752. https://doi.org/10.22237/jmasm/1493599140.

8

Performance and Sensitivities of Home Detection on Mobile Phone Data

Maarten Vanhoof[1], Clement Lee[2], and Zbigniew Smoreda[3]

[1] *The Bartlett Centre for Advanced Spatial Analysis, University College London, London, UK*
[2] *Department of Mathematics and Statistics, Lancaster University, Lancaster, UK*
[3] *SENSE, Orange Labs, Paris, France*

8.1 Introduction

8.1.1 Mobile Phone Data and Official Statistics

Recently, interest in the use of Big Data in official statistics has grown (Daas et al. 2015; Vanhoof et al. 2018a; Vanhoof 2018). Big Data sources can offer more timely, high-resolution information compared to standard statistics production. One example are large-scale location-based traces, such as mobile phone data, which is the focus of this chapter. Compared to standard official statistics that provide residential population figures every 5–10 years, mobile phone data can help to create snapshots of human presence at a high resolution for any given time and for, at least, partial populations.

In the case of call detailed record (CDR) data, the most basic type of mobile phone data, user traces are sourced by cell towers that have local coverage areas of limited dimensions but that, all together, cover entire nations. User traces are then captured by mobile phone operators every time a mobile phone uses a cell tower, resulting in a trace that contains the type of activity (call or text), the time, and the cell tower location. The collection of all traces from all users serviced by a single operator results in huge databases covering a substantial part of the population, although not all because users can be serviced by other operators or can simply choose to not use a mobile phone. Nevertheless, such CDR databases allow the study of human activities at unprecedented temporal and spatial scales and complement existing official statistics on population, migration, mobility, or tourism.

Several previous studies recognized the potential of CDR data to complement official statistics. Deville et al. (2014) demonstrated how CDR data can show

Big Data Meets Survey Science: A Collection of Innovative Methods, First Edition. Edited by Craig A. Hill, Paul P. Biemer, Trent D. Buskirk, Lilli Japec, Antje Kirchner, Stas Kolenikov, and Lars E. Lyberg.
© 2021 John Wiley & Sons, Inc. Published 2021 by John Wiley & Sons, Inc.

population presence at a national scale and for any given time period, an interesting addition to existing population and migration statistics. CDR data have also been used to estimate general commuting times and distances by Kung et al. (2014) to estimate directions of general mobility of populations during very short time frames (Balzotti et al. 2018) and to reproduce the French official urban area classification (Vanhoof, Combes, and De Bellefon 2017a). At a more individual level, individual users' movement patterns extracted from CDR data offer opportunities to create figures on domestic tourism trips (Vanhoof et al. 2017b), long-distance travel (Janzen et al. 2018), or even to impute purposes of long-distance travel (Janzen, Vanhoof, and Axhausen 2016), all of which offer great complementary sources to expensive travel surveys.

Other lines of research have revealed how nationwide indicators on human mobility, calling activities, and subscription purchases derived from CDR data relate to measures of deprivation, poverty, or even food security as provided by official statistics (Pappalardo et al. 2016; Eagle, Macy, and Claxton 2010; Frias-Martinez et al. 2013; Decuyper et al. 2014; Vanhoof et al. 2018c). These relationships have inspired some researchers to express the vision that mobile phone data could be used to nowcast or even predict socioeconomic indicators nationwide (Pappalardo et al. 2015; Giannotti et al. 2012; Pappalardo et al. 2016). This vision opens another potential avenue for the integration of Big Data sources in official statistics that, although seemingly promising, is still in an early phase and will undoubtedly face numerous methodological challenges.

In short, CDR data have manifested themselves as an interesting and promising addition to current official statistics. Still, incorporation of CDR data in official statistics has not (yet) been accomplished, despite substantial investments of governments and institutions alike (Vanhoof 2018). One reason is that Big Data sources, and in extension their related methodologies, often do not adhere to the standards of official statistics for coverage, representation, quality, accuracy, and precision (Daas et al. 2015; Vanhoof et al. 2018a). As such, the integration of new, large data sources in official statistics will require reflection on, and renegotiation of, official statistics' principles that demands an organizational reinvention of current official statistics offices.

Our work focuses on the assessment of home detection from French CDR data. This does not mean that population presence is the most important application for integrating mobile phone data in official statistics. Other applications such as the extraction of long-distance travel patterns, holiday movements, or urban areas might be more suitable for the information typically available in mobile phone datasets and, therefore, produce better results. Rather, the argument is that the validation of home detection is crucial for the integration of mobile phone data in official statistics for three reasons.

First, many analytical methods for mobile phone data (or other noncontinuous location traces) are based, either explicitly or implicitly, on home detection as a prerequisite. Quality assessment of this step is necessary to estimate errors in further analytical steps. As a cornerstone of mobile phone research, home detection methods are often obscured in academic literature – details on their exact application, related uncertainties, perceived performance, or even validation are minimally investigated and rarely communicated. Even more remarkable is that the propagation of error from home detection is, to the best of the authors' knowledge, seldom discussed.

Second, knowledge of the supposed home location of mobile phone users forms the crucial link between mobile phone data and other data sources such as census data. Home detection is thus a key enabler for integrating different types of information. Third, home detection is one of the few possible ways to enrich mobile phone data with socioeconomic information, be it at aggregated level. Still, such socioeconomic information is a first step in understanding the selection bias in using mobile phone data from single operators and to assess the representativity of the analysis.

Within this context, quality assessment is crucial because it forms the very core of the official statistics' public service. Quality assessment is also a necessity to safeguard the quality and transparency of Big Data practices. Both are not always guaranteed nowadays (not even in academic work) due to the rapid pace in which Big Data applications are being developed, the hegemony on data accessibility by a limited number of private enterprises and research institutions, and ever-changing privacy regulations.

In this chapter, we develop one such quality assessment for home detection methods from CDR data. We argue that little research exists on the validity and related errors of home detection methods and that the sensitivity of results to researcher choices when setting up home detection algorithms (HDAs) is poorly understood. For this reason, we present an extensive empirical analysis of home detection methods when performed on a nationwide CDR dataset of traces from about 18 million mobile phone users in France in 2007. We analyze the validity of nine different HDAs, and we assess different sources of uncertainty that relate to them and the obtained results. Based on our approach, we discuss different measures for validation and investigate the sensitivity of results to researcher choices such as HDA parameter choice and observation period restriction.

8.1.2 The Home Detection Problem

Quality assessment for detecting the home location from users whose digital traces are stored in Big Data sources is not well developed, especially for noncontinuous, geolocated traces such as mobile phone data or check-in data on location based social networks (such as Flickr, TripAdvisor, or Foursquare). In CDR data, for example detecting a home location for each individual user means that one cell tower – the one most likely to cover the actual living place of a user – must be identified as home. This identification is most commonly done by a so-called HDA deployed on a historical record of geolocations produced by the user in the database – the user trace so to say.

The basic problem is that assumed home locations produced by HDAs cannot be tested against decent ground truth data at the individual user's level. Although operators might have customer-related information such as billing addresses, privacy regulations in many countries prohibit pairing this data with mobile phone datasets. In countries where pairing is not forbidden (many African nations), collecting decent validation data on home locations for millions of users is extremely challenging and expensive. Consequently, as noted by Vanhoof et al. (2018a), validation of home detection has mostly been carried out by comparing aggregated user counts (x users presumably living in the area covered by cell tower y) with population counts available from census data. Such high-level validation, however, is general and does not allow validation at different sublevels, obscuring not only insights on correctness for individual users but also for different subgroups of users (Vanhoof et al. 2018a). Additionally high-level validation partly obscures the effect of researchers' decisions such as algorithm choice, criteria choice, parameter choice, duration of observation, and period of observation. Measuring the impact of such decisions on the correctness of home detection for different subpopulations might be as important as understanding the high-level differences between different algorithms but has, because of the absence of lower-level validation data, never been properly studied.

Notwithstanding the absence of decent validation, the detection of home locations from user traces has proven important in different ways for different strands of mobile phone data research. To infer long-distance travel, tourism trips, or commuting, home detection is needed to determine when a user is performing a specific type of mobility or not. To understand the relation between mobile phone indicators and socioeconomic indicators, home detection is needed too. Because socioeconomic indicators are mostly available at aggregated levels, mobile phone indicators need to be aggregated in space to become comparable with, for example census data. These aggregations are typically done using home detection, meaning mobile phone users' characteristics get aggregated based on their assumed home locations.

For two reasons, in-depth investigations on home detection methods are typically not part of studies that use them as a prerequisite. First, proper validation data at the individual level is almost impossible to obtain but even high-level validation data might, in some cases, be difficult. Second, multiple iterations are needed to investigate the performance of home detection. Due to the size of current CDR datasets, iterations are technically challenging, time-consuming, and computationally expensive, even with Big Data technologies, because of the many look-up functions required to collect observations from all individual users.

Still it remains inexplicable that, apart from Vanhoof et al. (2018a) and Bojic et al. (2015), no studies have focused on the performance of home detection methods and their sensitivity to, for example HDA choice or the duration of available data. Concerning HDA choice, Vanhoof et al. (2018a) and Bojic et al. (2015) found that the percentage of users attributed a different home location when a different HDA was deployed ranged from 1% to 9% when using data on credit card transactions in Spain, from 7% to 20% when using a worldwide Flickr data, and from 4% to 40% when using a CDR dataset in France (the same one we deploy). HDA choice, in other words, may significantly influence home detection at nationwide scale. Thus, the validity and sensitivities of current home detection methods must be investigated, especially when such methods are considered for official statistics.

The absence of validation studies on home detection methods has several consequences. It is unclear exactly what makes home detection methods perform with the correctness they have today. Is it the data fed into them (because this could change over time), is it the way these methods are built, or something else? The broader consequence is that many assumptions underlying current home detection methods remain unproven and unchallenged, even though they could be wrong. One assumption, for example, is that the period and duration of observations do not influence the quality of home detection. Common sense suggests that this is not the case, as does the research. Deville et al. (2014) and Vanhoof et al. (2017b), for example, show how during summer months mobile phone users in France tend to move to tourist areas along the coast or near the mountains. Performing home detection on mobile phone data collected during this period is more likely lead to erroneous results compared to using another period, proving one underlying assumption wrong.

In this chapter, we start research in this direction by empirically investigating the nationwide performance of different home detection methods in France. We focus on the sensitivity to researchers' choices such as the HDA choice, the chosen period of observation, and the chosen duration of observation. A clearer insight into the combined effects of these choices on the quality of home detection is desirable and can help improve future work.

8.2 Deploying Home Detection Algorithms to a French CDR Dataset

8.2.1 Mobile Phone Data

Mobile phone data are the registrations of all actions mobile phone users perform (hereafter called users) on the operator's cellular network. From a data(base)

Table 8.1 Example of potential records in a mobile phone dataset.

Event	Timestamp	Cell tower	User	Duration
...	...	...	...	...
Call	01 October 2007 23:45:00	15 988	33 647 956 872	3656s
Text	02 October 2007 01:12:04	2051	3 367 261 532	125c
...	...	...	...	...

perspective, each action on the network is stored by a tuple holding information on the timestamp, a user identifier, the event type (call, text, mobile data), the duration of the network activity, and a cell tower ID as illustrated in Table 8.1.

The most common type of mobile phone data is CDR data, which only capture call and text events. A more advanced type consists of data detailed records (DDR) data, which capture events related to the exchange of mobile data packages that, for example, allow users to surf the Internet. CDR and DDR data differ in that CDR data typically consists of smaller volumes of information. CDR data are only collected when a user makes or receives a call/text, which generally does not happen that often. DDR data, on the other hand, are larger in volume, mainly because users tend to leave their 2G, 3G, 4G connections on for longer time periods, resulting in the exchange of numerous data packages between the phone and the network and, therefore, large amounts of DDR data.

Another important difference is that CDR data normally store the intended, addressed user (Table 8.2). In other words, if user A attempts to contact user B (by call or text), CDR data will store the identifier of both user A and user B. The identifier is not stored for DDR data, because no specific person is addressed when user A turns on a mobile data connection. The consequence is that contact networks can be constructed from CDR data. Indeed, for each user A, a historical record of

Table 8.2 Example of call detailed records data.

Event	Timestamp	Cell tower	Location area	Initiating user	Receiving user	Duration
...	...	...	...	...	...	...
Call	2007/10/01 23:45:00	15 988	00080177U8	33 647 956 872	33 649 274 861	3656s
Text	2007/10/02 01:12:04	2051	00000001D1	3 367 261 532	33 632 415 523	125c
...	...	...	...	...	...	...

CDR data can be used to construct a full calling pattern or a so-called ego-network of contacts. In such an ego-network, all users B, C, D, ..., K that have contacted user A or have been contacted by user A are denoted as nodes while edges between user A and the contacted users B–K are weighted by, for example, the number of calls that have occurred between them.

Additionally, mobile phone data (both CDR and DDR data) can help to describe human mobility. Most mobile phone data store information on the cell tower that is deployed. Network operators know the location of each cell tower in their network, as well as an estimation of the covered area by each cell tower (often estimated by means of the Voronoi polygons created from the cell tower location points). So based on a historical record of mobile phone activities – the different areas a single user has visited over time – a movement pattern can be reconstructed.

The rest of our investigation focuses on CDR data only, but knowing about the similarities and differences between CDR and DDR data is useful because they may be used together more often in the future.

8.2.2 The French Mobile Phone Dataset

In our analysis, we use an anonymized mobile phone dataset recorded by the French Operator Orange. The dataset covers mobile phone usage of 18 million subscribers on the Orange network in France during 154 consecutive days in 2007 (13 May 2007–14 October 2007). Mobile phone penetration was estimated at 86% at that time and, given a population of 63.945 million inhabitants during the observed period, constitutes about 32% of all French mobile phone users and 28% of the total population.

The mobile phone dataset consists of CDR data, typically collected by mobile phone service providers for billing and network maintenance. Every time a call or text is initiated or received, CDR data store locational (the used cell tower), temporal (time and duration of usage), and interactional (who contacts whom) information for both correspondents. Location traces from CDR data are noncontinuous, as they are user-initiated and rather sparse in time. In compliance with ethical and privacy guidelines, CDR data are anonymized.

This dataset is one of the largest CDR datasets available worldwide in population-wide coverage and has been extensively studied (e.g. Sobolevsky et al. 2013; Deville et al. 2014; Grauwin et al. 2017; Janzen et al. 2018; Vanhoof et al. 2018a,2018b; Cottineau and Vanhoof 2019). It is the latest CDR dataset available for France that allows for such long-term, continuous temporal – but anonymized – tracking of users in France. More recent datasets are aggregated and/or re-anonymized every given time period in line with the French Data Protection Agency (CNIL), who is anticipating the EU General Data Protection

Regulation that does not allow collecting individual traces extensively as they are considered risky even if personal identification information is irreversibly recoded.

The spatial accuracy of the dataset is restricted to the spatial resolution of the network, that is, to the locations of the cell towers installed by the network provider. The spatial distribution of the 18 273 cell tower locations is known but not uniform. In general, higher densities of cell towers are found in more densely populated areas like cities or coastlines. Lower densities of cell towers occur in rural areas, as well as in mountainous or natural reserve areas. The Voronoi tessellation of all cell tower locations is shown in Figure 8.4 illustrating the coverage and the density of the network.

The temporal resolution of the analyzed dataset is inhomogeneous because CDR are created and stored only during calls, thereby generating records for both caller and recipient. For example, for one arbitrary day of the covered timespan (Thursday, 1 October 2007), the median number of records per user was four, relating to only two different locations. Such statistics are representative for CDR-based studies and can be rather high compared to other large-scale noncontinuous datasets like credit card transactions or Flickr photos (Bojic et al. 2015).

On the one hand, temporal sparsity in observations and spatially inhomogeneous distributions of covered areas are typical characteristics of CDR datasets and pose substantial challenges for their automated analysis and the quality of home detection. Conversely, the large-scale reach at population level without requiring users' active participation for location sharing while preserving anonymity as well as privacy is very attractive for many application areas. Aggregating data over extended periods of time enables complex analysis and diminishes influence from singular events and/or nonroutine behavior.

8.2.3 Defining Nine Home Detection Algorithms

Most HDAs deployed on CDR data consist of single-step approaches, which detect a home by selecting the cell tower that accords best to an imposed decision rule – as opposed to two-step approaches where spatial grouping of cell towers is performed as an extra step. The decision rules applied in HDAs can be simple or complex, the former based on one criterion, the later based on a combination of several criteria as extensively discussed in Vanhoof et al. (2018a). Here, we opt to use simple decision rules over complex decision rules, because we can better single out the effect of criteria choice. Examples of typical criteria are "home is the location where most calls are made" and "home is the location where most activity has been observed during nighttime." Clearly, some of these criteria are subject to a parameter choice. For example, for "nighttime" criteria, the definition of nighttime has to be specified as, for example between 21.00 and 07.00 hours.

8.2 Deploying Home Detection Algorithms to a French CDR Dataset

Based on Vanhoof et al. (2018a) and Bojic et al. (2015), we use three criteria to perform home detection. Note that Vanhoof et al. (2018a) elaborate on an extra criterion related to spatial grouping but because of a consistently lower performance with regard to the other criteria, we omit this criterion in our analysis.

- *The maximum amount of activities criterion (MA)*: home is the cell tower where most activities of the user occurred during a specific observation period.
- *The distinct days criterion (DD)*: home is the cell tower where the maximum active days of a user were observed during a specific observation period.
- *The time constraints criterion (TC)*: home is the cell tower where most activities of the user occurred between XX.xx and YY.yy hours during a specific observation period.

The advantage of the MA and DD criteria is that they do not require any parameter choice. The TC criterion demands a parameter choice on which time restriction to deploy. Despite this extra parameter choice, HDAs based on the TC criterion are popular, especially in restricting periods to nighttime and/or weekend days, because this restriction is intuitive and parameter choices for defining nighttime can sometimes be based on available time surveys, both of which lend some justification to parameter and criteria choice. Nevertheless, studies investigating the sensitivity of the TC criterion to its parameter choices are nonexistent, and it is not clear whether nighttime or weekend days are the best options. For this reason, we will investigate different parameters choices for the TC criterion, incorporating nighttimes, daytimes, week days, weekend days, or some combination. The parameters are listed in Table 8.3. Nine HDAs are defined by combining different criteria and parameter choices aforementioned. They are described in Table 8.3 and are used in our analysis. Next, we specify how we will apply them to different time periods with different durations, to assess the influence on performance.

8.2.4 Different Observation Periods

Although the performance of HDAs could depend on the period of observation, no studies have explored this effect. We investigate such an effect by analyzing the results of the nine HDAs when deployed to CDR data collected during various time periods that start at different dates and last different durations.

The French dataset we use comprises data from 13 May until 15 October 2007. The most straightforward duration to consider would thus be 154 days, or the entire dataset. The disadvantages of doing so, however, are that calculations are computationally expensive, and that it does not allow sensitivity to time period to be studied. No one has proven that the longest duration necessarily leads to the best performance of home detection methods. We therefore also investigate discrete months as time period as in Vanhoof et al. (2018a). Because using

Table 8.3 Description of deployed HDAs.

Criteria	Parameters	Description: "home is cell tower where:"	Name
Maximum amount	/	Most activities occurred	MA
Distinct days	/	The maximum amount of active days were observed	DD
Time constraints	19, 9	Most activities occurred between 19.00 and 09.00 hours (night-time)	TC-19-9
Time constraints	19, 9, weekend	Most activities occurred between 19.00 and 09.00 hours (night-time) and during weekend days	TC-19-9-WE
Time constraints	21, 7	Most activities occurred between 21.00 and 07.00 hours (night-time)	TC-21-7
Time constraints	21, 7, weekend	Most activities occurred between 21.00 and 07.00 hours (night-time) and during weekend days	TC-21-7-WE
Time constraints	9, 19	Most activities occurred between 09.00 and 19.00 hours (daytime)	TC-9-19
Time constraints	9, 19, week	Most activities occurred between 09.00 and 19.00 hours (daytime) during weekdays	TC 9 19 WK
Time constraints	Weekend	Most activities occurred during weekend days only (Saturday and Sunday)	TC-WE

discrete months obscures proper comparison because of different numbers of days in different months, we also investigate durations of exactly 14 and 30 days, representing the amount of two weeks and about one month of data.

The actual time periods that relate to the different durations are straightforward for the discrete months and the 154 days' duration, but not necessarily for the 14 and 30 days. For the latter, we start observations at the first day of the dataset (13 May 2007) and take a moving window of 14 and 30 days, respectively, from that point. For the 14-day duration, home detection is performed during 11 two-week periods; the first is 13–26 May, the second 27 May–9 June, and so on. The same strategy is used for the 30-day duration, resulting in five periods; the first is 13 May–11 June. The last eight days, 7–15 October 2007, are omitted. Note that, because the dataset starts in mid-May, the 30-day periods are more or less complementary to the discrete months, offering interesting opportunities for comparison. All time periods for all different durations used in the analysis are illustrated in Figure 8.1.

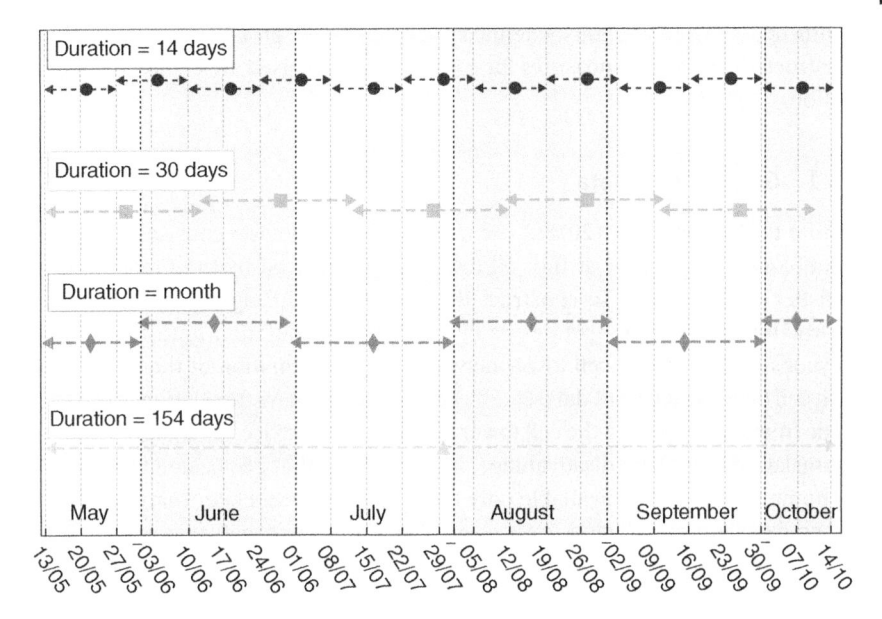

Figure 8.1 Different durations and related time periods used in the analysis.

8.2.5 Summary of Data and Setup

Our research setup performs home detection for each user in a French CDR dataset (around 18 million), based on nine HDAs (three different criteria, seven different parameter choices for the TC criterion), and for all 23 time periods (six discrete month periods, one entire observation period, five 30-day periods, and eleven 14-day periods). A total of around 3.7 billion home detections are performed based on user location traces. Before using the home location results to assess the influence of different user decisions (criteria choice, parameter choice, and time period) on performance in Section 8.4, we discuss how exactly we will measure performance.

8.3 Assessing Home Detection Performance at Nationwide Scale

Validation of HDAs at the individual level is not straightforward because collecting individual-level ground truth data is extremely expensive and has increased privacy risks. Consequently, researchers have to settle for high-level validation practices. In our analysis, we use aggregated population counts from census data as a ground truth dataset to compare against aggregated user counts that are the results of deploying previously defined HDAs. How the ground truth dataset was constructed and which measures for comparison were used are elaborated in this section.

8.3.1 Ground Truth Data

Similar to Vanhoof et al. (2018a), we use a validation dataset consisting of population counts aggregated at the cell tower level, prepared by the French official statistics office INSEE. To construct this dataset, INSEE aggregated geolocated information of the home addresses of the French population onto the Voronoi polygons of the Orange cell tower network, for an estimation of the coverage of each cell tower in the CDR dataset. The advantage is that no translations need to be made from census grid to the cell tower network grid (or vice versa), thus avoiding a translation error. The disadvantage, in our case, is that geolocated information on home addresses was available only for 2010, three years later than the mobile phone dataset was collected. As a result, any comparison between ground truth population counts and user counts from CDR data has to be relative also because Orange users represent only a share of the French population. Thus, our assumption is that, during a three-year period, the spatial distribution of the French population over the cell tower network does not change drastically.

8.3.2 Assessing Performance and Sensitivities

To measure the performance of the HDAs, we compare the outcome of each algorithm with the ground truth data. Specifically, we evaluate the degree of similarity between a vector of user counts (based on an HDA), denoted by x, and a vector of population counts (based on census data), denoted by y, both aggregated at cell tower level. Both vectors x and y thus have an equal length representing the 18 273 cell towers in the Orange network.

Because of the unknown spatial distribution of the 28% sample of Orange users, our assessment of similarity cannot be absolute. Therefore, we define performance measures based on the relative similarities between both vectors. Once a performance measure is calculated for all nine HDAs during all time periods, we can evaluate the influence of criteria choice, parameter choice, duration of observation, and period of observation on performance. The different parts of our methodology are illustrated in Figure 8.2. Each subfigure is explained in Section 8.4.

8.3.2.1 Correlation with Ground Truth Data

One direct way of quantifying (dis)similarities is to calculate the Pearson correlation coefficient (Pearson's R) between vectors x (user counts) and y (population

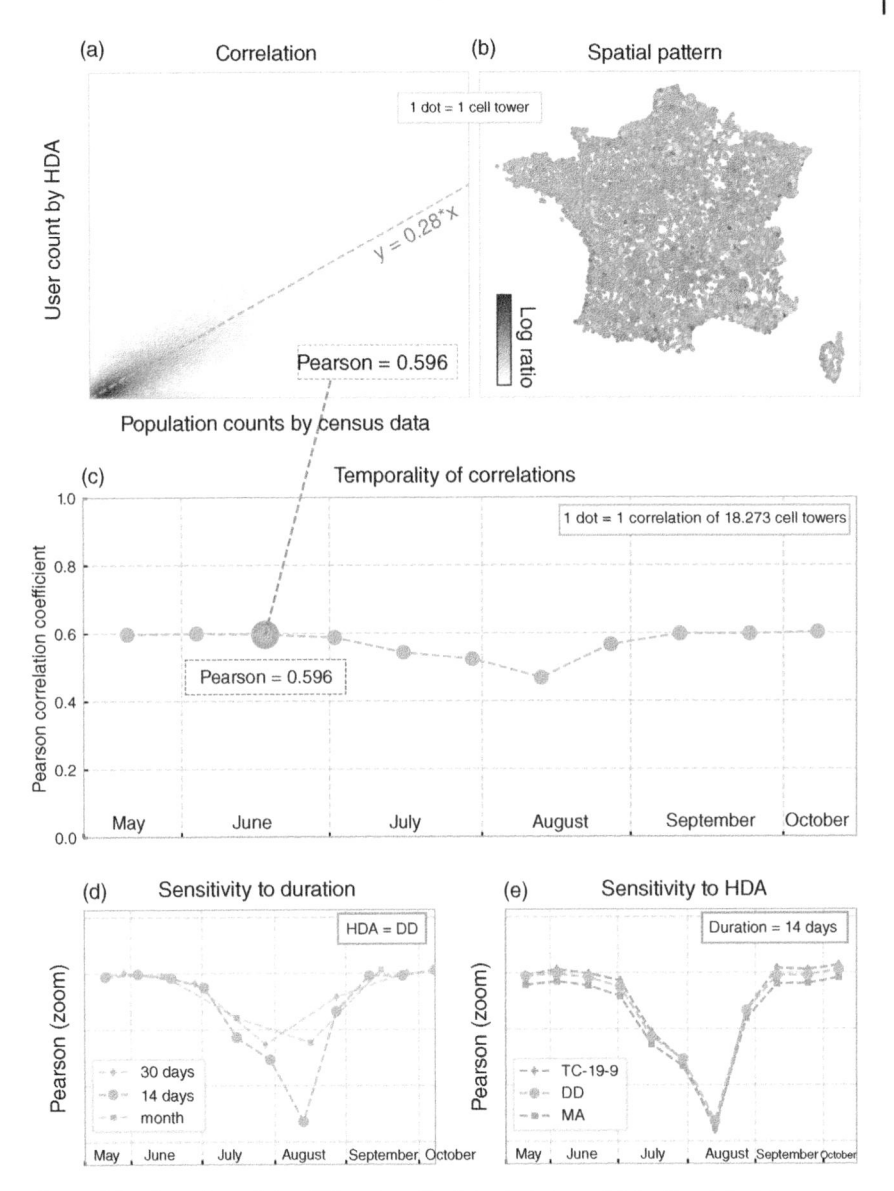

8.3 Assessing Home Detection Performance at Nationwide Scale | 257

Figure 8.2 Overview of the different methodological steps. (a) Scatterplot of the relation between user counts and ground truth data provided by population counts from census. Each dot represents a cell tower and is darkened according to the density of dots in its surrounding. A Pearson correlation coefficient for the point cloud is calculated. An expected (given the 28% overall market share) $y = 0.28x$ line is plotted as a guide to the eye. (b) Spatial pattern of the Log ratio between user counts and population counts from census data. (c) Temporality of the correlation between user counts and population counts from census data. (d) Sensitivity of the obtained correlations for duration choice given a chosen HDA (DD). (e) Sensitivity of the obtained correlations to HDA choice given a chosen duration (14-days).

validation count):

$$\text{Pearson's } R(\vec{x}, \vec{y}) = \frac{\sum (x_i - \bar{x})(y_i - \bar{y})}{\sqrt{\sum (x_i - \bar{x})^2 \sum (y_i - \bar{y})^2}} \qquad (8.1)$$

Pearson's R ranges between -1 and 1 representing, respectively, (perfect) opposition and similarity. Pearson's R values larger than 0 indicate a positive association between both vectors, whereas values smaller than 0 indicate negative association. Because the Pearson's correlation coefficient is only a general measure of the relation between both vectors, a visual investigation of the point cloud of both vectors is used as an additional tool in understanding their relation (see Figure 8.2a).

8.3.2.2 Ratio and Spatial Patterns

Although Pearson's R evaluates similarity between the vectors of population and user counts, it does not entirely allow for an assessment of the differences between ground truth and HDA results for each cell tower. To explore such individual differences, we calculate the ratio of the HDA user count to the ground truth population count (Figure 8.2b).

Note that, although local market shares of Orange can differ from cell tower to cell tower, ratios are distributed around 0.28, given the 28% overall market share. Large deviations from the expected 0.28 ratio can, therefore, be considered indicative for severe under- or overestimations. The ratio values for each HDA can be mapped to directly investigate the spatial pattern of differences between HDAs' user counts and the ground truth population counts to produce insights on the performance of HDAs in general.

8.3.2.3 Temporality and Sensitivity

To assess the sensitivity of HDAs, we deploy home detection for all combinations of criteria choice, parameter choice, and time periods previously defined and investigate performance measures over time (Figure 8.2c), between different HDAs (Figure 8.2d) and for different time periods (Figure 8.2e). As each summarizing measure describes the performance detecting homes for 18 million users, distributed over 18 273 cell towers, small differences in general performance relate to large absolute numbers of users allocated to a different home location.

8.4 Results

8.4.1 Relations between HDAs' User Counts and Ground Truth

After running the nine HDAs on all users in the CDR dataset for all time periods, we find the Pearson correlation coefficients (defined in Section 8.3.2.1) to

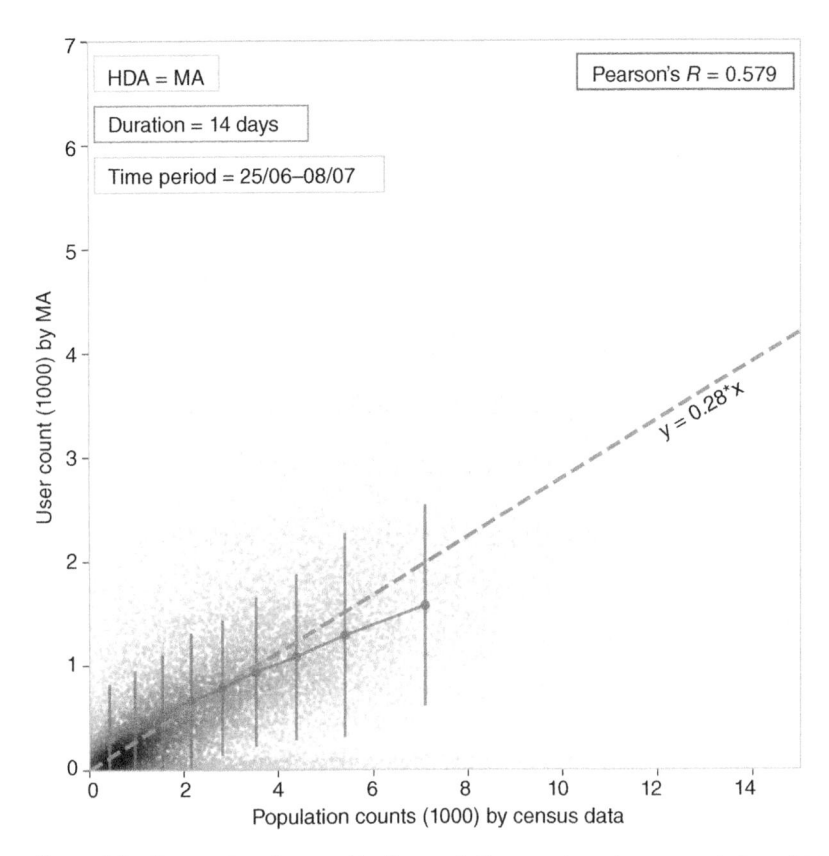

Figure 8.3 Scatterplot of ground truth population counts and user counts based on the MA algorithm for 14 days between 25 June and 7 August. Each dot represents one cell tower, and is darkened by density of the dots in its surrounding, in a gradient from black (high density) to light gray (low density). For each group of cell towers based on the deciles (except the 90–100 decile) of the population counts (x axis), the mean (black middle dot) and standard deviation (whisker) of the user counts (y axis) were calculated and plotted.

range between 0.45 and 0.60, which indicates a moderate performance (see also Figures 8.3, 8.5, 8.7, 8.8). Figure 8.3 helps explain the relation between user counts obtained from HDAs and the ground truth population counts. While it only depicts the results from the MA algorithm run for the 14 days between 25 June 2007 and 8 July 2007, other HDAs and time periods show similar relations. Three elements in Figure 8.3 deserve highlighting.

First, the majority of cell towers has rather low population and user counts (between 0 and 2000 persons). This effect is partly due to high densities of cell towers in urban areas. Second, cell towers are typically centered around the 0.28 line (dashed), which aligns with a 28% overall market share of the Orange operator, but divergence is high. This is indicated by the means (black dots) and the standard deviations (vertical error bars) of subgroups of cell towers grouped according to the deciles of the population counts. Overestimation typically occurs for cell towers with lower ground truth population, while underestimation is more related to cell towers that have a higher ground truth population. Without more contextual information on the cell towers such as location or typical usage by mobile phone users, it is impossible to properly account for this pattern. Third, one can clearly distinguish a group of cell towers with very low user counts. This group seems to be evenly distributed over the different ground truth population counts and can be considered an artifact of data collection. They correspond to cell towers that were (temporally) inactive during certain observation periods because they were, for example under repair or temporally dislocated.

8.4.2 Spatial Patterns of Ratios Between User Counts and Population Counts

Figure 8.4 shows the spatial pattern of how HDAs' user counts overestimate or underestimate population counts, by mapping the ratio between both for the MA algorithm deployed on the 14 days between 25 June 2007 and 7 August 2007 (similar to Figure 8.5). Again, this example is exemplary for other HDAs and time periods. HDAs underestimate populations in major city centers and among major roads compared to ground truth data, while overestimation occurs more in rural and tourist areas. Overestimation in tourist regions becomes even more prevalent during holiday periods as shown in Figure 8.6. Underestimation in city centers relates to local market shares of Orange because city centers are highly competitive locations between operators (with better services offered by smaller operators), resulting in smaller market shares for all operators. Overestimation in rural areas, then again, can be explained by reasons of (historical) coverage and brand loyalty of small communities.

8.4.3 Temporality of Correlations

Investigating Pearson's R values for different HDAs over time reveals that the performance of all HDAs is sensitive to the period of observation. In Figure 8.5, which shows the correlation coefficient of four different HDAs for all periods for 14 days, performance clearly drops during summer months July and August. This drop in performance is observed for all HDAs and is independent of the duration of observation (see also Figures 8.7 and 8.8). It is, in magnitude, the largest sensitivity that we observed during our experiments.

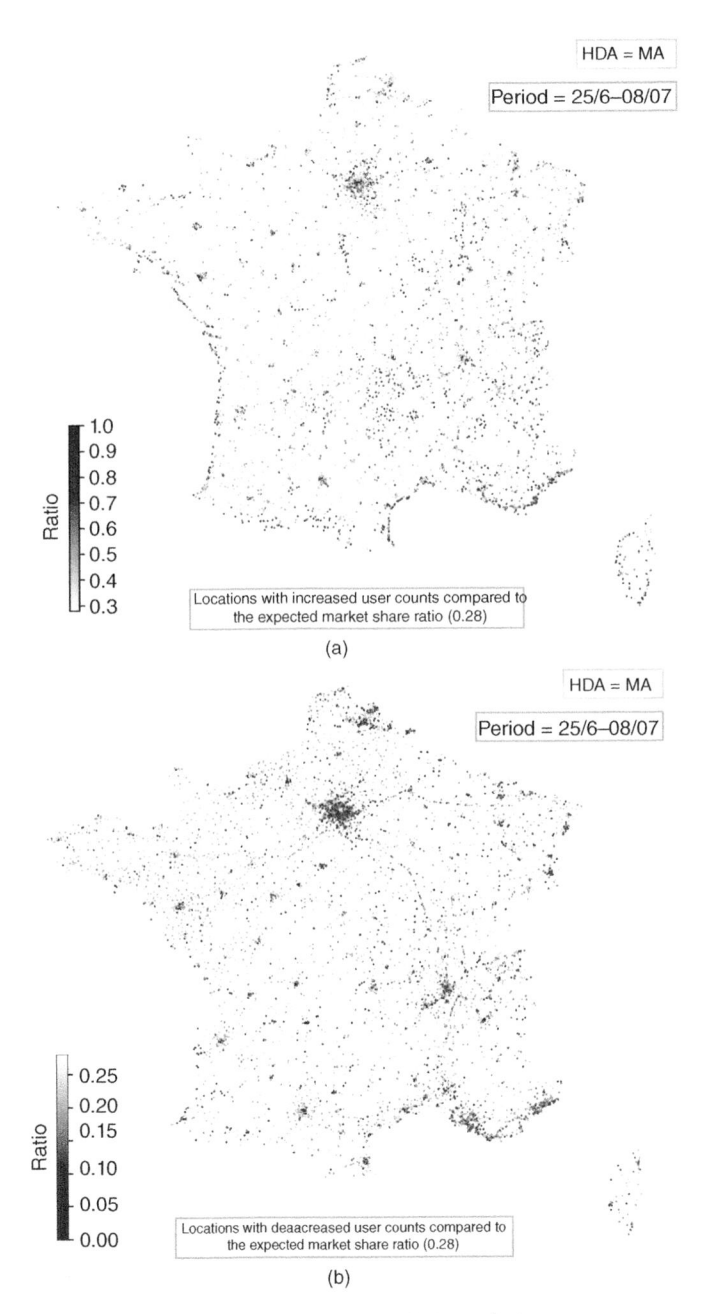

Figure 8.4 Maps for each cell tower with the ratio between user counts from the CDR data (based on the MA algorithm for 14 days between 25 June and 7 August) and population counts from the validation dataset. Cell towers with a ratio higher than the expected 0.28 based on the market share are on the left; towers with a lower ratio compared to 0.28 are on the right.

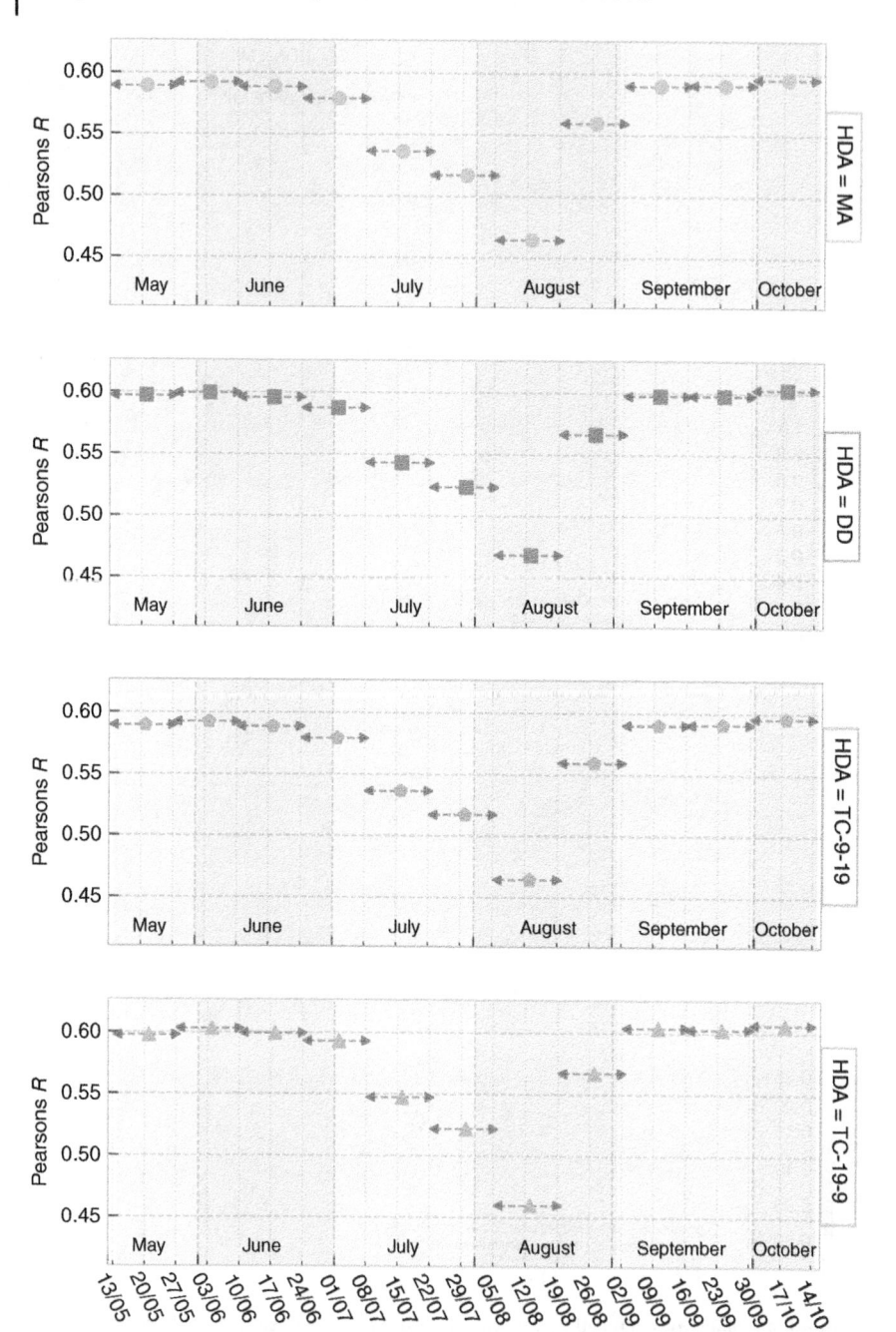

Figure 8.5 Performance over time of different HDAs for time periods with fixed duration of 14 days. The correlation measures were obtained from comparison with ground truth data (see Section 8.3.2.1) and are plotted in the middle of the observation periods, with dotted lines and arrows indicating the extent of the time period. Other HDAs depict similar temporal patterns.

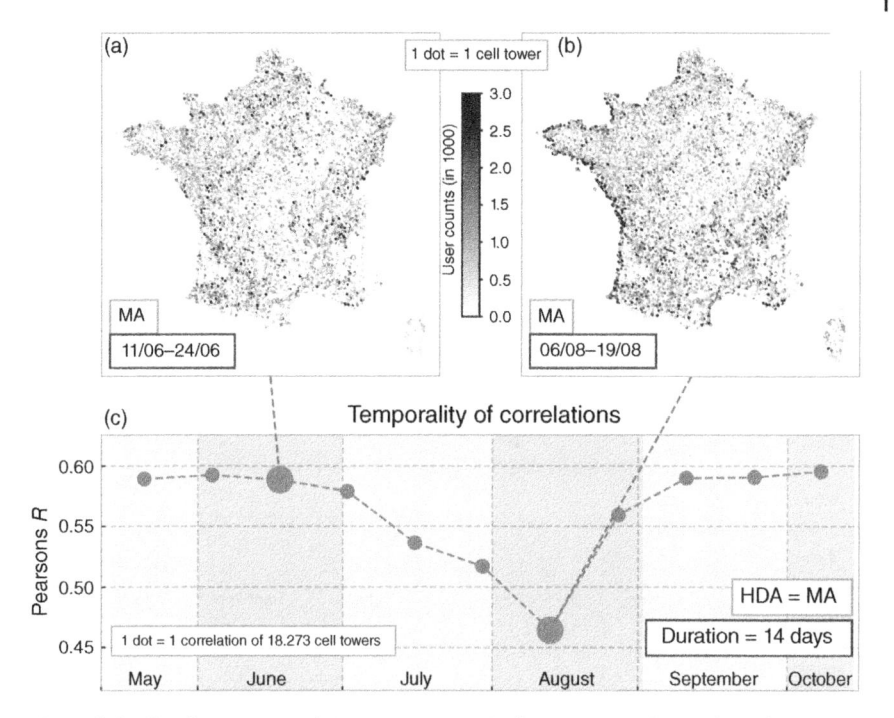

Figure 8.6 Spatial patterns of the user counts obtained by the MA algorithm for a non-summer (a) and a summer (b) period of 14 days. Home detection in summer periods results in higher user counts in tourist areas, which results in lower correlation with the ground truth dataset (c).

The limited performance of home detection during summer months is not surprising given that much of the French population travels to holiday destinations during this period (Deville et al. 2014; Vanhoof et al. 2017b, 2018a). It is, however, surprising that this mobility influences the results of HDAs to such a large degree, especially in comparison to the other sensitivities examined. The loss in performance of HDAs during summer periods because of (domestic) tourism[1] can be superbly illustrated by showing the spatial pattern of user counts obtained from a single HDA deployed on both a nonsummer and summer period in Figure 8.6. Clearly, during summer periods, user counts resulting from HDA go up drastically in tourist regions such as seaside locations, resulting in a significantly lower correlation with ground truth.

---

1 In 2015, 88.1% of all tourism trips performed by French people were estimated to be domestic tourism trips, making it one of the largest shares in Europe (Vanhoof et al. 2017b).

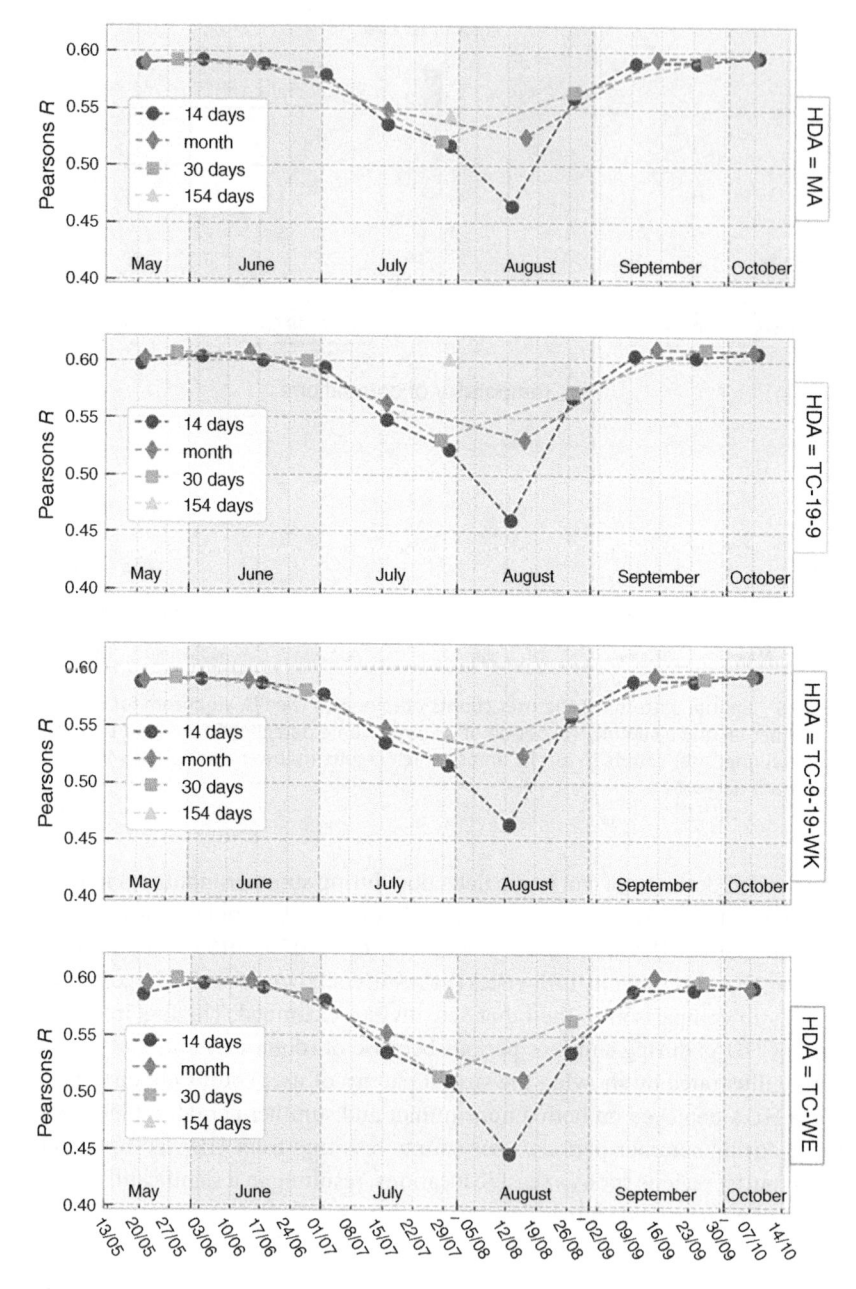

Figure 8.7 Performance over time of four algorithms for time periods characterized by different durations of observation.

8.4 Results | 265

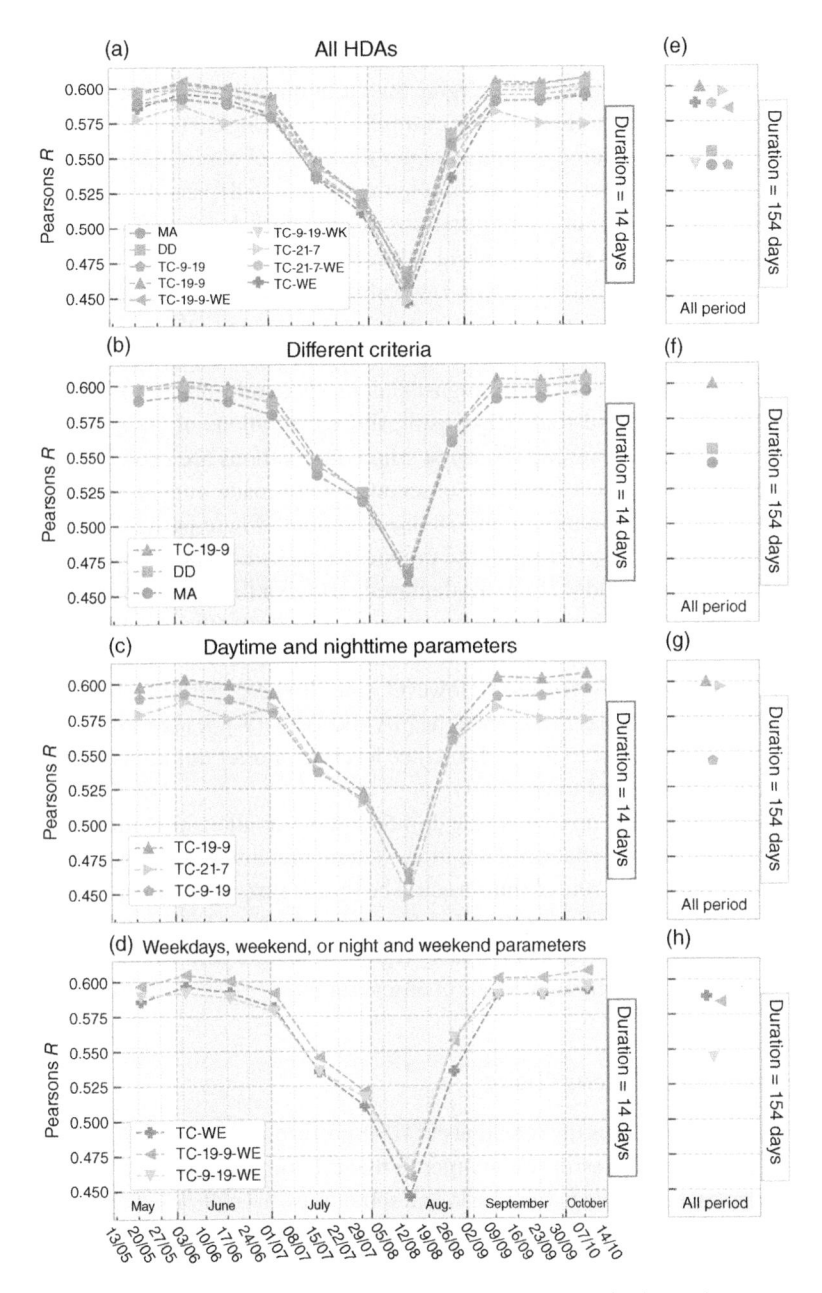

Figure 8.8 Performance over time of HDAs with different criteria and/or parameters for all time periods with a 14-day (a–d) and 154-day (e–h) duration of observation.

8.4.4 Sensitivity to the Duration of Observation

One outstanding question is to which degree the duration of the time period used influences the performance of HDAs. For example, it seems logical that while holiday mobility influences home detection, larger durations of observation periods could mitigate for this effect. As shown in Figure 8.7, which depicts the sensitivity of HDA performance to different durations of time periods for four different HDAs, longer observation periods indeed mitigate the summer drop in performance, although only to a certain extent. Interestingly, the sensitivity to the duration of observation is subordinate to the sensitivity to time period (in this case, summer periods), in that duration influences performance mainly by the proportion of the time period that occurs in August and, to a lesser degree, in July.

More specifically, we find that HDAs using shorter durations of observations (such as 14 days) perform among the worst when observations are made during summer but among the best when the observations are made outside summer months – in contrast to the month and 30-day durations, where performance is somewhere in between, depending on the proportion of the time period that is in July or August and independent from the deployed HDA. For the 154-day duration, we find that for some HDAs, the longer time period can mitigate the effect of summer holidays, similar to the best performance of shorter durations (for example, the TC-19-9 and TC-WE algorithms). However, not all HDAs perform this way. Performances for the 154-day duration of the MA and TC-9-19-WK algorithms, for example, are not even close to the performance levels of shorter duration periods that are not occurring in summer.

The consequence is that no clear single duration of observations performs best, and all depend on the combination of duration, general mobility of the population, and the chosen HDA. One rule of thumb could be that, if no insights are available on periods of general mobility, performing home detection on longer durations might be the safest choice, but will probably lead to moderate performance compared to shorter but well-chosen periods of observations.

8.4.5 Sensitivity to Criteria Choice

Final investigation concerns the sensitivity of HDA performance to criteria and/or parameter choice. An interesting observation is that criteria and parameter choice are less influential compared to time period or, sometimes, even duration of observation choice. For periods with a 14-day duration, for example, the effect of criteria choice is about 0.025 (expressed in Pearson's R), whereas the summer period effect is about 0.15, or an order higher (Figure 8.8b).

Still, some interesting observations can be made when comparing the performance of different HDAs, as in Figure 8.8. The TC criterion outperforms the MA and DD criteria for some parameters (such as the 19-9) but definitely not for all. In other words, parameter choice for the TC criterion has an impact on performance. For example, defining nighttime as 7–21 hours instead of 9–19 hours results in substantial performance loss for all 14-day periods investigated (Figure 8.8c). Even more remarkable is that the 7–21 parameter, at least for 14 days, is consistently outperformed by the 9–19 parameter, which is a daytime definition (Figure 8.8c). This finding drastically challenges the assumption that using nighttime would be better because people are at home then. The performance of different TC parameters is also influenced by the time period. Use of nighttime and weekends, for example, outperforms using weekdays during nonsummer periods, but this is not true for all 14-day duration periods in August (see Figure 8.8d).

The most remarkable finding regarding the sensitivity of performance to criteria and parameter choice is that it is strongly dependent on the duration of observation. While performance during 30-day and month durations are similar to the 14-day periods in Figure 8.8a–d, Figure 8.8e–h show how patterns of performance change drastically when considering the 154-day period. Note how similar the performance of the TC 9-19, TC 19-9, and TC 21-7 are for all 14-day periods (Figure 8.8c) and how different their performance is for the 154-day period (Figure 8.8g).

For the 154-day duration, the general logic is that the TC criterion with parameters restricted to nighttime and weekend days performs significantly better compared to other HDAs (Figure 8.8e). From our experiments, it is not clear what exactly is driving this gain in performance during longer observation periods, nor is it clear from which duration of observation this gain is occurring (although it has to be between 30 and 154 days). One possible explanation is that TC criteria need an observation period with sufficient duration to operate properly according to their semantics, but further inquiry is needed.

8.5 Discussion and Conclusion

Our experiments have revealed the different effects of criteria choice, parameter choice, duration of observation period, and time period on the performance of HDAs for a large French CDR dataset. After investigating 255 different setups, we find that HDAs in France perform moderately at best, with correlations with high-level ground truth data ranging between about 0.40 and 0.60. We call this performance moderate at best, since it is still a significant way from perfect accordance (correlation = 1). However, it is unclear whether correlations between 0.4 and 0.6 should be considered good or bad because many elements might influence these results. For example, better performances can likely be obtained when incorporating proper estimates of local market shares of the single operator, which would eliminate the local variances of market shares that are not accounted for in our analysis.

Our results show that there exists a structural uncertainty in home detection at a nationwide scale that has yet to be fully understood. This uncertainty is partly made up by researcher choices on the time periods used and the HDAs' criteria, which we set out to investigate in our research. And it is partly made up by elements that are not properly investigated yet, such as unknown local market shares, uneven representation of populations in a single operator dataset, differing definitions of home between validation data, and the methods used for home detection, and differing mobile phone usage between users. All of these elements are likely to influence the accuracy of home detection and deserve further investigation in future research.

Investigating the spatial pattern of performance, we observe that all nine HDAs for all 225 deployed time periods underestimate populations in city centers and among main roads, while overestimating population in tourist destinations and some rural areas. Our definitions of under- and overestimation are, however, based on an assumed market share of the operator of 0.28%, which is correct for the national level but can vary locally. In this perspective, the outstanding question remains to which degree the combination of CDR data from multiple operators (aiming at a 100% coverage of mobile phone users) would render similar spatial patterns. So far, little work has been published that combines data from several operators, but such combined datasets would be beneficial. The basic nature of traces captured in CDR data allow for such a combination of data between operators (even though each operator might have slightly different technical systems in place), and so this seems a good avenue for the near future.

For France, in 2007, we find HDA performance to be sensitive, in descending order of magnitude, to the deployed time period, the duration of observation, and to a small degree only, to criteria and parameter choice. The largest sensitivity is to the July and August periods, when performance drops significantly for all HDAs. During July and August, HDAs consistently overestimate population counts in tourist regions, suggesting that they are influenced by large number of French people traveling on holiday. The effect of the duration of observation is subordinate to this summer effect: performances of HDAs are directly related to the proportion of the time period occurring in July and August. Shorter periods outside the summer months outperform longer durations, where part of the observations were made in July and/or August. Consequently, there is no clear advice on what duration of observation to use. When periods of large-scale population mobility are unknown, longer durations might be the safest option. When such periods are known, however, avoiding them at all costs seems the best advice, even if this means giving up part of the dataset.

Our most remarkable finding is that criteria and parameter choice for HDAs seem of little influence, especially compared to the sensitivity to time period and duration of observation. For criteria, we find the distinct day-criterion slightly outperforms the amount of activities criterion. The performance of the popular TC is highly dependent on the chosen parameters. Remarkably, for example the 9 to 19-hour time constraint outperformed most algorithms, whereas 7 to 21-hour time constraint (only a few hours' difference) performed the worst of all tested algorithms. Additionally, the performance of HDAs based on the time constraints-criterion is rather inconsistent, with intuitive (e.g. nighttime and weekends) and contra-intuitive (e.g. only working days) constraints outperforming each other at different time periods and for different durations of observations. These results call into question why the TC, although popular in literature (Vanhoof et al. 2018a), should ever be used; if not for our one observation that, for the 154-day period, time-constraint HDAs with intuitive parameters outperformed all other HDAs, with performance equaling the best performances of other HDAs for other periods and durations in our experiment.

Thus, we find it difficult to recommend one HDA, criteria, or time period to use when performing home detection in France. Performance depends on a combination of factors, and future researchers should investigate the sensitivity of their results versus these researchers' choices. One outstanding question is the transferability of our findings. Because this work is the first to investigate the sensitivities of home detection methods, no one knows whether our findings can be replicated in datasets for other years and for other countries. Perhaps the largest sensitivity of home detection performance is in the way people user their mobile phones (and the type of information CDR data can capture), an element that can vary across location and time. We, as a research community, still have to duplicate this research setup to many different CDR datasets to fully understand how, when, and where home detection is a trustworthy step in our analysis of mobile phone data.

Our work offers an insight in the combined effect of user choices on the performance of home detection when deployed on a French CDR dataset. Our results can help other practitioners decide on suitable HDAs and time periods of observation. We strongly urge other researchers to reproduce our experiments on their own datasets. Additionally, our work can inform the assessment of uncertainty and error related to home detection methods when performed on CDR data or, to a lesser degree, other large datasets of geolocated traces for individual users. Ultimately, our work can contribute to the wider debate on integrating Big Data in official statistics in two ways. First, it serves as a reminder that, despite showing large potential, many Big Data sources and related methods are still in need of quality assessment. Second, our work shows that collaboration among academia, private sector, and official statistics offices can be extremely fruitful to overcome barriers experienced by one or multiple parties, even though the actual realization of such collaborations is never easy.

References

Balzotti, C., Bragagnini, A., Briani, M., et al. (2018). Understanding human mobility flows from aggregated mobile phone data. *arXiv* 1803.00814.

Bojic, I., Massaro, E., Belyi, A. et al. (2015). Choosing the right home location definition method for the given dataset. In: *Proceedings of the 7th International Conference on Social Informatics (SocInfo), Beijing, China (9-12 December)*, 194–208. Springer International Publishing.

Cottineau, C. and Vanhoof, M. (2019). Mobile phone indicators and their relation to the socioeconomic organisation of cities. *ISPRS International Journal of Geo-Information* 8 (1): 19. https://doi.org/10.3390/ijgi8010019.

Daas, P.J.H., Puts, M.J., Buelens, B. et al. (2015). Big data as a source for official statistics. *Journal of Official Statistics* 31 (2): 249–262. https://doi.org/10.1515/Jos-2015-0016.

Decuyper, A., Rutherford, A., Wadhwa, A., et al. (2014). Estimating food consumption and poverty indices with mobile phone data. *arXiv* 1412.2595.

Deville, P., Linard, C., Martin, S. et al. (2014). Dynamic population mapping using mobile phone data. *Proceedings of the National Academy of Sciences of the United States of America* 111 (45): 15888–15893. https://doi.org/10.1073/pnas.1408439111.

Eagle, N., Macy, M., and Claxton, R. (2010). Network diversity and economic development. *Science Translational Medicine* 328 (5981): 1029–1031. https://doi.org/10.1126/science.1186605.

Frias-Martinez, V., Soto, V., Virseda, J. et al. (2013). Can cell phone traces measure social development? *Proceedings of the Third International Conference on the Analysis of Mobile Phone Datasets, NetMob,* Boston, MA (1–3 May), pp. 62–65.

Giannotti, F., Pedreschi, D., Pentland, A. et al. (2012). A planetary nervous system for social mining and collective awareness. *European Physical Journal: Special Topics* 214 (1): 49–75. https://doi.org/10.1140/epjst/e2012-01688-9.

Grauwin, S., Szell, M., Sobolevsky, S. et al. (2017). Identifying and modeling the structural discontinuities of human interactions. *Scientific Reports* 7: 46677. https://doi.org/10.1038/srep46677.

Janzen, M., Vanhoof, M., and Axhausen, K.W. (2016). Purpose imputation for long-distance tours without personal information. Working paper published in ETH working series.

Janzen, M., Vanhoof, M., Smoreda, Z. et al. (2018). Closer to the total? Long-distance travel of French mobile phone users. *Travel Behaviour and Society* 11: 31–42. https://doi.org/10.1016/j.tbs.2017.12.001.

Kung, K.S., Greco, K., Sobolevsky, S. et al. (2014). Exploring universal patterns in human home-work commuting from mobile phone data. *PLoS One* 9 (6): e96180. https://doi.org/10.1371/journal.pone.0096180.

Pappalardo, L., Pedreschi, D., Smoreda, Z. et al. (2015). Using big data to study the link between human mobility and socio-economic development. *Proceedings of the 2015 IEEE International Conference on Big Data (Big Data)*, Santa Clara, CA (29 October–1 November), pp. 871–878.

Pappalardo, L., Vanhoof, M., Gabrielli, L. et al. (2016). An analytical framework to nowcast well-being using mobile phone data. *International Journal of Data Science and Analytics* 2 (1): 75–92. https://doi.org/10.1007/s41060-016-0013-2.

Sobolevsky, S., Szell, M., Campari, R. et al. (2013). Delineating geographical regions with networks of human interactions in an extensive set of countries. *PLoS One* 8 (12): e81707. https://doi.org/10.1371/journal.pone.0081707.

Vanhoof, M. (2018). Geographical veracity of indicators from mobile phone data. PhD thesis. Newcastle University, UK.

Vanhoof, M., Combes, S., and De Bellefon, M.-P. (2017a). Mining mobile phone data to detect urban areas. In: *Statistics and Data Science: New Challenges, New Generations, SIS 2017* (eds. A. Petrucci and R. Verde), 1005–1012. Florence, Italy: Firenze University Press.

Vanhoof, M., Hendrickx, L., Puussaar, A. et al. (2017b). Exploring the use of mobile phones during domestic tourism trips. *Netcom* 31 (3/4): 335–372.

Vanhoof, M., Reis, F., Ploetz, T. et al. (2018a). Assessing the quality of home detection from mobile phone data for official statistics. *Journal of Official Statistics* 3 (4): 935–960. https://doi.org/10.2478/Jos-2018-0046.

Vanhoof, M., Reis, F., Smoreda, Z., et al. (2018b). Detecting home locations from CDR data: introducing spatial uncertainty to the state-of-the-art. *arXiv*: 1–13.

Vanhoof, M., Schoors, W., Van Rompaey, A. et al. (2018c). Comparing regional patterns of individual movement using corrected mobility entropy. *Journal of Urban Technology* 25 (2): 27–61. https://doi.org/10.1080/10630732.2018.1450593.

Section 3

Big Data in Official Statistics

9

Big Data Initiatives in Official Statistics

Lilli Japec[1] and Lars Lyberg[2]

[1] *Statistics Sweden, Stockholm, Sweden*
[2] *Inizio, Stockholm, Sweden*

9.1 Introduction

Statistics production for official statistics and other areas are currently facing considerable challenges. Many of the challenges result from what we might describe as the changing survey landscape. Nonresponse rates are increasing and so are costs for traditional data collection. To varying degrees, users often want more timely and richer data, sometimes at the expense of data accuracy. Some research groups are promoting alternative inferential paradigms. Examples include Calibrated Bayes (Little 2015) and nonprobability sampling (Buelens, Burger, and van den Brakel 2018). During the last decade, much attention has been devoted to the issue of combining multiple data sources in official statistics production and the potential that Big Data might offer. Many prominent methodologists described these challenges in detail, e.g. Holt (2007), Groves (2011), Couper (2013), Baker et al. (2013), Landefeld (2014), Pfefferman (2015), Citro (2014), Hulliger et al. (2012), Kitchin (2015), Baker (2017), and Tam and Kim (2018). Most methodologists associated with official statistics agree that the traditional surveys have limitations because of increasing costs, increasing nonresponse rates, and changing user preferences. They also seem to agree that the potential of new data sources and data collection modes should be explored. This chapter concentrates on one of these developments: Big Data and its potential impact on current and future statistics production.

Section 9.2 describes some characteristics of the changing survey landscape and gives examples of initiatives that are currently under way. Section 9.3 describes various strategies to incorporate Big Data in official statistics. Some national sta-

---

Big Data Meets Survey Science: A Collection of Innovative Methods, First Edition. Edited by Craig A. Hill, Paul P. Biemer, Trent D. Buskirk, Lilli Japec, Antje Kirchner, Stas Kolenikov, and Lars E. Lyberg.
© 2021 John Wiley & Sons, Inc. Published 2021 by John Wiley & Sons, Inc.

tistical institutes (NSIs) are more advanced than others but most are doing at least some work in this area. Section 9.4 provides examples of actual attempts at producing statistics using Big Data thereby reducing costs, combining Big Data with administrative data and sample surveys to improve statistics, and using Big Data to explore new topics or refine existing concepts. Asking questions to measure a concept can be insufficient in many instances and to complement that kind of measurement by incorporating more data sources seems promising. Section 9.5 discusses the quality aspects of introducing Big Data. Researchers have attempted to develop frameworks and other quality assessment methods. We review these and point to some inherent problems with them (Biemer 2016; Biemer and Amaya 2020). Section 9.6 discusses some legal issues that Big Data might generate (Bender et al. 2017) and how these problems might differ across countries and regions. Section 9.7 speculates about future developments in data collection and analysis for official statistics in an era of Big Data.

9.2 Some Characteristics of the Changing Survey Landscape

The survey landscape is changing rapidly. When Jerzy Neyman published his seminal work on sampling methodology and classical inference in 1934 and 1937, respectively, it provided answers that many had wanted (Neyman 1934, 1937). To study a population, researchers and producers of statistics did not need to access the entire population. A probability sample is sufficient: based on that sample, one can make inferences about the entire population. This breakthrough was an enormous cost-saver and facilitated more research than before it was published. At the outset, however, Neyman and his peers clearly realized that the sampling theory only took the sampling error into account, and confidence levels of estimates might be overstated due to various other errors, such as those listed by Deming (1944). Our guess is that at the time it was more important to promote the probability sampling method among stakeholders than pointing out its possible limitations. Over the years, this emphasis on sampling error has prevailed although lots of work has been devoted to preventing, mitigating, and adjusting for nonsampling errors so that the total survey error (TSE) comes as close as possible to the sampling error. For several reasons, this strategy has become increasingly complicated, while at the same time, new survey data collection avenues have been created. Also, alternatives to the dominating frequentist inferential paradigm used in official statistics, such as Calibrated Bayes, have been suggested (Little 2015). Calibrated Bayes can be used to combine information from probability and nonprobability sources or applied when nonsampling errors need to be modeled, something that the classical inferential paradigm cannot do easily.

Thus, we have a new survey landscape formed by various problems, opportunities, and new developments that have direct or indirect impact on statistics production and on survey research. One problem is that costs of traditional data collection are increasing. For instance, in some research areas, face-to-face interviewing is no longer viable. Respondents do not respond to surveys as they formerly did, resulting in response rates that sometimes have reached unprecedented low levels. For instance, the Swedish Labor Force Survey's response rate dropped from 98% to approximately 50% during the last 50 years, a slow but steady decline. Similar developments have occurred in many other countries. Decreasing response rates have triggered research on nonprobability sampling – a method that is not new to survey research. Nonprobability sampling can be effective in pilot studies to prove the existence of certain phenomena but also in situations where probability sampling cannot be done, e.g. in some studies of hard-to-survey populations (Tourangeau et al. 2014). In general though, nonprobability sampling such as quota sampling and self-selection procedures have been largely avoided in statistics production because of unknown selection biases and no possibilities to calculate margins of error. Recently, however, researchers have shown renewed interest in such methods, triggered mainly by cost considerations, low response rates in probability surveys, user demands for quicker results, and the advent of various Big Data sources that do not easily lend themselves to probability sampling (e.g. Buelens, Burger, and van den Brakel 2018; Mercer et al. 2017; Baker et al. 2013; Valliant and Dever 2011). Currently, much of this research boils down to combining probability and nonprobability sampling and careful weighting adjustments of the latter.

Most producers of official statistics realize that modernization of survey data collection is necessary. It should be done in ways that keep the response burden as small as possible. This opens up opportunities for web modes and mobile devices as well as an abundance of data sources in the Big Data tent. Official statistics is steered by a mix of stakeholders consisting of owners (governments), different kinds of users who want different things, service providers (NSIs), and respondents. Holt (2007) summarized the demands on the service providers from owners and users as five formidable challenges: wider, deeper, better, quicker, and cheaper. Respondents, on the other hand, are in general not too eager to participate in data collection as manifested by low response rates and by their use of various strategies to make the survey task as easy as possible by practicing satisficing (Krosnick 1991) and motivated misreporting (Bach and Eckman 2018). More recently, Citro (2014) questioned the sample survey paradigm of the last 70 years and suggested it be replaced by a multiple data sources paradigm, where user needs for information are first identified, followed by determining the best combination of data sources that can satisfy these needs. Thus, some basic procedures in official statistics need to be changed to meet the demands to which Holt referred. One change is to embrace the opportunities that various forms of Big Data can offer in the production of official statistics.

Official statistics are constantly discussed in the survey literature. Typical topics include, but are not restricted to, their roles, challenges, core values and basic principles, user needs and user influence, the need for innovation, the risk of becoming redundant, trust, comparability, and data quality. Examples of such discussions are Desrosieres (1998) on the politics of large numbers, Stiglitz, Sen, and Fitoussi (2009) on the measurement of economic and social progress, Sturgeon (2013) on global value chains and economic globalization, Porter (1995) on trust in numbers, and standards such as the United Nations (UN) fundamental principles of official statistics (UN 1994), the European statistics code of practice (European Statistical System (ESS) 2017a), and US principles and practices for a federal statistical agency (Citro 2014).

In the last few years, much discussion has concerned various ways to modernize official statistics and widen its scope. At the opening of the BigSurv18 conference, Tom Smith (2018) from the UK Office for National Statistics (ONS) stated that surveys are the last resort. He claimed that we need multiple types of data to triangulate the "truth" and that surveys, which are constrained in many ways, as a sole source are not capable of using multiple data types. But already in 2014, Heeringa (2014) coined the notion of survey-assisted modeling. He discussed the information content of available data resources and stated that modeling, data mining, and analytics had the highest information content, followed by his notion of survey-assisted modeling, where a survey could provide model training and model refinement and also compensate for errors. Less information content is found in model-assisted surveys, whereas regular surveys provide the least information content. Heeringa found that existing data systems, big or small, can benefit from survey assistance. Official statisticians interested in Big Data currently agree with that idea.

Most NSIs are working with Big Data and other data sources, most notably administrative data, as a complement to surveys. For example, ONS has a Data Science Center and Statistics Netherlands plays a major role in the Big Data work that takes place within the European Statistical System (ESS). Eurostat recently released (van Sebille et al. 2018) its final report from the ESSnet Big Data project part 1, discussing the potential of various Big Data sources in statistics production. Tools such as webscraping, smart meters, Automatic Identification System (AIS) data, mobile phone data, and machine learning have been investigated for their potential to produce new official statistics either as standalones or in certain combinations. Other NSIs such as the Australian Bureau of Statistics (see Chapter 11) and the US Federal Statistical System (National Academies of Sciences, Engineering, and Medicine 2017) are treading new paths in this landscape of opportunities. The UN Big Data Global Working Group has a continuing inventory of Big Data projects in official statistics around the world. Examples include

- *Austria*: Webscraping for price collection
- *Belgium*: Geocoding static objects
- *Canada*: Smart meter electricity data
- *China*: Crop outputs using satellite data
- *Czech Republic*: Scanner data for price statistics and possibly for national accounts
- *Ecuador*: Social media data to create a happiness index
- *Finland*: Merging Big Data and official statistics to produce statistics on commuting
- *Hungary*: Webscraping to estimate job vacancies
- *Haiti*: Cellphone data to measure rainfall in data-scarce contexts
- *Ireland*: Mobile phone data for tourism statistics
- *Israel*: Road sensor data for transportation statistics
- *Italy*: Google trend data to nowcast unemployment
- *Norway*: Webscraping to estimate internet trade
- *Poland*: Webscraping to improve sampling frames
- *Republic of Korea*: Mobile data for estimating daily migration
- *Singapore*: Environmental sensors for real-time environmental information
- *Sweden*: AIS data for ship identification
- *United States*: Automated coding of payroll systems data to reduce response burden
- *Bangladesh*: Modeling Google cloud data to predict vulnerability to flooding
- *World Bank*: Machine learning to predict and target poverty
- *India*: Tracking light from satellites to monitor rural electrification
- *Colombia*: Using risk terrain modeling to evaluate crime
- *Guatemala*: Transaction and purchase data to enhance tax compliance.

Thus, what we witness in official statistics is an unprecedented aspiration to change, while keeping stakeholders happy and core values intact. Of course, one core value is good data quality. In many initiatives, tools and approaches are tested to determine if estimates can be produced using them. In terms of actually assessing the quality of these estimates or judging the limitations of Big Data in specific applications, much work remains to be done. Furthermore, history shows that innovation often can be slow (Dillman 1996) and uncoordinated (Kotz 2005), but many past innovations have become sustained improvements, because of the time and effort invested. However, now this scenario seems different from previous demands for change. Developments take place very rapidly and most users, owners, and, to some extent, respondents no longer accept tediousness, large costs, and high response burden. Thus, the pressure is on, which is manifested by the many initiatives described in this chapter and elsewhere.

One prevailing trend is the wish to combine data sources, such as surveys and censuses, administrative data, and Big and not-so-Big Data, including medical records systems, genetic profile data, commercially compiled data, financial data, transaction data, mobile devices, wearable measurement devices, webscraping, websites, social media, smart meters, satellites, global positioning system (GPS) and geographic information system (GIS), sensors, pictures and videos, vessel and flight data, and scanner data. Other research issues include how to combine sources and what sources to combine given the user needs (Daas et al. 2015). Currently, social media data seem to be the most difficult to use in statistics production (see Chapter 6, this volume).

Another trend is the ongoing development of methods for combining less costly nonprobability samples with more costly probability samples (Valliant, Dever, and Kreuter 2018; Brick 2014; Buelens et al. 2018; Tam et al. 2020) and to combine modeling with surveys, what Heeringa (2014, 2017) denoted as survey-assisted modeling. A more general trend is the increased use of mixed-mode data collection to combat costs, to enhance information on concepts of interest, and to accommodate respondents. Mixed-mode data collection has downsides since each mode has its own unique error structure, but there are methods to adjust for such effects on data quality (De Leeuw 2018).

A fourth trend is that concepts need to be examined from wider angles. It is not always sufficient to capture concepts via estimates of population parameters built on survey questions developed by subject matter researchers. Sources other than surveys can provide those wider angles (Radermacher 2017, 2018; MacFeely 2016). For instance, following and interpreting traditional concepts on employment and wages have become increasingly difficult. The world changes fast and statistics need to adjust to that pace by relying on a growing number of data sources. The pace of change will most likely accelerate, which means those involved in producing official statistics must have a sense of urgency. Holt's (2007) assessment of the situation for official statistics is as valid today as it was 13 years ago. But change calls for methodological research and implementation. Several authors have described the issues and suggested what needs to be done. A common theme is that they are convinced that Big Data and combinations of data sources are part of a new survey era (Groves 2011; Couper 2013; Pfefferman 2015; Vaccari 2014; Signorelli and Biffignandi 2018; Kalton 2018; Meng 2018; Biemer and Amaya 2020).

9.3 Current Strategies to Handle the Changing Survey Landscape

Many NSIs have recognized the challenge of increasing costs for data collection and the new survey landscape and have started to look for new data sources for official statistics production. These new data sources, however, come with new challenges such as getting access to data, legal issues, lack of know-how, and an insufficient IT infrastructure. Sections 9.3.1–9.3.7 discuss some examples of strategies that NSIs have adopted to cope with this new situation.

9.3.1 Training Staff

Traditionally, a statistical agency would have in-house analytical, statistical, and IT-skills, but additional skills are needed for big data sets such as statistical modelling methods, new techniques for data collection, processing, and storing, advance computer programming, and building and maintaining computation infrastructures to deal with large data sets (Japec et al. 2015).

Skills can be obtained via training courses on Big Data that are targeted toward production of official statistics and social research. One example is the Joint Program in Survey Methods at the University of Maryland that in its curricula from 2018 covered topics such as linking Big Data with survey data, coverage and measurement errors within the Big Data context, and concepts from machine learning as they apply to processing Big Data. EMOS (European Master in Official Statistics), a collaboration between a number of European NSIs, universities, and Eurostat, also offers courses and webinars on Big Data.

Recently, many of the conferences that professionals working in national statistical agencies attend have an artificial intelligence or Big Data track in their programs, e.g. at New Techniques and Technologies for Statistics (NTTS), American Association for Public Opinion Reporting (AAPOR) and American Statistical Association conferences. The BigSurv18 initiative is, to our knowledge, the first conference entirely devoted to Big Data in statistics production. The goal is to get professionals with different skills relevant to surveys and Big Data to meet, share experiences, and hopefully collaborate. The BigSurv conference is intended to be a continuing event.

9.3.2 Forming Partnerships

Many statistical agencies lack the new types of skills that they need to be able to work with artificial intelligence and Big Data. One strategy is to form partnerships with universities, private firms, and other statistical agencies to collaborate on projects of mutual interest. However, finding incentives for private firms to cooperate with an NSI needs careful consideration. One possibility is that a statistical agency could be incentivized to provide data that can help a private firm to understand a specific industry or sector. However, an NSI must avoid acting in ways that could be perceived as being commercial or favoring a particular organization or firm. Perhaps the biggest potential is that many private organizations today have an explicit strategy for assuming social responsibility, which might create opportunities for collaboration.

Another reason for an NSI to form a partnership is to get access to data. The partner's willingness to share data will vary depending on, for instance, how crucial the data are in a firm's business model and, if applicable, its interpretation of European Union's (EU) General Data Protection Regulation (GDPR). Statistics Netherlands has formed partnerships with national and international partners in both the private and public sectors. Partners include the Maastricht University, Georgetown University, De Nederlandsche Bank, IBM, Capgemini Nederland, Microsoft Netherlands, and other NSIs. Forming partnerships can bring knowledge and expertise to an NSI, which would be otherwise unavailable, for instance, access to data lakes and cloud platforms.

9.3.3 Cooperation Between European NSIs

In 2016, a European project began studying various Big Data sources to see if they could be used for production of official statistics (van Sebille et al. 2018). The project, ESSnet on Big Data, explored many facets: webscraping job portals for production of vacancy statistics, using data from smart electricity meters to produce energy statistics, and using AIS data to produce port statistics. The results from the project showed that these three data sources in particular had potential for use in production of official statistics. The second round of the project started in December 2018 (ESS 2019) and is exploring such technology as:

- data from smart farming generated by equipment used in livestock feeding and plant production,
- sensor data related to smart cities such as data on quality of air and road accidents,
- data from smart devices such as human wearables and smart homes,
- financial transaction data to measure the sharing economy, and
- combining earth observation data and administrative data to determine quality of housing and quality of life.

9.3.4 Creating Big Data Centers

To enhance creativity and speed development in official statistics, some NSIs have created Big Data centers that focus on how to use new data sources. These centers' mission is to address challenges such as producing more timely statistics and statistics on a more detailed level, developing new indicators and reducing response burden. Part of the concept is to collaborate with external partners. Another objective for the Big Data centers is to build capacity in data science and artificial intelligence. In these environments, researchers, data scientists, and subject matter specialists are working together developing new statistics using Big Data. Examples of NSIs with Big Data centers are Statistics Netherlands, ONS in the United Kingdom, and Statistics Canada. In the United Kingdom, the ONS focuses its research in five areas: the evolving economy, United Kingdom in the global context, urban and rural future, society, and sustainability.

9.3.5 Experimental Statistics

Statistics Netherlands, ONS, Statistics New Zealand, and Eurostat are examples of statistical agencies that publish so-called experimental statistics on their websites. These statistics are in a testing phase and are based on administrative or Big Data sources. ONS defined what it considers to be experimental statistics (ONS 2019): those statistics that are new and still subject to testing in terms of their volatility and ability to meet customers' needs. One situation could be that new methods are tested and that the statistics have only partial coverage. Furthermore, most experimental statistics do not meet ONS's quality standards. Users are cautioned about the limitations of experimental statistics. Statistical agencies working with experimental statistics are seeking user involvement by asking for feedback on the usefulness of the experimental statistics. At some stage, experimental statistics may become established (nonexperimental). ONS provides criteria that will help determine when experimental statistics can be considered nonexperimental. Examples of such criteria are: coverage of the statistics should reach a satisfactory level, users should find the statistics useful and credible, and the statistics are deemed to fulfill ONS's quality standards. ONS also has a four-step procedure for changing the experimental status to regular status.

9.3.6 Organizing Hackathons

A hackathon is an event in which a specific challenge or problem is presented and different teams consisting of, for instance, data scientists, computer programmers, and subject matter specialists compete with their solutions. These events are limited in time, often just a day or two, so the activities are quite intense. During recent years, NSIs have organized a number of hackathons, often in cooperation with other agencies or private firms. The tasks given to the teams vary, but the goal is to come up with a creative solution to a problem in a very short time period. Examples of problem solutions could be a tool that provides new insights by combining different datasets, a visualization of data in an innovative way, or an application program interface (API), a software program, or some other type of product. The UN Economic Commission for Europe and Statistics Netherlands in 2017 organized a hackathon entitled, *Telling Stories with SDG Data*. SDG, or

Sustainable Development Goals, refers to the UN 2030 Agenda adopted by all UN member states in 2015, which had 17 goals and 169 targets; UN members collected data to monitor progress toward these goals. One such target is: "By 2020, substantially reduce the proportion of youth not in employment, education or training" and an indicator to monitor progress is "Proportion of youth (aged 15–24 years) not in education, employment or training." The hackathon challenge was to come up with an innovative product that describes the youth population regarding some selected aspects of Agenda 2030. Another example is the hackathon that Eurostat organized in March 2019; the challenge was, "How can innovative solutions for data collection reduce response burden and enrich or replace the statistical information/data provided by the time use survey?" A third example is from Sweden where government agencies and the private sectors have organized Hack for Sweden for a number of years. The challenge in spring 2019 focused on sustainability and Agenda 2030. The final example is from BigSurv18, Green City Hackathon, which addressed bike use in the city of Barcelona using open data.

The goals of these hackathons are often manifold. Besides creating innovative products, they are also a way to create interest in official statistics.

9.3.7 IT Infrastructure, Tools, and Methods

Although NSIs have the capacity to handle large amounts of data, additional investments in IT infrastructure are needed to be able to use Big Data. Some NSIs have already made this investment. An increased capacity to store data and to process data are examples of components that contribute to these investment costs (Japec et al. 2015).

Even when an organization has upgraded its IT infrastructure, methods are still needed to deal with Big Data efficiently. Researchers need methods that handle such obstacles as a computer's memory being too small to hold Big Data so the computing task takes a very long time (Wang et al. 2016). Wang et al. gave an overview of statistical procedures that are scalable to big datasets and that can handle these obstacles. They discussed both subsampling-based methods and methods that first partition a big dataset into blocks, then process each block separately (or in parallel), and then aggregate the solutions from each block (so-called divide and conquer methods). They also discussed methods to use when data come in streams or large chunks, and thus, a sequentially updated analysis is desired without storing the data – otherwise known as online updating methods.

The official statistics community is willing to share tools and experiences about Big Data. "Awesome official statistical software" in the GitHub Repository (2019) provides open-source statistical software packages useful for creating and accessing official statistics. This repository has a number of webscraping packages.

9.4 The Potential of Big Data and the Use of New Methods in Official Statistics

In an article in *The American Statistician* published in 2007, Tim Holt, a former Director at the ONS in United Kingdom, described five challenges for official statistics: the demand for "wider, deeper, quicker, better, and cheaper" statistics. These user demands are still key challenges for all NSIs, and the use of Big Data for statistics production is one potential remedy. In this section, we give examples of studies carried out by NSIs using Big Data classified according to Holt's list of challenges. One caveat is that these are examples of initiatives to explore the *potential* of Big Data. To a large extent, Big Data in official statistics is still uncharted territory without much discussion of data limitations. However, these initiatives are attempts to serve users in better ways.

9.4.1 Wider and Deeper

Users like to have a wider, ever-growing range of statistics that cover broad aspects of a concept. They also want statistics to address new phenomena in society, which requires new concepts to be defined and measured, e.g. globalization, digital transformation, and migration. Social media data can help users and researchers get a better understanding of how phenomena in society are discussed and what wording potential data providers use (Weststrøm et al. 2011). Users also want deeper statistics, i.e. statistics with an increased level of geographic and other details.

9.4.1.1 Green Areas in the Swedish City of Lidingö

Combining different data sources can generate both wider and deeper statistics. An example from Statistics Sweden (2015) is statistics that describe the green structure of large urban areas and the extent to which the general public has access to these green areas (depicted as dark grey in Figure 9.1). In this example, several different data sources were combined, namely satellite images, land registry information, and data from the register of the total population. Figure 9.1a shows green areas in Lidingö, Sweden. By combining the different data sources, one can identify the green areas accessible to the general public (Figure 9.1b). Other green areas include golf courses, building land, lots, and areas that are privately owned and exempt from the right of public access.

9.4.1.2 Innovative Companies

An example of using Big Data to provide both wider and deeper statistics comes from Statistics Netherlands (van der Doef, Daas, and Windmeijer 2018). The agency investigated whether innovative companies could be identified by analyzing their websites. The number of innovative companies in a country is an

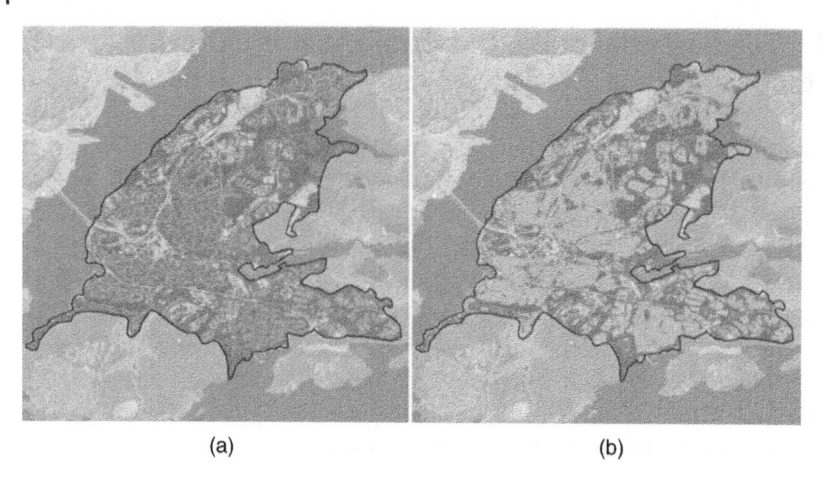

Figure 9.1 All green areas in Lidingö (a) and green areas accessible to general public (b) (depicted as dark grey). Source: SCB © Ortofoto © Lantmäteriet.

important strategic indicator, since innovation can create jobs and contribute to economic growth. In the EU, this information is collected from enterprises in the Community Innovation Survey (CIS). The enterprises included in the CIS have 10 or more employees. Statistics Netherlands analyzed the text on the company websites. To train the algorithm, the agency used information from the CIS about what companies are innovative. From the business register, they selected 500 000 companies with fewer than 10 employees, and the trained algorithm was used to classify the companies as innovative or not. The agency manually checked that the algorithm worked well and checked the results against the Innovation Top 100 for small and medium-sized enterprises. The algorithm accurately classified quite a large number of companies. These statistics were published as experimental. By adding these small companies, coverage was improved compared to CIS. By including geographical information for these companies, deeper information can be gained that is of interest to local governments, for example.

9.4.1.3 Coding Commodity Flow Survey

In the US Commodity Flow Survey, the US Bureau of Transportation collects information from establishments about the goods they ship. Examples of the type of information requested include value of the goods, weight, mode of transportation, and destination of shipments. The Bureau is currently studying whether shipment information could be extracted directly from companies' business systems to improve estimate precision, geographic granularity, and frequency of estimates (Parker and Sharp 2018). Furthermore, the Bureau is exploring if machine learning algorithms can be used to classify commodities according to the Standard Classification of Transported Goods. There are several hundreds of codes to choose from and if the code could be predicted based on the description of the commodity provided by the respondent, then the response burden could be substantially reduced. We should stress, though, that this task could be very challenging given what we know about the difficulties in both manual and automated coding of complex variables (Biemer and Lyberg 2003).

9.4.2 Better Statistics

Better statistics, that is, better quality in terms of increased accuracy or improved qualitative dimensions, such as relevance and accessibility, is important to many users. In this section, we provide some examples of how Big Data might be used to improve quality.

9.4.2.1 AIS

All vessels have an AIS device that frequently sends signals, about every three seconds, so that a ship's position can be followed in real time (Consten et al. 2018b). Every country has an agency responsible for these data. Consten et al. studied whether AIS data can be used to produce maritime statistics such as port statistics. The large amount of data makes it rather time-consuming to prepare the data before statistics can be produced. For instance, maritime ships must be filtered out since the AIS data contain information on fishing ships and yachts that should not be included in the statistics. This is part of the process to construct a reference frame of maritime ships. In this process, a number of identifiers in the datasets must be linked so that the frame can be constructed.

There are private providers that prepare and sell AIS data. One ESSnet study on Big Data, used AIS data to see whether port statistics, for instance, could be produced, and to improve statistics on emissions from maritime transports. The quality of the data was studied by comparing the national data from Denmark, Poland, and Greece with data from a private provider. The national data had better coverage and contained more observations. The data from the private provider did not cover all ports and the traveled distances were underestimated, which led to underestimation of emissions. The private provider filtered the data but it was not clear how they did it. The national AIS data might be a good source for producing official statistics. For instance, no source currently provides statistics on departing ships and their next destination, but one can estimate these numbers using AIS data. Quality can also be an issue because errors can occur (De Wit et al. 2017), e.g. technical errors related to the AIS device producing the wrong positions and speed of ships (Bošnjak, Šimunović, and Kavran 2012). Human errors can also occur related to the information manually entered into the AIS device, such as entering the wrong ship number, type, and length. Studying quality of the AIS data is therefore important.

9.4.2.2 Expenditure Surveys

Many countries have experienced an increase in nonresponse rates and costs in their consumer expenditure surveys (CESs). Traditionally, to collect data on expenditures, respondents in a country are asked to keep a diary for a number of weeks or send their receipts to the data collector, usually the NSI. In Norway (Zhang and Holgersson 2018) and Sweden, the most recent CES were both canceled due to high nonresponse rates. Amdam, Holgersen, and Buelens (2018) studied whether micro-level transaction data from retail chains could be used as an alternative data source. The authors studied a sample of receipt data, including information on loyalty card holders from one of the largest grocery retail chains in Norway. They compared expenditure patterns of card holders and noncard holders with the Norwegian consumption total that is known from Consumer Price Index (CPI) statistics. The study showed that card holders have a different spending pattern than noncard holders. The authors concluded that using micro-level transaction data would yield biased estimates of consumer expenditure so it was not a viable option.

9.4.2.3 Examples of Improving Statistics by Adjusting for Bias

Different error sources can hamper the quality and the usefulness of the traditional survey. In their paper on capture–recapture techniques for transport survey estimate adjustment using highway-sensors, Klingwort, Buelens, and Schnell (2018) demonstrated how combining Big Data, administrative data, and survey data can be used to estimate and correct for bias in the Dutch Road Freight Transport Survey (RTFS). The RTFS was a diary survey where data were collected from truck owners. Due to large response burden, underreporting was a problem in RTFS. The estimates were downward biased due to nonresponse and underreporting. In this study, weigh-in-motion (WIM) road sensor data from a number of locations were used to estimate and correct for the bias in the estimates of transported shipment weights and the number of days on which transport occurred. This estimation was possible since the WIM data license plate information was available and could be matched with the Dutch Vehicle Register (RWS). The RWS has information about ownership and truck details. The information from the RWS allows matching of the information with the Dutch Enterprise Register that contains information about for instance company size and classification of economic activity (NACE). They used capture–recapture techniques to estimate and correct for the bias due to nonresponse and underreporting.

9.4.3 Quicker Statistics

Quicker statistics are in high demand, especially for economic indicators. Many users want to be able to detect changes in the economy as quickly as possible. Most examples presented in this section (such as using AIS data to produce maritime statistics) can also improve timeliness.

9.4.3.1 Early Estimates

Statistics Finland explored whether more timely estimates of the quarterly gross domestic product (GDP) could be produced (van Sebille et al. 2018). They used firm-level data and machine learning methods to nowcast the Trend Indicator of Output (TIO). The TIO is a monthly indicator, highly correlated with the GDP, which describes the development of the volume of produced output in the economy. They used the TIO together with traffic loop data to nowcast the quarterly GDP. The premise was that there is a correlation between how much traffic there is on the roads in a country and how well the economy is doing. The conclusion from the study is that early estimates can be produced with similar accuracy as the official release but 1.5 months earlier. Statistics Slovenia (SURS) carried out a similar study with similar results (van Sebille et al. 2018). This work was carried out as part of the ESSnet on Big Data and is still in progress.

9.4.4 Cheaper Statistics

Many NSIs have experienced budget cuts so the ability to produce cheaper statistics is crucial.

9.4.4.1 Consumer Price Index (CPI)

Traditionally, interviewers have been sent to different stores to collect prices for the CPI. Since this process is very costly, some countries are now using scanner data from retail stores to replace parts of the data collection that interviewers did previously. Statistics Sweden (Norberg, Sammar, and Tongur 2011) was able to reduce costs for data collection while improving the quality in the CPI. Many European countries now use scanner data to produce CPI. Currently, this use of Big Data is probably the most common in the production of official statistics.

9.4.4.2 Smart Meter Data

In a European project (van Sebille et al. 2018), data from smart electricity meters were used to determine if energy statistics could be produced. Data from smart meters are generated frequently (every hour or more often). All EU member states have committed to deploy smart electricity meters, and the deployment rate by 2020 is expected to be 72%. Examples of challenges when using smart meters data include linking data to other datasets and representativity. The latter is, however, expected to improve once the deployment rate of smart meters in the EU increases. Using smart meters, data is expected to cut costs since energy statistics are produced via traditional surveys in many countries.

9.4.4.3 ISCO and NACE Coding at Statistics Finland

In the Finnish Labor Force Survey (LFS), respondents were asked about their occupation and the industry of their workplace (Kärkimaa and Larja 2018). These data were then coded according to the statistical classifications, ISCO and NACE, respectively. Often respondents are asked additional questions so the interviewer can choose the correct code; however, quite often the interviewer is not able to code so coders do the actual coding after the interview. Coding according to statistical nomenclatures is a very labor-intensive process. In the Finnish LFS, 15% of the labor hours was devoted to coding occupation and industry. To reduce costs, Kärkimaa and Larja (2018) studied whether artificial intelligence using machine learning methods could be used to automate the process. They combined register and survey data and tested different methods and models. They predicted industry and occupation with an accuracy of more than 85%. Implementing this new system is expected to reduce survey costs. It is, however, unclear how large the proportion left for manual coding is. Therefore, comparing their results with documented results from conventional automated coding was difficult. Also, methods for measuring accuracy were unclear. The main finding, we believe, is that artificial intelligence can be used for coding a complex variable.

9.5 Big Data Quality

The defining properties of Big Data all start with the letter V, a device most likely intended to be a memory jogger to characterize the dimensions of a new concept. Originally, Laney (2001) suggested three V's: volume, variety, and velocity. Gradually, the number of V's increased to include value and veracity. Now the list has 42 V's of Big Data and data science (Shafer 2017) and finding new V's has become an activity on its own. To define a field in this way is, of course, constraining and counterproductive. The additional V's that come closest to Big Data quality are veracity and validity. Veracity refers to what we usually call data quality, such as variances, biases, fitness for purpose, and process maintenance, whereas validity could mean rigor in analysis. In any case, different authors define identical V's differently, and official statistics has a tradition of presenting quality as frameworks consisting of dimensions such as accuracy, relevance, credibility, timeliness, accessibility, interpretability, comparability, coherence, and so on. Dimensions vary across organizations such as NSIs, Eurostat, the UN, OECD, and the

World Bank. A common element is that the accuracy component is quantitative and can, in principle, be estimated separately for each type of statistics. The other components are qualitative and might be viewed as summary indicators for a survey or even a system of surveys.

The components or dimensions are sometimes in conflict. High accuracy in terms of a small mean squared error, which is the sum of the variance and the squared bias for an estimate, might have a negative impact on timeliness. For instance, nonresponse follow-up might slow down the production thereby decreasing timeliness. Furthermore, different users have different trade-off priorities. What is optimal varies between users and what happens in practice is that it is up to the producer to strike a balance between different user demands. This work is particularly demanding in official statistics, which is supposed to serve so many purposes. Official statistics should also be high quality and cost-effective. These requirements are difficult to specify, and these features tend to be rather vague. In order to live up to high-quality standards, researchers have developed some principles and guidelines over the years, including principles and practices for the federal statistical system and individual agency guidelines in the United States, documents on survey methods and practices in Canada, Code of Practice in the ESS, quality frameworks in most NSIs, and the UN principles for official statistics. Experience shows imposing global standards in official statistics is difficult because of varying levels of know-how between NSIs and whether official statistics are centralized or decentralized in countries (Kotz 2005). In any case, these principles and documents have an important purpose since they can also be used to assess quality, not just serve as recommended procedures.

With the advent of Big Data, the tables are turned. After an initial hype with statements like "The end of theory. The data deluge makes the scientific method obsolete" (Anderson 2008) and long listings of V's, the situation has become more stable and service providers, decision-makers, and many methodologists realize that Big Data is here to stay and that it can improve statistics in ways we have described here, at least eventually.

The overarching issue, however, is the assessment of quality. Big Data sources are plentiful, but the development of quality assessment is in its infancy, as shown in this volume. Studies in recent years have evaluated the quality of a Big Data source by comparing Big Data estimates with survey estimates. In those studies, the survey estimate was considered to be the "gold standard." This approach should be contrasted to the more common procedure where administrative data are used as the gold standard to evaluate quality of survey estimates. Errors exist in all data sources whether they are Big Data, administrative data, or survey data. However, we can expect them to be different since the processes are very different and the amount of bias in each data source varies.

A number of different models describe how Big Data are generated (Consten et al. 2018a). One such example comes from the AAPOR report on Big Data (Japec et al. 2015) with the following steps:

(1) Generate
(2) Extract, transform, and load
(3) Analyze (filter/reduction [sampling] and computation/analysis [visualization])

Errors can occur in all these steps and they have to be considered in relation to the research objective and target population. Each Big Data source has its own error structure, where many components are similar to those used in regular surveys. Common error types include

- Specification error, meaning that Big Data concepts do not coincide with the concepts to be studied or they may vary across data sources.
- Missingness, e.g. when measuring traffic with sensors, some roads are not covered, computers might have downtime or sensors may malfunction (Daas et al. 2015) – or when measuring attitudes via social media, some people are excluded and only a fraction of users actually post something on a certain topic.
- Selectivity, in that Big Data subpopulations often do not coincide with target populations studied in official statistics.
- Measurement errors, such as noncalibrated sensors and the fact that social media posts do not reflect true opinions and attitudes.
- Processing errors, such as linking enterprises in a register to scraped units.
- Inaccurate modeling, resulting in coding errors when converting text to variables.
- Lack of insights regarding the maintenance of the Big Data sources. Issues such as reporting frequency, irregular updates of administrative registers, underreporting and overreporting of administrative data due to varying ambitions, and know-how on the part of the register provider.

Biemer (2016) and Biemer and Amaya, Chapter 4, have started to develop total error (TE) models to accommodate this new world of multiple data sources and combinations of probability and nonprobability sampling and sometimes no sampling at all. The authors use the notion of hybrid estimation to handle this situation with integrated and single source data. The components of these models are much the same as those in TSE models, i.e. coverage error, specification error, content error, missing data, and data processing error, but the structures and characteristics might differ from those in TSE models.

There are also frameworks for administrative data (Reid, Zabala, and Holmberg 2017; Australian Bureau of Statistics 2011), and Trepanier (2014) summarized methodologies for integrated use of administrative data across a number of organizations and development projects concerning official statistics. Those frameworks tend to be similar to the dimensional frameworks where accuracy is blended with qualitative dimensions such as timeliness and comparability. Hsieh and Murphy (2017) presented a quality framework for Twitter as a single source and discussed Twitter errors such as coverage, query, and interpretation error. Regarding tweets and sentiments, topic coverage seems more important than population coverage. Also, establishing the meaning of tweets using machine learning is imperative for them to be used as proxies for public opinion. Even though exceptions exist, it is hard to know ahead of time when this type of Big Data is biased (see Amaya et al. (2020), Chapter 6). The consequence is that most findings are impossible to generalize and hard to replicate. In all fairness, similar problems exist in traditional survey settings, where problems occur in replicating findings due to variations in essential survey conditions or incomplete information about experimental features.

9.6 Legal Issues

In many countries, statistical laws give the NSI the right to access and process data. Other laws also protect citizens in this context, such as the EU law and the EU GDPR. The aim of GDPR is to protect data and privacy for all individuals within the EU. Privacy means not only the "right to be left alone" but also "the ability to share information selectively" (Executive Office of the President's Council of Advisors on Science and Technology 2014). NSIs have a long tradition conforming to statistical laws and they have procedures in place to protect privacy. The current laws, however, do not explicitly mention the use of Big Data for official statistics production. It is up to each NSI (and each owner of Big Data) to interpret the laws in the Big Data context and to figure out if and how to use Big Data.

One advantage Big Data has compared to survey data is the possibility to produce more detailed statistics, e.g. for certain regions or subgroups. However, a trade-off still exists between disclosure risks and providing detailed statistics. Confidentiality, defined by McCallister, Grance, and Scarfone (2010) as "preserving authorized restrictions on information access and disclosure, including means for protecting personal privacy and proprietary information," poses a new challenge for NSIs in the Big Data context.

9.6.1 Allowing Access to Data

Many of the Big Data sources that could potentially be used for official statistics production, such as transactional and sensor data, are collected by private firms or other agencies. The sampled person or establishment is informed about the purpose of the survey so as to make an informed decision whether to participate. In the new setting with Big Data, the informed consent procedure is no longer that simple (Bender et al. 2017). With Big Data often used together with other data, for a purpose not foreseen when the data were collected, consent becomes more complicated. The traditional principle – that participants should get information about how the data will be used and that they give consent before they are part of the research – requires a new approach in the Big Data setting.

Private firms or other agencies collect many Big Data sources that could potentially be used for official statistics production, such as transactional and sensor data. Getting access to these privately held data for production of official statistics is not straightforward for many reasons. There could be legal uncertainties about data use, and the data can be in a format that requires a substantial investment before it can be used. In the EU, the ESS has recently taken an initiative to try to change the law so that NSIs would get access to privately held data for production of official statistics (European Statistical System Committee 2017, 2018). This situation is similar to that of administrative data, where many NSIs have access to administrative data from other agencies (European Statistical System (ESS) 2017b). Getting access to data can mean getting access to aggregated data or raw data.

Stateva et al. (2017) compared the laws and regulations in six European countries to find out whether there are some legal obstacles to collect data through webscraping for production of official statistics. Representatives of three countries in the study expressed some uncertainty about whether webscraping was allowed, whereas the other three had a more favorable interpretation that permitted webscraping. Stateva et al. concluded that laws and regulations were very similar in the six countries, but the interpretation of the laws varied. They specifically studied the Copyright Protection and Database Protection laws to see if and how these laws affected NSIs' possibilities to webscrape information. The Copyright law grants the creator of an original work exclusive rights for its use and distribution. Database rights are considered property rights and creating a database from webscraped data could be interpreted as breaching the database rights. The Copyright Protection law, however, makes an exception of the use of a database for nonprofit scientific research. Stateva et al. (2017) conclude that it is reasonable to argue that an NSI would fall into this latter category of use and that scraping the web does not breach the Copyright or the Database Protection law.

9.6.2 Providing Access to Data

Providing access to microdata that have been collected for production of official statistics to use them for research is a mission for many NSIs. There are different approaches to handle this task, including providing public use files or organizing research data centers where researchers can access microdata after signing a contract (Bender et al. 2017). Here again the Big Data setting poses some new challenges. For instance, data anonymization does not work since identification of individual patterns is easy; almost everyone in the file is unique, since information is so frequent or geographically detailed (Bender et al. 2017; Narayanan and Shmatikov 2008).

9.7 Future Developments

Big Data is here to stay and is to some extent already being used in the production of official statistics. The examples in this chapter and in other chapters in this volume show that the use of multiple data sources in the production of official statistics has become increasingly common. Some NSIs are more active than others, but everyone is aware that this resource cannot be ignored. Big Data from, for example, sensors, phones, satellites, and cameras seem promising for official statistics on road and marine traffic, commuting, tourism, CPI, crop yield, energy consumption, and so on. Big Data such as social media, user feedback, and blogs have potential to improve official statistics in other ways. Concepts such as employment, occupation, and wages change over time and must be adjusted to reflect the current lay of the land. Such Big Data can help identify how people and establishments communicate about these and other things. This type of data can also be used to create sampling frames, studying perceptions of survey respondents via sentiments expressed in social media (Torres van Grinsven and Snijkers 2015), provide auxiliary variables (Marchetti et al. 2015) for small area estimation much faster than is commonly the case, and to assist in exploring new areas of research.

The growth in data volumes is indeed breathtaking but that is not the only reason to use Big Data in official statistics. Traditional surveys have problems. It is difficult to recruit interviewers, surveys are very expensive, surveys are not good at capturing certain types of concepts such as hypothetical questions, vague quantifiers, and facts relying on respondents' memory. Furthermore, there is a general demand in society for decreased response burden, which implies shorter survey questionnaires, and nonresponse is steadily increasing in most countries, while users want richer official statistics. Part of this equation might be solved by using multiple sources of data in statistics production. Several authors admit that it is impossible for official statistics to ignore this development if NSIs want to stay relevant (Callegaro and Yang 2018; Daas et al. 2015; Radermacher 2014, 2017, 2018; Stiglitz et al. 2009; Sturgeon 2013; Pfefferman 2015; Signorelli and Biffignandi 2018; Vaccari 2014). Estimating population parameters is no longer always the sole purpose of statistics production. Users want new and innovative analyses (MacFeely 2016).

To be fair, Big Data also has problems. Survey data will be needed to answer questions that Big Data cannot. Survey data will be needed to address errors in Big Data. Thus, the imminent challenge is to develop methods that combine data sources, including surveys, in efficient ways and to assess the quality of the resulting statistical products. Such work has begun: Meng (2018), Biemer (2016), Heeringa (2017), and Biemer and Amaya (2020), Chapter 5, discuss possible frameworks for found data, probability or nonprobability. Big Data are found data and originally produced for purposes other than statistics production. Each source has its own error structure, some of it known, some unknown, and some that defy expression. Quality assessment seems to be the most important issue when moving to a multi-source mixed-mode paradigm. Correcting for errors needs modeling approaches. Traditionally, NSIs are not too keen on doing that even though it is practiced in model-assisted surveys, for instance in nonresponse adjustment. In 1996, Dillman wrote a provocative article on innovation resistance in NSIs. In 2001, Platek and Särndal asked if statisticians can deliver, alluding to the reality that all important error sources are not included in quality statements released by statistics producers (Platek and Särndal 2001). Quality assessments and quality profiles will be pressing issues in future adjustments of the production of official statistics. Big Data has been around for about a decade now, and NSIs have great interest in innovation. However, change has just started. NSIs need to invest in IT infrastructure and capacity building. For instance, machine learning and AI in general as well as modeling are urgent new areas for official statisticians to master. Methods for combining probability and nonprobability sampling will also be important (Buelens, Burger, and van den Brakel 2018). And finally, we need new design principles in a multi-data source environment.

References

Amaya, A., Bach, R., Kreuter, F. et al. (2020). Measuring attitude strength in social media data. In: *Big Data Meets Survey Science: A Collection of Innovative Methods*, Chapter 5.

Amdam, S., Holgersen, H., and Buelens, B. (2018). Consumer Expenditure Statistics from Retail Transaction Data. Paper presented at BigSurv18 conference in Barcelona, Spain (24–27 October 2018).

Anderson, C. (2008). The end of theory: the data deluge makes the scientific method obsolete. *Wired Magazine* (16 July).

Australian Bureau of Statistics (2011). Quality Management of Statistical Outputs Produced from Administrative Data. Catalogue number 1522.0, Canberra, Australia.

References

Bach, R. and Eckman, S. (2018). Motivated misreporting in web panels. *Journal of Survey Statistics and Methodology* 6 (3): 418–430. https://doi.org/10.1093/jssam/smx030.

Baker, R. (2017). Big data: a survey research perspective. In: *Total Survey Error in Practice*, Wiley Series in Survey Methodology (eds. P.P. Biemer, E. de Leeuw, S. Eckman, et al.), 47–67. Hoboken, NJ: Wiley.

Baker, R., Brick, J.M., Bates, N.A. et al. (2013). Summary report of the AAPOR task force on non-probability sampling. *Journal of Survey Statistics and Methodology* 1 (2): 90–143. https://doi.org/10.1093/jssam/smt008.

Bender, S., Jarmin, R., Kreuter, F. et al. (2017). Privacy and confidentiality. In: *Big Data and Social Science. A Practical Guide to Methods and Tools* (eds. I. Foster, R. Ghani, R.S. Jarmin, et al.), 299–311. Boca Raton, FL: CRC Press https://doi.org/10.1201/9781315368238.

Biemer, P. (2016). Errors and inference. In: *Big Data and Social Science. A Practical Guide to Methods and Tools* (eds. I. Foster, R. Ghani, R.S. Jarmin, et al.), 299–311. New York, NY: CRC Press/Taylor and Francis Group/Chapman and Hall.

Biemer, P. and Amaya, A. (2020). Total error frameworks for found data. In: *Big Data Meets Survey Science: A Collection of Innovative Methods*, Chapter 4.

Biemer, P.P. and Lyberg, L. (2003). *Introduction to Survey Quality*. Hoboken, NJ: Wiley.

Bošnjak, R., Šimunović, L., and Kavran, Z. (2012). Automatic identification system in maritime traffic and error analysis. *Transactions on Maritime Science* 1 (2): 77–84. https://doi.org/10.7225/toms.v01.n02.002.

Brick, M. (2014). Explorations in non-probability sampling using the web. *Proceedings of the Statistics Canada Symposium*, Ottawa, Canada (29–31 October).

Buelens, B., Burger, J., and van den Brakel, J. (2018). Comparing inference methods for nonprobability sampling. *International Statistical Review* 86 (2): 322–343. https://doi.org/10.1111/insr.12253.

Callegaro, M. and Yang, Y. (2018). The role of surveys in the era of 'Big Data'. In: *The Palgrave Handbook of Survey Research* (eds. D.L. Vannette and J.A. Krosnick), 175–192. Cham, Switzerland: Palgrave Macmillan.

Citro, C.F. (2014). From multiple modes for surveys to multiple data sources for estimates. *Survey Methodology* 40 (2): 137–161.

Consten, A., Chavdarov, V., Daas, P. et al. (2018a). *Report Describing the Quality Aspects of Big Data for Official Statistics*. ESSNet Big Data, Deliverable 8.2. Luxembourg: Eurostat https://webgate.ec.europa.eu/fpfis/mwikis/essnetbigdata/index.php/WP8_Reports,_milestones_and_deliverables1.

Consten, A., Puts, M., de Wit, T. et al. (2018b). *Consolidated Report on Project Results Including a Cost-Benefit Analysis of Using AIS-Data for Official Statistics*. ESSnet on Big Data, Deliverable 4.8. Luxembourg: Eurostat https://webgate.ec.europa.eu/

fpfis/mwikis/essnetbigdata/images/3/3f/WP4_Deliverable_4.8_31_05_2018_final .pdf.

Couper, M.P. (2013). Is the sky falling? New technology, changing media, and the future of surveys. *Survey Research Methods* 7 (3): 145–156.

Daas, P.J.H., Puts, M.J., Buelens, B. et al. (2015). Big data as a source for official statistics. *Journal of Official Statistics* 31 (2): 249–262. https://doi.org/10.1515/Jos-2015-0016.

De Leeuw, E. (2018). Mixed-mode: past, present and future. *Survey Research Methods* 12 (7): 75–89.

De Wit, T., Consten, A., Puts, M. et al. (2017). *Deriving Port Visits and Linking Data from Maritime Statistics with AIS-Data. ESSnet on Big Data, Deliverable 4.2*. Luxembourg: Eurostat https://webgate.ec.europa.eu/fpfis/mwikis/essnetbigdata/images/8/8d/WP4_Deliverable_4.2_2017_02_10.pdf.

Deming, E. (1944). On errors in surveys. *American Sociological Review* 9 (4): 359–369. https://doi.org/10.2307/2085979.

Desrosieres, A. (1998). *The Politics of Large Numbers. A History of Statistical Reasoning*. Cambridge, MA: Harvard University Press.

Dillman, D. (1996). Why innovation is difficult in government surveys. *Journal of Official Statistics* 12 (2): 113–124.

van der Doef, S., Daas, P., and Windmeijer, D. (2018). Identifying innovative companies from their website. Paper presented at BigSurv18 Conference, Barcelona, Spain (25–27 October 2018).

European Statistical System (ESS) (2017a). European statistics code of practice (16 November 2017). https://webgate.ec.europa.eu/fpfis/mwikis/essnetbigdata/index.php/ESSnet_Big_Data (accessed 06 March 2020).

European Statistical System (ESS) (2017b). Position paper on access to privately held data which are of public interest (12 October 2018). https://webgate.ec.europa.eu/fpfis/mwikis/essnetbigdata/index.php/ESSnet_Big_Data (accessed 06 March 2020).

European Statistical System (ESS) (2019). ESSnet on big data II. https://webgate.ec.europa.eu/fpfis/mwikis/essnetbigdata/index.php/ESSnet_Big_Data (accessed 21 March 2019).

European Statistical System Committee (2017). ESS Priorities Beyond 2020.

European Statistical System Committee (2018). Smart Statistics & Big Data Road Map. Work Program Objective 11.

Executive Office of the President's Council of Advisors on Science and Technology (2014). Report to the President. Big Data and Privacy: A Technological Perspective. https://bigdatawg.nist.gov/pdf/pcast_big_data_and_privacy_-_may_2014.pdf (accessed 27 March 2020).

GitHub Repository (2019). Awesome official statistical software. https://github.com/alexkowa/awesome-official-statistics-software (accessed 21 March 2019).

Groves, R.M. (2011). Three eras of survey research. *Public Opinion Quarterly* 75 (5): 861–871. https://doi.org/10.1093/poq/nfr057.

Heeringa, S. (2014). Survey research and big data: estrangement or a long-term relationship? Presentation at the Statistical Society of Canada Meetings, Toronto, Canada (26 May 2014).

Heeringa, S. (2017). Survey-assisted modeling: integration of sample survey designs and methods with big data systems. Presentation at 5th School on Sampling and Survey Methodology, Cuiaba, Brazil (18 October 2017).

Holt, D.T. (2007). The official statistics Olympic challenge. *The American Statistician* 61 (1): 1–8. https://doi.org/10.1198/000313007x168173.

Hsieh, Y. and Murphy, J. (2017). Total Twitter error: decomposing public opinion measurement on Twitter from a total survey error perspective. In: *Total Survey Error in Practice*, Wiley Series in Survey Methodology, vol. 74 (eds. P. Biemer, E. deLeeuw, S. Eckman, et al.), 23–46. Hoboken, NJ: Wiley.

Hulliger, B., Lehtonen, R., Münnich, R. et al. (2012). *Analysis of the Future Research Needs for Official Statistics. European Commission.* Luxembourgh: Eurostat.

Japec, L., Kreuter, F., Berg, M. et al. (2015). *AAPOR Report on Big Data*. Oakbrook Terrace, IL: American Association for Public Opinion Research https://www.aapor.org/Education-Resources/Reports/Big-Data.aspx.

Kalton, G. (2018). The past, present and the future of social surveys. Joint Program in Survey Methodology (JPSM) Distinguished Lecture, College Park, MD (27 April 2018).

Kärkimaa, J. and Larja, L. (2018). How to make AI do your job for statistical classification of industry and occupation. Paper presented at BigSurv18 Conference, Barcelona, Spain (25–27 October 2018).

Kitchin, R. (2015). The opportunities, challenges, and risks of big data for official statistics. *Statistical Journal of the IAOS* 31 (3): 471–481. https://doi.org/10.3233/SJI-150906.

Klingwort, J., Buelens, B., and Schnell, R. (2018). Capture-recapture techniques to validate survey with sensor data. Paper presented at BigSurv18, Barcelona, Spain (25–27 October 2018).

Kotz, S. (2005). Reflection on early history of official statistics and a modest proposal for global coordination. *Journal of Official Statistics* 21 (2): 139–144.

Krosnick, J. (1991). Response strategies for coping with cognitive demands of attitude measures in surveys. *Applied Cognitive Psychology* 5 (3): 213–236. https://doi.org/10.1002/acp.2350050305.

Landefeld, S. (2014). Uses of big data for official statistics. Paper presented at the International Conference on Big Data for Official Statistics, Beijing, China (20–30 October 2014).

Laney, D. (2001). 3D Data Management: Controlling Data Volume, Velocity and Variety. Technical Report META Group, In., File 949, Stanford, CT, USA.

Little, R. (2015). Calibrated Bayes, an inferential paradigm for official statistics in the era of big data. *Statistical Journal of the IAOS* 31 (4): 555–563. https://doi.org/10.3233/SJI-150944.

MacFeely, S. (2016). The continuing evolution of official statistics; some challenges and opportunities. *Journal of Official Statistics* 32 (4): 789–810. https://doi.org/10.1515/jos-2016-0041.

Marchetti, S., Giusti, C., Pratesi, M. et al. (2015). Small area model-based estimators using big data sources. *Journal of Official Statistics* 31 (2): 263–281. https://doi.org/10.1515/Jos-2015-0017.

McCallister, E., Grance, T., and Scarfone, K. (2010). *Guide to Protecting Confidentiality of Personal Identifiable Information (PII). SP 800-122*. Gaithersburg, MD: National Institute of Standards and Technology.

Meng, X. (2018). Statistical paradises and paradoxes in big data (I): law of large populations, big data paradox, and the 2016 U.S. presidential election. *Annals of Applied Statistics* 12 (2): 685–726. https://doi.org/10.1214/18-AOAS1161SF.

Mercer, A.W., Kreuter, F., Keeter, S. et al. (2017). Theory and practice in nonprobability surveys. *Public Opinion Quarterly* 81 (S1): 250–271. https://doi.org/10.1093/poq/nfw060.

Narayanan, A. and Shmatikov, V. (2008). Robust de-anonymization of large sparse datasets. In: *Proceedings of the 2008 IEEE Symposium on Security and Privacy*, 111–125. Oakland, CA, Washington DC, USA: IEEE Computer Society https://doi.org/10.1109/SP.2008.33.

National Academies of Sciences, Engineering, and Medicine (NASEM) (2017). *Federal Statistics, Multiple Data Sources, and Privacy Protection: Next Steps* (eds. R. Groves and B.A. Harris-Kojetin). Washington, DC: The National Academies Press https://doi.org/10.17226/24893.

Neyman, J. (1934). On the two different aspects of the representative method: the method of statistical sampling and the methods of purposive selection. *Journal of the Royal Statistical Society* 97 (4): 557–625. https://doi.org/10.2307/2342192.

Neyman, J. (1937). Outline of a theory of statistical estimation based on the classical theory of probability. *Philosophical Transactions of the Royal Society of London. Series A, Mathematical and Physical Sciences* 236 (767): 333–380. https://doi.org/10.1098/rsta.1937.0005.

Norberg, A., Sammar, M., and Tongur, C. (2011). A study of scanner data in the Swedish consumer price index. Paper presented at the Joint UNECE/ILO Meeting on Consumer Price Indices, Wellington, New Zealand (10–12 May 2011).

Office for National Statistics (2019). Guide to experimental statistics. https://www.ons.gov.uk/methodology/methodologytopicsandstatisticalconcepts/guidetoexperimentalstatistics (accessed 21 March 2019).

Parker, J. and Sharp, J. (2018). Alternative approaches for measuring the movement of goods in the United States. Paper presented at BigSurv18 Conference, Barcelona, Spain (25–27 October 2018).

Pfefferman, D. (2015). Methodological issues and challenges in the production of official statistics. *Journal of Survey Statistics and Methodology* 3 (4): 425–467.

Platek, R. and Särndal, C.-E. (2001). Can a statistician deliver? *Journal of Official Statistics* 17 (1): 1–20. with Discussion 21–127.

Porter, T.M. (1995). *Trust in Numbers: The Pursuit of Objectivity in Science and Public Life*. Princeton, NJ/Chichester: Princeton University Press.

Radermacher, W.J. (2014). New challenges facing official statistics. *Statistical Journal of the IAOS* 30: 3–16.

Radermacher, W.J. (2017). Official statistics 4.0 – learning from history for the challenges of the future. In: *Statistics and Data Science: New Challenges, New Generation* (eds. A. Petrucci and R. Verde), 800–820. Florence: Firenze University Press.

Radermacher, W.J. (2018). Official statistics in the era of big data – opportunities and threats. *International Journal of Data Science and Analytics* 6 (3): 225–231. https://doi.org/10.1007/s41060-018-0124-z.

Reid, G., Zabala, F., and Holmberg, A. (2017). Extending TSE to administrative data: a quality framework and case studies from Stats NZ. *Journal of Official Statistics* 33 (2): 477–511. https://doi.org/10.1515/Jos-2017-0023.

van Sebille, M., Struijs, P., Swier, N. et al. (2018). *ESSnet on Big Data. Final Technical Report*. Luxembourg: Eurostat.

Shafer, T. (2017). *The 42 V's of Big Data Science*. Charlottesville, VA: Elder Research, Inc.

Signorelli, S. and Biffignandi, S. (2018). From big data to information: statistical issues through a case study. In: *Classification, (Big) Data Analysis and Statistical Learning* (eds. F. Mola, C. Conversano and M. Vichi). Cham, Switzerland: Springer https://doi.org/10.1007/978-3-319-55708-3_1.

Smith, T. (2018). Keynote address. Delivered at BigSurv18 Conference, Barcelona, Spain (25–27 October 2018).

Stateva, G., ten Bosch, O., Maslankowski, J. et al. (2017). *Webscraping Enterprise Characteristics. Legal Aspects Related to Webscraping of Enterprise Websites. Deliverable 2.1, ESSnet on Big Data*. Luxembourg: Eurostat.

Statistics Sweden (2015). Green Space and Green Within Localities 2010. Statistiska Meddelanden, MI 12 SM 1501.

Stiglitz, J.E., Sen, A.K., and Fitoussi, J.-P. (2009). *Report by the Commission on the Measurement of Economic Performance and Social Progress*. Paris, France: Commission on the Measurement of Economic Performance and Social Progress.

Sturgeon, T. (2013). *Global Values Chains and Economic Globalization – Towards a New Measurement Framework*. Luxembourg: Eurostat.

Tam, S.-M. and Kim, J.K. (2018). Big data, selection bias and ethics – an official statistician's perspective. *Statistical Journal of the International Association for Official Statistics* 34: 577–588.

Tam, S.-M., Kim, J.K., Ang, L. et al. (2020). Mining the new oil for official statistics. In: *Big Data Meets Survey Science: A Collection of Innovative Methods*, Chapter 11.

Torres van Grinsven, V. and Snijkers, G. (2015). Sentiments and perceptions of business respondents on social media: an exploratory analysis. *Journal of Official Statistics* 31 (2): 1–24. https://doi.org/10.1515/jos-2015-0018.

Tourangeau, R., Edwards, B., Johnson, T.P. et al. (eds.) (2014). *Hard-to-Survey Populations*. New York: Cambridge University Press.

Trepanier, J. (2014). Methodologies for an Integrated Use of Administrative Data in the Statistical Process. Report from the Statistical Network MIAD, CROS. European Commission. Eurostat.

United Nations (1994). Fundamental Principles of Official Statistics. UN Statistical Commission, New York, NY, USA.

Vaccari, C. (2014). Big data in official statistics. PhD thesis. University of Camerino, Camerino, Italy.

Valliant, R. and Dever, J.A. (2011). Estimating propensity adjustments for volunteer web surveys. *Sociological Methods & Research* 40 (1): 105–137. https://doi.org/10.1177/0049124110392533.

Valliant, R., Dever, J.A., and Kreuter, F. (2018). Nonprobability sampling. In: *Practical Tools for Designing and Weighting Survey Samples* (eds. R. Valliant, J. Dever and F. Kreuter). New York: Springer https://doi.org/10.1007/978-3-319-93632-1_18.

Wang, C., Chen, M.-H., Schifano, E. et al. (2016). Statistical methods and computing for big data. *Statistics and Its Interface* 9 (4): 399–414. https://doi.org/10.4310/SII.2016.v9.n4.a1.

Weström, C., Bradbury, J., Grossenbacher, A., et al. (2011). Social media in statistical agencies. Eurostat working paper. Social-Media Subgroup of the Sponsorship Group on Communication.

Zhang, L.-C. and Holgersson, H. (2018). Consumer expenditure statistics and retail transaction data. Paper presented at the United Nations Economic Commission for Europe Conference of European Statisticians Workshop on Data Editing, Neuchâtel, Switzerland (18–20 September 2018).

10

Big Data in Official Statistics: A Perspective from Statistics Netherlands

Barteld Braaksma, Kees Zeelenberg, and Sofie De Broe

Statistics Netherlands, The Hague/Heerlen, The Netherlands

10.1 Introduction

In this chapter, which builds on Braaksma and Zeelenberg (2015, 2017), we describe and discuss opportunities for Big Data in official statistics. Big Data may be characterized by their high volume, high velocity, and high variety. These aspects have advantages and disadvantages when used in official statistics. On one hand, high volume of Big Data may lead to more detailed and more accurate statistics; on the other hand, Big Data may be very selective and the estimates based on them severely biased. Similarly, their high velocity may lead to more frequent, more timely statistical estimates, but discontinuities may occur as well as sudden jumps in time series that may be hard to explain. Also, with the advance of Big Data and open data, the risk for disclosure of individual data is much higher, which poses new challenges for statistical institutes.

Using such sources in official statistics requires innovative approaches not based on surveys and censuses. This chapter focuses on methodological challenges, in particular, on how official statistics may be produced from Big Data. Specifically, we discuss the best strategies for using Big Data in official statistics and develop a strategy, which may be used for assessing quality aspects and gives guidance how to develop official statistics with Big Data sources.

Basically, Big Data in official statistics can be handled in two ways. The first is to accept the Big Data for what they are: a perhaps imperfect, yet very timely, indicator of developments in society. In short, we might argue: these data exist and that is why they are interesting. A second way is to use formal models and extract information from these data in either a model-based or model-assisted approach. In the model-based approach we may make the most of many new methods for dealing with Big Data developed by mathematical and applied statisticians;

Big Data Meets Survey Science: A Collection of Innovative Methods, First Edition. Edited by Craig A. Hill, Paul P. Biemer, Trent D. Buskirk, Lilli Japec, Antje Kirchner, Stas Kolenikov, and Lars E. Lyberg.
© 2021 John Wiley & Sons, Inc. Published 2021 by John Wiley & Sons, Inc.

these methods are also very useful for conducting statistical analyses. In the model-assisted approach Big Data are regarded as auxiliary data, which is likely the most profitable way to use Big Data in official statistics.

In Section 10.2, we briefly describe the various types of data sources in official statistics. In Section 10.3, we give several examples of Big Data in official statistics. In Section 10.4, we present, as principles, the basic framework for assessing the use of Big Data in official statistics and how this leads to a strong preference for using Big Data as auxiliary data. In Section 10.5, we give several examples of this "integration" approach. In Section 10.6, we briefly describe how Big Data makes disclosure control of official statistics more difficult and indicate some ways how this may be researched further. In Section 10.7, we give a broader perspective showing how this work may lead to a fusion of paradigms in official statistics. In Section 10.8, we present some concluding remarks.

10.2 Big Data and Official Statistics

Official statistics have four types of data sources:

- *Survey data*: data collected by interviewing or by other types of questioning persons, households, and enterprises, selected by a probability sample from a well-defined population
- *Census data*: data based on a complete enumeration of a population
- *Administrative data*: data from official registrations of a well-defined population, such as a population register or a tax register
- *Big Data*: data generated by digital activities, e.g. activities on the internet (social media), communications between businesses and between businesses and consumers (e.g. shops, banking, and commercial transactions), and machine-generated data, e.g. from sensors (internet of things).[1]

Census data and administrative data may also be regarded as Big Data, in particular when referring to large populations, such as an entire country or large provinces. Also, Big Data may or may not refer to a well-defined population. So, an alternative distinction might be between

- data referring to a well-defined population
- data with unclear population references or that cannot be linked to a population, sometimes called *found data*.

Traditionally, producers of official statistics have relied on their own data collection, using paper questionnaires, face-to-face, and telephone interviews, or, in

---

[1] See UN-ECE (2013) for more detailed classifications and examples of big data.

recent years, web surveys. The classical approach originates from the era of data scarcity, when official statistical institutes were among the few organizations that were able to gather data, process it in a controlled way, and disseminate information. A main advantage of the survey-based approach is that it gives full control over questions asked and populations studied. Big disadvantages are that it is expensive and burdensome, both for the surveying organization and the respondents, and that there may be large measurement errors, nonresponse errors, mode effects, and other nonsampling errors.

More recently, statistical institutes have used administrative registers, usually assembled by government agencies. However, control over the data is reduced and overcoverage or undercoverage of the population of statistical interest may occur as well as errors, especially conceptual errors. In the Netherlands the official population register does not contain homeless persons or immigrants without official residence permit; and people may not actually live at their registered address. Therefore, the administrative population might not exactly match the statistical population. However, these data are cheaper to obtain than survey data; in some countries like the Netherlands, the access to and use of administrative data sources is regulated by law, so that statistical institutes have easy and free access to them.

Big Data sources are even more difficult to control. They typically consist of "organic data" (Groves 2011) collected by enterprises or institutes for other purposes than statistics. For example, a statistical organization might want to use retail transaction data to provide prices for their Consumer Price Index statistics, while the purpose of the data collector, e.g. a supermarket chain, is to track inventories and sales.

10.3 Examples of Big Data in Official Statistics

In this section, we provide four examples of Big Data in official statistics: scanner data, social media messages, traffic-loop data, and mobile phone data.

10.3.1 Scanner Data

Prices of purchases in Dutch retail stores have for decades been entered into the cash registers of stores by scanning a bar code (the EAN-13-code), which is assigned to each packaged product. Bar codes have replaced manual entering of prices by the cashier and have increased efficiency (less time spent on each customer), improved quality (fewer errors), and enhanced customer satisfaction (less time spent queuing). In the 1990s, Statistics Netherlands realized the potential of scanner data for price statistics but not until 2002 was the first contract with a supermarket chain store signed, which allowed the statistical use of scanner data. Since then the use of scanner data has gradually expanded to cover all supermarket chains and other chain stores in, e.g. clothing, hardware, and groceries.

The use of scanner data for price statistics can be considered a form of statistical Big Data use *"avant la lettre,"* because it had already started before the term Big Data became widely popular.[2] Use of scanner data increases efficiency, reduces response burden, and improves quality of statistics. Scanner data necessitated the development of completely new methodologies and production processes, which took some time. But now it has been firmly established as a major source for price statistics. Gradually, further statistical uses of scanner data are being explored, for example, the compilation of a "pepper nut index," showing the sales in autumn of seasonal cookies and candy associated with the popular Dutch children's feast of St. Nicholas (5 December). This small pilot project showed the potential of scanner data and inspired further ideas. As a follow-up, feasibility of a study on regional food patterns based on scanner data is being explored on the request of our National Institute for Public Health and the Environment (RIVM).

10.3.2 Traffic-Loop Data

In the Netherlands, approximately 100 million traffic detection loop records are generated each day. More specifically, for more than 30 000 detection loops on Dutch roads, the number of passing cars is recorded on a minute-by-minute basis. The data are collected and stored by the National Data Warehouse (NDW) for Traffic Information (www.ndw.nu), a government agency that provides the data to Statistics Netherlands. The detection loops discern length classes, enabling the differentiation between cars and trucks, for example. Their primary use is to detect traffic jams and provide information about road use for maintenance purposes. Harvesting the vast amount of data is a major challenge for statistics; however, it could result in speedier and more robust traffic statistics, including more detailed information on regional levels and increased resolution in temporal patterns.

Unfortunately, this source suffers from undercoverage and selectivity (Daas et al. 2015). Due to system failures, the number of vehicles detected is not available for every minute, and many Dutch roads, including some important ones, lack detection loops. The first problem can be corrected by smoothing, e.g. by imputing the absent data with data that is reported by the same loop during a five-minute interval before or after that minute. Furthermore, coverage is improving over

---

2 The term Big Data with its current meaning is believed to have been coined by Roger Magoulas from O'Reilly in 2005, but it is difficult to be sure because the term itself has been mentioned in other contexts long before that by several authors.

time, as gradually more and more roads have detection loops, enabling a more complete coverage of the most important Dutch roads and reducing selectivity. At the same time, the Dutch Road Authority (*Rijkswaterstaat*) is considering replacing the traffic-loop system altogether by new ways to collect the data they need, because maintenance of the traffic-loop sensors is relatively expensive and cumbersome. Alternatives are floating car data (FCD), where data is collected from car navigation systems, mobile phones, and surveillance by drones. The advantage of such methods is that surveillance is not confined to the static locations of the traffic loops, so that traffic on secondary and tertiary roads or inside cities can also be monitored (Klunder et al. 2017). Apart from the obvious opportunities of FCD for statistics, however, this reveals another issue with Big Data: the sources may change or disappear altogether with technological advances.

Some detection loops are linked to weigh-in-motion stations, which automatically measure the weight of the vehicle and are combined with cameras that record the license plates. One important weigh station is located on the highway connecting the port of Rotterdam to the rest of the Netherlands. In the future, these measurements may be used to estimate the weight of the transported goods.

Examples of statistical applications using these data include very rapid estimates of the amount of goods transported, exported and imported, and even a rough indicator of economic activity (van Ruth 2014; cf. Section 10.5.4). Another example concerns the effect of adverse weather conditions. From 4–6 January 2016, the first three working days of that year, the northern part of the Netherlands was hit by sleet, which affected all traffic and had a severe impact on public life. Only two days later, Statistics Netherlands published an analysis of the quantitative effect based on traffic-loop data. The analysis showed that on major roads the amount of traffic was reduced to half of the three-year average, while on minor roads it was only 25% of the normal intensity. Without the traffic-loop data this analysis would not have been possible and could not have been published so quickly.

10.3.3 Social Media Messages

Social media is a data source where people voluntarily share information, discuss topics of interest, and contact family and friends. More than 3 million public social media messages are produced daily in the Netherlands. These messages are available to anyone with internet access, but collecting them all is obviously a huge task. The social media data analyzed by Statistics Netherlands has been provided by the company Coosto (www.coosto.com), which routinely collects all Dutch social media messages. In addition, Coosto provides some extra information, like assigning sentiment scores to individual messages or adding information about the place of origin of a message.

To find out whether social media is a useful data source for statistics, Dutch social media messages have been studied from two perspectives: content and sentiment (Daas and Puts 2014). Studies of the content of Dutch Twitter messages, the predominant public social media message in the Netherlands at the time, revealed that nearly 50% of those messages were composed of "pointless babble." The remainder predominantly discussed spare time activities (10%), work (7%), media (5%), and politics (3%). Use of these more serious messages was hampered by the less serious "babble" messages. Thus, additional cleaning and filtering were needed to separate the signal from the noise.

After removing messages without real content, researchers found the sentiment in Dutch social media messages to be highly correlated with Dutch consumer confidence (Daas and Puts 2014). Facebook gave the best overall results. The observed sentiment was stable on a monthly and weekly basis, but daily figures displayed highly volatile behavior. Thus, it might become possible to produce useful weekly sentiment indicators, more frequently than the present monthly indicator of consumer confidence.

As a follow-up, a social tension indicator has been developed that aims to measure tensions and feelings of unrest in society (CBS 2018). This daily indicator is based on Twitter messages and shows a more or less stable baseline, with a slight upward trend from 2010 to 2013 and slightly decreasing since 2013. In addition, a number of large spikes were observed, which all seem to be related to clearly identifiable events that caused a heavy reaction in society, like the terrorist attacks in Paris and Brussels and the crash of the MH-17 plane over Ukraine. Reactions to domestic events were also observed such as the "Dam screamer" event when somebody started to shout during the two minutes of silence at the national commemoration of World War II, televised live throughout the country from the Dam square in Amsterdam. The social tension indicator was released as experimental statistics[3] and attracted a lot of attention from the media, with mixed reactions. In some cases, Statistics Netherlands was praised for coming up with these innovative statistics, while others criticized the use of Twitter.

10.3.4 Mobile Phone Data

Nowadays, people carry mobile phones with them everywhere and use their phones throughout the day. To manage the phone traffic, a large amount of data must be processed by mobile phone companies. This data is very closely associated with people's behavior that is of interest for official statistics. For example, phone traffic is relayed through geographically distributed phone masts, which enables

---

[3] Experimental statistics are statistics that are still under development and do not yet comply with all final quality specifications; they are released to obtain feedback from potential users.

determination of the location of phone users. The relaying mast, however, may change several times during a call, and so nontrivial location algorithms are needed to assess the caller's actual location and movements (Tennekes 2018).

Several uses for official statistics may be envisaged, including inbound tourism (Heerschap et al. 2014) and daytime population (Tennekes and Offermans 2014); see also UN (2017) for a survey of mobile phone data in official statistics. Little is known about the "daytime whereabouts" due to lack of data sources; in contrast to the "nighttime population" based on official (residence) registers. Obviously, we have to take into account several issues when considering statistical uses of mobile phone data. For example, in the European Union, the group of mobile phone users is selective when compared with the population: young children do not usually carry a mobile phone. In 2017 only 25% of people over 65 used a mobile phone for internet access, whereas almost 90% of young people (12–30 years) used a mobile phone (Eurostat 2018). Similarly, 45% of individuals with primary educational attainment used a mobile phone, whereas 80% of those with higher education used a mobile phone. Also, we may not have access to the data from all mobile phone providers, which will create additional selectivity. Thus, we have to be careful when interpreting the data or when developing processing methods.

10.4 Principles for Assessing the Quality of Big Data Statistics

The principles we use for evaluating Big Data are, following the EU Statistical Law (EU 2009), statistical quality (relevance, accuracy, timeliness, accessibility, comparability, and coherence) and statistical principles (independence, impartiality, objectivity, reliability, confidentiality, and cost effectiveness). In particular, we focus on

- accuracy, objectivity, and reliability, since these are fundamental for official statistics: if statistics do not describe society accurately enough or are not objective or reliable, they are essentially useless;
- relevance, timeliness, accessibility, comparability, and coherence.

In the discussion below, we distinguish between survey data, census data, administrative data, and Big Data (cf. Section 10.2).

Some work has already been done on developing Big Data quality frameworks in an international context, in particular the pioneering work done in the UN-ECE Big Data Quality Task Team (UN-ECE 2014), the American Association of Public Opinion Research (AAPOR) Task Force on Big Data (Japec et al. 2015a, Chapter 5; Japec et al. 2015b) and Biemer (2020). But as yet no authoritative, generally accepted framework exists while many agree that existing quality frameworks for official statistics are not sufficient because Big Data has specific characteristics (Consten et al. 2018), Therefore, we focus here on principles and aspects of quality for Big Data and we try to derive conclusions about the Big Data strategy for National Statistical Institutes (NSIs).

10.4.1 Accuracy

The accuracy of any statistic is measured by its sum of variance and the squared bias. To judge these, we have to know the process by which the data was generated. A total survey error (TSE) approach gives control over the major error sources, and the UN-ECE and AAPOR Task Forces as well as the ESSnet Big Data took this approach.[4] The TSE approach is a reminder that we should not compare an ideal version of surveys to the raw practice of administrative data and Big Data. It is important to keep this in mind when comparing statistics based on traditional methods and sources to those based on newer methods and sources.

Big Data may be highly volatile and selective: the coverage of the population to which the data refer may change from day to day, leading to inexplicable jumps in time-series. Furthermore, the individual observations in these datasets often lack linking variables and so cannot be linked to other datasets or population frames, which severely limits the possibilities for correction of selectivity and volatility using traditional methods.

For example, phone calls usually relate to persons, but how to interpret their signals is far from obvious. People may carry multiple phones or none, children use phones registered to their parents, phones may be switched off, and so on. Moreover, the way people use their phones may change over time, depending on changes in billing, technical advances, and preferences for alternative communication tools, among other things. For social media messages, similar issues may arise when trying to identify characteristics of their authors.

Many Big Data sources consist of event-driven observational data, which are not designed for data analysis. These "fuzzy" Big Data are often collected through some intermediary ("aggregator") such as Google, Facebook, and Coosto. They lack well-defined target populations, data structures, and quality indicators, making it hard to apply traditional statistical methods based on sampling theory. Indeed, statistical applications of these Big Data, such as the Google Flu index and the Billion Prices Project, always refer to, and will always have to refer to, official statistical series to establish their validity.

---

4 ESSnet Big Data (ESS 2019) is a project within the European statistical system (ESS) jointly undertaken by 28 partners. Its objective is the integration of Big Data in the regular production of official statistics, through pilots exploring the potential of selected Big Data sources, and through building and implementing concrete applications.

Accuracy of statistics based on Big Data has been studied more formally by Meng (2014, 2018). He shows that the mean squared error of any statistic based on a part of the population, whether it comes from a random sample or from a Big Data source, depends on three elements: a *data quality* measure (the correlation in the population between the variable of interest and the indicator function that shows whether an individual has responded or participated, or has been reported or recorded), a *data quantity* measure (varying inversely with the fraction of the population that is in the dataset), and the *population standard deviation* of the variable of interest. When combining various data sources, "... those relatively tiny but higher quality ones [such as from probabilistic samples] should be given far more weights than suggested by their sizes." Meng concludes that, when using Big Data for population inferences, additional information must be used, either from the Big Data source itself or from other data sources. The additional information must be sufficient to correct for the bias, perhaps not completely but so that the statistic will be useful to users. This information may consist of characteristics of the individuals in the dataset that make poststratification possible. For example, recent examples have shown the potential of linkage with sensor data (Klingwort, Buelens, and Schnell 2018). However, if some important part of the population is completely missing, correction will be impossible.

10.4.2 Models in Official Statistics

In Section 10.4.1, we pointed out that the use of Big Data in official statistics will often require modeling and additional information to correct for biases. Such models specify the relations between the statistics of interest and the additional information. Now, we will briefly review how models are often viewed in official statistics. In Section 10.4.3, we will look at the implications of the objectivity and reliability principles for the use of such models.

Here, we follow the well-known distinction between design-based methods, model-assisted methods, and model-based methods. Design-based methods strictly conform to a survey model, where respondents are sampled according to known probabilities, and the statistician uses these probabilities to compute an unbiased estimate of some population characteristic, such as average income. Model-assisted methods use a model that captures some prior information about the population to increase the precision of the estimates; however, if the model is incorrect, then the estimates are still unbiased when taking only the design into account. The examples of Big Data in official statistics provided in Section 10.3 rely mostly on the data as collected, with corrections for probabilities of observation, and thus fall in the categories of design-based or model-assisted methods.

Model-based methods, however, rely on the correctness of the model: the estimates are biased if the model does not hold. As an example, suppose we want to estimate consumer confidence in a certain period, and that we have a traditional survey sample for which consumer confidence according to the correct statistical concept is observed, but also a social media source where a sentiment score can be attached to individual messages by applying a certain algorithm. A model-assisted approach would be to use the social media source data as auxiliary variables in a regression estimator. Even if the model that relates consumer confidence to sentiment scores does not hold perfectly, the resulting estimator is still approximately unbiased under the sampling design. A simple example of a model-based estimator would be to aggregate all the individual sentiment scores in the social media source, and use this as an estimate of consumer confidence. The implicit model here is that sentiment in the social media source is equal to, or highly correlated with, consumer confidence in the statistical sense. If this model does not hold, then the resulting estimate will be biased. If both sample and the social media data were available, it would not be efficient to use only the latter data in a model-based estimator. But it may be much cheaper to refrain from sampling and to use only the Big Data source. The response burden on persons in the sample may also be a barrier to maintain a survey if a suitable alternative is available.

NSIs have always been reluctant to use model-based methods in official statistics. They have relied on censuses and surveys, using mostly design-based and model-assisted methods. Yet, in specific statistical areas, NSIs have used model-based methods, e.g. in making small area estimates, in correcting for nonresponse and selectivity, in computing seasonally-adjusted time series, and in making preliminary macroeconomic estimates. In fact, common techniques like imputation of missing data often rely on model assumptions. So, in a sense, models are already being used in official statistics. But very often, these models remain implicit and are not being emphasized in the documentation and the dissemination. So NSIs should not abstain from using model-based methods for handling Big Data sources. In subsections 10.4.3–10.4.5, we discuss how this might be done.

10.4.3 Objectivity and Reliability

NSIs must, as producers of official statistics, be careful in the application of model-based methods. The public should not have to worry about the quality of official statistics; objectivity and reliability are among the principles of official statistics in the European Statistical Law (EU 2009) "… meaning that statistics must be developed, produced and disseminated in a systematic, reliable and unbiased manner." The European Statistics Code of Practice (EU 2018, principle 12) says: "European Statistics accurately and reliably portray reality." Other international declarations, such as those of the International Statistical Institute (1985) and the United Nations (1991), and national statistical laws, such as those of the Netherlands, have similar principles.

Statisticians try to live up to these principles, but how to apply them is a matter of interpretation and is not always successful. Often, statisticians have to compromise between several principles. When using models, we can interpret these two principles as follows.

We take the principle of objectivity to mean that the data used to estimate the model should refer to the phenomenon that one is describing; in other words, the objects and the populations for the model should correspond to the statistical phenomenon at hand. Data from the past may be used to estimate the model, but official statistical estimates based on the model never go beyond the present time period; so, for an NSI, nowcasting is allowed, but not forecasting and policy analyses. Of course, this process is different for a forecasting agency or a policy-evaluation agency, whose purpose is exactly to go beyond the present period or present context. Even if official statistics and policy evaluation are combined in one report or, as is the case with some NSIs, in one organization, it is always desirable to distinguish official statistics, which describe what has actually happened, from policy evaluations, which deal with "what–if" situations.

In this context the principle of reliability means that revisions to official statistical data must not be made just because the model changes, e.g. because it breaks down (model failure). In particular for time-series models we must be on guard, because model failure may lead to an incorrect identification of turning points in the series.

Also, we should refrain from using behavioral models, which in essence are models describing choices by social agents such as enterprises and households. Such behavioral models are prone to model failure: any behavioral model is almost certain to fail in the future because behavior of economic and social agents has changed. For example, in economic policy, the famous Lucas (1976) critique states that any structural economic policy will be detected by economic agents, who will then adapt their behaviors. The consequence is "…that any change in policy will systematically alter the structure of econometric models" (Lucas 1976, p. 41). It is thus naïve to base predictions on models using aggregated time series.

An additional reason to avoid behavioral models is to prevent situations where an external researcher finds interesting results when fitting a certain model, but, unknown to the researcher, the NSI has used that same model to create the very data that the external researcher used. This dilemma might lead to the wrong conclusions and the wrong policy suggestions, and could moreover be dangerous for the reputation of the NSI. Also, the primary purpose of an NSI is to describe, not to predict, prescribe, or judge (as opposed to a forecasting agency or a policy-evaluation agency which are different).

The principles of objectivity and reliability lead to some methodological principles for model-based methods. In particular, model building should be accompanied by extensive specification tests to ensure that the model is robust. Any use of models must be made explicit: it should be documented and made transparent to users. Whenever official statistics that have been produced using a model-based approach are published, this fact should explicitly be mentioned in the publication. The models must be described in the statistical documentation, including information on the details of the model selection, the assumptions and the analyses regarding model fit and robustness. Such caution may help to avoid a situation where the model used to produce the statistics is being "discovered" by an outside researcher, which in turn could lead to incorrect conclusions.

Based on these principles, Statistics Netherlands developed guidelines (Buelens, de Wolf, and Zeelenberg 2014) for the use of models in the production of official statistics. There are three main principles, reflecting the discussion above:

1. The model should be used only for estimating missing data. That is, the model should only be used for the time period for which the data are available, which precludes forecasting and policy analysis.
2. The variables in the model should be directly related to the statistical topic for which the model is used. That is, both the entities and the populations related to the model should reflect those of the statistical phenomenon in question, which precludes the use of behavioral variables, since these are indirectly related.
3. The model specification should be extensively tested against alternative specifications, the model should be robust against outliers and breaks in the data, and the model should be stable over time.

The UK Office for National Statistics (McLaren and Drew 2015) has developed similar guidelines.

Many, if not most, topics in official statistics where models have been used, already conform to these guidelines. Some examples are: small area estimation in the labor force surveys, time-series modeling to improve the precision of the monthly unemployment rate, nonresponse adjustments (weighting and calibration under the missing at random assumption [MAR]), correction of mode effects in mixed-mode surveys, capture-recapture models to estimate hidden populations, and seasonal adjustments. So, despite these warnings, there is room for using models in the production of official statistics from Big Data.

10.4.4 Relevance

Timeliness of Big Data sources make them potentially relevant for current policy. However, even if we know that a Big Data source covers the whole population, the statistical information that can be extracted may be limited. For example, with traffic sensors one can observe that a car is passing, but we do not know who is in the car, who owns the car, and why he or she is driving at that spot. So, the relevance and the coherence with other statistics remain limited. These traffic-intensity statistics are important in themselves, but they become really useful if they can be linked with other data sources and surveys.

Another example relates to mobile phone data. We can observe that a phone is located in a certain neighborhood or has crossed a border, but we do not know who is carrying the phone, who the owner is, and why he or she is at that spot. Again, these data may be used to derive statistics about the daytime population (cf. Section 10.3.4) and about the number of tourists. But they would become particularly useful if they could be linked to expenditure patterns, for example.

An issue that inevitably arises when working with Big Data is the question of societal relevance versus relevance from an official statistics perspective. Mobile phone data may be used to detect the source of an outbreak of an infectious disease like legionella. Provided the infected persons give their consent and phone operators also agree to cooperate, statistical analysis of the whereabouts of these persons based on their mobile phone use might provide clues about the location of infection sources. Although the societal relevance is clear and statistical expertise comes into play, this task is probably not appropriate for a statistical institute.

With social media-based statistics the question of relevance becomes quite important, especially given recent accusations of manipulation by foreign powers through social media, fake accounts, fake news and the fact that use of social media is not homogeneous across the population.

10.4.5 Some Examples of Quality Assessments of Big Data Statistics

It has been shown (see Section 10.5.3) that the sentiment indicator based on social media messages, discussed in Section 10.3.3, is highly correlated with more traditional estimates of consumer confidence. Therefore, we may conclude that this indicator is relevant. However, the social media-based sentiment indicator does not track the traditional indicator exactly. On the other hand, because consumer confidence statistics are often the result of a telephone survey, these statistics will contain sampling errors, and also, often worse, nonsampling errors. The traditional consumer confidence indicator is, because of sampling errors, not an exact measure of consumer confidence, and most certainly has a bias because of nonsampling errors. Thus, it would be more appropriate to say that the social media sentiment indicator and the traditional indicator both are estimates of "the mood of the nation, albeit with different error structures" and thus both indicators are relevant.

Since the social media indicator clearly can be produced more quickly and much more frequently, it scores higher on the aspect of timeliness. However, comparability may be much harder to maintain, since participation in social media may change or even show large fluctuations over time; and methods similar to nonresponse adjustment in surveys may have to be used to compensate. Still, even if the social media sentiment indicator might score lower on relevance or accuracy, it may, because of its timeliness, still be useful for society if an NSI decides to present it as an official statistic.

The other examples of Big Data presented so far can also be judged according to these common quality dimensions. For example, traffic-loop data may be used to produce rapid estimates of traffic intensity and perhaps also of the quantity of goods transported, exported, and imported. Since quantities will be based on the weight of the transported goods, the bias component of its accuracy may be larger than that of the traditional estimate derived from a survey among transport companies, but because its coverage will be nearly complete, the variance component will be nearly zero. Such a very rapid estimate may be highly relevant.

With mobile phone data, more problems of representativeness may occur: some persons carry more than one mobile phone, some phones may be switched off, and background characteristics are not known or imperfect because of prepaid phones, company phones, and children's phones registered to parents. Accuracy can be an issue when mapping phone masts to statistically relevant geographical areas: often they do not overlap perfectly (cf. Beręsewicz et al. 2018, Section 3.1.5). Phone mast connections do not stop at administrative borders like those of municipalities and provinces, or even national borders: when crossing the border from the Netherlands to Belgium, you may still be connected to a Dutch phone mast for some time and vice versa. This problem becomes more pronounced with more detail, where to some extent model-based decisions need to be made for assigning phone calls to areas.

10.5 Integration of Big Data with Other Statistical Sources

10.5.1 Big Data as Auxiliary Data

Big Data may be highly volatile and selective: the coverage of the population to which they refer may change from day to day, leading to inexplicable jumps in time-series. And often, the individual observations in these Big Data sets lack linking variables and so cannot be linked to other datasets or population frames, which severely limits the possibilities for correction of selectivity and volatility.

In other words, with Big Data there is often insufficient information about the relationships of the data source to the statistical phenomena we want to describe (often caused by lack of information about the data-generating process itself). Models are then useful to formulate explicit assumptions about these relations and to estimate selectivity or coverage characteristics; see Beręsewicz et al. (2018) for an extensive survey of methods to correct selectivity in Big Data.

For example, one way to reduce possible selectivity in a social media source could be to profile individual accounts to find out more about background characteristics. If we can determine whether an account belongs to a man or a woman, we should be able to better deal with gender bias in sentiment. Such techniques have already been developed and are becoming increasingly sophisticated. The same applies to age distribution, education level, and geographical location. Coverage issues with individual social media sources can be reduced by combining multiple sources; the sensible way to do so is by using a model, for example, a multiple regression model or a logit model if the composition of the various sources is known. Another example is the use of time-series methods to reduce volatility (see Kapetanios, Marcellino, and Petrova 2018 for a survey).

For many phenomena with Big Data, we also have other information, such as survey data for a small part of the population, and prior information from other sources. One approach is to use Big Data together with such additional information to determine whether we can model the phenomenon that we want to describe. In recent years, mathematical statistics have been used to develop advanced new methods for Big Data; some examples are high-dimensional regression, machine-learning techniques, graphical modeling, data science, and Bayesian networks (Belloni, Chernozhukov, and Hansen 2014; Choi and Varian 2012; Gelman et al. 2013; Nickerson and Rogers 2014; Varian 2014; Berk 2016; Efron and Hastie 2016; Baumer, Kaplan, and Horton 2017). Also, more established methods, such as Bayesian analytics, time-series methods and multilevel (hierarchical) models (Gelman et al. 2013) as well as time-series models have appeared to be useful.

A third strategy is to take inspiration from the way national accounts are commonly compiled. Many sources that are, in themselves, incomplete, imperfect, and/or partly overlapping are integrated, using a conceptual reference frame to obtain a comprehensive picture of the whole economy while applying many checks and balances. In the same way, Big Data and other sources that, in themselves, are incomplete or biased may be combined to yield a complete and unbiased picture pertaining to a certain phenomenon.

To illustrate the fruitfulness of these strategies, we discuss in Sections 10.5.2–10.5.7 various examples where Big Data are used together with other sources.

10.5.2 Size of the Internet Economy[5]

The internet is clearly an important technology that acts as both a driver and a means for changes in the economy. The internet influences the economy in four main ways:

1. Means of communication: online presence on the internet with a website;

---

5 This subsection in based on Oostrom et al. (2016).

2. Online stores (e-commerce), e.g. Amazon and Zalando;
3. Online services, e.g. AirBnB, eBay, Booking.com, and dating sites;
4. Internet-related information and communication technology (ICT) such as web design, hosting, and internet marketing.

Estimating the size of the internet economy is not easy. Only the last group, internet-related ICT, is to some extent distinguished as a separate industry in statistical surveys. Online stores are, according to European rules, grouped in a single industry, so that hardly any information is available about the types of their activities. Traditional retail stores that have more and more sales online will probably not change the NACE category under which they first registered. Online services are subsumed in the industries corresponding to their output, so that, again, hardly any information exists about the type of their activities. No regular statistical information is available about the internet as a means of business communication. By combining Big Data, administrative data, and survey data, Statistics Netherlands (Oostrom et al. 2016) succeeded in estimating the size of the country's internet economy for each of the four classes. The data consisted of:

Big Data:

Big Data comprises a list of all Dutch websites, including (where applicable) business name, company registration number, size of site traffic, and other data; altogether over 100 attributes for each site. The list contains 2.5 million websites and is maintained by Dataprovider (https://www.dataprovider.com). When a website is owned by a company, it is legally obliged to publish its company registration number.

Administrative data:

The General Business Register (GBR) is a comprehensive list of all enterprises in the Netherlands and their ownership relations, based on administrative data from the company register and the tax registers.[6] About 1.5 million enterprises are in the GBR. Addresses and telephone numbers are included in the GBR and for many enterprises, a hostname of the website is included.

The short-term statistics provide turnover of enterprises based on the value added tax (VAT) register, giving a nearly complete census of enterprises.

---

6 An enterprise in official statistics is more or less the same as a business unit, and a legal unit is an entity officially registered as an economically active unit, such as a corporation and a self-employed person, whereas an enterprise group (a set of enterprises controlled by the same owner) is more or less the same as a company. See Eurostat (2016) for more details and references to implementation rules.

Survey data:

Structural business statistics are collected in an annual survey of enterprises on employment and financial data that includes all enterprises with more than 50 employees, and smaller enterprises are sampled.
Several other surveys such as those on ICT and wages are also useful.

Several keys have been used in linking all these databases: the company registration number, address and telephone number, and hostname.

The statistical results have been remarkable. About two thirds of all enterprises have no website; most of these are self-employed persons. Online stores, online services, and internet-related ICT comprise about 5% of the economy, comparable to construction and transportation. So, the internet economy is important, but its size is not large; in fact, it is much smaller than health services and education services. On the other hand, the use of ICT and internet is probably very extensive, since most enterprises use computers and the internet.

The study received a lot of coverage in Dutch media and the Dutch government and policy makers valued it. It also drew international attention. This example clearly shows both the viability and relevance of integration of Big Data with more traditional data sources.

10.5.3 Improving the Consumer Confidence Index

The consumer confidence index (CCI) measures the opinion of consumers about their present and expected own financial situation, the present and expected general economic climate, and intentions for spending on major durables. For each of the five questions in the survey, the percentages of positive answers and negative answers are balanced, and the CCI is the average of these five numbers (CBS 2018; EC 2019).

The social media sentiment index (SMI) is based on Big Data from Twitter and Facebook (see Section 10.3.3). The sentiment of a message is determined by classifying the words as positive, negative, or neutral (Daas and Puts 2014). The sentiment of the medium, Twitter and Facebook, is computed as the balance of the percentages of positive and negative answers, and the SMI as the average of the sentiment of the two media.

Here we try to improve the ordinary estimate from surveys or from registers with the help of Big Data. For example, we looked at the relationship between the CCI and the SMI (van den Brakel et al. 2017).

Figure 10.1a shows the CCI and Figure 10.1b shows the SMI; note that the vertical scales are different. The time period is 2009–2014 and the data are monthly. Both series move more or less together, which is confirmed by a formal statistical analysis using a structural time-series model. Both series appear to be

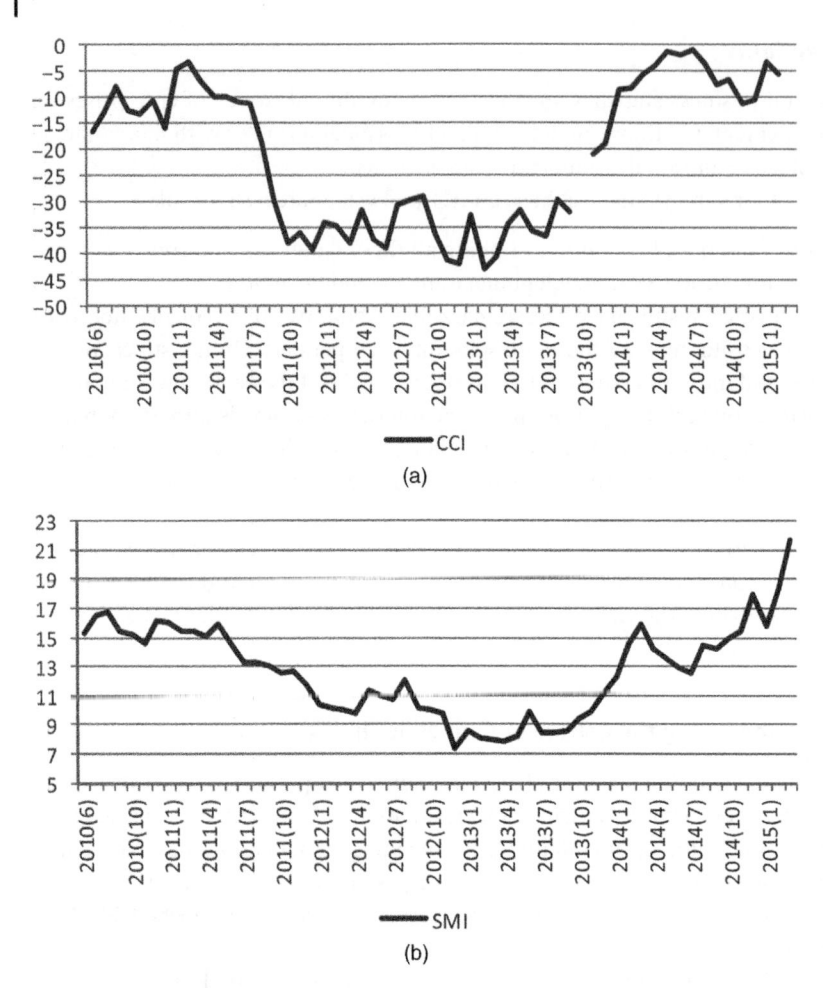

Figure 10.1 Consumer confidence index (a) and social media sentiment index (b), 2010–2015. Note: The vertical scale in both panels is the balance of positive and negative answers; cf. the text for more details.

co-integrated, which indicates that both series are driven by a common factor and thus represent the same phenomenon. Thus, the CCI can be improved with the help of the model. For example, one might use the higher frequency of the SMI to increase the frequency of the CCI by interpolating and extrapolating the CCI. Also, the much greater volume of SMI data might be used to estimate the CCI for specific subpopulations.

10.5.4 Big Data and the Quality of Gross National Product Estimates

Big Data may also help improve the quality of gross national product (GNP) estimates. This contribution is important, because the quality of the first estimate of the quarterly GNP, 45 days after the quarter (Zeelenberg 2016), needs improvement. In many countries, users need an even more timely first estimate, preferably within 30 days after the end of the quarter.

In a recent study at Statistics Netherlands, we considered four different Big Data sources of potential interest to address this need:

1. *Tax databases*: These are mainly tax data on wages and sales. They are not yet rapid enough for wide use: they lag about two months behind: one month for reporting taxes and one month for filling the databases.
2. *Company accounts*: In the next few years direct access to company accounts will be possible in that reporting modules for taxation and statistics are built into the accounting software. But it is not yet possible, and even when it has been implemented, will be for annual accounts only.
3. *Banking transactions of enterprises and households*: This source is clearly the most promising. Banks in the Netherlands have one clearinghouse, and it acts very rapidly. Banks have to report daily, weekly, and monthly to the central bank – and strong privacy and confidentiality constraints are involved. Thus, securing access to this source for statistical purposes will be difficult; even if successful, some time will be needed before this source is sufficiently analyzed and understood to be used in statistics production.
4. *Model-based estimates based on Big Data*: These are not a source as such, but provide a way to use Big Data. At the moment, this option appears to be the best.

van Ruth (2014) showed what model-based estimates from Big Data may have to offer; he analyzed the relationship between traffic intensity and economic activity in an important region of the Netherlands, the city of Eindhoven and its vicinity. Traffic intensity was measured from traffic sensors on the road surfaces, and economic activity was measured by expected production, taken from the monthly Manufacturing Sentiment Survey. The traffic intensity indicator tracked the expected production indicator amazingly well. Peaks and troughs coincided, meaning that the traffic intensity index should be able to signal important turning points in economic activity. Statistically, the series appeared to be coincident, and possibly seasonal adjustment and a trend-cycle decomposition may remove some noise and further improve the model. Now, traffic intensity data becomes available with a much shorter time lag than traditional survey data. From the model that relates output to traffic intensity, we may then make a preliminary estimate of output that, in turn, may be used to improve the first estimate of GNP.

Another example is Luomaranta et al. (2018), who used time-series models and statistical-learning techniques to improve early estimates of the Finnish gross domestic product (GDP). They considered firm-level data, from early respondents, as well as traffic data. The firm-level data, although strictly speaking not a Big Data source, gave the best results (see also Fornaro, Luomaranta, and Saarinen 2017, for a more detailed analysis), and apart from a single outlier, predicted the monthly and quarterly GDP very well. The traffic data performed less well in their study, but still predicted GDP reasonably well, a remarkable result given the rather unstructured and unedited nature of these Big Data. Luomaranta et al. (2018) also reported results for Slovenia using traffic-sensor data that were only roughly edited. Again, these results show that by using Big Data, GDP may be timelier and more accurately estimated. To summarize, time-series models, combined with machine-learning models, are a promising way to improve the first and preliminary estimates of GDP.

A third example is the use of the IVS90 (information and tracking) system for inland shipping in the Netherlands. Data from this sensor-based system were input into a model to estimate production and added value for improving flash estimates of quarterly GNP. The performance of this model is currently being evaluated. Potential bias is an important issue under investigation: not all shipping companies are using the IVS90 system so the IVS90 population is not equal to the population of shipping companies relevant from a national accounts perspective.

10.5.5 Google Trends for Nowcasting

Choi and Varian (2012) showed how to use search engine data from Google Trends to "predict the present," also known as nowcasting. They presented various examples of economic indicators including automobile sales, unemployment claims, travel destination planning, and consumer confidence.

In most cases, they applied simple autoregressive models incorporating appropriate Google Trends search terms as predictors. For nowcasting consumer confidence, they used a Bayesian regression model, since it was not clear in advance which search terms to use.

They found that even their simple models that included relevant Google Trends variables tended to outperform models that excluded these predictors by 5–20%. They made no claims to perfection or exhaustiveness, but these preliminary results indicate that pursuing this model-based path further is worthwhile.

Further studies have been published recently using Google Trends for nowcasting for topics such as consumer expenditure (Fasulo, Guandalini, and Terribili 2017), automobile sales (Nymand-Andersen and Pantelidis 2018), suicide

(Tran et al. 2017), and unemployment (Naccarato et al. 2018). Most of these studies conclude that Google Trends may be useful when combined with other data sources, but not on its own.

We should be cautious when interpreting search-term based results. Several years ago, there was a lot of enthusiasm concerning Google Flu, but more recently the nowcasting performance of Google Flu has decreased significantly (Lazer et al. 2014). Google has also been criticized for a lack of transparency. They have not revealed the search terms used in Google Flu, which prohibits a sound scientific debate and cross-validation by peers.

In fact, this last point has more general significance. One of the items in the European Code of Practice (EU 2018), is that NSIs should warn the public and policy makers when statistical results are being used inappropriately or are being misrepresented. As emphasized by Reimsbach-Kounatze (2015) and Fan, Han, and Liu (2014), finding spurious results is easy with Big Data, and NSIs can act as statistical authorities to offer best practices for analyzing Big Data.

10.5.6 Multisource Statistics: Combination of Survey and Sensor Data

Klingwort, Buelens, and Schnell (2018) dealt with the current problem of integrating Big Data into the production of official statistics; they conducted two case studies. In the first case study, they estimated underreporting in the Dutch Road Freight Transport Survey (RFTS) using sensor data of the weigh in motion (WIM) road sensor network. In the RFTS truck owners reported the days on which their trucks were used and the transported cargo weight. These responses were validated using the sensor data by linking the data sources one-by-one using the license plates of the trucks as the unique identifier. By enhancing both data sets with administrative data (the license plates are again used as the unique linking identifier), they modeled the capture probabilities (using logistic regression and log-linear models) of trucks in the survey and the sensor data using capture-recapture techniques. The derived capture–recapture estimate corrected for underreporting in the survey.

In the second application, only the sensor data was used to estimate the transported weight carried by Dutch trucks in the Netherlands. Because the survey data was based on a probability sample, its estimate is considered a benchmark. It is intended to estimate the transported cargo weight by pseudo-design-based methods, model-based prediction, and machine-learning algorithms independently for the sensor data. Each group of methods was applied to the sensor and survey data estimating the weight and outcomes were compared. The aim is the development or proposal of preferred and recommended methods in the context of survey methodology and official statistics and the guidance on method selection.

10.5.7 Combining Administrative and Open Data Sources to Complete Energy Statistics

The Centre for Big Data Statistics developed an excellent example of an experimental statistics application on energy transition (De Broe et al. 2019), a societal challenge that central government, provinces, and cities in the Netherlands and abroad are facing (Energyville 2017). They need to move from a strong dependence on fossil fuels toward an energy system where renewable energy plays a dominant role and reach their Climate Action Plan targets for energy use and emissions (EZ 2016). A possible scenario is that energy is produced and used locally in a self-sustaining way, where solar energy has an important role. Statistics Netherlands has, therefore, developed an experimental solar energy statistic. This work is an example of a complex societal phenomenon that requires a multisource approach in which Big Data sources and new analytical methods allow for new insights based on new statistical products. If smart meters were installed in most households generating solar power locally, making a good estimate would be fairly easy – but most Netherlands homes do not have them. We explored what could be done with existing data sources, such as administrative data on solar panels. However, the administrative sources on the number and location of domestic solar installations are not always completely up to date. To estimate the share of sustainable energy in the overall energy consumption, we opted for combining multiple data sources and approaches to get more reliable estimates.

There are four possible approaches. In the first two approaches we estimate the number and capacity, i.e. installed maximum power, of solar panel installations. In the first approach, we identify solar panels by combining administrative data on solar panel installations with data on VAT refunds[7] due to the installation of solar panels. In the second approach, we use aerial images in combination with intelligent pattern recognition software to identify solar panel installations that are not in administrative sources. The project aim was twofold: (i) automate the process to extract the location of solar panels from aerial or satellite images, and (ii), produce a map of solar panels along with statistics on the number of solar panels. In both approaches we estimated the produced solar power by multiplying capacity by a common factor that measures produced solar energy as a fraction of capacity. We tried to improve on this common factor by using detailed open-source data on location, inclination, and orientation as well as solar irradiance and energy output of a small group of solar panels. Because the aerial images give information on location, inclination, and orientation of nearly all solar panels and we also have

---

7 Because of intricacies of the value-added tax (VAT) rules, private households that install solar panels may apply for a refund of VAT. The advantage for statistical purposes is that this leads to a corresponding entry in the administrative VAT register.

localized data on solar irradiance from the Dutch Meteorological Institute as well as a height register of buildings, we can differentiate the common factor to a large number of classes.

The third approach is an indirect one. We use a time-series analysis of energy consumption and solar irradiance, together with variables such as daily temperature, to estimate the production of solar energy. A difference to the previous approaches is that the required input data on energy consumption is usually only available at some aggregated level, e.g. an electricity distribution station, so the estimated solar energy production for this approach is not on a micro level.

In a fourth approach we try to identify households that installed solar panels by measuring changes in their yearly consumption of electricity over multiple years. If electricity consumption increased, we expect it to be related to the installation of solar panels, and the size of this increase would provide some estimate of the power produced by these solar panels. However, this approach was not scientifically strong enough for our purposes.

All in all, a combination of the first two approaches, together with a refinement of the common production-power factor, will be a sound base for solar energy statistics, and we will most likely follow that path. In addition, if the quality of the third approach is good, it might be a good way to check the completeness of the first two approaches.

10.6 Disclosure Control with Big Data

Traditionally, statistical disclosure control (SDC) by NSIs has focused on tables and microdata collected and produced by the NSIs themselves. However, Big Data have enabled private data companies to assemble databases with detailed information on individuals and enterprises with data from many sources. These databases may be linked deterministically when identifiers such as names and addresses, social security numbers and bank account numbers are in the databases to be linked. These linkages are not without error, e.g. typing errors in the identifiers, more than one unit with the same identifier, and so on. Alternatively, they may be linked probabilistically, by using various characteristics in the databases and by calculating the probability that two records from different databases refer to the same unit; if this probability is higher than a certain threshold value, the records are assumed to refer to the same unit, and if it is lower, then the records are assumed to refer to different units (see Sayers et al. 2016, for a brief introduction). More details may be found in Christen (2012), Harron et al. (2015), and Herzog et al. (2007).

This abundance of data poses new problems for SDC – strategic, methodological, and ethical problems – that need to be addressed but for which no clear-cut solutions exist. For example, should NSIs, when protecting tables or data files against disclosure, account for the possibility that government agencies and private companies will use the NSI data to enrich their own databases and thereby get to know more about their citizens or customers? And what if these enriched data are used to profile citizens so that they may come under suspicion or are denied access to certain services such as loans? Should we use another methodological paradigm than the one we have used so far? Should we consider different disclosure scenarios? Does the changing attitude toward privacy influence the way we should treat our published data? How much existing as well as future data should we take into account when assessing disclosure risks?

Big Data are often characterized by the three Vs: volume (amount of data), velocity (speed of data in and out), and variety (range of data types and sources). Each V poses several questions and issues related to SDC. New techniques probably have to be developed that may have to depend on heuristic methods and sophisticated use of artificial intelligence and machine learning.

10.6.1 Volume

How will NSIs deal with huge amounts of data? In general, they will continue to publish aggregated information and, in that case, the current SDC techniques might still be applicable. However, when Big Data (or excerpts from them) are released as microdata, the current SDC techniques no longer apply: identity disclosure is almost certain. Then methods producing synthetic data may be preferable: use Big Datasets to estimate a model and use that model to generate a synthetic dataset that resembles the original Big Data. Alternatively, one might use other techniques that mask the true values of sensitive variables to just create enough uncertainty about the exact values to make them less sensitive.

10.6.2 Velocity

When data become available more quickly, processing also needs to occur faster. The current SDC techniques can be time consuming when the underlying datasets increase in size and number. Streaming data might lead to streaming statistics, but then we should be able to protect those statistics in real time.

10.6.3 Variety

Big Data may be unstructured, distributed over different places, indirect observations (events instead of units), unclear underlying population, selectivity, and so on. Current SDC methods rely on masking characteristics of individuals so that it seems as if there are more than one similar unit in the population. For example, information about the characteristic zip code might be replaced by information about the region of residence, so that there will be many more individuals with that characteristic, and identification of individuals in the dataset becomes much more difficult. But when the underlying population is not known, this option is not valid. Uncertainty should then be attained by introducing uncertainty on the sensitive information directly, for example, by rounding.

The new European General Data Protection Regulation (GDPR; see EU 2016) gives some general guidance on some of the questions in the previous paragraphs. The most relevant part of the GDPR is Recital 26, which implies that in assessing disclosure risks, NSIs have to consider the availability of external data. Therefore, when the combination of official statistics and external data would allow disclosure of individual data, the NSI, being the *controller* in the sense of the GDPR, would in principle be liable for breaching the GDPR, especially if the external data are more or less publicly available. In such a case, sharper disclosure rules should be applied.

That the combination of data may give rise to serious issues is shown by the discovery by the Australian student Nathan Ruser that the Strava app could be used to detect secret military camps (Hsu 2018). This example does not concern disclosure of individual information, but does show that unforeseen disclosure of sensitive information from readily available public data is already happening and also that with Big Data it is relatively easy to obtain information that from a societal perspective may be undesirable to reveal. Thus, developing further guidelines is important, both on the questions raised in the previous paragraphs and on techniques for preventing disclosure. There is definitely a role here for the European Data Protection Board, the successor to the former Article 29 Working Party.

10.7 The Way Ahead: A Chance for Paradigm Fusion

Big Data offers opportunities for new statistics or redesign of existing statistics:

- their high volume may lead to better accuracy and more details,
- their high velocity may lead to more frequent and more timely statistical estimates, and
- their high variety may give opportunities for statistics in new areas.

Some statistics based on Big Data are useful in their own right, because they are used in policy making or public discussion. An important caveat is that often a Big Data source does not cover the entire target population that is interesting from a statistics user's perspective. Selectivity may be introduced in statistical estimates, which limits the usefulness of Big Data from a statistical perspective. This chapter presented some possible solutions and workarounds. In a general sense, the best Big Data strategy for NSIs is to focus on the combination of all data available (Big

Data as auxiliary data) to give ample opportunities for increasing the frequency, timeliness, and relevance of official statistics.

Big Data also poses several challenges to existing paradigms and methodologies within official statistics. First, statisticians have to cope with features of the data such as abundance, variety, timeliness and dynamism, messiness and uncertainty, and the fact that much of what is generated has no specific question or purpose behind it. Second, new techniques, rooted in artificial intelligence and built into machine learning systems, can automatically detect patterns and build predictive models (Goodfellow, Bengio, and Courville 2016). Third, different algorithms can be applied to a dataset to determine the best model, a radically different approach to that traditionally used wherein analysts select an appropriate method based on their knowledge of techniques and the data (Kitchin 2014). It seems obvious that the approaches within different paradigms are not mutually exclusive. Data science requires computational science, models, and simulation, just as in the field of official statistics where data cannot be published without thorough checking that the intended concept is measured and validated, data are quality controlled, and methods are proven reliable. The strengths and weaknesses of the three types of data (survey, administrative, and Big Data) and associated methodologies offer an opportunity to tackle some existing methodological issues of bias (selection and measurement), causation, and inference as well as some statistical issues such as timeliness.

10.7.1 Measurement and Selection Bias

The strength of Big Data clearly lies in the direct measurement of the phenomenon as opposed to survey data with using a questionnaire and often interviewers leading to measurement errors. Survey data are representative of the study population, and the underlying statistical laws allow inference to the entire population based on the sample. However, survey data often do not allow focus on a lower regional level (if the sample was designed to do so) without great loss of precision and associated with the estimates due to small numbers in each of the cells. Due to the availability of Big Data, this lack of precision at the lower (regional) level decreases with more information obtained by incorporating these Big Data sources in models. Big Data can further help to improve the specificity of the sampling frame to focus samples on hard-to-reach or hard-to-count parts of the study population; this issue is similar to the increase in timeliness and refining of details discussed in Sections 10.4.4, 10.4.5, and 10.5.

The greatest weakness of some Big Data sources is the unknown population behind the source. Often, little information is available on which part of the study population is present in the data source, so one cannot make inferences about the study population. Some solutions are using feature extraction (one extracts features of the population in the source), pattern recognition (one tries to see whether certain patterns in the data can reveal something about the population in the source), and searches for clusters (a variant of the previous strategy, Kitchin 2014). Models are then useful to formulate explicit assumptions about these relationships and to estimate selectivity or coverage issues (Beręsewicz et al. 2018).

When a survey and a Big Data source independently measure an identical target variable and can be linked one-by-one using a unique identifier, the subset of the population in the Big Data source that matches a survey unit can be used. This matching subset of elements in the Big Data source can be used to validate the survey responses and vice versa; to estimate underreporting of the study population and to compare estimates of the outcome's variables, as shown in the previous example (Klingwort et al. 2018).

10.7.2 Timeliness

When a Big Data source is more timely or more frequent than the corresponding official statistics source, it may be used, as in the consumer confidence case (Section 10.5.3), to produce real-time experimental statistics that can later be validated through combination with other data available later to finally produce official statistics. This may also lead to so-called early warnings, giving early signals of imminent economic or social problems, such as a financial crisis (Aldasoro, Borio, and Drehmann 2018), famine, or imminent migrant crisis.

10.7.3 Quality

All types of data suffer from quality issues, and Big Data is no exception. By using established data cleaning methods and by linking with other data sources, we can investigate these data quality issues otherwise left undiscovered. A related difficultly is distinguishing noise from signal in Big Data. Modeling the data-generating process is one way of dealing with this uncertainty. In some cases, the study population is only narrowly represented in the dataset (sometimes known as unbalanced datasets). Oversampling the study population through a survey is one way of compensating for the lack of data on the study population in the Big Data source.

An additional problem may be that the delivery of Big Data sources can be unstable. These data sources, and their quality management, are often open or owned by private organizations. Legal agreements could be made to ascertain the delivery of the data (as was done for administrative data sources in the Netherlands). Meanwhile, one could opt to develop models that can run with or without the (big, open) data being available, in which case one can, depending on the data available, provide more or less precise estimates of the parameters. It is through the stability of the administrative and survey data that further delivery of the statistical information can be guaranteed.

10.7.4 Phenomenon-Oriented Statistics

The fusion of paradigms offers the greatest potential for new statistical output, new ways of measuring, presenting and visualizing societal phenomena, and bringing about a change of culture and mindset in official statistics to allow questions of current official statistics.

In many cases the combination of data will be hampered because some data sources are more likely to deal with units while other types of data are more likely to deal with events. Different sources cover a different part of the study population, and the combination potentially allows a more complete picture of the phenomenon. Additionally, different data will tell different stories (provide different estimates of the measured parameter). In these cases, the fusion may be more likely to be focused on the content to provide a coherent picture of a phenomenon in past and present figures.

Finally, new output based on the combination of large data sources requires an IT infrastructure that allows dealing with large unstructured data to store them and to develop algorithms and methods such as machine learning and deep learning. Simultaneously, one needs to address the skills required to deal with the data and develop the required data science methods. Therefore, training existing personnel is an important part of the process.

10.8 Conclusion

In this chapter we discussed the potential of combining different types of data, methods, and approaches reflected by the traditional (administrative and survey data) and new data sources (Big Data). A paradigm fusion will have to deal with combining data in time and space, develop new data visualization techniques, taking into account that different parts of the study population could be covered in the data, concepts are measured differently, and different data quality issues are at stake. It would also require a careful watch on measures of the privacy protection in the process.

The methods mean unraveling the black boxes of deep and machine learning, tackling the ever-present challenge of distinguishing correlation and causation, using strengths of statistical laws that allow statistical inference with hypothesis free data-driven pattern recognition, and integrating different types of data as part of smaller, more focused, specialized survey methodologies.

The fusion of paradigms (combining all the data and methods available) could mean large cost and response burden reductions. It would also mean a continuation of the present movement toward using more nonprobability samples, unstructured noisy data, and experimental products in a pre-official stage of the statistical production as well as toward further change in the culture and mindset of statisticians. Such fusion is also an excellent opportunity to work in a multi- and interdisciplinary fashion by training statisticians to acquire data science skills and to ensure that data scientists know about statistical laws and representativity, to install IT infrastructure and have IT and visualization experts, and to join sociologists to think about concepts and data governors to ensure data protection.

Finally, NSIs must continue to actively explore Big Data opportunities. Many more sources will emerge and may become available for production of statistics. In the near future, biological data, e.g. on genomes, and medical data, on health and care of individuals, will become available for scientific research and for linking with social data on income, crime, jobs, and so on.[8] The internet of things, consisting of all kinds of large and small devices, is expected to generate a tremendous amount of data from which information on personal behavior can be derived: movement patterns, health aspects, energy consumption, and much more. Sensors in the public space will provide information on the environment like air quality or noise pollution, contributing to the concept of a smart city. Smart manufacturing and smart agriculture refer to industries that take advantage of intensive generation and analysis of large amounts of data. And in addition to physical space, virtual, or cyberspace becomes an increasingly important study object in itself, giving rise to new phenomena like cybercrime or the internet economy. The exploration of opportunities will be accompanied by nontrivial challenges (as argued in this chapter), but especially the more advanced NSIs are in an excellent position to use their traditional experience and high-quality standards in innovative ways.

References

Aldasoro, I., Borio, C., and Drehmann, M. (2018). Early warning indicators of banking crises: expanding the family. *BIS Quarterly Review*: 29–45.

Baumer, B.S., Kaplan, D.T., and Horton, N.J. (2017). *Modern Data Science with R*. Boca Raton, FL: Chapman and Hall/CRC.

---

[8] The Royal Netherlands Academy of Arts and Sciences has placed a proposal (Boomsma et al. 2016) for such a database by universities and Statistics Netherlands on its *Academy Agenda for Large-scale Research Facilities* which must be in place by 2025. This Agenda lists research facilities that could produce new scientific breakthroughs (KNAW 2016).

Belloni, A., Chernozhukov, V., and Hansen, C. (2014). High-dimensional methods and inference on structural and treatment effects. *Journal of Economic Perspectives* 28 (2): 29–50. https://doi.org/10.1257/jep.28.2.29.

Berȩsewicz, M., Lehtonen, R., Reis, F. et al. (2018). *An Overview of Methods for Treating Selectivity in Big Data Sources*. Luxembourg: Eurostat https://doi.org/10.2785/312232.

Berk, R.A. (2016). *Statistical Learning from a Regression Perspective*, 2e. Berlin: Springer.

Biemer, P., and Amaya, A. (2020). Total error frameworks for found data. *In Big Data Meets Survey Science: A Collection of Innovative Methods*. (eds. C.A. Hill, P.P. Biemer, T. D. Buskirk, et al.), 133–162. Hoboken, NJ: Wiley.

Boomsma, D.I., Aarts, C.W.A.M., van Harmelen, F. et al. (2016). M3: from molecule to society and back. Contribution to the Academy Agenda for Large-scale Research Facilities of the Royal Netherlands Academy of Arts and Sciences (KNAW). https://www.knaw.nl/shared/resources/adviezen/bestanden/KNAWAgendaM3.pdf.

Braaksma, B. and Zeelenberg, K. (2015). "Re-make/re-model": should big data change the modelling paradigm in official statistics? *Statistical Journal of the IAOS* 31 (2): 193–202. https://doi.org/10.3233/SJI-150892.

Braaksma, B. and Zeelenberg, K. (2017). *Big Data in Official Statistics*. Hershey, PA: IGI.

Buelens, B., de Wolf, P.-P., and Zeelenberg, K. (2014). Model-based Estimation at Statistics Netherlands. Report. The Hague/Heerlen: Statistics Netherlands.

CBS (Statistics Netherlands) (2018). Social Tension Indicator Based on Social Media. https://www.cbs.nl/en-gb/about-us/innovation/project/social-tensions-and-emotions-in-society.

Choi, H. and Varian, H.A.L. (2012). Predicting the present with Google trends. *The Economic Record* 88: 2–9. https://dx.doi.org/10.1111/j.1475-4932.2012.00809.x.

Christen, P. (2012). *Data Matching: Concepts and Techniques for Record Linkage, Entity Resolution, and Duplicate Detection*. Berlin: Springer https://doi.org/10.1007/978-3-642-31164-2.

Consten, A., Chavdarov, V., Daas, P. et al. (2018). Report Describing the Quality Aspects of Big Data for Official Statistics. ESSNet Big Data, Deliverable 8.2. Luxembourg: Eurostat. https://webgate.ec.europa.eu/fpfis/mwikis/essnetbigdata/index.php/WP8_Reports,_milestones_and_deliverables1.

Daas, P.J.H. and Puts, M.J. (2014). Social Media Sentiment and Consumer Confidence, Statistics Paper Series no. 5. Frankfurt, Germany: European Central Bank. https://www.ecb.europa.eu/pub/pdf/scpsps/ecbsp5.en.pdf.

Daas, P.J.H., Puts, M.J., Buelens, B. et al. (2015). Big data as a source for official statistics. *Journal of Official Statistics* 31 (2): 249–262. https://doi.org/10.1515/Jos-2015-0016.

De Broe, S., Meijers, R., ten Bosch, O. et al. (2019). From experimental to official statistics: the case of solar energy. *Statistical Journal of the IAOS* 35 (3): 371–385.

Efron, B. and Hastie, T. (2016). *Computer Age Statistical Inference: Algorithms, Evidence, and Data Science*. Cambridge, MA: Cambridge University Press.

Energyville (2017). City portal. https://www.energyville.be/en/research/city-portal-your-building-stock-repository-primary-tabs.

European Commission (EC) (2019). Business and consumer surveys. https://ec.europa.eu/info/business-economy-euro/indicators-statistics/economic-databases/business-and-consumer-surveys_en.

European Statistical System (ESS) (2019). ESSnet big data. https://webgate.ec.europa.eu/fpfis/mwikis/essnetbigdata/index.php/ESSnet_Big_Data.

European Union (EU) (2009). Regulation on European statistics. *Official Journal of the European Union* L87 (31 March 2009): 164–173. http://data.europa.eu/eli/reg/2009/223/2015-06-08.

European Union (EU) (2016). General data protection regulation. *Official Journal of the European Union* L119 (4 May 2016): 90ff. http://data.europa.eu/eli/reg/2016/679/oj.

European Union (EU) (2018). *European Statistics Code of Practice*. Luxembourg: Eurostat http://ec.europa.eu/eurostat/web/quality/overview https://doi.org/10.2785/798269.

Eurostat (2016). Statistics explained—glossary: enterprise. http://ec.europa.eu/eurostat/statistics-explained/index.php/Glossary:Enterprise.

Eurostat (2018). Individuals—mobile internet access. http://appsso.eurostat.ec.europa.eu/nui/show.do?query=BOOKMARK_DS-056936_QID_-49726DCB_UID_-3F171EB0&layout=TIME,C,X,0;IND_TYPE,L,Y,0;INDIC_IS,L,Z,0;UNIT,L,Z,1;GEO,L,Z,2;INDICATORS,C,Z,3;&zSelection=DS-056936GEO,EU28;DS-056936INDICATORS,OBS_FLAG;DS-056936INDIC_IS,I_IUMP;DS-056936UNIT,PC_IND;&rankName1=UNIT_1_2_-1_2&rankName2=INDICATORS_1_2_-1_2&rankName3=GEO_1_2_0_1&rankName4=INDIC-IS_1_2_0_1&rankName5=TIME_1_0_0_0&rankName6=IND-TYPE_1_2_0_1&sortC=ASC_-1_FIRST&rStp=&cStp=&rDCh=&cDCh=&rDM=true&cDM=true&footnes=false&empty=false&wai=false&time_mode=NONE&time_most_recent=false&lang=EN&cfo=%23%23%2C%23%23.%23%23.

EZ (Ministerie van Economische Zaken: Ministry of Economic Affairs) (2016). *Energieagenda: Naar Een CO^2-arme Energievoorziening (Energy Agenda: Towards Zero-CO^2 Energy Supply)*. The Hague: Ministry of Economic Affairs https://www.rijksoverheid.nl/onderwerpen/duurzame-energie/documenten/rapporten/2016/12/07/ea.

Fan, J., Han, F., and Liu, H. (2014). Challenges of big data analysis. *National Science Review* 1 (2): 293–314. https://doi.org/10.1093/nsr/nwt032.

Fasulo, A., Guandalini, A., and Terribili, M.D. (2017). Google trends for nowcasting quarterly household consumption expenditure. *Rivista Italiana di Economia Demografia e Statistica* 71 (4): 5–14. http://www.sieds.it/index.php/2018/01/01/rivista-lxxi-4-ottobre-dicembre-2017.

Fornaro, P., Luomaranta, H., and Saarinen, L. (2017). Nowcasting Finnish turnover indexes using firm-level data. ETLA Working Paper 46. Helsinki: Research Institute of the Finnish Economy. https://www.etla.fi/en/publications/nowcasting-finnish-turnover-indexes-using-firm-level-data/.

Gelman, A., Carlin, J.B., Stern, H.S. et al. (2013). *Bayesian Data Analysis*. Boca Raton, FL: Chapman and Hall/CRC https://doi.org/10.1201/b16018.

Goodfellow, I., Bengio, Y., and Courville, A. (2016). *Deep Learning*. Cambridge, MA: MIT Press https://www.deeplearningbook.org.

Groves, R.M. (2011). Three eras of survey research. *Public Opinion Quarterly* 75 (5): 861–871. https://doi.org/10.1093/poq/nfr057.

Harron, K., Goldstein, H., and Dibben, C. (2015). *Methodological Developments in Data Linkage*. Chichester: Wiley https://doi.org/10.1002/9781119072454.

Heerschap, N.M., Ortega Azurduy, S.A., Priem, A.H. et al. (2014). Innovation of tourism statistics through the use of new big data sources. Paper prepared for the Global Forum on Tourism Statistics, Prague. http://www.tsf2014prague.cz/assets/downloads/Paper%201.2_Nicolaes%20Heerschap_NL.pdf.

Herzog, T.N., Scheuren, F.J., and Winkler, W.E. (2007). *Data Quality and Record Linkage Techniques*. Berlin: Springer https://doi.org/10.1007/0-387-69505-2.

Hsu, J. (2018). The Strava heatmap and the end of secrets. *Wired*. https://www.wired.com/story/strava-heat-map-military-bases-fitness-trackers-privacy.

International Statistical Institute (ISI) (1985). Declaration on Professional Ethics, revised edition 2010. http://www.isi-web.org/about-isi/professional-ethics.

Japec, L., Kreuter, F., Berg, M. et al. (2015a). *AAPOR Report on Big Data*. Oakbrook Terrace, IL: American Association for Public Opinion Research https://www.aapor.org/Education-Resources/Reports/Big-Data.aspx.

Japec, L., Kreuter, F., Berg, M. et al. (2015b). Big data in survey research. *Public Opinion Quarterly* 79 (4): 839–880. https://doi.org/10.1093/poq/nfv039.

Kapetanios, G., Marcellino, M., and Petrova, K. (2018). *Analysis of the Most Recent Modelling Techniques for Big Data with Particular Attention to Bayesian Ones*. Luxembourg: Eurostat https://doi.org/10.2785/679114.

Kitchin, R. (2014). Big data, new epistemologies and paradigm shifts. *Big Data & Society* 1 (1) https://doi.org/10.1177/2053951714528481.

Klingwort, J., Buelens, B., and Schnell, R. (2018). Capture-recapture techniques for transport survey estimate adjustment using road sensor data. Paper presented at BigSurv18, Barcelona, Spain (25–27 October).

Klunder, G.A., Taale, H., Kester, L. et al. (2017). Improvement of network performance by in-vehicle routing using floating car data. *Journal of Advanced Transportation* 2017: 1–16. https://doi.org/10.1155/2017/8483750.

Koninklijke Nederlandse Akademie van Wetenschappen (KNAW) (2016). *Thirteen Selected Facilities and Three Honourable Mentions*. Royal Netherlands Academy of Arts and Sciences https://www.knaw.nl/en/advisory-work/copy_of_knaw-agenda-grootschalige-onderzoeksfaciliteiten-13-geselecteerde-faciliteiten?set_language=en.

Lazer, D., Kennedy, R., King, G. et al. (2014). Big Data. The parable of Google flu: traps in big data analysis. *Science* 343 (6176): 1203–1205. https://doi.org/10.1126/science.1248506.

Lucas, R.E. (1976). *Econometric Policy Evaluation: A Critique*, Carnegie-Rochester Conference Series on Public Policy. New York: Elsevier.

Luomaranta, H., Puts, M., Grygiel, G. et al. (2018). *Report About the Impact of One (or More) Big Data Source (and Other) Sources on Economic Indicators. ESSNet Big Data, Deliverable 6.6*. Luxembourg: Eurostat https://webgate.ec.europa.eu/fpfis/mwikis/essnetbigdata/index.php/WP6_Reports,_milestones_and_deliverables1.

McLaren, C. and Drew, S. (2015). Practical guidance on modelling for the implementation of changes to National Accounts outputs. ONS Methodology Working Paper Series No. 2. https://www.ons.gov.uk/methodology/methodologicalpublications/generalmethodology/onsworkingpaperseries.

Meng, X. (2014). *A Trio of Inference Problems that Could Win You a Nobel Prize in Statistics (If You Help Fund It)*. Boca Raton, FL: CRC Press https://www.taylorfrancis.com/books/9781482204988/chapters/10.1201/b16720-52.

Meng, X. (2018). Statistical paradises and paradoxes in big data (I): law of large populations, big data paradox, and the 2016 U.S. presidential election. *Annals of Applied Statistics* 12 (2): 685–726. https://doi.org/10.1214/18-AOAS1161SF.

Naccarato, A., Falorsi, S., Loriga, S. et al. (2018). Combining official and Google trends data to forecast the Italian youth unemployment rate. *Technological Forecasting and Social Change* 130: 114–122. https://doi.org/10.1016/j.techfore.2017.11.022.

Nickerson, D.W. and Rogers, T. (2014). Political campaigns and big data. *Journal of Economic Perspectives* 28 (2): 51–74. https://doi.org/10.1257/jep.28.2.51.

Nymand-Andersen, P. and Pantelidis, E. (2018). Google Econometrics: Nowcasting Euro Area Car Sales and Big Data Quality Requirements. Statistics Paper 30, Frankfurt: European Central Bank.

Oostrom, L., Walker, A.N., Staats, B. et al. (2016). Measuring the Internet Economy in the Netherlands: A Big Data Analysis. Discussion Paper 2016-14. Heerlen: Statistics Netherlands. https://www.cbs.nl/nl-nl/achtergrond/2016/41/measuring-the-internet-economy-in-the-netherlands.

Reimsbach-Kounatze, C. (2015). The Proliferation of "Big Data" and Implications for Official Statistics and Statistical Agencies: A Preliminary Analysis. OECD Digital

Economy Papers 245. Paris, France: OECD.
https://doi.org/10.1787/5js7t9wqzvg8-en.

Sayers, A., Ben-Shlomo, Y., Blom, A.W. et al. (2016). Probabilistic record linkage. *International Journal of Epidemiology* 45 (3): 954–964.
https://doi.org/10.1093/ije/dyv322.

Tennekes, M. (2018). Statistical inference on mobile phone network data. Presentation at the 11th Conference of the European Forum for Geography and Statistics, Helsinki (17 October).
https://www.efgs2018.fi/index.html#subpage-199.

Tennekes, M. and Offermans, M.P.W. (2014). Daytime population estimations based on mobile phone metadata. Paper presented at the Joint Statistical Meetings, Boston, MA. http://www.amstat.org/meetings/jsm/2014/onlineprogram/AbstractDetails.cfm?abstractid=311959.

Tran, U.S., Andel, R., Niederkrotenthaler, T. et al. (2017). Low validity of Google trends for behavioral forecasting of national suicide rates. *PLoS One* 12 (8): e0183149. https://doi.org/10.1371/journal.pone.0183149.

UN-ECE (2013). Classification of types of big data. https://statswiki.unece.org/display/bigdata/Classification+of+Types+of+Big+Data.

UN-ECE (2014). A suggested framework for the quality of big data. https://statswiki.unece.org/download/attachments/108102944/Big%20Data%20Quality%20Framework%20-%20final-%20Jan08-2015.pdf?version=1&modificationDate=1420725063663&api=v2.

United Nations (UN) (1991). Fundamental principles of official statistics. Revised edition 2014. http://unstats.un.org/unsd/dnss/gp/fundprinciples.aspx.

United Nations (UN) (2017). Handbook on the use of mobile phone data for official statistics. Draft, UN Global Working Group on Big Data for Official Statistics. https://unstats.un.org/bigdata/taskteams/mobilephone.

van den Brakel, J., Söhler, E., Daas, P. et al. (2017). Social media as a data source for official statistics: the Dutch consumer confidence index. *Survey Methodology* 43 (2): 183–210.
https://www150.statcan.gc.ca/n1/en/catalogue/12-001-X201700254871.

van Ruth, F.J. (2014). Traffic Intensity as Indicator of Regional Economic Activity. Discussion paper 2014–2021. The Hague: Statistics Netherlands.
https://www.cbs.nl/nl-nl/achtergrond/2014/34/traffic-intensity-as-indicator-of-regional-economic-activity.

Varian, H.R. (2014). Big data: new tricks for econometrics. *Journal of Economic Perspectives* 28 (2): 3–28. https://doi.org/10.1257/jep.28.2.3.

Zeelenberg, K. (2016). Methodological challenges in official statistics. *Proceedings of the Statistics Canada 2016 International Methodology Symposium*, Gatineau, Québec, Canada: Statistics Canada (22–24 March).

Further Reading

Biemer, P., Trewin, D., Bergdahl, H., and Japec, L. (2014). A system for managing the quality of official statistics. *Journal of Official Statistics* 30 (3): 381–415. https://doi.org/10.2478/JOS-2014-0022.

CBS (Statistics Netherlands) (2017). *Nationale energieverkenning 2017 (National Energy Outlook 2017)*. The Hague: Statistics Netherlands https://www.cbs.nl/nl-nl/publicatie/2017/42/nationale-energieverkenning-2017.

Consten, A., Chavdarov, V., Daas, P. et al. (2018). Report Describing the Methodology of Using Big Data for Official Statistics and the Most Important Questions for Future Studies. ESSNet Big Data, Deliverable 8.4. Luxembourg: Eurostat. https://webgate.ec.europa.eu/fpfis/mwikis/essnetbigdata/index.php/WP8_Reports,_milestones_and_deliverables1.

Daas, P.J.H., Burger, J., Le, Q. et al. (2016). Profiling of Twitter Users: A Big Data Selectivity Study. Discussion Paper 2016-06. The Hague/Heerlen: Statistics Netherlands. https://www.cbs.nl/en-gb/background/2016/21/profiling-of-twitter-users-a-big-data-selectivity-study.

de Jonge, E., van Pelt, M., and Roos, M. (2012). Time Patterns, Geospatial Clustering and Mobility Statistics Based on Mobile Phone Network Data. Discussion Paper 2012-2014. Heerlen: Statistics Netherlands. https://www.cbs.nl/nl-nl/onze-diensten/methoden/onderzoeksomschrijvingen/aanvullende%20onderzoeksbeschrijvingen/time-patterns-geospatial-clustering-and-mobility-statistics.

De Meersman, F., Seynaeve, G., Debusschere, M. et al. (2016). Assessing the Quality of Mobile Phone Data as a Source of Statistics. Paper presented at the European Conference on Quality in Official Statistics, Madrid, 2 June 2016. http://www.ine.es/q2016/docs/q2016Final00163.pdf.

de Wolf, P.-P. and Zeelenberg, K. (2015). Challenges for Statistical Disclosure Control in a World with Big Data and Open Data. Invited paper for the 60th World Statistics Congress. http://isiwsc2015.org/components/com_users/views/registration/tmpl/media/uploadedFiles/paper/63/1973/IPS045-P1-S.pdf.

Lane, J., Stodden, V., Bender, S., and Nissenbaum, H. (2014). *Privacy, Big Data, and the Public Good: Frameworks for Engagement*. Cambridge: Cambridge University Press.

Struijs, P. (2016). *BIG Data for Official Statistics*. Vitoria-Gasteiz: Eustat http://www.eustat.eus/prodserv/seminario_i.html.

Struijs, P., Braaksma, B., and Daas, P.J.H. (2014). Official statistics and Big Data. *Big Data & Society* 1 (1): 1–6. https://doi.org/10.1177/2053951714538417.

UN-ECE (2013). What Does "Big Data" Mean for Official Statistics? High-Level Group for the Modernisation of Statistical Production and Services. http://www1.unece.org/stat/platform/pages/viewpage.action?pageId=77170622.

Vaccari, C. (2016). *Big Data in Official Statistics*. Saarbrücken: Lambert.

Xie, X. and Meng, X.-L. (2017). Dissecting multiple imputation from a multi-phase inference perspective: what happens when God's, imputer's and analyst's models are uncongenial? *Statistica Sinica* 27 (4): 1485–1544. https://doi.org/10.5705/ss.2014.067.

# 11

Mining the New Oil for Official Statistics[1]

Siu-Ming Tam[1,2], Jae-Kwang Kim[3], Lyndon Ang[1], and Han Pham[1]

[1] *Australian Bureau of Statistics, ABS House, Belconnen, ACT 2617, Australia*
[2] *School of Mathematics, National Institute for Applied Statistical Research, Australian University of Wollongong, Keiraville, NSW 2500, Australia*
[3] *Department of Statistics, Iowa State University, Ames, IA 50011, USA*

11.1 Introduction

At the 2006 Senior Marketers' Conference (Haupt 2016), a UK mathematician, Clive Humby, pronounced that "Data is the new oil. It's valuable, but if unrefined it cannot really be used. It has to be changed into gas, plastic, chemicals, etc. to create a valuable entity that drives profitable activity; so must data be broken down, analyzed for it to have value." We agree. Like oil, how the data is created initially and then how it is "refined" for statistics production will determine its public value. Indeed, in official statistics, data that are not representative of the population on which public and private decisions are made, or data that are susceptible to measurement errors, are of limited value at best. While official statisticians have been using administrative data in the production of official statistics for decades, only recently have they begun developing new ways of refining the ubiquitous Big Data, defined by Eurostat (2014) as "large amount of data produced very quickly by a high number of diverse sources," which include the Internet of Things, sensors, and social media.

Suppose we wish to estimate some finite population parameters, e.g. the finite population mean, of a target population based on a dataset, where the size of the target population is known. If the dataset comes from a probability sample, the estimation is straightforward, and we can draw on the extensive literature on survey sampling developed over the past 50 years, e.g. Cochran (1977),

---

1 The views expressed in this chapter are those of the authors' and do not necessarily reflect the views of the Australian Bureau of Statistics.

Big Data Meets Survey Science: A Collection of Innovative Methods, First Edition. Edited by Craig A. Hill, Paul P. Biemer, Trent D. Buskirk, Lilli Japec, Antje Kirchner, Stas Kolenikov, and Lars E. Lyberg.
© 2021 John Wiley & Sons, Inc. Published 2021 by John Wiley & Sons, Inc.

Fuller (2009), Särndal, Swensson, and Wretman (1992), or Chambers and Clark (2012) for estimation and analysis. However, if the dataset comes from a nonprobability sample, e.g. a Big Data source, the estimation is less straightforward, because the theory for making inference with nonprobability samples is still being developed. Tam and Clarke (2015) and Pfeffermann (2015) discussed the methodological challenges of using Big Data in producing official statistics, as well as Thompson (2018).

Methods that combine information of two independent data sources from the same target population for inference are referred to as data integration. Rivers (2007) proposed mass imputation based on nearest-neighbor methods for data integration. Zhang (2012) developed a statistical theory for register-based statistics and data integration. Assuming missing-at-random (Rubin 1976) for inclusion, or otherwise, of observations in the nonprobability sample, Bethlehem (2015) discussed practical issues in sample matching to address selection bias in the nonprobability sample; Kim and Wang (2019) considered a weighting adjustment method for handling Big Data based on parametric model assumptions on the selection mechanism for the Big Data source; and Chen, Li, and Wu (2018) developed a doubly robust estimator for nonprobability samples, assuming relevant auxiliary information is available from an independent random sample. Lohr and Raghunathan (2017) and Thompson (2019) provided reviews of issues with data integration. Where the variable of interest is binary, Tam and Kim (2018) developed a method to combine data from a nonprobability sample and a random sample, without assuming missing-at-random for the nonprobability sample inclusion mechanism. Combining data from different sources to overcome coverage issues in nonprobability or Big Data sources and to improve the efficiency of estimates is an emerging hot topic for statistical research.

In this chapter, we extend the results of Tam and Kim (2018) to continuous variables, again without making any missing-at-random assumptions on the inclusion mechanism for the nonprobability sample. In addition, we also extend data integration methods to address measurement errors in the data source (henceforth denoted as B), the simple random sample (denoted by A), and nonresponse biases in A. In Section 11.2, we briefly describe the methods Tam and Kim (2018) used. In Section 11.3, we show how the two data sources, B and A, can be combined to address undercoverage bias in B and improve the efficiency in estimating the population total of the target population using A. In Section 11.4, we discuss the estimation of the population total when measurement errors occur in data source B or in the probability sample A. In Section 11.5, we extend the results of Section 11.4, where unit nonresponses occur in the probability sample A. In Section 11.6, we present simulation results to illustrate the methods. Section 11.7 discusses two applications of the methods in official statistics. Section 11.8 discusses certain limitations and Section 11.9 offers conclusions.

11.2 Statistical Inference for Binary Variables from Nonprobability Samples

Couper (2013), Keiding and Louis (2016) and Elliott and Valliant (2017) are recent examples of the literature on challenges in using nonprobability samples for making inferences. One challenge is addressing undercoverage bias, which is essentially a missing data problem. Let the row vector, $Y' = (y_1, \ldots, y_N)$, summarize the value of each of the N units of the target population, $U = \{y_1, \ldots, y_N\}$. Also let the row vector, $\delta' = (\delta_1, \ldots, \delta_N)$, denote the inclusion indicator of the N units of the target population, where $\delta_i = 1$ if the unit is in the nonprobability sample, or 0 otherwise.

We now partition the population, U, into two strata, B and C, one comprising all the observations in the nonprobability sample (or a Big Data source) B, and the second component comprising the remaining units of the population, C, i.e. the complement of B in the target population. We can likewise partition Y into $Y' = (Y'_B, Y'_C)$, where the subscript B denotes the population units included in B, and C denotes the units in C. Following Smith (1983), it can be shown that if $f(\delta \mid Y_B, Y_C) = f(\delta \mid Y_B)$, i.e. the inclusion mechanism for the data in the nonprobability sample B does not depend on the data in C, it can be ignored for finite population inference. This condition, known as missing-at-random (Rubin 1976), holds if the data source B comes from a probability sample. However, for many nonprobability samples, e.g. social media sources, the above condition does not generally hold. Typically, these sources consist of data that self-selected participants have volunteered, and their participation, or otherwise, in the nonprobability sample may depend on Y_C. Where this is the case, inference has to allow for the generally unknown inclusion mechanism by using modeling assumptions.

Where the variable of interest, Y, is binary, the finite population mean becomes a proportion i.e. $p = \Pr(Y = 1)$, and it can be shown that the proportion of $Y = 1$ compiled from data source B is $p_B = \frac{\Re p}{\Re p + (1-p)}$, where $\Re = \frac{\Pr(\delta_i = 1 \mid Y_i = 1)}{\Pr(\delta_i = 1 \mid Y_i = 0)}$ measures the "representativeness" of the data source B in terms of the Y characteristic. Hence, the bias of p_B is $(p_B - p) = \frac{p(1-p)(\Re - 1)}{1 + (\Re - 1)p}$ (Puza and O'Neill 2006; Raghunathan 2015).

The bias vanishes when $\Re = 1$, i.e. when data source B is representative of the target population. However, when $\Re > 1$, units whose Y values equal to one are more represented than those whose Y values equal to zero in B, and consequently, the estimate of $p = \Pr(Y = 1)$ from B is biased upwards, i.e. the estimate p_B, is larger than the true p. Likewise, when $\Re < 1$, units whose Y values equal to one are less represented than units whose Y values equal to zero and the estimate, p_B, is smaller than the true p.

Assuming that there exists an independent (of B) simple random sample, A, of the target population U; that the sizes of data sources B, A and the target population, i.e. N_B, n and N respectively, are known; and that $\delta' = (\delta_1, \ldots, \delta_N)$ is fully observed for the units in A, i.e. through matching the units in A against those in B, we know which of the units in A are included in B, Tam and Kim (2018) showed that $\Re$ and p can be estimated, respectively, by:

$$\hat{\Re} = \frac{n_{B1}/n_1}{n_{B0}/n_0} \quad \text{and} \quad \hat{p} = \frac{p_B}{\hat{\Re} - p_B \hat{\Re} + p_B}$$

where $p_B = \frac{\sum_{i \in B} y_i}{N_B}$, n_{B1}, n_1, n_{B0} and n_0 are defined in Table 11.1.

Let the structure of the target population be represented by Table 11.2, where the counts, N_{B1}, N_{B0}, N_B, N_C and N are assumed known, but N_{C1}, N_{C0}, N_1 and N_0 are unknown.

Using the data structures in Tables 11.1 and 11.2, an alternative estimator of p is possible. From

$$p = \Pr(Y = 1 \mid \delta = 1) \Pr(\delta = 1) + \Pr(Y = 1 \mid \delta = 0) \Pr(\delta = 0)$$
$$= p_B W_B + p_C (1 - W_B)$$

where $p_B = N_{B1}/N_B$, $W_B = N_B/N$ and $p_C = \Pr(Y = 1 \mid \delta = 0)$, an alternative estimator of p is given by $\hat{p} = p_B W_B + \hat{p}_C (1 - W_B)$, where $\hat{p}_C = n_{C1}/n_C$.

The above equations outline two different approaches for mining the data source B for estimating p. In the first approach, through $\hat{\Re}$, a (nonlinear) adjustment is

Table 11.1 Breakdown of sample size, n, by δ and Y.

	$\delta = 1$	$\delta = 0$	Total
$Y=1$	n_{B1}	n_{C1}	n_1
$Y=0$	n_{B0}	n_{C0}	n_0
Total	n_B	n_C	n

Table 11.2 Breakdown of the target population size, N, by δ and Y.

	$\delta = 1$	$\delta = 0$	Total
$Y=1$	N_{B1}	N_{C1}	N_1
$Y=0$	N_{B0}	N_{C0}	N_0
Total	N_B	N_C	N

made to p_B to estimate p. In contrast, the second approach estimates p by taking a convex combination of p_B and $\hat{p}_C$, and the resultant $\hat{p}$ is known as a poststratified estimator (PSE). In the latter approach, the method implicitly recognizes that the target population consists of two strata, i.e. a stratum comprising data source B in which the data is fully observed, and a stratum C consisting of units in the population but not in the data source B, i.e. $C = U \cap \bar{B}$. The units in C are not observed. The stratifying variable to separate one stratum from another in this case is δ. In the sequel, we will use B to represent the fully observed stratum, and data source B, interchangeably. Estimation by poststratification extends naturally to nonbinary variables, and will be used in the sequel to extend the results of Tam and Kim (2018) to integrate data sources consisting of continuous variables.

11.3 Integrating Data Source B Subject to Undercoverage Bias

Recalling that the population is considered to be divided into two strata, B, which is fully observed, and C, which is not observed, the total of the variable of interest in U is the sum of the known total in B and the unknown total in C. The main idea of this section is to use a random sample, A, to estimate the total of the units in C. To illustrate ideas, we assume in this section that B is observed without measurement error, and A with no measurement error and no unit nonresponse. These assumptions will be relaxed in Sections 11.4 and 11.5, respectively.

Let the variable of interest, Y, be a continuous variable and the population total to be estimated is $T = \sum_1^N y_i$. Then $T = \sum_{i \in B} y_i + \sum_{i \in C} y_i = \sum_1^N \delta_i y_i + \sum_1^N (1 - \delta_i) y_i$. Using the sample units in $A \cap C$, the total for the stratum C can be estimated by

$$N_C \frac{\sum_{i \in A \cap C} d_i y_i}{\sum_{i \in A \cap C} d_i} = N_C \frac{\sum_{i \in A} d_i (1 - \delta_i) y_i}{\sum_{i \in A} d_i (1 - \delta_i)}$$

where $d_i = \pi_i^{-1}$ is the weight, and π_i is the first-order inclusion probability of unit i. Hence, the population total can be estimated by

$$\hat{T}_P = \sum_1^N \delta_i y_i + N_C \frac{\sum_{i \in A} d_i (1 - \delta_i) y_i}{\sum_{i \in A} d_i (1 - \delta_i)} \tag{11.1}$$

$\hat{T}_P$ is known in the literature as a PSE, with δ as the stratifying variable.

If the size of the simple random sample, n, is such that the sampling fraction, n/N, is small, it can be shown that

$$\text{Var}(\hat{T}_P) \approx (1 - W_B) \frac{N^2}{n} s_C^2$$

where $S_C^2 = N_C^{-1} \sum_1^N (1-\delta_i)(y_i - \overline{Y}_C)^2$, $\overline{Y}_C = N_C^{-1} \sum_1^N (1-\delta_i)y_i$. Let $S^2 = N^{-1} \sum_1^N (y_i - \overline{Y})^2$ and $\hat{T}_A = N\sum_{i \in A} y_i/n$. We have $\frac{\text{Var}(\hat{T}_P)}{\text{Var}(\hat{T}_A)} = (1-W_B)\frac{S_C^2}{S^2} \ll 1$, if $S_C^2 \approx S^2$. Hence, by treating stratum B as a fully observed stratum, and combining it with the sample units in $A \cap C$, we can effectively increase the sample size of A by a factor of $1/(1-W_B)$ if $S_C^2 \approx S^2$. For example, if $W_B = 0.5$, this factor is 2 and if $W_B = 0.8$ the factor is 5. The efficiency of the estimation can be significantly enhanced by ingesting Big Data into the random sample.

Define the Regression Data Integration (RegDI) estimator of T, $\hat{T}_{\text{RegDI}}$, by $\hat{T}_{\text{RegDI}} = \sum_{i \in A} w_i y_i$, for which the weights, w_i, are determined by minimizing $Q(d, w)$ where

$$Q(d, w) = \sum_{i \in A} d_i \left(\frac{w_i}{d_i} - 1\right)^2 \tag{11.2}$$

subject to

$$\sum_{i \in A} w_i x_i = \sum_1^N x_i \tag{11.3}$$

where $x_i = (1-\delta_i, \delta_i, \delta_i y_i)'$ for $i = 1, \ldots, N$. In this formulation, we require the weights, w_i, of $\hat{T}_{\text{RegDI}}$ to be close to the Horvitz–Thompson weights, d_i, so as to obtain asymptotic design unbiasedness, as well as calibrated to the known benchmarks, $\sum_1^N x_i = \left(N_C, N_B, \sum_1^N \delta_i y_i\right)'$.

$\hat{T}_{\text{RegDI}}$ is also known in the literature as a calibration estimator (Deville and Särndal 1992). There is a close relationship between a PSE and a calibration estimator. For example, Deville, Särndal, and Sautory (1993) observed that the PSE defined in Eq. (11.1) is a special case of the calibration estimator, and Zhang (2010) showed that "calibration is the relaxed stratification" in the sense that the interaction effects of a saturated model used for stratification are removed in the calibration model. Formally, it can be shown by tedious algebra (Kim and Tam 2018) that $\hat{T}_{\text{RegDI}}$ is algebraically equivalent to $\hat{T}_P$. This equivalence will be used in Sections 11.4 and 11.5 to extend the methods outlined in this section to other complex situations, e.g. measurement errors in the data of B, or A, by changing Eq. (11.3) suitably to calibrate the weights to other relevant benchmarks.

11.4 Integrating Data Sources Subject to Measurement Errors

In this section, we relax the assumptions that B and A are not subject to measurement errors. In the first case, B is subject to both undercoverage and measurement errors. However, noting in Eq. (11.3) that the role played by B in the RegDI estimator, $\hat{T}_{\text{RegDI}}$, is a benchmarking variable, all one needs to do is to replace $x_i = (1 - \delta_i, \delta_i, \delta_i y_i)'$ in Eq. (11.3) by $x_i = (1 - \delta_i, \delta_i, \delta_i y_i^*)'$ where y_i^* is observed instead of y_i in B.

Formally, we estimate T by $\hat{T}_{\text{RegDI}} = \sum_{i \in A} w_i y_i$, where w_i is still required to minimize $Q(d, w)$ of Eq. (11.2), but subject to a new calibration constraint: $\sum_{i \in A} w_i(1 - \delta_i, \delta_i, \delta_i y_i^*) = \sum_1^N (1 - \delta_i, \delta_i, \delta_i y_i^*)$. In this formulation, we "mine" the data from the nonprobability sample by calibrating the estimator to the benchmark, $\sum_1^N \delta_i y_i^*$ from B.

For the case where the units in A are measured with errors, while the w_i's derived from Eqs. (11.2) and (11.3) need no change, we now estimate T by $\hat{T}_{\text{RegDI}} = \sum_{i \in A} w_i \hat{y}_i$, where $\hat{y}_i$ is the predicted value for y_i based on a measurement error model for $i \in A$. How do we build the measurement error model? Assuming that $A \cap B$ is not an empty set – a reasonable assumption to make when the data source B is big – then for every $i \in A \cap B$, we have two observations, namely, y_i observed without measurement error in B, and y_i^* observed with measurement error in A. The set of (y_i^*, y_i) for $i \in A \cap B$ constitutes the training dataset for building the measurement error model.

The case of observing y_i^* but not y_i, in A may not be unusual, e.g. if the data in A is collected annually, and the data source B is available monthly, then the estimator using the observed data from A can be up to one year out of date for estimating the contemporary population total.

Formally, if $y_i^* = \beta_0 + \beta_1 y_i + e_i$, $e_i \sim (0, \sigma^2)$, then we estimate β_0 and β_1 by the following pseudo estimating equation for (β_0, β_1) using data from the training dataset:

$$\sum_{i \in A} w_i \delta_i (y_i^* - \beta_0 - \beta_1 y_i)(1, y_i) = (0, 0) \qquad (11.4)$$

The use of the training dataset in Eq. (11.4) is justified if the mechanism for $\delta_i = 1$ depends on y_i but not y_i^* (Pfeffermann, Krieger, and Rinott 1998). In some applications, e.g. estimating the yield of a crop using satellite imagery data, in which y_i is the yield of a crop for a small geographical area from agricultural surveys, and y_i^* is the corresponding satellite imagery data, the assumption of $\delta_i = 1$ depending on y_i and not y_i^*, is reasonable.

11.5 Integrating Probability Sample *A* Subject to Unit Nonresponse

Now consider the common situation where the probability sample, A, suffers from unit nonresponse. To illustrate, we assume that there are no measurement errors in B and A. In this case, undercoverage bias exists in B, and nonresponse bias in A.

Where an auxiliary variable, z_i, is available and observed throughout A, the literature (Särndal and Lundström 2005; Kim and Riddles 2012; Brick 2013) suggests using nonresponse weighting adjustment based on a missing-at-random assumption. Combining nonresponse adjustment with calibration, we propose a response-propensity-adjusted RegDI estimator of the form: $\hat{T}_{\text{RegDI2}} = \sum_{i \in A} r_i w_i y_i$, where r_i ($=0,1$) is a response indicator, and the weights, w_i are adjusted for nonresponse while fulfilling calibration constraints similar to Eq. (11.3). We will extend the weight adjustments to missing-not-at-random (MNAR) situations.

To begin, we consider the following MNAR model:

$$\Pr(r_i = 1 \mid z_i, y_i) = p(z_i, y_i \mid \phi) \tag{11.5}$$

where $0 < p(z_i, y_i \mid \phi) \leq 1$, and ϕ is an unknown parameter. If $\hat{\phi}$ is a consistent estimator of ϕ, we can use $\hat{p}^{-1}(z_i, y_i \mid \hat{\phi})$ as the nonresponse adjustment factor to the weights of the units in sample A – see Remark 11.1.

We use the two-step calibration approach outlined in Dupont (1995), i.e. first to determine the unknown parameter of the MNAR model, and second to determine the weights subject to certain calibration constraints. We illustrate the ideas using a logistic regression model for Eq. (11.5):

$$\Pr(r_i = 1 \mid z_i, y_i) = \frac{\exp(\phi_Z z_i + \phi_Y y_i)}{1 + \exp(\phi_Z z_i + \phi_Y y_i)}$$

Step 1: Estimate ϕ from the calibration equation

$$\sum_{i \in A} d_i \frac{r_i}{p(z_i, y_i; \phi)} (z_i, \delta_i y_i) = \sum_{i \in A} d_i (z_i, \delta_i y_i) \tag{11.6}$$

Noting that $\sum_{i \in A} d_i \delta_i y_i = \sum_{i \in A \cap B} d_i y_i$, even though y_i is missing from the random sample A, we can replace it by the corresponding value observed from B. Equation (11.6) requires that the unknown parameter, ϕ, be determined in such a way that the response-propensity-adjusted Horvitz–Thompson estimator (the left hand side of Eq. (11.6)) has the same numerical value as the Horvitz–Thompson estimator (the right hand side of Eq. (11.6)) with no nonresponse in A.

Step 2: Compute the calibration weight, w_i, by minimizing

$$Q_2(d_2, w) = \sum_{i \in A} r_i d_{i2} \left(\frac{w_i}{d_{i2}} - 1 \right)^2$$

subject to $\sum_{i \in A} r_i w_i x_i = \sum_1^N x_i$, where $x_i = (1 - \delta_i, \delta_i, \delta_i y_i)$, $d_{i2} = d_i / \hat{p}_i$ and $\hat{p}_i = \hat{p}(z_i, y_i; \hat{\phi})$. This step requires, as before, the calibration weight w_i to be "close" to the response-propensity-adjusted weight d_{i2}.

The final estimator, the two-step RegDI estimator, is then

$$\hat{T}_{\text{RegDI2}} = \sum_{i \in A} r_i w_i y_i$$

where w_i is derived from Step 2 above, and $\hat{\phi}$ from Eq. (11.6) for calculating d_{i2}.

Remark 11.1 If

$$r_i \perp \delta_i \mid (z_i, y_i) \tag{11.7}$$

that is, r_i is independent of δ_i, given z_i and y_i, we can show that the expectation of the left and right sides of Eq. (11.6) is identical, and hence $\hat{\phi}$ estimated from Eq. (11.6) is consistent. We can also show that Eq. (11.7) is satisfied if Eq. (11.5) is correctly specified, and there is no underspecification of variables in the model, or if the sampling mechanism for B depends only on (Z, Y) (Kim and Tam 2018). The use of Eq. (11.6) to estimate ϕ is similar in spirit to the methods in Kott and Chang (2010). Also, the approach used in this chapter does not require the nonresponse instrumental variable assumption for model identification made in Wang et al. (2014).

Remark 11.2 Modification to Steps 1 and 2 where a missing-at-random nonresponse model is used is straightforward, i.e. by dropping the y_s's in Eq. (11.5), and will not be further discussed here.

Remark 11.3 We have not included in this chapter the measures of uncertainties for the RegDI estimators outlined in Sections 11.2–11.5 as they are out of scope here. However, using Taylor expansion, we derived variance approximations for them in Kim and Tam (2018), which will be published elsewhere. Alternatively, they can be estimated by nonparametric bootstrap methods outlined in Rao and Wu (1988). See also Chipperfield and Preston (2007) for another bootstrap approach.

11.6 Empirical Studies

In this section, we evaluate the methods outlined in this chapter by using simulation under a number of scenarios, including measurement errors and nonresponse in the observations. We also evaluate the robustness of the MNAR propensity models used for adjusting nonresponse in A.

In the simulation study, observations on a continuous Y variable measured without error are generated from the following linear regression model:

$$y_i = 7 + 0.7(x_i - 2) + e_i$$

where $x_i \sim N(2, 1), e_i \sim N(0, 0.51)$ and e_i is independent of x_i. The simulated population has a mean and variance of 7 and 1.51 units, respectively. We generate a finite population of size $N = 1\,000\,000$ from this model. Also, we generate observations with measurement errors using the following linear regression model:

$$y_i^* = 2 + 0.9 \times (y_i - 3) + u_i$$

where $u_i \sim N(0, 0.5^2)$, independent of y_i. This population has a mean of 2.36 units and a variance of 26.51 units. The choice of the parameters in the above models are arbitrary and the x_i variable is introduced to enable us to choose a biased B sample to evaluate the methods.

To enable the evaluation of the methods proposed in this chapter, we repeatedly obtain two samples, denoted by A and B, by simple random sampling of size $n = 500$ and by an unequal probability sampling of size $N_B = 500\,000$, respectively. In selecting sample B, we create two strata, where stratum 1 consists of elements with $x_i \leq 2$, and stratum 2 consists of those with $x_i > 2$. Within each stratum, we select n_h elements by simple random sampling independently, where $n_1 = 300\,000$ and $n_2 = 200\,000$. Under this sampling scheme, the sample mean of B is smaller than the population mean. We assume that the stratum information is not available at the time of data analysis, as otherwise we could remove the bias of the sample mean of B by suitable weighting.

We consider the following three scenarios:

Scenario 1: No measurement errors in the two samples. Thus, we observe y_i in both samples.
Scenario 2: Measurement errors in sample B. Thus, we observe y_i in A and y_i^* in B.
Scenario 3: Measurement errors in sample A. Thus, we observe y_i^* in A and y_i in B.

We further assume that we observe δ_i for all units in sample A, and for all units i in $A \cap B$, we observe (y_i^*, y_i) in Scenario 3.

We consider the following four estimators for the population mean of Y:

1. *Mean A*: Mean of sample A observations.
2. *Mean B*: Mean of sample B observations.
3. *PSE*: Poststratified estimator of the form defined in Eq. (11.1).
4. *RegDI*: RegDI estimator of the form $\hat{T}_{\text{RegDI}} = \sum_{i \in A} w_i y_i$ as defined in Section 11.3 for Scenario 1 and Section 11.4 for Scenario 2, and $\hat{T}_{\text{RegDI}} = \sum_{i \in A} w_i \hat{y}_i$ for Scenario 3.

Furthermore, we generate two sets of r_i, independently from Bernoulli (p_i), where p_i is the response probability for unit i in A, and generated by the following logistic regression models:

$$p_i = \frac{\exp(-1 + 0.5 y_i)}{1 + \exp(-1 + 0.5 y_i)} \tag{11.8}$$

and

$$p_i = \frac{\exp\{-1.9 + 0.5 y_i + 0.2(y_i - 1)^2\}}{1 + \exp\{-1.9 + 0.5 y_i + 0.2(y_i - 1)^2\}} \tag{11.9}$$

respectively. The overall response rate is around 62%. We consider the following two additional scenarios:

Scenario 4: The response model Eq. (11.8) is correctly specified.
Scenario 5: The correct response model is Eq. (11.9) but Eq. (11.8) is used as it were the "correct" model.

We consider the following three estimators for the population mean of Y:

1. *CC*: Complete case estimator equal to the mean of sample A observations.
2. *IPW*: Inverse probability weight estimator defined by

$$\frac{\sum_{i \in A} r_i \hat{p}_i^{-1} y_i}{\sum_{i \in A} r_i \hat{p}_i^{-1}}$$

where $\hat{p}_i = p(y_i; \hat{\phi})$ using the response model defined in Eq. (11.8), and $\hat{\phi}$ is obtained by solving

$$\sum_{i \in A} d_i \left\{ \frac{r_i}{p(y_i; \phi)} - 1 \right\} (1, \delta_i y_i) = (0, 0) \qquad (11.10)$$

3. *RegDI2*: Two-step calibration estimator as defined in Section 11.5.

Results of the simulation for the five different scenarios, and different estimators used, are summarized in Table 11.3.

In Scenario 1, as expected, the performance of estimators PSE and RegDI is the same and, by integrating the data from A and B, is much more efficient than either Mean A or Mean B.

In Scenario 2, both Mean B and PSE are very inefficient, because no attempt is made to address the measurement errors in B. Although Mean A is unbiased, it is not as efficient as RegDI because the latter gains efficiency through integrating the data from A and B.

In Scenario 3, Mean A and PSE perform even poorer than Mean B, showing that the measurement error in this simulation has a bigger impact on Mean A than the undercoverage bias on Mean B. RegDI is shown to be a very efficient estimator.

In Scenario 4, the performance of IPW exceeds expectations, but RegDI2 is demonstrably more efficient.

In Scenario 5, the robustness of RegDI (and IPW) against mis-specification of the nonresponse model is a pleasant surprise. In this case, the price to pay for the mis-specification in the nonresponse model is a substantial increase in the variance of the estimator, due mainly to the increase in the variation of the weights. This is due to the IPW using only the first adjustment step of RegDI.

Table 11.3 Results based on a Monte Carlo sample of size 1000.

Scenario	Estimator	Bias	Std Var	Std MSE
I	Mean A	0.00	100	100
	Mean B	−0.11	0	1116
	PSE	0.00	47	47
	RegDI	0.00	47	47
II	Mean A	0.00	100	100
	Mean B	−1.10	0	63842
	PSE	−0.49	47	12895
	RegDI	0.00	62	58
III	Mean A	−1.00	108	52831
	Mean B	−0.11	0	668
	PSE	−0.50	51	13521
	RegDI	0.00	83	79
IV	No unit nonresponse case	0.00	100	100
	CC	0.18	159	1900
	IPW	0.00	191	192
	RegDI2	0.00	150	151
V	No unit nonresponse case	0.00	100	100
	CC	0.36	143	6984
	IPW	−0.01	1058	1068
	RegDI2	−0.01	686	692

Std Var (MSE) = standardized variance (mean squared error).

11.7 Examples of Official Statistics Applications

We give two examples of how the methods outlined in this chapter may be applied in the production of official statistics in Australia.

Example 11.1 In May 2015, Dairy Australia launched a national database, DairyBase, for Australian dairy farmers to store their farm performance information. DairyBase provides a web-based system and tools to help dairy farmers to manage their farms. Participation in DairyBase is voluntary and at the time of writing this chapter, has an estimated coverage of about 30% of the dairy farmers.

A recent comparison of the data items available in DairyBase with those in the agricultural census and survey programs conducted by the Australian Bureau of Statistics (ABS) revealed a number of (a) identical data items between the DairyBase and ABS collections, (b) data items whose definitions in the DairyBase and ABS collections differ; and (c) data items available in the DairyBase but not available in ABS collections. In addition, DairyBase, which is updated regularly by farmers, is more contemporary than the ABS collections. Farmers could save time if they could elect to provide data through DairyBase rather than having to provide the same information twice to the ABS.

The methods developed in Section 11.3 can be used to combine the DairyBase data items in (a) with ABS agricultural surveys to significantly improve the precision of agricultural statistics at a much-reduced cost. The methods developed in Section 11.4 can be used to combine the data items in (b) with the ABS agricultural surveys to deal with differences in the definitions of the agricultural terms from the two different sources, and also to address the fact that the ABS surveys are generally less contemporary than the DairyBase. Finally, the methods developed in Section 11.5 can be used to adjust for nonresponse bias in the ABS agricultural surveys, in conjunction with integrating the data items in (a) or (b) with the ABS collections.

Example 11.2 To test the methods using real-life data, we consider the data source B to comprise the ABS 2015-16 Agricultural Census (ABS 2017), which had a response rate of 85%. We use the 2014–15 Rural Environment and Agricultural Commodities Survey (REACS) (ABS 2016), which had a response rate of 78% as the probability sample A. In this study, we assume that both sources B and A have no measurement errors (though noting that the two data sources are one year apart). Our interest is to combine the Agricultural Census data with the REACS data to estimate the number of dairy cattle (DAIRY), the number of beef cattle (BEEF), and the number of tons of wheat for grain or seed produced (WHEAT) for 2015–2016. We must deal with undercoverage in B, and unit nonresponse in A; the methods developed in Sections 11.3 and 11.5 can be applied, respectively.

In this study, the x_i variable used in Eq. (11.3) is

$$x_i = (1 - \delta_i, \delta_i, \delta_i \times \text{AOH}_i, \quad \delta_i \times \text{DAIRY}_i, \quad \delta_i \times \text{BEEF}_i, \quad \delta_i \times \text{WHEAT}_i)'$$

where AOH_i is the Area of Holding held by the farm.

A logistic regression model was used to estimate the probability of response in probability sample A for the farms. A separate model was fitted for each of the eight states of Australia separately. The estimated propensity for inclusion in A is

$$\widehat{\pi}(z_i, y_i; \widehat{\phi}) = \frac{\exp(\widehat{\phi}_z z_i + \widehat{\phi}_y y_i)}{1 + \exp(\widehat{\phi}_z z_i + \widehat{\phi}_y y_i)}$$

Table 11.4 Estimates of $\hat{\phi}_z$ and $\hat{\phi}_y$, and their standard errors, for the Australian states.

Parameter	$\hat{\phi}_I$	$\hat{\phi}_O$	$\hat{\phi}_S$	$\hat{\phi}_{IN}$	$\hat{\phi}_{AOH}$
New South Wales	1.4 (1.1E−2)	8.3* (49.3)	5.2E−5 (8.2E−6)	−5.0E−5 (8.2E−6)	−4.0E−3* (3.4E−3)
Victoria	1.3 (1.4E−2)	8.4* (51.6)	5.0E−5 (1.0E−5)	−5.0E−5 (1.0E−5)	8.0E−5 (1.4E−5)
Queensland	1.2 (1.4E−2)	11.5* (255.5)	1.3E−4 (2.8E−5)	−1.3E−4 (2.8E−5)	7.8E−6 (1.4E−6)
South Australia	1.6 (2.2E−2)	8.3* (57.7)	3.5E−5 (1.0E−5)	−4.0E−5 (1/0E−5)	2.8E−6 (1.5E−6)
Western Australia	1.4 (2.4E−2)	10.4* (138.8)	3.5E−5 (1.0E−5)	−9.0E−5 (3.9E−5)	2.1E−7* (6.0E−7)
Tasmania	1.4 (2.4E−2)	9.3* (108.2)	7.1E−5* (6.3E−5)	−7.0E−5* (6.0E−5)	−7.0E−5 (3.3E−5)
Northern Territory	9.9E−1 (1.0E−1)	—	2.1E−5* (2.8E−5)	−2.0E−5* (2.8E−5)	2.1E−6 (8.8E−7)
Australian Capital Territory	4.0E−1* (3.1E−1)	—	2.3E−4* (4.1E−4)	−2.2E−4* (4.1E−4)	7.3E−4* (7.0E−4)

Notes: (i) Bracketed figures are estimated standard errors of the parameters; (ii) * denotes estimate not significant at the 95% confidence level.

where the auxiliary variable z_i comprises:

- an intercept term (I);
- an outlier flag (O_i) with the exception of the Northern Territory and the Australian Capital Territory;
- a size measure (S_i) of the farm in terms of the dollar value of the agricultural operation; and
- an interaction term between S_i and the presence of the unit in the Agricultural Census and REACS (IN_i).

The y_i variable used in the model is AOH_i. Table 11.4 summaries the estimates of $\hat{\phi}_z$ and $\hat{\phi}_y$, and their standard errors (SEs), for the eight states of Australia.

The results of this pilot study are summarized in Table 11.5.

In Table 11.5, the Agricultural Census data, in spite of its undercoverage bias, can be used to improve the precision of the REACS results by a factor of 13 and 8 in the estimation of the cattle and wheat, respectively.

Table 11.5 Bias, variance, and mean squared error of selected agricultural commodities at the Australian level.

Variable	Estimator from	Bias (×10³)	Var (×10⁹)**	MSE (×10⁹)
DAIRY	REACS only (A)	0.00	6.19	6.19
	Agricultural Census only (B)*	−362.45	0	131.37
	RegDI using (A) and (B)	0.00	0.43	0.43
BEEF	REACS only (A)	0.00	85.00	85.00
	Agricultural Census only (B)*	−2389.53	0	5709.86
	RegDI using (A) and (B)	0.00	6.79	6.79
WHEAT	REACS only (A)	0.00	171.29	171.29
	Agricultural Census only (B)*	−2043.52	0	4176.00
	RegDI using (A) and (B)	0.00	20.83	20.83

Notes: (i) * Estimated by the difference between the total from B and the published ABS estimate from the Agriculture Census adjusted for nonresponse. (ii) ** Bootstrap estimates (Chipperfield and Preston, 2007) from 100 bootstrap samples.

11.8 Limitations

Although the efficacy of the methods outlined in this chapter has been tested using simulated and real-life data, the following are limitations, i.e. conditions need to be fulfilled before applying the methods to other applications:

1. There is no overcoverage bias in B.
2. Identifiable information is available from units in A and B so matching of the units can occur to allow the observation of δ_i, for $i \in A$, i.e. determine which units in A are also in B, and allowing data linking to occur.
3. There is no matching or linking error.
4. Values of N, N_B, and $\sum_{i \in B} y_i$ are known.
5. A reasonably large nonprobability dataset is available so that $A \cap B$ is not empty for measurement error or unit nonresponse adjustment, where warranted.
6. At least one of the two sets of measurements in either A, or B, is correct.
7. Where needed, an adequate measurement error model is available to adjust for those errors in the observations in A; and δ_i is independent of y_i^* for $i \in A \cap B$.
8. Where needed, an adequate parametric MNAR model is available for unit nonresponse adjustment, although no knowledge is required on the parameters of the model; and r_i is independent of δ_i, given z_i and y_i, for $i \in A$.

11.9 Conclusion

Provided that the limitations are addressed, we have shown that a nonprobability sample and Big Data sources, in spite of undercoverage or self-selection bias, can be used as benchmarks to calibrate the Horvitz–Thompson weights of a random sample to provide a very efficient estimator of the finite population total. Using the methods in Section 11.3, we showed that the sample size, n, of a simple random sample, can be increased by a factor of $(1 - W_B)\frac{S_C^2}{S^2}$ which, as shown in Table 11.5, can be substantial, and allows official statisticians to reduce the cost of data collection by, if desired, reducing the sample size judiciously.

Observing that the PSE in Section 11.3 is equivalent to a calibration estimator with the Horvitz–Thompson weights calibrated to the known benchmarks N_C, N_B and $\sum_1^N \delta_i y_i$ simultaneously, we can apply the calibration idea to complex situations involving measurement errors or unit nonresponse. Indeed, when the data in B is measured with error, one can replace the third benchmark $\sum_1^N \delta_i y_i$ in $\sum_1^N x_i$ by $\sum_1^N \delta_i y_i^*$ to determine the weights, $w_i's$. However, when the data in A has measurement errors, we can use the same benchmarks N_C, N_B and $\sum_1^N \delta_i y_i$ for determination of weights, but we need to replace the estimator $\sum_{i \in A} w_i y_i^*$ by $\sum_{i \in A} w_i \hat{y}_i$ with $\hat{y}_i$ predicted using a measurement error model.

For the more typical case when the random sample suffers from unit nonresponse, we have to apply a response-propensity adjustment to the weight w_i to account for the nonresponse. In this chapter, we developed a procedure to adjust for the nonresponse bias from an MNAR model, and illustrate the idea using a logistic regression model.

Combining data from different sources to overcome coverage issues in nonprobability or Big Data sets, and to improve the efficiency of estimates, is an emerging hot topic for statistical research. Building on the methods proposed in the chapter, we will explore how the methods may be extended for small area estimation, and how the method may be affected by the accuracy, or otherwise, of matching and linking the data between A and B to inform the values of $\delta_i's$.

References

Australian Bureau of Statistics (2016). Agricultural Commodities, Australia 2014–15. ABS Catalogue Number 7121.0.

Australian Bureau of Statistics (2017). Agricultural Commodities, Australia 2015–16. ABS Catalogue Number 7121.0.

Bethlehem, J.G. (2015). Solving the nonresponse problem with sample matching? *Social Science Computer Review* 34: 59–77. https://doi.org/10.1177/0894439315573926.

Brick, J.M. (2013). Unit nonresponse and weighting adjustment: a critical review. *Journal of Official Statistics* 29: 329–353.

Chambers, R.L. and Clark, R. (2012). *An Introduction to Model-Based Survey Sampling with Applications.* London: Oxford University Press.

Chen, Y., Li, P., and Wu, C. (2018). Doubly robust inference with non-probability survey samples. *Journal of the American Statistical Association* https://www.tandfonline.com/doi/abs/10.1080/01621459.2019.1677241 (accessed 27 March 2020).

Chipperfield, J. and Preston, J. (2007). Efficient bootstrap for business surveys. *Survey Methodology* 33: 167–172.

Cochran, W.G. (1977). *Sampling Techniques.* New York: Wiley.

Couper, M.P. (2013). Is the sky falling? New technology, changing media, and the future of surveys. *Survey Research Methods* 7 (3): 145–156.

Deville, J.C. and Särndal, C.E. (1992). Calibration estimators in survey sampling. *Journal of the American Statistical Association* 87: 376–382.

Deville, J.C., Särndal, C.E., and Sautory, O. (1993). General raking procedures in survey sampling. *Journal of the American Statistical Association* 88: 1013–1020.

Dupont, F. (1995). Alternative adjustment where there are several levels of auxiliary information. *Survey Methodology* 21: 125–135.

Elliott, M. and Valliant, R. (2017). Inference for nonprobability samples. *Statistical Science* 32: 249–264.

Eurostat (2014). Feasibility Study on the Use of Mobile Positioning Data for Tourism Statistics – Consolidated Report.

Fuller, W.A. (2009). *Sampling Statistics.* Hoboken, NJ: Wiley.

Haupt, M. (2016). Who should get credit for the quote "data is the new oil"? Quora. https://www.quora.com/Who-should-get-credit-for-the-quote-data-is-the-new-oil (accessed 3 March 2019).

Keiding, N. and Louis, T.A. (2016). Perils and potentials of self-selected entry to epidemiological studies and surveys (with discussions). *Journal of the Royal Statistical Society A* 179: 1–28.

Kim, J.K. and Riddles, M. (2012). Some theory for propensity-scoring-adjustment estimators in survey sampling. *Survey Methodology* 38: 157–165.

Kim, J. K. and Tam, S. M. (2018). Data integration by combining big data and survey data for finite population inference. (Manuscript under preparation).

Kim, J.K. and Wang, Z. (2019). Sampling techniques for big data analysis in finite population inference. *International Statistical Review* 87: 177–191.

Kott, P.S. and Chang, T. (2010). Using calibration weighting to adjust for nonignorable unit nonresponse. *Journal of the American Statistical Association* 105: 1265–1275.

Lohr, S. and Raghunathan, T. (2017). Combining survey data with other data sources. *Statistical Science* 32 (2): 293–312. https://doi.org/10.1214/16-STS584.

Pfeffermann, D. (2015). Methodological issues and challenges in the production of official statistics: 24th Annual Morris Hansen Lecture. *Journal of Survey Statistics and Methodology* 3 (4): 425–483.

Pfeffermann, D., Krieger, A.M., and Rinott, Y. (1998). Parametric distributions of complex survey data under informative probability sampling. *Statistica Sinica* 8 (4): 1087–1114.

Puza, B. and O'Neill, T. (2006). Selection bias in binary data from voluntary surveys. *The Mathematical Scientist* 31: 85–94.

Raghunathan, T. (2015). Statistical challenges in combining information from big and small data sources. Paper presented to the Expert Panel meeting at the National Academy of Science (9 November 2015).

Rao, J.N.K. and Wu, C.F.J. (1988). Resampling inference with complex survey data. *Journal of the American Statistical Association* 83: 231–241.

Rivers, D. (2007). Sampling for web surveys. Presented at the Joint Statistical Meetings, Salt Lake City, UT.

Rubin, D.B. (1976). Inference and missing data. *Biometrika* 63: 581–590.

Särndal, C.E. and Lundström, S. (2005). *Estimation in Surveys with Nonresponse*. Chichester: Wiley.

Särndal, C.E., Swensson, B., and Wretman, J. (1992). *Model Assisted Survey Sampling*. New York: Springer-Verlag https://doi.org/10.1007/978-1-4612-4378-6.

Smith, T.M.F. (1983). On the validity of inferences from non-random sample. *Journal of the Royal Statistical Society A* 146: 394–403.

Tam, S.M. and Clarke, F. (2015). Big data, official statistics and some initiatives by the Australian Bureau of Statistics. *International Statistical Review* 83: 436–448.

Tam, S.M. and Kim, J.K. (2018). Big data, selection bias and ethics – an official statistician's perspective. *Statistical Journal of the International Association for Official Statistics* 34: 577–588.

Thompson, M.E. (2019). Combining data from new and traditional data sources in population surveys. *International Statistical Review* 87: 79–89.

Thompson, M.E. (2018). Dynamic data science and official statistics. *Canadian Journal of Statistics* 46: 10–23.

Wang, S., Shao, J., and Kim, J.K. (2014). An instrument variable approach for identification and estimation with nonignorable nonresponse. *Statistica Sinica* 24: 1097–1116.

Zhang, L.C. (2010). Post-stratification and calibration – a synthesis. *The American Statistician* 54: 178–184.

Zhang, L.C. (2012). Topics of statistical theory for register-based statistics and data integration. *Statistica Neerlandica* 66 (1): 41–63. https://doi.org/10.1111/j.1467-9574.2011.00508.x.

Further Reading

Hand, D.J. (2018). Statistical challenges of administrative and transaction data. *Journal of the Royal Statistical Society A* 181: 1–24.

Kim, J.K. and Park, M. (2010). Calibration estimation in survey sampling. *International Statistical Review* 78: 21–39.

Kim, J.K. and Rao, J.N.K. (2009). A unified approach to linearization variance estimation from survey data after imputation for item nonresponse. *Biometrika* 96: 917–932.

Rao, J.N.K. and Molina, I. (2015). *Small Area Estimation*. Hoboken, NJ: Wiley.

Skinner, C.J. and Rao, J.N.K. (1996). Estimation in dual frame surveys with complex designs. *Journal of the American Statistical Association* 91: 349–356.

Wu, C. and Sitter, R. (2001). A model-calibration approach to using complete auxiliary information from survey data. *Journal of the American Statistical Association* 96: 185–193.

12

Investigating Alternative Data Sources to Reduce Respondent Burden in United States Census Bureau Retail Economic Data Products

Rebecca J. Hutchinson

US Census Bureau, Economic Indicators Division, Washington, DC, USA

12.1 Introduction

Retail store closures, mergers, and acquisitions among major retailers, innovative industry disruptors, and the evolution of online shopping dominate the daily business news. Official statistics that accurately and consistently measure retail sales have long been closely watched economic indicators, but in this dynamic retail environment, they are even more thoroughly monitored. At the same time, response rates are declining for many United States Census Bureau surveys, including the retail surveys. Respondents often cite the burden of completing multiple surveys monthly and/or annually as one reason for nonresponse (Haraldsen et al. 2013). Recognizing these challenges and the growing needs of its data users, the Census Bureau is committed to exploring the use of Big Data or alternative data sources to produce high-quality data products while reducing respondent burden (U.S. Census Bureau 2018).

To reduce respondent burden, the Census Bureau has been exploring the use of third-party data in its retail survey programs. If a retailer is already providing another party with data similar to what the Census Bureau collects on surveys and censuses, can that data consistently be used to replace what a retailer is asked to provide to Census Bureau surveys?

This chapter details a proof-of-concept project undertaken by the Economic Directorate of United States Census Bureau using retailer point-of-sale data to test if the data could be used in place of data reported on survey instruments. The point-of-sale data includes sales tabulations at the store and product levels. To determine the data's quality and usability, the point-of-sale data are compared at the store and national levels against the Monthly and Annual Retail Trade Surveys and against the 2012 Economic Census. Additionally, product data from the Economic Census are compared to the product-level data provided by the third-party data source.

This chapter highlights the preliminary findings of the work at the store level and national level and details the challenges that the product-level work presented. Section 12.1 provides an overview of the Economic Directorate of the Census Bureau, focusing on the retail programs within the Directorate, the challenges the Directorate is facing, and the Big Data vision for using alternative data sources to address these challenges. Section 12.2 discusses respondent burden. Section 12.3 provides details on point-of-sale data and the point-of-sale data used in this project. Section 12.4 provides the background, description, and results of a project undertaken using point-of-sale data in conjunction with existing retail survey data. Section 12.5 highlights the lessons learned and issues identified when using third-party data in official government statistics as well as next steps for this work.

12.1.1 Overview of the Economic Directorate

The Economic Directorate of the Census Bureau is responsible for statistical programs that measure the economic activity of US businesses and government organizations. The Economic Directorate's mission is to collect quality economic data and provide statistics that are critical to understanding current conditions in the economy. These data are important to the preparation of key measures of economic activity by other agencies, including gross domestic product estimates, benchmark input–output accounts, producer price indexes, and measures of industrial production and manufacturing capacity utilization.

Every five years, the Economic Directorate conducts an Economic Census and a Census of Governments. Together these censuses cover all US nonagricultural businesses: manufacturing, wholesale trade, retail trade, mining, utilities, construction, transportation, finance and insurance, real estate, healthcare, and other services sectors, as well as local, state, and federal governments.

On a monthly, quarterly, or annual basis, the Directorate conducts 70 separate surveys. These collections include 12 principal economic indicators that provide the most timely official measurement of the US economy including housing starts; retail sales; wholesale sales; services revenue; manufacturers' shipments, inventories, and orders; new construction put in place; and corporate profits.

Additionally, the Economic Directorate is responsible for monthly merchandise export and import statistics, extensive compilations of administrative records, and numerous special research and technical studies.

12.1.2 Big Data Vision

Official economic statistics produced by the Census Bureau have long served as high-quality benchmarks for data users. However, demands for more timely and more granular data, a decline in respondent cooperation, increasing costs of traditional survey data collection, and a changing economic landscape create challenges for the Census Bureau to meet its data users' needs. To meet these needs, exploring nontraditional means of collecting and obtaining data is now being emphasized (Jarmin 2019).

The Census Bureau has initiated a number of exploratory projects using alternative data sources while remaining mindful of both the great possibilities and the great challenges that accompany the use of these sources. For measurement of the economy, these alternative data sources could include high-frequency and near real-time data such as point-of-sale data obtained from a retailer or a third party, building permit data obtained from an application programming interface (API), or commodity flow data collected by sensors. The Census Bureau envisions leveraging these alternative sources with existing survey and administrative data to provide more timely data products, to offer greater insight into the nation's economy through detailed geographic and industry-level estimates, and to improve efficiency and quality throughout the survey life cycle. Alternative data collection methods such as system-to-system data collection and web scraping could also play a large role in reducing burden on respondents and Census Bureau analysts (Dumbacher and Hanna 2017). Rather than conducting costly follow-up operations with respondents, analysts could instead use the data gathered through alternative data collection methods or through alternative data sources.

Incorporating these types of alternative data sources into official government statistics has promise but also raises concerns related to methodological transparency, consistency of the data, information technology security, public–private partnerships, confidentiality, and the general quality of the data. Statisticians who set policy and quality standards for official government statistics are now faced with various issues surrounding third-party data. The US Office of Management and Budget (OMB) and associations such as the American Association for Public Opinion Research (AAPOR) and the American Statistical Association have begun looking more closely at how to evaluate the quality of third-party data and statistics derived from them (AAPOR 2015).

12.1.3 Overview of the Census Bureau Retail Programs

The retail trade program currently covers retail companies as defined by the North American Industry Classification System (NAICS) and represents all retail companies (NAICS Sector 44-45) with and without paid employees. These retail businesses may be large retailers with many store locations, single-unit retailers with only one location, or retailers operating solely as e-commerce businesses.

The Census Bureau measures the retail economy every five years in the Economic Census and more frequently in monthly and annual surveys. In years ending in 2 and 7, the Economic Census – a mandatory survey – asks for detailed sales and product-level information as well as employment and payroll and business characteristics for each physical store location that a retailer operates. Data collected by the Economic Census are used to update the Census Bureau's Business Register from which the sampling frames for many economic surveys – including the annual and monthly retail trade surveys – are created. Each year, the Annual Retail Trade Survey (ARTS) collects data at the company or retailer level nationally; no store location data are collected. The ARTS collects annual sales, e-commerce sales, beginning and end-of-year inventories, and expenses data as well as some retailer characteristics; the annual data are released approximately 15 months after the data year ends.

Within the Economic Indicators Division of the Economic Directorate, two retail surveys are conducted. The Monthly Retail Trade Survey (MRTS) is a voluntary survey done at the retailer or company level and collects sales/receipts as well as end-of-month inventories and e-commerce sales from all retail industries. Estimates from this survey are released approximately six weeks after month's end. The MRTS is a subsample of the ARTS and a selection of the MRTS sample occurs approximately every five years to ensure the sample remains representative and to redistribute the burden for small and mid-size businesses.

The timeliest measurement of the retail economy and earliest indication of nominal consumer spending produced by the government is the Advanced Monthly Retail Trade Survey (MARTS). This survey measures only sales/receipts and estimates are published approximately two weeks after month's end. The MARTS is a subsample of the MRTS, and this sample is selected every two to three years, again to ensure a representative sample and to redistribute burden.

Table 12.1 provides a summary of the retail trade programs at the Census Bureau.

12.2 Respondent Burden

OMB has authority over information collected by federal agencies including surveys conducted by the Census Bureau. The Paperwork Reduction Act of 1995 grants OMB this authority with the goal of minimizing the burden on the public while simultaneously maximizing the public benefit of information collected and minimizing the costs of data and information collection to the federal government

Table 12.1 Overview of the Census Bureau's retail trade programs.

	Economic Census	Annual Retail Trade Survey (ARTS)	Monthly Retail Trade Survey (MRTS)	Advanced Monthly Retail Trade Survey (MARTS)
Frequency	Conducted every five years (years ending in 2 and 7)	Conducted annually	Conducted monthly	Conducted monthly
Reporting status	Required by law	Required by law	Voluntary	Voluntary
Sample source	Not applicable	Sampled from frame created by the Economic Census	Subsampled from the Annual Retail Trade Survey	Subsampled from the Monthly Retail Trade Survey
Data collection level	Establishment or store level	Company level	Company level	Company level
Data items collected	• Business characteristics • Employment and payroll • Detailed product-level sales	• Business characteristics • E-commerce sales • Sales • Inventories • Expenses	• Limited business characteristics • Reporting period information • Sales • Inventories • E-commerce sales	• Limited business characteristics • Reporting period information • Sales • E-commerce sales

(U.S. Office of Personnel Management 2011). Census Bureau surveys must be authorized by OMB and are typically reauthorized every three years. As part of this reauthorization, each survey must estimate the number of burden hours that the survey will place on an individual reporter and on the potential set of respondents as a whole; this burden estimate appears on survey instruments or in a letter to the respondent.

Respondent burden for business surveys is measured from two different perspectives: actual and perceived (Willeboordse 1997). Actual, measurable units of burden can be quantified by a dollar amount or by number of hours. Examples of these types of measurements include number of people involved in the survey completion, time spent to complete the survey, and salary cost of completing the survey (Haraldsen et al. 2013). This burden measurement can be complex for larger businesses where multiple people are involved in the completion of one or more survey instruments. In addition to Census Bureau surveys, businesses may also be receiving surveys from other government agencies. The decentralized nature of the US federal statistical programs hinders coordination of data collection and data sharing among over the 100 included agencies (U.S. Office of Management and Budget 2017). Each agency has its own set of legal and organizational barriers in place that can prevent interagency data-sharing activities that may reduce respondent burden.

Figure 12.1 displays estimates of the total burden hours for multi-unit establishments for completing Census Bureau retail trade program survey instruments in 2017. The survey instruments used in these estimates include the 2017 MRTS, the 2017 ARTS, and the 2017 Economic Census. The burden-hour estimates used were obtained through cognitive and other pretesting activities conducted with survey respondents. These estimates are required for OMB survey reauthorization. The MRTS takes seven minutes to complete but retailers have to complete it 12 times each year and may also receive more than one survey instrument each month if its operations include more than one kind of retail business as defined by NAICS. The ARTS can take up to 3 hours, 19 minutes to complete and is completed only once per year. The Economic Census is the most burdensome of these

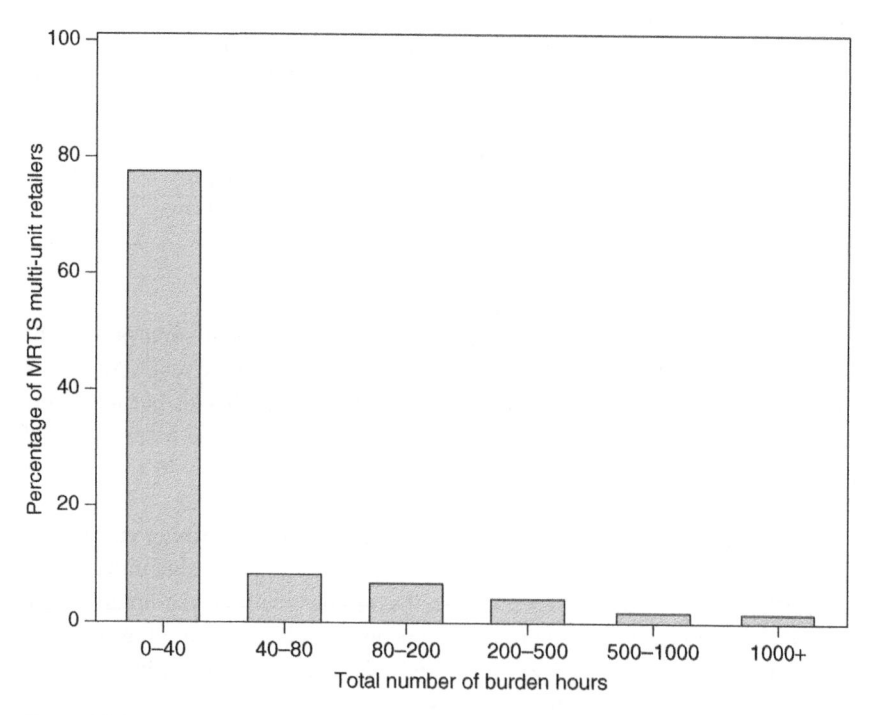

Figure 12.1 Estimated total burden hours to complete retail trade survey instruments in 2017. Source: MRTS form, 2017 ARTS form, and 2017 Economic Census initial letter to multi-units.

retail survey instruments where a separate survey instrument is completed for each store location. If a retailer has 100 store locations, then 100 survey instruments need to be completed. The estimated time burden for a single Economic Census survey ranges between 41 minutes and 5 hours, 36 minutes. The burden analysis discussed here is for multi-unit establishments who receive the MRTS. Multi-units are retailers with two or more establishments or store locations that often have the bookkeeping practices or software and staff in place to streamline government reporting; therefore, for the purposes of this analysis, the minimum reporting time for the Economic Census was used. As seen in Figure 12.1, over 70% of these multi-unit retailers could have spent 40 hours or less completing all of their Census Bureau retail survey instruments. On the other hand, over 7% of these businesses could have spent over 200 hours completing their survey instruments.

Although the analysis here focuses on the retail-specific burden, these same retailers may be part of larger, more diversified companies, and may be included in surveys in other industry trade areas including wholesale, manufacturing, and services. These retailers may also be receiving business surveys conducted by other government agencies including the Bureau of Labor Statistics and the Bureau of Economic Analysis. In many cases, individual companies providing data about their performance is essential to the production of these data. As respondents face increasing requests to provide data, respondent burden increases as does the risk for lower quality estimates due to low response rates (Haraldsen et al. 2013).

Perceived burden is harder to measure in well-defined units. Perceived burden measures the willingness of the respondents to participate in the survey (Willeboordse 1997). Perceived burden can include the usefulness of providing the data both to the respondent and to society (Haraldsen et al. 2013). Interviews conducted by Census Bureau researchers with 30 large businesses – both in retail and in other industries – found that work that benefits the business will take priority over work related to reporting to government surveys, especially those surveys that are voluntary and do not carry penalty for nonresponse (Willimack and Nichols 2010). Some businesses will even refuse to participate in any voluntary surveys, including the voluntary MRTS (the ARTS and the Economic Census are mandatory and required by law).

Ease of access to data and the ability to retrieve the requested data from across a company and across information systems are also perceived factors that play into a business's decision to complete a survey instrument (Willimack and Nichols 2010), especially relevant for instruments requesting more than just topline national sales estimates. For example, the Economic Census asks retailers for employment and payroll figures, class of customer, physical characteristics including square footage of an establishment, and sales by product types for each physical store location that a retailer is operating. Large businesses said that product-line sales information was particularly difficult to provide (Willimack and Nichols 2010).

12.3   Point-of-Sale Data

12.3.1   Background on Point-of-Sale Data

There are different approaches to reducing respondent burden. If the data needs to be collected via surveys, then improvements to the questionnaire can be made or the collecting agency or party can better communicate the importance of the data to the respondent (Haraldsen et al. 2013). However, if the respondent is already providing another party with data similar to what the Census Bureau collects on surveys and censuses, the survey form may no longer need to be completed.

Point-of-sale data, also known as scanner data, are one possible third-party source that may help reduce burden. Point-of-sale data are detailed data on sales of consumer goods obtained by scanning the barcodes or other readable codes of products at electronic points-of-sale both in brick and mortar retail stores and online. Point-of-sale data can provide information about quantities, product characteristics, prices, and the total value of goods sold and has the advantage that the data are available at the retailer, store, and product levels. Other third-party data sources, including credit card data or payment processor data, are often only available at an aggregated level. Due to confidentiality agreements, vendors of this data often cannot reveal which retailers are included in the aggregates. Additionally, point-of-sale data are more complete, capturing all purchases in a store whereas credit card data would only include purchases made with a credit card.

Much work has been done exploring the use of scanner data in producing price indices, and many official statistical agencies use scanner data for price index work. Eurostat (2017) identified a number of advantages of using scanner data when working with price indices, including that scanner data provides information on expenditures for all items sold over a continuous time period. Scanner data also can identify new product offerings faster than traditional price collection methods. The detailed product attribute data available in scanner data are also useful when working with price indices (Bird et al. 2014). The US Bureau of Labor Statistics has researched using scanner data to supplement the Consumer Price Index calculations and cited the potential of using alternative data sources to validate data collected through traditional operations (Horrigan 2013).

Data can also be used in creative non-price index efforts. IBM has used grocery store scanner data to locate the source of food-borne illnesses (IBM 2016). The National Cattleman's Beef Association uses scanner data to understand better the changing meat preferences of its customers (Krebs 2016).

The Census Bureau project also explores the use of point-of-sale data so that the focus is not on prices. Rather, the focus is on the theory that if all items that a retailer sells are collected in a point-of-sale data feed, then summing those sales across products and store locations over a month or a year should reflect total retail sales for a retailer. If the theory holds, the sales figure from the point-of-sale data should be comparable to what a retailer provides in the MRTS, the ARTS, and the Economic Census. To successfully test this theory, a point-of-sale dataset needs to meet the following requirements:

- Identify the data by retailer name.
- Provide product-level sales for each of the retailer's store locations.
- Have data available by month at a minimum.

Obtaining retailer scanner feeds can be done either directly through a retailer or through a third-party vendor. Although the raw scanner data from either source should be identical, both options have advantages and disadvantages (Boettcher 2014). First, the third-party vendor will clean the data and aggregate and curate the data in a consistent format to meet its data users' needs. This service comes at a high cost. While survey operations, specifically nonresponse follow-up, are themselves expensive to conduct, third-party data may also be expensive to purchase or the price of the data may limit the amount of data that can be purchased. The US Congress appropriates the budget of the Census Bureau and limited funds are available for alternative data source purchases in a given fiscal year. One of the primary challenges government agencies face with this type of effort is finding a solution that is scalable to the entire scope of the survey while operating within budget limitations (Jarmin 2019).

One other concern with using third-party data is that control of the raw data is relinquished. In traditional data collection through survey instruments, the Census Bureau controls the full data collection and data processing life cycle. Statistical agencies must be transparent in their methodologies; thus, if third-party data were used, the third party must also be transparent with its methodologies.

Though potentially cheaper in terms of purchasing data, obtaining data directly from a retailer can require extensive physical IT resources as well as staffing resources to ingest and clean the data. Monthly datasets with sales by store location and product type are large and can cause server slowness when processed. The Census Bureau would be interested in obtaining data feeds directly from retailers in the future, but staffing and IT limitations currently limit this effort from being implemented on a large scale. For the future of this project, cloud storage is being pursued. Additionally, the Census Bureau is currently developing an enterprise data lake. Data lakes are scalable storage repositories that bring together datasets of all sizes in a way that allows for easy access and sharing of the data (Miloslavskaya and Tolstoy 2016). At the time of this project, point-of-sale data from a third party are the more feasible option.

12.3.2 Background on NPD

Through the official government acquisitions process, we researched third-party data sources that would potentially be useful to this effort and selected the NPD Group, Inc. (NPD) as the third-party data source vendor for this project. NPD is a private market research company that collects point-of-sale data from over 1300 retailers representing 300000 stores and e-commerce platforms worldwide. To put that store count in perspective, the Census Bureau's 2016 County Business Patterns identified over one million establishments (or stores) in the Retail NAICS 44-45. Thus, one limitation of the NPD dataset is that it is not scalable to the entire economy because the NPD data represent less than one-third of the retail universe.

From each store location, NPD receives and processes weekly or monthly data feeds containing aggregated scanner transactions by product. By providing the data to NPD, retailers have access to NPD-prepared reports that help retailers measure and forecast brand and product performances as well as identify areas for improved sales opportunities.

At a minimum, each data feed includes a product identifier, the number of units sold, product sales in dollars, the average price sold, total store sales in dollars, and the week ending date. Sales tax and shipping and handling are excluded. Any price reductions or redeemed coupon values are adjusted for before NPD receives the feeds; thus, the sales figures in the feed reflect the final amount that the customer paid; these data should align to the net revenue total for the company. NPD does not receive data on individual transactions or purchasers.

NPD edits, analyzes, and summarizes the point-of-sale data feeds at detailed product levels and creates market analysis reports for its retail and manufacturing partners. NPD also curates datasets for customers like the Census Bureau. NPD's business model is not focused on delivering data for individual retailers and is based on aggregated product reports. NPD has had to modify existing processes and create new ones to deliver the curated retailer datasets to the Census Bureau.

NPD processes data for many product categories including apparel, small appliances, automotive, beauty, fashion accessories, consumer electronics, footwear, office supplies, toys, video games, jewelry, and watches. Although it receives a feed of total store point-of-sale activity that includes all purchased items, NPD only classifies data for those products in the product categories listed above. Any sales on items that do not belong in these categories are placed in an unclassified bucket. For example, NPD currently does not provide market research on grocery items; all grocery sales data are tabulated as unclassified. This is another limitation of the data: a whole-store picture is not available at the product level unless detailed information from the unclassified bucket can be provided as well.

Retailer datasets from NPD contain monthly data by store and product level, i.e. for a given month, sales for Product Z in Store Location Y for Retailer X. As part of the acquisitions process, the Census Bureau provided dataset requirements to NPD and NPD curated the datasets from their data feeds. The datasets are limited to stores located in the continental United States and include values for the following variables:

- Time period (month/year)
- Retailer name
- Store number
- Postal code of store location
- Channel type (brick and mortar or e-commerce)
- Imputation flag (indicates if sales figure is tabulated directly from a feed or derived using imputation methodology)
- Product classifications by industry, product category, and product subcategory
- Sales figures

One observation for each month and year for each store location includes a total sales value of the unclassified data. At this time, NPD only collects brick and mortar sales and e-commerce sales. If a retailer has business-to-business or catalog operations, those data can also be broken out. NPD does not collect other data items that the Census Bureau surveys do collect, including inventories and expenses. Thus, while the respondent burden can be reduced on reporting sales, retailers may still have to provide other data items via traditional surveys unless these other data items can also be collected in the NPD data feeds or by other data sources.

Additionally, NPD provides national-level datasets by month for each of the retailers. These national-level estimates could also be obtained by summing the sales data in the store-level datasets by month.

12.4 Project Description

With a point-of-sale data provider selected, the project's initial focus was to make a preliminary determination of the viability of point-of-sale data as a replacement for retail survey data. The project plan favors an incremental approach where data from a small number of retailers are purchased over a two-year research period. The research phase allowed for an exploratory review of a small amount of data for quality concerns and for exploring potential uses of the data. The goal of this research phase was to determine if the point-of-sale data could be used in a production environment where point-of-sale data are included in published estimates for the monthly and annual surveys as well as the Economic Census without sacrificing the quality of the estimates.

Recall that the driving question of this project was, "If a retailer is already providing another party with similar data to what the Census Bureau collects on surveys and censuses, can that data be used in place of what a retailer would be asked to provide on a Census Bureau form?" For each type of data, this project sought to answer that question by also answering these questions:

- *National-level data*: How well do national-level sales data tabulated from the point-of-sale data compare to data that retailers reported to the monthly and annual retail surveys? If the data aligned well for retailers who reported and survey data was available for comparison, how is the quality of the point-of-sale data for those retailers who do not report to the survey determined?
- *Store-level data*: How well do store-level sales and location data tabulated from the point-of-sale data compare to data that retailers reported the 2012 Economic Census?
- *Product-level data*: How well do the product categories in the point-of-sale data align to the product categories used in the Economic Census? If the mapping is possible, how well do the product sales compare between the NPD product data and Economic Census product data?

12.4.1 Selection of Retailers

At the beginning of the project, NPD provided a list of retailers that provide data feeds to NPD. From the list, the retailers were selected according to the following criteria:

- *Good reporting history to the MRTS*: The selection of retailers that are good reporters (i.e. retailers that consistently report to the survey) to the MRTS, the ARTS, and the 2012 and/or 2017 Economic Census allows for an initial baseline quality comparison to the NPD data.
- *Nonrespondents to the MRTS*: Priority was also given to selecting MRTS nonrespondents because this voluntary survey is one of the most timely measures of retail sales and response is critical to data quality.
- *High-burden retailers*: High burden-retailers identified by the burden calculation in Section 12.2 were also considered a priority because they have the potential to benefit from the project by reducing respondent burden.

Using these selection criteria, the Census Bureau provided NPD with prioritized lists of retailers to be included in the project. NPD has access to data from over 1300 retailers; however, they had to obtain signed agreements with the retailers to share these data with the Census Bureau. Because NPD has the client contacts for these retailers, NPD led the effort to have retailers agree to share their NPD data with the Census Bureau. The Associate Director of the Economic Directorate sent a letter to the retailers detailing the goals of the project, including reduced respondent burden and improved data accuracy. The letter informed retailers that any data from NPD would be protected by United States Code Title 13, which requires that data are kept confidential and only used for statistical purposes.

Both to uphold the confidentiality and privacy laws that guide Census Bureau activities and also to facilitate productive work with specific retailers, a small number of NPD staff working on this project completed background investigations and were granted Special Sworn Status. With this status, NPD staff are sworn to uphold the data stewardship practices and confidentiality laws put in place by United States Code Title 13 and Title 26 for their lifetimes.

Retailer participation in this effort is voluntary. NPD provided background to the retailers on the benefits of this project including reduced burden, but it is ultimately the retailers' decisions to participate or not. For the most part, retailers were enthusiastic about participating, often stating, "We've been waiting for something like this to happen!," that "something" being a way to use data that is already being collected and aggregated to eliminate the need to complete a survey instrument. However, some retailers declined to participate. Those that declined cited a variety of reasons ranging from legal and privacy concerns to difficulty understanding the purpose of the project. Others acknowledge that completing Census Bureau surveys is not that difficult for the retailer.

12.4.2 National-Level Data

For the initial national-level comparisons, data were purchased from NPD for three retailers that are good reporters to the MRTS, the ARTS, and the 2012 Economic Census. Good reported data are necessary to perform a baseline quality check of the NPD data. NPD reached out to their contacts at these retailers and obtained formal approval for the retailer's NPD data to be used in this research project.

Monthly data for 2012 through 2015 were obtained for the selected retailers. When conducting these types of comparisons, a year of data in which the Economic Census was conducted (2012 or 2017) is critical to successfully completing a baseline comparison of total retailer activity because the Economic Census collects total sales at the store location level.

Currently, no official or standardized quality measures are in place within the Economic Directorate to deem a retail third-party data source's quality acceptable. For this project, the focus is on how well the NPD data agree with the data that the retailer reported to the MRTS. Specifically, the focus is on determining if the data were consistently well correlated. The working quality metrics used in this project are the average and absolute average difference between the NPD data and the MRTS data as well as the number of months where the difference between the

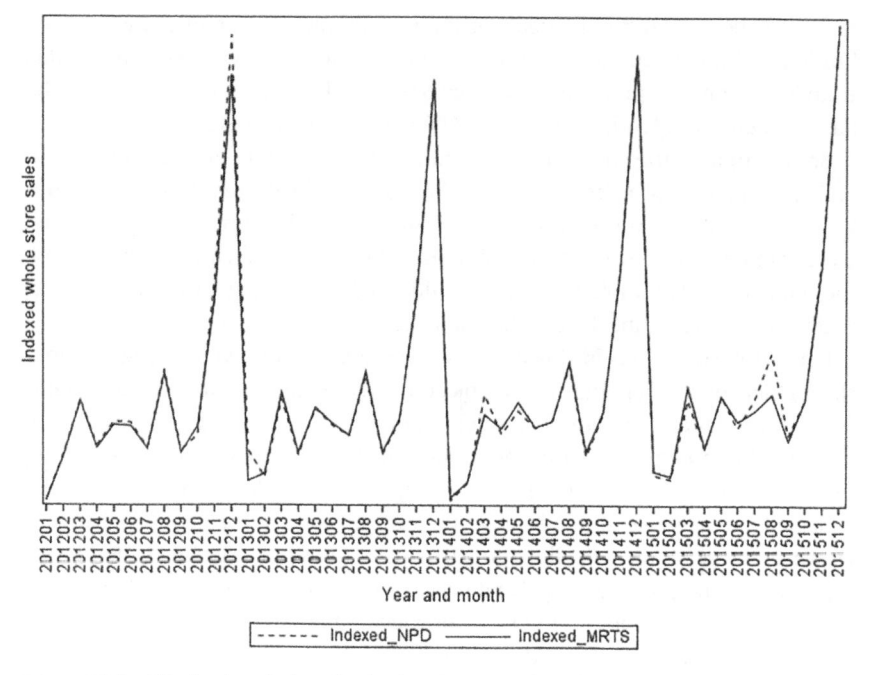

372 | *12 Investigating Alternative Data Sources to Reduce Respondent Burden*

Figure 12.2 Whole store indexed sales levels comparison for selected good reporting retailers by month, 2012–2015. Source: NPD and MRTS data.

NPD data and the MRTS data was less than 1%. At the national level, the NPD data for each of the retailers line up well when compared to the data reported by the retailers to the MRTS. Figure 12.2 shows a comparison of the indexed sum of whole store sales (brick and mortar sales plus e-commerce sales) between the NPD and MRTS data for the three retailers.

Table 12.2 displays the differences in sales at the national level between the NPD retailer data and the MRTS data; these differences were small and most months had absolute differences less than 1%.

The maximum absolute differences shown in Table 12.2 highlight that in some months, NPD data and MRTS data did not line up well. Because the data did line up during most months, the larger differences raised the question of determining which value was most accurate. The NPD feed could have been incorrect that month, or the retailer could have reported an incorrect value to MRTS. Of greater concern during this project are the months when the differences between the NPD data and the MRTS data were large and widespread. During this phase of the work, one year's worth of NPD data for one of the retailers was markedly different from the other three years of NPD data and exhibited a large deviation from the MRTS data that was not present in other years. NPD identified the source of the issue as a

Table 12.2 Descriptive statistics for differences between national retailer NPD data and Monthly Retail Trade Survey data.

	Retailer 1	Retailer 2	Retailer 3
Average difference between NPD and MRTS retail sales data levels (%)	−0.31	−0.11	0.60
Average absolute difference between NPD and MRTS retail sales data levels (%)	2.14	2.32	1.39
Median difference between NPD and MRTS retail sales data levels (%)	0.00	−0.55	0.13
Maximum absolute difference between NPD and MRTS retail sales data levels (%)	21.87	25.24	11.44
Minimum absolute difference between NPD and MRTS retail sales data levels (%)	0.00	0.02	0.05
Number of months out of the total 48 months where absolute difference between NPD and MRTS retail sales data levels was less than 1%	34	44	38

Source: NPD and MRTS data.

discrepancy that occurred when the retailer changed the format of its feed and an incorrect data feed overwrote the original, correct data. As a substitute, the retailer provided store-level totals for that year but no product-level information.

This issue also demonstrates one of the risks of relying on third-party data: occurrences of these problems could not be predicted if this effort moved from research to production. Additionally, if the NPD data were used in a production environment rather than research, time is critical to the MARTS and questions about the data must be resolved quickly. When a retailer provides a dollar value on a survey form that seems incorrect or questionable, retail analysts often follow up with the retailer via a phone call. When a questionable data value appears in a third-party dataset, the process for communicating questions is unclear. Are questions directed through the third-party vendor? How quickly can answers be obtained for indicator programs when time is limited?

Based on the comparisons between the NPD data and the MRTS data for good reporters, there was enough confidence in the national-level NPD data to expand the comparison to the purchase of two retailers who do not report to the MRTS. NPD secured permission from these two retailers to share data for this project; however, due to the limited availability of data that could be shared, only 2015, 2016, and 2017 data were available for purchase. These years differed from those used in the good reporter comparison but offered a substantial enough time series to study and draw preliminary conclusions.

Because these retailers did not report to the monthly survey, the comparison results were not as straightforward because there is not a known monthly baseline against which to compare. However, these retailers do report to the ARTS. These annual data provide an initial value to check the NPD data against the annual level. In a scenario where the retailer does not report to the annual survey as well, other comparison data could include the Economic Census or any publicly available financial filings.

Table 12.3 shows the differences for two years where reported ARTS data were available for these two retailers. These small differences provided a positive check in the confidence of the validity of the NPD data.

This portion of the project was not only a validation exercise of the NPD data but also of the imputation methodology used for the MRTS. The current imputation methodology estimates current month sales for a company. They are estimated based on the ratio of current month sales to prior month sales for companies in the same industry and of similar size that reported in both months. This ratio was applied to the company's prior month sales estimate to get current month sales. At the national level, the NPD data correlated well with the imputed MRTS data. Imputation methodology for the MRTS was based on having a consistent, repeatable process that reflects past information about the retailer as well as industry behavior from reporting companies each month. Thus, survey imputation will not often be successful in identifying retailer activity that is unusual. Point-of-sale data identify this unusual movement so differences between the NPD data and the imputed MRTS data were expected. That said, the primary goal of the MRTS is to generate the best month-to-month trends possible. There are little to no controls over the levels and levels change over time for a company that is consistently imputed. The ARTS data was used to adjust the levels annually using a benchmark operation at both a macro industry level and often at a micro company level. Since this is only done annually, imputed data levels can get off track over time so the most important quality metric for any consistently nonreporting retailer is how well the month-to-month changes compared between the NPD data and the MRTS data. As seen in Table 12.4, over half of month-to-month change differences were less than 1%.

Table 12.3 Differences between annual national retail sales in NPD data and Annual Retail Trade Survey data.

Difference between NPD and ARTS retail sales data levels	Retailer 1 (%)	Retailer 2 (%)
2015	−0.10	1.40
2016	−0.39	1.16

Source: NPD and ARTS data.

Table 12.4 Differences between month-to-month change in national sales in NPD data and Monthly Retail Trade Survey data.

	Retailer 1	Retailer 2
Average difference between NPD and MRTS retail sales data month-to-month change (%)	0.52	2.23
Average absolute difference between NPD and MRTS retail sales data month-to-month change (%)	5.30	8.53
Median difference between NPD and MRTS retail sales data month-to-month change (%)	−0.04	0.77
Maximum absolute difference between NPD and MRTS retail sales data month-to-month change (%)	12.32	29.89
Minimum absolute difference between NPD and MRTS retail sales data month-to-month change (%)	0.04	0.77
Number of months out of the total 35 months where the absolute difference between NPD and MRTS retail sales data month-to-month change was less than 1%[a]	21	18

a) Month-to-month change calculations require two months of data. For the first month of the time series, no prior month data were available so this calculation could not be done. So despite having 36 months of data, only 35 month-to-month changes were analyzed.
Source: NPD and MRTS data.

The results of these exercises provide confidence that the NPD data can be used in place of both reported and imputed monthly data at the national level for the MRTS. If a new retailer agrees to share its NPD data with the Census Bureau before that data was used in production, the full available time series from NPD needs to be analyzed and compared to the MRTS and the ARTS data to ensure confidence in these data extends to this retailer as well.

Additionally, timing and speed of delivery are critical to transitioning the use of this national point-of-sale data to production use. In order for the NPD data to be useful to the Census Bureau's MARTS and the MRTS, the data must be delivered promptly. For a retailer that is currently included in the MARTS sample, the NPD data must be delivered within 10 days of month's end to be included in the MARTS estimate. For inclusion in the MRTS estimate, the NPD data needs to be delivered within 30 days of month's end to be included in the estimate. NPD indicated it could deliver most retailer data within 10 days of month's end and deliver all retailer data within 20 days of month's end.

12.4.3 Store-Level Data

Unlike many of the Census Bureau surveys where data are collected at the company level, the Economic Census is conducted at the store or establishment level. A retailer with 100 store locations has to provide detailed product and business characteristic information for each individual location. Though only conducted every five years, Section 12.2 highlighted that the Economic Census is the most burdensome of the retail survey instruments; any third-party data source that could relieve even some of this burden would be welcomed. However, to reduce the respondent burden involved in the Economic Census, a third-party data source must have a similar, granular level of data collection: it must have detailed product sales information for each individual store location. One of the great features of the NPD data feeds is the rich, product-level data that they contain.

Using the three retailers from the Section 12.4.2 who were good reporters to the monthly, the annual, and the 2012 Economic Census, the store-level data from 2012 NPD were compared to the store-level data that each retailer provided to the 2012 Economic Census. The inclusion of the store number in the NPD datasets allows for a clean and logical match to the Economic Census database, which includes a store number variable in each store location record.

For the purposes of this work, the analysis focuses on how well the store locations and store sales correlated. Only one store location among all three retailers did not match between the NPD and Economic Census data. As shown in Table 12.5, the differences in sales at the store-level were on average under 2.5% and in most cases, were lower.

Based on the results of the store-level comparison above, data for 13 additional retailers were purchased and delivered in early 2017. Store-level tabulations of the NPD data were completed for these retailers before the initial mailing of the 2017 Economic Census. These tabulations from the NPD data will be compared to what the retailers ultimately report to the 2017 Economic Census. This effort will serve as a test to determine if by using a third-party source like NPD, Economic Census data could be collected earlier and at a lower burden to the retailer.

Table 12.5 Descriptive statistics for differences between store-level retailer NPD data and Economic Census data.

	Retailer 1	Retailer 2	Retailer 3
NPD/2012 Economic Census store location match rate (%)	100	99.9	100
Average percentage difference in store sales between NPD and 2012 Economic Census (%)	−2.36	−1.22	0.96
Median percentage difference in store sales between NPD and 2012 Economic Census (%)	−2.18	−1.18	0.31

Source: NPD and 2012 Economic Census data.

In addition to reducing respondent burden, store-level point-of-sale data has one other potential use: more timely updates to the Business Register, the database that houses the sampling frame for many of the economic surveys. When a retailer opens or closes a store location, there can be a lag until that information is updated in Census Bureau databases. Because NPD receives data weekly or monthly up to the point that a store location closes, the Census Bureau has the potential to know of closures sooner. Likewise, a store location opening would be identified in near real-time on the NPD feeds. This potential use will be explored more in the future.

12.4.4 Product Data

Every five years, the Economic Census collects detailed product-line sales, receipts, or revenues from retailers. Approximately three years after the end of the Economic Census year, product-level reports are made available to the public. The product-level data are valuable to Census Bureau data users but come at the cost of high respondent burden for retailers and of a delivery with a nearly three-year lag. Product-level data are one area where alternative data sources – including point-of-sale data – could help not only with reducing respondent burden but also in creating more timely product reports, since data would be available more frequently than every five years.

Point-of-sale data from NPD are collected at the stock-keeping unit (SKU) level, which allows retailers to track product inventories. By collecting data at the SKU level, NPD is able to assign detailed product attributes to each of these SKUs and place them into broader categories including apparel, small appliances, automotive, beauty, fashion accessories, consumer electronics, footwear, office supplies, toys, video games, and jewelry. These categories are defined differently than the product-level categories defined by the Census Bureau, which makes sense as the two organizations are serving two different – though likely somewhat overlapping – data user groups. For this reason, the product-line work focuses on whether or not a mapping between the NPD product lines and the Census Bureau product lines is even feasible.

This project falls during a time of transition for product-line data collection at the Census Bureau. Through the 2012 Economic Census, the Census Bureau collected product-level data at product lines defined for each industry (retail, wholesale, manufacturing, and so on) by the Census Bureau. With the 2017 Economic Census, the North American Product Classification System (NAPCS) was fully implemented. NAPCS moves product classification away from an industry-based system and into a demand-based, hierarchical classification system. The new system is consistent across the three North American countries of Canada, Mexico, and the United States.

This project began in 2016, before the start of the 2017 Economic Census data collection, and early datasets from NPD contained 2012 data. To keep the project moving along, the classification system used in the 2012 Economic Census was used to gain an early understanding of the NPD product classification system with the goal of applying this knowledge to mapping the NPD product catalog to NAPCS. The large number of product categories in the NPD data and in the Economic Census data required narrowing the scope of the effort to make the mapping exercise feasible while still gaining useful information. The project focused on the product category of apparel, because it was perceived to be the easiest category to map. However, this mapping exercise was not simple. During the proof-of-concept phase, a high-level product mapping of the apparel category was completed. Table 12.6 displays this mapping. Column 2 displays the NPD product categories; Column 3 displays the product lines used in the 2012 Economic Census. One-to-one matches are highlighted in black; partial matches are highlighted in light gray; nonmatches are white.

Notable issues highlighted by this mapping exercise include:

- *Level of comparison*: The 2012 Economic Census product lines were broken out by men's, women's, and children's apparel items. NPD's breakouts were by apparel type. By far, the biggest takeaway of this effort was that NPD had to provide additional attributes that would identify the apparel product types as men's or women's. This issue likely extends to other product categories as well.
- *Limited one-to-one mappings*: The lone perfect one-to-one product-line match between NPD and the 2012 Economic Census product lines was dresses. Smaller buckets were created to allow for more specific matching. For example, pants, jeans, shorts, shorts/skirts, and other bottoms were product-line categories in the NPD data that could be combined and compared to an aggregation of the men's tailored and dress slacks, men's casual slacks, jeans, shorts, etc., and women's slacks/pants, jeans, shorts, skirts from the 2012 Economic Census product lines. Additionally, the 2012 Economic Census product line for women's suits, pantsuits, sport jackets, and blazers included both the suit and suit separates and the jackets, blazers, and sports coat categories NPD used. These buckets would not be problematic provided that enough product-level detail was available to ensure the correct products were assigned to the correct buckets.

Product-level data from the 2012 Economic Census and product-level data from 2012 in the NPD data are available for most retailers included in the project.

Table 12.6 Initial NPD and Economic Census product mapping of apparel categories.

General category	NPD product category	2012 Economic Census product line
Accessories	Scarves/mufflers, headwear, handwear, handbags, totes/shoppers, checkbook holder, cosmetic bag, key fobs/cases, money accessories, wallet, wristlet	Men's hats, gloves, neckwear, handkerchief, and belts
		Women's handbags, wallets, neckwear, gloves, belts, rain accessories, hats, wigs, and hairpieces
Athletic wear	Active bottoms, athletic sets, bodysuit/leotards, swimwear	Men's sport apparel
		Women's sport apparel
Bottoms	Pants, jeans, shorts, skirts, skorts, other bottoms	Men's tailored and dress slacks, casual slacks and jeans, and shorts
		Women's slacks/pants, jeans, shorts, and skirts
Dresses	Dresses	Women's dresses
Outerwear	Outerwear bottoms, outerwear suits/sets, outerwear tops	Men's overcoats, topcoats, raincoats, and outer jackets
		Women's dressy and tailored coats, outer jackets, and rainwear
Tops	Dress shirts, knit shirts, sweaters, sweatshirts, woven shirts	Men's dress shirts, sport shirts, and sweaters
		Women's tops
Undergarments	Bras, cold weather undergarments, panties, shapewear, sheer hosiery, sleepwear, socks, tights, undershirts, underwear bottoms	Men's hosiery, pajamas, robes, and underwear
		Women's hosiery, bras, girdles, corsets, lingerie, sleepwear, and loungewear
Suits	Suits and suit separates Jackets, blazers, and sports coats	Men's suits and formal wear
		Men's sport coats and blazers
		Women's suits, pantsuits, sport jackets, and blazers
Children and infant clothing	Children's/infants' sets Special infants' wear	Boys' clothing and accessories
		Girls' clothing and accessories
		Infants' and toddlers' clothing and accessories

(Continued)

Table 12.6 (Continued)

General category	NPD product category	2012 Economic Census product line
Other	No comparable NPD product category	Men's other apparel
	No comparable NPD product category	Men's custom-made garments
	No comparable NPD product category	Men's career and work uniforms
	No comparable NPD product category	Women's fur garments
	No comparable NPD product category	Women's other apparel
	No comparable NPD product category	Women's sweat tops, pants, and warm-ups
	No comparable NPD product category	Women's custom-made garments

However, the complexities of the apparel product matching in Table 12.6 made it impossible to draw any meaningful conclusions from comparing the 2012 Economic Census apparel sales data to the NPD apparel sales data. Instead, the focus of the effort shifted to what additional information is needed from NPD to map its full product catalog to NAPCS, which would allow for meaningful comparisons of the NPD data to 2017 Economic Census product data.

NPD has since been able to provide additional product-level data. With this additional information, the strategy for the mapping was to assign a NAPCS code to each item in the NPD product catalog with assistance from classification staff at the Census Bureau as well as product-line experts at NPD. With this additional information from NPD, a NAPCS code was successfully assigned to every item in the NPD product catalog. Figure 12.3 uses an apparel example to demonstrate how this added level of detail helped with this exercise.

With this mapping successfully completed, sales in the NPD dataset could be tabulated by NAPCS code. As 2017 Economic Census data are collected from retailers included in the NPD project, comparisons between the NPD product-level data and the 2017 Economic Census data by NAPCS code will be completed. However, this is also the first Economic Census year that retailers were required to report data to the Economic Census using NAPCS classifications, so this may introduce uncertainty to any comparison results.

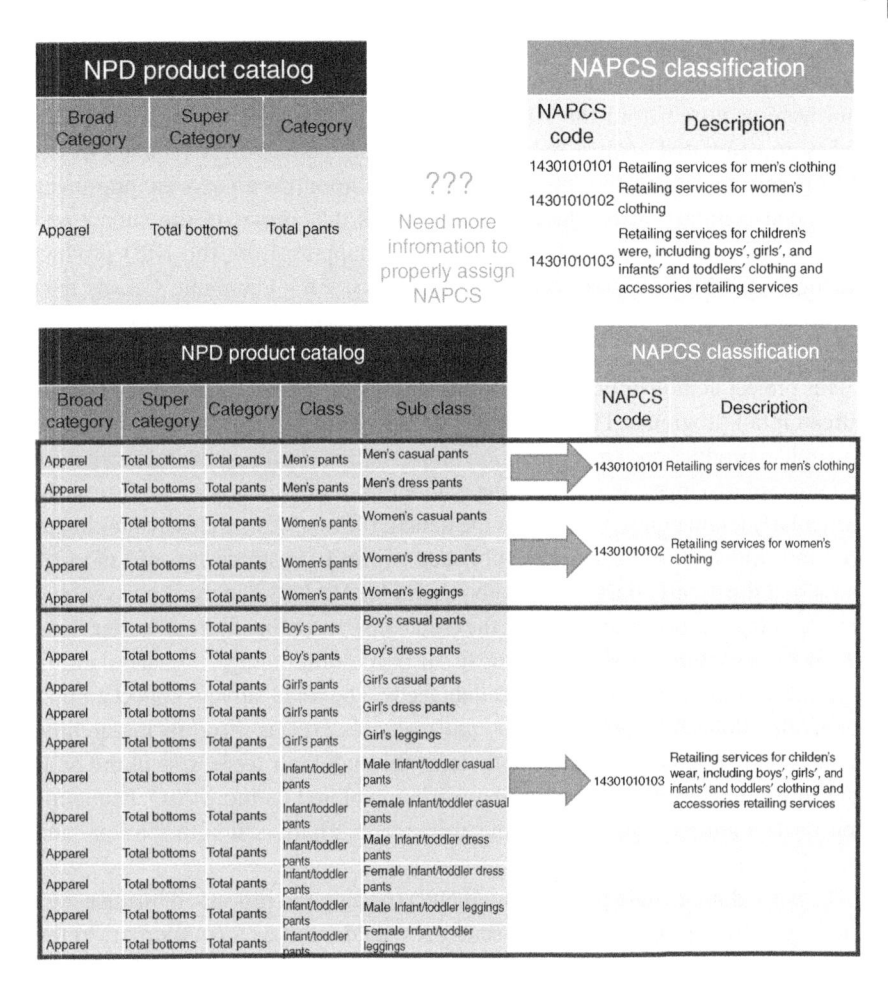

Figure 12.3 Final NPD and Economic Census product mapping of apparel categories.

12.5 Summary

In this chapter, we explored the use of alternative data sources to reduce respondent burden in Census Bureau retail surveys. The demand for more timely data in an evolving retail economy coincides with falling survey response rates often due to respondent burden. As part of its Big Data vision, the Census Bureau has begun exploring if alternative data sources could be used to reduce burden while maintaining the high quality of its official statistics. For the retail sector of the economy, point-of-sale data are one potential alternative data source. Point-of-sale data were acquired from the NPD Group, Inc. at the store and product levels and were compared against data currently being tabulated for retailers in the MARTS and the 2012 Economic Census. Results from this effort were promising with good comparison results for both retailers that report to the survey and retailers that are nonrespondents. A product mapping from the NPD product catalog to the NAPCS was also completed. Once 2017 Economic Census data are available for the purchased retailers, we will compare that data to the NPD data.

This project demonstrated great potential for using point-of-sale data in Census Bureau retail programs. The real challenge lies ahead in moving this work from research to production. The production phase requires building the infrastructure and processes to ingest and review the data for real-time use in the retail surveys. Particularly challenging is the use of the data in the MARTS – a closely monitored economic indicator – because it is published within 10 business days of a month's end. For a third-party data source to be useful for MARTS, the third-party would need to collect, process, and deliver the data consistently in an even shorter time, which is not something NPD has done in the past. Additionally, only sales data are currently available through the NPD data feeds. The retail surveys collect a number of other items including inventory and expenses. NPD is currently researching the feasibility of collecting other data items through their feeds. Use of the NPD data in the Economic Census will be further explored as more 2017 Economic Census data are reported and become available for analysis at both the store and product levels.

The work done to date has motivated NPD to begin the process of hiring a data scientist for this project. This data scientist would work as a counterpart to the analysis work done by the Census Bureau. Although NPD has technical staff dedicated to the project, no one is dedicated to helping with retailer data issues both proactively and reactively. If the NPD data were to be used in a production environment rather than research, time would be critical when using the NPD data for the MRTS – and questions regarding the data need to be resolved quickly. When a retailer provides a dollar value on a survey that seems incorrect or questionable, retail analysts often follow up with the retailer via a phone call or secure communication. When a questionable data value appears in a third-party dataset, the process for communicating questions is unclear. Are questions directed through the third-party vendor? How quickly can answers be obtained for indicator programs when time is limited? With NPD placing a dedicated staff member in this new role, the Census Bureau will work to determine the process to answer these questions.

The Big Data vision of the Census Bureau goes beyond using this type of data to reduce burden; it also seeks to leverage data sources like point-of-sale data with existing survey and administrative data to provide more timely data products, to offer greater insight into the nation's economy through detailed geographic and industry-level estimates, and to improve efficiency and quality throughout the survey life cycle. The NPD data offer an exciting opportunity to help fulfill this vision. Of particular interest are the product-level data. The Census Bureau currently only publishes product-level data every five years using data from the Economic Census. The NPD data has monthly product-level information that could be used to create more timely product-level data products. Additionally, the monthly datasets include store-level information, which means the NPD data can identify store openings and closures quicker than current Census Bureau survey operations. Developing a pipeline to use the NPD data to create a more up-to-date picture of retail economic turnover would be valuable both at the national level and at more granular geographies.

As exciting as its progress has been, the project still faces challenges to actual use in a production environment. First, only sales data are currently available through the NPD data feeds. The retail surveys collect a number of other items including inventories and expenses. NPD is currently working to check the feasibility of collecting other data items through their feeds and other non-NPD data sources that contain business operations data may also be able to provide additional data items. Until then, traditional survey collection instruments will need to collect the remaining items and respondents will still take on burden. Additionally, even if every retailer that works with NPD agrees to share its NPD data with the Census Bureau, this data still only makes up about 30% of the retail estimate. How the remaining 70% of the retail universe can benefit from a similar effort is a question that needs exploring.

In addition to the actual implementation and data product work, the Census Bureau continues to tackle the difficult issues and questions that accompany the use of third-party data sources, not just for retail but across trade areas. One question is how the risk of a change in availability of a retailer's data from a third party can be mitigated. If the contract ends or if a retailer's data are no longer available through a third party, how that retailer is placed back into traditional survey collection operations is a process that will need to be developed. Additionally, a third-party vendor could create its own data product comparable to an existing Census Bureau data product. Finally, there is not an official set of guidelines in place to determine if the quality of a third-party data source is good enough to use in place of survey data. Although determining quality will always have a subjective element, a checklist of objective measurements that could be followed and recorded for third-party data review would allow for a consistent review across the Census Bureau.

Disclaimer

Any views expressed are those of the author and not necessarily those of the United States Census Bureau.

Disclosure

The Census Bureau has reviewed this data product for unauthorized disclosure of confidential information and has approved the disclosure avoidance practices applied. (Approval ID: CBDRB-FY19-184)

References

American Association for Public Opinion Research (AAPOR) (2015). AAPOR report on Big Data, AAPOR Big Data Task Force 2015. AAPOR, https://www.aapor.org/Education-Resources/Reports/Big-Data.aspx (accessed 27 March 2020).

Bird, D., Breton, R., Payne, C., et al. (2014). Initial report on experiences with scanner data in ONS. https://www.ons.gov.uk/ons/guide-method/user-guidance/prices/cpi-and-rpi/initial-report-on-experiences-with-scanner-data-in-ons.pdf (accessed 21 August 2018).

Boettcher, I. (2014). One size fits all? The need to cope with different levels of scanner data quality for CPI computation. Paper from the UNECE Expert Group Meeting on CPI, Geneva (26–28 May 2014). https://www.unece.org/fileadmin/DAM/stats/documents/ece/ces/ge.22/2014/WS4/WS4_04_One_size_fits_all.pdf (accessed 21 August 2018).

Dumbacher, B.A. and Hanna, D. (2017). Using passive data collection, system-to-system data collection, and machine learning to improve economic surveys. Paper from the 2017 Joint Statistical Meetings, Baltimore, MD. http://ww2.amstat.org/meetings/jsm/2017/onlineprogram/AbstractDetails.cfm?abstractid=322018 (accessed 18 February 2019).

Eurostat (2017). Practical guide for processing supermarket scanner data. https://circabc.europa.eu/sd/a/8e1333df-ca16-40fc-bc6a-1ce1be37247c/Practical-Guide-Supermarket-Scanner-Data-September-2017.pdf (accessed 13 March 2020).

Haraldsen, G., Jones, J., Giesen, D. et al. (2013). Understanding and coping with response burden. In: *Designing and Conducting Business Surveys* (eds. G. Snijkers, G. Haraldsen, J. Jones, et al.), 219–252. Hoboken, NJ: Wiley.

Horrigan, M. (2013). *Big Data and Official Statistics*. Washington, DC: Bureau of Labor Statistics https://www.bls.gov/osmr/symp2013_horrigan.pdf.

IBM (2016). IBM researchers use grocery scanner data to speed investigations during early foodborne illness outbreaks. Press release (12 August).

Jarmin, R.S. (2019). Evolving measurement for an evolving economy: thoughts on 21st century US economic statistics. *Journal of Economic Perspectives* 33 (1): 165–184.

Krebs, A. (2016). What's in a number? Leveraging scanner data to understand the retail beef consumer. *Beef Issues Quarterly* (13 October 2016). http://www.beefissuesquarterly.com/CMDocs/BeefResearch/BIQ/Fall%202016%20Full%20BIQ.pdf.

Miloslavskaya, N. and Tolstoy, A. (2016). Big data, fast data, and data lake concepts. *Procedia Computer Science* 88: 300–305.

U.S. Census Bureau (2018). U.S. Census Bureau Strategic Plan – fiscal year 2018 through fiscal year 2022. https://www.census.gov/content/dam/Census/about/about-the-bureau/PlansAndBudget/strategicplan18-22.pdf (accessed 21 August 2018).

U.S. Office of Management and Budget (2017). Analytical perspectives. https://www.whitehouse.gov/wp-content/uploads/2018/02/ap_15_statistics-fy2019.pdf (accessed 26 June 2018).

U.S. Office of Personnel Management (2011). Paperwork Reduction Act (PRA) guide version 2.0. https://www.opm.gov/about-us/open-government/digital-government-strategy/fitara/paperwork-reduction-act-guide.pdf (accessed 17 August 2018).

Willeboordse, A. (1997). Minimizing response burden. In: *Handbook on Design and Implementation of Business Surveys* (ed. A. Willeboordse), 111–118. Luxembourg: Eurostat http://ec.europa.eu/eurostat/ramon/statmanuals/files/Handbook%20on%20surveys.pdf.

Willimack, D.K. and Nichols, E. (2010). A hybrid response process model for business surveys. *Journal of Official Statistics* 25 (1): 3–24.

Section 4

Combining Big Data with Survey Statistics: Methods and Applications

13

Effects of Incentives in Smartphone Data Collection

Georg-Christoph Haas[1,2], Frauke Kreuter[1,2,3], Florian Keusch[2,3], Mark Trappmann[1,4], and Sebastian Bähr[1]

[1] Institute for Employment Research, Nuremberg, Germany
[2] Joint Program in Survey Methodology, University of Maryland, College Park, MD, USA
[3] Department of Sociology, School of Social Sciences, University of Mannheim, Germany
[4] University of Bamberg, Bamberg, Germany

13.1 Introduction

Smartphone sensor data enable researchers to analyze phenomena that cannot be investigated with survey data alone (e.g. Sugie 2018). However, smartphone data may include very sensitive information, e.g. on geolocation or app usage, which users may perceive as too private to share with researchers. To date, very little research has systematically examined participation in studies that collect passive smartphone sensor data. To our knowledge, no study so far has examined whether the knowledge about the effectiveness of incentives in surveys also holds for smartphone sensor data collection. Common incentive amounts and incentive schemes traditionally used in surveys may not be sufficient to motivate participation in a study that collects data passively from smartphones, given that individuals may perceive sensor data as more valuable than survey data. However, since participation in passive data collection requires less effort from participants, burden (measured in time spent on data collection) is much reduced compared to regular surveys. Therefore, recruiting participants might be easier, and the effect of incentives on participation might be less pronounced. In either case, it is important for researchers to know whether vulnerable groups are particularly receptive to incentives, compared to majority groups in a population. Institutional review boards and ethics committees would likely hesitate to approve a study that – by using monetary incentives – places vulnerable populations, e.g. welfare recipients, at greater risk of providing sensitive data. For these reasons, we not only analyze effects of different incentive schemes on participation rates in a study

Big Data Meets Survey Science: A Collection of Innovative Methods, First Edition. Edited by Craig A. Hill, Paul P. Biemer, Trent D. Buskirk, Lilli Japec, Antje Kirchner, Stas Kolenikov, and Lars E. Lyberg.
© 2021 John Wiley & Sons, Inc. Published 2021 by John Wiley & Sons, Inc.

combining self-reports and passive data collection using smartphones but also break out these effects by economic subgroups. In Section 13.2, we start with a brief review of the literature on the effectiveness of incentives and the postulated mechanisms explaining these effects. Section 13.3 explains the study design with an emphasis on the experimental conditions (more details on study design features are described in Kreuter et al. (2018)). Section 13.4 displays the results, which we will discuss in Section 13.5 paired with suggestions for future research.

13.2 The Influence of Incentives on Participation

Providing some form of incentive, whether monetary or some other kind of token of appreciation, is common for studies recruiting respondents to answer survey questions (see, for example, James and Bolstein 1990; Church 1993; Willimack et al. 1995; Singer, Groves, and Corning 1999; Singer 2002; Toepoel 2012; Pforr 2016). Singer and Ye (2013) summarize the findings of two decades of research on this topic and state that monetary (cash) incentives are more effective in increasing response rates than are gifts or in-kind incentives, and prepaid incentives are more effective than are promised incentives. Although incentive amounts have increased over time, Singer and Ye (2013, p. 18) also report that research points to the nonlinear effect of monetary incentives, though generally higher incentives increase response rates more than lower ones do.

To gauge how findings from surveys translate to data collection on smartphones, it is helpful to review the different mechanisms suggested to explain the effect of incentives. Going all the way back to the 1960s, Singer and Ye (2013, p. 115) pointed to social exchange and the "norm of reciprocity" as an explanation for the effectiveness of prepaid incentives. Social exchange theory argues that prepaid incentives create an obligation to provide on individuals, which they can settle by responding to the survey. The effectiveness of promised incentives – paid conditionally after the survey has been completed – could be better explained by various "versions of utility theories" (Singer and Ye 2013, p. 115), arguing that people decide on a course of action if, in their view, the benefits of acting outweigh the costs. Since we only use promised incentives, we can only test the hypotheses of the utility theories framework – albeit, as we will explain below, we paid incentives continuously and respondents did not have to wait until the whole study was over.

In the context of utility theories, the question arises of what value a given incentive has for an individual. In their discussion of Leverage-saliency theory, Groves, Singer, and Corning (2000) emphasized the relative importance of various features of the survey in the decision-making process, together with how salient these features are to the sample case. Incentives can be used as leverage to increase survey participation, and Groves et al. (2006) demonstrated that people with low interest in a survey topic can be recruited by monetary incentives that compensate for the lack of interest. Therefore, higher incentives may be used to increase the leverage, whereby research suggests that, compared to lower incentives, higher incentives have a diminishing marginal utility to increase response rates (Singer and Ye 2013; Mercer et al. 2015).

Experiments in panel studies suggest that incentives also have a long-term effect on survey participation. Incentives only need to be paid in one wave to increase participation for the current and following waves, and larger incentives lead to higher response rates in later waves (Singer and Kulka 2002; Goldenberg, McGrath, and Tan 2009). For continuous data collection in a smartphone app study, this result could mean that a higher incentive for installing the app may increase participants' commitment throughout the data collection period to keep the app installed and lower attrition or that a higher incentive for installing the app may nudge participants to allow more passive data permissions.

Jäckle et al. (2019) are the first to evaluate the effect of incentives on installing a research app. The app served as a data collection instrument for a spending study in the United Kingdom. Participants had to download the app and upload receipts over the course of a month. The authors randomly assigned sample members into two groups and offered £2 or £6 for downloading the app. For each of the three examined outcomes (completion of the registration survey, proportion of individuals using the app at least once, and proportion of individuals using the app at least once per week over the data collection period), the £6 incentive produced higher rates than did the £2 incentive, but the differences were not statistically significant for any of the outcome variables. The lack of effect might have been a result of the small monetary difference between the two incentive groups.

A concern often voiced in the context of incentives is that the same monetary amount has a higher value for individuals with less wealth (Philipson 1997; Felderer et al. 2017). If this observation is indeed true, economically disadvantaged sample members might be more inclined to provide data in general and sensitive sensor data in particular.

If incentive payments are perceived as compensation for the time and effort a respondent provides (Philipson 1997), the opportunity cost for low-income individuals should be lower compared to high-income groups, and incentives should have a stronger effect on low-income individuals. This notion is supported by findings from Mack et al. (1998), who found that a US$20 incentive, compared to a US$10 incentive and to no incentive, disproportionately increased participation of individuals with less wealth. Singer et al. (1999) also found that incentives increased response propensities of low-income individuals.

In the context of a smartphone app study such as the one described below, it is not clear whether utility theories are applicable in a similar fashion. Compared to telephone and face-to-face interviews, relatively little time is needed to install an app and to have it run in the background for data collection. However, one could argue that in the case of research apps, data is exchanged for money rather than time. In general, individuals, if asked hypothetically, are concerned about their privacy when they are asked to share their data passively with researchers (Jäckle et al. 2019; Revilla, Couper, and Ochoa 2018; Keusch et al. 2017; Wenz, Jäckle, and Couper 2017). Those concerns may be tied to trust issues: individuals do not trust researchers to protect their data adequately. However, their concerns seem to decrease, i.e. their willingness to participate increases, if they are offered more control over when the data are collected, if the study is sponsored by a university (compared with a governmental institution), and if the study offers incentives (Keusch et al. 2017). Cantor, O'Hare, and O'Connor (2008) and Goldenberg, Smyth, and Christian (2014) pointed out that incentives can be used to establish trust and that trust is more important for gaining cooperation than the incentive value. If these observations describe the major mechanism, we would expect a certain threshold to be needed to establish trust but would not necessarily expect increasing incentive amounts to have a linear effect on participation.

The study presented in this chapter has several novel characteristics with respect to issuing incentives. First, incentives are paid to participants for installing an app that passively collects data (if the participant grants informed consent) and presents short surveys to participants. Second, incentives are paid for the actual permission to collect such passive data for 30 consecutive days. Without this permission, the app only collects survey and para data (i.e. time stamps and information on whether the data sharing is activated). Third, incentives are paid for answering survey questions. For the first two tasks, the amount and conditions of the incentives were randomly varied, and it is the effects of these variations on participation behavior we examine in detail.

Broadly speaking, we try to answer the following questions: Do we observe effects of different incentive amounts on the installation rate of a research app? Are these effects proportional to the incentive amounts provided? Do incentives affect participants' decisions to share passive data or to deinstall the app? Do we observe differential effects of incentives, with vulnerable (less wealthy) groups being more receptive to higher incentives than nonvulnerable groups? How much money is actually paid out, i.e. participants downloading vouchers from the app?

13.3 Institut für Arbeitsmarkt- und Berufsforschung (IAB)-SMART Study Design

The goal of the IAB-SMART study is to gain insights into the effects of long-term unemployment on social inclusion and social integration and to examine effects of network integration on reintegration into the labor market using a new data collection approach. For context, three sets of data are needed to achieve the substantive research goals: (i) a reliable data source about the employment status of the study participants (available at the IAB through social security administration records; see Jacobebbinghaus and Seth (2007)), (ii) background variables on the study participants (available through IAB surveys), and (iii) behavioral measures on the amount of social interaction and network activities (available through the IAB-SMART study). For more details on the overall study design and measurements, see also Kreuter et al. (2018).

13.3.1 Sampling Frame and Sample Restrictions

Participants for the IAB-SMART study were sampled from the German Panel Study Labour Market and Social Security (PASS), an annual household panel survey of the German residential population aged 15 and older that oversamples households receiving welfare benefits. PASS is primarily designed as a data source for research into the labor market, poverty, and the welfare state. However, PASS also focuses on the social consequences of poverty and unemployment, including social exclusion and health outcomes. At the time of the IAB-SMART study, PASS had been in the field for 12 years (more information on PASS can be found in the annual PASS methods and data reports available at https://fdz.iab.de/de/FDZ_Individual_Data/PASS.aspx). Due to the ability to match data collection outcomes of PASS against high-quality administrative records from social security notifications and labor market programs, extensive nonresponse studies are available for PASS, showing rather small biases for a range of variables such as benefit receipt, employment status, income, age, and disability (Kreuter, Couper, and Lyber 2010; Levenstein 2010; Sakshaug and Kreuter 2012). Foreign nationals were found to be considerably underrepresented in PASS (Kreuter, Couper, and Lyber 2010), but weighting can adjust for this underrepresentation.

All PASS respondents who participated in wave 11 (2017) and reported having an Android smartphone (see Figure 13.1) were eligible for the IAB-SMART app study. We restricted the study to Android devices because extensive passive data collection is restricted under iOS (Harari et al. 2016), and other operating systems had market shares that were too low to justify additional programming efforts. For the purposes of the incentive study, we do not expect the operating system to have any limiting factor, though we discuss this point in the discussion section. Keusch et al. (2020) examined issues of coverage and found that smartphone owners in Germany were younger, more educated, and more likely to live in larger communities than were non-smartphone owners, but the authors reported little coverage bias in substantial PASS variables due to smartphone ownership. These results hold even when limiting the sample to Android smartphone owners only.

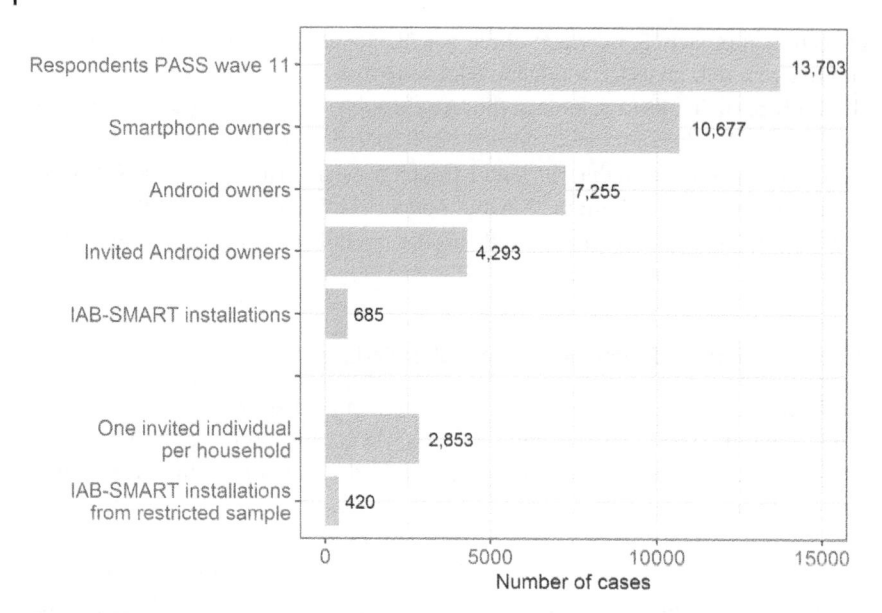

Figure 13.1 Sample size at each stage of the IAB-SMART selection process.

13.3.2 Invitation and Data Request

The invitation to participate in the IAB-SMART study was sent in January 2018 to a random sample of PASS Wave 11 participants aged 18–65 who reported owning an Android smartphone ($N = 4293$). To participate in the study, smartphone owners had to install an app on their smartphone and activate the data-sharing functions explained below. The field period of the study was six months.

Our initial goal was to recruit 500 participants. Because response rates to smartphone data collection with extensive data-sharing functionalities were hard to gauge from the literature, we sent invitations in two installments. We used the first round of invitations to 1074 PASS participants to monitor uptake rates. The second round of invitations was sent to an additional 3219 PASS participants.

The invitation package sent in both installments contained several pieces: a cover letter (explaining the goals of the study and how to find the app in the Google Play store), information on data protection and privacy, a description of the data-sharing functions, and an explanation of the incentives. Each letter contained a unique registration code. A reminder mailing was sent after 11 days, including an installation brochure, which explained the downloading and registration process to users step by step. In the second installment, the installation brochure was added to the first mailing. The addition of the installation brochure did not have a significant effect on installation rates. See the online appendix in Kreuter et al. (2018) for full documentation of the invitation materials.

Those willing to participate in the study had three tasks incentivized separately: (i) installing the app from the Google Play store using the QR code, using the link

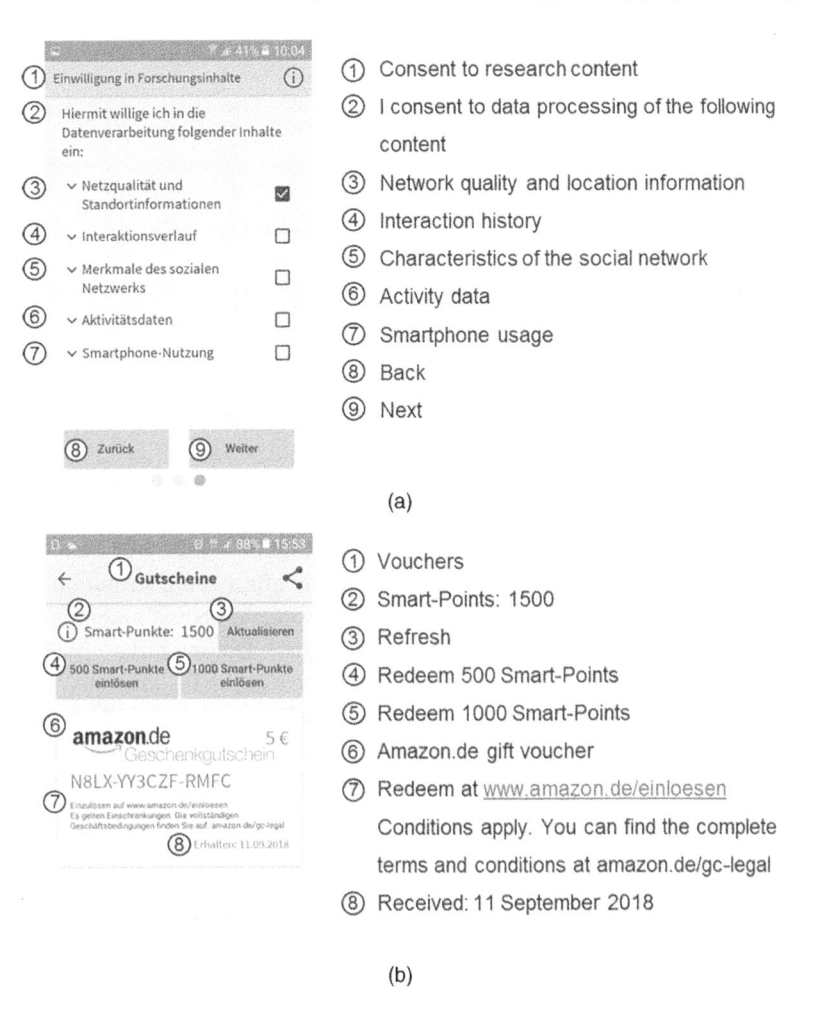

13.3 Institut für Arbeitsmarkt- und Berufsforschung (IAB)-SMART Study Design

① Consent to research content
② I consent to data processing of the following content
③ Network quality and location information
④ Interaction history
⑤ Characteristics of the social network
⑥ Activity data
⑦ Smartphone usage
⑧ Back
⑨ Next

(a)

① Vouchers
② Smart-Points: 1500
③ Refresh
④ Redeem 500 Smart-Points
⑤ Redeem 1000 Smart-Points
⑥ Amazon.de gift voucher
⑦ Redeem at www.amazon.de/einloesen
Conditions apply. You can find the complete terms and conditions at amazon.de/gc-legal
⑧ Received: 11 September 2018

(b)

Figure 13.2 Screen-shots showing the five data-sharing functions (a) and in-app Amazon.de vouchers (b). *Note*: The app was programmed and offered in German, but direct translations into English are provided in the figure.

provided in the invitation letter, or by searching for the app name directly in the store, (ii) allowing the app to collect sensor and other passive measurements, and (iii) answering survey questions launched through the app at predefined times or triggered by geo-locations. All participants were offered incentives in form of Amazon.de vouchers (see Figure 13.2b) based on the number of points earned (one point = one euro-cent). Vouchers were available for every 500 points earned (€5). The total amount a participant could earn varied between €60 and €100, depending on the incentive condition (see Section 13.3.3).

Experimental conditions were assigned randomly to the selected PASS participants. However, because PASS is a household panel, some households received

```
┌─────────────────────────┐   ┌─────────────────────────┐   ┌─────────────────────────┐   ┌─────────────────────────┐
│ Installation experiment │   │  Function experiment    │   │   Survey completion     │   │    Overall amount       │
└─────────────────────────┘   └─────────────────────────┘   └─────────────────────────┘   └─────────────────────────┘
```

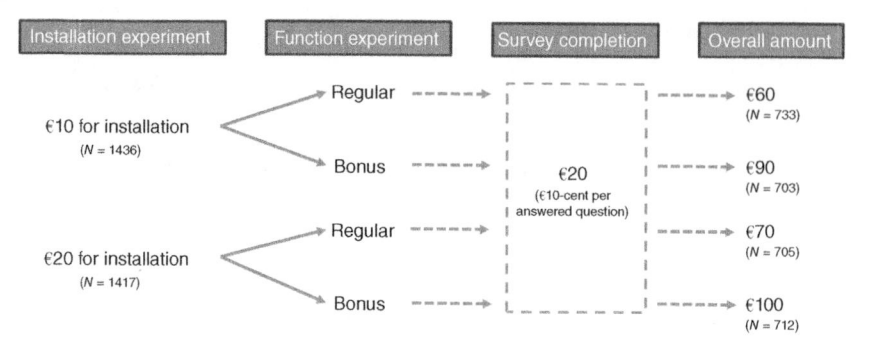

                          ──→ Regular ─ ─ ─ → ┌ ─ ─ ─ ─ ─ ─ ┐   ─ ─ ─ ─ → €60
      €10 for installation   (N = 733)
           (N = 1436)   │   €20   │
                          ──→ Bonus   ─ ─ ─ →   (€10-cent per ─ ─ ─ ─ → €90
                                                │answered question)│   (N = 703)
                          ──→ Regular ─ ─ ─ →   ─ ─ ─ ─ → €70
      €20 for installation   (N = 705)
           (N = 1417)   │   │
                          ──→ Bonus   ─ ─ ─ → └ ─ ─ ─ ─ ─ ─ ┘   ─ ─ ─ ─ → €100
                                                                               (N = 712)

Figure 13.3 Crossed experimental design with maximum incentive amounts for six-month data collection period (N = 2853).

different incentive conditions within the same household. To avoid any confounding due to family members talking to each other, we restricted our analysis to those households that had only one person selected into the IAB-SMART study (N = 2853). This restriction did not negatively affect the distribution of cases to incentive groups (see Figure 13.3, showing roughly equal amounts of cases in each condition within each of the two factors). However, the number of app installations we could use decreased from 685 to 420 app installations.

The data passively collected through IAB-SMART are grouped into five data-sharing functions. Individuals who installed the app could consent to sharing their data via any or all of these five functions. Participants could enable and disable data collection in any or all of the five functions at any point in time during the six-month study period (for more details on the consent process, see Kreuter et al. (2018)). We designed a separate screen for respondents to navigate their data sharing (Figure 13.2a). Allowing *Network quality and location information* issues a test every 30 minutes where Wi-Fi and mobile network data are collected. Those data allow estimates of the current geo-position of the smartphone. *Interaction history* records metadata from incoming and outgoing calls and text messages with hashed phone numbers (i.e. taking a string [phone number] of any length and output a nonpersonal random string of a fixed length). The *Characteristics of the social network* function allows, if enabled, access to the phone's address book and the classification of contacts into gender and nationalities using the following two websites: genderize.io and www.name-prism.com. Information is sent to the site, without any names stored on either provider's site. Resulting classification probabilities are retrieved and combined with the hashed phone book contact. The *Activity data* function collects measurements in two-minute intervals via the smartphone's accelerometer and pedometer. *Smartphone usage* captures the apps installed on the phone and the start/end-time of each app usage without recording any information about activities conducted within an app.

13.3.3 Experimental Design for Incentive Study[1]

We conducted a 2 × 2 experiment on the installation and the function incentives (see Figure 13.3). One random group of participants was promised €10 for installing the app, and the other group was promised €20. Independent of the installation incentive (completely crossed), one random group was promised one euro for each function activated for 30 consecutive days, and the other group was promised one euro for each function activated for consecutive 30 days plus five additional euro if all five data-sharing functions were activated for 30 days. Consequently, the first group would receive €5 and the second group €10 per month for activating all five data-sharing functions. For simplicity, we refer to the groups of the function experiment as the *regular* and *bonus* group. Additionally, all participants received up to €20 for answering survey questions in the app over the field period (10 euro-cent per answered question). Therefore, the maximum promised incentive varied between €60 and €100 depending on the assigned group. Participants could redeem their incentives directly in the app as Amazon.de vouchers.[2]

Because the invitation letter mentioned both the individual incentive amounts and the overall maximum amounts, respondents could have focused primarily on the overall maximum amounts and less on the differential incentives provided for installation and the app functions. Therefore, we report both marginal effects for each factor (installation experiment and function experiment, see Figure 13.3) and the combination of the two factors (maximum amounts of €60, €70, €90, and €100).

13.3.4 Analysis Plan

We will analyze the effect of incentives on four outcome variables: (i) installing the app on the smartphone (app installed vs. app not installed), (ii) number of initially activated data-sharing functions (0–5), (iii) deactivating functions during the field period (deactivated a function at least once vs. did not deactivate any functions), and (iv) retention (proportion of days out of field period until the app is deinstalled). For each of our four outcome variables, we use the following procedures. First, we use t-tests, χ^2 tests, and ANOVAs to examine the main effects of the incentive conditions in our three experiments, i.e. installation experiment,

---

[1] The invitation letter contained a flyer, which explained the incentive scheme (for the original flyer and English translation see Figures 13.A.1 and 13.A.2).
[2] When issuing the incentives, we allowed for discretion (e.g. due to network error, etc.). The IAB-SMART app checked whether each data collection function was activated at three random points in time each day. To receive points for activation, the app had to be able to execute the check on at least 10 out of 30 consecutive days. Furthermore, of the days the app was able to execute the check, the function was not allowed to be deactivated on more than three days. However, we did not explicitly mention this point to participants.

function experiment, and maximum amount, on the outcome variables. Second, we investigate effects of treatment heterogeneity across welfare status[3] (welfare recipients vs. nonwelfare recipients) to evaluate whether vulnerable groups are more affected by incentives. To do so, we examine differences in our outcome variables across welfare recipient status with t-tests, χ^2 tests, and ANOVAs.

We also analyze to what extent individuals installed the app and cashed-out the incentive without providing any data. We analyze how many points individuals actually redeemed in the experimental groups to study the influence of incentives on costs.

All analyses were conducted using Stata 14.2 (StataCorp 2015) and R version 3.4.0 (R Core Team 2017). Analysis code and data can be reviewed and accessed on request at the IAB (for more information, see here: https://www.iab.de/en/daten.aspx).

13.4 Results

13.4.1 App Installation

Figure 13.4 shows the overall effects of the different incentive treatments on app installation. A higher installation incentive resulted in a higher installation rate,

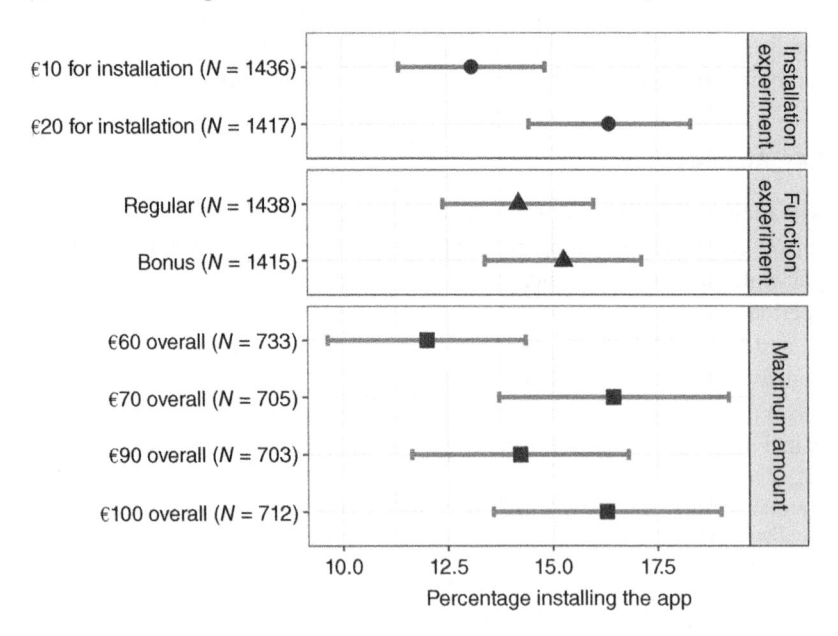

Figure 13.4 Percentage of app installations of invited individuals, with 95% confidence intervals ($N = 2853$), by incentive condition, maximum amount of incentives, and welfare status.

---

[3] Welfare benefits are paid to all households with insufficient income in which at least one person is of working age (15–65) and able to work, regardless of their labor market status.

at 16.4% of those offered €20 for installing the app compared to 13.1% of those offered only €10 ($\chi^2 = 5.8$, df = 1, $p = 0.01$). We do not observe a statistically significant marginal effect for the additional function experiment with a €5 bonus for activation of all five data-sharing functions for 30 consecutive days compared to the regular group ($\chi^2 = 0.58$, df = 1, $p = 0.447$). For the maximum incentive amount, we observe a higher installation rate (bottom panel) for the €70 (16.4%) and €100 group (16.3%) compared to the €60 (12.0%) and €90 (14.2%) group. However, the differences are not significant at the 5% level ($\chi^2 = 7.53$, df = 3, $p = 0.057$). Because the €70 and €100 groups include the €20 as an installation incentive, the installation experiment drives the differences in the installation rates by maximum amounts.

We do not find a differential installation rate based on welfare status ($\chi^2 = 0.37$, df = 1, $p = 0.541$). However, to understand a potentially differential effect of incentives on people with different welfare status, we analyze the effects of our incentives for nonwelfare and welfare recipients separately (see Figure 13.5). In the top panel of Figure 13.5, we observe that for both welfare status groups, the €20 incentive increases the installation rate compared to the €10 incentive (3.5% point increase for nonwelfare recipients and 2.7% point increase for welfare recipients). This difference is statistically significant for nonwelfare recipients only ($\chi^2 = 4.9$, df = 1, $p = 0.027$) but not for welfare recipients ($\chi^2 = 0.9$, df = 1,

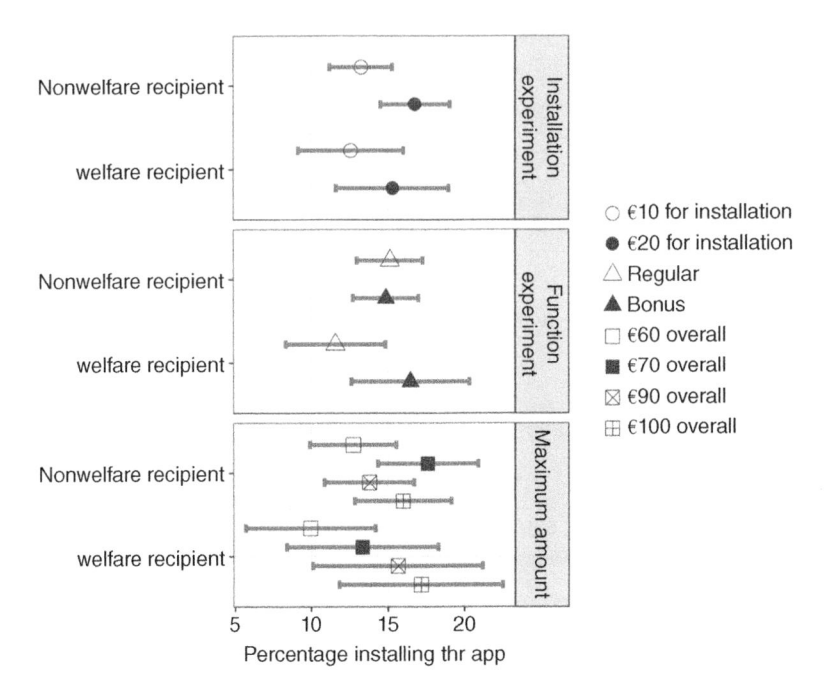

Figure 13.5 Percentage of app installations of invited individuals, with 95% confidence intervals ($N = 2853$), by experimental groups and maximum amount of incentives, by welfare status.

$p = 0.342$). Because the number of cases is lower for the welfare recipient group ($n = 729$) than for the nonwelfare recipient group ($n = 2118$), the nonsignificant effect for welfare recipients may be tied to smaller sample size. For the function experiment, we observe no difference in the installation rate between the regular and the bonus function incentive for nonwelfare recipients, while for welfare recipients, the bonus incentive leads to a higher installation rate than does the regular incentive. However, this effect is not statistically significant ($\chi^2 = 3.2$, df = 1, $p = 0.073$), potentially due to the relatively small sample size of welfare recipients. Similarly, there seems to be a linear increase in the installation rate with increasing maximum incentive amount for welfare recipients, but we do not observe a clear pattern for nonwelfare recipients. Again, none of the effects is statistically significant (χ^2 tests; all $p > 0.05$).

13.4.2 Number of Initially Activated Data-Sharing Functions

When installing the app, participants could choose to activate any of five data-sharing functions. One must keep in mind that the general installation of the app is a precondition for being able to receive any incentive for activating a function. In general, we observe high activation rates in all experimental groups (on average, between 4.1 and 4.3 initially activated data-sharing functions; see Figure 13.6). The already high activation rate does not change with a higher

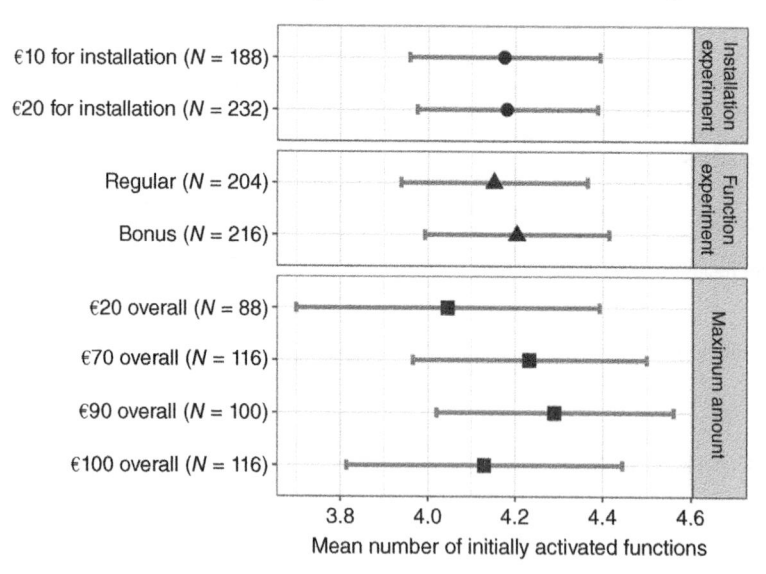

Figure 13.6 Mean number of initially activated data-sharing functions, with 95% confidence intervals, conditional on installation, by incentive condition and maximum amount of incentives ($N = 420$).

installation incentive ($t = -0.04$, df $= 407.8$, $p = 0.971$), the bonus incentive to have all five data-sharing functions activated ($t = -0.34$, df $= 417.3$, $p = 0.735$) or the resulting maximum amounts ($F_{ANOVA} = 0.46$; df $= 3$; $p = 0.707$). The bonus group incentive of the function experiment, however, does not primarily aim to increase the average number of initially activated data-sharing functions; instead, it aims to nudge participants to activate all five data-sharing functions. Although there is a 4%-point difference in activating all data-sharing functions between the experimental groups (70.8% for the bonus incentive vs. 66.2% for the regular incentive), this difference is not statistically significant ($\chi^2 = 0.85$, df $= 1$, $p = 0.356$).

We do not find significant differences in the mean number of initially activated data-sharing functions by welfare recipient status ($t = -1.58$, df $= 145.6$, $p = 0.115$). Figure 13.A.3 shows the effects of our incentives for nonwelfare and welfare recipients. We do not find any significant differences within the welfare subgroups (t-tests and ANOVA; all $p > 0.05$), suggesting that our incentives do not have differential effects within welfare status subgroups.

13.4.3 Deactivating Functions

To be compliant with the EU General Data Privacy Regulation, we made it easy for participants to change the settings of the data-sharing functions in the setting menu of the app during the field period. For the installation experiment and the maximum amount, we expect that higher incentives create a commitment to deactivate fewer data-sharing functions during the field period. For the function experiment, as participants in the bonus group gain an additional €5 by having all five functions activated for 30 consecutive days, the loss associated with deactivating a function is larger than for the regular group. Thus, we expect that fewer participants deactivate a data-sharing function in the setting menu for the bonus group.

Only approximately 20% of all participants changed their settings at least once during the field period. Of those participants who changed their function settings at least once, only 31 participants (approximately 7% of 420 participants) deactivated a function at least once. We have very few cases that we can compare over our experimental groups. As a result, we obtain large confidence intervals that overlap and make it hard to investigate effects (see Figure 13.7). Although there seems to be a pattern of less deactivation with higher installation incentive, bonus incentive (vs. regular incentive), and higher maximum amount, none of these differences were statistically significant (χ^2 tests; all $p > 0.05$; see Figure 13.7).

Because the proportion of participants who deactivated a function is very low, we do not further compare the effect of incentives within the two welfare status subgroups.

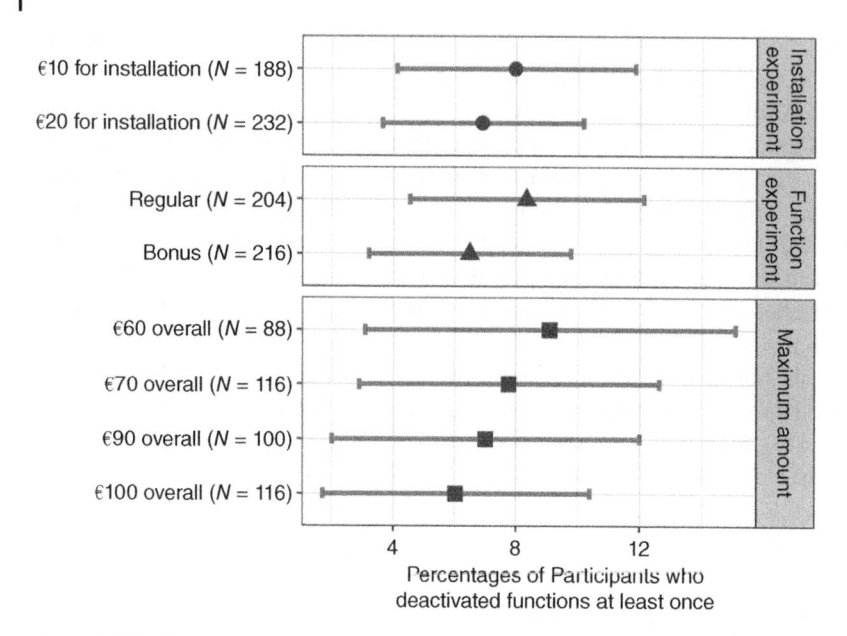

Figure 13.7 Percentages of participants who deactivated their function settings at least once, with 95% confidence intervals, conditional on installation, by incentive conditions, maximum amount of incentives and welfare status ($N = 420$).

13.4.4 Retention

It was possible for participants to just install the app and provide no or very little information by deinstalling the app rather quickly – but still cashing in an Amazon.de voucher for installing the app. On average, participants kept the app installed for 86% of the field period, meaning that if an individual decided to install the app exactly 100 days before the end of the field period, she kept the app installed for 86 days. Looking at the average percentage of days participants stayed in the study (see Figure 13.8), we observe patterns that may suggest that those who received lower incentives deinstalled the app earlier than did those who received higher incentives. Although the effect is not statistically significant in the installation and function experiments (t-tests; $p > 0.05$), it is for the maximum overall amount ($F_{ANOVA} = 3.13$, df $= 3$, $p = 0.026$). A post-hoc test reveals that those receiving up to €60 overall stayed on average 10 of 100 days fewer than did those receiving €70 or €90 (Tukey multiple comparisons of means tests; $p_{adjusted} < 0.05$). However, the difference between the €100 maximum amount group and the €60 group is not statistically significant (Tukey multiple comparisons of means test; $p > 0.05$).

We do not find a differential retention rate by welfare status ($t = 0.38$, df $= 158.0$, p-value $= 0.704$). Looking at effects of our incentive experiments within welfare

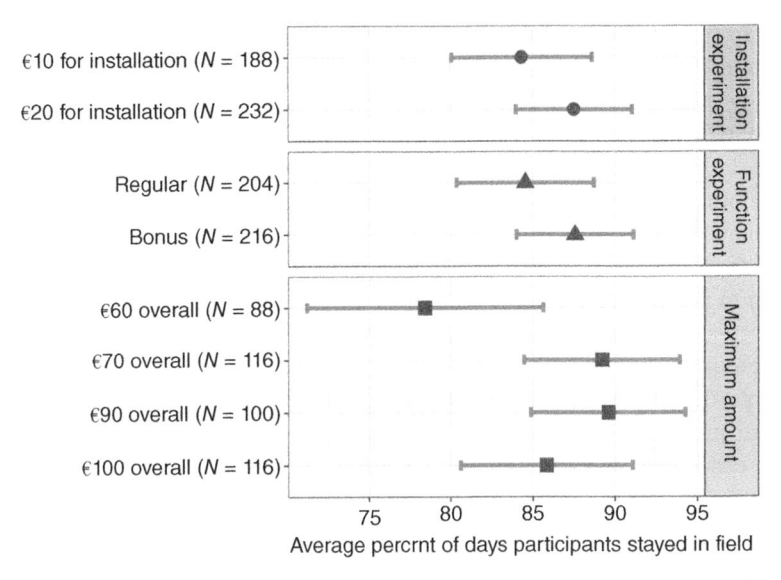

Figure 13.8 Average time participants stayed in field, with 95% confidence intervals, i.e. time between first installation and deinstallation in percent, by incentive conditions and maximum amount of incentives (N = 420).

status subgroups (see Figure 13.A.4, we find no significant differences (*t*-tests and ANOVA; all $p > 0.05$) except for the difference between the €60 maximum amount (82%) and the €70 maximum amount (91%) for nonwelfare recipients (Tukey multiple comparisons of means test; $p_{\text{adjusted}} = 0.032$).

Only 20 participants deinstalled the app within one week of installation. Unfortunately, our groups are too small to examine effects of our experimental treatment on the tendency to deinstall the app shortly after installing it.

13.4.5 Analysis of Costs

For any study designer, overall costs of data collection are of ultimate interest. In the final Section 13.4.5, we analyze how our experimental groups affect costs by examining the average proportion of collected points that participants redeemed.

Overall, 687 individuals installed the app. However, as previously, for the following analyses, we only consider participants from households in which only one member was selected (N = 420). Of 420 individuals who installed the app, 361 individuals redeemed at least one voucher, and 59 participants did not exchange their points for vouchers. One reason for not redeeming vouchers might be tied to technical issues within the app, i.e. participants received vouchers, but the app failed to store and upload voucher data to the data collection server.[4] Some individuals might not have exchanged any points for vouchers. However, for simplicity, we assign the value zero to all cases where we have no information on the amount paid out.

Individuals may be motivated to participate not only by the incentives we offered but also for other reasons, e.g. to help us collect innovative scientific data or due to curiosity about the new form of data collection. However, the higher the incentive, the higher should be the probability of attracting benefit maximizers whose major motivation to participate is receiving an incentive. If this prediction is true, we should observe that the proportion of redeemed voucher values is lower for smaller incentive groups.

Overall, participants redeemed 78.8% of their collected points. Figure 13.9 shows the average proportion of points that participants redeemed by experimental group. We observe an average proportion of 80.2% of redeemed points for those offered €20 for installing the app compared to 76.1% for those offered only €10. However, the difference is not significant ($t = -1.1$, df $= 388.5$, $p = 0.252$). For the function experiment, we observe a small nonsignificant difference of 0.4% points ($t = 0.1$, df $= 416.5$, $p = 0.917$). We also cannot find any significant effects for the maximum amount ($F_{ANOVA} = 1.19$, df $= 3$, $p = 0.313$).

Our argument that individuals may only participate because we offered incentives may especially affect the group of welfare recipients. Vulnerable groups may be more motivated to participate because of incentives instead of other reasons such as altruism or curiosity and thus have a higher average proportion of redeemed points compared to nonvulnerable groups who can afford to not redeem all points. However, we cannot find any significant effects of the welfare status on the redeeming of points ($t = 0.77$, df $= 157.5$, $p = 0.443$).

---

4 The data for received vouchers and credits has implausible gaps. For example, some participants received more money in vouchers than they actually collected points. The missing points appear to be caused by technical errors within the app or communication problems between the app and the server. For our analysis, we assume that missing points are equally distributed over our groups. For our full participant sample ($N = 685$), we spent €37 730 on vouchers but only have data for received vouchers of €36 070. Therefore, we cannot account for €1660 in voucher. For our restricted participant sample ($N = 420$), our data show that we have paid €21 420 in vouchers to our participants. Unfortunately, as we do not know what data is missing for participants who received one invitation per household and for participants who received more than one invitation per household, we have no means of evaluating how large the gap between the redeemed voucher value and the collected points is for our analysis sample. However, it is not possible to receive a higher voucher value than collected points; we therefore conclude that each participant who received more vouchers than collected points actually collected those points without the system storing this information. For example, a participant received a €10 voucher, but we have no information on collected points for this participant. To receive a voucher, however, (s)he must have collected at least 1000 points; we impute these 1000 points for the participant. Therefore, we adjust our data by adding the missing points to those who redeemed more money in vouchers than collected points. This process reduces the missing points to approximately 26 560 points (€265.60).

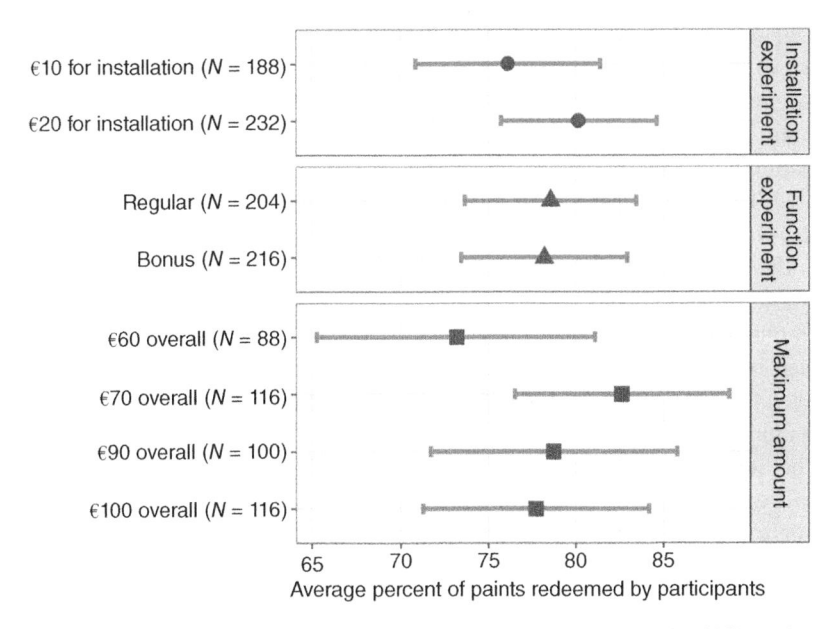

Figure 13.9 Average percent of points redeemed by participants, with 95% confidence intervals, by incentive conditions, maximum amount of incentives, and welfare status ($N = 420$).

We find no significant difference between our experimental groups within welfare status subgroups (see Figure 13.A.5; t-tests and ANOVA; all $p > 0.05$), suggesting that incentive conditions do not affect nonwelfare and welfare recipients differently in redeeming points.

13.5 Summary

In this chapter, we investigated the effects of monetary incentives on participation in a study collecting self-reports and sensor data from smartphones based on a completely crossed two-factor experimental design. Target persons sampled from the long-running PASS panel survey in Germany were promised either €10 or €20 conditional on installing the app and were promised either €1 for each passive data collection function activated for 30 consecutive days or €1 per function plus a €5 bonus if all five data-sharing functions were activated for 30 consecutive days. All incentives were provided as Amazon.de vouchers that could be redeemed by participants in the app.

The main finding is that well-known results from the survey literature on the effects of incentives on participation seem to carry over to invitations to share smartphone data. Although the task differs and is less time consuming for participants, we found similar patterns regarding the effects of different amounts of incentives.

A €20 installation incentive causes significantly more targeted individuals (16.4%) to install an app that passively collects smartphone data than does a €10 incentive (13.1%). In contrast, paying respondents a €5 bonus incentive if they grant researchers access to all five data-sharing functions neither increases installation rates nor has an effect on the number of data-sharing functions activated. This result is surprising, as the potential difference between the regular and the bonus incentive condition over the 180-day field period is three times higher than the installation incentive. We communicated the potential maximum amount to the respondents.

We argued that vulnerable groups such as welfare recipients may be more attracted by the monetary incentives and thus have a higher installation rate. However, for different subgroups defined by welfare status, we find no effect on installation rates.

In the literature, on survey nonresponse, one important issue is whether participants who require more recruitment effort produce data of lower quality, e.g. more item nonresponse. Applied to the research question at hand, one could ask whether participants in the high installation incentive group provide less passively collected data, i.e. initially activate fewer data-sharing functions, deactivate functions during the field period, and deinstall the app earlier. For the number of initially activated functions and deactivation of function settings during the field period, we find no evidence that different incentives have an effect. Similarly, for retention, we cannot tie any effect to our installation and function experiment. We find is that participants who were offered a maximum incentive of €70 and above had the app installed on average for a longer period than did their counterparts in the €60 group. Thus, it seems that between the €60 and €70 maximum incentive lies a threshold that affects participant's choice to keep the app installed. Our results indicate that the higher incentive does not encourage target persons to collect the incentive and then deinstall the app.

We do not find any effect for welfare status subgroups for the number of initially activated data-sharing functions, deactivating function settings during the field period or retention. Furthermore, we do not find evidence of differential effects of incentives across the different subgroups for those three outcome variables. From an ethical perspective, these results are good news because our results suggest that with offering different amounts of incentives, we do not coerce vulnerable groups to share their data. Our analyses, however, may suffer from a low number of cases (especially in the welfare recipient groups) that may mask existing effects. Furthermore, we have to keep in mind that finding no significant differences between vulnerable and nonvulnerable groups does not mean that no individuals felt constrained by being offered an incentive. Offering incentives is ethically problematic, even if only one individual was forced to participate because her situation did not allow her to decline the offered incentive.

13.5.1 Limitations and Future Research

This study comes with several limitations. First, we used data from only one study in Germany, and we do not know yet how results generalize to similar studies with different passive data collection requests or in different countries. All invited smartphone owners had participated in at least one prior wave of a mixed-mode (computer-assisted personal interview and computer-assisted telephone interview) panel survey. Thus, they are likely to have more positive attitudes toward scientific studies than does the general population. In addition, a trust relationship between the research institute conducting the study and the panel respondents has been established, and respondents have become used to receiving a cash incentive of €10 per survey wave. These factors might increase willingness to participate in general and modify the reaction to incentives compared to other populations who are not part of an ongoing panel study.

Second, for each type of incentive in our study, there were only two experimental groups and no control group without an incentive. Thus, we have no information on the effect of introducing an incentive vs. no incentive or on whether there are diminishing returns when the amount is further increased.

Third, smartphone data collection is still new. All invited PASS respondents are very unlikely to ever have been confronted with a similar request. This novelty factor could lead to different results than might be found once this form of data collection becomes more established. People might become more or less trusting or more or less interested in this kind of research in the future.

Fourth, our study's generalizability may be limited by the type of incentive we used. Throughout the study, we claim that we provided monetary incentives to participants, but participants never received actual money; instead, they received Amazon.de vouchers. Amazon is the largest online retailer in Germany (Ecommerce News 2017). One could argue that these vouchers are as good as money; however, these vouchers can only be used in the German Amazon online store. They cannot be used in brick-and-mortar shops, such as supermarkets, or in other online stores. Individuals may perceive that a €10 Amazon.de credit is harder to spend than €10 in cash. Against this background, the type of incentive may actually modify the effect of the amount of incentive. Furthermore, we have no information on how many of our participants do not have an Amazon.de account and whether those without an account differ from those with an account. Some participants might have preferred different online incentives, e.g. payments through PayPal, bank transfers, or donations. Therefore, our findings about the effect of incentives are limited to Amazon.de vouchers. Whether different incentives or combinations of incentives are more efficient has to be empirically tested in future research.

Fifth, so far, we have very little knowledge about the value of passively collected smartphone data; nor do participants have a benchmark to estimate their value.

Most target persons in our study probably share similar data with commercial providers without pay and without the benefits of anonymization to be able to use certain apps or other online services.

Sixth, our analyses may suffer from small sample sizes. With a higher number of cases in each experimental group, differences between groups may become more clear, and statistical tests may identify effects that are now covered.

Finally, it is not possible to identify whether sample members went to the Google Play store, looked at the app, but then decided not to download the app. We only have data from individuals who finished the onboarding process, i.e. the process between accessing the Google Play store and finishing all consent decisions. Only as the onboarding process was finished was the app able to collect data, and we do not have any information about the number of failed onboardings.

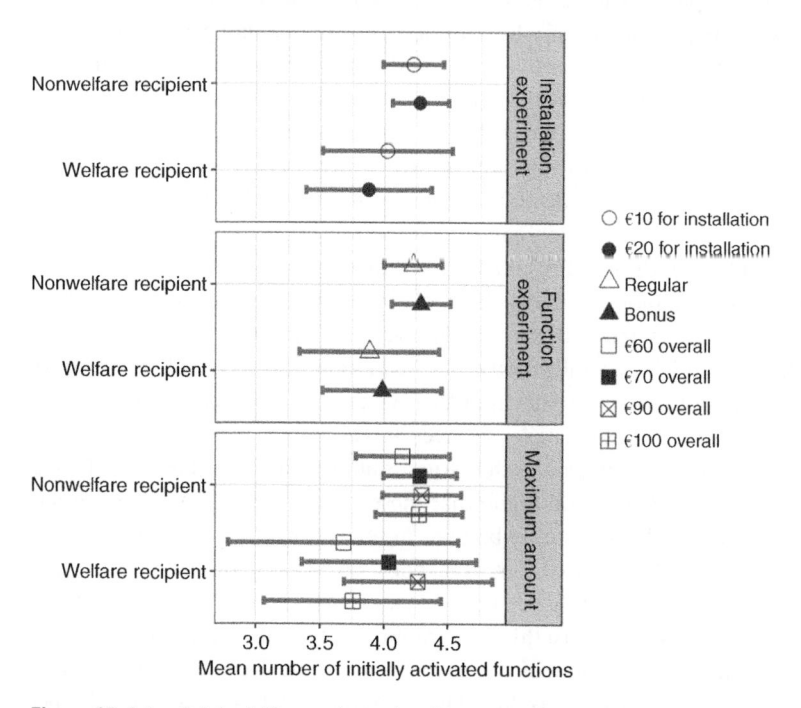

Figure 13.A.1 Original (German) voucher flyer; experimental conditions are highlighted in light grey.

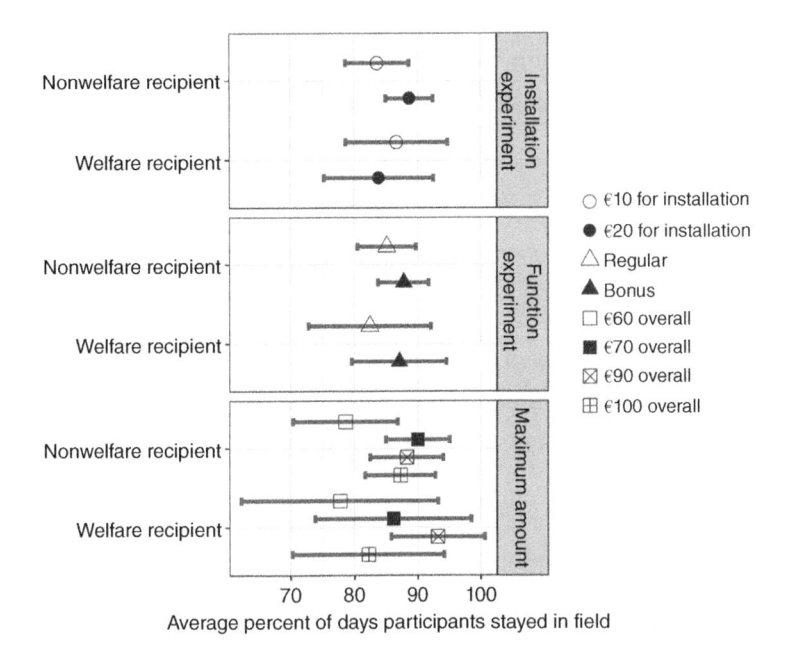

Figure 13.A.2 Voucher flyer (English translation); experimental conditions are highlighted in light grey

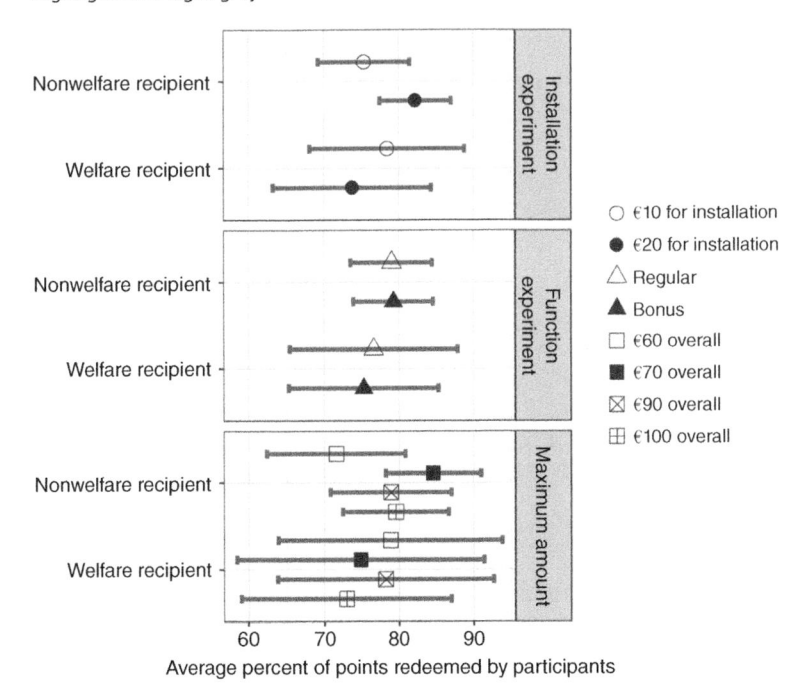

Figure 13.A.3 Mean number of initially activated data-sharing functions with 95% confidence intervals, by incentive conditions and maximum amount of incentive, by welfare status ($N = 420$).

Der Forschung helfen und Amazon.de Gutscheine* erhalten!

App downloaden

Als erstes Dankeschön für die Teilnahme an unserer Studie erhalten Sie von uns einen 10/20 Euro Amazon.de Gutschein nach erfolgreichem Download der IAB-SMART-App. Diesen können Sie sich in der App unter dem Menüpunkt „Gutscheine" sofort ausgeben lassen.

Innerhalb der App können Sie Punkte sammeln**. Haben Sie 500 Punkte gesammelt, können Sie diese in einen Fünf Euro Amazon.de Gutschein umwandeln. Punkte sammeln Sie durch

- Aktivierung von Funktionen der App
- Beantwortung von Fragen

Insgesamt können Sie so weitere bis zu 60/70/90/100 Euro in Gutscheinen erhalten.

Funktionen aktivieren

Bei der Installation der App, werden Sie gefragt, welche Funktionen der App Sie aktivieren möchten. Für jede aktivierte Funktion erhalten Sie alle 30 Tage 100 Punkte. Später können Sie jederzeit die einzelnen Funktionen unter dem Menüpunkt „Einstellungen" aktivieren bzw. deaktivieren.

Beispiel: Haben Sie die Funktion Aktivitätsdaten und Interaktionsverlauf aktiviert erhalten Sie alle 30 Tage 200 Punkte

Haben Sie alle Funktionen gleichzeitig aktiviert, erhalten Sie alle 30 Tage 500 Punkte. \ Haben Sie alle Funktionen gleichzeitig aktiviert, erhalten Sie alle 30 Tage 500 Extrapunkte, also insgesamt 1000 Punkte.

Bitte beachten Sie, dass bei der Deaktivierung einer Funktion Ihre angesammelten Tage verfallen.

Fragen beantworten

Im Zeitraum der gesamten Studie haben Sie die Chance Fragen zu arbeitsmarktrelevanten Themen zu beantworten. Für jede Frage, die Sie beantworten, erhalten Sie Zehn Punkte.

Punkte einlösen

Ihren aktuellen Punktestand finden Sie in der App unter „Gutscheine". Sobald Sie 500 Punkte gesammelt haben, können Sie diese in einen Fünf Euro Amazon.de Gutschein umwandeln.

*Es gelten Einschränkungen. Die vollständigen Geschäftsbedingungen finden Sie auf: amazon.de/gc-legal.
**diese Aktion gilt bis zum 31.07.2018.

Figure 13.A.4 Average time participants stayed in field with 95% confidence intervals, i.e. time between first installation and deinstallation in percent, by incentive conditions and maximum amount of incentive, by welfare status ($N = 420$).

Support research and receive Amazon.de vouchers*!

Download the App
The first gesture of appreciation for participating in our study is a 10/20 euro voucher from Amazon.de that you will receive after successfully downloading the IAB-SMART-App. You will immediately be able to access the voucher selecting menu item "Vouchers."

The app comes with a points-based system**. For each 500 points, you get a five euro Amazon.de voucher in exchange. You can earn points by

- Activating extended features in the app
- Answer questions

Overall, you can collect vouchers in the total amount of up to 60/70/90/100 euro

Activating extended features
During the installation process, the app asks you to activate extended features. For each feature you activate, you will receive 100 points after each 30 days. You are free to activate or deactivate the features to a later date by selecting the menu item "Settings."

For Example: If you activate the feature "Activity Data and Interaction History" you will gain 200 points every 30 days.

If you activate all five features, every 30 days you will receive 500 points. If you activate all five features, every 30 days you will receive 500 extra points, that means overall 1000 points!

Please note that the gathered days you achieved will decay when you disable this feature.

All features when they are activated.

Answer questions
While the study takes place, you will have the opportunity to complete surveys to labour market-related issues. For each answered question, you will receive 10 points.

Redeem points
To check your actual status points select "Vouchers" in the app menu. As soon as you reach 500 points you can convert them into a €5 voucher from Amazon.de.

* Limitations apply. For full details and terms of conditions please visit: amazon.de/gc-legal.
**This offer does apply until 31.07.2018.

Figure 13.A.5 Average percent of points redeemed by participants with 95% confidence intervals by incentive conditions and maximum amount of incentive, by welfare status ($N = 420$).

References

Cantor, D., O'Hare, B., and O'Connor, K. (2008). The use of monetary incentives to reduce non-response in random digit dial telephone surveys. In: *Advances in Telephone Survey Methodology* (eds. J.M. Lepowski, N.C. Tucker, J.M. Brick, et al.), 471–498. New York: Wiley.

Church, A.H. (1993). Estimating the effect of incentives on mail survey response rates: a meta-analysis. *Public Opinion Quarterly* 57 (1): 62–79. https://doi.org/10.1086/269355.

Dillman, D.A., Smyth, J.D., and Christian, L.M. (2014). *Internet, Phone, Mail and Mixed-Mode Surveys: The Tailored Design Method*, 4e. New York: Wiley.

Ecommerce News. (2017). Top 10 online stores in Germany. https://ecommercenews.eu/top-10-online-stores-germany/.

Felderer, B., Müller, G., Kreuter, F. et al. (2017). The effect of differential incentives on attrition bias. *Field Methods* 30 (1): 56–69. https://doi.org/10.1177/1525822X17726206.

Goldenberg, K. L., McGrath, D., and Tan, L. (2009). The effects of incentives on the consumer expenditure interview survey. *Proceedings of the Survey Research Methods Section, American Statistical Association*, 5985–5999. Available at: http://www.asasrms.org/Proceedings/y2009f.html

Groves, R.M., Couper, M.P., Presser, S. et al. (2006). Experiments in producing nonresponse bias. *Public Opinion Quarterly* 70 (5): 720–736. https://doi.org/10.1093/poq/nfl036.

Groves, R.M., Singer, E., and Corning, A. (2000). Leverage-saliency theory of survey participation: description and an illustration. *Public Opinion Quarterly* 64 (3): 299–308. https://doi.org/10.1086/317990.

Harari, G.M., Lane, N.D., Wang, R. et al. (2016). Using smartphones to collect behavioral data in psychological science: opportunities, practical considerations, and challenges. *Perspectives on Psychological Science* 11 (6): 838–854. https://doi.org/10.1177/1745691616650285.

Jäckle, A., Burton, J., Couper, M.P. et al. (2019). Participation in a mobile app survey to collect expenditure data as part of a large-scale probability household panel: coverage and participation rates and biases. *Survey Research Methods* 13 (1): 23–44. https://doi.org/10.18148/srm/2019.v13i1.7297.

Jacobebbinghaus, P. and Seth, S. (2007). The German integrated employment biographies sample IEBS. *Schmollers Jahrbuch. Zeitschrift für Wirtschafts- und Sozialwissenschaften* 127: 335–342.

James, J.M. and Bolstein, R. (1990). The effect of monetary incentives and follow-up mailings on the response rate and response quality in mail surveys. *Public Opinion Quarterly* 54 (3): 346–361. https://doi.org/10.1086/269211.

Keusch, F., Antoun, C., Couper, M. P., et al. (2017). Willingness to participate in passive mobile data collection. Paper presented at the AAPOR 72nd Annual Conference, New Orleans, LA, 18–21 May 2017.

Keusch, F., Bähr, S., Haas, G.-C. et al. (2020). Coverage error in data collection combining mobile surveys with passive measurement using apps * data from a German national survey. In: *Sociological Methods & Research*, online first, S. 1–38.

Kreuter, F., Couper, M. P., and Lyber, L. (2010). The use of paradata to monitor and manage survey data collection. *Proceedings of the Joint Statistical Meetings (JSM)*, Vancouver, British Columbia, Canada (31 July–5 August), pp. 282–296.

Kreuter, F., Haas, G.-C., Keusch, F. et al. (2018). Collecting survey and smartphone sensor data with an app: opportunities and challenges around privacy and informed consent. *Social Science Computer Review* https://doi.org/10.1177/0894439318816389.

Levenstein, R. (2010). Nonresponse and measurement error in mixed-mode designs. Doctor of philosophy dissertation. University of Michigan, Ann Arbor, MI. https://deepblue.lib.umich.edu/bitstream/handle/2027.42/78764/rmlev_1.pdf?sequence=1.

Mack, S., Huggins, V., Keathley, D. et al. (1998). Do monetary incentives improve response rates in the survey of income and program participation? In: *Proceedings of the Section on Survey Methodology*, 529–534. Alexandria, VA: *American Statistical Association*.

Mercer, A., Caporaso, A., Cantor, D. et al. (2015). How much gets you how much? Monetary incentives and response rates in household surveys. *Public Opinion Quarterly* 79 (1): 105–129. https://doi.org/10.1093/poq/nfu059.

Pforr, K. (2016). Incentives. In: *GESIS Survey Guidelines*. Mannheim, Germany: GESIS—Leibniz Institute for the Social Sciences https://doi.org/10.15465/gesis-sg_en_001.

Philipson, T. (1997). Data markets and the production of surveys. *The Review of Economic Studies* 64 (1): 47–72. https://doi.org/10.2307/2971740.

R Core Team (2017). *R: A Language and Environment for Statistical Computing*. Vienna, Austria: R Foundation for Statistical Computing. https://www.R-project.org/.

Revilla, M., Couper, M.P., and Ochoa, C. (2018). Willingness of online panelists to perform additional tasks. *Methods, Data, Analyses* 13 (2): 223–252. Advance Access publication June 2018. https://doi.org/10.12758/mda.2018.01.

Sakshaug, J. and Kreuter, F. (2012). Assessing the magnitude of non-consent biases in linked survey and administrative data. *Survey Research Methods* 6 (2): 113–122. https://doi.org/10.18148/srm/2012.v6i2.5094.

Singer, E. (2002). The use of incentives to reduce nonresponse in household surveys. In: *Survey Nonresponse* (eds. R.M. Groves, D.A. Dillman, J.L. Eltinge, et al.), 163–177. New York: John Wiley & Sons.

Singer, E. and Kulka, R.A. (2002). Paying respondents for survey participation. In: *Studies of Welfare Populations: Data Collection and Research Issues* (eds. M.V. Ploeg, R.A. Moffitt and C.F. Citro), 105–128. Washington, DC: National Academy Press.

Singer, E. and Ye, C. (2013). The use and effects of incentives in surveys. *The Annals of the American Academy of Political and Social Science* 645 (1): 112–141. https://doi.org/10.1177/0002716212458082.

Singer, E., Groves, R.M., and Corning, A.D. (1999). Differential incentives: beliefs about practices, perceptions of equity, and effects on survey participation. *Public Opinion Quarterly* 63 (2): 251–260.

Singer, E., van Hoewyk, J., Gebler, N. et al. (1999). The effect of incentives on response rates in interviewer-mediated surveys. *Journal of Official Statistics* 15 (2): 217–230.

StataCorp (2015). *Stata Statistical Software: Release 14*. College Station, TX: StataCorp LP.

Sugie, N.F. (2018). Work as foraging: a smartphone study of job search and employment after prison. *American Journal of Sociology* 123 (5): 1453–1491. https://doi.org/10.1086/696209.

Toepoel, V. (2012). Effects of incentives in surveys. In: *Handbook of Survey Methodology for the Social Sciences* (ed. L. Gideon), 209–223. New York, NY: Springer https://doi.org/10.1007/978-1-4614-3876-2_13.

Wenz, A., Jäckle, A., and Couper, M. P. (2017). Willingness to use mobile technologies for data collection in a probability household panel. ISER Working Paper 2017-10. https://www.understandingsociety.ac.uk/sites/default/files/downloads/working-papers/2017-10.pdf.

Willimack, D.K., Schuman, H., Pennell, B.-E. et al. (1995). Effects of a prepaid nonmonetary incentive on response rates and response quality in a face-to- face survey. *Public Opinion Quarterly* 59 (1): 78–92. https://doi.org/10.1086/269459.

14

Using Machine Learning Models to Predict Attrition in a Survey Panel

Mingnan Liu

Independent Researcher, San Mateo, CA, USA

14.1 Introduction

A longitudinal or panel survey differs from a cross-sectional survey in that it repeatedly collects data from the same group of respondents to monitor changes of attitudes, opinions, or behaviors over time. An alternative approach for measuring changes is to ask retrospective questions in a cross-sectional survey. That approach, however, is subject to recall error, so in many cases longitudinal or panel surveys are preferable to facilitate understanding changes and trends (Olsen 2018).

Although obtaining high or adequate response rates is increasingly challenging for any survey, longitudinal or panel surveys face the additional challenge of panel attrition – that is, respondents who participate in one interview but not subsequent interviews. Researchers who conduct these types of surveys not only have to recruit participants at the first stage but they must also essentially re-recruit these original respondents to participate in further surveys at later stages.

Lynn (2018) summarizes two main reasons why panel attrition is problematic. First, a high panel attrition rate can cause the sample size of subsequent waves of surveys to shrink rapidly, which hinders or prevents follow-up surveys to produce precise estimates for the survey population. Second, similar to survey nonresponse bias, panel attrition can introduce bias to survey estimates, especially if people who stop participating in the longitudinal study are systematically different from those who stay in the panel. Given these risks for survey estimates, it is important to predict and correct for panel attrition.

A variety of factors could cause survey attrition and may vary depending on the particular survey setting, context, and population. Lepkowski and Couper (2002)

Big Data Meets Survey Science: A Collection of Innovative Methods, First Edition. Edited by Craig A. Hill, Paul P. Biemer, Trent D. Buskirk, Lilli Japec, Antje Kirchner, Stas Kolenikov, and Lars E. Lyberg.
© 2021 John Wiley & Sons, Inc. Published 2021 by John Wiley & Sons, Inc.

examine survey attrition in the second wave of longitudinal studies and conclude that the three main reasons for survey attrition are nonlocation, noncontact, and refusal to participate.

Survey attrition due to nonlocation happens when respondents cannot be located for subsequent waves due to reasons like a change of address or telephone number. Even when respondents can be located for the following waves, they may not answer the phone when interviewers call or are not at home when interviewers visit the household, resulting in noncontact. Even after the participants are located and contacted, they may still refuse to participate in subsequent interviews. If any of those steps goes wrong, the survey will suffer from attrition.

Given the importance of repeatedly engaging respondents in longitudinal studies, many research efforts have been devoted to understanding survey attrition. Using the UK Understanding Society survey, Lagorio (2016) shows that wave 1 variables, such as call records, characteristics of the dwelling, demographics, interview experience, and cross-wave factors (for example, having the same interviewer for both waves of interviewing), can predict both contact and cooperation for waves 2–4. Several design features were tested, and some showed a positive impact on maintaining participants in the panel for subsequent waves. One such important feature for attrition is the mode of data collection. For example, a face-to-face survey almost guarantees a lower attrition rate than any other survey mode, but the cost can be prohibitive (Couper and Ofstedal 2009). An alternative approach is to use a mixed-mode survey to tackle survey attrition, which can be effective at a much lower cost (Lynn 2013).

Other design features that have been tested for reducing survey attrition include offering survey incentives (Zagorsky and Rhoton 2008), framing the survey request more effectively (Tourangeau and Ye 2009), changing the length of the interview (Hill and Willis 2001), requesting address updates between interviews (Fumagalli, Laurie, and Lynn 2013), assigning the same interviewer for subsequent waves (Hill and Willis 2001; Lynn, Kaminska, and Goldstein 2014), and keeping interviewer workload manageable (Nicoletti and Buck 2004), among others.

One limitation of this line of study is, as Lynn (2018) points out, that the focus has been on the mean effects of treatments, that is, the success metric for different techniques to reduce panel survey attrition is the overall sample mean impact of the techniques. In reality, different subgroups have different attrition rates (Lillard and Panis 1998; Olson and Witt 2011), and a technique that is effective in preventing attrition among one group may not be useful at all for another group. In that case, a targeted approach would be more effective (Lynn 2014). If one technique is more effective among one subgroup, it makes sense to apply that technique only to that group and not to others. This approach is most likely to result in a higher benefit-to-cost ratio. A crucial and necessary component to executing such an approach is the ability to identify such subgroups in terms of response patterns.

In this paper, I explore several methods for estimating propensities of attrition within a survey panel setting. In particular, I demonstrate the feasibility of predicting the likelihood of attrition at wave 2 for each wave 1 respondent based on four different modeling methods: logistic regression, random forests, support vector machines (SVMs), and least absolute shrinkage and selection operator (LASSO). Each model will be developed using information collected during the first wave, such as respondents' answers to the survey questions, interviewer observations, and demographics. When resources are constrained, which they typically are, this approach will enable researchers to focus their efforts on those individuals who are predicted to be least likely to participate in the wave 2 survey.

Given the complexity of panel attrition, we might expect that a model relying on only main effects might be underspecified. I explore both a traditional approach to modeling attrition commonly used in practice (i.e. logistic regression) along with three other machine learning methods that might be more aptly suited because they can each balance the complexity of the model with the available data to improve the prediction of panel attrition. Moreover, both the random forests and LASSO methods can provide a measure of variable importance that can help better prioritize or understand the drivers for accurately predicting panel attrition.

In Section 14.1.1 introduces the surveys of consumers (SoCs) used to demonstrate various prediction methodologies, followed a brief introduction to three machine learning methods and the metrics used to evaluate them. The performance of these models for predicting survey attrition is summarized in Section 14.3. The chapter concludes with a summary, a discussion of potential applications in other areas, and future research.

14.1.1 Data

The data used for this study come from the 2014 to 2015 SoC, a monthly telephone survey of about 500 US adults (in 48 states and the District of Columbia). The interviews include both a new monthly sample and a recontact sample of people who were interviewed six months prior. After completing the second interview, respondents are released from the panel, and no further reinterview is attempted; thus, the SoC is a rotating panel (Curtin 1982).

In this study, I predicted wave 2 participation (1 = attrition in wave 2; 0 = response in wave 2) using data available from the wave 1 survey. Across the entire dataset used for the analysis, about half did not participate in the second wave (4065 wave 2 respondents and 4094 nonrespondents). The variables in the survey can be summarized into three broader categories:

(1) demographic variables, such as sex, age, region, income, and home ownership;

(2) substantive variables of the survey consisting of the core SoC questions about personal finance, business conditions, inflation expectations, buying conditions, and gas price expectations; and

(3) interviewer observation data, including the interviewer's judgment about how well the respondent understood the questions and the respondent's attitude toward the interview.

For more information about the survey, see https://data.sca.isr.umich.edu/survey-info.php.

In total, there are 39 predictors available for the models: 26 are categorical variables and 13 are continuous variables. Details about the specific variables used in models discussed in this chapter, including question wordings, are included in Appendix 14.A.

14.2 Methods

This combination of variables and the complexity of panel attrition makes it difficult to know a priori which variables directly relate to attrition in a linear sense and which variables might relate to attrition in a nonlinear sense – and moreover which combination of variables might be related to attrition via an interactive effect. In other words, proper specification of panel attrition for these 39 variables might not be possible, and might render logistic regression, or similar methods that require the form of the model to be specified, impractical. Although underspecified models can still be useful for predicting attrition or other survey outcomes of interest, I also explored the use of machine learning methods that do not require prior specification of the model form and that can adapt the complexity of the model based on the available predictors and data. I compared the results using a traditional main-effects logistic regression, which is often applied in practice, to three other aforementioned machine learning methods. I chose these methods both because they are popular alternatives to logistic regression as well as for their strengths in modeling predictions that are not just linear. In Sections 14.2.1–14.2.4 introduces each method and then discusses how the models derived from these methods will be evaluated.

14.2.1 Random Forests

Random forests are an extension of the ideas of classification and regression trees (CART) developed by Breiman et al. (1984). A CART algorithm starts with the entire sample, making a series of splits of the sample and then making a specific decision in each subset to form final or terminal nodes that are relatively homogeneous to the desired binary outcome. In the final nodes, an observation is predicted based on the mean response of other observations in the same node or the most commonly occurring class. This approach is referred to as a "tree" because it splits the sample from the root node and branch recursively until the final nodes are reached, thus creating an upside-down tree; see (Buskirk 2018) for an illustration of a decision tree. The random forests technique is an ensemble-based method developed from the decision tree-based method (Breiman 2001). A random forest is a collection of trees, and each tree is grown using a bootstrap subsample of the original dataset, which has the same sample size as the original sample. Random forests need to grow a large number of trees, usually no fewer than 500, with bootstrapped samples. Trees in random forests are grown to the maximum size so that each terminal node only has one observation. By averaging estimates from many independently grown trees with different sets of predictors, random forests reduce the variance and bias of a very large decision tree.

Whereas a single decision tree considers all available predictors, each branch in each tree in a random forest considers only a random subset of all available predictors – typically around $\sqrt{p}$ for classification problems and $p/3$ for regression problems, where p is the total number of predictors. Limiting the number of predictors ensures that random forests grow decorrelated trees that can reduce the variance and make results more reliable. The number of predictors and the number of trees are the two tuning parameters for random forests. The random forest analysis in this chapter was conducted using the R randomForest package (Table 14.1).

14.2.2 Support Vector Machines

Second-wave survey attrition in this panel study was also predicted using SVM (Vapnik 2013). SVM finds a boundary (called hyperplane), defined by the values of the predictors, to separate the two binary outcomes. Depending on which side

Table 14.1 Tuning parameters used and previous studies for random forest, SVM, and LASSO.

Method	Tuning parameter	Previous studies using this method
Random forests	Number of predictors and number of trees	Breiman et al. (1984) and Buskirk (2018)
Support vector machine	The penalty (C) and the radial kernel tuning parameter (γ)	Vapnik (2013) and Signorino and Kirchner (2018)
LASSO	The penalty (λ)	Tibshirani (1996), Signorino and Kirchner (2018), and Kern, Klausch, and Kreuter (2019)

of the boundary an observation falls, analysts can predict the outcome, and in this case, we can predict if that respondent will participate in the second wave. When only two predictors exist, the boundary is a line. With three predictors, the boundary is a plane, and with more than three predictors, the boundary is a hyperplane.

In theory, an unlimited number of such hyperplanes can separate the binary outcome variable. The one hyperplane that we should choose to use is the maximal margin hyperplane, or the separating hyperplane farthest from the observations. A classifier based on the maximal margin hyperplane is called a maximal margin classifier. However, a clear drawback of the maximum marginal classifier is the restriction that a binary outcome must be separable by a linear function. SVMs overcome this limitation by enlarging the feature space to accommodate a nonlinear boundary (or a nonlinear function of predictors). More specifically, the SVM enlarges the feature space using kernels. The SVM uses polynomial and radial kernels, among others. A soft margin can be applied in the SVM as well, allowing for more flexibility. The SVM analysis is conducted using the R kernlab package.

14.2.3 LASSO

The final method we considered for modeling panel attrition is LASSO (Tibshirani 1996, 2011) and its variant. Unlike a regular ordinary least squares (OLSs) or logistic regression, LASSO shrinks the coefficient estimates of some predictors (or features) toward zero or forces them to be exactly zero. This model is also known as a penalized regression model because LASSO constrains or regularizes the coefficient estimates to be zero. This is achieved through a tuning parameter λ. A large λ will set some coefficients exactly equal to zero such that those variables are automatically eliminated from the model, leaving only those that are more predictive of the outcome variables.

Also, a nonlinear relationship may exist between the outcome variable and predictors, such as an interaction between two predictors or the second order of a predictor. In those cases, LASSO can be applied to a basis expansion of predictors in which the predictors are transformed in a nonlinear way, such as a polynomial expansion. The LASSO analysis is conducted using the R glmnet package.

14.2.4 Evaluation Criteria

A standard way to evaluate the performance of machine learning models, including those introduced previously, is through cross-validation where some observations are identified as the training set and the remaining observations as the testing set. In this analysis, I used a simple split sample cross-validation to evaluate the models, and under this approach, 80% of wave 1 respondents were randomly assigned to the training set (for developing the models), and the remaining 20%

are held back in a testing set to evaluate model performance. The same training and testing sets are used for all models. When tuning parameters existed, I used a 10-fold cross-validation in the training data to select the best tuning parameters.

Because the outcome in this study was binary (i.e. wave 2 attrition or not), I used several statistics to evaluate the performance of the models. They included the accuracy (percentage correctly classified), sensitivity (true positive rate – the rate of wave 2 attritors that were correctly classified as such), specificity (true negative rate – the rate of wave 2 respondents who were accurately classified as such), and balanced accuracy (the average of sensitivity and specificity). Each of these statistics can be derived from a confusion matrix or two-by-two cross-tabulation of actual value of attrition vs. predicted attrition, as illustrated in Table 14.2.

Table 14.2 Confusion matrix based on four models applied to test set.

Actual	Wave 2 respondent	Wave 2 nonrespondent	Total
a. Confusion matrix based on random forest model			
Random forest prediction			
Wave 2 respondent	475	329	804
Wave 2 nonrespondent	290	537	827
	765	866	1631
b. Confusion matrix based on SVM model			
SVM prediction			
Wave 2 respondent	491	313	804
Wave 2 nonrespondent	308	519	827
	804	827	1631
c. Confusion matrix based on LASSO model			
LASSO prediction			
Wave 2 respondent	512	292	804
Wave 2 nonrespondent	313	514	827
	825	806	1631
d. Confusion matrix based on logistic regression model			
Logistic regression prediction			
Wave 2 respondent	513	291	804
Wave 2 nonrespondent	322	505	827
	835	796	1631

I also computed the area under the receiver operating characteristic (ROC) curve for each method, which measures the area under a plot of the sensitivity vs. 1-specificity for predicting attrition. Values of area under the curve (AUC) close to 1 indicate more accurate classification models, and values of AUC close to 0.5 indicate poorly fitting classification models, because a random predictor has a value of AUC equal to 0.5. Note: the results for any of the methods were based on the model performance in the test dataset. After I developed the final model in the training data, I applied the exact model, using the test data to check its performance in prediction. Because the test data were not used in developing the model, the results in the test data were the same as applying the model to new data. Thus, the confusion matrices and area under the ROC curve statistics for each of the methods were based on the test dataset. Because the ultimate outcome of interest is the binary variable representing attrition (or not) in wave 2, I converted the propensity scores derived from each of the models (which lie on the 0–1 scale) to a predicted binary category. I adopted a simple, common approach for this conversion for all models that assigned attrition (as a binary outcome of 1) to any wave 1 respondent whose predicted propensity of attrition was greater than 0.5 and a binary outcome of 0 to any wave 1 respondent whose propensity for attrition was less than or equal to 0.5.

14.2.4.1 Tuning Parameters

For each of the three machine learning methods, the first step was to specify the models and determine the values for tuning parameters. This step was crucial from a methodological perspective although it is not usually of substantive interest. I present the tuning parameters for each method here.

Random forests: Recall that there are two tuning parameters for random forests: the number of trees and the number of variables considered for each tree. For the number of variables, I followed the default rule of $\sqrt{p}$ (rounded down) in which p is the number of variables. In this case, it was 6. To find the number of trees for the random forests, I first fitted a model with 2000 trees, which was sufficiently large. The model was fitted in a training dataset. The classification error decreased as the number of trees increased to about 1000, at which point the error rates started to level off. Consequently, I decided that the final random forest should have 1000 trees and six variables (randomly selected) for each tree.

SVM: I used a soft-margin SVM with a radial kernel. First, I used a 10-fold cross-validation (on the training dataset) to find the SVM tuning parameter C (the penalty) and the radial kernel tuning parameter γ. The results from the cross-validation show that $C = 2$ and $\gamma = 0.0173$. The final SVM model was fitted using these tuning parameters.

LASSO: LASSO has one tuning parameter, the penalty λ. A large λ will force more coefficients to be exactly zero while a small λ will allow more coefficients to be nonzero. As with SVM, I used 10-fold cross-validation on the training data to find the appropriate λ that minimized the mean squared error at $\lambda = 0.0043$.

14.3 Results

This section compares the results for the four methods. The logistic regression serves as the baseline benchmark.

The confusion matrix in Table 14.2 presents actual results in rows and predicted results in columns for the four methods used in the analysis. The data are based on the test set only. Numbers in the diagonal are correctly predicted (i.e. the predicted results match the actual results). The off-diagonal cases are incorrectly predicted.

Random forest: As described in Section 14.2, several statistics can be used in a classification model for evaluating the model performance. Table 14.2a explains how they are calculated, as the same statistics are used in the other three models. The accuracy is the percent of cases that are correctly predicted ($62.0\% = (475+537)/1631$). The sensitivity is the presence of actual positives (those respondents who actually did not participate in a wave 2 interview) that are correctly identified as such ($64.9\% = 537/827$). Specificity is the percentage of actual negatives (those respondents who actually participated in a wave 2 interview) that are correctly identified as such ($59.1\% = 475/804$). The balanced accuracy (62.0%) is the average of sensitivity and specificity. Finally, the area under the ROC curve is 67% (Figure 14.1). This result is moderately better than guessing by chance (which is 50%). For all of the statistics, the higher the numbers, the better the model predicts the outcomes. These statistics are summarized in Table 14.3.

SVM: Table 14.2b presents the confusion matrix that can be interpreted just as the random forest. The same model accuracy statistics for SVM are presented in Table 14.3. As shown, the SVM accurately predicted 61.9% of the observations. Overall, the model performance statistics show that the SVM performance is similar to random forests.

LASSO: The LASSO model was also applied to the test data and the confusion matrix is shown in Table 14.2c. As Table 14.3 shows, 62.9% of the observations are correctly predicted. The area under the ROC curve is 66%.

Logistic regression: Finally, I applied a main-effect logistic regression model to the same dataset, with best subset selection. The confusion matrix is presented in Table 14.2d. The model performance is presented in the last column in Table 14.3. As shown, the logistic model performs similar to the other methods tested.

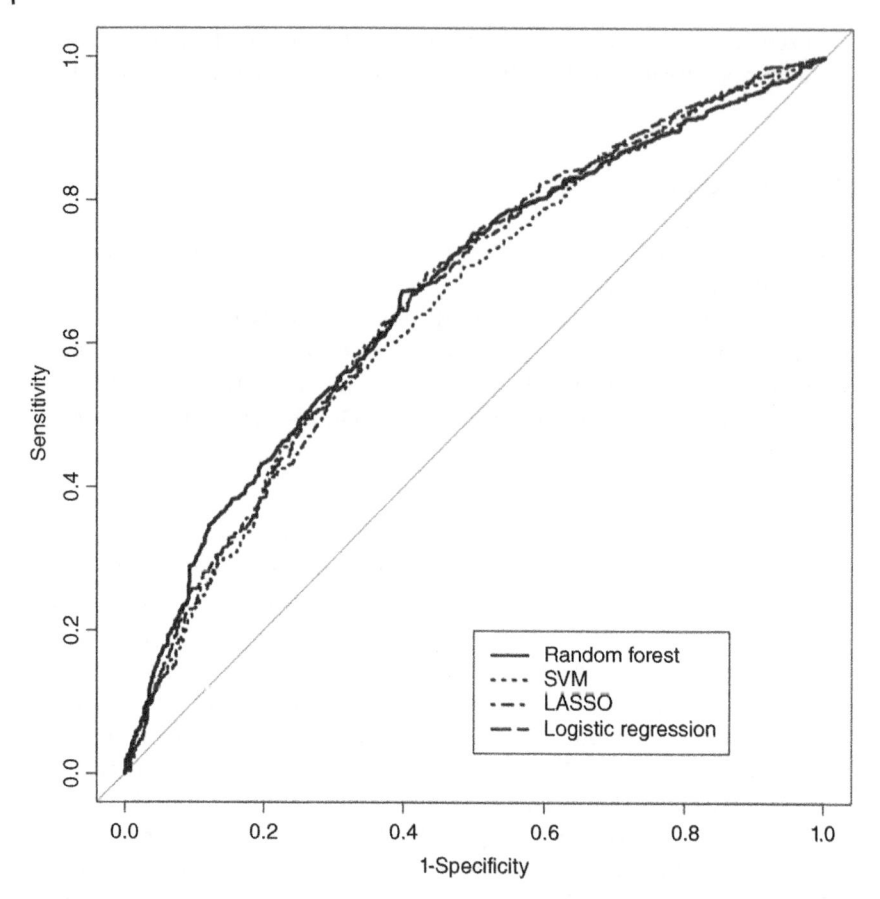

Figure 14.1 ROC curve for LASSO, random forest, SVM, and logistic regression.

As Table 14.3 shows, the LASSO is the only machine learning method that shows a slight advantage compared to the logistic regression. Random forests and SVM show no meaningful improvement compared to the logistic regression. This finding is also illustrated by the ROC curve where the four curves are very close to each other and at times overlap with one another, suggesting that these machine learning methods do not substantially and systematically improve the prediction of panel attrition. However, one advantage of machine learning methods is in identifying the importance of predictors. The random forest technique can naturally detect the importance of a predictor as it relates to both univariate and interactive effects. Similarly, one natural outcome of LASSO is the main-effect model reduction or higher order term identification. In Section 14.3.1 examines the variable importance across three methods (random forest, LASSO, and logistic regression).

Table 14.3 Statistics of model accuracy for predicting wave 2 participation by applying random forest, SVM, LASSO, and logistic regression models to test data.

Statistics (based on a 20% test sample)	Random forest	SVM	LASSO	Logistic regression
Accuracy (i.e. percentage correctly classified, %)	62.0	61.9	62.9	62.4
Sensitivity (i.e. true positive rate, %)	64.9	62.8	62.2	61.1
Specificity (i.e. true negative rate, %)	59.1	61.1	63.7	63.8
Balanced accuracy (mean of sensitivity and specificity, %)	62.0	61.9	62.9	62.4
Area under the ROC curve (%)	67.1	65.3	66.5	62.4

14.3.1 Which Are the Important Predictors?

This study has one advantage: it uses the relatively rich data collected from the first interview to predict the second interview. However, not all variables are equally important in predicting wave 2 participation. Note that these methods use very different technics in identifying a variable's importance. Since LASSO shrinks variable coefficients to zero if they are not predictive of the outcome variable, variables with nonzero coefficients are important in predicting the outcome. Random forests produce variable importance as part of their outcome. For logistic regression, I applied a best subset variable selection. The variables selected in this approach are considered to be important predictors to panel attrition. The purpose of this analysis was to examine which variables, if any, are consistently identified as important across each of these methods.

The LASSO model results in 15 nonzero coefficients (Table 14.4). Using that as the baseline, I compared the important predictors across random forest, logistic regression, and LASSO. Five variables were consistently important across the three methods: education, age, number of kids, income, and news heard about business condition changes. Another three variables that were also relatively important are whether respondents have investments, their attitudes toward the interview, and how well they understand the survey questions, as reported by the interviewer.

14.4 Discussion

One important objective of a longitudinal or panel survey is to measure changes of attitudes, opinions, or behaviors, which requires keeping respondents engaged in follow-up surveys. A number of studies have explored the causes of panel attrition

Table 14.4 Important predictors for random forest, LASSO, and logistic regression.

Predictor names	Random forest	LASSO	Logistic regression
Education	x	x	x
Age	x	x	x
Number of children <18 in household	x	x	x
News heard of changes in biz cond (1)	x	x	x
Gas price expectations 5 years		x	
Quantile of income	x	x	x
Economy good/bad next 5 years		x	
Home selling attitude		x	
Economy better/worse next year		x	
Vehicle buying attitudes		x	
Region		x	
Have investment	x	x	
Sex		x	
Respondent's attitude	x	x	
Respondent's understanding of questions	x	x	

and examined the effectiveness of various techniques for reducing it. This research shows that few studies have tried to predict the likelihood of panel attrition for each panel survey respondent. When resources are constrained, it is wise to focus on those observations that are least likely to respond to follow-up surveys to reduce attrition rate.

Four classification methods, including random forests, SVMs, LASSO, and logistic regression, are used in this study to predict panel attrition. The first three methods are common machine learning techniques frequently used in many fields, although survey researchers are just starting to use them. As this study shows, as have several recent publications (Buskirk et al. 2018), those techniques can be quite useful for answering survey research-related questions. Also, from my experience, some data analysis packages, such as R, have made it very user-friendly for survey researchers to adopt these techniques in their work. Since logistic regression is frequently used in the field of survey research and researchers are more familiar with this method, it is treated as the benchmark in the analysis.

Across the four methods used in this study, LASSO shows a slight advantage in predicting wave 2 survey participation, as indicated by the overall accuracy. The advantage is not substantial, however, and the other two methods (random forests and SVM) show similar predictive performance, judging from several statistics. But, when comparing these three methods to the logistic regression model, the three methods do not show a significant advantage over the logistic regression model. Judging from the AUC, LASSO has a slight advantage over logistic regression, although the difference is very small. One potential explanation for the similar model performance is in the important variable selection where only main effects are determined to be the important variables from both LASSO and random forests. One advantage of these machine learning methods is their ability to identify nonlinear relationships such as interaction and second-order predictors. Because the nonlinear relationship is not important in predicting the panel attrition, the alternative machine learning methods are not more advantageous than the logistic regression model.

Because they often face resource constraints, if researchers want to allocate more resources to those who are predicted to be nonrespondents in order to reduce panel attrition, we would like to have more confidence in the true positives to spend limited resources wisely: we would like to see a high sensitivity rate. Among these methods, random forest has the highest sensitivity, although the difference is not substantial.

The variable importance analysis sheds light on the variables that are most predictive of the outcome. This study shows that several demographic variables (such as education, age, number of kids, and income) and interviewer evaluation of respondents (such as respondent's attitudes toward the interview and how well they understand the survey questions) are important in predicting follow-up survey participation. Researchers should consider asking about these variables in a panel study and consider using them not only for subsequent survey prediction but also for weighting or nonresponse adjustment. The good news is that many of them are demographic variables that most surveys would collect regardless.

Several other related topics can be further explored to understand survey and panel participation. First, this study relies heavily on respondents' answers to the first interview when predicting wave 2 participation. However, paradata (such as call logs) are often included in similar analysis and could potentially increase the predictive power. Such data are not available for this study but future studies should consider adding paradata to the prediction model.

Second, the survey used in this study (SoC) has only two waves of data collection. Other longitudinal studies follow up with respondents more often. One potential topic for study is the question of how well one can predict panel attrition for later waves.

Third, another area of application for this study is in online web panels. Such panels recruit panel members and invite them to participate in surveys regularly. However, not all members will remain in the panel and members with certain characteristics are more likely to attrite from the panel than others. Researchers could benefit from the techniques used in this study to understand and predict who is likely to attrite from an online panel, and potentially take preventive methods to prevent them from attriting.

To conclude, in a panel study, the ability to predict which respondents are more likely to stop participating in the follow-up interviews has both operational and research implications. Operationally, practitioners can focus their resources, effort, and time on those who are least likely to participate in the follow-up study to minimize panel attrition. This study is one of several examining how we as survey researchers can unlock the power of parxsadata, substantive survey data, and machine learning to better understand, identify, and mitigate attrition within survey panels.

14.A Questions Used in the Analysis

Variable	Question wording
Demographic variables	
Region	Region of residence
Sex	Sex of respondent
Marital status	Are you currently married (living with a partner), separated, divorced, widowed, or have you never been married?
Education	Education of respondent
Age	Age of respondent
Number of children <18 in household	How many members of your household are 17 years of age or younger?
Number of adults 18+ in household	Counting yourself, how many members of your household are 18 or older?
Quantile of income	Quantile of income
Own/rent home	Do you (and your family living there) own your own home, pay rent, or what?
Have investment	The next questions are about investments in the stock market. First, do you (or any member of your family living there) have any investments in the stock market, including any publicly traded stock that is directly owned, stocks in mutual funds, stocks in any of your retirement accounts, including 401(K)s, IRAs, or Keogh accounts?

14.A Questions Used in the Analysis

Variable	Question wording
Survey substantive variables	
Personal finances between year ago	We are interested in how people are getting along financially these days. Would you say that you are better off or worse off financially than you were a year ago?
Reasons: finances between year ago (1)	Why do you say so? (Are there any other reasons?)
Reasons: finances between year ago (2)	Why do you say so? (Are there any other reasons?)
Personal finances between next year	Now looking ahead – do you think that a year from now you will be better off financially, or worse off, or just about the same as now?
Economy better/worse year ago	Would you say that at the present time business conditions are better or worse than they were a year ago?
Economy better/worse next year	And how about a year from now, do you expect that in the country as a whole business conditions will be better, or worse than they are at present, or just about the same?
Economy good/bad next year	Now turning to business conditions in the country as a whole – do you think that during the next 12 months we'll have good times financially, or bad times, or what?
Economy good/bad next 5 year	Looking ahead, which would you say is more likely – that in the country as a whole we'll have continuous good times during the next 5 years or so, or that we will have periods of widespread unemployment or depression, or what?
News heard of changes in biz condition (1)	During the last few months, have you heard of any favorable or unfavorable changes in business conditions? What did you hear?
News heard of changes in biz condition (2)	During the last few months, have you heard of any favorable or unfavorable changes in business conditions? What did you hear?
Unemployment more/less next year	How about people out of work during the coming 12 months – do you think that there will be more unemployment than now, about the same, or less?

Variable	Question wording
Government economic policy	As to the economic policy of the government – I mean steps taken to fight inflation or unemployment – would you say the government is doing a good job, only fair, or a poor job?
Interest rates up/down next year	No one can say for sure, but what do you think will happen to interest rates for borrowing money during the next 12 months – will they go up, stay the same, or go down?
Durables buying attitudes	Generally speaking, do you think now is a good or a bad time for people to buy major household items?
Home buying attitudes	Generally speaking, do you think now is a good time or a bad time to buy a house?
Home selling attitude	What about selling a house – generally speaking, do you think now is a good time or a bad time to sell a house?
Vehicle buying attitudes	Speaking now of the automobile market – do you think the next 12 months or so will be a good time or a bad time to buy a vehicle, such as a car, pickup, van, or sport utility vehicle?
Chance will have comfortable retirement	Compared with 5 years ago, do you think the chances that you will have a comfortable retirement have gone up, gone down, or remained the same?
Price expectations 1 year recoded	Price expectations for next 12 months recoded
Price expectations 5 years recoded	Price expectations for next 5 years recoded
Gas price expectations 5 years	Gasoline price expectations for next 5 years
Gas price expectations 12 months	Gasoline price expectations for next 12 months
Chance of income increase in 5 years	What do you think the chances are that your income will increase by more than the rate of inflation in the next 5 year or so?
Percent chance of income increase	Next I would like to ask you about your own personal income prospects in the next 12 months. What do you think is the percent chance that your income in the next 12 months will be higher than your income in the past 12 months?

Variable	Question wording
Chance will lose job in 5 years	During the next 5 years, what do you think the chances are that you (or your husband/wife) will lose a job you wanted to keep?
Chance will have social security	What do you think the chances are that when you retire, your income from Social Security and job pensions will be adequate to maintain your living standards?
Percent chance of invest increase 1 year	What do you think is the percent chance that a $1000 investment in a diversified stock mutual fund will increase in value in the year ahead, so that it is worth more than one thousand dollars one year from now?
Interviewer observation variables	
Respondent's understanding of questions	Was the respondent's understanding of the questions excellent, good, fair, or poor?
Respondent's attitude	In general, what was the respondent's attitude toward the interview?

References

Breiman, L. (2001). Random forests. *Machine Learning* 45 (1): 5–32. https://doi.org/10.1023/A:1010933404324.

Breiman, L., Friedman, J., Stone, C.J. et al. (1984). *Classification and Regression Trees*, 1e. New York, NY: Chapman & Hall/CRC.

Buskirk, T.D. (2018). Surveying the forests and sampling the trees: an overview of classification and regression trees and random forests with applications in survey research. *Survey Practice* 11 (1): 1–13. https://doi.org/10.29115/SP-2018-0003.

Buskirk, T., Kirchner, A., Eck, A. et al. (2018). An introduction to machine learning methods for survey researchers. *Survey Practice* 11 (1): 1–11. https://doi.org/10.29115/SP-2018-0004.

Couper, M.P. and Ofstedal, M.B. (2009). Keeping in contact with mobile sample members. In: *Methodology of Longitudinal Surveys* (ed. P. Lynn), 183–203. New York, NY: Wiley.

Curtin, R.T. (1982). Indicators of consumer behavior: the University of Michigan surveys of consumers. *Public Opinion Quarterly* 46 (3): 340–352.

Fumagalli, L., Laurie, H., and Lynn, P. (2013). Experiments with methods to reduce attrition in longitudinal surveys. *Journal of the Royal Statistical Society: Series A (Statistics in Society)* 176 (2): 499–519. https://doi.org/10.1111/j.1467-985X.2012.01051.x.

Hill, D.H. and Willis, R.J. (2001). Reducing panel attrition: a search for effective policy instruments. *The Journal of Human Resources* 36 (3): 416–438. https://doi.org/10.2307/3069625.

Kern, C., Klausch, T., and Kreuter, F. (2019). Tree-based machine learning methods for survey research. *Survey Research Methods* 13 (1): 73–93. https://doi.org/10.18148/srm/2019.v13i1.7395.

Lagorio, C. (2016). Call and response: modelling longitudinal contact and cooperation using wave 1 call records data. 37. *Understanding Society Working Paper Series*. No. 2016-01. Available at: https://www.understandingsociety.ac.uk/sites/default/files/downloads/working-papers/2016-01.pdf (accessed 23 March 2020).

Lepkowski, J.M. and Couper, M.P. (2002). Nonresponse in the second wave of longitudinal household surveys. In: *Survey Nonresponse* (eds. R.M. Groves, D.A. Dillman, J.L. Eltinge, et al.), 259–272. New York, NY: Wiley.

Lillard, L.A. and Panis, C.W.A. (1998). Panel attrition from the panel study of income dynamics: household income, marital status, and mortality. *The Journal of Human Resources* 33 (2): 437–457. https://doi.org/10.2307/146436.

Lynn, P. (2013). Alternative sequential mixed-mode designs: effects on attrition rates, attrition bias, and costs. *Journal of Survey Statistics and Methodology* 1 (2): 183–205. https://doi.org/10.1093/jssam/smt015.

Lynn, P. (2014). Targeted response inducement strategies on longitudinal surveys. In: *Improving Survey Methods: Lessons from Recent Research* (eds. U. Engel, B. Jann, P. Lynn, et al.), 322–338. Abingdon, UK: Psychology Press.

Lynn, P. (2018). Tackling panel attrition. In: *The Palgrave Handbook of Survey Research* (eds. D.L. Vannette and J.A. Krosnick), 143–153. Cham: Palgrave Macmillan https://doi.org/10.1007/978-3-319-54395-6_19.

Lynn, P., Kaminska, O., and Goldstein, H. (2014). Panel attrition: how important is interviewer continuity? *Journal of Official Statistics* 30 (3): 443–457. https://doi.org/10.2478/jos-2014-0028.

Nicoletti, C. and Buck, N. (2004). Explaining interviewee contact and co-operation in the British and German Household Panels. Working Paper No. 2004–2006. University of Essex. https://www.econstor.eu/handle/10419/92156.

Olsen, R. (2018). Panel attrition. In: *The Palgrave Handbook of Survey Research* (eds. D.L. Vannette and J.A. Krosnick), 509–517. Cham: Palgrave Macmillan https://doi.org/10.1007/978-3-319-54395-6_59.

Olson, K. and Witt, L. (2011). Are we keeping the people who used to stay? Changes in correlates of panel survey attrition over time. *Social Science Research* 40 (4): 1037–1050. https://doi.org/10.1016/j.ssresearch.2011.03.001.

Signorino, C.S. and Kirchner, A. (2018). Using LASSO to model interactions and nonlinearities in survey data. *Survey Practice* 11 (1): 1–10. https://doi.org/10.29115/SP-2018-0005.

Tibshirani, R. (1996). Regression shrinkage and selection via the lasso. *Journal of the Royal Statistical Society: Series B (Methodological)* 58 (1): 267–288.

Tibshirani, R. (2011). Regression shrinkage and selection via the lasso: a retrospective. *Journal of the Royal Statistical Society: Series B (Statistical Methodology)* 73 (3): 273–282. https://doi.org/10.1111/j.1467-9868.2011.00771.x.

Tourangeau, R. and Ye, C. (2009). The framing of the survey request and panel attrition. *Public Opinion Quarterly* 73 (2): 338–348. https://doi.org/10.1093/poq/nfp021.

Vapnik, V. (2013). *The Nature of Statistical Learning Theory*, 2e. New York, NY: Springer Science & Business Media.

Zagorsky, J.L. and Rhoton, P. (2008). The effects of promised monetary incentives on attrition in a long-term panel survey. *Public Opinion Quarterly* 72 (3): 502–513. https://doi.org/10.1093/poq/nfn025.

15

Assessing Community Wellbeing Using Google Street-View and Satellite Imagery

Pablo Diego-Rosell, Stafford Nichols, Rajesh Srinivasan, and Ben Dilday

The Gallup Organization, Washington, DC, USA

15.1 Introduction

American communities face significant health and wellbeing challenges. In addition to long-standing inequalities among minorities, mortality and morbidity rates have increased among whites since the turn of the century (Case and Deaton 2015). Increases in drug overdoses, suicides, and alcohol-related liver disease are mostly to blame for this ongoing trend (Case and Deaton 2017). Community health data in the United States are collected through expensive large-scale surveys, including the American Community Survey (ACS) and the behavioral risk factor surveillance system (BRFSS). Additionally, Gallup conducts a cross-sectional Daily Tracking survey (GDT) that covers both subjective wellbeing (SWB) and self-reported health variables. These data sources collect data relatively infrequently: smaller regions are only surveyed every three or five years in the ACS, and with much lower coverage at the community level in the BRFSS and GDT.

Over the last decade, computational methods have progressed remarkably, and deep learning applications are now able to leverage text data from social media and different types of satellite and panoramic imagery to reliably estimate statistics relating to race, gender, education, occupation, unemployment, and other demographics at the small-area level. Convolutional neural networks (CNNs) have been successfully deployed in several studies to map economic wellbeing by identifying physical features such as road characteristics, building, and shadows, and by using nightlight and land use data (Babenko et al. 2017). Using high-resolution daytime satellite imagery from Google Earth (GE), Jean et al. (2016) identified image features that could explain up to 75% of the variation in local consumption expenditures in Nigeria, Tanzania, Uganda, Malawi, and

Big Data Meets Survey Science: A Collection of Innovative Methods, First Edition. Edited by Craig A. Hill, Paul P. Biemer, Trent D. Buskirk, Lilli Japec, Antje Kirchner, Stas Kolenikov, and Lars E. Lyberg.
© 2021 John Wiley & Sons, Inc. Published 2021 by John Wiley & Sons, Inc.

Rwanda. They trained a CNN without direct supervision to identify semantically meaningful features that were predictive of local-level consumption, such as urban areas, roads, bodies of water, and agricultural areas. This approach proved more powerful than previous efforts. Acharya, Fang, and Raghvendra (2017) achieved similar results using Google Street View (GSV) imagery and transfer learning on pretrained VGG16 models (a CNN architecture named after the Visual Geometry Group from Oxford), and ResNet18 models to predict income levels at the US neighborhood level. In a more recent paper, Gebru et al. (2017) estimated socioeconomic characteristics in 200 US cities based on a CNN trained to classify car makes, models, and years. Taking labeled images of 2657 visually distinct cars from specialized websites such as edmunds.com, and expert annotations on GSV images, Gebru et al. (2017) accurately classified cars in a sample of 50 million GSV images. They then used the aggregate composition of the cars at the zip code level, including 88 car-related attributes such as average value, makes, models, year, foreign vs. domestic, etc., to determine socioeconomic statistics and political preferences in the US population. They found a strong correlation with actual voter preferences ($r = 0.73$), median household incomes ($r = 0.82$), and demographic indicators such as ethnicity (e.g. percentage of Asians, $r = 0.87$).

SWB and health outcomes could be similarly mapped to visible features from the built environment. Community aesthetics, such as the presence of graffiti, litter, or broken windows, correlated strongly with income (e.g., Thornton et al. 2016). The broken windows theory predicts that untidy community aesthetics engender crime (Keizer, Lindenberg, and Steg 2008), further eroding wellbeing. Neighborhood walkability affects health by influencing physical activity, obesity, and pollution (Frank et al. 2006). Kelly et al. (2014) further identified land use as a predictor of observed physical activity: mixed and nonresidential zones were more likely to show individuals engaged in physical activity. Segments with pedestrian infrastructure were also more likely to include individuals engaged in physical activity. Several authors identified housing type as a predictor of physical health (Berglund, Westerling, and Lytsy 2017) and mental health (McCarthy et al. 1985): individuals residing in apartments and high-rise buildings had a higher risk of psychological distress. Finally, Gebru et al. (2017) showed that the distribution of car makes, models, and years strong predicted income and demographics. The amount of traffic itself affected health, particularly through the effects of increased air pollution (Brunekreef and Holgate 2002) and environmental noise (Orban et al. 2016).

We propose a method to predict SWB and health outcomes at the census-tract level based on a combination of GSV/GE imagery and survey data from BRFSS and GDT. We first compiled a training set of GSV images, randomly selected through systematic global positioning system (GPS) sampling of the street grid in each of the 200 census tracts in Baltimore, and 195 census tracts in San Francisco. These images were then crowdsourced on MTurk and labeled according to several features identified in the literature as predicting SWB and health outcomes. Additionally, we incorporated predictors from GE images and freely available classified land cover data with a spatial resolution of 30 m. Using the processed imagery, we created aggregate measures of each feature by census tract and built a model to optimize a prediction of average SWB/health outcomes within the census tract, as measured from existing BRFSS and GDT survey data.

This chapter has three major sections, including a methods section describing the geospatial sampling approach for street-level imagery and the processing of all data sources (GSV images, satellite imagery, survey-based outcomes), followed by a results and discussion section describing the model development process and the application of results, and finally a conclusions section evaluating the proposed methods.

15.2 Methods

This section defines sampling units and frames, data sources used to identify outcomes and predictors, and data processing and transformation steps to generate the final variables used in the analysis.

15.2.1 Sampling Units and Frames

Statistical divisions in the United States include states, counties, census tracts, and, at the lowest level, census blocks. Census tracts are small, relatively permanent statistical subdivisions of a county, with an average population of about 4000 and range from a minimum of 1200 to a maximum of 8000. Census tracts are an ideal unit for small-area estimation (SAE) because all census data are available at that level. Additionally, census tracts have geographically desirable properties: they are perfectly nested within counties and cover a well-defined geographic area that is stable from census to census. Census tracts are in many ways preferable to zip codes, which are also sometimes used for SAE. Zip codes offer less granularity, large variability in size, little correspondence with existing official datasets, and hard-to-define, unstable boundaries. Our unit of analysis was therefore the census tract.

We used a general power analysis rule for multiple regression, $N = 50 + 8k$, where N = sample size, k = number of predictors, (around 20), to determine that 200 census tracts would provide sufficient data points to model the link between imagery features and indicators from survey data. We focused on the cities of Baltimore and San Francisco as our test cases. Both cities have an ideal number of census tracts, 200 and 195, respectively. Additionally, they both have SAE BRFSS data available at the tract level and have large income inequalities within and between them. In Baltimore, for example, many parts of the city are vacant and dilapidated, while other parts of the city are well developed and upscale (see Appendix 15.B).

15.2.2 Data Sources

To conduct the analyses outlined earlier, we relied on three data sources described in more detail in this section. Specifically, we used health and wellbeing outcome data from traditional surveys, built environment predictors obtained from GSV, and geospatial predictors using imagery from GE and the National Land Cover Database (Homer, Fry, and Barnes 2012).

15.2.2.1 Study Outcomes from Survey Data

We selected broad health and wellbeing outcomes from two major probability-based survey sources: BRFSS and the GDT poll. BRFSS is a health-related telephone survey managed by the US Centers for Disease Control and Prevention (CDC). BRFSS collects state data about US residents about their health-related risk behaviors, chronic health conditions, and use of preventive services in all 50 states, the District of Columbia, and three US territories, with more than 400 000 adult interviews conducted annually. The GDT surveys 1000 US adults each day, 350 days per year using a dual-frame design of landline and cellphone numbers. Demographic weighting targets for the United States and states are based on the most recent Current Population Survey figures for the US population aged 18 and older, while weighting targets for metropolitan areas and congressional districts are based on Nielsen Claritas statistics on the US population aged 18 and older. Phone status targets are based on the most recent National Health Interview Survey and population density targets are based on the most recent US decennial census.

Although both BRFSS and GDT collect large samples, they are not large enough to produce direct survey estimates at the small-area level. For our research, we used SAEs derived from both surveys using multilevel regression and poststratification. Model-based SAEs of SWB were calculated by Gallup, whereas SAEs from BRFSS had already been calculated since 2015 by CDC, CDC Foundation, and the Robert Wood Johnson Foundation as part of the 500 Cities Project. Census tract-level estimates were available for download directly from CDC's website.[1]

In 2010, 78.8% of US adults self-reported having good or better physical health, and 79.1% of US adults self-reported having good or better mental health (CDC 2010). Both physical health and mental health are important components of health-related quality of life (HRQOL), a multidimensional concept that focuses on the impact of health status on quality of life. We selected these two broad variables from the BRFSS SAEs at the census-tract level:

---

[1] See https://www.cdc.gov/500cities/.

15.2 Methods

- *Physical health*: Physical health not good for ≥14 days among adults aged ≥18 years
  - *Numerator*: Respondents aged ≥18 years who reported 14 or more days during the past 30 days during which their physical health was not good.
  - *Denominator*: Respondents aged ≥18 years who reported the number of days during the past 30 days during which their physical health was not good (i.e. excluding those who refused to answer, had a missing answer, or answered "don't know/not sure").
- *Mental health*: Mental health not good for ≥14 days among adults aged ≥18 years.
  - *Numerator*: Respondents aged ≥18 years who reported 14 or more days during the past 30 days during which their mental health was not good.
  - *Denominator*: Respondents aged ≥18 years who reported the number of days during the past 30 days during which their mental health was not good (i.e. excluding those who refused to answer, had a missing answer, or answered "don't know/not sure").

Gallup Computed Model-Based SAEs of SWB Using GDT Data

Following Organisation for Economic Co-operation and Development (OECD) international guidelines on measuring SWB (OECD 2013), we selected two broad indicators of SWB from the GDT: life evaluations (LE) and affect balance (AB). We operationalized these two indicators using an approach similar to the one described by Diego-Rosell, Tortora, and Bird (2016):

- LEs were measured with the Cantril Self-Anchoring Striving Scale (Cantril 1965). The question uses a 0–10 scale and asked respondents:
  Please imagine a ladder with steps numbered from zero at the bottom to ten at the top. Suppose we say that the top of the ladder represents the best possible life for you, and the bottom of the ladder represents the worst possible life for you. On which step of the ladder would you say you personally feel you stand at this time, assuming that the higher the step the better you feel about your life, and the lower the step the worse you feel about it? Which step comes closest to the way you feel?

AB was created using experiential measures of emotions, including two positive experience questions (smile or laugh, enjoyment) and three negative experience questions (worry, sadness, stress). The questions were introduced as follows:

Now, please think about yesterday, from the morning until the end of the day. Think about where you were, what you were doing, who you were with, and how you felt:

The positive affect questions were:

1. *Did you smile or laugh a lot yesterday?*
2. Did you experience the following feelings during A LOT OF THE DAY yesterday? How about enjoyment?

The negative affect questions were:

1. Did you experience the following feelings during A LOT OF THE DAY yesterday? How about worry?
2. How about sadness?
3. How about stress?

All five affect questions were dummy coded as 1 for a "Yes" answer and as 0 for "No," "Don't know" or "Refused" answer.[2] To obtain the overall AB index, we subtracted the sum of the negative affect questions from the sum of the positive affect questions.

We then estimated these two outcomes at the tract level with a multilevel regression and poststratification approach using data from the GDT and the 2016 ACS five-year estimates. We first estimated a multilevel linear regression model for each of the two outcomes, with random effects for the interaction of gender (male/female), age (18–24, 25–34, 35–44, 45–64, 65+), and educational attainment (less than 12th grade, high school graduate, some college, bachelor's degree, and graduate/professional degree), and state-level fixed effects for the log of mean income and the unemployment rate among the civilian population 16+. We applied poststratification with the ACS tract-level population counts by gender, age, and education, as well as tract-level estimates of income and unemployment, also from ACS. A full description of the estimation procedures is provided by Kastellec, Lax, and Phillips (2010).

All four outcomes variables were merged into a common dataset at the tract level. Although they represented distinct domains, the four outcomes were strongly correlated as shown in Table 15.1.

15.2.2.2 Study Predictors from Built Environment Data

Data gathered from GSV and GE about the built environment represented the most complex and labor-intensive process. This section presents these predictors in three stages: image sampling, image labeling, and quality control.

Table 15.1 Pearson correlations among outcome variables for the 395 total census tracts from Baltimore and San Francisco.

	Physical health	Mental health	Life evaluation
Mental health	0.93		
Life evaluation	−0.87	−0.92	
Affect balance	−0.72	−0.84	0.89

---

2 Given the smaller samples in the GDT, excluding these missing datapoints could potentially lead to sparse cells, so treatment of missing cases is different from the physical and mental health measures, which rely on larger samples and exclude DK/Refused answers.

Built Environment Data – Image Sampling

We divided city streets into segments and selected a sample of GPS locations. First, we defined which road segments to include and exclude from the sample frame. All roads within Baltimore and San Francisco city limits were included, except for interstates, bridges, tunnels, and major highways, because often no neighborhoods were visible from the GSV imagery captured on them. Small alleys that did not have GSV images were also excluded. Next, we generated GPS points every 30 m along the surface of all road segments across the cities. This 30-m interval was determined based on our estimation of the typical visible range in a GSV image, or the maximum distance from which image features were discernible. This process resulted in 98 817 total points for Baltimore, and 77 038 points for San Francisco spread evenly across each street in these cities. These points are depicted in Figures 15.1–15.4 as white dots with the black lines representing the census tract boundaries.

On average, each census tract contained about 500 points in Baltimore, and 400 points in San Francisco. We used systematic simple random sampling to select 60 points at an even interval throughout each census tract, sufficient for 90% confidence and ± 10pp error. Before selection, we sorted points by their longitude, and then latitude, to encourage a more even geographic spread of selected points.

Given a list of latitude and longitude values from the random sample generation process, we downloaded the corresponding images from GSV. The GSV application programming interface (API) takes the location, heading, pitch, and field-of-view as parameters. Similar to the approach that Andersson et al. (2017) used, we followed these steps:

- Generated an approximate 360° view by iterating through four heading directions (0°, 90°, 180°, 270°) for each latitude/longitude pair, using a field-of-view of 90°, and the default pitch of 0. Some researchers such as Andersson et al. (2017) also used this approach. The combination of latitude, longitude, heading, and pitch defined a unique, image-specific URL.
- Given a URL, the images were loaded using a GET request within the Python requests library. For archiving, each image was stored with a filename denoting latitude, longitude (rounded to six decimal digits), and heading.[3]

Built Environment Data – Image Labeling

The first step in the image labeling process was identifying features of the built environment commonly mentioned in the literature as predictive of health and/or wellbeing outcomes:

---

3 This process was executed under the Google API terms of service valid as of 7 February 2018. Recent updates to the terms of service explicitly prohibit image scraping for use outside Google-provided services, which would impede the replication of this process. See: https://cloud.google.com/maps-platform/termsSee: https://cloud.google.com/maps-platform/terms.

Figure 15.1 Universe of GPS points generated in Baltimore city. Powered by Google.

- Graffiti
- Litter/trash
- Parks, playgrounds, or recreation facilities
- Predominant type of home
- Maintenance of homes
- Broken/boarded-up windows
- Rooftop decks

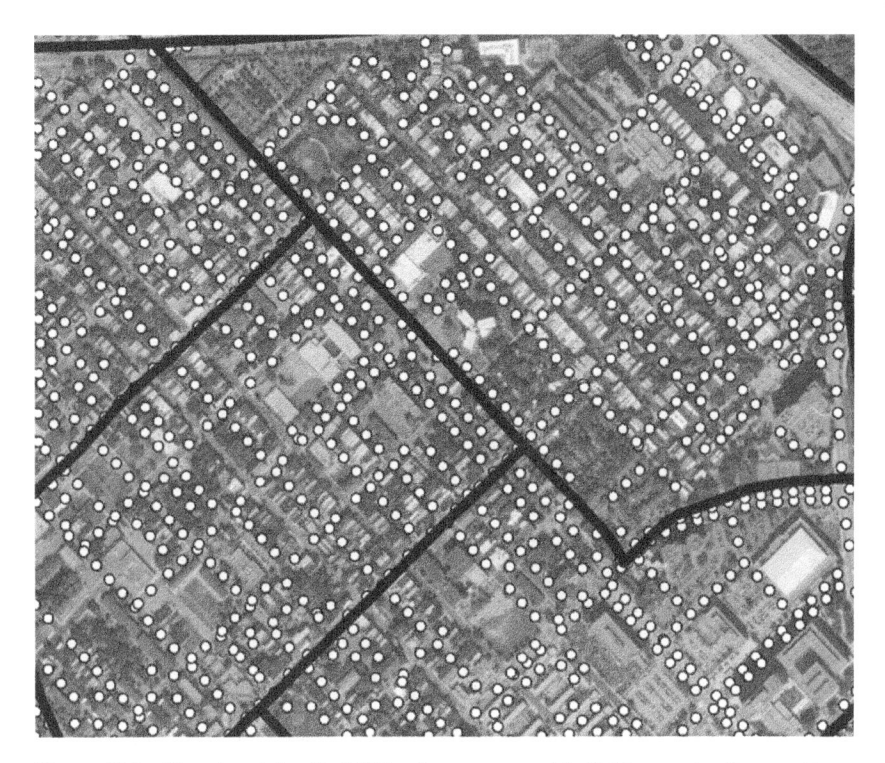

Figure 15.2 Tract-level detail of GPS points generated in Baltimore city. Powered by Google.

- Predominant type of nonresidential building
- Presence of weeds on the sidewalks
- Uneven/broken pavement on the sidewalks
- Benches or other places to rest along the sidewalks
- Strip of grass next to the sidewalks
- Trees on or next to the sidewalks
- Streetlights
- Pedestrian traffic
- Potholes or uneven or broken pavement on the road
- Oil stains on the road
- Traffic
- Predominant car age
- Predominant car type

The image labeling process involved presenting one of the sampled GSV images to MTurk workers, next to a form asking workers to identify the extent to

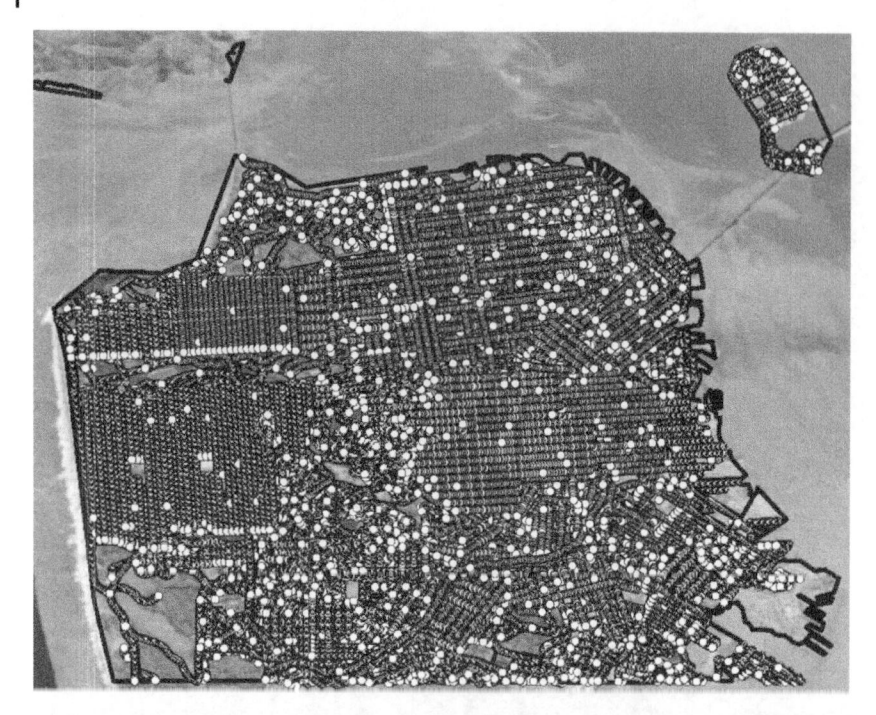

Figure 15.3 Universe of GPS points generated in San Francisco. Powered by Google.

Figure 15.4 Detail points generated in San Francisco. Powered by Google.

which the features above were present in the image (see Appendix 15.A for full questionnaire).

We first calibrated the reliability of the image labeling process with a soft launch on MTurk, including one random image per census tract in Baltimore, for a total of 200 images. Three independent raters using the same rating form labeled these images to assess the reliability of the labeling process. We obtained three ratings for a total of 197 tracts. Our reliability analysis of the initial form flagged Q2 (litter/trash) and Q17 (oil stains) as items with the poorest κ values (see Table 15.2). A closer inspection of images with high levels of disagreement showed that most had a small amount of either litter/trash or oil, which some raters chose to flag as meeting the criterion, while others disregarded it. To better measure these instances, we changed the rating scale for these items from binary to a Likert scale with the options "none," "some," "a lot." Additionally, we redesigned the data entry form to minimize scrolling and enforce skip patterns when a question was not applicable (e.g. if "no sidewalks are visible").

We retested for reliability using the updated form in the same set of images from Baltimore, and a second set of images, including one random image per census tract in San Francisco. We saw an improvement in average inter-rater agreement in both sets, increasing from 55% to 67% in Baltimore and 68% in San Francisco, and average κ, going from 0.33 to 0.51 in Baltimore and 0.48 in San Francisco. Agreement and reliability improved for all items, except for Q1 (presence of graffiti), which was low in San Francisco (0.20) even though its measure improved for Baltimore from 0.46 to 0.80. Only 3% of raters either set endorsed this item, so its κ value was highly influenced by a handful of responses – and therefore volatile. Other items including Q2 (litter/trash), Q3 (parks & rec facilities), Q10 (uneven or broken pavement on the sidewalks), Q17 (oil stains on the road), and Q19 (most cars new or old) still had low reliability ($\kappa < 0.4$ in both retest sets) using the updated form, possibly highlighting the inherent difficulty of labeling images according to these features. This exercise also provided further assurance that the reliability of the data labeling process in San Francisco and Baltimore was quite similar.

Built Environment Data – Quality Control

Using the updated data entry form, we proceeded to label an additional batch of 11 448 images in Baltimore and 11 700 in San Francisco to achieve the sample of 60 images per tract calculated in the *Built Environment Data – Image Sampling* section. Quality control (QC) was an important part of the image labeling process. The first QC measure was to limit our pool of MTurk workers to those with a "master" qualification. Although this qualification was not transparent, Amazon indicates that "these workers have consistently demonstrated a high degree of success in performing a wide range of human intelligence tasks (HITs)

Table 15.2 Inter-rater agreement (% agree) and reliability (κ) for MTurk labeling.

		% Agree			κ		
	Item	BMO (1)	BMO (2)	SFO (2)	BMO (1)	BMO (2)	SFO (2)
Looking at this image in general…							
Q1	Do you see any graffiti?	95	98	93	0.46	0.82	0.20
Q2	Do you see any litter/trash?	55	59	63	0.04	0.29	0.21
Q3	Do you see any parks, playgrounds or recreation facilities?	74	87	88	0.14	0.06	0.15
Looking at the buildings in this image…							
Q4	What is the predominant type of home?	44	57	55	0.44	0.60	0.54
Q5	Are the homes clean and well maintained?	59	70	72	0.44	0.60	0.58
Q6	Do you see any broken/boarded-up windows?	63	72	88	0.46	0.56	0.73
Q7	Do you see any rooftop decks?	70	80	80	0.53	0.66	0.64
Q8	What is the main type of nonresidential building?	65	65	75	0.38	0.48	0.65
Looking at the sidewalks in this image, do you see any…							
Q9	…weeds on the sidewalks?	44	45	69	0.33	0.38	0.54
Q10	…uneven or broken pavement on the sidewalks?	40	53	43	0.27	0.35	0.31
Q11	…benches or other places to rest along the sidewalks?	81	83	84	0.50	0.59	0.62
Q12	…strip of grass next to the sidewalks?	38	67	72	0.30	0.61	0.57
Q13	…trees on or next to the sidewalks?	42	68	69	0.32	0.63	0.60
Q14	…streetlights?	50	66	62	0.43	0.61	0.58
Q15	How many pedestrians do you see?	82	85	75	0.34	0.72	0.66
Looking at the roads in this image, do you see any…							
Q16	…potholes or uneven or broken pavement on the road?	42	63	60	0.23	0.37	0.41
Q17	…oil stains on the road?	38	33	37	0.16	0.22	0.25
Q18	How much traffic do you see in this image?	41	75	70	0.24	0.61	0.66
Q19	Would you say that most cars in this image are new or old?	38	49	41	0.32	0.43	0.34
Q20	Would you say that most cars in this image are… (econ, regular, lux)	36	73	61	0.31	0.65	0.44
Average		55	67	68	0.33	0.51	0.48

BMO 1 = Baltimore, initial form $n = 197$ images.
BMO 2 = Baltimore, updated form $n = 196$ images.
SFO 2 = San Francisco, updated form, $n = 195$ images.
All K = 3 raters per image.

across a large number of Requesters." Additionally, we flagged each individual submission according to its internal consistency, including short completion times (<30 seconds), response set patterns (all "yes" or all "no" responses), incoherence (e.g. a report of "well-maintained homes" followed by a report of "broken/boarded-up windows"), and unusual features (e.g. "rooftop decks" or "graffiti"). We also conducted in-depth spot checks, particularly for high-volume workers. In our Baltimore batch of 11 448 images, our QC led to rejecting and reposting 2458 of 13 942 submissions, or about 18% of all submissions. We had to block 12 workers out of 161 (7%) because of their extremely poor performance. These quality issues were concerning, particularly considering that we had already filtered the labor pool for quality. Shortly after completing the image labeling process in Baltimore, technology media began echoing these quality concerns, even referring to a "bot panic"[4] on Amazon MTurk. For our San Francisco batch of data collection, we further reinforced our QC by limiting workers to those with at least 1000 completed HITs, and a 97% acceptance rate or higher. We obtained a total of 9554 labeled images, out of the total of 11 700 submitted. The additional worker selection criteria led to improved quality, with only 73 rejections, representing 0.8% of all HITs.

We aggregated all variables by response category to create tract-level estimates by calculating a simple tract average. Not applicable or missing responses were eliminated from the denominator when we calculated tract averages. We merged these estimates with variables derived from the satellite imagery analysis, resulting in a total of 56 tract-level independent variables. The distribution of each aggregated variable is shown in the boxplots in Appendix 15.C. Tables 15.3 and 15.4 represent the unweighted, citywide percentages for each feature, along with the intracluster correlation coefficient (ρ), which is computed based on the tract as the clustering variable. Table 15.3 shows descriptive statistics for binary (yes/no) response items. For example, only 1% of the images in Baltimore contained any graffiti. Table 15.4 shows descriptive statistics for multinomial response items. For example, only 1% of the images in San Francisco showed "a lot" of trash.

15.2.2.3 Study Predictors from – Geospatial Imagery

We finally incorporated satellite imagery by clipping satellite images from GE, based on the outline of each census tract, to create a Triangular Greenness Index (TGI) for each tract. We also used the National Land Cover Database (2011) to classify pixels within each census tract into land use categories at a 30-m resolution. The National Land Cover Database was generated by US government agencies, using a modified Anderson Level II classification system. We calculated the following spatial variables:

- *Tract size*: We calculated size as a count of pixels within each tract.
- *TGI*: We calculated this index by first separating the image into red green blue (RGB) channels, then conducting a pixel-level subtraction of the R and B

---

4 See for example https://www.wired.com/story/amazon-mechanical-turk-bot-panic (accessed 24/8/2018).

Table 15.3 Descriptive statistics and intracluster correlation (ρ) for binary items.

		Baltimore				San Francisco			
	Item	Yes (%)	No (%)	N/A (%)	ρ	Yes (%)	No (%)	N/A (%)	ρ
Q1	Graffiti	1	99	—	0.01	2	98	—	0.09
Q3	Parks/recreation facilities	6	94	—	0.02	3	97	—	0.08
Q5	Homes clean/well-maintained	64	7	28	0.09	74	4	22	0.20
Q6	Broken/boarded-up windows	4	74	23	0.05	1	88	11	0.02
Q7	Rooftop decks	1	72	27	0.03	2	78	20	0.03
Q10	Uneven/broken pavement	20	69	11	0.05	13	77	10	0.03
Q11	Benches/places to rest	2	87	11	0.01	2	89	10	0.04
Q12	Strip of grass	44	45	11	0.19	7	83	10	0.15
Q13	Trees	59	30	11	0.05	58	33	10	0.20
Q14	Streetlights	46	44	10	0.02	38	52	10	0.06
Q16	Potholes	21	71	8	0.02	23	70	7	0.07

Descriptive statistics and ICC for 11 448 images from Baltimore and 9554 images from San Francisco.

channels from the G channel (green − 0.39 × red − 0.61 × blue, see for example McKinnon and Hoff (2017)), and averaging the resulting "greenness" factor over all the pixels in the image (see Appendix 15.B).

- *Land use*: We counted the number of pixels of each class/value in each tract,[5] over the total number of pixels in the tract, with the following land uses identified:
  - Open Water
  - Developed, Open Space
  - Developed, Low Intensity
  - Developed, Medium Intensity
  - Developed, High Intensity
  - Barren Land (Rock/Sand/Clay)
  - Deciduous Forest
  - Evergreen Forest
  - Mixed Forest
  - Shrub/Scrub
  - Grassland/Herbaceous
  - Woody Wetlands
  - Emergent Herbaceous Wetlands

---

5 See class definition: https://www.mrlc.gov/nlcd11-leg.php.

Table 15.4 Descriptive statistics and intracluster correlation (ρ) for multinomial items.

	Item	Response	Baltimore %	Baltimore ρ	San Francisco %	San Francisco ρ
Q2	Litter/trash	A lot	3	0.01	1	0.02
		Some	19	0.03	15	0.05
		None	78	0.04	85	0.06
Q4	Homes	Apartment	10	0.08	41	0.20
		Attached	36	0.15	22	0.16
		Detached	22	0.20	15	0.22
		Other	3	0.03	1	0.02
		N/A	28	0.12	22	0.22
Q8	Nonresidential buildings	Church	1	0.01	1	0.05
		Commercial	6	0.09	11	0.16
		Government	1	0.01	1	0.03
		Industrial	5	0.04	4	0.19
		Retail	6	0.03	14	0.22
		Other	9	0.02	4	0.03
		N/A	73	0.11	66	0.34
Q9	Weeds on the sidewalk	A lot	9	0.03	1	0.05
		Some	26	0.04	11	0.06
		None	55	0.05	79	0.13
		N/A	10	0.05	10	0.14
Q15	Pedestrians	0	87	0.03	72	0.16
		1–2	7	0.03	13	0.08
		3–10	1	0.01	5	0.19
		>10	0	0.00	1	0.09
		N/A	4	0.02	10	0.14
Q17	Oil stains	A lot	3	0.02	4	0.04
		Some	25	0.03	50	0.05
		None	64	0.03	39	0.06
		N/A	7	0.02	7	0.02
Q18	Cars in circulation	0	69	0.03	56	0.09
		1–2	18	0.01	24	0.04
		3–10	6	0.03	11	0.08
		>10	1	0.01	1	0.03
		N/A	6	0.00	8	0.04
Q19	Cars new/old	New	55	0.03	58	0.06
		Old	18	0.02	29	0.06
		N/A	27	0.04	12	0.09
Q20	Car types	Luxury	4	0.01	2	0.02
		Regular	51	0.02	76	0.05
		Economy	17	0.01	10	0.02
		N/A	28	0.04	13	0.01

Descriptive statistics and ICC for 11 448 images from Baltimore and 9554 images from SF.

15.2.2.4 Model Development, Testing, and Evaluation

We used the Baltimore labeled data to estimate the marginal returns in mean adjusted R^2 to each additional sampled image per tract. We simulated the marginal returns through a bootstrap estimate of model fit for increasing tract-level sample sizes, with sample sizes ranging from one image per tract, up to a maximum of 50 images per tract. For each sample size, we calculated tract-level summary statistics based on the available GSV images, e.g. for sample size $n = 1$, one image was used to represent each tract. Summary variables were then entered into an ordinary least squares (OLS) regression model to predict each of the four outcomes (Physical Health, Mental Health, Life Evaluations, and Affect Balance) for each bootstrap sample, with 100 replications per sample size (images selected with replacement). Figure 15.5 shows the gains in model fit (adjusted R^2) as the number of images sampled within a census tract increases, showing a clear logarithmic relationship (overlaid on the graph), with diminishing returns for each additional GSV image sampled.

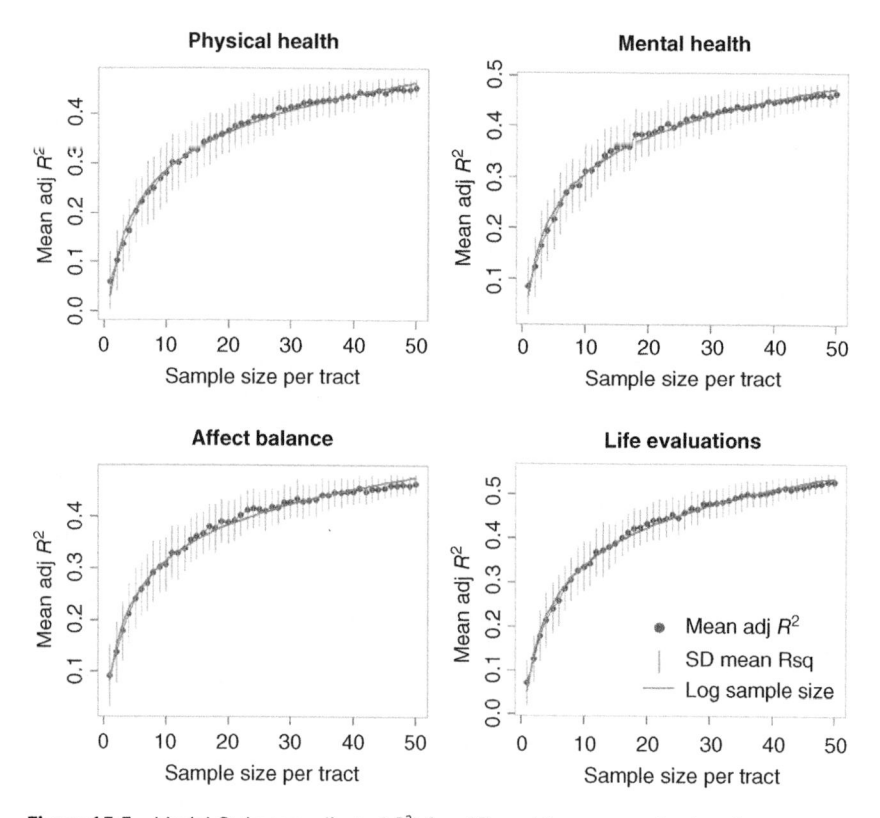

Figure 15.5 Model fit (mean adjusted R^2) for different image sample sizes (n range 0–50) at tract level.

Table 15.5 Estimated model fit (mean adjusted R^2) for different image sample sizes ($n = 60, 120, 180, 240$) at tract level.

	Sample size			
Outcome	60	120	180	240
Physical health	0.483	0.560	0.605	0.637
Mental health	0.493	0.566	0.608	0.638
Affect balance	0.494	0.563	0.604	0.633
Life evaluations	0.561	0.647	0.697	0.733

Given the highly predictable relationship between tract-level sample sizes and model fit, we can estimate the expected model fit for larger sample sizes (see Table 15.5). Keeping in line with the logarithmic relationship between sample size and sampling error, we estimated that each doubling of the sample size would improve model fit by about 10%. Since we were able to plot 98 817 GPS points in 200 census tracts, there are on average 494 GPS points per tract, so we estimated that sampling gains may accrue up to a maximum sample size of about 2000 images per tract (~500 GPS points per tract, four 90° screenshots per GPS point), at which point the tract would have been fully covered, and sampling additional images would not provide extra information. Given diminishing returns, we conclude that the initial sample of 11 448 images is sufficient to provide proof of concept while allowing us to estimate the potential gains in fit for larger sample sizes.

15.3 Application Results

We next examined the bivariate and multivariate relations between predictors and outcomes to ascertain the explanatory power of imagery-based variables. We conducted each analysis separately for Baltimore and San Francisco, and then evaluated the generalizability of results.

15.3.1 Baltimore

Using the labeled data for the sample of 11 448 images in Baltimore, aggregated at the tract level added to tract-level, satellite-based statistics, we proceeded to calculate the Pearson correlation between each of the 56 predictors and the four outcomes of interest[6] (full table in Appendix 15.C). Seven variables emerged as the strongest correlates of health and SWB outcomes (six of which are from the labeled data), including the presence of graffiti, broken windows, streetlights, trash/litter, weeds on the sidewalks, oil stains on the road, and the proportion of medium intensity development. A predominance of attached homes was a particularly strong predictor of AB.

We entered all predictors into an OLS regression model for each outcome. To facilitate interpretation of results, we implemented a stepwise selection of predictors based on the exact Akaike Information Criterion (AIC), combining both forward selection and backward elimination. Regression tables for the final models are shown in Appendix 15.D. Depending on the outcome, and on the basis of adjusted R^2 values in Table 15.6, our models explain anywhere between 56% of variance (Mental Health) and 63% of variance (LE). Based on our models, we estimated a synthetic outcome that will show a Pearson correlation with the true scores between $r = 0.79$ (AB) and $r = 0.82$ (LE), similar, for example, to the correlations shown by Gebru et al. (2017).

For robustness, we computed generalized linear models via penalized maximum likelihood least absolute shrinkage and selection operator (LASSO) with k-fold cross-validation. The resulting coefficients for the final models are shown in Appendix 15.E, yielding similar conclusions to the analysis above. R^2 values for the LASSO models are presented in Table 15.6, showing a lower fit ranging

Table 15.6 Estimated model fit (Baltimore).

	Dependent variable			
	Physical health (1)	Mental health (2)	Life evaluation (3)	Affect balance (4)
Observations	199	199	199	199
Adjusted R^2	0.587	0.564	0.626	0.565
Residual std. error	2.848 (df = 176)	2.147 (df = 171)	0.161 (df = 173)	0.082 (df = 172)
F statistic	13.781*** (df = 22; 176)	10.483*** (df = 27; 171)	14.278*** (df = 25; 173)	10.908*** (df = 26; 172)
R^2 LASSO	0.550	0.520	0.577	0.544

*$p < 0.1$; **$p < 0.05$; ***$p < 0.01$.
$df = R^2$.

---

6 Since some variables exhibited significant skewness, we conducted a Tukey transformation of all predictors using the –"transformTukey" function in the *rcompanion* package in R to produce a more-normally distributed vector of values.

from 0.520 to 0.577, equivalent to a Pearson correlation between $r = 0.72$ (Mental Health) and $r = 0.76$ (LE).

Although most multivariate relationships were as predicted, we had some unexpected findings. The presence of streetlights was associated with worse health and SWB outcomes, a potential case of reverse causality if unsafe areas were given priority by city planners when installing streetlights. The presence of rooftop decks, a sign of a gentrifying neighborhood (in the authors' own observations) in Baltimore, was very strongly associated with better outcomes across the board, both in bivariate and multivariate models. The absence of pedestrians, theoretically a sign of poorer walkability, was associated with slightly better health and SWB outcomes. "Greenness," as measured by the TGI, was a strong risk factor in the multivariate models, even though it had a weak bivariate correlation with all four outcomes, implying that its multivariate effect emerged in combination with other factors. The heat maps in Figure 15.6 show the original data source and the predictor scores for our best-fitting model (LE). Summary heat maps displaying the differences between observed and fitted values are presented in Appendix 15.F.

A visual analysis of the actual vs. fitted maps showed that the models were generally able to pick up major features of the human geography of Baltimore. Health and SWB outcomes were generally higher in the areas surrounding the inner harbor, including neighborhoods such as Federal Hill, Fells Point and Canton, and along the Charles Street corridor, particularly west of Charles Street.

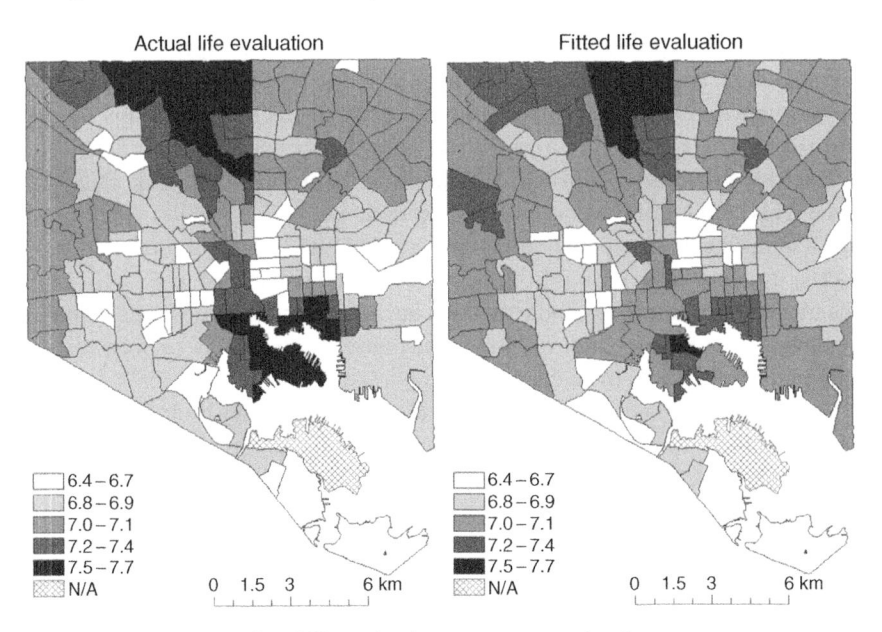

Figure 15.6 Actual vs. fitted life evaluation scores at tract level.

However, in some tracts, our fitted predictions were far from the actual outcomes. We conducted a Bonferroni outlier test with studentized residuals to identify major outliers, identifying four tracts where our predictions were quite different from the original data:

- Tract 2715.03 had better scores than predicted, particularly for LE, where the actual score (7.7) was much higher than the predicted score (7.0).
- Tracts 1003, 1304, and 1801 had worse outcomes than predicted across the board.

The satellite image for each tract, relative to its approximate location on the Baltimore map, is shown on satellite imagery (see footnotes for links). Tract 2715.03 is a sparsely populated (pop = 922) area in Roland Park neighborhood. This tract is home to the Baltimore Polytechnic Institute and the upscale Village of Cross Keys and is in the vicinity of the Cylburn Arboretum and the Baltimore Golf Club. This tract has a high median age (65.9[7], compared to 34.7 for Baltimore[8]) and a high median household income (US$ 71339 vs. US$ 44.262 for the city). These factors are consistent with a higher LE score, which tends to increase with income, and shows a U-shaped relationship with age (Diego-Rosell, Tortora, and Bird 2016). Although we can proxy income levels through our imagery analysis, the high median age in this tract was probably not picked up by any of our imagery-based features.

Tract 1003 is located between the Mt. Vernon and Lathrobe Homes neighborhood; the Baltimore Detention Center and its associated facilities are located there. The census counts prisoners as residents of the place they are imprisoned, and this population is also included in the ACS data, so it is likely that the factors from the physical environment are unlikely to pick up the characteristics of this unique population.

Tract 1304 includes Druid Hill Park and the Parkview/Woodbrook neighborhood. This tract is quite average, with a population of 2352, a median age of 32.6,[9] and a somewhat low-median household income of US$ 35 208. Our image analysis picked up some of the desirable properties of this neighborhood, e.g. with 14% of the images including parks and recreation facilities, a complete absence of graffiti or broken/boarded-up windows, which may have led the model to overestimate the health and SWB in the area.

Finally, tract 1801 is in downtown Baltimore, surrounded by route US40 and N. Martin Luther King Jr. Blvd. This tract has a young population (21.8 years,[10] compared to 34.7 for the city), and has a very low median household income

---

7 https://censusreporter.org/profiles/14000US24510271503-census-tract-271503-baltimore-md/.
8 https://factfinder.census.gov/faces/nav/jsf/pages/community-facts.xhtml?src=bkmk.
9 https://censusreporter.org/profiles/14000US24510130400-census-tract-1304-baltimore-md/.
10 https://censusreporter.org/profiles/14000US24510180100-census-tract-1801-baltimore-md/.

(US$ 15 270 vs. US$ 44.262 for the city). The tract includes the Lexington Terrace neighborhood, a public housing area, with a reputation for gang and drug-related violence.[11] Our imagery-based markers of community unsafety were not particularly high compared to city averages, e.g. graffiti and broken/boarded-up windows (both 1.7% vs. 3.6% for the average tract), or streetlights (51.7% vs. 45.5% for the average tract). It is possible that our models do not fully capture some of these extreme factors.

15.3.2 San Francisco

We next examined the performance of the San Francisco data, with a final sample of 154 census tracts. These data were Tukey-transformed and entered into an OLS model with stepwise predictor selection and complemented with a LASSO model as in Baltimore. Depending on the outcome, and on the basis of the adjusted R^2 values, our models presented in Table 15.7 explain anywhere between 53% of variance (Physical Health) and 65% of variance (Affect Balance). In other words, based on our models, we estimated a synthetic outcome that will show a Pearson correlation between $r = 0.77$ (Physical Health) and $r = 0.84$ (LE). The LASSO models showed a substantially lower explanatory power, with R^2 values ranging from 0.219 (Mental Health) to 0.508 (Affect Balance). The discrepancy between the LASSO and OLS results suggest that our available predictors are not as robust in San Francisco as in Baltimore.

Table 15.7 Estimated model fit (San Francisco).

	Dependent variable			
	Physical health (1)	Mental health (2)	Life evaluation (3)	Affect balance (4)
Observations	154	154	154	154
Adjusted R^2	0.5281	0.586	0.564	0.651
Residual std. error	2.302 ($df = 130$)	1.435 ($df = 128$)	0.106 ($df = 133$)	0.066 ($df = 126$)
F statistic	8.444*** ($df = 23; 130$)	9.658*** ($df = 25; 128$)	10.920*** ($df = 20; 133$)	11.560*** ($df = 27; 126$)
R^2 LASSO	0.428	0.219	0.312	0.508

*$p < 0.1$; **$p < 0.05$; and ***$p < 0.01$.
$df = R^2$.

---

11 Also former home of Donnie Andrews, who inspired *The Wire*'s Omar Little character: http://articles.baltimoresun.com/2011-07-09/news/bs-md-marbella-andrews-20110709-1-drug-lord-lexington-terrace-fran-boyd.

An examination of the multivariate coefficients for the San Francisco models showed some differences with Baltimore. For example, the presence of graffiti and tract greenness was associated with better outcomes in San Francisco than in Baltimore, while the presence of economy cars was associated with worse outcomes in San Francisco than in Baltimore. Other indicators that showed surprising effects in Baltimore were, on the other hand, confirmed in San Francisco. For example, the presence of pedestrians or streetlights was associated with worse outcomes.

15.3.3 Generalizability

Heat maps showing the difference between actual and fitted values for all four outcomes are available on Appendix 15.F. These maps illustrate that predictions tend to be more accurate in less dense areas. For Baltimore, the densest census tracts are those roughly in the center of the map. For San Francisco, they are in the north east (top right). These areas are the most underfitted and overfitted. Presumably, the imagery obtained from these areas does not explain the wellbeing of local residents as well as imagery in more suburban areas. This is perhaps due to the complex, diverse, high-rise, transient nature of downtown areas and suggests the built environment here does not factor into wellbeing as much as more suburban neighborhoods.

We calculated Moran's I to measure the spatial autocorrelation of each set of outcomes (see Table 15.8), showing that the actual and fitted measures result in similar spatial distributions within each outcome. In Baltimore, Physical Health had the highest degree of spatial correlation, while Affect Balance showed the lowest degree of spatial correlation. In San Francisco, Affect Balance showed the highest degree of spatial correlation, while Mental Health had the lowest.

Table 15.8 Moran's I.[a]

	Actual	Fitted
Baltimore physical health	0.346	0.354
Baltimore mental health	0.316	0.348
Baltimore life evaluation	0.318	0.295
Baltimore affect balance	0.235	0.264
San Francisco physical health	0.234	0.268
San Francisco mental health	0.200	0.207
San Francisco life evaluation	0.241	0.228
San Francisco affect balance	0.263	0.280

a) All figures significant at 0.01%. Based on Euclidean Distance method, and an Inverse Distance spatial conceptualization.

Table 15.9 Cross-validation results.

R^2 – random forests (all predictors)	Dependent variable			
	Physical health (1)	Mental health (2)	Life evaluation (3)	Affect balance (4)
Trained and tested on Baltimore data	0.545	0.566	0.511	0.449
Random forests (trained and tested on San Francisco data)	0.435	0.510	0.497	0.543
Random forests (trained on Baltimore, tested on San Francisco)	0.125	0.132	0.147	0.184

*$p < 0.1$; **$p < 0.05$; and ***$p < 0.01$.

We finally tested sample prediction error by incorporating a machine learning approach based on random forests with 10-fold cross-validation, with data randomly sorted and split into 10 equal subsets, followed by iterative training and testing (nine subsets used training and one for testing), and testing results averaged over all 10 possible subsets. The results of the random forests algorithm, trained on Baltimore data, and tested for out of sample fit using 10-fold cross-validation on the Baltimore data, showed R^2 values that were slightly lower than the earlier estimates, ranging from 0.449 to 0.566. We then conducted the equivalent exercise on the San Francisco data, and again obtained lower values of R^2, ranging from 0.435 to 0.543. Finally, when we trained the algorithm on Baltimore data and then tested it on the San Francisco data, we obtained low R^2 values ranging from 0.125 to 0.184 (Table 15.9).

15.4 Conclusions

Our results provide proof of concept for a remote/imagery-based approach to SAE of health and SWB outcomes. Depending on the outcome, our models explain a significant amount of outcome variance, ranging from 56% (Mental Health) to 63% (Life Evaluations) in Baltimore, and between 53% of variance (Physical Health) and 65% of variance (Affect Balance) in San Francisco. According to our estimations, the explanatory power of our models could be boosted by around 10% by doubling the sample size of images per tract, and by around 20% by quadrupling the sample size. Additional gains in model fit could be obtained by increasing the reliability of our measures, either through instrument redesign or multi-rater assessment, and by identifying features that further help mapping the built environment to health and SWB outcomes. This finding is particularly relevant for areas on both extremes of the health and SWB continuum, as highlighted by our analysis of outlier tracts.

Crowdsourced evaluation of GSV images can be fast, thanks to the massive amount of MTurk workers available on short notice, but it is still labor intensive, costly, and not scalable to higher geographic levels. The crowdsourced labeling exercise was initially conceived as an intermediate step, providing us with an annotated dataset to automatize the image labeling process via CNN algorithms. However, recent changes to Google's terms of service explicitly restrict scraping of Google Maps Content for use outside Google-provided services, which may potentially hinder this method.[12]

Besides the proof of concept, our analysis also helped us identify which features have greater predictive power. We will focus our algorithm development process on highly predictive features, such as home types, the presence of graffiti, broken windows, streetlights, trash/litter, weeds on the sidewalks, oil stains on the road, intensity of development and greenness.

Our research offers a series of lessons for future studies aiming to estimate community-level outcomes based on imagery. The first involves the need to ensure the reliability of the image labeling method, be it based on crowdsourcing to humans or a computer vision algorithm. Our study identified some features that were potentially useful, but unreliably labeled by humans. Some features, such as the age, make and model of cars, have already been shown as powerful predictors of local area-level sociodemographic variables but are unreliably labeled by MTurk workers in our study. We may be able to incorporate existing specialized algorithms to automatize the classification of cars. Further, we can expand our analysis of satellite imagery to go beyond generic land uses and focus on features that are strongly related to health and SWB.

A related lesson, also bearing on reliability, is the importance of strong QC measures for the image labeling exercise, particularly true when dealing with crowdsourcing platforms such as Amazon MTurk, which are liable to be exploited by bots or fraudulent human workers. Image labeling exercises should whenever possible incorporate gold standard QC measures. The first line of defense is worker qualifications. Our Baltimore batch required a master's degree qualification on Amazon MTurk, but still allowed a significant amount of fraudulent work to slip through. The more stringent criteria used in our San Francisco batch were highly effective: only workers with at least 1000 completed HITs and a 97% acceptance rate or higher were allowed to complete the work. Nonetheless, workers' output should be examined. In our exercise we flagged submissions based on time to complete an assessment, internal consistency of the answers, unusual combination of answers, and rare features. We also conducted in-depth

---

12 See new terms as of 2 May 2019: https://cloud.google.com/maps-platform/terms/.

spot checks, particularly for high-volume workers. Future research should consider the use of known answers to evaluate performance in an automated fashion, e.g. MTurk workers could asked to categorize six different photos, one of which has already been correctly labeled by an expert. The extent to which the worker's answers match the expert's answers for the prelabeled picture could be used to approve or reject the remaining five pictures.

A final lesson pertains to generalizability. Our out-of-sample error analysis calls for caution when extrapolating model predictions from one city to another. We find that our choice of variables is useful to predict health and wellbeing outcomes when the algorithm is trained and evaluated locally, but the predictions do not generalize to other cities. A robust model should be trained on multi-city samples to obtain a decent prediction. Also it is important to consider the generalizability of the chosen features when developing an image labeling strategy. Some markers of community wellbeing, such as the presence of rooftop decks, may represent a sign of gentrification when spotted on top of Baltimore's formerly gritty rowhomes, but this may not be the case in other cities.

An automated approach will help us reach massive scale to improve both geographic coverage and accuracy of model-based estimates of health and SWB. The automated approach will also allow us to determine whether imagery-based approaches are able to capture variations in health and SWB outcomes over time, potentially providing an alternative to costly traditional surveys.

15.A Amazon Mechanical Turk Questionnaire

Item #	Question	Response options
Q1	Looking at this image in general… Do you see any graffiti?	1. Yes, 2. No
Q2	Do you see any litter/trash?	1. None, 2. Some, 3. A lot
Q3	Do you see any parks, playgrounds or recreation facilities?	1. Yes, 2. No
Q4	Looking at the buildings in this image… What is the predominant type of home?	1. Single family – Detached, 2. Single family – attached (Rowhouses), 3. Multi-family (Apartments), 4. Other, 5. Homes not visible
Q5	Are the homes clean and well maintained?	1. Yes, 2. No, 3. Homes not visible
Q6	Do you see any broken/boarded-up windows?	1. Yes, 2. No, 3. No windows visible
Q7	Do you see any rooftop decks?	1. Yes, 2. No, 3. Homes not visible

Item #	Question	Response options
Q8	What is the main type of nonresidential building?	1. Retail (e.g. shops, bars, restaurants), 2. Industrial (e.g. factories, warehouses), 3. Commercial (e.g. offices, hotels, banks), 4. Church, temple or other place of worship, 5. Government, 6. Other, 7. Nonresidential buildings not visible
Q9	Looking at the sidewalks in this image, do you see any… …weeds on the sidewalks?	1. No, 2. Some, 3. A lot, 4. Sidewalks not visible
Q10	…uneven or broken pavement on the sidewalks?	1. Yes, 2. No, 3. Sidewalks not visible
Q11	…benches or other places to rest along the sidewalks?	1. Yes, 2. No, 3. Sidewalks not visible
Q12	…strip of grass next to the sidewalks?	1. Yes, 2. No, 3. Sidewalks not visible
Q13	…trees on or next to the sidewalks?	1. Yes, 2. No, 3. Sidewalks not visible
Q14	…streetlights?	1. Yes, 2. No, 3. Sidewalks not visible
Q15	How many pedestrians do you see?	1. None, 2. One-two pedestrians, 3. Three to ten pedestrians, 4. More than ten pedestrians, 5. Sidewalks not visible
Q16	Looking at the roads in this image, do you see any… …potholes or uneven or broken pavement on the road?	1. Yes, 2. No, 3. Roads not visible
Q17	… oil stains on the road?	1. No, 2. Some, 3. A lot, 4. Roads not visible
Q18	How much traffic do you see in this image?	1. No traffic (No motorized vehicles in circulation), 2. Light traffic (One-two motorized vehicles in circulation), 3. Medium traffic (Three to ten motorized vehicles in circulation), 4. Heavy traffic (More than ten motorized vehicles in circulation), 5. Roads not visible
Q19	Would you say that most cars in this image are new or old?	1. New (Less than 10 years old), 2. Old (10 years old or more), 3. No cars visible
Q20	Would you say that most cars in this image are…	1. Economy, 2. Regular, 3. Luxury, 4. No cars visible

15.B Pictures and Maps

Figure 15.B.1 Boarded-up homes – Baltimore. Border of Greenmount West and Oliver, 21 November 2009, by Dr. John 2005: https://www.flickr.com/photos/dr_john2005/4124337715/in/set-72157622850024572/.

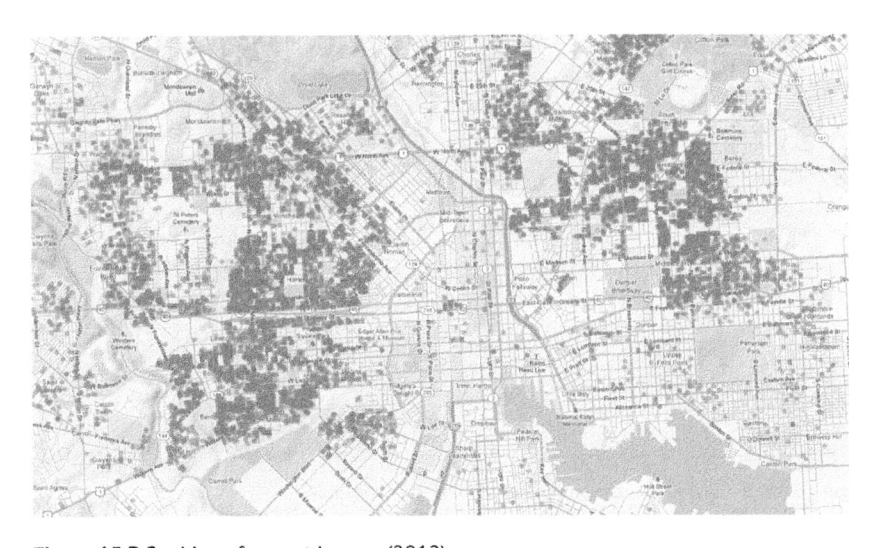

Figure 15.B.2 Map of vacant homes (2012).

Figure 15.B.3 Baltimore census tracts. Powered by Google.

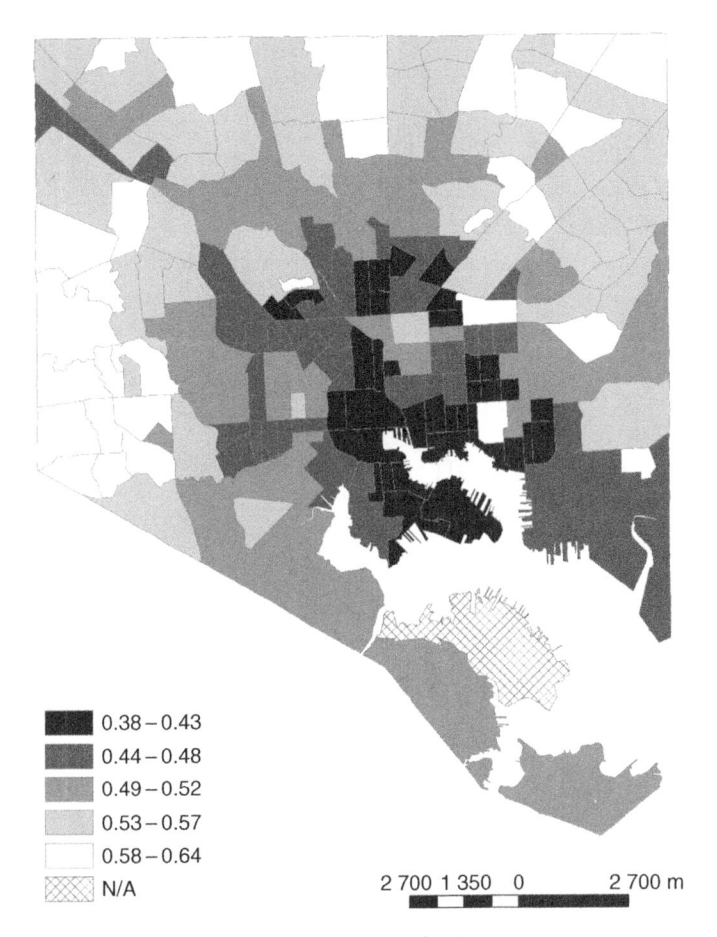

Figure 15.B.4 Normalized TGI values – Baltimore census tracts.

15.C Descriptive Statistics

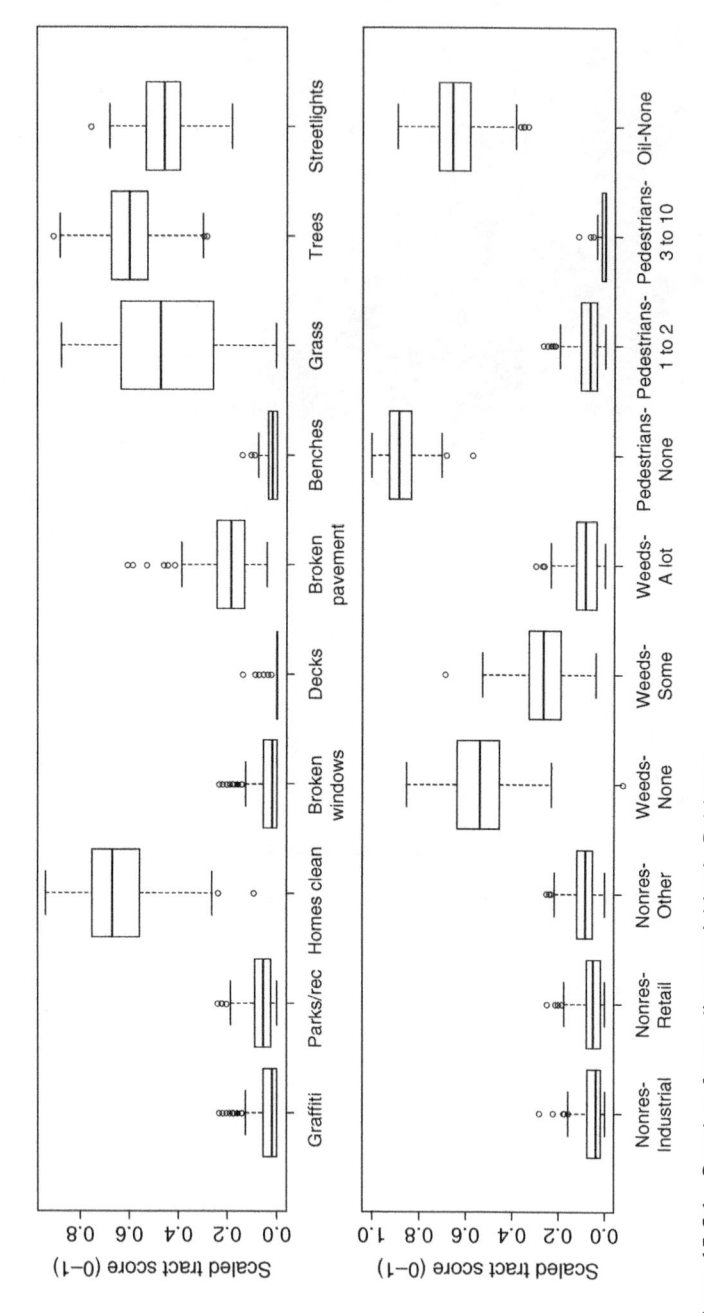

Figure 15.C.1 Boxplots for predictor variables in Baltimore.

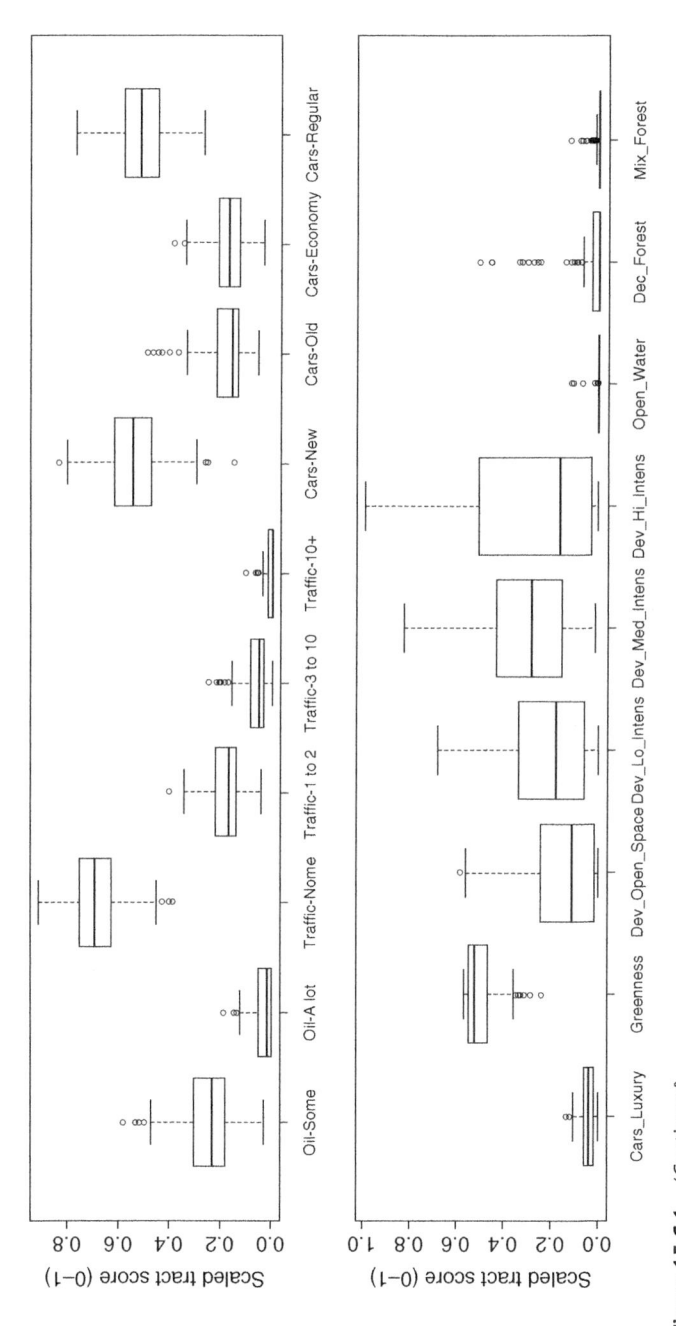

Figure 15.C.1 (Continued)

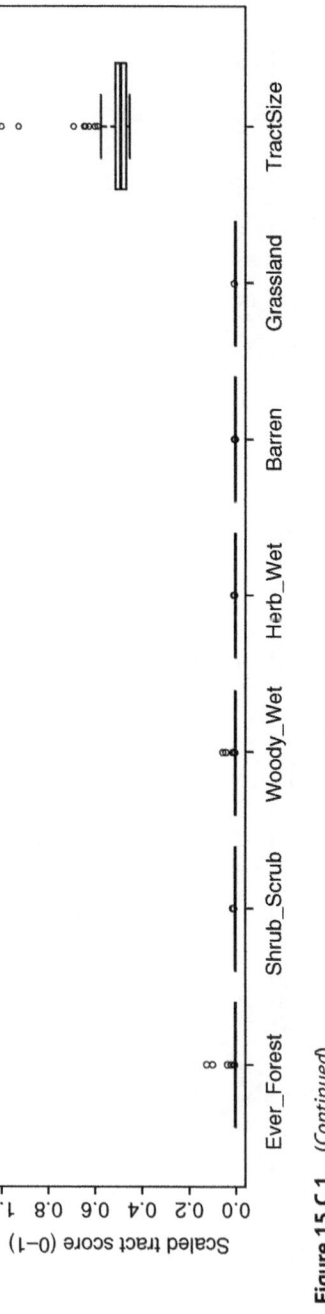

Figure 15.C.1 *(Continued)*

Table 15.C.1 Pearson correlation coefficient between Tukey-transformed predictor variables and outcomes.

Predictor	Physical health	Mental health	Life evaluation	Affect balance	Predictor	Physical health	Mental health	Life evaluation	Affect balance	Predictor	Physical health	Mental health	Life evaluation	Affect balance
Graffiti	0.41	0.46	−0.41	−0.46	Nonres-Commercial	−0.10	−0.06	0.14	0.11	Cars-Economy	0.12	0.17	−0.15	−0.17
Parks/rec	0.03	−0.02	0.00	0.10	Nonres-Industrial	0.16	0.28	−0.22	−0.33	Cars-Regular	0.07	0.08	−0.07	−0.05
Homes clean	−0.05	−0.07	0.03	0.04	Nonres-Retail	0.07	0.14	−0.06	−0.14	Cars-Luxury	−0.03	−0.06	0.11	0.13
Broken windows	0.41	0.46	−0.41	−0.46	Nonres-Other	0.15	0.22	−0.17	−0.21	TGI	0.03	−0.10	−0.03	0.08
Decks	−0.37	−0.27	0.31	0.17	Weeds-None	−0.32	−0.29	0.38	0.34	Dev-Open-Space	−0.04	−0.14	0.00	0.13
Broken pavement	0.24	0.24	−0.28	−0.24	Weeds-Some	0.37	0.36	−0.37	−0.34	Dev-Lo-Intens	0.46	0.43	−0.45	−0.40
Benches	−0.04	−0.01	0.02	0.01	Weeds-A lot	0.36	0.31	−0.41	−0.34	Dev-Med-Intens	0.08	0.21	−0.09	−0.22
Grass	0.04	−0.10	−0.04	0.13	Pedestrians-None	−0.17	−0.22	0.17	0.22	Dev-Hi-Intens	−0.09	−0.10	0.12	0.11
Trees	−0.13	−0.20	0.24	0.31	Pedestrians-1 to 2	0.28	0.30	−0.25	−0.25	Open-Water	−0.19	−0.28	0.19	0.29
Streetlights	0.42	0.45	−0.38	−0.38	Pedestrians-3 to 10	0.16	0.17	−0.13	−0.12	Dec-Forest	−0.21	−0.26	0.23	0.27

(Continued)

Table 15.C.1 (Continued)

Predictor	Physical health	Mental health	Life evaluation	Affect balance	Predictor	Physical health	Mental health	Life evaluation	Affect balance	Predictor	Physical health	Mental health	Life evaluation	Affect balance
Potholes	0.06	0.08	−0.19	−0.18	Oil-None	−0.19	−0.23	0.24	0.24	Mix-Forest	−0.24	−0.26	0.34	0.29
Trash-None	−0.44	−0.44	0.48	0.38	Oil-Some	0.27	0.31	−0.34	−0.30	Ever-Forest	−0.10	−0.15	0.16	0.23
Trash-Some	0.44	0.47	−0.50	−0.41	Oil-A lot	0.37	0.39	−0.40	−0.35	Shrub-Scrub	−0.04	−0.02	−0.02	0.01
Trash-A lot	0.17	0.10	−0.16	−0.07	Traffic-None	−0.03	−0.07	0.00	0.01	Woody-Wet	−0.08	−0.04	0.04	0.03
Homes-Apartment	0.02	0.06	0.02	0.01	Traffic-1–2	0.21	0.24	−0.21	−0.21	Herb-Wet	0.03	0.00	0.04	0.09
Homes-Attached	0.31	0.35	−0.39	−0.44	Traffic-3–10	0.03	0.04	0.01	0.03	Barren	−0.02	−0.08	0.07	0.11
Homes-Detached	−0.18	−0.27	0.20	0.28	Traffic-10+	−0.01	0.04	0.02	0.00	Grassland	−0.19	−0.27	0.20	0.26
Homes-Other	−0.03	0.03	0.06	−0.04	Cars-New	−0.04	0.00	0.09	0.08	Tract size	0.12	0.17	−0.15	−0.17
Nonres-Church	0.24	0.20	−0.14	−0.13	Cars-Old	0.21	0.21	−0.28	−0.23					

15.D Stepwise AIC OLS Regression Models

Table 15.D.1 Stepwise AIC OLS regression models in Baltimore city.

	Dependent variable			
	Physical health (1)	Mental health (2)	Life evaluation (3)	Affect balance (4)
Graffiti	3.62 (2.20)			−0.12* (0.07)
Homes-clean	−4.45*** (1.66)	−3.27** (1.50)	0.24** (0.11)	0.16** (0.07)
Decks	−10.55*** (2.45)	−5.69*** (1.85)	0.38*** (0.14)	0.12* (0.07)
Broken pavement		−5.42 (3.79)		0.24* (0.13)
Benches				−0.21* (0.11)
Trees	−3.72* (2.21)	−3.30** (1.61)	0.21* (0.12)	0.10 (0.06)
Streetlights	9.29*** (2.75)	7.27*** (2.25)	−0.50*** (0.16)	−0.29*** (0.08)
Trash-None	−5.53*** (1.90)	−6.32*** (1.54)	0.450*** (0.11)	0.16*** (0.06)
Trash-a-lot	−6.19 (3.77)	−7.42** (2.99)	0.53** (0.22)	0.37*** (0.11)
Homes-Attached			−0.21** (0.09)	−0.25*** (0.06)
Nonres-Commercial	−3.91** (1.94)	−3.67** (1.56)	0.24** (0.10)	
Homes-Detached				−0.12 (0.09)
Nonres-Industrial	4.20 (2.65)	4.40** (2.07)	−0.36** (0.15)	−0.25*** (0.08)
Nonres-Retail	−5.48* (2.83)	−3.82* (2.16)	0.30* (0.16)	
Nonres-Other		5.09** (2.45)	−0.41** (0.18)	
Weeds-None	12.48** (5.31)	6.17 (4.21)		
Weeds-Some	13.64*** (4.22)	8.56** (3.34)		
Weeds-a-lot	9.63*** (3.43)	5.20* (2.84)	−0.27 (0.17)	−0.15* (0.09)
Pedestrians-None	−4.37*** (1.63)	−2.77** (1.21)	0.18** (0.09)	0.12** (0.05)
Oil-None		10.48** (4.81)	−1.04*** (0.36)	
Oil-Some		14.26** (6.06)	−1.38*** (0.46)	
Oil-a-lot	4.37 (2.97)	9.21*** (3.15)	−0.77*** (0.23)	
Traffic-None		−9.77** (4.85)	0.65* (0.37)	
Traffic-1–2		−11.27* (5.95)	0.73 (0.46)	
Pedestrians-3–10				0.16 (0.10)
Traffic-3–10		−9.26** (3.79)	0.57** (0.29)	0.24*** (0.09)

(Continued)

Table 15.D.1 (Continued)

	Dependent variable			
	Physical health (1)	Mental health (2)	Life evaluation (3)	Affect balance (4)
Cars-New	5.68** (2.59)	3.56* (2.15)		0.39** (0.17)
Cars-Old				1.05* (0.58)
Cars-Economy	−5.60* (3.14)	−4.54* (2.44)	0.27 (0.18)	−0.32* (0.18)
Cars-Luxury	7.38** (3.45)			
Cars-Regular				−0.44** (0.21)
Greenness	97.55*** (17.60)	60.77*** (13.66)	−5.81*** (0.99)	−2.41*** (0.56)
Dev-Open-Space	−8.10*** (1.99)	−5.40*** (1.44)	0.37*** (0.11)	0.16*** (0.06)
Dev-Med-Intens	3.17** (1.60)			
Barren	6.32* (3.27)			
Dec-Forest		−1.92* (1.08)		
Mix-Forest			0.25** (0.12)	
Ever-Forest			0.22** (0.11)	
Grassland		−4.72* (2.66)	0.27 (0.20)	
Dev-Lo-Intens				−0.12* (0.07)
Dev-Hi-Intens				−0.13* (0.07)
Open-Water				0.07 (0.04)
Shrub-Scrub				0.21* (0.13)
Constant	−79.24*** (15.88)	−36.86*** (12.33)	11.96*** (0.87)	1.98*** (0.69)
Observations	199	199	199	199
R^2	0.633	0.623	0.674	0.622
Adjusted R^2	0.587	0.564	0.626	0.565
Residual std. error	2.85 (df = 176)	2.15 (df = 171)	0.16 (df = 173)	0.08 (df = 172)
F statistic	13.78*** (df = 22; 176)	10.48*** (df = 27; 171)	14.28*** (df = 25; 173)	10.91*** (df = 26; 172)

*$p < 0.1$; **$p < 0.05$; ***$p < 0.01$.

Table 15.D.2 Stepwise AIC OLS regression models in San Francisco.

	Dependent variable			
	Physical health (1)	Mental health (2)	Life evaluation (3)	Affect balance (4)
Graffiti	−8.65* (4.99)	−5.25* (3.16)		
Homes-clean	−2.47** (1.12)	−1.58** (0.76)	0.10* (0.06)	0.05 (0.03)
Decks	−10.34*** (3.23)	−9.58*** (2.07)	0.70*** (0.15)	0.41*** (0.09)
Benches	−4.47** (2.21)	−2.09 (1.40)	0.16 (0.10)	0.12* (0.06)
Trees	−3.98*** (1.09)	−2.64*** (0.71)	0.32*** (0.05)	0.21*** (0.03)
Streetlights	6.59** (2.59)	3.07* (1.61)	−0.19* (0.11)	−0.14* (0.07)
Trash-None	−4.23*** (1.22)			
Trash-Some		4.43*** (1.29)	−0.37*** (0.09)	−0.25*** (0.06)
Trash-a-lot	7.81* (4.25)	5.58** (2.52)		−0.28** (0.12)
Homes-Apartment		2.92*** (1.06)	−0.13* (0.08)	
Homes-Other				0.41** (0.18)
Nonres-Commercial	−3.36** (1.68)	−2.61** (1.08)	0.21*** (0.07)	0.20*** (0.05)
Nonres-Retail	−3.25** (1.40)	−1.45 (0.90)		0.11*** (0.04)
Weeds-Some	−3.75 (2.59)			0.11 (0.08)
Nonres-Other			0.31* (0.17)	
Pedestrians-None	−6.91** (2.86)	−4.56** (1.76)	0.22*** (0.06)	0.12*** (0.04)
Pedestrians-1–2	−7.42 (4.49)	−3.78 (2.81)		
Oil-None		3.52 (2.53)	−0.53*** (0.19)	
Oil-a lot		2.32 (1.59)	−0.21* (0.12)	−0.09 (0.07)
Traffic-3–10	−5.55*** (1.84)	−2.89** (1.13)	0.25*** (0.08)	0.16*** (0.06)
Traffic-10+				−0.12 (0.08)
Cars-New	−16.97** (7.43)	−5.00*** (1.43)	0.33*** (0.10)	0.71** (0.32)
Cars-Old	−15.67* (8.45)			0.66* (0.36)
Cars-Economy	17.55*** (6.52)	9.06*** (2.27)	−0.52*** (0.17)	−0.82*** (0.27)
Cars-Regular	15.58*** (5.27)	5.61*** (1.14)	−0.41*** (0.08)	−0.64*** (0.23)
Cars-Luxury				−0.32* (0.18)
Greenness	−15.17*** (3.78)	−4.70** (2.36)		0.22** (0.11)
Dev-Open-Space	−0.02*** (0.01)			0.00* (0.00)
Open-Water		0.02*** (0.00)	−0.00*** (0.00)	−0.00** (0.00)

(Continued)

Table 15.D.2 (Continued)

	Dependent variable			
	Physical health (1)	Mental health (2)	Life evaluation (3)	Affect balance (4)
Dev-Lo-Intens	0.03*** (0.01)	0.03*** (0.01)	−0.00** (0.00)	
Dev-Med-Intens	−0.01*** (0.00)	0.01*** (0.00)		0.00*** (0.00)
Shrub-Scrub	−0.08* (0.05)			
Dev-Hi-Intens		0.01*** (0.00)	−0.00*** (0.00)	
Mix-Forest				−0.00 (0.00)
Ever-Forest				0.00** (0.00)
TractSize		−66.15*** (16.28)	1.74** (0.67)	−0.44* (0.24)
Constant	34.07*** (4.48)	38.18*** (7.44)	7.23*** (0.34)	0.62*** (0.16)
Observations	154	154	154	154
R^2	0.599	0.654	0.621	0.712
Adjusted R^2	0.528	0.586	0.564	0.651
Residual std. error	2.30 (df = 130)	1.44 (df = 128)	0.11 (df = 133)	0.07 (df = 126)
F statistic	8.44*** (df = 23; 130)	9.66*** (df = 25; 128)	10.92*** (df = 20; 133)	11.56*** (df = 27; 126)

*$p < 0.1$; **$p < 0.05$; and ***$p < 0.01$.

15.E Generalized Linear Models via Penalized Maximum Likelihood with k-Fold Cross-Validation

Table 15.E.1 Generalized linear models via penalized maximum likelihood with k-fold cross-validation – Baltimore city.

	Dependent variable			
	Physical health (1)	Mental health (2)	Life evaluation (3)	Affect balance (4)
(Intercept)	13.43	9.26	7.10	0.74
Graffiti	2.67	1.93	0.00	−0.07
Parks-rec	—	—	—	—
Homes-clean	—	—	—	—
Broken windows	0.02	0.08	0.00	0.00
Decks	−9.54	−4.61	0.33	0.06
Broken pavement	—	—	—	—

Table 15.E.1 (Continued)

	Dependent variable			
	Physical health (1)	Mental health (2)	Life evaluation (3)	Affect balance (4)
Benches	—	—	—	—
Grass	—	—	—	—
Trees	−1.84	−1.43	0.24	0.13
Streetlights	10.06	7.34	−0.41	−0.21
Potholes	—	—	—	−0.01
Trash-None	−2.60	—	0.01	—
Trash-Some	1.48	7.19	−0.72	−0.17
Trash-a-lot	—	—	—	0.03
Homes-Apartment	—	—	—	0.01
Homes-Attached	—	0.47	−0.07	−0.09
Homes-Detached	—	—	—	—
Homes-Other	—	—	—	—
Nonres-Church	3.82	—	—	—
Nonres-Commercial	—	−0.43	0.04	0.03
Nonres-Industrial	1.00	3.65	−0.18	−0.22
Nonres-Retail	—	—	—	—
Nonres-Other	2.53	3.47	−0.25	−0.12
Weeds-None	—	−0.16	0.11	0.06
Weeds-Some	2.49	0.48	—	—
Weeds-a-lot	4.55	2.04	−0.26	−0.11
Pedestrians-None	−1.35	−0.50	0.03	0.03
Pedestrians-1–2	—	—	—	—
Pedestrians-3–10	—	—	—	—
Oil-None	—	—	—	—
Oil-Some	—	—	—	—
Oil-A-lot	2.48	2.34	−0.13	—
Traffic-None	—	—	—	—

(Continued)

Table 15.E.1 (Continued)

	Dependent variable			
	Physical health (1)	Mental health (2)	Life evaluation (3)	Affect balance (4)
Traffic-1–2	—	—	—	—
Traffic-3–10	—	−0.20	—	0.05
Traffic-10+	—	—	—	—
Cars-New	—	—	—	—
Cars-Old	—	—	—	—
Cars-Economy	—	—	—	—
Cars-Regular	—	—	—	—
Cars-Luxury	3.62	—	—	0.01
Greenness	2.62	1.69	−0.18	−0.09
Dev-Open-Space	—	−0.03	—	—
Dev-Lo-Intens	—	—	—	—
Dev-Med-Intens	2.34	0.63	−0.10	−0.02
Dev-Hi-Intens	—	—	—	—
Open-Water	—	—	—	—
Dec-Forest	—	—	—	—
Mix-Forest	—	—	—	—
Ever-Forest	−0.14	—	0.19	0.00
Shrub-Scrub	—	—	—	0.06
Woody-Wet	—	—	—	—
Herb-Wet	—	—	—	—
Barren	4.11	0.50	—	—
Grassland	—	—	—	—
TractSize	—	—	—	—
R^2	0.55	0.52	0.578	0.544

Table 15.E.2 Generalized linear models via penalized maximum likelihood with k-fold cross-validation – San Francisco.

	Dependent variable			
	Physical health (1)	Mental health (2)	Life evaluation (3)	Affect balance (4)
(Intercept)	18.26	10.87	7.44	0.69
Graffiti	—	—	—	—
Parks-rec	—	—	—	—
Homes-clean	—	—	—	—
Broken windows	—	—	—	—
Decks	−3.92	—	0.15	0.21
Broken pavement	—	—	—	—
Benches	—	—	—	—
Grass	—	—	0.03	0.01
Trees	−2.48	—	0.12	0.14
Streetlights	—	—	—	—
Potholes	—	—	—	0.06
Trash-None	−3.90	−2.16	0.18	0.13
Trash-Some	—	—	—	—
Trash-a lot	7.92	4.04	−0.10	−0.17
Homes-Apartment	—	—	—	—
Homes-Attached	—	—	—	—
Homes-Detached	—	—	—	0.00
Homes-Other	—	—	—	0.15
Nonres-Church	—	—	—	—
Nonres-Commercial	—	—	—	—
Nonres-Industrial	—	—	—	—
Nonres-Retail	—	—	—	—
Nonres-Other	—	—	—	—
Weeds-None	—	—	—	—
Weeds-Some	—	—	—	—
Weeds-a lot	—	—	—	—
Pedestrians-None	—	—	—	—
Pedestrians-1–2	—	—	—	—
Pedestrians-3–10	—	—	—	—

(Continued)

Table 15.E.2 (Continued)

	Dependent variable			
	Physical health (1)	Mental health (2)	Life evaluation (3)	Affect balance (4)
Oil-None	—	—	—	—
Oil-Some	—	—	—	—
Oil-A lot	1.35	—	—	−0.06
Traffic-None	—	—	—	—
Traffic-1–2	—	—	—	—
Traffic-3–10	—	—	—	—
Traffic-10+	—	—	—	—
Cars-New	—	—	—	—
Cars-Old	—	—	—	−0.11
Cars-Economy	—	—	—	—
Cars-Regular	—	—	—	−0.01
Cars-Luxury	—	—	—	—
Greenness	−11.15	—	—	0.06
Open-Water	—	—	—	—
Dev-Open-Space	—	—	—	—
Dev-Lo-Intens	—	—	—	0.00
Dev-Med-Intens	—	—	—	—
Dev-Hi-Intens	—	—	—	0.00
Shrub-Scrub	—	—	—	—
Mix-Forest	—	—	—	—
Ever-Forest	—	—	—	—
Barren	—	—	—	—
Grassland	—	—	—	0.00
Woody-Wet	—	—	—	—
Herb-Wet	—	—	—	—
Dec-Forest	—	—	—	—
TractSize	—	—	—	—
R^2	0.428	0.219	0.312	0.508

15.F Heat Maps – Actual vs. Model-Based Outcomes

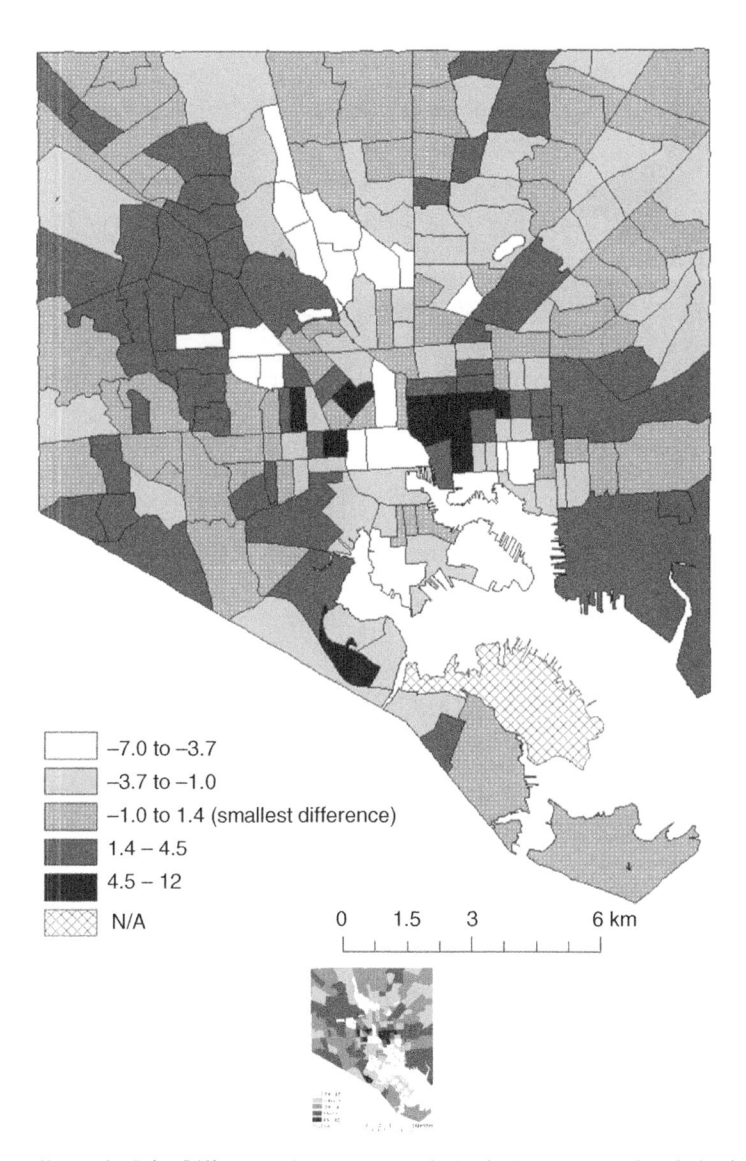

Figure 15.F.1 Differences between actual physical health and fitted physical health – Baltimore.

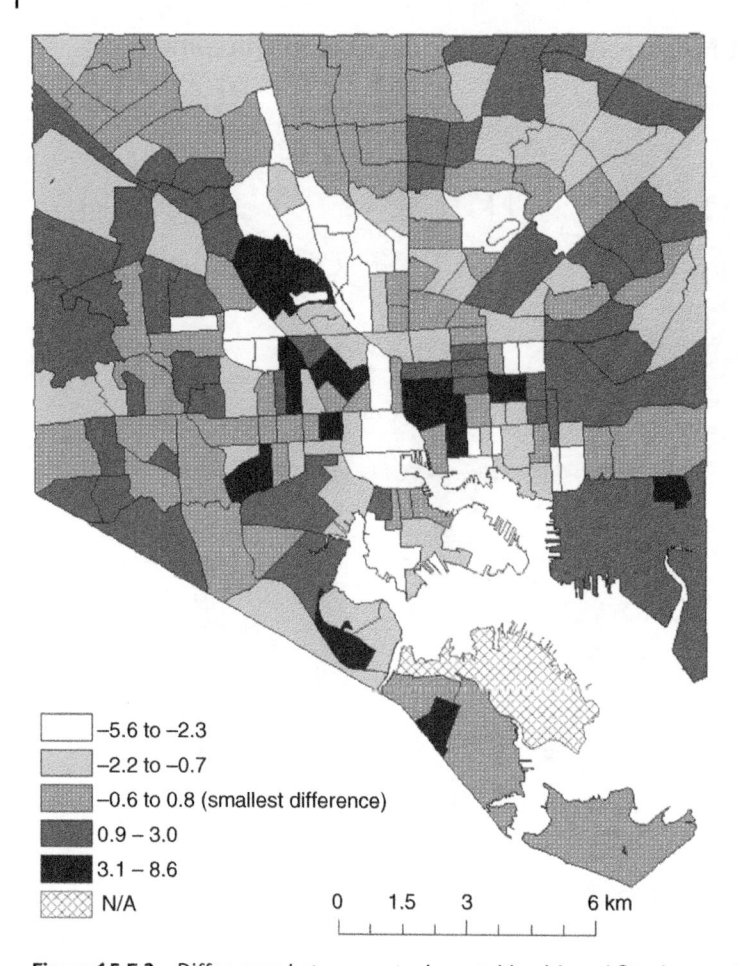

Figure 15.F.2 Differences between actual mental health and fitted mental health – Baltimore.

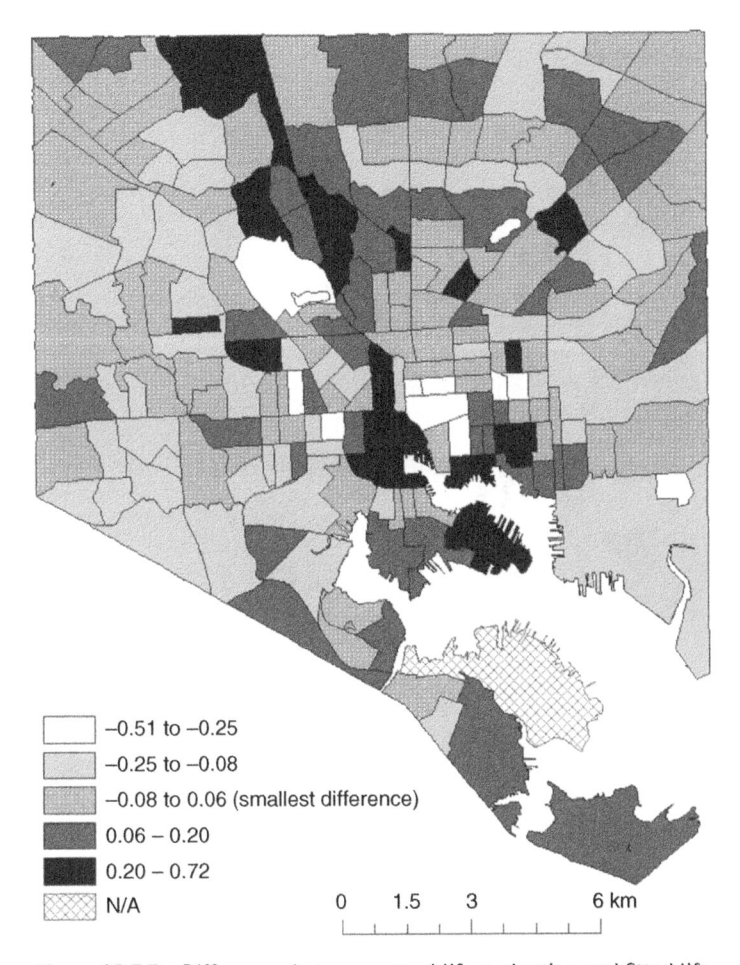

Figure 15.F.3 Differences between actual life evaluation and fitted life evaluation – Baltimore.

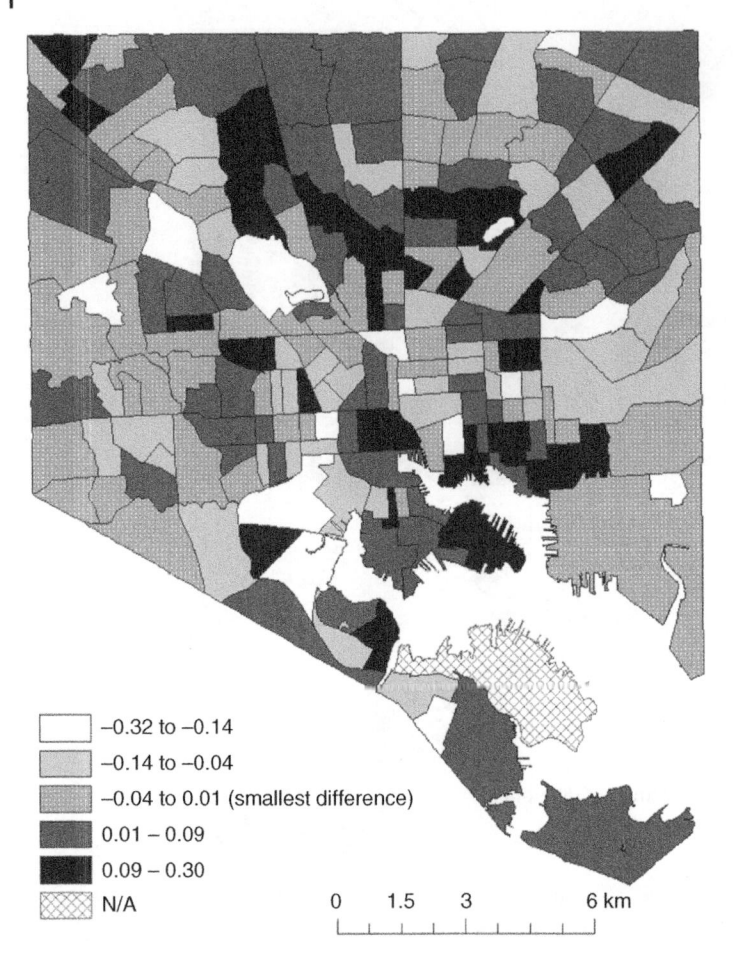

Figure 15.F.4 Differences between actual affect balance and fitted affect balance – Baltimore.

15.F Heat Maps – Actual vs. Model-Based Outcomes | 481

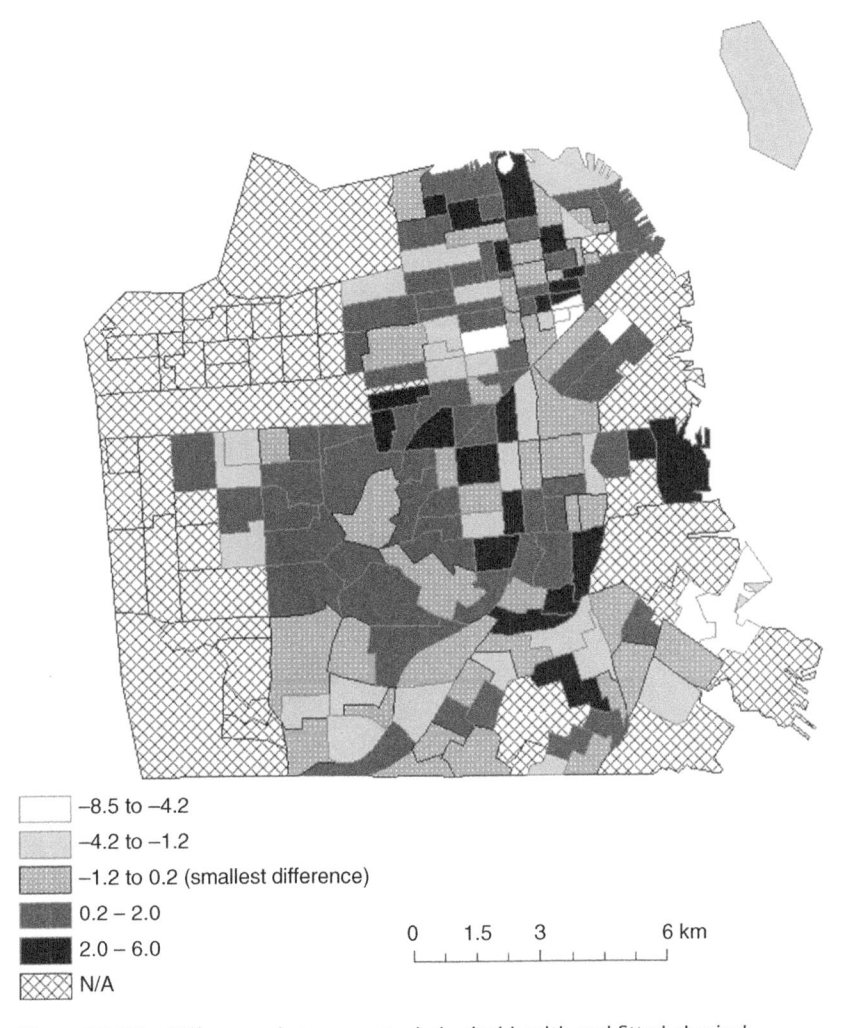

- ☐ −8.5 to −4.2
- −4.2 to −1.2
- −1.2 to 0.2 (smallest difference)
- 0.2 − 2.0
- 2.0 − 6.0
- N/A

Figure 15.F.5 Differences between actual physical health and fitted physical health – San Francisco.

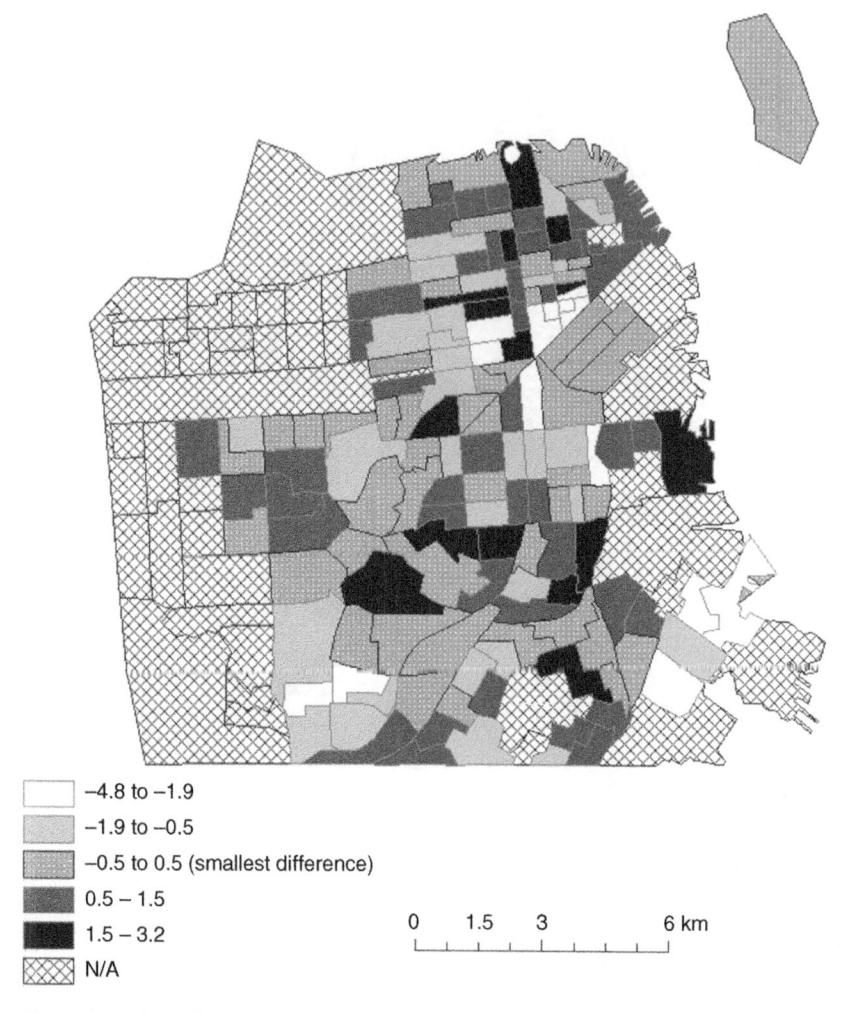

- −4.8 to −1.9
- −1.9 to −0.5
- −0.5 to 0.5 (smallest difference)
- 0.5 − 1.5
- 1.5 − 3.2
- N/A

0   1.5   3   6 km

Figure 15.F.6 Differences between actual mental health and fitted mental health – San Francisco.

15.F Heat Maps – Actual vs. Model-Based Outcomes

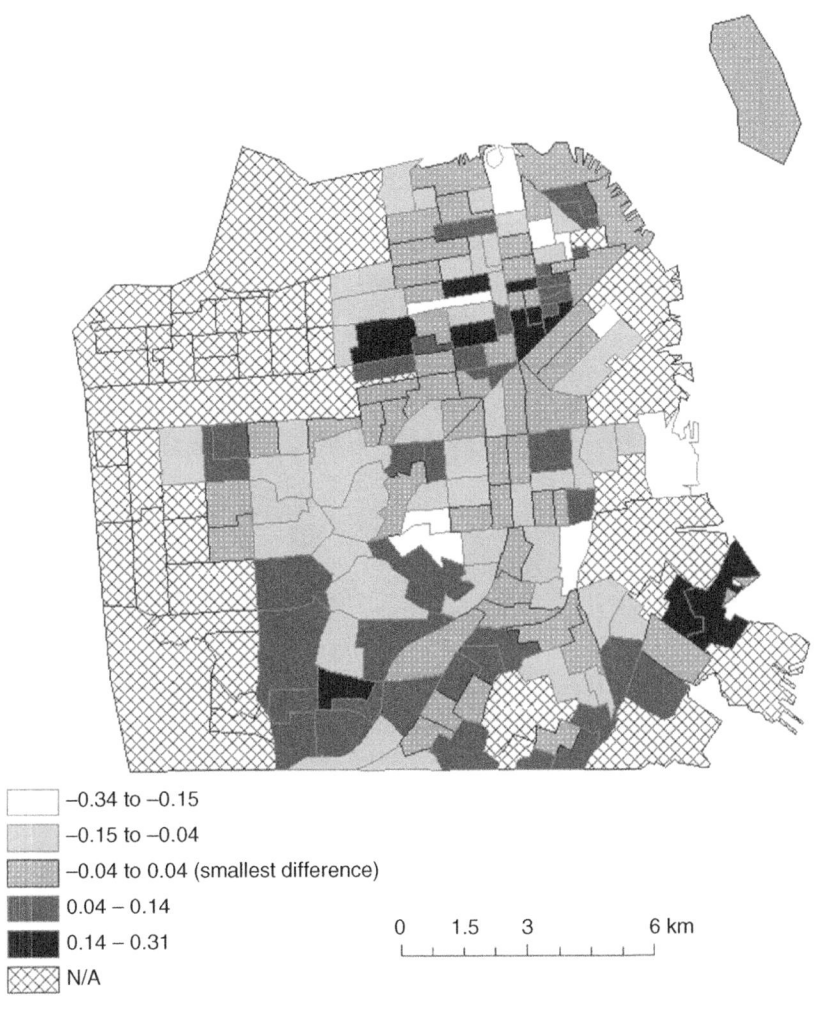

- ☐ −0.34 to −0.15
- −0.15 to −0.04
- −0.04 to 0.04 (smallest difference)
- 0.04 – 0.14
- 0.14 – 0.31
- N/A

0   1.5   3   6 km

Figure 15.F.7 Differences between actual life evaluation and fitted life evaluation – San Francisco.

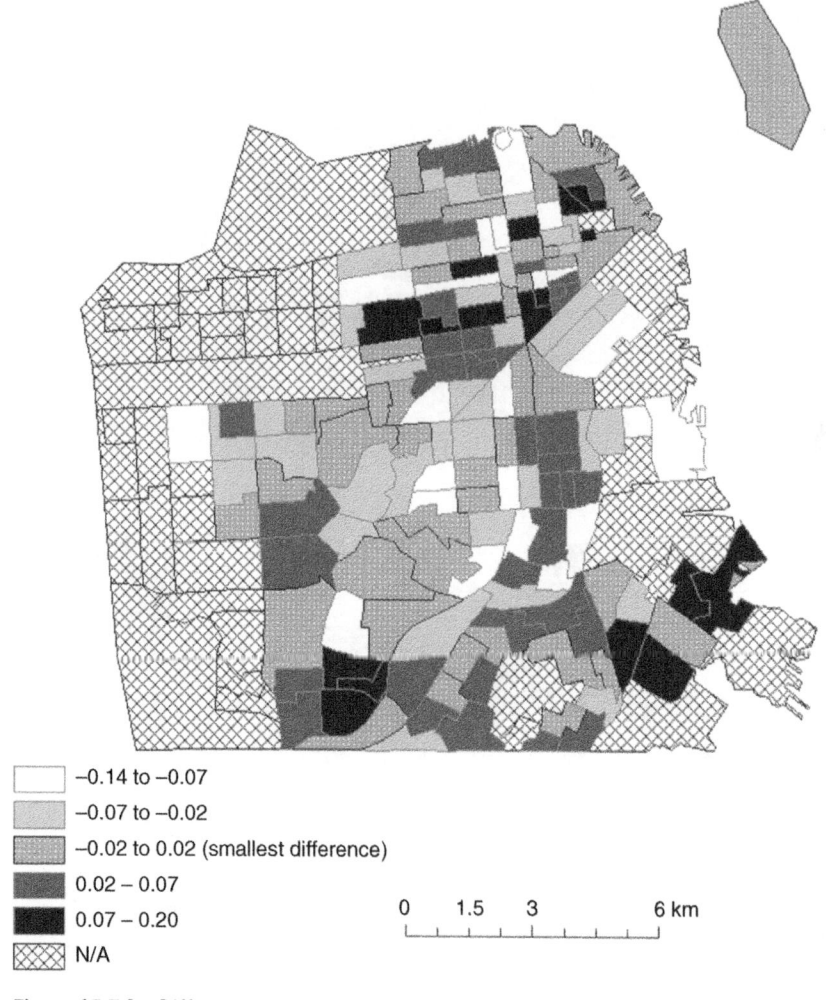

- –0.14 to –0.07
- –0.07 to –0.02
- –0.02 to 0.02 (smallest difference)
- 0.02 – 0.07
- 0.07 – 0.20
- N/A

Figure 15.F.8 Differences between actual affect balance and fitted affect balance – San Francisco.

References

Acharya, A., Fang, H., and Raghvendra, S. (2017). Neighborhood Watch: Using CNNs to Predict Income Brackets from Google Street View Images. http://cs231n.stanford.edu/reports/2017/pdfs/556.pdf.

Andersson, V.O., Birck, M.A.F., Araújo, R.M. et al. (2017). *Towards Crime Rate Prediction Through Street-Level Images and Siamese Convolutional Neural Networks. XIV Encontro Nacional de Inteligencia Artificial e Computacional*. Brasil, MG: Uberlândia.

Babenko, B., Hersh, J., Newhouse, D., et al. (2017). Poverty mapping using convolutional neural networks trained on high and medium resolution satellite images, with an application in Mexico (CoRR, abs/1711.06323). In: *Proceedings from NIPS 2017: Neural Information Processing Systems Workshop on Machine Learning for the Developing World*, Long Beach, CA, Preprint arXivarXiv:1711.06323.

Berglund, E., Westerling, R., and Lytsy, P. (2017). Housing type and neighbourhood safety behaviour predicts self-rated health, psychological well-being and frequency of recent unhealthy days: a comparative cross-sectional study of the general population in Sweden. *Planning Practice & Research* 32 (4): 444–465. https://doi.org/10.1080/02697459.2017.1374706.

Brunekreef, B. and Holgate, S.T. (2002). Air pollution and health. *The Lancet* 360 (9341): 1233–1242. https://doi.org/10.1016/S0140-6736(02)11274-8.

Cantril, H. (1965). *The Pattern of Human Concerns*. New Brunswick, NJ: Rutgers University Press.

Case, A. and Deaton, A. (2015). Rising morbidity and mortality in midlife among white non-Hispanic Americans in the 21st century. *Proceedings of the National Academy of Sciences of the United States of America* 112 (49): 15078–15083. https://doi.org/10.1073/pnas.1518393112.

Case, A. and Deaton, A. (2017). Mortality and morbidity in the 21st century. *Brookings Papers on Economic Activity* 2017 (1): 397–476. https://doi.org/10.1353/eca.2017.0005.

Centers for Disease Control and Prevention (CDC) (2010). *National Health Interview Survey*. Atlanta, GA: National Center for Health Statistics.

Diego-Rosell, P., Tortora, R., and Bird, J. (2016). International determinants of subjective well-being: living in a subjectively material world. *Journal of Happiness Studies* 19 (4): 1–21. https://doi.org/10.1007/s10902-016-9812-3.

Frank, L.D., Sallis, J.F., Conway, T.L. et al. (2006). Many pathways from land use to health: associations between neighborhood walkability and active transportation, body mass index, and air quality. *Journal of the American Planning Association* 72 (1): 75–87. https://doi.org/10.1080/01944360608976725.

Gebru, T., Krause, J., Wang, Y., et al. (2017). Using deep learning and Google Street View to estimate the demographic makeup of the us. *Preprint arXiv:1711.06323*.

Homer, C.H., Fry, J.A., and Barnes, C.A. (2012). The national land cover database. *US Geological Survey Fact Sheet* 3020 (4): 1–4.

Jean, N., Burke, M., Xie, M. et al. (2016). Combining satellite imagery and machine learning to predict poverty. *Science* 353 (6301): 790–794. https://doi.org/10.1126/science.aaf7894.

Kastellec, J. P., Lax, J. R., and Phillips, J. (2010). *Estimating state public opinion with multi-level regression and poststratification using R. Unpublished manuscript, Princeton University*. Available at: https://scholar.princeton.edu/sites/default/files/jkastellec/files/mrp_primer.pdf.

Keizer, K., Lindenberg, S., and Steg, L. (2008). The spreading of disorder. *Science* 322 (5908): 1681–1685. https://doi.org/10.1126/science.1161405.

Kelly, C., Wilson, J.S., Schootman, M. et al. (2014). The built environment predicts observed physical activity. *Front Public Health* 2: 52. https://doi.org/10.3389/fpubh.2014.00052.

McCarthy, P., Byrne, D., Harrison, S. et al. (1985). Housing type, housing location and mental health. *Social Psychiatry* 20 (3): 125–130. https://doi.org/10.1007/BF00583578.

McKinnon, T. and Hoff, P. (2017). Comparing RGB-based vegetation indices with NDVI for agricultural drone imagery. https://agribotix.com/blog/2017/04/30/comparing-rgb-based-vegetation-indices-with-ndvi-for-agricultural-drone-imagery/.

Orban, E., McDonald, K., Sutcliffe, R. et al. (2016). Residential road traffic noise and high depressive symptoms after five years of follow-up: results from the Heinz Nixdorf recall study. *Environmental Health Perspectives* 124 (5): 578–585. https://doi.org/10.1289/ehp.1409400.

OECD (2013). *OECD Guidelines on Measuring Subjective Well-being*. OECD Publishing https://doi.org/10.1787/9789264191655-en.

Thornton, C.M., Conway, T.L., Cain, K.L. et al. (2016). Disparities in pedestrian streetscape environments by income and race/ethnicity. *SSM—Population Health* 2: 206–216. https://doi.org/10.1016/j.ssmph.2016.03.004.

16

Nonparametric Bootstrap and Small Area Estimation to Mitigate Bias in Crowdsourced Data: Simulation Study and Application to Perceived Safety

David Buil-Gil[1], Reka Solymosi[1], and Angelo Moretti[2]

[1] *University of Manchester, Department of Criminology, Manchester, UK*
[2] *Manchester Metropolitan University, Department of Computing and Mathematics, Manchester, UK*

16.1 Introduction

Open and crowdsourced data are shaping a new revolution in social research methods. More social science researchers are applying crowdsourcing techniques to collect open data on social problems of great concern for governments and societies, such as crime and perceived safety (Salesses 2009; Salesses, Schechtner, and Hidalgo 2013; Solymosi and Bowers 2018; Solymosi, Bowers, and Fujiyama 2018; Williams, Burnap, and Sloan 2017). Crowdsourcing techniques are defined here as methods for obtaining information by enlisting the services of large crowds of people into one collaborative project (Howe 2006, 2008). Data generated through people's participation in these (generally) online platforms serving a variety of functions allow for analyzing social problems, examining their causal explanations, and even exploring their spatial and temporal patterns.

Such data already offer many advantages over traditional approaches to data collection (see Brabham 2008; Goodchild 2007; Haklay 2013; Surowiecki 2004). Some are highlighted later in this chapter (e.g. reduced cost of data collection, spatial information). Crowdsourced data could even provide cheaper, more accurate geographical information than most traditional approaches (e.g. sample surveys). However, to reliably use these data, we must be confident in addressing the biases introduced through their unique mode of production.

Crowdsourced data have been repeatedly criticized due to biases arising from participants' self-selection and consequent nonrepresentative data (Nielsen 2006; Stewart, Lubensky, and Huerta 2010). Studies examining unequal participation in crowdsourced data have found systematic overrepresentation of certain groups: men tend to participate more than women in such activities, as well as employed

Big Data Meets Survey Science: A Collection of Innovative Methods, First Edition. Edited by Craig A. Hill, Paul P. Biemer, Trent D. Buskirk, Lilli Japec, Antje Kirchner, Stas Kolenikov, and Lars E. Lyberg.
© 2021 John Wiley & Sons, Inc. Published 2021 by John Wiley & Sons, Inc.

people, citizens between ages 20–50, and those with a university degree are all more likely contributors (Blom et al. 2010; Solymosi and Bowers 2018). Moreover, small groups of users are sometimes responsible for most observations (Blom et al. 2010; McConnell and Huba 2006). As a consequence, although crowdsourced data allow renewed exploratory approaches to social problems, the level of representativeness of such data might be too small and the biases too large to produce direct analyses from these. Thus, new methods are required to analyze representativeness in crowdsourced data and to reduce their bias.

Elliott and Valliant explored some model-based techniques to increase the representativeness of crowdsourced samples, but most of these assume the availability of individual-level auxiliary information (e.g. age, gender, nationality, education level) about participants, which is needed to fit unit-level models (see Elliott and Valliant 2017). Although some crowdsourcing platforms record large samples of highly relevant variables, users do not provide auxiliary individual information apart from the measure of interest and the geographical information. Some examples are: Place Pulse 2.0, which records data from respondents answering "Which place looks safer?" between two images from Google Street View (Salesses, Schechtner, and Hidalgo 2013); FixMyStreet, a platform for reporting environmental issues, where over 90% of participations are anonymous and no auxiliary information is provided (Solymosi, Bowers, and Fujiyama 2018); and other online pairwise wiki surveys (Salganik and Levy 2015).

In this research, we propose an innovative approach to reduce biases in crowdsourced data when no auxiliary information – with the exception of geo-location – is available at the individual level. This chapter presents a nonparametric bootstrap followed by an area-level model-based small area estimation approach, which aims to increase the precision and accuracy of area-level estimates obtained from nonprobability samples in crowdsourced data. First, we use a nonparametric bootstrap to estimate pseudo-sampling weights and produce area-level bootstrap weighted estimates. The nonparametric bootstrap reduces the implicit bias in crowdsourced data to allow for more reliable estimates. Second, by fitting an area-level model with available area-level covariates and producing empirical best linear unbiased predictor (EBLUP) estimates, we borrow strength from related areas and produce estimates with increased precision (Fay and Herriot 1979; Rao and Molina 2015). In order to evaluate our approach, we conduct a simulation study and an application. The simulation study is based on a synthetic generated population, while in the application we produce estimates of perceived safety in Greater London from the Place Pulse 2.0 dataset (Salesses 2009; Salesses, Schechtner, and Hidalgo 2013).

This chapter is organized as follows. In Section 16.2, we introduce the rise of crowdsourcing and emphasize the implications for its use in social science research. In Section 16.3, we examine the main limitations associated with nonprobability samples generated through crowdsourcing. Section 16.4 briefly introduces some of the main approaches explored to reduce the bias in crowdsourced data, most of which rely on the availability of respondents' auxiliary information. Section 16.5 presents the nonparametric bootstrap approach followed by the area-level EBLUP. Section 16.6 is devoted to the simulation study, including the method to simulate the population and the evaluation of the estimator. In Section 16.7, we apply the new method to estimate perceived safety in Greater London. Finally, Section 16.8 draws conclusions and suggests future work.

16.2 The Rise of Crowdsourcing and Implications

Crowdsourcing is a term that has gained reasonable traction since it was coined in 2006 by Jeff Howe, referring to harnessing information and skills from large crowds into one collaborative project (Howe 2006, 2008). Since crowdsourcing originated in the open source movement in software, its definitions are rooted in online contexts, generally referring to it as an online, distributed problem-solving and production model (Brabham 2008). An early example of crowdsourcing is the photo-sharing website Flickr (www.flickr.com), where people upload their photographs and tag them with keywords. Others visiting the site can search through pictures using the assigned keywords. What is novel about the mode of production of these projects is that it is not reliant on a specific person to work or collect data until they meet certain requirements expected of them, but instead anyone can participate as much as they want. Then, the crowd's participation adds up to a complete output (Surowiecki 2004).

A specific subset of crowdsourcing projects encourages people to submit spatial information about their local areas onto a combined platform, resulting in spatially explicit data. Such data is referred to as Volunteered Geographical Information (VGI), where various forms of geodata are provided voluntarily by individuals (Goodchild 2007). The mechanism behind the creation of such VGI is "participatory mapping," which refers to the practice of map making by people who contribute to the creation of a map to represent the topic of their expertise. People contribute their insight to collaboratively produce a representation of an area (Haklay 2013).

Such community-based participatory research has been used to better understand social problems, and it has gained respect for aiming to highlight everyone's experiences in a space equally. These data collection approaches are not one-sided, instead they also serve to collect data to influence direct decision-making. The outputs from such data can be used to lobby for changes in their neighborhoods, contributing to a reversal of the traditional top-down approach to the creation and dissemination of geographic information (Goodchild 2007). For example, citizens involved with collecting data about noise pollution in their area can use that information as evidence-base when lobbying for interventions by local authorities (Becker et al. 2013). VGI created by citizens can provide an alternative to traditional authoritative information from mapping agencies, and it can even be used for emergency management. During wildfires in Santa Barbara, California, in 2007–2009, volunteer maps online (some of which accumulated over 6 00 000 hits) provided essential information about the location of the fire, evacuation orders, emergency shelters, and other useful information (Goodchild and Glennon 2010).

The above examples illustrate some benefits of the mode of production of data generated by crowdsourcing projects, alongside the bonus of their eliciting participation in large numbers. However, they also incur many biases in the sample of participants, which need to be taken into account, especially if such data are going to be used for research purposes. Traditional approaches to data collection for the purposes of drawing statistical inference have paid careful attention to addressing these biases. It is important that if crowdsourced data are used to answer research questions, then similar care should be taken. To support this, Section 16.3 discusses some of the limitations of crowdsourced data from the viewpoint of possible biases in the nonprobability samples of participants who generate the content in such projects.

16.3 Crowdsourcing Data to Analyze Social Phenomena: Limitations

Researchers are making increasing use of data produced via crowdsourcing, innovating in various fields across the social sciences. Some of these papers also acknowledge the biases inherent in the mode of production of these data (e.g. Malleson and Andresen 2014; Williams, Burnap, and Sloan 2017). While often acknowledged, these issues are usually lightly touched upon in a limitations section, and raised as something to be "kept in mind." However, processes to understand and account for these biases are required to make the best possible use of these data. To better understand their effect, we first consider some sources of bias in crowdsourced data.

16.3.1 Self-Selection Bias

Participation in crowdsourcing activities is driven by a variety of factors, some discussed above. Therefore, crowdsourced data might be affected by biases arising from people's self-selection: the sample that contributes to such data is self-selected, giving way for people more motivated to speak about the issue. As noted by Longley (2012), "self-selection is an enemy of robust and scientific generalization, and crowdsourced consultation exercises are likely to contain inherent bias" (p. 2233).

Beyond motivation as a driver of this bias, an entire body of work has explored the impacts of the digital divide, which refers to certain socioeconomic groups being overrepresented in these data due to technological literacy (e.g. Fuchs 2008; Yu 2016). These systematic biases need to be accounted for when analyzing crowdsourced data. Gender bias has been found, showing that men tend to participate more in such activities than women: Salesses, Schechtner, and Hidalgo (2013) examined Place Pulse 1.0 data and found that the 78.3% of participants who reported their gender were males. Further work on VGI participation has also shown unequal participation along many sociodemographic characteristics: employed people, citizens aged between 20 and 50, and those with a university degree are most likely to participate (Haklay 2010).

Further, area-level characteristics also have an effect; who participates and where people participate are influenced by various external factors. Mashhadi, Quattrone, and Capra (2013) find that socioeconomic factors, such as population density, dynamic population, distance from the center and poverty, all play an important role to explain unequal participation in Open Street Map, while analyses of data from FixMyStreet show more reports made in better-off areas measured using neighborhood-level measures of deprivation (Solymosi, Bowers, and Fujiyama 2018).

16.3.2 Unequal Participation

In crowdsourcing projects, it is often observed that few users are responsible for most crowdsourced information, while the majority participate only a few times. This concept is known as participation inequality. In economics and social sciences, this is sometimes referred to as the Pareto principle, which states that approximately 80% of the observed effect comes from 20% of the units observed (Sanders 1987). Such level of concentration is also observed in other social sciences, such as criminology, where crime calls concentrate in small units: 3.5% of the addresses in Minneapolis produced 50% of all calls to the police in a single year (Weisburd 2015).

In crowdsourcing projects, this discrepancy is even greater, as participation inequality has been noted to follow a 90–9–1 rule. Stewart, Lubensky, and Huerta (2010) identified that about 90% of users are "outliers," who read or observe, but do not contribute to the project. Then, 9% of users contribute occasionally (contributors), and 1% of users account for almost all the contributions (super contributors). For example, in 2006, Wikipedia had only 68 000 active contributors, which was 0.2% of the 32 million visitors it had in the United States, and the most active 1000 people (0.003% of its users) contributed about two-thirds of the site's edits (Nielsen 2006). Furthermore, Dubey et al. (2016) show that

6118 of the 81 630 users of Place Pulse 2.0 participated only once, while 30 users participated more than 1000 times and 1 user provided 7168 contributions. This is an extreme distribution of the Pareto principle, and it has been termed the "1% rule of the Internet" by McConnell and Huba (2006).

16.3.3 Underrepresentation of Certain Areas and Times

Interestingly, there is another bias that is introduced by the underrepresentation of certain areas and times. In VGI projects, users decide when and where to submit reports, and these decisions are reflected in the under- and over-representation of certain areas and times in the sample. For example, Antoniou, Jeremy, and Mordechai (2010) looked at the geographical distribution of geotagged photos uploaded to platforms such as Picasa and Flickr, and they found that these cluster in urban areas and tourist attractions, with sparse coverage in rural areas. Furthermore, crowdsourcing applications that wish to gain insight into people's perception of safety can also suffer from people's avoidance of areas which they perceive to be most unsafe (Solymosi, Bowers, and Fujiyama 2018). With respect to the underrepresentation of certain times, Blom et al. (2010) note that participation is five times higher at noon, while the number of participants during the night is almost nonexistent.

16.3.4 Unreliable Area-Level Direct Estimates and Difficulty to Interpret Results

Due to the biases described in this section, and other possible sources of bias such as nonresponse and attrition (see Elliott and Valliant 2017), it becomes probable that aggregating responses and producing area-level direct estimates from crowdsourced data might lead to biased and unreliable estimates. Such estimates are not only difficult to interpret but also can contribute to erroneous and spurious theoretical explanations of social phenomena. As crowdsourcing is a growing methodological approach, it becomes important to address these issues, in order to create a refined methodology. In Section 16.4, we discuss previous approaches to reweighting crowdsourced data, before we introduce a nonparametric bootstrap algorithm followed by an area-level EBLUP as one possible approach to address these biases when individual auxiliary information is not available.

16.4 Previous Approaches for Reweighting Crowdsourced Data

In cases of crowdsourced datasets that record auxiliary information from participants (e.g. gender, age, income, education level), different approaches have been used to reduce their sample bias and adjust the nonprobability samples to the target population distributions (see Elliott and Valliant 2017). Most of these approaches estimate pseudo-sampling weights to correct for the bias in nonprobability samples (e.g. Baker et al. 2013; Elliott 2009; Elliott et al. 2010). Selection bias in web-surveys can be corrected following a quasi-randomization approach (Valliant, Dever, and Kreuter 2013). Moreover, a reference survey with the same covariates of the nonprobability survey can be used to make statistical inference possible (Schonlau, van Soest, and Kapteyn 2007). Another strategy is sample matching (Baker et al. 2013). Sample matching can be performed at individual or aggregate level. Hierarchical regression modeling may also be used (see Elliott and Valliant 2017). Wang et al. (2015) propose a multilevel regression and poststratification (MRP) method, which is an extension of the hierarchical regression modeling. Other common techniques used to correct for selection bias are Bayesian Additive Regression Trees (BART), Inverse Probability Bootstrapping (Nahorniak et al. 2015), Propensity Score Adjustment (Lee 2006), and the Least Absolute Shrinkage and Selection Operator (LASSO; Chen 2016).

However, some crowdsourcing platforms do not record participants' auxiliary information other than the target variable and the geographical information of the target place or responding person (e.g. Place Pulse 2.0). For such cases, Arbia et al. (2018) propose a two-phase approach, which does not make use of individual-level auxiliary information, to reduce the bias and allow for statistical inference from crowdsourced data. In the first phase, which aims to reduce nonsampling errors, standard and spatial outliers are detected, removed, and replaced with the average of the neighboring observations. Spatial outliers are defined here as values that exceed r times the standard deviation of the average values in each area. The second postsampling phase aims to reweight the responses to let the data resemble an optimal spatial sample design. In each area, pseudo-sampling weights are calculated as the ratio between the number of observations available and the number of observations required by an optimal sampling design. The estimation of the outcome measure in each area is finally obtained as a weighted average using the pseudo-sampling weights. Here, we suggest and explore a different approach and present a nonparametric bootstrap algorithm followed by a model-based area-level small area estimation approach.

16.5 A New Approach: Small Area Estimation Under a Nonparametric Bootstrap Estimator

In order to reduce the biases in crowdsourced data and produce more reliable area-level estimates when no individual auxiliary information – besides the geographical information – is available, we introduce a nonparametric bootstrap followed by an area-level small area estimation approach. This is based on the nonparametric bootstrap technique studied in general by Efron and Tibshirani (1993), as well as the inverse probability bootstrap approach studied by Nahorniak et al. (2015). This method is designed to produce small area estimates from crowdsourced datasets that record only the outcome variable and the geographical information (of target place or respondent), but no other individual auxiliary information is available.

Let U be the finite target population, which is partitioned into D areas, $U_1, \ldots, U_D$, of sizes $N_1, \ldots, N_D$. Our aim is to estimate the population mean of a variable of interest Y given by the following formula:

$$\overline{Y}_d = \frac{\sum_{i \in U_d} y_{di}}{N_d}, d = 1, \ldots, D \tag{16.1}$$

where y_{di} is the observation of the variable of interest Y for unit i from area d, and N_d is the dimension population in area d.

Traditionally, the Horvitz–Thompson estimator (Horvitz and Thompson 1952) is used to provide unbiased direct estimates of $\overline{Y}_d$. This is defined as follows:

$$\widehat{\overline{Y}}_d^{HT} = \frac{\sum_{i \in s_d} w_{di} y_{di}}{\sum_{i \in s_d} w_{di}} \tag{16.2}$$

where w_{di} is the survey weight of unit i in area d given by the inverse of the first-order inclusion probability of unit i. Unfortunately, the Horvitz–Thompson estimator cannot be directly used due to the nonprobabilistic nature of crowdsourced data. In order to directly adjust the crowdsourced sample to the target population, unit-level auxiliary information (e.g. age, gender, ethnicity) is needed to calculate the pseudo-sampling weights (e.g. Elliott and Valliant 2017). Thus, in cases where there is no individual auxiliary information in crowdsourced data, we suggest following two steps to reduce the unrepresentativeness: a nonparametric bootstrap algorithm (Step 1) followed by an area-level EBLUP (Step 2).

16.5.1 Step 1: Nonparametric Bootstrap

First, a nonparametric bootstrap approach, which draws *stratified simple random samples with replacement* (SSRSWR) based on simplified optimal sample sizes per area (Yamane 1967), is used to estimate bootstrap pseudo-sampling weights and bootstrap weighted estimates. Weights are computed as the inverse of the first-order inclusion probability (Särndal, Swensson, and Wretman 1992). The nonparametric bootstrap estimates are the average bootstrap weighted estimate across all bootstrap replicates.

Nahorniak et al. (2015) use pseudo-sampling weights to generate weighted bootstrap samples, and they show that unequal probability samples can be transformed into equal probability data by using the inverse of the original sample

16.5 A New Approach: Small Area Estimation Under a Nonparametric Bootstrap Estimator

inclusion probabilities in a bootstrapping process. In our case, no auxiliary information (apart from the geographies) is available, and thus we estimate pseudo-sampling weights as the inverse of the first-order inclusion probability based on simplified optimal sample sizes per area in each bootstrap replicate.

The bootstrap algorithm steps are listed below:

From an observed nonprobability sample s_d selected from a finite population U_d, draw a sample $s_d^{*(b)}$ for each area $d = 1, \ldots, D$ using SSRSWR and obtain $y_{di}^{*(b)}$, which denotes the observation of variable Y for unit i in area d for the bth bootstrap replicate. Note that certain units of the original sample may be missing in the SSRSWR, and other elements might be present two or more times; this is due to the nature of sampling designs with repetition. The sample sizes per area selected in each replicate are obtained via the simplified optimal sample size: $n_d^{\text{Yamane}} = \frac{N_d}{1+N_d(h)^2}$, where N_d is the population size in area d and h is the chosen margin of error (Yamane 1967, p. 886). Here we suggest $h = 0.01$ (99% confidence interval) to maximize the bootstrap performance: this will be the chosen margin of error in the simulation study and application shown below. By selecting SSRSWR with n_d equal to the ideal sample size in each stratum, we adjust the bootstrap method to the optimal sample size in each area, and control that the new method can be applied regardless the size of the target population. The pseudo-sampling weights are calculated as the inverse of first-order inclusion probability (see Särndal, Swensson, and Wretman (1992) for details about first-order inclusion probabilities in case of sampling designs with repetitions). These are denoted by w_{di}^{boot}:

$$w_{di}^{\text{boot}} = \left[1 - \left(1 - \frac{1}{n_d}\right)^{n_d^{\text{Yamane}}}\right]^{-1} \quad (16.3)$$

where n_d is the original sample size in area d and n_d^{Yamane} refers to the calculated simplified optimal size in area d.

The adjusted estimates of $\overline{Y}_d$ in each bth replication are obtained by

$$\hat{\overline{Y}}_d^{*(b)} = \frac{\sum_{i \in s_d^{*(b)}} w_{di}^{\text{boot}} y_{di}^{*(b)}}{\sum_{i \in s_d^{*(b)}} w_{di}^{\text{boot}}} \quad (16.4)$$

We note that w_{di}^{boot} cancels out if all units in area d are defined by the same weight, but bootstrap weights would vary if we computed these to adjust, for example, for nonresponse and attrition (area for future work). Repeat this process for $b = 1, \ldots, B$ replicates and obtain the following Monte-Carlo approximation of the nonparametric bootstrap estimator:

$$\hat{\overline{Y}}_d^{\text{Boot}} = B^{-1} \sum_{b=1}^{B} \hat{\overline{Y}}_d^{*(b)} \quad (16.5)$$

which is the nonparametric bootstrap estimator of $\overline{Y}_d$.

16.5.2 Step 2: Area-Level Model-Based Small Area Estimation

Second, the traditional area-level EBLUP estimator, which is based on the Fay–Herriot model (Fay and Herriot 1979), is used to borrow strength from available area-level auxiliary information. In small area estimation, area-level models relate the area means or totals (in this case, the bootstrap estimates) to area-level covariates (Rao and Molina 2015). Thus, available area-level covariates with strong relations with our variable of interest are needed to increase the precision of our estimates (Rao and Molina 2015): this step relies on the availability of covariates strongly related to our outcome measure.

The original area-level EBLUP makes use of the Horvitz–Thompson estimator given in Eq. (16.2) and its variance. In this work, however, we use the bootstrap estimate (Eq. (16.5)) and assume

$$\hat{Y}_d^{Boot} = \overline{Y}_d + e_d, e_d \sim N(0, \psi_d), d = 1, \ldots, D \tag{16.6}$$

where ψ_d is the variance of bootstrap estimates (Eq. (16.4)) in area d. Then, we assume $\overline{Y}_d$ to be linearly related to a set of area-level covariates x'_d:

$$\overline{Y}_d = x'_d \beta + v_d, v_d \sim N(0, A), d = 1, \ldots, D \tag{16.7}$$

where v_d is independent from e_d. Thus,

$$\hat{Y}_d^{Boot} = x'_d \beta + v_d + e_d, \ v_d \sim N(0, A), \ e_d \sim N(0, \psi_d), \ d = 1, \ldots, D \tag{16.8}$$

The area-level best linear unbiased predictor (BLUP) of $\overline{Y}_d$ is computed as

$$\hat{Y}_d^{BLUP} = \hat{Y}_d^{Boot} - \frac{\psi_d}{A + \psi_d}[\hat{Y}_d^{Boot} - x'_d \hat{\beta}(A)] \tag{16.9}$$

where $\hat{\beta}(A)$ is the maximum likelihood estimator of β. If we replace $\gamma_d(A) = \psi_d/(A + \psi_d)$, then:

$$\hat{Y}_d^{BLUP} = [1 - \gamma_d(A)]\hat{Y}_d^{Boot} + \gamma_d(A)x'_d \hat{\beta}(A) \tag{16.10}$$

Since in real applications, A is unknown, we need to replace it by an estimator $\hat{A}$. In this case, $\hat{A}$ is obtained via restricted maximum likelihood (REML) method. After we replace A by $\hat{A}$ we obtain the EBLUP (Rao and Molina 2015):

$$\hat{Y}_d^{EBLUP} = [1 - \gamma_d(\hat{A})]\hat{Y}_d^{Boot} + \gamma_d(\hat{A})x'_d \hat{\beta}(\hat{A}) \tag{16.11}$$

16.6 Simulation Study

This simulation study is designed to explore the performance of the bootstrap (Eq. (16.5)) and EBLUP estimators (Eq. (16.11)) in terms of bias and mean squared error. The study is based on generating one fixed population and drawing random samples with replacement, which is a mixture between a design and model-based simulation approach.

16.6.1 Population Generation

The population is generated from the following unit-level linear mixed-effect model (Battese, Harter, and Fuller 1988):

$$y_{di} = x_{di1}\beta_1 + x_{di2}\beta_2 + e_{di} + u_d \quad (16.12)$$

where x_{di1} and x_{di2} are the values of the first and second covariates for unit i in area d, β_1 and β_2 are the regression coefficients of covariates 1 and 2, e_{di} refers to the individual error of unit i in area d, and u_d denotes the area effects of area d. The parameters used to fit the linear mixed-effect model have been obtained from a unit-level linear model of perceived safety using data from the European Social Survey 5 (ESS), where we use two covariates (age and gender). Age and gender have been highly analyzed in safety perceptions research and are known to be related to our outcome measure (see Hale 1996). The simulation parameters are then: $\beta_1 = 0.004$, $\beta_2 = 0.50$, $\sigma^2 = 0.50$, and $\sigma_u^2 = 0.02$. $e_{di} \sim N(0, \sigma^2)$ and $u_d \sim N(0, \sigma_u^2)$. x_{di1} values are produced from a normal distribution using parameters from the age distribution in the European Social Survey 5 ($\bar{x}_1 = 48.34$ and sd(x_1) = 46.69), while x_{di2} values are produced from a Bernoulli distribution with parameter 0.5 (equal probabilities for males and females). The population size is $N = \sum_{d=1}^{D} N_d = 30\,046$, in which N_d is produced from a uniform distribution between 100 and 300 (min(N_d) = 100, med(N_d) = 195, $\bar{N}_d = 200.3$, max(N_d) = 298), and $D = 150$. Table 16.1 shows a summary of the quantities used in the computations for generating the population.

16.6.2 Sample Selection and Simulation Steps

The simulation consists of the following steps:

1. Selection of $t = 1, \ldots, T$ ($T = 500$) samples from two-stage SSRSWR and an unequal probability selection design. Sampling probabilities were computed from the calibration of the proportion of units according to their age group and gender to such proportion in a real exemplar crowdsourced dataset: Place Pulse 1.0. Note that unlike Place Pulse 2.0, which does not record participants' auxiliary information, the Place Pulse 1.0 platform asked participants about their age, gender, and other information. Of the 97.1% respondents who reported their gender at Place Pulse 1.0, 76% were males and 21.1% identified themselves as females (78.3% males and 21.7% females); and the median

Table 16.1 Summary of the quantities used to generate the population.

Quantity	Description
d	Values between 1 and 150, in which each value refers to an area d. The population size per area is produced from a uniform distribution between 100 and 300.
x_{di1}	Normal distribution from $\bar{x}_1 = 48.34$ and $sd(x_1) = 46.69$ (obtained from ESS data).
x_{di2}	Bernoulli distribution with parameter 0.5.
β_1	0.004 (obtained from model fitted from ESS data).
β_2	0.50 (obtained from model fitted from ESS data).
σ^2	0.50 (obtained from model fitted from ESS data).
σ_u^2	0.02 (obtained from model fitted from ESS data).
e_{di}	Normal distribution from $\bar{e} = 0$ and $sd(e) = \sqrt{\sigma^2}$.
u_d	Normal distribution from $\bar{u} = 0$ and $sd(u) = \sqrt{\sigma_u^2}$.
y_{di}	$y_{di} = x_{di1}\beta_1 + x_{di2}\beta_2 + e_{di} + u_d$.

age was 38 years (Salesses, Schechtner, and Hidalgo 2013, p. 8). Let p_k be proportion of units in Place Pulse 1.0 falling within class k (defined by age group and gender) and P_k the proportion of simulated population in the same class. Thus, we compute the sampling probabilities as p_k/P_k to select nonprobability samples as a function of gender and age. These sampling probabilities reproduce two of the self-selection mechanisms observed in crowdsourced samples, where males are more represented than females and where young and middle-aged citizens are more represented than children and seniors. Sample sizes are drawn with the only constraint of at least two units selected per area (min(n_d) = 2, med(n_d) = 93.5, $\bar{n}_d$ = 117.9, max(n_d) = 296). Then, we select $T = 500$ samples biased according to the sample distribution noted by Salesses, Schechtner, and Hidalgo (2013) in Place Pulse 1.0. Hereby, we take control of the bias to make sure that poststratified estimates suffer from self-selection bias and low reliability as in real crowdsourced data.

2. In each sample, poststratified unweighted estimates are computed, as well as the bootstrap estimates (Eq. (16.5)) from $b = 1, \ldots, B$ ($B = 500$) replicates and the area-level EBLUP estimates (Eq. (16.11)). Area-level models, which are used to produce EBLUP estimates, are fitted from the area-level averaged gender and age obtained from the original population. The poststratified estimator (direct estimator, $\hat{\bar{Y}}_d(\text{pst})$), which is expected to produce highly biased and unreliable

estimates, is given by the sample mean:

$$\hat{\bar{Y}}_d(\text{pst}) = \sum_{i \in s_d} \frac{y_{di}}{n_d} \quad (16.13)$$

3. The results are then assessed by the empirical bias and the empirical root mean squared error, denoted by $\text{Bias}_d(\hat{\bar{Y}}_d)$ and the $\text{RMSE}_d(\hat{\bar{Y}}_d)$ (Petrucci and Salvati 2006), which are computed as:

$$\text{Bias}_d(\hat{\bar{Y}}_d) = \frac{1}{T} \sum_{t=1}^{T} (\hat{\bar{Y}}_{dt} - \overline{Y}_d) \quad (16.14)$$

$$\text{RMSE}_d(\hat{\bar{Y}}_d) = \sqrt{\frac{1}{T} \sum_{t=1}^{T} (\hat{\bar{Y}}_{dt} - \overline{Y}_d)^2} \quad (16.15)$$

where $\hat{\bar{Y}}_d$ denotes each estimate (either poststratified, bootstrap, or EBLUP) in area d, $\hat{\bar{Y}}_{dt}$ denotes each estimate in area d and sample t, and $\overline{Y}_d$ is the true value observed in the population in area d.

Then, summary statistics across the small areas are calculated and shown in Section 16.6.3. The simulation experiment has been coded in R software and the "sae" package was used to produce the EBLUP estimates (Molina and Marhuenda 2015).

16.6.3 Results

Table 16.2 shows the summary of the empirical values and the summary of the three estimates averaged across samples (i.e. poststratified, bootstrap, and EBLUP estimates). Figure 16.1 shows the Kernel density distribution of the empirical values and the three estimates across areas. Both Table 16.2 and Figure 16.1 show that while the poststratified estimator is skewed toward lower values due to the bias introduced in our samples, both the nonparametric bootstrap and the EBLUP estimator shrink the estimates toward the empirical mean; and their mean and median are closer to the empirical measures of central tendency. The minimum and the maximum values are also improved by the use of the bootstrap and EBLUP estimators in comparison with the original poststratified estimates, which show a large bias.

To assess the performance of the nonparametric bootstrap and EBLUP estimators, the estimates' median empirical $\overline{\text{Bias}}$ (Eq. (16.14)) and $\overline{\text{RMSE}}$ (Eq. (16.15)) are produced and shown in Table 16.3. The bootstrap estimator produces better estimates than the poststratified, both in terms of $\overline{\text{Bias}}$ and $\overline{\text{RMSE}}$, reducing these from $\overline{\text{Bias}(\hat{\bar{Y}}_d(\text{pst}))} = -0.142$ to $\overline{\text{Bias}(\hat{\bar{Y}}_d^{\text{Boot}})} = -0.115$ and from $\overline{\text{RMSE}(\hat{\bar{Y}}_d(\text{pst}))} = 0.192$

Table 16.2 Summary of empirical values $\overline{Y}_d$, and $\hat{\overline{Y}}_d(\text{pst})$, $\hat{\overline{Y}}_d^{\text{Boot}}$ and $\hat{\overline{Y}}_d^{\text{EBLUP}}$ estimates across areas.

	Min	First quart	Mean	Median	Third quart	Max
$\overline{Y}_d$	−0.012	0.206	0.330	0.319	0.444	0.837
$\hat{\overline{Y}}_d(\text{pst})$	−0.182	0.052	0.184	0.168	0.299	0.639
$\hat{\overline{Y}}_d^{\text{Boot}}$	−0.191	0.058	0.227	0.209	0.360	0.847
$\hat{\overline{Y}}_d^{\text{EBLUP}}$	−0.168	0.065	0.226	0.211	0.353	0.814

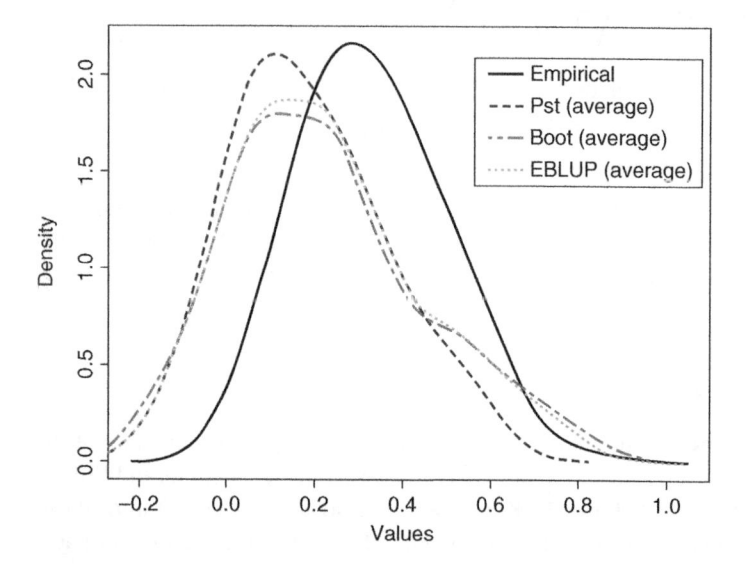

Figure 16.1 Kernel density plot of empirical values $\overline{Y}_d$, and $\hat{\overline{Y}}_d(\text{pst})$, $\hat{\overline{Y}}_d^{\text{Boot}}$ and $\hat{\overline{Y}}_d^{\text{EBLUP}}$ estimates across areas.

to $\overline{\text{RMSE}(\hat{\overline{Y}}_d^{\text{Boot}})} = 0.178$, respectively. In addition, after fitting the area-level models and producing the EBLUP estimates, both measures of precision and reliability decrease slightly ($\overline{\text{Bias}(\hat{\overline{Y}}_d^{\text{EBLUP}})} = -0.113$, $\overline{\text{RMSE}(\hat{\overline{Y}}_d^{\text{EBLUP}})} = 0.173$), showing a better performance than the two previous estimators.

However, area-level measures of bias and RMSE are also needed to examine the level of accuracy and precision of our estimates in each area, because our estimator might produce better estimates in some areas but not in others. Figure 16.2 shows the bias of the three estimates obtained in each area, and Figure 16.3 shows the area-level RMSE of the three estimates. Figure 16.2 shows that the bootstrap

Table 16.3 Estimates' median bias and RMSE across small areas.

Quality measure	$\hat{\bar{Y}}_d(\text{pst})$	$\hat{\bar{Y}}_d^{\text{Boot}}$	$\hat{\bar{Y}}_d^{\text{EBLUP}}$
Bias	−0.142	−0.115	−0.113
RMSE	0.192	0.178	0.173

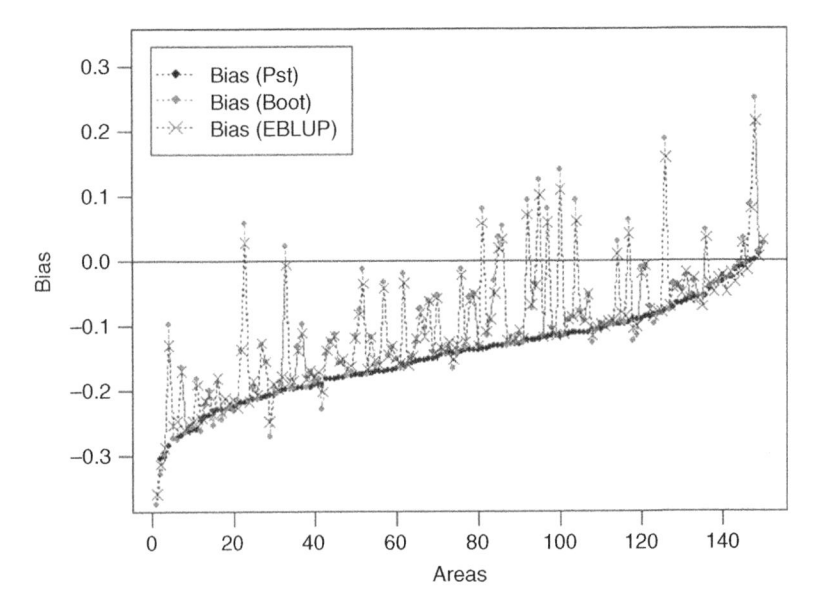

Figure 16.2 Bias of poststratified, bootstrap, and EBLUP estimates (ordered by poststratified estimates' bias).

estimates' bias is smaller than the poststratified estimates' bias in 119 areas out of 150 (73.9%). At the same time, EBLUP estimates' bias is smaller than the bootstrap estimates' bias in 103 of the 150 areas under study (68.7%). If we compare the final EBLUP estimates' bias against the original poststratified estimates' bias, we observe that the bias has been reduced in 124 areas in total (82.7%), and such reduction is larger than the 25% in 49 areas.

Figure 16.3 shows that the bootstrap estimates' empirical RMSE is reduced in 83 areas out of the 150 as compared to the poststratified estimates' RMSE, while the RMSE of the bootstrap estimates is slightly larger than the poststratified estimates' RMSE in 67 areas. Although the bootstrap estimates' median measure of RMSE is improved with respect to the poststratified estimates' RMSE (see Table 16.3), the bootstrap estimator does not provide better estimates (in terms of RMSE) than the

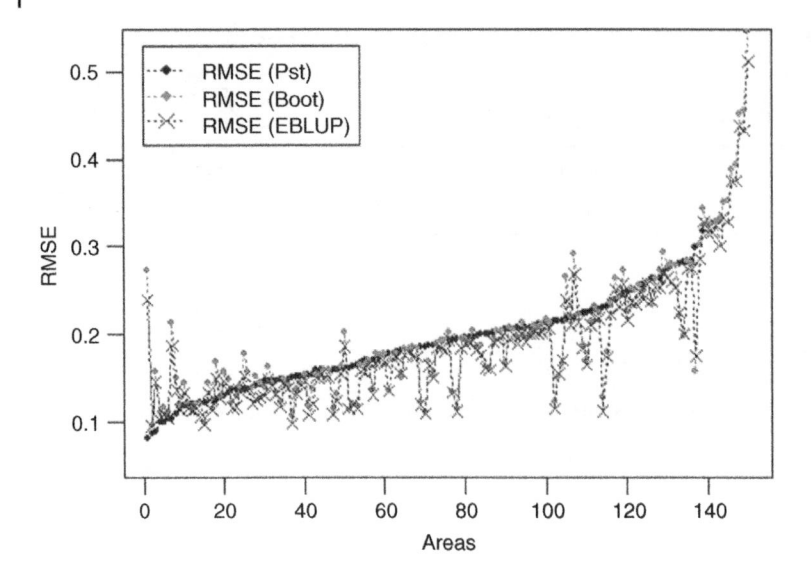

Figure 16.3 RMSE of poststratified, bootstrap, and EBLUP estimates (ordered by the poststratified estimates' RMSE).

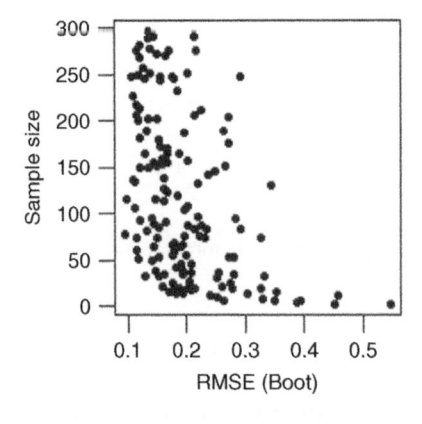

Figure 16.4 Sample size per area plotted against bootstrap estimates' RMSE.

poststratified estimator in 44.7% of areas. However, if we compare the final EBLUP with the original poststratified estimates, we obtain that the empirical RMSE is improved in 127 out the 150 areas (the 84.7%). The RMSE has been increased by more than 25% in three areas, and it has been reduced by more than 25% in 17 areas. The EBLUP estimates' RMSE is better than the bootstrap estimates' RMSE in 141 of the areas under study (94% of the total).

Finally, Figures 16.4 and 16.5 plot the RMSE of the bootstrap and EBLUP estimates, respectively, against the number of units sampled per areas, to examine if these estimators perform better when the area sample size increases. Both plots

Figure 16.5 Sample size per area plotted against EBLUP estimates' RMSE.

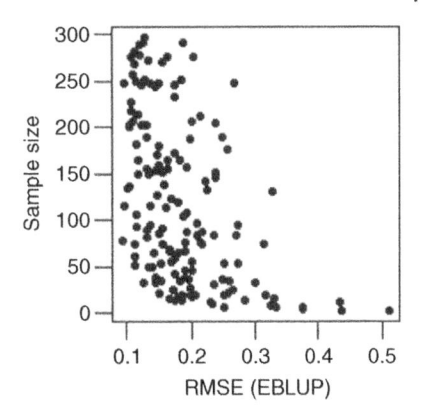

show a significant negative Spearman's rank correlation, denoted as ρ, between the sample size per area and the RMSE, which is $\rho = -0.49$ ($p < 0.001$) in the case of the bootstrap estimates and $\rho = -0.53$ ($p < 0.001$) in the case of the EBLUP estimates. Thus, there is a direct relation between the areas sample size and the estimators' performance.

16.7 Case Study: Safety Perceptions in London

Crowdsourced data can be used to "study people's perception of crime, disorder, and place at a resolution at which data were previously unavailable" (Solymosi, Bowers, and Fujiyama 2018, p. 964). Indeed, numerous researchers have explored the use of crowdsourced samples to map the worry about crime and perceived safety (e.g. Candeia et al. 2017; Harvey et al. 2015; Salesses, Schechtner, and Hidalgo 2013; Solymosi and Bowers 2018). Nevertheless, conclusions drawn from crowdsourced samples are likely affected by the biases discussed above (see Solymosi and Bowers 2018). The method outlined above can be used to reduce such biases. In this section, we use data from the Place Pulse 2.0 platform to produce and map the bootstrap (Eq. (16.5)) and EBLUP (Eq. (16.11)) estimates of safety perceptions in Greater London.

16.7.1 The Spatial Study of Safety Perceptions

Social scientists are increasingly interested in examining the geographical distribution of crime and perceptions of security at a detailed geographical level (e.g. Solymosi, Bowers, and Fujiyama 2018; Weisburd 2015). Both crime and safety perceptions are unequally distributed across cities, and their negative effects disproportionately affect certain areas and communities more than others.

By mapping these perceptions, researchers can better understand their causes, and ultimately design spatially targeted interventions to mitigate their effects. Section 16.2 showed that crowdsourced data provide new insights into the spatial distribution of social perceptions, and Section 16.3 presented some of the biases that limit their representativeness. For these reasons, innovative approaches are needed to produce more reliable estimates from crowdsourced data. Then, such estimates can be mapped to examine the spatial distribution of the target parameter. To fit area-level models to produce reliable model-based estimates, significant covariates at a small area level should be available. Furthermore, the selection of the covariates must be oriented by previous research results.

Prior research has shown that perceptions of security are driven by a series of individual factors that explain differences between citizens' perceived vulnerability, such as gender, age, employment status, education level, or income (Farrall et al. 1997; Hale 1996; Pantazis 2000). However, the unequal geographical distribution of perceived security has also been explained by a series of neighborhood variables that shape citizens' urban perceptions. First, higher crime rates have been associated with lower perceptions of security (Breetzke and Pearson 2014; Liska, Lawrence, and Sanchirico 1982; Rotarou 2017); although other research shows little or no relation between those. Second, different relative measures of deprivation, poverty, and socioeconomic development are known to be related to the geographical distribution of perceived safety: these perceptions tend to be lower in economically and socially deprived areas (Pantazis 2000; Rotarou 2017). According to Pantazis (2000), people living in poverty suffer the greatest from a range of insecurities "that relate to crime and the prospect of experiencing a number of non-criminal incidents including job loss, financial debts, and illness" (p. 433). And third, the ethnic composition of the area, and more particularly the proportion of ethnic minorities living in each neighborhood, is known to be a predictor of the spatial distribution of perceived insecurity (Liska et al. 1982). These findings influence our choice of area-level covariates for our model.

16.7.2 Data and Methods

16.7.2.1 Place Pulse 2.0 Dataset

The Place Pulse 2.0 platform recorded data from the question "Which place looks safer/wealthier/more beautiful/more boring/livelier/more depressing?" in which respondents were shown two random images from 56 cities across 28 countries (see Figure 16.6). Place Pulse 2.0 images were taken from Google Street View and were originally captured between 2007 and 2012. Place Pulse was hosted in an open website (http://pulse.media.mit.edu) and anyone could participate, but the platform closed in late 2019. The images were geocoded, and users answered either by choosing one of the two images or clicking on "equal." Respondents provided

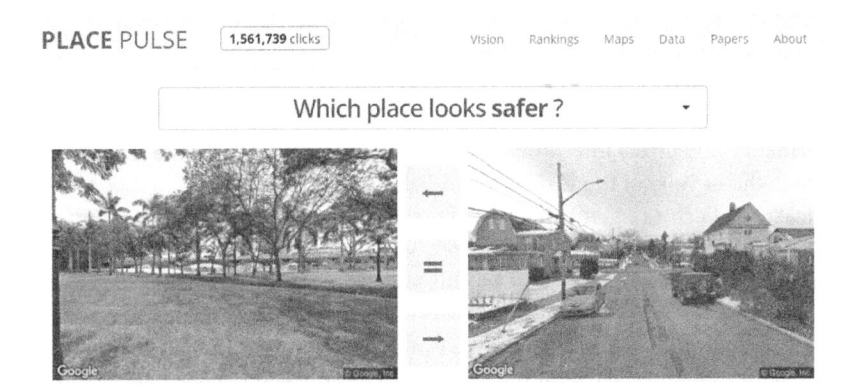

Figure 16.6 Place Pulse 2.0 website.

no auxiliary information about themselves (see Dubey et al. 2016). This platform functions in a very similar way than other online pairwise wiki surveys, such as All Our Ideas (http://www.allourideas.org) (Salganik and Levy 2015).

In this application, we used only Place Pulse 2.0 data recorded to measure perceived safety in Greater London. Reports were recorded between 2013 and August 2018. The total sample size was 17 766 responses distributed across 1368 lower layer super output areas (LSOAs) in Greater London. LSOAs are geographic units of analysis designed to improve the reporting of small area statistics in England and Wales: each LSOA contains between 1000 and 3000 citizens, and between 400 and 1200 households. The average number of responses per LSOA was $\bar{n}_d = 12.99$; the minimum sample size per small area was 1 (in 35 areas) and the maximum was 91.

The aim of this application was to produce reliable estimates of perceived safety at a low geographical level in Greater London. Each response was then a unit grouped within an LSOA: "safer" reports were coded as 1, while "less safe" and "equal" responses were coded as 0. Then, we produced poststratified estimates of the proportion of "safer" responses per area (min = 0.0, $Q1 = 0.5, \bar{x} = 0.6, Q2 = 0.6$, $Q3 = 0.7$, max = 1.0), as well as nonparametric bootstrap and EBLUP estimates from $B = 500$ replicates. By estimating the proportion of "safer" responses per area, not only could we examine the performance of the EBLUP (Eq. (16.11)) under the nonparametric bootstrap (Eq. (16.5)) when applied to a crowdsourced dataset but we could also produce a map of perceived safety at a low spatial level and analyze neighborhood predictors of perceived safety. Note that previous research suggests using 0 to 10 Q-scores per image, which are produced as fractions of times each image is selected over another image, corrected by the "win" and "loss" ration of all images with which it was compared (see Candeia et al. 2017; Harvey et al. 2015; Salesses, Schechtner, and Hidalgo 2013). In this research, we chose a more straightforward approach to estimate the proportion of "safer" responses per area. This reduced the computation time for data analysis, as only images from Greater London were used (instead of safety assessments for each image paired at least once to an image from London), and it allowed a better control of the method's performance and direct interpretations of final model-based estimates.

Due to the novelty of the EBLUP approach under the nonparametric bootstrap, no measure of error (e.g. mean squared error) has been developed yet to analyze the estimates' reliability. Future research will need to develop new methods to estimate the mean squared error of this estimator: this topic will be explored in our future research. However, to externally validate our results, we will be able to compare the estimates produced in this research to reliable estimates of perceived safety obtained from the Metropolitan Police Service Public Attitudes Survey (MPSPAS) 2011/12 (only available at the borough level). We expect a high correlation between the EBLUP estimates produced from crowdsourced Place Pulse 2.0 data and the direct estimates obtained from the MPSPAS dataset.

16.7.2.2 Area-Level Covariates

To fit an area-level model and produce the EBLUP estimates, we selected a set of five available covariates in line with the discussion earlier in this section: (i) proportion of black and minority ethnic citizens (BAME) 2011, (ii) crimes rate 2012, (iii) income deprivation score, (iv) employment deprivation score, and (v) education, skills, and training deprivation score (see Table 16.4). The proportion of BAME was obtained from the UK Census 2011, and the crime data were provided by the Metropolitan Police Service. The scores for income deprivation, employment deprivation and education, skills and training deprivation were items of the English Index of Multiple Deprivation 2015, which provides statistics about measures of relative deprivation in the small areas in England. After fitting the area-level model with our five covariates, all of them showed significant negative beta coefficients to estimate the area-level perceived safety.

16.7.3 Results

In Subsection 16.7.3.1, we assess our estimates, both internally and externally: first, we present the model diagnostics to assess our EBLUP model and, second, we compare our estimates (first produced at a borough level) with estimates of perceived security obtained from the MPSPAS. In Subsection 16.7.3.2 we present the EBLUP estimates of perceived safety and visualize these on the Greater London map.

16.7.3.1 Model Diagnostics and External Validation

Figure 16.7 shows the normal Q–Q plot of the area-level model standardized residuals, computed as in Petrucci and Salvati (2006). Most residuals follow a normal

Table 16.4 Summary measures of area-level covariates and correlation coefficients with bootstrap estimates of perceived safety.

	Min	First quart	Mean	Median	Third quart	Max	Spearman's rank correlation with perceived safety
Proportion BAME	0.02	0.22	0.39	0.37	0.54	0.96	−0.25***
Crimes rate	0.02	0.09	0.18	0.13	0.19	10.23	−0.19***
Income deprivation	0.01	0.09	0.17	0.15	0.23	0.47	−0.22***
Employment deprivation	0.00	0.07	0.11	0.10	0.15	0.36	−0.18***
Education, skills, and training deprivation	0.01	5.45	14.09	12.14	20.45	64.03	−0.21***

***$\alpha < 0.001$; **$\alpha < 0.01$; and *$\alpha < 0.05$.

Figure 16.7 Normal Q–Q plot of standardized residuals of EBLUP model.

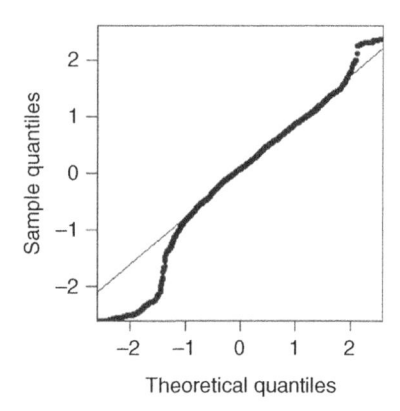

distribution, though there are some outliers at both tails. The Shapiro–Wilk test to check the normality of the standardized residuals also suggests no rejection of the null hypothesis of normal distribution ($W = 0.957$, $p = 0.612$).

To externally validate our estimates of perceived safety, we first produced EBLUP estimates at a borough level in Greater London, and compared these to the direct estimates of "perceived safety when walking alone after dark" obtained from MPSPAS 2011/2012 data. The MPSPAS recorded large representative samples at borough level in Greater London, with an average of 745.09 citizens sampled per area (min = 676, max = 792). MPSPAS 2011/2012 data were recorded between January 2011 and December 2012, but the proportion of MPSPAS respondents who feel "very safe" or "fairly safe" when walking alone after dark appears to be quite stable over time in most London boroughs (see Figure 16.8).

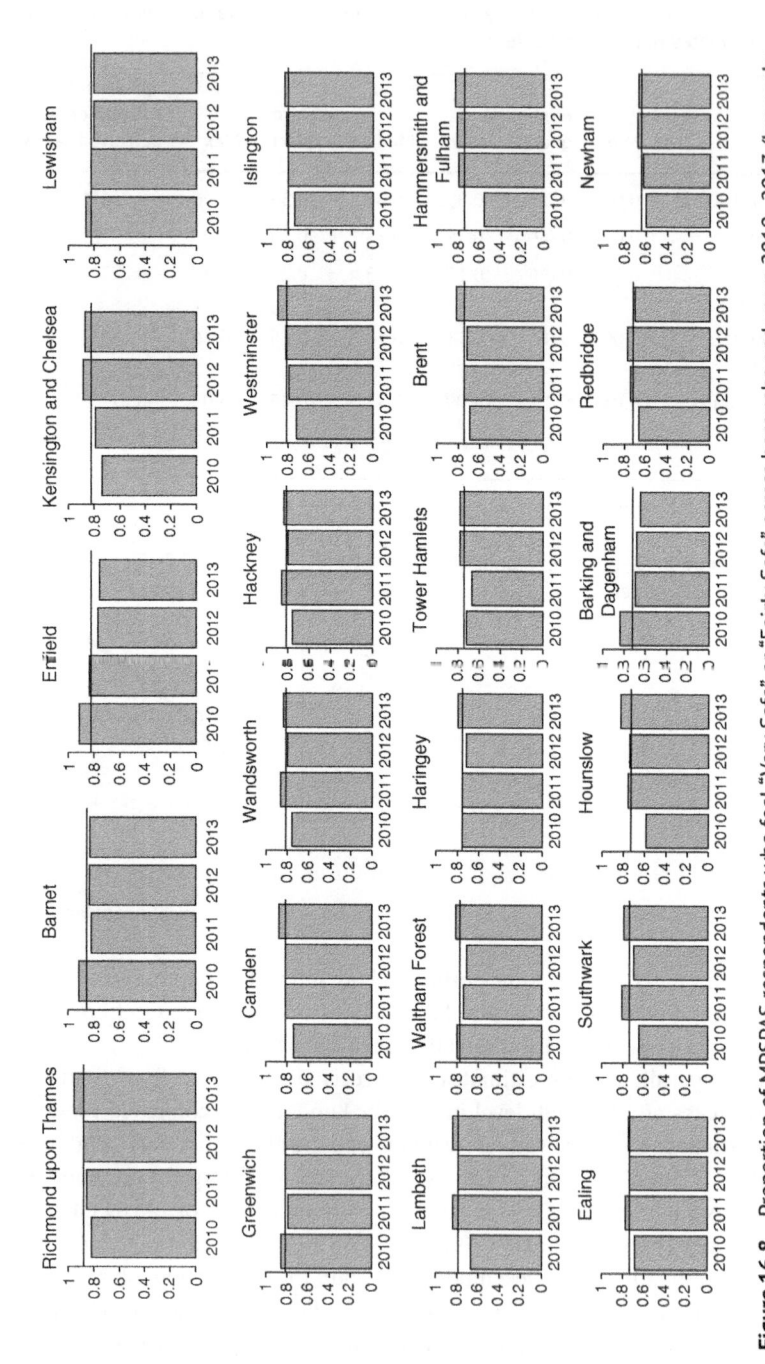

Figure 16.8 Proportion of MPSPAS respondents who feel "Very Safe" or "Fairly Safe" across boroughs and years 2010–2013 (boroughs included in Place Pulse 2.0).

16.7 Case Study: Safety Perceptions in London

Time stability shown in Figure 16.8 indicates that external validation results are likely to be similar regardless of the MPSPAS edition that is used. Thus, we feel confident comparing the direct estimates of perceptions of security obtained from the MPSPAS 2011/12 to externally validate our EBLUP estimates of perceived safety produced from Place Pulse data (2013–2018). The measure of "How safe do you feel walking alone after dark?" has been highly analyzed in criminological literature and, although it has been criticized as a measure of emotional fear of crime (e.g. Farrall et al. 1997), it provides consistent results to examine the geographies of perceived security (e.g. Luo, Ren, and Zhao 2016).

We produce direct estimates of the proportion of respondents who felt "very safe" or "fairly safe" (coded as 1), whereas "fairly unsafe" and "very unsafe" responses were coded as 0. "Refusal" to answer, "don't know" and "do not go out" responses were coded as "no answers" and deleted from the analysis. Then, we rescaled estimates obtained from MPSPAS and Place Pulse 2.0 to 0–1 values ($\frac{\hat{Y}_d - \min(\hat{Y})}{\max(\hat{Y}) - \min(\hat{Y})}$) to allow comparisons. Figure 16.9 shows the borough-level differences between MPSPAS direct estimates of feeling of safety when walking alone after dark and Place Pulse EBLUP estimates of perceived safety. Only 6 out of 24 areas show differences larger than −0.25 or 0.25, among which Place Pulse EBLUP estimates are larger than MPSPAS direct estimates in four cases, and MPSPAS estimates are larger than Place Pulse estimates in two areas. In most cases, however, differences between both datasets are small. Moreover, there is a medium–high significant Spearman's rank correlation between both estimates

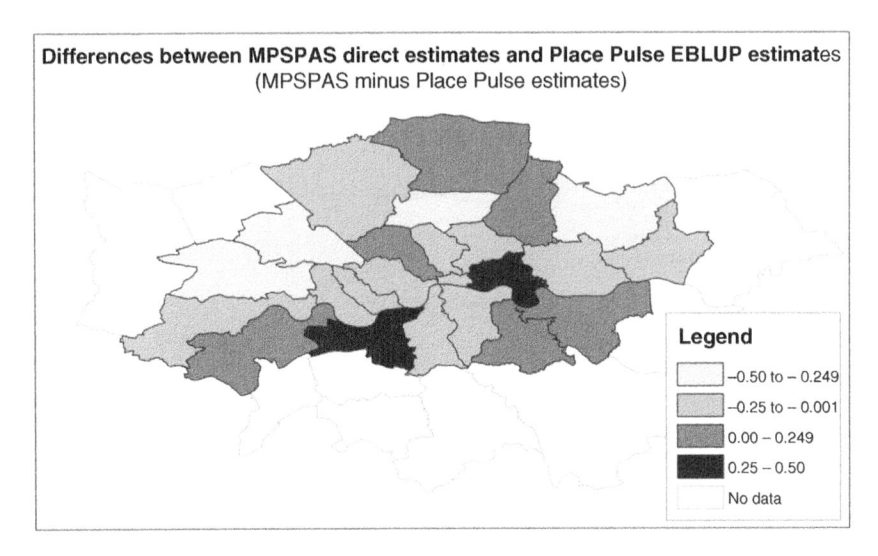

Figure 16.9 Differences between direct estimates of feeling of safety after dark obtained from MPSPAS data and EBLUP estimates of perceived safety produced from Place Pulse.

($\rho = 0.54$, $p < 0.05$) and a Bivariate Moran's I coefficient equal to 0.51 ($p < 0.01$). Thus, considering that the correlation is fitted from only 24 boroughs, we can expect our model-based estimates drawn from the Place Pulse data to represent a very similar construct than the variable of "feeling of safety when walking alone after dark" recorded from the MPSPAS survey.

16.7.3.2 Mapping Safety Perceptions at Neighborhood Level

Figure 16.10 shows the map of the EBLUP estimates of perceived safety in 1368 LSOAs across Greater London. Lighter color scales show a lower estimated perceived safety, while darker color scales show a higher perceived neighborhood security. Note that white areas indicate "no data." The Place Pulse 2.0 dataset only records data in an elliptic area around the London city center, which covers some complete boroughs and some LSOAs of incomplete boroughs. Estimates vary from a minimum of 0 and a maximum of 1, and the measures of central tendency are 0.49 (mean), 0.50 (median), and 0.50 (mode). The small area estimates show large differences within each Greater London borough. The lowest estimates

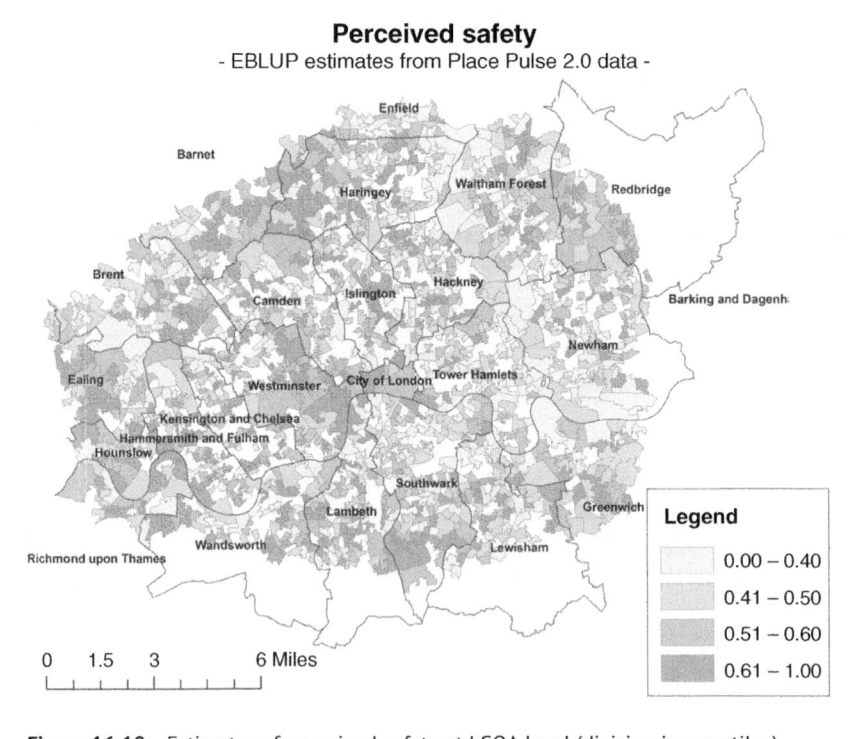

Figure 16.10 Estimates of perceived safety at LSOA level (division in quantiles).

of perceived safety are found in Eastern neighborhoods, especially in certain areas of Newham, Waltham Forest, and Tower Hamlets, whereas the highest estimates of perceived safety are in areas of the central boroughs of City of London and Westminster.

16.8 Discussion and Conclusions

Social science research is increasingly using open and crowdsourced data to analyze and map social phenomena, such as crime and safety perceptions (Salesses 2009; Salesses, Schechtner, and Hidalgo 2013; Solymosi and Bowers 2018; Solymosi, Bowers, and Fujiyama 2018; Williams et al. 2017). By using crowdsourced data, researchers can obtain larger samples less expensively than traditional approaches for data collection. In addition, some crowdsourced datasets record VGI that allow examining spatial patterns at a very detailed geographical scale. Although crowdsourced data can provide new insights into people's attitudes and perceptions, these are affected by a series of biases that limit the representativeness of the data (i.e. self-selection bias, unequal participation, underrepresentation of areas and times), and, thus, direct estimators might lead to unreliable area-level estimates.

Researchers have made several attempts to reduce biases and increase representativeness in crowdsourced data, most of which assume the availability of individual auxiliary information. Such approaches use individual covariates to allow for various unit-level modeling techniques aimed to compute pseudo-sampling weights and adjust the nonprobability samples to the target population (see Elliott and Valliant 2017). However, not all crowdsourcing projects record individual auxiliary information. In this chapter, we proposed and evaluated a two-phase approach aimed to produce reliable small area estimates from crowdsourced data with no individual auxiliary information (apart from the area of the target place or respondent). First, a nonparametric bootstrap algorithm selects repeated samples using an SSRSWR design and produces bootstrap weighted estimates. Then, the second phase is aimed to borrow strength from related areas by fitting an area-level model and producing EBLUP estimates (Fay and Herriot 1979; Rao and Molina 2015).

To evaluate this two-phase approach, we conducted a simulation study and an application. First, the simulation study is based on generating one fixed population and drawing SSRSWR with an unequal probability selection to reproduce the biases in crowdsourced data. Then, we compared poststratified unweighted estimates to the nonparametric bootstrap and the EBLUP estimates, which are expected to increase the estimates reliability. From the simulation experiment, we observe: first, the distribution and the summary measures of the EBLUP estimates are slightly closer to the empirical summary measures than the poststratified estimates. Second, the median bias and RMSE are reduced after producing the nonparametric and the EBLUP estimates. And third, the RMSE and the bias of the final EBLUP estimates are closer to zero (in most areas) than the poststratified estimates' RMSE and bias: the final EBLUP estimates are generally more reliable and less biased than the poststratified estimates. However, the nonparametric bootstrap estimator does not provide better estimates than the poststratified estimator, in terms of RMSE, in a large number of areas. Such limitation is clearly reduced after fitting the area-level models and producing the EBLUP estimates, which shows the need for the second step of the method.

Then, the EBLUP under the nonparametric bootstrap approach has been applied to produce small area estimates of perceived safety at LSOA level in Greater London from the Place Pulse 2.0 crowdsourced dataset. Our results have been validated externally by comparing these to reliable direct estimates drawn from the MPSPAS dataset. The final EBLUP estimates allow for reliably mapping the perceived safety at a very detailed micro geographical level.

Although the EBLUP approach under the nonparametric bootstrap has shown positive results, further simulation experiments with more complex sampling designs are needed to investigate whether this method produces reliable estimates when the sample biases are higher, smaller, or show different distributions. Moreover, the method needs to be applied to other crowdsourced datasets (e.g. FixMyStreet, All Our Ideas) to assess its performance under different nonprobability samples. Then, once the method performance has been assessed under different simulation experiments and real crowdsourced datasets, new software tools can be developed to facilitate and speed the computation of the estimates. A measure of uncertainty also needs to be developed to estimate the RMSE of the EBLUP estimates under the nonparametric bootstrap. Double bootstrap techniques will also be explored to further reduce the estimates' bias.

Small area estimation techniques are now well established not only to produce research results of academic and scientific relevance, but local and national authorities also use them to provide reliable local statistics at a small area level. In this chapter we have shown an application of the area-level EBLUP (under a nonparametric bootstrap) to reduce the bias and increase the reliability of crowdsourced datasets. Both academics and policy makers might benefit from the development of new methods to successfully bridge the gap between crowdsourcing techniques and small area estimation, as these techniques might be helpful to produce more reliable, spatially and temporally more precise and cheaper small area statistics. Reliable small area estimates are needed to improve our understanding of social dynamics, and to design and evaluate geographically targeted policies.

References

Antoniou, V., Jeremy, M., and Mordechai, H. (2010). Web 2.0 geotagged photos: assessing the spatial dimension of the phenomenon. *Geomatica* 64 (1): 99–110.

Arbia, G., Solano Hermosilla, G., Micale, F., et al. (2018). Post-sampling crowdsourced data to allow reliable statistical inference: the case of food prices in Nigeria. Paper presented at XLIX Riunione Scientifica della Società Italiana di Statistica, Palermo, Italy (20–22 June). http://meetings3.sis-statistica.org/index.php/sis2018/49th/paper/viewFile/1090/64.

Baker, R., Brick, J.M., Bates, N.A. et al. (2013). Summary report of the AAPOR task force on non-probability sampling. *Journal of Survey Statistics and Methodology* 1 (2): 90–143. https://doi.org/10.1093/jssam/smt008.

Battese, G.E., Harter, R.M., and Fuller, W.A. (1988). An error-components model for prediction of county crop areas using survey and satellite data. *Journal of the American Statistical Association* 83 (401): 2836. https://doi.org/10.1080/01621459.1988.10478561.

Becker, M., Caminiti, S., Fiorella, D. et al. (2013). Awareness and learning in participatory noise sensing. *PLoS One* 8 (12): e81638. https://doi.org/10.1371/journal.pone.0081638.

Blom, J., Viswanathan, D., Go, J. et al. (2010). Fear and the city—role of mobile services in harnessing safety and security in urban contexts. In: *Proceedings of the SIGCHI Conference on Human Factors in Computing Systems (CHI'10), Atlanta, GA (4 October)*, 1841–1850. New York: Association for Computing Machinery.

Brabham, D.C. (2008). Crowdsourcing as a model for problem solving. *Convergence: The International Journal of Research into New Media Technologies* 14 (1): 75–90. https://doi.org/10.1177/1354856507084420.

Breetzke, G.D. and Pearson, A.L. (2014). The fear factor: examining the spatial variability of recorded crime on the fear of crime. *Applied Geography* 46: 45–52. https://doi.org/10.1016/j.apgeog.2013.10.009.

Candeia, D., Figueiredo, F., Andrade, N. et al. (2017). Multiple images of the city: unveiling group-specific urban perceptions through a crowdsourcing game. In: *HT'17 Proceedings of the 28th ACM Conference on Hypertext and Social Media Pages*, Prague, Czech Republic (4–7 July), 135–144. New York: Association for Computing Machinery https://doi.org/10.1145/3078714.3078728.

Chen, K. T. (2016). Using LASSO to calibrate non-probability samples using probability samples. PhD thesis. University of Michigan, Ann Arbor, MI.

Dubey, A., Naik, N., Parikh, D. et al. (2016). Deep learning the city: quantifying urban perception at a global scale. In: *Computer Vision—European Conference on Computer Vision (ECCV)*, Amsterdam, The Netherlands (11–14 October), 196–212. Cham: Springer.

Efron, B. and Tibshirani, R. (1993). *An Introduction to the Bootstrap*. London, UK: Chapman and Hall https://doi.org/10.1007/978-1-4899-4541-9.

Elliott, M.R. (2009). Combining data from probability and non-probability samples using pseudo-weights. *Survey Practice* 2 (6): 1–7. https://doi.org/10.29115/SP-2009-0025.

Elliott, M. and Valliant, R. (2017). Inference for nonprobability samples. *Statistical Science* 32: 249–264.

Elliott, M.R., Resler, A., Flannagan, C.A. et al. (2010). Appropriate analysis of CIREN data: using NASS-CDS to reduce bias in estimation of injury risk factors in passenger vehicle crashes. *Accident Analysis and Prevention* 42 (2): 530–539. https://doi.org/10.1016/j.aap.2009.09.019.

Farrall, S., Bannister, J., Ditton, J. et al. (1997). Questioning the measurement of the 'fear of crime': findings from a major methodological study. *British Journal of Criminology* 37 (4): 658–679. https://doi.org/10.1093/oxfordjournals.bjc.a014203.

Fay, R.E. and Herriot, R.A. (1979). Estimates of income for small places: an application of James-Stein procedures to census data. *Journal of the American Statistical Association* 74 (366a): 269–277. https://doi.org/10.1080/01621459.1979.10482505.

Fuchs, C. (2008). The role of income inequality in a multivariate cross-national analysis of the digital divide. *Social Science Computer Review* 27 (1): 41–58. https://doi.org/10.1177/0894439308321628.

Goodchild, M.F. (2007). Citizens as sensors: the world of volunteered geography. *GeoJournal* 69 (4): 211–221. https://doi.org/10.1007/s10708-007-9111-y.

Goodchild, M.F. and Glennon, J.A. (2010). Crowdsourcing geographic information for disaster response: a research frontier. *International Journal of Digital Earth* 3 (3): 231–241. https://doi.org/10.1080/17538941003759255.

Haklay, M. (2010). How good is volunteered geographic information? A comparative study of OpenStreetMap and ordnance survey datasets. *Environmental and Planning B. Urban Analytics and City Science* 37 (4): 682–703.

Haklay, M. (2013). Citizen science and volunteered geographic information: overview and typology of participation. In: *Crowdsourcing Geographic Knowledge. Volunteered Geographic Information (VGI) in Theory and Practice* (eds. D. Sui, S. Elwood and M. Goodchild), 105–122. Dordrecht: Springer https://doi.org/10.1007/978-94-007-4587-2_7.

Hale, C. (1996). Fear of crime: a review of the literature. *International Review of Victimology* 4 (2): 79–150. https://doi.org/10.1177/026975809600400201.

Harvey, C., Aultman-Hall, L., Hurley, S.E. et al. (2015). Effects of skeletal streetscape design on perceived safety. *Landscape and Urban Planning* 142: 18–28. https://doi.org/10.1016/j.landurbplan.2015.05.007.

Horvitz, D.G. and Thompson, D.J. (1952). A generalization of sampling without replacement from a finite universe. *Journal of the American Statistical Association* 47 (260): 663–685. https://doi.org/10.1080/01621459.1952.10483446.

Howe, J. (2006). The rise of crowdsourcing. *Wired Magazine* 14 (06): 1–5.

Howe, J. (2008). *Crowdsourcing. How the Power of the Crowd Is Driving the Future of Business*. London, UK: Random House.

Lee, S. (2006). Propensity score adjustment as a weighting scheme for volunteer panel web surveys. *Journal of Official Statistics* 22 (2): 329–349.

Liska, A.E., Lawrence, J.J., and Sanchirico, A. (1982). Fear of crime as a social fact. *Social Forces* 60 (3): 760–770. https://doi.org/10.1093/sf/60.3.760.

Longley, P.A. (2012). Geodemographics and the practices of geographic information science. *International Journal of Geographical Information Science* 26 (12): 2227–2237. https://doi.org/10.1080/13658816.2012.719623.

Luo, F., Ren, L., and Zhao, J.S. (2016). Location-based fear of crime. *Criminal Justice Review* 41 (1): 75–97. https://doi.org/10.1177/0734016815623035.

Malleson, N. and Andresen, M.A. (2014). The impact of using social media data in crime rate calculations: shifting hot spots and changing spatial patterns. *Cartography and Geographic Information Science* 42 (2): 112–121. https://doi.org/10.1080/15230406.2014.905756.

Mashhadi, A., Quattrone, G., and Capra, L. (2013). Putting ubiquitous crowd-sourcing into context. In: *Proceedings of the 2013 Conference on Computer Supported Cooperative Work*, San Antonio, TX (23–27 February), 611–622. New York: Association for Computing Machinery https://doi.org/10.1145/2441776.2441845.

McConnell, B. and Huba, J. (2006). The 1% rule: charting citizen participation. Church of the customer blog. https://web.archive.org/web/20100511081141/http://www.churchofthecustomer.com/blog/2006/05/charting_wiki_p.html.

Molina, I. and Marhuenda, Y. (2015). sae: An R package for small area estimation. *The R Journal* 7 (1): 81–98. https://doi.org/10.32614/RJ-2015-007.

Nahorniak, M., Larsen, D.P., Volk, C. et al. (2015). Using inverse probability bootstrap sampling to eliminate sample induced bias in model based analysis of unequal probability samples. *PLoS One* 10 (6): e0131765. https://doi.org/10.1371/journal.pone.0131765.

Nielsen, J. (2006). The 90-9-1 rule for participation inequality in social media and online communities. https://www.nngroup.com/articles/participation-inequality.

Pantazis, C. (2000). 'Fear of crime', vulnerability and poverty. *British Journal of Criminology* 40 (3): 414–436. https://doi.org/10.1093/bjc/40.3.414.

Petrucci, A. and Salvati, N. (2006). Small area estimation for spatial correlation in watershed erosion assessment. *Journal of Agricultural, Biological, and Environmental Statistics* 11 (2): 169–182. https://doi.org/10.1198/108571106X110531.

Rao, J.N.K. and Molina, I. (2015). *Small Area Estimation*, 2e. Hoboken, NJ: Wiley https://doi.org/10.1002/9781118735855.

Rotarou, E.S. (2017). Does municipal socioeconomic development affect public perceptions of crime? A multilevel logistic regression analysis. *Social Indicators Research* 138 (2): 705–724. https://doi.org/10.1007/s11205-017-1669-2.

Salesses, M. P. (2009). Place Pulse. Measuring the collaborative image of the city. MSc thesis. Massachusetts Institute of Technology, Cambridge, MA.

Salesses, P., Schechtner, K., and Hidalgo, C.A. (2013). The collaborative image of the city: mapping the inequality of urban perception. *PLoS One* 8 (7): e68400. https://doi.org/10.1371/journal.pone.0068400.

Salganik, M.J. and Levy, K.E. (2015). Wiki surveys: open and quantifiable social data collection. *PLoS One* 10 (5): e0123483. https://doi.org/10.1371/journal.pone.0123483.

Sanders, R. (1987). The pareto principle: its use and abuse. *Journal of Services Marketing* 1 (2): 37–40. https://doi.org/10.1108/eb024706.

Särndal, C.E., Swensson, B., and Wretman, J. (1992). *Model Assisted Survey Sampling*. New York: Springer-Verlag https://doi.org/10.1007/978-1-4612-4378-6.

Schonlau, M., van Soest, A.H.O., and Kapteyn, A. (2007). Are 'Webographic' or attitudinal questions useful for adjusting estimates from web surveys using propensity scoring? *SSRN Electronic Journal* https://doi.org/10.2139/ssrn.1006108.

Solymosi, R. and Bowers, K. (2018). The role of innovative data collection methods in advancing criminological understanding. In: *The Oxford Handbook of Environmental Criminology* (eds. G.J.N. Bruinsma and S.D. Johnson), 210–237. New York: Oxford University Press.

Solymosi, R., Bowers, K.J., and Fujiyama, T. (2018). Crowdsourcing subjective perceptions of neighbourhood disorder: interpreting bias in open data. *The British Journal of Criminology* 58 (4): 944–967. https://doi.org/10.1093/bjc/azx048.

Stewart, O., Lubensky, D., and Huerta, J.M. (2010). Crowdsourcing participation inequality: a scout model for the enterprise domain. In: *Proceedings of the ACM SIGKDD Workshop on Human Computation*, Washington (25–25 July), 30–33. New York: Association for Computing Machinery https://doi.org/10.1145/1837885.1837895.

Surowiecki, J. (2004). *The Wisdom of Crowds: Why the Many Are Smarter than the Few and How Collective Wisdom Shapes Business, Economies, Societies, and Nations*. New York: Doubleday.

Valliant, R., Dever, J.A., and Kreuter, F. (2013). *Practical Tools for Designing and Weighting Survey Samples*. New York: Springer https://doi.org/10.1007/978-1-4614-6449-5.

Wang, W., Rothschild, D., Goel, S. et al. (2015). Forecasting elections with non-representative polls. *International Journal of Forecasting* 31 (3): 980–991. https://doi.org/10.1016/j.ijforecast.2014.06.001.

Weisburd, D. (2015). The law of crime concentration and the criminology of place. *Criminology* 53 (2): 133–157. https://doi.org/10.1111/1745-9125.12070.

Williams, M.L., Burnap, P., and Sloan, L. (2017). Crime sensing with big data: the affordances and limitations of using open-source communications to estimate crime patterns. *British Journal of Criminology* 57: 320–340.

Yamane, T. (1967). *Statistics. An Introductory Analysis*, 2e. New York: Harper and Row.

Yu, L. (2016). Understanding information inequality: making sense of the literature of the information and digital divides. *Journal of Librarianship and Information Science* 38 (4): 229–252. https://doi.org/10.1177/0961000606070600.

17

Using Big Data to Improve Sample Efficiency

Jamie Ridenhour, Joe McMichael, Karol Krotki, and Howard Speizer

RTI International, Research Triangle Park, NC, USA

17.1 Introduction and Background

Lists can provide good means of identifying members of a target population, but list frames are often incomplete in their coverage. To increase a frame's coverage, we may append or link additional data. Doing so, however, may decrease the efficiency of the sample by decreasing the eligibility rate, that is, the number of members of the target population for a fixed amount of sample. Improving the eligibility rate in a survey saves money because a smaller overall sample can be drawn to find a desired number of members of the target population. In the example we present here, our main purpose for using Big Data was to improve coverage (i.e. how much of our target population is on our frame) compared to an initial list frame. We then used data from the combined frame to model the likelihood that a given household would be eligible for the survey.

The National Recreational Boating Safety Survey (NRBSS), which RTI conducts on behalf of the United States Coast Guard, exemplifies our approach to increasing both coverage and efficiency. The NRBSS collects information via web or paper survey from boat-owning households on the number of registered and unregistered boats in the household along with additional information on boat trips within the prior month[1] to assess boat safety exposure risk.

The NRBSS target population is boat-owning households in all 50 states and the District of Columbia.[2] "Boat" includes specific boat types: power boat, cabin boat,

---

1 RTI fields a new sample cohort each month.
2 The Coast Guard included Puerto Rico in previous iterations of this survey but excluded it for this round, given the impact of Hurricane Maria not only on boating activity but also on the basic infrastructure of the island.

Big Data Meets Survey Science: A Collection of Innovative Methods, First Edition. Edited by Craig A. Hill, Paul P. Biemer, Trent D. Buskirk, Lilli Japec, Antje Kirchner, Stas Kolenikov, and Lars E. Lyberg.
© 2021 John Wiley & Sons, Inc. Published 2021 by John Wiley & Sons, Inc.

pontoon boat, air boat, house boat, sail boat, row boat, inflatable boat, and personal water craft (e.g. jet ski). All states and DC require registration of at least some if not all of these types of boats. The target population for the NRBSS also includes households that own boats that are not required to be registered which we refer to as "unregistered" throughout the chapter. These so-called unregistered boats include those whose type does not require registration such as canoes, kayaks, and paddle boards but can also include other types of boats that should be but are not registered. For example, a canoe may not have to be registered in a given state but, in that state, a canoe with a motor added should be registered. Although many boat-owning households can be identified by state registration lists, these lists will fail to include those households that only own unregistered boats or households that failed to register its boats or for which the registration information is not up to date.

For the purposes of this study, all households in the United States can be categorized into one of the following groups:

- Households with no boats
- Boat-owning households with only registered boats
- Boat-owning households with both registered and unregistered boats
- Boat-owning households with only unregistered boats

The ideal frame for this target population is a list of all households that includes owners of registered and/or unregistered boats, but such a list does not exist. Because some boat types, but not all, must be registered, we can access a list frame that applies to only a subset of the target population (i.e. those whose boats are registered), and it has the usual pitfalls of a list frame: some entries may be out-of-date or incorrect and some members who should be on the list are not. There is no reliable list of owners of unregistered boats. What we will refer to as the registry frame is the combined list of state boat registries from all states who permit their state boater registration information to be used for this purpose – eight states[3] do not permit their registration information to be used for the survey. Thus, the registry frame is a list of names and addresses of households that have registered at least one boat with a state that permits access to their data. The types of boats that must be registered, how often they must be registered, and the information provided to the registry varies from state to state. For example, some states distinguish between cabin motorboats and open motorboats in their registrations, but others do not. This is an important note

---

3 Colorado, Idaho, Louisiana, Minnesota, Montana, New Hampshire, Vermont, and West Virginia.

because exposure hours by boat type is an important study estimate. Although we know the boat registration lists are incomplete and potentially out-of-date, they remain a relatively efficient way to find households with registered boat owners, a key subset of the target population. While we refer to accessing the registry frame, note that we never had access to the complete frame but rather had to purchase samples from it as it is owned by a vendor.

The challenge in developing an appropriate frame for this survey was how to supplement the registry frame to cover the entire national population of boat-owning households, including those owning registered boat types, those owning unregistered boat types, and those owning both. Our solution was an ABS approach using RTI's Enhanced ABS Frame, which we will refer to as the Enhanced Frame.

RTI's Enhanced Frame comprises the Computerized Delivery Sequence (CDS) file from the United States Postal Service augmented with hundreds of variables from a consumer database. The CDS component of the Enhanced Frame provides near-complete coverage of all postal delivery points in the United States. There are over 140 million postal delivery points on the CDS and to enhance that dataset, we merged on consumer database variables from Acxiom InfoBase. The consumer database is at the person-level, containing more than 300 million records with hundreds of variables that we must roll up into address-level data and merge with the CDS.

Using consumer data in the survey process has become more common in recent years, and research has shown that surveys can potentially increase their sample efficiency by bringing in auxiliary information for defining sample strata (Ridenhour and McMichael 2017) and improving survey field operations (West et al. 2015).

Although the Enhanced Frame could have been used as the only frame for this survey, it would have been inefficient in that we would have needed to sample a larger number of households overall to obtain the desired number of boat-owning households. The proportion of all US households that own boats is unknown but one industry statistic[4] estimates there were 11.9 million registered boats in the United States as of 2016. This statistic does not tell us what proportion of households own registered boats (as households may own more than one registered boat), and there is no information on the number of unregistered boats or the proportion of households with only unregistered boats (households can own both registered and unregistered boats). Taking a conservative approach, fewer than 10% of US households own boats. Using the address frame without any additional infor-

---

4 https://www.growboating.org/toolkit/facts-and-figures.aspx.

mation would require a substantially larger overall sample to achieve the desired number of boat-owning households sufficient to compute the survey estimates required by the United States Coast Guard (USCG). If we had used the Enhanced Frame alone, we would expect 90% of addresses to be ineligible for the survey.

Thus, on one hand, we have the registry lists that are efficient but incomplete in their coverage and, on the other hand, the Enhanced Frame that is complete but not efficient. In other words, on the registry frame, a large proportion of any random sample would be eligible boat-owning households but not all boat-owning households are on the registry, and while the Enhanced Frame covers all households, any random sample would result in a large number of ineligible households, the very definition of sample inefficiency.

Figure 17.1 illustrates the multiple and overlapping target populations and the available frames. The target populations are represented by circles: long dashes surrounding a gray circle signify registered boat-owning households, and short dashes indicate households owning unregistered boats. There is overlap between the two populations because some boat-owning households have both registered and unregistered boats. Given the structure of both the state registries and the ABS (meaning that both are lists of addresses), the natural unit of selection is an address as a proxy for a household.

The squares in Figure 17.1 represent the available frames: the largest one for the Enhanced Frame, the smaller one for the registry frame. The Enhanced Frame is a complete set of addresses in the country and therefore, in theory, includes all boat-owning households, with both registered and unregistered boats.

As discussed previously, the registry frame is the compilation of the state registry frames from the 43 states allowing access each with its own specifications as to what data are available and how they can be used. The composite registry frame

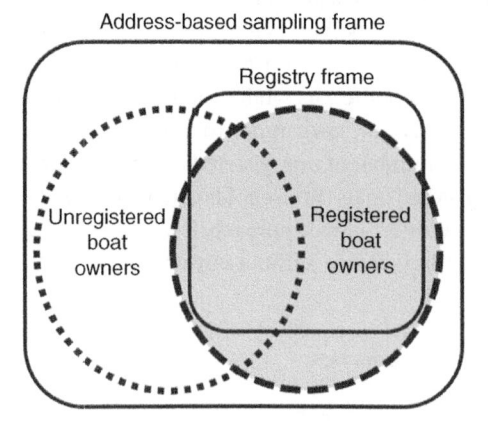

Figure 17.1 Frames and target population.

is a list of all registered boat-owning households in the country, which does not coincide perfectly with the total population of registered boat-owning households due to missing states and/or households that have not registered their boats.

Multiple frame surveys are most commonly used to increase coverage of the target population and/or decrease the costs associated with obtaining response from the target population. The frames involved may be overlapping, in which case care must be taken to adjust for the multiple chances of selecting units from the frame. Such an adjustment can be made at the time of sampling if the overlap is known at sample selection or during weighting if the overlap is unknown *a priori* but gathered during the survey. Although the concept of a multiple frame survey has been around for a long time (Hartley 1962), our application of it differs in its use of Big Data. The Enhanced Frame contains over 140 million records providing near-complete coverage of the household population and the registry frame is theoretically a proper subset of the Enhanced Frame; however, the two could not be merged and we could only purchase samples from the latter. Thus, we took a dual-frame approach using the strengths of each frame to find all boat owners. The challenge in the dual-frame approach (registry and ABS) involves determining how to use the ABS most effectively to augment the registry frame and to efficiently identify unregistered boat owners. The two frames could not be combined at any point in their entirety; rather, we selected a sample from the registry frame and a sample from the Enhanced Frame and deduplicated the two samples; all addresses in the registry sample were fielded as registry sample and the address sample from the Enhanced Frame was sent to the registry vendor so that any selected addresses from the Enhanced Frame subsequently identified as also being on the registry were not fielded given that these cases already had a chance of selection.

We discuss how we improved the efficiency of the Enhanced Frame, which in this case is our yield rate (i.e. the proportion of all sampled households that are eligible respondents) in Section 17.2.

17.2 Methods to More Efficiently Sample Unregistered Boat-Owning Households

As discussed previously, the Enhanced Frame is not efficient for finding boat-owning households. We wanted to increase the proportion of boat-owning households we would obtain from a fixed sample size, so we sought to combine multiple sets of data to improve the utility of the ABS Frame.

The obstacles we encountered in moving forward with combining multiple data sources may be common in the era of Big Data: access, usage, and complexity. Access was an obstacle because not all stakeholders have access to all of the data, and the multiple data sources cannot always be easily merged in their entirety.

For example, the provider of the state registry data does not have access to RTI's Enhanced Frame and, conversely, RTI does not have direct access to all addresses in the registry due to cost constraints (as detailed in the Model 2 description, we took a large sample from the registry). Similarly, team members at other institutions do not have direct access to RTI's Enhanced Frame. This challenge is not necessarily uncommon with large databases, particularly those maintained by different vendors. Contractual requirements may stipulate that datafiles from separate vendors cannot be stored in the same datafile simultaneously. Our situation was similar, so we had to build our propensity model as two separate modeling steps rather than one.

Complexity was an obstacle because the design and implementation of this survey involved working with several large datafiles, raising challenges in merging the files, measuring the degree of overlap, and ensuring that we had coverage of all members of the target population. To accomplish our goal, we had to establish a multistep approach to bringing components of data together when possible, managing the process through establishing a clear set of definitions and rules. When linking the different sources of data (e.g. addresses on the CDS and the consumer data), we had to decide which cases would be linked and what variable served as the linkage key (e.g. address, partial address, homeowner name, etc.). The consumer data portion of the Enhanced Frame is person-level and to be linked to the CDS, that information must be summarized to a single address. Not all person entries associated with an address may be current, resulting in decision rules about which person-level observations to keep and which to discard. Address information, like the city, may differ between the two sets of data necessitating decision rules about what constitutes a match and what does not (Brown and McMichael 2018).

We wanted to obtain an address-level prediction of boat ownership to find the owners of only unregistered boats who were not covered by the registry frame. To accomplish this goal of obtaining an address-level prediction of boat ownership, we relied on two separate predictive models; the first model used a third dataset containing a separate source of boat registration information along with geospatial data, due to data access limitations. We refer to this data as the "geospatial data" to distinguish it from the vendor-supplied registration data, but this dataset contained both boat registration information along with geospatial data such as distance to water variables. More specifically, we were not permitted to link the so-called geospatial data we suspected could be highly predictive of boat ownership (regardless of boat registration category/status) to the address data of the two other data sources. Thus, there were two modeling steps. First, we used geospatial data to develop a model (Model 1) that predicted boat ownership spatially (i.e. for an area of land). Then, we used the large registry sample and the results of Model

1 to develop Model 2: an address-level model predicting boat-owner propensity for all addresses on the Enhanced Frame. In an ideal world, we could have modeled everything at one time without the need for the output of one model to feed in as a predictor in the subsequent model. But these two models had to be developed separately because of restrictions relating to data access and linkage mentioned earlier.

Model 2 was based on a sample from the Enhanced Frame with *registered* boat households flagged by the boat registry vendor (InfoLink) – which is why we expected the Model 1 results to be so critical to the success of Model 2. We wanted to capture factors that may be related to propensity to own a boat (e.g. proximity to water) that would apply to boat owners regardless of boat type. The registry frame of boat owners was used to develop Model 2 parameters predicting boat ownership. This model was then applied to predict whether or not each household in the ABS Frame was a boat owner. The application of this model to the Enhanced Frame assumes that the underlying factors related to boat ownership for registered and unregistered boats are similar and that the relationships would be the same in the eight states whose registry data we could not use were similar to those within the 43 states we were able to use. For example, if proximity to large bodies of water is a predictor of a household being more likely to own a registered boat (e.g. a sailboat), it may also be a good predictor of households that own boats that do not have to be registered (e.g. canoes or kayaks). Also, as registration requirements vary by state, owner of certain boat types may have to be registered in one state and the auxiliary information that is predictive of that boat ownership may also transfer to another state where that boat type does not have to be registered. Thus, our overarching hypothesis here is that we can account for characteristics related to owning a boat, regardless of registration status, and model those with all of the available data.

17.2.1 Model 1: Spatial Boat Density Model

The goal of the spatial boat ownership model was to estimate the number of boats in a census block group (CBG). The number of boats was available in ZCTA-level data (ZIP Code Tabulation Areas maintained by the US Census Bureau), and we wanted to have that information at a smaller geography (CBG).

Predictors used in this linear modeling included other census and spatial variables that had to be available at both the ZCTA-level and the CBG-level to make the translation: population, population density, population of males, population ages 35–65, population of non-Hispanic whites, number of housing units, number of owner-occupied housing units, per capita income, and seven types of distance to water variables (e.g. distance to marinas, distance to boat ramps, etc.) – the list is shown in Table 17.1.

Table 17.1 Selected predictors for Model 1.

Source	Summary level	
American Community Survey (2012–2016)	Census block group and ZCTA	Population density
		% Population male
		% Population age 35–64
		% Non-Hispanic white
		% Owner-occupied housing units
		Per capita income
Esri	Census block	Distance to nearest boat ramp
		Distance to nearest Marina
		Distance to nearest body of water by surface area
		Area 0.5–10 mi^2
		Area 10–50 mi^2
		Area 50–100 mi^2
		Area 100–1000 mi^2
		Area 1000 + mi^2 (includes ocean and Great Lakes)

The model coefficients were developed for the ZCTA data, then applied to CBG, and then normalized to the total in ZCTA so that the output of this model was the predicted number of boats in the CBG. The resulting R^2 of this model was 0.641.

Model 1 provided information on the predicted number of boats in a CBG. The Enhanced Frame has the CBG of each address on it so the predicted number of boats from Model 1 became one of many candidate predictors for Model 2 – the model we developed to predict address-level boat-ownership propensity. The estimates from Model 1 were incorporated into Model 2 without incorporating the error associated with the Model 1 prediction because our interest was the predicted probability with no interest in precision.

17.2.2 Model 2: Address-Level Boat-Ownership Propensity

Because the composite registry file did not cover all of the United States as previously described and we did not purchase all 11M addresses on the registry, we could not flag all addresses on the Enhanced Frame that existed on the registry frame. Namely, we did not have information about boat ownership information from those states not included on the composite registry frame, and for fielding, we only purchased the boat registry sample needed to achieve our goals. For sample selection, this created the additional hurdle of needing to deduplicate our address sample against the registry sample to ensure that addresses did not have more than one chance of being selected for the survey. To improve the utility of the Enhanced Frame itself, we needed a sample from the registry that then could be merged to Enhanced Frame for the sole purpose of model development. Our goal was to develop a model for predicting address-level boat ownership propensity and our indication of which addresses owned boats was based on a sample of 350 000 addresses from the registry frame; we ensured the sample covered all available states and the District of Columbia.

Using our sample of 350k records (sampling 3% of the total registrations) from the Enhanced Frame with boat registry indicator appended along with the spatial prediction of boats (i.e. Model 1 results) and all variables available on the Enhanced Frame, we sought to develop a logistic regression model that would predict boat ownership at the address level and apply that model to the full address frame to make our sample more efficient at targeting likely boat-owning households. The list of candidate and selected variables for Model 2 are shown in Table 17.2.

To develop the Model 2 parameters, we assigned 10% of the sample data to a validation dataset and developed the model on the remaining 90% training data. We used stepwise selection in SAS PROC HPLOGISTIC (the "high performance" version of logistic for large data). We allowed for two-way interactions of main effects and used the validation data to measure the prediction error. Model building was terminated based on a stop criterion of minimum average square error. Any collinearity among predictors in the model was not a concern because the goal was the resulting boat-ownership propensity.

The final model included the proportion of households in a zip code that are registered boat-owning households, the boat-owning household rate by CBG (i.e. the output from Model 1), and other demographic variables.

The model selection statistics are shown in Table 17.3. The area under the receiver operating characteristic (ROC) curve is an index of the accuracy of the test. When this statistic is close to 1, it indicates a perfect model, whereas results close to 0.5 indicate that the model did not predict boat ownership. Although we would have preferred the model to be more in the neighborhood of 0.8, the resulting 0.71 is meaningful. The max-rescaled R^2 indicates how the model with the predictors compares to the null model (i.e. the model with just the intercept).

We applied Model 2 to all addresses on the Enhanced Frame, to enable calculation of boat-ownership propensity for all addresses. Propensity distributions varied substantially by state as shown in Figure 17.2. Because of this variation, the propensity strata were formed within state by grouping these propensities into 20 equally sized strata based on 5-percentile cut points. The sample was disproportionately allocated to the higher propensity strata: 75% of the ABS

Table 17.2 Candidate and selected predictors for Model 2.

Source	Append level	Candidate	Selected
Acxiom InfoBase	Address	Age 18–29	Y
		Age 30–34	Y
		Age 35–44	Y
		Age 45–54	—
		Age 55–64	—
		Age 65–74	Y
		Age 75+	—
		Age 18–37	—
		Age 38–57	Y
		Age 58–77	Y
		Male age 35–44	—
		Male age 45–54	Y
		Male age 55–64	Y
		Male age 65–74	Y
		Personicx Lifestage cluster code	
		Personicx Lifestage group	—
InfoLink	ZIP code	% Registered boats	Y
Model 1	Census block group	Estimated number of registered boats	Y
USDA	Census tracts	Rural–urban commuting area codes	—
Esri	Census tract	Tapestry urbanization group	—
		LifeMode group	—
US Census Planning Database (2012–2016)	Census block group	Numerous (150+ variables)	X vars in Model 1

Table 17.3 Key model selection statistics.

Statistic	Training	Validation
Area under the ROC	0.710	0.711
Average square error	0.068	0.069
Misclassification error	0.078	0.078
R^2	0.038	0.039
Max-rescaled R^2	0.091	0.093

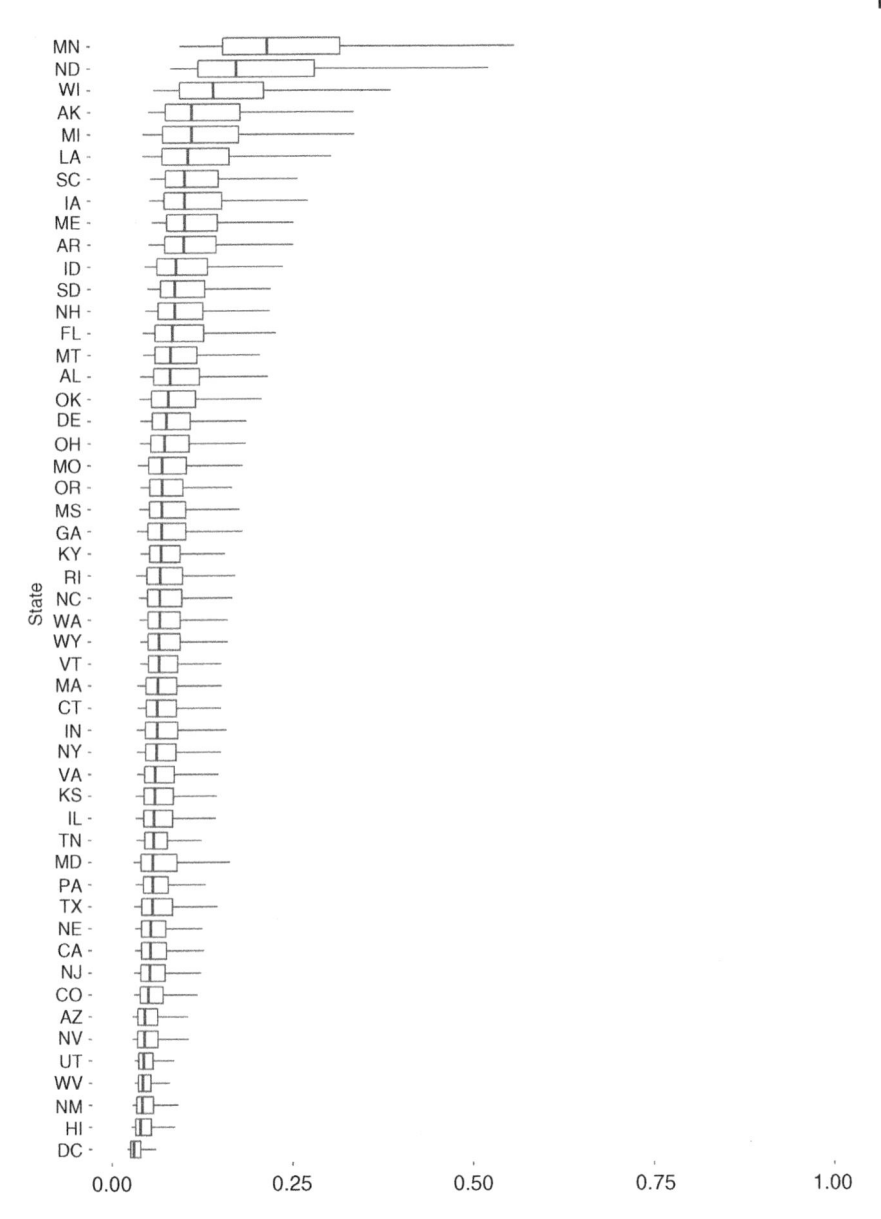

Figure 17.2 Boat ownership propensities by state. *Note*: Extreme values were removed from the plot to make the distributions across states easier to see.

sample was allocated to the highest five propensity strata, and the remaining 25% of the ABS sample came from the lower 15 propensity strata. The ABS sample was deduplicated against the registry frame so only addresses not on the registry frame could be fielded from the Enhanced Frame.

This approach helped us more efficiently target households that were more likely to be boat-owning, thus reducing the amount of screening needed. The goal was to optimize our eligibility and coverage rates.

17.3 Results

Results by frame from survey data collection are shown in Table 17.4. Because the study is still in the field, these results are based on 9 of 12 cohorts, those for which data collection is complete. The data support the conclusion that use of Big Data, in the form of the Enhanced Frame, significantly improved the survey's coverage. Based on the registry frame, we were able to identify a total of 19 237 eligible households. With the inclusion of the Enhanced Frame, we added an additional 6564 eligible households, a substantial increase of 34%. We should keep in mind that these additional households are made up of two parts. One part includes households with registered boats that should be on the registry frame but are not. (We sent the complete ABS sample to our registry vendor for deduplication against their entire database so all remaining ABS sample addresses should not have any registered boats.) The second part includes households that have only unregistered boats. We do not expect these households to be on the registry frame, but they represent an important part of the target population for the US Coast Guard.

Because we administered a single survey, eligibility was determined based on responses gathered from the questionnaire. As such, we define the screening

Table 17.4 Data collection results.[a]

	Registry frame		Enhanced Frame		Total (both frames)	
	Total	Rate (%)	Total	Rate (%)	Total	Rate (%)
Total sampled	62 216		100 544		162 760	
Screened	20 927	33.6	15 185	15.1	36 112	22.2
Eligible	19 237	91.9	6 564	43.2	25 801	71.4
Yield		30.9		6.5		15.9

a) Based on 9 of 12 completed cohorts.

rate[5] as the proportion of the selected sample that responded, regardless of their eligibility. The eligibility rate is the proportion of respondents that were deemed eligible, i.e. they reported boat ownership in the survey. The yield rate is the product of the screening rate and the eligibility rate. The yield rate from the registry frame (30.9%) was high, as expected. Table 17.4 presents the two components of the yield rate separately by frame. The screening rate for the registry sample is 33.6%, whereas for the Enhanced Frame, it is less than half, 15.1%. This indicates that members of the registry frame represent a population more vested in the survey topic, more likely to be interested in the survey topic, and thus more likely to participate. The screening rate for the Enhanced Frame resembles the screening rate we typically see with a general population survey. Finally, the eligibility rate, not surprisingly, is high (91.9%) for the registry frame, whereas for the Enhanced Frame, it is much lower, at 43.2%.

These figures provide an assessment of the extent to which the application and modeling of Big Data improved the quality of our sample. The Enhanced Frame completed the coverage of the target population but to have sampled from it alone would have been cost prohibitive because the yield rate is much lower, 6.5% compared to 30.9% for the registry frame. Most registered boat owners originated from the registry frame (save the eight states for which we could not access the registration list). Because boat owners may own both registered and unregistered boats, it is not surprising then that we get reports of unregistered boats from both frames: 55% of households with unregistered boats originate from the registry frame, while the remaining 45% originate from the Enhanced Frame.

Clearly, relying exclusively on the Enhanced Frame would have been exorbitantly expensive, but in combination with the registry fame, we were able to achieve an overall yield rate of 15.9%, i.e. we could count on finding an eligible household in almost every six sampled households. Thus, by combining the two frames, stratifying, and applying unequal selection proportions, we succeeded in not only increasing coverage but also did so with an increased screening rate.

To shed light on the degree to which the propensity strata helped in maximizing eligibility rates, Figure 17.3 presents the different rates by the propensity strata. The respondents in this graph are those who originated on the Enhanced Frame, so if the registry list perfectly covered registered boat owners, we would expect these eligible households to have unregistered boats only. The eligibility rate increases from a low of 30% to a high of close to 50%. Just as interesting is the pattern of change for the screening rates by propensity strata: from a low of 11% to a high of 17%. This range offers possibilities for optimal sample allocation thus

---

5 This rate could also be referred to as a cooperation rate. We use "screening" because although it was a single instrument that we wanted all respondents to return, boat owners were the population of interest.

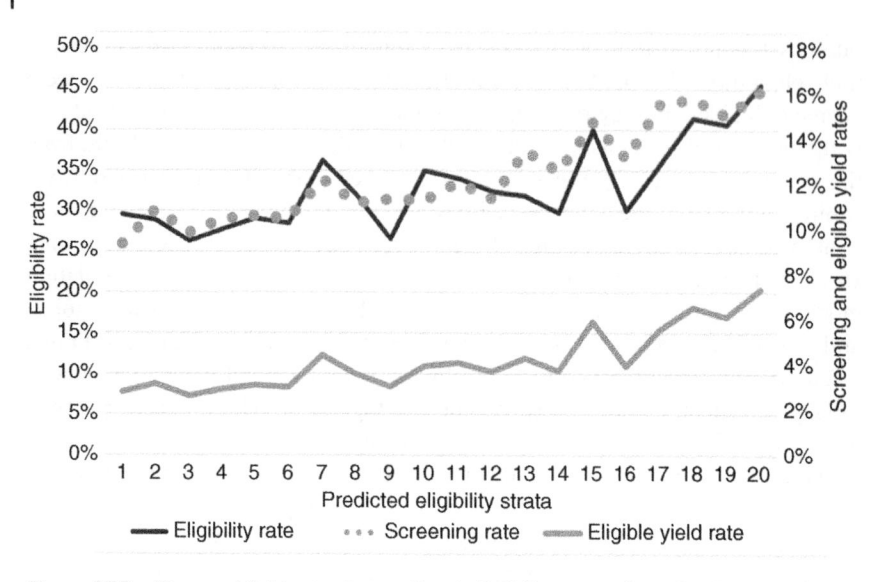

Figure 17.3 Observed field rates by predicted eligibility strata from the Enhanced Frame sample. *Note*: The coloring of the two *y*-axis corresponds to coloring of the different rates in the legend displayed at the bottom.

increasing sample efficiency. As with many sample designs for cross-sectional surveys, we were not able to optimally allocate this sample because we did not know what the realized rates would be; however, based on this obtained information, we could more optimally allocate a similarly designed sample in a future cross-sectional survey of the same population. Oversampling the high eligibility strata is beneficial for overall yield but oversampling leads to higher unequal weight effects (UWEs), which reduces sampling precision. We recommend a careful balance between oversampling high eligibility strata while keeping the UWE at an acceptable level. The eligibility rates displayed in Figure 17.3 show that 5 percentile cut points resulting in 20 propensity strata may not be the best approach if we were to do this again. Groups of strata may have resulted in similar enough eligibility rates and screening rates to be collapsed, which could reduce the overall weight variation.

We also note that the increase in the screening rates by propensity strata may indicate an avidity bias. That is, people who do not own boats are less likely to complete and return the survey than those that do. In a future iteration of the survey, we will consider ways in which to mitigate this potential bias.

Complete coverage of all boat owners, both registered and unregistered, is important not only for the survey to fully cover the target population but also because key attributes about boating behavior differ between owners of registered boats and owners of unregistered boats.

17.4 Conclusions

This project successfully sampled from two frames: a registry frame for a segment of the target population and an overlapping ABS Frame of all households in the country. The goals were twofold: to increase coverage of the target population and to control survey costs. Although population benchmarks of unregistered boat owners do not exist, based on the increasing eligibility rate of addresses sampled from the Enhanced Frame that were not on the registry frame, we see evidence that the model successfully identified characteristics of households, both geographic (e.g. proximity to water bodies of various sizes) and person attributes (e.g. age of adults in the household), that correlate to boat ownership generally, regardless of boat registration status. Adding the Enhanced Frame clearly resulted in higher coverage, not only picking up unregistered boat owners but also locating boat owners who, for various reasons, were not present on the registry frame. Furthermore, the propensity model stratification led to an increase in the eligibility rate and a resultant decrease in survey costs; however, the trade-off of higher eligibility resulted in larger weight variation due to the disproportionate allocation.

Although the context of this research involved a specific population and subject matter, we argue that the methodology described here could be replicated in similar situations, with different populations and topics. The ABS Frame is widely and readily available and can be used in several contexts in combination with specific list frames to increase sample design efficiency.

Although our specific goal was to find boat-owning households in the United States, our approach is generalizable. We started with an incomplete and partially inaccurate list frame that we supplemented with larger data. Our larger data included spatial data, census data, and auxiliary information though all three would not necessarily be needed for a different application. We drew a sample from the list frame and merged it to the Big Data to develop a model to predict eligibility. We then applied that model to the large data, created propensity strata, and allocated sample accordingly. This approach maximizes coverage while controlling screening costs.

We did encounter challenges that others doing similar work may want to carefully consider. Due to the confidentiality of several of our data sources, we had to break our approach into separate models (the first then used as predictors in the second). This added time to the project both in terms of the schedule as well as the person-time involved in getting to the end goal of address-level propensities for our survey population.

The limitation of developing the address-level boat ownership model based only on boat-owning households found on the registry was the assumption that boat-owning households have similar characteristics regardless of whether they own registered and/or unregistered boats. To the extent that households with only unregistered boats differed from those with registered boats, the model may have been less effective at predicting household ownership of unregistered boats (though we note that we did also find owners of registered boats from the ABS Frame). Now that the survey has been fielded, we have more ground truth for both types of households to improve the model for future iterations of the survey.

Acknowledgments

The authors wish to express their gratitude to the editors, Antje Kirchner and Trent Buskirk, for their invaluable feedback, which helped us make large improvements to this chapter. We also thank Karla McPherson for her keen editorial eye.

References

Brown, D. and McMichael, J. (2018). Give a second thought to the secondary city: new applications of the USPS city state file. In: *JSM Proceedings, Survey Research Methods Section*, Vancouver, British Columbia, Canada. 28 July–2 August. Alexandria, VA: American Statistical Association.

Hartley, H.O. (1962). Multiple frame surveys. In: *Proceedings of the Social Statistics Section*, 2. Minneapolis, MN, USA. 7–10 September 1962: American Statistical Association.

Ridenhour, J. L. and McMichael, J. P. (2017). Propensity stratification with auxiliary data for address-based sampling frames. *Proceedings of the American Association for Public Opinion Research*, New Orleans, LA, USA, 18–21 May 2017. http://www.asasrms.org/Proceedings/y2017/files/594100.pdf.

West, B.T., Wagner, J., Hubbard, F. et al. (2015). The utility of alternative commercial data sources for survey operations and estimation: evidence from the National Survey of Family Growth. *Journal of Survey Statistics and Methodology* 3 (2): 240–264. https://doi.org/10.1093/jssam/smv004.

Section 5

Combining Big Data with Survey Statistics: Tools

18

Feedback Loop: Using Surveys to Build and Assess Registration-Based Sample Religious Flags for Survey Research

David Dutwin

NORC at the University of Chicago, Chicago, IL 60603, USA

18.1 Introduction

Survey research has long utilized data appended to sample sources to effectively identify and survey specific populations of interest. Telephone sample providers have built partnerships with credit history companies to link telephone numbers to information about the person or household associated with that telephone number. Is she Hispanic? Young? Affluent? Not only have marketers utilized such appended data to target audiences, but survey researchers have used such data to more effectively survey populations of interest.

Although some appended data comes from direct linkages, i.e. a sample file of phone numbers matched to a concurrent data base of credit histories via phone number, other data is model-based. Examples are companies that aggregate voter registration lists[1] and provide registration-based samples (RBSs) to survey researchers, marketers, and of course, political campaign officials and pollsters. The typical RBS datafile contains data both direct and modeled. Voter file data are appended with listed telephone numbers, credit information, and other available data available for linkage directly by name and address. But other data is modeled as well: some states report party registration of individuals, others do not, and for such states, party identification is a modeled construct.

Voter registration lists have been available for some time, before Big Data was widely used. But Big Data and data science have given researchers an

---

1 In the United States, voter registration lists are used to establish eligibility to vote, specify which candidates persons can vote for, communicate to citizens about elections, validate people when they show up at the polls, and audit elections post-voting. Each state maintains their own list and private companies aggregate statewide lists into a national list for limited resale.

Big Data Meets Survey Science: A Collection of Innovative Methods, First Edition. Edited by Craig A. Hill, Paul P. Biemer, Trent D. Buskirk, Lilli Japec, Antje Kirchner, Stas Kolenikov, and Lars E. Lyberg.
© 2021 John Wiley & Sons, Inc. Published 2021 by John Wiley & Sons, Inc.

invigorated interest in these data, particularly how modern modeling techniques can be applied to further enhance and expand on the data available. For survey researchers, this opportunity is new, and works in both directions: if survey data can be matched to RBS, then survey data can be used to build new modeled appends into the RBS universe. In the other direction, survey-based self-reporting can assess the efficacy of models preexisting in RBS datafiles.

This chapter explores one such exercise, using self-reported survey data matched onto an RBS to build model-based variables across the entire RBS datafile and to use the survey data to assess the efficacy of preexisting modeled data in the RBS. For this exercise, we explore religion as a key metric. The rationale for choosing religion is that it is (i) a metric wholly modeled in RBS datafiles, and (ii) there is a small but vibrant field of religious research in social science that struggles to attain valid and affordable survey data of small religious groups. If there were a more effective way to identify persons of specific religious groups, such survey research could be executed more effectively. Given the expense of low-incidence population research in general, finding effective indicators for low-incidence groups like Jews, Muslims, and Mormons, as well as other low-incidence groups across socioeconomic status, racial and ethnic identities, low-prevalence health populations and other groups, would be a boon to the survey research community in general.

18.2 The Turn to Trees

For years, regression-based tools have dominated exercises like the one detailed in this chapter. For example, nonresponse modeling has up until recently almost exclusively utilized models built with logistic regression (Duffy et al. 2005; Rosenbaum and Rubin 1983; Schonlau et al. 2003). Regression, properly utilized, requires that a number of assumptions are met (Allison 1998). Models can fail to converge due to small sample sizes in specific cells (Allison 2008), and failure to satisfy key assumptions can lead to bias and general model misspecification.

Recursive partitioning algorithms and modern machine learning methods have recently become an increasingly common alternative, and in many respects, are more suited to models of classification (Lemon et al. 2003). There are many options and a quickly growing body of literature on these approaches, which include chi-square automatic interaction detection (CHAID) (Morgan and Sonquist 1963), classification and regression trees (CARTs) (Breiman et al. 1984), and random forests (Breiman 2001). Substantial literature explores the statistical properties of such approaches and ways to optimize and refine each method. Hastie, Tibshirani, and Friedman (2009), for example, explore relations between machine learning classification methods and regression methods that utilize flexible specifications such as generalized additive models and other basis function expansions and demonstrate the circumstances under which the two classes of methods yield comparable vs. distinct performance.

Less extensive is applied literature in the use of tree-based approaches to social science and Big Data. Cesare, Grant, and Nsoesie (2017) summarizes no fewer than 160 attempts to predict demographic attributes based on data available on Twitter. Pennacchiotti and Popescu (2011a,b) used classification trees to attempt to predict demographics and other metrics such as party identification. Simaki, Mporas, and Megalooikonomou (2016) explored age prediction for Twitter users utilizing random forests. Other researchers used a variety of techniques including Bayesian approaches, neural networks, regression, and k-nearest neighbors. Cesare overall reports general success in predicting gender but far less success with age and race/ethnicity.

Administrative data and patient records have already been used to assess future risk of disease or other health maladies. Ridinger (2002) used extensive patient information to build models predicting patients who may be at high risk of future conditions. Though they did not utilize their model to predict cases in a larger dataset, Cairney et al. (2014) used classification trees to more effectively identify determinants of mental health service use than linear regression models alone were able to attain due to the inherent intersectionality of the tree-based approach. Similarly, Kershaw et al. (2002) used classification trees to identify individuals with high risk of sexually transmitted diseases during pregnancy. Buskirk and Kolenikov (2015) specifically set out to test the efficacy of random forest compared to regression and did so in modeling a number of health measures including body mass index, smoking status, hypertension, and doctor's visits. Overall, recursive partitioning has become increasingly popular for classification and prediction; the remainder of the chapter explore the efficacy of this approach to classify sample cases on religion.

18.3 Research Agenda

This chapter reports on an applied example of using tree-based approaches to build models that predict whether a person (that is, the person's record) in a national voter file is Jewish, and to use predictions to better identify individuals' religious identification for survey research. Hundreds of models were constructed toward this effort, varied by key settings and variables, to discover which approaches and features result in the most effective models. Models considered effective do more than just succeed at prediction. One goal is to attain the best possible rate of predicting people who are in fact Jewish to be Jewish. But as with the use of modeling in medical and health applications, it is equally, if not more important, to prevent misclassification of non-Jews. In the parlance of sampling, prediction (specificity)

Table 18.1 Summary of terms.

Concept	Definition	Meaning in survey sampling context	Error type
Specificity	Probability that case in the model is a case in the population	Coverage	Type I
Sensitivity	Probability a case in population is a case in the model	Incidence and sampling efficiency	Type II

denotes coverage: what percentage of actual Jews will be identified as Jewish from the model? The concern with misclassification is, on the other hand, a concern of sensitivity, which from a sampling perspective is survey incidence: what percentage of those predicted to be Jewish will in fact be Jewish? Again, in many respects, this is a key goal of this exercise, given that the incidence of being Jewish is approximately 2% nationally (Pew Research Center 2013). Even increasing incidence twofold can save survey researchers substantial costs in fielding surveys of this low-incidence population. So a key research question is: which models both maximize specificity (coverage) and maximize sensitivity (incidence)? Table 18.1 defines these terms.

18.4 Data

The SSRS omnibus is a phone survey of 1000 adults in the United States, conducted at least once per week, using simple random samples of landlines and cellphones, in English and Spanish across all 50 states. Between 2013 and 2017, the SSRS omnibus interviewed 378 370 persons, 60% of them via cellphones. Response rate over that time was 7.5%. As an omnibus, every week the survey fields different questions. However, there is a common demographic battery that includes typical metrics like age and educational attainment, as well as expanded questions about the full age and gender of every child in households with children, religion, health insurance, millennial-specific questions, and questions specific to Hispanics. In theory, many variables of small groups could be modeled and scored onto a large dataset like the RBS. Importantly, the omnibus identifies Jews both by religion and not by religion (see Pew Research Center 2013 for a discussion on this topic).

There are a number of major RBS providers in the United States. SSRS partnered with L2 on this exercise because of their status as a nonpartisan RBS provider, as SSRS is similarly a nonpartisan survey research provider. The 2017 L2 RBS file contains 180 153 331 records, and hundreds of variables including detailed voting histories, geographic variables denoting all levels of political boundaries (Congressional District, etc.), and a host of variables either derived from the voter files themselves or third-party providers, or by modeling. Modeled variables range from demographics to consumer behavior and financial benchmarks.

While the goal is to develop models for a range of metrics, including specific Hispanic groups, households with children, households that are uninsured or on public assistance, and others, the first test again endeavored to model Jewish households. The decision admittedly was based on need and opportunity: Jewish demography is of particular interest to the author, and it provided an excellent opportunity to test the efficacy of the modeled estimate.

One final data source was the Jewish Community Survey of Metropolitan Detroit (JCSMD). This survey uses a highly stratified random-digit dial (RDD) design that incorporates listed sample sources and residual RDD telephone numbers to provide some nonzero probability of selection to all households with telephones in three Detroit-area counties (see www.Jewishdatabank.org for the methodology report on the JCSMD, forthcoming in late 2018). As part of the study, a small subset of the overall study utilized a stratified sample from the L2 voter file. Specifically, sample was stratified into voter file sample that was prepunched as Jewish, and then remaining sample was stratified into high- and low-incidence Jewish sample, based on an initial model of Jewish likelihood from the procedures described here.

18.5 Combining the Data

One challenge in combining large datasets is the difficulty in attaining effective matches. Voter files, for example, do not have telephone numbers for every state and must be merged using listed telephone directories. L2, like other providers, does its best to match telephones to as many records as possible, but in the end, as might be expected (given the percent of the United States that have listed phone numbers), only about two-thirds of the 2017 file had a telephone number appended with a record.

This consideration is important because telephone number is the primary data point in a telephone survey such as the SSRS omnibus for linkage with other data. Although some telephone surveys do attain address information, most do not, given its expense and for many surveys, limited utility. Other metrics can be leveraged as well. The omnibus has first name as well as the demographics it attained as part of the survey like age, gender, and race/ethnicity. As such, a general fuzzy logic matching algorithm was utilized to match as many omnibus records as possible to the L2 datafile.

The attrition in such a process is considerable. First, as mentioned, the L2 file does not have telephone number for 33% of cases. With telephone number as the principal match, there is no real possibly of matching to phoneless records. Second, not all Americans are registered to vote. According to the 2016 Current Population Survey, 91% of Americans aged 18 or older are citizens, and in total, 70% of US adults self-report being registered to vote. Third, the matched phone in the voter file may be a different phone than the number used to conduct an interview in the omnibus survey (for example, where the omnibus interviews on a cell phone and the RBS record has a landline number). Fourth, time is a concern because the SSRS omnibus data leveraged here spans five years, and the match rate could deteriorate with older data: people can change their phone numbers, drop their landline numbers (removing the match from phone to a registered voter), or could conversely register to vote (creating a missing match).

Overall, the matching was conducted in two phases. The first was a precise match on telephone number, age, zip code (self-reported in omnibus data), and name elements (a fuzzy logic algorithm that requires a 50% match rate on name to accommodate misspellings). This resulted in 61 972 matches. A second matching procedure developed dichotomous match/no match variables for seven metrics: zip code, first initial, age, gender, and race/ethnicity, assuming first an exact match on telephone number. Records with a match for five of the seven variables were considered a match, resulting in an additional 4512 matched for a total of 66 484 matches.

The result contains considerable attrition, as evidenced in Table 18.2. Attrition may not be a significant concern: much like the debate over whether to weight data in multivariate analyses (Dumouchel and Duncan 1983) non-matching does not have to necessarily impact the ability to effectively model. However, there are of course limitations. If, for example, a variable is predictive of a population, but a segment of that population is substantially lost due to systematic matching, there

Table 18.2 Data match rates.

Jewish	Matched		Total
	No	Yes	
No	302 752	66 374	369 126
	82.00%	18.00%	
Yes	7132	2110	9242
	77.50%	22.50%	
	309 884	68 484	378 368

may not be enough of that part of the distribution for the modeling technique to empirically establish a relationship. Worse still is the possibility that certain segments of a population distribution may be entirely missing due to extreme systematic match rates. And given related evidence that ignoring complex weights can yield significantly different results (Toth and Eltinge 2011), systematic matching might yield similar results. Later sections of this chapter include a brief match bias analysis to explore the extent to which systematic matching impacted the models.

18.6 Building Models

The general exercise of model building with large datasets is, in effect, to use one data source's variables to serve as independent variables with which to model a dependent variable from the other data source. This procedure can occur with either dataset serving either role; it all depends on the researcher's goals. Here, the goal was to score the full L2 dataset with a variable predicting whether a household is Jewish, using the self-reported data from the omnibus survey as the dependent variable.

We had to make several decisions about modeling: the first was model type. Three types were tested: CHAID, CART, and random forest, and each has relative merits. CHAID will grow trees until the data become devoid of significant interactions. Because overfitting can occur (whereby models attain high internal validity at the expense of external validity, see Breiman et al. 1984), many researchers now favor CART, and specifically CART with pruning procedures by which tree size is reduced to avoid issues in overfitting. A third type is random forest, which employs an ensemble method to aggregate different trees into an overarching prediction (Margineantu and Dietterich 1997). Overall, we tested CHAID, CART, and random forest, with pruning as a nested manipulation within the CARTs.

The second decision involved downsampling. Because being Jewish has a low-incidence prevalence (about 2–3%), running models with the full 66 484 cases would result in model decision points driven almost entirely by splits that would predict not being Jewish. On the other hand, downsampling is effectively throwing away good cases that could provide some further ability of the models to learn. Although a lack of downsampling will often predict all cases toward the predominant classification (non-Jewish), the specific probability of being Jewish should still often have variance. In short, if the population incidence of being Jewish is 3%, a model without downsampling could effectively indicate Jewish status based on a cut point of 0.03, not 0.5. To test the best approach, models were run at three levels of downsampling: none, a 3 : 1 ratio of non-Jew to Jew, and a full 1 : 1 ratio. I additionally tested models with no downsampling but a weight

Table 18.3 Downsampling sample sizes.

Downsampling	Non-Jews	Jews	Total
None	66 376	2110	68 486
3 : 1	6187	2110	8297
1 : 1	2134	2110	4244

applied to "prioritize" the outcome variable to a 50/50 distribution. Predictions based on these models were again manually set to cut points specific to the downsampling strategy, namely 0.031 for models without downsampling, 0.25 for those with a 3 : 1 downsample, and 0.5 for those with a 1 : 1 downsample (see Table 18.3).

CART and random forest models can be run to classify or to predict. In classification, the outcome variable is defined as a factor (nominal) variable, while in regression-based trees, the outcome variable is continuous (scale). CHAID models use classification outcomes only. CARTs and random forests were run with each type of outcome variable.

Fourth, half of the CART and CHAID models were tested containing a validation technique while half did not include validation. While we certainly do not recommend eschewing validation, we were curious as to the effects of forgoing validation in this specific application. Specifically, the concern was the 1 : 1 downsample model that contained only 4244 cases (see Table 18.3), which could result in limited ability to classify in great detail. Split sample (50/50) validation meant that only 2122 cases would reside in each of the training and test datasets.

A fifth test took all developed models and altered the cut point by which cases are predicted to be Jewish to a cut point that optimizes both specificity and sensitivity using the ROCR package in R.

Finally, we were concerned that two variables would dominate the models so we had to estimate that likelihood and what impact these variables would have. Specifically, the two variables in question were the already existing modeled Jewish estimate in the L2 data, and a variable that denotes whether the person has a distinctive Jewish last name (DJN). Given dozens of studies like the JCSMD, we know these two variables are highly correlated with Jewish status, and would potentially dominate any model (assuming even modest accuracy). Thus, we ran models both with and without each of these variables.

Overall, 368 models were run in total: model type (by pruning for CART) × downsampling × classification/regression × validation × cut point optimization × inclusion of the religion variable × inclusion of the DJN variable. The models were fitted on both the matched omnibus data and the JCSMD data.

18.7 Variables

The L2 dataset is a dataset rich with over 350 variables. Numerous considerations were involved in deciding which variables to include in the models. Many of these variables will likely have no predictive power on the dependent variable, and still others simply make no sense due to their repetitive nature, for example, geographical breaks by zip code, Congressional District, parish, etc.

The first step was to include available demographics: gender, race, number of persons in the household, gender of adults in the household (male only, female only, or mixed), marital status, presence of a child in the household, and dwelling type. Additional variables were political party affiliation, dwelling type (multi-unit, single, or other), estimated household income amount, homeownership, and voting history, specifically in the 2016 general election and the primary as well as in the 2014 general and primary elections. Also included were estimated home value and ranking of state affluence.

Additional variables in the L2 data were based on consumer behaviors and interests: dichotomous variables for gun ownership, veteran status, donated to animal causes, child causes, veteran causes, person has invested, donations made to wildlife causes, to the local community, cat ownership, dog ownership, other pet ownership, has a home office, interest in current affairs, in religious causes, the theater, in the arts, in auto work, in sewing, in woodworking, in crafts, in gardening, in home improvement, in domestic travel, in cruise travel, in auto racing, in football, baseball, basketball, hockey, golf, nascar, fishing, camping or hiking, shooting for sport, is a collector, is an art buyer, has donated to a charity, or has donated to an environmental cause.

In addition, since the L2 datafile has variables sufficient to identify Census block groups, data could be merged to the L2 file from the US Census Planning Database (https://www.census.gov/topics/research/guidance/planning-databases.html.)
The following variables were merged into the L2 data at the level of Census block group, and recoded into classes: urbanicity (terciles), rural status (terciles), incidence of Hispanics (quintiles), Caucasians (terciles), African–Americans (quintiles), American Indians (high/low), Asians (tertiary), non-English language prevalence (quartiles), no high school diploma (terciles), Spanish language (terciles), public assistance (terciles), and health insurance (quintiles).

18.8 Results

Before moving on to the full results of the models and their efficacy, we considered to what degree the preexisting L2 data is a useful indicator of Jewish persons. Table 18.4 shows that overall, 25% of those indicated to be Jewish in the L2 data

Table 18.4 Incidence and coverage, L2 religion variable.

	Omnibus	JCSMD
Self-reported Jewish	2110	123
L2 Jewish	3367	333
L2 Jew and self-reported Jewish	842	23
Incidence	25.0%	6.9%
Coverage	39.9%	18.7%

were found to be Jewish in omnibus data. Notably, this percentage is considerably lower in the JCSMD data, where only 6.9% were found to be Jewish. More so, while the L2 Jewish variable attains a 40% incidence in the omnibus data, it is only 18.7% in the JCSMD data. These differences are perhaps to be expected, given there are likely significant differences in the makeup of Jews in Detroit compared to Jews nationally.

Overall, 20 out of 368 models did not provide predictions because the trees failed to make any significant splits. All of these were CART models with pruning, all but four with no downsampling strategy, and all but four using a categorical outcome.

Models were assessed by ranking them by order of their ability to attain high specificity and sensitivity in both sets of data. These four rankings are explored individually, as well as clustered by metric (specificity or sensitivity) and data set, and overall. Overall, the random forests produced far superior models; the best-ranked 39 models overall were random forest. Fifteen models attained perfect predictions in the omnibus data, though in many cases, but not all, at the expense of sensitivity, as they attained sensitivity scores below the overall mean ranking. Some forests did extremely well with omnibus data but then performed poorly in the JCSMD data, though others did well in both.

Overall, models varied from 100% to 8% (an outlier, the next worst model was 36%) of correctly predicting Jewish status in the omnibus data. In terms of incidence, omnibus models ranged from a high of 100% to a low of 5.7%. Eight random forests attained near perfect (99.3% or higher) scores on both specificity and sensitivity in the omnibus data.

Within the JCSMD, results were more mixed: the best-performing models were a mix of random forests, CARTs, and CHAIDs. Specificity ranged from 88% to 0%; and sensitivity from 33% to 0%.

Given the number of models, the table of models and their outcomes are a useful data frame to explore potential significant results by the key variants of the modeling, such as downsampling and mode type. The overarching research question remains: What is the best combination of settings to develop a model identifying Jews? Again, it is not enough to predict Jewish status; it is critically important to maximize incidence as well. Developing a model with both high internal and external validity is also preferable. Internal validity equals success in the omnibus data, and high external validity equals success in the JCSMD data or in validated omnibus data. Thus, we focus on understanding the best model in the omnibus data alone, as well as in both omnibus and JCSMD combined. That said, rankings in the JCSMD data is of interest as a test "in the wild."

To assess the best models, classification is the best tool to use, specifically, CART. However, this exercise is different: here the sole purpose is to assess the best model, so no validation or pruning is needed. Rather, it is more important to grow large trees to allow for the assessment of many combinations of settings. As before, each model was ranked in order of its performance on a given metric, and mean rankings were used across dataset, by specificity/sensitivity, and overall. In short, the trees predict the ranking of the models, with varying model features as the predictors. As is typical of tree analyses, each branching is given a node number, simply in the order of the branching. Terminal nodes are nodes in which no further branching can be attained. Trees were allowed to grow to branch nodes no smaller than 15, though a minimum of 10 was tested as well, showing no difference in overall results.

Figure 18.1 provides the tree for the overall ranking of models. Nodes 5 and 6 are the terminal nodes for all random forest variables, and these two nodes were the two best overall sets of predictive models in the tree, as illustrated in the overall mean rankings in Table 18.5. The overall best model, node 6, contains 24 models, and the only prior split is on religion (with node 6 specifying that models are better when the religion model is included). No other features were found to split those forests into better performing forests (even when the minimum node size was set to 10).

To better understand the results of predicting overall rank, we used additional trees of each type of ranking. The first summative outcome presented on these trees is provided in Table 18.6, which shows the results of nine trees, each predicting rank, starting with overall ranking and then breaking down rank for the omnibus overall, JCSMD overall, incidence overall, coverage overall, and each of the four combinations of dataset and incidence/coverage. Table 18.6 specifically explores which features are most important in the models, using the normalized independent variable importance outcome of each tree. For the tree predicting overall ranking, model type was the most important variable, followed by religion at 54% the importance of model type. From there importance drops significantly for the next most important variable, sensitivity, at just over 7%. Table 18.6 illustrates that this ranking is not consistent across all models. Model type is the most important variable for many models, but religion, downsampling,

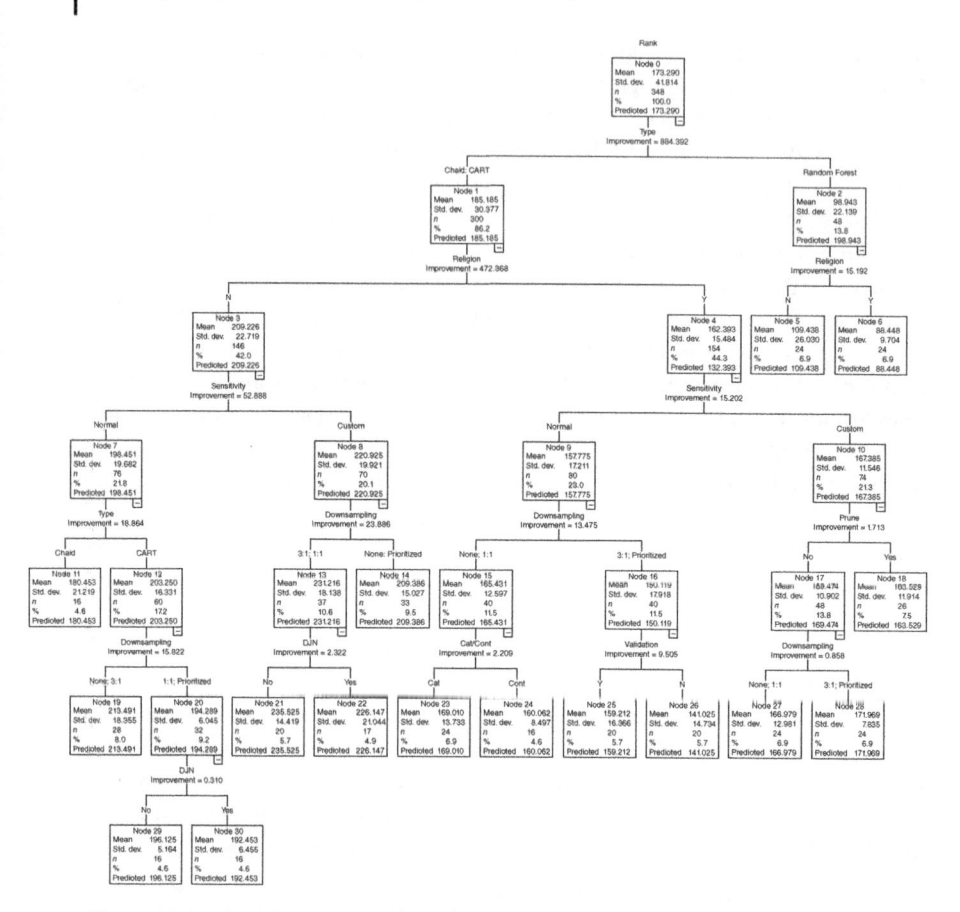

Figure 18.1 Tree of trees, overall.

and sensitivity also play significant and often predominant roles depending on the situation.

That said, when exploring the best node of each model, we found that random forest performs better than other model types, resulting in both superior and significant models. Table 18.7 illustrates that no matter what is being ranked, clusters of random forest models perform the best. Each of the highest-ranked nodes in Table 18.7 contains 24 models. With 368 models overall, the average possible rank is 184, and as illustrated in the table, the best-ranked nodes all perform substantially better than the mean. This is true no matter which ranking is tested. In addition to overall mean rankings of the best modes, Table 18.7 provides the splits

Table 18.5 Mean rank by node.

Node	Mean
6	88
5	109
26	141
25	159
24	160
18	164
27	167
23	169
28	172
11	180
30	192
29	196
14	209
19	213
22	226
21	236

that occurred in arriving at these terminal nodes. Although random forest was clearly superior overall, further splitting by religion improved rankings for four of the nine tests. Sensitivity was a significant split in seven of nine, but did not significantly lean toward a normal vs. customized setting. No other feature splits were found to consistently improve the models.

Overall, how do the best models fare in terms of incidence and coverage? The first decision is to define what is "best." Given that the models here are built with omnibus data, and that JCSMD serves are only a test, we should only determine the best models using omnibus modeling. That said, the 24 models in node 6 in the overall rankings test are the same 24 models in node 6 of the omnibus ranking, and 12 of these models are also in node 6 in the overall JCSMD rankings. Again as noted in Table 18.7, the difference is in the specific splits within random forests, in JCSMD data, which split on sensitivity rather than religion. The point here is that overall it is generally the case that the best models in the omnibus turned out to also be the best models in the JCSMD data.

Table 18.6 Adjusted importance measures.

Variable	Overall (%)	Omnibus (%)	Detroit (%)	Incidence (%)	Omni incidence (%)	JCSMD incidence (%)	Coverage (%)	Omnibus overage (%)	JCSMD coverage (%)
Type	100.0	100.0	24.0	29.4	75.8	2.8	44.8	100.0	27.2
Religion	54.0	55.4	100.0	100.0	70.8	98.1			6.0
Sensitivity	7.0	7.3	31.0	89.7	42.9	100.0	100.0	63.0	100.0
Downsampling	6.0	6.6	24.0	95.3	100.0	50.2	49.3	21.8	65.5
Validation	1.1	0.4	7.8	6.6			1.0	0.4	
DJN	0.3	0.3	3.1	4.7		5.2			1.8
Categorical/Continuous	0.2		2.4	1.5				1.8	
Prune	0.2	0.2			4.9	3.4	12.3	17.5	6.7

Table 18.7 Highest-ranked nodes.

	Type	Religion	Down-sampling	Sensitivity	Mean rankings
Overall	RF	Yes			88
Omnibus	RF	Yes			88
JCSMD	RF			Custom	83
Incidence	RF			Custom	45
Omni incidence	RF			Custom	22
JCSMD incidence	RF	Yes		Custom	40
Coverage	RF			Normal	19
Omni coverage	RF			Normal	6
JCSMD coverage	RF or CART	Yes	1 : 1	Normal	20

Table 18.8 provides results on the node 6 models that were best in the omnibus data. It is difficult to say that there is a model clearly superior to other models. Models 15, 18, 21, and 24 attained perfect or near perfect predictions in omnibus data, but subsequently resulted in the lowest coverage attained in the JCSMD data, though also a significantly higher incidence in JCSMD data than most other models. If we go simply by ranking, models 15 and 21 attain the best mean ranking on JCSMD data. However, these models cover only a small percent of Jews in Detroit. From a practical sampling perspective, it would be preferable to find more common ground across incidence and coverage than are furnished by these four models. Indeed, models 16, 18, and 22 are optimal at JCSMD coverage while still attaining relatively high incidences; while models 13 and 17 attain still higher coverage rates of around 40% in JCSMD data, though while attaining significantly lower incidences. Overall, while models 15 and 21 both attain perfect predictions in the omnibus data, their performance is less than desirable in the JCSMD data; whereas from this author's perspective, models 16 and 18 are the best models for JCSMD data.

These models vary in the features they employed. Models 15 and 21 both included religion; both did not employ any downsampling or prioritization; used a categorical outcome variable; and customized their sensitivity setting. Models 16 and 18 also utilized the L2 religion variable, did not use the DJN variable, employed customized sensitivity setting, and only varies by their downsampling strategy, with model 16 utilizing a 3 : 1 downsampling ratio and model 18 using the full sample but prioritized.

Table 18.8 Node 6 results.

Model	Omnibus coverage (%)	Omnibus incidence (%)	JCSMD coverage (%)	JCSMD incidence (%)
1	100.0	19.4	73.2	3.6
2	99.9	14.3	80.5	3.4
3	100.0	29.2	78.0	2.9
4	100.0	18.8	74.0	3.6
5	100.0	14.3	79.7	3.3
6	100.0	29.9	78.9	2.9
7	100.0	19.9	71.5	3.7
8	99.8	14.7	78.9	3.4
9	100.0	29.2	78.0	2.9
10	100.0	19.3	70.7	3.5
11	100.0	14.6	78.9	3.4
12	100.0	30.4	75.6	2.9
13	99.5	36.6	42.3	5.3
14	97.3	21.2	69.9	4.3
15	100.0	100.0	6.5	33.3
16	99.7	62.2	19.5	11.0
17	98.9	32.5	40.7	4.8
18	100.0	99.3	17.1	14.5
19	99.3	37.1	40.7	5.5
20	97.7	20.9	68.3	4.1
21	100.0	100.0	5.7	30.4
22	99.5	62.2	17.1	10.9
23	99.3	31.4	46.3	5.1
24	99.9	100.0	5.7	18.9

18.9 Considering Systematic Matching Rates

As noted earlier, cases that were and were not successfully matched to L2 data had a significant degree of difference. Differences in those matched and nonmatched are provided in Figure 18.2.

One principal difference was that older respondents were about twice as likely to match as young respondents. There were significant differences as well by race.

18.9 Considering Systematic Matching Rates

Significant Differences in Matched and Nonmatched Respondents

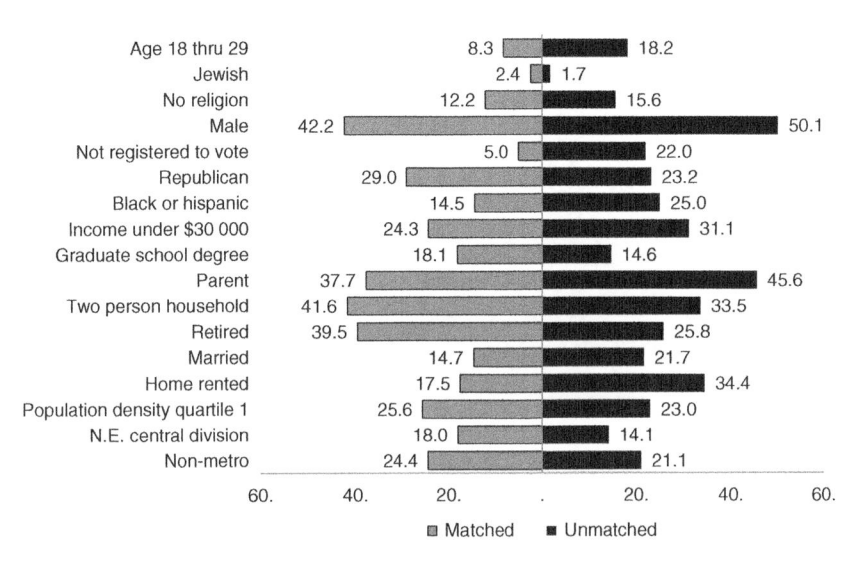

Demographic	Matched	Unmatched
Age 18 thru 29	8.3	18.2
Jewish	2.4	1.7
No religion	12.2	15.6
Male	42.2	50.1
Not registered to vote	5.0	22.0
Republican	29.0	23.2
Black or hispanic	14.5	25.0
Income under $30 000	24.3	31.1
Graduate school degree	18.1	14.6
Parent	37.7	45.6
Two person household	41.6	33.5
Retired	39.5	25.8
Married	14.7	21.7
Home rented	17.5	34.4
Population density quartile 1	25.6	23.0
N.E. central division	18.0	14.1
Non-metro	24.4	21.1

Figure 18.2 Demographics by match rates.

Though many other differences are apparent, age and race are likely the principal drivers of differences in marital status, number of persons in the household, and tenure, as well as religion, education, and income. Interestingly, Jews attained a higher match rate than non-Jews. This finding is not particularly surprising, however, given that Jews are much more likely to be registered to vote (Pew 2013: 84% for Jews, 74% non-Jews), and are older, more educated, and more affluent. These household and individual characteristics typically lead to higher match rates.

To assess the degree to which matching bias effects the modeling, we compared a full spectrum of Jewish identity measures. First, we compared the overall distribution of Jews from the omnibus against matched omnibus Jews, Jews from the L2 variable, and Jews from the best model predictions from the Section 18.7. As these models attained perfect predictions, we found no differences between the Jews matched and those modeled; the model and matched metrics in Table 18.9 are identical. The mean absolute bias (MAB) was calculated on 16 available omnibus demographics and then with the grand MAB for these 16 variables. Specifically, the point estimates for a given subset of Jewish (those matched, L2 Jews, and best model Jews) were subtracted from the weighted point estimates for all omnibus Jews interviewed over the five-year period of data used in this study. These differences for each point estimate within a variable (for example, differences in political affiliation were attained for Republicans, Democrats, and Independents) were then averaged together to attain a single overall MAB for each metric. Overall,

Table 18.9 Mean absolute bias of three Jewish variables.

Demographic characteristics	Matched (%)	L2 (%)	Model (%)
Metro status	1.2	4.5	1.2
Division	0.8	3.5	0.8
Home ownership	3.7	5.6	3.7
Number of adults	0.8	0.4	0.8
Parent	1.1	1.0	1.1
Political affiliation	2.5	8.5	2.5
Registered to vote	6.5	8.9	6.5
Gender	4.1	3.6	4.1
Age	1.3	3.2	1.3
Race	1.0	1.4	1.0
Income	0.7	1.6	0.7
Education	1.1	5.9	1.1
Employment	1.6	2.3	1.6
Marital status	2.2	3.9	2.2
No religion	1.1	1.8	1.1
Denomination	1.3	4.3	1.3
Total	1.9	3.8	1.9

the MAB for matched and modeled Jews was just under 2% (1.9%). Cases flagged as Jewish in the L2 variable attained a significantly higher bias at 3.8%.

18.10 Discussion and Conclusions

Given the "turn in nonresponse" in survey research (Pew Research Center 2012; Curtin, Presser, and Singer 2005; Dutwin and Lavrakas 2016), survey research has become increasingly, if not prohibitively, expensive. Survey researchers, by necessity, are pushed to find more and more efficient ways to effectively sample populations. And for surveys of low-incidence populations, these costs are compounded since nothing is more expensive and wasteful in survey research than screening out nonqualified households. Sample stratification has long been a staple in the toolbelts of sampling methodologists (Kalton and Anderson 1986), and given the cost of screening in low-incidence research, is in many respects an outright prerequisite.

18.10 Discussion and Conclusions

But many populations do not lend well to stratification. One might think, for example, of age, which from a geographic perspective can be almost fruitless to attempt to stratify. Depending on the type of geographic breakdown, stratification of many community-level variables, including educational attainment and income, is not effective (many zip codes, for example, have both high- and low-income neighborhoods). Although there is certainly variation by religion for many religious groups (e.g. Mormons in Utah or to a lesser extent, Jews in New York City), finding low-incidence populations for more specific, often smaller, geographies can be exceedingly difficult. To the extent that new sampling stratification opportunities present themselves, survey researchers will find valuable uses for them. Such is the case in Jewish research, where researchers commonly conduct surveys from synagogue lists and the like, but then find it truly challenging to interview Jews that do not show up on these lists. Typically, the cost per interview from such lists is under $50, while the cost to find Jews not on any lists can easily exceed $500 and even $1000 per interview; the lion's share of the cost is buried in screening. In these "residual RDD" strata, survey incidences of 1% or less, are not uncommon. Finding stratification opportunities within this residual RDD that can double the incidence just from 1% to 2% on average, can save thousands of dollars.

The random forest models (or more precisely, aggregation of models since random forest is an ensemble method) were far superior to CHAID or CART. This finding is not unexpected since random forest should be able to use its ability to learn across the 1000 trees explored in each prediction. But within the forests, it was unclear that any one model was superior to others. As reported earlier, models 15 and 21 both performed perfect predictions, but models 16 and 18 resulted in better on-the-ground performance in the JCSMD data. But again, in the building of the models with omnibus data, JCSMD results would be unknown. Since model 18 attained near perfect predictions in the omnibus data, and did fairly well in the JCSMD data, it is the best model overall (that is, with the advantage of "hindsight" in being able to explore JCSMD results).

It is important to note the significant degree of difference between prediction in the L2 data and the JCSMD data. In this situation, models may perform extremely well in training data but less efficaciously in real-world applications. But in this case, there is more to the story, if not a different story entirely. First, the L2 data served as both training and test, and in such conditions, the test data performed entirely comparably to the training data. So, in some sense, pound for pound, the JCSMD data should not have performed any less effectively than the test omnibus data. In each application, the models were applied to real-world cases, one to the omnibus data, and the second to the JCSMD data. However, some important differences exist between these data. First and foremost, the omnibus data is national, and the JCSMD data is specific to three counties: this difference has a range of implications. The distribution of Jews in Detroit may not be the same as Jews nationwide. And the results of the model were on par with the results of the preexisting L2 Jewish indicator, which similarly was found to be 40% predictive in omnibus data but only 25% predictive in JCSMD prediction, and worse still attained 19% coverage in the omnibus data dropped to just under 7% in JCSMD data. Those results compare with model 18 that was nearly perfect in both incidence and coverage in the omnibus data, and attained 17% and 14% incidence and coverage, respectively, in the JCSMD data. So the random forest models performed about as well in JCSMD incidence as the L2 Jewish variable but were about twice as effective at attaining coverage. Overall, the models are far more successful at correctly classifying Jews than the L2 Jewish variable is capable of alone. And in both cases, when a national model is built and then applied to a local application, as is now commonly said, your mileage may vary.

Of course, one may view the results of the models in the JCSMD data both pessimistically and optimistically. On the one hand, any researcher would like the predictive results in these data to match what was found in the omnibus dataset. But from a practical standpoint, these models afford a significant improvement over RDD. The end goal is to produce an indicator to increase the survey incidence over the population incidence, and these models can do so – perhaps not to the same degree as the omnibus results but still to a degree that greatly increases the probability of reaching Jewish households in surveys.

One can conceive of using local data to improve the predictive efficacy of these models. For example, in Jewish research, local information is often available, such as lists of synagogue members or lists of persons with likely Jewish last names. Such lists can serve as additional indicators to improve model accuracy. Additionally, for larger geographies, one could develop models specific to the geography in question, for example, in large metropolitan areas like New York City, Chicago, and Los Angeles.

Certainly an area of further research will be to explore more deeply the impact of matching bias and then specifically ways to mitigate against it impacting the results. More work is required to more effectively assess whether predictions can be improved with some match bias mitigation strategy.

Overall, the use of classification trees and machine learning applications like random forest offer great potential in developing models that predict low-incidence populations. There are many branches along the tree of decision-making in determining which settings maximize prediction and incidence. And one can make many choices in deciding which models work best; this chapter explains just a few of the choices and analyses. These models, warts and all, target populations significantly better than chance alone and can provide significant screening cost savings in survey research. The future holds even greater promise. With continued matching with other datasets or future years of omnibus data, the predictions of these models can improve and offer not just prediction at the household level but also perhaps estimation on a national scale and in certain applications, smaller geographies.

Big Data is not a replacement for survey research. Rather, survey research can play a crucial role and offer key data to enlarge the potential of Big Data. The exercise detailed here underscores the value of survey data and its potential power to develop effective models for large datasets, as well as to document many of the challenges and choices faced when endeavoring to blend these two data together.

References

Allison, P. (1998). *Multiple Regression: A Primer*. New York: Sage.

Allison, P. (2008). Convergence failures in logistic regression. *Proceedings of the SAS Global Forum, Paper 360*. http://www2.sas.com/proceedings/forum2008/360--2008.pdf (accessed 30 March 2016).

Breiman, L. (2001). Random forests. *Machine Learning* 45 (1): 5–32. https://doi.org/10.1023/A:1010933404324.

Breiman, L., Friedman, J., Stone, C.J. et al. (1984). *Classification and Regression Trees*, 1e. New York, NY: Chapman & Hall/CRC.

Buskirk, T.D. and Kolenikov, S. (2015). Finding respondents in the forest: a comparison of logistic regression and random forest models for response propensity weighting and stratification. *Social Science Open Access Repository*. https://doi.org/10.13094/SMIF-2015-00003.

Cairney, J., Veldhuizen, S., Vigod, S. et al. (2014). Exploring the social determinants of mental health service use using intersectionality theory and CART analysis. *Journal of Epidemiology and Community Health* 68: 145–150.

Cesare, N., Grant, C., and Nsoesie, E.O. (2017). Detection of user demographics on social media: a review of methods and recommendations for best practices. *The Computing Research Repository (CoRR), /abs/1702.01807*. Available from: https://arxiv.org/abs/1702.01807.

Curtin, R., Presser, S., and Singer, E. (2005). Changes in telephone survey nonresponse over the past quarter century. *Public Opinion Quarterly* 69 (1): 87–98. https://doi.org/10.1093/poq/nfi002.

Duffy, B., Smith, K., Terhanian, G. et al. (2005). Comparing data from online and face-to-face surveys. *International Journal of Market Research* 47 (6): 615–639.

Dumouchel, W. and Duncan, G. (1983). Using sample survey weights in multiple regression analyses of stratified samples. *Journal of the American Statistical Association* 78 (383): 535–543. https://doi.org/10.1080/01621459.1983.10478006.

Dutwin, D. and Lavrakas, P. (2016). Trends in telephone outcomes, 2008–2015. *Survey Practice* 9 (3): 1–11.

Hastie, T., Tibshirani, R., and Friedman, J. (2009). *The Elements of Statistical Learning: Data Mining, Inference, and Prediction*, 2e. New York: Springer https://doi.org/10.1007/b94608.

Kalton, G. and Anderson, D.W. (1986). Sampling rare populations. *Journal of the Royal Statistical Society: Series A (Statistics in Society)* 149 (1): 65–82. https://doi.org/10.2307/2981886.

Kershaw, T.S., Lewis, J., Westdahl, C. et al. (2002). Using clinical classification trees to identify individuals at risk of STDs during pregnancy. *Perspectives on Sexual and Reproductive Health* 39 (3): 141–148.

Lemon, S.C., Roy, J., Clark, M.A. et al. (2003). Classification and regression tree analysis in public health: methodological review and comparison with logistic regression. *Annals of Behavioral Medicine* 26 (3): 172–181. https://doi.org/10.1207/S15324796ABM2603_02.

Margineantu, D. and Dietterich, T. (1997). Pruning adaptive boosting. *ICML* 97: 211–218.

Morgan, J. and Sonquist, J. (1963). Problems in the analysis of survey data and a proposal. *Journal of the American Statistical Association* 58: 415–434.

Pennacchiotti, M. and Popescu, A.M. (2011a). Democrats, republicans and Starbucks aficionados: user classification in Twitter. In: *Proceedings of the 17th ACM SIGKDD International Conference on Knowledge Discovery and Data Mining*, 430–438. San Diego, CA: ACM.

Pennacchiotti, M. and Popescu, A.M. (2011b). A machine learning approach to Twitter user classification. In: *Proceedings of the Fifth International AAAI Conference on Weblogs and Social Media*, 281–288. Menlo Park, CA: Association for the Advancement of Artificial Intelligence https://www.aaai.org/ocs/index.php/ICWSM/ICWSM11/paper/view/2886.

Pew Research Center (2012). Assessing the representativeness of public opinion surveys. http://www.people-press.org/2012/05/15/assessing-the-representativeness-of-public-opinion-surveys (accessed 11 March 2020).

Pew Research Center (2013). A portrait of Jewish Americans. http://assets.pewresearch.org/wp-content/uploads/sites/11/2013/10/jewish-american-full-report-for-web.pdf (accessed 11 March 2020).

Ridinger, M. (2002). American Healthways uses SAS to improve patient care. *DM Review* 12: 139.

Rosenbaum, P.R. and Rubin, D. (1983). The central role of propensity score in observational studies for casual effects. *Biometrika* 70: 41–55.

Schonlau, M., Zapert, K., Simon, L.P. et al. (2003). A comparison between responses from a propensity-weighted web survey and an identical RDD survey. *Social Science Computer Review* 21: 1–11.

Simaki, V., Mporas, I., and Megalooikonomou, V. (2016). Age identification of twitter users: classification methods and sociolinguistic analysis. *Proceedings of the 17th*

International Conference on Intelligent Text Processing and Computational Linguistics (CICLing), Montreal, Canada.

Toth, D. and Eltinge, J.L. (2011). Building consistent regression trees from complex sample data. *Journal of the American Statistical Association* 106 (496): 1626–1636. https://doi.org/10.1198/jasa.2011.tm10383.

19

Artificial Intelligence and Machine Learning Derived Efficiencies for Large-Scale Survey Estimation Efforts

Steven B. Cohen and Jamie Shorey

RTI International, Research Triangle Park, NC, USA

19.1 Introduction

"End-product" analytic resources used to inform policy, and action must have rigorous statistical integrity. To achieve this goal, statistical and analytic staff devote substantial time and effort to implement estimation and associated imputation tasks, which are essential components of the end-product analytic databases derived from national or subnational surveys and related data collections. These efforts require a substantial commitment of project funds to achieve, and significant lag times often exist from the time data collection is completed to the time the final analytic data file is released. This chapter focuses on the development and implementation of artificial intelligence (AI)- and machine learning (ML)-enhanced applications to imputation for national surveys that achieve cost and time efficiencies while satisfying well-defined levels of accuracy that ensure data integrity. We emphasize enhanced processes as an alternative to manual, repetitive, or time-intensive tasks; operationalize decisions based on predefined outcome preferences and on access to input data that sufficiently inform the decisions; and facilitate real-time interpretation and interactions for accessing and acting on the AI-derived decisions so users can focus on higher-order thinking and problem resolution. Our approach includes the framing of predictions of criterion variables and their distributions as a multitask learning (MTL) problem. MTL jointly solves multiple learning tasks by exploiting the correlation structure across tasks. Consideration is also given to the application of random forest (RF) methods that use an ensemble of decision trees (DTs) to facilitate predictions.

To illustrate our approach, we provide examples with applications to national surveys, including the Medical Expenditure Panel Survey (MEPS), a large-scale

Big Data Meets Survey Science: A Collection of Innovative Methods, First Edition. Edited by Craig A. Hill, Paul P. Biemer, Trent D. Buskirk, Lilli Japec, Antje Kirchner, Stas Kolenikov, and Lars E. Lyberg.
© 2021 John Wiley & Sons, Inc. Published 2021 by John Wiley & Sons, Inc.

annual longitudinal national survey that collects data on health-care use, expenditures, payment sources, and insurance coverage for the US civilian, noninstitutionalized population. This research effort focuses on harnessing AI/ML techniques to yield MEPS expenditure data and estimates that are closely aligned with the actual results that require several months to produce and are provided in the MEPS final analytic files. The method performance is evaluated based on the medical expenditure datasets released as public use files, which are the reference standard in the evaluation phase of this study.

19.2 Background

Demand continues to grow for more timely, efficient, and higher-quality survey and statistical designs, data collection efforts, data analytics, products, decision tools, and more effective research efforts. To maintain a competitive stance and capacity, adapting to new technologies and approaches is essential. Thus, this research initiates the development of an infrastructure to stimulate the formulation and activation of AI-dependent disruptive innovations, to enhance and fast-track core estimation and imputation procedures. Rather than cover a wide range of applications at its inception, this activity focuses on imputation, an essential component of the development of analytic data files that yield survey estimates and research findings. When successfully completed, this effort can be appropriately scaled to enhance the effectiveness, timeliness, and/or efficiency of targeted applications.

The two core categories of AI caliber are as follows:

1. *Artificial narrow intelligence (ANI)*: The primary objective is to specialize in a specific area or task.
2. *Artificial general intelligence*: The primary objective is to develop a computer system that can perform general intellectual tasks that people usually perform.

This effort focuses on specific ANI tasks, supporting the integration of innovations in statistics, data-enabled science, and AI to develop unique optimized solutions to analytical problems and research efforts necessary to satisfy sponsor needs.

Our research intends to develop AI-derived processes that are an alternative to manual, repetitive, or time-intensive tasks; operationalize decisions based on predefined outcome preferences and on access to input data that sufficiently inform the decisions; facilitate real-time interpretation and interactions for accessing and acting on the AI-derived decisions so users can focus on higher-order thinking and problem resolution; and improve on, take to scale, or make less opaque new AI innovations.

19.2.1 Project Goal

Statistical and analytic staff devote substantial time and effort to implement the estimation and imputation tasks that are essential components of the end-product analytic databases derived from national or subnational surveys and related data collections. Sponsors demand rigorous statistical integrity in the end-product analytic resources used to inform policy and action. To achieve the targeted level of quality in the final estimation weights and imputation procedures for critical key analytic measures and other core survey data elements, a significant time lag occurs from completion of data collection to release of the final analytic data file.

Demand is increasing for fast-track preliminary/beta versions of the analytic file(s) generated from survey data. The survey estimates and preliminary analytic findings based on multivariate analyses conducted by internal research staff that could be derived by these early deliveries would provide analysts with invaluable insights as to the stability of prior trends or serve as bellwether alerts of likely significant departures/impending issues that could benefit from swift corrective actions. For this study, the national MEPS will be used as the platform for developing the AI solution(s) to generating the fast-track survey estimation and imputed analytic files. The primary objectives of this effort are to achieve reductions in time and cost for sponsor deliverables while achieving data quality standards.

Our research team has emphasized the imputation process for MEPS to fast-track the production of analytic files of acceptable levels of statistical quality and accuracy. For example, the current MEPS imputation process requires substantial time and resources to ensure that data quality thresholds are achieved. This project uses AI- and ML-derived solutions to determine whether the observed data and imputed data have acceptable quality to allow the overall process to proceed to analytic file production. These AI-/ML-derived approaches are specified to determine whether quality thresholds are achieved for the resultant survey estimates and, if not, to facilitate adjustments to the imputation process iteratively until acceptable accuracy in estimates is achieved.

19.3 Accelerating the MEPS Imputation Processes: Development of Fast-Track MEPS Analytic Files

This initiative component focused on accelerating the MEPS imputation processes to yield fast-track estimates that serve as early alerts to inform health policy efforts. MEPS collects data on health-care use, expenditures, sources of payment (SOP), and insurance coverage for the US civilian, noninstitutionalized population. The survey is sponsored by the Agency for Healthcare Research and Quality (AHRQ). Since its inception, MEPS data have supported a highly visible set of descriptive and behavioral analyses of the US healthcare system (Cohen, Cohen, and Banthin 2009). These include studies of the population's access to, use of, and expenditures and SOP for health care; the availability and costs of private health insurance in the employment-related and nongroup markets; the population enrolled in public health insurance coverage and those without health-care coverage; and the role of health status in health-care use, expenditures, and household decision-making, and in health insurance and employment choices. As a consequence of MEPS breadth, the data have informed the nation's economic models and projections of health-care expenditures and utilization. The level of the cost and coverage detail collected in MEPS has enabled public- and private-sector economic models to develop national and regional estimates of the impact of changes in financing, coverage, and reimbursement policy, as well as estimates of who benefits and who bears the cost of a change in policy (Cohen and Cohen 2013; Cohen and Buchmueller 2006).

MEPS is a family of three interrelated surveys: Household Component (MEPS-HC), Medical Provider Component (MEPS-MPC), and Insurance Component (MEPS-IC). MEPS-IC also collects establishment-level data on insurance programs. Through a series of interviews with household respondents, MEPS-HC collects detailed information at the individual respondent level on demographic characteristics, health status, health insurance, employment, and medical care use and expenditures. These data support estimates for individuals and for families in the United States. Respondents identify medical providers from whom they have received services.

The set of households selected for MEPS-HC is a subsample of 15 000 households/35 000 individuals participating in the National Health Interview Survey (NHIS). NHIS is an ongoing annual household survey of 40 000 households conducted by the National Center for Health Statistics, Centers for Disease Control and Prevention, to obtain national estimates of health-care utilization, health conditions, health status, insurance coverage, and access for the civilian, noninstitutionalized population. In addition to the cost savings achieved by eliminating the need to independently list and screen households, selecting a subsample of NHIS participants led to enhanced analytical capacity of the resultant survey data. Using NHIS data in concert with the data collected for MEPS provides greater capacity for longitudinal analyses not otherwise available. Furthermore, the large number and dispersion of the primary sampling units in MEPS resulted in more precise expenditure survey designs. MEPS-HC consists of an overlapping panel design in which any given sample panel is interviewed a total of five times in person over 30 months to yield annual use and expenditure data for two calendar years. These rounds of interviewing are conducted at about five- to six-month intervals. They are administered through a computer-assisted personal interview with a family respondent who reports for him/herself and for other family members. Data from two panels are combined to produce estimates for each calendar year. Westat is the data collection organization for MEPS-HC.

MEPS-MPC is a survey of the medical providers, facilities, and pharmacies that provided care or services to sample individuals. The primary objective is to collect detailed data on the expenditures and SOP for the medical services provided to individuals sampled for MEPS. Such data are essential to improve the accuracy of the national medical expenditure estimates derived from MEPS, given that household respondents are not always the most reliable sources of information on medical expenditures. MPC data are collected a year after the household health-care event information is collected to allow adequate time for billing transactions to be completed. MPC collects data on dates of visits/services, use of medical care services, charges, SOPs and amounts, and diagnoses and procedure codes for medical visits/encounters. Only providers for whom a signed permission form was obtained from the household authorizing contact are eligible for data collection in MPC. The categories of providers in MPC include (i) office-based medical doctors; (ii) hospital facilities providing inpatient, outpatient, and emergency room care; (iii) health maintenance organizations (HMOs); (iv) physicians providing care during a hospitalization; (v) home care agencies; and (vi) pharmacies. RTI International is the data collection organization for MEPS-MPC.

This effort focused on employing AI/ML techniques to yield imputed MEPS expenditure data that are aligned with the results that required several months to produce in order to release the MEPS final analytic public use files. We evaluated the method's performance based on the AHRQ-derived imputed dataset, which was regarded as the reference standard.

The evaluation was done in several phases:

1. Understanding the data
2. Attempting to reproduce the imputation strategy employed in prior MEPS cycles
3. Evaluating the performance of AI/ML methods
4. Enhancing the performance of the adopted AI/ML methods.

To initiate the development of the fast-track imputation estimation methodology for MEPS applications, we concentrated on the medical expenditures and associated SOP related to office-based physician visits experienced by the US civilian, noninstitutionalized population. The data were further restricted to visits that are not associated with a flat fee or capitation. In examining the current MEPS data, for the 2014 physician-based visits, we found that approximately 50% of the expenditure data were completely or partially missing.

The first phase of this effort to develop the fast-track imputation strategy required an initial imputation of the missing data using conventional imputation methods, such as weighted sequential hot deck (WSHD), which uses survey estimation weights to select donor records that adjust for the missing content in the recipient cases in cells where the donors and recipients share similar profiles on correlated factors (Cox and Cohen 1985; Cox 1980). This imputation method aligns the weighted distributions of the imputed data with the estimates obtained from the donor records (Iannacchione 1982; Andridge and Little 2010). Alternative imputation procedures included model-based and multiple imputation strategies (Rubin 1987; van Buuren 2018). Following the WSHD approaches used in prior MEPS expenditure imputation efforts, we conducted analyses to fit regression models to identify the most salient factors about expenditures for physician office visits (Zodet, Wobus, and Machlin 2007). These were important imputation class variables. The measures were prioritized via results from the regression models employed, then recategorized as necessary to define the final imputation class variables. We then applied WSHD imputation procedures to impute the missing payments based on the defined imputation class associated with the medical expenses. Finally, we compared the quality of the newly imputed data with the complete data and the existing MEPS imputed data via summary statistics and payment distributions.

19.3.1 MEPS Data Files and Variables

We downloaded the 2014 MEPS-HC data and office-based medical provider data from the AHRQ website at https://meps.ahrq.gov/mepsweb/data_stats/download_data_files.jsp. We then extracted person-level variables from the HC, including demographic, geographic, perceived health status, and insurance coverage variables. We extracted event-level variables from the MEPS event-level files, including test procedures performed at the visit, total charge, and various SOPs. The subset variables from the HC file were merged onto the medical event file by person ID (DUPERSID) to form an initial working dataset for subsequent imputation. In MEPS, an individual's medical expenditures for a given health encounter are decomposed into the 12 source of payment measures: (i) out-of-pocket payment (family); (ii) Medicare; (iii) Medicaid; (iv) private insurance; (v) veterans/Civilian Health and Medical Program of the Department of Veterans Affairs (CHAMPVA); (vi) TRICARE, formerly known as the Civilian Health and Medical Program of the Uniformed Services (CHAMPUS); (vii) other federal payment; (viii) state and local government; (ix) workers' compensation; (x) other private sources; (xi) other public insurance; and (xii) all other sources.

The sum of these SOP for a medical event constitutes the overall medical expenditure for that specific health-care utilization encounter. In addition to the sum of payments for a given medical event, there is an associated charge, which is often negotiated down by health insurance arrangements. In our modeling efforts, we used this related measure as a potential predictor of the respective SOP and over medical expenditure associated with that charge. In MEPS, this variable is imputed before directing attention to the imputation of missing values in the associated source of payment variables.

As indicated previously, we restricted our data to all respondents with positive weights (PERWT14F > 0), visits to physicians only (MPCELIG = 1), not a flat fee (FFEEIDX = −1), complete HC and MPC data, and fully or partially imputed data (IMPFLAG[1] = 1, 2, 3, 4). We considered only fully imputed medical expenditures on the public use files (where IMPFLAG = 3) for re-imputation in this analysis.

19.3.2 Identification of Predictors of Medical Care Sources of Payment

The variables required to implement the WSHD procedure are typically key predictors of the data to be imputed. Initially, we fit linear regression models to assess the association between the predictors and the outcome measure. The overall medical expenditure for medical events served as the outcome variable in the model, which is the sum of all individual payments from the 12 sources noted previously. Potential explanatory variables considered in the models were determined based on findings from previous studies, which include total charge; whether surgery was performed; any additional medical services; whether received anesthesia [ANESTH]; age, sex, race/ethnicity, region, insurance coverage status, whether covered by Medicare, Medicaid, an HMO, or by TRICARE/CHAMPVA; and perceived health status.

To account for the complex survey design, we ran PROC REGRESS from the statistical software package SUDAAN. Results from the regression models are shown in Table 19.1.

Data show that total charge and whether surgery was performed at the visit were highly correlated with the total payments ($p < 0.0001$). Other variables that were strongly associated with the total expenditure are some of the medical test variables relating to whether a procedure was received (e.g. EKG/ECG), whether anesthesia was received, and type of insurance coverage, including Medicare and Medicaid ($p < 0.05$). Sex and region were also significant factors at the 0.10 significance level.

---

1 Imputation status in the MEPS office-based medical provider visits data: 1 = complete HC data, 2 = complete MPC data, 3 = fully imputed data, and 4 = partially imputed data. Values 0 (not eligible for imputation) and 5 (capitation imputation) are not considered in this analysis.

Table 19.1 Linear regression of the overall sum of medical payments for visits to office-based physician providers, 2014 Medical Expenditure Panel Survey: β coefficients, 95% confidence intervals of β coefficients, and *p* values from the Wald *F* test.

Predictors	Visits to physician providers (MPCELIG = 1, n = 75 272, R^2 = 0.2021)		
	β coefficient	95% CI[a] of β	Wald *Fp* value (*df*)[b]
Event-level variables			
Total charge[c]			
$0.00–$76.38	0.00	—	<0.0001 (9)
$76.39–$105.00	24.95	[16.10, 33.81]	
$105.01–$132.00	40.38	[31.35, 49.40]	
$132.01–$159.00	53.69	[44.60, 62.78]	
$159.01–$195.00	64.54	[55.04, 74.03]	
$195.01–$235.00	78.75	[69.51, 88.00]	
$235.01–$300.00	99.67	[89.19, 110.15]	
$300.01–$425.00	130.40	[119.01, 141.78]	
$425.01–$879.20	216.20	[204.51, 227.89]	
$879.21–$271 000.00	977.20	[898.09, 1056.3]	
Surgery was performed			
Yes	263.51	[178.79, 348.22]	<0.0001 (1)
No	0.00	—	
Had an EEG[d]			
Yes	−15.92	[−207.1, 175.23]	0.8697 (1)
No	0.00	—	
Had an EKG[e] *or ECG*[f]			
Yes	74.35	[10.44, 138.26]	0.0228 (1)
No	0.00	—	
Had laboratory tests			
Yes	−6.42	[−23.11, 10.26]	0.4487 (1)
No	0.00	—	
Had a mammogram			
Yes	−5.45	[−35.26, 24.35]	0.7186 (1)
No	0.00	—	

Table 19.1 (Continued)

	Visits to physician providers (MPCELIG = 1, $n = 75\,272$, $R^2 = 0.2021$)		
Predictors	**β coefficient**	**95% CI[a) of β**	**Wald F_p value (df)[b)**
Had an MRI/CAT[g) scan			
Yes	8.64	[−99.33, 116.61]	0.8748 (1)
No	0.00	—	
Had other diagnostic test/exam			
Yes	13.36	[−9.94, 36.67]	0.2596 (1)
No	0.00	—	
Received anesthesia			
Yes	306.35	[78.22, 534.47]	0.0087 (1)
No	0.00	—	
Household component variables			
Age			
0–4	0.00	—	0.2124 (5)
5–17	15.60	[−8.85, 40.06]	
18–24	1.20	[−25.84, 28.24]	
25–44	−6.48	[−24.22, 11.27]	
45–64	6.34	[−9.92, 22.60]	
65+	52.10	[−11.65, 115.85]	
Sex			
Male	0.00	—	0.0829 (1)
Female	−16.07	[−34.26, 2.11]	
Race/ethnicity			
Hispanic	0.00	—	0.4036 (4)
Non-Hispanic white only	12.93	[−5.90, 31.77]	
Non-Hispanic black only	23.55	[−5.56, 52.66]	
Non-Hispanic Asian only	17.69	[−16.13, 51.52]	
Non-Hispanic other race or multiple race	20.32	[−9.09, 49.74]	

(continued)

Table 19.1 (Continued)

Predictors	Visits to physician providers (MPCELIG = 1, $n = 75\,272$, $R^2 = 0.2021$)		
	β coefficient	95% CI[a)] of β	Wald Fp value (df)[b)]
Region			
Northeast	0.00	—	0.0983 (3)
Midwest	7.31	[−15.04, 29.66]	
South	−15.53	[−34.18, 3.11]	
West	0.67	[−24.51, 25.85]	
Veteran status			
Yes	−11.21	[−38.45, 16.03]	0.4180 (1)
No	0.00	—	
Health insurance coverage			
Any private	12.20	[−23.96, 48.36]	0.5530 (2)
Public only	−1.66	[−49.46, 46.15]	
Uninsured	0.00		
Medicare			
Yes	−87.94	[−156.80, −19.11]	0.0125 (1)
No	0.00	—	
Medicaid			
Yes	−48.98	[−78.70, −19.26]	0.0014 (1)
No	0.00	—	
Covered by private HMO[h)]			
Yes	−5.79	[−27.50, 15.93]	0.5998 (1)
No	0.00	—	
Any time covered by TRICARE/CHAMPVA[i)]			
Yes	−30.19	[−74.72, 14.34]	0.1827 (1)
No	0.00	—	

Table 19.1 (Continued)

Predictors	Visits to physician providers (MPCELIG = 1, n = 75 272, R^2 = 0.2021)		
	β coefficient	95% CI[a] of β	Wald Fp value (df)[b]
Perceived health status			
Poor	−16.46	[−66.16, 33.25]	0.5146 (1)
Other	0.00	—	

—, Covariate reference level; CI, not applicable.
The 2014 office-based medical provider visits file and the full Medical Expenditure Panel Survey Household Component (MEPS-HC) file were downloaded from the following websites: https://meps.ahrq.gov/data_stats/download_data_files_detail.jsp?cboPufNumber=HC-168G and https://meps.ahrq.gov/mepsweb/data_stats/download_data_files_detail.jsp?cboPufNumber=HC-171, respectively.
This analysis was restricted to events where there was not a flat fee (FFEEIDX = −1), visits to physician providers (MPCELIG = 1), and respondents with positive weights who had completed MEPS-HC and MEPS Medical Provider Component data or partially imputed data (IMPFLAG = 1, 2, 4).
a) CI = confidence interval.
b) df = degrees of freedom.
c) The total charge (OBTC14X) was recoded into decile categories based on the data where FFEEIDX = −1 and IMPFLAG = 1, 2, 4; MPCELIG = 1; and PERWT14F > 0.
d) EEG = electroencephalogram.
e) EKG = electrocardiogram.
f) ECG = electrocardiogram.
g) MRI/CAT = magnetic resonance imaging/computerized tomography.
h) HMO = health maintenance organization.
i) CHAMPVA = Civilian Health and Medical Program of the Veterans Affairs.
Source: 2014 MEPS, AHRQ.

19.3.2.1 Class Variables Used in the Imputation

To reduce the number of imputation classes, we combined the medical test procedure variables to make a composite test variable. The insurance coverage variables were also collapsed.

Although veteran status was not significant and was not retained in the regression model selection for the total expenditure as the dependent outcome, it is a key variable in determining whether a payment should have been possibly received from veterans/CHAMPVA in the imputation. Therefore, veteran status was added to the list of imputation class variables:

1. Recoded health insurance coverage
2. Whether a payment was received from veterans/CHAMPVA
3. Total charge categorized by deciles
4. Whether surgery was performed

5. Whether a test or a procedure was performed
6. Perceived poor health status
7. Region

We used the following additional sorting variables for the implementation of the WSHD imputation methodology to help select the nearest neighbor as the donor in the HD imputation: total charge, continuous version, age, race/ethnicity, and sex.

19.3.3 Weighted Sequential Hot Deck Imputation

Next, we used PROC HOTDECK from SUDAAN to perform WSHD imputation for records whose data status was fully imputed in the MEPS dataset (Research Triangle Institute 2012). The imputations were implemented in imputation classes defined by variable combinations determined to be strongly correlated with the measures requiring imputation. Similar to stratification, imputation classes were specified to be internally homogeneous on the criterion measures, and records between classes should be as heterogeneous as viable. Data for donors and recipients were further sorted by the second-tier variables listed previously. When donors could not be defined in an imputation class, we collapsed imputation classes in the least important imputation class variable. For the MEPS data, we ran the following imputation scenario: using complete or partially imputed data as donors (IMPFLAG = 1, 2, or 4) and fully imputed records as recipients (IMPFLAG = 3).

To assess the impact of imputation on data quality, we compared estimates and distributions of medical expenditures at the following levels:

1. Overall, existing MEPS data vs. HD imputed data, for all records with IMPFLAG = 1, 2, 3, 4
2. Existing MEPS data where IMPFLAG = 1, 2, 4 (donors) vs. existing MEPS data where IMPFLAG = 3 (recipients)
3. Existing MEPS data where IMPFLAG = 1, 2, 4 (donors) vs. HD imputed data where IMPFLAG = 3 (recipients)
4. 2014 estimates vs. the previous year's estimates

19.4 Building the Prototype

We initiated the imputation process with 2007 MEPS data and compared it with the actual data on the final 2007 file. We assessed the quality of the imputation and implemented corrective strategies that achieved specified levels of alignment. Using 2012 as an example, levels of permissible variation in overall expenditures and SOP were initially determined based on the observed differentials in estimates between actual 2010 and 2011 MEPS data. We also compared the adjusted newly imputed 2012 data with the prior year 2011 actual data on overall expenditures and SOP to inform specifications for levels of permissible variations over time.

We repeated the process for the 2013 MEPS data and compared results with the actual data on the final 2013 file. We assessed the quality of the imputation and implemented corrective strategies that achieved specified levels of alignment. This knowledge of necessary additional adjustments to the imputation process is one of the additional adjustment strategies from which the AI/ML imputation procedures will draw, based on the patterns of missingness observed. The process was also implemented for 2007–2011 and 2014 MEPS data, and the AI and ML techniques employed will incorporate the prior knowledge acquired in improving the imputation procedures for all 2007–2014 MEPS data. We compared the quality of the newly imputed data with that of the complete data and the existing MEPS imputed data via summary statistics and payment distributions. The imputation process is summarized in the following section using the 2012 MEPS data as an example.

19.4.1 Learning from the Data: Results for the 2012 MEPS

The **first pass** used the standard HD imputation described previously. Results aligned well for overall payments, where the mean and total of the overall medical expenditures from HD imputation are quite close to the actual data. However, more effort is needed to improve the SOPs estimates. Most notable deviations observed from the actual imputed data on the public use file were for the following SOPs: family, veterans, other federal sources, and workers' compensation (Table 19.2).

A **second pass** was implemented building on the results of the first imputation: The top 1% of the WSHD-imputed source of payments, including family, veterans, other federal, state and local government, workers' compensation, and other private, were re-imputed using top 1% donors from the 2011 recipient data (i.e. the 2011 actual fully imputed data), and the total payments were adjusted accordingly. We imposed this strategy after observing that the overall distributions of the imputed SOPs on the 2012 MEPS public use event files for the recipient records at the upper tails of the respective payment distributions aligned much closer to the prior year's imputed recipient data than the donor records. Cases with values at or above the 99th percentile were included in the re-imputation dataset. However, if the 99th percentile was zero, only cases with respective values greater than the 99th percentile were included. Imputations were performed separately for each payment measure, and only the respective value was replaced in each imputation.

A **third pass** of the medical expenditure event-level imputations continued to build on the results of the second-pass imputation. The top 10% of HD imputed

Table 19.2 Means and standard errors of the medical expenditures of visits to physicians by existing data and first pass weighted sequential hot deck imputed data, 2011–2012 Medical Expenditure Panel Survey.

Expenditure	2012 Existing data (n = 107 659)			2012 WSHD[a] imputed data (n = 107 659)			2011 Existing data (n = 101 152)		
	Unweighted	Weighted		Unweighted	Weighted		Unweighted	Weighted	
	Mean	Mean	SE[b] mean	Mean	Mean	SE[b] mean	Mean	Mean	SE[b] mean
Amount paid by									
Family	22.79	25.73	0.69	29.28	32.10	0.73	23.15	26.15	0.79
Medicare	46.61	49.21	2.86	47.03	49.09	2.65	51.97	53.38	2.47
Medicaid	23.75	15.72	1.24	24.54	16.43	1.25	26.05	16.06	1.01
Private insurance	90.13	103.94	3.64	93.23	104.74	3.63	88.97	103.52	3.98
Veterans/CHAMPVA[c]	6.04	6.46	0.66	2.48	2.76	0.43	5.34	6.14	1.11
TRICARE	2.14	2.51	0.46	1.72	2.15	0.39	3.00	3.16	0.66
Other federal	0.44	0.33	0.08	0.05	0.03	0.01	0.54	0.40	0.10
State and local government	3.40	1.77	0.21	2.39	1.25	0.15	2.56	1.87	0.27
Workers' compensation	3.56	3.45	0.71	1.34	1.27	0.21	4.06	3.99	0.59
Other private	3.78	5.49	1.16	4.42	5.32	0.87	4.76	4.03	0.39
Other public	0.89	0.59	0.16	0.38	0.25	0.06	1.11	0.62	0.16
Other insurance	5.63	4.27	0.56	4.93	3.89	0.57	3.60	2.90	0.42
Total paid	**209.17**	**219.46**	**4.43**	**211.81**	**219.27**	**4.36**	**215.12**	**222.22**	**3.72**

a) WSHD = weighted sequential hot deck.
b) SE = standard error.
c) CHAMPVA = Civilian Health and Medical Program of the Veterans Affairs.
Source: 2011–2012 MEPS, AHRQ.

family payments from previous adjustment (i.e. top 1% of the initial HD imputed source of payment adjustments on family, veterans, other federal, state and local government, workers' compensation, and other private) were further re-imputed by considering the actual prior year (2011) imputed MEPS data as donors and implementing an inflator for increases in medical spending over time obtained from the Centers for Medicare and Medicaid Services' National Health Expenditure Accounts. A prioritization was made for the family payment component because it exhibited a larger departure from the MEPS imputed data and contributed a substantial amount to the overall expenditure total. The linked donor records for this imputation pass were identified based on values derived from applying a predictive model for family payments to the prior year imputed MEPS data subset. The record with the closest distance between the predictive values of a recipient from the current year (2012) data and the donor from the prior data was chosen as a donor for the current year. If more than one donor record was identified as having tie distance values, the average values of the actual donors' payment data were used as donor values. Table 19.3 summarizes the results, where the mean and total of the overall medical expenditures from HD imputation remain quite close to the actual data. We also saw notable improvements to the alignment of the source of payment estimates at this stage, particularly for family as a payer. Here, the overall mean family payment after third-pass imputation ($26.21) was more aligned with the actual 2012 and 2011 estimates (i.e. $25.73 and $26.15, respectively) than the first- and second-pass imputations (i.e. $32.10 and $31.12, respectively). Departures still exist for veterans/CHAMPVA as a payer.

19.5 An Artificial Intelligence Approach to Fast-Track MEPS Imputation

Armed with a better understanding of the nuances and impact of alternative fast-track MEPS imputation strategies, we then considered AI-/ML-type algorithms to estimate health-care expenditures for application to MEPS. Our predictor variables included basic demographic information, categorized insurance costs for the current year, and more than 80 condition and provider categories, listing medical conditions and provider variables. To tackle the large number of covariates and the highly nonlinear health-care costs, we used hierarchical statistical regression methods. We investigated the use of classification and regression trees (CARTs) and RFs to estimate unknown variables related to health-care costs for office-based provider visits (Breiman et al. 1984; Shah et al. 2014). We demonstrated that (i) ML approaches can approximate the standard imputation process in much shorter time; (ii) although ML algorithms

Table 19.3 Means and standard errors of the medical expenditures of visits to physicians by existing data and third pass weighted sequential hot deck/predicted mean matching imputed data, 2011–2012 Medical Expenditure Panel Survey.

Expenditure	2012 Existing data (n = 107 659)			2012 WSHD[a] imputed data (n = 107 659)				2011 Existing data (n = 101 152)			
	Unweighted	Weighted		Unweighted		Weighted		Unweighted	Weighted		
	Mean	Mean	SE[b] mean	Mean	Mean	Mean	SE[b] mean	Mean	Mean	Mean	SE[b] mean
Amount paid by											
Family	22.79	25.73	0.69	23.33	26.21	26.21	0.65	23.15	26.15	26.15	0.79
Medicare	46.61	49.21	2.86	47.62	49.92	49.92	2.72	51.97	53.38	53.38	2.47
Medicaid	23.75	15.72	1.24	24.81	16.59	16.59	1.24	26.05	16.06	16.06	1.01
Private insurance	90.13	103.94	3.64	94.31	106.52	106.52	3.62	88.97	103.52	103.52	3.98
Veterans/CHAMPVA[c]	6.04	6.46	0.66	4.08	4.47	4.47	0.42	5.34	6.14	6.14	1.11
TRICARE	2.14	2.51	0.46	2.39	2.80	2.80	0.41	3.00	3.16	3.16	0.66
Other federal	0.44	0.33	0.08	0.15	0.13	0.13	0.02	0.54	0.40	0.40	0.10
State and local government	3.40	1.77	0.21	2.63	1.45	1.45	0.15	2.56	1.87	1.87	0.27
Workers' compensation	3.56	3.45	0.71	2.79	2.76	2.76	0.30	4.06	3.99	3.99	0.59
Other private	3.78	5.49	1.16	4.16	5.19	5.19	0.87	4.76	4.03	4.03	0.39
Other public	0.89	0.59	0.16	0.45	0.30	0.30	0.05	1.11	0.62	0.62	0.16
Other insurance	5.63	4.27	0.56	5.41	4.34	4.34	0.58	3.60	2.90	2.90	0.42
Total paid	209.17	219.46	4.43	212.14	220.67	220.67	4.29	215.12	222.22	222.22	3.72

a) WSHD = weighted sequential hot deck.
b) SE = standard error.
c) CHAMPVA = Civilian Health and Medical Program of the Veterans Affairs.
Source: 2011–2012 MEPS, AHRQ.

are also limited by skewed cost distributions in health care, for a large fraction of health-care events in the population, we could predict with higher accuracy using these algorithms; and (iii) our methods can also be used to evaluate future costs for segments of the population with reasonably low error. Our analysis shows that RF is a promising method for predictive modeling, providing the best performance across a range of other regression methods we tried.

19.5.1 Why Artificial Intelligence for Health-Care Cost Prediction

Predicting health-care costs and conducting statistical analysis of health-care cost data are challenging for several reasons. A small fraction of individuals accounts for the bulk of population health-care expenditures in the United States (Cohen 2014). As such, medical expenditure data are characterized by highly non-Gaussian distributions, which are typically difficult to use with standard ML or regression approaches. The data exhibit a skewed distribution with a long right-hand tail and a large number of zero-valued elements. There are also significant correlations among the predictors.

MEPS final data are produced from more than 50 tables and 4000 variables. Processing involves the extensive development of constructed variables, coding of information reported as text strings, merging of matched health-care events and prescribed medications collected from medical providers and pharmacies, imputation for missing data, and weighting.

Additional challenges in modeling health-care costs include the following:

1. Medical billing technology has advanced over the years into a highly complex system that exhibits game theoretic aspects.
2. Negotiated rates between medical systems and insurers are unknown.
3. Eligibility expansion of the Medicaid and Children's Health Insurance Programs, with differential eligibility rules for children, parents, and nonparents.
4. Individuals can choose between comprehensive and high-deductible plans, and public plan options.
5. Levels of employer subsidization differ.
6. Tax credits and other subsidies are difficult to measure.
7. Copayments, deductibles, and other flat rates are dependent on multiple factors that highly influence the amount paid (Figure 19.1).
8. A bill may involve multiple visits over multiple years or multiple costs for the same visit.

A survey of the literature for algorithmic prediction of health-care costs revealed a bias toward multiple linear regression models and by rule-based approaches, which involve the incorporation of specific domain knowledge (Morid et al. 2017).

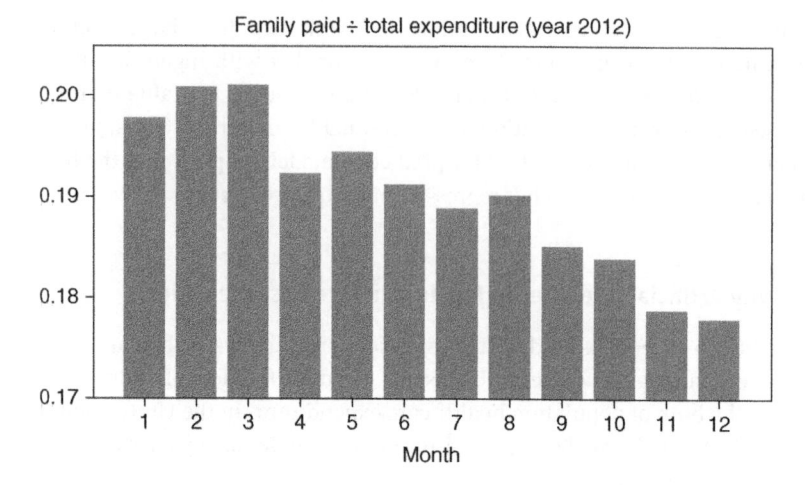

Figure 19.1 Family paid as a proportion of total expenditures (2012). Source: 2012 MEPS.

More recently, researchers have explored ML approaches like clustering and classification for this purpose.

Figure 19.1 displays the year/month effects on total out-of-pocket expenditures. The out-of-pocket percentage of the bill paid declines over the year, month by month. We hypothesize that this decline occurred because payers reached their deductible over the year and reached maximum out-of-pocket amounts. Any deductible and cumulative payment amounts were incorporated in the model.

In their comprehensive review, Mihaylova et al. (2011) outlined statistical methods to accommodate the skewness observed in health-care data, such as general linear models and Markov models.

19.5.1.1 Imputation Strategies

Over the last decade, researchers have developed various computational approaches to better deal with missing data. An ML approach to approximate existing imputation methods is difficult because of constraints in the form of edit restrictions that have to be satisfied by the data. Examples of such edits are known logical relationships based on *a priori* knowledge of the system (in this case, insurance) being modeled. Records that do not satisfy these edits are inconsistent and are considered incorrect. In some cases in the data, variables are derived from other variables, such as totals based on other variables. Designing an ML approach that factors in these edit restrictions is complex (Coutinho, de Waal, and Shlomo 2013; Kim et al. 2014).

Substantive and statistical staff at AHRQ applied logical edits to many variables before the datasets were available to the public. In some cases, missing values were imputed from other available data. AHRQ has developed standardized procedures for coding these missing values. One challenge is developing ML approaches that can approximate the procedures these experts use in cleaning the data.

As noted, MEPS expenditure data have used the WSHD method for imputation (Zodet, Wobus, and Machlin 2007). The method assumes a probability distribution for using donor i a certain number of times d_i (i.e. $\Pr(d_i = t)$ for $t = 0, 1, \ldots, n$). This probability distribution is based on the survey weights assigned to the units. The probabilities are chosen so that means and proportions estimated using the imputed data in well-defined homogeneous imputation cells will be equal in expectation to the weighted means or proportions estimated using respondent data only. The totals for the imputed data will generally not be exactly equal to known or previously estimated totals. For these data, which contain a mix of categorical and continuous data, we observed strong partitioning effects over the predictor variables, such that the values of the associated target variable are similar in these partitions.

Many works address aspects of using decision, classification, and regression trees to predict response propensities (Toth and Eltinge 2011; Toth and Phipps 2014; Buskirk and Kolenikov 2015). Regression trees have typically not been used for imputation because of the perceived instability of estimates derived from them and general bias against nontraditional methods. DTs make it difficult to calculate traditional metrics such as standard error, and no similar notion has been developed that is yet accepted by the statistical community. DTs have been applied to many large surveys including MEPS and the National Household Education Survey (Wun et al. 2004; Roth, Montaquila, and Chapman 2006). The US Census Bureau recently studied the use of CART as applied to the US Consumer Expenditure Survey and found that DTs compared favorably to likelihood methods, especially where the number of variables is large (Lohr, Hsu, and Montaquila 2015).

CART is a tree-based method most often used for classification or prediction. CART models exhibit more flexibility than other tree-type models in that they can be applied to categorical and continuous data (Breiman et al. 1984; Breiman 2001; Burgette and Reiter 2010). DTs are invariant under strictly monotone transformation of the individual predictors; they are robust to predictor outliers and often obtain good prediction results without needing extensive parameter tuning. DTs work by searching for precisely such groups; the algorithm aims to partition the predictor space into high-dimensional rectangles so that values of the target variable are as similar as possible. DTs have a great advantage in interpretability. The logic of how the predictor space is partitioned and the associated purity of all terminal nodes are easily assessed and examined. However, a major problem with DTs is their high variance. A small change to the input data could alter the series of splits in the building process, which in turn changes the interpretation of the overall tree, which could decrease the prediction accuracy on unseen data.

19.5.1.2 Testing of Imputation Strategies

Imputation strategies have different goals depending on the survey objectives. Hastie, Tibshirani, and Friedman (2009) discussed bias variance trade-offs in detail. For example, when individual data are released, such as in MEPS, preservation of these individual values is very important.

The following are examples of survey requirements used in selecting imputation methods:

1. *The ability of the imputation procedure to preserve the individual item values*: measured by calculating the (weighted) average deviation of the imputed data from the true data for continuous variables.
2. *The ability of the imputation method to preserve population estimates*: the average deviation of the mean and dispersion estimates based on the imputed data and the true data can be calculated for this purpose.
3. *The ability of the imputation procedure to preserve the distribution of the data*: assessed by comparing the Kolmogorov–Smirnov distance between the imputed and the true data.

19.5.1.3 Approach

Figure 19.2 shows the high-level research workflow. The first (and most difficult) step was preprocessing that included raw data extraction, attribute selection, and the creation of multiyear test and training datasets with a select set of pertinent attributes used in DT and neural network classifiers and K-means clustering models. The next step was to implement various modeling techniques in which we built, trained, and ran multiple models on test sets to get the results. Finally, we analyzed the model performance using relevant measures.

We first trained a DT, regression, and RF regression model. Of the three models, RF exhibited the best characteristics in initial tests. We followed ML best practice (e.g. using cross-validation for hyper-parameter fitting – to choose the number of estimators in the RF model) to predict total health-care expenditures and source of payment distributions based on historical and current expenditure data. The overall RF regression model, considering all utilization features, exhibits reasonable performance ($r^2 = 0.46$, nrmse $= 1.68$). When we examined an individual feature's predictive power (i.e. using one feature at a time to train the RF model), the amount of workers' compensation income and INSURC were relatively more important than other features in predicting a patient's total health-care expenditure.

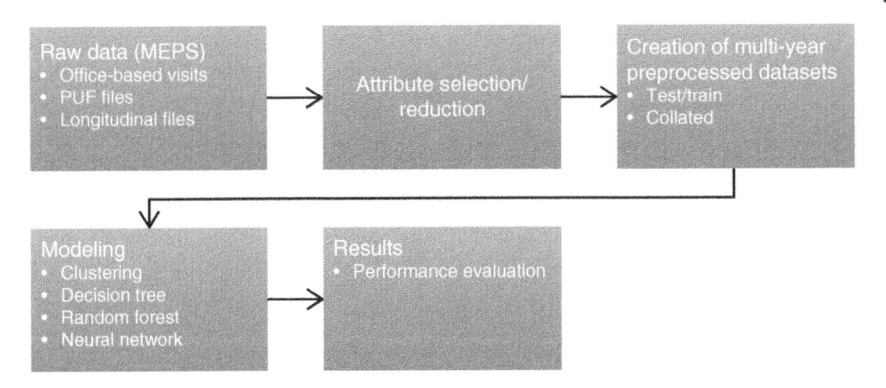

Figure 19.2 Research design. Source: RTI International.

19.5.1.4 Raw Data Extraction

The 2010–2015 MEPS database was used to collect the full-year consolidated data files, the office-based medical provider visit files, and the public use files from each year in the study. The ASCII format of the MEPS-HC full-year consolidated file for the US noninstitutionalized population in 2006–2015 is available. It is a large dataset with records containing 5255 columns that represent the values of 1823 variables. Adding to the difficulty, many of the variables represent values in different rounds or time-specific measurements.

We first developed software to automatically download and parse the codebook information and the data file, and we used the information to label data types for columns into Boolean, continuous, or categorical. For this part, we used a programming language, Python. Finally, we store the combined data file into a Python data frame object. Where possible, we converted data from categorical to Boolean unless the categories made sense as a continuous variable.

Person-level files: Each record in the person-level files represents a person and includes (i) demographic characteristics, such as age, gender, race/ethnicity, marital status, educational level, family relationship, and occupation; (ii) income variables; (iii) employment variables, such as employment status, hours worked, job tenure, wages, types of business, whether health insurance was offered, industry code, number of employees, union status, reasons for not working, job change status, paid vacation, paid sick leave, and pension plan; (iv) health status variables, such as overall physical and mental health status and activity and functional limitations; and (v) disability variables, such as work loss days, days missed from school, and days stayed in bed due to illness, are also obtained for each person.

Event-level files: Each record in the event-level files represents a unique medical event and includes characteristics associated with that event. In each of the event-level files, some respondents may have multiple events (e.g. more than one office-based visit), so they will have multiple records in the file. Each office-based provider visit record includes date of the event, type of provider seen, time spent with the provider, medical conditions (ICD-9/10 codes), type of care received, types of treatments (e.g. physical therapy, occupational therapy, speech therapy, chemotherapy, radiation therapy) received during the event, types of services received during the event (e.g. laboratory test, sonogram, ultrasound, X-rays), medications prescribed during the visit, flat fee, SOPs, total payment and total charge of the office-based event expenditure, and full-year person-level weight.

The data file contains a person weight variable that was used to derive national estimates to assess the prevalence nationwide. To obtain analytic variables, the records on this file were linked to the MEPS public use data files using the sample person identifier (DUPERSID). Information about health-care service utilization and expenditures associated with utilization events is collected during every round through the MEPS-HC component. Expenditures are defined in MEPS as the amount that was actually paid from all sources for care provided. Office-based and outpatient visits include visits to physicians and nonphysician providers (e.g. chiropractors, nurse practitioners, optometrists). For this study, we included only visits to physicians in the analysis.

We preprocessed the data by removing zero-weighted records, relabeling attribute values, removing highly correlated variables, and normalizing.

19.5.1.5 Attribute Selection

We reduced the original dataset containing hundreds of variables to a more manageable size. Based on a literature survey, we chose about 20 categories of variables from these classes of variables present in the MEPS-HC dataset, including the following:

1. Demographic variables
2. Health status variables
3. Income and tax filing variables
4. Veteran and workers' compensation status variables
5. Access to care variables
6. Employment variables
7. Health insurance variables

We selected our cost, demographic, expenditure, insurance, and clinical characteristic features from the combined merged datasets. Data from 2010 to 2015 were cleaned, and variable names were renamed (e.g. PERWT07F changed to PERWT) to be able to merge with other yearly files. Descriptive statistics were computed to

Table 19.4 General categories of variables used for this evaluation.

Income	Insurance
• Wage/salary • Unemployment • Worker's compensation • Interest, dividends • Business income, including farms • VA pensions • Private pensions • Alimony, child support • OASDI,[a] SSI,[b] welfare (TANF[c] and GA[d]) • Capital gains, tax refunds • Receipt of food stamps or other public assistance • Social Security Disability Income	• Monthly insurance coverage indicator for all classes of insurance • Medicare Parts A and B • Medicaid • Self-employed insurance • Union insurance • Workers' compensation insurance • State and local coverage • Other federal • Type of insurance: managed, health maintenance organization, limited • Prior year coverage variables • Employer establishment characteristics (type of business, numbers of employees, whether establishment offers health insurance as an employee benefit) • Characteristics of plans offered (type of plan, specific medical services covered, enrollment, whether plan was self-insured, stop loss coverage, administrative costs) • Deductible and coinsurance amounts, maximum coverage amounts, coverage of preexisting conditions • Total premiums (single and family coverage)

a) OASDI = Social Security.
b) SSI = Supplemental Security Income.
c) TANF = Temporary Assistance for Needy Families.
d) GA = general assistance.
Source: MEPS, AHRQ.

examine the data for out-of-range values. Frequencies, minimum and maximum values, means, and standard errors (continuous variables) for each of the variables were determined. Overall, 107 variables were used in the final set. Table 19.4 summarizes the general categories of variables.

The software developed uses the monthly insurance coverage variables to update each event in the MEPS medical office visits files iteratively. Additional variables were created to indicate the type of coverage during the month of the event. Additional health insurance coverage variables were created to represent cross-sectional (date of medical event) and full-year insurance status. Using a series of tests, we identified the following MEPS demographic variables as most relevant to insurance status: age, race (most significantly, identified as Native American), dependent status, family size, geographic region of residence, month, and reported health status.

19.5.1.6 Inter-Variable Correlation

The Spearman correlation evaluates the monotonic relationship between two continuous or ordinal variables. This value was calculated for the 50 most significant variables and used to remove highly correlated variables from the sample. The two-year panels were pooled by variable names common to all panels. The prediction process incorporated prior year variables of total expenditures. Where prior year cost data were used, we adjusted using historical medical cost data from the US Bureau of Labor Statistics (Table 19.5).

Some of the predictor variables may be correlated with each other (such as education and occupation). Therefore, multicollinearity between these predictor variables could be a problem. From the 718 variables, we performed a variable selection technique using Spearman's rank-order correlation to create a correlation matrix of all variables. We dropped variables with a high degree of correlation (>0.9) with others and retained the most salient predictors.

19.5.1.7 Multi-Output Random Forest

The prediction of medical expenditure composition can be framed as an MTL problem. MTL jointly solves multiple learning tasks by exploiting the correlation

Table 19.5 Medical component of the Consumer Price Index, 2004–2014, percentage change over previous year.

Year	Percentage change
2004	4.4
2005	4.2
2006	4.0
2007	4.4
2008	3.7
2009	3.2
2010	3.4
2011	3.0
2012	3.7
2013	2.5
2014	2.5

Source: US Bureau of Labor Statistics.

structure across tasks. We implemented a *multi-output RF* in Python as our imputation technique. RF builds on aggregating the prediction from an ensemble of DTs, and it has a proven record in survey data analysis (Buskirk et al. 2018). DTs are independently trained with a bootstrap sample of the training data, often referred to as the *bagging* technique (Hastie, Tibshirani, and Friedman 2009; Dietterich 2000a,b). Each tree is constructed in a recursive fashion. A subsample of the training data falls on a tree node, and a (possibly random) subset of the features is selected. Then, for each feature, the algorithm enumerates all possible splitting points (decision boundaries) and computes an impurity score based on the splitting. The impurity scores, usually the information gain or Gini score, reflect the homogeneity of the sample given the split (Dixon et al. 1987). The mean decrease in Gini coefficient is a measure of how each variable contributes to the homogeneity of the nodes and leaves in the resulting RF.

If the splitting condition is satisfied, the best split based on the impurity score will be executed, which makes the node a decision node; otherwise, the node becomes a leaf node. For multi-output, the impurity score is usually computed on a task-based fashion, then aggregated to make the decision. The final ensemble averaging step turns a swarm of diversified, potentially unstable, weak learners into robust strong learners. The impurity score, on which the splitting rule hinges, usually does not rely on a particular statistical model. This adds to the robustness of the multi-output RF model.

19.5.2 Evaluation

The *multi-output RF* model was trained on prior year MEPS data; we then estimated the values for the source of payment vector using a trained RF model. Then, we implemented this ML-based imputation method to correct for item nonresponse for the 2014 MEPS source of payment data. Next, we compared the MEPS source of payment estimates derived from this ML imputation strategy with the existing MEPS event-level expenditure data released on the MEPS office-based physician visit public use files to assess the performance of the methodology employed. The comparisons focused on the alignment of the source of payment and overall expenditure estimates for summary statistics, expenditure distributions, and model-based results.

Table 19.6 demonstrates the effectiveness of this imputation approach in yielding results comparable with those based on the detailed imputation procedures implemented in the 2014 MEPS for office-based medical provider visit expenditures. Results are well aligned for overall payments: the mean and total of the overall medical expenditures from ML imputation approach were quite close to the 2014 MEPS estimates obtained from the public use files. Similarly, the ML-derived mean estimates for the two largest payment sources for office-based physician

Table 19.6 Means and standard errors of the medical expenditures of visiting physicians by existing data and AI/ML[a] imputed data, 2014 Medical Expenditure Panel Survey.

Expenditure	2014 Existing data (n = 120 893)			2014 AI/ML[a] imputed data (n = 120 893)		
	Unweighted Mean	Weighted Mean	SE[b] mean	Unweighted Mean	Weighted Mean	SE[b] mean
Amount paid by						
Family	21.19	25.98	0.95	27.96	31.81	0.94
Medicare	54.72	57.30	3.04	55.81	58.59	3.11
Medicaid	30.32	18.88	1.08	29.48	18.46	1.00
Private insurance	75.59	87.02	3.35	76.31	86.88	3.24
Veterans/CHAMPVA[c]	6.71	6.48	1.13	1.87	1.51	0.43
TRICARE	1.94	1.99	0.44	1.77	1.79	0.37
Other federal	0.64	0.52	0.20	0.17	0.09	0.04
State and local government	3.04	1.82	0.34	1.79	1.20	0.17
Workers' compensation	3.37	2.37	0.34	1.59	1.18	0.15
Other private	4.58	5.21	1.09	5.03	5.33	0.99
Other public	0.56	0.30	0.05	0.56	0.35	0.05
Other insurance	3.67	3.00	0.43	3.04	2.61	0.32
Total paid	206.33	210.86	3.85	205.38	209.81	3.80

a) AI/ML = artificial intelligence/machine learning.
b) SE = standard error.
c) CHAMPVA = Civilian Health and Medical Program of the Veterans Affairs.
Source: 2014 MEPS, AHRQ.

events, private insurance and Medicare, close aligned with the final 2014 MEPS estimates derived by AHRQ. Although additional model fine tuning is needed for achieving closer alignment for family and veterans/CHAMPVA as SOPs, the aggregate impact of these components on total payments serve to counterbalance each other.

We downloaded the 2014 Office-Based Medical Provider Visits File and Household Component file from the following websites: https://meps.ahrq.gov/data_stats/download_data_files.jsp. Our analysis was restricted to data where weights are positive (PERWT14F > 0) and data that are completed and imputed (IMPFLAG = 1, 2, 3, 4), not a flat fee (FFEEIDX = −1), and visits to physicians (MPCELIG = 1). The AI/ML data were created by combining the ML-imputed data for cases where IMPFLAG = 3 with the original MEPS data where IMPFLAG = 1, 2, 4.

Table 19.7 Person-level comparison of percentage of the total expenditures and mean expenditures among the population between actual office-based physician visit event data and AI/ML[a] imputed data ($n = 21\,399$), 2014 Medical Expenditure Panel Survey.

Percentile	Actual data				AI[a] imputed data			
	Percent	SE[b] percent	Mean	SE mean	Percent	SE[b] percent	Mean	SE[b] mean
Top 1%	21.66	1.42	27 906	1234	21.68	1.46	27 621	1209
Top 5%	43.92	1.27	11 327	383	43.69	1.25	11 213	390
Top 10%	57.46	1.07	7413	213	57.19	1.06	7339	212
Top 20%	72.95	0.74	4704	115	72.77	0.75	4670	113
Top 25%	78.14	0.62	4032	96	77.99	0.62	4004	94
Top 30%	82.26	0.50	3538	83	82.12	0.51	3514	80
Top 40%	88.33	0.37	2849	63	88.23	0.38	2831	62
Top 50%	92.51	0.24	2387	54	92.42	0.24	2373	53

a) AI/ML = artificial intelligence/machine learning.
b) SE = standard error.
Source: 2014 MEPS, AHRQ.

We also assessed the convergence in the estimated medical expenditure distributions and their concentration between the fast-track and existing MEPS-imputed estimates. Table 19.7 demonstrates the convergence in distributional estimates of person-level medical expenditures based on the fast-track imputation strategy for 2014. Specific to the overall payment variable, we implemented this by calculating the distribution of total payments among the population. First, we aggregated the event payment data, restricted to not-a-flat-fee visits to physician providers only, to the person-level data. Then, using the weights, we determined the percentage of overall office-based expenditures attributable to the top 1%, 5%, 10%, 20%, 25%, 30%, 40%, and 50% of the population with office-based visits. In addition, we calculated the mean expenses for each of these percentiles and their standard errors. These results indicate that the estimated medical expenditure distributions and their concentration between the fast-track and existing MEPS imputed estimates have a good level of agreement. Note that the number of observations used for these estimates is generally less than the number of person-level records with positive weights from the HC file because they are only a subset of the event data that were restricted to not-a-flat-fee office-based physician visits in the fast-track imputation.

We also assessed alignment of statistically significant measures in analytic models predicting medical expenditures. Table 19.8 presents results of the fast-track imputation procedure applied to 2014 MEPS data comparing the correspondence of significant predictors of individuals with the highest 5% aggregated totals of medical expenditures for office-based physician visits. As shown, the β coefficients, their standard errors, and their level of significance derived from the fast-track imputations are aligned with those derived from the actual imputed data.

We downloaded the 2014 MEPS-HC data and MEPS-MPC data from the following website: https://meps.ahrq.gov/data_stats/download_data_files.jsp. This analysis was restricted to physician office visits only (MPCELIG = 1) where there was not a flat fee (FFEEIDX = −1), and all respondents had positive weights with completed or partially/fully imputed HC and MPC data (IMPFLAG = 1, 2, 3, 4). The comparison data for column "ML-imputed data" was created by combining the ML-imputed data for cases where IMPFLAG = 3 with the original MEPS data where IMPFLAG = 1, 2, 4. We then aggregated both event-level data to personal-level data for regression analysis.

This initiative demonstrated the capacity to reengineer the imputation tasks associated with the MEPS that often have taken more than six months to complete. The resultant methodology allowed accelerated production of the MEPS event imputation process in less than one-third of the time of the current processing. The following diagnostic criteria were used to assess the quality and accuracy of the imputation procedures:

1. Statistical tests were used to assess the convergence in the expenditure estimates between the fast-track and existing MEPS imputed estimates.
2. Statistical tests were used to assess the convergence in the estimated medical expenditure distributions and their concentration between the fast-track and existing MEPS imputed estimates.
3. Assessments of the alignment of statistically significant measures in analytic models were used to predict medical expenditures.

The results observed in our evaluations were of acceptable quality levels to support preliminary estimates. Furthermore, once the underlying methodology was developed, future applications of this medical expenditure imputation process could be implemented in a much shorter period, reducing the process to a matter of weeks.

19.6 Summary

This research effort was initiated to help facilitate the formulation and activation of innovations benefiting by advances in AI, ML, and predictive analytics to enhance and fast-track core estimation and imputation procedures. More specifically, our objective was to fast-track the generation of survey estimates from national surveys

Table 19.8 Logistic regression comparison for individuals likely to be in the top 5% of the total health-care expenditure distribution using the 2014 Medical Expenditure Panel Survey data restricted to office-based physician provider visits and AI/ML-imputed data ($n = 21\,399$).

Measures	MEPS actual data ($R^2 = 0.1201$)			ML[a)] imputed data ($R^2 = 0.1220$)		
	β coefficient	SE[b)] of β	Wald Fp value	β coefficient	SE[b)] of β	Wald Fp value
Age	−0.0013	0.0045	0.7719	−0.0008	0.0045	0.8494
Sex						
Male	0.0000	0.0000	0.0126	0.0000	0.0000	0.0619
Female	−0.2777	0.1103		−0.2050	0.1092	
Race/ethnicity						
Hispanic	0.0000	0.0000	0.7521	0.0000	0.0000	0.6647
Non-Hispanic white	−0.0424	0.1424		−0.0640	0.1494	
Non-Hispanic black	0.1070	0.1685		0.1145	0.1761	
Non-Hispanic other	0.0335	0.2231		−0.0172	0.2211	
Marital status						
Married	0.7912	0.2640	0.0045	0.7559	0.2610	0.0050
Widowed	1.2668	0.3508		1.2543	0.3473	
Divorced/separated	1.1008	0.3132		1.0481	0.3082	
Never married	0.8880	0.2720		0.8876	0.2753	
Younger than 16	0.0000	0.0000		0.0000	0.0000	
Family size						
One	0.0000	0.0000	0.1440	0.0000	0.0000	0.2149
Two or more	0.2414	0.1646		0.2077	0.1669	
Region						
Northeast	0.0000	0.0000	<0.0001	0.0000	0.0000	<0.0001
Midwest	0.5280	0.1568		0.4887	0.1580	
South	−0.3967	0.1312		−0.4679	0.1289	
West	0.0020	0.1466		−0.0057	0.1361	
Family income classification						
Poor	0.0000	0.0000	0.3635	0.0000	0.0000	0.1655
Near poor	0.1864	0.3322		0.1106	0.3381	

(continued)

Table 19.8 (Continued)

Measures	MEPS actual data ($R^2 = 0.1201$)			ML[a] imputed data ($R^2 = 0.1220$)		
	SE[b] of β	Wald Fp value	SE[b] of β	Wald Fp value	SE[b] of β	Wald Fp value
Low income	−0.0195	0.2046		−0.1103	0.1957	
Middle income	0.1956	0.1936		0.1852	0.1816	
High income	0.3088	0.2076		0.3258	0.2049	
Health insurance coverage						
Any private	0.3705	0.3416	0.5182	0.4464	0.3604	0.3963
Public only	0.2610	0.3220		0.2975	0.3380	
Uninsured	0.0000	0.0000		0.0000	0.0000	
Health status						
Excellent	0.0000	0.0000	0.0085	0.0000	0.0000	0.0166
Very good	0.4055	0.1818		0.3352	0.1744	
Good	0.6591	0.1821		0.5906	0.1732	
Fair	0.5461	0.2336		0.5254	0.2293	
Poor	0.6753	0.3085		0.5391	0.3023	
Limitation in activity						
Yes	0.0763	0.1907	0.6896	0.1414	0.1965	0.4725
No	0.0000	0.0000		0.0000	0.0000	
Cancer						
Yes	0.5212	0.1610	0.0014	0.4998	0.1650	0.0028
No	0.0000	0.0000		0.0000	0.0000	
Heart disease[c]						
Yes	−0.1347	0.1452	0.3546	−0.2026	0.1586	0.2030
No	0.0000	0.0000		0.0000	0.0000	
High blood pressure						
Yes	−0.2524	0.1312	0.0558	−0.2704	0.1308	0.0400
No	0.0000	0.0000		0.0000	0.0000	
Inpatient events	0.0676	0.0725	0.3524	0.0631	0.0710	0.3753
Number of prescribed medicine purchases	0.0029	0.0022	0.1769	0.0037	0.0021	0.0714
Number of ambulatory visits	0.1770	0.0075	<0.0001	0.1795	0.0077	<0.0001

a) ML = machine learning.
b) SE = standard error.
c) Heart disease was defined as "Yes" if a respondent had a diagnosis of coronary heart disease, heart attack, or other heart disease.
Source: 2014 MEPS, AHRQ.

before data collection completion and final analytic data file production while satisfying well-defined levels of accuracy and ensuring data integrity. This capability would (i) satisfy the demand from current and future survey sponsors for early alerts regarding new trends and unexpected findings; (ii) automate manual tasks by using input data and establishing predefined outcome preferences; (iii) permit the user to focus energy on higher-order problem resolution; and (iv) achieve gains in timeliness, cost, and quality in final survey products by the earlier identification and resolution of estimation and imputation issues that have surfaced.

MEPS served as the host national survey to develop and fine tune the methods necessary to yield gains in the efficiency and the timeliness of the release of preliminary survey estimates. To initiate the development of a fast-track estimation methodology for MEPS applications as a prototype, we concentrated on the medical expenditures and associated SOPs related to office-based physician visits experienced by the US civilian, noninstitutionalized population. Relative to overall MEPS medical expenditure estimates, nearly 25% of the total spending is attributable to this component of health-care utilization. In examining the more recent MEPS data, we found that approximately 50% of the expenditure data for the physician-based visits are completely or partially missing. The method's performance was evaluated based on the fully imputed MEPS public use expenditure datasets, which were regarded as the reference standard. The evaluation was done in several steps:

- Data transformation for compatibility with modern AI/ML tools
- Evaluation of the performance of alternative AI methods
- Modification of the AI/ML approaches to address MEPS estimation/imputation needs

Several national survey efforts comparable in scale, periodicity, and policy relevance to the MEPS have significant lag times from completion of data collection to release of the final analytic data files to the research community, policymakers, and the public. There is a clear benefit to survey sponsors for the production of fast-track preliminary/beta versions of the analytic files generated from survey data. The availability of preliminary survey estimates and analytic findings based on descriptive and multivariate analyses of these expedited data resources would provide the research and health policy community with invaluable insights. Specifically, these early deliveries could signal the stability of prior trends or serve as bellwether alerts of likely significant departures or impending issues that could benefit from swift corrective actions.

The fast-track hot deck and AI-/ML-based applications to the MEPS imputation process uncovered underlying structures to the final data on the public use files produced. The final results were achieved by a hybrid approach that combined statistical profile matching and high-level AI (RF)-based imputation. For several of the years under study, these fast-track imputation methods produced comparable survey estimates relative to those produced from the MEPS final imputed data, which we considered the gold standard. Consequently, these study results demonstrated the potential to reengineer survey estimation tasks that formerly took more than six months to complete to accelerate production to less than half the time and within acceptable quality levels to support preliminary estimates. The resultant preliminary data and associated analytical tools could then be made publicly available to the research community.

We presented our findings at several national conferences that highlighted advances in statistical research and survey practice: the Joint Statistical Meetings of the American Statistical Association, the annual meetings of the American Association for Public Opinion Research, the recent BigSurv18 Conference, and the AcademyHealth DataPalooza. At those meetings and subsequent briefings, leaders responsible for large national survey efforts in health, health care, education, and business were informed about this initiative's purpose and results. Project directors and data managers that we communicated with recognize that timely data releases would facilitate better policy formulation and practice. Such benefits could be realized by national survey efforts that are successful in fast tracking data releases to the public and the research community at large.

We encountered several challenges in our research initiative that needed resolution to complete the project. First and foremost was the acquisition of the essential expertise in AI and ML techniques that would help solve the analytical problems at hand. We benefitted significantly by having a large staff of data scientists within our statistical program and were successful in hiring a senior PhD computational scientist with expertise in AI. Another significant challenge was having the necessary substantive expertise to help select relevant predictive measures strongly associated with the criterion variables and the ability to discern resultant data anomalies and analytic results. Care in the selection of the host dataset for this project was also essential, with criteria that included strong substantive, analytical and substantive internal knowledge of the national survey, the inherent estimation and data processes, and the existing challenges confronting data production. Although several advances that our approach achieved to fast-track the imputation and data release strategies for the MEPS should be transferable to comparable initiatives, challenges similar to those we have confronted will be operational and will need resolution to improve the likelihood of a successful outcome.

Acknowledgments

Special acknowledgments go to Feng Yu and Georgiy Bobashev at RTI International for their contributions.

References

Andridge, R. and Little, R. (2010). A review of hot deck imputation for survey non-response. *International Statistical Review* 78 (1): 40–64. https://doi.org/10.1111/j.1751-5823.2010.00103.x.

Breiman, L. (2001). Random forests. *Machine Learning* 45 (1): 5–32. https://doi.org/10.1023/A:1010933404324.

Breiman, L., Friedman, J., Stone, C.J. et al. (1984). *Classification and Regression Trees*, 1e. New York, NY: Chapman & Hall/CRC.

Burgette, L.F. and Reiter, J.P. (2010). Multiple imputation for missing data via sequential regression trees. *American Journal of Epidemiology* 172 (9): 1070–1076. https://doi.org/10.1093/aje/kwq260.

Buskirk, T. D. and Kolenikov, S. (2015). Finding respondents in the forest: a comparison of logistic regression and random forest models for response propensity weighting and stratification. *Survey Insights: Methods from the Field, Weighting: Practical Issues and 'How to' Approach*. http://surveyinsights.org/?p-5108, https://doi.org/10.13094/SMIF-2015-00003.

Buskirk, T., Kirchner, A., Eck, A. et al. (2018). An introduction to machine learning methods for survey researchers. *Survey Practice* 11 (1): 1–11. https://doi.org/10.29115/SP-2018-0004.

van Buuren, S. (2018). *Flexible Imputation of Missing Data*, 2e. Boca Raton, FL: Chapman & Hall/CRC Interdisciplinary Statistics https://doi.org/10.1201/9780429492259.

Cohen, S.B. (2014). *The Concentration and Persistence in the Level of Health Expenditures Over Time: Estimates for the US Population, 2011–2012. Statistical Brief #449*. Rockville, MD: AHRQ http://www.meps.ahrq.gov/mepsweb/data_files/publications/st449/stat449.shtml.

Cohen, S.B. and Buchmueller, T. (2006). Trends in medical care costs, coverage, use and access: research findings from the Medical Expenditure Panel Survey. *Medical Care* 44 (5): 1–3. https://doi.org/10.1097/01.mlr.0000208145.39467.6a.

Cohen, S.B. and Cohen, J.W. (2013). The capacity of the Medical Expenditure Panel Survey to inform the Affordable Care Act. *Inquiry* 50 (2): 124–134. https://doi.org/10.1177/0046958013513678.

Cohen, J.W., Cohen, S.B., and Banthin, J.S. (2009). The Medical Expenditure Panel Survey: a national information resource to support healthcare cost research and inform policy and practice. *Medical Care Research and Review* 47 (7 Suppl. 1): 44–50. https://doi.org/10.1097/MLR.0b013e3181a23e3a.

Coutinho, W., de Waal, T., and Shlomo, N. (2013). Calibrated hot-deck donor imputation subject to edit restrictions. *Journal of Official Statistics* 29 (2): 299–321. https://doi.org/10.2478/jos-2013-0024.

Cox, B.G. (1980). The weighted sequential hot deck imputation procedure. In: *Proceedings of the Survey Research Methods Section, Houston, TX*, 721–726. Alexandria, VA: The American Statistical Association.

Cox, B.G. and Cohen, S.B. (1985). *Methodological Issues for Health Care Surveys*. New York/Basel: Marcel Dekker.

Dietterich, T. G. (2000a). Ensemble methods in machine learning. Presented at the International Workshop on Multiple Classifier Systems, Cagliari, Italy (12–23 June 2000). https://doi.org/10.1007/3-540-45014-9_1.

Dietterich, T.G. (2000b). An experimental comparison of three methods for constructing ensembles of decision trees: bagging, boosting, and randomization. *Machine Learning* 40 (2): 139–157. https://doi.org/10.1023/A:1007607513941.

Dixon, P.M., Weiner, J., Mitchell-Olds, T. et al. (1987). Bootstrapping the Gini coefficient of inequality. *Ecology* 68 (5): 1548–1551. https://doi.org/10.2307/1939238.

Hastie, T., Tibshirani, R., and Friedman, J. (2009). *The Elements of Statistical Learning: Data Mining, Inference, and Prediction*, 2e. New York: Springer https://doi.org/10.1007/b94608.

Iannacchione, V. (1982). Weighted sequential hot deck imputation macros. In: *Proceedings of the Seventh Annual SAS User's Group International Conference*. Cary, NC: SAS Institute.

Kim, H.J., Reiter, J.P., Wang, Q. et al. (2014). Multiple imputation of missing or faulty values under linear constraints. *Journal of Business & Economic Statistics* 32 (3): 375–386. https://doi.org/10.1080/07350015.2014.885435.

Lohr, S., Hsu, V., and Montaquila, J. (2015). Using classification and regression trees to model survey nonresponse. In: *Proceedings of the Joint Statistical Meetings, 2015 Survey Research Methods Section*, 2071–2085. Alexandria, VA (8–13 August): American Statistical Association.

Mihaylova, B., Briggs, A., O'Hagan, A. et al. (2011). Review of statistical methods for analysing healthcare resources and costs. *Health Economics* 20 (8): 897–916. https://doi.org/10.1002/hec.1653.

Morid, M.A., Kawamoto, K., Ault, T. et al. (2017). Supervised learning methods for predicting healthcare costs: systematic literature review and empirical evaluation. *AMIA Annual Symposium Proceedings* 2017: 1312–1321.

Research Triangle Institute (2012). *SUDAAN Language Manual, Volumes 1 and 2, Release 11*. Research Triangle Park, NC: Research Triangle Institute.

Roth, S., Montaquila, J., and Chapman, C. (2006). *Nonresponse Bias in the 2005 National Household Education Surveys Program* (Technical Report NCES 2007-016). U.S. Department of Education, National Center for Education Statistics. Washington, DC: U.S. Government Printing Office.

Rubin, D. (1987). *Multiple Imputation for Nonresponse in Surveys*. New York, NY: Wiley https://doi.org/10.1002/9780470316696.

Shah, A.D., Bartlett, J.W., Carpenter, J. et al. (2014). Comparison of random forest and parametric imputation models for imputing missing data using MICE: a CALIBER study. *American Journal of Epidemiology* 179 (6): 764–774. https://doi.org/10.1093/aje/kwt312.

Toth, D. and Eltinge, J.L. (2011). Building consistent regression trees from complex sample data. *Journal of the American Statistical Association* 106 (496): 1626–1636. https://doi.org/10.1198/jasa.2011.tm10383.

Toth, D. and Phipps, P. (2014). Regression tree models for analyzing survey response. In: *Proceedings of the Government Statistics Section*, 339–351. Alexandria, VA: American Statistical Association.

Wun, L.M., Ezzati-Rice, T.M., Baskin, R. et al. (2004). *Using Propensity Scores to Adjust Weights to Compensate for Dwelling Unit Level Nonresponse in the Medical Expenditure Panel Survey* (Working Paper No. 04004). Rockville, MD: Agency for Healthcare Research and Quality.

Zodet, M.W., Wobus, D.Z., and Machlin, S.R. (2007). *Class Variables for MEPS Expenditure Imputations* (Methodology Report No. 20). Rockville, MD: Agency for Healthcare Research and Quality http://www.meps.ahrq.gov/mepsweb/data_files/publications/mr20/mr20.shtml.

20

Worldwide Population Estimates for Small Geographic Areas: Can We Do a Better Job?

Safaa Amer[1], Dana Thomson[2,3], Rob Chew[1], and Amy Rose[4]

[1] *RTI International, Research Triangle Park, NC, USA*
[2] *WorldPop, University of Southampton, UK*
[3] *Flowminder Foundation, Stockholm, Sweden*
[4] *Oak Ridge National Laboratory, Oak Ridge, TN, USA*

20.1 Introduction

Conducting surveys in low- and middle-income countries (LMICs) is particularly challenging because many areas lack a complete sampling frame, have outdated census information, or have limited data available for designing and selecting a representative sample. Fortunately, with developments in geographic information systems (GISs), remote sensing, and machine learning, tools have emerged to disaggregate and update the distribution of census data to support survey sampling methodology and improve population estimates. In this chapter, we discuss the basis for these population estimates, scope, and limitations based on experiences in development of massive global population datasets and usage of these datasets as a basis for sampling design. We also present tools and approaches for using these georeferenced population estimates for complex household survey sampling (i.e. Geo-Sampling, GridSample R, and GridSample2.0). Finally, we discuss challenges with geographic population distributional assumptions within these georeferenced areas that are operationally relevant for conducting household surveys in LMICs, with approaches to help address them using deep neural network models, gridded enumeration area (EA) creation, and attempts to further improve both settlement layers and population estimates.

Big Data Meets Survey Science: A Collection of Innovative Methods, First Edition. Edited by Craig A. Hill, Paul P. Biemer, Trent D. Buskirk, Lilli Japec, Antje Kirchner, Stas Kolenikov, and Lars E. Lyberg.
© 2021 John Wiley & Sons, Inc. Published 2021 by John Wiley & Sons, Inc.

20.2 Background

Every country needs accurate population estimates because they support essential functions such as national and local policy development, service delivery planning for public and private sectors, investment planning, needs assessments, and distributing aid. Censuses and surveys have historically been the main approach for estimating population size, spatial distribution, and population attributes such as socioeconomic demographics. However, the cost of conducting a census presents a significant burden, and usually only conducted at 5- or 10-year intervals, with many developing countries struggling to secure the budget and resources needed even for a 10-year cycle.[1]

Although censuses are valuable and provide a snapshot in time of the population, they suffer from many problems. Because populations are dynamic, estimates from censuses are already outdated by the time data are processed and released. Researchers often resort to projection models to update population estimates between consequent censuses where the accuracy of the projection depends on sensitive modeling assumptions such as population growth rate. Furthermore, although census data provide high-level estimates of the population's spatial and demographic distribution, the scope of additional population characteristics reported in censuses is limited.

Surveys allow for a deeper dive into specific phenomena and characteristics of the general population or of targeted subpopulations. In addition, primarily because of advances in sampling design and weighting, surveys can provide representative estimates of a population in a more timely, cost-effective manner than a full census can. However, surveys often rely heavily on census information, such as population estimates, to create sampling frames and leverage sampling designs such as probability proportional to size (PPS). In many LMICs, where census data are outdated and sampling frames are incomplete, traditional survey methods relying on census data have been of limited use, hindering communities with arguably the most to gain from being represented in accurate, timely surveys.

To fill this gap, survey researchers working in LMICs have started adopting alternative population data, such as gridded population estimates (Fotheringham and Rogerson 1993; Tobler et al. 1997), to aid in sampling and weighting. Unlike census datasets that use EAs that rarely conform to the spatial extent of analysis regions required for actionable interventions (Goodchild, Anselin, and Deichmann 1993), gridded population estimates are reported in square grids (ranging from 1 km × 1 km to 30 m × 30 m) that are small and uniform enough to be analyzed. Additionally, gridded population estimates are more frequently and consistently

---

[1] For a comprehensive list of census dates, visit https://unstats.un.org/unsd/demographic-social/census/censusdates (United Nations Statistics Division 2019).

Table 20.1 Gridded population datasets.

Method	Name	Coverage	Resolution[a]	Years
Top-down direct disaggregation	GPWv4	Global	30″ (1 km × 1 km)	2000, 2005, 2010, 2015, 2020
Top-down informed disaggregation	GRUMP	Global	30″ (1 km × 1 km)	1990, 1995, 2000
	GHS-POP	Global	250 m × 250 m	1975–2015
	HRSL	18 countries	1″ (30 m × 30 m)	2015
Top-down complex model	LandScan Global	Global	30″ (1 km × 1 km)	1998–2017
	WorldPop	Countries on 4 continents	3″ (100 m × 100 m)	2010, 2015, 2020
	WorldPop Global	Global	30″ (100 m × 100 m)	2000, 2020
Bottom-up	GRID3	3 countries	3″ (100 m × 100 m)	Varying (ground condition)
	LandScan HD	23 countries	3″ (100 m × 100 m)	Varying (ground condition)

a) Because the gridded data are in a spherical coordinate system, cell widths decrease with the cosine of the latitude of the cell, but cell heights do not vary. Thus, the uniform area measurement of the cell is in arc-seconds or arc-minutes, and the area in meters or kilometers can only be approximated.

updated than most censuses and large surveys in LMICs (see Table 20.1). Although these datasets offer promise, few works are aimed at the survey research community that unpack the landscape of different gridded population datasets or discuss the challenges and advances in survey methods and field protocol for using these data effectively. This chapter provides a unified resource for understanding current gridded population datasets, their use in survey research, and promising areas of future work toward improved population estimates.

Section 20.3 includes an overview of popular gridded population datasets, common methodological frameworks for developing gridded population estimates, and a discussion of pros and cons worth considering for selecting a gridded population dataset from a survey perspective. Section 20.4 provides a more targeted view, focusing on survey methods that use gridded population estimates specifically. This section also highlights differences between census population estimates and gridded population estimates that may be relevant when planning data collection. Section 20.5 presents a case study of gridded population data and sampling methods in Nigeria. Section 20.6 ends the chapter with a discussion on future developments on gridded population datasets and how that may affect surveys in LMICs going forward.

20.3 Gridded Population Estimates

20.3.1 Data Sources

Data sources used to generate gridded population estimates are achieved either through total population counts such as census data disaggregated into finer geographic areas (top-down) or through aggregation of population counts from smaller geographic areas to larger areas (bottom-up) through micro-censuses, survey household listings, or small area estimation for targeted subpopulations (Janicki and Vesper 2017; Joyce and Malec 2009). Additionally, geographic vector data such as roads, water bodies, and building locations; satellite raster data such as temperature, elevation, and nighttime lights; and other modeled spatial data layers such as urban extent boundaries (Lloyd, Sorichetta, Tatem 2017) can be used to help predict population distributions at fine spatial resolutions. Table 20.1 highlights some existing gridded population datasets. Several gridded population datasets incorporate Big Data such as geotagged tweets or Facebook accounts (Facebook Connectivity Lab 2016; Patel et al. 2017) and mobile phone call detail records (Deville et al. 2014; Wilson et al. 2016; Lu et al. 2016) as other ancillary data.

Until recently, geostatistical techniques used to model gridded population data ranged in complexity from uniform disaggregation of total population counts (Doxsey-Whitfield et al. 2015; Pesaresi et al. 2016); to informed disaggregation of total population counts using areal weighting with ancillary data (Balk et al. 2015) to advanced disaggregation using complex models (Stevens et al. 2015; Dobson et al. 2000; Rose and Bright 2014; Azar et al. 2010). All of the aforementioned modeling techniques are considered top-down approaches because they involve disaggregating administrative area census population totals to smaller grid cells. All top-down gridded datasets are also "pycnophylactic" (Tobler 1979), that is, cell counts reaggregate to administrative area counts. Although top-down gridded population models may improve the relative distribution and detail of population totals within smaller areas, they are constrained to circumstances when the input population data and spatial covariates are reasonably accurate and detailed and cover the entire population. These conditions do not occur in data-limited settings in LMICs (e.g. Somalia, Democratic Republic of Congo, and Afghanistan).

"Bottom-up" modeling techniques are thus being developed to model population totals independent of census data. Bottom-up gridded population models combine population counts from a selection of small areas (e.g. micro-census) and spatial covariates to predict population counts in areas of the country where population was not counted (Wardrop et al. 2018; Weber et al. 2018). In combination with representative small-area samples of population data (Rao and Molina 2015), bottom-up approaches rely on highly resolved spatial constraints, such as building footprints or settlement areas to predict population where the total for any geographic area is unknown.

Rapid advances in remote sensing, machine learning, and the ever-increasing availability of high-quality spatial datasets continue to provide opportunities to improve global gridded population distribution databases.

20.3.2 Basic Gridded Population Models

The earliest gridded population datasets were based on top-down direct disaggregation approaches including simple areal weighting and a uniform distribution assumption where each cell was assigned the same population count within a census administrative unit (e.g. GPW; Doxsey-Whitfield et al. 2015). Basic dasymetric methods soon followed using one or two ancillary datasets, such as urban settlement area boundaries or landcover type, to inform the location and density of the disaggregated population taking into account the differential population density across urban and rural areas (e.g. GHS-POP [Pesaresi et al. 2016]; HRSL [2016]; and GRUMP [Balk et al. 2015]).

Areal weighting and basic dasymetric methods remain in use today, although when compared to actual population counts, areal weighting and basic dasymetric methods consistently produce less accurate cell-level population estimates than advanced dasymetric modeling techniques (e.g. LandScan Global [Dobson et al. 2000; Rose and Bright 2014], WorldPop [Stevens et al. 2015], and Demobase [Azar et al. 2010]), which exploit multiple covariates related to human activity.

20.3.3 LandScan Global

LandScan Global is a global population database depicting an ambient (24-hour average) population distribution. It was conceived as an improved resolution global population distribution for estimating populations at risk and has been updated annually since 1998. The LandScan Global methodology is a top-down approach, disaggregating subnational census information through a multivariable dasymetric modeling approach that exploits spatial data and imagery analysis technologies (Dobson et al. 2000; Rose and Bright 2014). A co-kriging model (Matheron 1979; Journel and Huijbregts 1978; Cressie 1986) is used to spatially disaggregate subnational census counts to approximately $1\,km \times 1\,km$ grid squares using ancillary datasets including land cover and land use type, slope, transportation networks, exclusion areas including water bodies and national parks, and settlement locations and extents. LandScan Global cell values are reported as integers with uninhabited areas represented.

Unlike other gridded population datasets that represent only residential population, LandScan Global data represent an average (i.e. ambient) population that integrates diurnal movements and encapsulates the range of human activity throughout a day into a single measure (Dobson et al. 2000). Because natural or manmade crises may occur at any time of the day, the purpose of LandScan Global is to develop a population distribution surface in totality, not just the locations of where people sleep (i.e. residential). In this way, LandScan Global data are analogous to mapping biological habitat where the species total environment (e.g. nests, feeding areas, travel pathways, density gradients, and boundary conditions) are considered. Although not specifically developed for household survey sampling, LandScan Global was used for this purpose for several years, especially in countries where other gridded population datasets were not available (Oak Ridge National Laboratory 2017).

Because LandScan Global is ambient, its use as a sample frame may result in oversampling residential populations in city center locations, although major differences might not be observed in rural areas far from cities where population density is not expected to fluctuate in a 24-hour period. Documentation and metadata that discuss attribute and spatial input datasets and their vintage are available; however, LandScan Global does not fit a single model globally. Instead the basic model is adapted to distinct geographic areas, accounting for cultural variations in the way people live and move. Thus, publishing the comprehensive LandScan Global model would encumber the annual update cycle of the dataset itself. Further, there are no ground truth data for ambient population counts in contrast to residential (e.g. census), which makes developing measures of accuracy challenging. For this reason, LandScan's internal accuracy evaluations have been against earlier, simpler methods developed by the US government to model global gridded populations between 1965 and 1995 (Dobson et al. 2000), but not other contemporary gridded (residential) population datasets.

20.3.4 WorldPop

WorldPop data are country-level datasets generated for most LMICs reflecting residential population in approximately 100 m × 100 m grid cells. The first WorldPop datasets – initially developed under separate AfriPop, AsiaPop, and AmeriPop projects – used a land cover-based dasymetric model (Linard, Gilbert, and Tatem 2011; Gaughan et al. 2013). By the time the three projects were being combined as WorldPop in 2013, the team had developed and adopted a new random forest modeling method with dozens of publicly available spatial covariates, including transportation network, infrastructure, rivers and water bodies, national reserve areas, slope, precipitation, temperature, and settlements that produced more accurate estimates than basic gridded population modeling methods (Stevens et al. 2015; Sorichetta et al. 2015).

Random forest modeling is a highly flexible, nonparametric ensemble machine-learning algorithm that grows a "forest" of decision trees during the modeling process (Breiman 2001). As a nonparametric model, datasets derived from random forest models reflect complex relationships between population and covariates without a priori assumptions. Further, the random forest model accommodates both continuous and categorical variables allowing many diverse covariates, and the model is capable of dealing with collinear covariates and nonlinear associations. The random forest model can only estimate population values present in the input census training data; thus, in countries with highly aggregated census data, a second country in the same region with more detailed census data may be included in the training model to introduce a wider, more realistic, range of population values that can be assigned to 100 m × 100 m cells in the country of interest (Gaughan et al. 2015). WorldPop data include metadata with links to publicly available input datasets and model prediction errors at the geographic scale of the training data (WorldPop 2017). The WorldPop model is also well documented and publicly available (Stevens et al. 2015). In early 2019, a new WorldPop Global dataset was released with annual estimates from 2000 to 2020 for the globe. The WorldPop Global dataset is built from a standardized set of covariates using a random forest model and includes a settlement growth model and age-sex structures.

With global settlement mapping not yet accurate enough to capture all small settlements and isolated residential buildings, WorldPop population estimates are modeled on a logarithmic scale, which produces nonzero population predictions for all cells with land cover. Consequently, a small fraction of the census population is allocated to uninhabited areas, for example in deserts and forests, where the estimated cell population might be 0.000 01 persons, but also where settlement datasets are not refined enough to be sure that all residential areas are captured. Such allocation may be problematic where the census administrative units used to train WorldPop models are both very aggregated and comprised vast areas of unsettled land. However, in evaluations, the use of random forest models with or without restriction to built settlements produced comparable results and more accurate results than simple allocation of populations to mapped settlements (Reed et al. 2018).

20.3.5 LandScan HD

Taking advantage of new technological and methodological advancements, the LandScan population distribution project at Oak Ridge National Laboratory

(ORNL) has continued to evolve over the last two decades. LandScan HD adapts population modeling methods developed for LandScan Global, settlement mapping research and production in high-performance computing environments, land use, and neighborhood mapping through image segmentation, and population density models that are specific to a variety of building uses (e.g. restaurants, museums, single family residential) and land use types.

ORNL is now taking advantage of the petabytes of very high-resolution satellite imagery collected every day, a highly effective approach for generating accurate human settlement maps. It allows for characterization of population from settlement structures by exploiting image texture and spectral features. Recent research using machine learning and high-performance geocomputation defined a new standard for rapid analysis of high-resolution imagery to map the spatial extent of human activity on earth (Graesser et al. 2012; Yuan 2018; Yang et al. 2018). These settlement structures and accompanying neighborhood segmentations are now the foundation for LandScan HD, where modeling is tailored to the unique geography and data conditions of individual countries or regions by combining social, cultural, physiographic, and other distinguishing geographic characteristics. Similarities are curated among these geographic areas to leverage existing training data and machine learning algorithms to rapidly scale development (Lunga et al. 2018).

Beyond the geospatial footprint of settlement features derived from imagery, the LandScan HD model also considers the spatial, temporal, and sociocultural variation of occupancy. A Bayesian learning framework, population density tables (PDT), probabilistically estimates ambient occupancy in units of people/1000 ft^2 for more than 50 building types at the national and subnational levels to provide global coverage (Stewart et al. 2016). These estimates of how people occupy various facility types worldwide are combined with spatial and locational data including the above-mentioned settlement structure data and neighborhood segmentations and points of interest (POI) data and other volunteered geographic information (VGI; Thakur et al. 2015) to establish bottom-up population estimates at the cell level.

As with all population estimates, LandScan HD has limitations in the quality and availability of input data used in modeling. However, the inclusion of very high-resolution settlement or building detection, at or near-native resolution of the input imagery used for derivation, significantly aids the population mapping problem in that the geographic area for which population must be estimated is substantially reduced. To date, LandScan HD has been completed in 23 countries in Africa, Asia, North America, and South America.

20.3.6 GRID3

Finally, the most recent bottom-up high-resolution population estimate is the Geo-Referenced Infrastructure and Demographic Data for Development (GRID3), which aims to support national sectoral development priorities, humanitarian efforts, and the United Nations' Sustainable Development Goals. GRID3 is a multicountry and multidonor partnership initiated in 2018 to produce bottom-up gridded population estimates to support national statistical agencies to plan census and supplement population estimates between censuses (GRID3 2018).

Using a Bayesian modeling framework, GRID3 integrates micro-census training data counts with a settlement type layer and other spatial covariates (e.g. schools, health facilities, and socioeconomic and demographic characteristics derived from demographic and health surveys such as household size) to predict population numbers in $100\,m \times 100\,m$ grid cells (Wardrop et al. 2018). These estimates are constrained to high-resolution maps of settled areas. To date, GRID3 micro-census data have been designed and collected for the explicit purpose of bottom-up mapping, collecting household and population counts in small areas sampled across settlement types and administrative regions of a country. The Bayesian modeling framework allows uncertainty to be modeled separately at the cell level, meaning that uncertainty estimates can also be calculated for any aggregation of cells (Wardrop et al. 2018). Larger uncertainty estimates occur when a particular settlement type has widely varying population density, or when the micro-census sample in a settlement type is limited. Because of the recent initiation of GRID3, its coverage is currently limited to Mozambique, Zambia, and Democratic Republic of Congo, although additional countries are expected to join the GRID3 project.

20.3.7 Challenges, Pros, and Cons of Gridded Population Estimates

The rest of this chapter focuses on four datasets: LandScan Global and WorldPop, which have been used as alternate population frame to a census in surveys, LandScan HD, and GRID3, which could potentially be used as population sample frames in the near future. First, we address the challenges faced during design and creation of these datasets and then we explain how they have been used as an alternate frame to census or to avoid full listing efforts in sampling for surveys.

One fundamental difference between these datasets is that each captures a different representation of population: WorldPop and GRID3 represent residential population locations, LandScan Global models daily ambient population including residents and commuters, and LandScan HD can be tailored to represent residential, nonresidential, or ambient population. Despite these differences, all of these datasets share some common challenges and potential opportunities for improvement.

One often undiscussed challenge with gridded population datasets is effective spatial resolution. In the development of top-down and bottom-up population layers, data inputs at varying resolutions are harmonized, both in the spatial components of the distribution model (e.g. infrastructure data, land cover) and the population count constraints (e.g. census or micro-census enumeration units). Thus, average covariate or population counts in a larger area may be used to model population counts in smaller grid cells. Furthermore, the various modeling techniques used to estimate population counts are based on different assumptions and parameters potentially yielding different results for a given cell (Stevens et al. 2015).

In addition to the modeling techniques, errors in top-down gridded population estimates are influenced by (i) inaccuracy of the input population data; (ii) the geographic scale of the input population data; (iii) the age, accuracy, completeness, and type of covariate data; and (iv) the geographic size of the output grid cell. Top-down gridded population datasets are usually derived from third-, fourth-, or fifth-level administrative units from the most recent census. As a general rule, the closer in size the input population data unit and output grid cell unit, the more accurate cell-level estimates will be. Thus, estimates in larger grid cells (e.g. 1 km × 1 km) will, on average, be more accurate in a given cell than smaller grid cells (e.g. 100 m × 100 m). However, smaller cells (e.g. 100 m × 100 m) are often needed for analysis and field-based activities in densely populated urban areas where 1000 people might occupy a single city block.

Top-down population estimates such as LandScan Global and WorldPop face two key challenges. First, the countries with the greatest need for gridded population data – where census or other official data sources are outdated, inaccurate, or highly aggregated – are the most challenging to generate accurate top-down gridded population estimates. Second, assessment of accuracy at a cell level for specific datasets would require a partial or full census, thus obfuscating the need for a gridded population model in the first place, and thus is never done.

Census-independent gridded population datasets may help to overcome errors related to outdated or inaccurate input population data. These bottom-up gridded population datasets are usually derived from a micro-census collected in areas roughly 3 km^2 explicitly for bottom-up mapping activities and are often close in size to the output grid cells and collected relatively recently. However, the distribution and number of micro-census units across settlement types can influence the accuracy of final estimates. Furthermore, like top-down gridded population modeling, the age, accuracy, completeness, and type of covariate data can also influence bottom-up gridded population estimates. Academic-government collaborations in Sierra Leone (Hillson et al. 2014), Northern Nigeria (Weber et al. 2018), and Afghanistan (Wardrop et al. 2018) have released a handful of ad hoc bottom-up gridded population datasets. Table 20.2 provides a side-by-side comparison of these four population frames reflecting availability, accuracy, pros, and cons of each dataset.

20.3 Gridded Population Estimates

Table 20.2 Pros and cons of three gridded population datasets for use as survey sample frame.

Name	Cell size	Pros	Cons
LandScan Global (Dobson et al. 2000)	1 km × 1 km	• Global coverage • All geographic areas are updated annually	• Represents an ambient rather than residential population • Grid size is often too large to use directly for analysis or field-based activities • Prediction error is not evaluated at either the scale of input population data or output
WorldPop (Stevens et al. 2015)	100 m × 100 m	• Prediction error is reported at the scale of the input population dataset • Provide a sufficient scale for analysis and field-based activities in densely populated urban areas • Represents residential population	• Prediction error is not available at the scale of output • Not constrained to built settlements
LandScan HD	100 m × 100 m	• Error estimates available at the scale of output • Provide a sufficient scale for analysis and field-based activities in densely populated urban areas • Represents residential and/or ambient population • Independent of outdated or inaccurate census data	• Error estimates are not available at the scale of output • This dataset is not yet publicly available
GRID3	100 m × 100 m	• Error estimates available at the scale of output • Provide a sufficient scale for analysis and field-based activities in densely populated urban areas • Independent of outdated or inaccurate census data	• This dataset is not yet publicly available

20.4 Population Estimates in Surveys

Conducting surveys in LMICs is often challenging because many areas lack a complete sampling frame, have outdated census information, or have limited data available for designing and selecting a representative sample especially in rural areas (Kalton 1983). To select a household survey from gridded population data, WorldPop and LandScan Global have been used as sample frames in 14 countries across Africa, Asia, and South America (Cajka et al. 2018), Nigeria (Chew et al. 2018), Iraq (Galway et al. 2012; Hagopian et al. 2013), Myanmar (Muñoz and Langeraar 2013), and subnationally in surveys in eastern Democratic Republic of Congo (Thomson et al. 2012), Kathmandu Valley Nepal (Elsey et al. 2016), and Chin State Myanmar (Sollom et al. 2011). The World Bank, World Food Programme, World Vision International, municipal governments, and academic teams have conducted dozens of additional unpublished gridded population surveys.

Gridded population datasets cannot be used in exactly the same way as census sample frames for household survey selection. This is because gridded population datasets are composed of cells each with a similar size and shape, and highly variable population estimates, whereas a typical census sample frame has units of different sizes and shapes, but each with a similar population total. Several tools and methods have been developed to feasibly use gridded population datasets as a survey sample frame. Two general approaches are available depending on the geographic size of grid cells. Groups that sampled from LandScan $1\,km \times 1\,km$ grid cells developed tools and methods to disaggregate high-population cells into smaller areas either manually (Muñoz and Langeraar 2013; Thomson et al. 2017) or automatically (Chew et al. 2018), while groups that started with WorldPop $100\,m \times 100\,m$ grid cells have developed tools and methods to aggregate low-population cells into larger areas before sampling or after sampling (Thomson et al. 2017). These approaches are discussed in detail below in Sections 20.4.1–20.4.4.

20.4.1 Standard Sampling Strategies

In standard sampling strategies, we start with a preexisting sampling frame such as the census or via area probability sampling methods if we do not have access to the frame or if an appropriate frame does not exist (Üstun et al. 2005). Sampling generally consists of multiple stages. The first stage starts with creating a list of primary sampling units (PSUs), which are usually administrative units or census EAs from the last census (UNSD 2005; ICF International 2012). Using a probability sampling method, we then select a sample of PSUs. If the PSUs have large populations, smaller units called secondary sampling units (SSUs) may be identified and sampled to avoid high levels of clustering in the sample or for manageable field work logistics. SSUs might consist of smaller administrative units such as districts or census EAs containing housing units (Moser and Kalton 1971; Häder and Gabler 2003; Kish 1994).

Once the last stage of sampling clusters is completed, we generate the final frame, or a full list of households, for screening or random selection. With the lack of a complete and detailed frame at such lower stages of sampling, the standard strategies include listing and random walks. The choice of strategy is driven by the need for uncertainty estimates, cost, and time available. Listing entails a census of households within the cluster, a time- and resource-intensive activity that allows the use of sample probability weights to calculate uncertainty around estimates and adjust for nonresponse (O'Muircheartaigh, Eckman, and Weiss 2002). Meanwhile, random walks represent a quick, less expensive alternative where field staff are given a set of starting points using landmarks, a direction, and a step size to identify households following field rules. Listing is considered the gold standard, yet it could still suffer from main street bias and missing some of the units (Lepkowski 2005). Random walks are known to suffer from bias and do not provide sufficient information for sample weight adjustments (Bauer 2016).

20.4.2 Gridded Population Sampling from 1 km × 1 km Grid Cells

Muñoz and Langeraar suggested manual segmentation of LandScan grid cells into areas of approximately 100 households based on high-resolution satellite imagery (Muñoz and Langeraar 2013); however, this approach requires a tremendous time investment for a tedious task that is both difficult (in counting buildings) and highly subjective (in judging which buildings are residential and number of households per building). Thomson et al. (2012) used a much less time-consuming, but still subjective, method to manually delineate clusters of approximately 40 nearest, accessible households to a point location within a LandScan grid cell. Object detection techniques have been used to automate the identification and extraction of buildings from aerial imagery (Amer et al. 2016) and use of drone imagery whenever possible to enhance the capability of extracting field information for listing and sampling (Amer et al. 2016). Thus far, because of the lack of easy unbiased methodologies to divide geography into areas with equal population size, an alternate way is to divide the area into standard size grid cells and use the population size within these grids for sampling weights in the analysis to account for varying density across grid cells, as discussed in Section 20.4.2.1.

20.4.2.1 Geosampling

Geosampling is a probability-based, gridded population sampling method that addresses some of these issues by using GIS tools to create logistically manageable area units for sampling. GIS grid cells are overlaid to partition a country's existing administrative boundaries into 1 km × 1 km primary grid cells, which are further divided into area units – secondary grid cells – that vary in size from 50 m × 50 m to 150 m × 150 m depending on density estimate from LandScan population estimates (Cajka et al. 2018). Once smaller grid cells are selected in the sample, a census of all households within these secondary grid cells is conducted.

This strategy allows more accurate population estimates within the smaller grid cells and use of the weights to generalize to the larger population. The accuracy of the estimates at the smaller grid cells stems from areas that are clearly delineated geographically and manageable by the field staff with information about geolocations captured to validate field work and conduct quality assurance steps.

Furthermore, additional efforts have been conducted toward operational improvements of geosampling and automation of the process to the extent possible. Because geosampling was developed using LandScan Global for gridded population data with 1 km × 1 km cells, additional modifications and quality procedures were required to effectively implement data collection at the secondary grid cells where households were sampled. For example, to avoid sending interviewers to unoccupied areas, researchers visually inspected aerial images of secondary grid cells to determine if the area was residential or nonresidential prior to field work. Because this process of manually classifying sampling units can be labor intensive, is prone to human error, and can create the need for simplifying assumptions during calculation of design-based sampling weights, Chew et al. (2018) developed deep learning classification models to predict whether aerial images are residential or nonresidential at accuracies comparable to a human-level baseline. Although the study only developed models for Guatemala and Nigeria, the authors' findings suggest that by adopting a transfer learning approach, similar models can work well in other areas with relatively modest amounts of new training data.

Additionally, to create units that are operationally relevant for conducting household surveys in LMICs, sometimes population estimates and household counts are needed at areas smaller than typically found in gridded population datasets with a global coverage. To further enhance geosampling, machine learning models designed for object detection tasks were developed to identify and count the number of structures per grid cell, to use these counts as a proxy for soft population estimates (Amer et al. 2016). Sampling buildings within smaller grid cells, rather than covering all households within the original sampled cells, will lead to lower levels of clustering. In this case, the size of the cluster is estimated through the number of buildings detected within each of the grid cells, the approximate building footprint for detected structures, and assumptions about the average number of households per building, allowing for the use of PPS sampling and enhanced calculation of weights (Brewer and Hanif 2013; Unangst and Amer 2017; Valliant and Dever 2017).

20.4.3 Gridded Population Sampling from 100 m × 100 m Grid Cells

In many cities, 100 m × 100 m cells are approximately the size of a city block and thus can be feasibly used as a smallest geographic unit. However, when starting with 100 m × 100 m grid cells, the key issue is to find methods to combine grid cells into larger sampling units as shown in two GridSample tools below.

20.4.3.1 GridSample R Package

The GridSample R package is a free, publicly available tool in comprehensive r archive network (CRAN; http://cran.r-project.org) for selecting sampling areas for household probability surveys (Thomson et al. 2018). The package is also described in a paper to guide users to selects clusters (i.e. PSUs) from any specified gridded population dataset and survey coverage boundary (Thomson et al. 2017). The GridSample R package uses several libraries including *rgdal* and *raster* to sample with common complex household survey design features including probability proportionate to estimated size (PPES) sampling with serpentine selection of cells, stratification with equal allocation, and oversampling in urban populations (ICF International 2012; Kalton 1983). The GridSample R package offers an additional feature to oversample in space that may be useful to improve small area estimates derived from household survey data (Gething et al. 2015). In the algorithm, the user selects whether to treat cells as clusters, or whether to "grow" clusters after sample selection by adding neighboring cells until population and area thresholds are met (Thomson et al. 2017).

A proxy sample weight could be calculated using the population estimate of the final grown cluster; however, the proxy weight will be biased if the population in initial "seed" cell is much smaller than the population in the final "grown" cluster. Instead, adaptive design-based sample weights can be calculated for the grown clusters (e.g. Thompson 1991).

Although free and publicly available, the GridSample R package requires survey planners to use R programming language. Furthermore, use of a detailed gridded population sample frame for a large coverage area (e.g. the country of Brazil, Democratic Republic of Congo, or India) will max out the RAM on any personal computer. Thus, the R package is best used in surveys with a smaller coverage area, and by survey planners with intermediate programming skills.

20.4.3.2 GridSample2.0 and www.GridSample.org

GridSample2.0 is an optimized algorithm developed in Python programming language that gives users the features available in the GridSample R package (e.g. PPES sampling, stratification, oversampling) and several additional features. The algorithm was built with 100 m × 100 m WorldPop, bottom-up GRID3, or Land-Scan HD estimates of residential population in mind. Given that cells will often need to be aggregated to achieve a cluster target population, the algorithm provides two options to create EAs based on gridded population data. First, the user can leverage the gridEA algorithm to group cells into larger units according to population and area constraints (Dooley 2019). The gridEA algorithm works like other EA creation tools such as AZTool (Cockings et al. 2011) but is tailored to gridded population rasters in data-sparse contexts. Second, if users have existing census EA boundaries or similar small area boundaries with missing or outdated census counts, they can use a gridded population dataset to update population counts in the census EA sample frame. Additional features in GridSample2.0 include implicit stratification by settlement type, proportional or custom allocation of clusters to strata, and optional exclusion of areas classified as unsettled.[2]

The ability to define gridded EAs of any target population size from 100 m × 100 m cells opens new possibilities for micro-census (one-stage) survey designs in which the household listing and interviews are performed on the same day in small clusters (e.g. 20 households). Particularly in urban settings, micro-census samples are an attractive alternative to standard two-or three-stage sample designs because mobile, nontraditional, and vulnerable households are often unintentionally excluded because of the months – or even years – of time gap between household listing and interviews, biasing estimates toward middle-class families in those urban settings (Elsey et al. 2016, 2018). Micro-census designs are also attractive among survey teams performing rapid assessment in LMICs seeking robust survey methods that only require one field visit to reduce cost and time, or minimize security risks (VAM Unit 2018).

To ensure that GridSample2.0 can support gridded population surveys across LMICs, the algorithm was given an online user-friendly interface, www.GridSample.org,[3] and a supercomputer for data processing by Flowminder Foundation with funding from Gates Foundation and the Department for International Development (DFID)[4]. For survey planners with limited experience working with geographic data, www.GridSample.org contains preloaded WorldPop datasets to create a sample frame and preloaded administrative and urban–rural boundaries to define survey coverage or strata boundaries. Alternatively, users can upload their own sample frame, strata, or coverage boundaries as shapefiles.

More advanced users can download the GridSample2.0 Python script to run the algorithm offline or with custom gridded datasets. Thus, GridSample2.0 is well suited to use LandScan HD and GRID3 population and settlement type layers for

---

[2] Release date in GitHub in early 2019. Contact dana.thomson@flowminder.org for more information.
[3] GridSample.org website launch date in early 2019. Beta version visible before launch.
[4] GRID3 website coming online soon, placeholder citation: https://unstats.un.org/unsd/statcom/49th-session/side-events/20180307-1M-GRID3-Launch-Concept%20Note.pdf (United Nations Statistics Division 2018).

household survey sampling when they become available. The output of both www.GridSample.org and the GridSample2.0 Python script includes a file of cluster boundaries (both as a shapefile and keyhole markup language (KML) file) that can be viewed in ArcGIS, QGIS, or Google Earth. Users also receive a detailed report of the sample frame, input datasets and parameters, description of the sample selection process, and an Excel file with precalculated design weights.

20.4.4 Implementation of Gridded Population Surveys

Regardless of the tool used, sampling from gridded population data often results in clusters consisting of one or more grid cells often with block-shaped boundaries unrelated to physical features identifiable in the field (e.g. roads, rivers, land plots). Implementation of a gridded population survey generally involves the use of satellite imagery, printed on a paper map or preloaded on a tablet, to navigate in the field. Protocols must also be established to decide whether buildings on a cluster boundary should be included or excluded from the sample. For example, buildings on the north and east cell boundary might be included, while buildings on the south and west cell boundaries are excluded. Manual segmentation of clusters along roads, rivers, and land plots into approximately equal-population segments using a GIS and satellite imagery is also an option to ensure that at least some cluster boundaries are identifiable in the field. Manual segmentation may be necessary in rural settings if the cluster is large and buildings are divided by a major barrier such as a large river or mountain. Several example field manuals and step-by-step processes to implement gridded population surveys are available (Elsey et al. 2018; Hagopian et al. 2013; Amer 2015).

20.5 Case Study

To demonstrate the benefit of population estimates using the tools discussed throughout this chapter, consider a survey of childhood health in Nigeria. Nigeria is the most populous country in Africa and one of the 10 largest countries in the world, where population estimates are targeted both at the national level and for specific subpopulations of interest. The last two population censuses in Nigeria took place in 2006 and 1991 (United Nations Statistics Division 2019), both of which were widely contested with accusations of undercounts of rural populations and women and overcounts in the north of the country (Okolo 1999; Yin 2007). Because the country is so large, with a growing population, diverse population characteristics across different states, and a wide range of housing development occurring in both urban and rural areas, accurate population estimates are necessary to support decision-making at the governmental level and to guide international development resources. Based on the 2006 census, the total population of Nigeria in 2006 was 140 431 790, consisting of 28 197 085 households (Nigeria Data Portal 2019). However, as of January 2019, the United Nations estimates the current population of Nigeria to be 198 434 606 and is forecasted to reach 206 152 701 by 2020 (Worldometers 2019). These estimates are generally based on an estimated annual growth rate since the 2006 census. For top-down approach, models are derived from the most recent census population count, normalized to current population projections (LandScan Global uses US State Department projections, WorldPop uses United Nations projections), with proportional allocation of the projected population by administrative area and prorating by age-sex group. Additional modifications to population projections may made if additional rates of population growth or decline are available. For bottom-up approach to estimate the population in Nigeria, efforts are currently ongoing across several organizations.

Consider a study on breastfeeding and child nutrition that targets women with children 0–24 months old. With such a large population, no reliable frame, and lack of information on the subpopulation distribution, standard population estimation tools are not sufficient to provide the relevant information. Thus, a survey is needed to estimate this target subpopulation of women. To conduct such a survey, any researcher would look into a sophisticated sampling design to capture the variance in the population and provide an unbiased subpopulation estimate. Standard survey protocols would start with a sample that would either consider Nigerian states (36 states and the federal capital territory) as strata or select a sample of states depending on resources available for the study (e.g. time, money, logistics). Within states, districts, also known as local government areas (LGAs), would be sampled. Once LGAs are sampled, census EAs with approximately 100–300 households each would be the next sampling unit where either listing or random walks would be conducted to screen households toward identifying women with children 0–24 months old. Listing would require a tremendous effort and resources, and random walk is expected to suffer from bias. Furthermore, the sampling process would usually depend on population estimates and projections at state, LGA, and EA levels, which might suffer from error. As an alternate, we can use geosampling or www.GridSample.org within the sampled LGAs as follows.

If geosampling is used, 1 km × 1 km grid cells will be overlaid on each LGA. Population estimates for the 1 km × 1 km grid cells can be based on either LandScan or WorldPop data. Aerial imagery of the 1 km × 1 km grid cell is then processed through a machine learning classification algorithm to identify whether it is a residential or nonresidential cell – thus excluding grid cells with no buildings (e.g. national parks) to increase field work efficiency. Residential grid cells are considered for the next stage of sampling for a random subsample of 1 km × 1 km grid cells within each targeted LGA. A smaller grid is then overlaid on each sampled 1 km grid cell to construct the secondary grid cells with grid cells of size 50 m × 50 m in urban areas, 100 m × 100 m in peri-urban areas, and 150 m × 150 m in rural areas to account for differential population density to reduce clustering and keep field logistics manageable for field staff. These secondary grid cells are then run through the classification algorithm again to exclude nonresidential grid cells. Only households in residential grid cells are then screened to identify women with children 0–24 months old to conduct the survey. A design-based approach is then used to estimate the target subpopulation.

If GridSample is used, the researcher would log onto http://www.gridsample .org/tool to use dropdown menus and preloaded datasets to select his or her sample. The website breaks the sample selection process into seven steps, each of which is accompanied by guidance text and links to preloaded datasets if the researcher wishes to download and inspect source data. In the first step (Coverage), the user selects the coverage area from a list of countries; up to four levels of subnational administrative areas from the Database of Global Administrative Areas (GADM, https://gadm.org) then appear allowing the user, in the case of Nigeria, to optionally constrain the coverage area to a random subset of states or LGAs or urban/rural areas, or to define a custom coverage area by uploading a shapefile. In Step 2 (Frame), the user defines the sample frame by selecting a preloaded gridded population dataset (currently, only WorldPop top-down estimates are included) and whether to sample from cells directly, three sized gridded EAs, or a frame of small areas defined with an uploaded shapefile. In our scenario, the user would likely select gridEAs with a target of 500 people (100–150 households) and maximum area of 3 km × 3 km, excluding areas defined as unsettled by the European Commission the global human settlement model (GHS-SMOD) dataset. A histogram of sample frame unit counts is provided with this step, allowing the researcher to evaluate the quality of the sample frame before moving on. In Step 3 (Design), the researcher can specify whether the survey will use a one- or two-stage design, whether stratification or spatial oversampling will be applied, and whether he or she is able to input a random number to replicate the exact sample later. In this scenario, a two-stage design and stratification would probably be specified, although specification of smaller gridEAs (e.g. target 75 people, 1 km × 1 km) in the Frame step and selection of one-stage sampling in the Design step is also possible, allowing household listing and interviews to occur on the same day during field work.

The Steps 4 (Strata) and 5 (Spatial) are optional, and only the Strata step would be enabled in this scenario because it was selected during the Design step. Samples can be stratified by urban/rural areas, the subnational administrative units (same as Coverage step), and self-defined strata boundaries with an uploaded shapefile. Admin 1 units – states – would be a sensible level of stratification for this scenario. In Step 6 (Target), the researcher enters a target population label such as "Children

0–24 months," indicates the average number of target population members per household, for example 0.1 as estimated from a recent survey, and average household size nationwide or by strata. The final step (Sample Size) requires different inputs depending on number of sample stages and whether the survey is stratified to calculate the number of PSUs to be selected and how they will be allocated to strata (e.g. equally, proportionally, or custom). All parameters have now been entered; thus, the researcher would submit the job. After the sample is processed (selected) on a remote super computer, the user receives an e-mail with a link to download the shapefile of PSU boundaries, a report, and the sample design weights after the sample selected.

Before starting field work, the research should review each PSU over satellite imagery, manually segmenting any PSUs with populations clearly much larger than the target 150 households or PSUs with a physical barrier. After preparing geographically accurate field maps from using satellite imagery, optionally with road and building data (e.g. from OpenStreetMap), the research team would proceed with a typical household mapping and listing process and screen households for children age 0–24 months.

20.6 Conclusions and Next Steps

Efforts are ongoing to improve population estimates both at the general population level and for targeted subpopulations.[5] Both countries and international development organizations are working together in LMICs to refine census processes by integrating spatial tools and GIS and benefiting from refined aerial imagery. Multiple efforts are under way to use feature extraction methods from satellite imagery to delineate local areas of similar population types to include settlement classification (Weber et al. 2018), land use classification datasets (Grippa et al. 2018), and unplanned settlement classification (Kuffer, Pfeffer, and Slizas 2016). It may be possible to generate survey sampling units and census EAs with sensible geographic boundaries (e.g. following roads, rivers) using these types of feature extraction methods in combination with gridded population totals.

In parallel, ongoing efforts are taking place to improve population estimates at the national level or in small areas through gridded population datasets. Both census improvement and gridded population estimates at the national level provide better frames for survey sampling and improve the sample allocation and weights. Furthermore, sampling designs using GIS and gridded population are improving methodologies to reduce error and account for potential sources of bias. The creation of clusters that meet custom population and geographic size constraints

---

5 Contact samer@rti.org for more information or for potential contributions.

via disaggregation or aggregation of grid cells allows for survey designs that are not typically possible with a census EA sample frame. Namely, gridded population sampling opens up the possibility of micro-census sampling such that all households in a cluster are listed and interviewed on the same day during field work. Furthermore, as gridded population sampling surveys become more popular, designs that perform full household enumeration at the last stage of sampling can be used as training data for bottom-up gridded population datasets.

Better understanding of systematic errors in population estimates will allow researchers to more effectively select sample grids that fit survey goals and improve weighting procedures (Eckman, Himelein, and Dever 2019).

Acknowledgments

The authors would like to acknowledge the efforts of several contributors who provided support on research, development, review, and edits. From the RTI team, Karol Krotki, Kasey Jones, Jamie Cajka, Jennifer Unangst, and Justine Allpress made contributions on research development and implementation. From Oak Ridge National Laboratory, Budhendra Bhaduri, Eric Weber, and Jacob McKee contributed to the research, content development, and chapter review. From University of Southampton and Flowminder Foundation, Claire Dooley, Dale Rhoda, and Ian Waldock contributed to the research, and Andrew Tatem and Warren C. Jochem reviewed the chapter and gave valuable feedback.

References

Amer, S.R. (2015). *Geo-Sampling: From Design to Implementation*. Tampa, FL: AAPOR.

Amer, S.R., Krotki, K., Evans, J. et al. (2016). *Using Drones for Household Enumeration and Estimation*. Austin, TX: AAPOR.

Azar, D., Graesser, J., Engstrom, R. et al. (2010). Spatial refinement of census population distribution using remotely sensed estimates of impervious surfaces in Haiti. *International Journal of Remote Sensing* 31 (21): 5635–5655. https://doi.org/10.1080/01431161.2010.496799.

Balk, D., Brickman, M., Anderson, B., et al. (2015). *Mapping global urban and rural population distributions: estimates of future global population distribution to 2015*. Environment and Natural Resources Working Paper 24.

Bauer, J.J. (2016). Biases in random route surveys. *Journal of Survey Statistics and Methodology* 4 (2): 263–287. https://doi.org/10.1093/jssam/smw012.

Breiman, L. (2001). Random forests. *Machine Learning* 45 (1): 5–32. https://doi.org/10.1023/A:1010933404324.

Brewer, K.R.W. and Hanif, M. (2013). *Sampling With Unequal Probabilities*. New York: Springer Science & Business Media.

Cajka, J., Amer, S., Ridenhour, J. et al. (2018). Geo-sampling in developing nations. *International Journal of Social Research Methodology* 21 (6): 729–746. https://doi.org/10.1080/13645579.2018.1484989.

Chew, R.F., Amer, S., Jones, K. et al. (2018). Residential scene classification for gridded population sampling in developing countries using deep convolutional neural networks on satellite imagery. *International Journal of Health Geographics* 17 (1): 12. https://doi.org/10.1186/s12942-018-0132-1.

Cockings, S., Harfoot, A., Martin, D. et al. (2011). Maintaining existing zoning systems using automated zone-design techniques: methods for creating the 2011 census output geographies for England and Wales. *Environment and Planning A: Economy and Space* 43 (10): 2399–2418. https://doi.org/10.1068/a43601.

Cressie, N.A.C. (1986). Kriging nonstationary data. *Journal of the American Statistical Association* 81 (395): 625–634. https://doi.org/10.2307/2288990.

Deville, P., Linard, C., Martin, S. et al. (2014). Dynamic population mapping using mobile phone data. *Proceedings of the National Academy of Sciences of the United States of America* 111 (45): 15888–15893. https://doi.org/10.1073/pnas.1408439111.

Dobson, J.E., Bright, E.A., Coleman, P.R. et al. (2000). LandScan: a global population database for estimating populations at risk. *Photogrammetric Engineering & Remote Sensing* 66 (7): 849–857.

Dooley, C. (2019). gridEZ: an algorithtm for generating enumeration zones with user-defined target population and geographic size. Available from: https://github.com/cadooley/gridEZ (accessed 26 March 2020).

Doxsey-Whitfield, E., MacManus, K., Adamo, S.B. et al. (2015). Taking advantage of the improved availability of census data: a first look at the gridded population of the world, version 4. *Papers in Applied Geography* 1 (3): 226–234. https://doi.org/10.1080/23754931.2015.1014272.

Eckman, S., Himelein, K., and Dever, J.A. (2019). Sample designs using GIS technology for household surveys in the developing world. In: *Advances in Comparative Survey Methods: Multicultural, Multinational and Multiregional Contexts (3MC)* (eds. T.P. Johnson, B.-E. Pennell, I.A.L. Stoop, et al.). New York, NY: Wiley.

Elsey, H., Thomson, D.R., Lin, R.Y. et al. (2016). Addressing inequities in urban health: do decision-makers have the data they need? Report from the Urban Health Data Special Session at International Conference on Urban Health Dhaka 2015. *Journal of Urban Health* 93(3): 526–537. https://doi.org/10.1007/s11524-016-0046-9.

Elsey, H., Poudel, A.N., Ensor, T. et al. (2018). Improving household surveys and use of data to address health inequities in three Asian cities: protocol for the surveys for Urban equity (SUE) mixed methods and feasibility study. *BMJ Open* 8 (11): e024182. https://doi.org/10.1136/bmjopen-2018-024182.

Facebook Connectivity Lab and Center for International Earth Science Information Network (CIESIN) (2016). *High Resolution Settlement Layer (HRSL). Source Imagery for HRSL 2016 DigitalGlobe*. New York: Columbia University https://ciesin.columbia.edu/data/hrsl.

Fotheringham, A.S. and Rogerson, P.A. (1993). GIS and spatial analytical problems. *International Journal of Geographical Information Systems* 7 (1): 3–19. https://doi.org/10.1080/02693799308901936.

Galway, L., Bell, N., Sae, A.S. et al. (2012). A two-stage cluster sampling method using gridded population data, a GIS, and Google Earth(TM) imagery in a population-based mortality survey in Iraq. *International Journal of Health Geographics* 11: 12. https://doi.org/10.1186/1476-072X-11-12.

Gaughan, A.E., Stevens, F.R., Linard, C. et al. (2013). High resolution population distribution maps for Southeast Asia in 2010 and 2015. *PLoS One* 8 (2): e55882. https://doi.org/10.1371/journal.pone.0055882.

Gaughan, A.E., Stevens, F.R., Linard, C. et al. (2015). Exploring nationally and regionally defined models for large area population mapping. *International Journal of Digital Earth* 8 (12): 989–1006. https://doi.org/10.1080/17538947.2014.965761.

Gething, P., Tatem, A., Bird, T. et al. (2015). *Creating Spatial Interpolation Surfaces with DHS Data*. DHS Spatial Analysis Reports No. 11. Rockville, MD: ICF International.

Goodchild, M.F., Anselin, L., and Deichmann, U. (1993). A framework for the areal interpolation of socioeconomic data. *Environment and Planning A: Economy and Space* 25 (3): 383–397. https://doi.org/10.1068/a250383.

Graesser, J., Cheriyadat, A., Vatsavai, R.R. et al. (2012). Image based characterization of formal and informal neighborhoods in an urban landscape. *IEEE Journal of Selected Topics in Applied Earth Observations and Remote Sensing* 5 (4): 1164–1176. https://doi.org/10.1109/JSTARS.2012.2190383.

GRID3. (2018). About us. http://grid3.org (accessed 14 March 2020).

Grippa, T., Georganos, S., Zarougui, S. et al. (2018). Mapping urban land use at street block level using OpenStreetMap, remote sensing data, and spatial metrics. *ISPRS International Journal of Geo-Information* 7 (7) https://doi.org/10.3390/ijgi7070246.

Häder, S. and Gabler, S. (2003). Sampling and estimation. In: *Cross-Cultural Survey Methods* (eds. J.A. Harkness, F.J.R. van de Vijver and P.M. Mohler), 117–136. Hoboken, NJ: Wiley.

Hagopian, A., Flaxman, A.D., Takaro, T.K. et al. (2013). Mortality in Iraq associated with the 2003–2011 war and occupation: findings from a national cluster sample survey by the university collaborative Iraq mortality study. *PLoS Medicine* 10 (10): e1001533. https://doi.org/10.1371/journal.pmed.1001533.

Hillson, R., Alejandre, J.D., Jacobsen, K.H. et al. (2014). Methods for determining the uncertainty of population estimates derived from satellite imagery and limited survey data: a case study of Bo city, Sierra Leone. *PLoS One* 9 (11): e112241. https://doi.org/10.1371/journal.pone.0112241.

ICF International (2012). *Demographic and Health Survey Sampling and Household Listing Manual*. Calverton, MD: ICF International.

Janicki, R. and Vesper, A. (2017). Benchmarking techniques for reconciling Bayesian small area models at distinct geographic levels. *Statistical Methods & Applications* 26 (4): 557–581. https://doi.org/10.1007/s10260-017-0379-x.

Journel, A.G. and Huijbregts, C.J. (1978). *Mining Geostatistics*. London: Academic Press.

Joyce, P. and Malec, D. (2009). *Population Estimation Using Tract Level Geography and Spatial Information*, Research Report Series (Statistics #2009-3). Washington, DC: Statistical Research Division, U.S. Census Bureau.

Kalton, G. (1983). *Introduction to Survey Sampling*. Newbury Park, CA: Sage Publications https://doi.org/10.4135/9781412984683.

Kish, L. (1994). Multipopulation survey designs: five types with seven shared aspects. *International Statistical Review* 62 (2): 167–186. https://doi.org/10.2307/1403507.

Kuffer, M., Pfeffer, K., and Sliuzas, R. (2016). Slums from space – 15 years of slum mapping using remote sensing. *Remote Sensing* 8 (6): 1–29. https://doi.org/10.3390/rs8060455.

Lepkowski, J. (2005). Non-observation errors in household surveys in developing countries. In: *Household Sampled Surveys in Developing and Transition Countries*. Department of Economic and Social Affairs, Statistics Division, Studies in Methods, Series F No.96, Chapter 8. New York, USA: United Nation Statistics Division https://unstats.un.org/unsd/HHsurveys/pdf/Chapter_8.pdf.

Linard, C., Gilbert, M., and Tatem, A.J. (2011). Assessing the use of global land cover data for guiding large area population distribution modelling. *GeoJournal* 76 (5): 525–538. https://doi.org/10.1007/s10708-010-9364-8.

Lloyd, C.T., Sorichetta, A., and Tatem, A.J. (2017). High resolution global gridded data for use in population studies. *Science Data* 4: 170001. https://doi.org/10.1038/sdata.2017.1.

Lu, X., Wrathall, D.J., Sundsøy, P.R. et al. (2016). Detecting climate adaptation with mobile network data in Bangladesh: anomalies in communication, mobility and consumption patterns during cyclone Mahasen. *Climatic Change* 138 (3–4): 505–519. https://doi.org/10.1007/s10584-016-1753-7.

Lunga, D., Yang, H.L., Reith, A. et al. (2018). Domain-adapted convolutional networks for satellite image classification: a large-scale interactive learning workflow. *IEEE Journal of Selected Topics in Applied Earth Observations and Remote Sensing* 11 (3): 962–977. https://doi.org/10.1109/JSTARS.2018.2795753.

Matheron, G. (1979). *Recherche de Simplification Dans un Problem de Cokrigeage*. Fontainebleau: Centre de Geostatistique.

Moser, C. and Kalton, G. (1971). *Survey Methods in Social Investigation*. London: Routledge.

Muñoz, J. and Langeraar, W. (2013). A census-independent sampling strategy for a household survey in Myanmar. http://winegis.com/images/census-independent-GIS-based-sampling-strategy-for-household-surveys-plan-of-action%20removed.pdf (accessed 14 March 2020).

Nigeria Data Portal (2019). Nigeria Census. http://nigeria.opendataforafrica.org/xspplpb/nigeria-census (accessed 14 March 2020).

Oak Ridge National Laboratory (2017). LandScan documentation. http://web.ornl.gov/sci/landscan/landscan_documentation.shtml (accessed 14 March 2020).

Okolo, A. (1999). The Nigerian census: problems and prospects. *American Statistician* 53 (4): 321–325. https://doi.org/10.2307/2686050.

O'Muircheartaigh, C., Eckman, S., and Weiss, C. (2002). Traditional and enhanced listing for probability sampling. http://works.bepress.com/stephanie_eckman/11 (accessed 14 March 2020).

Patel, N.N., Stevens, F.R., Huang, Z. et al. (2017). Improving large area population mapping using geotweet densities. *Transactions in GIS* 21 (2): 317–331. https://doi.org/10.1111/tgis.12214.

Pesaresi, M., Ehrlich, D., Florczyk, A.J. et al. (2016). *Operating Procedure for the Production of the Global Human Settlement Layer from Landsat Data of the Epochs 1975, 1990, 2000, and 2014*. JRC Technical Report EUR 27741 EN. Ispra, Italy: European Union.

Rao, J.N.K. and Molina, I. (2015). *Small Area Estimation*, 2e. Hoboken, NJ: Wiley https://doi.org/10.1002/9781118735855.

Reed, F., Gaughan, A., Stevens, F. et al. (2018). Gridded population maps informed by different built settlement products. *Data* 3 (3) https://doi.org/10.3390/data3030033.

Rose, A.N. and Bright, E. (2014). The LandScan global population distribution project: current state of the art and prospective innovation. *Proceedings of the Population Association of America Annual Meeting*, Boston, MA.

Sollom, R., Richards, A.K., Parmar, P. et al. (2011). Health and human rights in Chin state, Western Burma: a population-based assessment using multistaged household cluster sampling. *PLoS Medicine* 8 (2): e1001007. https://doi.org/10.1371/journal.pmed.1001007.

Sorichetta, A., Hornby, G.M., Stevens, F.R. et al. (2015). High-resolution gridded population datasets for Latin America and the Caribbean in 2010, 2015, and 2020. *Scientific Data* 2: 150045. https://doi.org/10.1038/sdata.2015.45.

Stevens, F.R., Gaughan, A.E., Linard, C. et al. (2015). Disaggregating census data for population mapping using random forests with remotely-sensed and ancillary data. *PLoS One* 10 (2): e0107042. https://doi.org/10.1371/journal.pone.0107042.

Stewart, R., Urban, M., Duchscherer, S. et al. (2016). A Bayesian machine learning model for estimating building occupancy from open source data. *Natural Hazards* 81 (3): 1929–1956. https://doi.org/10.1007/s11069-016-2164-9.

Thakur, G.S., Bhaduri, B.L., Piburn, J.O. et al. (2015). PlanetSense: a real-time streaming and spatio-temporal analytics platform for gathering geo-spatial intelligence from open source data. In: *Proceedings of the 23rd SIGSPATIAL International Conference on Advances in Geographic Information Systems*. Seattle, WA: Association for Computing Machinery (ACM). https://doi.org/10.1145/2820783.2820882.

Thompson, S.K. (1991). Adaptive cluster sampling: designs with primary and secondary units. *Biometrics* 47 (3) https://doi.org/10.2307/2532662.

Thomson, D.R., Hadley, M.B., Greenough, P.G. et al. (2012). Modelling strategic interventions in a population with a total fertility rate of 8.3: a cross-sectional study of Idjwi Island, DRC. *BMC Public Health* 12 (1): 959. https://doi.org/10.1186/1471-2458-12-959.

Thomson, D.R., Stevens, F.R., Ruktanonchai, N.W. et al. (2017). GridSample: an R package to generate household survey primary sampling units (PSUs) from gridded population data. *International Journal of Health Geographics* 16 (1): 25. https://doi.org/10.1186/s12942-017-0098-4.

Thomson, D.R., Ruktanonchai, N., Stevens, F.R., et al. (2018). Gridsample: tools for grid-based survey sampling design v0.2.1. https://cran.r-project.org/web/packages/gridsample/index.html (accessed 14 March 2020).

Tobler, W.R. (1979). Smooth pycnophylactic interpolation for geographical regions. *Journal of the American Statistical Association* 74 (367): 519–530. https://doi.org/10.1080/01621459.1979.10481647.

Tobler, W., Deichmann, U., Gottsegen, J. et al. (1997). World population in a grid of spherical quadrilaterals. *International Journal of Population Geography* 3 (3): 203–225. https://doi.org/10.1002/(SICI)1099-1220(199709)3:3<203::AID-IJPG68>3.0.CO;2-C.

Unangst, J. and Amer, S.R. (2017). A review of weighting assumptions for geosampling-based survey designs: a case study in Nigeria. In: *Proceedings of the Joint Statistical Meetings, Baltimore, MD*. Alexandria, VA: The American Statistical Association.

United Nations Statistics Division (2005). Household Sample Surveys in Developing and Transition Countries. Department of Economic and Social Affairs Statistics

Division Studies in Methods, Series F No. 96. Available from: https://unstats.un.org/unsd/hhsurveys/pdf/Household_surveys.pdf.

United Nations Statistics Division (2018). *Launch Event: GRID 3 – Geo-Referenced Infrastructure and Demographic Data for Development – Within the 49th Session of the United Nations Statistical Commission*. New York, NY: UNSD https://unstats.un.org/unsd/statcom/49th-session/side-events/20180307-1M-GRID3-Launch-Concept%20Note.pdf.

United Nations Statistics Division (2019). *Demographic and Social Statistics*. New York: UNSD https://unstats.un.org/unsd/demographic-social/census/censusdates.

Üstun, T.B., Chatterji, S., Mechbal, A. et al. (2005). Quality assurance in surveys: standards, guidelines, and procedures. In: *Household Surveys in Developing and Transition Countries* (ed. United Nations Statistical Division, United Nations Department of Economic and Social Affairs), Chp. X, 199–230. New York, NY: United Nations http://unstats.un.org/unsd/HHsurveys/pdf/Household_surveys.pdf.

Valliant, R. and Dever, J.A. (2017). *Survey Weights: A Step-by-Step Guide to Calculation*. College Station, TX: StataPress.

Vulnerability Analysis and Mapping (VAM) Unit (2018). *Urban Essential Needs Assessment in the Five Communes of Kimbanseke, Kinsenso, Makala, N'sele and Selembao (Kinshasa)*. Rome, Italy: World Food Programme.

Wardrop, N.A., Jochem, W.C., Bird, T.J. et al. (2018). Spatially disaggregated population estimates in the absence of national population and housing census data. *Proceedings of the National Academy of Sciences of the United States of America* 115 (14): 3529–3537. https://doi.org/10.1073/pnas.1715305115.

Weber, E.M., Seaman, V.Y., Stewart, R.N. et al. (2018). Census-independent population mapping in northern Nigeria. *Remote Sensing of Environment* 204: 786–798. https://doi.org/10.1016/j.rse.2017.09.024.

Wilson, R., Zu Erbach-Schoenberg, E., Albert, M. et al. (2016). Rapid and near real-time assessments of population displacement using mobile phone data following disasters: the 2015 Nepal earthquake. *PLoS Currents* 8: 1–26. https://doi.org/10.1371/currents.dis.d073fbece328e4c39087bc086d694b5c.

Worldometers (2019). Nigeria population (LIVE). http://www.worldometers.info/world-population/nigeria-population (accessed 14 March 2020).

WorldPop (2017). Data availability. www.worldpop.org.uk/data/data_sources (accessed 14 March 2020).

Yang, H.L., Yuan, J., Lunga, D. et al. (2018). Building extraction at scale using convolutional neural network: mapping of the United States. *IEEE Journal of Selected Topics in Applied Earth Observations and Remote Sensing* 11 (8): 2600–2614. https://doi.org/10.1109/JSTARS.2018.2835377.

Yin, S. (2007). Objections surface over Nigerian census results. Population Reference Bureau. http://www.prb.org/Publications/Articles/2007/ObjectionsOverNigerianCensus.aspx (accessed 14 March 2020).

Yuan, J. (2018). Learning building extraction in aerial scenes with convolutional networks. *IEEE Transactions on Pattern Analysis and Machine Intelligence* 40 (11): 2793–2798. https://doi.org/10.1109/TPAMI.2017.2750680.

Section 6

The Fourth Paradigm, Regulations, Ethics, Privacy

21

Reproducibility in the Era of Big Data: Lessons for Developing Robust Data Management and Data Analysis Procedures

D. Betsy McCoach[1], Jennifer N. Dineen[2], Sandra M. Chafouleas[1], and Amy Briesch[3]

[1] *The Neag School of Education, University of Connecticut, Storrs, CT, USA*
[2] *The Department of Public Policy, University of Connecticut, Storrs, CT, USA*
[3] *Bouve College of Health Sciences, Northeastern University, Storrs, CT, USA*

21.1 Introduction

In recent years, options for survey data collection mode and sample sources have increased, and technological advances for data collection have blossomed (Couper 2013, 2017; Hill and Dever 2014). Current technology allows for ubiquitous, almost continuous data collection on the web, smart devices, and beyond. These technological advances have ushered in a new era in survey research methods: Big Data meets survey data. This chapter focuses on the challenges and opportunities of using structured data from administrative and publicly available data sources, such as school records; demographic data; or public health records, in conjunction with traditional survey data. We illustrate several issues associated with managing large, multifaceted, multisource datasets with our recent educational research project, which incorporated both traditional surveys and preexisting administrative data gathered from multiple sources. We close with a set of recommendations for researchers who wish to integrate Big Data and survey data.

21.2 Big Data

Over the last decade, the term "Big Data" has gained enormous popularity. Even so, the term lacks a consistent definition (Ward and Barker 2013). Early on, it referred to data that were so large and complex that the information could not be stored or analyzed using traditional techniques. However, the capacity to work

---

Big Data Meets Survey Science: A Collection of Innovative Methods, First Edition. Edited by Craig A. Hill, Paul P. Biemer, Trent D. Buskirk, Lilli Japec, Antje Kirchner, Stas Kolenikov, and Lars E. Lyberg.
© 2021 John Wiley & Sons, Inc. Published 2021 by John Wiley & Sons, Inc.

with large quantities of data has exploded in recent years, which may render such a context-dependent definition obsolete. Big Data differs from traditional survey data in its volume (the amount of information gathered), velocity (the speed of data collection), and variety (the multitude of possible data formats) (Callegaro and Yang 2018; Johnson and Smith 2017; Laney 2001). Big Data also differ in their chronicity, veracity (accuracy), and complexity (Callegaro and Yang 2018; Chen and Wojcik 2016; Johnson and Smith 2017). Common forms of Big Data include internet data, transaction data, administrative data, commercially available databases, publicly available data, and paradata.

Although some researchers view Big Data as a possible replacement for conventional surveys (Anderson 2008), it typically acts as a supplement to traditional survey methodology, allowing researchers to ask fewer questions and reduce error related to false reporting, misinterpretation, fatigue, and unit nonresponse (Couper 2013; Lazer et al. 2014; Mishkin 2014). The currently evolving literature in this area focuses on the differentiation of Big Data methods and traditional survey designs (Cukier and Mayer-Schoenberger 2013), the benefits and challenges of using Big Data (Japec et al. 2015), and/or the general role of Big Data as a complement to survey designs (Wells and Thorson 2016). However, specific frameworks or guidelines for the combined application of Big Data and survey methodology remain limited.

Data collected with conventional survey research methods generally includes variables measured with a questionnaire under the time and resource constraints imposed when gathering information from human respondents. These approaches force researchers to grapple with finite resources, time constraints, and survey fatigue. In contrast, the volume, variety, and velocity of Big Data sources can give researchers more analysis options and unique insights (Couper 2013, 2017; Hill and Dever 2014; Meyer and Mittag 2019; Raghupathi and Raghupathi 2014; Wang, Kung, and Byrd 2018). Big Data can also save valuable resources and reduce respondent burden (Couper 2017; Perez, Greco, and Sermonetaa 2017). It is now feasible to build expansive, customized databases by selecting any and all variables from a variety of Big Data sources deemed relevant for research purposes.

In addition, the widespread availability of Big Data sources expands options for addressing research questions of interest. Big Data provides potential solutions to challenges facing the survey research industry: the increasing cost of high-quality data collection, declining response rates, and respondent fatigue (Adams and Umbach 2012; Couper 2013; Lavrakas 2008). These issues limit the amount of information that researchers can accumulate and cast doubt on the validity of the data they do gather. Because researchers utilizing Big Data methods do not directly collect the information (instead using it for a secondary research purpose), they often display less concern about veracity issues, such as response bias, participant nonresponse, and attrition (Couper 2017; Savage and Burrows 2016). However, validity and data quality are equally important when working with Big Data.

21.3 Challenges Researchers Face in the Era of Big Data and Reproducibility

Given that Big Data sources are often collected for nonresearch purposes, researchers face various challenges when incorporating Big Data into their analyses. The validity of using data to conduct inferential research in an area unrelated to the initial data collection may be questionable. Both the manner of data collection and the current state of the data help investigators to determine whether and how to use the data to answer research questions.

Big Data is often larger in volume and complexity; thus, managing Big Data is often more difficult than data from traditional survey designs. This complexity creates both statistical and logistical challenges for researchers. One of the most salient challenges of working with Big Data sources is the plethora of choices researchers have at every stage of data management. The researcher may struggle to manage the inherent messiness of the data (Cukier and Mayer-Schoenberger 2013), and must constantly engage in, and document, all aspects of the decision-making process. In addition, the current lack of theory and frameworks about how to manage Big Data sources likely contribute to numerous options that researchers face throughout the research process. For example, because data are typically initially collected for use outside of research and are often unstructured, researchers must decide which data sources to use and how much data to acquire, as well as how to link and adapt data to make it amenable for analysis. As such, although researchers initially save time and resources by not collecting original data, they often must engage in a lengthier data management and preparation process (Japec et al. 2015). Furthermore, options for managing, analyzing, and interpreting the results from Big Data will likely increase as databases grow in size, requiring even more resources and human capital to manage future efforts. Because Big Data often possess different characteristics than information gathered with traditional survey designs, working with these datasets often requires researchers to learn and utilize new technical skills (Callegaro and Yang 2018; Chen and Wojcik 2016). For example, data management in this new world often requires advanced computing skills, potentially incorporating multiple programming languages. The burgeoning field of data science is a testament to this new reality.

21.4 Reproducibility

Calls for increased methodological transparency and greater reproducibility and replicability of research results have swept the biological and social sciences over the past decade (Miller 2010; Royal Society 2012; Pashler and Wagenmakers 2012; Science International 2015). Such concerns have radically changed expectations about the research process and its research products (Pashler and Wagenmakers 2012; Hill and Dever 2014; Leek and Peng 2015; Nosek et al. 2015; Open Science Collaboration 2015). Methodological transparency is necessary to ensure accurate interpretation and reproducibility of research results. Increasingly, researchers must furnish datasets and robust input files that allow reviewers, editors, and other researchers to reproduce their findings. The breadcrumb trail from initial sources of raw data to finished analyses should be completely traceable. In other words, an independent researcher should be able to recreate all analytic results from the initial raw data, ideally with minimal effort. Ensuring reproducible results requires systematic procedures for data preparation, statistical analysis, and documentation (Mair 2016).

Reproducibility techniques have several advantages. First, conducting analyses in this manner allows researchers to make changes anywhere in the data collection, data management, or data analysis process and generate new set of results quickly. Imagine that a researcher has just closed out a large survey study and analyzed the data. Suddenly, she discovers that several additional participants recently responded to the survey; obviously, these new respondents did not appear in the original analytic sample. If the researcher automated all data management, analysis, and reporting procedures, then she can update the analyses and recreate the final report by simply clicking a button.

Second, mistakes are more easily traced and remediated when researchers use reproducible techniques (Munafò et al. 2017; Servick 2018). Errors are always possible and occur occasionally, whether or not researchers build the capacity for reproducibility into their data management/analysis/reporting systems. However, investigators are more likely to detect these errors if they employ reproducible techniques. When another person can seamlessly duplicate the results of a study, checking for errors becomes easier and occurs more frequently. In fact, several top journals in the natural and social sciences now require authors to submit data and code when they submit a research paper for review, and many publishers have developed data-sharing guidelines. For example, *Science* requires authors to provide "all data necessary to understand, assess, and extend the conclusions of the manuscript" (https://www.sciencemag.org/authors/science-journals-editorial-policies). *Nature* stipulates that: "Datasets must be made freely available to readers from the date of publication, and must be provided to editors and peer-reviewers at submission, for the purposes of evaluating the manuscript" (https://www.nature.com/authors/policies/availability.html).[1]

Third, reproducibility allows other researchers to more easily replicate research results. The increased transparency afforded by such a process allows researchers to more easily build upon the findings of prior research studies. The Reproducibility Project conducted replications of 100 studies published in three well-respected psychology journals in 2008. Only 39% of the new studies replicated the original results, and the mean effect size for the replication studies was only half as large as the mean effect size for the original studies (Open Science Collaboration 2015). In response to this phenomenon, the National Science Foundation (NSF) and the Institute of Education Sciences (IES) recently published a companion to the *Common Guidelines for Education Research and Development*, which outlines principles for promoting reproducible and replicable research. Reproducibility refers to "the ability to achieve the same findings as another investigator using extant data from a prior study" (NSF/IES 2018, p. 1). When results are reproducible, they are no longer researcher dependent. Instead, they are captured in perpetuity. Therefore, the methods and results of a study are clearly elaborated for future generations. Replication studies are new and designed to determine whether new findings are similar to those from a previous study. Replication studies depend on access to detailed information about all aspects of a study's design and analysis (NSF/IES 2018) and, therefore, depend on reproducibility of the original results.

Sandve et al. (2013) recommended that "as a minimal requirement, you should at least be able to reproduce the results yourself." Although such a statement could induce a chuckle or chortle, how many of us have spent considerable time and effort piecing together the results of prior analyses? Often, the process of finding the data and syntax files and reproducing the original analyses feels as if it takes longer than starting from scratch. Ideally, researchers should be able to locate and reproduce their own research results quickly and effortlessly. Even when the syntax and data are well organized, researchers often fail to sufficiently document for future researchers (or for themselves at a later date) the myriad decisions that arise during the data management, variable creation, and data analysis stages. In the throes of a large project, we make countless decisions thoughtfully. However, if we do not record those decisions in an easily accessible way, the rationale(s) for those decisions may be lost (or, at the very least, separated from the data itself). The datafile and accompanying data manual should contain all the information that an unaffiliated researcher requires to analyze the data independently. A syntax file

---

1 See also *Journal of Accounting Research*, https://onlinelibrary.wiley.com/page/journal/1475679x/homepage/forauthors.html; *Frontiers*, https://www.frontiersin.org/about/author-guidelines; and *Journal of Economic Studies*, http://www.emeraldgrouppublishing.com/products/journals/author_guidelines.htm.

can use the master datafile to create a data manual that contains all necessary data cleaning and transformation decisions.

21.5 Reliability and Validity of Administrative Data

In survey research, we often distinguish between reliability and validity. Applying the framework of reliability and validity to administrative data provides a useful lens for understanding the variety of data quality issues that can plague such data.

Reliability is the consistency or precision of responses. Reliability of administrative data is a function of the precision with which it was gathered and documented. Multiple factors influence its reliability. For example, the coarseness with which continuous data such as percentages are reported influences the reliability of the data: reporting continuous data as a smaller number of ordered categories decreases precision and compromises the reliability of the administrative data.

Validity refers to the appropriateness of inferences made from data. It is a function of the degree to which the administrative data match the constructs of interest. In other words, are the data at hand an adequate proxy for the constructs we want to measure? There is no guarantee that found data can provide the necessary information to measure the constructs or answer the research questions of interest. At the outset of every study, investigators should carefully consider the validity of the specific inferences they want to make. A variety of factors may influence validity, including the closeness of the proxy variable to the true variable of interest, the timing of data collection, and the level of data aggregation. Ironically, data that are easy to collect and measure reliably are often poor proxies for the underlying construct of interest. For example, in the search to explain factors that predict teacher effectiveness, number of years of teaching experience and receipt of a master's degree often serve as proxy variables because the two variables are easily (and reliably) measured in most research studies of teachers. Unfortunately, neither variable is a good proxy for teacher quality: experience and advanced degrees are only weakly related to teacher quality (Harris and Sass 2010).

21.6 Data and Methods

21.6.1 The Case

Discussion of Big Data within mainstream educational research literature is relatively recent and generally limited to guidance on protecting student privacy or the increased analytic options available for large datasets (Vance 2016; Figlio 2017; Ho 2017). To date, few existing practical examples or relevant guidelines specifically address the organizational and analytic challenges of combining Big Data and survey data for education research (Laney 2001).

In this chapter, we explore the challenges researchers face in the era of Big Data and reproducibility. Our experiences during the National Exploration of Emotional/Behavioral Detection in School Screening (NEEDs[2]) project gave us important insights and examples. NEEDs[2] is an exploratory project funded by the US Department of Education, IES (R305A140543). The project's goal was to better understand the landscape of social, emotional, and behavioral (SEB) health screening in US public schools and to examine whether educational outcomes vary as a function of district-level approaches to SEB screening. Specifically, we investigated both the degree to which use of SEB screening in US public schools predicts positive student academic and behavioral outcomes, and whether the use of SEB screening is associated with enhanced outcomes when compared to other, more common, identification approaches. School-based mental health is a niche policy area, but the project researchers encountered at least six potential challenges in using Big Data in combination with traditional survey research. For this reason, our lessons learned apply broadly to research in other policy areas that utilize other sources of administrative data and other data formats. Using the NEEDs[2] project as our backdrop, we describe the fallacies that surrounded our initial approach to using Big Data in combination with traditional survey data and provide recommendations for developing robust data management and data analysis procedures.

21.6.2 The Survey Data

This investigation utilized findings from five stakeholder surveys administered to a nationally representative sample of US school districts. We created the survey sampling frame using the 2013–2014 Common Core of Data Local Education Agency (School District) universe. We selected typical local school districts within the 50 states and Washington, DC for participation. We excluded special districts (e.g. under the Bureau of Indian Education or the Department of Defense), districts whose boundaries had changed, and districts with fewer than 100 students. Thus, our finale sampling frame included a total of 12 315 eligible districts. From these districts, 1217 district administrators (DAs) completed the NEEDs[2] DA survey.[2,3]

---

2 Instances of districts not being qualified include district consolidation, charter school districts, closed districts, duplicate listings, and other specialized reasons. In all, 155 districts were eliminated.
3 The response rate for this survey is 10%. We calculated an unweighted response rate based on standards adopted for establishment surveys by the U.S. Bureau of Labor Statistics (2004) and the U.S. Census Bureau (1993). See https://www.bea.gov/about/pdf/ Responseratesnonresponseinestablishmentsurveys FESAC121404.pdf and https://s3.amazonaws.com/sitesusa/wp-content/uploads/sites/242/2014/05/IGEN-ices3_final.pdf.

After administering the DA survey, we randomly selected one elementary and one secondary school from each participating district. Once we selected a school into the sample, we located contact information for the school administrator through internet searches and/or phone calls to the school. Cooperating building administrators completed the Building Administrator survey and distributed links for surveys to three additional stakeholder populations: student support staff (e.g. school psychologist, social workers, or guidance counselors), teachers, and parents.

21.6.3 The Administrative Data

To reduce respondent burden and measurement error in outcome variables, the NEEDs^2 project also utilized administrative data from three national databases and district publications: the 2013–2014 National Center for Education Statistics (NCES) Common Core of Data (CCD), the 2013–2014 Civil Rights Data Collection (CRDC), the Stanford Education Data Archive (SEDA), and district-procured special education data.

The NCES CCD Local Education Agency (District) Universe Survey is an annually released database that includes data for all public school districts across the United States. Data contain district-level frequencies of students by grade, sex, race/ethnicity, disability, and English-Language Learner status (NCES 2005). Stanford's Center for Education Policy Analysis created the publicly available SEDA (Reardon, Kalogrides, and Shores 2017). SEDA gathers and disseminates data to inform educational policies and practices for US students. The archive includes data from districts, schools, communities, geographic areas, etc. by variables such as grade, race, socioeconomic status (SES), academic subject, and standardized test scores (Fahle et al. 2018). The United States Department of Education has collected information on education and civil rights issues in US public schools through the CRDC since 1968. The CRDC collects information on student enrollment, educational programs and services, limited English proficiency, and disability. For this study, we also utilized special education data. For example, we gathered information on the number of students served in the least-restrictive environment (LRE) 80% of the time, from individual states and districts. For consistency with the school years for which standardized testing data was available, we requested data from the 2011–2012, 2012–2013, and the most recent school year for which data were available.[4]

---

[4] The response rate for this survey is 10%. We calculated an unweighted response rate based on standards adopted for establishment surveys based on Shimizu (2000). See https://s3.amazonaws.com/sitesusa/wp-content/uploads/sites/242/2014/05/IGEN-ices3_final.pdf

21.6.4 The Six Research Fallacies

21.6.4.1 More Data Are Better!

Historically, researchers joked that there was no such thing as too much data. Perhaps that axiom was true at the turn of the century, but it is certainly no longer true (and we have stopped making that joke). Current technology allows us to collect and store copious amounts of data relatively quickly, without too much effort. Amassing large quantities of information rapidly is so easy that we now face the issue of compiling data without regard to its quality or utility. For example, when test takers complete surveys or assessments online, we record vast quantities of process data on their behaviors, including (but not limited to) the number of seconds they spend on each screen; which screens they return to (and for how long); all selected responses to a given question (not just the final answer); mouse movements throughout the testing session; etc. Paradata describe the data collection process (Lavrakas 2008). In our test-taking example, paradata generated during the assessment process may provide important insights about the survey process and may help to improve research efficiency and reduce bias (Kreuter, Couper, and Lyber 2010; Nicolaas 2011; Kreuter 2013; Krueger and West 2014). Thus, the inclusion of paradata may enhance the validity of survey research.

However, even though paradata may improve the quality of survey research, working with paradata creates its own set of challenges (Kreuter 2013; Kyle et al. 2016). The quality of this information may be questionable. In addition, the files that record this nano-level data can be quite large and cumbersome. For certain research questions, having access to such microdata is essential. However, for other investigations, such data may represent a large and deep rabbit hole, which diverts the researcher from his/her main question(s) of interest. To utilize paradata effectively, preprocessing the information is essential, creating smaller subsets of usable analytic data from the vast quantities collected during the research process (Kreuter 2013).

When we first began creating master databases for the NEEDs[2] project, we decided to incorporate all possible variables into our master datafile. In this way, we thought that we could keep all of our options open and be flexible in our exploratory analyses. However, such a strategy ultimately proved counterproductive. Although the inclination to merge all possible datasets and interesting variables into one master file was understandable, this intuition was wrong. Rather than providing flexibility and maximizing options for later data analyses, such "greedy" approaches proved to be messy and inefficient. Trying to incorporate many variables, from many datasets, from multiple data sources created a variety of logistical and analytic issues.

First and foremost, such large and cumbersome datafiles can cause confusion among research team members and will certainly be confusing for external users of the datafile. It is also time-consuming and inefficient to document the provenance of variables that are never used in the analyses. However, given the complexity of the dataset, documentation of all variables (even those not ultimately included in the data analyses) is of the utmost importance. For example, researchers who run experiments at CERN's Large Hadron Collider particle accelerator discard more than 99% of the data generated (Siegel 2018). The collider produces 30 million events per second, translating to almost 400 000 PB of data per year (Starr 2019). Although it seems reasonable to only use a sample of these events, since data of this volume and velocity is almost impossible to store, analyze, and manage (Starr 2019), physicists now wonder what discoveries may have been discarded with the unstored data (Siegel 2018). Developing a thoughtful system for selecting, curating, merging, storing, and documenting data is essential. Ideally, these discussions and plans should begin at the outset of the study.

Our experiences with the NEEDs[2] project changed our perspective on dataset creation and maintenance; we now recommend creating smaller, more selective datasets. First, do not import all possible variables into a master dataset and wait to confront the difficult decisions about which variable(s) to incorporate into the analyses later. Instead, create a lean, well-documented master datafile that can easily be merged with various other auxiliary datafiles when needed. Second, avoid creating a master datafile that features multiple versions of the same variable. For example, do not include three different versions of a race variable in your master datafile if you do not plan to use all three versions in your analyses. Instead, decide if a variable or dataset is necessary before you incorporate it into your master datafile. Then, code variables in the simplest, most efficient manner for the master datafile and recode each variable (as needed) prior to the particular data analysis you want to execute. Before deciding whether to incorporate a variable or supplementary dataset in the master datafile, spend time exploring the original source variables. Carefully examine each auxiliary variable of interest in the administrative dataset and review all documentation related to it: what is the original source of the variable, what is its level of measurement and distribution, how was the variable constructed, and how does that variable match your theoretical needs? Although doing the legwork to make these tough decisions up front is time-consuming, it ultimately saves time and increases analytic efficiency.

As an example, for the NEEDs[2] project, we needed a variable that captured the SES of a school district to use in our analyses. There were several district-level SES variables or proxies for SES variables across the administrative datafiles we merged with our survey responses (such as the percentage of free and reduced price lunch students in the district, or the percentage of children aged 5–17 who lived in poverty in the district). Before incorporating multiple variables from several different datasets, we should have vetted the data more thoroughly and made the tough decisions regarding variable inclusion/exclusion. Instead, we created the master file and then faced the task of deciding, which SES variable/proxy to use as our covariate. In an effort to make this determination, multiple members of the research team conducted preliminary analyses using different SES variables, which emanated from various administrative datafiles. Ultimately, we had a teamwide conversation about which variable to use. This decision was multifaceted, including both conceptual and empirical considerations. Conceptual considerations included which of the district SES variables most closely aligned with our definition of the concept and our reason for including it as a covariate in the model. Empirical considerations included our examination of the sampling distribution and descriptive statistics for each variable to ensure that they seemed reasonable; contained no or few problematic observations/outliers; had a low percentage of missing data; etc. Finally, we selected the SES variable that conceptually matched our analytic needs and exhibited good data quality and utility. In retrospect, we should have conducted those analyses prior to creating the master datafile. Instead, our master datafile now contains several different SES variables, only one of which we used in our analyses. This redundancy boosts the potential for error (e.g. someone mistakenly uses the wrong SES variable in analyses), increases the size of the datafile unnecessarily, and creates preventable confusion, both inside and outside of the research team. Additionally, incorporating superfluous variables in the master datafile can require analysts to engage in post-analysis data cleaning procedures prior to sharing the project's final datasets, as many journals/publishers and funding agencies currently mandate. Therefore, large datafiles with redundant variables both complicate and hinder efforts to ensure the reproducibility of research results and data analyses.

21.6.4.2 Merging Is About Matching by IDs/Getting the Columns to Align

The first intuition might be to merge early and clean later. However, the process of screening and cleaning your data helps to better understand and vet the data. This work ultimately aids in the quest to create smaller, tighter master datafiles (see fallacy one). Instead, we suggest that you harmonize your data. "Data harmonization refers to all efforts to combine data from different sources and provide users with a comparable view of data from different studies" (DSDR 2019). "The goal of data harmonization is to create 'harmony' between different sources of data to create a complete, cohesive picture" (Guess 2017). Often, we use the term "data harmonization" to describe the process of integrating multiple studies or datasets across time. However, even seemingly cross-sectional data needs to be harmonized. If we collect administrative data during the same general timeframe on the same variables, and those variables are imperfectly correlated, how can we explain the disconnection between the two different sources? Understanding why the same variable is not perfectly replicated (or correlated) across two seemingly comparable data sources may provide insight regarding how to better interpret patterns of relationships among conceptually related variables across two different data sources.

Merging Big Data with traditional survey data presents methodologists with an additional set of challenges. The 2018 NIH Strategic Plan for Data Science identified several data science challenges for the National Institutes of Health (NIH). One central challenge is that "datasets exist in many different formats and are often not easily shared, found, or interoperable" (NIH 2018). As previously noted, compared to traditional survey data, Big Data often consist of preexisting data from a variety of sources. In general, these data may or may not have been initially collected for any sort of formal analysis; the quality (i.e. validity and reliability) of each data source may vary. Thus, found data pose substantial research challenges. Relative to survey research, big databases typically require more time and resources to link together due to greater complexity (Callegaro and Yang 2018; Johnson and Smith 2017).

The NEEDs^2 project was incredibly complex, requiring research team members to merge data from five stakeholder surveys, three federal databases, and a variety of online repositories. In doing so, we encountered multiple variable formats and various levels of measurement. This provided numerous opportunities for data from one source to be out-of-date and/or out-of-sync with other sources. For example, the project's survey data collection occurred during 2016 and 2017. However, several available administrative data sources that provided compelling outcome variables lagged by two to four years.

We also had to consider the commonality of data definitions and concepts when merging data sources (FlyData 2019). The research questions for the NEEDs^2 project pertained to regular school districts ("Locally governed agency responsible for providing free public elementary or secondary education; includes independent school districts and those that are a dependent segment of a local government such as a city or county") and component districts ("Regular local school district that shares its superintendent and administrative services with other school districts participating in the supervisory union") (https://nces.ed.gov/ccd/ccddata.asp/). Initially, we decided to exclude all nonregular school districts, including supervisory unions (SUs). By CCD definition, an SU is "an education agency that performs administrative services for more than one school district, providing a common superintendent for participating districts."[5] We examined SUs and found large proportions of the districts in three states – Vermont, New Hampshire, and Montana – and in one of the largest school districts in the country, New York City. Vermont and New Hampshire had dozens of districts that shared superintendents with other districts. Those

---

5 School district definitions are copied from the U.S. Department of Education, National Center for Education Statistics CCD (2018b).

states interpreted their district organizational structures as consistent with the NCES definition of SUs, rather than component districts. And, almost all of the school districts in Montana were organized in SUs. Removing the classification would have made the chance of selection for Montana local education agencies (LEAs) close to zero, underrepresented school districts in Vermont and New Hampshire, and made the probability of selection for New York City Public Schools (NYCPS) zero.

We revisited the varying definitions of SUs when merging the data as well. Traditionally, NCES treated NYCPS as a single district in their reporting; but, since 2005 when the district became an SU, NCES gathered data from the 33 component districts under the single SU. Thus, NYCPS had 33 separate LEA identifiers, and simply merging on the LEA ID became problematic. Traditional data management strategies and processes were not adequate for keeping the various data sources and formats synchronized. This example illustrates the importance of using the research goals and theoretical model to drive decisions about data inclusion/exclusion and data management. It also highlights the importance of spending time researching and understanding the variety of contexts and the nuances of the data when making preprocessing decisions.

21.6.4.3 Saving Your Syntax Is Enough to Ensure Reproducibility

Creating a master datafile from multiple sources creates challenges for both reproducibility and documentation. Documentation of variable creation/cleaning procedures and provenance can become unwieldy. How can researchers make a dataset robust and reproducible enough to allow other researchers to use the data independently?

Although carefully preserved and thoroughly commented syntax files are essential to ensuring reproducibility, they are often not enough because many data-related decisions are not syntax-based. For example, why did the research team choose the SES variable from dataset A rather than the variable from dataset B? Why did they choose to recode a variable from seven categories into five? The syntax/code and data dictionaries carefully document the creation and current state of all variables in the datafile. In that sense, they provide detailed records of *what* resides in the datafile and *how* those data were created, collected, or manipulated. However, syntax files and data dictionaries generally do not include information about *why* data were generated, selected, or modified in a particular fashion. For example, the syntax and data dictionaries should provide detailed documentation that explains how the researchers pooled seven items on a measurement instrument to create a composite variable. However, there is no place to store a multi-paragraph description that defends the rationale for excluding item 8 from the scale. So, where should we store the methodological and substantive details about how and why that decision was made? The most common solution to this problem is to create a separate text document that describes the methodology behind variable creation as well as a detailed record of why such decisions were made and what other alternatives were considered, but not ultimately chosen. Such a text document should be stored with and should accompany the data at all times. For users of Stata, an even more elegant option is available: *variable notes*. In addition to allowing variable labels and value labels, Stata allows users to generate notes that attach to individual variables in the dataset. The maximum number and size of the variable notes is quite high. Thus, users can store pages of metadata about the creation, provenance, manipulation, and current state of a given variable in text that is tied directly to the variable within the Stata dataset. Typing "notes" in the Stata command window returns a complete, unabbreviated list of all notes on all variables in the datafile, creating a methodological document that is linked to both the datafile and the individual variables. In our opinion, this is one of the most unique aspects of Stata, and it is one of the great advantages of using Stata for data management.

For R users, a well-organized R markdown file can serve essentially the same purpose. R markdown provides an integrated platform for writing and executing code, displaying and saving output, and writing and formatting text. Analysts use knitr to execute the code within the markdown file and display results within the text document. R markdown can easily create text documents in .html, .pdf, or .docx formats. Therefore, R markdown can serve as a data journal, chronicling all pre-analysis discussions and decisions in the same document that contains the analysis code and the output. R markdown can also produce publication-quality documents, with all tables and references to analytic results coded into the text so that the document can easily be updated. Essentially, R markdown creates a single pipeline from the initial data source to the final product. Such a streamlined process enhances transparency and reproducibility. R markdown has only one shortcoming compared to Stata's notes: the metadata contained in the text portion of the R markdown file are unavailable to others if the data frame is downloaded into a .csv file. Otherwise, the tremendous advantages of R markdown for reproducibility and transparency are unparalleled.

In addition, the CharmStats suite of products represents another attempt to enhance research transparency and reproducibility. QuickCharmStats 1.1. is a free, open-source software that helps organize, document, and publish data harmonization projects (Winters and Netscher 2016). The QuickCharmStats platform allows users to import and combine multiple types of metadata along with any additional information used to harmonize the data (Winters and Netscher 2016). This software starts with concepts, moves to operationalization of target and source variables, facilitates recoding, stores information in a relational database, and ultimately produces data recoding syntax in multiple statistical languages (Winters and Netscher 2016). The QuickCharmStats workflow ensure[s] transparency through the careful documentation of the harmonization process, including information on the variable name, label and its values, the question wording, and information about the source studies. QuickCharmStats provides space to note any literature or publications that guided the recoding and allows researchers to make notes on the logic behind coding decisions that might not be obvious. All the information from a project can be published as a report, and it is this report that is submitted for peer review and published with a DOI at GESIS

(Winters and Netscher 2016).

CharmStatsPro allows teams of researchers to easily work together on large-scale projects by creating a database accessible to multiple team members. There, researchers can include technical notes about coding, research decisions, data issues and solutions, as well as attach hyperlinks to other codebooks, questionnaire documents, or relevant study notes. In addition, CharmStatsPro generates searchable digital codebooks, syntax, and other research documentation (Winters and Netscher 2016).

21.6.4.4 Transparency in Your Process Ensures Transparency in Your Final Product

The notion of transparency is central for establishing the quality of a research project and producing credible results. At a minimum, transparency requires a thorough write-up of the research process, analysis, and dissemination. However, concerns about the challenges of reproducibility cross many academic disciplines (Playford et al. 2016; Janke, Asher, and Keralis 2012), including survey methodology. The survey community has pushed for transparency for decades (AAPOR 2018), and scholars routinely share information regarding sample source, strategy, and size, along with data collection mode, field period, and question wording. However, transparency in projects that involve both traditional survey research and Big Data has an extra level of complexity. In projects that use data gathered from multiple modes and methodologies, multiple types, formats, and sources of data need to be documented.

In addition to the need for more extensive documentation when using traditional surveys with administrative data, researchers face the challenge of being fully transparent about the provenance of data they did not create. Unlike survey data, administrative data are found (not made), leaving researchers who want or need to be transparent at the mercy of the original data collectors. As we worked with NEEDs[2] administrative data, one reality became apparent: we could exhibit complete transparency regarding data sources/methods and unambiguously and thoroughly document variable provenance, but we could not make the data more transparent than it was at the original source. If the original data collectors did not clearly convey the procedures they used to measure, collect, and assemble the source data, subsequent investigators would find it impossible to conduct secondary analyses to remove the murkiness from their own research products.

In the NEEDs[2] project, we often worked with variables whose names did not adequately describe the construct being measured or whose documentation was limited. For example, we included the percentages of students receiving special education services and the percentages of students classified as having 504 plans (having health impairments) as outcome variables. In both cases, the numbers did not include all students receiving intervention services because many districts provide struggling, non-identified students with services through the Response to Intervention framework in the hope of improving their skills and avoiding formal identification. Additionally, identification practices and eligibility criteria vary between districts and between states, creating measurement error. Similarly, we collected data on the percentage of students with Individualized Education Programs in the district who spend 80% of their time in the least-restrictive educational environment (LRE80) and the percentage who spend 40% of their time in the least restrictive environment (LRE40) in our models. These data were not readily available, so we collected the information from the individual districts in our sample. Approximately 15% of our sample suppressed the information because too few students were in these placements and 14% of the sample did not report the data at all. Because districts decide what data to report and what to suppress, the criteria for reporting such information varied greatly. Some districts decided to not report LRE40 and LRE80 when fewer than 5% of students were in such a placement; other districts reported ranges such as less than 5% or less than 1%, and some reported very small percentages (1% and 0.94%, for example). Additionally, the definition or criteria for LREs were not included in the data reported by the districts. The definition time in an LRE40 occurs at the district or even the building level, introducing unexplainable (error) variance, and thus decreasing the reliability of the administrative data. The lack of clarity and consistency in measuring and reporting suppression standards and exact definitions across districts makes it impossible to be fully transparent when using this variable. In addition, the lack of a standard response format and consistent reporting criteria make meaningful interpretations of findings related to these variables challenging, at best.

Before deciding which data to include, researchers must thoroughly vet administrative data and its documentation to ensure that the included measures actually capture the desired information with adequate precision. If, as demonstrated in fallacy one, there is too much data, eliminating poorly constructed or weakly documented measures can help reduce the size of the final dataset.

21.6.4.5 Administrative Data Are Higher Quality Than Self-Reported Data

Prior literature is filled with admonitions about self-reported data (Brenner and DeLamater 2016; McCoach, Gable, and Madura 2013; Spencer et al. 2002; Vavreck 2007). Therefore, there is a temptation to assume that administrative data are of higher quality and potential utility than self-reported data. Certainly, this could be true; however, administrative data can also be lower quality. As mentioned earlier, administrative data may be unreliable and/or suffer from invalid uses and interpretations. Issues related to inadequate reliability and validity of administrative data can be more difficult to combat, given that they are "found," or preexisting, data. Therefore, the researcher may have no choice but to use suboptimal administrative data and force-fit it into the research project.

Another complication is that the timing of data collection for survey data and administrative data are often disconnected, leading to validity issues. For example, although US Census data are high quality, they are only collected once every 10 years. If the demographics in a geographic area change rapidly, Census data from several years ago may not adequately capture the construct of interest in the present. For the NEEDs[2] project, we wanted to examine whether behavioral assessment practices (BAPs) were related to dropout rates or high school completion rates. However, as we ended the four-year project, dropout rates for the year in which we collected the survey data were still unavailable. Often, when survey and administrative data are not captured within the same time frame, researchers must decide whether to use administrative data that were collected before or after the survey data, and neither choice is optimal.

Furthermore, misalignment between the level at which researchers gather data and the level at which they report data occurs often. Relatedly, the levels of data collection and dissemination may not be appropriate to answer the research questions posed in the study. For example, we were interested in knowing whether BAPs were related to special education identification and placement rates. The administrative data contained a district variable that reported the percentage of students in the district who were identified as requiring special education services. However, this variable was aggregated across 13 years of schooling (kindergarten through 12th grade) and all schools within the district. Therefore, a change in educational policy in one year would likely be undetectable for several years after implementation of the change, even if the policy actually did have an effect. This would be particularly problematic if trying to detect the effect of a policy targeting a particular grade level. Furthermore, inter-district differences in policy implementation and outcomes are impossible to examine with a district-level variable. In another study, we wanted to ascertain the percentage of students identified as gifted within a school system. Again, we had similar problems. The percentage of gifted students was aggregated across all the grades in the school. However, the comparability of these metrics was even more compromised. Given that gifted education is not federally mandated as special education is, schools differed in terms of the grade level at which they first identified students as gifted and they differed in terms of the number of grade levels represented in the school. The aggregate percentage of gifted students in the school, therefore, depended on both the grade level at which they began identifying students as gifted and the grade levels contained within the school. Without those two critical pieces of information, we could not compare the percentages of gifted students across schools. In fact, we could not even determine the percentage of students who were identified as gifted by the end of elementary school.

21.6.4.6 If Relevant Administrative Data Exist, They Will Help Answer Your Research Question

The validity of administrative data also leads to fallacy number 6, which is highly related to fallacy 5 (*administrative data are higher quality than self-reported data*). Researchers who use secondary datasets have a standing joke: "these data have every possible variable, except the one that *you* need!" Unfortunately, that statement has a great deal of truth. The variables available in the administrative dataset are often ill-suited to detect the effect of interest. Often, researchers try to use available data, even though they do not clearly map onto the investigator's theoretical framework. Even more frustrating, researchers often seek variables that are almost impossible to collect in an administrative dataset. So, they turn to proxies for those variables of interest. Although this approach may work reasonably well in some cases, using poor proxies can be dangerous: researchers may fail to find a relationship between two constructs because they used the wrong variables to measure one or more of the constructs. This represents a clear validity threat: it challenges the validity of possible data-based inferences on several fronts. First, administrative data often exist as composite variables that cannot be disentangled. The aggregation may occur because categories are collapsed together to generate one value or because multiple variables make unique contributions to a larger construct (as in the case of SES). For example, administrative data may report the percentage of students with 504 plans.[6] However, they may not disaggregate the data by the Americans with Disabilities Act accommodations category addressed within the 504. Knowing that 5% of the students in a school have 504 plans is far less informative than knowing that 4% of the students in a school

---

6 A 504 plan refers to a civil rights statute, Section 504 of the Rehabilitation Act of 1973, which requires recipients of federal financial assistance to provide students with documented disabilities "appropriate educational services designed to meet the individual needs of such students to the same extent as the needs of students without disabilities are met" (U.S. Department of Education 2018a).

have 504 accommodations for attention deficit hyperactivity disorder and 1% of the students in the school have 504 accommodations for physical ailments or disabilities. Additionally, aggregation may occur across meaningful subdivisions of the data. For example, knowing that 5% of students in a school have 504 accommodations is far less informative than knowing that 1% of kindergarteners and 8% of fifth graders receive 504 accommodations. Similarly, knowing that 10% of the students in a district receive special education services may be less useful than knowing the percentage of special education students in each of the schools in the district.

Second, administrative data often lacks information about quality, dosage, or degree of implementation. For example, even when they contain information about the percentage of students within a grade level who have learning disabilities, such data almost never contain meaningful details about the quality, quantity, and substance of the services that students receive. Therefore, even when disaggregated, administrative data often lack nuanced information about the specific constructs that researchers seek to measure.

We experienced these issues in the NEEDs^2 project. Although we had a wealth of administrative data at our disposal, when we tried to map the administrative data to our conceptual framework and theory of change, we realized just how inadequately the existing data captured our true outcomes of interest. For example, for one research question, we sought to examine the effects of district behavioral assessment policies on district behavioral outcomes. Commonly collected administrative data on behavioral outcomes include the percentage of in-school suspensions, the percentage of out-of-school suspensions, and the number of expulsions. First, all three of these variables are rare occurrences within a school system. They featured low base rates within districts and low between-district variability. Second, as mentioned under fallacy 5, the level of aggregation was problematic. More suspensions and expulsions occurred in higher grades; however, the district-level metric did not report rates by grade level, making it even less likely that we would be able to detect differences in the rates across districts. Third, districts have varying policies about whether, when, and how to institute suspensions and expulsions, and districts differ in the behavioral threshold that results in a suspension or an expulsion. Consequently, making direct comparisons across states is rather tenuous.

Although we had district-level information about the percentage of students receiving special education services, variables that disaggregated the percentage of special education students, both by disability status and by grade level would have been more useful. Even more importantly, we realized that improved BAPs could theoretically influence special education identification in two opposing manners. Improved BAP could help to identify students who had previously gone undetected, thereby increasing identification rates. However, improved BAP could also help school personnel to intervene earlier, before problems became so severe that special education identification was necessary. In this way, improved BAP could reduce the number of students identified for special education services. Detecting such a nuanced, two-pronged, indirect effect of BAP on student outcomes proved impossible with the administrative data accessed for the NEEDs^2 project.

Ideally, we sought an administrative measure that would indicate the degree to which student behavior represented a problem in the school district. Ultimately, we found that no available administrative data could serve as a reasonable proxy for the construct that we wanted to measure. In reality, a set of survey questions asking administrators about their perceptions of students' behavior and the degree to which behavior represented a problem in the school/district would have been more useful than the preexisting data that we had, even though such self-reported data are fraught with their own problems.

21.7 Discussion

The data management strategies for incorporating Big Data into traditional survey research are more extensive and diverse than those used when working with survey data alone. Furthermore, the process needs to be clearly articulated if researchers are to conduct high-quality, reproducible research using a combination of survey and administrative data. Data management and data analysis must be carefully and thoughtfully integrated. With large projects that merge multiple data sources, attempts to create one flat master datafile may be a fruitless endeavor. Instead, thoughtfully developing a relational database or an integrated set of datafiles that can be pulled together for analyses may ultimately be more efficient and reproducible. Planning for data management and data analysis within this complex framework should begin prior to data collection, and the research team must devote considerable time and effort to data management, data curation, and research reproducibility issues throughout the entire research process.

We recommend the following steps for creating reproducible datasets and data analyses:

1. Spend time with each original data source first. Get acquainted with the data in the source datafile, thoroughly read its documentation, run descriptives, and graphically inspect the variables that you may consider merging into the master datafile. Inspect frequencies, cross-tabulations, histograms, and bar charts for categorical variables. Examine means, standard deviations, correlations, and bivariate scatterplots for continuous variables. Scrutinize patterns of missing data, both within and across variables. Then, create a smaller datafile with the variables that you plan to merge into your master datafile(s).

2. In each smaller datafile you create, conduct any necessary recoding. Also, ensure that the variables feature the appropriate scale of measurement for the analyses you plan to conduct.
3. Determine the optimal number of master datafile(s) for your project and establish a suitable level of aggregation for these file(s). The goals of the research and the structure of the multiple datasets should guide decisions about how to create, merge, and store master datafiles.
4. Merge each of the cleaned smaller datafiles into the master datafile(s). Use one .Rmd file (in R) or master .do or .stmd file (in Stata) to document the process of cleaning, trimming, and recoding the variables from the external files and creating the master datafile(s).
5. Conduct additional screening, cleaning, and other necessary data management steps for the master file(s). Be sure to carefully label all variables and value codes. Create notes in the datafile or the .Rmd file to document the provenance of each variable. Be sure to document the source of the variable, and any recoding or cleaning that resulted in changes from the original source variable to the variable that currently exists in the master file(s). Including descriptive information about the number of missing cases and the descriptive statistics for the variable may also be useful.
6. Save the master datafile(s), the syntax and all other supporting documentation in a well-labeled master data folder with a completion date. The master datafile(s) should never be altered. If you need to correct a master datafile after you post it, create a new file with a separate name. Clearly mark it as the current master datafile in a new folder with a later completion date. The folders should be uncluttered and easily sorted by date, so that the newest master datafile appears at the beginning (or the end) of the file list.
7. Any analysis-specific recoding, centering, variable creation, or variable manipulation should occur within the analysis file. Create and use analysis-specific variables (such as aggregated or centered variables) in the data analyses, but do not save these variables within the master datafile. Clearly label all data analysis syntax files and structure them so that you can run the data analyses for a given research project from the master datafile with just the click of a button.
8. Choose and use common tools, and set up systems to use them consistently. Researchers often have strong preferences about statistical software packages and other data utilities. In reality, reproducibility can be accomplished using virtually any conventional statistical software program. Whereas no one tool is a magic bullet, some tools facilitate reproducibility better than others. It is crucial, both for project management and for future reproducibility, to use commonly agreed-upon tools consistently. We faced unanticipated inefficiencies when one member of the team chose to merge datafiles in R and another member of the team conducted the data management tasks in

Stata. In reality, either Stata or R could have easily handled our data merging and management tasks. However, combining the two programs resulted in many headaches that could have been easily avoided. Whatever efficiencies we gained by allowing researchers on the team to use their tool of choice were lost because we needed to recode and redocument many variables during the transition from R to Stata.

9. Develop a set of team-based norms. We cannot overstate the importance of training and establishing commonalities across your team, starting on day one. Everyone needs to agree on naming and labeling conventions for each created document, from the first administrative datafile to the master data to the final report/manuscript. We recommend short (but informative) variable names, and longer, more descriptive variable and value labels. Be sure that everyone adheres to the data management and data analysis steps above, and be sure that everyone follows the same naming, file organization, and syntax organization structures. We recommend hosting a meeting at the beginning of the project to establish: norms for file organization and structure; file/folder naming standards and organizational plans; and variable creation, naming, labeling and storage conventions. If multiple people plan to work on the same analysis tasks, it is imperative that you develop consistent practices related to file naming, document storage, and organizational structure that allow different people to access the same files and add syntax that all team members understand. We have also found that as the project progresses, "booster shot" meetings help to ensure that the data systems we put in place at the beginning of the study continue throughout the remainder of the project. Long (2009) presents some excellent and thorough suggestions for these types of conventions.

Researchers need to develop standards for, and to evaluate the quality of, data gathered from outside sources early in the process. Education research lacks a standard set of guidelines to evaluate the quality of data gathered from outside sources. Our NEEDs[2] project highlights the importance of considering several quality dimensions when deciding whether to use administrative Big Data in conjunction with traditional survey data. Part of the data vetting process should include questions, such as:

- Are the data collection processes transparent?
- Are the data complete?
- Do the available data allow for valid inferences?
- Are the data reliable/accurate?
- Are the data timely?

When deciding whether and how to include Big Data in a project, researchers must assess the quality of the data vs. the quantity of the data. As we pointed out in fallacy one, sometimes less is more, even regarding data. Researchers who primarily use quantitative data can be lured by the amount of data available in big datasets. Used in conjunction with traditional survey research, Big Data has the potential to give researchers a broader look at the question with more analytical power or provide insights into small, low-incidence populations difficult and costly to reach via traditional survey methods. These additional data are only helpful, however, if they are high quality and a good fit with the research question. Creating extremely large datasets presents a number of challenges. Specifically, very large datafiles can be slow to load and run (especially when you work with them remotely), taxing the limits of available software and hardware. When such large datasets yield useful results, the benefits of incorporating Big Data into survey studies far outweigh the costs. However, when primary data collection gets bogged down by countless useless variables, Big Data can distract from – rather than enhance – the research process. As Hill et al. aptly stated, survey researchers need to develop deeper understanding about the sources, limitations, and potential errors of the vast quantity of extant accessible data (Hill and Dever 2014). We hope that our suggestions provide helpful advice for survey researchers who wish to incorporate large administrative datasets into their own research projects.

References

Adams, M.J.D. and Umbach, P.D. (2012). Nonresponse and online student evaluations of teaching: understanding the influence of salience, fatigue, and academic environments. *Research in Higher Education* 53 (5): 576–591. https://doi.org/10.1007/s11162-011-9240-5.

American Association for Public Opinion Research (AAPOR) (2018). Transparency initiative. https://www.aapor.org/transparency_initiative.htm (accessed 17 September 2018).

Anderson, C. (2008). The end of theory: the data deluge makes the scientific method obsolete. *Wired Magazine* 16: 16-07.

Brenner, P.S. and DeLamater, J. (2016). Lies, damned lies, and survey self-reports? Identity as a cause of measurement bias. *Social Psychology Quarterly* 79 (4): 333–354. https://doi.org/10.1177/0190272516628298.

Callegaro, M. and Yang, Y. (2018). The role of surveys in the era of 'Big Data'. In: *The Palgrave Handbook of Survey Research* (eds. D.L. Vannette and J.A. Krosnick), 175–192. Cham, Switzerland: Palgrave Macmillan.

Chen, E.E. and Wojcik, S.P. (2016). A practical guide to big data research in psychology. *Psychological Methods* 21 (4): 458–474. https://doi.org/10.1037/met0000111.

Couper, M.P. (2013). Is the sky falling? New technology, changing media, and the future of surveys. *Survey Research Methods* 7 (3): 145–156.

Couper, M.P. (2017). New developments in survey data collection. *Annual Review of Sociology* 43 (1): 121–145. https://doi.org/10.1146/annurev-soc-060116-053613.

Cukier, K. and Mayer-Schoenberger, V. (2013). The rise of big data: how it's changing the way we think about the world. *Foreign Affairs* 92: 28.

Data Sharing for Demographic Research (DSDR) (2019). Data harmonization. https://www.icpsr.umich.edu/icpsrweb/content/DSDR/harmonization.html (accessed 14 March 2020).

Fahle, E.M., Shear, B.R., Kalogrides, D., et al. (2018). Stanford education data archive: technical documentation v2.1. https://stacks.stanford.edu/file/druid:db586ns4974/SEDA_documentation_v21.pdf.

Figlio, D. (2017). *Rule of Administration Data in Education Research: Panel Summary ("Panel 1 Summary")*. Washington, DC: National Academy of Education.

FlyData (2019). The 6 challenges of big data integration. https://www.flydata.com/the-6-challenges-of-big-data-integration/ (accessed 14 March 2020).

Guess, A.R. (2017). Five steps to data harmonization with absolutdata CEO Anil Kaul. http://www.dataversity.net/depth-interview-five-steps-data-harmonization-abolutdata-ceo-anil-kaul/ (accessed 10 March 2019).

Harris, D.N. and Sass, T.R. (2010). What makes for a good teacher and who can tell? https://pdfs.semanticscholar.org/4b83/3fb726a400ebe12c2560482caca15c580478.pdf.

Hill, C.A. and Dever, J. (2014). The future of social media, sociality, and survey research. In: *Social Media, Sociality, and Survey Research* (eds. C.A. Hill, E. Dean and J. Murphy), 295–317. Research Triangle Park, NC: RTI International.

Ho, A. (2017). *Advancing Educational Research and Student Privacy in the "Big Data" Era ("Ho Workshop Paper")*. Washington, DC: National Academy of Education.

Janke, L., Asher, A., and Keralis, S. (2012). *The Problem of Data. Council on Library and Information Resources (CLIR) Report. Pub. #154*. Washington, DC: Council on Library and Information Resources.

Japec, L., Kreuter, F., Berg, M. et al. (2015). Big data in survey research. *Public Opinion Research* 79 (4): 839–880. https://doi.org/10.1093/poq/nfv039.

Johnson, T.P. and Smith, T.W. (2017). Big data and survey research: supplement or substitute? In: *Seeing Cities Through Big Data* (eds. P. Thakuriah (Vonu), N. Tilahun and M. Zellner), 113–125. Cham: Springer https://doi.org/10.1007/978-3-319-40902-3_7.

Kreuter, F. (2013). Facing the nonresponse challenge. *The Annals of the American Academy of Political and Social Science* 645 (1): 23–25.

Kreuter, F., Couper, M.P., and Lyber, L. (2010). The use of paradata to monitor and manage survey data collection. In: *Proceedings of the Joint Statistical Meetings*

(JSM), Vancouver, British Columbia, Canada, 282–296. American Statistical Association.

Krueger, B.S. and West, B.T. (2014). Assessing the potential of paradata and other auxiliary data for nonresponse adjustments. *Public Opinion Quarterly* 78 (4): 795–831. https://doi.org/10.1093/poq/nfu040.

Kyle, T., Frascino, N., Prosviryakova, M., et al. (2016). Paradata production post-data collection: challenges and best practices. The United States Census Bureau. https://www.census.gov/fedcasic/fc2016/ppt/1_7_Paradata.pdf (accessed 9 January 2019).

Laney, D. (2001). 3D Data Management: Controlling Data Volume, Velocity and Variety. Technical Report META Group.

Lavrakas, P.J. (2008). *Encyolpedia of Survey Research Methods.* Thousand Oaks, CA: Sage Publications, Inc. https://doi.org/10.4135/9781412963947.

Lazer, D., Kennedy, R., King, G. et al. (2014). Big data. The parable of Google flu: traps in big data analysis. *Science* 343 (6176): 1203–1205. https://doi.org/10.1126/science.1248506.

Leek, J.T. and Peng, R.D. (2015). Opinion: reproducible research can still be wrong: adopting a prevention approach. *Proceedings of the National Academy of Sciences of the United States of America* 112 (6): 1645–1646. https://doi.org/10.1073/pnas.1421412111.

Long, S. (2009). *The Workflow of Data Analysis.* College Station, TX: Stata Press.

Mair, P. (2016). Thou shalt be reproducible! A technology perspective. *Frontiers in Psychology* 7: 1079. https://doi.org/10.3389/fpsyg.2016.01079.

McCoach, D., Gable, R., and Madura, J. (2013). *Instrument Development in the Affective Domain.* New York, NY: Springer.

Meyer, B.D. and Mittag, N. (2019). Using linked survey and administrative data to better measure income: implications for poverty, program effectiveness, and holes in the safety net. *American Economic Journal: Applied Economics* 11 (2): 176–204. https://doi.org/10.1257/app.20170478.

Miller, P.V. (2010). Presidential address: the road to transparency in survey research. *Public Opinion Quarterly* 74 (3): 602–606. https://doi.org/10.1093/poq/nfq038.

Mishkin, G. (2014). Integrating big data with traditional research. Quirks. https://www.quirks.com/articles/integrating-big-data-and-traditional-research (accessed 10 April 2018).

Munafò, M.R., Nosek, B.A., Bishop, D.V.M. et al. (2017). A manifesto for reproducible science. *Nature Human Behaviour* 1: 0021. https://doi.org/10.1038/s41562-016-0021.

National Center for Education Statistics (NCES) (2005). *Directory of Public Elementary and Secondary Education Agencies. U.S. Department of Education, National Center for Education Statistics.* Washington, DC: U.S. Government Printing Office.

National Institues For Health (NIH) (2018). NIH strategic plan for data science. https://datascience.nih.gov/sites/default/files/NIH_Strategic_Plan_for_Data_Science_Final_508.pdf.

National Science Foundation/Institute of Education Sciences (NSF/IES) (2018). Companion Guidelines on Replication and Reproducibility for Education Research and Development. https://www.nsf.gov/pubs/2019/nsf19022/nsf19022.pdf.

Nicolaas, G. (2011). Survey paradata: a review. National Center for Social Research. http://eprints.ncrm.ac.uk/1719/1/Nicolaas_review_paper_jan11.pdf (accessed 7 January 2019).

Nosek, B.A., Alter, G., Banks, G.C. et al. (2015). Scientific standards. Promoting an open research culture. *Science* 348 (6242): 1422–1425. https://doi.org/10.1126/science.aab2374.

Open Science Collaboration (2015). Psychology. Estimating the reproducibility of psychological science. *Science* 349 (6251): aac4716. https://doi.org/10.1126/science.aac4716.

Pashler, H. and Wagenmakers, E.J. (2012). Editors' introduction to the special section on replicability in psychological science: a crisis of confidence? *Perspectives on Psychological Science* 7 (6): 528–530. https://doi.org/10.1177/1745691612465253.

Perez, M., Greco, M., and Sermonetaa, C. (2017). Integration of administrative and survey data to reduce respondent burden: the Italian experience in the field of agriculture statistics. *Paper presented to the Conference of European Statisticians Workshop on Statistical Data Collection*, Ottawa, Canada WP (10–12 October 2017).

Playford, C.J., Gayle, V., Connelly, R. et al. (2016). Administrative social science data: the challenge of reproducible research. *Big Data & Society* 3 (2): 1–13. https://doi.org/10.1177/2053951716684143.

Raghupathi, W. and Raghupathi, V. (2014). Big data analytics in healthcare: promise and potential. *Health Information Science and Systems* 2: 3. https://doi.org/10.1186/2047-2501-2-3.

Reardon, S.F., Kalogrides, D., and Shores, K. (2017). *The Geography of Racial/Ethnic Test Score Gaps (CEPA Working Paper No. 16-10)*. Stanford, CA: Stanford Center for Education Policy Analysis http://cepa.stanford.edu/wp16-10.

Royal Society (2012). Science as an open enterprise. http://royalsociety.org/policy/projects/science-public-enterprise/report/ (accessed 14 January 2018).

Sandve, G.K., Nekrutenko, A., Taylor, J. et al. (2013). Ten simple rules for reproducible computational research. *PLoS Computational Biology* 9 (10): e1003285. https://doi.org/10.1371/journal.pcbi.1003285.

Savage, M. and Burrows, R. (2016). The coming crisis of empirical sociology. *Sociology* 41 (5): 885–899. https://doi.org/10.1177/0038038507080443.

Science International (2015). Open data in a big data world. https://www.icsu.org/publications/open-data-in-a-big-dataworld (accessed 19 January 2018).

Servick, K. (2018). 'Generous' approach to replication confirms many high-profile social science findings. *Science* https://doi.org/10.1126/science.aav2151.

Shimizu, I. M. (2000). Response in Federal Establishment Surveys. https://s3.amazonaws.com/sitesusa/wp-content/uploads/sites/242/2014/05/IGEN-ices3_final.pdf (accessed 14 March 2020).

Siegel, E. (2018). Has the Large Hadron Collider accidentally thrown away the evidence for new physics? Forbes. https://www.forbes.com/sites/startswithabang/2018/09/13/has-the-large-hadron-collider-accidentally-thrown-away-the-evidence-for-new-physics/#28cafaac9270 (accesseed 13 September 2018).

Spencer, E.A., Appleby, P.N., Davey, G.K. et al. (2002). Validity of self-reported height and weight in 4808 EPIC-Oxford participants. *Public Health Nutrition* 5 (4): 561–565. https://doi.org/10.1079/PHN2001322.

Starr, M. (2019). Less than 1% of large Hadron Collider data ever gets looked at. Science Alert. https://www.sciencealert.com/over-99-percent-of-large-hadron-collider-particle-collision-data-is-lost (accessed 06 January 2019).

U.S. Department of Education (2018a). Protecting students with disabilities. https://www2.ed.gov/about/offices/list/ocr/504faq.html (accessed 10 March 2019).

U.S. Department of Education, National Center for Education Statistics CCD (2018b). School and district glossary. https://nces.ed.gov/ccd/commonfiles/glossary.asp (accessed 25 September 2018).

Vance, A. (2016). Panel Handout: Lessons Learned from Education Stakeholders. National Association of State Boards of Education. Vance Handout.

Vavreck, L. (2007). The exaggerated effects of advertising on turnout: the dangers of self-reports. *Quarterly Journal of Political Science* 2 (4): 325–343. https://doi.org/10.1561/100.00006005.

Wang, Y., Kung, L., and Byrd, T.A. (2018). Big data analytics: understanding its capabilities and potential benefits for healthcare organizations. *Technological Forecasting and Social Change* 126: 3–13. https://doi.org/10.1016/j.techfore.2015.12.019.

Ward, J. S. and Barker, A. (2013). Undefined by data: a survey of big data definitions. https://arxiv.org/pdf/1309.5821.pdf.

Wells, C. and Thorson, K. (2016). Combining big data and survey techniques to model effects of political content flows in Facebook. *Social Science Computer Review* 35 (1): 33–52. https://doi.org/10.1177/0894439315609528.

Winters, K. and Netscher, S. (2016). Proposed standards for variable harmonization documentation and referencing: a case study using QuickCharmStats 1.1. *PLoS One* 11 (2): e0147795. https://doi.org/10.1371/journal.pone.0147795.

Further Reading

Biemer, P.P. (2010). Total survey error: design, implementation, and evaluation. *Public Opinion Quarterly* 74 (5): 817–848.

Boyd, D. and Crawford, K. (2012). Critical questions for big data: provocations for a cultural, technological, and scholarly phenomenon. *Information, Communication & Society* 15: 662–679.

Cai, L. and Zhu, Y. (2015). The challenges of data quality and data quality assessment in the big data era. *Data Science Journal* 14: 2. https://doi.org/10.5334/dsj-2015-002.

Calude, C.S. and Longo, G. (2017). The deluge of spurious correlations in big data. *Foundations of Science* 22: 595–612.

Dresner Advisory Services, LLC (2017). Big Data Analytics Market Study. https://www.microstrategy.com/getmedia/cd052225-be60-49fd-ab1c-4984ebc3cde9/Dresner-Report-Big_Data_Analytic_Market_Study-WisdomofCrowdsSeries-2017 (accessed 14 March 2020).

Fan, J. and Liao, Y. (2014). Endogeneity in high dimensions. *Annals of Statistics* 42: 872.

Fan, J., Han, F., and Liu, H. (2014). Challenges of big data analysis. *National Science Review* 1 (2): 293–314.

Gandomi, A. and Haider, M. (2015). Beyond the hype: big data concepts, methods, and analytics. *International Journal of Information Management* 35: 137–144.

Harford, T. (2014). Big data: are we making a big mistake? FT Magazine. 2014-03-28. https://www.ft.com/content/21a6e7d8-b479-11e3-a09a-00144feabdc0.

Harris, D.N. and Sass, T.R. (2011). Teacher training, teacher quality, and student achievement. *Journal of Public Economics* 95: 798–812.

Kamaruddin, S.K. and Ravi, V. (2016). Credit card fraud detection using big data analytics: use of PSOAANN based one-class classification. In: *Proceedings of the International Conference on Informatics and Analytics*. Association for Computing Machinery https://doi.org/10.1145/2980258.2980319.

Kataria, M. and Mittal, M.P. (2014). Big data: a review. *International Journal of Computer Science and Mobile Computing* 3: 106–110.

Khoury, M.J. and Ioannidis, J.P. (2014). Big data meets public health. *Science* 346: 1054–1055.

Laha, A. (2016). Statistical challenges with big data in management science. In: *Big Data Analytics* (eds. S. Pyne, B.L.S.P. Rao and S.B. Rao), 41–55. New Delhi: Springer https://doi.org/10.1007/978-81-322-3628-3_3.

Lohr, J. (2013). The origins of 'Big Data': an etymological detective story. *New York Times* (1 February). https://bits.blogs.nytimes.com/2013/02/01/the-origins-of-big-data-an-etymological-detective-story/.

Maxwell, S.E., Lau, M.Y., and Howard, G.S. (2015). Is psychology suffering from a replication crisis? What does "failure to replicate" really mean? *American Psychologist* 70: 487.

Schmidt, S. (2009). Shall we really do it again? The powerful concept of replication is neglected in the social sciences. *Review of General Psychology* 13 (2): 90–100.

Schultze, C.L. and Newlon, D.H. (2011). Expanding access to administrative data for research in the United States. In: *Ten Years and Beyond: Economists Answer the NSF's Call For Long-Term Research Agendas* (eds. C.L. Schultze and D.H. Newlon), 81–84. American Economic Association https://ssrn.com/abstract=1886598.

22

Combining Active and Passive Mobile Data Collection: A Survey of Concerns

Florian Keusch[1,2], Bella Struminskaya[3], Frauke Kreuter[1,2,4], and Martin Weichbold[5]

[1] Department of Sociology, School of Social Sciences, University of Mannheim, Germany
[2] Joint Program in Survey Methodology, University of Maryland, College Park, MD, USA
[3] Department of Methodology and Statistics, Utrecht University, The Netherlands
[4] Institute for Employment Research, Nuremberg, Germany
[5] University of Salzburg, Austria

22.1 Introduction

Smartphones have become deeply ingrained into people's daily lives: users take pictures and videos, communicate through text messaging and calls, and use their phones to navigate around cities. Although technology adoption varies by country, the growing importance of smartphones is indisputable when one examines the rates of smartphone ownership and mobile Internet use. For example, 77% of US adults report owning a smartphone (Pew Research Center 2017b), and 91% of adults in the Netherlands, 84% of adults in Germany, and 79% of adults in Austria use the Internet on a mobile device (Eurostat 2018). Similarly high rates of smartphone ownership are reported for some countries in the Asia-Pacific area (eMarketer Report 2017). The levels of smartphone ownership in Africa are substantially lower, but they vary considerably among countries (Afrobarometer 2018). The popularity of smartphones creates new opportunities for researchers who can use them to collect data through self-reports in mobile web surveys (e.g. Couper, Antoun, and Mavletova 2017), but also recruit respondents to perform additional tasks such as taking pictures, recording audio and video, granting access to contact lists, allowing logging of calls and text messages, tracking app usage, Internet browsing behavior, and collecting users' activity and GPS location information (Link et al. 2014; Raento, Oulasvirta, and Eagle 2009). Researchers use data collected through smartphone sensors and other mobile devices, for example, to link emotional well-being to geographic locations (MacKerron and

Big Data Meets Survey Science: A Collection of Innovative Methods, First Edition. Edited by Craig A. Hill, Paul P. Biemer, Trent D. Buskirk, Lilli Japec, Antje Kirchner, Stas Kolenikov, and Lars E. Lyberg.
© 2021 John Wiley & Sons, Inc. Published 2021 by John Wiley & Sons, Inc.

Mourato 2013; York Cornwell and Cagney 2017), map social networks and ties (Eagle and Pentland 2006; Kassarnig et al. 2017; Stopczynski et al. 2014), measure job search behavior (Kreuter et al. 2018; Sugie 2018) and consumer expenditure (Jäckle et al. 2017), or study mobility and travel behavior (Evenson and Furberg 2017; Goodspeed et al. 2018; Greene et al. 2016; Scherpenzeel 2016).

When using smartphones for data collection, Wenz, Jäckle, and Couper (2017) distinguished between active and passive roles of participants. Mobile data collection that involves *active* engagement by the participant include tasks such as responding to survey questions or taking photos, and give participants maximum control over what data they share. Other forms of mobile data collection are passive in that data collection runs in the background (e.g., tracking GPS location, activity data, call logs). Especially if data is collected continuously and at high frequencies, participants have little or no control during the data collection process other than turning off the measurement.

Due to the large volume of data, the high velocity and frequency of measurement, and the variety of data formats that can be collected through apps and sensors, these products of passive measurement can be considered Big Data (Callegaro and Yang 2018), with all its advantages and disadvantages for both researchers and smartphone users. The added utility of these data for the researcher arises from the richness of the data that can be collected at much higher frequency than self-reports from surveys without much, if any, burden for participants. Another advantage of passive measurement is that sensor data can lead to more accurate estimates than self-report (e.g., Boase and Ling 2013; Evenson, Goto, and Furberg 2015; Scherpenzeel 2016; Stopher, FitzGerald, and Xu 2007). However, the increased size of the data collected requires the researcher to set up infrastructure (including storage, computing power, analytical skills) to store, manage, and process these data. For the smartphone user, providing these data poses risks; for example, data streams could be intercepted by an unauthorized party. Connecting multiple streams of data from different sources could also create detailed profiles of users' habits, demographics, or well-being that would not only allow someone to reidentify previously anonymous users but also use this information to impact credit, employment, or insurability (van Deursen and Mossberger 2018; Bender et al. 2017).

The premise under which social and market research can function effectively is that research participants provide relevant, accurate information without fear of the adverse effects mentioned above, and the continued success of social and market research relies on the public's trust that these data will be handled responsibly and ethically (Joe, Raben, and Phillips 2016). However, smartphone users are increasingly concerned about the privacy of their information (Pew Research Center 2014, 2015, 2017a). Especially for participants of passive mobile data collection, anticipating all the purposes for which the data collected can be used might be difficult. Yet, precisely the unanticipated secondary uses often constitute the "crown jewels" of passive data (Tene and Polonetsky 2013). For the researcher, the challenge lies in how to balance the risk to the participants with the utility of the collected data, the so-called privacy-utility trade-off (Bender et al. 2017).

Against this background, we studied users' concern with different forms of active and passive data collection on smartphones, utilizing data from probability and nonprobability samples in two countries. We answer the following two research questions:

- Does concern about participating in smartphone data collection differ by type of data collected on a smartphone?
- Does concern about smartphone data collection vary across subgroups of smartphone users with different levels of smartphone skills and smartphone use habits?

In the remainder of this chapter, we first review existing literature on concern with and willingness to engage in active and passive forms of mobile data collection. We then describe four online surveys conducted in two countries that all administered a similar set of questions on concern with five different forms of mobile data collection. We use these data to analyze differences in concern across the five tasks and study correlates of concern. We conclude with a discussion of our findings, their practical implications, and suggestions for further research.

22.2 Previous Research

22.2.1 Concern with Smartphone Data Collection

When asked to perform additional tasks for research that go beyond answering survey questions on their mobile devices, smartphone users have shown varying rates of willingness to perform such tasks. For example, Revilla et al. (2016) found that stated willingness of online panel members was much higher for taking pictures (25–49% in seven countries) than for sharing GPS location (19–37%). Wenz, Jäckle, and Couper (2017) and Revilla, Couper, and Ochoa (2018) confirmed lower stated willingness of respondents to allow various types of passive tracking (e.g., GPS, online behavior) compared to actively completing tasks (e.g., taking photos, completing online questionnaires, scanning barcodes). Keusch et al. (2019) found that giving participants more control over when data are shared with researchers increased willingness for downloading a research app that would passively collect data from the smartphone compared to data collection that the participant could not temporarily turn off.

An example of a seemingly contradictory finding is demonstrated by Struminskaya et al. (2018) who asked smartphone users in the Dutch Longitudinal Internet Studies for the Social Sciences (LISS) panel about their willingness to provide GPS location and to wear a fitness bracelet. Respondents' stated willingness to share their GPS location on the smartphone was considerably lower (30% "definitely yes" and "probably yes") than the willingness to wear a fitness bracelet (60%), despite both tasks using GPS sensors. Revilla, Couper, and Ochoa (2018) reported similar findings of a fitness bracelet eliciting higher willingness than GPS on the smartphone (although not when the question asked to track the location of respondents' children). These examples led us to believe that the decisions about stated willingness and actual consent to allow passive data collection seem to be based on heuristics. Perhaps respondents associated a fitness bracelet with health, while GPS tracking was associated with surveillance (Pew Research Center 2016). Another explanation might be that users were not even aware that a fitness bracelet tracks their GPS location. Balebako et al. (2014) showed that smartphone users often do not understand the terminology used in standard descriptions of different data types collected on their devices, and even experts tend to disagree on their meaning. Concerns with data collection might also influence willingness and actual consent to allow passive data collection. Privacy concerns affected stated willingness to perform additional tasks and allow passive data collection on smartphones (Jäckle et al. 2017; Keusch et al. 2019; Revilla, Couper, and Ochoa 2018; Struminskaya et al. 2018; Wenz, Jäckle, and Couper 2017). Thus, users might attach different levels of concern to different forms of mobile data collection. High concern might be assumed for tasks involving passive mobile data collection (e.g., using GPS or downloading an app for smartphone usage tracking) where the user has little control over when and what data are actually shared with the researcher. Lower concern might be assumed for tasks that allow users to curate what data are actually shared, such as completing online questionnaires or sharing pictures.

Concerns associated with a relatively new technology are not unique to passive data collection: Singer and Couper (2011) argued that perceived lack of security of Internet transactions can influence respondents willingness to participate in Internet surveys (p. 138). In several experimental vignette studies, Couper and Singer (2013) found that any mention of paradata, that is, passively collected data about respondents' answering behavior (e.g., survey duration, keystroke information, navigation within the questionnaire, changing the answer, screen resolution, etc.) lowered the willingness to participate in online surveys. However, to date little is known about privacy concerns that participants might have when engaging in new forms of mobile data collection.

22.2.2 Differential Concern across Subgroups of Users

In addition to concern with mobile data collection varying by type of data collection, perceptions of concern might vary by user characteristics. From research on how people engage with the Internet and other technologies, we know that access to a technology does not necessarily mean that everybody is able and willing to use the technology to its full potential. Hargittai (2002) uses the term "second-level digital divide" for this phenomenon. For example, a study by the Pew Research Center (2017a) found that education is highly correlated with knowledge about IT-related topics such as cybersecurity. Thus, people with higher education might have a higher familiarity with technology, potentially because they engage more with it and, thus, might feel more comfortable using it and have lower concerns. Those with lower levels of education might have high concerns as they do not use the technology as often or they might have lower concerns due to the lack of understanding. The same report found that Americans 50 and older expressed greater concern over personal data security than younger people. Recent research also found that smartphone skills and the use of smartphones for different activities correlated with reported willingness to participate in smartphone-based data collection tasks that went beyond responding to mobile web surveys (Couper, Antoun, and Mavletova 2017; Keusch et al. 2019; Struminskaya et al. 2018; Wenz, Jäckle, and Couper 2017). Similarly, education, age, smartphone skills, the frequency of smartphone use, and the diversity of activities that users engaged in with their smartphones might be correlated with concerns about the use of smartphones for research. Higher educated users, younger users, users who are more skilled in their use of a smartphone, who are using the smartphone more frequently, and who use the smartphone for more different activities might have fewer concerns with mobile data collection.

22.3 Methods and Data

To answer our research questions, we collected survey data about concerns when using a smartphone to participate in research among respondents in four web surveys; two German nonprobability online panels, one German probability-based online panel, and one probability-based web survey in Austria. Measuring the same constructs in different samples, both based on probability and nonprobability methods, allowed us to replicate our findings under different conditions and provided a measure of reliability of our findings. We first briefly introduce the four surveys and then describe the measures that were collected in these surveys and how we analyzed the data.

22.3.1 Sample 1

In December 2016, 9000 email invitations were sent to members of a German non-probability online panel; 3144 people started the survey. Quotas for gender and age were used; only smartphone owners were able to proceed to the main questionnaire. A total of 404 panel members who started the survey were screened out because of the quotas; 32 were screened out because they said they did not own a smartphone. Of the 2708 remaining respondents, 61 broke off the survey (2.2%), while 24 respondents had duplicated IDs and were dropped from the dataset. The remaining 2623 respondents completed the survey, constituting Sample 1 in our study (Keusch 2019b).

22.3.2 Sample 2

In December 2017, members of another German nonprobability online panel were invited through a survey-router system to participate in a web survey, and 1398 people started the survey. Again, quotas for gender and age were used, and only smartphone owners were able to proceed to the main questionnaire. Eighty-two panel members who started the survey were screened out because of the quotas or because they reported they did not own a smartphone. Of the 1316 remaining respondents, 102 broke off the survey (7.8%), and 1214 respondents completed the questionnaire, constituting Sample 2 in our study (Keusch 2019a).

22.3.3 Sample 3

The third sample came from Wave 32 of the German Internet Panel (GIP), administered in November 2017 (Herzing and Blom 2018; Blom et al. 2018). GIP is a probability-based longitudinal online survey based on a sample recruited face-to-face and representative of both the online and the offline population in Germany aged 16–75 years. People who did not have a computer and/or no access to the internet were provided with a basic laptop/tablet computer to participate. Panel members are invited on a bimonthly basis to participate in web surveys on political and economic attitudes and reform preferences (Blom, Gathmann, and Krieger 2015). A total of 2648 GIP panel members participated in the Wave 32 survey with a completion rate of 53.3% and a cumulative response rate of 10.9%. Both owners and nonowners of smartphones participated in Wave 32, but only respondents who reported owning a smartphone were asked the relevant questions for our analysis. Thus, Sample 3 was limited to the 2186 smartphone owners who completed the GIP Wave 32 questionnaire.

22.3.4 Sample 4

The fourth dataset came from a web survey conducted by the Austrian statistical office (Statistics Austria) in spring 2018. The data was collected as part of Wave V.2 of the PUMA (Plattform für Umfragen, Methoden und empirische Analysen) project (PUMA 2018, 2019). A random sample of 1500 Austrian residents aged 16–74 years was drawn from the Austrian central registry (Zentrales Melderegister, ZMR) and invited to complete an online questionnaire. Of the 695 people who completed the web questionnaire, 632 reported owning a smartphone, constituting Sample 4 in our study.

22.3.5 Measures

The four studies described in Sections 22.3.1 to 22.3.4 collected information on a variety of topics, but in all four surveys, we administered an identical set of questions that will help us answer our research questions. The main outcome variables for our study came from a question on concern with five different forms of mobile data collection[1]:

> Smartphones can collect a variety of data that provide researchers with information of the everyday life of the users. Below you will see a number of activities that you could do with your smartphone. How concerned would you be about the security of providing information in the following ways for research? (Scale: not at all concerned, a little concerned, somewhat concerned, very concerned)
>
> (1) Complete an online questionnaire on your smartphone.
> (2) Download an app which collects data about how you use your smartphone.
> (3) Use the camera of your smartphone to take photos or scan barcodes (for example, photos of receipts, barcodes of purchased products).
> (4) Allow built-in features of your smartphone to measure the frequency and speed at which you walk, run, or cycle.
> (5) Share the GPS position of your smartphone (for example, to measure time spent in urban vs. green spaces).

For our logistic regression models predicting concern, we dichotomized the response to each of the five tasks to "low concern" (combining "not at all

---

[1] This question is modeled after a question on willingness to carry out specific research-related tasks on a smartphone that was asked by Wenz et al. (2017) in the UK Understanding Society Innovation Panel.

concerned" and "a little concerned") vs. "high concern" (combining "somewhat concerned" and "a lot concerned").

In addition to the questions on concern when using smartphones for various forms of mobile data collection, respondents were asked about frequency of smartphone use, smartphone skills, smartphone activities, general privacy concern, and sociodemographics (see Appendix 22.A for full question wording). We asked respondents about their frequency of smartphone use for activities other than phone calls or text messaging using a fully labeled 5-point scale. To measure smartphone skills, respondents had to rate themselves on a scale from 1 Beginner to 5 Advanced. For the analysis, we dichotomized the responses to these two variables to "every day" vs. "less than every day" for frequency of smartphone use and "high" (4 or 5 on the original scale) vs. "low" (1, 2, or 3 on the original scale) for self-reported smartphone skills. We further asked respondents whether they used their smartphones for 12 different activities such as browsing websites, reading and/or writing emails, reading and posting content on social media, making purchases, and installing new apps. We summed up the answers into a count of smartphone activities (range: 0–12).

In addition, we collected information on general privacy concern, age, gender, and education of respondents, and we used these measures as control variables in our analysis. General privacy concern was measured based on the question, "In general, how worried are you about your personal privacy?" using the same 4-point fully labeled response scale as our main dependent variables. For the analysis, we collapsed responses into two groups: low concern vs. high concern for general privacy concern. Table 22.1 provides descriptive statistics of all measures used in our analysis.

22.3.6 Analysis Plan

We start our analysis with providing descriptive statistics for the responses on the original 4-point scale of the main measure of interest: concern when engaging in mobile data collection. We then specify five models for each of the datasets from our four samples with dichotomized concern (high vs. low) for the five tasks as the dependent variable. We regress concern on frequency of smartphone use ("every day" vs. "less than every day"), self-reported smartphone skills ("high" vs. "low"), and number of smartphone activities controlling for general privacy concern ("high" vs. "low"), and sociodemographics using logistic regression. All analyses for this study were done in R version 4.0.0 (R Core Team 2020).[2]

---

[2] All code for the analyses can be found at https://github.com/fkeusch01/mobile-data-concern.

Table 22.1 Descriptive statistics.

	Sample 1		Sample 2		Sample 3		Sample 4	
	%	Miss	%	Miss	%	Miss	%	Miss
DV: High concern with								
Online questionnaire	44.4	5	34.7	1	63.0	3	54.4	1
Smartphone usage	79.0	18	67.7	9	83.4	4	84.8	1
Camera	49.3	10	41.4	5	57.8	2	58.0	3
Activity data	50.9	11	42.0	5	51.9	5	43.4	1
GPS	70.7	12	60.0	6	73.8	4	72.4	1
Use smartphone every day	90.3	5	84.8	1	83.6	1	85.6	1
High smartphone skills	71.0	2	72.8	0	52.4	1	60.4	0

	Sample 1				Sample 2				Sample 3				Sample 4			
	Med	Mean	SD	Miss	Med	Mean	SD	Miss	Med	Mean	SD	Miss	Med	Mean	SD	Miss
Number of smartphone activities	9	8.5	2.9	0	9	8.7	3.0	0	5	5.8	3.2	0	8	7.5	2.9	0

	Sample 1		Sample 2		Sample 3		Sample 4	
	%	Miss	%	Miss	%	Miss	%	Miss
High general privacy concern	61.0	2	64.7	3	64.8	1	54.4	0
Female	49.9	0	50.0	0	49.2	1	48.9	0
Age		0		0		1		2
Less than 30 years	28.9		29.2		19.5[a]		29.7	
30–49 years	47.5		47.4		40.2[a]		36.8	
50 years and older	23.6		23.5		40.4[a]		33.5	
Without HS degree	48.4	31	49.0	28	46.7	37	51.6	0
n	2623		1214		2186		632	

DV = dependent variable; Med = median; SD = standard deviation; Miss = missing values.

a) In the GIP (Sample 3), age is reported in five-year birth cohorts, thus the age categories used here are "less than 33 years," "33–52 years," and "53 years and older."

22.4 Results

Figure 22.1 plots the concern for the five forms of mobile data collection from the four samples. In all four samples, downloading an app that collects data about how users engage with their smartphone yields the highest concern. For example,

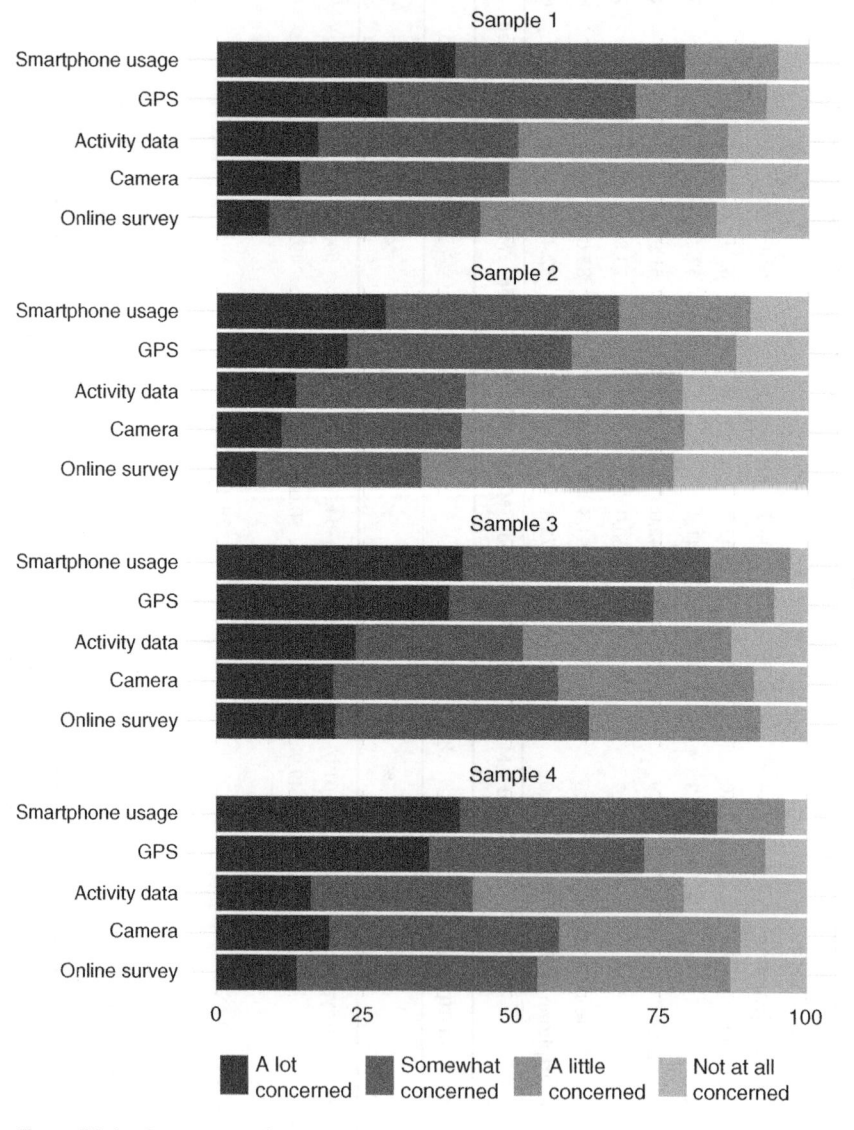

Figure 22.1 Percentage of respondents reporting concern with five forms of mobile data collection by sample.

79% of Sample 1 respondents (Sample 2: 68%; Sample 3: 83%; and Sample 4: 85%) reported that they would be a lot or somewhat concerned if an app tracked their smartphone usage data. GPS tracking for research also yielded high concern in all four samples: 70% of Sample 1 respondents (Sample 2: 60%; Sample 3: 74%; and Sample 4: 72%) reported a lot or somewhat concern about GPS tracking. Less concern was reported when allowing built-in sensors of the smartphone to measure activity, such as the frequency and speed of walking, running, or cycling (Sample 1: 51%; Sample 2: 42%; Sample 3: 52%; and Sample 4: 43%), using the camera of the smartphone to take photos or scan barcodes (Sample 1: 49%; Sample 2: 41%; Sample 3: 58%; and Sample 4: 58%), and completing an online questionnaire on the smartphone (Sample 1: 44%; Sample 2: 35%; Sample 3: 63%; and Sample 4: 54%). Although the level of concern differs between respondents in the four samples, tracking smartphone usage always yields the highest concern followed by GPS data collection, regardless of whether the data comes from a nonprobability online panel or a probability online sample.

We next turn to the results from logistic regression models predicting concern (combining "a lot concerned" and "somewhat concerned" vs. combining "a little concerned" and "not at all concerned") when engaging in the five forms of mobile data collection based on general privacy concern, frequency of smartphone use, self-rated smartphone skills, number of smartphone activities, gender, age, and education. Figure 22.2 presents the average marginal effects from these models

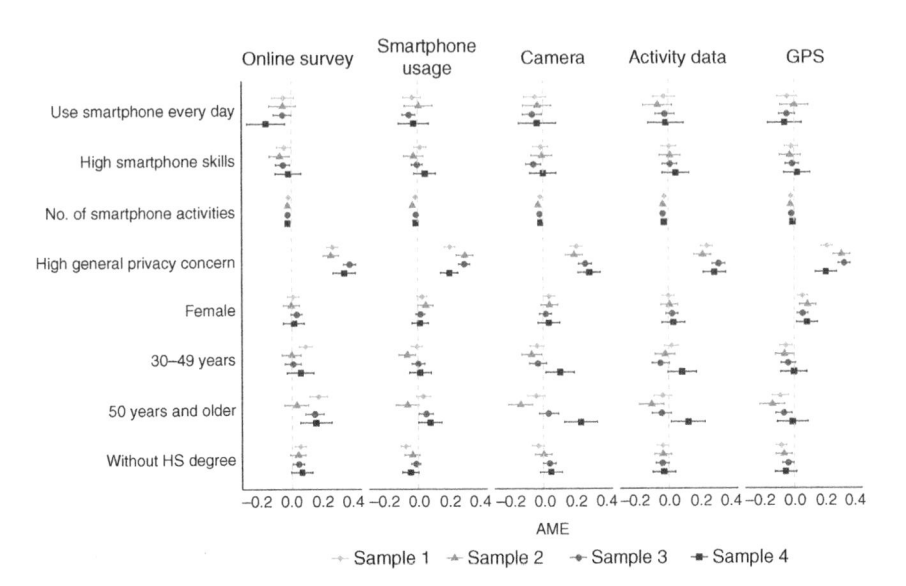

Figure 22.2 Average marginal effects (AME) and 95% confidence intervals from logistic regression predicting concern with five forms of mobile data collection.

using the *margins* package in R (Leeper 2018). Detailed model results can be found in Tables 22.B.1 through 22.B.4.

We again find rather comparable results for all four samples. For all five tasks and in all four samples, the more activities a respondent reported to do on their smartphone, the lower the likelihood for high concern for all five tasks. With each additional smartphone activity reported, the likelihood of having high concerns decreases by about two percentage points (p.p.). The effect for one additional smartphone activity ranges from a one- (GPS tracking in Sample 4) to a four-percentage point (activity data in Sample 2) decrease in likelihood to report high concern.

Since smartphone activities are measured as counts (range 0–12) on a different scale than the other predictors in our models (all binary), the small coefficients in the tables in the Appendix 22.B and the average marginal effects (AMEs) close to zero in Figure 22.2 do not provide a full picture of the true effect of smartphone activities on concern. We thus plotted the concern for the five forms of mobile data collection by number of reported smartphone activities. Figure 22.3 shows a steady decrease of concern when the number of smartphone activities reported increases across all five tasks and in all four samples.

For the other predictors in Figure 22.2, using the smartphone at least once a day for tasks other than calling and texting is negatively correlated with concerns for online survey on the smartphone in Sample 4 only (−16 p.p.) and with concern for camera (−7 p.p.) and smartphone usage tracking (−6 p.p.) in Sample 3. For all other outcome measures, the frequency of smartphone use is not significantly correlated with concern. Self-reported smartphone skills are significantly negatively correlated with concern when completing online questionnaires on the smartphone in Samples 1 (−5 p.p.), 2 (−8 p.p.), and 3 (−6 p.p.) but not in Sample 4 and not with the other four tasks (exception: use of camera in Sample 3 with −6 p.p.).

For all five tasks and across all four samples, we find that general privacy concern is significantly positively correlated with concern when participating in mobile data collection. For example, in Sample 1 respondents who reported high general privacy concerns have on average a 26-percentage point higher likelihood to report high concern with completing an online survey on their smartphone compared to respondents with low general privacy concerns. For other samples and other tasks, the AMEs for general privacy concern range between 0.21 (concern when using the camera in Sample 2) and 0.38 (concern with online surveys in Sample 3).

The demographic control variables seem to have differential influence on concern depending on the task. In all four samples, women are more likely than men to report high concern with GPS data collection (Sample 1: +5 p.p., Sample 2:

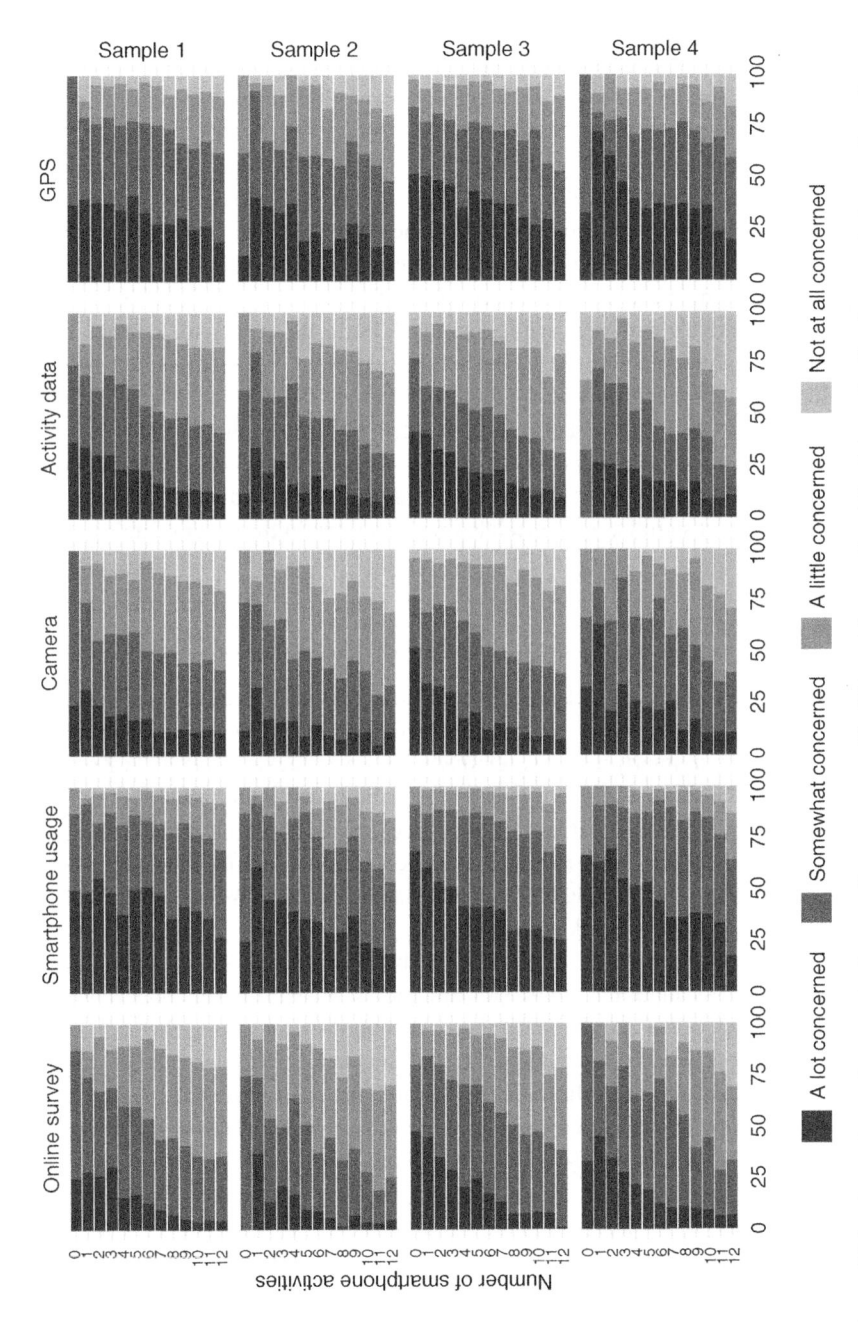

Figure 22.3 Percentage of respondents reporting concern with different forms of mobile data collection by sample by number of smartphone activities reported.

+9 p.p., Sample 3: +5 p.p., Sample 4: +8 p.p.). Gender is not significantly correlated with concern for the other four tasks in any of the four samples. Regarding age, concern with online surveys completed on smartphones increases with age in three samples (n.s. in Sample 2), and concern with smartphone usage tracking increases in two samples (Samples 3 and 4). On the contrary, concern for GPS tracking decreases with age (n.s. in Sample 4). Age seems to have an inconsistent influence on concern when allowing tracking of smartphone usage, using the camera, and collecting activity data via smartphone sensors. Concern for downloading an app that tracks smartphone usage increases with age in Samples 3 and 4, but decreases in Sample 2. For using the camera and tracking activity data, higher age correlates positively with concern in Sample 4, but is the reverse in Sample 2. In Sample 1, respondents without a high school degree are eight percentage points less likely to report high concern when asked to allow GPS tracking, eight percentage points less likely to report high concern with smartphone usage tracking (−7 p.p. in Sample 2), and six percentage points more likely to report high concern with online surveys than respondents with a high school degree. Educational attainment is not significantly correlated with concern in the other samples.

22.5 Conclusion

Researchers are increasingly leveraging the broad capabilities of smartphones for data collection in the social sciences, but willingness of users to participate in studies with their smartphones is relatively low (e.g., Jäckle et al. 2017; Kreuter et al. 2018). Based on data from two nonprobability and two probability online samples in two German-speaking countries, we find that users have high concerns when asked to participate in mobile data collection. In addition, we find that the level of concern differs by the type of data that is collected. We consistently find the highest concern for tracking smartphone usage via a research app followed by collection of geolocation data via GPS, both forms of passive mobile data collection. Across all four samples, smartphone users report lower concern when asked to participate in active mobile data collection, such as using the camera to take photos or scan barcodes and when responding to a mobile web survey. Mobile web surveys and sharing photos with researchers allow users to curate what data are actually transferred to researchers. Passive data collection, however, is always working, and participants usually can only decide to share all or nothing. Our data shows that smartphone users make clear distinctions between the different forms of mobile data collection and that concern might be related to the sense of control over data that are provided and the perceived sensitivity of these data (see Table 22.2); the more control people give up over when and what data are collected, the more concern they have. In general, our findings are in

Table 22.2 Level of concern, role of participant, control, and sensitivity of data by type of smartphone data collection.

Data	Concern	Role of participant	Control	Sensitivity of data
Smartphone usage, GPS	High	Passive	Low	High
Activity data	Medium	Passive	Low	Low
Online survey, Camera	Low	Active	High	High/low

line with earlier research (e.g., Revilla, Couper, and Ochoa 2018; Struminskaya et al. 2018; Wenz, Jäckle, and Couper 2017) showing that active mobile data collection – allowing the user to curate potentially sensitive information before sharing with the researcher – leads to higher stated willingness to participate in research using smartphones than passive mobile data collection where the user has little control during the data collection process.

Consistent with what Revilla, Couper, and Ochoa (2018) and Struminskaya et al. (2018) reported for willingness to participate in mobile data collection, we find in our study that requests of collecting activity data, such as the frequency and speed at which users walk, run, or cycle, via built-in sensors of a smartphone produce much less concern than the other two forms of passive data collection (i.e., GPS, smartphone usage). One possible explanation for this finding is that users might further differentiate within passive data collection methods not only based on the control they have over the data collection process but also based on the perceived sensitivity of the information collected. The number of steps a user walks in a day might be perceived as less sensitive than geo-coordinates that provide information about actual locations. More research is needed on the perceived sensitivity of these different data sources.

We also find that the number of different activities for which people report to use their smartphone correlates negatively with the level of user concern for both passive and active mobile data collection. Familiarity with technology reduces concern. On the other hand, self-reported smartphone skills do not predict concern in our study when controlling for the number of smartphone activities. We take this as an indication that asking users about activities for which they use their smartphone is more valid measure of familiarity and comfort with smartphones than having users rate their skills of use. We also find that educational attainment does not correlate with concern about mobile data collection when controlling for the number of smartphone activities.

Interestingly, we find very similar patterns of concern across the four samples used in our study. On the one hand, concern in the two samples from nonprobability online panel samples is lower than in the two probability samples. The difference in concern levels between the two types of samples is not surprising, given that members of nonprobability online panels volunteered for research and might be more inclined to participate in other types of research. On the other hand, the ranking of concerns is highly comparable across all four samples with tracking of smartphone usage and GPS location yielding higher concerns than the use of the camera, collecting activity data, and responding to mobile web surveys. Of course, even for probability-based online panels, self-selection occurs as nonresponse at different stages of the recruitment process (Lee 2006). A recent study by Herzing and Blom (2018) showed that the propensity to become a member of the probability-based GIP increases with digital affinity, a composite measure of device ownership, Internet usage, and attitudes toward technology. Thus, the level of concern for mobile data collection is most likely even higher in the general population than in the two probability samples reported in our study. Given the clear differences in concern between the different forms of active and passive mobile data collection we find in four samples, we consider our findings to be reliable.

The findings from our study have various implications for researchers who want to use smartphone technology for data collection. First, researchers need to be aware that users have considerable concern about collecting data through smartphones, especially for passive mobile data collection that limits the amount of control users have over the data collection process. Giving users' access to their data and allowing them to control when and what data are passively shared with the researcher could reduce concern and increase willingness to participate in passive mobile data collection (Keusch et al. 2019). However, providing participants with information on their data during the data collection process might bias the results because (i) smartphone users with higher interest in learning about their own behavior might be more likely to participate in passive mobile data collection (self-selection) and (ii) smartphone users might change their behavior based on the feedback provided (reactivity).

A second implication of our findings for implementing passive mobile data collection studies pertains to the high correlation between concerns for smartphone data collection and the number of different activities that users engage in on their device. Due to differential nonparticipation of smartphone user groups, bias in passive measurement of these activities is expected. Thus, researchers have to account for an overrepresentation of heavy smartphone users when estimating smartphone activities through passive mobile data collection.

Third, users might have different reasons for their concerns with mobile data collection, so researchers need to address those specific reasons when they invite smartphone users to participate in a study. Some users might be concerned that the data they are asked to share with the researcher are too sensitive, for example, because they contain highly private information on location and behaviors. Other users might not have a problem with sharing the same data with researchers for a scientific study but they might be concerned about a potential data breach that would expose their information to unauthorized third parties.

Finally, some users might express concerns about mobile data collection because they do not fully understand what data can be collected passively from a smartphone and what conclusions researchers would be able to draw based on these data; thus, they would rather not participate at all instead of taking a risk.

On a final note, our data are observational; thus, we cannot draw any conclusions on causal effects of concern on actual participation in mobile data collection (i.e., downloading an app that collects smartphone usage data and location information) or how the researcher could address these concerns. Future research should measure concern for different forms of active and passive mobile data collection and how they can be reduced in the communication with users in an experimental setting that would ideally also measure a behavioral outcome, that is, not only hypothetical willingness but also actual participation in a study. In addition, we need to better understand how concerns about privacy differ from other factors that lead to nonparticipation in such studies, for example, concerns about potential data breaches and confidentiality or technical limitations that smartphone users might perceive.

22.A Appendix

22.A.1 Frequency of Smartphone Use

> How often do you use a smartphone for activities other than phone calls or text messaging?
> Several times a day
> Every day
> Several times a week
> Several times a month
> Once a month or less

22.A.2 Smartphone Skills

> Generally, how would you rate your skills of using your smartphone?
> Beginner
> 2
> 3
> 4
> Advanced

22.A.3 Smartphone Activities

Do you use your smartphone for the following activities?
(a) Yes
(b) No
(c) Browsing websites
(d) Reading and/or writing email
(e) Taking photos
(f) Looking at content on social media websites/apps (for example looking at text, images, videos on Facebook, Twitter, Instagram)
(g) Posting content to social media websites/apps (for example posting text, images, videos on Facebook, Twitter, Instagram)
(h) Making purchases (for example buying books or clothes, booking train tickets, ordering food)
(i) Online banking (for example checking account balance, transferring money)
(j) Installing new apps (for example from iTunes, Google Play Store)
(k) Using GPS/location-aware apps (for example Google Maps, Foursquare, Yelp)
(l) Connecting to other electronic devices via Bluetooth (for example smartwatches, fitness bracelets, step counter)
(m) Playing games
(n) Streaming videos or music

22.A.4 General Privacy Concern

In general, how worried are you about your personal privacy?
Not at all concerned
A little concerned
Somewhat concerned
Very concerned

22.B Appendix

Table 22.B.1 Sample 1 multiple logistic regression estimates and standard errors (s.e.) for predicting concern with five forms of mobile data collection.

	Online questionnaire estimate (s.e.)		Smartphone usage estimate (s.e.)		Camera estimate (s.e.)		Activity data estimate (s.e.)		GPS estimate (s.e.)	
Intercept	−0.38 (0.21)		1.88 (0.27)	***	0.47 (0.20)	*	0.55 (0.20)	**	1.87 (0.23)	***
Use smartphone every day	−0.25 (0.17)		−0.25 (0.22)		−0.22 (0.16)		−0.13 (0.16)		−0.25 (0.19)	
High smartphone skills	−0.22 (0.11)	*	0.10 (0.13)		−0.07 (0.10)		0.02 (0.11)		−0.10 (0.11)	
Number of smartphone activities	−0.09 (0.02)	***	−0.10 (0.02)	***	−0.08 (0.02)	***	−0.11 (0.02)	***	−0.11 (0.02)	***
High general privacy concern	1.22 (0.09)	***	1.25 (0.10)	***	0.90 (0.08)	***	1.03 (0.09)	***	1.05 (0.09)	***
Female	0.04 (0.09)		0.18 (0.10)		0.15 (0.08)		0.01 (0.08)		−0.27 (0.09)	**
Age (Ref = less than 30 years)										
30–49 years	0.42 (0.11)	***	−0.05 (0.12)		−0.17 (0.10)		0.09 (0.10)		−0.30 (0.11)	**
50 years and older	0.80 (0.13)	***	0.23 (0.16)		−0.20 (0.13)		−0.16 (0.13)		−0.49 (0.14)	**
Without HS degree	0.26 (0.09)	**	−0.54 (0.11)	***	−0.14 (0.08)		−0.16 (0.09)		−0.44 (0.09)	**
Delta deviance (df)	394.3 (8)	***	216.6 (8)	***	168.2 (8)	***	218.3 (8)	***	219.6 (8)	***
n	2581		2569		2576		2575		2574	

*$p < 0.05$, **$p < 0.01$, and ***$p < 0.001$.

Table 22.B.2 Sample 2 multiple logistic regression estimates and standard errors (s.e.) for predicting concern with five forms of mobile data collection.

	Online questionnaire estimate (s.e.)		Smartphone usage estimate (s.e.)		Camera estimate (s.e.)		Activity data estimate (s.e.)		GPS estimate (s.e.)	
Intercept	−0.11 (0.31)		1.94 (0.35)	***	0.73 (0.30)	*	0.94 (0.31)	***	0.99 (0.31)	**
Use smartphone every day	−0.28 (0.22)		0.03 (0.25)		−0.17 (0.21)		−0.31 (0.21)		−0.01 (0.22)	
High smartphone skills	−0.38 (0.16)	*	−0.15 (0.18)		−0.04 (0.16)		0.05 (0.16)		−0.13 (0.17)	
Number of smartphone activities	−0.13 (0.03)	***	−0.19 (0.03)	***	−0.15 (0.03)	***	−0.17 (0.02)	***	−0.12 (0.03)	***
High general privacy concern	1.37 (0.16)	***	1.47 (0.14)	***	0.91 (0.14)	***	1.01 (0.14)	***	1.36 (0.13)	***
Female	−0.01 (0.14)		0.27 (0.14)		0.19 (0.13)		0.03 (0.13)		0.41 (0.13)	**
Age (Ref = less than 30 years)										
30–49 years	−0.01 (0.16)		−0.40 (0.16)	*	−0.34 (0.15)	*	−0.11 (0.15)		−0.31 (0.16)	*
50 years and older	0.16 (0.21)		−0.39 (0.22)		−0.69 (0.20)	***	−0.52 (0.20)	**	−0.67 (0.20)	***
Without HS degree	0.21 (0.13)		−0.21 (0.14)		−0.19 (0.13)		−0.03 (0.13)		−0.32 (0.13)	*
Delta deviance (df)	176.8 (8)	***	194.8 (8)	***	112.0 (8)	***	133.9 (8)	***	170.8 (8)	***
n	1181		1173		1177		1177		1176	

$^*p<0.05$, $^{**}p<0.01$, and $^{***}p<0.001$.

Table 22.B.3 Sample 3 multiple logistic regression estimates and standard errors (s.e.) for predicting concern with five forms of mobile data collection.

	Online questionnaire estimate (s.e.)		Smartphone usage estimate (s.e.)		Camera estimate (s.e.)		Activity data estimate (s.e.)		GPS estimate (s.e.)	
Intercept	0.11 (0.24)		1.50 (0.31)	***	0.48 (0.22)	*	0.41 (0.22)	*	1.35 (0.25)	***
Use smartphone every day	−0.33 (0.17)		−0.57 (0.23)	*	−0.34 (0.15)	*	−0.11 (0.14)		−0.31 (0.18)	
High smartphone skills	−0.30 (0.13)	*	−0.03 (0.16)		−0.29 (0.11)	*	0.05 (0.12)		−0.08 (0.13)	
Number of smartphone activities	−0.14 (0.02)	***	−0.10 (0.02)	***	−0.11 (0.02)	***	−0.17 (0.02)	***	−0.12 (0.02)	***
High general privacy concern	1.90 (0.11)	***	2.26 (0.14)	***	1.22 (0.10)	***	1.43 (0.10)	***	1.37 (0.11)	***
Female	0.19 (0.11)		0.16 (0.13)		0.08 (0.10)		0.11 (0.10)		0.33 (0.11)	**
Age (Ref = less than 33 years)										
33–52 years	0.04 (0.14)		0.02 (0.18)		−0.16 (0.13)		−0.24 (0.14)		−0.26 (0.16)	
53 years and older	0.83 (0.16)	***	0.46 (0.21)	*	0.17 (0.15)		−0.21 (0.15)		−0.43 (0.18)	
Without HS degree	0.25 (0.11)	*	−0.13 (0.14)		0.25 (0.18)		−0.19 (0.10)		−0.25 (0.11)	
Delta deviance (df)	557.8 (8)	***	380.5 (8)	***	298.0 (8)	***	328.1 (8)	***	343.3 (8)	***
n	2145		2143		2145		2142		2143	

$*p < 0.05$, $**p < 0.01$, and $***p < 0.001$.

Table 22.B.4 Sample 4 multiple logistic regression estimates and standard errors (s.e.) for predicting concern with five forms of mobile data collection.

	Online questionnaire estimate (s.e.)		Smartphone usage estimate (s.e.)		Camera estimate (s.e.)		Activity data estimate (s.e.)		GPS estimate (s.e.)	
Intercept	0.53 (0.47)		1.84 (0.64)	**	−0.35 (0.45)		−0.48 (0.43)		1.08 (0.47)	**
Use smartphone every day	−0.88 (0.35)	*	−0.26 (0.50)		−0.19 (0.32)		−0.08 (0.28)		−0.34 (0.33)	
High smartphone skills	−0.10 (0.22)		0.40 (0.30)		0.01 (0.22)		0.23 (0.21)		0.10 (0.23)	
Number of smartphone activities	−0.13 (0.04)	**	−0.12 (0.05)	*	−0.09 (0.04)	*	−0.13 (0.04)	***	−0.05 (0.04)	
High general privacy concern	1.64 (0.19)	***	1.82 (0.27)	***	1.40 (0.18)	***	1.32 (0.18)	***	1.07 (0.18)	***
Female	0.08 (0.19)		0.13 (0.24)		0.19 (0.18)		0.15 (0.18)		0.44 (0.19)	*
Age (Ref – less than 30 years)										
30–49 years	0.30 (0.23)		0.12 (0.28)		0.51 (0.22)		0.42 (0.22)		−0.01 (0.23)	
50 years and older	0.82 (0.27)	***	0.72 (0.36)	*	−1.19 (0.27)	***	0.59 (0.26)	*	−0.06 (0.27)	
Without HS degree	0.34 (0.19)		−0.44 (0.25)		0.25 (0.18)		−0.14 (0.18)		−0.30 (0.19)	
Delta deviance (df)	169.1 (8)	***	73.8 (8)	***	124.1 (8)	***	93.6 (8)	***	49.6 (8)	***
n	628		628		626		628		628	

$^*p < 0.05$, $^{**}p < 0.01$, and $^{***}p < 0.001$.

Funding

This work was supported by the German Research Foundation (DFG) through the Collaborative Research Center SFB 884 Political Economy of Reforms (Project A9) (139943784 to Markus Frölich, Florian Keusch, and Frauke Kreuter) and the Austrian Federal Ministry of Science, Research and Economy through the project Platform for Survey Research, Methods and Empirical Analyses (PUMA) (to F.K. and M.W.).

References

Afrobarometer (2018). Afrobarometer. A pan-African series of national public attitude surveys on democracy, governance, and society. http://afrobarometer.org (accessed 16 March 2020).

Balebako, R., Shay, R., and Cranor, L.F. (2014). Is your inseam a biometric? A case study on the role of usability studies in developing public policy. *Proceedings of the USEC '14*, San Diego, CA (February 23).

Bender, S., Jarmin, R., Kreuter, F. et al. (2017). Privacy and confidentiality. In: *Big Data and Social Science. A Practical Guide to Methods and Tools* (eds. I. Foster, R. Ghani, R.S. Jarmin, et al.), 299–311. Boca Raton, FL: CRC Press https://doi.org/10.1201/9781315368238.

Blom, A.G., Gathmann, C., and Krieger, U. (2015). Setting up an online panel representative of the general population: the German internet panel. *Field Methods* 27 (4): 391–408. https://doi.org/10.1177/1525822x15574494.

Blom, A.G., Felderer, B., Höhne, J.K. et al. (2018). *German Internet Panel, Wave 32 (November 2017) (ZA6906 Data File Version 1.0.0)*. Cologne: GESIS Data Archive https://doi.org/10.4232/1.13043.

Boase, J. and Ling, R. (2013). Measuring mobile phone use: self-report versus log data. *Journal of Computer-Mediated Communication* 18 (4): 508–519. https://doi.org/10.1111/jcc4.12021.

Callegaro, M. and Yang, Y. (2018). The role of surveys in the era of 'Big Data'. In: *The Palgrave Handbook of Survey Research* (eds. D.L. Vannette and J.A. Krosnick), 175–192. Cham, Switzerland: Palgrave Macmillan.

Couper, M.P. and Singer, E. (2013). Informed consent for web paradata use. *Survey Research Methods* 7 (1): 57–67.

Couper, M.P., Antoun, C., and Mavletova, A. (2017). Mobile web surveys: a total survey error perspective. In: *Total Survey Error in Practice* (eds. P.P. Biemer, E. de Leeuw, S. Eckman, et al.), 133–154. Hoboken, NJ: Wiley.

van Deursen, A.J.A.M. and Mossberger, K. (2018). Any thing for anyone? A new digital divide in Internet-of-things skills. *Policy & Internet* 10 (2): 122–140. https://doi.org/10.1002/poi3.171.

Eagle, N. and Pentland, A. (2006). Reality mining: sensing complex social systems. *Personal and Ubiquitous Computing* 10 (4): 255–268. https://doi.org/10.1007/s00779-005-0046-3.

eMarketer Report (2017). Internet and mobile users in Asia-Pacific: eMarketer's country-by-country forecast for 2017–2021. https://www.emarketer.com/Report/Internet-Mobile-Users-Asia-Pacific-eMarketers-Country-by-Country-Forecast-20172021/2002155 (accessed 25 September 2018).

Eurostat (2018). Digital economy and society: ICT usage in households and by individuals. http://ec.europa.eu/eurostat/web/digital-economy-and-society/data/database (accessed 30 May 2018).

Evenson, K.R. and Furberg, R.D. (2017). Moves app: a digital diary to track physical activity and location. *British Journal of Sports Medicine* 51 (15): 1169–1170. https://doi.org/10.1136/bjsports-2016-096103.

Evenson, K.R., Goto, M.M., and Furberg, R.D. (2015). Systematic review of the validity and reliability of consumer-wearable activity trackers. *International Journal of Behavioral Nutrition and Physical Activity* 12: 159. https://doi.org/10.1186/s12966-015-0314-1.

Goodspeed, R., Yan, X., Hardy, J. et al. (2018). Comparing the data quality of global positioning system devices and mobile phones for assessing relationships between place, mobility, and health: field study. *JMIR mHealth and uHealth* 6 (8): e168. https://doi.org/10.2196/mhealth.9771.

Greene, E., Flake, L., Hathaway, K., et al. (2016). A seven-day smartphone-based GPS household travel survey in Indiana. Paper presented at the Transportation Research Board 95th Annual Meeting, Washington, DC (10–14 January 2016).

Hargittai, E. (2002). Second-level digital divide: differences in people's online skills. *First Monday* 7 (4) http://firstmonday.org/issues/issue7_4/hargittai/index.html.

Herzing, J.M.E. and Blom, A.G. (2018). The influence of a person's digital affinity on unit nonresponse and attrition in an online panel. *Social Science Computer Review* https://doi.org/10.1177/0894439318774758.

Jäckle, A., Burton, J., Couper, M.P., et al. (2017). Participation Is a Mobile App Survey to collect expenditure data as part of a large-scale probability household panel: response rates and response biases. Understanding Society Working Paper 2017-09.

Joe, K., Raben, F., and Phillips, A. (2016). The ethical issues of survey and market research. In: *The SAGE Handbook of Survey Methodology* (eds. C. Wolf, D. Joye, T.W. Smith, et al.), 77–86. Los Angeles, CA: Sage.

Kassarnig, V., Bjerre-Nielsen, A., Mones, E. et al. (2017). Class attendance, peer similarity, and academic performance in a large field study. *PLoS One* 12 (11): e0187078. https://doi.org/10.1371/journal.pone.0187078.

Keusch, F. (2019a). *Willingness to Participate in Passive Mobile Data Collection (ZA6977 Data File Version 1.0.0)*. Cologne: GESIS Data Archive https://doi.org/10.4232/1.13246.

Keusch, F. (2019b). *Mobile Data Collection – Incentive Experiment (ZA6978 Data File Version 1.0.0)*. Cologne: GESIS Data Archive https://doi.org/10.4232/1.13247.

Keusch, F., Struminskaya, B., Antoun, C. et al. (2019). Willingness to participate in passive mobile data collection. *Public Opinion Quarterly* 83 (S1): 210–235. https://doi.org/10.1093/poq/nfz007.

Kreuter, F., Haas, G.-C., Keusch, F. et al. (2018). Collecting survey and smartphone sensor data with an app: opportunities and challenges around privacy and informed consent. *Social Science Computer Review* https://doi.org/10.1177/0894439318816389.

Lee, S. (2006). An evaluation of nonresponse and coverage errors in a prerecruited probability web panel survey. *Social Science Computer Review* 24 (4): 460–475. https://doi.org/10.1177/0894439306288085.

Leeper, T.J. (2018). Margins: Marginal Effects for Model Objects. R package version 0.3.23. https://cran.r-project.org/web/packages/margins/margins.pdf.

Link, M.W., Murphy, J., Schober, M.F. et al. (2014). Mobile technologies for conducting, augmenting and potentially replacing surveys: executive summary of the AAPOR task force on emerging technologies in public opinion research. *Public Opinion Quarterly* 78 (4): 779–787. https://doi.org/10.1093/poq/nfu054.

MacKerron, G. and Mourato, S. (2013). Happiness is greater in natural environments. *Global Environmental Change* 23 (5): 992–1000. https://doi.org/10.1016/j.gloenvcha.2013.03.010.

Pew Research Center (2014). *Public Perceptions of Privacy and Security in the Post-Snowden Era*. Washington, DC: Pew Research Center.

Pew Research Center (2015). *Americans' Privacy Strategies Post-Snowden*. Washington, DC: Pew Research Center.

Pew Research Center (2016). *Privacy and Information Sharing*. Washington, DC: Pew Research Center.

Pew Research Center (2017a). *Americans and Cybersecurity*. Washington, DC: Pew Research Center.

Pew Research Center (2017b). *Mobile Fact Sheet*. Washington, DC: Pew Research Center.

PUMA (2018). *PUMA Survey V.2. Modulberichte. Einblicke in Österreichs gesellschaftlichen Wandel*. Vienna, Austria: University of Vienna & Statistik Austria.

PUMA (2019). *PUMA Survey 5.2. Insights in societal changes in Austria. (V1.0) AUSSDA*. https://doi.org/10.11587/NHWVOO.

R Core Team (2020). *R: A Language and Environment for Statistical Computing*. Vienna, Austria: R Foundation for Statistical Computing https://www.R-project.org.

Raento, M., Oulasvirta, A., and Eagle, N. (2009). Smartphones: an emerging tool for social scientists. *Sociological Methods & Research* 37 (3): 426–454. https://doi.org/10.1177/0049124108330005.

Revilla, M., Toninelli, D., Ochoa, C. et al. (2016). Do online access panels need to adapt surveys for mobile devices? *Internet Research* 26: 1209–1227.

Revilla, M., Couper, M.P., and Ochoa, C. (2018). Willingness of online panelists to perform additional tasks. *Methods, Data, Analyses* https://doi.org/10.12758/mda.2018.01.

Scherpenzeel, A. (2016). Mixing online panel data collection with innovative methods. In: *Methodische Probleme von Mixed-Mode-Ansätzen in der Umfrageforschung* (eds. S. Eifler and F. Faulbaum), 27–49. Heidelberg: Springer.

Singer, E. and Couper, M.P. (2011). Ethical considerations in Web surveys. In: *Social Research and the Internet* (ed. M. Das), 133–162. New York, NY: Taylor and Francis.

Stopczynski, A., Sekara, V., Sapiezynski, P. et al. (2014). Measuring large-scale social networks with high resolution. *PLoS One* 9 (4): e95978. https://doi.org/10.1371/journal.pone.0095978.

Stopher, P., FitzGerald, C., and Xu, M. (2007). Assessing the accuracy of the Sydney household travel survey with GPS. *Transportation* 34 (6): 723–741. https://doi.org/10.1007/s11116-007-9126-8.

Struminskaya, B., Toepoel, V., Lugtig, P., et al. (2018). Willingness to collect smartphone sensor data in a Dutch probability-based online panel of the general population. Paper presented at the 73rd AAPOR Annual Conference, Denver, Colorado (16–19 May 2018).

Sugie, N.F. (2018). Utilizing smartphones to study disadvantaged and hard-to-reach groups. *Sociological Methods & Research* 47 (3): 458–491. https://doi.org/10.1177/0049124115626176.

Tene, O. and Polonetsky, J. (2013). Big data for all: privacy and user control in the age of analytics. *Northwestern Journal of Technology and Intellectual Property* 11: 240–273.

Wenz, A., Jäckle, A., and Couper, M.P. (2017). Willingness to use mobile technologies for data collection in a probability household panel. ISER Working Paper 2017-10. www.understandingsociety.ac.uk/sites/default/files/downloads/working-papers/2017-10.pdf.

York Cornwell, E. and Cagney, K.A. (2017). Aging in activity space: results from smartphone-based GPS-tracking of urban seniors. *Journals of Gerontology, Series B: Psychological Sciences and Social Sciences* 72 (5): 864–875. https://doi.org/10.1093/geronb/gbx063.

23

Attitudes Toward Data Linkage: Privacy, Ethics, and the Potential for Harm

Aleia C. Fobia, Jennifer H. Childs, and Casey Eggleston

US Census Bureau, Center for Behavioral Science Methods, Washington, DC, USA

23.1 Introduction: Big Data and the Federal Statistical System in the United States

Big Data offers both challenges and opportunities for national statistical systems (U.N. Economic and Social Council 2014). For the United States Federal Statistical System (USFSS), one of those opportunities is the use of existing administrative records. Administrative records are a subset of Big Data that include data collected as part of administering state, local, and federal programs (Connelly et al. 2016). Current uses of administrative records by federal agencies in the United States include construction of sampling frames, improving survey design, imputation for missing responses, and weighting to known population totals (NASEM 2017b). The 2020 Decennial Census will use administrative records to reduce the field workload for in-person follow-up for those who do not self-respond to the census. Administrative records will help identify vacant units, units that do not meet the definition of a housing unit and will also help optimize the number and timing of contact attempts necessary to successfully enumerate a household. The data sources include both government and commercial sources (U.S. Census Bureau 2017).

Recent legislation proposes to expand the use of administrative records in the United States to help improve federal government policies and programs (CEP 2017). As part of this proposal, the capacity for sharing and linking existing data for statistical purposes would be expanded. Legal and policy challenges to the use of existing records in the USFSS have received much attention, as have data quality challenges (Prell et al. 2009; NASEM 2017a,b). For example, when state, local, and federal programs in the United States collect data, the use of that data

---

Big Data Meets Survey Science: A Collection of Innovative Methods, First Edition. Edited by Craig A. Hill, Paul P. Biemer, Trent D. Buskirk, Lilli Japec, Antje Kirchner, Stas Kolenikov, and Lars E. Lyberg.
© 2021 John Wiley & Sons, Inc. Published 2021 by John Wiley & Sons, Inc.

is often restricted by law (NASEM 2017b). Another critical issue is how the use of existing data, which would include sharing and linking data from various federal programs, affects privacy and confidentiality concerns.

Privacy and confidentiality concerns have a long history of tension with government data collection (National Research Council 1993; Garfinkel 2000; Allen and Rotenberg 2016). Efforts toward increased use of administrative records, linking data for research and statistical purposes, and sharing data between federal agencies raise questions about how survey respondents understand the privacy and confidentiality of their information in this arena of shared administrative records. This chapter explores four research questions:

1. What do respondents say they expect and believe about the federal government's stewardship of data?
2. How do these expectations and beliefs change or remain when respondents are asked about data linkage or sharing?
3. Under what circumstances do respondents support sharing or linking data?
4. When respondents are asked about data sharing in the federal government, what fears and preoccupations (if any) do they express?

Using qualitative and quantitative data collected over a six-year period (2012–2018), we give a broad overview of participants' concerns and expectations about data sharing in the US federal government. We conclude with suggestions for a potential ethical framework that might guide government use of administrative data.

23.2 Data and Methods

This chapter focuses on results from both qualitative and quantitative projects. The quantitative data comes from questions asked as part of the Gallup Daily Tracking Survey. The qualitative data comes from a series of cognitive interviews, focus groups, and web probing studies on issues of privacy and confidentiality that Census Bureau staff conduct.[1]

Since 2008, Gallup has conducted the Gallup Daily Tracking Survey, which asks US adults about various topics. The Gallup Daily Tracking Survey consists of computer-assisted telephone interviews with randomly sampled respondents from all 50 US states and the District of Columbia. Data is collected almost daily (350 days/year), and on average 500 interviews are completed per day. In 2012, the Census Bureau and other federal statistical agencies established a contractual

---

[1] Data for this publication has been approved by the Census Bureau's Disclosure Review Board by this number CBDRB-FY19-CED001-B0007.

relationship with Gallup to add questions to the Daily Tracking Survey on public opinion toward the USFSS that we label the Census Module (Childs et al. 2012). Data for the Census Module were collected periodically between February 2012 and July 2018. Table 23.1 displays the subset of questions and responses that were asked as part of the Census Module that we use for analysis in this chapter. The questions cover a range of topics including perceptions of privacy and confidentiality, experience with using government data, support for the use of administrative records, and oversight of combined data.

The Gallup Daily Tracking Survey relies on dual-frame sampling, which includes random-digit-dial (RDD) list-assisted landline interviewing and RDD wireless phone sampling to reach those in wireless-only and wireless-mostly households. Each nightly sample collected during this time frame included a quota of 70% cell phone respondents and 30% landline respondents. Additional quotas were also in place for region and time zone within region. Landline respondents were selected at random using the next birthday method for within household selection. All interviews were conducted in English.

To compensate for disproportionalities in selection probabilities, duality of the sample frames, and nonresponse, Gallup weights the data on a daily basis. Gallup further poststratifies the data using an iterative proportional fitting (i.e. raking) algorithm to account for nonrandom nonresponse by phone status, age, sex, region, education, population density, ethnicity, and race. Demographic weighting targets are based on the most recent Current Population Survey figures, phone status targets are based on the most recent National Health Interview Survey, and population density targets are from the most recent census (Gallup 2018). The American Association for Public Opinion Research (AAPOR)-III response rate averaged 8–12% during the time period reported on in this study (AAPOR 2016). Although the Gallup Daily Tracking Survey is nationally representative, the low response rate is a limitation to our findings in this study. The Census Bureau does not use this data to generalize to the larger population, but rather uses the results from this survey to monitor awareness and attitudes, and as an indicator of the impact of potential negative events and for potential changes in communication campaigns. Qualitative data were collected from a series of focus groups, cognitive interviews, and web probing studies focused on respondents' views toward data security, privacy, and confidentiality conducted between 2015 and 2018. Table 23.2 provides details on location and number of respondents for each individual study.

23.2.1 Focus Groups 2015 and 2016

The goal of the focus groups was to gather qualitative data on public opinion of potential census methods and issues, such as privacy and confidentiality,

Table 23.1 Census module survey items.

Item	Item text	Answer choice
Data user	The census, the number of deaths in the United States by different diseases, the crime rate, and unemployment rate are examples of federal statistics produced by federal statistical agencies that are part of the federal government. Have you ever used federal statistics for study or work?	Yes No Don't know Refused
Trust in statistical products	Personally, how much trust do you have in the federal statistics in the United States? Would you say that you tend to trust federal statistics or tend not to trust them?	Tend to trust them Tend not to trust them Don't know Refused
Central database	Next, a question about the US government as a whole. Do you think federal government agencies share a single central database of the name, address, and date of birth of US residents?	Yes No Don't know Refused
Trust in confidentiality	People can trust federal statistical agencies to keep information about them confidential	Strongly disagree Somewhat disagree Neither agree nor disagree Somewhat agree Strongly agree Don't know Refused
Respect for privacy	Would you say that federal statistical agencies often invade people's privacy or generally respect people's privacy?	Often invade Generally respect Don't know Refused
Security of combined data by government or private company	If government information about people's jobs, earnings, and participation in government programs were combined, do you think the information would be more secure if it was kept by the government or kept by a private company?	The government A private company Don't know Refused
Independent oversight support	Would you be more likely or less likely to support combining the data sources if there was an independent group, separate from the federal government, in charge of making sure the data were kept confidential and privacy was respected?	More likely to support Less likely to support (Would make no difference)[a] not read aloud Don't know Refused

a) Survey analysts will want to know that an answer recorded as "would make no difference" was not actually read aloud to respondents.

Table 23.1 (Continued)

Item	Item text	Answer choice
"Cold Ask" question about support of administrative records	For the next census in 2020, if the Census Bureau got information, [like your DATA ITEM], that you already provided to the Social Security Administration, they may not need to ask you for this information on a questionnaire. If you knew that this information was being obtained from the Social Security Administration only to produce statistics, and that your personal information would remain unavailable to the anyone outside the Census Bureau, would you be strongly in favor of the Census Bureau getting your information from the Social Security Administration, somewhat in favor of it, neither in favor nor against it, somewhat against it, or strongly against it? There were four DATA ITEM fills: 1) generic "information," 2) name and age, 3) income, and 4) contact information.	Strongly against it Somewhat against it Neither in favor nor against Somewhat in favor of it Strongly in favor of it Don't know Refused
Framed question about support of administrative records (Save government money: High overall cost)	Now I will read you some reasons why some people like the idea of the Census getting your [DATA ITEM] from the [AGENCY] and ask for your opinion. The 2010 Census cost over $10 billion dollars. Getting your [DATA ITEM] directly from the [AGENCY] could reduce the cost for the 2020 Census and save government money. Does this reason make you strongly in favor of the Census getting your [DATA ITEM] from the [AGENCY], somewhat in favor of it, neither in favor or against it, somewhat against it, or strongly against it?	Strongly against it Somewhat against it Neither in favor nor against Somewhat in favor of it Strongly in favor of it Don't know Refused
Framed question about support of administrative records (Save government money: Cost per household)	Now I will read you some reasons why some people like the idea of the Census getting your [DATA ITEM] from the [AGENCY] and ask for your opinion. The 2010 Census cost about $100 dollars per household. Getting your [DATA ITEM] directly from the [AGENCY] could reduce the cost for the 2020 Census and save government money. Does this reason make you strongly in favor of the Census getting your [DATA ITEM] from the [AGENCY], somewhat in favor of it, neither in favor or against it, somewhat against it, or strongly against it?	Strongly against it Somewhat against it Neither in favor nor against Somewhat in favor of it Strongly in favor of it Don't know Refused

Table 23.1 (Continued)

Item	Item text	Answer choice
Framed question about support of administrative records (Social good: Local)	Now I will read you some reasons why some people like the idea of the Census getting your [DATA ITEM] from the [AGENCY] and ask for your opinion. Because some people choose not to respond to the Census, getting [DATA ITEM] from the [AGENCY] could help the Census Bureau get a better idea of population sizes informing where the community should build new schools, hospitals, roads, and firehouses. Does this reason make you strongly in favor of the Census getting your [DATA ITEM] from the [AGENCY], somewhat in favor of it, neither in favor or against it, somewhat against it, or strongly against it?	Strongly against it Somewhat against it Neither in favor nor against Somewhat in favor of it Strongly in favor of it Don't know Refused
Framed question about support of administrative records (Social good: National)	Now I will read you some reasons why some people like the idea of the Census getting your [DATA ITEM] from the [AGENCY] and ask for your opinion. Because some people choose not to respond to the Census, getting [DATA ITEM] from the [AGENCY] could help the Census Bureau get a better idea of population sizes informing how to distribute the seats in the U.S. House of Representatives. Does this reason make you strongly in favor of the Census getting your [DATA ITEM] from the [AGENCY], somewhat in favor of it, neither in favor or against it, somewhat against it, or strongly against it? *There were 8 DATA ITEM with AGENCY fill combinations: 1) Social Security Administration with a generic reference to "information," 2) Social Security Administration with name and age, 3) Social Security Administration with income, 4) Internal Revenue Service with name and age, 5) Internal Revenue Service with income, 6) Public Records with name and age, 7) Public records with contact information, and 8) Department of Motor Vehicles with contact information.*	Strongly against it Somewhat against it Neither in favor nor against Somewhat in favor of it Strongly in favor of it Don't know Refused

Table 23.2 Description of qualitative studies analyzed in this chapter.

Year	Name of study	N	Type of study	Location	Description
2015	Privacy and confidentiality census test focus group	52	Focus groups	Georgia and Arizona	Investigate privacy and confidentiality concerns
2015	Respondent messaging	303	Web probing	Online	Test respondent-facing privacy and confidentiality messaging
		40	Cognitive interviews	Washington, DC Metro Area	
2016	Privacy and confidentiality census test focus group	57	Focus groups	California and Texas	Investigate privacy and confidentiality concerns
2017	Re-identification survey cognitive test	28	Cognitive interviews	Washington, DC Metro area	Test questionnaire about privacy concerns
2018	Privacy act cognitive testing	38	Cognitive interviews	Washington, DC Metro area	Test legally required language

alternative contact methods, Internet response options, and administrative records use. The groups were conducted as follow-ups to census site tests.[2] In Georgia, we held four focus groups separated by race and age. In Arizona, we held four focus groups separated by race and Hispanic origin.

In 2016, census site tests were conducted in Texas and California. Follow-up focus groups were separated by language and ethnicity. In Texas, we held four focus groups with people who had responded to the census test, separated by ethnicity and language spoken at home. In California, we conducted three focus groups, also separated by ethnicity and language spoken at home.

23.2.2 Cognitive Interviews

This chapter draws on cognitive interview data from three projects. The first project conducted in 2015, Respondent Messaging, was designed to test privacy and confidentiality messaging that the Census Bureau uses in its respondent-facing materials. For this study, we used a think-aloud protocol and

---

[2] In the decade leading up to the decennial Census where the United States conducts a full census of all residents, smaller site tests are periodically conducted to test planned operations. For more information on Census tests see: www.census.gov.

asked respondents to react to messages and paraphrase their meaning. This project also included a web probing component. We used an online survey platform to show respondents examples of messages. Then respondents were asked, "In your own words, what is this message telling you?" and were given a text box in which to write their answers. The sample for the web study came from the Census Bureau's opt-in research panel, which is a nonprobability panel that allows visitors to the Census website to sign up to participate in research studies. Since March 2013, the sign-up has been available through the Census Bureau website and over 15 000 respondents have signed up to participate. For this study, we selected 4000 e-mail addresses and sent up to three e-mails with a link to the instrument. After cleaning the data to remove duplicate responses and respondents under the age of 18, 303 completed responses remained for analysis, which represents an 8% response rate.

The second cognitive interview project, the Re-Identification Survey Cognitive Test in 2017, was designed to test new questions about the sensitivity of decennial census data items. Respondents were asked to complete a decennial census form and then asked a series of questions to measure how sensitively they perceived each item. This study used a retrospective probing method with a think-aloud protocol. The third cognitive interview project, the Privacy Act Cognitive Test in 2018, tested messages that the Census Bureau is required to communicate to respondents. This study also used a think-aloud approach as well as paraphrase probes to investigate respondent understanding of privacy and confidentiality notifications.

23.3 Results

In this section, we present both qualitative and quantitative data to address our four research questions. We discuss each question in turn.

23.3.1 What Do Respondents Say They Expect and Believe About the Federal Government's Stewardship of Data?

Three broad themes from questions asked in the Census Module and qualitative data are discussed in this section: confidentiality, privacy, and trust in statistics.

23.3.1.1 Confidentiality
One of the items in the Census Module asked respondents if they agreed that the USFSS keeps their data confidential (see Table 23.3).

We then examined the characteristics of respondents who agreed and disagreed with the confidentiality statement and found that a variety of individual characteristics predicted positive perceptions of the confidentiality protections provided by statistical agencies (see Table 23.4). A logistic regression predicting

Table 23.3 Public trust of federal statistical agencies to keep information about them confidential.

	Weighted frequency	Weighted percentage
Strongly agree	18 747	14.9
Somewhat agree	42 188	33.5
Neither agree nor disagree	7986	6.3
Somewhat disagree	23 441	18.6
Strongly disagree	32 007	25.4
Don't know	877	0.7
Refused	876	0.7
Total	126 122	100

Source: Gallup daily tracking survey, January 2014–July 2018. See Table 23.1: Trust in confidentiality. Percentages may not add up to 100 due to rounding.

agree/neutral responses to the confidentiality item by data user status, sex, race, age, education, and income found a significant association with all predictor variables. Of these, the strongest predictors (indicated by odds ratios farther from a value of 1 and higher F-values for the overall effect) were age, data user status, and education, in that order. Age was most strongly related to perceptions of confidentiality: the youngest respondents (18–24 years old) were substantially more likely to agree that statistical agencies protect confidentiality compared to the oldest respondents (65+ years old). The middle-age groups (25–44 years old and 45–64 years old) were also somewhat more likely to have positive perceptions of confidentiality compared to the oldest group of respondents. As might be expected, data users and individuals with high education (at least some postgraduate work or higher) also reported more positive perceptions of confidentiality protections compared to those who had never been data users and those with less education, respectively. Though other differences were smaller (that is, the odds ratio between the comparison group and the reference group were closer to 1, and F-values were not as high), the results also indicated that being female, identifying as black or Hispanic, and responding "Don't Know" or "Refused" to the income item were all associated with a greater tendency to agree that statistical agencies protect privacy.

In qualitative data, some respondents tended to report that they trusted the government with their data. Trust in confidentiality of data was often associated with positive perceptions of how government used the data. As one participant said:

> Like decisions about hospitals and schools and all that kind of information has to have data to base decisions on if good decisions are going to be

Table 23.4 Odds ratios from logistic regression predicting agree/neutral responses to trusting federal statistical agencies to keep data confidential.[a]

Variable	Comparison	Odds ratio (95% CI)	F-value	df	p-value
Data user			450.42	1	<0.0001
	User vs. nonuser	1.44 (1.39, 1.49)			
Sex			71.39	1	<0.0001
	Female vs. male	1.13 (1.10, 1.16)			
Race			11.51	3	<0.0001
	Black vs. white	1.14 (1.08, 1.19)			
	Hispanic vs. white	1.08 (1.02, 1.14)			
	Other vs. white	0.95 (0.90, 1.01)			
Age			839.68	3	<0.0001
	18–24 vs. 65+	3.57 (3.36, 3.79)			
	25–44 vs. 65+	1.96 (1.88, 2.03)			
	45–64 vs. 65+	1.16 (1.12, 1.20)			
Education			359.01	2	<0.0001
	No college vs. more than college	0.56 (0.54, 0.59)			
	Some college vs. more than college	0.65 (0.63, 0.68)			
Income			11.79	3	<0.0001
	Low vs. don't know/refused	0.92 (0.85, 0.99)			
	Medium vs. don't know/refused	0.88 (0.85, 0.93)			
	High vs. don't know/refused	0.93 (0.87, 0.99)			

Weighted $N = 119\,774$

a) The modeled event is reporting "Somewhat Agree" or "Strongly Agree" or "Neither Agree nor Disagree" to the confidentiality perception question (see Table 23.1, Trust in Confidentiality). Odds ratios higher than 1 indicate that the comparison group was more likely to agree with the statement "People can trust statistical agencies to keep information about them confidential" compared to the reference group. For simplicity of interpretation, we treat "Don't Know" and "Refuse" responses as missing; including them did not alter the general pattern of results. We also ran the regression with "Neither Agree nor Disagree" responses collapsed with the "Disagree" category. It did not alter the pattern of results.

Source: Gallup daily tracking survey, January 2014–July 2018.

made. And I'm not sure I don't trust the government. I don't trust all the people serving in the government but that doesn't mean I don't trust that the process has to happen.

(50+, white, Georgia, 2015)

The above quote is characteristic of participants who tended to report they trusted federal statistics. The relationship between being a data user and positive perceptions of confidentiality in the quantitative data is mirrored by the association of mentioning trust in federal statistics along with uses of statistical data in the focus groups and cognitive interviews. One participant in a focus group mentioned that she had used census data in the past and that her experience played a role in her support of federal statistics. She also said she trusted federal statistics and the government more generally.

As discussed, the Gallup study found that 44% of respondents disagreed that people can trust federal statistical agencies to keep their data confidential. This lack of trust was expressed in qualitative data as a sentiment about the vulnerability of government data. Large-scale data breaches emerged as a salient reference point for participants when discussing the vulnerability of government data. Participants mentioned data breaches from both government agencies and private companies when discussing how they thought all data was vulnerable. The dominant theme was that all data is vulnerable and that data breaches are inevitable. Some participants seemed to distinguish between the government and private companies, as in the quote below:

> In the last 18 months, how many companies have been broken into digitally? We would like to hope that the government has better security than a normal hacker would [be able to break into], but, I mean ...
>
> (18–29, black, Georgia, 2015)

Here the participant distinguished between companies and the government. The participant expressed that he hopes the government has stronger security but at the same time expressed doubt that data can be kept safe from hackers. In the next quote, a respondent familiar with databases identified a trust issue with data security.

> There is certainly a trust issue. I think ... I make my living working databases and stuff. I understand perhaps better than some how you can privatize and secure some of that data. But I'm also aware that one of the biggest industries in the world is becoming cracking into data you're not supposed to have, whether it's corporate or government data, you know, anywhere.
>
> (50+, white, Georgia, 2015)

Again, this respondent made a distinction between corporate and government data, but he also grouped them together. These examples show that while corporate and government data are understood as distinct, many participants view all data as vulnerable.

Although differences between the public and private sector are somewhat salient for participants, there is less differentiation between government agencies. Participants view data breaches in one sector of the government as examples that all federal data is vulnerable. As one participant said, "I guess everything is in the cloud now. The facilities aren't necessarily that secure. Kids can hack into DoD computers. NSA people leak information. Is there a safe place to store it? I don't know" (Washington, DC metro area, 2014). This quote also shows that respondents do not necessarily distinguish between federal statistical agencies and other types of federal government agencies when using past data breaches as a frame of reference. Breaches and hacks at the Department of Defense and the National Security Agency are given as evidence of data vulnerability across all sectors of government. In focus groups and interviews, participants also mentioned data breaches at the Office of Personnel Management and the Internal Revenue Service (IRS) as examples of government breaches.

Another theme from qualitative data is that respondents do not believe that the federal government will always keep its promise to keep data confidential. In focus groups and interviews, some participants expressed that they believe laws protecting privacy and confidentiality are subject to change. These participants were adamant that things can change based on who is in political power. They mentioned that laws protecting confidentiality can change. Some believe that, if needed, law enforcement agencies will be able to obtain individual data despite what laws currently allow. As one participant stated, "To be honest, I could see executive orders being given that would attempt to get this information. I think that's an extreme thing. I don't think it's necessarily going to happen…" (Privacy Act Cognitive Testing, 2018). Another respondent said, "Yeah, like you would say it, but I feel like if there was an extreme situation where the IRS needed the information from census, I'm sure [they'd pass it along]" (18–29, black, Georgia, 2015).

Overall, both quantitative and qualitative data show that some people trust the government with their data and that trust is associated with the belief that the data will be put to good use. However, people also think that data is vulnerable. This belief is supported by past data breaches that they used as examples when talking about the vulnerability of data. People mentioned breaches in both the private and public sector as examples and to support their beliefs that data collected by the government is vulnerable. There are some nuances in how people think data collected and held by the government is distinct from private companies, but within government participants do not tend to think of differences between agencies. Another theme is that respondents believe that laws protecting confidentiality and privacy are subject to changing politics.

Table 23.5 People who believe the government invades privacy vs. respects privacy.

	Weighted frequency	Weighted percentage
Often invades	52 468	41.6
Generally respects	66 932	53.1
Don't know	4568	3.6
Refused	2153	1.7
Total	126 121	100

Source: Gallup daily tracking survey, January 2014–July 2018. See Table 23.1: Respect for privacy. Percentages may not add up to 100 due to rounding.

23.3.1.2 Privacy

To get at the privacy concept, we turn to one item in the Census Module that asks whether respondents believe the federal government invades or respects people's privacy. A slight majority (53%) said they believe privacy is "generally respected," while 42% said the government "often invades" privacy (see Table 23.5).

In focus groups and interviews, one of the dominant themes was that the federal government has information on everyone and already knows everything. As one participant noted, "The government can access any information they'd like … whether I allow them to or not" (non-Hispanic, Texas, 2016). The assumption that the federal government knows everything despite their preferences or permission supports the quantitative finding about invasion of privacy by the government. When asked what happens to government data after it is collected, another participant said, "It goes in their computer memory banks and they can pull up anything on you" (50+, black, Georgia, 2015).

A related theme about privacy that emerged from qualitative data is a belief that much information is "already out there." Many participants said they did not believe that they had much privacy. This perception of low levels of privacy included both the federal government and private companies. As one participant said, "I have a friend whose got a degree in IT and if you just go on Google and put your own name in there and some real simple things like your address, or your age, or real, very minimal information, you'd be surprised how much stuff comes up on you" (50+, white, Arizona, 2015). Another participant described the type of information he believed was accessible. He said,

> All they're going to find out is I really like cherries a lot and I shop a lot. I'm a shop-a-holic and they know what I buy, and they know what I eat. And it doesn't bother me. Everything. It doesn't matter. They know exactly … you know, if they want to know, they know. You're going to go to a hospital, they can get your records. They could read about it. Anything medically or

whatever you're doing, a reprimand at work, they'll know about it. So it doesn't matter. You've got to accept [it]. That's the society we live in and it's been that way since I was born. I've been here all my life, and, you know, it's just something that I've accepted. But it doesn't really bother me.

(non-Latino, California, 2016)

Although this participant said he believed most information is available to those who want to find it, he also said that he is not worried that this information is available. Not all participants felt similarly about their lack of privacy. Many participants' expectations of privacy depended on the type of data they thought was accessible. One participant said,

I don't think really I do [have privacy or confidentiality issues] because the questions that they ask me are stuff like if someone was good at hacking computers or anything they could probably find that through Facebook – and those are just questions that don't necessarily get too personal with me as a person.

(18–29, white, Arizona, 2015)

This participant referred to the demographic questions asked on 2000 US decennial census forms (e.g. age, race, sex, and ethnicity). She felt that since these types of personal data are generally available on social media, she did not mind if they are accessible otherwise as well.

Throughout the qualitative data, participants expressed nuanced positions about what type of data they thought was personal and private and in what contexts they would be willing to risk loss of privacy. Some participants said that they had "nothing to hide" and therefore were not bothered by their data or information being known or accessible. One participant said, "And the federal government, they help us. They have no reason to harm us. If you don't owe anything, you have nothing to fear. You should help them when you can so that they help us too" (40+, Hispanic, Arizona, 2015).

As in the quote above, when participants said they had nothing to hide, they often expressed a tradeoff where their loss of privacy came with some type of benefit. One participant expressed that he was willing to accept a loss of privacy in exchange for safety from terrorists. He said,

Yeah. I think for our country we have blurred the lines, and that's just like telecommunication and the privacy of when they were looking for terrorists and all of this, and they were collecting all this data. I do believe that he had … they have a right to do that. I feel safe knowing that somebody … I'm not gonna talk about anything on the phone that you can't hear. I'm not living bad. I'm not living illegal. But when you got people who are trying to blow up our country, who are selling drugs, who are doing this and doing that, by all means, any means necessary. And that's my true feelings.

(50+, black, Georgia, 2015)

Other participants said they were willing to lose some privacy in return for helping others.

But if ... and if the government is gonna do something with that to better their life. Because when one person's life is better, that makes the next person's life better. And we want a better life, and that's the bottom line. If we gonna use it for the betterment of mankind here and in the future, honey, you could ... and then you could give me two or three social security numbers if you want to. You can get all of my business. You can come to my house. I will Skype with you. I have no problems.

(50+, black, Georgia, 2015)

Together, the themes of context or data-dependent privacy expectations and the tradeoff between privacy and benefits are evidence that people's opinions on the subject are complex. This complexity helps to somewhat explain the almost-even split between respondents who reported that they believe the government invades privacy and those who reported that the government respects privacy. Expectations and perceptions of privacy for many are a risk-benefit calculation that depends on the type of data and the benefits they or others might receive. As one participant noted, "Really, like with everything else, you answer it and you have faith that the benefits outweigh the risks, right?" (Hispanic, Texas, 2016).

23.3.1.3 Trust in Statistics

As part of the Gallup question series, we asked respondents about whether they trust federal statistics (see Table 23.6).

Respondents were almost evenly divided: 48.6% reported that they tended to trust federal statistics and 48.4% reported that they tended to mistrust federal statistics. Reasons given for mistrust of federal statistics from open-ended follow-ups to this question were revealing. Many answered that they believed that statistics were inaccurate. Others answered that statistics were politically motivated or that they believed that the government is dishonest as a whole. Inaccuracy was another concern of respondents who tended to distrust federal statistics. Some respondents connected this concern with distrust of confidentiality protections. They suggested that concerns about individual confidentiality can lead some respondents to lie on surveys and other forms and that distorts the statistics that are reported. In other work, we found that being a data user

Table 23.6 Trust in federal statistics in the United States.

	Weighted frequency	Weighted percentage
Tend to trust federal statistics	61 250	48.6
Tend not to trust federal statistics	61 035	48.4
Don't know	2267	1.8
Refused to answer	1569	1.2
Total	126 121	100

Source: Gallup daily tracking survey, January 2014–July 2018. See Table 23.1, Trust in statistical products. Percentages may not add up to 100 due to rounding.

increased trust in federal statistics and that attitudes toward the federal statistical system were significant predictors of trust in federal statistics (Childs et al. 2019). Trust in government has also been shown to predict favorability toward data sharing (Singer, Schaeffer, and Raghunathan 1997).

The public holds the government to a higher standard than it does the private sector in keeping their information confidential. However, there is a perception that data breaches are inevitable despite the protections promised by the government and steps taken to ensure data security. Respondents had low expectations of privacy, particularly with the government. Many believe that the government has access to a wide variety of data about individuals despite their preferences about privacy. In Section 23.3.2, we discuss how these beliefs and expectations change when participants are asked about administrative records or data sharing in government.

23.3.2 How Do Expectations and Beliefs About the Federal Government's Stewardship of Data Change or Remain When Asked About Data Linkage or Sharing?

To gather qualitative data on data linkage and sharing, focus groups began with more general questions about perceptions of privacy and confidentiality and government data collection. Then we asked participants more specific questions about data that is shared between federal agencies. When they were asked about the use of administrative records, some participants expressed opinions and perceptions similar to their opinions about government data collection in general. Participants stood by their assumptions that the federal government already has their data and extended that assumption to data sharing. Participants expressed a similar opinion about a tradeoff between benefits or uses of data and privacy loss or risk to privacy. Another similarity between general government data collection and administrative records was the theme that support for data sharing depended on the context and the data that participants thought would be shared. One difference was an increased sense of privacy loss when participants considered data shared between agencies.

In both qualitative and quantitative data, many participants said that they already believe that the government shares data and that any government agency can access their data at will. In its most recent fielding (fall 2016), 53.9% of respondents answered yes to this item: "Do you think federal government agencies share a single central database of the name, address, and date of birth of US residents, or not?"

In focus groups and interviews, many participants said they thought government agencies already shared data. Many participants also expressed a sense of resignation about government data sharing: they could not do anything to prevent data sharing and expected that it would happen with or without their consent. As one participant said,

> Down the line, it's going to get passed through the different agencies. It's just going to get so many privacy policies like going to the hospital or even signing up for healthcare—that was a big deal a couple of years ago. That's probably where they got my phone number from. So—I'm pretty sure. So it's all interconnected where there's nothing we can do to stop it, so we might as well just get used to it.
>
> (18–29, white, Georgia, 2015)

When asked a question they have not considered previously, participants drew on broader beliefs to form opinions (Schuman and Presser 1981). Broader beliefs about government were used to form opinions on favorability toward administrative records. The participant quoted here drew his opinions about data sharing between agencies from his broader beliefs about government practices. He said, "It has been proven that the NSA was caught spying on Americans illegally so. I think it's safe to assume that the government is sharing the information between agencies. I mean, that's a given" (50+, white, Georgia, 2015). This use of broader beliefs about government is similar to how participants used past data breaches to inform their opinions about the vulnerability of government data discussed earlier.

Some participants supported data sharing, particularly when they saw a benefit for themselves or their communities. As one participant said, "I hope [data sharing] means that if there are other agencies that are developing new programs or modifying existing programs, they can use my responses to help do it in a way that will benefit the country and the majority of the citizens" (Privacy Act Cognitive Testing, 2018). Many participants mentioned efficiency or decreased respondent burden as a particular benefit of government data sharing. For some, having prefilled forms was seen as increasing efficiency of data collection and reducing the time burden for respondents. The two quotes below are characteristic of this theme about the benefits of data sharing between agencies.

> If you are talking about the census obtaining some information from other areas and giving you a partially filled out form, or saying "can you confirm, you know, this information is still accurate or whatever." As a time-saver, I think people might accept that as long as it wasn't too intrusive in what you were collecting.
>
> (50+ white, Georgia, 2015)

> I mean sometimes I wish, as someone who has filled out forms in life, sometimes I think, "gosh, it's there already." You know, like who are we kidding? They have this already. Just let's put it together.
>
> (non-Latino, California, 2016)

Another similarity between general data collection and data sharing was the theme that support depended on the context and the type of data that participants thought would be shared. Although some respondents reacted positively to the idea of data sharing between federal agencies, others questioned whether the statistics produced from administrative records would be accurate. When asked for reactions to the Census Bureau using information from other agencies for the next census, a few participants pointed out that accuracy might be an issue for certain groups. One person pointed out that with data sharing, "You're not going to get stuff on undocumented residents" (non-Latino, California, 2016). This sentiment, that certain groups will not be represented in administrative records or perhaps misrepresented, mirrors larger concerns about representation in Big Data more generally (Barocas and Selbst 2016). When focus groups discussed whether records would be obtained from the IRS, participants said that tax records were particularly subject to accuracy problems since people have incentive to be untruthful with tax agencies. Later, we explore the ethics of this issue of missingness from administrative records.

One difference between participants' reactions to general government data collection and data sharing between agencies was an increased sense of privacy loss associated with data sharing. Some participants expressed the expectation that they should have control over their information and that giving it out themselves was not a problem but sharing seemed to violated their sense of privacy. One respondent said,

> But if I don't give my personal information to anyone, then I don't feel like the next person ought to be doing it either. I want to be the one that gives

it out and not just your random person or organization or whatever. If I give it to specific people or whatever then that's where it should stay until I authorize for it to be elsewhere.

(Re-identification Cognitive Testing, 2018)

Similar comments from other respondents expressed a sense of discomfort with data sharing between agencies and a sense that consent did not matter much.

Overall, there were many similarities in how participants reacted to general government data collection and sharing between agencies. A sense that the government already has information and already shares is pervasive. However, opinions are mixed on whether people support data collection and sharing. Another common thread is that support for both data collection and use of existing records depends on the context and the type of data being shared. In Section 23.3.3, we delve deeper into support and opposition to data sharing and linkage.

23.3.3 Under What Circumstances Do Respondents Support Sharing or Linking Data?

In this section, we explore the results of the Gallup Survey questions on support or opposition to the use of administrative records. We asked respondents about their support for getting data from various sources, different data items, and gave respondents different reasons for sharing data between agencies.

Between February 2012 and March 2014, we asked respondents whether they supported using administrative records in the decennial census and varied the different sources from which the records would be shared (Social Security Administration, IRS, Department of Motor Vehicles, Public Records) and the type of information collected (contact information, name and age, income, see Table 23.1 for question wording). As shown in Figure 23.1, we found that respondents were more likely to support the use of administrative records when they were from the Social Security Administration as opposed to data from the IRS. Also, respondents were more favorable toward using records to obtain personal information, such as name and age, than they were toward using records to obtain income information as shown in Figure 23.1. Both findings demonstrate that respondents are less comfortable with administrative records when it concerns data that they perceive could harm them financially. Respondents viewed income and IRS data as potentially harmful to them financially, which mirrors the qualitative finding that participants were concerned about financial loss and harm.

As reported in King et al. (2013), support for the use of administrative records was predicted by knowledge of federal statistics, trust in federal statistics, belief that policymakers need good statistics to make decisions, and belief that federal statistical agencies keep information confidential.

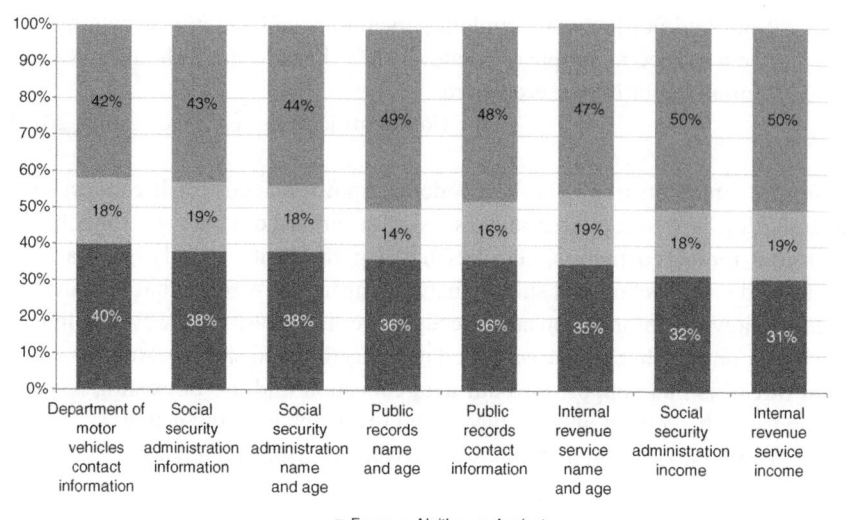

23 Attitudes Toward Data Linkage: Privacy, Ethics, and the Potential for Harm

Figure 23.1 Favorability of administrative record use by source and information type. Source: Gallup daily tracking survey, February 2012–March 2014. See Table 23.1: Cold ask. Not intended for point estimates. Percentages may not add up to 100 due to rounding.

Source	Favor	Neither	Against
Department of motor vehicles contact information	40%	18%	42%
Social security administration information	38%	19%	43%
Social security administration name and age	38%	18%	44%
Public records name and age	36%	14%	49%
Public records contact information	36%	16%	48%
Internal revenue service name and age	35%	19%	47%
Social security administration income	32%	18%	50%
Internal revenue service income	31%	19%	50%

We also asked an open-ended probe following the question about support of administrative records use by the Census Bureau. After a period of verbatim recording of answers, we then coded responses separately for those who answered positively to the support question and for those who answered negatively to the support question. For those who answered negatively, each open-ended response was coded into one of four categories: privacy, accuracy, trust, and other. We found that 39% of respondents who answered negatively to the support question cited privacy concerns (see Figure 23.2). Accuracy was another concern; however, when probed only 8% of respondents mentioned this issue. In qualitative data, participants seemed to communicate that this issue was a more significant concern with administrative records than the quantitative data suggests. About 20% of respondents who said that they do not support administrative records said it was because they do not trust the government.

Results from the open-ended probe asked of those who tended to favor administrative records were similar to reasons for the support of administrative records from focus groups and interviews. After a period of verbatim recording of answers, we coded responses into five categories: saving money, easier/time, accuracy, social good, and other. Respondents reported that saving money (23%), making data collection easier and saving time (19%), increased accuracy (18%), and social good (7%) were reasons they supported the use of administrative records.

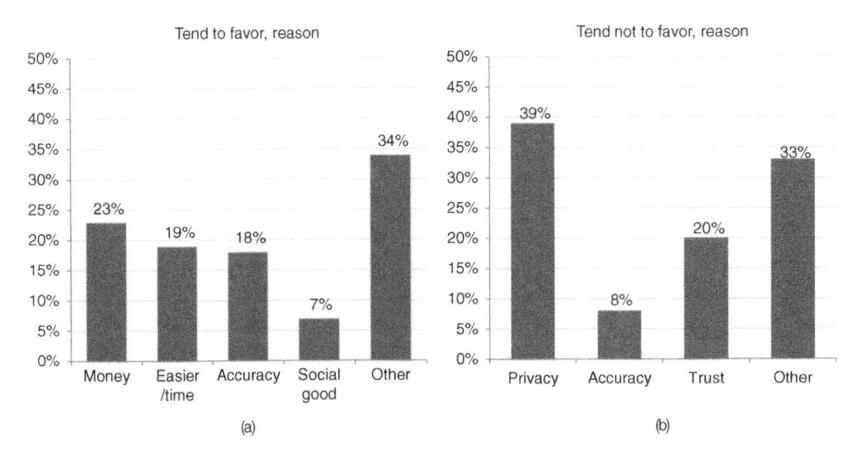

Figure 23.2 Distribution of reasons why respondents (a) tend to favor or (b) tend not to favor use of administrative records in the decennial census. Source: Gallup daily tracking survey, September 2013–October 2013. Percentages might not add up to 100 due to rounding.

After asking respondents about their support for administrative records in the census, we gave them reasons why they might support administrative records and asked if those reasons would make them support the use of existing records. Using the same set of sources and types of data, we used two different question frames with two variations of each frame (see Table 23.1, framed question about support of administrative records). The first frame informed respondents that administrative records could save the government money. One variation mentioned the high overall costs of the decennial census (US$ 10 billion) and the other mentioned the cost per household (US$ 100 per household). The second frame informed respondents about social good that could come from the use of administrative records. One variation used an example about local social good (i.e. new schools, hospitals, roads, and firehouses) and the other variation had an example of national good (i.e. distribution of seats in the US House of Representatives).

We found that when the benefits of data sharing and linkage are made clear to respondents, they were more likely to support these practices. Both question frames improved rates of favorability by an average of about 15% (compared to favorability when no benefit is described). Frames about local social good resulted in higher rates of favorability than the national social good frame (see Figure 23.3). This result was amplified for income data from the IRS, where 49% of respondents supported administrative records for local good. This number dropped to 38% when the question was framed as a national social good. In other work, where we experimented with question frames, we found that respondents were less favorable to administrative records when the purpose was for informed

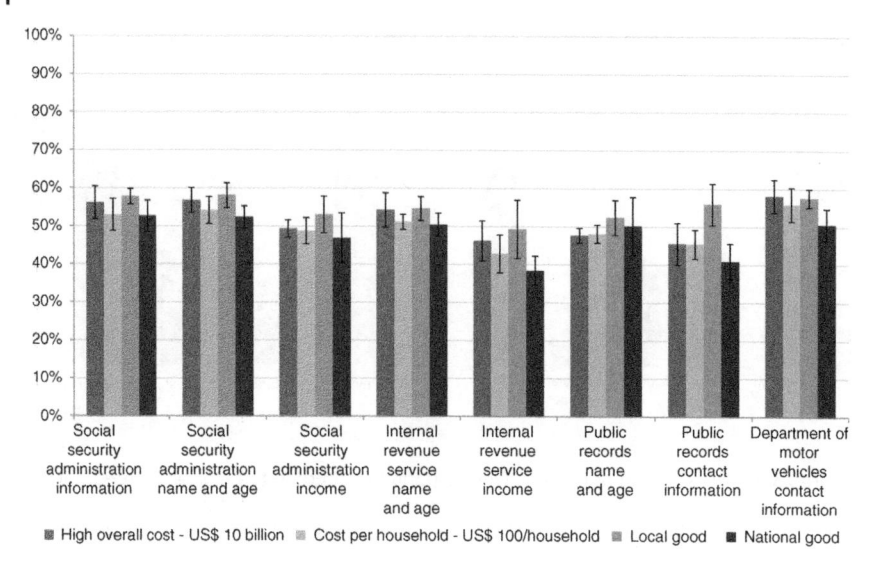

Figure 23.3 Percentage who favor use of administrative records by frame, source, and information type. Source: Gallup daily tracking survey, February 2013–June 2013. See Table 23.1: Framed question about support. Percentages may not add up to 100 due to rounding.

decision-making than for efficient use of taxpayer money, government accountability, or for community benefits (Fobia et al. 2019). These findings support similar work on framing and consent (see Pascale 2011; Bates, Wroblewski, and Pascale 2012).

Between 10 February and 22 May 2017, we asked two questions on public oversight of data linkage (see Table 23.1, Security of combined data by government or private company and independent oversight support). The first question asked about confidentiality and privacy protection and the second question asked about data security. Responses to these questions provided mixed results. Respondents said they were more likely to support combining data if an independent group would be overseeing confidentiality (62%) as opposed to the government providing oversight (27%; 8% said would make no difference; see Table 23.7). They were divided about whether the government (43%) or a private company (47%) would be more likely to keep information safe (see Table 23.8). This result is interesting in light of previous work by Singer et al. (2011), which found that only 23% of respondents favored using administrative records for the census if information was acquired from a private credit rating agency. Perhaps the specific private organization providing oversight is important to public perception or public opinion may be evolving – although almost 7% of respondents answered "Don't Know" to this question and another 3% refused to answer. Further research could

Table 23.7 Public's perceived willingness to support combining data, using an independent group in charge of ensuring confidentiality and privacy is respected.

Willingness response option	Weighted frequency	Weighted percentage
More likely to support	7170	62.0
Less likely to support	3131	27.1
Would make no difference	906	7.8
Don't know	250	2.2
Refused	116	1.00
Total	11 573	100

Source: Gallup daily tracking survey, February 2017–May 2017. See Table 23.1: Independent oversight support. Percentages may not add up to 100 due to rounding.

Table 23.8 Public's perception on which institution will keep data more confidential, government vs. private company.

Type of institution	Weighted frequency	Weighted percentage
Government	4941	42.7
A private company	5493	47.5
Don't know	759	6.6
Refused	380	3.3
Total	11 573	100

Source: Gallup daily tracking survey, February 2017–May 2017. See Table 23.1: Security of combined data. Percentages may not add up to 100 due to rounding.

explore this issue of oversight and its relationship with attitudes toward data sharing.

To account for context effects, we randomly assigned the order of these two oversight questions. For the question asking about confidentiality/privacy protection oversight, the order in which these questions were asked did not make a significant difference (X^2 [4, $N = 11\,573$] $= 7.68$, $p = 0.104$). However, when the data security question was asked first rather than following the oversight question, more people responded that the government would do a better job keeping the data safe (X^2 [3, $N = 11\,573$] $= 20.78$, $p = 0.0001$). We suspect that the difference may be attributed to respondents thinking about the value of independent oversight based on the first question; that idea seems to have affected their response to the question on data security.

23.3.4 What Fears and Preoccupations Worry Respondents When Asked About Data Sharing in the Federal Government?

In the Gallup Survey and qualitative studies, we asked participants about their privacy and confidentiality concerns with government data collection as well as their specific concerns about data sharing in the federal government. In the Re-Identification Survey Cognitive Test, we specifically asked participants what types of concerns they were thinking about in a questionnaire about data breaches and hacking. In focus groups, we asked participants if they had concerns about data sharing between federal agencies in particular. We found that when participants were asked what types of harm they are thinking about regarding their privacy and confidentiality, their responses can be categorized into two types: (i) individual harm and (ii) community harm. Individual harm is an occurrence that might hurt just one person. Examples respondents gave in this category included financial loss, identity theft, and personal safety or personal privacy. Community harms are those that affect a group of people that share a particular characteristic, for example, race or ethnic groups, or age groups. The concepts are not mutually exclusive: often, what might be considered community harm to one person, would certainly be an individual harm to another. This section explores the individual and community harms that make up the fears and preoccupations that participants expressed about government data collection in general as well as their fears specific to data sharing and linkage.

23.3.4.1 Individual Harm

One major theme of individual harm is financial loss. Overwhelmingly, participants tended to first think about financial loss when asked about their concerns about their data being stolen or breached. Participants were concerned with identity theft, credit card fraud, and fraudulent loans. One participant commented, "Concerns that I think about are an identity theft, stealing of sorts. The safety, for instance for my daughter" (Re-identification Survey Cognitive Test, 2018). This type of fear about financial loss was typical of most respondents' reaction.

Participants also associated the threat of financial loss with perceptions of security of their social security number. Many said that they are most worried when they are asked for their social security number. One participant commented when asked about data sharing, "I think I share all the information as long as my social security number is protected. As long as somebody doesn't steal it to get credit cards, they can share whatever. I don't mind" (non-Latino, California, 2016). This preoccupation with harm from financial loss could partly explain why respondents in the Gallup Survey did not favor the use of administrative records when associated with the IRS and income data (see Figure 23.1).

When participants were asked about their concerns about data sharing in particular, many mentioned concerns about violations of privacy, another theme of individual harm. As mentioned in Section 23.3.2, participants expressed an increased sense of privacy loss when discussing sharing data between agencies. One aspect of privacy harm related to data linkage and sharing was the perception that it removes people's control over their data. As one participant noted, "I think they should ask permission first, before giving information to, to anyone asking for information about me, they should talk to me first and ask my permission, to give, give information to someone" (40+, Hispanic, Arizona, 2015). Other participants echoed this sentiment about their desire to give consent for their data to be shared. However, since many participants thought that government agencies already share their data, they also expressed a sense that they have lost control of their personal information.

Participants mentioned other types of individual harm less often, including information obtained by stalkers, bill collectors, and marketers. Personal safety is another theme of individual harm. Some participants said they were concerned about their personal safety and their children's (as in the quote above where the participant mentioned her daughter's safety).

23.3.4.2 Community Harm

Although financial concerns about identity theft are foremost, qualitative data shows that community-level concerns are another common type of harm that people mentioned when asked about breaches of privacy and confidentiality. Community harm themes include harmful decisions based on data, use of data for targeting or discrimination, fear of data sharing with law enforcement, and populations missing from administrative records and surveys.

Harmful decision-making based on data is an example of community harm. One participant explained that she was concerned that someone might use her data to harm to her community. She said, "Someone [might be] gathering data to make decisions out of my control [such as] raising property taxes based on a percentage of people of color living in this community, which would have a negative effect on my children and myself as well" (Re-Identification Survey Cognitive Test, 2018). A related type of community harm is use of data for targeting or discrimination. As one participant said,

> Someone [could be] seeking to target people with disabled children or anything of that sort, or even elderly. My mother gets calls in the nursing home and that's not even a published number – scam calls. Things like that. If I were elderly and poor, I might be concerned. I would feel like maybe I could be a target if the data was breached.
>
> (Re-Identification Survey Cognitive Test, 2018)

Like the participant quoted above, many people expressed concerns about harm to communities of which they were not members. Participants expressed concerns about groups that could potentially be targeted. One participant said, "But if you are, for instance, if you're Latino, even if you're here with papers and all that, just the fact that somebody could get the [data], there could be adverse consequences to you in terms of harassment" (Re-Identification Survey Cognitive Test, 2018). This sentiment, that groups could potentially be harmed, was typical of how participants talked about community harm.

Another community harm theme was fear of data sharing with law enforcement. Participants often expressed this fear as a specific concern about data sharing with immigration enforcement agencies. As one participant said, "Then you have the immigrants, the illegal immigrants and I think they are not going to want to fill everything on here. Because they do not want to get deported or have someone else deported in their family" (Re-Identification Survey Cognitive Test, 2018). This participant connected the concern with data being shared for law enforcement purposes with the theme of missingness from administrative records. Concern about certain groups missing from administrative records was a dominant theme in the qualitative data. As one participant noted, "There are certain groups within our society you're just… you're not going to find in government databases very well at all" (50+, white, Georgia, 2015). This participant mentioned homeless people as an example of a group that would likely be hard to find in government databases.

The distinction between individual and community harms could help guide messaging about the use of administrative records. For example, although participants seemed to understand that groups missing from administrative records was problematic, the emphasis in the data was not on how that missingness could result in losing out on the benefits of government data collection. Rather, participants emphasized how the participation of some groups might be harmful to those groups. Focusing messaging on community benefits of inclusion in administrative records could balance concerns about potential harms. In Section 23.4, we discuss how the findings from these studies can inform an ethical framework around the use of administrative records.

23.4 Discussion: Toward an Ethical Framework

Previous work has used public perceptions to guide an ethical framework for the government's use of Big Data (Drew 2016). Similarly, our findings suggest three principles that could guide an ethical framework for government use of administrative data: (i) data security, (ii) transparency in needs and potential uses of data, and (iii) connection of data collection to outcomes. In this section, we discuss each of these principles, concluding with two areas where additional research is necessary.

23.4.1 Data Security

This research clearly shows that participants are concerned about the security of their data. Fears about financial harm are most salient for many. However, in this new era of decreased privacy, the types of harm that the public is concerned about could evolve (Garfinkel 2000). Assurances of data security and individual privacy are important elements of an ethical framework for use of administrative data. Messaging for privacy and data security requires a balance between too much notification and not enough information (Singer, Hippler, and Schwarz 1992). As we found in this research, many people already believe that any data being collected is vulnerable, despite any assurances that it is safe. As part of this framework, data security assurances should address both individual and community harms that respondents associate with government data and data sharing, including assurances concerning fears of law enforcement and sharing between government agencies responsible for enforcement.

23.4.2 Transparency in Need for Data and Potential Uses of Data

One major finding from this work is that support of administrative record use and of government data collection more generally depend highly on context. Here and in other work, we have found that question framing matters when asking respondents about their support for use of administrative records (Fobia et al. 2019; Singer, Bates, and Van Hoewyk 2011; Kreuter, Sakshaug, and Tourangeau 2015; Tourangeau and Ye 2009). Other studies have shared similar results: it matters to participants why data is being collected or shared and for what purpose it will be used (Ipsos MORI 2016). Transparency in the need for data becomes another important element of a potential ethical framework. Respondents want to know why government needs their data and the reasons for sharing between agencies.

This element of transparency raises one issue that needs further work. Public support for the use of Big Data in government hinges on clarity about specific data uses. However, restrictions about data use are one of the largest hurdles preventing the US government from leveraging much of the data it already collects. Further work on how to resolve this issue in public support for administrative record use would help clarify this element of an ethical framework.

23.4.3 Connecting Data Collections to Benefits

One of this project's findings – the public's apparent willingness to risk some loss of privacy for the benefits of government data collection and use of administrative records – underscores the last principle of a potential ethical framework. Explicit connections between data collection or sharing and their benefits to communities could help increase support of administrative record use. Participants want to know how sharing their data or allowing their data to be shared between agencies has had tangible benefits for their community. This knowledge is particularly important for groups who are more likely to be missing from administrative records. This element raises another issue for further research and exploration.

Moving toward increased use of administrative records creates coverage issues that are both similar and distinct from those issues faced by traditional survey methods. Respondents are aware of these issues and at times withhold support of administrative records use due to the potential for missing certain populations. Coverage in administrative records and Big Data more generally is not new and has been flagged as a significant problem for this field of research (Barocas and Selbst 2016; Barocas 2014; Crawford 2013). Further research on how to navigate these issues is needed. Ensuring that the benefits of data sharing and use of administrative records are fairly distributed across all groups should be a critical piece of any potential ethical framework for the use of administrative records.

References

Allen, A.L. and Rotenberg, M. (2016). *Privacy Law and Society*, 3e. St. Paul, MN: West Academic Publishing.

American Association for Public Opinion Research (AAPOR) (2016). *Standard Definitions: Final Dispositions of Case Codes and Outcome Rates for Surveys*, 9e. Deerfield, IL: AAPOR.

Barocas, S. (2014). Data mining and the discourse on discrimination. https://dataethics.github.io/proceedings/DataMiningandtheDiscourseOnDiscrimination.pdf (accessed 10 March 2020).

Barocas, S. and Selbst, A. (2016). Big data's disparate impact. *California Law Review* 104: 671–732. https://doi.org/10.15779/Z38BG31.

Bates, N., Wroblewski, M.J., and Pascale, J. (2012). Public Attitudes Toward the Use of Administrative Records in the U.S. Census: Does Question Frame Matter? Technical Report. Survey Methodology Series #2012-04, United States Census Bureau. https://www.census.gov/content/dam/Census/library/working-papers/2012/adrm/rsm2012-04.pdf.

Childs, J.H., Fobia, A.C., King, R. et al. (2019). Trust and credibility in the U.S. Federal Statistical System. Survey Methods: Insights from the Field. https://surveyinsights.org/?p=10663.

Childs, J.H., Willson, S., Martinez, S.W. et al. (2012). Development of the federal statistical system public opinion survey. Paper presented at the 67th Annual Conference of the American Association for Public Opinion Research. Orlando,

FL. http://ww2.amstat.org/sections/SRMS/Proceedings/y2012/Files/400242_500695.pdf.

Commission of Evidence-Based Policymaking (CEP) (2017). The promise of evidence-based policymaking. https://www.cep.gov/content/dam/cep/news/2017-09-06-news.pdf (accessed 10 March 2020).

Connelly, R., Playford, C.J., Gayle, V. et al. (2016). The role of administrative data in the big data revolution in social science research. *Social Science Research* 59: 1–12. https://doi.org/10.1016/j.ssresearch.2016.04.015.

Crawford, K. (2013). The hidden biases in big data. *Harvard Business Review*, 01 April 2013.

Drew, C. (2016). Data science ethics in government. *Philosophical Transactions of the Royal Society of London. Series A, Mathematical and Physical Sciences* 374 (2083) https://doi.org/10.1098/rsta.2016.0119.

Fobia, A.C., Holzberg, J., Childs, J.H. et al. (2019). Attitudes towards data linkage for evidence-based policymaking. [Special Issue]. *Public Opinion Quarterly* 83 (S1): 264–279. https://doi.org/10.1093/poq/nfz008.

Gallup (2018). How does the gallup U.S. poll work: methodology. http://www.gallup.com/224855/gallup-poll-work.aspx?utm_source=link_analyticsv9&utm_campaign=item_213755&utm_medium=copy (accessed 10 March 2020).

Garfinkel, S. (2000). *Database Nation: The Death of Privacy in the 21st Century*. Sebastopol, CA: O'Reilly and Associates.

Ipsos MORI (2016). Data science ethics dialogue. https://www.ipsos.com/ipsos-mori/en-uk/data-science-ethics-dialogue (accessed 10 March 2020).

King, R., Childs, J.H., Wroblewski, M. et al. (2013). Attitudes towards the use of administrative records. Paper presented at the 66th Annual Conference of the American Association for Public Opinion Research, Boston, MA. http://ww2.amstat.org/sections/SRMS/Proceedings/y2013/Files/400285_500783.pdf (accessed 10 March 2020).

Kreuter, F., Sakshaug, J.W., and Tourangeau, R. (2015). The framing of the record linkage consent question. *International Journal of Public Opinion Research* 28 (1): 142–152. https://doi.org/10.1093/ijpor/edv006.

National Academies of Sciences, Engineering, and Medicine (NASEM) (2017a). *Federal Statistics, Multiple Data Sources, and Privacy Protection: Next Steps* (eds. R. Groves and B.A. Harris-Kojetin). Washington, DC: The National Academies Press https://doi.org/10.17226/24893.

National Academies of Sciences, Engineering, and Medicine (NASEM) (2017b). *Innovations in Federal Statistics: Combining Data Sources While Protecting Privacy* (eds. R. Groves and B.A. Harris-Kojetin). Washington, DC: The National Academies Press https://doi.org/10.17226/24652.

National Research Council (1993). *Private Lives and Public Policies: Confidentiality and Accessibility of Government Statistics* (eds. G.T. Duncan, T.B. Jabine and V.A.

De Wolf). Washington, DC: The National Academies Press https://doi.org/10.17226/2122.

Pascale, J. (2011). *Requesting Consent to Link Survey Data to Administrative Records: Results from a Split-Ballot Experiment in the Survey of Health Insurance and Program Participation (SHIPP).* (Study Series in Survey Methodology #2011-03). Washington, DC: U.S. Census Bureau http://www.census.gov/srd/papers/pdf/ssm2011-03.pdf.

Prell, M., Bradsher-Fredrick, H., Comisarow, C. et al. (2009). Profiles in success of statistical uses of administrative data. http://www.bls.gov/osmr/fcsm.pdf (accessed March 2019).

Schuman, H. and Presser, S. (1981). *Questions and Answers in Attitude Surveys*. New York: Academic Press.

Singer, E., Bates, N., and Van Hoewyk, J. (2011). Concerns about privacy, trust in government, and willingness to use administrative records to improve the decennial census. Paper presented at the 66th Annual Conference of the American Association for Public Opinion Research, Phoenix, AZ (12 May 2011). http://ww2.amstat.org/sections/SRMS/Proceedings/y2011/Files/400168.pdf.

Singer, E., Hippler, H.-J., and Schwarz, N. (1992). Confidentiality assurances in surveys: reassurance or threat? *International Journal of Public Opinion Research* 4 (3): 256–268. https://doi.org/10.1093/ijpor/4.3.256.

Singer, E., Schaeffer, N.C., and Raghunathan, T. (1997). Public attitudes toward data sharing by federal agencies. *International Journal of Public Opinion Research* 9 (3): 277–285. https://doi.org/10.1093/ijpor/9.3.277.

Tourangeau, R. and Ye, C. (2009). The framing of the survey request and panel attrition. *Public Opinion Quarterly* 73 (2): 338–348. https://doi.org/10.1093/poq/nfp021.

U.N. Economic and Social Council (2014). Report of the global group on big data for official statistics. https://unstats.un.org/unsd/statcom/doc15/2015-4-BigData-E.pdf (accessed 10 March 2020).

U.S. Census Bureau (2017). 2020 census operational plan: a new design for the 21st century. Version 3.0. https://www.census.gov/programs-surveys/decennial-census/2020-census/planning-management/planning-docs/operational-plan.html (accessed 10 March 2020).

24

Moving Social Science into the Fourth Paradigm: The Data Life Cycle

Craig A. Hill

RTI International, Research Triangle Park, NC, USA

Professor Sir John Taylor, Director General of the UK Research Councils, coined the term "eScience" almost two decades ago, which he defined as, "science increasingly done through global collaboration enabled by the Internet, using very large data collections, terascale computing resources, and high-performance visualization." He went on to elaborate that these collaborations in key areas of science would have to be enabled by a "next generation of infrastructure" – and, by that, he did not mean only hardware and software but also culture. A few years later, Hey, Tolle, and Tansley (2009) emphasized this point in the concluding chapter of their book: "at the heart of scientific computing in this age of the fourth paradigm is a need for scientists and computer scientists to work collaboratively… to make significant progress, the research community must be supported by an adequate cyberinfrastructure comprising not only the hardware… but also the software tools and middleware."

Microsoft researcher Jim Gray recognized all of this – and more. In 2007, he spoke at the US National Research Council (NRC), outlining his fourth paradigm view – a shift in the way in which scientific research would be conducted in the future. In this view, science was poised to advance into its *next*, fourth paradigm: that is, after starting with (i) empiricism, graduating to (ii) theoretical, and eventually embracing (iii) computational methods, science had the potential to combine all three and become data-intensive, or data-enabled science, or, alternatively, become "eScience" (see Figure 24.1).

Specifically, Gray (and then Hey et al. 2009) described the history of science as having had four relatively distinct phases, eras, or paradigms, starting about 1000 years ago. When empirical science – the first paradigm – was "invented," science was strictly observational. The only real tools available to budding scientists at the time were small-scale experiments, allowing them to observe (mostly) natural

Big Data Meets Survey Science: A Collection of Innovative Methods, First Edition. Edited by Craig A. Hill, Paul P. Biemer, Trent D. Buskirk, Lilli Japec, Antje Kirchner, Stas Kolenikov, and Lars E. Lyberg.
© 2021 John Wiley & Sons, Inc. Published 2021 by John Wiley & Sons, Inc.

EMPIRICAL

Renaissance/enlightenment
(1,000 years ago)

- Small-scale experiments
- **TOOLS**
  - Observation
  - Censuses
- **PRODUCTS**
  - Papers/books
  - Counts

THEORETICAL

19th/20th century
(100 years ago)

- Theory development
- Hypothesis-testing
- Explanatory/nowcasting
- **TOOLS**
  - SAS/SPSS
  - Multiple regression/logit
  - Survey Research (data-rich case-poor)
- **PRODUCTS**
  - Estimates
  - Inference
  - Nowcasting
  - Official statistics

COMPUTATIONAL

- Computational chemistry
- Bioinformatics
- High-performance computing
- **TOOLS**
  - HPC
  - Hadoop
  - R
  - d3
  - Data Science
- **PRODUCTS**
  - Simulation
  - Synthetic data
  - Models

THE FOURTH PARADIGM

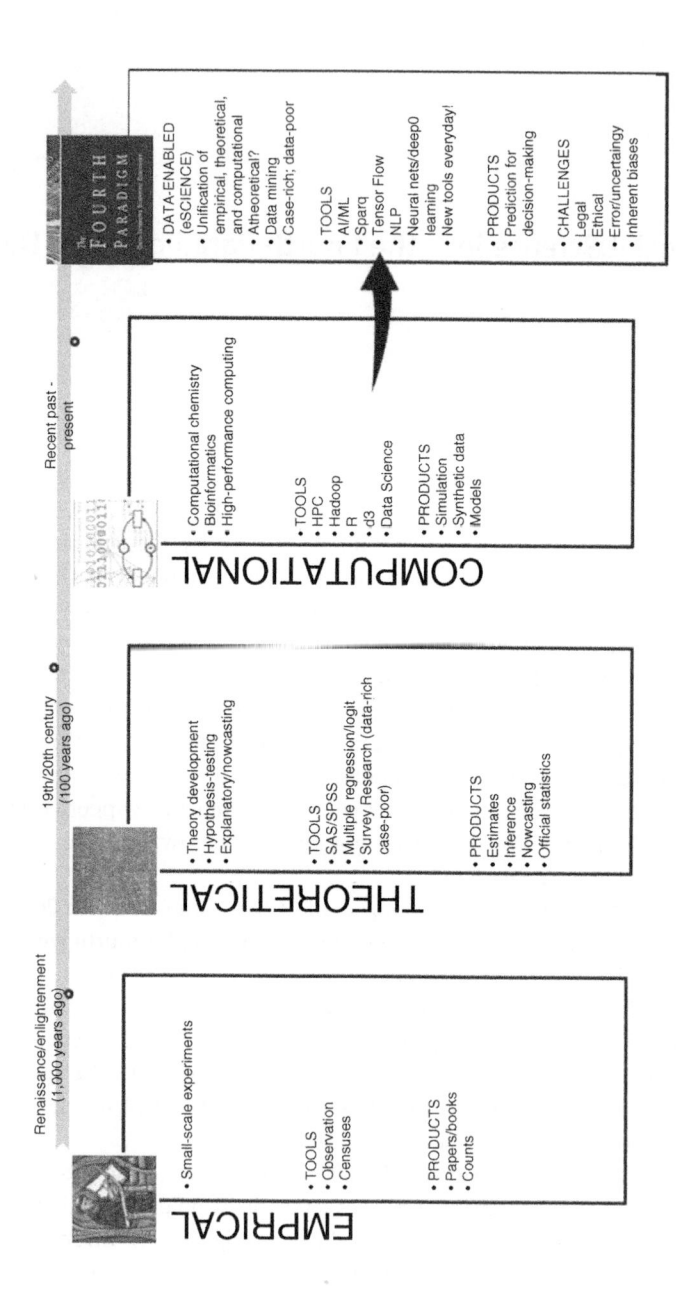

Recent past - present

- **DATA-ENABLED (eSCIENCE)**
  - Unification of empirical, theoretical, and computational
  - Atheoretical?
  - Data mining
  - Case-rich; data-poor
- **TOOLS**
  - AI/ML
  - Sparq
  - Tensor Flow
  - NLP
  - Neural nets/deep0 learning
  - New tools everyday!
- **PRODUCTS**
  - Prediction for decision-making
- **CHALLENGES**
  - Legal
  - Ethical
  - Error/uncertaingy
  - Inherent biases

Figure 24.1 The four paradigms of science.

phenomena – in their natural states. In social science, virtually the only tool available was counts or censuses. The result, in essence, was that scientists could systematically characterize or organize what they were able to observe. The products of these small experiments or counts were talks, papers, books, and ledgers, containing, for example, taxonomies or standardized chemical terminology.

Beginning about 100 years ago, however, science entered the second paradigm – science became theoretical. At that time, scientists started with a theory about the natural world (or even human behavior), developed hypotheses designed to prove (or disprove) that theory, designed experiments to test the hypotheses, and then explained the results. The scientific method was critical to the development of our ability to explain the cause of what we observed and allowed us to make estimates of what (variable) had the largest effect on what we observed. Most scientists and researchers were trained in this version of the scientific method and were fortunate enough to take advantage of new tools being developed to aid in this approach. In the social sciences, for example, software such as SAS and SPSS allowed us to ingest data, easily calculate frequencies and measures of central tendency, and even perform sophisticated analyses around correlation and causation, such as multiple regression and factor analysis. And, coincident with the dawn of the second paradigm, those in our field saw, and leveraged, probability-based survey research that resulted in data-rich, but case-poor datasets; that is, survey research allowed us to create an analysis plan that would collect, via a questionnaire, *exactly* that data we needed (data-rich), but, at the same time, because of the time and expense involved, we applied probability-based sampling strategies to ask those questions of relatively small numbers of people (case-poor). Applying survey research techniques in an attempt to understand human behaviors and attitudes afforded us the ability to make inferences from a small population to a larger population, derive estimates of the behavior or attitude for that larger population, and even create official statistics at the national level.

Gray's third paradigm is labeled computational and began to take hold about 20 years ago – although not so much in the social sciences, where it has only recently gained steam. In other fields, though, such as chemistry and biology, the presence of high-performance computing and massive amounts of data, created a platform for *simulating* real-world data and results. In chemistry, for example, one could search for new molecules that might have therapeutic value on a computer, instead of methodically combining elements by hand in a laboratory. In short, scientific data could be obtained or generated computationally – that is, created or simulated without actually having to perform an experiment. The social sciences are only recently beginning to grasp the potential power of such an approach. So, we can see, for example, the "emerging intersection of the social and computational sciences, an intersection that includes analysis of web-scale observational data, virtual lab-style experiments, and computational modelling" (Watts 2016). We can now employ computational approaches to studying social phenomena by analyzing human (i.e. social media)-generated Big Data and/or by model-building using simulated data to analyze social networks, for example.

Creating or generating (or, in a more practical sense, leveraging massive amounts of extant) data about human behavior has the potential to solve the case-poor dilemma referenced just above. Indeed, some social scientists got on board and started to avail themselves of new tools, such as Hadoop (enabling the integration and organization of large numbers of large datasets) and R, an open-source, community-authored and -improved suite of statistical software tools, or d3, to visualize their results, and so on. In fact, we started to see the rise of data science and an ensuing (and ongoing) battle between statisticians and computer scientists about who owned that space and who would define it. This conflict has not yet been settled, but is likely to become a moot point in the not-too-distant future (see π-shaped researchers below).

In Gray's aforementioned talk at the NRC, he espoused the view that science is now entering the fourth paradigm – a state that, embracing data-intensive principles and practices, would unite the empirical, theoretical, and computational methods, creating eScience (or data-enabled science or data-intensive science). As the fourth paradigm takes hold, it should – and must – give rise to new ways of communicating and collaborating among scientists and new ways of funding science and new ways of publishing and disseminating results (new "products").

Social scientists want to make theoretically sound inference. It should be noted, though, that some in the social science community criticize an eScience approach as being atheoretical: that is, when the day arrives (or is it already here?) that conclusions can be reached without theory development, strict and strenuous hypothesis testing, and statistical proof, we will all become heretics. Some social scientists unjustifiably conflate eScience with data mining, operationalized as applying massive compute power to Big Data and letting the machine "see" what patterns emerge; and, they fret, those patterns become "conclusions" made without regard to existing theory or even human interpretation. And, indeed, it is true that today, anyone can "do" artificial intelligence (AI) or machine learning without knowing anything more than how to perform a search on Google, which easily returns all the tools one needs to "run" AI on her data. But that is an oversimplification (and quite likely wrong-headed); instead, as noted above, the fourth paradigm should *unify* all of the previous paradigms/methods/approaches.

Our major challenge is bringing together computers and humans in a way that improves the human condition. Arriving at such an idealized future state (the fourth paradigm) in which data are shareable, discoverable, and accessible by virtually connected communities of researchers will require that we face and overcome numerous challenges. For the most part, this chapter concentrates on the challenges and reality presented by *data* – and not the challenges associated with computing or processing power. There is plenty of literature elsewhere about advances in network architecture, grid-style computing, quantum computing, and neuro-architecture, so we leave the latter to others. Here, we detail a few of the hurdles that social scientists and survey researchers who are on the verge of entering the fourth paradigm will face. None of these are intractable, or even insurmountable; rather, they represent research *opportunities*.

24.1 Consequences and Reality of the Availability of Big Data and Massive Compute Power for Survey Research and Social Science

Obviously, the changes in the amount and scale of both data and computer processing power laid the groundwork for all sciences, social sciences included, to change the methods by which it attempts to conduct science. In *The Third Wave* (1980), Alvin Toffler describes three waves of civilization, beginning with the agricultural wave, followed by the industrialization wave, and now supplanted by the information wave. Toffler further notes that the advent of each wave brings uncertainty, upheaval, and change. Those willing to embrace the change can not only acquire power and wealth but also fashion fundamental alterations of civilization. We will not, however, have achieved a state of ubiquity until we no longer notice the roles that computers and technology play in our everyday lives (Hill, Dean, and Murphy 2013). The ubiquity of computers, new technology, and ever-present data has been the stuff of science fiction for decades, but we are now close. This state of ever-present, ever-growing data is often codified as the four Vs.[1]

24.1.1 Variety

Many heavily computer-dependent transactions and interactions occur daily, even if we do not take direct notice. Making a phone call, sending a (SMS) text message, making a bank deposit, swiping a loyalty card at Starbucks or Walmart, paying for a meal with a credit card, passing in front of a CCTV camera in London, posting a video on YouTube, querying Google, tweeting on Twitter, and a hundred other seemingly innocuous activities that we perform every day – all involve a vast network of computers humming away behind the scenes, generating vast amounts of data. The sweeping digitization of almost every facet of everyday life results in bytes of information posted or transacted from seemingly everywhere, all the time.

---

[1] Favorite infographic for the four Vs is at https://www.ibmbigdatahub.com/infographic/four-vs-big-data.

24.1.2 Volume

As computers and computer-based technology nears ubiquity, the amount of transactional and interactional data created grows exponentially. The Visual Capitalist has created a popular, easily digestible way of visualizing this concept, shown in its "What Happens in an Internet Minute" infographic (Desjardins 2019). The 2019 version shows that every minute, for example 188 million e-mails are sent, 1 million people log in to Facebook, and 4.5 million videos are viewed on YouTube. As our cities, cars, homes, and household objects become digitally connected, the amount of data will only continue to grow (Davies 2017). As another example Microsoft's network more than doubles each year, and it has added more than 250 data centers to that network (Lee 2018).

24.1.3 Velocity

Computers do the work they do at an ever-increasing pace, contributing to the generation of more and more data. It is now possible to analyze some particular set of variables of interest daily, or even hourly or by the second, if preferred. Faster data processing and faster data transmission rates make for shorter and shorter feedback loops.

24.1.4 Validity

With all that being said, we all know that there's a lot of junk out there, too. People create Facebook pages for their cats, sensors capture false positives, and data elements go missing. One of the biggest roles that social science researchers can play in this arena is helping to make sense of it all. Revolutions in science have often been preceded by revolutions in measurement, and the explosion of data and data accessibility are necessitating new ways of measuring human behavior.

24.2 Technical Challenges for Data-Intensive Social Science Research

The four Vs present a tremendous opportunity for social science researchers: data from everywhere, including humans and devices, and a constant parade of new technologies[2] (variety); a tremendous amount of data, eliminating the case-poor problem (volume); new data every day, every hour, every second – no need to wait for a survey to be fielded and completed (velocity); but, also, a lot of challenges in

---

2 See, for example, the Gartner Hype Cycle, published annually: https://www.gartner.com/en/research/methodologies/gartner-hype-cycle.

interpretability, arising from still using old methods on new data types and sources (validity). But social scientists still need to address several aspects: here, we offer a short treatise on just a few: (i) the "long tail"; (ii) uncertainty characterization and quantification, which affects our ability to make robust inference from massive, new data sources; and (iii) reproducibility.

24.2.1 The Long Tail

Above, we noted the staggering volume of data being produced every day by mundane human transactions and interaction. Add to this that data being created by *scientists* alone (not to mention the vast amounts of every-second data you are creating on your mobile device) is growing phenomenally quickly. Figure 24.2 is taken from a talk at the National Science Foundation in 2013 (Suresh 2013), but the story remains the same now and in the future – the amount of data being created by sensors, instruments, and other data-producing devices is not only creating Big Data, it is creating a Big Problem, often referred to as the "long tail." Look at the bubble size of, for example, the Large Hadron Collider (LHC). Approximately 98% of the data generated by the activities at the LHC are not actually useful or used (no event). Since the introduction of the first microarrays for genomics data

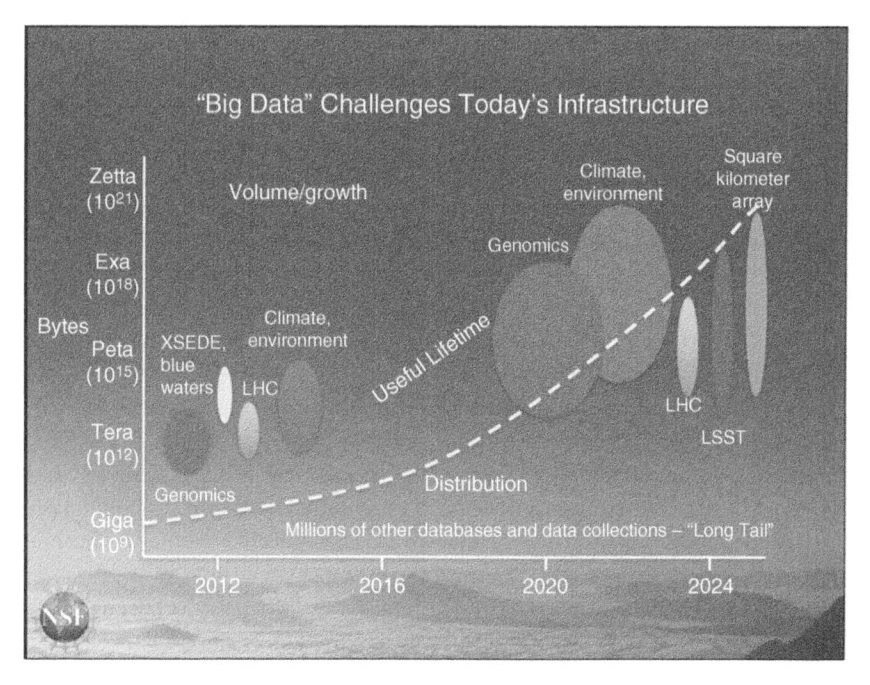

Figure 24.2 Data volume and the "Long Tail."

to the now readily available next generation whole genome sequencing, aided by the open-source movement, the amount and availability of genomics data are exploding.

One of the most fundamental challenges for eScience is simply being able to store, manage, curate, access, and process all of this information, not to mention making decisions about whether and when to delete any of it.

Charles Rothwell, director of the US National Center for Health Statistics (NCHS), noted, in an address to the Council of Professional Associations on Federal Statistics, that "we need larger and more flexible computing platforms" suitable for analyzing million and millions of electronic health records or genomic data, whether these are secure cloud-based solutions or government-controlled environments (Rothwell 2018).

24.2.2 Uncertainty Characterization and Quantification Or True, Useful, and New Information: Where Is It?

Many social science researchers are not yet familiar enough with methods and approaches to handle Big Data and, thus, have trouble making sense of it. Computerized methods could streamline and accelerate important discoveries in the social sciences, but only if we develop new methods and approaches for making sense and inference from these data types. If we want to make or create societal-scale inference- and decision-making algorithms and systems, we will need new thinking about how to do that. Many in the mainstream media espouse the view that Big Data equals complete information, but, in truth, many Big Data sources are incomplete – and messy, rife with missing values, missing Xs (the wrong data), and measurement error. Most Big Data are generated opportunistically, as opposed to intentionally, which can result in uncertainty due to lack of controls, inherent biases, and irregular data elements. Surely, a favorite definition of Big Data would be one were $N = $ All. But, really, this does not ever obtain. As noted by Robert Groves, our current state is referred to as the era of Big Data, not Big Information (Groves 2012).

In the fourth paradigm, we will have access to (Big) Data that are not necessarily collected from (only) a target population; more likely, our target population's data is inside a larger set – and, just as likely, these data will not look remotely like the tidy, designed data from a random or representative sample of the population. We have the opportunity to create new methods to handle bias, confounding, and missing data in these new datasets.

A subtle, but often overlooked, truth is that the human brain is hard-wired to look for patterns. Much of the power of fourth paradigm science emanates from scientists' ability to link data from disparate sources, creating the opportunity to find new patterns in the data. However, without the proper training, or the proper approach or method, it is oh-so-easy for a data-owner to find patterns in a big dataset. Entertaining evidence of this phenomenon exists at Tyler Vigen's website,[3] where he shows, for example, that the correlation (Pearson's R) between total revenue generated by arcades and the number of computer science PhDs awarded over the years 2000–2009 is 0.985065 – almost perfect. In the hands of people with access to data and tools, these kinds of patterns can emerge as moments of serendipity, giving rise to algorithm-based decision-making machines that can be misleading or flat out wrong. If not carefully constructed, algorithms can make mistakes because they pick up on features of the environment that are correlated with outcomes, even when there is no causal relationship between them. In the algorithmic world, this is called overfitting. (When this happens in a brain, we call it superstition.) The by-now infamous Google Flu Trends cautionary tale fell prey to just such an approach: Google engineers did not actually know what links, if any, there were between search terms and the spread of influenza; rather, they were merely finding patterns (correlation) in the data – and were not looking for causation.

In addition, traditional correlational analyses can be fooled, and thus produce overestimates, by the characteristics of high-dimensional and unstructured data (Fan, Han, and Liu 2014), such as genomic and biological data. Now, with high-throughput computing available to analyze, for example, genomic data, scientists can do large-scale hypothesis testing, assessing millions of hypotheses simultaneously. In such a scenario, classical statistical methods have low power, and new methods must be developed that can leverage the computing power (Benjamini and Hochberg 1995). In addition, biomedical researchers will want to use data that describe phenomena across orders of magnitude in temporal and spatial scales: there is much potential in creating datasets that combine genomic data or data indicative of subcellular processes (e.g. gene and protein expression panels) with, say, electronic health records or data from longitudinal studies, but there must be further research on how best to connect and integrate these multiscale datasets.

The US National Academies of Science recognized these perils of dealing with massive data as far back as 2013, noting that documents, pictures, videos, and sensor data could be sources of discovery and knowledge, but only if we were ready and able to adopt and develop new and sophisticated analysis techniques that went beyond "classical indexing and keyword counting (Committee on the Analysis of Massive Data, 2013)." To do so, the authors wrote that we, as scientists, would have to meet many challenges, including (but not limited to): tracking data provenance; coping with sampling biases and heterogeneity; ensuring data integrity; and developing scalable and incremental algorithms. Although Big Data has "small data"

---

3 https://www.tylervigen.com/spurious-correlations.

problems (and those have to be addressed, too), all of these challenges, if met, would help to create both characterization and quantification of uncertainty.

One step in characterizing uncertainty is data cleaning (or munging). Although social scientists, statisticians, and programmers have been cleaning and editing data for decades, at issue now is scalability: developing cleaning processes that can be applied to millions (or billions) of data records or elements presents a magnitude-change not dealt with by many social scientists. For example, when Statistics Netherlands undertook to publish official statistics using road sensor and public comments data, they needed to clean 105 billion and 3 billion records, respectively (Puts, Daas, and de Waal 2015).

Another aspect of the difficulty in arriving at sound and solid quantification of uncertainty is that our traditional notions or concepts of data quality may not apply to user-generated content. Streaming or social media-based content, for example, is produced by users of all stripes, not scientists, without regard to what we would think of as quality. Ascertaining provenance or truth from these data is yet another challenge. Some in the computer science community are adopting the precepts of the credibility model (Fogg and Tseng 1999) as one way to gauge uncertainty; typically and originally, the credibility assessment framework was applied to open-source software development, but it may be useful as a way of assessing the quality of user-generated data. As of now, at least, we should be able to interpret, explain, and communicate the significance or uncertainty level of any findings we disseminate from exploratory analyses.

24.2.3 Reproducibility

For the fourth paradigm to truly take hold, collaborative research must be reproducible. Many researchers now believe that science is undergoing a reproducibility crisis, but questions of reproducibility and related principles date back nearly 80 years. It does seem, however, that quite a few controversies have arisen lately – or maybe we just hear about them more easily and frequently now – across a wide array of disciplines stemming from a failure to reproduce results or findings. More people have more access to data than has ever been the case; however, it is also true that more people using near-ubiquitous data and off-the-shelf tools seem to result in findings that are neither replicable nor reproducible.

Again, in a fourth paradigm spirit, the scientific community will need widely accepted definitions, terms, and constructs as regards reproducibility, will benefit from common or standard protocols, and will welcome transparency in publications that can support reproducible research goals. Pellizzari et al. (2017) exhort scientists to embrace these concepts and model good stewardship behavior.

So, too, does the US National Institutes of Health (NIH). It noted the need to improve the infrastructure supporting the reuse of scholarly data; as a result, NIH brought together a wide array of interested parties to design the FAIR Data Principles: data should be Findable, Accessible, Interoperable, and Reusable (Wilkinson et al. 2016), hoping that this guideline would enhance the reusability and reproducibility of scholarly work. An important distinction or extension from previous work in this area is that the FAIR principles specifically emphasize enhancing the ability of machines to automatically find and use data.

In a similar vein, McCoach et al. (2018) are aligned with the importance of thoroughly thinking through one's data management approach from the outset of a study, and outline several lessons learned from a case study in field of education research. They noted that concerns over reproducibility have changed expectations about the research process and the products of research to the point where researchers are frequently required to make their data and code available; as a result, and as noted above, researchers will want to carefully document data provenance, the data management workflow, and any automation steps or approaches.

24.3 The Solution: Social Science Researchers Become "Data-Aware"

Increasingly, science – even social science – is a team sport, requiring close collaboration across multiple institutions and researchers (and their data). At the heart of scientific computing in the fourth paradigm is a need for domain scientists, statisticians, and computer/data scientists to work collaboratively (Hey et al. 2009). Bringing researchers from the computational and statistical disciplines together with researchers from other disciplines, such as social sciences, cognitive sciences, humanities, is what the fourth paradigm is all about. All science has become more and more computational (third paradigm), able now to harness the abilities of ever more powerful computers and abundant, ubiquitous data, leveraging techniques such as simulation and modeling. Arriving at the fourth paradigm (also known as eScience or data-enabled science or data-intensive scientific discovery) will only occur if scientists and researchers are willing to consider, *a priori*, adopting a data management life cycle approach as they plan and execute their studies. More specifically, because of the integral role that data play now in scientific breakthroughs, researchers need to plan – upfront – for the ultimate dissemination and stewardship of the study's data (in addition to the usual analytic plan).

Table 24.1 is meant to be illustrative, as opposed to exhaustive. Many examples of the data life cycle exist in the literature (cf. Agrawal et al. 2012), but here, we make two main points with respect to current state of social science – and, more specifically, the intersection between computer science and survey research as a

Table 24.1 The data life cycle, as applied to social science and survey research.

Acquire/create/collect	Munge	Use/reuse/statistical analysis/analytics	Disseminate	Steward/Govern

• Primary data collection
  – In-person
  – Telephone
  – Mail
  – Online
• Laboratory
• Field observation
• Administrative records
• Video/audio
• Internet of Things (IoT)
  – Sensors
  – Smart devices
  – Wearables
• Crowdsourcing
• UAVs/drones
• Social media
• Webscraping
• Commercial datasets
	• **Extract**
	• **Transfer**
	• **Load**
	• **Organize**
	• **Filter**
	• **Clean**
	• **Annotate**
	• **Label**
		• Derive
		• Analyze
		• Estimate
		• Impute
		• Model
		• Interpret
		• Uncertainty
		  – Characterization
		  – Quantification
		• Visualize
		• **Train**
		• **Algorithmize**
		  – AI
		  – ML
			• Publish
			• Patent/IP
			• **Share**
			  – **Code**
			  – ***Raw data***
			  – ***Workflow***
			• ***Portals***
			• ***DBs***
			• ***Repository***
				• Store
				  – Subset
				  – Compress
				• Index
				• Curate
				• *Discoverable*
				• Destroy

INTEGRATE: "LAKE"/PLATFORM.
Plain text: domain scientists + statisticians.
Bold text: computer/data scientists.
Italicized text: library scientists/informaticists.
Source: Adapted from Agrawal et al. (2012).

major tool for social scientists: (i) all of us need to become *data-aware* – that is, fully recognize that the data we acquire (whether that be through primary data collection, i.e. "designed" data or from other, extant sources, i.e. organic data), manage and clean, and then analyze also have a life – and, more often than not, may live on in near-perpetuity; (ii) currently, the different steps or aspects of the data life cycle require many different skill sets and experiences and there is a need to bridge the gap between silos.

24.4 Data Awareness

24.4.1 Acquire/Create/Collect

Social scientists can now create or access data from an ever-increasing variety of sources. Survey researchers are most accustomed to *designing* their own data, writing a questionnaire, and then asking questions of a carefully constructed sample of individuals, households, establishments, or institutions. Indeed, there are many modes and methods for generating or creating data in this way: in-person, telephone, online/web, mail, etc. Now, however, data are accumulating so fast (velocity) and from so many sources (variety) that identifying and accessing all of it are formidable challenges. Nonetheless, increasingly, survey researchers and social scientists are acquiring data from administrative records; from sensors (worn by humans or sitting in a static location in the environment); from devices, such as drones, built specifically to collect data (including, but not limited to, pictures and videos); from social media and other data on the World Wide Web; or by purchasing data from, again, a wide variety of commercial data aggregators and integrators. Thus far, this kind of work is typically done by a domain scientist, perhaps aided by a statistician (if designing a probability-based sample, for example), and perhaps aided by a computer scientist if acquiring data from an extant source.

24.4.2 Munge

All of these data – regardless of source – require management: they must be brought together, transformed, and loaded (E-T-L). They must be cleaned, annotated, and labeled. Often, this work is referred to as occurring "below the water line," that is, if the collection and analysis is the tip of the iceberg, all of the necessary E-T-L tasks are invisible – and often comprise 80%, by some estimates, of the total amount of labor/time in completing a study. Almost always, this work is performed by computer or data scientists.

24.4.3 Use/Reuse

At the heart of every scientific discipline, whether we are studying biological or behavioral characteristics of humans or the underpinnings of the physical environment, we (typically) use statistical analysis – a methodology to systematically analyze our data and draw conclusions about what the data are telling us. The overall objective of statistical analysis is now sometimes described as "sense-making." We generate or acquire observations about the world (which is vast, complex, and full of uncertainty), convert those observations into numbers, clean, manipulate, and organize those numbers, then apply techniques that allow us to interpret and translate back to the world what we have found. Making sense of cleaned and annotated data is often the most exciting step in the process. Getting from the (cleaned) raw data to a point from which we can make an estimate, or inference, or a (statistical) model about the world is why we do this work in the first place.

Although the basic principles and concepts of statistical analysis remain more or less constant (since the second paradigm), thousands of specific analytic techniques are now available to cope with different types of data problems or characteristics. One of the biggest challenges (opportunities) is for domain scientists, statisticians, and data scientists to put their collective heads together to recognize which analytic technique is most appropriate for the data type and size, and how to interpret and apply the results. In general, we want to (i) summarize our data (data reduction) – start with a vast amount (volume) of data; (ii) reduce it to smaller sets (without sacrificing critical or nuanced information), sacrificing, perhaps, some detail in exchange for parsimony and salience; or use statistical analysis or analytics as an inferential measuring tool, able to quantify the degree of confidence about the accuracy and precision of an estimate we have made; or (iii) discover and describe associations, relationships, and patterns (that may allow us to predict behaviors or outcomes).

24.4.4 Disseminate

Often, the goal of a research undertaking is to publish one's work in a well-respected journal (or book!). However, such a publication should *not* be the end; rather, as Table 24.1 indicates there are many other additional considerations for dissemination, especially in a fourth paradigm world. One of the fundamental precepts in the original fourth paradigm thinking is that scientists would share both their results and their *data* (and code and other descriptive information); in fact, the FAIR principles, described earlier, operationalize this idea. Dissemination can take many forms, and there are now any number of repositories for datasets, accessible and findable for both domain and computer/data scientists.

24.4.5 Stewardship

The often overlooked last step in the data life cycle is making arrangements for one's data to live on and become reusable by others. Library scientists and informaticians have long thought about this step, but it is now incumbent on us fourth paradigm scientists to ensure that we are thinking, from the outset of our study, about our plans for storing, indexing, and curating data. And, as mentioned above, the "long tail" for data implies that we also be thinking about when and if we decide to destroy or expunge data.

The key point, when considering the entire range of the data life cycle as depicted in Table 24.1, is to treat the data life cycle as an *outcome itself*. To be truly data-aware – and thus to become a fourth paradigm scientist – one needs to think about, and have a plan for the entire range of activities in the life cycle at the beginning of any research study. Just as one would develop – at the outset – an analytic plan, one should also develop a data management/life cycle plan as one of the first steps in planning a study.

24.5 Bridge the Gap Between Silos

Much of the power in Big Data analytics comes from integrating and analyzing multiple, heterogeneous datasets. On a single study, for example, one could conceivably combine data from Internet of Things (IoT) sensors, documents and text, video, and many other types of both structured and unstructured data. We need more research on how best to integrate multiple sources of data when, for example unique identifiers in each dataset do not exist, which will often be the case. Research on this topic is more often conducted in the computer science and informatics fields, but applying statistical and data science thinking to this problem could benefit all. As denoted by the bold and italicized text in Table 24.1, many different skills and expertise are currently needed across the data life cycle for social science, including domain scientists (subject matter experts, or SMEs), statisticians, data scientists, computer scientists, and informatics specialists.

Silos can be built, inadvertently, between the columns in Table 24.1, however. For example, statisticians trained in previous cohorts lack facility/familiarity with programming, machine learning, distributed computing, and data management attributes and thus run the risk of being able to contribute to smaller and smaller slices of the life cycle – and being replaced by data scientists who have both the statistical and programming training. Data science is on the rise; although one can (and many do) still debate the definition of data science or data scientist, the great majority would agree that data science incorporates some statistical training

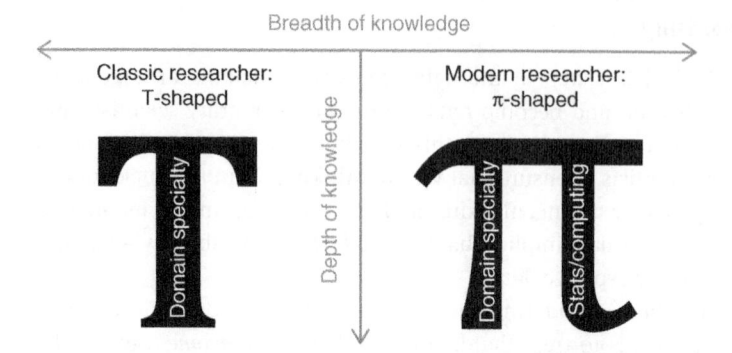

Figure 24.3 π-shaped researcher. Source: Faris et al. (2011).

and expertise, along with data munging and data visualization skills (Schutt and O'Neil 2014) – at least three, if not four, of the columns in Table 24.1.

The *future's so bright, I gotta wear shades: π-shaped social scientists.* In the near future (if not already), the tools of data-enabled science will be commonplace, free, and easily accessible, but SMEs will still be driving the science. And, so, in the near future, we will see SMEs who are π-shaped instead of T-shaped (see Figure 24.3); in short, graduate-level training in a particular discipline – be it physics, history, and everything in between – will include solid training in both statistics and computing. Put another way, all disciplines will recognize that they should be producing a workforce that can use data to its best advantage as those disciplines become more and more data-enabled (Berman et al. 2018). The practice of data science will infiltrate every discipline so that it can support the increasing role of data in an eScience world, including, training in programming, software engineering, version control, the subtleties of stewardship, and digital scholarship.

It is increasingly evident – obvious, even – to developers of college-level curricula that data skills must be incorporated in every discipline, at both undergraduate and graduate levels. We can already see evidence and signals of this thinking in many different settings. The Moore Foundation[4] started its Data-Driven Discovery Initiative, designed to drive and advance academic data science in 2013, and has many grants in excess of $20 million aimed at scaling-up specific data-driven software and methods. The US National Science Foundation has long had a program called the Interactive Graduate Education and Research Traineeship and recent grants have focused on data science. The University of Washington recently hired several interdisciplinary postdocs to do multidisciplinary data-intensive research, positions designed especially to attract π-shaped researchers, and it also houses an eScience institute on general computational and data science methods. Michigan State University has now started an Applied Computation and Mathematics

---

4 https://www.moore.org/initiative-strategy-detail?initiativeId=data-driven-discovery.

Department, where interdisciplinary tenure-track faculty will have joint appointments in a home department and in this new department.

24.6 Conclusion

The fourth paradigm holds promise as an Eden-like environment where scientists from all disciplines make all of their clean data and code available to all, and we can all share it and access it to apply to our own particular research pursuits. Although that idyllic state is some ways off, we can see it on the horizon.

The fourth paradigm, especially as applied to the intersection of Big Data and survey research, would require cross-discipline sharing of data, code, and knowledge; in many ways, this book represents a small step in that direction. Even so, there are technical challenges to meet and overcome, including data management, storage, and accessibility issues; convincing statisticians and data scientists and computer scientists to put their heads together to define and operationalize uncertainty characterization and quantification; and taking all the necessary steps to ensure that our work is reproducible. These are just a few of the challenges – but all of these challenges (and others) represent research opportunities – opportunities that could be best met using a collaborative, cross-disciplinary mix of researchers.

We are, despite the challenges, getting closer to the fourth paradigm. Social scientists, however, must become completely "data aware," that is, they must recognize that the data they collect or acquire, manage and munge, use and reuse, and disseminate and share must be properly stewarded – and, more importantly, that plans for the future of their data must be built at the *beginning* of a research study. We can see increasing evidence that these data-aware protocols are being taught to the students of today, who will, in turn, become the scientists of tomorrow.

References

Agrawal, D., Bernstein, P., Bertino, E. et al. (2012). *Challenges and Opportunities with Big Data. A white paper prepared for the Computing Community Consortium committee.* Washington, DC: Computing Research Association http://cra.org/ccc/resources/ccc-led-whitepapers/.

Benjamini, Y. and Hochberg, Y. (1995). Controlling the false discovery rate: a practical and powerful approach to multiple testing. *Journal of the Royal Statistical Society: Series B (Methodological)* 57: 289–300.

Berman, F., Rutenbar, R., Hailpern, B. et al. (2018). Realizing the potential of data science. *Communications of the ACM* 81 (4): 67–72. https://doi.org/10.1145/3188721.

Committee on the Analysis of Massive Data (2013). *Frontiers in Massive Data Analysis*. Washington, DC, USA: The National Academies Press.

Davies, W. (2017). How statistics lost their power – and why we should fear what comes next. *The Guardian* (19 January) https://www.theguardian.com/politics/2017/jan/19/crisis-of-statistics-big-data-democracy.

Desjardins, J. (2019). What happens in an Internet minute in 2019? https://www.visualcapitalist.com/what-happens-in-an-internet-minute-in-2019/ (accessed 16 March 2020).

Fan, J., Han, F., and Liu, H. (2014). Challenges of big data analysis. *National Science Review* 1 (2): 293–314. https://doi.org/10.1093/nsr/nwt032.

Faris, J., Kolker, E., Szalay, A. et al. (2011). Communication and data-intensive science in the beginning of the 21st century. *OMICS* 15 (4): 213–215. https://doi.org/10.1089/omi.2011.0008.

Fogg, B. and Tseng, H. (1999). The elements of computer credibility. In: *CHI '99: Proceedings of the SIGCHI conference on Human Factors in Computing Systems, Pittsburgh, PA (May 1999)*, 80–87. Association for Computing Machinery https://doi.org/10.1145/302979.303001.

Groves, R. (2012). What happens when big data meets official statistics. World Bank. http://live.worldbank.org/what-happens-when-big-data-meets-official-statistics-live-webcast (accessed 16 March 2020).

Hey, T., Tansley, S., and Tolle, K. (2009). *The Fourth Paradigm: Data-Intensive Scientific Discovery*. Redmond, WA: Microsoft Research.

Hill, C.A., Dean, E., and Murphy, J. (2013). *Social Media, Sociality, and Survey Research*. Hoboken, NJ: Wiley.

Lee, P. (2018). A talk at the American Association for the Advancement of Science (AAAS) Forum on Science & Technology Policy (21 June 2018).

McCoach, D. B., Dineen, J., Chafouleas, S., et al. (2018). Reproducibility in the era of big data: lessons for developing robust data management and data analysis procedures. Paper presented at the Big Data Meets Survey Science Conference, Barcelona, Spain (October 2018).

Pellizzari, E., Lohr, K., Blatecky, A. et al. (2017). *Reproducibility: A Primer on Semantics and Implications for Research* (RTI Press Publication No. BK-0020-1708). Research Triangle Park, NC: RTI Press https://doi.org/10.3768/rtipress.2017.bk.0020.1708.

Puts, M., Daas, P., and de Waal, T. (2015). Finding errors in Big Data. *Significance* 12 (3): 26–29. https://doi.org/10.1111/j.1740-9713.2015.00826.x.

Rothwell, C. (2018). NCHS director addresses challenges for federal statistical agencies. *AmStatNews* (18–20 August) https://magazine.amstat.org/blog/2018/08/01/nchsdirector/.

Schutt, R. and O'Neil, C. (2014). *Doing Data Science*. Sebastapol, CA: O'Reilly Media, Inc.

Suresh, S. (2013). Innovation in the new era of global science & engineering. Presented at TMS Annual Meeting, National Science Foundation, San Antonio, TX (5 March 2013).

Toffler, A. (1980). *The Third Wave*. New York, NY: Bantam Books.

Watts, D. (2016). Computational Social Science: Exciting progress and future challenges. In: *Proceedings of the 22nd ACM SIGKDD International Conference on Knowledge Discovery and Data Mining*, 419–419. Microsoft Research.

Wilkinson, M.D., Dumontier, M., Aalbersberg, I.J. et al. (2016). The FAIR Guiding Principles for scientific data management and stewardship. *Scientific Data* 3: 160018. https://doi.org/10.1038/sdata.2016.18.

Index

a

activated data-sharing functions 400–401, 409
active data collection 83–84
active mobile data collection 658, 670–671 *see also* mobile data collection; smartphones
activity data function 396
ad blockers 77
address-level prediction, of boat ownership, Enhanced Frame
  data collection results 530
  limitation 533
  oversampling 532
  propensities by state 527, 529
  registered boat households flagged by boat registry vendor (InfoLink) 525–530
  screening and eligibility rate 530, 531
  spatial boat density model 525–526
administrative data
  ASPIRE 218
  behavioral assessment practices 643, 645–646
  bias/variance 223
  budgetary and time constraints 219
  cost/schedule efficiencies 99
  data collection procedures 218
  data linkage

  confidential identifiers 103
  control group portion 103
  data quality requirements 102
  demographic characteristics 101
  determinants of spell length 101
  gold standard administrative data item 102
  longitudinal datafiles 102
  self-reports 101
  survey data 102
  survey respondent 103
  suspected survey error 101
  systematic errors 103
  unemployment insurance (UI) records 102
  verbatim responses 101
data processing and estimation procedures 217
data quality 218
data quality assessment
  cell errors 226–227
  column errors 226
  coverage errors 228–229
  data table 224–225
  errors in data integration process 227–228
  invalid, unknown, and missing values 230–231
  nonresponse errors 229–230

Big Data Meets Survey Science: A Collection of Innovative Methods, First Edition. Edited by Craig A. Hill, Paul P. Biemer, Trent D. Buskirk, Lilli Japec, Antje Kirchner, Stas Kolenikov, and Lars E. Lyberg.
© 2021 John Wiley & Sons, Inc. Published 2021 by John Wiley & Sons, Inc.

administrative data (*contd.*)
  row errors   225
  definition   217
  efficiencies/quality improvements   99
  external data sources
    data quality assessment   234
    population counts   235–236
  FBI UCR program   223
  Framingham Health Study   100
  Gallup survey research questions, on data sharing
    respondents favorable to   701–704
    respondents less favorable to   703–704
  General Business Register (GBR)   318
  hybrid strategy   99
  imputations   233–234
  law enforcement agencies (LEAs)   219
  linking datafiles   100
  NEEDs² project   634
  NIBRS Database
    administrative crime statistics and the history of   220–221
    construction   221–222
    row-column-cell errors   227
  NSECE Household Survey
    analytical motivation   125
    characteristics   124
    continuous variables   121
    CoreLogic data   126
    data collection outcomes   120
    eligibility   105
    government program participation records   105
    interview nonresponse   120
    large-scale US surveys   105
    logistic regression   120
    lot-level analyses   122
    overall weighted response rate   105
    parental consents   105
    policy and practice data   105
    predict screener and interview nonresponse   121, 122
    screener nonresponse   120
    standard errors   123
    survey error   120
    t-tests   123
    two-stage probability design   105
    unit-level and lot-level matching   123
    Zillow proprietary datafiles   107–116
  official statistics   217
  Pilot Study on Crime in Bakken Region   238–239
  product-specific assessment   222, 223
  quality   643–644
  reliability of   632
  row-column-cell framework   223
  sample-based method   231–232
  secondary data users   223
  source and linkage   100
  source-specific assessment   222, 223
  specification errors   218
  statistical weighting   232–233
  vs. survey data for crime statistics   236–238
  survey interviews   99
  survey responses   99
  total survey error (TSE) paradigm   218
  usage, ethical government framework for
    connecting data collections to community benefits   709–710
    data security   709
    transparency element   709
  validity of   632, 644
  Zillow data files
    assessed value   117

distribution of state mean values 118
duplicate records 116
market segments 106
market transactions 106
public records 106
rates of completeness, for categorical variables 118
residential property tax assessments 106
total market value 117
total market value *vs.* tax amount 119
transactions data 106
variables 106
ZTRAX variables 117
Agricultural Resource Management Survey (ARMS) 30
algorithm-based decision-making machines 721
Algorithmic biases 1
Amazon.de vouchers 395, 402, 407, 410, 411
Amazon Mechanical Turk Questionnaire 459–460
Amazon MTurk 458
American Association for Public Opinion Research (AAPOR) 361, 685
AAPOR Task Force on Big Data 6
American Community Survey (ACS) 435
American Statistical Association 361
Annual Retail Trade Survey (ARTS) 362
annual retail trade survey data 374
app installations, percentage 398–400
application programming interface (API) 361
areal population sampling 5
artificial intelligence 562, 592, 716
 data science 7
 and machine learning 5
artificial narrow intelligence (ANI) 562
artificial neural networks (ANNs) 27
augmenting traditional survey data 4, 12
Australian Bureau of Statistics 278

b

bagging technique 585
Bayesian Additive Regression Trees (BART) 493
Bayesian learning framework 604
Bayesian models 183
behavioral assessment practices (BAPs) 643, 645–646
behavioral models 313
behavioral risk factor surveillance system (BRFSS) 435, 438–439
Big Data 133, 658, 683, 719
 challenges 629
 creating reproducible datasets/data analyses, steps for 646–648
 definition 627
 era of 720
 legal issues 293–295
 NEEDs[2] project
  administrative data 634, 643–644
  behavioral assessment practices 643, 645–646
  creating master databases for 635
  data harmonization 637
  dataset creation and maintenance, perspective on 636
  merging data sources 638
  quality dimensions 648–649
  research questions, for regular school and component districts 638, 639
  social, emotional, and behavioral health screening 633

Big Data (contd.)
  socioeconomic status variables/proxies 636, 637
  survey data 633–634
  syntax/code and data dictionaries 639
  transparency 641–642
 in official statistics 2
  accuracy 310–311
  administrative data 304
  AIS 287–288
  auxiliary data 316–317
  bias 288
  calibrated Bayes 276
  census data 304
  changing user preferences 275
  consumer confidence index 319–320
  consumer price index (CPI) 289
  costly probability samples 280
  economic and social progress 278
  European Statistical System (ESS) 278
  expenditure surveys 288
  face-to-face interviewing 277
  found data 304
  global value chains and economic globalization 278
  Google trends for nowcasting 322–323
  gross national product (GNP) 321–322
  innovation 279
  internet economy 317–319
  ISCO and NACE coding 290
  measurement and selection bias 328–329
  methodological research and implementation 280
  mixed-mode data collection 280
  mobile phone data 308–309
  models in 311–312
  multisource statistics 323
  nonprobability sampling 275, 277
  nonresponse rates 275
  objectivity and reliability 312–314
  open data sources 324–325
  phenomenon-oriented statistics 330
  probability sample 276
  quality 329–330
  quality assessments 315–316
  quicker statistics 289
  relevance 314–315
  sample survey paradigm 277
  scanner data 305–306
  smart meter data 289–290
  social media messages 307–308
  statistical disclosure control (SDC) 325–327
  statistics production 280
  survey-assisted modelling 278, 280
  survey-based approach 305
  survey data 304
  survey landscape 280–284
  survey task 277
  timeliness 329
  tools and approaches 279
  total survey error (TSE) 276
  traffic-loop data 306–307
  web modes and mobile devices 277
  wider and deeper statistics 285–287
 public opinion 12
 quality 290–293
 reproducibility 630–632
 scientific domain and business sector 2
 survey and social sciences 1, 2
 survey researchers and government officials 3

vs. traditional survey data   628
vision   361
Bonferroni outlier test   454–455

C

call detailed record (CDR) data   245
CART models   575, 579
cell error   140–141, 226–227
Census Bureau Retail Programs   361–363
Census Module research questions
 confidentiality   690–694
 data linkage/sharing (*see* data sharing in federal government)
 privacy   695–697
 trust in federal statistics   697–698
Census Module survey items   685–688
CharmStatsPro   641
CharmStats suite of products   640
chi-square automatic interaction detection (CHAID) models   38, 538, 543, 544, 546
Civil Rights Data Collection (CRDC)   634
classification and regression trees (CARTs)   32, 538, 543, 544, 546
classification trees   539
cognitive interviews   66, 689–690
Coleman Report on Equality of Educational Opportunity   100
column error   140, 226
commercial data *see* administrative data
community-based participatory research   489
composite registry frame   522–523
computational science   715, 716
computational social science   12
computational tools   5
computer, definition   11
computer-assisted coding   27

Computerized Delivery Sequence (CDS) file   521
confidentiality (data)   684, 690–694, 704, 705
confidentiality and privacy issues   4
consumer confidence index   319–320
consumer price index (CPI)   289
convolutional neural networks (CNNs)   435, 436
coverage errors   228–229
credibility assessment framework   722
crowdsourced data
 criticism   487
 nonparametric bootstrap technique
  area-level EBLUP   496
  bootstrap algorithm steps   495
  Horvitz–Thompson estimator   494
  pseudo-sampling weights   493–495
  SSRSWR   494
 representativeness   488
 safety perceptions in London
  area-level covariates   506
  mapping safety perceptions, at neighbourhood level   510–511
  model diagnostics and external validation   506–510
  Place Pulse 2.0 dataset   504–506
  spatial study   503–504
 self-selection bias   490–491
 simulation study   496
  area-level measures, of bias and RMSE   500–502
  bootstrap and EBLUP estimators   499
  Kernel density distribution, of empirical values   499, 500
  population generation   497
  sample selection and simulation steps   497–499
  sample size *vs.* RMSE (EBLUP)   500–502

crowdsourced data (*contd.*)
  underrepresentation of certain areas and times   492
  unequal participation   491–492
  unreliable area-level direct estimates   492
crowdsourcing
  data, limitations   490–492
  definition   489
  techniques   487
cybersecurity   661

d

DairyBase data items   350–351
data awareness
  acquire/create/collect   725
  data cleaning (munging)   725
  dissemination   726
  statistical analysis   726
  stewardship   727
  use/reuse   726
data cleaning (or munging)   722, 725
Data-Driven Discovery Initiative   728
data encoding error (DEE)   142, 156
data encoding process   144
data harmonization   637
data integration and estimation
  hybrid estimation process   135
  integration process   137
  source datasets   135–137
  unified dataset   137
data-intensive social science research, technical challenges for   718–723
data management life cycle approach   723–725, 727
data poverty issues   1
data processing error   145
data science challenges, for National Institutes of Health (NIH)   638
data science methods   47

dataset error framework   145
data-sharing functions   394–395
data sharing in federal government
  administrative data/record sharing, Gallup survey on   701–704
  community harm   707–708
  government *vs.* private company
    managing data confidentiality   704, 705
    security of combined data by   704, 705
  individual harm   706–707
  participants' expectations and beliefs about   698–701
data sharing with law enforcement   707
data sources
  public opinion and social phenomena   11
data triangulation   7
data validity   718
data variety   717
data velocity   718
data volume   718
deactivating data functions   401–402
decision trees (DTs)   561, 579
decompositions   143
density-based spatial clustering algorithms   28
density-based spatial clustering of applications with noise (DBSCAN)   23
digital trace data   193

e

Economic Directorate   360
economic indicators   360
eligibility rate, in survey   519
empirical best linear unbiased predictor (EBLUP) estimates   488
empirical science   713
end–product analytic resources   561

Energy Information Agency (EIA)   148
Enhanced Frame
  address-level prediction, of boat ownership
    data collection results   530
    limitation   533
    oversampling   532
    propensities by state   527, 529
    registered boat households flagged by boat registry vendor (InfoLink)   525–530
    screening and eligibility rate   530, 531
    spatial boat density model   525–526
  CDS component of   521
  composite registry frame   522–523
  data obstacles   523–524
  and target population   522
errors
  administrative records   134
  cell errors   226–227
  column errors   226
  coverage errors   228–229
  data encoding process   146
  data-generating mechanism   134
  data generation process   157
  in data integration process   227–228
  in datasets
    cell error   140–141
    column error   140
    harmonization process   138
    row/column/cell model   138
    row error   139
  error-generating processes
    data encoding error (DEE)   142
    data encoding process   144
    data processing error   145
    dataset error framework   145
    decompositions   143
    gross domestic product (GDP)   142
    invoice value   142
    measurement error   145
    noncoverage error   144
    nonprobability datasets   144
    populations and sample recruitment systems   144
    population unit   143
    recruitment process   143
    sample recruitment error (SRE)   142
    sample recruitment process   143
    specification error   145
    statistical adjustment errors   145
    statistical value   142
    statistical value vs. invoice value   145
    survey noncontacts   144
  error mitigation
    data encoding error   156
    sample recruitment error   153–156
  frame deficiencies   134
  identification and treatment   3
  illustration
    CAPI response rate   148
    DEE bias   149
    interviewer measurements   149
    RECS square footage data   149–150
    RelMSE of survey and Zillow data   151, 152
    square footage of housing units   149
    Zillow data   149
  integrated-data movement   134
  mean squared error (MSE)   145, 150, 233
  measurement errors   173, 344–345
  nonresponse errors   229–230
  nontraditional data sources   134
  observation and nonobservation error   157
  probability samples   146

errors (*contd.*)
  row/column/cell framework   157
  row errors   225
  sample recruitment mechanism   146
  simple random sampling   146
  specification, measurement, and data processing error   157
eScience   713
  challenges for   720
EU General Data Privacy Regulation   401
European Statistical System's ESSnet on Big Data   3
event–level files   581–582

f

Facebook   65
FAIR Data Principles   723
fast-track MEPS imputation strategy
  applied to 2014 MEPS data   587–590
  attribute selection   582–584
  CART models   579
  decision trees   579
  effectiveness   585, 586
  health-care costs
    algorithmic prediction   577
    CARTs and random forests   575
    machine learning approach   578–579
    modeling challenges   577
  high-level research workflow   580, 581
  inter-variable correlation   584
  multi-output random forest   584–585
  person-level medical expenditures, estimates of   587
  probability distribution   579
  raw data extraction   581–582
  testing of   580
  WSHD method   579
financial loss, threat of   706

"Fit-for-purpose" paradigm   2
FixMyStreet   488
floating car data (FCD)   307
focus groups   689
  goal of   685
four paradigms of science   713, 714
fourth paradigm science, power of   720
Framingham Health Study   100

g

Gallup Daily Tracking Survey   684, 685
  data sharing in federal government
    administrative data/record sharing   701–704
    community harm   707–708
    government vs. private company   704, 705
    individual harm   706–707
Geographic information system (GIS)
  grid frames   5
Geo–Referenced Infrastructure and Demographic Data for Development (GRID3)   604–605
geosampling   609–610
German ESS Questions   184–185
German Panel Study Labour Market and Social Security (PASS)   393
German voucher flyer   408, 409
Gini coefficient   585
Google Street View (GSV) images   436
  in Baltimore
    actual vs. fitted affect balance maps   480
    actual vs. fitted health maps   477, 478
    actual vs. fitted life evaluation scores   453, 479
    Bonferroni outlier test   454–455
    cross-validation results   457
    estimated model fit   452

generalized linear models via penalized maximum likelihood with *k*-fold cross-validation 472–474
heat maps 453
Moran's I|i calculation 456
Pearson correlation 451, 467–468
pictures and maps 461–463
predictor variables, boxplots for 464–466
stepwise AIC OLS regression models 469–470
data sources
BRFSS surveys 438–439
GDT surveys 438
health-related quality of life, components of 438–439
survey data study outcomes 438–440
model development, testing, and evaluation 450–451
predictors from built environment data
image labeling process 441–443, 445
image sampling 441–444
quality control 445, 447–449
predictors from Geospatial Imagery
land use 448
TGI 447–448
tract size 447
sampling units and frames 437–438
in San Francisco
actual *vs.* fitted affect balance 484
actual *vs.* fitted health maps 481, 482
actual *vs.* fitted life evaluation 483
estimated model fit 455
generalized linear models via penalized maximum likelihood with *k*-fold cross-validation 475–476

Moran's I|i calculation 456
stepwise AIC OLS regression models 471–472
government statistical programs 73
Gray, Jim 713
gridded population estimates 598, 599
areal weighting and basic dasymetric methods 601
challenges 605–606
data sources 600–601
GRID3 604–605
LandScan Global 601–602
LandScan HD 603–604
in Nigeria 613–616
population sampling
from 1 km × 1 km grid cells 609–610
from 100 m × 100 m grid cells 611–613
pros and cons of 606, 607
in surveys
implementation of 613
population sampling 609–613
standard sampling strategies 608–609
WorldPop data 602–603
gridEA algorithm 612
GridSample2.0 611–613
GridSample R package 611
gross domestic product (GDP) 142
Groves, Robert 720

h

harmful decision-making based on data 707
harmonization process 138
hashtag 65
hierarchical regression modeling 493
high-throughput computing 721
home detection algorithms (HDA)
call detailed records data 250

home detection algorithms (HDA) (*contd.*)
   correlation with ground truth data 256–258
   counts and population counts 260
   data and setup 255
   data packages 250
   distinct days criterion (DD) 253
   ego-network of contacts 251
   French mobile phone dataset 251–252
   ground truth data 256
   maximum amount of activities criterion (MA) 253
   network operators 251
   observation periods 253–255
   performance and sensitivities 256
   potential records 250
   ratio and spatial patterns 258
   sensitivity to criteria choice 266–267
   sensitivity to duration of observation 266
   temporality and sensitivity 258
   temporality of correlations 260, 262–265
   time constraints criterion (TC) 253
   user counts and ground truth 258–260
Horvitz–Thompson estimator 494

i

incentives
   smartphone data collection 390–392
Instagram 65
installation brochure 394
Institut für Arbeitsmarkt-und Berufsforschung (IAB)–SMART study
   experimental design 397
   incentives effect of 397–398
   invitation and data request 394–396
   sampling frame and restrictions 393–394
   selection process 394
interaction history records 394
Interactive Graduate Education and Research Traineeship 728
internet of things 11, 64
intricate variables 73
Inverse Probability Bootstrapping 493
invoice value 142

j

Jewish Community Survey of Metropolitan Detroit (JCSMD) 541, 547, 549, 551, 555–556
just-in-time adaptive interventions (JITAIs) 30

l

LandScan Global 601–602
LandScan HD 603–604
large-scale survey estimation *see* Medical Expenditure Panel Survey (MEPS)
law enforcement agencies (LEAs) 219
Least Absolute Shrinkage and Selection Operator (LASSO) 14, 31, 45, 417, 419, 420, 422–427, 452, 455, 493
leverage-saliency theory 390
linear regression model 347
list frames 519
location information 396
logistic regression 120
long tail and data volume 719
lot-level analyses 122
low-and middle-income countries (LMICs) 597
   gridded population estimates 598, 599
   areal weighting and basic dasymetric methods 601

challenges   605–606
data sources   600–601
GRID3   604–605
LandScan Global   601–602
LandScan HD   603–604
in Nigeria   613–616
pros and cons of   606, 607
in surveys   608–613
WorldPop data   602–603

m

machine learning methods (MLMs)   4
  algorithmic optimization
    clustering algorithms   21
    data collection cost constraints   21
    final segmentation   21
  alternative data sources   28
  confusion matrices   16
  cross-validation   15
  data error
    Big Data sources   23
    categorical and continuous variables   22
    density–based spatial clustering of applications with noise (DBSCAN)   23
    k-nearest neighbors algorithm   22
    k-prototypes clustering algorithm   22
    sampling designs   22, 23
    scaling binary or nominal variables   22
  explanation *vs.* prediction   15
  explanatory models   15
  hierarchical cluster analysis (HCA)   14
  high-dimensional data   14
  instrumentation and interviewer training   27–28
  k-means clustering   14
  longitudinal settings   31

  model error
    data collection costs   22
    false positive misclassification error   21
    misclassification errors   21
  ordinary least squares regression   14
  prediction or classification models   15
  predictive accuracy   16
  question wording
    Cox survival model   25
    evaluation and testing   26–27
    Markov chains   25
    recurrent neural networks (RNN)   25
    Survey Quality Predictor (SQP)   24
  reimagining traditional survey research   12
  sample design development
    ANOVA   17
    cross-validation information   18
    Gaussian mixture models (GMMs)   16
    k-means clustering   16, 17
    random digit-dial (RDD) sample   17
    unsupervised learning methods   16
  sample frame construction
    convolutional neural networks (CNNs)   19
    gridded samples   18
    human coders   19
    neural networks model   20
    object recognition tasks   19
    primary grid units (PGUs)   18
    residential units   19
    sample partitions/subsets   18
    sampling frame   19, 20
    sampling units   20
    secondary grid units (SGUs)   18
    two–category classification   18

744 | Index

machine learning methods (MLMs) (*contd.*)
    uniform record locator (URL) 18
    sample weighting and survey adjustments
        propensity score estimation 37–41
        sample matching 41–43
    specification of hyperparameters 14
    supervised and unsupervised machine learning technique 14
    survey data analysis and estimation
        continuous and categorical auxiliary data 45
        finite population inference 46–47
        fuzzy forests method 44
        LASSO and adaptive LASSO approaches 45
        model-assisted approaches 45
        poststratification adjustment cells 45
        probability-based RDD survey 45
    survey data coding and processing
        coding unstructured text 32–35
        data validation and editing 35
        imputation 35–36
        record linkage and duplicate detection 36
    survey recruitment and data collection
        monitoring and interviewer falsification 29
        responsive and adaptive designs 29–32
    validation sample 15
Markov chains (MC) 25
mean absolute bias (MAB) 553–554
mean squared error (MSE) 145, 150, 233
measurement error 145, 173, 344–345
Medical Expenditure Panel Survey (MEPS)
    description 561–562
    expenditures, defined 582
    imputation processes (*see also* fast-track MEPS imputation strategy)
        Agency for Healthcare Research and Quality 563
        class variables 571–572
        cost and coverage detail 564
        data files and variables 566–567
        evaluation phases 565
        means and standard errors, of medical expenditures 574, 576
        medical payments, predictors identification of 567–571
        MEPS–HC 564–565
        MEPS–IC 564
        MEPS–MPC 565
        quality assessment 572, 573
        results 573–575
        WSHD procedure 565–566, 572, 579
    objectives/goals 563
Medical Expenditure Panel Survey–Household Component (MEPS–HC) 564–565
Medical Expenditure Panel Survey–Insurance Component (MEPS–IC) 564
Medical Expenditure Panel Survey–Medical Provider Component (MEPS–MPC) 565
missingness 171–173
missing-not-at-random (MNAR) 346
mobile data collection
    active 658, 670–671
    passive 658, 670–672
    privacy concerns 660
    research concerns 659–661
    second-level digital divide 661
    web surveys
        and age influence 670

analysis plan   664–665
Austrian statistical office   663
average marginal effects   667–668
confidence intervals   667–668
demographic control variables
      668, 670
descriptive statistics for the
      responses   664–665
German Internet Panel   662
German nonprobability online
      panel   662
multiple logistic regression
   estimates and standard errors
      675–678
outcome variables   663
questions on concern   663–664
respondents reporting concern,
      percentage of   666–667, 669
results from logistic regression
      models   667–668
willingness rate for research tasks
      659, 671
mobile phone data
   home detection algorithms (HDA)
      call detailed records data   250
      correlation with ground truth data
         256–258
      counts and population counts   260
      data and setup   255
      data packages   250
      distinct days criterion (DD)   253
      ego-network of contacts   251
      French mobile phone dataset
         251–252
      ground truth data   256
      maximum amount of activities
         criterion (MA)   253
      network operators   251
      observation periods   253–255
      performance and sensitivities   256
      potential records   250

ratio and spatial patterns   258
sensitivity to criteria choice
      266–267
sensitivity to duration of observation
      266
temporality and sensitivity   258
temporality of correlations   260,
      262–265
time constraints criterion (TC)   253
user counts and ground truth
      258–260
home detection problem
   CDR data   247
   census data   248
   consequence   249
   customer-related information   248
   decent validation data   248
   high-level validation   248
   in-depth investigations   248
   individual user's level   248
   mobile phone indicators and
      socioeconomic indicators   248
   validity and sensitivities   249
official statistics
   analytical methods   246
   Big Data applications   247
   call detailed record (CDR) data
      245
   home detection   247
   home detection algorithms (HDAs)
      247
   socioeconomic indicators   246
   socioeconomic information   247
   user traces   245
Monthly Retail Trade Survey (MRTS)
      362
   descriptive statistics   373
   high-burden retailers   370
   national-level data   371–372
   nonrespondents   370
   reporting history   370

MTurk 458
  labeling, inter-rater agreement and reliability 445, 446
multi-armed bandits (MABs) 30
multilevel regression and poststratification (MRP) method 493
multi-output random forest 584–585
multiple frame surveys 523
multitask learning (MTL) problem 561

n

Naïve Bayesian classifiers 28
National Incident-Based Reporting System (NIBRS) database 219
National Institutes of Health (NIH)
  data science challenges for 638
national-level data 370
National Recreational Boating Safety Survey (NRBSS) 519
  registry frame 520, 521
  RTI's Enhanced Frame (see Enhanced Frame)
  target population 519–520, 522
natural language processing 7, 27, 28, 32–34
NCES CCD Local Education Agency (District) Universe Survey 634
NEEDs² project, Big Data
  administrative data 634, 643–644
  behavioral assessment practices 643, 645–646
  creating master databases for 635
  data harmonization 637
  dataset creation and maintenance, perspective on 636
  merging data sources 638
  quality dimensions 648–649
  research questions, for regular school and component districts 638, 639

social, emotional, and behavioral health screening 633
socioeconomic status variables/proxies 636, 637
survey data 633–634
syntax/code and data dictionaries 639
transparency 641–642
network quality 396
noncoverage error 144
nonparametric bootstrap technique 488
  crowdsourced data
    area-level EBLUP 496
    bootstrap algorithm steps 495
    Horvitz–Thompson estimator 494
    pseudo-sampling weights 494–495
    SSRSWR 494
nonprobability datasets 144
nonprobability sample
  missing-at-random assumptions 340
  statistical inference, binary variables
    breakdown of sample size 342
    social media sources 341
    target population 342, 343
nonprobability surveys 71
nonresponse errors 229–230
nonresponse model 349
nonsurvey data
  augmenting traditional survey data 12
"norm of reciprocity," 390
North American Industry Classification System (NAICS) 361
NPD Group, Inc. (NPD) 368–369, 372–373
NSECE Household Survey
  CoreLogic data 126
  eligibility 105
  government program participation records 105
  large-scale US surveys 105

overall weighted response rate   105
parental consents   105
policy and practice data   105
two-stage probability design   105
Zillow proprietary datafiles
   identify matches   110–114
   intended analyses   114–116
   misalignment of units of observation   110
   nonuniqueness of matches   107–109

o

official statistics   133, 359
   applications   350–353
   data integration   340
   empirical studies   347–350
   integrating data source
      measurement errors   344–345
      undercoverage bias   343–344
   integrating probability sample   345–347
   limitation   353
   nonprobability sample (see nonprobability sample)
   probability sample   339
   public and private decisions   339
online influencers   79–80
open-ended questions   27, 199
overfitting   721

p

paid social media advertising   76–77
Panel Study Labour Market and Social Security (PASS)   393
Paperwork Reduction Act   362
paradata   65, 635
participatory mapping   489
PASS see Panel Study Labour Market and Social Security (PASS)
passive mobile data collection   658, 670–672 see also mobile data collection; smartphones
Pearson's correlation coefficients   207
personal safety, threat of   707
person-level files   581
petabytes of data   2
π-shaped researcher   728
point-of-sale data   359, 382
political campaigns   210
population density tables (PDT)   604
primary sampling units (PSUs)   38
privacy (data)   684, 695–697
   community harm   707–708
   individual harm   706–707
Privacy Act Cognitive Test   690
privacy loss, threat of   707
privacy-utility trade-off and data collection   659
private online community   86, 87
probability sample   146, 339
probability surveys   71
product data   377–381
product-level data   370
propensity score adjustment   493
propensity score estimation
   Bayesian Adaptive Regression Trees   40
   chi-square automatic interaction detector (CHAID) models   38
   direct and stratification approaches   39
   Laplace correction   41
   occupational employment statistics survey   38
   primary sampling units (PSUs)   38
   survey researchers   38
pseudo-sampling weights   493
public agenda   196
public attention assumption   197
public opinion   193
public responses   194

q

qualitative data   684, 685
qualitative survey activities   66
quantitative data   684
QuickCharmStats   640–641

r

random-digit-dial (RDD) list-assisted landline interviewing   685
random-digit-dial (RDD) wireless phone sampling   685
random forest (RF)   561, 575
random forest models   538, 543, 544, 548, 555
recurrent neural networks (RNN)   25
recursive partitioning algorithms   538
Reddit data   167–170, 186–188
Reddit survey   169, 181
registration-based sample (RBS) religious flags, for survey research   537
  challenge in combining large datasets   541
  data match rates   542
  data source   540–541
  downsampling sample sizes   544
  JCSMD data   541, 547, 549, 551, 555–556
  L2 dataset   545, 546, 550, 555–556
  modeling decisions   543–544
  research agenda   539–540
  results   545–552
  sensitivity   539, 540, 547–549
  specificity   539, 540, 547
  SSRS omnibus   540–541
  systematic matching rates   552–554
regularization networks   27
Re-Identification Survey Cognitive Test   690
  data sharing in federal government   706–708

reliability of administrative data   632
reproducibility   630–632, 722–723
  CharmStatsPro   641
  QuickCharmStats platform   640–641
  R markdown   640
  syntax/code and data dictionaries   639
  variable notes (Stata users)   640
Residential Energy Consumption Survey (RECS)   148
ResNet18 models   436
respondent burden
  business's decision   365
  business surveys   363
  data collection and data sharing   364
  Economic Census   364, 365
  low response rates   365
  MRTS   364
  point-of-sale data
    brick and mortar retail stores and online   366
    confidentiality agreements   366
    credit card data/payment processor data   366
    data lakes   367
    IBM   366
    monthly datasets   367
    scanner data   366
    statistical agencies   367
respondent-driven sampling (RDS)   70–71
  and advertising   67
Respondent Messaging   689–690
restricted maximum likelihood (REML) method   496
retailer datasets   368–369
retention, app   402–403
reuse of scholarly data   722
R markdown file   640
row error   139, 225, 227, 236, 237

S

sample matching   493
  curse of dimensionality   41
  demographic and political variables   42
  nonprobability samples   43
  proximity measures   41–43
  random forest models   42
  supervised *vs.* unsupervised applications of random forest models   42–43
  synthetic sample   42
  variables   42
sample recruitment error   142, 153–156
sample recruitment mechanism   146
scanner data   305–306
second-level digital divide   661
selection bias, in web–surveys   493
Shapiro–Wilk test   507
simple random sampling   146
small area estimation techniques   512
smart devices   11
smart meter data   289–290
smartphone data collection
  activated data-sharing functions   400–401
  app installation   398–400
  costs analysis   403–405
  deactivating functions   401–402
  future research   407–408
  influence of incentives   390–392
  Institut für Arbeitsmarkt-und Berufsforschung (IAB)
    experimental design   397
    incentives effect of   397–398
    invitation and data request   394–396
    sampling frame and restrictions   393–394
  limitations   407–408
  retention   402–403

smartphones   657
  activities   674
  for data collection (*see also* mobile data collection)
    active   658, 670–671
    passive   658, 670–672
    and second-level digital divide   661
    and education levels   661
    frequency of usage   673
    and privacy   658, 660, 674
    skills, rating of   673
smartphone sensor data   389
smartphone usage   396
social expressions   194
social media
  administrative procedures   65
  communication   63
  hashtag   65
  identifying people
    government statistical programs   73
    intricate variables   73
    outstanding challenges   73–74
    publicly key demographic variables   73
    screening process   73
  internet of things   64
  interviewing people
    active data collection   83–84
    passive social media data mining   82–83
    private online community   86, 87
    Twitter's API   84–85
  locating people
    ad blockers   77
    paid social media advertising   76–77
    tracing   75–76
  mass migration and population displacement   63
  paradata   65

social media (*contd.*)
  persuasion
    aid social media advertising 78–79
    online influencers 79–80
    paid social media campaign 80
  practical and ethical considerations 66
  qualitative survey activities 66
  respondent-driven sampling (RDS) and advertising 67
  sample people
    outstanding challenges 71–72
    respondent-driven sampling 70–71
    venue-based, time-space sampling (VBTS) 68–70
  slang/code terms 65
  social networking sites, active users 64
  survey research typology 88
  survey responses 65
  unstructured and messy 65
  user knowledge of consent 66
social media data 4
  attitude distributions 180
  coding 173–174, 179–180
  coding error 165
  community of social media users 194
  contemporary news event 196
  data-generating process 194, 195
  data sources 197–198
  data streams
    event-related terms 207
    event-related words 206
    event-style terms 205
    open-ended survey responses 209
    Pearson's correlation coefficients 207
    political campaigns 210
    Trump *vs.* Clinton event–related words 208–209
  Twitter and survey maximums 205
  Twitter data stream 205
  decompose error 164
  dichotomous indicators 164
  European Social Survey Data 166–167
  event detection
    distinct events 199
    events and attention metrics 200–203
    open-ended questions 199
    restrictive parameters 199
    text preprocessing 199
  forecast election outcomes 195
  key research decisions 195
  measurement error 173, 177–179
  misestimated flu prevalence 163
  missingness 171–173, 175–177
  official statistics 164
  public attitudes and behaviors 194
  public responses 194
  Reddit data 167–170, 186–187
  Reddit survey 169, 181
  research objective 171
  sentiment models 182
  social expressions 194
  specification error and traditional measurement error 165
  survey questions 195
  survey respondents and Twitter users
    data-generating processes 212
    event-related words 212
  Total Survey Error (TSE) framework 165
  t-tests 171
  tweets
    measure of attention 196, 197
    public agenda 196
    public attention assumption 197
    public concern 196
    tweets-as-attention model 196

Index | 751

Twitter data   163
social media sentiment index (SMI)   319
social network function   394
social science research   4
social sciences   715, 723
socioeconomic indicators   246
spatial boat density model   525–526
spatial outliers   493
Spearman correlation   584
specification error   145
SSRS omnibus   540–541
Stanford Education Data Archive (SEDA)   634
Stata, for data management   640
statistical agencies   5
statistical analysis   726
statistical disclosure control (SDC)   325
   variety   326–327
   velocity   326
   volume   326
statistical estimation   3
store-level data   370, 375–377
stratified simple random samples with replacement (SSRSWR)   494
subjective well-being (SWB)   435
   assessment (see Google Street View (GSV) images)
   Gallup computed model-based small-area estimation   439–440
   and health outcomes   436
supervisory unions (SUs)   638, 639
survey data   12, 304, 319, 628
   administrative data linkage   102
   analysis and estimation
      continuous and categorical auxiliary data   45
      finite population inference   46–47
      fuzzy forests method   44
      LASSO and adaptive LASSO approaches   45
      model-assisted approaches   45

      poststratification adjustment cells   45
      probability-based RDD survey   45
   coding and processing
      coding unstructured text   32–35
      data validation and editing   35
      imputation   35–36
      record linkage and duplicate detection   36
   costs for survey data collection   5
   NEEDs^2 project, Big Data   633–634
   study outcomes, GSV images   438–440
   traditional data collection   4
survey landscape
   Big Data centers   282–283
   European NSIs   282
   experimental statistics   283
   forming partnerships   281–282
   IT infrastructure, tools, and methods   284
   organizing hackathons   283–284
   training staff   281
survey questions   195
survey research   537
   agenda   539–540
   challenge in combining large datasets   541
   data match rates   542
   data source   540–541
   downsampling sample sizes   544
   JCSMD   541, 547, 549, 551, 555–556
   L2 dataset   555–556
      L2 religion variable, incidence and coverage   545, 546
      variables   545, 550
   modeling decisions   543–544
   results   545–552
   sensitivity   539, 540, 547–549
   specificity   539, 540, 547

752 | Index

survey research (*contd.*)
  SSRS omnibus   540–541
  systematic matching rates   552–554
survey research techniques   715
survey responses   65
Sysomos firehose access tool   198
system-to-system data collection   361

t

Taylor, John   713
technology-related issues   3
test-time feature acquisition   27
text preprocessing   199
theoretical science   715
The Third Wave   i, 717
time-series methods   317
Toffler, Alvin   717
topic modelling   34–35
tracing   75–76
traditional survey data collection   4
transparency, NEEDs² project   641–642
Triangular Greenness Index (TGI)   447
t-tests   123, 171
tweets-as-attention model   196
Twitter   65

u

undercoverage bias   343–344
UNECE Big Data project   3
unemployment insurance (UI) records   102
The United Nations Economic Commission for Europe (UNECE)   217
United States Federal Statistical System (USFSS)   683
unsupervised techniques   36

user traces   245
US Federal Statistical System   278
US National Science Foundation   728

v

validity of administrative data   632, 644
variable notes (Stata users)   640
venue-based, time-space sampling (VBTS)
  advertisements   70
  asynchronous communication and interaction   69
  Facebook-recruited men   70
  Facebook sampling   70
  venue-date-time units   70
  web-based approaches   70
Volunteered Geographical Information (VGI)   489, 490

w

web-based system   350
web scraping   361
web surveys, in mobile data collection
  and age influence   670
  analysis plan   664–665
  Austrian statistical office   663
  average marginal effects   667–668
  confidence intervals   667–668
  demographic control variables   668, 670
  descriptive statistics for the responses   664–665
  German Internet Panel   662
  German nonprobability online panel   662
  multiple logistic regression estimates and standard errors   675–678

outcome variables   663
questions on concern   663–664
respondents reporting concern, percentage of   666–667, 669
results from logistic regression models   667–668
WeChat   65

weighted sequential hot deck (WSHD) imputation procedure   565–566, 572, 579
WorldPop data   602–603
WSHD procedure *see* weighted sequential hot deck (WSHD) imputation procedure